ANNUAL REVIEW OF ANTHROPOLOGY

ANNUAL REVIEW OF ANTHROPOLOGY

VOLUME 30, 2001

WILLIAM H. DURHAM, *Editor*
Stanford University

E. VALENTINE DANIEL, *Associate Editor*
Columbia University

BAMBI B. SCHIEFFELIN, *Associate Editor*
New York University

www.AnnualReviews.org   science@AnnualReviews.org   650-493-4400

ANNUAL REVIEWS
4139 El Camino Way • P.O. BOX 10139 • Palo Alto, California 94303-0139

ℛ

ANNUAL REVIEWS

Palo Alto, California, USA

International Standard Serial Number: 0084-6570
International Standard Book Number: 0-8243-1930-3
Library of Congress Catalog Card Number: 72-821360

TYPESET BY TECHBOOKS, FAIRFAX, VA
PRINTED AND BOUND IN THE UNITED STATES OF AMERICA

Readers of the *Annual Review of Anthropology* (*ARA*) often ask, "How can I make a course reader of selections from the *ARA*, or at least include *ARA* chapters in a more general packet of readings? How long does it take and what does it cost to get access and permission?" Happily, online publication makes it possible for us to give the best-ever answers to these questions. Provided that the instructor and the students are at an institution (college, university, museum, NGO, etc.) with an institutional subscription to the *ARA*, or a more inclusive Annual Reviews site license, any *ARA* chapter can now be included in an online course reader in a way that is quick, requires no separate request for permission, and is free of additional cost.

What good news! A custom-designed reading packet of *ARA* material could hardly be more affordable or easier to assemble. The secret is that you can add *ARA* abstracts and/or chapters to your online syllabus, reading list, or other Web-based course materials simply by constructing free and easy Web links direct to the *ARA* online. Again, at subscribing institutions this requires no special permission from Annual Reviews and can be done in a matter of minutes from your own desk, or from the desk of a teaching assistant—who, in this day and age, can probably show you how. I thank my Stanford TA, Vernita Ediger, for proving to me that the process really is quick and simple. In brief, here's how it works: You simply add to your own online source document (such as a course syllabus, reading list, table of contents) a direct Web link to the abstract and/or full text of every online chapter you would like to use from the *ARA*. Currently, the Annual Reviews Web site, http://anthro.annualreviews.org, lists chapters and abstracts for all *ARA* volumes from 1996 to present, which amounts to over 130 chapters—a total that grows by more than 20 chapters per year. The present total includes more than 20 worthy chapters from each subfield the series handles, some of which have already been assembled into theme sections on particular topics (for example, the themes of the present volume are two: "AIDS" and "Diasporas"; themes from past volumes are listed at the back of each volume in the Cumulative Index of recent chapter titles). For teachers at institutions with an Annual Reviews site license, the news is still better: You can add to your reading list free links to any Annual Reviews publication, including chapters from the *Annual Review of Sociology*, the *Annual Review of Political Science*, or the *Annual Review of Ecology and Systematics*, for example.

The steps you'll take on your handy-dandy computer are approximately as follows (some details may need adjusting to suit your particular page editing software—I used the Composer® program that comes with Netscape Communicator, just to give you an example):

1. Using your page editor, open the source page to which you would like to add direct links. This could be any online page such as a course syllabus or list of readings that includes (or is about to include) at least one Annual Review chapter published since 1996. The source page usually bears an .htm suffix. If the *ARA* chapter is not already listed, type into an appropriate place on the source page the citation information (author, title, etc.), including the *ARA* volume and page numbers of the chapter(s) you wish to link.

2. Leave your online course page open. Now use your Web browser to visit the *Annual Review of Anthropology* home page (http://anthro.annualreviews. org; or, if your institution has an Annual Reviews site license, go to the corresponding home page for any Annual Reviews publication that has a chapter you want to include). By browsing tables of contents or using the search functions, navigate to the abstract or the full text chapter to which you wish to link. Copy to your clipboard the Web location (URL) of that page (the destination of your link), or jot it down: You will need it again momentarily.

3. Leaving the browser open to the destination page, click back to the source page and highlight the *ARA* citation information (e.g., journal name, volume, and page numbers). Then click on "Link" (in most editors this operation is available on a toolbar button or from a pull-down menu); an input box will appear. Prompted for a "Link to a page location or local file," copy from your clipboard the URL for the corresponding Annual Review chapter. (Note: The URL should end with identifying information for the chapter you have chosen—you'll see something like "26/1/567," which represents the volume number, issue number, and starting page number for the article you've chosen. If the URL goes on beyond this information, delete any excess characters so that the URL ends with the appropriate starting page number.) Click "Apply" to establish the link. It is that simple.

4. Repeat steps 1 through 3 for all the links you wish to create to Annual Review chapters. Then click "Save" to keep your hard work. Now visit your revised course page as your students will; check all the links (now colored blue) to make certain that they take users to the intended locations. If you are working on a copy of the source page, please remember to repost your updated code to the live server when you have finished editing. Voilà—you're done!

Although it may sound a bit intricate as outlined here, I'm certain that with practice it will prove about as painless a process of course reader creation as you have ever known. After a few minutes of practice, it took me only about 15 minutes to include six *ARA* links in the reader for my class on the Amazon—less time than it used to take me to find and deliver just the first chapter for a "custom published" reader to a local (permissions-paying!) xerocopier. Try it. I'd love to hear how it goes.

Readers who frequent the *ARA* home page will also notice that one can now access at any time "The 50 Most-Frequently-Read Articles" in the *ARA* (meaning the 50 that are most commonly viewed online, which I hope means "read") as well as "The 50 Most-Frequently Cited." Simply click on these entries on our home page—yet more helpful input when you are getting ready to prepare that next online course reader!

Fellow members of the Editorial Committee and I are always pleased to send a new volume off to the publisher, and that this volume marks the third decade of the *ARA* is particularly exciting. In addition to a bevy of fine chapters in the "AIDS" and "Diaspora" theme sections mentioned above, this volume is full of "don't miss" chapters, including those on ecotourism, kuru and prions, adaptation to altitude, and biodiversity prospecting. It is also a volume of transitions for the Editorial Committee, as Val Daniel and Bambi Schieffelin each complete their second terms of duty as Associate Editors. I am sure that many readers join in my salute to Val for all the intellectual strength and insight he has brought to these pages, especially to our section of Sociocultural Anthropology. Likewise, I know that I am not alone in appreciating the years of careful stewardship and intellectual guidance that Bambi has brought to many areas of our work, most notably to our section of Linguistics and Communicative Practices. Hats off to both of these colleagues for their years of dedicated editorial service. I am happy to report that the broad roles Val and Bambi have played will be filled in future years by Jean Comaroff (University of Chicago) and Jane Hill (University of Arizona), both of whom we are pleased to welcome back to the *ARA* in these new capacities. As always, I want again to express the gratitude that surely every Annual Review editor feels for the help of the production editor. More than any other person, Claire Insel deserves heaps of credit for pulling together this stimulating and worthwhile thirtieth anniversary volume.

William H. Durham
Editor

ERRATUM

Erratum for: Annu. Rev. Anthropol. 2000. 29:467–92.

**THE VISIBLE EVIDENCE OF CULTURAL PRODUCERS,
MAUREEN MAHON**

Please note, the acknowledgments should read:

A fall 1999 faculty fellowship at the Wesleyan University Center for the Humanities gave me the time and resources to complete this article. I thank the other Center fellows, Kate Brown, Michael Halberstam, Tom Huhn, and Sean McCann, and especially Center Director Elizabeth Traube for their stimulating conversations about aesthetics and politics. Keefe Murren provided valuable assistance, identifying sources and helping to compile the bibliography. I am grateful to Lila Abu-Lughod, Steve Feld, Faye Ginsburg, Brian Larkin, Meg McLagan, Fred Myers, Tim Raphael, Elizabeth Traube, and Jennifer Tucker for sharing manuscripts, sources, and inspiration along the way. Omissions and mistakes are, of course, my responsibility.

Annual Review of Anthropology
Volume 30, 2001

CONTENTS

ERRATA

An online log of corrections to *Annual Review of Anthropology*
chapters may be found at http://anthro.AnnualReviews.
org/errata.shtml

Related Articles

From the *Annual Review of Ecology and Systematics*, Volume 31, 2000:

  The Kinship Theory of Genomic Imprinting, David Haig

From the *Annual Review of Genetics*, Volume 35, 2001:

  Sir Francis Galton and the Birth of Eugenics, Nicholas W. Gillham

  The Genetic Architecture of Quantitative Traits, Trudy Mackay

  Informed Consent and Other Ethical Issues in Human Population Genetics, Henry Greely

From the *Annual Review of Genomics and Human Genetics*, Volume 2, 2001:

  Hundred-Year Search for the Human Genome, Frank Ruddle

  Human Genetics: Lessons from Quebec Populations, Charles R. Scriver

  Human Population Genetics: Lessons from Finland, Juha Kere

  Human Genetics on the Web, Alan E. Guttmacher

  The Genomics and Genetics of Human Infectious Disease Susceptibility, Adrian V. S. Hill

  The Genetics of Aging, Caleb E. Finch and Gary Ruvkun

From the *Annual Review of Neuroscience*, Volume 24, 2001:

  Prion Diseases of Humans and Animals: Their Causes and Molecular Basis, John Collinge

From the *Annual Review of Nutrition*, Volume 21, 2001:

  Nutritional Consequences of the African Diaspora, Amy Luke, Richard S. Cooper, T. Elaine Prewitt, Adebowale A. Adeyemo, and Terrence E. Forrester

  Dietary Regulation of Expression of Glucose-6-Phosphate Dehydrogenase, Lisa M. Salati and Batoul Amir-Ahmady

From the *Annual Review of Political Science*, Volume 4, 2001:

  Religion and Comparative Politics, Anthony Gill

  Biology and Politics: Linking Nature and Nurture, R. D. Masters

From the *Annual Review of Psychology*, Volume 52, 2001:

Sentence and Text Comprehension: Roles of Linguistic Structure, Charles Clifton Jr. and Susan A. Duffy

Psycholinguistics: A Cross-Language Perspective, Elizabeth Bates, Antonella Devescovi, and Beverly Wulfeck

Disrespect and the Experience of Injustice, Dale T. Miller

Evolutionary Psychology: Toward a Unifying Theory and a Hybrid Science, Linnda R. Caporael

From the *Annual Review of Public Health*, Volume 22, 2001:

The Social Ecology of Child Health and Well-Being, Felton Earls and Mary Carlson

Small-Community-Based Surveys, Ralph R. Frerichs and Magda A. Shaheen

Minisymposium on Obesity: Overview and Some Strategic Considerations, Shiriki K. Kumanyika

From the *Annual Review of Sociology*, Volume 27, 2001:

Urban Poverty After The Truly Disadvantaged: The Rediscovery of the Family, the Neighborhood, and Culture, Mario Luis Small and Katherine Newman

The Great Agricultural Transition: Crisis, Change, and Social Consequences of Twentieth Century US Farming, Linda Lobao and Katherine Meyer

Religious Nationalism and the Problem of Collective Representation, Roger Friedland

Socioeconomic Status and Class in Studies of Fertility and Health in Developing Countries, Kenneth A. Bollen, Jennifer L. Glanville, and Guy Stecklov

Is Globalization Civilizing, Destructive, or Feeble? A Critique of Five Key Debates in Social Science Literature, Mauro F. Guillén

Collective Identity and Social Movements, Francesca Polletta and James M. Jasper

Social Implications of the Internet, Paul DiMaggio, Eszter Hargittai, W. Russell Neuman, and John P. Robinson

Birds of a Feather: Homophily in Social Networks, Miller McPherson, Lynn Smith-Lovin, and James M. Cook

Early Traditions of African-American Sociological Thought, Alford A. Young Jr. and Donald R. Deskins, Jr.

ANNUAL REVIEWS is a nonprofit scientific publisher established to promote the advancement of the sciences. Beginning in 1932 with the *Annual Review of Biochemistry*, the Company has pursued as its principal function the publication of high-quality, reasonably priced *Annual Review* volumes. The volumes are organized by Editors and Editorial Committees who invite qualified authors to contribute critical articles reviewing significant developments within each major discipline. The Editor-in-Chief invites those interested in serving as future Editorial Committee members to communicate directly with him. Annual Reviews is administered by a Board of Directors, whose members serve without compensation.

Audrey Smedley

Annu. Rev. Anthropol. 2001. 30:xvii–xxxii

Travels and Adventures in an Unchartable Field

Audrey Smedley

Department of Sociology and Anthropology, Virginia Commonwealth University
Richmond, VA 23284; e-mail: asmedley@mail1.vcu.edu

Key Words   history, human variation, race, racism, culture, theory

■ **Abstract**   There was considerable optimism about the future of anthropology when I came into the field over forty years ago, at a time when World War II was still a meaningful memory, the Korean War was a subject of great agony, and Vietnam was not yet part of our consciousness. During the late 1950s I had developed an interest in experiencing other cultures, and this led me to the field of international studies and indirectly to anthropology. Anthropology seemed a very positive way to get to know about other peoples and their ways of life. Such knowledge would create greater understanding among all peoples, and particularly, it had the potential for reducing friction and avoiding conflict. Naively, I think, some of my contemporaries and I believed that the field would grow and become a powerful influence in international relations, providing the knowledge and strategies for establishing communication among peoples and promoting peaceful coexistence. We were very young then and inexperienced. In this overview I touch on only some of the high points of my experiences in anthropology over the past decades and briefly comment on some of my reactions to developments in the field.

INTRODUCTION TO ANTHROPOLOGY

Unlike many others I did not begin training in the discipline because of great interests in exotic people or bizarre customs. I knew nothing about the field of anthropology when I made my first journey abroad on a junior year program that turned out to be much more. A friend at the University of Michigan had discovered a special course in French civilization for foreign students that she said was really cheap and would allow us to live in Paris on $50 per month as students and travel extensively by hitchhiking during holidays. I had just finished a third year in a program of letters and law offered at the university and was planning on entering the law school. But my experiences at a university where there were only about 200 black students (out of over 25,000) had begun to frazzle and to erode the psychological strength I had been able to muster just to go there.[1]

---

[1]It is deliciously ironic that the University of Michigan is today one of a few universities that is fighting in the courts to keep affirmative action.

0084-6570/01/1021-xvii$14.00

Until the early 1950s, black students could not eat in any of the restaurants, get their hair cut in a barbershop, or try on clothing in some of the stores on State Street in the heart of the university. Until 1949 when some dorms were opened to them, black men and most black women lived in private homes in segregated communities off campus. On campus, housing was usually segregated and some dorms were restricted to whites only. During my second year, after the graduation of my black roommate, there was a major dilemma in my dorm when no other black female was available to share my room. When finally a white student with no apparent problems offered to room with me, it set off a minor scandal that left her defending that decision to her friends. I think that she lost some of them but did not appear to care. During that same year, I had run and been elected to the student legislature, which exposed me to many more incidents of overt and subtle prejudice. By the end of the third year I was exhausted from the weight of such racist experiences from both students and faculty, not to mention the many incidents of insults, rudeness, hatred, and contempt from the public. I decided that I needed to experience a society in which racism did not exist. (The daily onslaught of racially motivated insults and slights have been called by some psychologists "micro-aggressions." They now study these to understand their influence on the mental and physical health of low-status racial minorities.)

Paris was indeed a haven for American blacks who had established a fairly substantial ex-patriot presence after World War II. No one looked at you with the kind of irrational and unmitigated contempt that you could find in the United States. Salespeople, waiters, and waitresses did not belittle, ignore, or insult you, nor did anybody else, and no one was deliberately rude to you because of your "race." Black Americans learned to relinquish that guarded behavior that we have often been forced to bring to relationships with the white "others." More than anything else, one learned something about the nature of one's own humanity while experiencing an almost indescribable freedom that we knew we could never realize in the United States. Once while visiting the black writer Richard Wright, who had long lived in Paris, I heard someone describe this experience as "elevating, uplifting, liberating, like going to heaven!" Few people knew as well as black Americans, especially at that time, the meaning of "yearning to breathe free."

Yet Paris was more than that. For the first time I met people from different parts of Africa, from Haiti, Tahiti, and other South Seas islands, and from areas of the world that I had not even heard about. What amazed me was that they were French! It did not occur to me at the time, but I made a connection with a profound truth that was to become a significant part of my anthropological perspective. Biological features, especially in a society where "race" was of little importance, have nothing to do with a person's behavior or culture. Of the seven or eight thousand black African students at the University of Paris, none spoke or acted like "Negroes" in my country. They walked like Frenchmen, spoke like Frenchmen, acted like Frenchmen, and thought like Frenchmen. I had never experienced black men and women with such a sense of wholesome self-confidence.

At one point in my stay in Paris, I met a young man in the American library who looked like an ordinary black American, a nice-looking brown-skinned man with crinkly hair and a nice smile. Happy to see someone from "my" background, I started up a conversation. He spoke English like an American and told me he was from Chicago. We started hanging out together, and it was weeks before I began to realize that something was unusual about "Jimmy" from Chicago. I discovered that he spoke several different languages fluently and knew many students from different cultures. At the same time he seemed strange in his comings and goings. Finally after an afternoon in a Moroccan market it all became clear. "Jimmy" was really Jenah, was actually Moroccan, had never been to Chicago or any other place in the United States, and had learned his American-style English from watching American movies. He had taken pleasure in knowing that he could deceive even Americans by his mannerisms and speech. This taught me another lesson about learned behavior, how easy it is to acquire the behavioral traits of another culture (at least for some people). This experience undoubtedly inspired in me some of the first glimpses of a new way of looking at the world. For one thing, it raised questions about the meaning of race. As a Moroccan, Jenah was classified as an Arab and thus "white" in the American scheme of racial ideology. In Chicago, he most certainly would have been seen as "black."

I cite these experiences to convey a sense of the wider social contexts in which minority scholars have had to maneuver their lives and careers. Native Americans and blacks are generally always conscious of their low-status racial identity. To achieve any degree of success, it often takes an enormous effort to transcend the identities imposed on us and the stereotypes too many people deal us (Campbell 1998, Churchhill 1998, Jaimes 1994, Harrison 1995, Harrison & Harrison 1999). This is particularly true in the world of academia where there are always a few whites who feel the need to provide us with frequent reminders that we do not really belong. It is part of the possessive investment in whiteness that dictates constant reaffirmation of such social placement (Lipsitz 1998).

UNIVERSITY OF MICHIGAN AND THE NEO-EVOLUTIONISTS

When I returned to the United States after hitchhiking through much of western Europe and even crossing the Straits of Gibraltar and wandering around in North Africa, I was a very different person. Changing my major, I took a degree in letters and law and history, a field in which I already had many courses, and later enrolled in the master's program in anthropology at the University of Michigan. Simultaneously, I continued studies in history. Albert Hourani's courses in the history of Islam proved to be extremely valuable as well as enjoyable. So also were courses in English and American constitutional history. Leslie White and Elman Service were my mentors in anthropology.

It was perhaps fortunate that I began my career in a department where evolutionary theory was the major focus. Not only was the evolutionary perspective compatible with my general orientation toward, and interest in, history, but from the beginning I was able to grasp how evolution—essentially a process of change over time—could explain much of human cultural development. The works of White (1959, 1969) and Steward (1955) revealed the heuristic potential of the ecological perspective, an approach that recognized interconnections among cultural realities, the natural and social environments, and events of the past.

At the same time, the degree to which evolutionary theory could be construed to reflect notions of European "racial" superiority was not lost in the academic enterprise. One could not read Tyler, Morgan, Maine, not to mention Spencer, Galton, Darwin, and other writers of the nineteenth century, without recognizing the hubris of European male dominance and the elite view of world realities. The problem with too many of the evolutionists is that they imposed a value system on the changes and presumed that significant transformations in technology meant progress. Progress was defined in terms of all those recognizable stages that came closer by degrees to contemporary European societies, or at least to the educated upper-class elements of those societies. Thus, whether it was changes in the forms of marriage (from polygyny to monogamy), or improvements in the weapons of warfare, European evolutionists were prone to see evolutionary change as mimicking the historical trajectory of Europe. I did not know it at the time, but there was some irony in the fact that this late nineteenth-century era of developments in the social sciences also corresponded to the peak period of the development of racial ideology under which all human achievements were interpreted as products of race identity (Gossett 1997, Hannaford 1996, Smedley 1999). Still, my interests in the history of the field were stimulated even as I recognized the racial ideology that subsumed the works of so many of the early writers in anthropology.

At the same time, it was under the influence of scholars like Leslie White, Elman Service, and Marshall Sahlins that many elements came together in my thinking about the human condition. White's conception of evolutionary change did not depend on the racial science of the previous generations of evolutionists. His theory of the nature of culture and his promotion of a field of study that he called culturology, separated the domain of culture (a phenomenon based on the use of the symbol) from its connection to biology (White 1969, White & Dillingham 1973). He took Boas' (1940) distinction of race, language, and culture to its highest degree, identifying a realm of reality that was a thing sui generis. He helped us to see that virtually no aspect of human behavior, from the most intimate and basic to the most remote and abstract, was uninfluenced by some cultural (learned) meaning, norm, value, belief, or sentiment.

It was tantamount to a minor epiphany for me; the idea of culture as learned behavior had an enormous impact on me because such a revelation explained and confirmed my own empirical experiences. White argued that one can hold the biological variations in the human species constant and that human behavior consists of learned acts, thoughts, and ways of looking at the world that are superorganic.

Culture itself was presumed to have evolved following laws of change that were external to the biology of the people who carried that culture. The task of the evolutionary anthropologist was to identify the laws of cultural change. White saw these laws largely as arising from the techno-economic sphere of culture in which major variations could be explained by differentials in the harnessing of energy or by the efficiency in the use of energy. All of this could and should be studied independently of the biological characteristics of human populations or the psychological propensities of individuals. White emphasized Tyler's definition of culture and transformed it by adding the caveat "and based upon the use of the symbol." (White 1969, 1959). Symboling, the attribution of (arbitrary) meaning to things and events in the outside world, is a product of our evolved human nature; that it is shared by all of the human species is manifest in the fact that all normal humans can learn any culture. This concept of culture was sustained by Kroeber, Lowie, and other early anthropologists, even as they and other experts began to debate the multiple meanings of culture (Harris 1968).

Whatever their other failings, many of the early evolutionists and diffusionists appeared to have an understanding of culture as a phenomenon that should be studied separately from the biological beings who carry specific cultures. This view was often expressed, even by German and other European scholars, in terms of the "psychic unity of mankind" and by early Enlightenment philosophers who strongly promoted the idea of learning or enculturation. But the principle of treating culture as existing in a domain independent of biology was not well developed, and it is likely that many of those who expressed this view never fully comprehended its implications. Later generations of anthropologists did not seem to go beyond the simple assertion that culture was not related to biology or to language. Thus Leslie White's theoretical perspectives never really took hold among professional anthropologists; his vision of culturology as the science of culture never materialized as the new field he proposed, not even among most of his students. The major critique of culturology was that it ignored human agency and did not provide for the operation of individual free will. Many of White's critics failed to understand the multilayered, multifaceted nature of his evolutionism; he clearly recognized that humans make choices, but always in the context of a limited range of culturally created options. His critics also saw his theories as too materialistic and deterministic.

In time, however, I came to realize that the implications of structuring a field that ignored biological or biogenetic variations in humans as causative factors in human behavior are totally inconsistent with the prevailing ways by which Americans have interpreted human behavior. That is, it contradicts our racial ideology, what I have called the racial worldview (Smedley 1999). Since race ideology reached its zenith at about the same time that the various schools of anthropology emerged, the progenitors of the field could not have operated outside of this worldview that depended heavily on hereditarian ideas. Racial explanations, as a component of the developing sciences, appeared as the Enlightenment declined at the end of the eighteenth century and soon superseded all other causal explanations in human affairs. It subsequently became a powerful and deeply embedded facet of Western consciousness.

Because of the power of the racial worldview, various strands of our anthropological enterprise have reflected continuing opposition to White's contributions and the ramifications of his theories, although there continue to be some anthropologists who are concerned with developing a science of culture (see for a recent example O'Meara 1997, Harris 1997). Some subfields or trends, like sociobiology, have emerged as significant themes in the continuing effort to identify biological causes of social behavior. Although not an overtly racist position, what many sociobiologists appear to assume is that inherited group tendencies or differences, as well as individual ones, may well determine how various subgroups act and function in society. But the ways in which people are grouped are virtually always socially determined, and genetic inheritance may have nothing to do with it. No one has yet found genes that directly determine any form of social behavior, kinship or otherwise (Sahlins 1976, Lewontin et al 1984, Lewontin 1992, Rose 1979). Those ethologists or evolutionary biologists who are researching species-specific human behavior and their possible genetic correlates, or tracing patterns of immune processes, or examining the health consequences of public policy decisions are on much sounder ground (Goodman & Leatherman 1998).

The "neo-evolutionists" were outstanding theorists of the first half of the twentieth century. Although today some colleagues may eschew their categories of "bands," "tribes," and "chiefdoms," they introduced us to a new approach for understanding so-called pre-industrial societies based on the complex ways that such societies interacted with their natural and social environments. Many who refined this approach to the study of culture(s) have been called cultural ecologists, and their perspective has led to numerous insights into the causal factors behind many behavioral/cultural variations, both institutionalized and idiosyncratic (Bates 1998, Cronk 1991, Harris 1988, Rappaport 1968, Sahlins 1964). Barth (1969, 1981) for example, has provided us with models of multiple strands of interaction and decision-making, in given habitats, that have taken place in the past and led to conventionalized customs and actions. The use of the concept adaptive interaction opens up a wealth of possibilities for investigating connections among cultural customs, features of the environment, and interactive processes. In later years I turned to the perspective of cultural ecology in large part because so much of the general view regarding the adaptive interactions of societies within a particular kind of environment made sense to me. This approach has been seminal for my own work on the Birom, where I introduced new insights and ways of explaining habits and customs that I believe have been overlooked (see below).

FROM EVOLUTION TO BRITISH FUNCTIONALISM

The transition from an evolutionary school to one most notably identified with English functionalists may have been perceived by some as an experience in contradictions. For me, the experience at the University of Manchester was enlightening and enriching. In the 1950s and 1960s, social anthropology at Manchester had achieved the pinnacle of academic prominence. Its faculty and students under the leadership of Max Gluckman, who had been appointed to develop the department in 1949, had produced dozens of outstanding books and numerous articles that gave it a distinct reputation. Most of their work had been in Africa where I also wanted to do field research. Although I considered enrolling at Cambridge, virtually everyone who knew of the extraordinary works of British anthropologists declared that Manchester was the place to be. Kathleen Gough and David Aberle were particularly influential in my decision to go to Manchester.

The British approach in anthropology, unfortunately criticized by many Americans, introduced us to a way of looking at and analyzing social systems that to me was compatible with the perspective of the neo-evolutionists. If evolution is perceived as changes in form or function of an organism over time, one could hardly understand or research evolutionary processes without some form of functionalist understanding of social systems. Intellectually, I welcomed the analytic approach of the functionalists; it clearly made sense to tease apart relationships among social features and to be able to discern their interconnections with other aspects of culture. Unlike many of its critics, I saw structural-functionalism as a necessary and dynamic approach to the understanding of human social systems.

The social anthropologists at Manchester were about much more than simple structural-functionalism. All had done intensive field research and were known for their mastery of ethnographic details. Many (e.g., Elizabeth Colson, J.C. Mitchell, and John Barnes) had lived and worked under the auspices of the Rhodes-Livingtone Institute in East Africa while Gluckman was director (M. Gluckman, unpublished manuscript). Among other scholars at Manchester, some for varying periods, were Emrys Peters, Bill Watson, Victor Turner, Ian Cunnison, Scarlett and A.L. Epstein, Mary Douglas, Clyde Mitchell, Aiden Southall, Abner Cohen, Jay Singh, Martin Southwold, Richard Werbner, Tom Lupton, Emmanuel Marx, Paul Baxter, Richard Antoun, and many others. A unique aspect of the training at Manchester were the long seminars in which different scholars discussed their own work and benefited from the criticisms and comments of others. We often started in the mid-afternoon in the department and ended up late in the evening, still discussing critical matters, in the local pub. We had thoroughgoing discussions of the importance of social networks, the use of social dramas, the analysis of social conflict, the documentation of economic and social changes, politics and political processes, the nature and significance of ritual, lineage relationships, the stability of marriage, studies of customary law and its response to social change, and numerous other topics. Rather than static structural-functionalist analyses, we were drawn to the recognition of social *processes* and their transformations over time. It was this emphasis on the social process that helped to make Manchester unique and that attracted many visiting scholars from Oxford, Cambridge, London, and other universities.

Even as we delved into the ethnographic materials on social relations, at the back of my mind was the important connection with the habitat, especially with the production of strategic resources necessary for survival. The logical significance of environmental features to the strategies by which peoples organize themselves and make a living was obvious and comprehensible. I was intrigued by the intricate ways around which human beings sort out their lives and garner meaning from the process. I was eager to get into the field, somewhere in Africa. I applied for and received a Ford Foundation research fellowship for two years of field research.

FIELD RESEARCH

The decision to do field research in northern Nigeria was influenced by a number of things. I had read about the opening of tin mines in northern Nigeria earlier in the twentieth century along with descriptions of local populations that had seemingly been little touched by the outside world. It was not a pristine laboratory situation, but the remoteness of the Jos plateau and the small scale of these societies appealed to me. The fact that the climate was mild without the moist tropical heat of southern regions also factored into that decision. I looked forward with great anticipation to field research and thought I was well prepared for it.

The hospitality with which I was received warmed me to the Birom people. Every day was too short for learning all the things I wanted to know. I loved the lilt of the Birom language and found that children were the best teachers. In time I settled into a compound with an agnatic kin group of 30 people (one child was born while I was there but died soon after birth). Although some of the kinspeople gave me a Birom name (Katchallom = bush cow, referring to a hearty survivor!), I think it was always clear that I was a guest, an outsider, who had come to live among them. They did not expect that I would assume an identity within their culture. For my part I never felt alone, alienated, or fearful, a fact that surprised some people from the outside world. I had thought that the proverbial culture shock would be more jarring for someone who had always lived with some degree of creature comforts, but physical adjustment was not too difficult. However, culture shock and that broad-ranging phenomenon we call homesickness can take many forms and produce unanticipated results.

Initially I thought that I would focus my research on the impact of tin-mining on the plateau. However, circumstances guided more of my attention to the inner workings of social life. Living in a compound, I had access day and night to the kin group and shared in their observations about many things. Numerous customs, such as the levirate and cicisbeism, fascinated me, and the more I learned about the nature of kinship and the interlinkages among individuals, the more fascinating these things became. I did collect a great deal of information about the tin-mining community along with statistics on the employment of indigenous peoples in the mines. Yet it was the entire society, inclusive of their experiences in the minesfield, that prompted my greater interests and concerns. I concentrated on the daily lives of the Birom people, who happened to live in some of the poorest communities in all of Nigeria. The poverty was fundamentally a product of an environment in which few food crops would grow well. The Jos plateau provided an unremittingly harsh human habitat; people had to eke a living out of soils of very low fertility, exacerbated by the fact that mining activities had destroyed some of the richest soils in the river valleys. It was in this context that I formulated my research for understanding how people coped and survived.

ENTERING THE PROFESSION

After returning from the field, I was hired at Wayne State University in Detroit and began my first real acquaintance with the profession of American anthropology and with anthropologists. As was customary with new people, I began teaching introductory courses and advanced courses in social and cultural anthropology. My interests in the history of anthropology and the history of theory led to these courses being added to the repertoire as I submerged myself in the literature.

Because of my courses on African ethnography, I also became involved with the development of Afro-American studies. Like many black scholars, I had long been aware of the distorted and sanitized versions of American history and the negative portrayals of Africans and African-Americans conveyed to American students. As a result of my English experiences, I discovered British writers of African history like Basil Davidson and archaeologists who had begun the important corrective to the way in which Western history has dealt with Africa (Arkell 1961, Bovill 1968, Caton-Thompson 1971, Chittick 1974, Curtin 1964, Connah 1987, Davidson 1970, Ross 1979, Shinnie 1965, Thompson 1969, and many others). At the request of students I began teaching African history along with ethnography. I also began to read a great deal about colonialism, the role of anthropologists in the colonial setting, and African responses to colonialism (Boahen 1987). My curiosity had been triggered by experiences with English colonial representatives in West Africa. Like many anthropologists I often found that the English colonial "types" were ethnographically more interesting in many ways than the "natives." Along with evangelical fundamentalist American missionaries, they were some of the more strange and exotic peoples living in Third World communities.

Misgivings about the field of anthropology soon emerged and caused me much anguish, especially as I contemplated publishing the results of my field research. Would my work be received as just another description of some "primitive" people to be catalogued away with all the others and misinterpreted as some form of denigration of people long exploited and ignored? Recent publications have acknowledged the acquiescence in and often direct participation of some of the first anthropologists in colonial governments (Asad 1988, Kuklick 1991, Salamone 2000). Would my work be identified with this category of early anthropologists? Would I be accused of complicity in the exploitation of the people among whom I lived? Is it possible that what I might publish would ultimately cause these people some harm? What was my responsibility to them, to the discipline (if any), and to my own sense of integrity and honor? While in the field I had never been asked to provide any sort of information to any government official. Indeed, I rarely saw or met anyone with a position responsible to either the colonial government or the independent government after October 1960. Even when I was permitted to look at the records of the mining companies, no one ever sought information from me. Most assumed that they already knew everything worth knowing about the "pagans." I had access to many government records but never participated in any discussion about them or the people of the plateau.

The generation of anthropologists with and by whom I was trained were extraordinary for their often stated opposition to policies of the colonizing nations and even for their radical political beliefs (Burton 1992, Kuklick 1991, Kuper 1988). Yet I still felt uneasy about my role as a Western anthropologist and observer.

One of the realities that bothered me was the critics' confusion of the methodology and theoretical orientation of early British anthropologists with their personal roles vis-à-vis the colonial presence. Functionalism should be interpreted as merely a guiding theory about the nature of human societies everywhere and not as a characterization of a political stance. To argue, as some of its critics did, that functionalists cannot deal with social or cultural change and therefore that the interests of British functionalists were only in features that maintained social stability and order and that supported colonial regimes, is to impose on functionalism unnecessary and irrelevant qualities and characteristics. It also means damning the method because of the individuals who use and promote it. If one wants to understand how any society works at any point in time, one must take a functionalist perspective. This is what all of the social sciences are supposed to do when they are analyzing social systems (Hempel 1959). The organic analogy, if not taken too far, has provided many useful insights into social systems, but it should not be confused with conservative political values. That some early anthropologists saw their work as a means of supporting colonial regimes does not invalidate the functionalist approach. Functionalism is not and cannot reveal anything about change until one also incorporates a dynamic dimension and observes how things interact and relate to one another over time. In the same way, history is not evolution; that is, reconstructions of historical events cannot tell us much about how societies undergo change unless we know how particular elements interrelate at different points in time.

Much of the criticism of the structural-functionalist school comes from the American school of anthropology, identified as the historical-particularist school associated with Boas and some of his students. It is an unfortunate part of the history of anthropology that scholars following different methods or theories or trends of thought have felt it necessary to debunk previous theories and to focus on magnifying differences in order to legitimize their own perspectives (Harris 1968, Stocking 1968). Perhaps because of my eclectic background I have never felt it necessary to become an adherent to any of the exclusive schools of anthropology. Rather I chose to see developments in the field as a cumulative enterprise under which different theories may provide useful insights or perhaps new ways of approaching and formulating information about the rich legacy of human cultures for different purposes.

COMING TO "RACE" AND THE RACIAL WORLDVIEW

In the early 1970s, I had an opportunity to spend two years at the Radcliffe (now Bunting) Institute, an event that was to change my life and the focus of my interests. While in Cambridge I prepared a book manuscript based on my field research among the Birom that had part of its emphasis on the social construction of gender roles. This occurred at a time when the feminist movement was on the rise and some scholars were drawing great attention to women in society. Numerous publications examining the roles of women in different cultures and attempting to establish theories about gender and sex suddenly appeared on the scene. A newly crafted feminist philosophy, for which I had much sympathy, appeared and tended to dominate virtually all scholarly works on gender. When several publishers reviewed my description of the Birom manuscript, however, they let it be known that this book would not sell for a simple reason. My work did not reflect the prevailing feminist philosophy regarding the universal oppression of women. In fact, the study even suggested that women, at least in some societies, may have been instrumental in creating some of the features of patrilineal ideology. Such a heretical approach, as this was seen at the time, could not be entertained by publishers who were already under stress because of the oil crises of the mid-1970s and the steep rise in the costs of publishing. Although I published a few papers on Birom women (Smedley 1974, 1980), the larger ethnographic study was eventually put aside as other matters commanded my attention. I later regretted that I had not continued to pursue the publishing of this manuscript at that time. Max Gluckman had read and recommended it for publication before his death, writing that he was "stunned and amazed" by the analysis and declaring that it was a first-class job. Also I was pleased when I later learned that Paul Bohannan, whom I have never met but for whom I have great respect, had been asked to read the manuscript, and that he called it "superb."

While living in Cambridge I met some of the black faculty then teaching at Harvard. During some of our discussions, Preston Williams, a professor of divinity at Harvard, thought it might be useful to gather together a few black scholars and do something on race. This was a topic to which I had already given considerable thought, and in fact I had read a paper at the American Anthropological Association meetings in the early 1960s on the history of racism in anthropology. I continued to discover new materials from the research for my courses in the history of anthropology. At William's urging I agreed to prepare a manuscript on the history of the idea of race as a working paper that might profitably be used for discussions of new approaches to the treatment of race.

After leaving Cambridge and taking a position at the State University of New York at Binghamton, I made use of funds we had from a Ford Foundation grant to hire students to continue research on this history. Within several years we had amassed a great amount of materials, developed some new insights into U.S. history, and in 1978 I decided to introduce a new course on the origin and evolution of the idea of race. Recognizing that there was no textbook covering all the materials for the course, by the mid-1980s I had decided to write my own. The result was *Race in North America: Origin and Evolution of a Worldview*, first published in 1993. Although it was designed to be primarily a textbook, I thought such information could also be useful for the educated public. There have long been thousands of books on the subject of race, mostly written by sociologists and historians, but few within or outside of anthropology had ever looked at the history of the idea or questioned the biological reality of race.

It was interesting to discover later that a number of other scholars in different disciplines were also becoming interested in the history of the idea and especially in the reality of race as a cultural invention. Whereas the anthropologist Ashley-Montagu (1969) had questioned the reality of biological races as early as 1941, few in our field had followed his leadership (some exceptions are Barkan 1992, Brace 1969, Livingstone 1962, and Stepan 1982). Indeed, anthropologists had become timid about race and racism. Little attention was given to the problem during and after the decades of the Civil Rights Movement. More than that, I became aware that anthropologists were really no different from individuals in other fields who would rather not deal with the phenomenon of race. One anthropologist even admitted to me, unabashedly, that he was "uncomfortable with blacks and Indians." He reflected the attitudes of the general white public, which by the 1970s and 1980s was weary of black activism and ignorant of the realities of the lived experience of racism and the distortions of history and social realities that have so denigrated blacks and other "racial" minorities and profoundly influenced white behavior (see Gregory & Sanjek 1994, Omi & Winant 1994, Smedley 1998a).

Minority scholars have long known that most of our white friends and colleagues have little knowledge or experience of racism. They are not even aware that they view the world through a racialized lens and consider that their beliefs about human variation are normal and shared with all others. Most people, blacks as well as whites, have no sense of the pathology reflected in the racial worldview, or how abnormal racial designations and race as a form of social identity actually are. It is only with recent publications about the nature of white race identity that some scholars have begun to question the whole phenomenon of race and what it has meant in American society and elsewhere (Allen 1994, 1997; Brodkin 1994; Ignatiev 1995; Jacobson 1998; Lipsitz 1998). We have only begun to realize how strange and aberrant has been the attribution of social identity based on physical appearance and ancestry in a world of thousands of specialized occupations, skills, interests, diverse knowledge, and value orientations that more clearly define who we are (Smedley 1998b).

It was during the decade before the publication of the race book that I terminated my membership in the American Anthropological Association and other organizations and distanced myself from developments in the field. In the meetings that I had attended, it seemed that the interests of most people had veered toward matters that to me were esoteric, irrelevant, and uninteresting. The emergence of the post-modernists, or some of them, seemed to me an exercise in ego-involvement that not only was not productive, but was more reflective of the self-centered nature of American individualism than anything else. Even the discussions and debates over theory that had been so absorbing in my student years seemed to have been lost or subverted.

It was also during this time that newly established black studies departments and programs were languishing, and many black scholars turned to developing or supporting these new fields. In this era numerous new publications on the histories and experiences of minority peoples convinced us that there were far more significant and meaningful things to learn than to focus on the intricacies of some remote culture. I devoted most of my time, energy, and attention to preserving and protecting our small department of black faculty at Binghamton University in the face of much opposition or indifference from white academics and numerous internal problems. Faculty in every black studies program or department in the United States were always aware that we were prejudged by most whites as incompetent or mediocre at best. Some of us constantly felt the need to insist on the credibility, validity, and academic value of the field. And all of this was very stressful. The unfortunate truth is that many universities felt pressured to acquire black faculty as rapidly as possible, and some of those hired to constitute such programs were not well trained and had little experience with university policies and practices at the faculty level.

RETURNING TO INTERESTS IN SOCIAL ANTHROPOLOGY: WOMEN AND PATRILINY

However, my interests in social systems and especially in theory have not diminished. After the completion of the revised and enlarged second edition of the "race" book (1999), I decided to revisit the manuscript on the Birom. This decision was inspired in part by the appearance of new studies by African and black American women anthropologists that have raised questions about the application of Western feminist theory to African societies (see the preface to Amadiume 1987, the papers in Mikell 1997, Mullings 1997, and Oppong 1983). I found myself in agreement with Amadiume that the feminist presupposition of women's universal inferiority and subordination is in fact ethnocentric; the universal subordination of women was not a conclusion that I could make based on my readings and research in Africa. Moreover, the similarities in the observations and interpretations of women's roles by African women scholars to my much earlier work have encouraged me to publish the Birom study (Smedley 2002). The data and conclusions from my study have also precipitated an interest in a related and much larger question; that is, whether some features of patrilineal systems that we have interpreted as oppressive to women may have been introduced by women themselves in furtherance of their own interests as they saw them. Most societies in the world organize themselves on the principle of patriliny, and their cultures manifest varying features and intensities of patrilineal ideology. In some occasional lectures, I have hypothesized that one explanation for the predominance of patrilineal structure and ideology is that women themselves may have invented them. Although my anthropological concerns in the past have not focused primarily on women, this is a fascinating question that I hope to research more fully in the future.

In the meantime, I have been called upon for numerous other publications, articles, book chapters, encyclopedia entries, and lectures on race and racism, on slavery, and other related topics. Race is a subject that will not disappear at any time in the predictable future, and we all need to confront it. Harrison (1995, 1997) and other anthropologists (Baker 1998, Blakey 1987, Shanklin 1994, Smedley 1998a, Williams 1991) have brilliantly informed us about the ways in which race has been treated in anthropology and other social sciences. In many publications, too numerous to mention, we have seen attempts to dilute the significance of race, or to conflate and confuse race with ethnicity, or to incorporate within ethnic territory certain biological attributes formerly used to refer to race. Even as geneticists and biologists conclude that there are no races, an insidious transformation in discourses explaining social inequities is occurring. "Culture" has been reified as the new explication for black backwardness and poverty, and "black culture" has become a euphemism for innate inferiority.

Of all scholars, anthropologists should understand the limitations that race and class impose on the lifestyles of subgroups in our society and combat those trends that perpetuate elements of hereditarian ideology. We also need to use our introspective skills to examine the deeply entrenched feelings that prevent scholars from transcending racial thought. Race is not an abstraction nor a matter of individual private opinions. Race is a substantive institutionalized reality that Americans experience every day and we need to treat it as such. But before anthropology can hope to provide solutions to human problems or even inform us much about the nature of such problems, it must divest itself of the racial elements that often rest just below the surface of its own imaginations.

Visit the Annual Reviews home page at www.AnnualReviews.org

LITERATURE CITED

Allen TW. 1994. *The Invention of the White Race*, Vol. 1. London/New York: Verso

Allen TW. 1997. *The Invention of the White Race*, Vol. 2. London/New York: Verso

Amadiume I. 1987. *Male Daughters, Female Husbands: Gender and Sex in an African Society*. London: Zed Books

Arkell AJ. 1961. *A History of the Sudan from the Earliest Times to 1821*. London: Univ. London Press. 2nd ed.

Asad T, ed. 1988. *Anthropology and the Colonial Encounter*. Atlantic Highlands, NJ: Humanities Press

Baker LD. 1998. *From Savage to Negro: Anthropology and the Construction of Race, 1896–1954*. Berkeley: Univ. Calif. Press

Barkan E. 1992. *The Retreat of Scientific Racism*. Cambridge/New York: Cambridge Univ. Press

Barth F. 1969. *Ethnic Groups and Boundaries: The Social Organization of Cultural Differences*. London: Allen Unwin

Barth F. 1981. *Process and Form in Social Life*. London: Routledge Kegan Paul

Bates DG. 1998. *Human Adaptive Strategies*. Boston, MA/London: Allyn Bacon

Blakey ML. 1987. Skull doctors: intrinsic social and political bias in the history of American physical anthropology, with special reference to the work of Ales Hrdlicka. *Crit. Anthropol.* 7(2):7–35

Boahen AA. 1987. *African Perspectives on Colonialism.* Baltimore, MD: Johns Hopkins Univ. Press

Boas F. 1940. *Race, Language and Culture.* New York: Oxford Univ. Press

Bovill EW. 1968. *The Golden Trade of the Moors.* London: Oxford Univ. Press. 2nd ed.

Brace CL. 1969. A nonracial approach towards the understanding of human diversity. In *The Concept of Race*, ed. A Montagu, pp. 103–52. New York: Collier Books

Brodkin K. 1994. *How Jews Became White Folks and What that Says about Race in America.* New Brunswick: Rutgers Univ. Press

Burton JW. 1992. Representing Africa: colonial anthropology revisited. *J. Asian Afr. Studies.* 27:3–4

Campbell G, ed. 1998. *Many Americas: Critical Perspectives on Race, Racism, and Ethnicity.* Dubuque, IA: Kendall/Hunt

Caton-Thompson G. 1971. *The Zimbabwe Culture: Ruins and Reactions.* London: Cass. 2nd ed.

Chittick HN. 1974. Kilwa: An Islamic trading city on the East African Coast. Nairobi: Gov. Print. Off.

Churchhill W. 1998. *Fantasies of the Master Race.* San Francisco, CA: City Lights Books

Connah G. 1987. *African Civilizations.* New York: Cambridge Univ. Press

Cronk L. 1991. Human behavioral ecology. *Annu. Rev. Anthropol.* 20:25–53

Curtin PD. 1964. *The Image of Africa: British Ideas and Action, 1780–1850.* Madison: Univ. Wisc. Press

Davidson B. 1970. *The Lost Cities of Africa.* Boston: Little, Brown

Goodman AH, Leatherman TL. 1998. *Building a New Biocultural Synthesis: Political-Economic Perspectives on Human Biology.* Ann Arbor: Univ. Mich. Press

Gossett T. (1965) 1997. *Race: the History of an Idea in America.* New York: Oxford Univ. Press

Gregory S, Sanjek R, eds. 1994. *Race.* New Brunswick: Rutgers Univ. Press

Hannaford I. 1996. *Race: the History of an Idea in the West. Washington, DC: Woodrow Wilson Cent. Press.* Baltimore: Johns Hopkins Univ. Press

Harris M. 1968. *Rise of Anthropological Theory.* New York: Thomas Y. Crowell

Harris M. 1988. *Culture, People, Nature: An Introduction to General Anthropology.* New York: Harper

Harris M. 1997. "Comment" on "Causation and the struggle for a science of culture," by Tim O'Meara. *Curr. Anthropol.* 38:410–14

Harrison FV. 1995. The persistent power of "race" in the cultural and political economy of racism. *Annu. Rev. Anthropol.* 24:47–74

Harrison FV, ed. 1997. *Decolonizing Anthropology: Moving Further Toward an Anthropology of Liberation.* Washington: Am. Anthropol. Assoc. 2nd ed.

Harrison FV, Harrison IE. 1999. *African American Pioneers in Anthropology.* Urbana/Chicago: Univ. Ill. Press

Hempel CG. 1959. *The logic of functional analysis*, ed. L Guse. Symp. Soc. Theory. New York: Harper Row

Ignatiev N. 1995. *How the Irish Became White.* New York: Routledge

Jacobson MF. 1998. *Whiteness of a Different Color: European Immigrants and the Alchemy of Race.* Cambridge, MA: Harvard Univ. Press

Jaimes MA. 1994. American racism: The impact on American-Indian identity and survival. In *Race*, ed. S Gregory, R. Sanjek, pp. 41–61. New Brunswick, NJ: Rutgers Univ. Press

Kuklick H. 1991. *The Savage Within: The Social History of British Anthropology, 1885–1945.* Cambridge, UK: Cambridge Univ. Press

Kuper A. 1988. *The Invention of Primitive Society: Transformations of an Illusion.* London/New York: Routledge

Lewontin RC. 1992. *Biology as Ideology: the Doctrine of DNA.* New York: Harper-Collins

Lewontin RC, Rose S, Kamin L. 1984. *Not in our Genes: Biology, Ideology and Human Nature.* New York: Pantheon Books

Lipsitz G. 1998. *The Possessive Investment in Whiteness: How White People Profit from Identity Politics.* Philadelphia, PA: Temple Univ. Press

Livingstone FB. 1962. On the non-existence of human races. *Curr. Anthropol.* 3:279–81

Mikell G, ed. 1997. *African Feminism: the Politics of Survival in Sub-Saharan Africa.* Philadelphia, PA: Univ. Penn. Press

Montagu A, ed. 1969. *The Concept of Race.* New York: Collier Books

Mullings L. 1997. *On Our Own Terms: Race, Class, and Gender in the Lives of African-American Women.* New York: Routledge

O'Meara T. 1997. Causation and the struggle for a science of culture. *Curr. Anthropol.* 38:399–410

Omi M, Winant H. 1994. *Racial Formation in the United States: From the 1960s to the 1990s.* New York/London: Routledge. 2nd ed.

Oppong C. 1983. *Female and Male in West Africa.* New York: Allen Unwin

Rappaport RA. 1968. *Pigs for the Ancestors: Ritual in the Ecology of a New Guinea People.* New Haven, CT: Yale Univ. Press

Rose S. 1979. It's only human nature: the sociobiologist's fairyland. *Race Class* 20(3):277–88

Ross S. 1979. *Racism and Colonialism: Essays on Ideology and Social Structure.* The Hague: Martinus Nijhoff

Sahlins M. 1964. Culture and environment: the study of cultural ecology. In *Horizons in Anthropology*, ed. S Tax, pp. 132–47. Chicago, IL: Aldine

Sahlins M. 1976. *The Use and Abuse of Biology: an Anthropological Critique of Sociobiology.* Ann Arbor: Univ. Mich. Press

Salamone F. 2000. The International African Institute: the Rockefeller Foundation and the development of British social anthropology in Africa. *Transform. Anthropol.* 9(1):19–29

Shanklin E. 1994. *Anthropology and Race.* Belmont, CA: Wadsworth

Shinnie M. 1965. *Ancient African Kingdoms.* London: Arnold

Smedley A. 1974. Women of Udu: survival in a harsh land. In *Many Sisters: Women in Cross-Cultural Perspective*, ed. C Matthiesson, pp. 205–28. Glenco: Free Press

Smedley A. 1980. The implications of Birom cicisbeism. In *Women With Many Husbands: Polyandrous Alliance and Marital Flexibility in Africa and Asia.* In *J. Comp. Fam. Stud.* (Spec. issue)

Smedley A. (1993) 1999. *Race in North America: Origin and Evolution of a Worldview.* Boulder, CO: Westview Press. 2nd ed.

Smedley A. 1998a. Science and the cultural construction of the idea of race. In *Many Americas: Critical Perspectives on Race, Racism, and Ethnicity*, ed. G Campbell, pp. 41–61. Dubuque, IO: Kendall/Hunt

Smedley A. 1998b. Race and the construction of human identity. *Am. Anthropol.* (Spec. ed.) 100(3):690702

Smedley A. 2002. *Gender and Adaptation on the Jos Plateau: A Historical and Ecological Study of a West African People.* In press

Stepan N. 1982. *The Idea of Race in Science: Great Britain, 1800–1960.* London: Macmillan

Steward J. 1955. *Theory of Culture Change: the Methodology of Multilinear Evolution.* Urbana: Univ. Ill. Press

Stocking GW Jr. 1968. *Race, Culture, and Evolution: Essays in the History of Anthropology.* New York: Free Press

Thompson L, Ferguson J, eds. 1969. *Africa in Classical Antiquity.* Ibadan, Nigeria

White L. 1959. *The Evolution of Culture: The Development of Civilization to the Fall of Rome.* New York: McGraw Hill

White L. (1949)1969. *The Science of Culture: A Study of Man and Civilization.* New York: Farrar, Straus Giroux. 2nd ed.

White L, Dillingham B. 1973. *The Concept of Culture.* Minneapolis, MN: Burgess

Williams B. 1989. A class act: anthropology and the race to nation across ethnic terrain. *Annu. Rev. Anthropol.* 18:401–44

Annu. Rev. Anthropol. 2001. 30:1–18

CROSS-CULTURAL COMPARATIVE
APPROACHES IN ARCHAEOLOGY

Peter N. Peregrine

Department of Anthropology, Lawrence University, Appleton, Wisconsin 54911-5798;
e-mail: peter.n.peregrine@Lawrence.edu

Key Words   archaeological method and theory, cross-cultural research,
cultural evolution, ethnology, history of archaeology

■ **Abstract**   Cross-cultural comparative approaches have been used widely in archaeological research, yet to date none seem to have achieved their full potential.
Synchronic cross-cultural comparisons have provided a number of material correlates
of behavior, as well as a few causal and noncausal associations that allow behavior to
be inferred from material remains. However, large areas of material culture, such as ceramics and lithics, have not yet been subject to extensive comparative analysis, and thus
large areas of archaeological research that might be aided by synchronic comparative
findings have been left unassisted. Diachronic cross-cultural comparisons have been
used extensively to chart and analyze cultural evolution. However, these comparisons
are typically based on grab-bag samples and only rarely employ statistics to aid in the
discovery or testing of evolutionary patterns. New research tools providing a statistically valid sampling universe and information resources for coding archaeological
data are being developed to facilitate cross-cultural comparisons.

INTRODUCTION

One of the basic problems faced by archaeologists is that our subjects cannot
speak to us. We must listen to them through the material remains they left behind,
and even these cannot tell us how or why they were made or what they mean.
Although a few archaeologists have run away from this problem by suggesting
that archaeological sites are little more than mirrors reflecting ourselves and not
the past (Shanks & Tilley 1992), most archaeologists maintain a deep concern for
interpreting and understanding those who went before. To understand the past,
archaeologists must find ways of making material remains speak, speak reliably,
and speak in a language we can understand. In this paper I suggest that cross-
cultural comparisons provide a powerful method for making the archaeological
record speak to us, and I review both past uses and future directions of cross-cultural
comparisons in archaeology.

0084-6570/01/1021-0001$14.00

COMPARATIVE ETHNOLOGY VERSUS
ETHNOGRAPHIC ANALOGY

Ethnographic analogy has been the primary method used to make the material record speak from the very beginnings of archaeology. Indeed, because we can never actually see the past, one could argue that analogy must be a part of archaeological interpretation (Bloch 1953, p. 48). However, the attempt to construct systematic methods for applying ethnographic information to the interpretation and analysis of the archaeological record has only occupied archaeologists since the 1950s (see Wylie 1985 for an overview of pre-1950s use of analogy).

One of the first to propose a systematic method for constructing analogies was Graham Clark (1951, 1953). He suggested that analogies might be most accurately and appropriately drawn from ethnographically-known cultures with subsistence technologies and ecological settings similar to those of the archaeological culture of interest. Wylie (1985, p. 71) terms this a "neo-evolutionist" approach, as it has its roots in an older method of drawing analogies from cultures in similar positions within an evolutionary typology [particularly Morgan's (1877)], but adds to it the idea that environment may play an important role in shaping a culture.

In 1961 Robert Ascher took up Clark's ideas and summarized problems many had found with them, including their overt environmental-determinist assumptions. He suggested that a method of "direct historic" analogy might be more appropriate than a neo-evolutionist one. By direct historic analogy Ascher (1961, pp. 323–24) meant that analogies should be drawn only from ethnographic cases that could be directly linked to the archaeological cultures being interpreted. Ascher believed that where cultural continuity could be demonstrated, features of prehistoric lifestyles could be expected to be retained, and hence, analogy would be more appropriate than in cases where cultural continuity could not be demonstrated.

Many archaeologists remained critical of the use of analogy. One reason was that a method similar to Ascher's, called the "direct historic approach" to archaeology, had been in use in North America for over 30 years and was beginning to be critically questioned (Trigger 1989, pp. 300–1). The direct historic approach proposed that archaeologists work back into the past from historically known cultures, basing interpretations on the previous period (see Steward 1942). It was quickly realized, however, that once one went past the latest prehistoric period, one was still completely removed from empirical analogy to known peoples and one ran the danger of compiling interpretive mistakes as one moved further into the past (Trigger 1989, pp. 391–95). Gary Feinman and his colleagues (Feinman et al 2000) recently illustrated this problem by demonstrating that reliance on direct historic analogy limits our understanding of variation and change in prehistoric Puebloan sociopolitical organization by disallowing interpretations suggesting prehistoric Puebloan groups were organized differently from contemporary ones, even though the archaeological record shows periods of dramatic change.

In the 1970s a movement, linked to the "new" archaeology and its emphasis on "middle-range" research (i.e. research focused on linking artifacts and artifact patterns to human behaviors), was initiated involving field research among living peoples designed specifically to develop means to interpret the archaeological record. Many saw this approach, termed "ethnoarchaeology" or "living archaeology," as the answer to the long-standing problem of ethnographic analogy in archaeological interpretation (Gould 1980, Gould & Watson 1982). It didn't take long, however, for archaeologists, even proponents of ethnoarchaeology, to realize that this method had many of the same problems the direct historic approach had (Wylie 1982). As one moved into the past, one still became completely removed from empirical analogy to known peoples, and as in the case of Puebloan sociopolitical organization mentioned above, one might not know when one was inappropriately limiting the range of possible interpretations.

It is interesting that in all this discussion and debate about the use of ethnographic analogy in archaeological interpretation, few have put forward the idea that findings from cross-cultural research might provide an appropriate source for drawing inferences (Peregrine 1996a). As McNett (1979, p. 40) succinctly put it "one is rather at a loss to explain why this method has not been used more for archaeological purposes." One reason McNett (1979, p. 41) offers is that archaeologists are simply unaware of the findings of cross-cultural research. McNett (1979) and Ember & Ember (1995) have compiled empirical findings of cross-cultural research with implications for archaeological interpretation. Both provide excellent overviews of the literature, and I only offer a brief summary here.

RESULTS FROM CROSS-CULTURAL RESEARCH

Cross-cultural research, as used here, refers specifically to the statistical testing of theories or hypotheses against data from a large (often worldwide) and clearly defined sample of societies. As Ember & Ember (1995, p. 88) put it, underlying cross-cultural research is the fundamental assumption "that if an explanation (theory or hypothesis) has merit, measures of the presumed causes and effects should be significantly and strongly associated synchronically." The importance of this approach is that if one can find a strong association in a worldwide sample of cultures, then one can assume that the association fits human behavior in general and not just the customs of a particular culture or historically related group of cultures (Sanderson 1990, pp. 211–12). Also, particularly important for the archaeologist, there is no a priori reason for this generalization not to hold for prehistoric cultures as well (but cf. Ember & Ember 1995, pp. 95–96).

It is important to point out that cross-cultural research is not only different from other methods of cross-cultural comparison [e.g., the California and Indiana schools of ethnology (see McNett 1979, pp. 42–46)], but it is also quite different from the theoretically based attempts to predict associations between behavior and material culture that have been used in archaeological interpretation. These theoretically based arguments were developed to avoid the presumed problem of the ethnographic record lacking information on material culture and/or being so heavily biased that material culture indicators of behavior are necessarily flawed (McNett 1979, pp. 46–54). A good example is a paper by Christopher Peebles and Susan Kus (1977) in which the authors suggest archaeological correlates of social ranking and chiefdom political organization. Based on the theoretical works of Service (1962) and Fried (1967), Peebles & Kus suggest that an important archaeological indicator of ranking and chiefdoms will be the presence of communal storage facilities used for redistribution. Unfortunately, a cross-cultural study of the New World (Feinman & Neitzel 1984) has shown that redistribution is actually rare in rank and chiefdom societies and, when it is present, is a highly diverse activity, possibly lacking in material indicators. Peebles & Kus's indicator was flawed because the theory they based it on was flawed. The method of cross-cultural research avoids this problem by empirically testing for indicators, differences, and correlations. The tremendous value of the cross-cultural method is precisely this: Material indicators of behavior are both developed through theoretical modeling and empirically demonstrated to hold true across a range of cultures (Ember & Ember 1995, pp. 105–6).

Cross-cultural research is based on several underlying assumptions that are also important to understand. First, it is assumed that cases for comparisons are drawn from a statistically valid sample representing the entire range of variation in the subject of interest. A number of such samples have been developed for cross-cultural research, including the Standard Cross-Cultural Sample (Murdock & White 1969) and the Human Relations Area Files (HRAF) Probability Sample (Naroll 1967). The entire HRAF Collection of Ethnography is itself a more than 30% sample of the ethnographic record. Second, it is assumed that the units of analysis are comparable. Whereas ethnologists claim to compare cultures, the actual units of analysis are most commonly individual communities within a larger cultural system, typically called "focal communities," each with specific pinpointing dates (see Ember & Ember 1988, 2001). Finally, cross-cultural research relies on the use of inferential statistics to determine empirically whether apparent associations or trends are indeed present (Ember & Ember 1998, 2001).

Ember & Ember (1995) outline two kinds of archaeologically useful findings from cross-cultural research. The first of these are material correlates of human behaviors (Ember & Ember 1995, p. 98), which McNett (1979, pp. 59–64) discusses as "proxy measures" of human behaviors. For McNett, these are the most important findings that cross-cultural research has to offer—ways to view human behavior by using material remains as proxy measures of those behaviors. For the Embers, material correlates are certainly valuable for archaeological interpretations in and of themselves, but they are more valuable when used to apply causal and noncausal associations to the archaeological record.

Causal and noncausal associations refer to situations in which one variable can be used to predict variation in another (Ember & Ember 1995, p. 97). Causal associations suggest a causal relationship between the variables (i.e. that variation in one causes variation in the other), whereas noncausal associations suggest simple covariation (either direct or inverse) between them. In either case, these are the most powerful findings for archaeological interpretation, because if two variables can be shown to be significantly associated in a diversity of cultures, then it would be difficult to argue that the same relationship would not hold for prehistoric cultures as well (see Wylie 1985, p. 101 for a discussion). Indeed, this is exactly the kind of predictive ability many involved in ethnoarchaeology are seeking (see, e.g., Gould 1980, pp. 109–10; Gould & Watson 1982, pp. 357–58, 363), but have apparently either missed or neglected in the results of cross-cultural research.

A few examples may serve to illustrate this point. In terms of causal and non-causal associations, the causes of variation in postmarital residence have been the subject of intense cross-cultural study, and a number of the identified predictors might be applicable to the archaeological record. For example, bilocal residence among foragers is predicted by three conditions: sudden depopulation, small community size, and high rainfall variability around a low mean (Ember 1975). Finding evidence of these conditions would allow an archaeologist to hypothesize bilocal residence in an archaeologically known foraging population. In nonforaging populations severe depopulation from disease appears to predict bilocal (or, more accurately, multilocal) residence (Ember & Ember 1972). Ember (1975) suggests that the likelihood of matrilocal versus patrilocal residence for foragers can be estimated based on the relative importance of fishing (a predictor of patrilocal residence) and gathering (a predictor of matrilocal residence) to subsistence. Thus, careful analysis of subsistence with regard to cross-cultural predictors might allow an archaeologist to hypothesize the type of postmarital residence practiced by the peoples occupying a given archaeological site or region.

In terms of material correlates of behavior, a well-known one is that between total living floor area and population (Naroll 1962). Replications by other researchers (e.g., Brown 1987, Peregrine 1994) suggest that the correlation is robust and that archaeologists can confidently predict site population by estimating 6 square meters of floor area per person. This finding has been used extensively in archaeology to estimate the population of sites and regions. Though perhaps the most widely used, the relationship between floor area and population is not the only material correlate discovered through cross-cultural research that has potential utility in archaeology. For example, several studies have demonstrated strong associations between house form and aspects of social organization, particularly postmarital residence. Specifically, dwellings with floor areas larger than roughly 80 square meters are likely to be matrilocal, whereas those with floor areas less than 40 square meters are likely to be patrilocal (Brown 1987, Divale 1977, Ember 1973). The internal divisions within houses also appear to correlate with social organization (Kent 1990). The presence of wealth differences, for example, correlates with multi-room dwellings (Whiting & Ayres 1968, Blanton 1993), and room size within multi-room dwellings appears to correlate with postmarital residence (James 1994). Clearly, an abundance of information about the social organization of prehistoric societies can potentially be obtained through material correlates.

DISCUSSION OF SYNCHRONIC CROSS-CULTURAL COMPARISONS

Cross-cultural research has generated a number of useful predictors and material correlates of behavior, but clearly more can be done. There has been virtually no research on material correlates of the two most prevalent items in the archaeological record: ceramics and lithics (but see Odell 1988, 1998). Only a handful of studies have focused specifically on behaviors associated with artistic styles and decoration (e.g., Fischer 1961, Blanton 1993). Very little research has been done on causal models or material correlates of religious beliefs and practices (but see Kamp 1998, Peregrine 1996b, Swanson 1960). Although finding material correlates for such things as religious beliefs may seem an impossible task—as Marc Bloch (1953, p. 194) put it, "there can be no psychology which confines itself to pure consciousness"—there must be material behaviors associated with such things as religious beliefs, and the task is to discover them. However, the task is also to use these findings, and to date, archaeology has not done a very good job at that. Cross-cultural research holds a unique and important key to the archaeological record, a key to unlock the voices of the material record, a key that allows these objects to speak to us from the past, and we should be more aggressive about using its results (see Blanton & Taylor 1995).

Thus far, the discussion of cross-cultural research has referred only to the ethnographic record, but what of the archaeological record? Much of archaeological interpretation involves comparison of archaeological materials across sites and regions. Indeed, such vital areas of archaeological interpretation as culture history, relative dating, and diffusion, to name only a few, are rooted in the comparison of archaeological materials between sites and regions. The point I would like to emphasize is that such comparisons are almost universally made along the lines of ethnographic analogy; that is, they are uncontrolled comparisons. Causal and non-causal associations, developed through rigorous statistical analysis, have not been developed based on archaeological cases, and only rarely have material correlates of behavior been discovered [e.g., alteration in habitation with sedentarism (see Kent 1999)]. Thus, although systematic, controlled comparisons have been common using the ethnographic record, they have been rare using the archaeological record.

DIACHRONIC CROSS-CULTURAL COMPARISONS

That the archaeological record has not been used as the ethnographic record has is not surprising—the two differ in important ways. After all, finding material correlates for behavior is impossible if one does not know the behavior was present in the first place. However, the archaeological record has been used for systematic comparison of a kind that is difficult, if not impossible, to perform within the ethnographic record: the comparison of a single society over time. In most cases the limited time depth of the ethnographic record prevents such diachronic comparisons, and if they are possible at all, the length of time over which stability and change can be examined is quite brief. The archaeological record, on the other hand, is uniquely suited to such diachronic analyses and, indeed, has been the subject of systematic diachronic comparisons for at least 150 years.

Diachronic cross-cultural comparison was a staple method among the founders of anthropology. In *Principles of Sociology*, for example, Herbert Spencer (1896–1899) attempted to construct a general law of cultural evolution in part by providing examples of various stages of cultural evolution that included pre-Columbian Mexico, Pharonic Egypt, and the Roman Empire, among others. Similarly, Edward Tylor, in *Primitive Culture* (1871), used diachronic comparison to trace cultural "survivals" and build evolutionary sequences. Lewis Henry Morgan also attempted to use diachronic comparison, in *Ancient Society* (1877), to establish a universal sequence of cultural evolution. Unfortunately, these early attempts at diachronic comparison were doomed to fail because the archaeological data available to these scholars were crude and lacked absolute dates, preventing the establishment of an empirical sequence of change. This lack of true diachronic data was a significant flaw in the work of the early evolutionists, a flaw that was rightly seized upon by Boas and his students, who launched a damning criticism of both comparative analyses and evolutionary theory [a critical perspective that continues to this day (see, e.g., Nisbet 1969, Hodder 1982, Shanks & Tilley 1992)].

Although the paucity of data and the Boasian reaction against these early evolutionists halted diachronic cross-cultural comparisons for a time, a second generation of evolutionists followed with comparisons based on better data and more rigorous theory (see Hallpike 1986, Harris 1968, Sanderson 1990, Trigger 1998 for reviews). Foremost among these scholars was Vere Gordon Childe, whose *Social Evolution* (1951) provides something of a blueprint for diachronic cross-cultural comparisons using archaeological data. His basic position is that "archaeology can establish sequences of cultures in various natural regions. And these cultures represent societies or phases in the development of societies. Potentially, therefore, archaeological sequences reveal the chronological order in which kinds of society did historically emerge" (Childe 1951, p. 17). To unleash this potential, Childe (1951, pp. 22–29) suggested that archaeologists needed to focus their efforts on clarifying archaeological sequences based on what can be most clearly observed in the archaeological record: technology and economy. Such changes in technology and economy, Childe argued, led to changes in other aspects of culture and, in turn, to cultural evolution. To illustrate this point, Childe (1951, pp. 166–79) examined and compared the archaeological sequences of temperate and Mediterranean Europe, the Nile valley, and Mesopotamia and concluded that innovation and diffusion are the major processes underlying cultural evolution. He also pointed out that it is only through diachronic comparison that diffusion can be empirically examined and measured (Childe 1951, p. 170).

In the United States the cultural anthropologist Julian Steward argued along similar lines. He posited that "a legitimate and ultimate objective [of anthropology] is to see through the differences of cultures to the similarities, to ascertain processes that are duplicated independently in cultural sequences, and to recognize cause and effect in both temporal and functional relationships" (Steward 1949, p. 3). Steward made suggestions about methodology for accomplishing this objective similar to those put forward by Childe, but also argued, in a manner similar to Murdock (1957), that synchronic comparison could also yield valuable information about cultural regularities. Steward's major contribution to diachronic cross-cultural research was an examination of Karl Wittfogel's hypothesis that the control of irrigation facilities led to the rise of states. Steward (1949, 1955, 1977) compared cases of state origins in Mesopotamia, Egypt, North China, Peru, and Mesoamerica and found support for the idea that control of irrigation systems was an important element in the emergence of centralized authority. Although Wittfogel's irrigation hypothesis has since been heavily criticized, Steward's cross-cultural attempt to evaluate it proved influential.

Whereas Childe and Steward planted the seeds for diachronic cross-cultural comparison using the archaeological record, Elman Service's *Origins of the State and Civilization* (1975) brought the method to fruition. Service compared five historically known cases of state origin and six archaeologically known cases to test a variety of theories of state origin against the data. Although his sample was a grab-bag and his methods of analysis wholly informal [Service (1975, p. 18) tells us, rather matter-of-factly, "There is no problem here that requires any statistical or sampling procedures because the instances of state formation that are documented well enough to be useful are so few"], Service conducted a clear and direct diachronic comparison of archaeological sequences in order to identify repeated patterns and processes—exactly the type of analysis envisioned by Childe and required by cross-cultural research. And although some of Service's conclusions have not fared well (e.g., his identification of redistribution as a central process in the origins of chiefdoms), the work itself has been tremendously influential.

What Service, Steward, Childe, and others (e.g., Adams 1966, Fried 1967, Parsons 1966, White 1959) demonstrated is that diachronic cross-cultural comparison is the most appropriate way to study cultural evolution (see Yoffee 1993 for a more recent discussion). It is only through diachronic comparison that presumed causes can be demonstrated to precede presumed effects, and it is only through diachronic comparison that evolutionary processes can be identified and studied over time.[1] These conclusions are in no way groundbreaking; indeed, historians and evolutionary biologists had been working under this assumption for generations, but as a consequence of the Boasian reaction against comparative research, it took

---

[1]A somewhat contradictory perspective is offered by Robert Carneiro. Carneiro (1962) argued that Guttman scaling can be an effective tool for examining cultural evolution, particularly with synchronic data. Carneiro (1970) put forward a methodology for performing such analyses (which included a list of 618 traits to be used in scaling) along with some promising results, but few have followed-up on his ideas.

anthropology much longer to recognize the necessity of comparative methodology (see Harris 1968, Sanderson 1990 for further discussion).

In recent years more sophisticated cross-cultural research using the archaeological record has produced innovative studies of cultural evolution in an explicitly comparative framework. For example, in *Ancient Mesoamerica: A Comparison of Change in Three Regions* (1992) Richard Blanton and his colleagues examined the evolution of complex societies in Mesoamerica. They compared and contrasted the evolutionary sequences in the Valley of Mexico, the Valley of Oaxaca, and the eastern Maya lowlands specifically because "controlled comparison and contrast... can illustrate very well some of the critical features pertinent to the dynamics of early complex societies" (Blanton et al 1992, p. 35). Such comparison allowed Blanton and this colleagues to draw several strong conclusions about cultural evolution in Mesoamerica, for example, that population pressure was not a primary factor in the evolution of complex polities, and that early states in Mesoamerica had strong commonalities that only became varied in the Classic and Postclassic periods, especially as market systems developed and expanded (Blanton et al 1992, pp. 222–42).

Similarly, in *How Chiefs Come to Power* (1997) Timothy Earle used diachronic cross-cultural comparison to examine the evolution of chiefs in Hawaii, the Andes, and Denmark. Unlike Blanton and his colleagues, Earle's cases are wholly independent of one another, coming from different parts of the world and from time periods when interaction was nonexistent. Thus, Earle's cases are explicitly intended to elucidate common processes in cultural evolution (Earle 1997, p. 17). What Earle found is that while these cases vary significantly in most ways, within each of them chiefs can be seen to be actively manipulating sources of power for their own benefit. Thus, what Earle identified as a primary process in cultural evolution is the development and manipulation of available power sources by emergent political leaders. As he put it, "The multiplicity of lines of social evolution should not obscure the common principles and processes of power politics. Attempts to extend and resist central power characterize social evolution...." (Earle 1997, p. 211).

Whereas these examples certainly do not represent all the diachronic cross-cultural comparative studies that have been performed by archaeologists (other examples include Connah 1987, Kirch 1984, Lamberg-Karlovsky & Sabloff 1979, Tainter 1988, Trigger 1993, Wenke 1980), they do illustrate that these and other comparative studies using the archaeological record are not truly controlled in the way sound cross-cultural studies are. The examples given here lack a valid sample representing the entire range of variation—Blanton and his colleagues examine only well-known Mesoamerican cases, and Earle restricts his analysis to cases on which he has personally worked. The units of analysis employed are not necessarily comparable: Although it might appear that the Valley of Oaxaca, the Maya lowlands, and the Basin of Mexico are roughly similar, two (the Valleys of Oaxaca and Mexico) were politically unified, but the other (Maya lowlands) was not; similarly the Teotihuacan polity was apparently expansionistic, whereas the Oaxaca and Maya lowland polities were less so. Thus, one might reasonably question the comparability of these regions, at least in terms of political evolution. Finally, neither study employs statistical techniques to determine unique and significant patterns or associations. Thus, these comparisons, while insightful and well-conducted, are nonetheless informal, and their results must be taken as largely subjective.

DISCUSSION OF DIACHRONIC CROSS-CULTURAL COMPARISONS

The lack of truly controlled diachronic cross-cultural comparisons in archaeology is a significant one, for it has become clear that diachronic cross-cultural comparison is the best means to study cultural evolution.[2] Diachronic cross-cultural comparison can examine change over a long period of time to determine empirically whether unilinear trends are present and test explanations for those trends by determining whether presumed causes actually precede presumed effects. Similarly, multilinear evolutionary processes, those that create the specific features of different societies within the larger, unilinear trends, can be tested diachronically to see if presumed causes precede assumed effects. Diachronic cross-cultural comparisons can also be employed to examine patterns of migration, innovation, and diffusion and to investigate the roles of these processes in cultural evolution. A synchronic study of a given region might suggest that a trait diffused through cultures in a region, and might suggest the nature of the source and path of the diffused traits. Only a diachronic study can demonstrate diffusion empirically, pinpoint the source of a given trait, and chart the path of its diffusion through time. However, diachronic cross-cultural comparison as it is being performed in archaeology today appears incapable of rigorously or objectively producing such results. What the examples reviewed above seem to lack are the very things that give cross-cultural research its strength: valid samples, clearly defined units of analysis, and appropriately employed statistics (but see Graber 1995 for one example of a statistical method).

NEW DIRECTIONS

Within the past decade, problems inherent in doing diachronic comparison of the archaeological record have begun to be addressed by the Human Relations Area Files (HRAF). As a first step in developing diachronic comparative methods for archaeology, HRAF commissioned a sampling universe of archaeological cases with comparable cases. Such a sampling universe must meet several conditions. First, the cases included must all be equivalent on some set of defining criteria.

---

[2]Again, Carneiro (1962, 1970) offers an interesting alternative to this position.

Second, the criteria used to define cases must be sensitive enough to variables of interest that patterns within and among them can be recognized. Third, the universe should include all possible cases. Fourth, the universe must allow random samples large enough for hypothesis tests, taking into account the loss of cases owing to missing data. Fifth, the universe must allow the use of basic information for stratified or cluster sampling, or for eliminating cases with specific characteristics in all cases.

The *Outline of Archaeological Traditions* (Peregrine 2001) was designed to fulfill these criteria and to serve as a sampling universe for comparative archaeological research. The *Outline of Archaeological Traditions* is an attempt to catalogue all archaeologically known human societies, covering the entire globe and the entire prehistory of humankind, using comparable units of analysis termed "archaeological traditions." An archaeological tradition is defined as a group of populations sharing similar subsistence practices, technology, and forms of sociopolitical organization, which are spatially contiguous over a relatively large area and which endure temporally for a relatively long period. Minimal areal coverage for an archaeological tradition can be thought of as something like 100,000 square kilometers. Minimal temporal duration can be thought of as something like five centuries. However, these figures are meant to help clarify the concept of an archaeological tradition, not to formally restrict its definition to these conditions. At present, the *Outline of Archaeological Traditions* defines a sampling universe of 298 major archaeological traditions, but it is designed to be a work in process, to be revised and updated as new information about human prehistory is generated and as existing information is synthesized and reinterpreted.

As a second step in developing a diachronic comparative methodology for archaeology, HRAF has developed the *Encyclopedia of Prehistory* (Peregrine & Ember 2001), a nine-volume work providing descriptive information and basic references for all the cases in the *Outline of Archaeological Traditions*. It is designed to be a basic tool to assist a researcher in initiating a diachronic cross-cultural comparative project. There are three types of entries in the *Encyclopedia of Prehistory*: major tradition entries, regional subtradition entries, and site entries. The major tradition entry is a general summary of information about a single major tradition. It provides descriptive information about the environment and culture of the people whose lifeways comprised the tradition. Although the geographic and temporal range of the major tradition entry was stipulated for authors, they were given the freedom to define regional subtraditions and sites on the basis of their own interpretations of the archaeological record. Regional subtradition and site entries, then, focus on archaeological areas and locales that are conventionally distinguished in the archaeological record for a given major tradition.

Finally, HRAF has also developed the Collection of Archaeology to parallel the Collection of Ethnography, arguably the most widely used tool in cross-cultural research. Like the Collection of Ethnography, the Collection of Archaeology provides indexed, searchable, full-text primary source documents for comparative research. (The documents are available on the World Wide Web at institutions that belong to the nonprofit HRAF consortium.) The cases for which primary sources have been included in the Collection of Archaeology have been selected by random sampling from the *Outline of Archaeological Traditions* and thus provide a statistically valid sample of cases for comparative archaeological research. With this resource, archaeologists may finally begin to undertake objective and rigorous diachronic comparative studies.

AN EXAMPLE

Despite the suggestion by Giddens (1984), Lowie (1966), Nisbet (1969), and others that there are no unilinear trends in cultural evolution, and of Shanks & Tilley (1992) that if unilinear trends are identified they are simply the product of contemporary politics, generations of anthropologists have noted that human cultures do appear to have changed over time in fairly common ways (see Trigger 1998, pp. 159–85). Over the past 40,000 years societies appear to have become larger in scale, more complex in terms of social and political roles and statuses, and more integrated in the means by which these different roles relate (Blanton et al 1992). Even the staunch historical particularist Goldenweiser admitted that "there is an element of truth in the conception that the development of culture has been an unfoldment, that the different aspects of culture are interconnected, that certain phases of culture cannot materialize unless certain other phases have preceded them" (Goldenweiser 1937, pp. 519–20). And yet, as Goldenweiser and others (e.g., Nisbet 1969, pp. 195–96) have pointed out, empirical data demonstrating these trends are lacking. With the research tools now being developed for diachronic cross-cultural comparative research, however, the empirical data are becoming available.

   To demonstrate empirically that unilinear trends in cultural evolution do exist, I coded all the cases in the *Outline of Archaeological Traditions* dating from the last 40,000 years on Murdock & Provost's (1973) 10-item index of cultural complexity. The variables comprising the index are listed in Table 1. Each is scored on an ordinal scale, and for this particular study the original five-point scales were recoded into three point scales for ease of coding. Scale values for each variable are summed for each case to create its index score. These data are preliminary, as they are the product of a single coder (myself) and hence have not been subject to a reliability analysis [although the scale itself has (see Chick 1997, pp. 294–95)]. The validity of the index as a single measure of cultural complexity has also been the subject of some debate. Chick (1997) questions whether it is more an index of technological complexity and societal scale than cultural complexity, although Levinson & Malone (1980, pp. 31–37) have demonstrated that it correlates with a number of other measures of cultural complexity. Finally, the data are based on information gleaned from draft entries submitted for publication in the *Encyclopedia of Prehistory*. These had not been revised by the authors and so may contain erroneous information. However, one would expect such errors to be random rather than systematic across the nearly 300 entries consulted, and hence any errors are

TABLE 1   Scales comprising the Murdock & Provost (1973) index of cultural complexity, recoded for use with archaeological cases

Scale 1: Writing and records
  1 = None
  2 = Mnemonic or nonwritten records
  3 = True writing

Scale 2: Fixity of residence
  1 = Nomadic
  2 = Seminomadic
  3 = Sedentary

Scale 3: Agriculture
  1 = None
  2 = 10% or more, but secondary
  3 = Primary

Scale 4: Urbanization (largest settlement)
  1 = Fewer than 100 persons
  2 = 100–399 persons
  3 = 400+ persons

Scale 5: Technological specialization
  1 = None
  2 = Pottery
  3 = Metalwork (alloys, forging, casting)

Scale 6: Land transport
  1 = Human only
  2 = Pack or draft animals
  3 = Vehicles

Scale 7: Money
  1 = None
  2 = Domestically usable articles
  3 = Currency

Scale 8: Density of population
  1 = Less than 1 person/square mile
  2 = 1–25 persons/square mile
  3 = 26+ persons/square mile

Scale 9: Political integration
  1 = Autonomous local communities
  2 = 1 or 2 level above community
  3 = 3 or more levels above community

Scale 10: Social stratification
  1 = Egalitarian
  2 = 2 social classes
  3 = 3 or more social classes or castes

TABLE 2   Linear regression of cultural complexity with years before present

Sample	R	Adjusted R-square	Significance
1	−0.557	0.291	0.000
2	−0.464	0.183	0.017
3	−0.469	0.187	0.016
4	−0.706	0.480	0.000
5	−0.525	0.252	0.002
6	−0.509	0.230	0.007
7	−0.392	0.107	0.087
8	−0.416	0.143	0.022
9	−0.419	0.143	0.029
10	−0.355	0.097	0.046

likely to reduce the probability of finding a statistically significant trend in the data.

To determine if a unilinear trend in cultural complexity is present through human history, I conducted a regression analysis with the cultural complexity index as the dependent variable and the midpoint of the time period of each archaeological tradition as the independent variable. I ran 10 regression analyses in all, each on a 10% random sample drawn from the 283 valid cases. The results are listed in Table 2. All but one demonstrate a statistically significant linear relationship between cultural complexity and time in years before present. I argue that this empirically demonstrates the reality of unilinear trends in cultural evolution. One cannot discount this study, as the Boasians did with previous studies coming to similar conclusions. Here the data are neither synchronic nor biased—they are diachronic and current, and the analyses were performed on statistically valid samples. Nor can one reasonably argue that the trend is an artifact of a particular social or political agenda, as the information the analyses were based on was provided by over 200 scholars working in over 20 different nations. Unless they all share the same social and political agenda (which seems unlikely, given Shanks & Tilley's arguments that the past is unique to each nation and, ultimately, to each individual), then their different perspectives should have created a random or nearly random pattern—certainly not a statistically significant linear relationship.[3]

---

[3]Before accepting this result, however, it should stand the test of a replication by another scholar. It is important, then, to realize that research tools are currently being developed that will allow other scholars to test this result. I suggest that these new research tools may usher in a new era of research on cultural evolution, one in which true diachronic cross-cultural comparative studies can be performed with relative ease and with methodological sophistication. I, for one, look forward to seeing the results of such studies.

CONCLUSIONS

Cross-cultural comparative approaches have been used widely in archaeological research, yet to date none seem to have achieved their full potential. Synchronic cross-cultural comparisons have provided a number of material correlates of behavior, as well as a few causal and noncausal associations that allow behavior to be inferred from material remains. However, large areas of material culture, such as ceramics and lithics, have not yet been subject to extensive comparative analysis, and thus large areas of archaeological research that might be aided by synchronic comparative findings have been left unassisted. Diachronic cross-cultural comparisons have been used extensively to chart and analyze cultural evolution. However, these comparisons are typically based on grab-bag samples and only rarely employ statistics to aid in the discovery or testing of evolutionary patterns. New research tools providing a statistically valid sampling universe and information resources for coding archaeological data are being developed to facilitate cross-cultural comparisons. One example of research employing these tools was presented here, and a unilinear trend in the evolution of cultural complexity was identified. Thus, although the contributions of cross-cultural comparative approaches to archaeology have been modest to date, their future appears promising.

ACKNOWLEDGMENTS

A first draft of this article was read and commented on by Richard Blanton, Timothy Earle, Carol Ember, and Melvin Ember. Not all of their suggestions were incorporated, but their efforts are deeply appreciated.

Visit the Annual Reviews home page at www.AnnualReviews.org

LITERATURE CITED

Adams RM. 1966. *The Evolution of Urban Society*. Chicago: Aldine

Ascher R. 1961. Analogy in archaeological interpretation. *Southwest. J. Anthropol.* 17: 317–25

Blanton RE. 1993. *Houses and Households: A Comparative Study*. New York: Plenum

Blanton RE, Kowalewski SA, Feinman GA, Finsten L. 1992. *Ancient Mesoamerica: A Comparison of Change in Three Regions*. Cambridge: Cambridge Univ. Press

Blanton RE, Taylor J. 1995. Patterns of exchange and the social production of pigs in highland New Guinea: their relevance to questions about the origins and evolution of agriculture. *J. Archaeol. Res.* 3:113–45

Bloch M. 1953. *The Historian's Craft*. New York: Vintage

Brown BM. 1987. Population estimation from floor area: a restudy of "Naroll's constant." *Behav. Sci. Res.* 21:1–49

Carneiro RL. 1962. Scale analysis as an instrument for the study of cultural evolution. *Southwest. J. Anthropol.* 18:149–69

Carneiro RL. 1970. Scale analysis, evolutionary sequences, and the rating of cultures. In

Handbook of Method in Cultural Anthropology, ed. R Naroll, R Cohen, pp. 834–71. Garden City, NY: Nat. Hist. Press.

Chick G. 1997. Cultural complexity: the concept and its measurement. *Cross-Cult. Res.* 31:275–307

Childe VG. 1951. *Social Evolution*. London: Watts & Co.

Clark JGD. 1951. Folk-culture and the study of European prehistory. In *Aspects of Archaeology in Great Britain and Beyond*, ed. WF Grimes, pp. 49–65. London: Edwards

Clark JGD. 1953. Archaeological theories and interpretations: Old World. In *Anthropology Today*, ed. AL Kroeber, pp. 343–60. Chicago: Univ. Chicago Press

Connah G. 1987. *African Civilizations*. Cambridge: Cambridge Univ. Press

Divale WT. 1977. Living floors and marital residence: a replication. *Behav. Sci. Res.* 12:109–15

Earle TK. 1997. *How Chiefs Come to Power*. Stanford, CA: Stanford Univ. Press

Ember CR. 1975. Residential variation among hunter-gatherers. *Behav. Sci. Res.* 10:199–227

Ember CR, Ember M. 1972. Conditions favoring multilocal residence. *Southwest. J. Anthropol.* 28:382–400

Ember CR, Ember M. 1988. *Guide to Cross–Cultural Research Using the HRAF Archive*. New Haven, CT: Hum. Relat. Area Files

Ember CR, Ember M. 1998. Cross-cultural research. In *Handbook of Methods in Cultural Anthropology*, ed. HR Bernard, pp. 647–87

Ember CR, Ember M. 2001. *Cross-Cultural Research Methods*. Walnut Creek, CA: Alta Mira

Ember M. 1973. An archaeological indicator of matrilocal versus patrilocal residence. *Am. Antiq.* 38:177–82

Ember M, Ember CR. 1995. Worldwide cross-cultural studies and their relevance for archaeology. *J. Archaeol. Res.* 3:87–111

Feinman GM, Lightfoot KG, Upham S. 2000. Political hierarchy and organizational strategies in the Puebloan Southwest. *Am. Antiq.* 65:449–70

Feinman GM, Neitzel J. 1984. Too many types: an overview of sedentary prestate societies in the Americas. In *Advances in Archaeological Method and Theory*, ed. MB Schiffer, 7:39–102. Orlando, FL: Academic

Fischer J. 1961. Art styles as cultural cognitive maps. *Am. Anthropol.* 63:80–83

Fried M. 1967. *The Evolution of Political Society: An Essay in Political Anthropology*. New York: Random House

Giddens A. 1984. *The Constitution of Society: Outline of a Theory of Structuration*. Berkeley: Univ. Calif. Press

Goldenweiser A. 1937. *Anthropology*. New York: Crofts

Gould RA. 1980. *Living Archaeology*. Cambridge: Cambridge Univ. Press

Gould RA, Watson PJ. 1982. A dialogue on the meaning and use of analogy in ethnoarchaeological reasoning. *J. Anthropol. Archaeol.* 1:355–81

Graber RB. 1995. *A Scientific Model of Social and Cultural Evolution*. Kirksville, MO: Thomas Jefferson Univ. Press

Hallpike CR. 1986. *The Principles of Social Evolution*. Oxford: Clarendon

Harris M. 1968. *The Rise of Anthropological Theory*. New York: Harper & Row

Hodder I. 1982. Theoretical archaeology: a reactionary view. In *Symbolic and Structural Archaeology*, ed I Hodder, pp. 1–16. Cambridge, UK: Cambridge Univ. Press

James SR. 1994. *Regional variation in prehistoric pueblo households and social organization: a quantitative approach*. PhD. thesis, Ariz. State Univ. Tempe

Kamp KA. 1998. Social hierarchy and burial treatments: a comparative assessment. *Cross-Cult. Res.* 32:79–115

Kent S. 1990. A cross-cultural study of segmentation, architecture, and the use of space. In *Domestic Architecture and the Use of Space*, ed. S Kent, pp. 127–52. Cambridge: Cambridge Univ. Press

Kent S. 1999. The archaeological visibility of storage: delineating storage from trash areas. *Am. Antiq.* 64:79–94

Kirch PV. 1984. *The Evolution of Polynesian*

Chiefdoms. Cambridge: Cambridge Univ. Press

Lamberg-Karlovsky CC, Sabloff JA. 1979. *Ancient Civilizations: The Near East and Mesoamerica.* Menlo Park, CA: Benjamin/ Cummings

Levinson D, Malone MJ. 1980. *Toward Explaining Human Culture: A Critical Review of the Findings of Worldwide Cross-Cultural Research.* New Haven, CT: Hum. Relat. Area Files

Lowie RH. 1966. *Culture and Ethnology.* New York: Basic Books

McNett CW. 1979. The cross-cultural method in archaeology. In *Advances in Archaeological Method and Theory*, ed. MB Schiffer, 2:39–76. Orlando: Academic

Morgan LH. 1877. *Ancient Society.* New York: Holt

Murdock GP. 1957. Anthropology as a comparative science. *Behav. Sci.* 2:249–54

Murdock GP, Provost C. 1973. Measurement of cultural complexity. *Ethnology* 12:379–92

Murdock GP, White DR. 1969. Standard cross-cultural sample. *Ethnology* 8:329–69

Naroll R. 1962. Floor area and settlement population. *Am. Antiq.* 27:587–89

Naroll R. 1967. The proposed HRAF probability sample. *Behav. Sci. Notes* 2:70–80

Nisbet RA. 1969. *Social Change and History.* New York: Oxford Univ. Press

Odell GH. 1988. Addressing prehistoric hunting practices through stone tool analysis. *Am. Anthropol.* 90:335–56

Odell GH. 1998. Investigating correlates of sedentism and domestication in prehistoric North America. *Am. Antiq.* 63:553–71

Parsons T. 1966. *Societies: Evolutionary and Comparative Perspectives.* Engelwood Cliffs, NJ: Prentice-Hall

Peebles C, Kus S. 1977. Some archaeological correlates of ranked societies. *Am. Antiq.* 42:421–48

Peregrine PN. 1994. Raoul Naroll's contribution to archaeology. *Cross-Cult. Res.* 28:351–63

Peregrine PN. 1996a. Ethnology versus ethnographic analogy: a common confusion in archaeological interpretation. *Cross-Cult. Res.* 30:316–29

Peregrine PN. 1996b. The birth of the gods revisited: a partial replication of Guy Swanson's 1960 cross-cultural study of religion. *Cross-Cult. Res.* 30:84–112

Peregrine PN. 2001. *Outline of Archaeological Traditions.* New Haven, CT: Hum. Relat. Area Files

Peregrine PN, Ember M, eds. 2001. *Encyclopedia of Prehistory.* New York: Kluwer Acad./Plenum. 9 vols.

Sanderson S. 1990. *Social Evolutionism.* Oxford: Blackwell

Service E. 1962. *Primitive Social Organization: An Evolutionary Perspective.* New York: Random House

Service E. 1975. *Origins of the State and Civilization: The Process of Cultural Evolution.* New York: Norton

Shanks M, Tilley C. 1992. *Re-Constructing Archaeology.* London: Routledge

Spencer H. 1896–1899. *Principles of Sociology.* New York: Appleton. 3 vols.

Steward JH. 1942. The direct historic approach to archaeology. *Am. Antiq.* 7:337–43

Steward JH. 1949. Culture causality and law: a trial formulation of early civilizations. *Am. Anthropol.* 51:1–27

Steward JH, ed. 1955. *Irrigation Civilizations: A Comparative Study.* Washington, DC: Pan Am. Union

Steward JH. 1977. Wittfogel's irrigation hypothesis. In *Evolution and Ecology*, ed. JC Steward, RF Murphy, pp. 87–99. Urbana: Univ. Ill. Press

Swanson G. 1960. *The Birth of the Gods.* Ann Arbor: Univ. Mich. Press

Tainter JA. 1988. *The Collapse of Complex Societies.* Cambridge: Cambridge Univ. Press

Trigger BG. 1989. *A History of Archaeological*

Thought. Cambridge: Cambridge Univ. Press

Trigger BG. 1993. *Early Civilizations: Ancient Egypt in Context.* Cairo: Am. Univ. Cairo Press

Trigger BG. 1998. *Sociocultural Evolution.* Oxford: Blackwell

Tylor EB. 1871. *Primitive Culture.* London: Murray. 2 vols.

Wenke RJ. 1980. *Patterns in Prehistory.* Oxford: Oxford Univ. Press

White LA. 1959. *The Evolution of Culture.* New York: McGraw-Hill

Whiting JM, Ayres B. 1968. Inferences from the shape of dwellings. In *Settlement Archae-*
ology, ed. KC Chang, pp. 117–33. Palo Alto, CA: Natl. Press Books

Wylie A. 1982. An analogy by any other name is just as analogical: a commentary on the Gould-Watson dialogue. *J. Anthropol. Archaeol.* 1:382–401

Wylie A. 1985. The reaction against analogy. In *Advances in Archaeological Method and Theory,* ed. MB Schiffer, 8:63–111. Orlando, FL: Academic

Yoffee N. 1993. Too many chiefs? (or, Safe texts for the '90s). In *Archaeological Theory: Who Sets the Agenda?,* ed. N Yoffee, A Sherratt, pp. 60–78. Cambridge: Cambridge Univ. Press

Annu. Rev. Anthropol. 2001. 30:19–39

COLONIAL LINGUISTICS

Joseph Errington

Yale University, New Haven, Connecticut 06520; e-mail: j.errington@yale.edu

Key Words language ideology, philology, sociolinguistics, language contact

■ **Abstract**   Academic knowledge of human linguistic diversity owes much to descriptions written, over four centuries ago, under the aegis of European colonial regimes around the world. This comparative review considers a small part of that body of linguistic descriptive work relative to its conditions of production: authorial interests that animated such writings, ideological and institutional milieux that enabled and shaped them, and the authoritative character they took on as natural symbols of colonial difference. European technologies of literacy enabled missionary and nonmissionary linguistic work that resulted in representations of languages as powerful icons of spiritual, territorial, and historical hierarchies that emerged in colonial societies. As descriptions of languages traveled from exotic colonial peripheries to European metropoles, they came under the purview of comparative philology. This disciplinary precursor to modern linguistics helped to legitimize colonial linguistic projects and legislate colonial difference on a global scale.

INTRODUCTION

Around the world, from the sixteenth to the early twentieth century, Europeans wrote about alien languages that they encountered in pursuit of their diverse colonial interests. The result is a group of writings with disparate geohistoric origins that can be gathered under the rubric of "linguistics" only if each is thought to be grounded in common presuppositions about languages' writability and so also about patterned relations between meanings of talk, on one hand, and speech sounds or their orthographic counterparts on the other. Such presuppositions make plausible the expository strategies that helped colonial (proto)linguists move from time-bound human speech to language objects, abstractable in textual form from communities and verbal conduct. However, the work of writing these descriptions was done in hugely different "landscapes in the colonial world" (Breckenridge & van der Veer 1993), so attention is required here to these diverse conditions of production (Fabian 1985): extrinsic interests and political circumstances that licensed authors' alien presences among speakers, institutional grounds, and readerships for their descriptive work, and so on.

"Colonialism" is a rubric for hugely different exploitative purposes, institutional configurations, and modes of subordination; so the work of linguistic description

0084-6570/01/1021-0019$14.00   **19**

done under the aegis of various colonial regimes needs to be considered with an eye to conditions that enabled it and social interests inscribed in it. Metalinguistic representations of alien speech, framed in languages more familiar to Europeans, recurringly made possible the figuring of language among the "cultural and representational feature[s] of colonial authority" (Cooper & Stoler 1997a, p. 18). To address these joined concerns—how representations of linguistic structure and colonial interests shaped and enabled each other—I center this review on collateral uses of these descriptive projects and their enabling assumptions, such that language difference could become a resource—like gender, race, and class—for figuring and naturalizing inequality in the colonial milieux (Breckenridge & van der Veer 1993, Gal & Irvine 1995, Irvine & Gal 2000). In this respect, the writings of linguists can be scrutinized as other colonial texts by historians, cultural anthropologists, literary theorists, and others have been. Insofar as the label "colonial linguistics" covers texts that reduced complex situations of language use and variation to unified written representations, it can be considered here under a broadly ideological profile (Woolard & Schieffelin 1994, Kroskrity 2000).

Actions of colonial agents outran their own intent, and colonial linguistic work likewise had uses and effects beyond those foreseen or intended by its authors. It was grounded in institutions and animated by interests that legitimized simple views of enormously complex situations and that licensed what were often "fantasmatic representation[s] of authoritative [linguistic] certainty in the face of spectacular ignorance" (Greenblatt 1991, p. 89). At issue here are the sources of such "certainty," because they are bound up with enabling ideologies about hierarchies of languages and peoples on colonial territory and in precolonial pasts.

If this review were restricted to linguistic descriptive work in peripheral colonial locales, to the exclusion of the study of language in European centers of colonial power, it would effectively reproduce the notion that colonialism was a project created by but not shaping of European political cultures. Writings on the political economy of the world system (Wallerstein 1974) and postcolonial political culture (e.g. Stoler 1989) suggest the need to consider colonial linguistic writings here with an eye to the colonial infrastructures that enabled their circulation between peripheries and European centers. For this reason, European philology has a place here as an academic venue that was central for legislating colonial and human differences, and so for mediating the broadest "tensions of empire" (Cooper & Stoler 1997b).

ORTHOGRAPHY AND ORTHODOXY

Greenblatt (1991, p. 88) observes of sixteenth century accounts of travels in the New World that their authors aimed to reduce the "opacity of the eye's objects . . . [human and natural] . . . by rendering them transparent signs." As narrative projects, they are subject to critical interpretive scrutiny. However, the transient opacity of alien talk required a semiotically distinct deployment of European writing; to be rendered "transparent," its speech sounds had to be fixed and made representable with familiar orthographic conventions. "[B]onding stranger denisons of other tongues 'to the rules of our writing'"—called "enfranchisement" by Mulcaster, a sixteenth century writer whom Greenblatt quotes (1991, p. 89)—was the only alternative to "kidnapping languages" through the living bodies of speakers. Such re-presentations of alien speech, at once iconic and narratively framed, served to mitigate linguistic otherness in (proto)colonial encounters.

Four centuries later, Kenneth Pike (1947) subtitled *Phonemics*, his well-known, barely postcolonial linguistics text, "a technique for reducing languages to writing." His use of the word "technique" signals a scientific framing of acoustic and articulatory properties of speech and a scientific goal of developing empirically accurate, isomorphic mappings of artificial written symbols onto speech sounds. Samarin (1984, p. 436) sees this self-consciously modern, scientific enterprise as a part and culmination of colonialism's "experimental civilization," a discipline that developed as Europeans dealt with alien ways of speaking in colonial situations and that provided experimental tests for Europeans' ideas about language. Colonial milieux counted as arenas for applying techniques of science, at least in some eyes, for the good of humankind.

However, assumptions about the status of linguistics as a science elide enduring, widespread links between the work of linguistic description and Christian proselytizing, nowhere more evident than in Pike's own comments on his object of study, phonemics, as "a control system blessed of God to preserve tribes from chaos" (quoted in Hvalkof & Aaby 1981, p. 37). As a leading figure of the Summer Institute of Linguistics, the single largest organization of linguists and missionaries working in the world today, he can be considered a postcolonial American successor to colonial-era missionizing linguists. This continuity between colonial past and postcolonial present is very clear in missionary linguistic work now ongoing in marginal communities all over the world, with collateral goals and effects both obvious and intimate (Schieffelin 2000). Late colonial era missionaries left another sort of mark on contemporary linguistic scholarship if, as Gaeffke (1990) asserts, disproportionate numbers of their offspring are now scholars of Oriental languages.

Colonial linguistics needs to be framed here, then, as a nexus of technology (literacy), reason, and faith and as a project of multiple conversion: of pagan to Christian, of speech to writing, and of the alien to the comprehensible. So too missionaries' linguistic work is salient here less for its empirical value than for its role in the assertion of spiritual dominion through language. Samarin observes (1984, p. 436–37) of religious doxa and linguistic descriptive practice that Protestant missionaries in Africa tended to be better linguists than Catholics. Whether or not this observation holds for nineteenth-century sub-Saharan Africa, it lacks portability to contexts such as early colonial Latin America, where early Catholic missionaries' exhaustive linguistic work has proven to be of enduring value (see Lockhart 1991). The shaping effects of religious doxa thus need to be considered in relation to the broader social biographies of missionaries—what Samarin calls their "cultural baggage"—together with extrinsic local conditions. When Samarin notes, for instance, that French missionaries in Africa tended to be inferior linguists to their German and Flemish counterparts, he tacitly alludes to effects of nationalist ideologies on linguistic work. Meeuwis (1999a,b) addresses this issue more directly in his comments on ethnonationalist sentiment and conflict among French and Flemish missionaries in the Congo in the mid-nineteenth century. He suggests (1999a, p. 385) that a Herderian "ideology of the natural" left its traces in missionary linguistic description and policy. Such examples testify to the need for caution in reading historiographies of missionary linguists that reproduce assumptions about the autonomy of religious faith, and consequently elide powerful shaping contingencies (Bendor-Samuel 1944, Hanzeli 1969, Hovdhaugen 1996, Wonderly & Nida 1963).

Rafael's compelling study (1993) of late sixteenth and early seventeenth century Spanish descriptions of Tagalog, written in the early, tribute-based colony of the Philippines, offers a useful entree to the broadest theological and semiotic grounds of missionary linguistic work. He foregrounds the hierarchy of languages and the "politics of translation" that grounded Latin's double significance as sanctioner and enabler of Catholic missionary descriptive work. As a Truth-language, metonymically bound up with the transcendent message it conveyed (Anderson 1991), Latin legitimized these descriptive projects both as means and ends for propagating faith. As the paradigm of written language, Latin was a descriptive resource: an ideal icon, template, and source of analytic categories for written (mis)representations of Tagalog speech. Castillian mediated this theolinguistic hierarchy as the language of secular authority, used to frame discursively the "reduction" of Tagalog to writing. A hierarchy of languages was legitimized by the exchange it enabled, as written appropriation of Tagalog speech served the production of written religious materials in that "same" language.

Rafael argues that a shift in Tagalog voice and subjectivity was engendered by Spanish colonialism and diagnoses this shift from missionary linguists' rejection of the native Tagalog script, *baybayin*. This is evidence for him of that script's dangerous elusiveness for missionaries' "totalizing signifying practices," owing to phonetic indeterminacies of *baybayin*, which presumably permitted a passing over of "sense in favor of sensation" (1993, p. 53). Rafael's move from orthographic convention to positioned subjectivity is influenced by Derrida's grammatology, but has earlier antecedents in, for instance, Herder's reading of the emblematic character of Hebrews from their orthography's phonetic indeterminacies (Herder 1966). On the other hand, seemingly analogous indeterminacies of Arabic orthography do not preclude a kind of Derridean "metaphysics of presence," at least in Messick's view (1993).

Alternatively, *baybayin's* marginal status might be considered with an eye to Spanish missionaries' ignorance of contexts and genres that may have served to disambiguate such orthographic ambiguities in use. Herzfeld (1987, pp. 51–52) observes in this vein that context dependence of language is a recurring mark of subordinate otherness in literate European eyes. Missionaries' blindness to generic shapings of *baybayin* literacy practices (Hanks 2000) would have deprived them of access to contextual factors that made it possible to disambiguate use of the writing.

For Mignolo (1994), analogous readings of fifteenth- and sixteenth-century Spanish missionary confrontations with Mayan speech and "writing without words" are overly parochial. Arguing against the grain of received opinion on early Spanish humanist thought (K. Woolard, personal communication), he traces political influence back from that peripheral colonial locale to contemporaneous debates on the Iberian peninsula about political and theological relations between Castillian and Latin. However, Mignolo's broader account (1995) resonates broadly with Rafael's theosemiotic critique of the "normativity" (Fabian 1986, p. 78) that was crucial for Spanish missionary linguistic work. In both, Latin texts licensed descriptive deployment of Latin categories, grounding the division of linguistic descriptive labor in which written European vernaculars mediated between pagan tongues and sacred writ.

LINGUISTIC TERRITORIALITY

In the nineteenth century, colonial regimes promoted invasive plantation and extractive economies, creating milieux in which the linguistic descriptions that missionaries wrote had recurring motivations, uses, and effects. I foreground here the naturalizing force such linguistic descriptions lent to colonial categories of social difference and their saliences as models of and for ethnocultural identities. Historiographic reviews of colonial linguistics in sub-Saharan Africa and insular Southeast Asia recurringly point to the capacity of linguistics to concretize and normalize the territorial logic of power exercised by English (Alberto 1997; Carmody 1988; Chimhundu 1992; Fardon & Furniss 1994b; Giliomee 1989; Harries 1988, 1989; Pennycook 1998; Samarin 1984, 1989; Tomas 1991), French and Belgian (Fabian 1985, 1986; Irvine 1993, 1995; Joseph 2000; Meeuwis 1999a,b; Raison-Jourde 1977; Samarin 1984, 1989; Yates 1980), and Dutch colonial states (Anderson 1991, Giliomee 1989, Groeneboer 1997, Kipp 1990, Kuipers 1998, Moriyama 1995, Smith-Hefner 1989, Steedly 1996).

Whatever their sectarian differences, missionaries were obliged to accede to the geographic divisions of spiritual labor enforced by the colonial states that accorded to each an exclusive jurisdiction. These preestablished boundaries, crucially distinct from frontiers (Fardon & Furniss 1994a), were understood to be categorical and not permissive of interpenetrating influences. In this way colonial rule reproduced on smaller scales European modes of territoriality—a "strategy for controlling people and their relationships by delimiting and asserting control over geographic area" (Sack 1986, p. 19)—which assumed bounded linguistic *cum* cultural homogeneity among national citizenries within sovereign European states (Balibar 1991, Gellner 1983). Anderson (1991) takes up this ideological commonality in his discussion of technologies of colonial surveillance.

"Territoriality" in this sense differs from Mignolo's use of the term (1995, p. 66) for "a sense of being and belonging beyond the administrative and legal apparatus by which the land is owned by a handful of people and the nation symbolically construed by its intellectuals." For present purposes, following accepted sociolinguistic usage (Gumperz 1971), I refer to Mignolo's territoriality—which I take to be the extrainstitutionally and interactionally grounded dimension of sociality—as "community."

Colonial states and missionary jurisdictions thus shared a territorial logic that was similarly inscribed in colonial linguistic work, presupposing mappings of monolithic languages onto demarcated boundaries (cf. Urciuoli 1995). Within those bounded confines were conceived to be ethnolinguistically homogeneous groups that were localized, and naturalized, as "tribes" or "ethnicities."

Assumptions about the naturalness of monoglot conditions helped Europeans grapple with bewildering linguistic diversity, which they could frame as a problematic, Babel-like condition to be subjected to regulation (Fabian 1986) or balkanization (Calvet 1974). Historiographies of missionaries show how the linguistic descriptions they authored, augmented by print literacy, served as a means for powerfully yet intimately "[c]onceptualizing, inscribing, and interacting with [colonialized people] on terms not of their own choosing" (Comaroff & Comaroff 1991, p. 15).

Prior to the British colonial presence at the turn of the previous century, what later became southern Rhodesia and then Zimbabwe was spanned by a graded continuum of Shona dialects. By 1930, Protestant and Catholic missions had produced three mutually distinct languages within their territorially delimited spheres of spiritual influence. Though Jesuit and Trappist Mariannhill missionaries shared the Catholic faith, they produced languages—Zezuru and Chimanyika, respectively—sufficiently different that removal of territorial boundaries between the two missionary districts in 1923 engendered active resistance among converts. Methodist, Episcopal, and Anglican missionaries were able together to "create . . . rather than merely reflect . . . one specific dialect of Shona" (Ranger 1989, p. 127) because their spheres of influence were economically and geographically complementary (large-scale maize producers and smallholders, respectively). (See also Chimhundu 1992.)

Protestant missionary linguists of different sects also worked in bounded domains or "fields" of operation in the East Sumatran part of the Dutch East Indies empire in the late nineteenth century. They developed print-literate codifications of Karo and Toba, languages that were previously undistinguished but were soon to count as the clearest marks of ethnic differences up to the postcolonial Indonesian present (Kipp 1990, Steedly 1996). In retrospect, such missionary work appears as a kind religiously inspired language engineering that fits well, for instance, Haugen's account of the process of dialect selection, codification, elaboration, and dissemination that culminates in a national language (Haugen 1972).

Missions of conversion, colonial territoriality, and print literacy thus converged in the work of colonial linguists who produced powerful icons of ethnolinguistic sharedness, identity markers that became central items for colonial "cultural package[s]." (Vail 1989, p. 11) The products of missionary linguistic work could be multiply naturalizing: emblematic of communities, assimilable as individual conduct, and mappable onto colonial territory. Henson (1974) observes that work by missionary linguists in British colonial Africa did not differ in kind from that of professional linguists. However, it could subserve the territorial and administrative logic of colonial states even if it was animated by utopian visions of spiritually and linguistically unified communities.

SOCIOLINGUISTIC HIERARCHIES

As missionary linguists proselytized and educated, antecedent social formations came to be supplanted by new ethnolinguistic groupings that were consonant with broader projects of conversion. The spread of the missionary lingua franca that became nativized as Tsonga, for instance, accompanied the breakdown of complex, interpenetrating translocal linkages of chieftanship and kinship (Harries 1988, 1989). So too missionary-constructed, "pared-down" Karo came into ascendance over its "dialectal" variants as a reified, territorially grounded mark of Karo-ness. Ethnicity progressively superseded antecedent webs of kinship characterized by social asymmetry, defined and restricted forms of social intercourse, and established rights and obligations (Steedly 1996).

However, missionary work that effaced precolonial social formations also gave rise to new, language-linked socioeconomic stratification that subserved political and economic agendas of the colonial states that sanctioned their work. Their new languages were spoken first by converts who were also members of literate proto-bourgeoisies, salariats, or literate colonialized compradores (Calvet 1974; Fabian 1985, 1986; Harries 1989; Samarin 1989). Emergent sociolinguistic hierarchies involved class-like differences between social fractions, which grounded the process Calvet (1974) calls "glottophagy," as missionary-supported forms of speech subsumed their "degenerate" variants.

These hierarchies bear broad comparison with others in Europe, where literate, urban, bourgeoisies viewed peasants and workers at their own geopolitical, economic, and linguistic margins in similar ways (Calvet 1974, Mazrui 1975, Pennycook 1998, Raison-Jourde 1977, Samarin 1989). Their images of languages and speakers a bit closer to home—on the Celtic fringe of Great Britain (Lauzon 1996) for instance, or at various of France's territorial peripheries (Weber 1976)—had broad parallels in the "grammars of difference" (Cooper & Stoler 1997a) that missionary linguists created along with grammars of foreign languages.

Ranger notes that though missionary linguistic work in southern Rhodesia was augmented by print literacy, it did not exert what Anderson calls the "vernacularizing thrust" of print capitalism, which helped to level prenational language hierarchies in Europe (Anderson 1991). Deployed outside a market-based system, it promoted instead a superposed codification, or model for speech, which indirectly contributed to the distinctiveness of an emergent, native, literate class. Harries (1989, p. 43) similarly characterizes print-mediated Tsonga's elite character in a colonially "imagined community," noting that it defined a linguistic hierarchy that lent dominant symbolic force to newly "spatial" (i.e., territorial) political identities.

Insofar as missionary centers offered unequal access to print-mediated forms of speech, they engendered differential senses of language-linked identities. As socioeconomic conditions came to confer more value on some forms of linguistic and symbolic capital than others (Bourdieu 1991, Irvine 1989), those differences grew in salience for asserting or contesting colonial power. Largely undescribed and perhaps undescribable in the historiographic literature are the linguistic "microprocesses" that mediated these social changes, particulars of variation that would have stemmed from and been diagnostic of new hierarchies as they were internalized and resisted within and across emerging lines of class, territorial, and gender difference. In this respect, the broadest findings of variationist sociolinguistic research in contemporary Western societies (e.g., Labov 1972) provide grounds for speculation about complex dynamics of language and social identity at the most mundane levels of colonial influence.

At the same time, social effects of colonial linguistic work need to be framed under "macro" profiles of political and economic interest, which varied over time and space, from regime to regime. Dutch recognition of Sundanese as a language and ethnicity distinct from Javanese only came in the mid-nineteenth century, for instance, as a direct upshot of moves to train indigenous officials to administer a plantation economy (Moriyama 1995). Political cultural conditions led the Dutch to fear the effects of Christian missions in this largely Islamic area, and so they took a socially restricted linguistic interest in Sundanese and Javanese. The upshot was a colonial linguistics focused on noble elite usage, yielding print-mediated codifications that reinforced rather than undermined antecedent politico-symbolic hierarchies (Errington 1998).

Instructive in this regard is missionary linguistic work done in Madagascar under the aegis of a native ruler rather than a colonial regime. Prior to the ascendance of the French, linguists of the Protestant London Missionary Society described the Merina language and translated the Bible at the behest of King Radama I. Quick to grasp the potential significance of this work, he supported it with the labor of two hundred of his soldiers. The resulting English/Malagasy, Malagasy/English dictionary of 1829 was "a foreign scientific project, in the best tradition of English academies or German universities of the eighteenth and nineteenth centuries" (Raison-Jourde 1977, p. 644). These missionaries invested an elite-but-local dialect with quasi-national significance, strengthening and affirming the royal center's territorial control over coastal peripheries. Raison-Jourde's acute description of this "scholarizing" project anticipates Bourdieu's economistic tropes of linguistic inequality (1991), tracing the elevation of new, codified linguistic norms and "laws of linguistic exchange." Print-mediated norms, licensed by the royal center, could be internalized by a newly literate Merina elite in the absence of a colonial regime. However, the emergence of those norms appeared to have exerted broadly analogous forces, creating inequality between varieties of the Merina language, class-like links to royal power, and the abstraction of linguistic conventions from the give and take of everyday life.

LINGUISTIC PICTURES OF PRECOLONIAL PASTS

It is no coincidence that Terence Ranger, historiographer of Rhodesian colonial linguistics discussed above, coedited a seminal collection of articles on invented traditions (Hobsbawm & Ranger 1983). This scholarly connection helps to broach the enabling paradox of colonial linguistics noted by Fabian (1985, p. 78): It presupposed contemporary versions of "traditional culture" that had to be invented in order to be defended. To discuss languages as colonially invented traditions, I foreground here the kinds of purist ideologies (Shapiro 1989) that made linguistic diversity into a legitimizing resource for colonial missionaries' regulatory efforts "from above."

Primevalness and purity were convergent, overdetermined aspects of missionary language ideologies. The perceived primitivity of the communities they encountered resonated in the first place with Biblical narratives of (monolingual) Eden, and the theology of dispersal from (multilingual) Babel. Linguistic diversity within and across communities could be perceived in this way as a puzzling sign of barbarism (Mannheim 1991), whereas linguistic homogeneity in Pacific island communities summoned up paradisiacal images of noble, if savage, societies (Schutz 1994). By the same token, secular understandings of human and language origins (Herzfeld 1987) helped to legitimize colonial efforts to reduce linguistic diversity. I discuss below late nineteenth-century positivist visions of language that licensed attacks on linguistic heterogeneity as parts of the broader confrontation of European reason with non-European confusion (Harries 1989) and helped augment heroic images of colonial agents in imperial history (Herzfeld 1987, Breckenridge & van der Veer 1993).

Images of originary purity helped most practically to develop just-so stories justifying missionary efforts to describe and propagate unitary, territorially distinct languages. However tenuous the historical evidence for such narratives, they legitimized linguists' selections and marginalizations of dialects as more or less similar to imagined local ur-languages. Purism thus served the glottophagic "recovery" of missionary languages that subsumed their degenerate variants.

Herzfeld (1987, p. 116) points to the dependence of such purist visions of language not just on ur-forms' locations in a distant past, but also their relations to some perduring place. He thus emphasizes what Bakhtin would call the chronotopic character of language purism; the usefulness of such chronotopes for colonial linguistics can be illustrated with two brief examples. According to Harries (1988, 1989), Swiss missionaries in the Spelonken district of southeast Africa codified Tsonga, a language they attributed to people who in reality were fairly recent immigrants from neighboring regions. However, to "systematize" the language, as they understood it, required that they construct it first as a written lingua franca, which in turn required explanations of the great structural variation in speech that they encountered. They had recourse to a story of coastal invaders who brought foreign forms into Tsonga-speaking areas, sullying the language that had been a "great bond" between clans in past centuries.

Cast in the idiom of invasion and coercion—"framing movement as displacement, rather than exchange or transformation" (Fabian 1986, p. 78)—such narratives made the past into an ideological operator and legitimizing resource for colonialist reductions of linguistic complexity. This can be seen likewise in Irvine & Gal's report (2000) of the French military's legitimizing of their own invasion of the Senegambia area of West Africa. They viewed speakers of the Sereer language as resistant to Islam, unwarlike, and "primitive;" so they could diagnose the relatively widespread bilingualism in Wolof that they found among Sereer speakers as evidence that they had in the past fallen prey to that more aggressive, sophisticated, Islamic group. Bilingualism, diagnosed as the residue of past conquest and present tyranny, motivated the French answer to the call of their own *mission civilatrice*.

However, such interested constructions of linguistic history could be pirated by colonial subjects, because the transhistorical purity and autonomy of such images of language allowed them to traverse "ambiguous lines that divided [colonial] engagement from appropriation" (Cooper & Stoler 1997a, p. 6). Two striking examples are worth citing here. Tamil, learned and described by Europeans beginning in the mid-sixteenth century (James 1991), became an object of native purism in the late nineteenth century after publication of a missionary's comparative grammar that foregrounded its previously unrecognized structural distinctness from North Indian languages, including Sanskrit, the dominant religious Truth language. Newly understood as first among members of the newly named Dravidian language family, Tamil became a symbolic resource in struggles for cultural autonomy that crosscut ethnic, caste, and religious lines of difference. Segments of a colonialized society appropriated colonizers' versions of linguistic descent and mobilized them in politically fraught struggles over legitimate genres of liturgical speech (Appadurai 1981, Schiffman 1996).

Similarly "modular," identitarian conceptions of originary language are described by Mannheim as having been mobilized in colonial Peru (1991). In precolonial times the language of the Inka had been a lingua franca of empire, distributed in an "eggshell thin overlay" (1991, p. 16) over local Quechua languages. Its appropriation by Spaniards for administrative and missionizing purposes was apparently legitimized by chronotopic associations with Cuzco, that empire's former sacred political center. However, by the seventeenth century, a local *criolla* elite justified its claims to a privileged Andean identity by invoking that same chronotope, mobilizing a dominant ideology of language to assert their autonomy relative to a dominant colonial regime. Such examples show how the iconic character of such images of language made them susceptible to appropriation in unanticipated ways, across lines of sociopolitical interest.

LANGUAGES OUT OF PLACE: DESCRIBING
AND USING LINGUA FRANCAS

Colonial linguists helped to create such lingua francas—language varieties used non-natively, at least initially, across lines of native language difference—which they understood to be originary, "normal" versions of the languages whose degenerate variants they encountered. Conversely, colonial regimes created conditions that engendered creole languages, but which linguists largely ignored. Most obvious are what Chaudenson (1977) calls exogenous creole languages, which arose in "plantocratic" colonies, like those of the Caribbean. (An important exception to this generalization is Hugo Schuchardt, a linguist who also resisted dominant nineteenth-century philological conceptions of language discussed in the next section.)

This superficial paradox is symptomatic of the ideological marginality of lingua francas and creoles under colonial regimes. Notwithstanding their high utility, they lacked both originary chronotopes and native speakers. Similar paradoxes emerged along with the lingua francas used in Europeans' early commercial contacts in Africa. Sango, Lingala, and Ngbanda, crucial for business but low in prestige, went largely undescribed (Morrill 1997), partly because Europeans had only transient contact with them and partly because they were vehicular versions of native languages, in use between Africans more than between Europeans and Africans (Samarin 1989).

However, two lingua francas—Swahili in central Africa and Malay in the Dutch East Indies—can be considered here with an eye to the ways their anomalous statuses shaped them as objects of colonial linguistics. Both became objects of descriptive, codifying attention because of their growing salience for regimes that progressively penetrated territories and communities. Linguistic work on both offers evidence of underlying tensions between colonial needs for effective communicative praxis across lines of sociolinguistic difference on one hand, and colonial ideologies of languages as marks of identity on the other.

Fabian reads such a dilemma from the two distinct genres of descriptive writing about Swahili that developed in the nineteenth century (1985). One, grounded in military/economic realities of colonial exploitation, emphasized Swahili's simplicity and utility in context-bound, limited purpose communication, and resonated with assumptions about the primitivity of native thought. The other literature, serving the colonial civilizing mission, foregrounded Swahili's grammatical and lexical subtleties as evidence of its suitability, under European cultivation, for elevation to the status of a language of education for, among others, native missionaries.

This generic difference indexed a split that could only be recast as a hierarchical relation between literacy-linked "high" and oral "low" varieties of Swahili. Descriptively appropriated as colonialists' "own" language, Swahili could serve restricted purposes of communication across the colonial divide, while the oral varieties of subaltern communities were residualized or placed under erasure (Gal & Irvine 1995) for political purposes. Fabian reads colonial linguistic management of "high" Swahili as a strategy of containment, animated by French anxieties about its use in linguistically plural communities of Africans working in their mine-based economies.

Broadly similar social tensions accompanied Malay's double development in the Dutch East Indies. National insecurity in Europe, linguistic diversity in the archipelago, and conflicted politics of commerce and conversion led the Dutch to forgo use of their own language with natives (Groeneboer 1998; Hoffman 1973, 1979). As a plantation economy superceded trade, colonialists had increased need for a medium of administrative communication across lines of territorial and linguistic difference. The upshot was the elevation of Malay, a lingua franca that had been in use throughout the area prior to Europeans' arrival in the sixteenth century. As it became an object of colonial linguistic treatment, Malay's useful but low-status oral varieties were superceded by one that was determined on scientific/philological grounds (discussed later) to have been originary. Cut off historically from its (putative) native speakers in the Riau islands, but also institutionally from Islam and Arabic orthography, this invented variety of Malay was codified and disseminated by a special class of colonial language officers. (Teeuw 1971).

The upshot was another broadly diglossic split (Ferguson 1959) between the print-mediated "high" Malay of colonial administration and heterogeneous "low" varieties of "market Malay" (Hoffman 1973, 1979), which were important as the verbal glue binding segments of an economically and ethnolinguistically plural society. Even as dialects of "low" Malay became useful for a native literate community, their speakers found themselves in the curious position of speaking a language that, under ideological erasure (Gal & Irvine 1995, Irvine & Gal 2000) by the colonial regime, did not exist (Siegel 1997). The reification of this high/low split mirrored hardening racial and gender divisions in late nineteenth-century urban milieux. The mystique of science so important to Dutch colonialism's legitimacy operated in the sphere of language to create models of Malay that helped eliminate intermediate, "hybrid" speech that incorporated elements of Dutch (Maier 1997).

So colonial linguistic work enhanced the practical and ideological usefulness of both languages by hierarchizing and mediating problematic linguistic diversity. Languages became targets for anxieties projected out of contradictory demands of pragmatic colonial policy on one hand, and ideas about linguistic identity on the other.

ORIENTALISM AND COMPARATIVE PHILOLOGY

As linguistic writings circulated beyond their originary colonial circumstances, they came to be read in Europe as windows on the most directly writable aspects of colonial otherness. They could also be brought together under the academic *cum* scientific purview of comparative philology, which developed contemporaneously with colonial penetration and domination of Africa, the Middle East, and parts of Asia over the nineteenth century. Colonial linguists provided grist for the mill of philological science, which in turn developed guiding images for the sorts of late nineteenth century colonial linguistic work sketched earlier. So comparative philology needs to be considered here as theoretically complementary to descriptive linguistics as practiced in disparate colonial locales.

The colonial origins of comparative philology—and, some would, say of modern linguistics more generally (Newmeyer 1986)—can be read from Sir William "Oriental" Jones' 1786 demonstration of structural commonalities between Latin, Greek, and Sanskrit (Aarsleff 1983). However, those affinities had been known to Europeans as early as the sixteenth century (Mukherjee 1968), and the comparative method that Jones demonstrated in rudimentary form had been developed independently by scholars in Europe (Gulya 1974). So it is worth foregrounding here instead the rhetorical force that accrued to his work as it traveled from India to a European readership.

Inscribed in Jones' *Third Discourse on the Hindus* can be seen two "modalities of colonial knowledge" (Cohn 1996). In an investigative modality he wrote as a judge who needed access to versions of native legal texts less "degenerate" than those initially available to him. This animated scholarship in the tradition of classical philology, aimed at recovering "pure," originary forms of texts. Though this project may have resonated with Hindu Puranic senses of a normative textual past (Rocher 1993), it primarily served and legitimized British rule.

However, the transposition of comparative strategies from the structure of texts to language systems took Jones' work into a historiographic modality. It demonstrated what Cohn calls the "ontological power" of "assumptions about how real social and natural worlds are constituted" (1996, p. 4). Jones accomplished this by transposing the strategies of classical philological scholarship from the domain of authored (and mistransmitted) texts to the domain of authorless linguistic structure. In this way, the comparative method opened up prehistory to empirical, inductive reasoning.

The ideological and political salience of this shift, and the enormous intellectual prestige it lent to the discipline of comparative philology that arose from it, can be characterized by adapting Chatterjee's observations (1986) on relativism and reason in (post)colonial encounters. Comparative philology brought into convergence the exercise of distinctively European reason and distinctively European power, allowing intellectual relations between European rationality and its (linguistic) object to be conflated with political relations between colonializing and colonialized peoples. This made philology central for scholarly figurings of colonial "dialectics of inclusion and exclusion" (Cooper & Stoler 1997a, p. 3), because it elided the gap between scientific study of abstract language structures and political control of human conduct. In this way the science of language (difference) simultaneously served to "transmute . . . polyglot agonies of Babel into a cult of transcendent European erudition" (Herzfeld 1987, p. 31).

Chatterjee's critique bears the imprint of Foucault's writing on power and knowledge, which influenced Said's earlier, formative account of philological and colonial interest in *Orientalism* (Said 1978; see also Said 1995). His critique of French comparative philology of Semitic languages is a powerful argument by example about the linguistic appropriation of Semitic (pre)history, which, purified by dint of (European) reason, could be returned in suitably domesticated form to its original inheritors. Said has been too influential for even those who resist his argument most to ignore (e.g., Gaeffke 1990) and his critique has been transposed effectively to other scenes of colonial philological work (Breckenridge & van der Veer 1993, Florida 1995). However, it has also been recurringly criticized in a manner reminiscent of Said's own criticism of Foucault (1978, p. 23) as having accorded too little attention to individual authors or texts (Ahmed 1992, Ludden 1993, Rocher 1993, Loomba 1998).

In the realm of (colonial) linguistic historiography, this recurring criticism points to the need to reread philological scholarship, paying explicit attention to political, intellectual, and biographical conditions of its production, as well as the ideologically salient metaphors it incorporates. Recent work under such a critical profile includes Irvine's work on the gendered politics of French philology of African languages (Irvine 1993, 1995), Joseph's study of language and scientific racism in relation to assimilationist and associationist colonial policies in French Indochina (Joseph 2000), and Olender's account (1992) of the philologist Renan's road from the seminary, through Semitic philology, to a "scientific" recuperation of the life of Christ.

The central, enduring philological trope that must be noted here is of language as organism, associated with the early, post-Biblical reflections on human origins of Herder and other German Romantics, who likewise were engaged in the crisis of national authenticity in Europe (Bauman & Briggs 2000, Blackall 1978). The trope powerfully informed images of language change in natural, entelechial processes of articulation, predetermined by languages' originary conditions and communities. This radically naturalized understanding of linguistic *cum* human difference grounded radically relativized views of historical change, what Fabian calls the allochronic "denial of coevalness" (1983, p. 30).

The spread of an axiomatic grammatical distinction between isolating, agglutinating, and inflecting methods of word formation, for instance, helped particularize and scientize studies of more or less "organic" language families. The Schlegel brothers, von Humboldt, and other early nineteenth-century philologists hypostasized these "empirical" categories to frame grammatical comparisons between languages in a natural-historical mode (Alter 1999, Davies 1998, Perceval 1987). Deployed in scientistic framings of grammatical structure, they served various and sometimes conflicting purposes, for instance, setting off Indo-European and Semitic languages from others (for Schlegel), or the former from the latter (for Renan, the linguistic theorist of scientific Racism) (Olender 1992).

Crucial here is the culmination of organismic tropes of language in Schleicher's diagrammatic, family tree (*stammbaum*) image of language change (Hoenigswald 1974, Calvet 1974) in the mid-nineteenth century. This image of branching descent was directly instrumental for inventing the kinds of linguistic pasts described earlier and for reifying colonial languages as unitized counters out of multilingual conditions of encounter (Silverstein 1997, p. 127). Worth noting here is Hoenigswald's observation (1974, p. 352) that the *stammbaum* model rehearses the classical philological image of textual transmission in the domain of language structure. This resonates with Wells' observations (1987) on the acmenistic character of comparative philology, because it contributed to visions of languages as decaying (along with their duly reified cultures) once past their apogees of development (see also Nielsen 1989, Perceval 1987), much as originary texts could only become corrupt through transmission.

Schleicher's empirically threadbare, Hegelian, gendered metaphysics of language is now largely forgotten. However, its professedly empirical, inductive framing of language difference served as a powerful license for global legislations of difference between the West and the Rest, and so between colonializing and colonialized peoples (Said 1995). The *stammbaum* model took on novel significance as used by Darwin to motivate his very different, evolutionary view of natural history and selection. Alter traces reciprocal influences between scientific thought about languages and species to show how, around 1870, the *stammbaum* model of orders and levels came to represent an "ascending staircase of social-cultural evolution" rather than the "tree of ethnological descent" (1999, p. 141; see also Fabian 1983, Burrow 1967, Jeffords 1987). The science of language then helped to naturalize evolutionism, making it an ideology that both legitimized colonialism generally, and enabled the work of colonial linguistics particularly.

POSTCOLONIAL POSTSCRIPT

Saussure's *Course in General Linguistics* (1966), cited by many as the founding document of modern linguistic science, contains the observation that "there is no other field in which so many absurd notions, prejudices, mirages, and fictions have sprung up" (1966, p. 7). With an eye to the developments just noted, those errors might be viewed as much from an ideological as a "psychological viewpoint" (as Saussure puts it). So too, the thrust of Saussure's exposition—the radical autonomy of linguistic systems, the methodological priority of language states over mutations, the nonteleological character of language change, etc.—works quite directly against the grain of comparative philology as just sketched. Because it brackets such issues, Saussure's linguistic metier appears, in Blommaert's words, "to be immune to ideological influences" and integrable into any kind of political context (Blommaert 1999, p. 183). However, the saliences of this later version of linguistic science for late colonial and postcolonial linguistics need to be noted here.

Notwithstanding Saussure's stature, evolutionist biology shaped the thinking of many of his contemporaries in European and colonial milieus. Most notable may be Otto Jespersen's influential, positivist vision of language progress, shaped by both Spencer and Darwin (Jespersen 1894; see McCawley 1992). His metric for measuring inequality between languages, which emphasized conceptual precision and communicative efficiency (Jespersen 1922), was understood to measure accumulated effects of the operation of reason, social progress, and a "wise natural selection." Though reminiscent of Vico's vision of the progression of language from the senses to the intellect (see Pennycook 1998), Jespersen's argument was buttressed by rigorous descriptions of linguistic categories. The upshot was a newly scientized version of the difference between modern Europe (languages) and communities of speakers of less evolved languages.

The ideological salience of such metrics should not be underestimated. Euroamerican developmentalist writings on postcolonial language politics have had enduring effects on language policy and linguistic work in plural postcolonial nations (e.g. Fishman 1968). They presuppose viewpoints largely congruent with Jespersen's. Swahili's place in a Tanzanian "political linguistics" (Blommaert 1999), for instance, has been linked to developmentalist notions of efficiency and simplicity; Indonesian linguists have promoted their national language—successor to Malay, the lingua franca of the Dutch East Indies—in a similar mode, figuring the language in a teleological developmentalist ideology (Errington 1998, Heryanto 1985, Keane 1997). These two languages' lack of originary chronotopes, noted earlier, may throw special ideological weight onto developmentalist legitimations of their statuses as national languages.

A central leitmotif running through the different kinds of linguistic work reviewed here, as suggested by Fardon & Furniss, is a common objectifying thrust that simultaneously brackets "politically charged expository strategies" (1994a, p. 16) of language use, including the very strategies of descriptive objectification that those works presuppose.

Suitably objectified, languages could be powerful naturalizing instruments for colonial power. Their hegemonic status, Fardon & Furniss suggest, can be read from their endurance even in critiques of colonialism such as Asad's, who demonstrates the power-laden character of colonial-era ethnographic "cultural translation" with recourse to essentialized understandings of "weak" and "strong" languages (Asad 1986). The necessary but recurringly disguised incompleteness of such work can be linked with its doubly interested character, vis-à-vis immediate authorial concerns and broader ideological stances. However, it is not legitimate to read such partialness as evidence of the wholly illusory or fictive character of the structures represented in that work; the production of linguistic knowledge cannot always and everywhere be dissolved into the reproduction of colonial interest. If the texts that colonial linguists produced were not the transparent windows on human-yet-natural reality they were intended to be, they can nonetheless be read critically, with an eye to their metalinguistic strategies for framing talk's patterned character. Read in critically relativized ways, colonial linguistic texts can be more meaningful than their authors knew, moving beyond while also incorporating knowledge they provide—in some cases, the only knowledge available—about massively variable yet underlyingly human talk.

ACKNOWLEDGMENTS

My sincere thanks for advice and information to James Lockhart, Harold Schiffman, and Kathryn Woolard. All shortcomings of this article are my doing.

Visit the Annual Reviews home page at www.AnnualReviews.org

LITERATURE CITED

Aarsleff H. 1983. Sir William Jones and the new philology. In *The Study of Language in England 1780–1860*. Minneapolis: Univ. Minn. Press

Ahmed A .1992. *In Theory: Classes, Nations, Literatures*. London/New York: Verso

Alberto P. 1997. Emperor's English: language as a technology of rule in British West Africa. *Penn Hist. Rev.* http://www.history.upenn.edu/phr/spring97/ess2.html

Alter SG. 1999. *Darwinism and the Linguistic Image: Language, Race, and Natural Theology in the Nineteenth Century*. Baltimore: Johns Hopkins Univ. Press

Anderson BR. 1991. *Imagined Communities: Reflections on the Origin and Spread of Nationalism*. New York: Verso. 2nd ed.

Appadurai A. 1981. *Worship and Conflict Under Colonial Rule: A South Indian Case*. Cambridge, UK: Cambridge Univ. Press

Asad T. 1986. The concept of cultural translation in British social anthropology. In *Writing Culture: The Poetics and Politics of Ethnography*, ed. J Clifford, GE Marcus, pp. 141–64. Berkeley: Univ. Calif. Press

Balibar E. 1991. The nation form: history and ideology. In *Race, Nation, Class: Ambiguous Identities*, ed. E Balibar, I Wallerstein, pp. 86–106, transl. C Turner. London/New York: Verso (from French)

Bauman R, Briggs CL. 2000. Language philosophy as language ideology: John Locke and Johann Gottfried Herder. See Kroskrity 2000, pp. 139–204

Bendor-Samuel J. 1994. Summer institute of linguistics. In *The Encyclopedia of Language and Linguistics*, ed. R Asher, pp. 4405–10. Oxford: Pergamon

Blackall E. 1959. *The Emergence of German as a Literary Language, 1700-1775*. Cambridge, UK: Cambridge Univ. Press

Blommaert J. 1999. *State Ideology and Language in Tanzania*. Koln, Ger.: Rudiger Koppe

Bourdieu P. 1991. *Language and Symbolic Power*. Cambridge, MA: Harvard Univ. Press

Breckenridge CA, van der Veer P, eds. 1993. *Orientalism and the Postcolonial Predicament: Perspectives on South Asia*. Philadelphia: Univ. Penn. Press

Burrow JW. 1967. The uses of philology in Victorian England. In *Ideas and Institutions of Victorian Britain*, ed. R Robson, pp.180–204. London: Bell & Sons

Calvet L-J. 1974. *Linguistique et Colonialisme: Petit Traite de Glottophagie*. Paris: Payot

Carmody B. 1988. Conversion and school at Chikuni, 1905–39. *Africa* 58(2):93–209

Chatterjee P. 1986. *Nationalist Thought and the Colonial World: A Derivative Discourse?* London: Zed Books UN Univ.

Chaudenson R. 1977. Toward a reconstruction of the social matrix of creole languages. In *Pidgin and Creole Linguistics*, ed. A Valdman, pp. 259–76. Bloomington: Indiana Univ. Press

Chimhundu H. 1992. Early missionaries and the ethnolinguistic factor during the 'Invention of Tribalism' in Zimbabwe. *J. Afr. Hist.* 33:87–109

Cohn BS. 1996. *Colonialism and Its Forms of Knowledge: The British in India*. Princeton, NJ: Princeton Univ. Press

Comaroff J, Comaroff J. 1991. *Of Revelation and Revolution*. Chicago: Univ. Chicago Press

Cooper F, Stoler AL. 1997a. Between metropole and colony. See Cooper & Stoler 1997b, pp. 1–56

Cooper F, Stoler AL, eds. 1997b. *Tensions of Empire: Colonial Cultures in a Bourgeois World*. Berkeley: Univ. Calif. Press

Davies AM. 1998. *Nineteenth-Century Linguistics*. Vol. 4. *History of Linguistics Ser.*, ed. G Lepschy. London: Longman

de Saussure F. 1966 (1916). *Course in General Linguistics*, ed. C Bally, A Sechehaye, transl. W Baskin. New York: McGraw-Hill (from French)

Errington J. 1998. Indonesian('s) development: on the state of a language of state. In *Language Ideologies*, ed. K Woolard, B Schieffelin, P Kroskrity, pp. 271–84. New York: Oxford Univ. Press

Fabian J. 1983. *Time and the Other: How Anthropology Makes Its Object*. New York: Columbia Univ. Press

Fabian J. 1985. *Language on the Road: Notes on Swahili in Two Nineteenth Century Travelogues. Sprache und Geschichte in Afrika Ser.* Hamburg: Buske

Fabian J. 1986. *Language and Colonial Power: The Appropriation of Swahili in the Former Belgian Congo 1880–1938*. Berkeley: Univ. Calif. Press

Fardon R, Furniss G. 1994a. Introduction: frontiers and boundaries—African languages as political environment. See Fardon & Furniss 1994b, pp. 1–32

Fardon R, Furniss G, eds. 1994b. *African Languages, Development and the State*. London: Routledge

Ferguson C. 1959. Diglossia. *Word* 15:325–40

Fishman J. 1968. Nationality-nationalism and nation-nationism. In *Language Problems of Developing Nations*, ed. J Fishman, J Ferguson, J DasGupta, pp. 39–51. New York: Wiley & Sons

Florida NK. 1995. *Writing the Past, Inscribing the Future: History as Prophecy in Colonial Java*. Durham, NC: Duke Univ. Press

Gaeffke P. 1990. A rock in the tides of time: Oriental studies then and now. *Acad. Quest.* Spring:67–74

Gal S, Irvine JT. 1995. The boundaries of languages and disciplines: how ideologies construct difference. *Soc. Res.* 62(4):967–1001

Gellner E. 1983. *Nations and Nationalism*. Ithaca, NY: Cornell Univ. Press

Giliomee H. 1989. The beginnings of Afrikaner ethnic consciousness, 1850–1915. See Vail 1989, pp. 21–54

Greenblatt S. 1991. Kidnapping language. In *Marvelous Possessions: The Wonder of the New World*, pp. 86–118. Chicago: Univ. Chicago Press

Groeneboer K, ed. 1997. *Koloniale Taalpolitiek in Oost en West: Nederlands-Indie, Suriname, Nederlandse Antillen en Aruba*. Amsterdam: Amsterdam Univ. Press

Groeneboer K. 1998. *Gateway to the West: The Dutch Language in Colonial Indonesia 1600–1950*, transl. M Scholz. Amsterdam: Amsterdam Univ. Press (from Dutch)

Gulya J. 1974. Some eighteenth century antecedents of nineteenth century linguistics: the discovery of Finno-Ugrian. See Hymes 1974, pp. 258–76

Gumperz JJ. 1971. The speech community. In *Language and Social Groups*, ed. AS Dil, pp. 114–27. Stanford, CA: Stanford Univ. Press

Hanks WF. 2000. Discourse genres in a theory of practice. In *Intertexts: Writings on Language, Utterance, and Context*, pp. 103–32. Oxford: Rowman & Littlefield

Hanzeli VE. 1969. *Missionary Linguistics in New France*. The Hague: Mouton

Harries P. 1988. The roots of ethnicity: discourse and the politics of language construction in South-East Africa. *Afr. Aff.* 87(346):25–52

Harries P. 1989. Exclusion, classification and internal colonialism: the emergence of ethnicity among the Tsonga-speakers of South Africa. See Vail 1989, pp. 82–117

Haugen E. 1972. Dialect, language, nation. In *The Ecology of Language*, ed. AS Dil, pp. 237–54. Stanford, CA: Stanford Univ. Press

Henson H. 1974. *British Social Anthropologists and Language: A History of Separate Development*. Oxford: Clarendon

Herder JG. 1966 (1787). Essay on the origin of language. In *On the Origin of Language*, pp. 85–166, transl. J Moran. New York: F Ungar (from German)

Heryanto A. 1985. The language of development and the development of language. transl. N Lutz. Indonesia. 40:1–24 (from Indonesian)

Herzfeld M. 1987. *Anthropology Through the Looking-Glass: Critical Ethnography in the Margins of Europe.* Cambridge, UK: Cambridge Univ. Press

Hobsbawm E, Ranger T, eds. 1983. *The Invention of Tradition.* Cambridge, UK: Cambridge Univ. Press

Hoenigswald HM. 1974. Fallacies in the history of linguistics: notes on the appraisal of the nineteenth century. See Hymes 1974, pp. 346–58

Hoenigswald HM, Wiener L, eds. 1987. *Biological Metaphor and Cladistic Classification: An Interdisciplinary Perspective.* Philadelphia: Univ. Penn. Press

Hoffman J. 1973. The Malay language as a force for unity in the Indonesian archipelago 1815–1900. *Nusantara* 4:19–35

Hoffman J. 1979. A foreign investment. *Indonesia* 27:65–92

Hovdhaugen E. 1996. *And the Word Was God.* Munster, Ger.: Nodus

Hvalkof S, Aaby P. 1981. *Is God an American? An Anthropological Perspective on the Missionary Work of the Summer Institute of Linguistics.* Copenhagen: Int. Work Group Indig. Aff.

Hymes D, ed. 1974. *Studies in the History of Linguistics: Traditions and Paradigms.* Bloomington: Indiana Univ. Press

Irvine JT. 1989. When talk isn't cheap: language and political economy. *Am. Ethnol.* 16(2):773–90

Irvine JT. 1993. Mastering African languages: the politics of linguistics in nineteenth-century Senegal. *Soc. Anal.* 33:27–46

Irvine JT. 1995. The family romance of colonial linguistics: gender and family in nineteenth-century representations of African languages. *Pragmatics* 5(2):139–53

Irvine JT, Gal S. 2000. Language ideology and linguistic differentiation. See Kroskrity 2000, pp. 35–84

James G. 1991. *Tamil Lexicography.* Tübingen, Ger.: Niemeyer

Jeffords S. 1987. The knowledge of words: the evolution of language and biology in nineteenth-century thought. *Centen. Rev.* 31(1):66–83

Jespersen O. 1894. *Progress in Language with Special Reference to English.* London: Swan Sonnenschein

Jespersen O. 1922. *Language.* London: Allen & Unwin

Joseph JE. 2000. Language and 'psychological race': Léopold de Saussure on French in Indochina. *Lang. Commun.* 20:29–53

Keane W. 1997. Knowing one's place: national language and the idea of the local in Eastern Indonesia. *Cult. Anthropol.* 12(1):37–63

Kipp RS. 1990. *The Early Years of a Dutch Colonial Mission: The Karo Field.* Ann Arbor: Univ. Mich. Press

Kroskrity P, ed. 2000. *Regimes of Language: Ideologies, Polities, and Identities.* Santa Fe: SAR

Kuipers JC. 1998. *Language, Identity, and Marginality in Indonesia.* Cambridge, UK: Cambridge Univ. Press

Labov W. 1972. *Sociolinguistic Patterns.* Philadelphia: Univ. Penn. Press

Lauzon M. 1996. Savage eloquence in America and the linguistic construction of a British identity in the 18th century. *Hist. Linguist.* 23(1/2):123–58

Lockhart J. 1991. *Nahuas and Spaniards: Postconquest Central Mexical History and Philology.* Stanford, CA: Stanford Univ. Press

Loomba A. 1998. *Colonialism/Postcolonialism.* London: Routledge

Ludden D. 1993. Orientalist empiricism: transformations of colonial knowledge. See Breckinridge & van der Veer 1993, pp. 250–278

Maier H. 1997. Nederlands-Indie en Het Maleis. See Groeneboer 1997, pp. 13–54

Mannheim B. 1991. *The Language of the Inka*

Since the European Invasion. Austin: Univ. Tex. Press

Mazrui A. 1975. *The Political Sociology of the English Language: An African Perspective.* The Hague: Mouton

McCawley JD. 1992. The biological side of Otto Jespersen's linguistic thought. *Hist. Linguist.* 19:97–110

Meeuwis M. 1999a. Flemish nationalism in the Belgian Congo versus Zairian anti-imperialism: continuity and discontinuity in language ideological debates. In *Language Ideological Debates,* ed. J Blommaert, pp. 381–424. Berlin: Mouton de Gruyter

Meeuwis M. 1999b. The White Fathers and Luganda. To the origins of French missionary linguistics in the Lake Victoria region. *Ann. Aequat.* 20:413–43

Messick B. 1993. *The Calligraphic State: Textual Domination and History in a Muslim Society.* Berkeley: Univ. Calif. Press

Mignolo W. 1994. Afterword: writing and recorded knowledge in colonial and post-colonial situations. In *Writing Without Words,* ed. E Boone, W Mignolo, pp. 293–313. Durham, NC: Duke Univ. Press

Mignolo W. 1995. *The Darker Side of the Renaissance: Literacy, Territoriality, and Colonization.* Ann Arbor: Univ. Mich. Press

Moriyama M. 1995. Language policy in the Dutch Colony: on Sundanese in the Dutch East Indies. *Southeast Asian Stud.* 32(4):446–54

Morrill CH. 1997. *Language, culture, and society in the Central African Republic: the emergence and development of Sango.* PhD thesis, Indiana Univ., Bloomington. 356 pp.

Mukherjee S. 1968. *Sir William Jones: A Study in Eighteenth-Century British Attitudes to India.* Cambridge, UK: Cambridge Univ. Press

Newmeyer FJ. 1986. *The Politics of Linguistics.* Chicago: Univ. Chicago Press

Nielsen HF. 1989. On Otto Jespersen's view of language evolution. In *Otto Jespersen: Facets of His Life and Work,* ed. A Juul, HF Nielsen, pp. 61–78. Philadelphia: Benjamins

Olender M. 1992. *The Languages of Paradise: Race, Religion, and Philology in the Nineteenth Century,* trans. A Goldhammer. Cambridge, MA: Harvard Univ. Press (from French)

Pennycook A. 1998. *English and the Discourses of Colonialism.* London: Routledge

Perceval W. 1987. Biological analogy before comparative grammar. See Hoenigswald & Wiener 1987, pp. 3–38

Pike KL. 1947. *Phonemics: A Technique for Reducing Languages to Writing.* Ann Arbor: Univ. Mich. Press

Rafael VL. 1993. *Contracting Colonialism.* Durham, NC: Duke Univ. Press

Raison-Jourde F. 1977. L'échange inégale de la langue: la pénétration des techniques linguistiques dans une civilisation de l'oral. *Annales* 32(4):639–69

Ranger T. 1989. Missionaries, migrants and the Manyika: the invention of ethnicity in Zimbabwe. See Vail 1989, pp. 118–50

Rocher R. 1993. British Orientalism in the eighteenth century: the dialectics of knowledge and government. See Breckenridge & Van der Veer 1993, pp. 215–45

Sack R. 1986. *Human Territoriality: Its Theory and History.* Cambridge, UK: Cambridge Univ. Press

Said E. 1978. *Orientalism.* London: Vintage

Said E. 1995. Secular interpretation, the geographical element, and the methodology of imperialism. In *After Colonialism,* ed. G Prakash, pp. 21–39. Princeton, NJ: Princeton Univ. Press

Samarin WJ. 1984. The linguistic world of field colonialism. *Lang. Soc.* 13:435–53

Samarin WJ. 1989. *The Black Man's Burden: African Colonial Labor on the Congo and Ubangi Rivers, 1880–1900.* Boulder, CO: Westview

Schieffelin B. 2000. Introducing Kaluli literacy: a chronology of influences. See Kroskrity 2000, pp. 293–328

Schiffman HF. 1996. *Linguistic Culture and Language Policy.* New York: Routledge

Schutz AJ. 1994. *The Voices of Eden: A History of Hawaiian Language Studies.* Honolulu: Unvi. Hawai'i Press

Shapiro M. 1989. A political approach to language purism. In *The Politics of Language Purism*, ed. B Jernudd & M Shapiro, pp. 21–30. Berlin: Mouton de Gruyter

Siegel JT. 1997. *Fetish, Recognition, Revolution*. Princeton, NJ: Princeton Univ. Press

Silverstein M. 1997. Encountering language and languages of encounter in North American ethnohistory. *J. Linguist. Anthropol.* 6(2):126–44

Smith-Hefner N. 1989. A social history of language change in mountain East Java. *J. Asian Stud.* 48:258–71

Steedly MM. 1996. The importance of proper names: language and "national" identity in colonial Karoland. *Am. Ethnol.* 23(3):447–75

Stoler A. 1989. Rethinking colonial categories: European communities and the boundaries of rule. *Comp. Stud. Soc. Hist.* 31:134–61

Teeuw A. 1973. *Pegawai Bahasa Dan Ilmu Bahasa [Language Officers and Indonesian Linguistics]*, transl. J Polak. Jakarta: Bhratara (from Dutch)

Tomas D. 1991. Tools of the trade: the production of ethnographic observations on the Andaman Islands, 1858–1922. In *Colonial Situations: Essays on the Contextualization of Ethnographic Knowledge*, ed. G Stocking, pp. 75–108. Madison: Univ. Wisc. Press

Urciuoli B. 1995. Language and borders. *Annu. Rev. Anthropol.* 24:525–46

Vail L, ed. 1989. *The Creation of Tribalism in Southern Africa*. Berkeley: Univ. Calif. Press

Wallerstein I. 1974. The rise and future demise of the world capitalist system. *Comp. Stud. Soc. Hist.* 16:387–415

Weber EJ. 1976. *Peasants Into Frenchmen: The Modernization of Rural France, 1870–1914*. Stanford, CA: Stanford Univ. Press

Wells R. 1987. Life and the growth of language: metaphors in biology and linguistics. See Hoenigswald & Wiener 1987, pp. 39–80

Wonderly WL, Nida EA. 1963. Linguistics and Christian missions. *Anthropol. Linguist.* 5(1):104–44

Woolard K, Schieffelin B. 1994. Language ideology. *Annu. Rev. Anthropol.* 23:55–82

Yates BA. 1980. The origins of language policy in Zaïre. *J. Mod. Afr. Stud.* 18 (2):257–79

Annu. Rev. Anthropol. 2001. 30:41–64

THE ORIGIN OF STATE SOCIETIES IN SOUTH AMERICA

Charles Stanish

Department of Anthropology, University of California, Los Angeles, Los Angeles, California 90095–1553; e-mail: stanish@ucla.edu

Key Words state formation, cultural evolution, Andes, chiefdoms, states

■ **Abstract** The earliest states developed in the central Andean highlands and along the central Pacific coast of western South America. The consensus in the archaeological literature is that state societies first developed in the central Andes in the early part of the first millennium C.E. A minority opinion holds that first-generation states developed as early as the late second millennium B.C.E. in the same area. The Andean region constitutes one of a few areas of first-generation state development in the world. This area therefore represents an important case study for the comparative analysis of state formation. This article outlines the arguments for state formation in South America, presents the evidence, analyzes the underlying assumptions about these arguments, and assesses the South American data in terms of contemporary anthropological theory of state evolution.

SOUTH AMERICA

South America, a continent approximately 17,870,000 km^2 in size, has been divided into as few as three and as many as two dozen different cultural areas by anthropologists (Willey 1971, pp. 17–24). Borrowing on the earlier work of Wissler (1922, pp. 245–57) and Bennett (1946, p. 1), Lumbreras (1981, p. 42) provides the most common cultural geographical division of South America: the Andes, the Llanos, Amazonia, the Chaco, the Pampas, and Patagonia (Figure 1). First-generation states evolved only in the central and south central part of one area, the Andes. This area, referred to collectively as the central Andes, would correspond to parts of Wissler's Inca area and to all of Willey's Peruvian cultural area (Willey 1971, p. 4). Bordered on the west by the Pacific Ocean, this culturally precocious region stretches from roughly the Peru-Ecuador border in the north, to the low forests of Peru and Bolivia in the east, and south to the southern part of the Titicaca Basin in Bolivia.

0084-6570/01/1021-0041$14.00

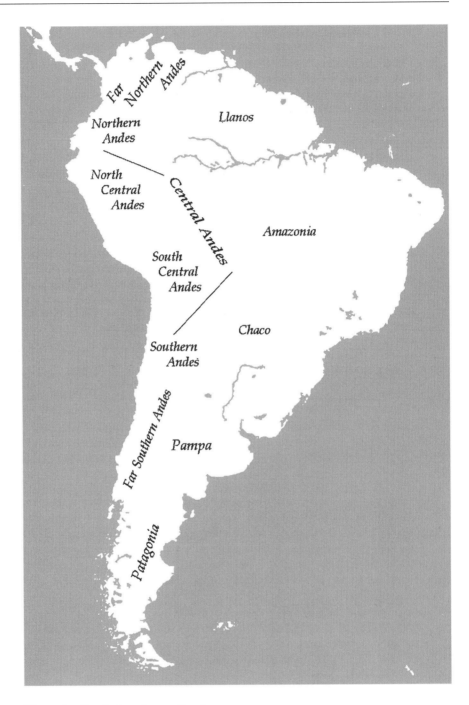

Figure 1   South American cultural areas.

THE CENTRAL ANDES

The central Andes extends over 1,000,000 km^2 and includes some of the world's driest deserts, rugged mountainsides and peaks, highland grasslands, and low forests (Figure 2). At the time of European contact, the central Andes was home to several dozen distinct ethnic and linguistic groups. In spite of this diversity, the idea that the central Andes is culturally unified and homogenous has been a subtext in anthropological and historical studies since at least the European conquest. A good argument can be made that such a bias developed directly out of Inca and Spanish

1-Aspero,   2-Cahuachi,   3-Cardal,   4-Cerro Blanco,   5-Cerro Sechín, 6-Chankillo,   7-Chavin,   8-Chiripa,   9-Chupacigarro,   10-El Paraíso, 11-Huaca La Florida, 12-Huacaloma, 13-Huaca Prieta , 14-Huaricoto, 15-Huaynuná, 16-Kotosh, 17-Kuntur Wasi, 18-La Galgada, 19-La Pampa, 20-Las Haldas,   21-Mina Perdida,   22-Moche,   23-Pachacamac, 24-Pacopampa,   25-Pampa de las Llamas - Moxeke,   26-Pikillacta, 27-Piruru, 28-Poro Poro, 29-Pucara, 30-Putina, 31-Qaluyu, 32-Salinas de Chao,   33-San Jacinto, 34-Sechín Alto, 35-Sechín Bajo, 36-Sipán, 37-Taukachi-Konkan, 38-Tiwanaku, 39-Wari

Figure 2   The central Andes.

imperial propaganda that promoted the cultural unity of empire. It is therefore not surprising that many definitions of the Andean or central Andean cultural area correspond rather neatly to the Incan imperial boundaries in the 1530s.

If one used the political and linguistic boundaries of the later first millennium C.E., there would be a very different picture. Around C.E. 600 there were three relatively distinct cultural, linguistic, political, and geographical areas in the central Andes. The Moche culture developed in the northern coastal desert. In this area, people spoke Mochica and related dialects (Torero 1990). In the central highlands, the Wari state dominated the political landscape. Most likely, an ancestral form of Quechua was spoken in this region. The people of Tiwanaku ruled the south central Andean *altiplano*, or high plains. In this region, Aymara, Pukina, and related dialects were the dominant languages in the sixteenth century, and we presume that some form of proto-Aymara (Aru) and/or Pukina was spoken in this area at the time of Tiwanaku. Each of these areas has its own research traditions. Given that this discussion focuses on the origin of the state and that many archaeologists point to these three regions as home to the earliest states, these areas structure this discussion.

DEFINING THE STATE

Flannery (1998, pp. 15–16; 1999) makes the essential point that the definition of the state is a task for anthropologists and political scientists working with ethnographic or historical data. The role of archaeologists, in contrast, is to define the material indicators of this phenomenon and then assess the data to define the emergence of the state. The anthropological definitions of the state, as well as its material indicators in the archaeological record, are closely linked to the theoretical framework in which the concept of the state is developed. Definitions that focus on political power and social classes tend to define states broadly, with many archaeological cases fitting into the definition. In most neomarxist frameworks, the existence of social classes in and of itself is the defining feature of state organization. Silva Santisteban (1997, p. 22), for instance, argues that the existence of any monument that is significantly large or elaborate enough to indicate group labor above the household, is evidence for state organization. In his words, ". . . the presence of a ceremonial center [is] tangible evidence of the sociopolitical formation that we call a State" (Silva Santisteban 1997, p. 101). A theoretically similar position is advocated by Haas (1987, p. 32), who also sees the exercise of economic power to be the essential variable in the definition of the state. In the Andes according to this definition, large earthen constructions reflect concentrated economic power and a state organization (Haas 1987, p. 22).

A more common view is that monumental architectural construction precedes the state in western South America. In this view, nonstate societies are fully capable of amassing sufficient labor to build large monuments, usually through religious or "theocratic" means (Burger 1995, p. 37; Fung Pineda 1988, p. 80; Moseley 1975,

1992). Moseley refers to complex, prestate societies as "civilizations," in which hierarchy can exist without hereditary rank (M.E. Moseley, personal communication). In this context, the ideology represents the community, not individuals or elite groups, and corporate architecture is created to provide focus for community rituals and the materialization of chief ideologies (e.g. DeMarrais et al 1996, Dillehay 1992).

In models that emphasize the religious functions of early monumental constructions, the state develops after the shift from a kin-based, chief "hierarchy at the service of the collectivity" (Albarracin-Jordan 1996, p. 70) to a hierarchy headed by a state elite that acts largely in its own interest. The state is defined by a series of factors that distinguish it from chief, kin-based organization. The relative importance of these factors is based upon the particular theoretical framework in which they are proposed. In the Andes, factors that have been proposed are generally consistent with the literature on state formation from around the world.

THE EMERGENCE OF COMPLEX SOCIETY IN THE LATE PRECERAMIC PERIOD

At the beginning of the fourth millennium B.C.E., all peoples in South America lived in small hunting, gathering, and horticultural camps, or, on rare occasions, in small semipermanent villages. By 3000–2500 B.C.E., the first fully sedentary and complex societies developed on the Pacific coast of Peru. Social complexity in the Andean archaeological record is generally indicated by the existence of large monuments that have functions beyond domestic residence and subsistence. Andean archaeologists refer to such architecture by several terms, including corporate, civic-ceremonial, elite-ceremonial, ritual, or public architecture. Settlements that have pyramids, courts, walled plazas, and so forth are considered to be organizationally more complex than politically egalitarian villages. The theoretical link between corporate architecture, a term first proposed by Moseley (1975), and cultural complexity rests on the premise that the monuments were built by, and meant to be seen and used by, a social group larger than a few families.

The Coast

Beginning around 3000 B.C.E., a few societies with a predominantly nonagricultural subsistence base built corporate monuments on the Peruvian coast. The site of Aspero, located on the northern edge of the Supe River adjacent to the Pacific Ocean, represents one of these early settlements. The earliest phases of corporate construction began around 2800–2000 B.C.E. (Feldman 1987, p. 12; Moseley 1992a, p. 117) (dates uncorrected unless noted otherwise). One large monument is the Huaca de los Idolos, a flat-topped pyramid 1500 m^2 in size used for ritual display (Feldman 1987, p. 11; Moseley 1992a, p. 115). Along with this pyramid, Aspero has 12–15 hectares (ha) of domestic midden areas, and 17 other pyramids between 1.0 and 4.0 m high. Excavations at the site reveal a pattern of continually rebuilt constructions by a resident population, a pattern found at many sites throughout the coastal valleys at this time.

Perhaps the largest settlement of this time period is located 2 km from the coast in the Chillón valley and is known as El Paraíso. According to Quilter (1985, p. 294) and Moseley (1992a, p. 119), the major construction at the site was in progress by 2000 B.C.E., and it continued to be occupied for two to four centuries. The 100,000 tons of stone masonry construction is found in at least seven mounds that form a giant U shape over 58 ha (Quilter 1985, p. 279). It has a huge, 7.0-ha plaza located between the arms of the U. Many structures were elaborately decorated. In particular, one structure was painted red and had a bright orange burnt floor with evidence of fire rituals. Moseley (1992a, p. 120) notes that artifacts include red pigment grinders, bird feathers, unfired figurines, and fruit tree branches. Earlier, we believed that there was little evidence for permanent habitation at the site. However, later work indicates that it indeed had a resident population (Fung Pineda 1988; Quilter 1991b, p. 427; Quilter 1991a; Quilter et al 1991).

Another large Preceramic site is known as Chupacigarro or Caral. Located inland in the Supe valley, the site is an impressive 50-ha Preceramic settlement that includes circular structures with ramps 50–80 m in diameter (Engel 1987), 25 pyramids up to 25 m high, and evidence of a sedentary population (Silva Santisteban 1997, pp. 103–4).

The three sites of Chupacigarro, Aspero, and El Paraíso are located in different ecological zones. They represent the geographically broad settlement distribution of major Preceramic sites, including the immediate coast, a site within a short walk from the ocean, and an inland site well away from the marine resources. These three examples indicate that the first monumental architecture was constructed in different ecological zones, where access to marine and agricultural resources varied greatly.

The Central Highlands

During the late Preceramic, a widespread building and ritual tradition developed among a number of formerly egalitarian highland communities as well. This has been called the "Kotosh Religious Tradition" by Burger & Burger (1980). At the type site of Kotosh, Burger (1995, p. 47) describes two artificial mounds and a series of superimposed temples. The highest mound was 14 m high and had a three-tiered platform with numerous chambers built into the base. There are at least 11 chambers and possibly up to 100 chambers at Kotosh itself (Burger 1995, p. 48; Izumi & Terada 1972). A prominent feature of this architectural tradition is small buildings, usually plastered and decorated with firepits in the floor. One of the most spectacular of these Preceramic structures is the Temple of the Crossed Hands at Kotosh. Other sites in the highlands, such as Huaricoto, La Galgada (Grieder et al 1988b), and Piruru (Bonnier & Rozenberg 1988), have similar ritual constructions, but the amount of labor and architectural complexity of each site varies. Paintings of serpents, niches in the walls, fire ritual, and repeated burying and rebuilding of the structures are some of the salient features of the Kotosh Religious Tradition.

La Galgada is a particularly important Preceramic period site that participated in the Kotosh tradition. Around 2300 B.C.E., the people at this site constructed elaborate round chambers with fire pits. Significant features of La Galgada include a circular court 17 m in diameter, the existence of "megalithic shaft tombs" (Grieder 1988, p. 73; Grieder & Bueno 1985, p. 108), and exotic objects in the fire pits.

The architecture of the Kotosh Religious Tradition is different from contemporary coastal sites. In the highlands, corporate architecture is characterized by single, free-standing buildings with separate entrances and no internal connections. There is no evidence for site planning, restricted access, or formal designs that were replicated across sites (Burger 1995, p. 51). In contrast, coastal traditions were characterized by much larger buildings with patterns of restricted access, although at least one site, Huaynuná in the Casma, has a ventilated hearth similar to the Kotosh Tradition (Pozorski & Pozorski 1990). Certainly, in both coast and sierra, monumental architecture was widespread by the beginning of the second millennium B.C.E.

Late Preceramic States?

The late Preceramic period witnessed the emergence of the first nonegalitarian societies in South America. On the Pacific coast, it is clear that some of the earliest settlements did not rely on agriculture for a significant proportion of their diet. Moseley (1975, 1985, 1992a, 1992b) has persuasively argued that many Preceramic coastal populations were based predominantly on the exploitation of marine resources. His "maritime hypothesis" has been supported by excavations at Aspero, Huaca Prieta, and other sites (Quilter & Stocker 1983, but see Wilson 1981). This work indicates that an economy based heavily on marine products was sufficient to support the construction of monumental architecture.

It is significant that cultigens are also found in Preceramic period middens. While marine resources were the staple in coastal Preceramic sites, the inhabitants also utilized both wild and cultivated food and industrial crops (Feldman 1987, p. 9; Pozorski & Pozorski 1990; Quilter & Stocker 1983) such as cotton, gourd, legumes, *achira*, and squash. Other Preceramic period sites were located away from the littoral. Settlements such as Chupacigarro exploited a mix of plant agricultural products and the collection wild foods. Marine resources at the site were obtained by exchange with other groups and/or direct exploitation.

In the highlands large Preceramic monuments were constructed in economies based largely on rain-fed and small-scale irrigation agriculture, plus the elaboration of exchange networks (Fung Pineda 1988, p. 71). Burger (1995, p. 32, 53) notes that marine fish bone and shell have been found at all Preceramic highland sites that have corporate architecture and notes that the population of Salinas de Chao controlled salt production and exchange (but cf. Pozorski & Pozorski 1990,

p. 24). In short, there are solid cultural links between the highlands, coast, and even eastern slopes in the late Preceramic (Bonavia & Grobman 1979; Quilter & Stocker 1983, pp. 554–55).

The consensus in the literature is that the late Preceramic period represents at most the development of ranked society typical of simple chiefdoms in the evolutionary anthropological literature. Terms used to describe this organization include "chiefdoms" (Feldman 1987), "societies with labor organizing leaders" (Bawden 1999, p. 172) "centralized, nonstate polities," and "regional centers" (Quilter 1991a). Certainly, the data indicate that there was no one site that was a center of a regional polity. Rather, there were a series of autonomous settlements of varying complexity up and down the coast. Few scholars argue that any political organization as complex as the state developed in the Preceramic. One exception is Silva Santisteban (1997, pp. 100–2), who argues that the pristine state had formed by 2300 B.C.E. on the Peruvian coast.

THE INITIAL PERIOD

The Coast

The Initial period dates from circa 2000–1800 B.C.E. to circa 900–600 B.C.E. The Initial period witnessed a rapid growth in the size of sites, development of architectural complexity, and general social complexity based on late Preceramic period antecedents. Several regional architectural styles emerged in this period. One of these is known as the U-shaped architectural tradition, first described by Williams (1971, also see Carrión Sotelo 1998 for an example of a recent field study). The ideal layout was composed of a high, flat-topped pyramid mound flanked in the front by two projecting linear structures to form a large U.

The site of Huaca La Florida, located 11 km inland in the Rímac valley, is one of the oldest of the classic U-shaped structures so far studied (Von Hagen & Morris 1998, p. 51). The main pyramid is 17 m high and the two projecting structures rise 4 m from base for approximately 500 m. Construction at the site began in the eighteenth century B.C.E. Burger estimates that the site required 6.7 million person-days of labor. He notes that it is not even the largest of the U-shaped sites on the coast. The little-known site of San Jacinto in the Chancay valley is four times as large, with a 30-ha plaza and two million cubic meters of fill (Burger 1995, p. 61). While centered on the central coast of Peru, this U-shaped architectural tradition has been noted as far south as the Lake Titicaca Basin (Stanish & Steadman 1994, p. 13) and as far north as Piura (Guffroy 1989, pp. 161–207).

A second architectural tradition of the Initial period centers on the construction of sunken, circular courts usually next to pyramids. This tradition, concentrated north of the Chancay valley, has been found in at least 50 sites. Many of these are located in the Supe valley (Burger 1995, p. 76). A third architectural tradition is known as Cupisnique, characterized by low platform pyramids, large stairways, and rectangular courts. Colonnades and elaborate painted sculptures distinguish this architecture (Burger 1995, p. 92). The architectural complex known as Huaca de los Reyes at the site of Caballo Muerto is emblematic of this late Initial period style. Ware-feline motifs executed as adobe friezes adorn this huaca (Conklin 1996).

One of the richest areas of the Initial period culture is the Casma valley. By 1400 B.C.E. or perhaps earlier, the site of Sechin Alto was the largest settlement in the Western Hemisphere (Burger 1995, p. 80, Moseley 1992a, pp. 123–24, Tello 1956). It is dominated by a huge, stone masonry platform 300 m in length and 250 m in width that forms the base of a U-shaped center.

Located near Sechin Alto is the site of Cerro Sechin. The oldest construction at Cerro Sechin was built on a stepped platform with three levels (Samaniego et al 1985, p. 173). In this early Initial period, the site covered only about 5 ha. A possible sunken court was located in the front of this pyramid and noted long ago by Tello. Perhaps the most outstanding feature of Cerro Sechin is the numerous carvings in stone on the outer wall of the pyramid. These early Initial period carvings depict macabre scenes of war, including decapitations, trophy heads, and body parts, plus warriors and victims in various states of subjugation.

The Casma valley site of Pampa de las Llamas-Moxeke stands as one of the most important Initial period sites in the Andes. The site has two huge artificial mounds, plaza areas, other buildings, and a substantial habitation area. The Moxeke mound measures $160 \times 170 \times 30$ m and is decorated with elaborate friezes along its flanks. The second mound, known as Huaca A, measures 140×140 m at its base and reaches up to 9 m in height. Both of the mounds are aligned along a central axis. These two aligned pyramids demarcate high-walled enclosures, a pattern that suggests a surprisingly high degree of site planning. Pozorski & Pozorski (1994, p. 67) note that middens up to 1.5 m deep are found at the edges of the corporate architecture. This residential debris, at least 110 "administrative" buildings, plus the mounds and enclosures cover up to 200 ha, although the total area of purely residential midden and corporate architecture is less that 75 ha.

The Casma valley data, as well as that from other valleys, indicate that the north Pacific coast was a major area of cultural development in the Initial period. However, the highlands also witnessed the rise of architecturally complex and large settlements as well.

The Central Highlands

U-shaped structures were built at sites throughout the highlands during the Initial period. At La Galgada, ritual architectural styles shifted away from the earlier fire-pit tradition. Likewise, this period witnessed the construction of a U-shaped building on a Preceramic temple mound, and the continuation of large burials (Grieder et al 1988b, pp. 202–3). Significant architectural monuments were erected at Kuntur Wasi in Huacaloma, Poro Poro, at the site of Chavín, and at dozens of other highland settlements (Burger 1995, pp. 109–112; Shady 1993). Construction at Chavín began by at least 900 B.C.E., and possibly earlier (Rick et al 1998, p. 208). The settlement witnessed the building of a number of corporate architectural features. During this period Chavín was the center of a highland style of elite pottery, textile, and stone art.

The South Central Highlands

The first construction of corporate architecture in the south central Andean highlands began in the Titicaca Basin around 1300 B.C.E. Hastorf (1999) and her colleagues have uncovered corporate structures at the site of Chiripa, located in Bolivia in the south Titicaca Basin. These early small rooms were built with uncut stone, had plastered floors and walls, and were sometimes built low into the ground. Over time, this architectural style became more elaborate. The plastered area became larger, rooms were added to the exteriors, the floors were sunk deeper into the ground, and walled terraces were built around the entire architectural complex. By 900 B.C.E., Chiripa was a nucleated habitation and ceremonial center spread over 7.5 ha (Bandy 1999, p. 26).

By the first centuries of the first millennium B.C.E., many peoples built elaborate sunken courts in the entire Titicaca region. Along with the corporate architecture, a new suite of ritual artifacts was introduced. These include ceramic trumpets, flat-bottomed bowls, and stone carvings (Chávez & Mohr Chávez 1975). In the north basin, the Qaluyu culture flourished from as early as 1300 B.C.E. up to 500 B.C.E. The type site of Qaluyu is a large mound and associated domestic habitation areas that cover at least 7 ha. There are a number of sunken courts on the mound. A stone temple wall was discovered in Qaluyu levels at the site of Pucara, located a few kilometers to the south (Wheeler & Mujica 1981). Other large Qaluyu sites are found in Ayaviri and Putina in the north (Plourde 1999). In short, throughout the Titicaca Basin from 1300 B.C.E. to circa 500 B.C.E., a few peoples in some villages started constructing elaborate court complexes, intensified interregional exchange, and intensified ritual behavior.

Initial Period States?

There is a wide difference of opinion regarding the level of political complexity in the Initial period. According to Pozorski (1987, p. 15) and Pozorski & Pozorski (1994, p. 70), early Initial period Pampa de las Llamas-Moxeke was the center of a "simple theocratic state" with a population of 2500–3000. It was linked to other sites in the Casma valley, placing Pampa de la Llamas-Moxeke at the top of a sitesize hierarchy. They point to numerous elite objects on Huaca A, including turquoise beads, figurines, and textiles, which suggests that this was a palace. They likewise argue that there was both elite- and low-status housing at the site and that the entire settlement was planned. Instead of one single site that can be identified as the first state, they argue that states developed among a number of polities in the Moche, Casma, Supe, and Chillón valleys in the north and central Peruvian coast (Pozorski & Pozorski 1987, p. 45).

Burger (1995, p. 75) views the Initial period as characterized by 20 or so "weakly stratified small-scale societies with highly developed religious institutions."

Burger notes that there is no state architecture typical of known states in the Andes, little evidence of economic specialization, an absence of workshops, and a great deal of variation between settlements. Schreiber (2001) agrees, viewing the Initial period as a time of simple chiefdom development. It is important to emphasize our lack of systematic regional research in the area. In those regions where surveys are conducted, we find dozens of early sites with monumental architecture (e.g. Vega-Centeno et al 1998). In short, the Initial period cultural landscape was populated with thousands of corporate buildings on hundreds of sites of varying sizes and complexity. The evidence suggests the existence of local polities with little regional integration with no single site that can be described as a political center of a multivalley polity.

THE EARLY HORIZON

The Early Horizon dates from circa 900 B.C.E. to 200 B.C.E. and corresponds to the first pan-Andean art style known as Chavín in the central highlands and the coast. This period corresponds to the last half of the Middle Formative (1300–500 B.C.E.) and the early part of the Upper Formative (500 B.C.E. to C.E. 400) in the south central Andes.

The Coast and Central Highlands

There was a widespread collapse of coastal polities just prior to the Early Horizon. Construction of architectural monuments was halted in progress at sites such as Cardal, Mina Perdida, Taukachi-Konkan, Sechín Bajo, Sechín Alto, and Las Haldas (Burger 1995, pp. 183–85; Fung Pineda 1988, p. 89; Greider 1975, p. 101). Likewise, a number of sites with different architectural and pottery styles were established in Casma, such as Pampa Rosario, San Diego, and Chankillo. Chankillo has traditionally been interpreted as a fortress, but some recent interpretations suggest that it served ritual purposes instead. Other unequivocal defensive sites were established throughout the region. In the Santa valley during the Early Horizon, Wilson discovered a number of fortified settlements (1988, p. 100). Some argue for an invasion of highlanders into the coast during the Early Horizon (Pozorski 1987), while others feel that the evidence points to local changes (Burger 1995, p. 189).

In contrast to the coastal cultures, the cultures of the highlands prospered during the Early Horizon. The site of Chavín increased in size and power. Construction at Chavín continued up to at least 400 B.C.E. and possibly two centuries later (Rick et al 1998, p. 208). Regional data suggest an aggregation of the surrounding sites into a 42-ha settlement by 400–200 B.C.E. with a population of 2000–3000 (Burger 1995, p. 168). At 20 times larger than any surrounding settlement, Chavín emerged as a true political center. Exchange with other Andean regions, including the coast, flourished, and there is evidence of the importation of prestige goods and local economic specialization. The prosperity was not limited to Chavín. Pacopampa, Kotosh, La Pampa, Kuntur Wasi, and other highland sites grew in size and complexity as well (Silverman 1996, p. 120).

The South Central Highlands

From approximately 400 B.C.E. to C.E. 200, the site of Pucara dominated the northern Titicaca Basin. Estimates of the size of Pucara range from 2.0–4.0 km^2 (Erickson 1988). The main architectural feature of Pucara is a series of massive terraces that lead up to a flat area with three, stone-slab–lined, sunken courts. The largest court measures about 16×16 m in size and is 2.2 m deep (Chávez 1988, Kidder 1943). A dense habitation area is located in front of the large terraces. Likewise, there are a number of mounds that most likely held sunken courts as well. Pucara pottery and sculpture show links to contemporary coastal Paracas and Early Tiwanaku, with antecedents in Chavín (Cook 1994, p. 186; Conklin & Moseley 1988; Silverman 1996).

The site of Tiwanaku, located in the southern Titicaca Basin, was occupied at this time as well. We do not know the size and complexity of Upper Formative period Tiwanaku because later constructions covered 4–6 km^2 with temples, pyramids, and other buildings. Limited test excavations at the site suggest that Tiwanaku was probably about as large as Pucara during the Upper Formative, but this remains speculative.

Early Horizon States?

Obviously, for those who view Chupacigarro and Pampa de las Llamas-Moxeke as states, polities such as Chavín and Pucara would be second-generation states. Many argue that the Early Horizon ceremonial centers were centers of regional cults or pilgrimage destinations that, while complex, do not meet the definition of a state society (Burger 1989, pp. 557–60; 1995, pp. 193–200). Schreiber (2001) views the Early Horizon coastal and north highland polities as complex chiefdoms, and Moseley (1992a, p. 159) suggests the existence of two regional political spheres, Chavín in the north and Pucara-Paracas in the south, that dominated the area as oracle centers.

The regional cult model was developed by Silverman using the site of Cahuachi as a case study (1990, 1991). Silverman (1995, p. 27) argues that this Nasca settlement did not have a urban population. She views it as a "complex non-state society or ranked society or chiefdom-level society," but not a state-level organization. This model provides a means by which a large settlement, with substantial architecture, could be constructed in a nonstate context. Burger (1988) likewise argues that the Early Horizon centers could be analogous to the historically documented pilgrimage center at Pachacamac. In the pilgrimage center model, many of the surface attributes of state organization can exist—large centers, widespread distribution of art styles, and so forth—without the actual socioeconomic hierarchies that anthropologists see as central to state organization.

THE EARLY INTERMEDIATE AND MIDDLE HORIZON

A poorly understood culture that is known as Gallinazo developed on the north coast during the Early Intermediate period. In the Virú valley, the Gallinazo Group was a town of several thousand people (Bawden 1999, p. 187). There was a substantial Gallinazo occupation in the Moche valley as well. Gallinazo is usually believed to antedate the Moche, although some evidence suggests at least some chronological overlap between the two (Bawden 1999, p. 190). With large settlements, impressive platform pyramids, extensive agricultural systems, and the like, some scholars have argued that Gallinazo was in fact a state-level society (e.g., Fogel 1993). Certainly, many of the cultural patterns seen in the Moche culture have direct antecedents to Gallinazo.

The Coastal Moche

In the north coast, the late Early Intermediate period Moche culture developed as a multivalley political entity by the fourth century C.E. (Bawden 1999; Shimada 1994, p. 95; Wilson 1988). The capital of the Moche polity is located in the Moche valley at the site of Moche. It is dominated by two main pyramids—the Huaca del Sol and Huaca de la Luna. The largest of these two, the Huaca del Sol, measures about 160×340 m in size and stands 40 m in height. It was one of the largest prehispanic monuments constructed in the Western Hemisphere. The Moche capital is unequivocally an urban settlement, perhaps the first true city in the Andes. It is characterized by a system of streets, canals, plazas, architectural groups, areas of craft specialization, and so forth (Uceda & Mujica 1998).

Moche-related sites are found throughout the north coast. Some scholars have suggested that there were two Moche spheres, a northern and a southern (Shimada 1994). The famous site of Sipán in the northern valley of Lambayeque contained one of the most elaborate Moche burials yet discovered. The date of the Lord of Sipán burial is early in Moche culture, around C.E. 150–200, which suggests the simultaneous emergence of elite centers of power that shared Moche iconography. Bawden provides a map of the early and middle Moche polity that suggests a discontinuous territory until Moche V, again reinforcing the notion of a simultaneous rise of the state culminating in Moche as its capital.

The South Central Highlands

The Upper Formative period site of Pucara ended as a political center no later than C.E. 400. Around C.E. 600, the Tiwanaku state began an aggressive expansion out of the southern Titicaca Basin. The site of Tiwanaku is a vast, planned urban capital that sprawled over the altiplano landscape in the southern Titicaca Basin. At its height in C.E. 800–900, Tiwanaku boasted an impressive architectural core of pyramids, temples, palaces, streets, and state buildings. Surrounding the core of the capital was an urban settlement of nonelite artisans, laborers, and farmers who lived in adobe structures up and down the valley (Janusek 1999). Current estimates suggest that the total urban settlement covers 4–6 km^2 in area, with a population in the Tiwanaku valley ranging from 30,000 to 60,000 (Janusek 1999, Kolata & Ponce 1992). Large areas of intensified agricultural production are associated with Tiwanaku and pre-Tiwanaku populations around the basin (Erickson 1988, Kolata 1986, Stanish 1994). The combined population of these settlements and the capital itself would have been quite substantial at the height of the Tiwanaku state, possibly reaching 100,000 people in the Tiwanaku and adjacent Katari valleys.

Tiwanaku artifacts and colonies are found throughout the circum-Titicaca basin and beyond. A well-documented Tiwanaku colony is found in Moquegua (Goldstein 1993). In the Cochabamba region of Bolivia, Anderson & Cespedes Paz (1998) argue for a Tiwanaku colony (but see Higueras-Hare 1996). Probable colonial areas have been identified in the Larecaja region of Bolivia (Faldín 1990), the Arequipa area, and Azapa (Goldstein 1995/1996). Recent settlement archaeology in the Titicaca Basin suggests that the Tiwanaku selectively controlled areas throughout the region. Tiwanaku did not, or could not, practice a small version of Inca statecraft by incorporating large, contiguous areas. Rather, it appears to have controlled economically and militarily strategic areas, including roads, rich agricultural areas, and resource-rich zones.

The Central Highlands

The site and culture of Wari represent an autochthonous expansive state that emerged in the middle of the first millennium C.E. in the central highlands roughly parallel in time to Tiwanaku. The capital site contains about 200 ha of stone architecture and another 300 ha of domestic residence around this architectural core (Schreiber 1987; 1992, p. 80). Up to 15 km^2 of site area has been cited as being part of the Wari urban complex (Isbell et al 1991, Schreiber 2001). The proportion of core architecture to domestic, nonelite architecture, and the overall size of the site is quite similar to contemporary Tiwanaku.

Wari stretches from the Cuzco area in the south to Cajamarca in Middle Horizon 1B (Schreiber 1992, p. 77). There are several provincial Wari settlements. Pikillacta, located near Cuzco, is built on a grid, has 700 individual structures, is 2 km^2 in size, and is the center of intrusive garrisons of Wari settlements in the Lucre valley (McEwan 1991, p. 93–100). Likewise, the site of Jincamocco in the Carhuarazo valley represents an intrusive Wari settlement that differs from local sites based on size, artifact inventory, and architectural plan (Meddens 1991; Schreiber 1992, p. 165). Like Pikillacta, the main enclosure was laid out as a single unit. The site conforms to Wari architectural canons with large, subdivided compounds of patios surrounded by peripheral galleries inside a single, large, and well-defined rectangular enclosure with a thick outer wall (Schreiber 1992, p. 200). These and other Wari sites indicate a rigidity of overall plan in Wari provincial architecture.

The Early Intermediate and Middle Horizon States?

The consensus in the archaeological literature is that states existed in the Andes by the middle of the first millennium C.E. (e.g. Berdichewsky 1995/1996, Flannery

1995, 1998, Isbell 1987, Lumbreras 1999, Marcus 1998). For the first time in the Andes, as represented by Moche, we have unequivocal evidence of royal tombs built in restricted-access temples, clear economic specialization, the existence of a road system, palaces, a warrior-based elite, a regional polity beyond a single valley, and a fully urbanized capital. Likewise both Wari and Tiwanaku have palaces, planned urban capitals, high populations, evidence of socioeconomic classes, site-size hierarchies, expansionist policies, agricultural intensification, economic specialization, and colonial enclaves. The state originated in Moche, Wari, and Tiwanaku in the first half of the first millennium C.E.

SOUTH AMERICA IN COMPARATIVE CONTEXT

Two assumptions about the nature of Andean culture and history underlie archaeological research in the region. One position views the Andes as culturally and historically unique. The position was developed as a coherent theory by Murra (1968, 1972) and continues to hold considerable influence, particularly among ethnohistorians and ethnographers. This body of theory is known as "verticality" or "zonal complementarity." The basic principle behind this theory is that the "vertical" stratification of ecological zones in the Andes has affected the political and economic strategies of the pre-Hispanic populations. It furthermore assumes that this is unique to the Andes and, as such, has promoted the development of a culture understandable only in its own terms.

According to verticality models, people strategically locate colonies to control a diverse set of ecological zones even in nonstate contexts. This geographical pattern allows the "complementary" ecozones to be exploited by a single group or polity. Hypothetically, the resulting distribution of colonies creates an archipelago of isolated landholdings over a number of ecological zones. The overlap of archipelagos results in a complex patchwork of different ethnic groups and political units, creating a socioeconomic system unique to the Andes. Recent work suggests that this perspective is not supportable. Throughout the world where the geography is characterized by a close juxtaposition of different ecological zones, complex polities have secured economic access by similar strategies.

The opposing perspective assumes that much of Andean history can be understood as an example of anthropological processes typical of all human societies. From this perspective, the Andes provides a rich corpus of data to refine our models of the evolution of state societies. It provides a number of parallels and contrasts to other areas of first-generation state development.

Geography

One difference stands out between the Andes and other areas of first-generation state evolution. The Andean cultural area, defined conservatively as the limits of the Inca state in 1532, is exceptionally long and covers a very rugged territory. It stretches for over 4000 km up and down western South America. To place this in context, this is about the same distance east-west from the Nile to the Indus river, an area that covers three regions of pristine state development in the Old World (including Mesopotamia).

Given the vast distances in the Andean cultural area, a legitimate question can be raised as to whether we should view western South America as having not one but three different areas of first-generation state development represented by Moche, Wari, and Tiwanaku. Perhaps the very notion of "pristine" state development must be challenged, and instead we should find a better control for the relative degrees of cultural autonomy in the formation of archaic states around the world.

Political and Economic Structure

The argument that there were state societies prior to the Middle Horizon is weak. In particular, we can point to the lack of evidence of state-level regional integration prior to Moche. The model that best characterizes the pre–Middle Horizon political landscape is a series of autonomous and semiautonomous polities without any evidence of complexity beyond that of a chiefdom society.

In contrast, the Moche, Tiwanaku, and Wari polities are similar to other first-generation states around the world. There is good evidence for the replication of distinctive artistic, mortuary, and architectural styles in distant regions. Unlike earlier periods there is unequivocal evidence for an urbanized capital city. Marcus & Flannery's (1996) description of Uruk and Teotihuacán can also be used to characterize these Andean state polities: the existence of "hyperurban" capital cities, "direct control of an irregular and noncontiguous territory, and distant 'colonies' or 'enclaves.'"

Moche, Tiwanaku, and Wari also exhibit classic site-size hierarchies typical of first-generation states. Albarracin-Jordan (1996) and McAndrews et al (1997) demonstrate a four-tiered site-size hierarchy for Tiwanaku in its core territory. Using more flexible criteria, a six-tiered one is noted in a nearby provincial territory (Stanish et al 1997). Isbell & Schreiber (1978) argue for a four-tiered hierarchy for Wari. For a major Moche area, Wilson (1988, p. 336) defines a hierarchy of sites that includes five tiers. In all cases, the number of site-size tiers is greater than the preceding periods, which suggests a differentiation of the settlement pattern and administrative complexity at the time of state formation.

Population Sizes

The population estimates for Initial period or Early Horizon sites such as Pampa de las Llamas-Moxeke and Chavín are quite low, around 2000–3000. In contrast, estimates for the later polities such as Moche, Wari, and Tiwanaku are higher, with published populations in the 50,000–200,000 range (Kolata 1993, Schreiber 1992).

Johnson & Earle (1987, pp. 230–46) and Earle (1997) offer baseline data on chiefdom and state demographics at the high end of the literature. Simple chiefdoms have population levels in the low thousands to tens of thousands. Complex chiefdoms, at least in Hawaii, have populations between 30,000 and 100,000, while states number in the hundreds of thousands to millions. At the other end, Renfrew (1982) has suggested that some small states have as few as 2000 people. Feinman & Neitzel (1984), using comparative data from the Americas, note that almost all middle-range societies have a maximum of 31,000 people. An intermediate estimate by Baker & Sanders (1972) suggests a figure of 48,000 as the threshold between chiefdoms and states. In this regard, the population estimates for hypothesized state societies in the Initial and Early Horizon periods is at the very low end of population estimates for archaic states from around the world. The demographic size proposed for the Middle Horizon polities is more consistent with the average populations estimates in the literature.

Circumscription and Population Pressure

The Pacific coastal valleys can be viewed as incredibly rich "linear oases" that pierce a virtually uninhabitable desert. These valleys occur at somewhat regular intervals that average around 30 km and constitute classic examples of a circumscribed environment. The highlands and altiplano, in contrast, are far less circumscribed. In particular, camelid pastoralism is not restricted to narrow zones but can be practiced over a very wide area. Unlike the coast, populations had alternatives to a single, rich, and restrictive ecological zone.

Systematic surveys provide data on population growth and densities. Earle (1997, p. 65) notes that in Mantaro valley, ". . . the populations . . . expanded and declined in erratic cycles that were not evidently related to resource conditions," a pattern similar to two other case studies he cites in Denmark and Hawaii. The data fit the circumscription model only after the Wari state developed. In the Titicaca Basin, there is a pattern of very slow, continuous growth with a spike in Inca period (Albarracin-Jordan & Mathews 1990, Stanish et al 1997). The data from these two highland areas support a political economic model (Earle 1987; 1997, p. 119), as opposed to strict population pressure models. Likewise, even on the coast, there remains little evidence of direct population pressure. Wilson (1988, p. 357), for instance, notes that in the Santa valley, "there is little evidence of population pressure *per se* in the pre-state systems . . .," although he goes on to suggest that it may have been a factor in other valleys.

In spite of the circumscribed nature of the coastal environment, there is little evidence for direct population pressure as a factor in state development. This also appears to be the case in the highlands. In short, localized population pressure does not appear to be a sufficient or necessary cause in Andean state formation. However, at a regional level, there are correlations between population size and state formation that remain subject to future testing.

Conflict and Warfare

Intergroup conflict is recognized as one of the key factors in the development of political complexity (e.g., Marcus & Flannery 1996, p. 157; Redmond 1994).

Warfare is present on the Andean coast from at least the Early Horizon. Wilson (1999) argues that conflict was present in the Santa valley from the Early Horizon until the development of Moche. Pozorski (1987) agrees that warfare was central to the formation of the first states in Santa and Nepeña but argues that in Casma, little conflict preceded the development of the first "theocratic" states. Conflict does occur later on in the Casma with the arrival of a "secular, militaristic state" around 1000 B.C.E. (Pozorski 1987). Therefore, if Pampa de las Llamas-Moxeke is considered to be an Initial period state, then warfare was not a factor. If, however, the state did not develop until the late Early Intermediate period, then conflict indeed was a factor in the rise of the state in the Casma valley as well. Iconographic evidence and physical remains unequivocally indicate that conflict and human sacrifice, probably of prisoners, was common in Moche society (Bourget 1997; Donnan & McClelland 1999; Verano et al 1999).

There is little doubt that militarism was a major strategy in Moche expansion on the coast. In the Santa valley, Wilson (1988, p. 333) and Shimada (1987) argue for a military conquest by the Moche displacing the earlier Gallinazo populations. Defensive architecture is common on Moche period sites throughout the north coast.

In the highlands, Earle (1997, p. 119) notes that warfare began early in the Mantaro valley, subsided with the Wari conquest, then increased again prior to Inca conquest. In the Titicaca region, evidence of conflict and the development of complex chiefly society are strongly correlated. In the Early and Middle Formative periods, there is little evidence of conflict. Then, in the Upper Formative, many sites were located in defensive positions (but see Topic & Topic 1987), and there is a pronounced introduction of trophy head and other militaristic iconography on stone stelae and pottery.

Wealth Finance

D'Altroy & Earle (1985) and Earle (1997) argue that central to development of complex society is the creation of a system of finance for state political economies. The key factors include the existence of surplus-producing subject peoples and potential efficiency in production. From this perspective, the emergence of archaic states in South America can be understood as a conjunction of favorable environmental zones in a context of gradual population growth. Population spikes tend to occur after state development, not before. The areas where states first developed have the greatest capacity for sustained demographic increase and the intensification of production. As a general rule, the north coast rivers where states took root are large, while the south coast rivers are not. The few exceptions support the rule; large southern rivers tend to be deeply entrenched and provide less opportunity for irrigation, while smaller northern rivers are connectable by intervalley canals.

As mentioned above, perhaps some of the richest areas in South America are found on the north Peruvian coast where these large rivers discharge into the sea. Here, the rich riverine resources are combined with the marine resources in the delta areas. In the highlands, there are many productive zones outside of the Titicaca Basin and north central highlands. However, it is in these two areas where a suite of highly productive natural features combine. The Lake Titicaca region has the lake itself, vast grasslands, rivers, and relatively close access to the eastern slopes. The use of raised fields near the lake provide the capacity for agricultural intensification, a technique not available in other areas of the highlands. In the north central Andes, the availability of irrigable land is often cited as one of the primary factors in the development of complexity and the state in the Andes. Likewise, the highland areas have access to pasture lands, rivers, and the eastern slopes. All three cases of Moche, Tiwanaku, and Wari state formation are correlated with agricultural intensification, intensification of exchange relationships, and intensification of commodity production, observations that conform to the wealth finance model.

Dynamic Cycling

Marcus (1992, 1993) and Marcus & Flannery (1996) have proposed a dynamic model of episodic expansion and collapse of archaic states. State polities emerge through the incorporation of other groups, creating at least a four-tiered hierarchy of settlement. As one polity peaks and begins to break down, former lower-level settlements regain their autonomy, after which the process of consolidation, expansion, and dissolution continues again (Marcus 1998). This model works not only for the Maya area, where it was originally proposed, but can be successfully used in many areas of state development around the world, including the Andes.

Data from the Andes support this model. In the Titicaca Basin, Tiwanaku developed after a period of Pucara contraction. After the Tiwanaku collapse, smaller Aymara-speaking polities developed throughout the area. Over a 1500-year period, polities expanded and contracted for four cycles, ending with the Inca conquest of the region. Likewise, in the north coast, regional research by Billman (1999) and Wilson (1988) outline a series of valleys and peaks beginning before the emergence of the Moche state.

Summary

South America provides an excellent case study for defining the processes of first-generation state formation. The data indicate that several factors were significant, including competition and war, high resource concentration in circumscribed environments, interregional exchange, the materialization of elite ideologies, and ecological conditions conducive to population increases. Factors that do not appear to be significant include local population pressures in circumscribed environments, direct control of irrigation, or other agricultural technologies by an elite. Localized population spikes appear after the development of state societies. Irrigation systems long predate the development of states. Moche, Wari, and Tiwanaku are not organizationally identical. There is virtually no evidence for any direct links between Tiwanaku and Moche, except for the most superficial of iconographic data. There are greater links between Moche and Wari, but these are largely iconographic as well and related to the fact that Wari seems to have had some political access to former Moche territory. Moche culture emphasized platform mounds with continual rebuilding, probably on the accension of a new ruler or dynasty. Elaborate elite burials are found in these pyramids. In contrast, we have yet to define a significant elite burial in Tiwanaku. Likewise, the focus of political ritual appears to be the "kalasasayas" (stone enclosures) and sunken courts, and not the pyramids themselves in Tiwanaku. The highlands and coast have different evolutionary trajectories, based in large part on the nature of resource distribution and availability and political finance (T. Earle, personal communication). In general, models that incorporate dynamic cycling and political economic theoretical frameworks best explain the evolution of the state in western South America.

ACKNOWLEDGMENTS

I thank B. Bauer, T. Earle, J. Haas, J. Marcus, M. Moseley, H. Silverman, and K. Schreiber for their gracious assistance on this article.

Visit the Annual Reviews home page at www.AnnualReviews.org

LITERATURE CITED

Albarracin-Jordan J, Mathews JE. 1990. *Asentamientos Prehispánicos del Valle de Tiwanaku*, Vol. 1. La Paz: Producciones CIMA

Albarracin-Jordan J. 1996. *Tiwanaku. Arqueología regional y dinámica segmentaria*. La Paz: Editores Plural

Anderson K, Cespedes Paz R. 1998. *Late Formative to Middle Horizon transition in Cochabamba, Bolivia*. Presented at Annu. Meet. Soc. Am. Archaeol., Seattle, WA

Baker P, Sanders W. 1972. Demographic studies in anthropology. *Annu. Rev. Anthropol.* 1:151–78

Bandy M. 1999. Systematic surface collection. See Hastorf 1999, pp. 23–26.

Bawden G. 1999. *The Moche*. Cambridge, UK: Blackwell

Bennett W. 1946. The Andean highlands: an introduction. In *Handbook of South American Indians, the Andean Civilizations*, ed. J Steward, 2:1–60. Washington, DC: Smithsonian Inst.

Berdichewsky B. 1995/1996. Surgimiento y caracter del estado Andino. *Diálogo Andino* 14/15:75–96

Billman B. 1999. Settlement pattern research in the Americas. Past, present, and future. In *Settlement Pattern Studies in the Americas. Fifty Years since Virú*, ed. B Billman, G Feinman, pp. 1–5. Washington, DC: Smithsonian Inst.

Bonavia D, Grobman A. 1979. Sistema de depósitos y almacenamiento durante el periodo precerámico en la costa del Perú. *J. Soc. Am.* 66:21–45

Bonnier E, Rozenberg C. 1988. Del santuario al caserío. Acerca de la neolitización en la Cordillera de los Andes centrales. *Bull. Inst. Fran. d'etudes And.* 17(2):23–40

Bourget S. 1997. La colère des ancêtres: découverte d'un site sacrificie à la Huaca de la Luna, vallé de Moche. In *À L'Ombre du Cerro Blanco, Nouvelles Découvertes dur la Culture Moche, Côte Nord du Pérou*, ed. C Chapdelaine, pp. 83–99. Montréal: Cah. Anthropol. 1, Univ. Montréal, Dép. Anthropol.

Burger R. 1988. Unity and heterogeneity within the Chavín horizon. See Keatinge 1988, pp. 99–144

Burger R. 1989. El horizonte Chavín: quimera estilística o metamorfosis socioeconómica? *Rev. And.* 7(2):543–73

Burger R. 1995. *Chavín and the Origins of Andean Civilization*. New York: Thames Hudson

Burger R, Burger LS. 1980. Ritual and religion at Huaricoto. *Archaeology* 33(6):26–32

Carrión Sotelo L. 1998. Excavaciones en San Jacinto, templo en U en el valle de Chancay. *Bol. Arq. PUCP* 2:239–50

Chávez K. 1988. The significance of Chiripa in Lake Titicaca Basin developments. *Expedition* 30(3):17–26

Chávez SJ, Mohr Chávez KL. 1975. A carved stela from Taraco, Puno, Peru and the definition of an early style of stone sculpture from the altiplano of Peru and Bolivia. *Ñawpa Pacha* 13:45–83

Conklin WJ. 1996. La arquitectura de la Huaca de Los Reyes. *Arkinka* 10:88–100

Conklin WJ, Moseley ME. 1988. The patterns of art and power in the Early Intermediate Period. See Keatinge 1988, pp. 145–63

Cook AG. 1994. *Wari y Tiwanaku: entre el estilo y la imagen*. Lima: Pont. Univ. Católica Peru Lima

D'altroy T, Earle T. 1985. Staple finance, wealth finance, and storage in the Inka political economy. *Curr. Anthropol.* 26(2):187–206

DeMarrais E, Castillo LJ, Earle T. 1996. Ideology, materialization, and power strategies. *Curr. Anthropol.* 37:15–31

Dillehay TD. 1992. Widening the socioeconomic foundations of Andean civilizations: prototypes of early monumental architecture. *Andean Past* 3:55–65

Donnan C, ed. 1985. *Early Ceremonial Architecture in the Andes*. Washington, DC: Dumbarton Oaks

Donnan C, McClelland D. 1999. *Moche Fineline Painting: its Evolution and its Artists*. Los Angeles: Fowler Mus. Cult. Hist.

Earle T. 1987. Specialization and the production of wealth: Hawaiian chiefdoms and the Inka empire. In *Specialization, Exchange, and Complex Societies*, ed. EM Brumfiel,

TK Earle, pp. 64–75. Cambridge, UK: Cambridge Univ. Press

Earle T. 1997. *How Chiefs Come to Power: the Political Economy in Prehistory*. Stanford, CA: Stanford Univ. Press

Engel F. 1987. *De las begonias al maíz. Vida y producción en el Perú antiguo*. Lima: Univ. Nac. Agrar. Molina

Erickson C. 1988. Raised field agriculture in the Lake Titicaca Basin. *Expedition* 30(3):8–16

Faldín A JD. 1990. La provincia Larecaja y el sistema precolombino del norte de La Paz. In *Larecaja, Ayer, Hoy y Mañana*, pp. 73–90. La Paz: Com. Cult.

Feinman G, Neitzel J. 1984. Too many types: an overview of sedentary prestate societies in the Americas. *Adv. Archaeol. Theory Method* 7:39–102

Feinman G, Marcus J, eds. 1998. *Archaic States*. Santa Fe, NM: Sch. Am. Res.

Feldman R. 1987. Architectural evidence for the development of nonegalitarian social systems in coastal Peru. See Haas et al 1987, pp. 9–14

Flannery KV. 1995. Prehistoric social evolution. In *Research Frontiers in Anthropology*, ed. M Ember, pp. 1–26. Englewood Cliffs, NJ: Prentice Hall

Flannery KV. 1998. The ground plans of archaic states. See Feinman & Marcus 1998, pp. 15–57

Flannery KV. 1999. Process and agency in early state formation. *Cambridge Arch. J.* 9:(1):3–21

Fogel JA. 1993. *Settlements in time: a study of social and political development during the Gallinazo occupation of the north coast of Peru*. PhD diss. Yale Univ., New Haven, CT

Fung Pineda R. 1988. The late Preceramic and Initial period. See Keatinge 1988, pp. 67–96

Goldstein P. 1993. Tiwanaku temples and state expansion: a Tiwanaku sunken-court temple in Moquegua, Peru. *Lat. Am. Antiq.* 4(1):22–47

Goldstein P. 1995/1996. Tiwanaku settlement patterns of the Azapa Valley, Chile. New data, and the legacy of Percy Dauelsberg. *Diálogo Andino* 14/15:57–73

Grieder T. 1975. A dated sequence of building and pottery at Las Haldas. *Ñawpa Pacha* 13:99–112

Grieder T. 1988. Burial patterns and offerings. See Grieder et al, 1988a, pp. 73–102

Grieder T, Bueno Mendoza A. 1985. Ceremonial architecture at La Galgalda. See Donnan 1985, pp. 93–109

Grieder T, Bueno Mendoza M, Smith CE Jr, Malina RM, eds. 1988a. *La Galgada, Peru. A Preceramic Culture in Transition*. Austin: Univ. Texas Press

Grieder T, Bueno Mendoza M, Smith CE Jr, Malina RM. 1988b. La Galgada in the world of its time. See Grieder et al 1988a, pp. 192–203

Guffroy J. 1989. Un centro ceremonial formativo en el Alto Piura. *Bull. Inst. Fran. d' etudes And.* 18(2):161–207

Haas J. 1987. The exercise of power in early Andean state development. See Haas et al 1987, pp. 31–35

Haas J, Pozorski S, Pozorski T, eds. 1987. *The Origins and Development of the Andean State*. Cambridge, UK: Cambridge Univ. Press

Hastorf C, ed. 1999. *Early Settlement at Chiripa, Bolivia*. Berkeley: Contrib. Univ. Calif. Archaeol. Res. Facil.

Higueras-Hare A. 1996. *Prehispanic settlement and land use in Cochabamba*. PhD diss. Univ. Pittsburgh, Pittsburgh, PA

Isbell W. 1987. State origins in the Ayacucho Valley, central highlands, Peru. See Haas et al 1987, pp. 83–90

Isbell W, Brewster-Wray C, Spickard L. 1991. Architecture and spatial organization at Huari. See Isbell & McEwan 1991, pp. 19–53

Isbell W, McEwan G, eds. 1991. *Huari Administrative Structure: Prehistoric Monumental Architecture and State Government*. Washington, DC: Dumbarton Oak

Isbell W, Schreiber K. 1978. Was Huari a state? *Am. Antiq.* 43:372–89

Izumi S, Terada K. 1972. *Andes 4: Excavations at Kotosh, Peru, 1963 and 1966*. Tokyo: Univ. Tokyo Press

Janusek JW. 1999. Craft and local power: embedded specialization in Tiwanaku cities. *Lat. Am. Antiq.* 10(2):107–31

Johnson A, Earle TK. 1987. *The Evolution of Human Society*. Stanford, CA: Stanford Univ. Press

Keatinge R, ed. 1988. *Peruvian Prehistory*. Cambridge, UK: Cambridge Univ. Press

Kidder A II. 1943. *Some Early Sites in the northern Lake Titicaca Basin*. Pap. Peabody Mus., Harvard Univ.:1

Kolata A. 1986. The agricultural foundations of the Tiwanaku state: a view from the heartland. *Am. Antiq.* 51(4):748–62

Kolata A. 1993. *The Tiwanaku*. London: Blackwell

Kolata A, Ponce S C. 1992. Tiwanaku: the city at the center. In *The Ancient Americas*, ed. R Townsend, pp. 317–33. Chicago: Art Inst. Chicago

Lumbreras LG. 1981. *Arqueología de la América Andina*. Lima: Editorial Milla Batres

Lumbreras LG. 1999. Andean urbanism and statecraft (CE 550–1450). In *The Cambridge History of the Native Peoples of the Americas,: South America, Part 1*, Vol. 3, ed. F Salomon, SB Schwartz, pp. 518–76. Cambridge, UK: Cambridge Univ. Press

Marcus J. 1992. Dynamic cycles of Mesoamerican states: political fluctuations in Mesoamerica. *Natl. Geog. Res. Explor.* 8:392–411

Marcus J. 1993. Ancient Maya political organization. In *Lowland Maya Civilization in the Eighth Century A.D.*, ed J Sabloff, J Henderson, pp. 111–83. Washington, DC: Dumbarton Oaks

Marcus J. 1998. The peaks and valleys of ancient states: an extension of the dynamic model. See Feinman & Marcus 1998, pp. 59–94

Marcus J, Flannery K. 1996. *Zapotec Civilization: How Urban Society Evolved in Mexico's Oaxaca Valley*. London: Thames Hudson

McAndrews T, Albarracin-Jordan J, Bermann B. 1997. Regional settlement patterns in the

Tiwanaku Valley of Bolivia. *J. Field Arch.* 24:67–83

McEwan G. 1991. Investigations at the Pikillacta site: a provincial Huari center in the valley of Cuzco. See Isbell & McEwan 1991, pp. 93–119

Meddens F. 1991. A provincial perspective on Huari organization viewed from the Chicha/Soras Valley. See Isbell & McEwan 1991, pp. 215–31

Moseley ME. 1975. *The Maritime Foundations of Andean Civilization.* Menlo Park, CA: Cummings

Moseley ME. 1985. The exploration and explanation of early monumental architecture in the Andes. See Donnan 1985, pp. 29–57

Moseley ME. 1992a. *The Incas and their Ancestors.* London: Thames Hudson

Moseley ME. 1992b. Maritime foundations and multilinear evolution: retrospect and prospect. *Andean Past* 3:5–42

Murra JV. 1968. An Aymara Kingdom in 1567. *Ethnohistory* (15):115–51

Murra JV. 1972. El'control vertical' de un máximo de pisos ecológicos en la economía de las sociedades Andinas. In *Visita de la Provincia de León de Huánuco en 1562. Documentos por la Historia y Etnología de Huánuco y la Selva Central* 2:427–76. Huánuco: Univ. Nac. Hermilio Valdizan

Plourde A. 1999. *The role of inter-regional exchange in Pucara and Tiwanaku state formation and expansion, northeastern Titicaca Basin, Perú.* Presented at the Annu. Meet. Soc. Am. Arch., Chicago, IL

Pozorski S. 1987. Theocracy vs. militarism: the significance of the Casma Valley in understanding early state formation. See Haas et al 1987, pp. 15–30

Pozorski S, Pozorski T. 1994. Early Andean cities. *Sci. Am.* 270(6):66–72

Pozorski T, Pozorski S. 1987. Chavin, the Early Horizon and the Initial Period. See Haas et al 1987, pp. 36–46

Pozorski T, Pozorski S. 1990. Huaynuná, a Late Cotton Preceramic site on the north coast of Peru. *J. Field Arch.* 17:17–26

Quilter J. 1985. Architecture and chronology at El Paraíso, Peru. *J. Field Arch.* 12:279–97

Quilter J. 1991a. Problems with the late Preceramic of Peru. *Am. Anthropol.* 93:450–54

Quilter J. 1991b. Late Preceramic Peru. *J. World Prehist.* 5:387–438

Quilter J, Ojeda EB, Pearsall DM, Sandweiss DH, Jones JG, Wing ES. 1991. Subsistence economy of El Paraíso, an early Peruvian site. *Science* 251:277–83

Quilter J, Stocker T. 1983. Subsistence economies and the origins of Andean complex societies. *Am. Anthropol.* (85):545–62

Redmond EM. 1994. External warfare and the internal politics of northern South American tribes and chiefdoms. In *Factional Competition and Political Development in the New World*, ed. EM Brumfiel, JW Fox, pp. 44–54. Cambridge, UK: Cambridge Univ. Press

Renfrew C. 1982. Polity and power: interaction, intensification, and exploitation. In *An Island Polity: The Archaeology of Exploitation in Melos*, ed. C Renfrew, M Wagstaff, pp. 264–90. Cambridge, UK: Cambridge Univ. Press

Rick JW, Kembel SR, Mendoza Rick R, Kembel JA. 1998. La arquitectura del complejo ceremonial de Chavín de Huantar: documentación tridimensional y sus implicancias. *Bol. Arq. PUCP* 2:181–214

Samaniego L, Vergara E, Bischof H. 1985. New evidence on Cerro Sechín, Casma Valley, Peru. See Donnan 1985, pp. 165–90

Schreiber K. 1987. Conquest and consolidation: a comparison of the Wari and Inka occupations of a highland Peruvian valley. *Am. Antiq.* 52:266–84

Schreiber K. 1992. *Wari Imperialism in Middle Horizon Peru, Anthropol. Pap. No. 87.* Ann Arbor: Mus. Anthropol. Univ. Mich.

Schreiber K. 2001. The Wari empire of Middle Horizon Peru: the epistemological challenge of documenting an empire without documentary evidence. In *Empires*, eds. S Alcock, T D'Altroy, K Morrison, C Sinopoli, pp. 70–92. Cambridge, UK: Cambridge Univ. Press

Shady R. 1993. Del Arcaico al Formativo en los Andes Centrales. *Rev. And.* 21:103–32

Shimada I. 1987. Horizontal and vertical dimensions of prehistoric states in north Peru. See Haas et al 1987, pp. 130–44

Shimada I. 1994. *Pampa Grande and the Mochica Culture.* Austin: Univ. Texas Press

Silva Santisteban F. 1997. *Desarrollo político en las sociedades de la civilización Andina.* Lima: Univ. Lima

Silverman H. 1990. The Early Nasca pilgrimage center of Cahuachi and the Nasca lines: anthropological and archaeological perspectives. In *The Lines of Nasca,* ed. A Aveni, pp. 209–304. Philadelphia: Am. Phila. Soc.

Silverman H. 1991. The ethnography and archaeology of two Andean pilgrimage centers. In *Pilgrimage in Latin America,* ed. NR Crumrine, A Morinis, pp. 215–28. Westport, CT: Greenwood

Silverman H. 1995. Recent archaeological investigations on the south coast of Peru: critique and prospects. *J. Steward Anthropol. Soc.* 23(1,2):13–41

Silverman H. 1996. The formative period on the south coast of Peru: a critical review. *J. World Prehist.* 10(2):95–146

Stanish C. 1994. The hydraulic hypothesis revisited: a theoretical perspective on Lake Titicaca Basin raised field agriculture. *Lat. Am. Antiq.* 5(4):312–32

Stanish C, de la Vega E, Steadman L, Chávez JC, Frye KL, et al. 1997. *Archaeological Survey in the Juli-Desaguadero Area, Lake Titicaca Basin, Peru.* Fieldiana Anthropol., NS 29. Chicago, IL: Field Mus.

Stanish C, Steadman LH. 1994. *Archaeological Research at the Site of Tumatumani Juli, Peru.* Fieldiana Anthropol., NS 23, Chicago, IL: Field Mus.

Tello JC. 1956. *Arqueología del valle de Casma: culturas Chavín, Santa o Huaylas Yunga, y sub-Chimú.* Pub. Antropol. Arch. "Julio C Tello". Lima: Univ. Nac. Mayor San Marcos

Topic J, Topic T. 1987. The archaeological investigation of Andean militarism: some cautionary observations. See Haas et al 1987, pp. 47–55

Torero A. 1990. Procesos lingüísticos e identificación de dioses en los Andes centrales. *Rev. And.* 8(1):237–63

Uceda S, Mujica E. 1998. Nuevas evidencias para viejos problemas: a manera de introducción. In *Investigaciones en la Huaca de la Luna 1996,* ed. S Uceda, E Mujica, R Morales, pp. 9–16. Trujillo: Facult. Cienc. Soc. Unin. Nac. Lib.

Vega-Centeno R, Villacorta LF, Cáceres LE, Marcone G. 1998. Arquitectura monumental temprana en el valle medio de Fortaleza. *Bol. Arq. PUCP* 2:219–38

Verano JW, Uceda S, Chapdelaine C, Tello R, Paredes MI, Pimentel V. 1999. Modified human skulls from the urban sector of the pyramids of Moche, northern Peru. *Lat. Am. Antiq.* 10(1):59–70

Von Hagen A, Morris C. 1998. *The Cities of the Ancient Andes.* New York: Thames Hudson

Wheeler J, Mujica E. 1981. Prehistoric pastoralism in the Lake Titicaca Basin, Peru 1979–1980 field season. *Natl. Sci. Found. Final Rep.*

Willey GR. 1971. *An Introduction to American Archaeology,* Vol. 2. *South America.* Englewood Cliffs: Prentice Hall

Williams C. 1971. Centros ceremoniales tempranos en el valle de Chillón, Rímac y Lurín. *Apuntes Arqueol.* 1:1–4

Wilson D. 1981. Of maize and men: a critique of the maritime hypothesis of state origins on the coast of Peru. *Am. Antiq.* 83:93–120

Wilson D. 1988. *Prehispanic Settlement Patterns in the Lower Santa Valley, Peru: A Regional Perspective on the Origins and Development of Complex North Coast Society.* Washington, DC: Smithsonian Inst.

Wilson DJ. 1999. *Indigenous South Americans of the Past and Present: an Ecological Perspective.* Boulder, CO: Westview

Wissler C. 1922. *The American Indian.* New York: Oxford Univ. Press.

Annu. Rev. Anthropol. 2001. 30:65–83

TOWARD AN ANTHROPOLOGY OF PRISONS

Lorna A. Rhodes

Department of Anthropology, University of Washington, Seattle, Washington 98195;
e-mail: lrhodes@u.washington.edu

Key Words   imprisonment, history of confinement, institutions, subjection, ethnography of incarceration

■ **Abstract**   The late twentieth century saw an intense expansion of the prison system in the United States during the same period in which Foucault's *Discipline and Punish* influenced academic approaches to power and subjection. This article reviews the history, sociology, and anthropology of the prison, as well as some recent popular critiques of the current situation. It highlights critical perspectives on modern forms of punishment and reform and suggests areas in which an anthropology of prisons might take up questions of modernity, subjection, classification, social suffering, and ethnographic possibility in the context of an increasingly politicized and racialized system of incarceration.

INTRODUCTION

In the United States today almost two million people are in prison. The expansion of the prison system began in the early 1980s, continues despite years of falling crime rates (Blumstein & Wallman 2000), and has resulted in the highest rate of incarceration in the world (Blumstein & Beck 1999, Caplow & Simon 1999, Donziger 1996, Mauer 1999). Most of today's prisons are a far cry from those of the earlier decades of the twentieth century, in which the occasional sociologist could ply his trade remarkably undisturbed (Tonry & Petersilia 1999a). Contemporary penology involves an increasingly managerial and technological orientation, psychologically and sociologically based forms of classification, and tight control over information and access (DiIulio 1987, Rhine 1998). A huge corrections industry depends on prison growth and promotes new technologies of enforcement, surveillance, and restraint (Christie 1994; Dyer 2000; Parenti 1999, pp. 211–244).

The past 20 years of prison expansion are the same years in which "the prison"— that space of regimentation and surveillance described in *Discipline and Punish*— has come to figure prominently in contemporary scholarship (Foucault 1979, Gordon 1991). The drawing of the kneeling prisoner that illustrates Foucault's discussion of Bentham's panopticon remains an icon of disciplinary subjection and an omnipresent subtext in discussions of the modern interpenetration of power and knowledge. Yet the extent to which Foucault's prison either serves as a guide

0084-6570/01/1021-0065$14.00

to the historical prison or represents any particular form of institutional discipline is unclear. Twenty-five years ago the development of a massive prison complex by the end of the century was beyond the horizon of the historians and social scientists then engaged in a wide-ranging critique of institutions of social control (e.g. Morris 1974). Today a large and growing body of work alludes to, but does not explore, the prison as a central site for the exercise of disciplinary power (e.g. Butler 1990, Santner 1996), while other literature, less theoretically driven, describes and critiques a rapidly metastasizing "prison industrial complex" (Burton-Rose 1998, Tonry & Petersilia 1999a, see also Parenti 1999, Duguid 2000, Alford 2000).

Little work in anthropology concerns prisons. Other disciplines, however, have an overwhelmingly productive historical involvement with crime and punishment. Psychiatry and psychology, sociology, criminology, and to some extent modern philosophy emerged as "disciplines" in relation to nineteenth-century institutions and are deeply implicated in their classificatory and normalizing impulses (Foucault 1965, 1979, 1988; Kittler 1990; Leps 1992). These fields share with the prison itself two features of modernity described by Giddens. The first is a "hidden compulsiveness," a "drive to repetition" (Giddens 1994, pp. 68–70) that can already be seen in Weber's discussion of the Protestant work ethic. The same ethic drove Bentham and Howard when they invented the penitentiary as a means of producing conscience through repetitive and meaningless work (Bentham 1948[1789], Semple 1993, Southwood 1958). The long engagement of the "disciplines" with the prison is nothing if not repetitive, a point that troubles any attempt to critique or contribute to these discourses. The second feature of modernity is reflexivity, the "pervasive filter-back" (Giddens 1994, p. 91) through which academic discourses affect the objects they describe. This looping of influence produces a "haunting double" (Lash 1994, p. 112; Beck et al 1994) in almost all areas in which disciplinary knowledges intersect with the practice of incarceration (for a more general discussion of reflexivity in relation to prisons see Caplow & Simon 1999, pp. 97–110).

Much writing on prisons consists of normalizing discourses enmeshed in this dynamic (see, e.g. Mays & Winfree 1998). A smaller literature attempts more self-reflective and problematizing approaches, while also revealing the difficulty of escaping the prison's disciplinary orbit. In this review I consider this second form of prison writing, which I have divided into four general types: (*a*) contemporary critiques directed against the numbing effects of the current situation; (*b*) efforts, particularly following Foucault, to revisit and revise our understanding of prison history; (*c*) sociological and anthropological work that attempts an entry into and a direct engagement in the interior life of the prison; and (*d*) work that addresses women as prisoners and problematizes the predominance of masculine perspectives in and on the prison. I end with a discussion of prospects and difficulties for future anthropological work. Though I discuss some European sources, my primary emphasis is the prison in the United States. For general overviews of US prisons see McShane & McShane (1996), Christianson (1998), and Tonry &

Petersilia (1999b); for studies of historical and contemporary prisons worldwide see, for example, O'Brien (1982), Spierenburg (1991), Morris (1998), and Stern (1998). On the recent spread of US practices to Europe, see Wacquant (1999).

WRITING AGAINST THE CONTEMPORARY PRISON

A growing critical literature meets the current prison boom head-on by questioning its premises and contextualizing the political emphasis on crime and punishment that supports it. Over half of prisoners in the United States are African American and three fourths are people of color; a rapidly growing number are women, also three fourths of color (Currie 1998, Donziger 1996, Mauer 1999, Miller 1996, Tonry 1995). Critics contend that prisons perform a kind of social, economic, and political "magic" by "disappearing" large numbers of poor and minority people (A Davis in Gordon 1998/1999, Donziger 1996, Hallinan 2001, Irwin & Austin 1993, Miller 1996, Tonry 1995, Walker et al 2000). This process occurs on many levels. One is political: repression of "disorder" and dissent through increasingly draconian methods of policing and control, including the war on drugs (Baum 1996, Dowker & Good 1995, Kennedy 1997, Kerness 1998, Miller 1996, Parenti 1999, Perkinson 1994). Another is economic: Prisons create jobs both in the rural areas where they are sited and in the growing prison-related industrial sector, remove the unemployed from statistical visibility, add to the census of depopulated counties, and disenfranchise current and former prisoners (Christie 1994, Davis 1998b, Dyer 2000, Gilmore 1998, 1998/1999, Gordon 1998/1999, Western & Beckett 1999, Western Prison Project 2000). The public discourse on crime reinforces this prison magic. Containing a barely concealed subtext in which danger to "law-abiding citizens" is located in African-American and other men of color, it "reproduces racism . . . in [an] ideologically palatable fashion" (Parenti 1999, p. 242), serves to "mobilize ... fears ..." (Davis 1998b, p. 62), and "relieves us of the responsibility of seriously engaging ... the problems of late capitalism" (A Davis in Gordon 1998/1999, p. 148; see also Baum 1996, Dyer 2000, Parenti 1999, Reiman 1998, Tonry 1995). Analysts of media representations of crime and imprisonment point to the political, economic, and cultural work these representations perform in supporting policies that lead to increasing rates of incarceration (Chambliss 1999, pp. 13–59; Baum 1996; Beckett 1997; Caplow & Simon 1999; Currie 1998; Dyer 2000; Ferrell & Websdale 1999). The proliferation of "supermaximum" high security facilities is a parallel form of magic within prisons, serving to further "disappear" some prisoners, again disproportionately African-American and other men of color, through new forms of high-tech solitary confinement (Abu-Jamal 1995, Dowker & Good 1995, Grassian 1983, Haney 1993, Human Rights Watch 1997, Kerness 1998, Parenti 1999, Perkinson 1994).

Ranging from pragmatic to visionary, from experience-near to sweeping, critiques of the prison problematize its role in the production of an "enemy within" (Duguid 2000, pp. 147–77). Prisoners also participate in this critical tradition of resistance to the prison's "dual function: to keep *us* [non-prisoners] out as well as *them* in" (Wicker 1998, p. xi). One former prisoner writes, "Most Americans remain ignorant . . . that they live in a country that holds hostage behind bars another populous country of their fellow citizens" (Baca 1998, p. 363). Among many voices from that second country are Himes (1998[1953]), Rideau (1992), Abbott (1981), and Genet (1964), as well as contributors to Franklin (1998b), Chevigny (2000), Arriens (1997), and Leder (2000). A prisoner newsletter and website report on prison conditions, legal actions, and the political climate (*Prison Legal News*, with links to many other prison sites; see also Burton-Rose 1998). Prisoners' accounts of current conditions, especially of solitary confinement in supermax prisons, describe a "nether-world of despair" (Abu-Jamal 1995, p. 12) and are "far more bleak and desperate than the prison literature of any earlier period" (Franklin 1998a, p. 17).

Many critics of the prison aim to "interrupt the conversation"—both popular and academic—that frames contemporary forms of incarceration as inevitable (Gordon 1998/1999, p. 156). They take on what Feldman, writing about the media imagery surrounding Desert Storm and Rodney King, calls "cultural anesthesia": "the banishment of disconcerting, discordant, and anarchic sensory presences and agents that undermine the normalizing and often silent premises of everyday life" (Feldman 1994, p. 405; cf. Daniel 1998, Kleinman & Kleinman 1997). Anesthesia results from evading the "embodied character of violence," not only through denial, but also through numbingly repetitive media images that engage the viewer in "material complicity" with its terms. Like police brutality and war, the prison enacts on the bodies of "others" a violence camouflaged by its position as what Davis calls an "abstract site" in the public imagination (A Davis in Gordon 1998/1999, p. 147; cf. Benjamin 1986[1920], Davis 1999, Santner 1996). At the same time, however, this national "secret" is highly fetishized, both as the spoken or unspoken complement to crime and in many of its public representations (cf. Sloop 1996). The academic study of prisons is enmeshed in this contradiction: On the one hand, the appearance of "objectivity" contributes to the abstraction that protects these sites from view, while on the other, intense engagement runs the danger of a compulsive intimacy with the terms provided by the prison itself.

REVISITING THE MARCH OF PROGRESS

In 1939 Rusche & Kirchheimer asked, "To what extent is the development of penal methods determined by . . . social relations?" (Rusche & Kirchheimer 1939). This question had great impact in the years following the reissue of their work in 1968, the same year in which the Paris student uprising struck Foucault with the realization, he later said, that he had been talking about power all along (Foucault 1980, pp. 115–16; also see Bright 1996, pp. 15–18). In *Discipline and Punish* Foucault turned Rusche & Kirchheimer's question on its head to offer the prison as an originary ground for the analysis of power (Foucault 1979). Other scholars, influenced by the same moment, produced less generalizable accounts that also direct attention to the contingent nature of the prison and its embeddedness in particular social and political conditions (Howe 1994, pp. 63–64). Like Foucault, they challenge conventional or "march of progress" accounts (Howe 1994, Cohen 1988; for examples of conventional histories see Am. Correct. Assoc. 1983, Keve 1991).

The more materialist of these approaches, and the closest to Rusche, considers prisons in direct relationship to labor conditions. Writing about American penitentiaries of the early nineteenth century, Melossi sees them as a response to economic dislocation in a society in which "Pauperism . . . came to be intimately connected with the problem of . . . criminal behavior" and a "voluntaristic explanation of 'being poor' [was] conducive to a 'punitive' approach" (Melossi & Pavarini 1981, p. 119). At the Auburn penitentiary—one of the first American prisons—a combination of factory-style labor during the day and isolation at night created "work structured in the same way as the dominant form of factory work" (Melossi & Pavarini 1981, p. 129; Melossi 1978). This approach can be criticized for its insistence on the primacy of the economic (as, e.g. by Howe 1994), but as a demystification of the rhetoric of reform it also highlights the compulsive temporal and spatial arrangements of modernity. Prison labor mimics the factory not because the factory is the primary institution from which prison derives, but because the configuration of bodies, work, and architecture in the postcolonial prison constitutes a form of power peculiar to the new democratic regime (Foucault 1979, Gordon 1991).

This configuration is central to three histories written in the 1970s that join *Discipline and Punish* in regarding the "architecture of mind" as central to the modern prison (Bender 1987). Rothman considers the asylums and penitentiaries of the Jacksonian era less in economic terms than as the consequence of a political response to widespread fear of social disorder (Rothman 1971; see also Rothman 1980). This response rested on the assumption that architecture was "one of the most important of the *moral* sciences" (Rothman 1971, p. 83). Evans explores the parallel development in England of the belief that "architecture [was] . . . a serviceable weapon in the war . . . against vice . . . as a vessel of conscience and as pattern giver to society . . ." (Evans 1982, p. 6). The intent to make "each individual . . . the instrument of his own punishment," in the words of one proponent (Rothman 1971), was most fully realized at Pentonville in England. Ignatieff describes the enforcement, in this mid-nineteenth-century penitentiary, of total isolation sustained by an impersonal "bureaucratic formalism" (Ignatieff 1978, p. 113). "Men came apart in the loneliness and the silence [and] . . . were taken away to the asylum" (Ignatieff 1978, p. 9).

Further unpacking of the social context and moral contingency of the nineteenth-century prison has followed these critical histories. Important, though so far scanty, is work that makes clear the central relationship between slavery and the American prison. The coexistence of slavery with the new penitentiary system was theorized by prison advocates (some of whom were involved in the antislavery movement) in terms of the beneficial effects of labor on the mind (soul). Slaves were not subject to reform of character, but the position of the prisoner as a "slave of the state" came both to substitute for slavery and to serve as an impetus for the rationalization of prison discipline (Hirsch 1992, p. 76; Davis 1998a, p. 99; Lichtenstein 1996; Oshinsky 1997; Wacquant 2000). One reading of the relationship between the prison and the construction of self (that is, the soul or mind that was considered absent in slaves) locates the intent to rewrite the "character" of prisoners in the earlier context of eighteenth-century literary conventions that portray the newly modern individual. "Both the realist novel and the penitentiary pretend that character is autonomous, but in both cases invisible authority . . . fosters the illusion [of a] consciousness . . . as free to shape circumstance as to be shaped by it" (Bender 1987, p. 212; cf. Foucault 1979). Individual "freedom to shape circumstance," this foundational "pretense" of the historical prison, continues to be the most familiar contemporary defense of prison discipline and labor, masking both racially disproportionate incarceration and the use of inmate workers in the global economy (e.g. Alford 2000, Bennett et al 1996; cf. Cole 1999 Davis 1998b, 1999).

A pervasive rhetoric of reform is built into the modern prison from the outset (Foucault 1979; e.g. Bookspan 1991, Pisciotta 1994). Ignatieff ends his grim account of Pentonville by hopefully suggesting that to "pierce through the rhetoric . . . [of] carceral power as 'reform'" is to prevent this "suffocating vision of the past" from "adjust[ing] us to the cruelties of the future" (Ignatieff 1978). Instead, a new set of reforms was springing up even as he wrote, including a conservative "new realism" that eschews utilitarian (rehabilitative) approaches in favor of incapacitation (e.g. Bennett et al 1996, DiIulio 1987). Today's supermaximum prisons isolate inmates much as Pentonville did, but have largely abandoned any gestures toward rehabilitation. Cohen noted in 1983 that in Orwell's dystopia the "proles" were subject more to segregation than to thought control. He speculated prophetically that we might be headed for a similar division between those subject to normalization (through various therapeutic strategies) and those simply encapsulated and policed (Cohen 1983, p. 121; cf. Hamm et al 1994, Parenti 1999).

Nevertheless, the penological and criminological literature depends on proposals for change, and in making them critics are drawn into an inevitable relationship to the rhetoric they hope to "pierce." Cohen quotes Adorno's remark that "One must belong to a tradition to hate it properly" (Cohen 1988, p. 5). Reflecting (from the perspective of 1985) on his career as a critical criminologist, he writes that "Every attempt I ever made to distance myself from the subject, to criticize it, even to question its very right to exist, has only got me more involved in its inner life" (Cohen 1988, p. 8). One consequence of this ambivalence on the part of critical theorists has been a series of shifting identifications of "where" power is. Is the enemy centralized authority, in which case "community" corrections and treatment offer a way out? Or is community itself a euphemism for intrusive surveillance and normalization? (Cohen 1983, 1985; cf. Torrey 1997). Such oppositions are enmeshed in a repetitive cycle of reform that seems to draw all who enter—whether self-consciously or not—into the strategies through which power/knowledge reconfigures and disguises itself.

Following the publication of *Discipline and Punish*, numerous historians weighed in with objections, though there seems to be general agreement about the moment when the modern disciplinary apparatus took shape (Howe 1994, Ignatieff 1983, Megill 1987). Leaving this aside, however, both conventional and critical histories of the prison show that "discipline" in prisons has in fact been erratic and temporary (Beaumont & de Tocqueville 1964[1833], pp. 162–163; cf. Hamm et al 1994, O'Brien 1982). We are misled about the implications for theory if we take too seriously administrative schemes for the prison and miss the extent and implications of slippage away from them (Ransom 1997, p. 33; cf. Alford 2000, Garland & Young 1983). The contemporary prison calls out for analysis along the lines suggested by the work of Ransom, Feldman, and others who ask how disciplinary power has those gaps and openings suggested by Foucault's comments on power's inevitable link to resistance (Feldman 1991, Ransom 1997; for a compelling recent example, see Jackson & Burke 1999). Studies of the historical prison lend depth to our understanding of the "deep struggle ... between discipline and its objects" (Bright 1996, p. 26) and suggest that the contemporary prison be seen not only as shaped but also as haunted by the past (Gordon 1997, pp. 3–28).

ENTERING THE PRISON: THE SOCIOLOGICAL TRADITION

Beginning in 1933, the Stateville Penitentiary in Illinois had an official job title called sociologist-actuary. Although the academics who held it had "no impact whatever" on day-to-day prison operation, it was symbolic of the decades-long relationship between the prison and University of Chicago sociologists (Jacobs 1977, p. 19). Classic works by these scholars considered the prison of the 1930s and 1940s a "small society" or a "society of captives," best understood in terms of roles and hierarchies. This view was reinforced by the isolated and relatively homogeneous character of prison populations at the time (Clemmer 1958, Sykes 1958; for a prisoner's account of this era at Stateville, see Leopold 1957).

By the 1970s it had become clear that prisons were in a state of flux and less at the "margins" than these accounts suggest (Irwin 1988). Jacobs, a member of the next generation of Chicago sociologists, approached Stateville through a combination of archival research and participant observation with inmates. Influenced by Rusche & Kirchheimer and Rothman, as well as his Chicago mentors, he viewed the prison "developmentally" as it moved away from the rigidly authoritarian regime of the 1930s and 1940s (Jacobs 1977, cf. Erickson 1957). Irwin studied the prison in Soledad, California, where he had himself been incarcerated earlier (Irwin 1970, 1980). Both Jacobs and Irwin attributed the decline of the "Big House" prisons of the previous era to "penetration" by legal, social welfare, and gang influences. The old order of authority decayed through successive periods of reform as links to the outside, particularly to the civil rights movement, increased (cf. Cummins 1994).

Both Jacobs and Irwin point to some reasons why little additional ethnographic work has been done in US prisons (cf. Tonry & Petersilia 1999a, p. 10). The period of relative permeability to academics had subsided by the early 1980s with the increased bureaucratization and rationalization of prison management described at its inception by Jacobs (see also Irwin & Austin 1993). His appendix on "participant observation among prisoners" recounts his unsuccessful struggle to avoid identification with any particular group and the threats leveled against him when he failed (Jacobs 1977, pp. 215–229). Such an unpredictable situation would be avoided by most prison administrators today (for exceptions see Fleisher 1989, Thomas 1988, Owen 1998 and, for journalism, Bergner 1998). In addition, the sociologists and other reform-minded entrants into the prisons of the 1950s, 1960s, and 1970s were engaged in a reflexive "loop" in which their perspective on human nature—particularly their belief in rehabilitation and enthusiasm for prison "subcultures"—contributed to experimental programs throughout the country; these were largely abandoned after the violent inmate uprisings of the 1970s and early 1980s (Unseem & Kimball 1989, Braswell et al. 1994; but for Canada and Great Britain see Duguid 2000 and Waldram 1997).

Some continuing sociological research explores the socialization and role adaptation of correctional officers (guards), reminding us that prison workers are worthy of study in their own right (Crouch 1980, Philliber 1987, Zimmer 1989). One researcher became a guard in a Texas prison. His description of his own socialization and subsequent witnessing of extreme violence toward inmates suggests both the difficulty of entering this world and the ethical hazards encountered once in it (Marquart 1986; for an excellent contemporary account by a journalist see Conover 2000). Violence is also at the center of *States of Seige*, which describes in detail the social dynamics of prison riots (Unseem & Kimball 1989). Another heir to the sociological tradition is the social psychologist Toch, who has developed an ecological approach that considers prisoners' lives in terms of adaptation and coping styles (Toch 1977; also see Johnson 1987, Morris 1998, Toch & Adams 1994). Toch's perspective is helpful for its emphasis on the interactive aspects of prison work and developmental orientation to the experience of being imprisoned.

ENTERING THE PRISON: ANTHROPOLOGY

The anthropological work that has been conducted in and about prisons is more self-conscious than the sociological perspectives just described, and reveals contradictions perhaps less obvious in more accessible ethnographic contexts. Analytic and critical possibilities that emerge by virtue of the prison's "confinement" of resistance within a (presumably) observable space are fraught with difficulty in coming to know this resistance as an outsider (cf. Bright 1996, pp. 1–31). Not least of these difficulties is that observation itself is what is being resisted. Feldman's account of political violence in Northern Ireland relies on former prisoners' descriptions of extremes of brutality and resistance, a context in which the usually submerged kinship between "informant" and "informer" was an explicit danger. Feldman notes that in "a culture of surveillance, participant observation is . . . a form of complicity with those outsiders who surveil" (Feldman 1991, p. 12). He chose instead to gather oral histories that describe how larger structures of authority and domination are both expressed in and resisted by political action at the level of the body. This move gives him compelling access to the prisoner's (retrospective) bodily relation to the prison, while offering some protection from the political implications of telling and listening.

The now-classic Stanford Prison Experiment has come to stand for the possibility that the individuals who make up the prison are susceptible to being "made up" by it according to their positions in a structure of domination (Haney et al 1981; cf. Butler 1990, Hacking 1986, Morris 1995). Two ethnographic monographs written in the 1980s suggest the susceptibility of the anthropologist to this dynamic. In striking contrast to Feldman's approach, Fleischer enlisted the support of the Bureau of Prisons to become a correctional officer at the Federal Penitentiary at Lompoc, California. He describes a period in which "I began to think of myself as a correctional worker . . . I was becoming lost . . . what hacks [guards] did was right, what convicts did was wrong" (Fleisher 1989, p. 112). The result, *Warehousing Violence*, is a vividly realist account supporting the "warehousing" of violence. Fleischer contends that the "profit-making maximum-security penitentiary" can, under good management, become a "peaceful" solution to violence by hard-core offenders. Thomas, whose participant observation in a prison drew him toward what he came to see as a slippery slope of identification with inmates, describes the pull in the opposite direction. "In ten years of research, many informants became close friends . . . there was a danger that I might begin to romanticize [them]" (Thomas 1993, p. 46). His decision to write on topics "less vulnerable to distortion by emotional attachment" resulted in an ethnography centered on the studied resistance of jailhouse lawyering (Thomas 1993, p. 47; Thomas 1988).

Both of these ethnographers are acutely aware of how their subjects are positioned and show how the formation of self and "others" proceeds at multiple levels within the hierarchical structure of the prison. They do not, however, see how these positions entail a cumulative investment in performances that must be repeatedly developed and asserted in practice. Thus, they describe the bedrock drive to legitimate the institution through repetitive acts of domination but tend to attribute the results to the "character" of either inmates or staff. Feldman is helpful here because, though he does not observe these interactions, he grounds his understanding in the body with the aim of "fractur[ing] the appearance of lawful continuity between centers of legitimation and local acts of domination" (Feldman 1991, p. 2). Though the accounts of Fleischer and Thomas are rich in an awareness of "local acts," they do not engage the tension underlying "lawful continuity" as it emerges in both the effort of legitimation and the need to conceal its fundamental instability (cf. Benjamin 1986[1920], Santner 1996). Without this element, however, it is difficult to situate the prison beyond its internal preoccupations with who has power and why, and to ask, instead, how they have it and what supports and legitimates its expression (Rhodes 1998; LA Rhodes in preparation).

CONSIDERING GENDER

The majority of prison studies describe male inmates without reflecting on the implications of this depiction or the language in which it is framed (Howe 1994). Feminist writers point to a double invisibility here that applies to both women and men. Women prisoners have been largely ignored by historical and sociological work, though a rather scant gender-sensitive literature runs parallel to the approaches discussed thus far. The critical history and sociology of women prisoners suggest that they may be simultaneously neglected and subjected to specifically intrusive and abusive forms of discipline (Belknap 2000; Carlen 1983, 1998; Dobash et al 1986; Freedman 1981; Rafter 1985; Zedner 1998; for an anthology of writing by women prisoners see Scheffler 1986). Many observers note that norms of female domesticity influence the discipline imposed on women and intensify the pain of imprisonment when they are separated from families (Howe 1994), so that even in prison there is "no place where (women) . . . can be considered as family-immune" (Carlen 1998, p. 86). Several contemporary scholars and journalists explore the life stories of women prisoners, connections between women's imprisonment and the general increase in incarceration, and the social dynamics of women's prisons (Girshick 1999, Owen 1998, Rierden 1997, Watterson & Chesney-Lind 1996). Concurrent with this effort to bring attention to women's imprisonment, feminist scholars have also become increasingly aware of the danger of reproducing a normative category of "women" and "repeat[ing] criminology's 'will to truth'" in relation to it (Howe 1994, p. 214).

The second invisibility pertains to the fact that the maleness of prisons is so taken for granted in penal history and contemporary criminology. This suggests that "rather than looking at men as prisoners we might look at prisoners as men" (Sim 1994, p. 101; cf. Howe 1994, Naffine 1996). Such a perspective, so far barely visible in the expanse of prison literature, opens up questions of the prison's various displays of masculine power, men as victims of violence in prison, the influence of gendered popular representations of crime and prisons, and the exploration of unconscious gender assumptions in criminology and penology (Naffine 1996, Sim 1994).

INTERRUPTING THE TERMS OF DEBATE

The increasing impact of prisons on growing numbers of people is a compelling reason for turning anthropological attention to these institutions. Many issues have arisen or become more acute in the years of expansion and are in need of fresh insight and analysis. Prominent among them are racism in the criminal justice system, including the prison (Cole 1999, Davis 1998b, Donziger 1996, Walker et al 2000); the increasing numbers and long sentences of women in prison (Donziger 1996); increasing numbers of mentally ill inmates (Kupers 1999, Torrey 1997), including those in supermax prisons (Lovell et al 2000); an expansion of policing that overlaps the operation of the prison (Parenti 1999); economic globalization and changes in employment patterns that affect both prison staff and prisoners (Gilmore 1998/1999); high-tech forms of solitary confinement (Dowker & Good 1995, Parenti 1999); and the impact of imprisonment on families and neighborhoods (Gilmore 1998, Wacquant 2000). Although I have indicated some of the available analyses of these issues, few include either general anthropological or specifically ethnographic perspectives.

The most pressing need for the study of prisons is to challenge the terms of the discourse that frames and supports them. One possibility I have mentioned is to extend to contemporary prisons the kinds of questions that have been applied to their history. For example, Foucault queried the production and "utility" of the nineteenth-century discourse on the "dangerous individual" as the object of new forms of policing and confinement (Foucault 1980, p. 47, 1988). This discourse has since multiplied exponentially (see, e.g. Hare 1993, Meloy 1997), and its current version figures heavily in prison management. Antidotes can be found in recent works that explore the development of classificatory systems within and outside institutions in the late nineteenth and early twentieth centuries (Donzelot 1997, Kittler 1990, Leps 1992) and in the critical unpacking of the contemporary classificatory and criminological impulse (Knox 1998, Lesser 1993, Seltzer 1998, Tithecott 1997). These authors suggest avenues for exploring the construction of criminality and madness in the practices of prisons and in the criminal justice system more generally. What effect does classification have on those classified and on those doing the classifying? How does the productivity of classification intersect with other practices, such as prison industry (labor) and education, in institutions based on principles of transparency and rationality? (cf. Carlen 1983; Hacking 1986; Nuckolls 1998; Rhodes 1998, 2001; Sloop 1996).

A second possible challenge to the prevailing discourse centers on the link between transparency (surveillance) and subjection. It is possible to simply critique the contemporary prison as a site of visual power, but doing so produces a rather static and functionalist argument that fails to take into account the play of visibility and opacity in these settings (cf. Alford 2000). More helpful is to take Foucault's critique of vision beyond its use as a metaphor for reflexivity. Ransom (1997) suggests that power/knowledge offers the possibility of interception, a fluid and sometimes fragile overlapping and disjunction. This perspective can be used, for example, to understand the complex dynamics of the relationship between psychiatry, "treatment," and the prison (Carlen 1998; Duguid 2000; Kupers 1999; Lunbeck 1994; Rhodes 1998, 2000). We can thus discover a less automatically reflexive, more complex site for resistance in the form of unexpected subjective, interpersonal and/or bodily identifications (Bright 1996, Rhodes 1998).

These possibilities must be seen, however, in relation to the specifics of the current political economy and the haunting of the American prison by slavery, as well as in light of the use of force in contemporary prisons (Davis 1998a,b; Gilmore 1998/1999; Kerness 1998; Reiman 1998; Wacquant 2000). Power/knowledge is not, as Foucault himself noted, intended to encompass conditions more closely resembling slavery or torture, both of which can also be found in (some) US prisons (Hamm et al 1994, Kerness 1998). Thus, we need to ask, not only about the "fit" of power, knowledge, and the prison, but about those areas in which other forms of domination need to be addressed. The close connection between incarceration and policing, the use of electronic weapons and restraints, and the preventive detention of reputed "gang members" within prisons all point to hybrid forms of power with particularly problematic implications in light of the current massive incarceration of people of color (Parenti 1999).

The entanglement of the prison with the intellectual history of the West also calls out for exploration through ethnographic and oral history approaches to those directly involved as prisoners, families of prisoners, correctional workers, administrators, architects, and manufacturers. The premise of much analysis of prison history is that internal contradictions and certain paradoxical elements of practice can be discovered in institutional structures. Those in "the system" struggle with the terms of these contradictions and may have something to tell us about how this struggle unfolds. If arguments about prisons are happening in prisons and expressed in daily practice, then we might expect them to shed some light on how such discourses become so hard to dislodge.

CONCLUSION

A few of the prison researchers described here have approximated "traditional" ethnography, and without their work we would know less about prisons than we do. Fundamentally, however, no outsider/observer can "participate" in the situation of the prisoner. Prison workers are well aware that this is the case for all visitors, often offering enthusiastic tours of their facilities that reveal and conceal in the same gesture. The ethnographer may get past the tour to an extent, but prisons are pervaded by an interpersonal opacity that thwarts even those who govern, manage, or live in them (cf. Bergner 1998, Conover 2000). To forget one's position as an outsider is to be in danger, not only from interpersonal trouble of various kinds but, more enduringly, from alarming emotional and intellectual identifications. Here the ethnographic desire for (perhaps fantasized but nonetheless compelling) alignment with one's subject(s) must be relinquished or at least bracketed (Daniel 1985, p. 246). Nor can one discount the element of coercion that dogs the acquisition of "knowledge" in this setting (cf. Hornblum 1998). The structure of relations inside the prison should disabuse us of the hope—often held in spite of ourselves—that knowledge of power/knowledge can trump power/knowledge itself (Feldman 1991).

This undermining of ethnographic identification is counterbalanced by the potential for an anthropology of prisons to engage us in other ways. Although the inaccessibility and opacity of the prison make ethnography difficult, they do not necessarily preclude it. In a thoughtful discussion of what she calls "quasi-ethnography" in a women's prison, Owen points out that the necessity for restraint on her part—for example, her recognition that prisoners may have too little privacy to tolerate the intrusion of a researcher—also deepened her understanding of the situation she was studying (Owen 1998). Restraints imposed on research by prison staff may be similarly folded into the process through which the ethnographer comes to appreciate the larger dynamics of restraint governing these institutions (cf. Waldram 1998). This kind of work, so obviously partial and so inescapably part of the historical context it aims to illuminate (Feldman 1991), forces an awareness of the paradoxical entanglements that snag us in the very categories and problems we set out to study.

Although no single work of anthropology will resolve this conundrum, we are increasingly aware that social suffering—in wars, illness, and as a result of a myriad of forms of social injustice—raises the issue of how we might speak to and against cultural anesthesia without contributing to its perpetuation (Daniel 1998, Feldman 1994, Kleinman & Kleinman 1997, Scheper-Hughes 1995). The dramatically bounded space of that "other country" of prisoners (Baca 1998) demands that we engage the haunted and saturated quality of specific routines of domination while not losing sight of the "prison nation" in which they occur (Hallinan 2001). We may hope that an anthropology thus grounded can offer some resistance to the historical undertow of compulsive repetition. The task of steering between abstract and fetishized representation is delicate, but it contains the possibility of a necessary confrontation with the brute facts of domination as they play out in institutions that have become ubiquitous, if partially veiled, features of our cultural and political landscape.

ACKNOWLEDGMENTS

I am grateful to Michelle Barry for her assistance and to David Allen, David Lovell, Kristin Cloyes, Cheryl Cooke, and Val Daniel for their comments.

Visit the Annual Reviews home page at www.AnnualReviews.org

LITERATURE CITED

Abbott J. 1981. *In the Belly of the Beast*. New York: Vintage

Abu-Jamal M. 1995. *Live From Death Row*. Reading, MA: Addison-Wesley

Alford CF. 2000. What would it matter if everything Foucault said about prisons were wrong? *Discipline and Punish* after twenty years. *Theory Society* 29:125–46

Am. Correct. Assoc. 1983. *The American Prison: From the Beginning*. College Park, MD: ACA

Arriens J. 1997. *Welcome to Hell: Letters and*

Writings from Death Row. Boston: Northeastern Univ. Press

Baca JS. 1998. Past present. See Franklin, 1998b, pp. 358–64

Baum D. 1996. *Smoke and Mirrors: The War on Drugs and the Politics of Failure.* New York: Little, Brown

Beaumont G, de Tocqueville A. 1964[1833]. *On the Penitentiary System in the United States and Its Application in France.* Carbondale: Southern Ill. Univ. Press

Beck U, Giddens A, Lash S. 1994. *Reflexive Modernization: Politics, Tradition and Aesthetics in the Modern Social Order.* Stanford, CA: Stanford Univ. Press

Beckett K. 1997. *Making Crime Pay: Law and Order in Contemporary American Politics.* New York: Oxford Univ. Press

Belknap J. 2000. *The Invisible Woman: Gender, Crime and Justice.* Belmont, CA: Wadsworth

Bender J. 1987. *Imagining the Penitentiary: Fiction and the Architecture of Mind in Eighteenth Century England.* Chicago: Univ. Chicago Press

Benjamin W. 1986[1920]. Critique of violence. In *Walter Benjamin: Essays, Aphorisms, Autobiographical Writings*, ed. P Demetz, pp. 277–300. New York: Schocken

Bennett WJ, DiIulio JJ, Walters JP. 1996. *Body Count: Moral Poverty and How to Win America's War Against Crime and Drugs.* New York: Simon & Schuster

Bentham J. 1948[1789]. *An Introduction to the Principles of Morals and Legislation.* New York: Hafner

Bergner D. 1998. *God of the Rodeo: The Search for Hope, Faith, and a Six-Second Ride in Louisiana's Angola Prison.* New York: Crown

Blumstein A, Beck AJ. 1999. Population growth in U.S. prisons: 1980–1986. See Tonry & Petersilia 1999b, pp. 17–61

Blumstein A, Wallman J. 2000. The recent rise and fall of American violence. In *The Crime Drop in America*, ed. A Blumstein, J Wallman, pp. 1–12. Cambridge: Cambridge Univ. Press

Bookspan S. 1991. *A Germ of Goodness: The California State Prison System, 1851–1944.* Lincoln: Univ. Neb. Press

Braswell C, Montgomery RH, Lombardo LX. 1994. *Prison Violence in America.* Cincinnati, OH: Anderson

Bright C. 1996. *The Powers That Punish: Prison and Politics in the Era of the "Big House," 1920–1955.* Ann Arbor: Univ. Mich. Press

Burton-Rose D, ed. 1998. *The Celling of America: An Inside Look at the U.S. Prison Industry.* Monroe, ME: Common Courage

Butler J. 1990. *Gender Trouble: Feminism and the Subversion of Identity.* New York: Routledge

Caplow T, Simon J. 1999. Understanding prison policy and population trends. See Tonry & Petersilia 1999b, pp. 63–120

Carlen P. 1983. *Women's Imprisonment: A Study in Social Control.* London: Routledge

Carlen P. 1998. *Sledgehammer: Women's Imprisonment at the Millenium.* London: MacMillan

Chambliss WJ. 1999. *Power, Politics and Crime.* Boulder, CO: Westview

Chevigny BG, ed. 2000. *Doing Time: 25 Years of Prison Writing.* New York: Arcade

Christianson S. 1998. *With Liberty for Some: 500 Years of Imprisonment in America.* Boston: Northeastern Univ. Press

Christie N. 1994. *Crime Control as Industry: Toward Gulags, Western Style.* London: Routledge

Clemmer DR. 1958. *The Prison Community.* New York: Holt, Rinehart & Winston

Cohen S. 1983. Social-control talk: telling stories about correctional change. In *The Power to Punish*, ed. D Garland, P Young, pp. 101–29. Atlantic Highlands, NJ: Humanities

Cohen S. 1985. *Visions of Social Control: Crime, Punishment and Classification.* Cambridge: Polity

Cohen S. 1988. *Against Criminology.* New Brunswick, NJ: Transaction

Cole D. 1999. *No Equal Justice: Race and Class in the American Criminal Justice System.* New York: New Press

Conover T. 2000. *Newjack: Guarding Sing Sing*. New York: Random House

Crouch BM. 1980. *The Keepers: Prison Guards and Contemporary Corrections*. Springfield, IL: Thomas

Cummins E. 1994. *The Rise and Fall of California's Radical Prison Movement*. Stanford, CA: Stanford Univ. Press

Currie E. 1998. *Crime and Punishment in America: Why the Solutions to America's Most Stubborn Social Crisis Have Not Worked and What Will*. New York: Henry Holt

Daniel EV. 1985. Review of A Crack in the Mirror: Reflexive Perspectives in Anthropology (Jay Ruby, ed). Urban Life 14(2):240–48

Daniel EV. 1998. The limits of culture. In *In Near Ruins: Cultural Theory at the End of the Century*, ed. NB Dirks, pp. 67–91. Minneapolis, MN: Univ. Minn. Press

Davis AY. From the prison of slavery to the slavery of prison: Frederick Douglass and the convict lease system. See James 1998, pp. 74–95

Davis AY. 1998b. Race and criminalization: black Americans and the punishment industry. See James 1998, pp. 61–73

Davis AY. 1999. A world unto itself: multiple invisibilities of imprisonment. In *Behind the Razor Wire: A Portrait of a Contemporary Prison*, ed. M Jacobson-Hardy, pp. ix-xvii. New York: New York Univ. Press

DiIulio JJ. 1987. *Governing Prisons: A Comparative Study of Correctional Management*. New York: MacMillan

Dobash RP, Dobash RE, Gutteridge S. 1986. *The Imprisonment of Women*. London: Blackwell

Donzelot J. 1997. *The Policing of Families*. New York: Pantheon

Donziger SR, ed. 1996. *The Real War On Crime: The Report of the National Criminal Justice Commission*. New York: Harper-Collins

Dowker F, Good G. 1995. The proliferation of control unit prisons in the United States. In *Prison Crisis: Critical Readings*, ed. EP Sharboro, RL Keller, pp. 34–46. New York: Harrow & Heston

Duguid S. 2000. *Can Prisons Work? The Prisoner as Object and Subject in Modern Corrections*. Toronto: Univ. Toronto Press

Dyer J. 2000. *The Perpetual Prison Machine: How America Profits From Crime*. Boulder, CO: Westview

Erickson G. 1957. *Ragen of Joliet*. New York: Dutton

Evans R. 1982. *The Fabrication of Virtue: English Prison Architecture, 1750–1840*. Cambridge: Cambridge Univ. Press

Feldman A. 1991. *Formations of Violence: The Narrative of the Body and Political Terror in Northern Ireland*. Chicago: Univ. Chicago Press

Feldman A. 1994. On cultural anesthesia: from Desert Storm to Rodney King. *Am. Ethnol.* 21(2):404–18

Ferrell J, Websdale N, eds. 1999. *Making Trouble: Cultural Constructions of Crime, Deviance, and Control*. New York: Aldine De Gruyter

Fleisher MS. 1989. *Warehousing Violence*. Newbury Park, CA: Sage

Foucault M. 1965. *Madness and Civilization: A History of Insanity in the Age of Reason*. New York: Vintage

Foucault M. 1979. *Discipline and Punish: The Birth of the Prison*. New York: Vintage

Foucault M. 1980. Truth and power. In *Power/Knowledge: Selected Interviews and Other Writings 1972–1977*, ed. C Gordon, pp. 109–33. New York: Pantheon

Foucault M. 1988. The dangerous individual. In *Michel Foucault: Politics, Philosophy, Culture*, ed. LD Kritzman, pp. 125–50. New York: Routledge

Franklin HB. 1998a. Introduction. See Franklin 1998b, pp. 1–18

Franklin HB, ed. 1998b. *Prison Writing in 20th-Century America*. New York: Penguin

Freedman EB. 1981. *Their Sisters' Keepers: Women's Prison Reform in America, 1830–1930*. Ann Arbor: Univ. Mich. Press

Garland D, Young P. 1983. Towards a social analysis of penality. In *The Power to Punish*, ed. D Garland, P Young, pp. 1–36. Atlantic Highlands, NJ: Humanities

Genet J. 1964. *The Thief's Journal*. New York: Grove

Giddens A. 1994. Living in a post-traditional society. See Beck et al. 1994, pp. 56–109

Gilmore RW. 1998. *From military keynesiasm to post-keynesian militarism: finance capital, land, labor and opposition in the rising california prison state*. PhD thesis, Rutgers Univ. 305 pp.

Gilmore RW. 1998/1999. Globalisation and US prison growth: from military Keynesianism to post-Keynesian militarism. *Race Class* 40(2/3):171–88

Girshick LB. 1999. *No Safe Haven: Stories of Women in Prison*. Boston: Northeastern Univ. Press

Gordon AF. 1997. *Ghostly Matters: Haunting and the Sociological Imagination*. Minneapolis: Univ. Minn. Press

Gordon AF. 1998/1999. Globalism and the prison industrial complex: an interview with Angela Davis. *Race Class* 40(2/3):145–57

Gordon C. 1991. Governmental rationality: an introduction. In *The Foucault Effect: Studies in Governmentality*, ed. G Burchell, C Gordon, P Miller, pp. 1–51. Chicago: Univ. Chicago Press

Grassian S. 1983. Psychopathological effects of solitary confinement. *Am. J. Psychiatry* 140(11):1450–54

Hacking I. 1986. Making up people. In *Reconstructing Individualism: Autonomy, Individuality and the Self in Western Thought*, ed. TC Heller, S Morton, DE Wellbery, pp. 222–36. Stanford, CA: Stanford Univ. Press

Hallinan JT. 2001. *Going Up the River: Travels in a Prison Nation*. New York: Random House

Hamm MS, Coupez T, Hoze FE, Weinstein C. 1994. The myth of humane imprisonment: a critical analysis of severe discipline in U.S. maximum security prisons, 1945–1990. See Braswell et al., pp. 167–200

Haney C. 1993. "Infamous punishment": the psychological consequences of isolation. *Nat. Prison Proj. J.* Spring: 3–21

Haney C, Banks C, Zimbardo P. 1981. Interpersonal dynamics in a simulated prison. In *Prison Guard/Correctional Officer*, ed. RR Ross, pp. 137–68. Ontario, Canada: Butterworths

Hare RD. 1993. *Without Conscience: The Disturbing World of the Psychopaths Among Us*. New York: Pocket Books

Himes C. 1998 (1953). *Yesterday Will Make You Cry*. New York: Norton

Hirsch AJ. 1992. *The Rise of the Penitentiary: Prisons and Punishment in Early America*. New Haven, CT: Yale Univ. Press

Hornblum AM. 1998. *Acres of Skin: Human Experiments at Holmesburg Prison: A True Story of Abuse and Exploitation in the Name of Medical Science*. New York: Routledge

Howe A. 1994. *Punish and Critique: Towards a Feminist Analysis of Penality*. New York: Routledge

Human Rights Watch. 1997. *Cold Storage: Super-Maximum Security Confinement in Indiana*. New York: Human Rights Watch

Ignatieff M. 1978. *A Just Measure of Pain: The Penitentiary in the Industrial Revolution 1750–1850*. London: Macmillan

Ignatieff M. 1983. State, civil society and total institutions: a critique of recent social histories of punishment. In *Social Control and the State: Historical and Comparative Essays*, ed. S Cohen, A Scull, pp. 75–105. Oxford: Robertson

Irwin J. 1970. *The Felon*. Englewood Cliffs, NJ: Prentice-Hall

Irwin J. 1980. *Prisons in Turmoil*. Boston: Little, Brown

Irwin J. 1988. Donald Cressey and the sociology of the prison. *Crime Delinq.* 34(3):328–37

Irwin J, Austin J. 1993. *It's About Time: America's Imprisonment Binge*. Belmont, CA: Wadsworth

Jackson J, Burke WF. 1999. *Dead Run: The Shocking Story of Dennis Stockton and Life on Death Row in America*. New York: Walker

Jacobs JB. 1977. *Stateville: The Penitentiary in Mass Society*. Chicago: Univ. Chicago Press

James J. 1998. *The Angela Y. Davis Reader*. Oxford: Blackwell

Johnson R. 1987. *Hard Time: Understanding*

and Reforming the Prison. Monterey, CA: Brooks/Cole

Kennedy R. 1997. *Race, Crime, and the Law.* New York: Vintage

Kerness B. 1998. Permanent lockdown in the United States. *Prison Focus* 2(2):4–7

Keve PW. 1991. *Prisons and the American Conscience: A History of U.S. Federal Corrections.* Carbondale: Southern Ill. Univ. Press

Kittler FA. 1990. *Discourse Networks, 1800/1990.* Stanford, CA: Stanford Univ. Press

Kleinman A, Kleinman J. 1997. The appeal of experience; the dismay of images: cultural appropriations of suffering in our times. In *Social Suffering,* ed. A Kleinman, V Das, M Locke, pp. 1–23 Berkeley: Univ. Calif. Press

Knox SL. 1998. *Murder: A Tale of Modern American Life.* Durham, NC: Duke Univ. Press

Kupers T. 1999. *Prison Madness: The Mental Health Crisis Behind Bars and What We Must Do About It.* San Francisco: Jossey-Bass

Lash S. 1994. Reflexivity and its doubles: structure, aesthetics, community. See Beck et al. 1994, pp. 110–73

Leder D. 2000 *The Soul Knows No Bars: Inmates Reflect on Life, Death and Hope.* Lanham, MD: Rowman Littlefield

Leopold N. 1957. *Life Plus Ninety Nine Years.* New York: Doubleday

Leps M-C. 1992. *Apprehending the Criminal: The Production of Deviance in Nineteenth-Century Discourse.* Durham, NC: Duke Univ. Press

Lesser W. 1993. *Pictures at an Execution.* Cambridge, MA: Harvard Univ. Press

Lichtenstein A. 1996. *Twice the Work of Free Labor: The Political Economy of Convict Labor in the New South.* New York: Verso

Lovell D, Cloyes K, Allen D, Rhodes L. 2000. Who lives in supermaximum custody? A Washington State study. *Fed. Probation* 64(2):33–38

Lunbeck E. 1994. *The Psychiatric Persuasion: Knowledge, Gender and Power in Modern America.* Princeton, NJ: Princeton Univ. Press

Marquart JW. 1986. Doing research in prisons: the strengths and weaknesses of full participation as a guard. *Justice Q.* 3(1):15–32

Mauer M. 1999. *Race to Incarcerate.* New York: New Press

Mays GL, Winfree LT. 1998. *Contemporary Corrections.* Belmont, CA: Wadsworth

McShane MD, McShane F. 1996. *Encyclopedia of American Prisons.* New York: Garland

Megill A. 1987. The reception of Foucault by historians. *J. Hist. Ideas* 48(1):117–41

Melossi D. 1978. Georg Rusche and Otto Kirchheimer: punishment and social structure. *Crime Soc. Justice* 9:73–85

Melossi D, Pavarini M. 1981. *The Prison and the Factory: Origins of the Penitentiary System.* London: Macmillan

Meloy JR. 1997. *The Psychopathic Mind: Origins, Dynamics, and Treatment.* Northvale, NJ: Aronson Inc.

Miller JG. 1996. *Search and Destroy: African-American Males in the Criminal Justice System.* Cambridge: Cambridge Univ. Press

Morris N. 1974. *The Future of Imprisonment.* Chicago: Univ. Chicago Press

Morris N. 1998. The contemporary prison: 1965–present. See Morris & Rothman 1998, pp. 202–31

Morris N, Rothman DJ, eds. 1998. *The Oxford History of the Prison: The Practice of Punishment in Western Society.* New York: Oxford Univ. Press

Morris RC. 1995. All made up: performance theory and the new anthropology of sex and gender. *Annu. Rev. Anthropol.* 24:567–92

Naffine N. 1996. *Feminism and Criminality.* Philadelphia: Temple Univ. Press

Nuckolls CW. 1998. *Culture: A Problem That Cannot Be Solved.* Madison: Univ. Wisc. Press

O'Brien P. 1982. *The Promise of Punishment: Prisons in Nineteenth-Century France.* Princeton, NJ: Princeton Univ. Press

Oshinsky DM. 1997. *Worse Than Slavery: Parchman Farm and the Ordeal of Jim Crow Justice.* New York: Free Press

Owen B. 1998. *In the Mix: Struggle and*

Survival in a Women's Prison. New York: SUNY Press

Parenti C. 1999. *Lockdown America: Police and Prisons in the Age of Crisis*. New York: Verso

Perkinson R. 1994. Shackled justice: Florence Federal Penitentiary and the new politics of punishment. *Soc. Justice* 21(3):117–31

Philliber S. 1987. Thy brother's keeper. *Justice Q.* 4(1):9–37

Pisciotta AW. 1994. *Benevolent Repression: Social Control and the American Reformatory-Prison Movement*. New York: New York Univ. Press

Prison Legal News. http.//www.prisonlegalnews.org

Rafter NH. 1985. *Partial Justice: Women in State Prisons 1800–1935*. Boston: Northeastern Univ. Press

Ransom JS. 1997. *Foucault's Discipline: The Politics of Subjectivity*. Durham, NC: Duke Univ. Press

Reiman J. 1998. *The Rich Get Richer and the Poor Get Prison: Ideology, Class and Criminal Justice*. Boston: Allyn & Bacon

Rhine EE, ed. 1998. *Best Practices: Excellence in Corrections*. Lanham, MD: Am. Correct. Assoc.

Rhodes LA. 1998. Panoptical intimacies. *Public Cult.* 10(2):285–311

Rhodes LA. 2000. Taxonomic anxieties: axis I and axis II in prison. *Med. Anthropol. Q.* 14(3):346–73

Rhodes LA. 2001. Utilitarians with words: "psychopathy" and the supermaximum prison. Ethnography. In press

Rideau W, Wilkber R. 1992. *Life Sentences: Rage and Survival Behind Bars*. New York: Times Books

Rierden A. 1997. *The Farm: Life Inside a Women's Prison*. Boston: Univ. Mass. Press

Rothman DJ. 1971. *The Discovery of the Asylum: Social Order and Disorder in the New Republic*. Boston: Little, Brown

Rothman DJ. 1980. *Conscience and Convenience: The Asylum and its Alternatives in Progressive America*. Boston: Little, Brown

Rusche G, Kirchheimer O. 1939. *Punishment and Social Structure*. New York: Columbia Univ. Press

Santner EL. 1996. *My Own Private Germany: Daniel Paul Schreber's Secret History of Modernity*. Princeton, NJ: Princeton Univ. Press

Scheffler JA, ed. 1986. *Wall Tappings: An Anthology of Writings by Women Prisoners*. Boston: Northeastern Univ. Press

Scheper-Hughes N. 1995. The primacy of the ethical: propositions for a militant anthropology. *Curr. Anthropol.* 36(3):409–40

Seltzer M. 1998. *Serial Killers: Death and Life in America's Wound Culture*. New York: Routledge

Semple J. 1993. *Bentham's Prison: A Study of the Panopticon Penitentiary*. New York: Oxford Univ. Press

Sim J. 1994. Tougher than the rest? Men in prison. In *Just Boys Doing Business? Men, Masculinities and Crime*, ed. T Newburn, EA Stanko, pp. 100–17. London: Routledge

Sloop JM. 1996. *The Cultural Prison: Discourse, Prisoners and Punishment*. Tuscaloosa: Univ. Alabama Press

Southwood M. 1958. *John Howard: Prison Reformer*. London: Independent

Spierenburg P. 1991. *The Prison Experience: Disciplinary Institutions and Their Inmates in Early Modern Europe*. New Brunswick: Rutgers Univ. Press

Stern V. 1998. *A Sin Against the Future*. Boston: Northeastern Univ. Press

Sykes G. 1958. *The Society of Captives*. New York: Rinehart

Thomas J. 1988. *Prisoner Litigation: The Paradox of the Jailhouse Lawyer*. Totowa, NJ: Rowman & Littlefield

Thomas J. 1993. *Doing Critical Ethnography*. Newbury Park, CA: Sage

Tithecott R. 1997. *Of Men and Monsters: Jeffrey Dahmer and the Construction of the Serial Killer*. Madison: Univ. Wisc. Press

Toch H. 1977. *Living in Prison: The Ecology of Survival*. New York: Free Press

Toch H, Adams K. 1994. *The Disturbed Violent Offender*. Washington, DC: Am. Psychol. Assoc.

Tonry M. 1995. *Malign Neglect: Race, Crime and Punishment in America*. New York: Oxford Univ. Press

Tonry M, Petersilia J. 1999a. American prisons at the beginning of the twenty-first century. See Tonry & Petersilia 1999b, pp. 1–16

Tonry M, Petersilia J. 1999b. *Prisons*. Chicago: Univ. Chicago Press

Torrey EF. 1997. *Out of the Shadows: Confronting America's Mental Illness Crisis*. New York: Wiley & Sons

Unseem B, Kimball P. 1989. *States of Seige: U.S. Prison Riots, 1971–1986*. New York: Oxford Univ. Press

Wacquant L. 1999. How penal common sense comes to Europeans: notes on the transatlantic diffusion of the liberal doxa. *Eur. Soc.* 1(3):319–51

Wacquant L. 2000. The new "peculiar institution": on the prison as surrogate ghetto. *Theor. Criminol.* 4(3):377–89

Waldram JB. 1997. *The Way of the Pipe: Aboriginal Spirituality and Symbolic Healing in Canadian Prisons*. Peterborough: Broadview Press

Waldram JB. 1998 Anthropology in prison: negotiating consent and accountability with a "captured" population. *Human Org.* 57(2):113–238

Walker S, Spohn C, DeLone M. 2000. *The Color of Justice: Race, Ethnicity and Crime in America*. Belmont, CA: Wadsworth

Watterson K, Chesney-Lind M. 1996. *Women in Prison: Inside the Concrete Womb*. Boston: Northeastern Univ. Press

Western B, Beckett K. 1999. How unregulated is the U.S. labor market? The penal system as a labor market institution. *Am. J. Sociol.* 104:1030–60

Western Prison Project. 2000. Census turns prisoners into commodoties—to the benefit of rural prison towns. *Justice Matters* 2(2):12–3

Wicker TG. 1998. Forward. See Franklin 1998b, pp. xi–xv

Zedner L. 1998. Wayward sisters: the prison for women. See Morris & Rothman 1998, pp. 295–324

Zimmer LE. 1986. *Women Guarding Men*. Chicago: Univ. Chicago Press

Annu. Rev. Anthropol. 2001. 30:85–108

THE BIOLOGY AND EVOLUTION OF HIV

Janis Faye Hutchinson
University of Houston, Department of Anthropology, Houston, Texas 77204-5020;
e-mail: Jhutchinson@uh.edu

Key Words HIV, AIDS, SIV

■ **Abstract** This review examines the current state of knowledge about HIV/AIDS in terms of its origins, pathogenesis, genetic variation, and evolutionary biology. The HIV virus damages the host's immune system, resulting in AIDS, which is characterized by immunodeficiency, opportunistic infections, neoplasms, and neurological problems. HIV is a complex retrovirus with a high mutation rate. This mutation rate allows the virus to evade host immune responses, and evidence indicates that selection favors more virulent strains with rapid replication. While a number of controversial theories attempt to explain the origin of HIV/AIDS, phylogenetic evidence suggests a zoonotic transmission of HIV to humans and implicates the chimpanzee (*Pan troglodytes troglodytes*) as the source of HIV-1 infection and the sooty mangabey as the source of HIV-2 infection in human populations. New therapies provide hope for increased longevity among people living with AIDS, but the biology of HIV presents significant obstacles to finding a cure and/or vaccine. HIV continues to be a threat to the global population because of its fast mutation rate, recombinogenic effect, and its use of human defenses to replicate itself.

INTRODUCTION

This review examines the current state of knowledge on the biology of HIV in terms of protein synthesis, genetic variation, mutation rate, and recombinogenic effect. An understanding of the genetics of HIV provides a context for understanding the short- and long-term impact of HIV on the physiology of the human body in terms of the pathogenesis of HIV disease, and associated cofactors that eventually produce AIDS. Examination of HIV's genomic variation also provides clues concerning selective pressures and temporal changes in the evolution of the virus.

A number of controversial theories to explain the origin of HIV/AIDS are considered. These theories include biological warfare, human experimentation gone wrong, and the most controversial idea that AIDS does not exist. Although these theories are considered, a more likely explanation examined involves zoonotic transmission from nonhuman primates to human populations.

0084-6570/01/1021-0085$14.00

85

Finally, implications for drug therapies and the future spread of HIV/AIDS are considered in relation to HIV's fast mutation rate, recombinogenic effect, and its use of human defenses to replicate itself. New therapies promise hope for increased longevity among people living with AIDS, but the death toll continues to rise. Examination of the biology, genetics, and evolution of HIV disease indicates that HIV/AIDS is a continual threat to the human population.

In order to understand the biology and evolution of HIV/AIDS, we must first have a working definition of the disease and understand its modes of transmission. The ensuing discussion defines HIV/AIDS in children and adults and gives the distinguishing characteristics of HIV and AIDS, and identifies its modes of transmission.

HIV/AIDS DEFINED

Acquired immune deficiency syndrome (AIDS) is characterized by progressive loss of the $CD4^+$ helper/inducer subset of T lymphocytes. Loss of T cells leads to severe impairment of immune function, constitutional diseases, opportunistic infections, neurological complications (AIDS dementia complex), and neoplasms that seldom occur in persons with intact immune function (Ho et al 1987; Fauci 1988, 1993; Greene 1993; Levy 1993; Weiss 1993; Natl. Inst. Allergy Infect. Dis. 1995; Clavel et al 1986; Fisher et al 1988; Price et al 1988). While the precise mechanisms that result in destruction of the immune system are not completely understood, an abundance of epidemiologic, virologic, and immunologic data support the conclusion that infection with HIV (human immunodeficiency virus) is the underlying cause of AIDS (Ho et al 1987; Fauci 1988, 1993; Greene 1993; Levy 1993; Weiss 1993; Natl. Inst. Allergy Infect. Dis. 1995; Darby et al 1995).

HIV was originally designated human T lymphotropic virus (HTLV)-III, lymphadenopathy-associated virus (LAV), or AIDS-associated retrovirus (ARV) (Fauci 1988). AIDS is induced by the HIV virus. Therefore, it is specifically referred to as HIV/AIDS because other factors such as corticosteroids, cancer chemotherapy, and alkylating agents can also produce AIDS-like symptoms (Stine 2000).

The Centers for Disease Control (CDC) provides criteria for defining HIV/AIDS in adults, children, and in developing countries. The CDC currently defines AIDS in an adult or adolescent age 13 years or older as HIV infection with a $CD4^+$ T cell count less than 200 cells per cubic millimeter of blood and/or HIV infection and the presence of one of 25 AIDS-indicator conditions, such as Kaposi's sarcoma, *Pneumocystic carinii* pneumonia, or disseminated *Mycobacterium avium* (MAC) (CDC 1987a). In children younger than 13 years, the definition of HIV/AIDS is similar to that in adults and adolescents, except that lymphoid interstitial pneumonitis and recurrent bacterial infections are included in the AIDS-indicator list (CDC 1987b). In developing countries, where diagnostic facilities could be limited, a case definition based on the presence of certain clinical symptoms associated with immunosuppression and the exclusion of other known causes of immune deficiency such as malnutrition or cancer are used in AIDS surveillance (Ryder & Mugewrwa 1994, Davachi 1994).

LENTIVIRUSES

HIV is a member of the lentivirus subfamily of retroviruses that produces chronic infection in the host and gradually damages the host's immune system (Dimmock & Primrose 1987, Hu et al 1996, Fauci 1988, Hahn et al 2000, De Cock et al 1993, Clavel et al 1986, Grez et al 1994, Beer et al 1999). Three major types of lentiviruses have been characterized in primates: simian immunodeficiency virus (SIV) and among humans, HIV-1, the predominant type in the world, and HIV-2, primarily found in West Africa and India (De Cock et al 1993, Clavel et al 1986, Grez et al 1994, Beer et al 1999).

TRANSMISSION

The clustering of AIDS cases and the occurrence of cases in diverse groups can only be explained by transmission of a virus, HIV, in a manner similar to hepatitis B virus: by sexual contact, by inoculation with blood or blood products, and by perinatal transmission from mother to newborn infant (Quinn 1987; Francis et al 1983; Curran et al 1984; CDC 1982, Fauci 1988). Exchange of fluids is necessary for transmission. Preliminary evidence suggests selective transmission of certain maternal HIV-1 variants for mother-infant pairs. That is, only a minor subset of maternal strains is transmitted to infants (Wolinsky et al 1992, Wike et al 1992). Also, mother-to-infant transmission rates are lower for HIV-2 than HIV-1 (Andreasson et al 1993).

HIV is not transmitted through contact with inanimate objects, through vectors, or through daily contact with infected people. Kissing is low risk for HIV infection (one documented case). Antibodies have been detected in saliva, suggesting that these antibodies neutralize HIV to produce HIV seronegative status (Stine 2000).

THE BIOLOGY OF HIV

The HIV virus is roughly spherical and about one ten-thousandth of a millimeter across. Its outer envelope or coat is composed of a double layer of lipid envelope that bears numerous spikes. Each spike is composed of four molecules of gp120 and the same number of gp41 embedded in the membrane. Beneath the envelope is a layer of matrix protein that surrounds the core (capsid). The capsid has a hollow, truncated cone shape and is composed of another protein, p24, that contains the genetic material of the HIV virus. Two strands of RNA consisting of about 9200 nucleotide bases, integrase, a protease, ribonuclease, and two other proteins, p6 and p7, fit inside the viral core (Greene 1993, Stine 2000, Fauci 1988).

Retroviruses like HIV reverse the usual direction of genetic information within the host cell to produce protein. The process of protein synthesis in regular gene expression results from the DNA being copied into RNA and the RNA being translated into specific proteins. With retroviruses the RNA is copied using its reverse transcriptase (RT) enzyme. In the cytoplasm RT migrates along the RNA to produce a complementary strand of DNA. After completion of the first DNA strand the RT begins constructing a second strand, using the first one as a template (Dimmock & Primrose 1987, Stine 2000, Greene 1993, Fauci 1988).

The double-stranded retroviral HIV DNA moves into the nucleus, where it inserts into the host DNA and becomes a provirus. Infection of the cell is then permanent. The provirus can remain dormant for a long time. Its genes cannot be expressed until RNA copies are made by the host cell's transcription machinery. Transcription starts when genetic switches at the ends of the provirus' long terminal repeats (LTRs) activate the cell's RNA polymerase II. Regulatory proteins known as NF-kB/Rel (in almost all human cells) bind with the LTRs at the ends of the provirus to activate the cell's RNA polymerase and thereby cause transcription of the provirus to RNA. NF-kB/Rel regulatory proteins increase in production when the cell is exposed to foreign proteins or by hormones that control the immune system (Dimmock & Primrose 1987, Stine 2000, Greene 1993, Fauci 1988). One member of this family, c-Rel, actually hinders HIV transcription, but it is produced more slowly than the ones that stimulate transcription (Greene 1993).

There are two phases of transcription after infection of a cell by HIV. After proviral DNA makes complementary copies of RNA strands some of the strands are cut into segments by cellular enzymes and spliced into a length of RNA appropriate for protein synthesis. These RNA strands become messenger RNA, producing regulatory proteins necessary for the production of HIV. By the time they migrate out of the nucleus to the cytoplasm they are about 2000 nucleotides long. The first phase lasts about 24 hours. In the second phase unspliced RNA transcripts become new viral strands (genome RNA or structural genes) and migrate out of the nucleus into the cytoplasm. Two new size classes of RNA are produced in this phase: long-unspliced strands of 9749 bases that comprise the genome RNA and medium-length (singly spliced) transcripts of about 4500 bases (virion assembly) that encode HIV's structural and enzymatic proteins. This material is enclosed within the viral core protein to become new viruses that migrate out of the cell (Greene 1993, Stine 2000).

THE GENETICS OF HIV

All retroviruses have a somewhat homogeneous structure and contain the same three genes, *gag, pol,* and *env,* encoding the structural proteins and enzymes used in the replication cycle (Dimmock & Primrose 1987, Stine 2000, Greene 1993,

Fauci 1988). HIV and SIV are different from other retroviruses in having more genes with complex interactions. The common and assumed ancestral genetic structure for primate lentiviruses, HIV and SIV, is *LTR-gag-pol-vif-vpr-tat-rev-env-nef-LTR* (Beer et al 1999, Stine 2000, Greene 1993). The function of each gene is not fully understood, but the gag gene codes for the manufacture of the dense cylindrical core proteins, the viral nucleocapsid. The *Gag* gene can direct the creation of virus-like particles in the absence of *pol* and *env*, and when it is nonfunctional HIV loses its ability to migrate out of the host cell (Dimmock & Primrose 1987, Wills & Craven 1991). The *pol* gene codes for reverse transcriptase, protease, ribonuclease, and integrase, which cuts the cell's DNA and inserts the HIV DNA (Dimmock & Pimrose 1987, Greene 1993). The *env* gene codes for the two envelope proteins gp120 and gp41, the transmembrane that binds gp120 with the exterior of HIV (Dimmock & Primrose 1987, Stine 2000). The *tat* gene produces a regulatory protein that increases transcription of the HIV provirus. *Nef* may modify the cell to make it able to manufacture HIV virions later. *Rev* appears to be responsible for switching the processing of viral RNA transcripts to the pattern that dominates after the cell has been infected for over 24 hours (when two new size classes of RNA are created) (Greene 1993, Rosen 1991). The long terminal repeats are not part of the 9749 bases of the HIV genome but contain sequences that help the regulatory genes control *gag-pol-env* gene expression. *Vif* is required for complete reverse transcription of viral RNA into HIV DNA. *Vpu* helps HIV bud out of the cell by destroying the CD4 protein within T4 lymphocytes, and *vpr* is related to the transmission of cytoplasmic viral DNA into the nucleus (Dimmock & Primrose 1987, Stine 2000).

HIV-infected cells contain from 400,000 to 2,500,000 copies of viral RNA per cell. Viral RNA can use as much as 40% of total protein synthesis for the production of gag viral protein, and there are high levels of viral RNA and protein synthesis prior to cell death. HIV produces viral RNAs at a level that has the potential to inhibit or compete for host protein synthesis (Somasundaran & Robinson 1988).

HIV GENOMIC VARIATION AND EVOLUTION

Mutations

Within a single cell HIV could make thousands of copies and some of them will be mistakes—mutations. Whereas some of these mutants may be inactive copies, others will be HIV mutants with enhanced survival and/or replication abilities. Both mutant and parent HIV replicate in the same manner, but over time as mutants are transmitted to other individuals and undergo more mutations these variants could evolve into a new viral strain such as HIV 3 (Stine 2000).

HIV has a high mutation rate (Dimmock & Primrose 1987, Ho et al 1995, Preston et al 1988, Vartanian et al 1992, Dougherty & Temin 1988, Hahn et al 1986, Saag et al 1988, Nowak 1990), but the mechanisms for producing HIV mutations are not completely understood. According to Levy (1988), new RNA strands accumulate in the host-cell cytoplasm, where they exchange parts with each other to produce new varieties of HIV (recombination). Another theory posits that HIV variants are the product of error-prone RT enzymes of HIV (Preston et al 1988, Nowak 1990). RT makes 1–10 errors on average during the replication of the HIV genome (Nowak 1990, Dougherty & Temin 1988, Preston et al 1988). In other words, there is a nucelotide mistransmission such as substitution, addition, and deletion when RT composes proviral DNA. Other ways to create HIV genetic diversity involve any steps in the reproductive cycle (Stine 2000). Vartanian and associates (1992) reported that each HIV-infected cell carries mutant HIV that is genetically unique, causing high genetic diversity among isolates of HIV.

Mutation rates and selection rates vary for different components of the HIV genome. *Gag* and *pol* genes are less variable than the *env* gene. Within the *env* gene there are five hypervariable regions, V1 to V5. The V3 region, about 30 amino acids within the envelope protein gp120, is highly mutable, and changes of one amino acid in this region can restrict recognition by neutralizing antibodies (Looney et al 1988, Nowak 1990, Shaper & Mullins 1993, Kliks et al 1993).

Collections of genetically distinct HIV variants can evolve from the initial infection. Populations of these closely related genomes, called quasispecies (Shioda et al 1991), vary increasingly over time (Hahn et al 1986) and are the products of mutation and selection (Bonhoeffer et al 1995). Different mutants within these quasispecies can exhibit very different biological properties such as cell tropisms (affinity), cytopathic properties, surface antigen traits, and replication rates (Shioda et al 1991). Quasispecies can migrate into new cellular populations by acquiring mutations that facilitate adaptation (Doms & Moore 1997). That is, some mutants may be able to infect previously uninfected tissues.

The genetic diversity of the HIV virus results in drug resistance and evasion from immune responses and makes development of a vaccine a challenge (Bonhoeffer et al 1995, Korber et al 1998). For example, some HIV mutants can evade the immune response and thrive (Stine 2000). As such, the immune response is a major force in positive selection pressure generating genetic diversity (Nowak 1990). The high mutation rate also results in the production of viral strands that are not susceptible to drug therapy. This process explains why drugs such as AZT are efficacious only temporarily (Greene 1993, Korber et al 1998) and why some HIV-1 strains are not reliably detected by all antibody screening tests currently in use (Loussert-Ajaka et al 1994, Schable et al 1994). Drug therapies, therefore, are also a force in positive selection and in creating genetic diversity in HIV. This genetic diversity makes it extremely difficult to develop a drug that can kill all HIV viruses.

Recombination

Because HIV is diploid (carries 2 RNA molecules), there can be genetic recombination (exchange of parts) between these strands and other strands in the area (Stine 2000, Levy 1988). HIV is highly recombinogenic, but recombination can only take place between genomes packaged within the same virion (Robertson et al 1997). Recombination in HIV is facilitated by coinfection with different subtypes of HIV and/or in cells with different susceptibilities for various subtypes and by geographic intermixing of subtypes (Laurence 1997). Recombination is probably involved in genetic diversity and selection pressures at every level, although it is only detected when distinct strains are present, for example two distinct strains in the same person (Korber et al 1998).

Temporal Changes in HIV Genotype

Variation in the rate of HIV evolution may be determined by differences in host-mediated selection pressures (Wolinsky et al 1996, Nowak et al 1995). For instance, upon infection, the individual has a homogeneous viral population (Bonhoeffer et al 1995, Wolinsky et al 1996, Nowak 1995). Stable viral population equilibrium is found when the initial virus is relatively fit and replicating in a relatively constant environment. In this environment a particular genetic variant, regardless of its pathogenic ability, would be preferentially increased (Wolinsky et al 1996). Early in the infection the immune response reacts quickly and strongly against common viral variants (Boyd et al 1993). As HIV infects different cells and tissues, rare mutants escape surveillance (the immune response) and increase in frequency (Wolinsky et al 1996). This provides strong selection pressure for HIV viral diversification (Boyd et al 1993, Bonhoeffer et al 1995, Saag et al 1988). HIV variants can evolve rapidly in parallel and coexist during chronic infection (Delwart et al 1993, Stine 2000).

After the virus generates many variants with specific cell tropism (affinity) there is a decline of the immune response and selection pressures are weaker (Boyd et al 1993, Bonhoeffer et al 1995). Individuals who progress to AIDS usually have a more homogeneous viral population. Slow evolution may represent the apparent predominance of an optimally adapted variant (Wolinsky et al 1996).

Mathematical models of the interaction between $CD4^+$ cells and HIV-1 indicate that selection favors more virulent strains (Anderson 1989, 1991), and more virulent strains appear later in the asymptomatic or incubation period (Levy 1990, Fenyo et al 1989). HIV-1 isolates from asymptomatic individuals grow slowly and have low titers of reverse transcriptase activity, whereas isolates from patients with AIDS grow rapidly, show high reverse transcriptase activity, and induce cell death more often (Fenyo et al 1989, Nowak et al 1991).

HIV Subtypes/Clades

Based on phylogenetic relationships, HIV-1 viruses can be divided into three major subtypes or clades: M, N, and O (Simon et al 1998, Gao et al 1999, Louwagie et al 1993, Leitner et al 1997, Sharp et al 1994). The predominant M group consists of 11 clades denoted subtypes A through K (Los Alamos Natl. Lab. 1998). Multiple strains are found in many countries, but in the United States the majority of isolates have been subtype B. The occasional presence of HIV-2 and HIV-1 subtypes other than B indicates multiple HIV introductions to North America (Hu et al 1996, Delwart et al 1993). Subtypes from Africa belong to four clades (A–D). Subtype C is found mainly along the south and east coast of Africa and the west coast of India (Delwart et al 1993, Stine 2000). E, B, and C are found in Southeast Asia (Louwagie et al 1993). One, subtype E, almost exclusively infects heterosexuals in northern Thailand, whereas both genotypes B and E are found in injection drug users in Bangkok (Moore & Anderson 1994, Kunanusont et al 1995).

Clines were shown for three of the genotypes. For instance, genotypes A and D were found in an east-to-west belt across sub-Saharan Africa from Senegal to Kenya. A north-to-south pattern was found for genotype C in Africa (Louwagie et al 1993).

Consideration of N and O groups reveals that nucleoside sequencing of the N group is restricted to Cameroon (Simon et al 1998). HIV-1 variants outside the M and N groups have been provisionally categorized as group O (De Leys et al 1990, Gurtler et al 1994). Within group O strains may differ as much from each other as the variants within group M subtypes differ from each other (Sharp et al 1994). Group O is primarily found in Cameroon (DeLeys et al 1990, Gurtler et al 1994), but it accounts for less than 10% of HIV infections (Gurtler et al 1994).

It must be recognized that the subtypes identified for HIV are provisional and reflect those isolates that have been collected and characterized (Hu et al 1996). Coinfection (Pieniazek et al 1995) and genetic recombination between different viral strains (Hu & Temin 1990) complicate identifying HIV variants. It is possible that difficult-to-detect divergent HIV strains have entered human populations (Hu et al 1996).

A major fraction of HIV-1 strains are intersubtype recombinants (Robertson et al 1997). For instance, a subtype from Cyprus, I, appears to be a recombinant of at least three subtypes, A, G, and I (it is not known if it originated in Africa or Cyprus) (Kostrikis et al 1995). Some exchanges may not be viable because certain combinations may not survive at either the RNA level or after translation of the RNA product (Robertson et al 1997).

HIV-2 comprises six distinct phylogenetic lineages, subtypes A through F (Los Alamos Natl. Lab. 1998, Gao et al 1994). HIV-2 predominates in West Africa and is also found in India (Hu et al 1996, Clavel et al 1986). HIV-1 and HIV-2 share about 60% nucleotide homology for *gag* and *pol* genes but much less for *env* and the other viral genes (Shaper & Mullins 1993).

Recombinant viruses are also found among HIV-2 strains (Gao et al 1994) and among SIVs (Chen et al 1996). So far, no viruses are known to be the product of recombinants of two highly divergent major groups of HIV-1, nor have recombinants of HIV-1 and HIV-2 been found in individuals dually infected with HIV-1 groups M and O (Takehisa et al 1997) or both HIV-1 and HIV-2 (Grez et al 1994).

HIV AND THE IMMUNE SYSTEM

Basic Immunology

HIV infects several cell types in the human body, but the more important cells are in the immune system. The immune system fights foreign substances, removes dead and damaged cells, and destroys mutant and cancerous cells. The human immune system is able to fight foreign entities never seen before because of the number of different kinds of cells called lymphocytes. The two types of lymphocytes are B and T cells that recognize foreign substances or nonself. B cells produce and secrete antibodies in response to an antigen (Pantaleo et al 1993a, Stine 2000). The three major types of T cells are cytotoxic or killer T cells, suppressor T cells, and helper T cells. Killer T cells eliminate virus-infected cells and are responsible for recovery from a viral infection. T suppressor/cytotoxic cells suppress the immune response after the foreign substance is eliminated. Helper T cells alert the immune system to antigens and signal other cells in the system to attack it. T4 cells do not kill cells but interact with B cells and killer T cells to help them attack foreign particles (Dimmock & Primrose 1987, Stine 2000).

There are specialized receptors on the surface of T cells to identify one of many millions of possible antigens that may invade the body. Each T cell expresses a receptor that binds with the complementary antigen on the foreign particle to neutralize or destroy it. Killer and suppressor T cells carry the CD8 receptor (T suppressor cells are called T8 cell), and the helper T cells (T4 cell) carry the CD4 receptor. Collectively, T8 and T4 cells regulate the body's immune response to foreign antigens (Dimmock & Primrose 1987, Stine 2000).

HIV Infection and the Immune System

HIV-1 mainly targets CD4$^+$T lymphocytes and CD4$^+$ cells of monocyte/macrophage lineage (Dimmock & Primrose 1987, Connor & Ho 1994). T4 cells may be lost through a number of processes. For instance, defects in T4 cells caused by HIV infection may produce activation-induced cell death or apoptosis (normal cell death) (Pantaleo et al 1993a). HIV also may trick the immune system into attacking itself (Kion & Hoffmann 1991). Another method is syncytia formation, which involves the massing of healthy T cells around a single HIV-infected T4 cell resulting in loss of immune function (Stine 2000, Hoxie et al 1986, Sodroski et al 1986, Gelderbloom et al 1985). Death of cells could be due to direct membrane disruption involving calcium channels (Gupta & Vayuvegula 1987) and/or phospholipid synthesis (Lynn et al 1988). A buildup of unintegrated proviral copies of HIV DNA may cause cytopathology, because it is associated with cell death in other retroviral systems (Levy 1988). It is believed that depletion of T4 cells is insufficient to cause AIDS because not enough T4 cells are destroyed. Equally important may be T4 cell infection of monocytes and macrophages that engulf and destroy antigens (Bakker et al 1992).

HIV usually puts a portion of its virus on the surface of the cell that it infects. Killer cells, cytotoxic T lymphocytes, search out and destroy infected cells. However, HIV escapes detection by cytotoxic T lymphocytes because *Nef* gets cells to remove a protein that indicates to the killer cells that the T cell is infected. This makes it possible for HIV-infected cells to evade killer T cells (Cohen 1997).

HIV, Macrophages, and T cells

There is a temporal change in viral tropism during the course of HIV-1 infection. Early in infection macrophage tropic (M-tropic) HIV viruses have the ability to infect macrophages and are nonsyncytium-inducing (NSI) owing to their inability to form syncytia on T-cell lines (Connor et al 1993, Zhu et al 1993, Fenyo et al 1988, Schuitemaker et al 1992). Usually, about 4–5 years after infection virus strains evolve in some individuals (about 50%) that can infect T-cell lines in addition to primary T-cells (Tersmette et al 1989, Milich et al 1993, Shioda et al 1991). In this change in tropism the virus sometimes loses the ability to infect macrophages, but more often they retain this property and are referred to as dual tropic (Collman et al 1992). HIV-1 viruses that can infect T-cell lines are referred to as T-tropic and are syncytium-inducing (SI). Viruses that can grow on transformed cell lines by continual passage are called T-cell line adapted (TCLA) (Doms & Moore 1997). Others consider tropism as a range where, for example, macrophages are infected efficiently and T cell lines are less efficiently infected (Moore & Ho 1995, Sullivan et al 1995, Fenyo et al 1997). This switch may be related to colonization of different types of cells or a product of natural selection in which certain phenotypes are selected for and escape the immune response (Weiss 1996).

CD4 receptors alone are sufficient for binding HIV to T4 lymphocyte membranes, but coreceptors are required to mediate entry of HIV-1 into cells. The best-known HIV-1 coreceptors are CXCR4 and CCR5, members of the CXC and CC chemokine receptor subfamilies, respectively (the number of coreceptors used by SIV and HIV is now 14) (Doms & Moor 1997, Fenyo et al 1997, Dragic et al 1996). CCR5 is the primary coreceptor for HIV-1 isolates with the NSI phenotype (Fenyo et al 1997, Deng et al 1996, Dragic et al 1996), whereas SI phenotypes are associated with the use of CXCR4 alone or in conjunction with CCR5 (Simmons et al 1996, Zhang et al 1996, Fenyo et al 1997). Studies show that in the presence of CD4 and the appropriate coreceptor, both SI and NSI viruses can induce syncytium formation. Therefore, the terms SI and NSI are not absolute but are related to coreceptor expression levels on target cells (Fenyo et al 1997, Feng et al 1996). All HIV-1, HIV-2, and SIV strains use one or both of these main receptors (Dragic et al 1996).

CD8 T lymphocytes partly control HIV infection by the release of HIV-suppressive factors, beta chemokines, that are active on monocytes and lymphocytes. Beta chemokines MIP-1α, MIP-1β, and RANTES are most active against HIV-1 in combination and inhibit infection of CD4$^+$ T cells by primary, NSI HIV-strains at the virus entry stage. However, TCLA/SI HIV-1 strains are insensitive to beta-chemokines. Therefore, some CD4$^+$ T-helper cells from HIV-1-exposed uninfected individuals resist infection with NSI strains (secrete high levels of beta chemokines) but are infected by TCLA/SI strains. It is unknown if high levels of these chemokines can delay HIV disease progression (Cocchi et al 1995).

Some exposed-uninfected individuals harbor identical mutations on both chromosomal copies of CC-chemokine receptor 5 (CCR-5) (Hill & Littman 1996, Samson et al 1996). A frameshift mutation, 32-base-pair deletion, generates a nonfunctional receptor that does not allow membrane fusion or infection by macrophage- and dual-tropic HIV-1 strains (Liu et al 1996, Samson et al 1996). This polymorphism has an allele frequency of 0.092–0.098 among whites but is absent among blacks from West and Central Africa and in Japanese populations. About 15–29% of whites are heterozygous, whereas about 1% are homozygous. The prevalence of heterozygotes was lower in an HIV-infected sample compared with the uninfected population. This indicates a possible partial protection from infection among individuals with a single copy of the mutant allele. However, both groups showed that those heterozygous for the CCR-5 mutation were susceptible to viral infection, although at reduced levels. It is not clear if transmission of HIV or progression to AIDS is affected by heterozygosity for the CCR-5 mutation (Samson et al 1996, Hill & Littman 1996).

PATHOGENESIS OF HIV/AIDS

Initial infection with HIV virus is followed by high viral replication with or without clinical symptoms (Daar et al 1991, Tindall & Cooper 1991, Ho et al 1989). In acute HIV infection there is typically a mild, flu-like illness with fever and muscle aches that lasts a few weeks (Greene 1993, Stine 2000, Fauci 1988). HIV antibodies are detected between 6–18 weeks after initial infection (Stine 2000). Then antibodies appear in the blood serum (seroconversion), after which it is difficult to isolate the virus. This asymptomatic period is distinguished by low viral replication interspersed with periods of increases in viremia (virus in blood) and by slow but constant decreasing numbers of CD4$^+$ cells (Tindall & Cooper 1991, Ho et al 1989, Fauci 1988, Fauci et al 1991).

Longitudinal studies of HIV-1-infected individuals indicate a long and variable incubation period (about 10 years) between infection and development of AIDS (Biggar 1990, Nowak et al 1991, Fauci et al 1991, Fauci 1988). A long asymptomatic period may be due to latent infection. During latent infection very little viral protein or RNA is produced (Rojko et al 1982). Research suggests that the *orf-B* gene of HIV is responsible for latency. This gene product interacts with cellular factors to slow down viral replication in a continuum that can proceed to latency (Levy 1988).

Another explanation for latency is related to the dichotomy between viral levels and viral replication in lymphoid organs versus peripheral blood. HIV is expressed in the lymphiod tissue throughout clinical latency even when there is minimal viral activity in the blood (Pantaleo et al 1993b, Fauci 1993). Follicular dentritic cells in the lymph nodes are exposed to HIV early in infection, requiring the nodes to work hard to eliminate the virus. Latency may be due to the interplay between the envelope protein and immune system, where initially the lymph nodes contain the virus, but eventually the virus gains the upper hand when it evolves a variant that evades the immune system response (Dimmock & Primrose 1987, Fauci 1993). In AIDS collapsing nodes may no longer be able to remove the virus, allowing its escape into the bloodstream (Fauci 1993, Greene 1993, Embretson et al 1993). Latently infected lymphocytes and macrophages are reservoirs for immune depletion in AIDS (Embretson et al 1993).

In rare cases HIV-seropositive individuals become seronegative. In some of these individuals latent HIV in peripheral mononuclear cells were detected by polymerase chain reaction, but in others no HIV was detected (Farzadegan et al 1988). This suggests that HIV infection could be eliminated completely by the immune response, but more likely the virus is hiding at other sites in the body (Levy 1988, Farzadegan et al 1988).

AIDS is the end stage of a progressive and continuous pathogenic process involving profound immune deficiency, opportunistic infections, and neoplasms (Ho et al 1987; Fauci 1988, 1993; Weiss 1993; Natl. Inst. Allergy Infect. Dis. 1995). There is a slow and steady reduction in $CD4^+$ T-helper or inducer lymphocytes during this period in those who develop AIDS (Tindall & Cooper 1991; Fauci 1988, 1993; Nowak 1991). The number of T4 lymphocytes in the blood decreases during this chronic infection from 1000 per cubic millimeter to less than 100 (Ho et al 1989, Greene 1993).

Although the pathogenesis of HIV is similar in those with HIV-2 and HIV-1 (De Cock et al 1990, Le Guenno et al 1991), the immunologic deficiency is less severe and the disease progression is slower in HIV-2 (Le Guenno et al 1991, Whittle et al 1994, Marlink et al 1994). The virulence of HIV-2 is known to vary significantly and range from relative attenuation to great pathogenicity. Differences in clinical manifestations may be partly related to genetic differences among infecting viral strains (Gao et al 1994).

COFACTORS IN HIV INFECTION

HIV infection alone can cause immunodeficiency in the absence of other infections, but coinfection can hasten immune deficiency (Greene 1993) by aiding in the depletion of T4 cells. Concomitant viral infections with Epstein-Barr virus, cytomegalovarius, herpes simplex virus, hepatitis B infection (Jordan 1991, Cohen & Herbert 1996, Anderson 1995, Catania et al 1994, Walker et al 1989), infection with *Mycoplasma fermentans* (incognitus strain) (Lo et al 1991), respiratory infection such as tuberculosis (Zacarias et al 1994, Braun et al 1993, Snider et al 1991), and sexually transmitted diseases such as chancroid, gonorrhea, chlamydia, and syphilis (Baqi et al 1999, Levine et al 1998, Erbelding et al 2000, Lankoande et al 1998, Ndinya et al 1997) are associated with HIV expression. Other cofactors including drugs used by injection-drug users such as heroin and other morphine-based derivatives (Walters & Simoni 1999, Reilley et al 2000, Eicher et al 2000), blood and blood products (Berkman 1984, Blumberg et al 1985), traumatic lacerations of the rectal mucosa (portal of entry for the virus) (Ratnam 1994), and stress, mental or physical (Siegel et al 1996, Puskar et al 1999, Wagner et al 1998, Cole et al 1996), can impair the immune system.

HIV, SIV, AND EVOLUTION

HIV-1 and HIV-2 represent cross-species (zoonotic) infections (Clavel et al 1986; Gao et al 1992, 1999; Ewald 1996; Hahn et al 2000; Dolittle 1989; Nzilambi et al 1988; Chakrabarti et al 1987). Five sources of evidence support a zoonotic transmission of primate lentiviruses, such as similarities in viral genome, phylogenetic relatedness, prevalence in the natural host, geographic coincidence, and plausible routes of transmission. HIV-1 and HIV-2 satisfy these criteria (Hahn et al 2000, Huet et al 1990, Hirsch et al 1989).

HIV-2 is closely related to SIVs isolated from macaques (SIV_{mac}) and sooty mangabeys (SIV_{sm}) (Clavel et al 1986, Gao et al 1992, Hahn et al 2000, Hirsch et al 1989). SIV_{sm} has been isolated from free-ranging and pet sooty mangabeys (*Cercocebus atys*) in West Africa (Chen et al 1996). However, no macaques in the wild in Asia and very few macaques in captivity are infected with SIV (Wu et al 1991). The close relationship between HIV-2 in humans and SIV_{sm} suggest that feral SIV-infected sooty mangabeys in West Africa are the natural source for HIV-2 infection in humans and macaque infection (Hirsch et al 1989; Gao et al 1992, 1999; Ewald 1996; Hahn et al 2000; Peeters et al 1989; Sharp et al 1994).

Examination of nucleotide sequence of HIV-2 and SIV indicate HIV-2 is more closely related to SIV_{sm} than it is to HIV-1 (Clavel et al 1986). For instance, HIV-2 and SIV_{sm} share an identical genomic structure (both have a protein, V_{px}, that is not found in any other primate lentiviruses) (Hirsch et al 1989) and the HIV-2 subtypes are not more closely related to one another than they are to SIV_{sm} (Chen et al 1996). Rather, SIV_{sm} and HIV-2 lineages are phylogenetically interspersed. This suggests that the different HIV-2 clades are not the result of a single mangabey-to-human transmission but are due to multiple independent cross-species transmission of SIV_{sm} into the human population (Hahn et al 2000). Transmission is possible because sooty managbeys are often hunted for food or kept as pets (Chen et al 1996, Marx et al 1991, Hahn et al 2000). SIV_{sm} has also been transmitted to humans after accidental exposure to monkey blood (Khabbaz et al 1994).

It is not known whether the chimpanzee is the natural reservoir for HIV-1, because only four animals tested SIV seropositive (Peeters et al 1989, Huet et al 1990, Janssens et al 1994, Vanden Haesevelde et al 1996). However, $SIV_{cpz\text{-}GAB}$ (Gabon), $SIV_{CPZ\text{-}GAB2}$ (Gabon), $SIV_{CPZ\text{-}ANT}$ (Zaire), and a new SIV_{cpz} sequence (SIV_{cpzUS}) (United States) indicate that SIV_{CPZ} and HIV-1 have the same genetic organization containing a gene, V_{pu}, not present in other lentiviruses (Huet et al 1990; Peeters et al 1989, 1992; Gao et al 1992, 1999; Ewald 1996; Hahn et al 2000).

Gao et al (1999) found that two chimpanzee subspecies in Africa, the eastern *Pan troglodytes schweinfurthii* and *Pan troglodytes troglodytes*, harbor SIV_{cpz}, but that they form two highly divergent but suspecies-specific phylogenetic lineages. Such findings are consistent with the ancestor of SIV_{cpz} strains infecting the common ancestor of *P. troglodytes* followed by host-dependent viral diversification (Hahn et al 2000). HIV-1 strains known to infect humans, including the HIV-1 groups M, N, and O, are closely related to only the SIV_{cpz} lineage found in *P.t. troglodytes* (Gao et al 1999, Beer et al 1999, Hahn et al 2000, Huet et al 1990). Compared with SIV_{CPZ}, the three groups of HIV-1 are not each other's closest relatives, so they must have each arisen from a separate cross-species transmission (Simon et al 1998, Gao et al 1999). Also, it is only in this region that HIV-1 group M viruses show the greatest diversity (Nkengasong et al 1994). The natural range of *P.t. troglodytes* coincides with areas of HIV-1 groups M, N, and O endemicity, which suggests that *P.t. troglodytes* is the primary reservoir for HIV-1 and that it is the source of at least three independent introductions of SIV_{cpz} into the human population (Gao et al 1999, Beer et al 1999, Hahn et al 2000, Simon et al 1998, Peeter et al 1997). A possible route of transmission is hunting because chimpanzees are commonly hunted for food in Africa, especially in the west equatorial region (Gao et al 1999, Hahn et al 2000).

Based on stored samples, humans in central Africa have been infected with HIV-1 group M viruses since 1959 (Zhu et al 1998). Multiple phylogenetic analyses authenticate the 1959 sample from the Democratic Republic of the Congo (formerly Zaire) as the oldest known HIV-1 infection. The initial zoonotic transmission is placed at the sequence very near the ancestral node of the B, D, and F clades of the M group. This suggests that diversity in these clades arose after 1959. Based on molecular clocks, with consideration of the peculiarities of HIV, the origin of zoonotic transmission to humans is placed at around 1930 (range 1910 to 1950) (Korber et al in Hahn et al 2000). The major-group viruses that dominate the AIDS pandemic shared a common ancestor in the 1940s or the early 1950s.

CONTROVERSIAL THEORIES ON THE ORIGIN OF HIV/AIDS

Since the inception of AIDS there have been a number of controversial theories about its origins. For example, one such theory suggests that AIDS was created by a biological warfare experiment that went wrong. It was suggested that researchers in the United States with Defense Department sponsors released a genetically engineered virus into Central Africa to study its impact on humans. A variant hypothesis is that it escaped from a laboratory where researchers tested the virus on prisoners who could increase their chances of parole by volunteering for the experiment.

When the prisoners were released, some became injection drug users and AIDS flourished (Adams 1989).

Gilks (1991) suggested zoonotic transmission in which the AIDS virus entered the human population through inoculation of prison volunteers with malaria-infected blood. Others suggested such transmission through grafts of simian testicles to humans in the early 1920s when some people believed it could delay or avert physical and mental disabilities (Gosden 1992), or that contaminated polio vaccine administered in the late 1950s in Africa was responsible for zoonotic transmission (Koprowski 1992). Another theory is that AIDS spread through reuse of unsterilized needles in vaccination programs. An offshoot of this hypothesis is that "inoculators" (used where people believe in the potency of injections over pills) sold injections in markets and bars and spread the virus. Other theories stated that AIDS was spread to the West by activities of international plasma dealers (Adams 1989), or that ritual scarification contributed to transmission (Pela & Platt 1989).

Early in the AIDS epidemic, because homosexual men comprised the initial population with AIDS in the United States, it was speculated that a homosexual lifestyle was the cause of the disease (Sonnabend et al 1983, Mavligit et al 1984). Peter Duesberg popularized this hypothesis. Duesberg, a molecular biologist at the University of California at Berkeley and a member of the National Academy of Sciences, put forth the most controversial hypothesis that HIV is a harmless passenger virus that does not cause AIDS (Duesberg 1989, 1994). Duesberg proposed a drug-AIDS hypothesis for the acquisition of AIDS. It predicts that (*a*) AIDS in the United States will be restricted to intravenous and oral users of recreational drugs and of AZT, (*b*) AIDS in the United States will predominantly affect adult males because they are the main users of recreational drugs and AZT, (*c*) US AIDS is new because the drug-use epidemic is new, (*d*) only the heaviest drug abusers will get AIDS, just like emphysema usually occurs among the heaviest smokers, (*e*) specific drugs cause group-specific AIDS disease (e.g. he says nitrites, used by homosexual men, are some of the best-known mutagens and carcinogens), and (*f*) most pediatric AIDS cases are caused by mothers who abuse drugs during pregnancy (Duesberg 1987, 1989, 1990, 1992, 1994, 1995). However, virologic, epidemiologic, and immunologic evidence supports the conclusion that HIV causes AIDS.

THE FUTURE OF HIV/AIDS

HIV may continue to be virulent because of its fast mutation rate, recombinogenic effect, and its use of human defenses to replicate itself. For instance, superinfection by viruses of different lineages has the potential for generating recombinant viruses with considerable genetic complexity. Such recombination could occur in humans to produce, for example, HIV-3 because biological mechanisms that usually constrain the evolution of viruses may not apply to HIV. That is, HIV may be evolutionarily free of constraints that could reduce its virulence.

Vaccine efficacy is strain or subtype specific (Hu et al 1996). As a result, developing a vaccine that protects 80% or more of those vaccinated has failed for pathogens that display extensive genetic variation both within and between hosts (Moore & Anderson 1994, Larder et al 1989, Larder & Kemp 1989). While researchers continually develop new drugs to attack the virus, HIV continually produces new variants that are already standing by to circumvent the drug. In addition, replacement of susceptible strains can occur rapidly (Wei et al 1995), and drug-resistant strains can be transmitted producing "primary" resistance in newly infected individuals (Erice et al 1993, Siegrist et al 1994). Therefore, immune system and drug-related selection may broaden the clinical expression of HIV/AIDS to include uncommon infections and constitutional diseases. Eventually, surveillance of drug-resistant HIV strains may be necessary, similar to surveillance of drug-resistant gonorrhea, malaria, and tuberculosis (Hu et al 1996).

While new therapies provide hope for increased longevity among people living with AIDS, the focus of drug therapies has not been in areas with the highest prevalence of HIV/AIDS. For instance, clinical trials for vaccines have been based on subtype B (found in the United States) and not on subtypes prevalent in the hardest hit countries such as those in Africa (Lurie et al 1994). In these areas and where multiple HIV strains are present, development of vaccines is problematic. However, in order to develop a vaccine and drug therapies, and to eventually end the HIV/AIDS pandemic, we must understand the biology and evolution of HIV.

Visit the Annual Reviews home page at www.AnnualReviews.org

LITERATURE CITED

Adams J. 1989. *AIDS: The HIV Myth.* New York: St. Martin's. 223 pp.

Anderson C. 1995. Childhood sexually transmitted diseases: one consequence of sexual abuse. *Public Health Nursing* 12:41–46

Anderson RM. 1989. Mathematical and statistical studies of the epidemiology of HIV. *AIDS* 3:333–46

Anderson RM. 1991. Populations and infectious diseases: ecology or epidemiology? *J. Anim. Ecol.* 60(1):1–50

Andreasson P, Dias F, Naucler A, Andersson S, Biberfeld G. 1993. A prospective study of vertical transmission of HIV-2 in Bissau, Guinea-Bissau. *AIDS* 7:989–93

Bakker LJ, Nottett SLM, deVos NM, de Graff L, Van Strijp JAG, et al. 1992. Antibodies and complement enhance binding and uptake of HIV-1 by human monocytes. *AIDS* 6:35–41

Baqi S, Shah SA, Baig MA, Mujeeb SA, Memon A. 1999. Seroprevalence of HIV, HBV and syphilis and associated risk behaviours in male transvestites (Hijras) in Karachi, Pakistan. *Int. J. STD AIDS* 10:300–4

Beer BE, Bailes E, Sharp PM, Hirsch VM. 1999. *Diversity and Evolution of Primate Lentiviruses.* http://hiv-web.lanl.gov/compendium

Berkman SA. 1984. Infectious complications of blood transfusions. *Semin. Oncol.* 11(1):68–76

Biggar RJ. 1990. AIDS incubation in 1,891 HIV seroconverters from different exposure groups. International registry of seroconverters. *AIDS* 4(11):1059–66

Blumberg N, Agarwal MM, Chuang C. 1985. Relation between occurrence of cancer of the colon and blood transfusion. *Br. Med. J.* 290:1037–39

Bonhoeffer S, Holmes EC, Nowak MA. 1995. Causes of HIV diversity. *Nature* 376:125

Boyd MT, Simpson GR Cann AJ, Johnson MA, Weiss RA. 1993. A single amino acid substitution in the V1 loop of human immunodeficiency virus type 1 gp120 alters cellular tropism. *J. Virol.* 67(6):3649–52

Braun MM, Cote TR, Robkin CS. 1993. Trends in death with tuberculosis during the AIDS era. *JAMA* 269(22):2865–68

Catania JA, Coates TJ, Kegeles S. 1994. A test of the AIDS risk reduction model: psychosocial correlates of condom use in the AMEN cohort survey. *Health Psychol.* 13(6):548–55

CDC. 1982. CDC task force on Kaposi's sarcoma and opportunistic infections. *N. Engl. J. Med.* 306:248–52

CDC. 1987a. Revision of the surveillance case definition of acquired immunodeficiency syndrome. *MMWR* 36:3S–15S

CDC. 1987b. Classification for human immunodeficiency virus (HIV) infection in children under 13 years of age. *MMWR* 35:224–35

Chakrabarti L, Guyader M, Alizon M, Daniel MD, Desrosiers RC, et al. 1987. Sequence of simian immunodeficiency virus from macaque and its relationship to other human and simian retroviruses. *Nature* 328:543–47

Chen Z, Telfer P, Gettie A, Reed P, Zhang L, et al. 1996. Genetic characterization of new West African simian immunodeficiency virus SIV$_{sm}$: geographic clustering of household-derived SIV strains with human immunodeficiency virus type 2 subtypes and genetically diverse viruses from a single feral sooty mangabey troop. *J. Virol.* 70:3617–27

Clavel F, Guyader M, Guetard D, Salle M, Montagnier L, Alizon M. 1986. Molecular cloning and polymorphism of the human immune deficiency virus type 2. *Nature* 324:691–95

Cocchi F, DeVico AL Garzino-Demo A, Arya SK, Gallo RC, Lusso P. 1995. Identification of RANTES, MIP-1α, and MIP-1β as the major HIV-suppressive factors produced by CD8+ T cells. *Science* 270:1811–15

Cohen J. 1997. Looking for leads in HIV's battle with immune system. *Science* 276:1196–97

Cohen S, Herbert TB. 1996. Health psychology: psychological factors and physical disease from the perspective of human psychoneuroimmunology. *Annu. Rev. Psychol.* 47:113–42

Cole SW, Kemeny ME, Taylor SE, Visscher BR. 1996. Elevated physical health risk among gay men who conceal their homosexual identity. *Health Psychol.* 15:243–51

Collman R, Balliet JW, Gregory SA, Friedman H, Koson DL, et al. 1992. An infectious molecular clone of an unusual macrophage-tropic and highly cytopathic strain of human immunodeficiency virus type 1. *J. Virol.* 66:7517–21

Connor RI, Ho DD. 1994. Human immunodeficiency virus type 1 variants with increased replicative capacity develop during the asymptomatic stage before disease progression. *J. Virol.* 68(7):4400–8

Connor RI, Mohri H, Cao Y, Ho DD. 1993. Increased viral burden and cytopathicity correlate temporally with CD4$^+$ T-lymphocyte decline and clinical progression in human immunodeficiency virus type 1-infected individuals. *J. Virol.* 67:1772–77

Curran JW, Lawrence DN, Jaffe H, Kaplan JE, Zyla LD, et al. 1984. Acquired immunodeficiency syndrome (AIDS) associated with transfusions. *N. Engl. J. Med.* 310(2):69–75

Daar ES, Moudgil T, Meyer RD, Ho DD. 1991. Transient high levels of viremia in patients with primary human immunodeficiency virus type 1 infection. *New. Engl. J. Med.* 324(14):961–64

Darby SC, Ewart DW, Giangrande PLF, Dolin PJ, Spooner RJD, Rizza CR. 1995. Mortality before and after HIV infection in the complete UK population of haemophiliacs. *Nature* 377:79–82

Davachi F. 1994. Pediatric HIV infection in Africa. In *AIDS in Africa*, ed. M Essex, pp. 439–62. New York: Raven. 728 pp.

De Cock KM, Adjorlolo G, Ekpini E, Sibailly T, Kouadio J, et al. 1993. Epidemiology and transmission of HIV-2—why there is no HIV-2 pandemic. *JAMA* 270:2083–86

De Cock KM, Odehouri K, Colebunder RL, Adjorlolo G, Lafontaine M, et al. 1990. A comparison of HIV-1 and HIV-2 infections in hospitalized patients in Abidjan, Côte d'Ivoire. *AIDS* 4:443–48

De Leys R, Vanderborght B, Vanden Haesevelde M, Heyndrickx L, van Geel A, et al. 1990. Isolation and partial characterization of an unusual human immunodeficiency retrovirus from two persons of West-Central African origin. *J. Virol.* 64:1207–16

Delwart EL, Shpaer EG, Louwagie J, McCutchan FE, Grez M, et al. 1993. Genetic relationships determined by a DNA heteroduplex mobility assay: analysis of HIV-1 *env* genes. *Science* 262:1257–61

Deng HK, Liu R, Ellmeier W, Choe S, Unutmaz D, et al. 1996. Identification of a major co-receptor for primary isolates of HIV-1. *Nature* 381:661–66

Dimmock NJ, Primrose SB. 1987. *Introduction to Modern Virology.* Oxford: Blackwell Sci. 362 pp.

Dolittle RF. 1989. The simian-human connection. *Nature* 339:338–39

Doms RW, Moore JP. 1997. HIV-1 coreceptor use: a molecular window into viral tropism. In *Human Retroviruses and AIDS.* http://hiv-web.lanl.gov/compendium

Dougherty JP, Temin HM. 1988. Determination of the rate of base-pair substitution and insertion mutations in retrovirus replication. *J. Virol.* 62(8):2817–22

Dragic T, Litwin V, Allaway G, Martin SR, Huang Y, et al. 1996. HIV-1 entry into CD4(+) cells is mediated by the chemokine receptor CC-CCKR-5. *Nature* 381:667–73

Duesberg P. 1987. Retroviruses as carcinogens and pathogens: expectations and reality. *Cancer Res.* 47:1199–220

Duesberg P. 1989. Human immunodeficiency virus and acquired immunodeficiency syndrome: correlation but not causation. *Proc. Natl. Acad. Sci. USA* 86:755–64

Duesberg P. 1992. The role of drugs in the origin of AIDS. *Biomed. Pharmacother.* 46:3–15

Duesberg P. 1994. Infectious AIDS—stretching the germ theory beyond its limits. *Int. Arch. Allergy Immunol.* 103:118–27

Duesberg P. 1995. Duesberg on AIDS causation: the culprit is noncontagious risk factors. *Scientist* 9:12

Duesberg PH. 1990. AIDS: non-infectious deficiencies acquired by drug consumption and other risk factors. *Res. Immunol.* 141:5–11

Eicher AD, Crofts N, Benjamin S, Deutschmann P, Ridger AJ. 2000. A certain fate: spread of HIV among injecting drug users in Manipur, North-East India. *AIDS Care* 12(4):497–504

Embretson K, Zupancic M, Ribas JL, Burke A, Racz P, et al. 1993. Massive covert infection of helper T lymphocytes and macrophages by HIV during the incubation period of AIDS. *Nature* 362:359–62

Erbelding EJ, Stanton D, Quinn TC, Rompalo A. 2000. Behavioral and biologic evidence of persistent high-risk behavior in an HIV primary care population. *AIDS* 14:297–301

Erice A, Mayers DL, Strike DG, Sannerud KJ, McCutchan FE, et al. 1993. Primary infection with zidovudine-resistant human immunodeficiency virus type 1. *N. Engl. J. Med.* 328:1163–65

Ewald PW. 1996. *Evolution of Infectious Disease.* Oxford: Oxford Univ. Press. 298 pp.

Farzadegan H, Polis MA, Wolinsky SM, Rinaldo CR, Sninsky JJ, et al. 1988. Loss of human immunodeficiency virus type 1 (HIV-1) antibodies with evidence of viral infection in asymptomatic homosexual men. *Ann. Int. Med.* 108(6):785–90

Fauci AS. 1988. The human immunodeficiency virus: infectivity and mechanisms of pathogenesis. *Science* 239(3840):617–22

Fauci AS. 1993. Multifactorial nature of human immunodeficiency virus disease: implications for therapy. *Science* 262:1011–18

Fauci AS, Schnittman SM, Poli G, Koenig S, Pantaleo G. 1991. Immunopathogenic mechanisms in human immunodeficiency virus

(HIV) infection. *Ann. Int. Med.* 114(8):678–93

Feng Y, Broder CC, Kennedy PE, Berger EA. 1996. HIV-1 entry cofactor: functional cDNA cloning of a seven-transmembrane, G protein-coupled receptor. *Science* 272:872–77

Fenyo EM, Albert J, Asojo B. 1989. Replicative capacity, cytopathic effect and cell tropism of HIV. *AIDS* 3 (Suppl. 1):S5–12

Fenyo EM, Morfeldt–Mansson L, Chiodi F, Lind A, von Gegerfelt A, et al. 1988. Distinct replicative and cytopathic characteristics of human immunodeficiency virus isolates. *J. Virol.* 62:4414–19

Fenyo EM, Schuitemaker H, Asjo B, McKeating J, Sattentau Q. 1997. *The History of HIV-1 Biological Phenotypes: Past, Present and Future.* http://hiv–web.lanl.gov/compendium

Fisher AG, Ensoli B, Looney D, Rose A, Gallo RC, et al. 1988. Biologically diverse molecular variants within a single HIV-1 isolate. *Nature* 334:444–47

Francis DP, Curran JW, Essex M. 1983. Epidemic acquired immune deficiency syndrome: epidemiologic evidence for a transmissible agent. *J. Natl. Cancer Inst.* 71(1):1–4

Gao F, Bailes E, Robertson DL, Chen Y, Rodenburg CM, et al. 1999. Origin of HIV-1 in the chimpanzee *Pan troglodytes troglodytes. Nature* 397:436–41

Gao F, Yue L, Robertson DL, Hill SC, Hui H, et al. 1994. Genetic diversity of human immunodeficiency virus type 2: evidence for distinct sequence subtypes with differences in virus biology. *J. Virol.* 68:7433–47

Gao F, Yue L, White AT, Pappas PG, Barchue J, et al. 1992. Human infection by genetically diverse SIV$_{sm}$-related HIV-2 in West Africa. *Nature* 358:495–99

Gelderbloom HR, Reupke H, Pauli G. 1985. Loss of envelope antigens of HTLV III/LAV, a factor in AIDS pathogenesis. *Lancet* 2:1016–17

Gilks C. 1991. AIDS, monkeys and malaria. *Nature* 354:262

Gosden RG. 1992. AIDS and malaria experiments. *Nature* 355:305

Greene WC. 1993. AIDS and the immune system. *Sci. Am.* 269(3):98–105

Grez M, Dietrich U, Balfe P, von Briesen H, Maniar JK, et al. 1994. Genetic analysis of human immunodeficiency virus type 1 and 2 (HIV-1 and HIV-2) mixed infections in India reveals a recent spread of HIV-1 and HIV-2 from a single ancestor for each of these viruses. *J. Virol.* 68:2161–68

Gupta S, Vayuvegula B. 1987. Human immunodeficiency virus-associated changes in signal transduction. *J. Clin. Immunol.* 7(6):486–89

Gurtler LG, Hauser PH, Eberle J, von Brunn A, Knapp S, et al. 1994. A new subtype of human immunodeficiency virus type 1 (MVP-5180) from Cameroon. *J. Virol.* 68:1581–85

Hahn BH, Shaw GM, De Cock KM, Sharp PM. 2000. AIDS as a zoonosis: scientific and public health implications. *Science* 287:607–14

Hahn BH, Shaw GM, Taylor ME, Redfield RR, Markham PH, et al. 1986. Genetic variation in HTLV-III/LAV over time in patients with AIDS or at risk for AIDS. *Science* 232:1548–53

Hill CM, Littman DR. 1996. Natural resistance to HIV? *Science* 382:668–69

Hirsch VM, Omsted RA, Murphey-Corb M, Purcell RH, Johnson PR. 1989. An African primate lentivirus (SIV$_{sm}$) closely related to HIV-2. *Nature* 339:389–92

Ho DD, Moudgil T, Alam M. 1989. Quantitation of human immunodeficiency virus type 1 in the blood of infected persons. *N. Engl. J. Med.* 321(24):1621–25

Ho DD, Neuman AU, Perelson AS, Chen W, Leonard JM, Markowitz M. 1995. Rapid turnover of plasma virions and CD4 lymphocytes in HIV-1 infection. *Nature* 373:123–26

Ho DD, Pomerantz RJ, Kaplan JC. 1987. Pathogenesis of infection with human immunodeficiency virus. *N. Engl. J. Med.* 317:278–86

Hoxie JA, Alpers JD, Rackowski JL, Huebner K, Haggarty B, et al. 1986. Alterations in T4 (CD4) protein and mRNA synthesis in cells infected with HIV. *Science* 234:1123–27

Hu DJ, Dondero TJ, Rayfield MA, George R, Schochetman G, et al. 1996. The emerging genetic diversity of HIV: the importance of global surveillance for diagnostics, research, and prevention. *JAMA* 275(3):210–16

Hu WS, Temin HM. 1990. Retroviral recombination and reverse transcription. *Science* 250:1227–33

Huet T, Cheynier R, Meyerhans A, Roelants G, Wain-Hobson S. 1990. Genetic organization of a chimpanzee lentivirus related to HIV-1. *Nature* 345:356–59

Janssens W, Fransen K, Peeters M, Heyndrickx L, Motte J, et al. 1994. Phylogenetic analysis of a new chimpanzee lentivirus $SIV_{cpz-gab2}$ from a wild-captured chimpanzee from Gabon. *AIDS Res. Hum. Retroviruses* 10:1191–92

Jordan WC. 1991. Sexual abstinence in patients with HIV infection: a 2-year follow-up study. *J. Natl. Med. Assoc.* 83(12):1102–3

Khabbaz RF, Heneine W, George JR, Parekh B, Rowe R, et al. 1994. Brief report: infection of a laboratory worker with simian immunodeficiency virus. *N. Engl. J. Med.* 330:172–77

Kion T, Hoffmann GM. 1991. Anti-HIV and anti-anti-MHC antibodies in alloimmune and autoimmune mice. *Science* 253:1138–40

Kliks SC, Shioda T, Haigwood NL, Levy JA. 1993. Variability can influence the ability of an antibody to neutralize or enhance infection by diverse strains of human immunodeficiency virus type 1. *Proc. Natl. Acad. Sci. USA* 90:11518–22

Koprowski H. 1992. AIDS and the polio vaccine. *Science* 257:1024–27

Korber B, Theiler J, Wolinsky S. 1998. Limitations of a molecular clock applied to considerations of the origin of HIV-1. *Science* 280:1868–71

Kostrikis LG, Bagdades E, Cao Y, Zhang L, Dimitriou D, Ho DD. 1995. Genetic analysis of human immunodeficiency virus type 1 strains from patients in Cyprus: identification of a new subtype designated subtype I. *J. Virol.* 69:6122–30

Kunanusont C, Foy HM, Kreiss JK, Supachai RN, Praphan P et al. 1995. HIV-1 subtypes and male-to-female transmission in Thailand. *Lancet* 345:1078–83

Lankoande S, Meda N, Lassana S, Compaore I, Catraye J. 1998. Prevalence and risk of HIV infection among female sex workers in Burkina Faso. *Int. J. STD AIDS* 9(3):146–50

Larder BA, Darby G, Richman DD. 1989. HIV reduced sensitivity to zidovudine (AZT) isolated during prolonged therapy. *Science* 243:1731–34

Larder BA, Kemp SD. 1989. Multiple mutations in HIV-1 reverse transcriptase confer high-level resistance to zidovudine (AZT). *Science* 246:1155–58

Laurence J. 1997. HIV vaccine conundrum. *AIDS Reader* 7:2, 27

Le Guenno BM, Barabe P, Griffet PA, Guiraud M, Morcillo RJ, et al. 1991. HIV-2 and HIV-1 AIDS cases in Senegal: clinical patterns and immunological perturbations. *J. Acquired Immune Defic. Syndr.* 4:421–27

Leitner T, Korber B, Robertson D, Gao F, Hahn B. 1997. *Updated Proposal of Reference Sequences of HIV-1 Genetic Subtypes.* http://hiv-web.lanl.gov/compendium

Levine WC, Revollo R, Kaune V, Vega J, Tinajeros F, et al. 1998. Decline in sexually transmitted disease prevalence in female Bolivian sex workers: impact of an HIV prevention project. *AIDS* 12:1899–906

Levy JA. 1988. Mysteries of HIV: challenges for therapy and prevention. *Nature* 339:519–22

Levy JA. 1990. Changing concepts in HIV infection: challenges for the 1990s. *AIDS* 4:1051–58

Levy JA. 1993. Pathogenesis of human immunodeficiency virus infection. *Microbiol. Rev.* 57(1):183–289

Liu R, Paxton WA, Choe S, Ceradini D, Martin SR, et al. 1996. Homozygous defect in HIV-1 coreceptor accounts for resistance of some multiply-exposed individuals to HIV-1 infection. *Cell* 86:367–77

Lo SC, Tsai S, Benish JR, Shih JW, Wear DJ, Wong DMl. 1991. Enhancement of HIV-1 cytocidal effects in CD4 lymphocytes by the AIDS-associated mycoplasma. *Science* 251:1074–76

Looney DJ, Fisher AG, Putney SD, Rusche JR, Redfield RR, et al. 1988. Type-restricted neutralization of molecular clones of human immunodeficiency virus. *Science* 241:357–59

Los Alamos Natl. Lab. 1998. *Human Retroviruses and AIDS 1998: A Compilation and Analysis of Nucleic Acid and Amino Acid Sequences.* http://hiv-web.lanl.gov

Loussert-Ajaka I, Ly TD, Chaix ML, Ingrand D, Saragosti S, et al. 1994. HIV-1/HIV-2 seronegativity in HIV-1 subtype O infected patients. *Lancet* 343:1393–94

Louwagie J, McCutchan FE, Peeters M, Brennan TP, Sanders BE, et al. 1993. Phylogenetic analysis of *gag* genes from 70 international HIV-1 isolates provides evidence for multiple genotypes. *AIDS* 7:769–80

Lurie P, Bishaw M, Chesney MA, Cooke M, Fernandes MEL, et al. 1994. Ethical behavioral and social aspects of HIV vaccine trials in developing countries. *JAMA* 271:295–301

Lynn WS, Tweedale A, Cloyd MW. 1988. Human immunodeficiency virus (HIV-1) cytotoxicity: perturbation of the cell membrane and depression of phospholipid synthesis. *Virology* 163:43–51

Marlink R, Kanki P, Thior I, Travers K, Eisen G, et al. 1994. Reduced rate of disease development after HIV-2 infection as compared to HIV-1. *Science* 265:1587–90

Marx PA, Li Y, Lerche NW, Sutjipto S, Gettie A, et al. 1991. Isolation of a simian immunodeficiency virus related to human immunodeficiency virus type 2 from a West African pet mangabey. *J. Virol.* 65:4480–85

Mavligit GM, Talpaz M, Hsia FT, Wong W, Lichtiger B, et al. 1984. Chronic immune stimulation by sperm alloantigens: support for the hypothesis that spermatozoa induce immune dysregulation in homosexual males. *JAMA* 251(2):237–41

Milich L, Margolin B, Swanstrom R. 1993. V3 loop of the human immunodeficiency virus type 1 env protein: interpreting sequence variability. *J. Virol.* 67(9):5623–34

Moore J, Anderson R. 1994. The WHO and why of HIV vaccine trials. *Nature* 372:313–14

Moore JP, Ho DD. 1995. HIV-1 neutralization: the consequences of viral adaptation to growth on transformed T cells. *AIDS* 9(Suppl. A):S117–36

Natl. Inst. Allergy Infect. Dis. 1995. *The Relationship of the Human Immunodeficiency Virus and the Acquired Immunodeficiency Syndrome.* Bethesda, MD: Natl. Inst. Health

Ndinya AJO, Ghee AE, Kihara AN, Krone MR, Plummer FA, et al. 1997. High HIV prevalence, low condom use and gender differences in sexual behaviour among patients with STD-related complaints at a Nairobi health care clinic. *Int. J. STD AIDS* 8(8):506–14

Nkengasong JN, Janssen W, Heyndrickx L, Fransen K, Ndumbe PM, et al. 1994. Genotype subtypes of HIV-1 in Cameroon. *AIDS* 8:1405–12

Nowak M. 1990. HIV mutation rate. *Nature* 347:522

Nowak R. 1995. How the parasite disguises itself. *Science* 269:755

Nowak MA, Anderson RM, McLean AR, Wolfs TFW, Goudsmit J, May RM. 1991. Antigenic diversity thresholds and the development of AIDS. *Science* 254:963–69

Nzilambi N, De Cock KM, Forthal DN, Francis H, Ryder RW, et al. 1988. The prevalence of infection with human immunodeficiency virus over a 10-year period in rural Zaire. *N. Engl. J. Med.* 318:276–79

Pantaleo G, Graziosi C, Fauci AS. 1993a. The immunopathogenesis of human immunodeficiency virus infection. *N. Engl. J. Med.* 328:327–35

Pantaleo G, Graziosi C, Demarest JF, Butini L, Montroni M, et al. 1993b. HIV infection is active and progressive in lymphoid tissue during the clinically latent stage of disease. *Nature* 362:355–58

Peeters M, Fransen K, Delaporte E, Vanden Haesevelde M, Gershy-Damet GM, et al. 1992. Isolation and characterization of a new chimpanzee lentivirus (simian immunodeficiency virus isolate cpz-ant) from a wild-captured chimpanzee. *AIDS* 6:447–51

Peeters M, Honore C, Huet T, Bedjabaga L, Ossari S, et al. 1989. Isolation and partial characterization of an HIV-related virus occurring naturally in chimpanzees in Gabon. *AIDS* 3:625–30

Pela AO, Platt JJ. 1989. AIDS in Africa: emerging trends. *Soc. Sci. Med.* 28(1):1–8

Pieniazek D, Janini LM, Ramos A, Tanuri A, Schechter M, et al. 1995. HIV-1 patients may harbor viruses of different phylogenetic subtypes: implications for the evolution of the HIV/AIDS pandemic. *Emerg. Infect. Dis.* 1:86–88

Preston BD, Poiesz BJ, Loeb LA. 1988. Fidelity of HIV-1 reverse transcriptase. *Science* 242:1168–71

Price RW, Brew B, Sidtis J, Rosenblum M, Scheck AC, Cleary P. 1988. The brain in AIDS: central nervous system HIV-1 infection and AIDS dementia complex. *Science* 239:586–92

Puskar KR, Tusaie MK, Sereika S, Lamb J. 1999. Health concerns and risk behaviors of rural adolescents. *J. Community Health Nursing* 16(2):109–19

Quinn TC. 1987. AIDS in Africa: evidence for heterosexual transmission of the human immunodeficiency virus. NY State *J. Med.* 87(5):286–89

Ratnam KV. 1994. Effect of sexual practices on T cell subsets and delayed hypersensitivity in transsexuals and female sex workers. *Int. J. STD AIDS* 5(4):257–61

Reilley B, Burrows D, Melnikov V, Andreeva T, Bijl M, Veeken H. 2000. Injecting drug use and HIV in Moscow: results of a survey. *J. Drug Issues* 30(2):305–21

Robertson DL, Gao F, Hahn BH, Sharp PM. 1997. *Intersubtype Recombinant HIV-1 Sequences.* http://hiv-web.lanl.gov/compendium

Rojko JL, Hoover EA, Quakenbush SL, Olsen RG. 1982. Reactivation of latent feline leukaemia virus infection. *Nature* 298:385–88

Rosen CA. 1991. Regulation of HIV gene expression by RNA-protein interactions. *Trends Genet.* 7:9–14

Ryder RW, Mugewrwa RW. 1994. The clinical definition and diagnosis of AIDS in African adults. In *AIDS in Africa*, ed. M Essex, pp. 269–81. New York: Raven. 728 pp.

Saag MS, Hahn BH, Gibbons J, Li Y, Parks ES, et al. 1988. Extensive variation of human immunodeficiency virus type-1 in vivo. *Nature* 334:440–44

Samson M, Libert F, Doranz BJ, Rucker J, Liesnard C, et al. 1996. Resistance to HIV-1 infection in Caucasian individuals bearing mutant alleles of the CCR-5 chemokine receptor gene. *Nature* 382:722–25

Schable C, Zekeng L, Pau CP, Hu D, Kaptue L, et al. 1994. Sensitivity of United States HIV antibody tests for detection of HIV-1 group O infections. *Lancet* 344:1333–34

Schuitemaker H, Koot M, Kootstra NA, Dercksen MW, Goede REY, et al. 1992. Biological phenotype of human immunodeficiency virus type 1 clones at different stages of infection: progression of disease is associated with a shift from monocytotropic to T-cell-tropic virus population. *J. Virol.* 66:1354–60

Shaper EG, Mullins JI. 1993. Rates of amino acid change in the envelope protein correlate with pathogenicity of primate lentiviruses. *J. Mol. Evol.* 37:57–65

Sharp PM, Robertson DL, Gao F, Hahn BE. 1994. Origins and diversity of human immunodeficiency viruses. *AIDS* 8(Suppl. 1):S27–42

Shioda T, Levy JA, Cheng-Mayer C. 1991. Macrophage and T cell-line tropisms of HIV-1 are determined by specific regions of the envelope gp120 gene. *Nature* 349:167–69

Siegel K, Karus D, Epstein J, Raveis V. 1996. Psychological and psychosocial adjustment of HIV-infected gay/bisexual men: disease stage comparisons. *J. Community Psych.* 24(3):229–43

Siegrist CA, Yerly S, Kaiser L, Wyler CA, Perrin L. 1994. Mother to child transmission of zidovudine-resistant HIV-1. *Lancet* 344:1771–72

Simmons G, Wilkinson D, Reeves JD, Dittmar MT, Beddows S, et al. 1996. Primary, syncytium-inducing human immunodeficiency virus type 1 isolates are dual-tropic and most can use either Lestr or CCR5 as coreceptors for virus entry. *J. Virol.* 70:8355–60

Simon F, Mauclere P, Roques P, Loussert-Ajaka I, Muller-Trutwin C, et al. 1998. Identification of a new human immunodeficiency virus type 1 distinct from group M and group O. *Nat. Med.* 4:1032–37

Snider DE, Seggerson JJ, Hutton MD. 1991. Tuberculosis and migrant farm workers. *JAMA* 265(13):1732

Sodroski J, Goh WC, Rosen C, Campbell K, Haseltine W. 1986. Role of the HTLV-III/LAV envelope in syncytium formation and cytopathicity. *Nature* 322:470–74

Somasundaran M, Robinson HL. 1988. Unexpectedly high levels of HIV-1 RNA and protein synthesis in a cytocidal infection. *Science* 242:1554–56

Sonnabend J, Witkin SS, Purtilo DT. 1983. Acquired immunodeficiency syndrome, opportunistic infections, and malignancies in male homosexuals. A hypothesis of etiologic factors in pathogenesis. *JAMA* 249(17):2370–74

Stine GJ. 2000. *AIDS Update 2000: An Annual Overview of Acquired Immune Deficiency Syndrome.* Englewood Cliffs, NJ: Prentice Hall. 486 pp.

Sullivan N, Sun Y, Li J, Hofmann W, Sodroski J. 1995. Replicative function and neutralization sensitivity of envelope glycoproteins from primary and T-cell line-passaged human immundeficiency virus type 1 isolates. *J. Virol.* 69:4413–22

Takehisa J, Zekeng L, Miura T, Ido E, Yamashita M, et al. 1997. Triple HIV-1 infection with group O and Group M of different clades in a single Cameroonian AIDS patient. *J. AIDS Hum. Retrovirol.* 14:81–82

Tersmette M, de Goede REY, Eeftink-Schattenkerk JKM, Schellekens PTA, Coutinho RA, et al. 1989. Association between biological properties of human immunodeficiency virus variants and risk for AIDS and AIDS mortality. *Lancet* 1:983–85

Tindall B, Cooper DA. 1991. Primary HIV infection: host responses and intervention strategies. *AIDS* 5:1–14

Vanden Haesevelde MM, Peeters M, Jannes G, Janssens W, Van der Groen G, et al. 1996. Sequence analysis of a highly divergent HIV-1-related lentivirus isolated from a wild captured chimpanzee. *Virology* 221:346–50

Vartanian JP, Meyerhans A, Henry M, Wain-Hobson S. 1992. High-resolution structure of an HIV-1 quasispecies: identification of novel coding sequences. *AIDS* 6:1095–98

Wagner G, Rabkin J, Rabkin R. 1998. Exercise as a mediator of psychological and nutritional effects of testosterone therapy in HIV$^+$ men. *Med. Sci. Sports Exerc.* 30(6):811–17

Walker DG, Itagaki S, Berry K, McGeer PL. 1989. Examination of brains of AIDS cases for human immunodeficiency virus and human cytomegalovirus nucleic acids. *J. Neurol. Neurosurg. Psychiatry* 52(5):583–90

Walters K, Simoni J. 1999. Trauma, substance use, and HIV risk among urban American Indian women. *Cultural Diversity Ethnic Minority Psychol.* 5(3):236–48

Wei X, Ghosh SK, Taylor ME, Johnson VA, Emini EA, et al. 1995. Viral dynamics in human immunodeficiency virus type 1 infection. *Nature* 373:117–22

Weiss RA. 1993. How does HIV cause AIDS? *Science* 260:1273–79

Weiss RA. 1996. HIV receptors and the pathogenesis of AIDS. *Science* 272:1885–86

Whittle H, Morris J, Todd J, Corrah T, Sabally S, et al. 1994. HIV-2-infected patients survive longer than HIV-1-infected patients. *AIDS* 8:1617–20

Wike CM, Korber BTM, Daniels MR, Hutto C, Munoz J, et al. 1992. HIV-1 sequence variation between isolates from mother-infant transmission pairs. *AIDS Res. Hum. Retroviruses* 8:1297–300

Wills JW, Craven R. 1991. Form, function, and use of retroviral Gag protein. *AIDS* 5:639–54

Wolinsky SM, Korber BTM, Newumann AU, Daniels M, Kunstman KJ, et al. 1996. Adaptive evolution of human immunodeficiency virus-type 1 during the natural course of infection. *Science* 272:537–42

Wolinsky SM, Wike CM, Korber BTM, Hutto C, Parks WP, et al. 1992. Selective transmission of human immunodeficiency virus type-1 variants from mothers to infants. *Science* 255:1134–37

Wu XX, Tu XM, He FQ, Shi HJ, Wei CZQ, et al. 1991. Studies on the monitoring of viruses in Chinese rhesus monkeys (*Macaca mulatta*). *Chin. J. Lab. Anim. Sci.* 1:179–83

Zacarias F, Gonzalez RS, Cuchi P, Yanez A, Peruga A, et al. 1994. HIV/AIDS and its interaction with tuberculosis in Latin America and the Caribbean. *Bull. Pan Am. Health Org.* 284):312–23

Zhang L, Huang Y, He T, Cao Y, Ho DD. 1996. HIV-1 subtype and second receptor use. *Nature* 383:768

Zhu T, Korber BT, Nahmias AJ, Hooper E, Sharp PM, Ho DD. 1998. An African HIV-1 sequence from 1950 and implications for the origin of the epidemic. *Nature* 391:594–97

Zhu T, Mo H, Wang N, Nam DS, Cao Y, et al. 1993. Genotypic and phenotypic characterization of HIV-1 in patients with primary infection. *Science* 261:1179–81

Annu. Rev. Anthropol. 2001. 30:109–37

LANGUAGE AND AGENCY

Laura M. Ahearn

Rutgers University, New Brunswick, New Jersey 08901; e-mail: ahearn@rci.rutgers.edu

Key Words   practice, grammar, dialogic, gender, literacy

■ **Abstract**   This review describes and critiques some of the many ways agency has been conceptualized in the academy over the past few decades, focusing in particular on practice theorists such as Giddens, Bourdieu, de Certeau, Sahlins, and Ortner. For scholars interested in agency, it demonstrates the importance of looking closely at language and argues that the issues surrounding linguistic form and agency are relevant to anthropologists with widely divergent research agendas. Linguistic anthropologists have made significant contributions to the understanding of agency as it emerges in discourse, and the final sections of this essay describe some of the most promising research in the study of language and gender, literacy practices, and the dialogic construction of meaning and agency.

WHY AGENCY NOW?

The term agency, variously defined, has become ubiquitous within anthropology and other disciplines. This essay describes and critiques some of the many ways agency has been conceptualized in the academy over the past few decades. While I propose a skeletal definition for the term, my purpose is not to dictate how scholars should define agency, or even to insist that they should use the term at all. Rather, my purpose is to survey the scholarship on agency and to suggest how important it is for scholars interested in agency to look closely at language and linguistic form. I argue that the issues surrounding language and agency are relevant to anthropologists with widely divergent research agendas because most anthropologists—whether archaeological, biological, cultural, or linguistic—are concerned, in one form or another, with what people say and do. Linguistic anthropologists have made significant contributions to the understanding of agency as it emerges in discourse, and in the final sections of this essay, I describe some of the most promising research in the study of language and gender, literacy practices, and the dialogic construction of meaning and agency.

Before turning to definitional issues, it is worthwhile to reflect for a moment on our own intellectual practice and ask ourselves why so many scholars in so many fields are currently interested in the concept of agency. Messer-Davidow poses this question directly, asking, "Why agency now?" (1995, p. 23). While there are undoubtedly many answers to this question, one is that there is a clear connection

0084-6570/01/1021-0109$14.00

between the emergence of interest in approaches that foreground practice on the one hand, and the social movements of the 1960s and 1970s on the other (Ortner 1984, p. 160). In addition, the social upheavals in central and eastern Europe in the late 1980s and early 1990s led many scholars to articulate more clearly their ideas about human agency and social structures (Sztompka 1991). As a result of witnessing or participating in actions aimed at transforming society, then, many academics have begun to investigate how practices can either reproduce or transform the very structures that shape them. I believe it is no coincidence that the recent agentive[1] turn, an outgrowth of the trends Ortner identified in 1984, follows on the heels not only of the social movements of the past few decades but also of postmodern and poststructuralist critiques within the academy that have called into question impersonal master narratives that leave no room for tensions, contradictions, or oppositional actions on the part of individuals and collectivities. It is because questions about agency are so central to contemporary political and theoretical debates that the concept arouses so much interest—and why it is therefore so crucial to define clearly.

DEFINITIONAL STARTING POINTS

In most scholarly endeavors, defining terms is half the battle. This is especially true for a word like language, which is so commonplace that researchers often mistakenly assume its meaning is self-evident (Williams 1977, pp. 21–44). Precise definitions are equally essential for words such as agency that have taken on new meanings on entering academic discourse. As a starting point for this review, I discuss language as a form of social action, which is the approach to language that many linguistic anthropologists take, and then present a provisional definition of agency.

Language as Social Action

Whereas most linguists follow de Saussure (1986) and Chomsky (1965, 1986) in studying language as a set of formal structures set apart from everyday interactions ("langue" rather than "parole," and "competence" rather than "performance"), most linguistic anthropologists regard language as a form of social action, a cultural resource, and a set of sociocultural practices (Schieffelin 1990, p. 16). People do things with words (Austin 1962, Searle 1969, cf. Butler 1997). Brenneis & Macaulay (1996), Duranti (1997), and Hanks (1996) present persuasive and thorough explications of this approach to language. Linguistic anthropologists consider language, whether spoken or written, to be inextricably embedded in networks of sociocultural relations. When scholars treat language, culture, and society as mutually constituted, one of their main responsibilities then becomes to study how

---

[1]There is no unanimity in the choice of an adjectival form for agency. While other writers use agential or agentic, I prefer agentive.

discourse both shapes and is shaped by sociocultural factors and power dynamics (Urban 1991). There are no neutral words, Bakhtin (1981, p. 293) reminds us: "All words have the 'taste' of a profession, a genre, a tendency, a party, a particular work, a particular person, a generation, an age group, the day and hour. Each word tastes of the context and contexts in which it has lived its socially charged life. . . ." Unequal power relations can result in—and be the result of—symbolic violence (symbolic power, symbolic domination), which, Bourdieu (1991, p. 170) maintains, occurs when individuals mistakenly consider a standard dialect or style of speaking to be truly superior to the way they themselves speak, rather than an arbitrary difference afforded social significance. Language and power are therefore commonly intertwined.

Note that in this view, language is not defined as a conduit that merely conveys information (Reddy 1979), and it is not a transparent vehicle carrying only referential meaning (Goodwin 1990, p. 4). In order to understand how linguistic anthropologists approach language, we have to set aside this vehicular metaphor—unless, that is, we say that linguistic anthropologists view language as a vehicle that people themselves are continually in the process of building together. According to this approach to language, meanings are co-constructed by participants, emergent from particular social interactions. Scholars have proposed various strategies for understanding how this works. Early work in the ethnography of communication encouraged researchers to look for patterns in actual speech (Gumperz & Hymes 1964, Bauman & Sherzer 1989). Scholars grounded in fields as diverse as ethnomethodology, sociolinguistics, the sociology of language, linguistic anthropology, and conversation analysis have contributed to an understanding of how meanings emerge in conversations by focusing on the microprocesses of linguistic interactions (Garfinkel 1967; Goffman 1974, 1981; Ochs et al 1996; Sacks 1992). The appropriate unit of analysis for many scholars who treat language as social action is not the sentence, the individual, or even the conversation but rather speech acts (Austin 1962, Searle 1969), speech events (Jakobson 1960, Hymes 1972), participant structures (Philips 1972), participation frameworks (Goffman 1981), participant frameworks and situated activities (Goodwin 1990), or communities of practice (Eckert & McConnell-Ginet 1992). Within these contexts, as meanings are coconstructed, social reality is also constructed. In the approach advocated here, then, language does not merely reflect an already existing social reality; it also helps to create that reality (Gumperz & Levinson 1996, Hill & Mannheim 1992, Lucy 1992, Sapir 1949, Spender 1980, Whorf 1956, Williams 1977).

With such a dialogic, coconstructed view of language as a form of social action, linguistic anthropologists face the challenge of interpreting fluid, often ambiguous linguistic data with important sociocultural implications. How can this task best be accomplished? Both text and context must be taken into consideration, and they must be understood to be intrinsically interwoven (Duranti & Goodwin 1992). We must acknowledge the inevitability of a certain degree of interpretive indeterminacy while also recognizing that indeterminacy is not limitless (Derrida

1972). Elsewhere I have argued that we should espouse what I call a practice theory of meaning constraint (Ahearn 1998, 2001). According to this perspective, we must shift our focus away from searching for definitive interpretations and instead concentrate on looking for constraints on the kinds of meanings that might emerge from an event such as a song performance or a text such as a love letter. Meanings might be infinite in number, but they are very tightly bounded. As Eco (1990, p. 42) notes, "If it is very difficult to decide whether a given interpretation is a good one, it is, however, always possible to decide whether it is a bad one." Appadurai (1991, p. 472) takes a similar view of language, calling for a new "theory of reception" that incorporates an understanding of intertextuality and situatedness. In advocating a practice theory rather than a theory of reception, however, I emphasize how individuals, including scholars, actively construct and constrain—rather than passively receive—interpretations that are both socially mediated and intertextually situated within a bounded universe of discourse.

From the foregoing discussion of language, it should be clear that as linguistic anthropologists increasingly treat language as a form of social action, the task of developing a theoretically sophisticated understanding of agency becomes ever more urgent. We turn therefore to the challenge of defining the concept.

A Provisional Definition of Agency

Jean and John Comaroff have called agency "that abstraction greatly underspecified, often misused, much fetishized these days by social scientists" (1997, p. 37; cited in Ortner 2001, p. 1). While this assessment may be a bit harsh, it is true that scholars often fail to recognize that the particular ways in which they conceive of agency have implications for the understanding of personhood, causality, action, and intention. Agency therefore deserves "deeper consideration and more extensive theoretical elaboration" (Dobres & Robb 2000, p. 3).

Let me propose, then, a provisional definition of the concept: Agency refers to the socioculturally mediated capacity to act.

According to this bare bones definition, all action is socioculturally mediated, both in its production and in its interpretation. Although this definition provides us with a starting point, it leaves many details unspecified. The following are some questions to ponder—questions that may be answered in different ways by different scholars. Must all agency be human? Can nonhuman primates (Small 1993), machines (Pickering 1995), technologies (Dobres 2000), spirits (Keane 1997, pp. 64–66), or signs (Colapietro 1989, pp. 95–97; Peirce 1955) exercise agency? Must agency be individual, leading to charges of unwarranted assumptions regarding Western atomic individualism (Ortner 1996)? Or can agency also be supraindividual—the property, perhaps, of families, faculties, or labor unions? Conversely, can agency be subindividual—the property of "dividuals" (Daniel 1984, p. 42; Marriott 1976; McElhinny 1998, p. 181), as when someone feels torn within herself or himself? What does it mean to be an agent of someone else? Must agency be conscious, intentional, or effective? What does it mean for an act to be conscious, intentional, or effective?

We might begin to answer some of these questions by considering, as Karp (1986) does, what distinguishes an "actor" from an "agent." In Karp's view, an actor refers to a person whose action is rule-governed or rule-oriented, whereas an agent refers to a person engaged in the exercise of power in the sense of the ability to bring about effects and to (re)constitute the world (Karp 1986, p. 137). Actor and agent should be considered two different aspects of the same person, according to Karp, or two different perspectives on the actions of any given individual. Ortner (2001) proposes differentiating among various types of agency, such as "agency of power" and "agency of intention," though she is careful to note that any such distinction is purely heuristic because types of agency are often inseparable in practice. Some scholars, such as Wertsch et al (1993), advocate a nonindividualistic notion of agency. Drawing on Vygotsky (1978, 1987) and paraphrasing Bateson (1972), they argue that agency "extends beyond the skin" because it is frequently a property of groups and involves "mediational means" such as language and tools (Wertsch et al 1993, p. 352).

It is especially important for anthropologists to ask themselves how conceptions of agency may differ from society to society, and how these conceptions might be related to notions of personhood and causality (Jackson & Karp 1990, Skinner et al 1998). Pickering suggests that "within different cultures human beings and the material world might exhibit capacities for action quite different from those we customarily attribute to them" (1995, p. 245). Desjarlais presents an illustration of this within the United States itself in his study of a homeless shelter in Boston, in which he argues that the forms of agency he observed emerged out of a specific sociocultural context. Agency was not ontologically prior to that context but arose from the social, political, and cultural dynamics of a specific place and time (Desjarlais 1997, p. 204). In my own work, I have maintained that it is important to ask how people themselves conceive of their own actions and whether they attribute responsibility for events to individuals, to fate, to deities, or to other animate or inanimate forces. In the case of Junigau, Nepal, people's conceptions of their own and others' actions are changing rapidly, demonstrating the need for anthropologists to ask not only what agency means for themselves as theorists, but what it means for the people with whom they work, and how those meanings may shift over time (Ahearn 2000b, 2001).

PROBLEMS IN DEFINING AGENCY

Several uses of agency that are common in the literature are, in my opinion, of questionable use to anthropologists (though perhaps not to scholars in other disciplines). In the following overview, which draws from several fields but does not purport to be a full delineation of the debates within any given discipline, examples are discussed in which agency is defined too simplistically, too narrowly, or too opaquely.

Agency as Free Will

One of the most common tendencies in discussions of agency is the treatment of it as a synonym for free will. This is especially evident in what philosophers call action theory. Within action theory, philosophers attempt to distinguish an "action" from an "event." Davidson (1980[1971], p. 43) begins his famous essay, "Agency," with the following question: "What events in the life of a person reveal agency; what are his deeds and his doings in contrast to mere happenings in his history; what is the mark that distinguishes his actions?" Twenty years later, Segal (1991, p. 3) echoes Davidson as he explains philosophical action theory: "Hitting a ball is an action, falling down a flight of stairs is not. A theory of action seeks, among other things, to explain the distinctions we make." In attempting to explain human agency, action theorists and other philosophers generally argue that agency requires some sort of concomitant mental state, such as "intention" (Davidson 1980[1971], p. 46), "presence of the self" (Segal 1991, p. 113), a "rational point of view" and a "domain of intentional control" (Rovane 1998, p. 85), or "motivation, responsibility, and expectations of recognition or reward" (Mann 1994, p. 14).

The main weakness in treating agency as a synonym for free will is that such an approach ignores or only gives lip service to the social nature of agency and the pervasive influence of culture on human intentions, beliefs, and actions. Even Taylor (1985, pp. 1–44), a philosopher whose writings on language and agency are extremely thought provoking, locates agency inside the mental processes of particular individuals when he connects agency with "second-order desires," "strong evaluation," and "a vocabulary of worth." Similarly, Ludwig Wittgenstein, the famous philosopher of language to whom linguistic anthropologists increasingly look for inspiration, fails to theorize adequately the sociocultural nature of language and action. While Wittgenstein (1958) recognizes the degree to which language and social forms are intertwined, he leaves the details of this interrelationship unexplained. Giddens (1979, p. 50) notes this shortcoming in Wittgenstein's work on language and action, stating, "Wittgensteinian philosophy has not led towards any sort of concern with social change, with power relations, or with conflict in society. Other strands in the philosophy of action have operated at an even further distance from such issues, focusing attention almost exclusively upon the nature of reasons or intentions in human activity."

Traces of this tendency to equate agency with socially unfettered free will can be found in many other disciplines, including anthropology, psychology, political science, and history. Sometimes scholars contend that only certain individuals "have agency," while others have little or none. Some historians, for example, locate agency solely in the power of individual "Great Men." A recent debate surrounds the publication of comparative political scientist Daniel J. Goldhagen's (1996) book, which argues that ordinary Germans played an active, agentive role in the Holocaust. Moses (1998) states, "Having raised the question of the perpetrators' choice, Goldhagen must convince the reader that they were not 'just following orders,' that is, that these actors possessed agency" (p. 205). According to Moses, however, Goldhagen's implicit methodological underpinnings are contradictory. On one hand he espouses rational choice models[2] to stress that ordinary Germans had "agency," which he equates with free will, and yet on the other hand he relies on behaviorism to account for the prevalence of antisemitism in German society (Moses 1998, p. 209).

Some scholars, especially those studying colonialism and postcolonialism, have been moving away from approaches that treat agency as a synonym for free will as exercised by completely autonomous individuals (e.g., Cooper 1994, Cooper & Stoler 1997, Pieters 2000, Pomper 1996, Scott 1988, Sewell 1992). Historian Lalu (2000, pp. 50–51) offers an observation that applies equally well to historians, philosophers, anthropologists, and all other scholars interested in agency: "[T]he question of agency, it seems, may be posed in ways other than in terms of the autonomous subject or authorial subject.... [We] may have to think of the ways in which agency is constituted by the norms, practices, institutions, and discourses through which it is made available." Such a linguistically and socioculturally mediated conception of agency is discussed further below.

Equating Agency with Resistance

Another misguided approach to agency is to consider it a synonym for resistance. This approach is characteristic of the work of some anthropologists, many scholars in subaltern studies, and feminist theorists in a number of fields. Feminism has always addressed issues of agency, if only implicitly (Mann 1994, p. 14), but recently the term has been cropping up with increasing frequency (Andermahr 1997, Davies 1991, Dissanayake 1996, Gardiner 1995, Goddard 2000, Kumar 1994, McNay 2000). Fraser (1992, pp. 16–17) explains that agency has become a problem in recent feminist theory because of two equally important goals. On the one hand, feminists have sought to establish the seriousness of their struggle by demonstrating the pervasiveness and systematicity of male dominance. This has led to the development of theories that emphasize the constraining power of gender structures and norms, while downplaying the resisting capacities of individuals and groups. On the other hand, feminists have also sought to inspire women's activism by rediscovering lost or socially invisible traditions of resistance in the past and present. In some scholars' work (both feminist and nonfeminist), instead of a balance between these two countervailing tendencies, there is an overemphasis on resistance (Abu-Lughod 1990). According to many feminist theorists, in order to demonstrate agency, a person must resist the patriarchal status quo (e.g., Goddard 2000, p. 3). While one can certainly understand the impulse behind equating agency with resistance, agency should not be reduced to it. Oppositional agency is only one of many forms of agency.

Many scholars interested in other forms of social and economic oppression also equate agency with actions that resist domination (Pruyn 1999; Scott 1985,

---

[2]See Burns (1994) for a critique of rational choice models of agency.

1990). As useful as many of these studies are, I take to heart Abu-Lughod's (1990) caution against the "romance of resistance" and second Ortner's (1995) conclusion that there is no such thing as pure resistance; motivations are always complex and contradictory (Ahearn 2000a, Gamburd 2000, Jeffery & Jeffery 1996, Jeffery & Basu 1998). I find MacLeod's work very helpful in conceptualizing both women's and men's agency. She notes that women, "even as subordinate players, always play an active part that goes beyond the dichotomy of victimization/acceptance, a dichotomy that flattens out a complex and ambiguous agency in which women accept, accommodate, ignore, resist, or protest—sometimes all at the same time" (MacLeod 1992, p. 534). Such a nuanced understanding of the multiplicity of motivations behind all human actions should be at the core of our definition of agency.

The Absence of Agency?

Another approach to agency that presents challenges to scholars is that of Foucault (1977, 1978). On one level, Foucault can be read as stating that omnipresent impersonal discourses so thoroughly pervade society that no room is left for anything that might be regarded as agency, oppositional or otherwise. In *The History of Sexuality*, Volume I, for example, Foucault (1978, pp. 93, 95) writes,

> Power is everywhere; not because it embraces everything, but because it comes from everywhere. And "Power," insofar as it is permanent, repetitious, inert, and self-reproducing, is simply the over-all effect that emerges from all these mobilities, the concatenation that rests on each of them and seeks in turn to arrest their movement . . . there is no power that is exercised without a series of aims and objectives. But this does not mean that it results from the choice or decision of an individual subject . . .

There have been numerous critiques of Foucault's definition of power, many of them focusing on the problematic implications it has for human agency (Bartky 1995, Hoy 1986). Even though Foucault states that "[w]here there is power, there is resistance," he continues on to say, "and yet, or rather consequently, this resistance is never in a position of exteriority in relation to power" (Foucault 1978, p. 95). The problem is that in *History of Sexuality*, Volume I, Foucault never explains how power is enforced or personified, and the processes of resistance remain similarly opaque. Nor, despite the centrality of Foucault's work to scholars of colonialism, does he examine colonial politics in any detail in that volume (Stoler 1995). Many scholars agree with Said (1983, p. 246), who argues that "[t]he disturbing circularity of Foucault's theory of power is a form of theoretical overtotalization. . . ."

Others, however, have maintained that Foucault's definition of power does not eliminate the possibility for agency, however defined. O'Hara (1992, p. 66), drawing largely on Foucault's later work, argues that Foucault proposes a model of agency that is "a matter of plurality, mobility, and conflict." According to Halperin (1995, pp. 16–17), Foucault's notion of power is not a substance but a relation, a dynamic situation; it produces not only constraints on, but also possibilities for, action. Nevertheless, even if Foucault's formulations do leave room for agency, his focus is more on pervasive discourses than on the actions of particular human beings.

PRACTICE THEORY

Consider Marx's famous words in "The Eighteenth Brumaire of Louis Bonaparte":

> Men make their own history, but they do not make it just as they please; they do not make it under circumstances chosen by themselves, but under circumstances directly found, given and transmitted from the past. The tradition of all the dead generations weighs like a nightmare on the brain of the living (Marx 1978[1852], p. 595).

How can we reconcile the fact that, as Marx noted almost a century and a half ago, individuals appear to create society even as they are created by it? Berger & Luckmann turn this question into a trilogy of paradoxical statements in their famous book, *The Social Construction of Reality: "Society is a human product. Society is an objective reality. Man is a social product"* (1966, p. 61; emphasis in the original). The most promising approach for understanding these seemingly contradictory statements is practice theory, which Ortner (1989, p. 11; 1984, 1996) defines as "a theory of the relationship between the structures of society and culture on the one hand and the nature of human action on the other." The emphasis in practice theory is on the social influences on agency; human actions are central, but they are never considered in isolation from the social structures that shape them.

Structuration Theory

Giddens is perhaps the central figure in the debate about agency and structure and is considered one of the founders of practice theory (Giddens 1979, 1984, Archer 1988, Burns & Dietz 1994, Karp 1986). Explicitly drawing on the insights of ethnomethodologists such as Garfinkel and interactionist sociologists such as Goffman, Giddens attempts to breathe life into social structures and bring social structures into contact with human actions (Giddens 1979, p. 57, 68, 83; Bryant & Jary 1991, Sewell 1992). Unlike scholars who treat agency as a synonym for free will or resistance, Giddens consistently links agency to structure through his discussion of rules and resources. Central to Giddens' theory of structuration is the understanding that people's actions are shaped (in both constraining and enabling ways) by the very social structures that those actions then serve to reinforce or reconfigure. Given this recursive loop consisting of actions influenced by social structures and social structures (re)created by actions, the question of how social change can occur is crucial and is taken up below in the context of other practice theorists.

Some sociologists prefer to use the term practice or praxis (drawing on and redefining the Marxist term) in addition to, or instead of, agency (Giddens 1979, p. 56; Sztompka 1994). Sztompka, for example, distinguishes the two terms in the following manner: "Agency and praxis are two sides of the incessant social functioning; agency actualizes in praxis, and praxis reshapes agency, which actualizes itself in changed praxis" (Sztompka 1994, p. 276). Thus, agency can be considered the socioculturally mediated capacity to act, while praxis (or practice) can be considered the action itself.

Agency and the Habitus

Aside from Giddens, the most influential theorist within practice theory is Bourdieu, a professor of sociology who has conducted ethnographic fieldwork in Algeria. Bourdieu borrows and redefines the term habitus, first used in anthropology by Marcel Mauss to refer to a habitual condition, particularly of the body (Farnell 2000, p. 399). Bourdieu's definition refers to a generative process that produces practices and representations that are conditioned by the "structuring structures" from which they emerge. These practices and their outcomes—whether intended or unintended—then reproduce or reconfigure the habitus (Bourdieu 1977, p. 78). The recursive nature of this process mirrors that found in Giddens' theory of structuration. The habitus generates an infinite but bounded number of possible actions, thoughts, and perceptions, each one of which is imbued with the culturally constructed meanings and values embodied by the habitus. These actions, thoughts, and perceptions in turn then recreate and/or challenge the culturally constructed meanings and values.

With this analysis of agency, Bourdieu moves us far from the concept of free will. Although he defines the habitus as "an endless capacity to engender products," Bourdieu emphasizes dispositions in order to preclude any assumption of absolute free will on the part of actors, repeatedly pointing out how far removed his concept of the habitus is from a creation of unpredictable novelty. What prevents the creation of unpredictably novel sociocultural products are the (pre)dispositions the habitus embodies in its many forms and structures. Of the infinite thoughts, meanings, and practices that the habitus can produce at any given historical moment, there is only a minimal probability that any will ever be thought or practiced because individuals are predisposed to think and act in a manner that reproduces the existing system of inequalities.

As necessary and helpful as his reminders are of the constraints on individuals' actions and thoughts, Bourdieu, like Giddens, faces the dilemma of explaining how social reproduction becomes social transformation (Sewell 1992). Bourdieu emphasizes the reproductive tendencies of the habitus, which, because it is sturdy and well-rooted, located in the physical environments containing actors, and embodied mentally and physically within the actors themselves, can be applied in new as well as familiar situations to reinforce the status quo. Despite the theoretical possibility of social transformation resulting from actions generated by the habitus, Bourdieu's framework leaves little room for resistance or social change.

The microprocesses of resistance are taken up in the *Practice of Everyday Life*, written by another theorist commonly associated with practice theory, historian Michel de Certeau. De Certeau encourages other scholars to attend to the actions of ordinary people, especially when they engage in "la perruque" (literally, "the wig"), a French idiomatic expression that refers to the work one does for oneself in the guise of work done for an employer (de Certeau 1984, p. 25). De Certeau uses the trope of la perruque to describe how individuals use strategies and tactics to carve out a semi-independent domain of practice within the constraints placed on them by the powerful.

Although de Certeau, Bourdieu, and Giddens offer us theories with significant explanatory power in regard to the persistence of deeply embedded relations of inequality, they give insufficient attention to the question of how any habitus or structure can produce actions that fundamentally change it. In an attempt to understand more fully how social change occurs, let us look at the work of other practice theorists working within anthropology.

Anthropological Contributions to Practice Theory

In his *Historical Metaphors and Mythical Realities*, Sahlins sets for himself the task of understanding how an attempt at social reproduction can become social transformation (Sahlins 1981, Obeyesekere 1992). Sahlins, unlike Bourdieu, attends closely to the processes of social transformation and emphasizes the importance of history in his historical and ethnographic account of the transformation that Hawaiian society underwent in the wake of Captain Cook's arrival and his subsequent murder. Noting (perhaps too perfunctorily) that such transformations can occur even without intercultural collisions, Sahlins nevertheless focuses on how these cross-cultural contacts may facilitate unprecedented change. When individuals bring their cultural understandings, as derived from structural principles (what Bourdieu would call their habitus), to bear on new situations, the dynamics of practice [what Sahlins calls "the structure of the conjuncture" (1981, p. 35)] can cause unintended outcomes. What starts as an attempt to reproduce social structure may end in social transformation. By interweaving history and structure in this manner, Sahlins not only highlights the importance of agency and its often unintended consequences, he also emphasizes the temporality of agency and throws into question the concept of resistance as conscious activity. Nevertheless, because Sahlins' work, like Bourdieu's, evinces traces of its structuralist roots, the processes of social reproduction/transformation he posits are rather mechanistic, and his "permanent dialectic of structure and practice" (Sahlins 1981, p. 54) has little room in it for tensions inherent within social structure itself.

Addressing this very issue, Ortner (1989) builds on the theories of both Sahlins and Bourdieu in *High Religion: A Cultural and Political History of Sherpa Buddhism*. In her elucidation of the terms practice, structure, actor, and history, Ortner sets out the four cornerstones on which her ethnography is built, thereby sidestepping the dualistic, mechanistic formulations of Bourdieu and Sahlins. Practice for

Ortner entails the recognition of asymmetry and domination in particular historical and cultural settings, along with an awareness of the cultural schemas and constraints within which individuals act. Departing from the claims of both Bourdieu and Sahlins, Ortner emphasizes the existence of inherent structural contradictions that keep a simple reproduction of the hegemonic social order from being a foregone conclusion. As Williams (1977, p. 113) notes, "The reality of any hegemony, in the extended political and cultural sense, is that, while by definition it is always dominant, it is never either total or exclusive." Because of the tensions and contradictions inherent in the habitus, actors are neither free agents nor completely socially determined products. Instead, Ortner (1989, p. 198) suggests that they are "loosely structured." The central question for practice theorists, then, is determining how such loosely structured actors manage at times to transform the systems that produce them.

Such loose structuring can occur linguistically as well as socioculturally. Speakers of a given language are constrained to some degree by the grammatical structures of their particular language, but they are still capable of producing an infinite number of grammatically well-formed utterances within those constraints. Moreover, languages, like cultures, change over time through drift and contact despite their supposedly self-reproducing structures (DeGraff 1999, Lightfoot 1999, Sapir 1933[1949], de Saussure 1986). It is therefore helpful to look closely at language (both its grammatical structures and its patterns of use) in order to gain a more thorough understanding of how people reproduce and transform both language and culture. The following section describes some of the grammatical constraints, either universal across all languages or particular to a smaller set of languages, that may predispose people to conceptualize agency and subjecthood in certain ways.

GRAMMATICAL AGENTS

Any discussion of agency and language must consider how grammatical categories in different languages distinguish among types of subjects, for such categories, "to the extent that they are obligatory and habitual, and relatively inaccessible to the average speaker's consciousness, will form a privileged location for transmitting and reproducing cultural and social categories" (Hill & Mannheim 1992, p. 387). Although each language has its own set of linguistic resources that can be used to exercise, attribute, or deny agency, there are also some features that can be found in every language (Comrie 1981). According to Dixon (1994, p. 6), for example, all languages work in terms of three basic relations–*S*, *A*, and *O*—defined as follows:

> *S*—*S*ubject of an intransitive verb (e.g., **Sita** went to Kathmandu);
>
> *A*—*A*gent, or subject, of a transitive verb (e.g., **Parvati** loves Shiva); and
>
> *O*—*O*bject of a transitive verb (e.g., Maya ate **rice**).

Semantically, there are various roles the subject of a sentence can take, such as the following (cf. Duranti 1994, pp. 122–123; Keenan 1984):

Agent	**Pabi** read the book.
Actor	**Shiva** danced.
Perceiver	**Tika** heard the news.
Instrument	**The stone** broke the window.
Patient/Undergoer	**The old woman** died.

These semantic roles can be treated in various ways syntactically. Defining the linguistic subject in a way that applies to all languages turns out to be a challenging and controversial topic over which linguists differ (Comrie 1981, pp. 98–101). In the majority of languages, including most of the languages of Europe, the subjects of transitive and intransitive verbs are treated the same way syntactically, while the object of a transitive verb is treated differently. This pattern is known as accusativity (Dixon 1994, pp. 16–17).[3] In about a quarter of the world's languages, however, a complementary pattern obtains in which the subject of an intransitive verb and the object of a transitive verb are treated the same way syntactically, while the subject of a transitive verb is treated differently. This pattern is known as ergativity (Bittner & Hale 1996, Dixon 1994, Plank 1979). In ergative languages, there is usually a grammatical marker that distinguishes Agents (of transitive verbs) from Subjects (of intransitive verbs) and Objects (of transitive verbs). Consider the following examples in Samoan, taken from Duranti (1994, p. 122), in which the ergative marker $\underline{e}$ is present only in (a), before the Agent of the transitive verb, and not before the Subject of the intransitive verb in (b):

(a) *'ua fa'atau $\underline{e}$ $\underline{le}$ $\underline{tama}$ le suka.*
TA[4] buy ERG ART boy ART sugar
The boy has bought the sugar.

(b) *'ua alu $\underline{le}$ $\underline{tama}$ 'i le maketi.*
TA go ART boy to ART market
The boy has gone to the market.

---

[3]Languages in which the subjects of transitive and intransitive verbs are treated the same way syntactically while the transitive object is treated differently are also called "nominative-accusative." Languages in which the subjects of intransitive verbs and the objects of transitive verbs are treated the same way syntactically are also called "ergative-absolutive." I follow Dixon (1994) in shortening these terms to "accusativity" and "ergativity," respectively, in order to emphasize which case is being treated uniquely; with accusativity, Objects are placed in the accusative case and are treated differently from Subjects and Agents, whereas with ergativity, Agents are placed in the ergative case and are treated differently from Subjects and Objects.

[4]The abbreviations used in the interlinear glosses have the following meanings: TA refers to a marker of verb tense or aspect; ERG refers to an ergative marker; ART refers to an article (Duranti 1994, pp. 177–78).

Some languages have "split" grammatical systems in which speakers follow an accusative pattern in some cases and an ergative pattern in other cases. In standard Nepali, for example, the ergative marker _le_ is obligatorily used with the Agents of transitive verbs in the past tense only—not in the present or future tense. In the dialect of Nepali spoken in the village of Junigau, Nepal, however, people use the ergative marker _le_ in nonobligatory ways in the present and future tenses when they want to place emphasis on the Agent, as can be seen in the following example taken from a Junigau woman's narrative of marriage (Ahearn 2001):

(c)   _mai le pani mān garchhu._
      I ERG too respect do
      I, too, respect [my husband].

A related sort of split appears in languages that have grammatical systems in which the subjects of some intransitive verbs are categorized with transitive subjects, while the subjects of other intransitive verbs are still considered intransitive. In Guaraní, for example, when "I" is used with more agentive intransitive verbs, such as "go" and "get up," it is placed in the same (ergative) case as when "I" is used with the transitive verb "bring" (Mithun 1991, p. 511). "I" is placed in a different case in Guaraní when used with less agentive intransitive verbs, such as "to be"— the same case that is used for the direct object pronoun "me." In these languages, attributions of agency are built right into their semantic and syntactic structures.

Let me emphasize, however, that in none of these cases is it possible to draw a simplistic connection between the presence of ergative case markings and "more" or "less" agency.[5] Nevertheless, ergative languages present researchers with a valuable tool they can use to explore notions of subjectivity and action in other cultures.

While languages may encode agency differently in their grammatical categories, there are some universal patterns that can be discerned regarding the types of nouns most likely to appear in the Agent position. Drawing on linguistic data from Chinook and Dyirbal, both of which are split ergative systems that use an ergative pattern of case-marking for certain types of noun phrases and an accusative pattern for other types of noun phrases, Silverstein (1976, pp. 116–122) proposes an animacy hierarchy that predicts where on the spectrum of noun phrases the split between ergativity and accusativity will occur.

Dixon generalizes from Silverstein's animacy hierarchy, a revised version of which is shown in Figure 1, arguing that in all languages, the items toward the right of the spectrum are more likely to be in the Agent function, and the items to the left of the spectrum are more likely to be in the Object position. Dixon (1994, p. 84) summarizes this important linguistic universal as follows:

---

[5]It is not useful, in my opinion, to talk of having "more," "less," or even "no" agency. As I hope I have demonstrated in this essay, agency is not a quantity that can be measured. Rather, researchers should focus on delineating different kinds of agency, or different ways in which agency is socioculturally mediated in particular times and places.

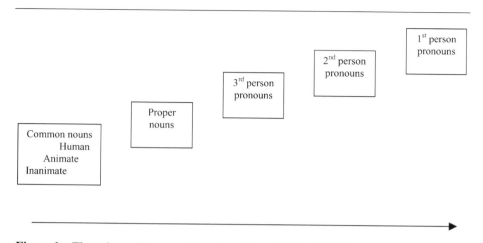

Figure 1   The animacy hierarchy (based on Dixon 1994, p. 85; Foley 1999, p. 210; revised from Silverstein 1976, p. 122).

> Put very roughly, a speaker will think in terms of doing things to other people to a much greater extent than in terms of things being done to him. In the speaker's view of the world, as it impinges on him and as he describes it in language, he will be the quintessential agent.[6]

In other words, from the universal grammatical principles underlying all languages, we know that the most salient person in a linguistic interaction is the speaker, "I" (Foley 1999, p. 210). The second most salient person is the addressee, "you." Both "I" and "you" are more salient, and therefore more likely to be found in the Agent position, than the absent participants in the interaction, ranked in the following order: third person pronouns, proper nouns, common nouns referring to humans, common nouns referring to animate nonhumans, and common nouns referring to inanimate objects. While there have been some challenges and revisions to this model (cf. Dixon 1994, pp. 83–94), the implications of a possibly universal tendency regarding the attribution of linguistic agency are worth considering. Note carefully, however, that we are talking about grammatical, not social, definitions of agency here. There are times when the grammatical and social categories of Agent will overlap, but this remains to be determined in each particular context (cf. Duranti 1994, p. 124).

How can the grammatical details regarding Agent, Subject, and Object in particular languages be relevant to scholars interested in the social aspects of agency?

---

[6]Dixon's use of the masculine generic demonstrates yet another example of how grammatical categories predispose speakers to attribute agency more often to certain kinds of subjects. See McConnell-Ginet (1979), Silverstein (1985), and Waugh (1982) for analyses of markedness in the use of masculine and feminine pronouns.

As DuBois (1987) notes, ergativity originates in discourse itself, in other words, in naturally occurring conversations. Derbyshire (1987, p. 319), for example, reports that in many Amazonian languages, when a noun phrase describing a highly ranked person is the subject in a transitive clause, the accusative pattern is followed, whereas when a noun phrase describing the higher ranked person is the object (a more marked, or unexpected, occurrence), the ergative pattern is followed. In English, LaFrance (1992) has shown that when subjects are asked to supply plausible scenarios of events that might have preceded and followed a set of sentences alternating male and female subjects and objects, they demonstrate a linguistic bias against women that she calls "the disappearing agent effect." Her findings indicate that if a sentence is phrased such that a female is described as doing something or feeling something, especially with respect to a male, then she fades from causal view, but when she is on the receiving end of someone else's actions, then the subject or source of these events, rather than she herself, is highlighted (LaFrance 1992, p. 341). Although these responses were elicited rather than taken from naturally occurring conversations, ethnographically informed investigations of this phenomenon demonstrate exactly how these linguistic usages reflect, reinforce, and sometimes reconfigure agency and status hierarchies in the society.

Duranti's *From Grammar to Politics: Linguistic Anthropology in a Western Samoan Village* (1994) provides just such an ethnographically rich example of how attention to linguistic forms can shed light on human agency.[7] Duranti maintains that the Samoans' use of ergative markers reveals how they attribute agency, especially in cases of praise or blame. Powerful individuals are more likely to use the ergative marker when they want to accuse someone of a malicious act, whereas less powerful individuals try to resist such accusations by suggesting alternative linguistic definitions of events. Thus, Duranti's "grammar of praising and blaming" demonstrates how agency is expressed in, and shaped by, the linguistic forms that a socially and linguistically embedded speaker uses.

AGENCY IN LINGUISTIC ANTHROPOLOGY

Linguistic anthropologists seek to understand how grammatical categories "loosely structure" speakers and therefore look carefully at how speech both shapes and reflects social and cultural realities. For these reasons, they are well situated to contribute to the scholarship on agency. Indeed, long before Giddens first popularized the term agency, linguistic anthropologists (and some scholars in related fields such as discourse analysis, ethnomethodology, and sociolinguistics) were writing about language as a form of social action. For years, linguistic anthropologists have examined specific speech events in order to illuminate how people think about their own and others' actions. By analyzing grammatical markers, pronoun use,

---

[7]See also Duranti & Ochs (1990).

turn taking, narrative structures, dispute resolution, overlapping utterances, and other linguistic features, linguistic anthropologists have looked to language for concrete examples of effective (and ineffective) social action. In the sections that follow, I present several paths linguistic anthropologists have taken to show how culture in all its forms emerges from everyday linguistic agency that is itself shaped by sociocultural formations. There are several bodies of literature not dealt with here, for although they make contributions to the study of language and agency, they are summarized well elsewhere. The burgeoning area of language ideology research, for example, is summed up in Kroskrity (2000) and Schieffelin et al (1998). Language change, creolization, and bilingualism are also not treated here (cf. DeGraff 1999, Lightfoot 1999, Romaine 1995). Nevertheless, while the following sections touch on only some of the many areas relevant to language and agency that have been explored by linguistic anthropologists, they illustrate the important contributions linguistic anthropology has to make to social theory as a whole.

Language and Gender

One of the areas within linguistic anthropology most centrally concerned with questions of agency is the field of language and gender. The scholarship in this area generally avoids relying on a definition of agency as resistance, which can be found in much of the gender literature in other fields, and instead draws on more nuanced understandings from within linguistics and sociology of language as social action. While many of the language and gender scholars do not use the term agency in their work, they explore the relationship between linguistic practices and social structures in ways that contribute to our understanding of the concept of agency. Dozens of articles demonstrating how gender as a social construct emerges from particular linguistic interactions are contained within a handful of indispensable anthologies (Bergvall et al 1996, Bucholtz et al 1994, 1999, Hall & Bucholtz 1995, Hall et al 1992, Livia & Hall 1997, Philips et al 1987, Roman et al 1994, Tannen 1993). The interested reader can find within these volumes studies that describe, for example, how phone sex workers exercise ambiguous agency by using traditionally "powerless," stereotypically feminine speech to become economically independent (Hall 1995); how preschoolers' dispute resolution practices reflect and shape their developing gendered identities (Sheldon 1993); and how gay men produce coming-out narratives full of references to personal agency regarding the learning of distinctively gay ways of talking (Leap 1999).

In an insightful essay that traces the intersections between practice theory and feminist theory, McElhinny (1998) identifies four scholars in the field of language and gender—Goodwin, Ochs, and the writing team of Eckert & McConnell-Ginet—who have made important contributions to both theoretical realms, and she urges that they be added to the canon. Goodwin, deservedly well known for her meticulously researched book, *He-Said-She-Said: Talk as Social Organization among Black Children*, focuses on "situated activities" rather than on whole societies or particular individuals because such a unit of analysis enables her to demonstrate how stereotypes about women's speech become untenable when moving from one activity to another (Goodwin 1990, p. 9). Goodwin discovered that the girls on Maple Street did indeed use talk for different purposes than boys did when interacting among themselves, but when interacting with boys, they frequently took on the boys' speech patterns, at times even outperforming them in verbal contests. She concludes, "This analysis has examined ways in which aspects of gender are manifested in speech activities, but more important, I have investigated how speech events can themselves *provide for* social organization, shaping alignment and social identities of participants to the present interaction" (Goodwin 1990, p. 286; emphasis in the original). Goodwin's work calls attention to the many different ways that agency can be exercised linguistically and to the importance of looking closely at linguistic as well as sociocultural contexts when attempting to understand social dynamics and social change.

Ochs' work treating language socialization as a lifelong activity also provides us with important insight into the microprocesses of social change and continuity (Ochs 1988, 1992, 1996; McElhinny 1998, p. 168). Because people are constantly learning new ways to speak and act for particular sociocultural contexts, a close examination of this learning process in children and adults can shed light on the slippage between social reproduction and social transformation (to which practice theorists such as Bourdieu and Giddens allude but fail to elucidate). Citing Bourdieu and Giddens, Ochs notes, "This focus on language practices as resources for socializing social and cultural competence links language socialization research to post-structural sociological paradigms that portray *social structures as outcomes of social practices . . .*" (Ochs 1996, p. 408; emphasis in the original). Ochs, often in collaboration with Schieffelin, looks closely at indexicality, honorific pronoun use, word order, case-markings, and other grammatical features to investigate how linguistic practices encode and socialize information about society and culture (Ochs & Schieffelin 1983, 1984, Schieffelin & Ochs 1986). In her research on Kaluli children's language socialization, Schieffelin (1990, p. 239) concludes that, "The microethnographic methods used in this study enable one to specify and interpret the words, interactions, relationships, and contexts in which cultural meanings are displayed to young children and reproduced by them. . . . This study shows how language is a resource for social theory." This latter statement, while true, is too modest. Linguistic anthropologists do not merely provide social theorists with the "resource" of linguistic data; they also contribute unique insights to the process of theory building. In focusing on language acquisition and socialization, Ochs & Schieffelin contribute to our understanding of the microprocesses of social reproduction, thereby helping us identify the potential slippages between social reproduction and social transformation.

Eckert & McConnell-Ginet also advance our understanding of linguistic and social practices in their individual and joint research on gendered social categories in a Detroit area high school (Eckert 1989, Eckert & McConnell-Ginet 1992, 1995; cf. McElhinny 1998, p. 171ff.). They write, "Language is a primary tool people use in constituting themselves and others as 'kinds' of people in terms of which attributes, activities, and participation in social practice can be regulated" (Eckert & McConnell-Ginet 1995, p. 470). Perhaps their most significant contribution to practice theory is their emphasis on a "community of practice" (cf. Lave & Wenger 1991), which they define as "an aggregate of people who come together around mutual engagement in an endeavor. Ways of doing things, ways of talking, beliefs, values, power relations—in short, practices—emerge in the course of this mutual endeavor" (Eckert & McConnell-Ginet 1992, p. 464). The concept of communities of practice offers scholars a processual yet structural unit that can easily be viewed as both constitutive of, and constituted by, its participants. In placing linguistic and social practices within the contexts of communities of practice, Eckert and McConnell-Ginet contribute to a more nuanced view of the varying ways in which agency is socioculturally constrained and enabled.

Literacy Practices

Language, of course, can be written as well as spoken. Another field of scholarship well situated to make significant contributions to our understanding of language and agency, therefore, is the study of literacy practices. Within linguistic anthropology and related disciplines in recent years there has been a theoretical debate, summarized nicely by Besnier (1995), Collins (1995), and Street (2001), regarding how literacy should be defined and studied. On one side of the issue are scholars like Goody & Watt (1963), who were early proponents of what Street (1984, 1993, 2001) has called the "autonomous" model of literacy. Goody and other supporters of the autonomous model maintain that the advent of literacy in a society will cause the same social and psychological effects, no matter which society is being studied. These scholars "conceptualise literacy in technical terms, treating it as independent of social context, an autonomous variable whose consequences for society and cognition can be derived from its intrinsic character" (Street 1984, p. 5). Another proponent of the autonomous model, Ong (1982, pp. 14–15), asserts boldly that "without writing, human consciousness cannot achieve its fuller potentials, cannot produce other beautiful and powerful creations. In this sense, orality needs to produce and is destined to produce writing." Ong, Goody, and others who espouse the autonomous model see a "Great Divide" separating "oral" societies from "literate" ones—a gap similar to the one turn-of-the-century anthropologists used to claim existed between "primitive" and "civilized" societies.

On the opposing side of the issue are those scholars engaging in what Street (2001, p.10) calls New Literacy Studies. Researchers such as Street himself (1984, 1993, 2001), Basso (1989[1974]), Baynham (1995), Besnier (1995), and Finnegan (1988) favor an "ideological" model for studying literacies, an approach that has benefited from, and contributed to, practice theory. Besnier (1995, p. 5) describes the goals of this approach as follows: "Rather than seeking an overarching and context-free characterization of the cognitive and social consequences of literacy, proponents of the ideological model focus on the activities, events, and ideological constructs associated with particular manifestations of literacy." This approach examines the specific ramifications of the advent of literacy in each society, claiming that there are no universal attributes of literate societies and maintaining that it is impossible for literacy skills to be acquired neutrally. Most anthropologists agree with Baynham (1995, p. 71) that it is important to understand literacy as a form of social practice (or agency), and to investigate the way it interacts with ideologies and institutions to shape and define the possibilities and life paths of individuals.

My own work on Nepali love letters derives inspiration from the work of Barton, Besnier, Street, and others who have explored the manifestations of various literacies in their social contexts (Barton & Hall 2000, Barton & Hamilton 1998, Barton et al 2000). In Junigau, Nepal, newly literate young women are applying their literacy skills in a novel form of courtship: love letters that echo the development discourses and changing notions of agency that can be found elsewhere in the society (Ahearn 2000b, 2001). This scholarship is an example of what Besnier (1995, p. 9) calls "event-centered studies" of literacy. He defines such studies as ethnographic investigations into the ways that literacy derives its meaning from the broader context in which it is practiced, and the ways that aspects of the situation acquire meaning from acts of reading and writing.

Because cultural meanings are often constituted through literacy practices as well as through verbal interactions, scholars interested in the role of different types of agency (oral and literate) in the reproduction and transformation of cultural meanings can benefit from the work of researchers in this field.

Dialogic Approaches

Many linguistic anthropologists interested in agency (including some mentioned in previous sections) are taking a dialogic approach following Bakhtin (1981, 1984, 1993) and, in a few cases, the Soviet psychologist Vygotsky (1978, 1987, Holland et al 1998, Wertsch et al 1993). In a statement that summarizes the approach to language and agency espoused by these scholars, Bakhtin (1984, p. 183) notes that "Language lives only in the dialogic interaction of those who make use of it." Mannheim & Tedlock (1995, p. 4) explain that dialogue, which etymologically refers to talk (*logos*) that goes back and forth (*dia*), can involve any or all of the following: straightforward verbal exchange, a social field across which multiple voices and multiple cultural logics contend, or a text that is multivocal and egalitarian rather than univocal and authoritarian. In all cases, however, the traditional relationship between structure and action, in which action is treated as a reflection of a prior structure, is rejected in favor of one in which structure emerges through situated action. Words or texts are socially situated by, not created by, individuals (Mannheim & Tedlock 1995, p. 5).

Locating language, culture, and agency in the interstices between people, rather than within individuals themselves, requires a different way of thinking about and studying linguistic and cultural interactions. While it may appear that a dialogic approach precludes the possibility of studying individuals, in their edited volume, *The Dialogic Emergence of Culture*, Tedlock & Mannheim (1995) provide numerous examples of how scholars can study the words and actions of particular people while also situating those individuals within sociocultural fields that are always fluid and in process. In Hill's contribution to the volume, for example, she draws on Bakhtin's notion of heteroglossia to analyze how the narrator Don Gabriel, a native Mexicano speaker, tells of his son's murder. The narrative contains dysfluencies when he speaks in Spanish of profit motives for the murder, but it remains elegantly fluent when he speaks in Mexicano about the loss of his son. "The narrative reveals a veritable kaleidoscope of 'emotional selves,' which are all art, distributed in fragments across the rhetorical systems of the narrative," writes Hill (1995, p. 139). Among these selves is one that positions itself squarely within the "domain of ongoing ideological resistance to a capitalist ideology," an ideology indexed by the use of Spanish. By locating multiple socially embedded voices among and within individuals in this narrative, Hill demonstrates the usefulness for linguistic and cultural anthropologists alike of a dialogic approach to the study of language and agency.

Another contribution to the Tedlock & Mannheim volume, a reprint of a 1983 paper by McDermott & Tylbor (1995[1983]), looks at how one short classroom interaction among several students and a teacher produces an outcome not predictable from analysis of the words alone. Rosa, a first-grade student who cannot read, constantly calls out for a turn at reading aloud—and yet on close examination, Rosa, her classmates, and the teacher all seem to be colluding through the use of subtle gestures and timing cues in order not to give Rosa a chance to read aloud (McDermott & Tylbor 1995[1983], p. 223). This collusional approach to understanding language and agency "refers to how members of any social order must constantly help each other posit a particular state of affairs, even when such a state would be in no way at hand without everyone so proceeding" (McDermott & Tylbor 1995[1983], p. 219). Just as meanings and outcomes are coconstructed, so is agency.

Basso (1996) explores the dynamics of "place-making" among the Western Apache, whose storytelling activities dialogically produce and reproduce historical knowledge and moral wisdom. Place-making through storytelling, Basso claims (1996, p. 7), is a way of constructing social traditions and identities, a way of "doing human history." Drawing on Bakhtin's (1981, p. 7) notion of chronotopes, which are places where time and space have fused to create culturally and historically charged locations, Basso describes how historical tales themselves have agency and shape the moral judgments that Apaches make about themselves and other people (Basso 1996, p. 62). The landscape itself also exercises agency in this process, as the historically and morally significant places serve to remind Apaches of the stories associated with them. Through telling stories associated with particular places, the Western Apache coconstruct a spatial, temporal, and cultural world that then serves to shape their future conduct. This is truly an instance of agency extending "beyond the skin" (Bateson 1972, Wertsch et al 1993).

Another important work that takes a dialogic approach to understanding language and agency is Hill & Irvine's anthology, *Responsibility and Evidence in Oral Discourse* (1993). Hill & Irvine write that the connection between knowledge and agency is of central importance to an approach that emphasizes dialogicality and the social construction of meaning. Interpreting events, establishing facts, conveying opinion, and constituting interpretations as knowledge are all activities involving socially situated participants, who are agents in the construction of knowledge and agents when they act on what they have come to know, believe, suspect, or opine (Hill & Irvine 1993, p. 2). As one example of such activities, Besnier's contribution to this volume demonstrates how residents on Nukulaelae Atoll in Polynesia take advantage of the multifunctionality of reported speech in order to inject a greater or lesser amount of affect into an utterance, thereby manipulating the audience's perception of the quoted individual (Besnier 1993). Besnier argues that the meanings of Nukulaelae utterances—like those of everyone else—cannot be understood without locating the speakers in temporally specific sociocultural fields of relationality. Linguistic agency is molded by these sociocultural fields, which it then proceeds to recreate or reconfigure.

CONCLUSION

To conclude, let me reiterate two points I have attempted to make throughout this review. First, scholars who choose to use the term agency should define it carefully. The provisional definition I offered at the outset of this essay—that agency refers to the socioculturally mediated capacity to act—leaves a great deal unspecified. For example, where is agency located? Must agency be human, individual, collective, intentional, or conscious? Some studies of agency reinforce received notions about western atomic individualism, while others deny agency to individuals, attributing it instead only to discourses or social forces. It is absolutely crucial that theorists consider the assumptions about personhood, desire, and intentionality that might unwittingly be built into their analyses. No matter how agency is defined—and it can be defined in any number of ways—implications for social theory abound. Scholars using the term must define it clearly, both for themselves and for their readers. For anthropologists in particular, it is important to avoid treating agency as a synonym for free will or resistance. One fruitful direction for future research may be to begin to distinguish among types of agency—oppositional agency, complicit agency, agency of power, agency of intention, etc.—while also recognizing that multiple types are exercised in any given action. By doing this, we might gain a more thorough understanding of the "complex and ambiguous agency" (MacLeod 1992) that always surrounds us.

Second, I hope I have demonstrated how focusing on linguistic interactions can provide important clues for scholars interested in the micro- and macro-processes of agency. Because language and culture are so tightly interwoven, neither should be studied in isolation from the other, especially when a researcher seeks to understand a concept as complex as agency. While practice theory offers several promising avenues that treat agency and structure as mutually constitutive, I maintain that attending closely to linguistic structures and practices can shed even more light on practice theorists' main dilemma: how social reproduction becomes social transformation. Because grammatical categories within particular languages construct the roles of Subject, Agent, and Object differently, researchers can benefit from examining such categories carefully when listening to how people attribute responsibility, credit, or blame for an event. Three areas in which scholars are skillfully combining a close examination of language with a concern for broader social issues are the fields of language and gender, literacy practices, and dialogic approaches to language. Such nuanced treatments of language and action serve as excellent models for the development of a more sophisticated understanding of agency.

ACKNOWLEDGMENTS

Many people read and commented on earlier drafts of this essay, including my wonderful in-house editor, Rick Black; my eloquent and loyal critic, Peter Laipson; and the following generous and knowledgeable colleagues: John Adams, Anne Blackburn, Marcia-Anne Dobres, Michele Gamburd, Karl Heider, Louise Jennings, Alice Kasakoff, Ann Kingsolver, Bruce Mannheim, and Gail Wagner. I am grateful to Sherry Ortner for introducing me to practice theory, to Bruce Mannheim for pointing out to me the connection between language and agency, and to Tom Fricke for helping me understand how agency works in Nepal. I also benefited enormously from the lively discussions of the Agency Reading Group at the University of South Carolina and from the research assistance of Gail Davis, Changyong Liao, and Jennifer Whetstone. This review is a product of collective rather than individual agency, but only I am to blame for any weaknesses that remain.

Visit the Annual Reviews home page at www.AnnualReviews.org

LITERATURE CITED

Abu-Lughod L. 1990. The romance of resistance: tracing transformations of power through Bedouin women. *Am. Ethnol.* 17(1):41–55

Ahearn LM. 1998. "A twisted rope binds my waist": locating constraints on meaning in a Tij songfest. *J. Ling. Anthropol.* 8(1):60–86

Ahearn LM. 2000a. Agency. *J. Ling. Anthropol.* 9(1):9–12

Ahearn LM. 2000b. True traces: love letters and social transformation in Nepal. See Barton & Hall 2000, pp. 199–207

Ahearn LM. 2001. *Invitations to Love: Literacy, Love Letters, and Social Change in Nepal.* Ann Arbor: Univ. Michigan Press. Forthcoming

Andermahr S. 1997. Agency. In *A Concise Glossary of Feminist Theory*, ed. S Andermahr, pp. 11–12. New York: Arnold

Appadurai A. 1991. Afterword. In *Gender,*

Genre, and Power in South Asian Expressive Tradition, ed. A Appadurai, FJ Korom, MA Mills , pp. 467–76. Philadelphia: Univ. Penn. Press

Archer MS. 1988. *Culture and Agency: The Place of Culture in Social Theory.* Cambridge, UK: Cambridge Univ. Press

Austin JL. 1962. *How to Do Things with Words.* London: Oxford Univ. Press

Bakhtin MM. 1981. *The Dialogic Imagination: Four Essays*, ed. M Holquist. Transl. C Emerson, M Holquist. Austin: Univ. Texas Press (From Russian)

Bakhtin MM. 1984. *Problems of Dostoevsky's Poetics.* Theory and History of Literature, Vol. 8. Transl. C Emerson. Minneapolis: Univ. Minn. Press (From Russian)

Bakhtin MM. 1993. *Toward a Philosophy of the Act*, ed. V Liapunov, M Holquist. Transl. V Liapunov. Austin: Univ. Texas Press (From Russian)

Bartky SL. 1995. Subjects and agents: the question for feminism. See Gardiner 1995, pp. 194–207

Barton D, Hall N, eds. 2000. *Letter Writing as a Social Practice.* Amsterdam: Benjamins

Barton D, Hamilton M, eds. 1998. *Local Literacies: Reading and Writing in One Community.* London: Routledge

Barton D, Hamilton M, Ivanič R, eds. 2000. *Situated Literacies: Reading and Writing in Context.* London: Routledge

Basso K. 1989(1974). The ethnography of writing. See Bauman & Sherzer 1989, pp. 425–32

Basso K. 1996. *Wisdom Sits in Places: Landscape and Language Among the Western Apache.* Albuquerque: Univ. New Mexico Press

Bateson G. 1972. *Steps to an Ecology of Mind: A Revolutionary Approach to Man's Understanding of Himself.* New York: Ballantine

Bauman R, Sherzer J, eds. 1989(1974). *Explorations in the Ethnography of Speaking.* New York: Cambridge Univ. Press. 2nd ed.

Baynham M. 1995. *Literacy Practices: Investigating Literacy in Social Contexts.* London: Longman

Berger PL, Luckmann T. 1966. *The Social Construction of Reality: A Treatise in the Sociology of Knowledge.* New York: Doubleday

Bergvall VL, Bing JM, Freed AF, eds. 1996. *Rethinking Language and Gender Research: Theory and Practice.* London: Longman

Besnier N. 1993. Reported speech and affect on Nukulaelae Atoll. See Hill & Irvine 1993, pp. 161–81

Besnier N. 1995. *Literacy, Emotion, and Authority: Reading and Writing on a Polynesian Atoll.* New York: Cambridge Univ. Press

Bittner M, Hale K. 1996. Ergativity: toward a theory of a heterogeneous class. *Ling. Inq.* 27(4):531–604

Bourdieu P. 1977. *Outline of a Theory of Practice.* Cambridge, UK: Cambridge Univ. Press

Bourdieu P. 1991. *Language and Symbolic Power.* Transl. G Raymond, M. Adamson. Cambridge, MA: Harvard Univ. Press (From French)

Brenneis D, Macaulay RKS, eds. 1996. *The Matrix of Language: Contemporary Linguistic Anthropology.* Boulder, CO: Westview

Bryant GA, Jary D, eds. 1991. *Giddens' Theory of Structuration: A Critical Appreciation.* New York: Routledge

Bucholtz M, Liang AC, Sutton LA, eds. 1999. *Reinventing Identities: The Gendered Self in Discourse.* New York: Oxford Univ. Press

Bucholtz M, Liang AC, Sutton LA, Hines C, eds. 1994. *Cultural Performances: Proceedings of the Third Berkeley Women and Language Conference.* Berkeley, CA: Berkeley Women Language Group

Burns TR. 1994. Two conceptions of human agency: rational choice theory and the social theory of action. See Sztompka 1994, pp. 197–249

Burns TR, Dietz T. 1994. Introduction to the series. See Sztompka 1994, pp. vii–xiv

Butler J. 1997. *Excitable Speech: A Politics of the Performative.* New York: Routledge

Chomsky N. 1965. *Aspects of the Theory of Syntax.* Cambridge, MA: MIT Press

Chomsky N. 1986. *Knowledge of Language: Its Nature, Origin and Use.* New York: Praeger

Colapietro VM. 1989. *Peirce's Approach to the*

Self: A Semiotic Perspective on Human Subjectivity. Albany: SUNY Press

Collins J. 1995. Literacy and literacies. *Annu. Rev. Anthropol.* 24:75–93

Comaroff J, Comaroff JL. 1997. *Of Revelation and Revolution,* Vol. 2. Chicago, IL: Univ. Chicago Press

Comrie B. 1981. *Language Universals and Linguistic Typology: Syntax and Morphology.* Oxford, UK: Blackwell

Cooper F. 1994. Conflict and connection: rethinking colonial African history. *Am. Hist. Rev.* 99:1515–45

Cooper F, Stoler AL, eds. 1997. *Tensions of Empire: Colonial Cultures in a Bourgeois World.* Berkeley: Univ. Calif. Press

Daniel EV. 1984. *Fluid Signs: Being a Person the Tamil Way.* Berkeley: Univ. Calif. Press

Davidson D. 1980(1971). Agency. In *Essays on Actions and Events,* ed. D Davidson, pp. 43–61. Oxford: Clarendon Press

Davies B. 1991. The concept of agency: a feminist poststructuralist analysis. *Soc. Anal.* 30:42–53

de Certeau M. 1984. *The Practice of Everyday Life.* Transl. S Rendall. Berkeley: Univ. Calif. Press (From French)

DeGraff M, ed. 1999. *Language Creation and Language Change: Creolization, Diachrony, and Development.* Cambridge, MA: MIT Press

Derbyshire DC. 1987. Morphosyntactic areal characteristics of Amazonian languages. *Int. J. Am. Ling.* 53:311–26

de Saussure F. 1986. *Course in General Linguistics,* ed. C Bally, A Sechehaye, with collab. A Riedlinger. Transl., annot. R Harris. La Salle, IL: Open Court (From French)

Derrida J. 1972. Signature, event, context. *Glyph* 1:172–97

Desjarlais R. 1997. *Shelter Blues: Sanity and Selfhood Among the Homeless.* Philadelphia: Univ. Penn. Press

Dissanayake W, ed. 1996. *Narratives of Agency: Self-Making in China, India, and Japan.* Minneapolis: Univ. Minn. Press

Dixon RMW. 1994. *Ergativity.* New York: Cambridge Univ. Press

Dobres M-A. 2000. *Technology and Social Agency: Outlining a Practice Framework for Archaeology.* Oxford: Blackwell

Dobres M-A, Robb J, eds. 2000. *Agency in Archaeology.* New York: Routledge

DuBois J. 1987. The discourse basis of ergativity. *Language* 63:805–55

Duranti A. 1994. *From Grammar to Politics: Linguistic Anthropology in a Western Samoan Village.* Berkeley: Univ. Calif. Press

Duranti A. 1997. *Linguistic Anthropology.* Cambridge, UK: Cambridge Univ. Press

Duranti A, Goodwin C, eds. 1992. *Rethinking Context: Language as an Interactive Phenomenon.* Cambridge, UK: Cambridge Univ. Press

Duranti A, Ochs E. 1990. Genitive constructions and agency in Samoan discourse. *Stud. Lang.* 14(1):1–23

Eckert P. 1989. *Jocks and Burnouts: Social Categories and Identity in High School.* New York: Teach. College

Eckert P, McConnell-Ginet S. 1992. Think practically and look locally: language and gender as community-based practice. *Annu. Rev. Anthropol.* 21:461–90

Eckert P, McConnell-Ginet S. 1995. Constructing meaning, constructing selves: snapshots of language, gender, and class from Belten High. See Hall & Bucholtz 1995, pp. 469–507

Eco U. 1990. *The Limits of Interpretation.* Bloomington: Indiana Univ. Press

Farnell B. 2000. Getting out of the *habitus*: an alternative model of dynamically embodied social action. *J. R. Anthropol. Inst.* 6:397–418

Finnegan R. 1988. *Literacy and Orality: Studies in the Technology of Communication.* Oxford, UK: Blackwell

Foley WA. 1999. Information structure. In *Concise Encyclopedia of Grammatical Categories,* ed. K Brown, J Miller, consulting ed. RE Asher, pp. 204–13. Amsterdam: Elsevier

Foucault M. 1977. *Discipline and Punish: The Birth of the Prison.* New York: Pantheon

Foucault M. 1978. *The History of Sexuality,* Vols. 1, 2. New York: Pantheon

Fraser N. 1992. Introduction: revaluing French feminism. In *Revaluing French Feminism: Critical Essays on Difference, Agency, and Culture*, ed. N Fraser, SL Bartky, pp. 1–24. Bloomington: Indiana Univ. Press

Gamburd MR. 2000. *The Kitchen Spoon's Handle: Transnationalism and Sri Lanka's Migrant Housemaids.* Ithaca, NY: Cornell Univ. Press

Gardiner JK, ed. 1995. *Provoking Agents: Gender and Agency in Theory and Practice.* Urbana: Univ. Illinois Press

Garfinkel H. 1967. *Studies in Ethnomethodology.* Englewood Cliffs, NJ: Prentice-Hall

Giddens A. 1979. *Central Problems in Social Theory: Action, Structure and Contradiction in Social Analysis.* Berkeley: Univ. Calif. Press

Giddens A. 1984. *The Constitution of Society: Outline of the Theory of Structuration.* Berkeley: Univ. Calif. Press

Goddard VA, ed. 2000. *Gender, Agency and Change: Anthropological Perspectives.* New York: Routledge

Goffman E. 1974. *Frame Analysis: An Essay on the Organization of Experience.* New York: Harper Row

Goffman E. 1981. *Forms of Talk.* Philadelphia: Univ. Penn. Press

Goldhagen DJ. 1996. *Hitler's Willing Executioners: Ordinary Germans and the Holocaust.* New York: Knopf

Goodwin MH. 1990. *He-Said-She-Said: Talk as Social Organization Among Black Children.* Bloominton: Indiana Univ. Press

Goody J, Watt I. 1963. The consequences of literacy. *Comp. Stud. Hist. Soc.* 5:306–26, 332–45

Gumperz JJ, Hymes D, eds. 1964. *The Ethnography of Communication.* (*Am. Anthropol.* 66(6), Special Publication) Washington, DC: Am. Anthropol. Assoc.

Gumperz JJ, Levinson SC, eds. 1996. *Rethinking Linguistic Relativity.* Cambridge, UK: Cambridge Univ. Press

Hall K. 1995. Lip service on the fantasy lines. See Hall & Bucholtz 1995, pp. 183–216

Hall K, Bucholtz M, eds. 1995. *Gender Articulated: Language and the Socially Constructed Self.* New York: Rutgers

Hall K, Bucholtz M, Moonwomon B, eds. 1992. *Locating Power: Proceedings of the Second Berkeley Women and Language Conference.* Berkeley, CA: Berkeley Women Language Group

Halperin DM. 1995. *Saint Foucault: Towards a Gay Hagiography.* New York: Oxford Univ. Press

Hanks WF. 1996. *Language and Communicative Practices.* Boulder, CO: Westview

Hill JH. 1995. The voices of Don Gabriel: responsibility and self in a modern Mexicano narrative. See Tedlock & Mannheim 1995, pp. 97–147

Hill JH, Irvine JT, eds. 1993. *Responsibility and Evidence in Oral Discourse.* Cambridge, UK: Cambridge Univ. Press

Hill JH, Mannheim B. 1992. Language and world view. *Annu. Rev. Anthropol.* 21:381–406

Holland D, Lachicotte W Jr, Skinner D, Cain C. 1998. *Identity and Agency in Cultural Worlds.* Cambridge, MA: Harvard Univ. Press

Hoy DC, ed. 1986. *Foucault: A Critical Reader.* Oxford: Blackwell

Hymes D. 1972. Models of the interaction of language and social life. In *Directions in Sociolinguistics: The Ethnography of Communication*, ed. JJ Gumperz, D Hymes, pp. 35–71. New York: Holt, Rinehart, Winston

Jackson M, Karp I, eds. 1990. *Personhood and Agency: The Experience of Self and Other in African Cultures.* Washington, DC: Smithsonian Inst.

Jakobson R. 1960. Closing statement: linguistics and poetics. In *Style in Language*, ed. T Sebeok, pp. 398–429. Cambridge, MA: MIT Press

Jeffery P, Basu A, eds. 1998. *Appropriating Gender: Women's Activism and Politicized Religion in South Asia.* New York: Routledge

Jeffery P, Jeffery R. 1996. *Don't Marry Me to a Plowman!: Women's Everyday Lives in Rural North India.* Boulder, CO: Westview

Karp I. 1986. Agency and social theory: a

review of Anthony Giddens. *Am. Ethnol.* 13(1):131–37

Keane W. 1997. Religious language. *Annu. Rev. Anthropol.* 26:47–71

Keenan EL. 1984. Semantic correlates of the ergative/absolutive distinction. *Linguistics* 22:197–223

Kroskrity PV, ed. 2000. *Regimes of Language: Ideologies, Polities, and Identities*. Santa Fe, NM: School Am. Res. Press

Kumar N, ed. 1994. *Women as Subjects: South Asian Histories*. Charlottesville: Univ. Virginia Press

LaFrance M. 1992. When agents disappear: how gender affects the implicit causality of interpersonal verbs. See Hall et al. 1992, pp. 338–43

Lalu P. 2000. The grammar of domination and the subjection of agency: colonial texts and modes of evidence. *Hist. Theory* 39(4):45–68

Lave J, Wenger E. 1991. *Situated Learning: Legitimate Peripheral Participation*. Cambridge, UK: Cambridge Univ. Press

Leap W. 1999. Language, socialization, and silence in gay adolescence. See Bucholtz et al. 1999, pp. 259–72

Lightfoot D. 1999. *The Development of Language: Acquisition, Change, and Evolution*. Malden, MA: Blackwell

Livia A, Hall K, eds. 1997. *Queerly Phrased: Language, Gender, and Sexuality*. Oxford, UK: Oxford Univ. Press

Lucy JA. 1992. *Language Diversity and Cognitive Development: A Reformulation of the Linguistic Relativity Hypothesis*. Cambridge, UK: Cambridge Univ. Press

MacLeod AE. 1992. Hegemonic relations and gender resistance: the new veiling as accommodating protest in Cairo. *Signs* 17(3):533–57

Mann PS. 1994. *Micro-Politics: Agency in a Postfeminist Era*. Minneapolis: Univ. Minn. Press

Mannheim B, Tedlock D. 1995. Introduction. See Tedlock & Mannheim 1995, pp. 1–32

Marriott McK. 1976. Hindu transactions: diversity without dualism. In *Transaction and Meaning: Directions in the Anthropology of Exchange and Symbolic Behavior*, ed. B Kapferer, pp. 109–42. Philadelphia: Inst. Study Hum. Issues

Marx K. 1978(1852). The eighteenth brumaire of Louis Bonaparte. In *The Marx-Engels Reader*, ed. RC Tucker, pp. 594–617, 2nd ed.

McConnell-Ginet S. 1979. Prototypes, pronouns, and persons. In *Ethnolinguistics: Boas, Sapir, and Whorf Revisited*, ed. M Mathiot, pp. 63–83. The Hague: Moulton

McDermott RP, Tylbor H. 1995(1983). On the necessity of collusion in conversation. See Tedlock & Mannheim 1995, pp. 218–36

McElhinny B. 1998. Genealogies of gender theory: practice theory and feminism in sociocultural and linguistic anthropology. *Soc. Anal.* 42(3):164–89

McNay L. 2000. *Gender and Agency: Reconfiguring the Subject in Feminist and Social Theory*. Oxford, UK: Blackwell

Messer-Davidow E. 1995. Acting otherwise. See Gardiner 1995, pp. 23–51

Mithun M. 1991. Active/agentive case marking and its motivations. *Language* 67(3):510–46

Moses AD. 1998. Structure and agency in the Holocaust: Daniel J. Goldhagen and his critics. *Hist. Theory* 37(2):194–222

Obeyesekere G. 1992. *The Apotheosis of Captain Cook: European Myth-Making in the Pacific*. Princeton, NJ: Princeton Univ. Press

Ochs E. 1988. *Culture and Language Development: Language Acquisition and Language Socialization in a Samoan Village*. Cambridge, UK: Cambridge Univ. Press

Ochs E. 1992. Indexing gender. See Duranti & Goodwin 1992, pp. 335–58

Ochs E. 1996. Linguistic resources for socializing humanity. See Gumperz & Levinson 1996, pp. 406–37

Ochs E, Schegloff EA, Thompson SA, eds. 1996. *Interaction and Grammar*. Cambridge UK: Cambridge Univ. Press

Ochs E, Schieffelin BB. 1983. *Acquiring Conversational Competence*. Boston: Routledge & Kegan Paul

Ochs E, Schieffelin BB. 1984. Language acquisition and socialization: three developmental stories. In *Culture Theory: Essays on Mind,*

Self, and Emotion, ed. RA Shweder, RA Levine, pp. 276–320. Cambridge, UK: Cambridge Univ. Press

O'Hara DT. 1992. *Radical Parody: American Culture and Critical Agency After Foucault.* New York: Columbia Univ. Press

Ong WJ. 1982. *Orality and Literacy: The Technologizing of the Word.* London: Methuen

Ortner SB. 1984. Theory in anthropology since the sixties. *Comp. Stud. Soc. Hist.* 26(1):126–66

Ortner SB. 1989. *High Religion: A Cultural and Political History of Sherpa Buddhism.* Princeton, NJ: Princeton Univ. Press

Ortner SB. 1995. Resistance and the problem of ethnographic refusal. *Comp. Stud. Soc. Hist.* 37(1):173–93

Ortner SB. 1996. Toward a feminist, minority, postcolonial, subaltern, etc., theory of practice. In *Making Gender: The Politics and Erotics of Culture*, pp. 1–20. Boston, MA: Beacon

Ortner SB. 2001. Specifying agency: the Comaroffs and their critics. *Interventions.* Forthcoming

Peirce CS. 1955. *Philosophical Writings of Peirce.* New York: Dover

Philips SU. 1972. Participant structures and communicative competence: Warm Springs children in community and classroom. In *Functions of Language in the Classroom*, ed. CB Cazden, VP John, D Hymes, pp. 370–94. New York: Columbia Teach.

Philips SU, Steele S, Tanz C, eds. 1987. *Language, Gender, and Sex in Comparative Perspective.* Cambridge, UK: Cambridge Univ. Press

Pickering A. 1995. *The Mangle of Practice: Time, Agency, and Science.* Chicago: Univ. Chicago Press

Pieters J. 2000. New historicism: postmodern historiography between narrativism and heterology. *Hist. Theory* 39(1):21–38

Plank F, ed. 1979. *Ergativity: Towards a Theory of Grammatical Relations.* London: Acad. Press

Pomper P. 1996. Historians and individual agency. *Hist. Theory* 35(3):281–308

Pruyn M. 1999. *Discourse Wars in Gotham-West: A Latino Immigrant Urban Tale of Resistance and Agency.* Boulder, CO: Westview

Reddy M. 1979. The conduit metaphor—a case of frame conflict in our language about language. In *Metaphor and Thought*, ed. A Ortony, pp. 284–324. Cambridge, UK: Cambridge Univ. Press

Romaine S. 1995. *Bilingualism.* Oxford, UK: Blackwell. 2nd ed.

Roman C, Juhasz S, Miller C, eds. 1994. *The Women and Language Debate: A Sourcebook.* New York: Routledge

Rovane C. 1998. *The Bounds of Agency: An Essay in Revisionary Metaphysics.* Princeton, NJ: Princeton Univ. Press

Sacks H. 1992. *Lectures on Conversation*, Vols. 1,2. Cambridge, UK: Blackwell

Sahlins M. 1981. *Historical Metaphors and Mythical Realities: Structure in the Early History of the Sandwich Islands Kingdom.* Ann Arbor: Univ. Mich. Press

Said EW. 1983. *The World, the Text, and the Critic.* Cambridge, MA: Harvard Univ. Press

Sapir E. 1933(1949). Language. See Sapir 1949, pp. 7–32

Sapir E. 1949. *Selected Writings of Edward Sapir*, ed. D Mandelbaum. Berkeley: Univ. Calif. Press

Schieffelin BB. 1990. *The Give and Take of Everyday Life: Language Socialization of Kaluli Children.* Cambridge, UK: Cambridge Univ. Press

Schieffelin BB, Ochs E. 1986. *Language Socialization Across Cultures.* Cambridge, UK: Cambridge Univ. Press

Schieffelin BB, Woolard K, Kroskrity PV, eds. 1998. *Language Ideologies.* Oxford, UK: Oxford Univ. Press

Scott JC. 1985. *Weapons of the Weak: Everyday Forms of Peasant Resistance.* New Haven, CT: Yale Univ. Press

Scott JC. 1990. *Domination and the Arts of Resistance: Hidden Transcripts.* New Haven, CT: Yale Univ. Press

Scott JW. 1988. *Gender and the Politics of History.* New York: Columbia Univ. Press

Searle JR. 1969. *Speech Acts: An Essay in the Philosophy of Language.* Cambridge, UK: Cambridge Univ. Press

Segal JM. 1991. *Agency and Alienation: A Theory of Human Presence.* Savage, MD: Rowman Littlefield

Sewell WH. Jr. 1992. A theory of structure: duality, agency, and transformation. *Am. J. Sociol.* 98(1):1–29

Sheldon A. 1993. Pickle fights: gendered talk in preschool disputes. See Tannen 1993, pp. 83–109

Silverstein M. 1976. Hierarchy of features and ergativity. In *Grammatical Categories in Australian Languages,* ed. RMW Dixon, pp. 112–71. Canberra: Aust. Inst. Aborig. Stud.

Silverstein M. 1985. Language and the culture of gender: at the intersection of structure, usage, and ideology. In *Semiotic Mediation: Sociocultural and Psychological Perspectives,* ed. E Mertz, RJ Parmentier, pp. 219–59. Orlando, FL: Acad.

Skinner D, Pach A III, Holland D. 1998. *Selves in Time and Place: Identities, Experience, and History in Nepal.* Lanham, MD: Rowman Littlefield

Small MF. 1993. *Female Choices: Sexual Behavior of Female Primates.* Cornell, NY: Cornell Univ. Press

Spender D. 1980. *Man Made Language.* Boston: Routledge Kegan Paul

Stoler AL. 1995. *Race and the Education of Desire: Foucault's History of Sexuality and the Colonial Order of Things.* Durham, NC: Duke Univ. Press

Street B. 1984. *Literacy in Theory and Practice.* Cambridge, UK: Cambridge Univ. Press

Street B, ed. 1993. *Cross-cultural approaches to literacy.* Cambridge, UK: Cambridge Univ. Press

Street B, ed. 2001. *Literacy and Development: Ethnographic Perspectives.* New York: Routledge

Sztompka P. 1991. *Society in Action: The Theory of Social Becoming.* Chicago: Univ. Chicago Press

Sztompka P, ed. 1994. *Agency and Structure: Reorienting Social Theory.* International Studies in Global Change, Vol. 4. Langhorne, PA: Gordon Breach

Tannen D, ed. 1993. *Gender and Conversational Interaction.* New York: Oxford Univ. Press

Taylor C. 1985. *Human Agency and Language: Philosophical Papers,* Vol. 1. Cambridge, UK: Cambridge Univ. Press

Tedlock D, Mannheim B. 1995. *The Dialogic Emergence of Culture.* Urbana, IL: Univ. Ill. Press

Urban G. 1991. *A Discourse-Centered Approach to Culture: Native South American Myths and Rituals.* Austin, TX: Univ. Texas Press

Vygotsky LS. 1978. *Mind in Society: The Development of Higher Psychological Processes,* ed. M Cole, S Scribner, E Souberman. Cambridge, MA: Harvard Univ. Press

Vygotsky LS. 1987. *Thinking and Speech,* ed., transl. N Minick. New York: Plenum (From Russian)

Waugh LR. 1982. Marked and unmarked: a choice between unequals in semiotic structure. *Semiotica* 38:299–318

Wertsch JV, Tulviste P, Hagstrom F. 1993. A sociocultural approach to agency. In *Contexts for Learning: Sociocultural Dynamics in Children's Development,* ed. EA Forman, N Minick, CA Stone, pp. 336–56. New York: Oxford Univ. Press

Whorf BL. 1956. *Language, Thought, and Reality: Selected Writings of Benjamin Lee Whorf.* Cambridge, MA: MIT Press

Williams R. 1977. *Marxism and Literature.* New York: Oxford Univ. Press

Wittgenstein L. 1958. *Philosophical Investigations.* Transl. GEM Anscombe. Oxford: Blackwell. 2nd ed.

Annu. Rev. Anthropol. 2001. 30:139–61

THE ANTHROPOLOGY OF REFORM AND THE REFORM OF ANTHROPOLOGY: Anthropological Narratives of Recovery and Progress in China

Stevan Harrell

*Burke Museum of Natural History and Culture, University of Washington, Seattle,
Washington 98195-3010; e-mail: stevehar@u.washington.edu*

Key Words history of anthropology, reform and opening, communities, lives,
nationlism

■ **Abstract** Since the beginning of China's Reform and Opening policy in 1978,
the anthropological study of China has revived, and anthropology as a discipline has
revived in China. Chinese anthropologists have become part of the world community
of anthropologists. Anthropology in and about China has described a society occupied both with recovery from the cultural devastation of High Socialism and with
progress toward an uncertain modernity. These narratives of recovery and progress can
be followed through the anthropological study of communities—rural, urban, and in
between—of individuals' lives, including gender and sexuality, family and marriage,
childhood and education, consumption and leisure, and of the nation and its constituent
ethnic and regional parts.

THE GREAT TRANSFORMATION

In 1978 society in China[1] was closed to outsiders and closed in upon itself; similarly, Chinese anthropology was discredited and practically out of contact with
anthropology in the rest of the world. Now China has undergone the social process
of *gaige kaifang*, or "reform and opening," hereafter Reform, which has been a
profound revolution away from the Revolution. Chinese anthropology has opened
up as well. The movement away from the study of bounded cultures and discrete
communities that has marked anthropology in the past two decades has run parallel
to the opening up of China's society and communities, so that Chinese and foreign
anthropologists have begun to participate in an evermore integrated conversation
about an ever more integrated society.

---

[1]Throughout this article, I use "China" to refer to the People's Republic of China. Taiwan
is called Taiwan and Hong Kong is called Hong Kong. Due to lack of space, the article
concentrates on China.

0084-6570/01/1021-0139$14.00   **139**

As anthropologists write about this transformation, they write about two grand, dialectically interlocked sets of themes: themes of recovery from the social and intellectual devastation of High Socialism and themes of progress toward a vaguely defined but highly desired modernity. Like society in general, the anthropology of China has its narratives of recovery and narratives of progress. I first narrate these changes in the institutions of anthropology, and then in the content of anthropological research and writing.

THE INSTITUTIONS OF ANTHROPOLOGY

The Prehistory of the New Anthropology

Ethnography, in the sense of describing the lives of cultural others, was a long and developed tradition in Imperial China (Hostetler 2001). But social and cultural anthropology (*shehui wenhua renleixue*) and ethnology (*minzuxue*) did not develop until the 1930s, when mostly foreign-trained scholars began to apply such paradigms as British functionalism and American historicism both to the study of minority peoples and to the study of Han villages. The works of these Chinese anthropologists, along with those of a few foreign scholars who had conducted fieldwork in China, were well integrated into the cosmopolitan discourse of immediate postwar anthropology.

All this was cut short by the founding of the Communist-ruled People's Republic in 1949. Anthropology and sociology were abolished as "bourgeois social sciences," and anthropologists were redefined as ethnologists and given the task of using Soviet-style ethnological analysis to determine who the non-Han minority populations of China were and to describe their societies according to the Soviet historical teleology (Chen 1998, Guldin 1994, Wang et al 1998). This collective patriotic task produced great volumes of ethnographic description, all fitted to the Soviet paradigm of social evolution, but Chinese ethnologists had little contact with their foreign counterparts. During the period from 1949 through 1979, very few foreigners did anthropological fieldwork in China; cosmopolitan anthropological knowledge of China came only from the reports of journalists and from emigré interviews conducted by sociologists in Hong Kong. During the Great Proletarian Cultural Revolution (1966–1976) almost all ethnological research stopped (Chen 1998, pp. 33–36). During this time the peripheries of Sinic civilization in Hong Kong and Taiwan became surrogates for China itself, laboratories for the study of "Chinese Society and Culture;" research done under those conditions continues to form a backdrop to research on the mainland since 1978.

Mao Zedong died in 1976, and by the end of 1978 Deng Xiaoping had consolidated power as China's "Paramount Leader." With the coming of his regime began the process of China's Reform and, importantly for us, the revival of anthropology.

The Revival of Anthropology, the Recovery of Old Paradigms, and the Discovery of the New

In 1980 the Chinese Anthropological Association was re-established, and soon thereafter two officially named departments of anthropology were created, one at Zhongshan University in Guangzhou in 1981 and one at Xiamen University in Xiamen in 1984 (Chen 1997, p. 47). Ethnology was established as an undergraduate major at the Central, Guangxi, and Yunnan Nationalities Colleges, and ethnology research institutes were created at several colleges. In 1993 the Institute of Sociology at Beijing University was renamed the Institute of Sociology and Anthropology (Chen 1997, p. 48). Once again, anthropology and ethnology (disputes about the name continue) were in full swing.

At this early stage, however, anthropology was still being practiced very much according to the Soviet-inspired model using detailed fieldwork data to authenticate the orthodox paradigm of social evolutionary stages. But the isolation of Chinese native anthropology could not last. Field research by foreign anthropologists had begun even before anthropology was officially re-established as a discipline in China, and not long afterwards, Chinese college graduates began to travel to the West to take anthropology degrees. They maintained contact with their colleagues at home, and whether they returned to China or stayed abroad, their ability to take concepts from primarily English-language discourses and transplant them to a Chinese scholarly and institutional context was crucial to the broadening of paradigms that began in earnest in China's anthropology in the late 1980s. A crucial juncture was reached when Tong Enzheng finally challenged the Morganian paradigm directly as rigid, overly deductive, and empirically indefensible (Tong 1988).

Since the mid-1990s there has been a further shift, with the establishment of more anthropology programs, at Yunnan University and at Qinghua University in Beijing, and the return of a large number of foreign-educated scholars to faculty positions at those and other institutions. At this writing, anthropology in China is still hampered by the relative lack of synthetic and theoretical materials in Chinese, but the gap is closing rapidly, and many scholars of Chinese origin, whether currently employed in China or elsewhere, are fully entangled in the cosmopolitan discourses of the discipline. At the same time, it has become progressively easier for foreigners to conduct field research in China. The result is that Chinese anthropology and the anthropology of China are once more part of world anthropology.

TOPICS OF ANTHROPOLOGICAL RESEARCH

As Chinese society and culture have experienced both institutional and epistemic movements of recovery and progress, anthropologists have narrated these movements in many areas including communities, lives, and the nation and its parts.

Communities

Earlier anthropology was concentrated in villages, with a minority of studies examining urban communities. Recent work adds migrant communities, spread between the place of origin and the place of destination.

VILLAGE COMMUNITIES   Anthropologists studying China have never given up what Feuchtwang (1998, p. 48) has described as the attempt to answer the question of "with what strength and shared sense of definition do rural residents treat where they live as a place of shared or common identity?" Great changes in the scale and content of local identity took place during the Revolutionary years, as Feuchtwang has pointed out, but they were studied only rarely, and usually from a distance or by nonanthropologists. In the 1980s there appeared a series of studies tracing the history of villages through the successive periods of land reform, collectivization, people's communes, the post–Great Leap famine, the nutritional and economic recovery of the early 1960s, the varying traumas of the Cultural Revolution, and the beginnings of the era of Reform. Initially, some of this research was done with emigré villagers in Hong Kong, (Chan et al 1984), but such ethnography at a distance was soon supplanted by direct ethnography (Potter & Potter 1990, Friedman et al 1991, Huang 1989), as well as the updated work of Chan et al (1992). In addition, Chinese anthropologists in particular have conducted a large number of restudies of villages that were the subject of pre- or immediately postwar ethnography, including Zhuang (2000) on the Fujian village studied in the 1940s by Lin (1944) and Zhou's study (2001) of the eastern Guandgong community studied by Kulp (1925).

These studies share a common theme: They show villagers reacting, sometimes helplessly, sometimes creatively, to twists and turns (hence Huang's felicitous title, *The Spiral Road*) of revolutionary political and economic policy, providing a villagers'-eye view of the policy changes, and of the meaning of such abstract terms as class struggle, Mao thought, bad class elements, basic-level cadres, workpoint systems, or learning from Dazhai, in actual practice. They also allow us to assess the extent to which the revolutionary events of the 1950s constituted a real historical break, and the extent to which pre-existing ideas of kinship, community, gender, and work persisted across the great historical divide. Also, most of these studies support the thesis first advanced by Skinner (1971) that the village as a bounded solidarity waxes and wanes with the opening and closing of the national and regional economies. In the collective period, when what Gates (1996) calls "the tributary mode of production" held strong sway over its subordinately articulated "petty-capitalist mode of production," the village closed in on itself and became a more bounded unit than it was in the early part of the twentieth century or certainly than it has been since the Reform and Opening. Ruf (1998), in fact, shows that in an area of Sichuan where the village was not a salient unit for most rural residents before the revolution, something like the village was created by the imposition of administrative structures.

All these studies treat the theme of the village as a moral community, which is taken up most explicitly in a series of works stemming from Richard Madsen's 1984 *Morality and Power in a Chinese Village*. Madsen portrays Chen Village as a place of contestation between the "Confucian" morality of graded obligations within a kinship system, which Madsen shows survived until the Cultural Revolution, and the "Maoist" mentality of class-struggle-based moral absolutism. The latter discredited the former in the late 1960s, but itself was bankrupted in villagers' minds by the bitter battles fought over empty fantasies of "class struggle" in the 1970s, leaving the villagers at the start of Reform with a kind of vacuous, utilitarian nonmorality (see also Chan 1985).

Indeed, the moral wasteland left by the failure of absolutist Maoism provides a background to the study of the phase of recovery. The attempt to recover a moral universe is viewed as having variable success in the Reform period. Jing Jun, for example, sees Gansu villagers' rebuilding of a temple to Confucius as has having re-created, through the manipulation of historical memory in ritual, "a strong, alternative base of power and authority ... tied to the increasingly noticeable assertion of local identity, voluntary associations, and community autonomy ..." (1996, p. 176). Ruan Yunxing reports a similar attempt to reconstruct a kin-based moral order in Yixu, a lineage village first studied by Lin Yaohua in the 1930s (Ruan 2000). Liu Xin, working in Shaanbei, by contrast, sees a retreat to utilitarianism reminiscent of that described by Madsen: "A formal structure of meaning, a system of signification, that used to guide action when interpreted by a local authority has collapsed: the meaning of an action is now reduced solely to its effects" (X. Liu 2000, p. 156). Intermediate between these extremes, Erik Mueggler's (2001) analysis of Lipuo (Yi) villagers in northern Yunnan sees them emerging from their self-described "age of wild ghosts" with a sense that there is a moral universe, however threatened, residing in an ethnically distinct sphere of meaning and morals, but that this sphere can never be autonomous from the larger, national culture in which it is embedded.

Other scholars suggest that the shift from revolutionary to reform structures is a shift from group to network as the focus of action, a conceptual distinction that resonates with Fei Xiaotong's 1949 dichotomy of a *tuanti geju* (group structure) and *chaxu geju* (hierarchical structure) (1992). Specifically, Yan Yunxiang, working in Heilongjiang, and Andrew Kipnis, working in Shandong, describe the re-creation of a moral economy based on the cultivation of personal networks of gifts and favors (Yan 1996, Kipnis 1997).

Many scholars have studied variability in village political economy and its relation to family and gender. Judd (1994), for example, shows how the role of women and men in household and collective management varies with the degree of commercialization and industrialization in three Shandong villages, a point also made by Wu Ga for Nuosu (Yi) women in Yunnan (2001). Feuchtwang and his colleagues (1998) undertook a systematic study of variability in 10 villages in 5 provinces, and Wang Mingming compared two of these villages in Fujian with a village in northern Taiwan (earlier the object of Feuchtwang's ethnography) to show how the political economy has influenced the forms of cooperation: A combination of increased village autonomy and exhortations toward "modernization" have in fact led to "primarily the restoration of traditional forms" of economic organization and cooperation (Wang 1997, pp. 164–67).

Villages, of course, are embedded in regions, whatever their current state of autonomy or integration. Regional studies have thus provided a fruitful and perhaps more controlled context for intercommunity comparisons than the more widespread samples discussed above. An important focus for such studies has been the Pearl River Delta in Guangdong, the location of Helen Siu's pioneering study of intraregional variation in village political organization (1989) and in marriage markets (1993) and Faure & Siu's study of historical variation in community organization (1995).

BIG CITY COMMUNITIES   As Skinner (1977, p. 258) long ago pointed out, the strict rural-urban dichotomy was not a feature of the traditional Chinese economic or conceptual landscape; cities were nodes of regional political and economic systems more than they were culturally separate places. It was under Western imperialist influence in the nineteenth and twentieth centuries that the city became equated with modernity and progress while the villages were seen as backwaters of tradition and superstition (Pannell 1992, Johnson 1992). The Communists, paradoxically, exalted the peasants ideologically while investing most of their developmental resources in the city and reinforced the distinction with a rigid system of household registration and ration controls (Cheng & Selden 1994). Rural people became *nongmin*, literally "farming commoners," but universally translated as "peasants," and their homes *nongcun* or "farm villages" (Cohen 1993), terms that were rarely if ever used before the Revolution or outside the People's Republic.

On the upside of this contrast there emerged in the early years of the People's Republic an urban form characterized by the cellular state *danwei* or work-unit: one or more compounds consisting of part or all of a city block, surrounded by a wall and approached through a gate with a gatehouse, and including in its most developed form workshops, residences, meeting rooms, clinics, bathhouses, childcare centers, and sometimes even schools. *Danwei* of this sort provided not only the physical but also the institutional space for urban people's lives during the period of High Socialism (Whyte & Parish 1984, Walder 1986, Li 1992). The Reforms in urban areas have consisted more than anything of the removal of both the physical and the institutional walls.

William Jankowiak (1993) described Huhhot in Inner Mongolia during the early and mid-1980s, a time when *danwei* culture was just beginning to erode and individual life still consisted of a public sphere in which one negotiated the *danwei* and its bureaucratic extensions and a separate private sphere of family, friends, romance, and ritual. The bulk of anthropological research on big cities, however, has come during the period when China's cities opened up, when the walls of many of the old *danwei* came down to make way for commercial emporia and skyscrapers with ground-level stores, restaurants, and beauty salons, and the dominance of state-owned industrial enterprises slowly gave way to joint ventures, small-scale entrepreneurship (Bruun 1993, Gold 1989), and increasingly larger private enterprise. Pieke (1996) documented the interconnections between life and personal strategies of people in state *danwei* and life in other sectors during the late 1980s, a period when the transition was in full force, though not far along. Rofel (1999) studied gender dynamics in a surviving state enterprise in Hangzhou during this process, and Ikels (1996) documented the development of a market economy and the concomitant cultural changes in Guangzhou at the same time.

In addition to comprehensive studies such as these, other researchers have concentrated on the reconstruction of social space, both geographical and class or occupational, during this time. For example, Hertz (2001) deals with the erosion of public morality as the crowd becomes more anonymous; Davis (2000, pp. 9–10) looks at the increasing emphasis on home and home decoration with the rise of consumer culture; and Junghans (2001) considers the paradoxes of shifting social hierarchies between the ideologically privileged state workers and currently wealthier entrepreneurs. Hertz (1998) contextualizes the rise of a new social group, stock market people, as dependents of the tributary state's (Gates 1996) entry into the market in order to raise capital. Mayfair Yang (1994) neatly sums up these historical changes through tracing shifts in the culture of *guanxixue*, or "relation-ology," the practice of building and drawing on personal networks to get things in general done. In the revolutionary years this was a way of maneuvering around bureaucratic rigidity, but it has adapted once again to the more networked social structure of the Reform years.

THE TERTIUM QUID: MIGRATION AND RURAL URBANIZATION   The imposed rigid rural-urban dichotomy of the Revolutionary years is now increasingly disturbed by two trends: renewed migration of rural people to the cities and creation of zones in the former countryside that are no longer quite rural yet not really urban either.

China's leaders recognized in the 1980s that transition to a market economy would require some loosening of the previously strict limits on migration, but they probably did not expect to have the currently estimated 100,000,000 or more people in what is called the *liudong renkou*, or "floating population," people who have left their rural homes to take up work or entrepreneurship in the cities.

Cities such as Beijing (Zhang 2001) Shanghai, and Guangzhou (Johnson 1992, Zhou 1997a, Zhou & Zhang 1997) now have large communities of migrants, as do newly urbanized and semi-urban areas in broad regions such as the Pearl River Delta and the area around Dalian (Zhou & Zhang 1997, Hoffman & Liu 1997). As in earlier times, migrants to a particular city from a particular region tend to cluster together in certain neighborhoods and to pursue certain occupations. In present-day Beijing, clothing makers and entrepreneurs come from southern Zhejiang, garbage collectors from Hebei, maids and other service workers from Anhui, and ethnic restauranteurs from Xinjiang (Zhang 2001). Much of the construction workforce in Kunming comes from Sichuan, and the manual labor force of the whole urbanizing Pearl River region comes from Hunan, Jiangxi, Guangxi, and remote parts of Guangdong (Guldin 1992, p. 158).

Migrants are necessary to urban construction and service industries, but they immediately excite prejudice from more established urban residents. They are blamed for crime, though they are most often its victims (Zhang 2001), and it is often said that their "quality" or *suzhi* is low (Zhang 2001; Anagnost 1997a, pp. 122–25). The poorest workers in Guuangzhou live in horrendous conditions, have no time for recreation, and are beholden to local officials and gangs for permission to stay. Typically, they associate primarily with fellow provincials and know nothing of the local language or of the culture of the area in which they work; they hope to return to their overpopulated homes to marry and not to return (Zhou 1997a). In addition, female migrants have special problems: They often end up poorly paid, ill-accommodated in crowded factory dormitories, and under pressure to marry before they get "old"; they thus rarely effect any structural change in gender concepts or marriage (Pun 1999), and their resistance sometimes takes symbolic but psychologically disruptive forms. At the same time, not all migrants are lower class; Zhang (2001) describes a migrant entrepreneurial elite and a middling class of small producers with their own complex structures of community and social networking.

The second trend, the creation of not-quite-urban spaces in the former countryside, is described in the Yangtze Delta area and also in the Shenyang-Anshan corridor and the area around Dalian (Hoffman & Liu 1997) in the Northeast, but particularly in the South: in southwestern Fujian (Shi 1997) and the Pearl River Delta, where Johnson (1992), Guldin (1992; 1997, pp. 47–70), Zhou (1997a), Zhou & Zhang (1997), and Zhou & Guo (1996) have seen processes of de-agriculturalization, where villagers stay in place but take up industrial occupations; townization of the countryside, in which small agglomerations, or *desakotas* (Ginsburg et al 1991), rise in formerly rural areas; and the citization of towns, in which medium-sized cities are created. In all these processes, changes in occupation, organization of time, and lifestyles are just as important indicators of urbanization as moving to a city (Guldin 1997, Zhou & Guo 1996, Shi 1997).

In urbanizing regional systems, villages, towns, and cities also display a changed hierarchy of desirability, as Guldin (1997, pp. 47–70) points out: In areas of rapid urbanization and increasing income, *desakotas* and even villages are increasingly seen as equally desirable with small cities; the same amenities are available, and there are more and less crowded living conditions (Shi 1997). Nevertheless, they still lack the cultural life of the large cities such as Guangzhou even though improved transportation now means that near-suburbanites can partake in the urban amenities without the noise and pollution.

Lives

Lives have changed greatly in the past 20 years: Physically, they are easier, a prominent part of the overall narrative of progress; socially and psychologically, they have recovered their private space in some ways, but have become more public in others. Almost nobody would go back to the revolutionary times, but the uncertainty and complexity of today's life have given rise to nostalgia for the "simpler" times of the revolution, and particularly for the only dimly imagined prerevolutionary days. Anthropologists have dealt with individual lives primarily in the urban areas; here I deal with several of their topics of interest.

GENDER AND SEXUALITY   Historian Tani Barlow observed that twentieth-century radical intellectuals, including the Communist Party, transformed Chinese understanding of womanhood from a relational one, in which women were seen as mothers, sisters, wives, and daughters, to an absolute one, in which women were seen as a biological category (*nüxing*) or as an undifferentiated political mass (*funü*) (Barlow 1991). In adopting this understanding, the Revolution claimed to have liberated women through their participation in labor, as predicted in the nineteenth century by Engels. The recent anthropology of gender in China begins with the first field studies, (Stacey 1983, Johnson 1983, Wolf 1985) showing that participation in the workforce did not bring equality of wealth and power. Instead, two other historians (Honig & Hershatter 1988) and one anthropologist (Croll 1983) began narrating the complexities of the gender system as it replaced the revolutionary narrative of progress both with conservative ideas of recovery of "natural" traditional gender and with narratives of a new kind of progress toward modernity.

Recent studies have explored the gendering of practically every aspect of life in Reform era China. Village studies have shown that women's power in family and community varies with political economy (Judd 1994), but there is a general agreement that there is a recovery in the villages of patriarchal domination, expressed in patrilocal arranged marriage, in expected household roles, and in the subordination of women in family and community ritual (X. Liu 2000, Jing 1996), with the very important differences that the patriarchal state now controls women's fertility as never before (Huang 1989, Mueggler 2001, Chan et al 1994) and that women often form the primary labor force in communities where men migrate to outside jobs (Shi 1997). In these situations, some women have gained de facto power even in the face of explicit ritual and political subordination. And things are changing in some areas: the generations have begun to struggle over love marriages even in the villages (Ruan et al 1998).

Students of urban China, by contrast, present a much more varied picture of different kinds of gendering in different aspects of life and different social groups. Brownell (1995, pp. 213–62) shows how sport is less explicitly gendered in China than in Western countries because sport was not part of traditional masculinity in the Confucian tradition. Rofel shows how three generations of female workers in a Hangzhou silk factory have operated with three different gender concepts: socialist equality for the grandmothers, gendered engagement with state power for the mothers, and "exciting new horizons in postsocialist discussions of nature, feminine bodies, and sexuality" for the daughters (1999, p. 279). Erwin (2000) shows how the fluid discourses of sexuality and gender in Shanghai have led to a hotline and talk-radio culture in which advice-mongers set the tone not only for their callers but for a large listening public. Farrer (2000) describes the generational differences between middle-aged social dancers, who skip work to express desire in a staid manner, and young, hip disco habitués, who go out at night to flaunt desirability in a daring way. Zhang (2001, Ch. 5) documents the difference between the ornamental, shopping-and-mahjongg life of the rich and the behind-the-scenes managerial life of the middle class among women in the Zhejiang migrant garment community. Once again, much of the field is tied together by Yang (1994, 1999, Ch. 1), who shows how men and women must construct their *guanxi* in ways consonant with the social expectations of modesty and relationality for women and of assertiveness and manipulativeness for men; this is one reason that Hertz (1998) gives for much higher male than female participation in Shanghai's stock market. In this whole discourse, recovery and progress are inextricably mixed: Progress toward modernity involves the recovery and valorization of gender difference; what this difference should be remains contested.

FAMILY, MARRIAGE, AND POPULATION   There is perhaps nowhere else in the anthropology of Reform Era China where there is as little narrative of recovery as with the patrilocal joint family. As Davis & Harrell pointed out (1993), the withdrawal of the state from so many aspects of Chinese life with the start of the Reforms came at the same time that the state penetrated more deeply than ever before into the reproductive lives of its citizens with the policy of planned birth.

It is not that Chinese women necessarily always wanted lots of children (Greenhalgh 1993; Gates 1993, 1996), but that their position in the patriarchal family system gave them little leeway to control their fertility (but see Stockard 1989). Now the state gives them almost no leeway not to control their fertility, and this intrusion of the state occasions great resentment and opposition (Mueggler 2001, Huang 1989). This restricted fertility, along with the limited return of property rights to rural families, has meant that not even the nostalgic semblance of the patrilocal joint household can be retained anywhere in China. What has replaced it in rural areas has been a kind of "networked family" (Unger 1993), in which sons and their wives, with sometimes a short initial period of residence in their parents' house (Wang 2001, X. Liu 2000), move out to form independent households, but households that retain close cooperative links in productive and childcare activities. In the big cities, except for the small population of private entrepreneurs, there is little productive cooperation among related families because most people are salaried, but there is still a lot of cooperation in childcare and a lot of help with consumption (Davis 1993). However, smaller and more divided families have also meant less insurance; when families have special needs to care for the elderly (Ikels 1993) or for disabled persons (Phillips 1993, Kohrman 2000) their network-building skills are strained to the utmost.

Despite the lack of common residence after marriage, the bond between the generations remains strong; despite the increasing mobility of family members in economic and political migration, much of this individual activity is conducted in the context of providing for marriage and the family. Whether a marriage is arranged by the parents or based on free choice, it is expensive. Dowries and bridewealth have skyrocketed since the Reforms, partly because the state no longer controls them (though it still formally forbids them) and partly because people have much more disposable income. More than anything else, though, marriage is an aspect of *guanxi* building, and lavish ceremonies and payments not only reinforce bonds between the parties but expand the social networks of both the bride's and the groom's families (Kipnis 1997, Yan 1996, Siu 1993). Perhaps here there is still a narrative of recovery, at least in village communities where marriage once again provides an opportunity to create and strengthen social networks.

CHILDHOOD AND EDUCATION   Smaller families, together with more resources available for schools and other sites of enculturation, have meant that individual children now mean more than ever before. Anagnost (1997b) has referred to the recent phenomenon as "the fetishization of the child"; it is as if the hopes of the family, and in some case of the nation, rest heavily on the narrow shoulders of the little emperors and empresses. This individual and collective anxiety has become embodied in the extraordinary proliferation of activities to train the child for success, as well as in the concern that children are being provided with the best food, beginning with campaigns to encourage breastfeeding (Gottschang 2000), and proceeding through making sure that children have what their peers consider appropriately up-to-date snacks and meals out (Chee 2000, Lozada 2000) and appropriately nutritious food at home (Guo 2000). In addition, parents and grandparents often feel obligated to provide a wide range of consumer goods for their children (Davis & Sensenbrenner 2000) so that they will not fall behind either educationally or socially. This has resulted in the frequent comment among urbanites that China has moved from a society in which children are filial to their parents to one in which parents serve their children.

Serving the children, however, does not consist exclusively or even primarily of indulging their material wishes or peer-pressured needs. It also means getting them the best possible education, and this means lessons from an early age, competition for the best schools, and cram schools when they are ready to compete for admission to better schools at higher levels. Schools become a filtering mechanism for social mobility (Tang & Parish 2000, pp. 56–58), and competition for elite schools is intense (Schoenhals 1993, p. 7).

What actually happens in schools is the subject of few ethnographic studies, many of those conducted in minority regions and emphasizing the ways in which formal education intends to make good Chinese citizens out of minority children, who often receive a mixed message (Borchigud 1995, Hansen 1999, Upton 1999). The only full-scale ethnography of what happens in the classroom is by Schoenhals (1993), who studied an elite school through classroom observation and student interviews and found that peer culture was a strong check on the intended hierarchical nature of teacher-student interaction, and that even the best students resisted this implicit hierarchy even as they strove for educational advancement.

CONSUMPTION AND LEISURE   Since 1978 the Chinese economy has made the physical and conceptual shift from a revolutionary economy based on heavy industry and re-investment to a Reform economy based on consumer goods, export to Europe and America, and more than anything else on turning China's population into consumers (Lu 2000). There is a narrative of recovery here, particularly directed toward the economic culture of petty-capitalist production and accumulation (Gates 1996). But the primary direction of anthropology has been toward a Bourdieuvian analysis of consumption.

Consumption begins at home, and Fraser has documented the advertising process that creates residential desire for emerging middle classes (2000), while Davis (2000, pp. 8–10) has documented the importance of interior decorating. Rising incomes and the reforms in agriculture have created a burgeoning variety of available foodstuffs for urban markets (Veeck 2000), food that not only supplies the increasingly elaborate banquets necessary to effective *guanxi* building (Yang 1994), but also makes home meals more complex, culinarily and sociologically, than ever before (Guo 2000) and raises for the first time as a cultural issue the question of the social and nutritional value of snacks (Gillette 2000, Chee 2000). People also eat out more than ever before (Yan 2000), often at American-style fast food restaurants, particularly McDonalds and Kentucky Fried Chicken. Watson (1997) and his colleagues have shown how, in China as in other East Asian societies, "foreign" food and the spaces in which it is consumed take on specific cultural meanings very different from what those foods mean in the United States or Europe. In Beijing in the 1990s, eating at McDonalds or KFC was expensive, prestigious, and except at peak hours, rather leisurely (Lozada 2000, Yan 2000). McDonalds is also credited with helping popularize the concept of the clean toilet (Yan 2000).

In the consciously Bourdieuvian world of present-day urban China, consumption exists not only for the intrinsic enjoyment of the conusmable but also for the furthering or solidification of social status. Wank (2000) has demonstrated how this works in the exchange of premium cigarettes between entrepreneurs and officials, and G. Wang (2000) narrates the way in which dancing, karaoke, and bowling rapidly succeeded each other in Shenzhen as venues in which one could woo possible business associates or solidify already existent relationships, which on a lower level of outlay are also helped by sending New Year, Christmas, and sometimes birthday cards (Erbaugh 2000). Alternative consumption styles of the young are experienced as productive of alternative value systems, as with the underground rock scene in Beijing described by Efird (2001). Even ethnicity can be demonstrated in selective and selectively valorized consumption of "modern" goods, as demonstrated for Xi'an Muslims by Gillette (2000).

In all these arenas, the value of cultural capital involves an idea of modernity, mainstream or alternative, which more often than not includes an element of foreignness. But consumption also serves the resurgent nationalism of the 1990s and beyond. Anagnost (1997a, Ch. 7) has shown how playing in theme parks can recreate the nation as a physical and conceptual space, and Krauss (2000) shows how enjoying public parks and monuments involves interacting with sculptural representations of various stages of the revolution and the Reform. Even the recent history of revolutionary hardship is now consumed in spaces of nostalgia, including restaurants where one eats like a sent-down youth (Hubbert 1999, pp. 230–284) and stores and markets that do a booming business in real and fake Mao buttons and cultural-revolution era posters and calendars (Hubbert 1996).

The Nation and Its Component Parts

Since the Chinese state gave up class and class struggle as a means of legitimation, it has turned to the construction of the nation as the prime means of inducing people to identify with its policies and programs (Duara 1995; Gladney 1991, pp. 87–93). The foundational text comes once again from Fei Xiaotong, who in 1989 was a vice-chair of the National People's Congress when he wrote *Zhonghua Minzu Duoyuan Yiti Geju* (the *E Pluribus Unum* structure of the Chinese nation or Chinese people) (Fei 1989). Before this, Chinese ethnology was about *minzu*, or nationalities, from a Stalinist historical evolutionary perspective, whereas Western anthropology was concerned about ethnic groups from a perspective influenced by Barth, Anderson, and Gellner. Since then, the whole discourse, including things written before 1989, has been more explicitly about unity and diversity, both within the Han *minzu* and between the Han and the minorities, with scholars both constructing and deconstructing nationalist and localist narratives.

BUILDING LOCAL ETHNIC IDENTITIES THROUGH SCHOLARSHIP   Ethnology has played an important part in the construction of ethnic identities in the Reform period. To recover what they saw as their rightful place in the Chinese family of nationalities, localist and nativist scholars had to convert from a Marxist ethnology of normalization and staging to a nativist ethnography of ethnic assertion. Soviet-style ethnology and its staged paradigm coincided closely with pre-Revolutionary sinocentric culturalism (Harrell 1995, pp. 3–36), with the result that the old ethnology implicitly demeaned local cultures simply by classifying them. The nativist reaction to this invidious paradigm involved the creation of fields of study—with conferences, edited volumes, and professional associations—named after the specific *minzu* whose cultures were being redefined and promoted: Tibetology or *Zang xue*, the study of the *Zang minzu* or Tibetan nationality within China (Upton 2000); *Yao xue* (Litzinger 2000), *Zhuang xue* (Kaup 2000), *Yi xue* (Bamo & Huang 2000, Harrell 2001), and many others.

Yi studies can serve as an example. Yi revisionists never deny that the Yi are part of China; rather, they attempt to show that their place in China was underestimated by the previous paradigm. This they do in several ways. First, they break out of the Morgan-Engels paradigm by denying that "slave society" is an accurate characterization of the society of the Nuosu, considered by many to be the most representative of true Yi culture, finding alternative models of stratification by clan membership or categories of purity and pollution (Pan WC 1987, Ma 1993, Liu 2001). Second, they demonstrate that the Yi have contributed more to Chinese civilization than their relegation to inferior minority status would indicate. Liu Yaohan, for example, has written that the 10-month calendar of the Yi was one of the historic foundations of Chinese civilization (1985), and others have attempted to show that the ancestors of the Yi developed the world's first writing system (Z.Y. Liu 2000). There has been a recent movement to assert that the Yi are the direct descendants of the early hominids found in the Yunnan region (Gelong 1996). Finally, they attempt to assert that Han dominance is recent in China, showing that the Yi had a culture of great refinement during the first millennium C.E. (Wu Gu 2001).

A rich literature has also grown up among Naxi intellectuals, which as Chao (1996) and White (1998) have shown both valorizes a vanishing, and vanishingly small, "pure Naxi" culture of the remote high-mountain villages and promotes the Naxi as a "civilized" *minzu* with long connections to high culture, music (Rees 2000), and education. Local groups not recognized as *minzu* can develop culturalist claims to separate status, as has been done by the Baima of northwestern Sichuan through their own nativist scholarship that demonstrates their lack of relations with the Tibetan *minzu* in which they are officially classified (Sichuan 1980). At the same time, scholarly members of the larger *minzu*, such as the Tibetans, can make counter-claims ridiculing what they see as the pretensions of local, breakaway groups (Upton 2000). A small number of intellectuals among the Naze or Mosuo, a matrilineal group straddling the Sichuan-Yunnan border, has attempted a revisionist scholarship that denies the primitivity attributed by Soviet-style ethnology to their social system (He 1991).

Scholarship is not the only area for localist ethnic cultural promotion. As Schein has richly demonstrated for the Miao of Southeast Guizhou (1999), ethnic tourism promotion is not just about bringing in money but is also about developing local self-respect among Miao cadres, intellectuals, and cultural performers. The Ge of Guizhou, a small group, most of whose members reject their state designation as Miao, have also asserted a separate entity through selective participation in the politics of cultural performance (Cheung 1996). For the Sani of eastern Yunnan, whose classification as Yi has at times been a matter of dispute, tourism partly concentrates on making local cultural products, such as the Sani myth of "Golden Girl" Ashima, into a key component of Yi culture, not just for locals and tourists but for the general Chinese educated public (Swain 2001).

DECONSTRUCTING BOTH THE OLD AND NEW PROJECTS   Both the revolutionary project of Soviet-style classification and the Reform project of recovery of local pride and history are unreflectively essentialist: People may argue about who is Yi or who is Tibetan, but they rarely consider that the categories may be historically situated, cultural constructions. This is where the cosmopolitan, deconstructive discourse enters the arena.

The pioneer in this area was Gladney (1991), who showed through ethnographic accounts that the Hui, or as he calls them Muslim Chinese, are as a category the creation of modernist politics, and the content of their local identity varies from community to community and changes from period to period. Gladney (1991, pp. 261–91) and, in more detail, Fan (2001) have shown that the Hui in Fujian have evolved an ethnic identity and even a Muslim identity as a result of the ethnic politics of the Reform Era. Gladney (1990) has gone further in his analysis of Uighur ethnogenesis, pinpointing the period in the 1920s when Uighurs became a group, as Kaup (2000) has also shown for the Zhuang in the 1950s. Diamond (1995) has performed a similar analysis of the category of Miao, and McKhann has done the same for the Naxi (1995) and Wu for the Bai (1990). Often the purpose of these deconstructive analyses is simply to demonstrate the artificiality or arbitrariness of the categories (McKhann 1995), but deconstructive scholars have also begun to realize that the categories have entered not only into scholarship and tourism promotion, as mentioned above, but also into school curricula (Harrell & Bamo 1998, Upton 1999) and ordinary journalistic discourse, so that what was socially constructed is nevertheless real for most of the participants, though they may disagree about the details.

Scholars working among ethnic groups that have more claim to historical nationhood and less assumption that they are part of China have special reasons to try to deconstruct the discourse of unity in diversity. For example, Bulag (1998, 2000) has shown how Inner Mongolian Mongols are caught between a Chinese evaluation as peripheral and underdeveloped and a Halh Mongolian evaluation as hopelessly Sinified. Borchigud (1995) has demonstrated how the state's educational policies have unintentionally engendered ethnic consciousness and passive resistance, and Khan (1996) has shown how an essentialist discourse of pastoral Mongols has both been adopted enthusiastically by Mongolian cultural entrepreneurs and left Mongolian farmers, who may not even ride horses, no culture with which they can identify. Williams (2000) uses what he sees as fundamentally different views of landscape and the human relation with it to explain both ethnic conflict and ecological degradation in Inner Mongolia since the Reform period.

It is not only the cultural essentialism of Soviet-style ethnology that this new anthropology attempts to revise. For example, both Shih (2001) and Weng (1995) have composed new portraits of Mosuo or Naze family and gender systems that are free of the classificatory primitivity assigned to them by the old ethnology, instead couching their discussions in the categories of anthropology of kinship and gender. Du (2001) has done the same thing for the gender system of the Lahu, using their system of gender complementarity to address questions of the possibility of equality between the genders. ZS Wang (1997) has used ethnography of minority groups to enter China into long-standing arguments about kinship and ethnicity, with a reinterpretation of the Kachin system studied by Leach, done on the basis of field research in Yunnan.

Some recent works on ethnicity and identity are less concerned with direct deconstruction of either Soviet-style or nativist approaches to the problem, and more focused on using empirical scholarship and models derived from cosmopolitan anthropology to approach ethnicity from different angles. Mueggler (2001) uses ritual models of houses, fields, and landscapes to examine how Lipuo people in central

Yunnan conceptualize and manage their relations with the ever-threatening Han. Dautcher (2001), by contrast, is more concerned with men's everyday practices in a poor periurban Uighur neighborhood, through which the participants create a spatiotemporal world that is both masculine and ethnically Uighur. Litzinger (2000) concentrates on the ethnic elites who produce the explicit models of ethnicity and history, and shows how their construction of what it means to be Yao has changed from prerevolutionary times through the present. Tapp (2001) shows through detailed analysis of kin relations and rituals that the Hmong, both in China and after migrating overseas, are a kind of Chinese whose entire identity is constructed in reactive opposition to the hegemonic practices of central governments and Han people.

REGIONAL CULTURES AND THE NATURE OF THE HAN   The study of regional variants of Han cultures is relatively free from the task of breaking out of the Morgan-Engels paradigm, because Han culture is presumed to be advanced, modern, and well-documented. But cultural or folkloristic aspects of regional variation are a rich topic for investigation and contribute to the construction of localist identities, particularly in South China (Friedman 1995). For example, studies of the variants of marriage practices investigated by the authors collected in Ma et al (1994) and the material culture and folk customs of the fishing folk of the central Fujian coast, analyzed in a series of monographs by scholars from Xiamen University and Hong Kong Chinese University (Chen & Qiao 1993, Qiao et al 1992), have used ethnographic description to establish or describe a cultural basis for local identities, as has Huang (1999b) for the Guangdong area.

Hakka identity has long been a topic of interest beginning with Lo Xianglin's claims of a kind of hyper-Chineseness of the Hakka compared with their neighbors in the South, a self-identifier that was quickly picked up by Hakka intellectuals all through the twentieth century. Recent localistic studies such as that of Li on gender relations (1996) reinforce this kind of cultural claim to uniqueness. Sow-Theng Leong's historical investigation of the context of Hakka and Hakka-speaking "shed people's" ethnic identity (1997), however, begins the critical examination of the nativist discourse, showing the contextual and historically variant content of Hakka identity, a theme reinforced by the essays collected in Constable (1997), which systematize and contextualize the Hakka identity, showing that what makes one Hakka is very different in Hong Kong (Constable 1997, pp. 98–123; Johnson 1997), Taiwan (Martin 1997), and overseas.

These regional assertions of identity take place against a background that assumes that the Han as a whole are a historically evolved group with economic, psychological, and other aspects of a unified culture (Xu 1999). Watson (1987) suggested that the unity comes from orthopraxy, in particular from performing funeral rites that all share common elements, while Ebrey (1996) found the dividing line between those who have Chinese surnames and those who do not. Brown (2001) inclines toward a more composite view, demonstrating that the process of "Hanification" may occur either first in culture, then in identity, or the other way around, depending on variation in the political economy and in the practices of intermarriage.

THE WHOLE NATION   One final trend in the deconstructionist project of contemporary anthropologists is to analyze critically the discourses of the whole nation, whether they are the culturalist discourses of self-orientalizing put forth by those who see a special cultural Chineseness in the resistance to demands for a popular voice in government (Lee 2000, Pye 1992) or the multiculturalist discourses of a nation with diverse roots and a common body (Fei 1989). In response to the first discourse, Anagnost (1997a) has undertaken a detailed critique of the philosophical foundations of "speaking bitterness" as a popular practice designed to create a docile if active communist citizen, whereas Weller (1999) has taken a political economy approach, along with a comparison to Taiwan's democratizing experience, to show that "Chinese culture" is no barrier to the development of institutions of civil society and political democracy. In response to the second discourse are many of the localist ethnic discourses mentioned above.

More broadly, Chinese anthropologists have attempted to find the proper place for anthropology in China. Many native anthropologists perceive their discipline as something that China has taken from the outside, usually from an unexamined and essentialized "West"—first as China was the object of research by foreigners and foreign-trained natives, and later as more and more natives learned anthropological theory and method outside China and brought it back to conduct research in their homeland (Rong & Xu 1997, Zhou 1997b, Naranbilik 1997). If, these scholars contend, anthropology is truly to flourish as a discipline in China, it must be a Chinese anthropology, and one of the most important current projects is thus one of *bentu hua*, or "nativization."

Scholars agree that one aspect of nativization is bringing Chinese anthropology up to the level where it makes a contribution to anthropology in general (Huang 1999a, Chang 2000). At the same time, however, there is a feeling that Chinese anthropology must be, to paraphrase Deng Xiaoping, "an anthropology with Chinese characteristics" or "an anthropology suited to Chinese conditions." This means, first of all, that nativized Chinese anthropology ought to be about China, because China needs anthropology to solve its problems of development, political change, and social morality (Wang & Feuchtwang 1997, Ji 2000). It also means that Chinese anthropology is applied anthropology (Zhou 1997b). In addition, Chinese scholars feel that by studying China they move the discipline away from its colonial origins. The irony is that so much of Chinese anthropology's roots lie in the Soviet-style ethnology of normalizing and scaling minority peoples that has involved Han scholars and Han-educated scholars acting in what many would still call an "internal-colonialist" context (Gladney 1994).

Finally, nativized anthropology seems to be making a unique contribution through moving away from intensive work in a single village and toward large-scale, collaborative regional and interregional projects, sometimes undertaken exclusively by domestic scholars and sometimes conducted with the collaboration of foreigners. Noteworthy results have come from the Zhongshan University project on rural urbanization (Zhou & Guo 1996); the Xiamen University project on local cultures and social change in Fujian (Chen & Cai 1993, Qiao et al 1992); and the project on the village economy under the reforms, undertaken under the direction of Stephan Feutchtwang and Wang Mingming (Feuchtwang 1998). In a very real sense, Chinese anthropology has accomplished its recovery and its integration into world anthropology. In the next few years the narrative of anthropology in China will be exclusively one of progress, though in what direction we do not know.

ACKNOWLEDGMENTS

There was no way to include everything I would have liked to in this review. For help and advice on what to put in and leave out, thanks to JJ, Wenbin, Ann, Lorna, Ralph, Louisa, Hairong, and especially Fan Ke.

Visit the Annual Reviews home page at www.AnnualReviews.org

LITERATURE CITED

Anagnost AS. 1997a. *National Past-Times.* Durham: Duke Univ. Press

Anagnost AS. 1997b. Children and national transcendence in China. In *Constructing China*, ed. K Lieberthal, SF Lin, EP Young, pp. 195–222. Ann Arbor: Univ. Mich. Cent. Chin. Stud.

Bamo A, Huang JM. 2000. *Guowai Yixue Lunwen Ji.* Kunming: Yunnan Jiaoyu

Barlow T. 1991. Theorizing woman: *funü, guojia, jiating. Genders* 10:132–60

Borchigud W. 1995. The impact of urban ethnic education on modern Mongolian ethnicity. See Harrell 1995, pp. 278–300

Brown MJ. 2001. *Is Taiwan Chinese?* Berkeley: Univ. Calif. Press

Brownell S. 1995. *Training the Body for China.* Chicago: Univ. Chicago Press

Bruun O. 1993. *Business and Bureaucracy in a Chinese City.* Berkeley: Univ. Calif. Inst. E. Asian Stud.

Bulag UE. 1998. *Nationalism and Hybridity in Mongolia.* Oxford: Oxford Univ. Press

Bulag UE. 2000. Colonial contradictions of class and ethnicity in "socialist" China. *Cult. Stud.* 14(3/4):532–82

Chan A. 1985. *Children of Mao.* Seattle: Univ. Washington Press

Chan A, Madsen R, Unger J. 1984. *Chen Village Under Mao and Deng.* Berkeley: Univ. Calif. Press. 1st ed.

Chan A, Madsen R, Unger J. 1992. *Chen Village Under Mao and Deng.* Berkeley: Univ. Calif. Press. 2nd ed.

Chang XQ. 2000. Xueshu guifan, xueshu duihua yu pingdeng kuanrong. *Guangxi Minzu Xueyuan XB* 22(4):7–14

Chao E. 1996. Hegemony, agency, and representing the past. In *Negotiating Ethnicities in China and Taiwan*, ed. MJ Brown, pp. 208–39. Berkeley: Univ. Calif. Inst. E. Asian Stud.

Chee BWL. 2000. Eating snacks and biting pressure: only children in Beijing. See Jing 2000, pp. 48–70

Chen GQ. 1997. Zhongguo renleixue fazhan shilüe. In *Renleixue Bentu Hua zai Zhongguo*, ed. SX Rong, JS Xu, pp. 43–48. Nanning: Guangxi Renmin

Chen GQ, Cai YZ. 1993. *Chongwu Jingjiang Cun.* Fuzhou: Fujian Jiaoyu

Chen NN, Clark CD, Gottschang SZ, Jeffrey L,

eds. 2001. *China Urban*. Durham, NC: Duke Univ. Press

Chen YL. 1998. The history of Chinese ethnology. In *A Collection of Chinese Ethnological Studies*, pp. 1–47. Taipei: Hong-Yih

Cheng TJ, Selden M. 1994. The origins and social consequences of China's *hukou* system. *China Q.* 139:644–68

Cheung SW. 1996. Representation and negotiation of Ge identities in southeast Guizhou. In *Negotiating Ethnicities in China and Taiwan*, ed. MJ Brown, pp. 240–73. Berkeley: Univ. Calif. Inst. E. Asian Stud.

Cohen ML. 1993. Cultural and political inventions in modern China: the case of the Chinese peasant. *Daedalus* 122:151–70

Constable N. 1997. *Guest People*. Seattle: Univ. Washington Press

Croll E. 1983. *Chinese Women Since Mao*. London: Zed

Dautcher JT. 2001. *Down a Narrow Road*. Cambridge, MA: Harvard Inst. E. Asian Stud. In press

Davis D. 1993. Urban households: supplicants to a socialist state. See Davis & Harrell 1993, pp. 50–76

Davis D, Harrell S. 1993. *Chinese Families in the Post-Mao Era*. Berkeley: Univ. Calif. Press

Davis DS. 2000. *The Consumer Revolution in Urban China*. Berkeley: Univ. Calif. Press

Davis DS, Sensenbrenner JS. 2000. Commercializing childhood. See Davis 2000, pp. 54–79

Diamond N. 1995. Defining the Miao. See Harrell 1995, pp. 92–116

Du SS. 2001. *Chopsticks Only Work in Pairs*. New York: Columbia Univ. Press. In press

Duara P. 1995. *Rescuing History from the Nation*. Chicago: Univ. Chicago

Ebrey PB. 1996. Surnames and Han Chinese identity. In *Negotiating Ethnicities in China and Taiwan*, ed. MJ Brown, pp. 19–37. Berkeley: Univ. Calif. Inst. E. Asian Stud.

Efird R. 2001. Rock in a hard place: music and the market in nineties Beijing. See Chen et al 2001, pp. 67–86

Erbaugh MS. 2000. Greeting cards in China. See Davis 2000, pp. 171–200

Erwin K. 2000. Heart to heart; phone to phone. See Davis 2000, pp. 145–70

Fan K. 2001. The reciprocity of tradition and modernity: identity politics in south Fujian. In *Tradition and Change in South and East Fujian*, ed. CB Tan. Hong Kong: Oxford Univ. Press. In press

Farrer J. 2000. Dancing through the market transition. See Davis 2000, pp. 226–49

Faure D, Siu HF, eds. 1995. *Down to Earth*. Stanford, CA: Stanford Univ. Press

Fei XT. 1989. *Zhonghua Minzu Duoyuan Yiti Geju*. Beijing: Zhongyang Minzu Xueyuan

Fei XT. 1992 (1949). *From the Soil: The Foundations of Chinese Society*. tr. G Hamilton, Z Wang. Berkeley: Univ. Calif. Press

Feuchtwang S. 1998. What is a village? In *Cooperative and Collective in China's Rural Development*, ed. EB Vermeer, FN Pieke, WL Chong, pp. 46–74. Armonk, ME: Sharpe

Fraser D. 2000. Inventing oasis. See Davis 2000, pp. 25–53

Friedman E. 1995. *National Identity and Democratic Prospects in Socialist China*. Armonk, ME: Sharpe

Friedman E, Pickowicz PG, Selden M. 1991. *Chinese Village, Socialist State*. New Haven, CT: Yale Univ. Press

Gates H. 1993. Cultural support for birth limitation in post-Mao China. See Davis & Harrell 1993, pp. 251–74

Gates H. 1996. *China's Motor*. Ithaca, NY: Cornell Univ. Press

Gelong A. 1996. *Yizu Gudaishi Yanjiu*. Kunming: Yunnan Minzu

Gillette MB. 2000. *Between Mecca and Beijing*. Stanford, CA: Stanford Univ. Press

Ginsburg N, Koppel B, McGee TB, eds. 1991. *The Extended Metropolis: Settlement Transition in Asia*. Honolulu: Univ. Hawaii Press

Gladney DC. 1990. The ethnogenesis of the Uighur. *C. Asian Survey* 9(1):1–28

Gladney DC. 1991. *Muslim Chinese*. Cambridge, MA: Harvard Univ. Press

Gladney DC. 1994. Representing nationality in China: refiguring majority/minority identities. *J. Asian Stud.* 53(1):92–123

Gold TW. 1989. Guerilla interviewing among the *getihu*. In *Unofficial China*, ed. P Link, R Madsen, PG Pickowicz, pp. 175–92. Boulder, CO: Westview

Gottschang SK. 2000. A baby-friendly hospital and the science of infant feeding. See Jing 2000, pp. 160–84

Greenhalgh S. 1993. The peasantization of population policy in Shaanxi. See Davis & Harrell 1993, pp. 219–50

Guldin GE, ed. 1992. *Urbanizing China.* New York: Greenwood

Guldin GE. 1994. *The Saga of Anthropology in China.* Armonk, ME: Sharpe

Guldin GE. 1997. *Farewell to Peasant China.* Armonk, ME: Sharpe

Guo YH. 2000. Family relations: the generation gap at the table. See Jing 2000, pp. 94–113

Hansen MH. 1999. *Lessons in Being Chinese.* Seattle: Univ. Wash. Press

Harrell S, ed. 1995. *Cultural Encounters on China's Ethnic Frontiers.* Seattle: Univ. Wash. Press

Harrell S, ed. 2001. *Perspectives on the Yi of Southwest China.* Berkeley: Univ. Calif. Press

Harrell S, Bamo A. 1998. Combining ethnic heritage and national unity: a paradox of Nuosu (Yi) language textbooks in China. *Bull. Concern. Asian Schol.* 30(2):62–71

He XW. 1991. Yongning Mosuo ren de hunyin ji qi xisu. In *Ninglang Wenshi Ziliao Xuanji.* Ninglang, Yunnan: Ninglang Zhengxie

Hertz E. 1998. *The Trading Crowd.* Cambridge: Univ. Cambridge Press

Hertz E. 2001. Face in the crowd: the cultural construction of anonymity in urban China. See Chen et al 2001, pp. 274–93

Hoffman L, Liu ZQ. 1997. Rural urbanization on the Liaodong peninsula. See Guldin 1997, pp. 151–82

Honig E, Hershatter G. 1988. *Personal Voices: Chinese Women in the 1980s.* Stanford, CA: Stanford Univ. Press

Hostetler L. 2001. *Qing Colonial Enterprise: Ethnography and Cartography in Early Modern China.* Chicago: Univ. Chicago Press

Huang SM. 1989. *The Spiral Road.* Boulder, CO: Westview

Huang SP. 1999a. Renleixue Zhongguohua de lilun, shixian he rencai. *Guangxi Minzu Xueyuan XB* 21(4):17–20

Huang SP. 1999b. *Guangdong Zuqun yu Quyu Wenhua Yanjiu.* Guangzhou: Guangdong Gaoji Jiaoyu

Hubbert J. 1996. *(Re) Collecting Mao: memorabilia and modernization.* Presented at Annu. Meet. Am. Anthropol. Assoc., San Francisco

Hubbert J. 1999. *The long march to modernity: intellectuals, generations and moral authority in post-Mao China.* Ph.D. diss., Cornell Univ., Ithaca, NY

Ikels C. 1993. Settling accounts: the intergenerational contract in an age of reform. See Davis & Harrell 1993, pp. 307–33

Ikels C. 1996. *The Return of the God of Wealth.* Stanford, CA: Stanford Univ. Press

Jankowiak WB. 1993. *Sex, Death, and Hierarchy in a Chinese City.* New York: Columbia Univ. Press

Ji GX. 2000. Fazhan yu lunzheng: renleixue shiye zhong de tianye gongzuo. *Guangxi Minzu Xueyuan XB* 22(4):21–24

Jing J. 1996. *The Temple of Memories.* Stanford, CA: Stanford Univ. Press

Jing J. 2000. *Feeding China's Little Emperors.* Stanford, CA: Stanford Univ. Press

Johnson EL. 1997. Hakka villagers in a Hong Kong city. See Constable 1997, pp. 80–97

Johnson G. 1992. The political economy of Chinese urbanization. See Guldin 1992, pp. 157–84

Johnson KA. 1983. *Women, the Family, and Peasant Revolution in China.* Chicago: Univ. Chicago Press

Judd E. 1994. *Gender and Power in Rural North China.* Stanford, CA: Stanford Univ. Press

Junghans L. 2001. Railway workers between plan and market. See Chen et al 2001, pp. 183–200

Kaup KP. 2000. *Creating the Zhuang.* Boulder, CO: Rienner

Khan A. 1996. Who are the Mongols? In *Negotiating Ethnicities in China and Taiwan*, ed. MJ Brown, pp. 125–59. Berkeley: Univ. Calif. Inst. E. Asian Stud.

Kipnis AB. 1997. *Producing Guanxi*. Durham, NC: Duke Univ. Press

Kohrman M. 2000. Grooming *que zi. Am. Ethnol.* 26(4):890–909

Krauss RC. 2000. Public monuments and private pleasures in the parks of Nanjing. See Davis 2000, pp. 287–311

Kulp DH. 1925. *Country Life in South China.* New York: Teachers' College Columbia Univ.

Lee KY. 2000. *From Third World to First.* New York: Harper Collins

Leong ST. 1997. *Migration and Ethnicity in Chinese History.* Stanford, CA: Stanford Univ. Press

Li B. 1992. *Danwei* culture as urban culture in modern China. In *Urban Anthropology in China*, ed. G Guldin, pp. 345–52. Leiden, Neth.: Brill

Li YJ. 1996. *Xingbie yu Wenhua.* Guangzhou: Guangdong Renmin

Lin YH. 1944. *The Golden Wing: a Family Chronicle.* New York: Inst. Pac. Rel.

Litzinger RA. 2000. *Other Chinas.* Durham, NC: Duke Univ. Press

Liu X. 2000. *In One's Own Shadow.* Berkeley: Univ. Calif. Press

Liu Y. 2001. On the heroic age of the Liangshan Yi. See Harrell 2001, pp. 104–16

Liu YH. 1985. *Zhongguo Wenming Yuantou Xintan.* Kunming: Yunnan Renmin

Liu ZY. 2000. Gu Yiwen xichuan de kaocha. Presented at 3rd Int. Conf. Yi Stud., Kuming, Yunnan

Lozada EP. 2000. Globalized childhood?: Kentucky Fried Chicken in Beijing. See Jing 2000, pp. 114–34

Lu HL. 2000. To be relatively comfortable in an egalitarian society. See Davis 2000, pp. 124–41

Ma EZ. 1993. Dui jiu Liangshan Yizu shehui jiegoude zai renshi ji "Heiyi" "Baiyi" de bianxi. *Liangshan Minzu Yanjiu* 2:38–48

Ma JZ, Qiao J, Thoraval J, eds. 1994. *Huanan Hunyin Zhidu yu Fünu Diwei.* Nanning: Guangxi Minzu

Madsen R. 1984. *Morality and Power in a Chinese Village.* Berkeley: Univ. Calif. Press

Martin HJ. 1997. The Hakka ethnic movement in Taiwan, 1986–1991. See Constable 1997, pp. 176–95

McKhann CF. 1995. The Naxi and the nationalities question. See Harrell 1995, pp. 39–62

Mueggler E. 2001. *The Age of Wild Ghosts.* Berkeley: Univ. Calif. Press

Naranbilik. 1997. Zhongguo renleixue de dubai yu duibai: keti yu wenti. See Rong & Xu 1997, pp. 25–32

Pan WC. 1987. Shilun Liangshan Yizu nuli shehui de dengji huafen. In *Xinan Minzu Yanjiu, Yizu Zhuanj*, ed. Zhongguo Xinan Minzu Yanjiu Hui. Kunming: Yunnan Renmin

Pannell C. 1992. The role of great cities in China. See Guldin 1992, pp. 11–39

Phillips MR. 1993. Strategies used by Chinese families coping with schizophrenia. See Davis & Harrell 1993, pp. 277–306

Pieke F. 1996. *The Ordinary and the Extraordinary.* London: Kegan Paul

Potter SH, Potter JM. 1990. *China's Peasants.* New York: Cambridge Univ. Press

Pun N. 1999. Becoming dagongmei (working girls). *China J.* 42:1–20

Pye LW. 1992. *The Spirit of Chinese Politics.* Cambridge, MA: Harvard Univ. Press. 2nd ed.

Qiao J, Chen GQ, Zhou LF, eds. 1992. *Huidong-ren Yanjiu.* Fuzhou: Fujian Jiaoyu

Rees H. 2000. *Echoes of History.* New York: Oxford Univ. Press

Rofel L. 1999. *Other Modernities.* Berkeley: Univ. Calif. Press

Rong SX, Xu JS, eds. 1997. *Renleixue Bentuhua zai Zhongguo.* Nanning: Guangxi Minzu

Ruan XB, Luo PL, He YY. 1998. *Hunyin, Xingbie yu Xing.* Hong Kong: Global

Ruan YX. 2000. Yixu: Xiri "zongzu xiangcun" de minsu jieqing. *Guangxi Minzu Xueyuan XB* 22(3):20–26

Ruf G. 1998. *Cadres and Kin.* Stanford, CA: Stanford Univ. Press

Schein L. 1999. *Minority Rules*. Durham, NC: Duke Univ. Press

Schoenhals M. 1993. *The Paradox of Power in a People's Republic of China Middle School*. Armonk, ME: Sharpe

Shi YL. 1997. One model of urbanization: the urbanization process in Xiamen city's Caitang village. See Guldin 1997, pp. 123–50

Shih CK. 2001. *In Pursuit of Harmony*. Stanford, CA: Stanford Univ. Press

Sichuan Sheng Minzu Yanjiu Suo. 1980. *Baima Zangren Zushu Wenti Taolunji*. Chengdu

Siu HF. 1989. *Agents and Victims in South China*. New Haven, CT: Yale Univ. Press

Siu HF. 1993. Reconstructing dowry and brideprice in South China. See Davis & Harrell 1993, pp. 165–88

Skinner GW. 1971. Chinese peasants and the closed community. *Comp. Stud. Soc. Hist.* 13(3):270–81

Skinner GW, ed. 1977. Introduction: urban and rural in Chinese society. In *The City in Late Imperial China*, pp. 253–73. Stanford, CA: Stanford Univ. Press

Stacey J. 1983. *Patriarchy and Socialist Revolution in China*. Berkeley: Univ. Calif. Press

Stockard JM. 1989. *Daughters of the Canton Delta*. Stanford, CA: Stanford Univ. Press

Swain MB. 2001. Desiring Ashima, sexing landscape, in China's Stone Forest. In *Seductions of Place: Geography and Touristed Landscapes*, ed. C Cartier, A Lew. London: Routledge. In press

Tang WF, Parish WL. 2000. *Chinese Urban Life Under Reform*. Cambridge, UK: Cambridge Univ. Press

Tapp N. 2001. *The Hmong of China: Context, Agency, and the Imaginary*. Leiden, Neth.: Brill.

Tong EZ. 1988. Moergen de moshi yu Makesi zhuyi. *Shehui Kexue Yanjiu* 12(2):177–96

Unger J. 1993. Urban families in the eighties: an analysis of Chinese surveys. See Davis & Harrell 1993, pp. 25–49

Upton JL. 1999. The development of modern school-based Tibetan language education in the PRC. In *China's National Minority Education*, ed. GW Postiglione, pp. 281–340. New York: Falmer

Upton JL. 2000. Notes toward a native Tibetan ethnology. *Tibet. J.* 25(1):3–26

Veeck A. 2000. The revitalization of the marketplace. See Davis 2000, pp. 107–23

Walder AF. 1986. *Communist Neo-Traditionalism*. Berkeley: Univ. Calif. Press

Wang DY. 2001. Ritualistic coresidence and the weakening of filial practice in rural China. In *The Practice of Filial Piety in East Asia*, ed. C Ikels. In press

Wang G. 2000. Cultivating friendship through bowling in Shenzhen. See Davis 2000, pp. 250–67

Wang JM, Zhang HY, Hu HB. 1998. *Zhongguo Minzuxue Shi*. Kunming: Yunnan Jiaoyu. 2 Vols.

Wang MM. 1997. *Cunluo Shiye zhong de Wenhua yu Quanli*. Beijing: Sanlian

Wang MM, Feuchtwang S. 1997. Guanyu Zhongguo renleixue fazhan quxiang de duihua. See Rong & Xue 1997, pp. 39–42

Wang ZS. 1997. *The Jingpo Kachin of the Yunnan Plateau*. Tempe: Prog. SE. Asian Stud., Ariz. State Univ.

Wank DL. 2000. Cigarettes and domination in Chinese business networks. See Davis 2000, pp. 268–86

Watson JL. 1987. The structure of Chinese funerary rites. In *Death Ritual in Late Imperial and Modern China*, ed. JL Watson, ES Rawski, pp. 3–19. Berkeley: Univ. Calif. Press

Watson JL. 1997. *Golden Arches East*. Stanford, CA: Stanford Univ. Press

Weller RP. 1999. *Alternate Civilities*. Boulder, CO: Westview

Weng NQ. 1995. *The mother house*. Ph.D. thesis, Univ. Rochester, Rochester, NY

White SD. 1998. State discourses, minority policies, and the politics of identity in the Lijiang Naxi people's autonomous county. In *Nationalism and Ethnoregional Identities in China*, ed. W Safran. London: Cass

Whyte MK, Parish WL. 1984. *Urban Life in Contemporary China*. Chicago: Univ. Chicago Press

Williams DM. 2000. Representations of nature on the Mongolian steppe. *Am. Anthropol.* 102(3):503–19

Wolf M. 1985. *Revolution Postponed: Women in Contemporary China.* Stanford, CA: Stanford Univ. Press

Wu DYH. 1990. Chinese minority policy and the meaning of minority cultures: the example of the Bai in Yunnan. *Hum. Org.* 49(1):1–13

Wu Ga. 2001. Nuosu women's economic role in Ninglang, Yunnan under the Reforms. See Harrell 2001, pp. 256–66

Wu Gu. 2001. Reconstructing Yi history from Yi records. See Harrell 2000, pp. 21–34

Xu JS. 1999. *Xueqiu: Han Minzu de Renleixue Fenxi.* Shanghai: Shanghai Renmin

Yan YX. 1996. *The Flow of Gifts.* Stanford, CA: Stanford Univ. Press

Yan YX. 2000. Of hamburger and social space: consuming McDonald's in Beijing. See Davis 2000, pp. 201–25

Yang MMH. 1994. *Gifts, Favors, and Banquets.* Ithaca, NY: Cornell Univ. Press

Yang MMH, ed. 1999. *Spaces of their Own.* Minneapolis: Univ. Minn. Press

Zhang L. 2001. *Strangers in the City.* Stanford, CA: Stanford Univ. Press

Zhou DM. 1997a. Investigation and analysis of "migrant odd-job workers" in Guangzhou. In *Farewell to Peasant China*, ed. GE Guldin, pp. 227–47. Armonk, ME: Sharpe

Zhou DM. 1997b. "Zhongguo shi" renleixue yu renleixue de bentuhua. See Rong & Xu 1997, pp. 68–74

Zhou DM. 2001. *Fenghuang Cun de Bianqian.* Beijing: Sanlian. In press

Zhou DM, Guo ZL. 1996. *Zhongguo Nongcun Dushihua.* Guangzhou: Guangdong Renmin

Zhou DM, Zhang YQ. 1997. Rural urbanization in Guangdong's Pearl River Delta. See Guldin 1997, pp. 71–122

Zhuang KS. 2000. *Yin Yi.* Beijing: Sanlian

Annu. Rev. Anthropol. 2001. 30:163–79

SEXUALITY, CULTURE, AND POWER IN HIV/AIDS RESEARCH

Richard Parker

Institute of Social Medicine, State University of Rio de Janeiro; Brazilian Interdisciplinary AIDS Association; and Sociomedical Sciences Division, Joseph L. Mailman School of Public Health, Columbia University, New York, New York 10032-2603; e-mail: rgp11@columbia.edu

Key Words   sexual practices, cultural analysis, political economy

■ **Abstract**   This article examines the development of anthropological research in response to AIDS. During the first decade of the epidemic, most social science research focused on the behavioral correlates of HIV infection among individuals and failed to examine broader social and cultural factors. By the late 1980s, however, pioneering work by anthropologists began to raise the importance of cultural systems in shaping sexual practices relevant to HIV transmission and prevention. Since the start of the 1990s, this emphasis on cultural analysis has taken shape alongside a growing anthropological research focus on structural factors shaping vulnerability to HIV infection. Work on social inequality and the political economy of HIV and AIDS has been especially important. Much current research seeks to integrate both cultural and structural concerns in providing an alternative to more individualistic behavioral research paradigms.

INTRODUCTION

Like many other disciplines, anthropology largely failed to distinguish itself in its initial responses to the HIV/AIDS epidemics. Certain other social science disciplines—in particular, psychology—were quick to mobilize themselves internally during the mid-1980s in order to lobby the U.S. federal government for funding and to offer institutional responses to the epidemic through the foundation of HIV/AIDS research centers (typically based in academic departments of psychiatry or psychology and well-integrated into largely epidemiological research efforts). However, anthropologists for the most part contributed only irregularly to such early research mobilization, largely on the basis of their own individual research initiatives and publications rather than as part of a formal or organized research response. This is not to say that no important anthropological contributions were made to the study of HIV and AIDS during this time (e.g., Bolognone 1986; Conant 1988a,b; Feldman 1985; Feldman & Johnson 1986; Feldman et al 1987;

0084-6570/01/1021-0163$14.00   **163**

E. Gorman 1986; M. Gorman 1986; Herdt 1987; Lang 1986; Nachmann & Dreyfuss 1986; Sindzingré & Jourdain 1987; Stall 1986; for further references to early anthropological work on HIV/AIDS, see Bolton et al 1991). But the dominant paradigm for the organization and conduct of AIDS research—both in the United States, where the epidemic was most intense at the time, and internationally, where its size and shape were only beginning to be perceived—was established in large part independently of anthropological contributions. The paradigm was characterized by a heavily biomedical emphasis and a largely individualistic bias in relation to the ways in which the social sciences might contribute meaningfully to the development and implementation of an HIV/AIDS research agenda.

This historical context proved to be especially important in shaping the dominant tendencies in the study of sexuality in relation to HIV and AIDS. One of the most immediate consequences of the HIV/AIDS epidemic was a remarkable increase in concern with (and funding for) research on sexuality—as well as a growing awareness of the extent to which the widespread neglect and even marginalization of sex research over much of the twentieth century had left virtually all countries largely unprepared to respond to an epidemic that appeared to be driven, above all else, through the sexual transmission of a viral infection (Herdt 1987; Herdt & Lindenbaum 1992). As policy makers and planners found themselves returning to the Kinsey surveys of sexual behavior—carried out in the United States more than fifty years earlier but now often invoked as if they applied to the historical present or, even more problematically, to the sexual practices found in radically different cultural traditions—new emphasis was placed on the urgent need for more adequate, current data on the nature of sexual behavior (see Turner et al 1989).

Indeed, much of the social science research activity that emerged in response to AIDS, not only during the mid- to late 1980s, but up to the present time, focuses on surveys of risk-related sexual behavior and on the knowledge, attitudes, and beliefs about sexuality that might be associated with the risk of HIV infection. Most of these studies have aimed to collect quantifiable data on numbers of sexual partners, the frequency of different sexual practices, previous experience with other sexually transmitted diseases, and any number of other similar issues that were understood to contribute to the spread of HIV infection (e.g., Carballo et al 1989; Chouinard & Albert 1989; Turner et al 1989; Cleland & Ferry 1995). On the basis of such data, the primary goal was to point the way for prevention policies and intervention programs designed to reduce behaviors associated with increased risk for HIV infection. By focusing on the links between empirical data on sexual behavior and largely psychological theories of individual behavior change (such as the Health Belief Model, the Theory of Reasoned Action, or the Stages of Change Model), it was assumed that more broad-based prevention programs could be developed in order to persuade individuals to change their behaviors in ways that would ultimately reduce the risk of HIV infection (e.g., Turner et al 1989).

Increasingly, however, as behavioral research and behavioral interventions began to be developed in a growing range of diverse social and cultural settings, the relative effectiveness of both the research instruments and intervention strategies came to be questioned, notably by anthropologists (see Herdt et al 1991, Parker et al 1991). The difficulties of translating or adapting research protocols for cross-cultural application quickly became apparent in the face of often radically different understandings of sexual expression and practices in different societies and cultures—and even in different subcultures within the same society (Bibeau 1991, Bolton et al 1991, Singer 1992, ten Brummelhuis & Herdt 1995, Clatts 1994, Herdt & Lindenbaum 1992, Parker 1994, Pollak 1988). The limitations of behavioral interventions based on information and reasoned persuasion as a stimulus for risk reduction also quickly became evident. In study after study, the finding that information in and of itself is insufficient to produce risk-reducing behavioral change was repeated, and the relative limitations of individual psychology as the basis for intervention and prevention programs became apparent (see Carrier & Magaña 1991, Clatts 1989, Herdt & Boxer 1992, Herdt et al 1991). By the late 1980s, therefore, on the basis of both research findings and practical experience around the world, it had become clear that a far more complex set of social, structural, and cultural factors mediate the structure of risk in every population group, and that the dynamics of individual psychology cannot be expected to fully explain, let alone produce, changes in sexual conduct without taking these broader issues into account (see Bolton & Singer 1992; Carrier 1989; Flowers 1988; Herdt & Lindenbaum 1992; Herdt et al 1991; Obbo 1988; Parker 1987, 1988; Schoepf et al 1988).

FROM BEHAVIORAL RISKS TO CULTURAL MEANINGS

Although anthropological work has played only a very limited role during the 1980s in the development of HIV/AIDS research agendas and initiatives focusing on sexual behavior, quite the opposite is the case for anthropology in the 1990s, in relation to finding the most important alternative approaches to research on sexuality and AIDS. While there has in fact been increasing convergence between these approaches over time, it is nonetheless possible to identify at least two major tendencies that, by the early 1990s, had begun to mount a serious challenge to the dominance of biomedically and epidemiologically driven behavioral research agendas for the study of HIV and AIDS, as well as to the psychological approach to sexuality described above.

On the one hand, particularly during the early 1990s, there was a growing focus on the interpretation of cultural meanings (as opposed to the calculus of behavioral frequencies) as central to a fuller understanding of both the sexual transmission of HIV in different social settings and the possibilities that might exist for responding to it through the design of more culturally appropriate prevention programs (Treichler 1999). On the other hand, emerging at the same time but gaining greater attention over the mid- to late 1990s, there was increasing concern with the impact of a range of wider structural factors that could be seen as shaping vulnerability to HIV infection as well as conditioning the possibilities for sexual risk reduction in specific social contexts (see Farmer 1992; Farmer et al 1996; Schoepf 1992a,b,c; Schoepf et al 1988; Treichler 1999).

By the early 1990s, a range of broader cultural factors began to be identified as centrally important to an adequate understanding of the social dimensions of HIV and AIDS. Furthermore, the limitations of traditional behavioral research approaches in public health had begun to become apparent, particularly with regard to the development of prevention and intervention activities (see Bolton & Singer 1992; Herdt & Lindenbaum 1992; Herdt et al 1991). Heavily influenced by developments within interactionist sociology and interpretive cultural anthropology, as well as by insights emerging from fields such as women's and gay and lesbian studies, attention turned to the broader set of social representations and cultural meanings that could be understood as shaping or constructing sexual experience in different contexts (Alonso & Koreck 1989; Carrier & Magaña 1991; Daniel & Parker 1993; Gorman 1991; Herdt & Boxer 1991, 1992; Obbo 1993; Schoepf 1992a,b). Stimulated by such social constructionist concerns, an important shift of emphasis began to take place from an earlier focus on individual psychology and individual subjectivity to a new concern with intersubjective cultural meanings related to sexuality (Brummelhuis & Herdt 1995; Gagnon & Parker 1995; Herdt & Lindenbaum 1992; Paiva 1995; Parker 1991; Parker & Aggleton 1999).

Fundamentally informed by anthropological approaches to other cultural phenomena (such as religious belief and political ideology), this new attention to sexual meanings emphasized their shared or collective character—their constitution not as the property of atomized or isolated individuals but rather of social persons who are integrated in the context of specific cultural settings (Herdt & Lindenbaum 1992). This new wave of anthropological research on HIV and AIDS thus sought to go beyond the calculation of behavioral frequencies. In order to examine and explicate what sexual practices mean to the persons involved, the significant contexts in which they take place, the social scripting of sexual encounters, and the diverse sexual cultures and subcultures that are present or emergent within different societies, the research also sought to go beyond the identification of statistical correlates aimed at explaining sexual risk behavior (e.g., Bolton & Singer 1992; ten Brummelhuis & Herdt 1995; Herdt & Lindenbaum 1992; Parker 1994, 1996a). It is perhaps not surprising that much of this work first emerged in cross-cultural research and in analyses of the situation in non-Western settings in which the biomedical categories used in epidemiological analysis failed to be fully applicable (Carrier 1989; Parker 1987, 1988; Wilson 1995; de Zalduondo et al 1991). Increasingly, cultural analysis has also been applied when considering specific sexual cultures or subcultures in the industrialized West, offering important new insights even in settings where extensive behavioral research had already been carried out (see Alonso & Koreck 1989; Clatts 1995; Henriksson 1995; Irvine 1994; Kane & Mason 1992; Magaña 1991; Sobo 1993, 1995a).

The focus of much important research on sexuality in relation to HIV and AIDS over the course of the past decade has thus moved from behavior, in and of itself, to the cultural settings within which behavior takes place—and to the cultural symbols, meanings, and rules that organize it (see Bolton 1992; González Block & Liguori 1992; Henriksson 1995; Henriksson & Mansson 1995; Herdt 1997a,b,c; Herdt & Boxer 1991, 1992; Hogsborg & Aaby 1992; Kendall 1995; Lyttleton 2000; Paiva 1995, 2000; Setel 1999). Special emphasis has been given to analyzing indigenous cultural categories and systems of classification that structure and define sexual experience in different social and cultural contexts—with particular stress on the cross-cultural diversity that exists in the construction of same-sex interactions (Alonso & Koreck 1989; González Block & Liguori 1992; Carrier 1989; Carrier et al 1997; Carrillo 1999; Lichtenstein 2000; Ligouri & Aggleton 1999; Preston-Whyte et al 2000; Tan 1995, 1996). Indeed, it has become increasingly apparent that many of the key categories and classifications [not only "homosexuality," but also categories such as "prostitution," or "female sexual partner" (of male injecting drug users)] that have typically been used in biomedicine to describe sexual behaviors, or account for vectors of infection of interest to public health epidemiology, are in fact not relevant in all cultural contexts. Indeed, the meanings of these concepts are not stable even in those contexts in which these categories are in wide circulation (e.g., Alonso & Koreck 1989; Avila et al 1991; Carrier 1989, 1995, 1999; Carrier et al 1997; Carrillo 1999; Díaz 1998; Herdt 1997b,c; Herdt & Lindenbaum 1992; Irvine 1994; Jenkins 1996; Kane & Mason 1992; Larvie 1997, 1999; Law 1997; Lichtenstein 2000; Liguori & Aggleton 1999; Liguori et al 1996; Preston-Whyte 1995; Preston-Whyte et al 2000; Silva 1999; Tan 1995, 1996, 1999, 2000; Wright 1997; de Zalduondo 1991). By focusing more carefully on local categories and classifications, the cultural analysis of sexual meanings has thus sought to move from what, in other areas of anthropological or linguistic investigation, have been described as an "etic" or "outsider" perspective, to an "emic" or "insider" perspective—or, perhaps even more accurately, from the "experience-distant" concepts of biomedical science to the "experience-near" concepts and categories that the members of specific cultures use to understand and interpret their everyday lives (see Geertz 1973, 1983; Parker 1991).

This shift of emphasis from the study of individual behaviors to the investigation of cultural meanings has drawn attention to the socially constructed (and historically changing) identities and communities that structure sexual practice within the flow of collective life (see Bolton 1992; Carrillo 1999; Herdt & Boxer 1992; Klein 1999; Rubin 1997; Tan 1995; 1999; Terto 2000). On the basis of such work, an important reformulation of the very notion of intervention has begun to take place. It has become increasingly apparent that the idea of a behavioral intervention may in fact be a misnomer, since HIV/AIDS prevention interventions almost never function at the level of behavior but rather at the level of social or collective representations (Parker 1996a). New knowledge and information about perceived sexual risk will always be interpreted within the context of pre-existing systems of meaning—systems of meaning that necessarily mediate the ways in which such information must always be incorporated into action. Because action has increasingly come to be understood as socially constructed and fundamentally collective in nature, earlier notions of behavioral intervention have given way to ethnographically grounded AIDS education and prevention programs that are community-based and culturally sensitive—programs aimed at transforming social norms and cultural values, and thus at reconstituting collective meanings in ways that will ultimately promote safer sexual practices (see Altman 1994; Bolton & Singer 1992; Paiva 1995, 2000).

FROM CULTURAL MEANINGS TO STRUCTURAL VIOLENCE

Such ethnographically grounded descriptive and analytic research on the social and cultural construction of sexual meanings provides important insights to the representations shaping HIV-related risk and offers the basis for the development of culturally sensitive and culturally appropriate, community-based HIV/AIDS prevention programs. However, since the start of the 1990s it has also become increasingly evident that the range of factors influencing the construction of sexual realities is far more complex than previously perceived. It has become evident that not just cultural, but also structural, political, and economic factors shape sexual experience (and hence constrain the possibilities for sexual behavior change) to a far greater extent than had previously been understood (Singer et al 1990; Farmer 1992; Schoepf 1991). In particular, research has emphasized that political and economic factors have played a key role in determining the shape and spread of the epidemic and has emphasized that these same factors have been responsible for many of the most complex barriers to effective AIDS prevention programs (Baer et al 1997; González Block & Liguori 1992; Farmer 1992, 1999; Farmer et al 1996; Lindenbaum 1997, 1998; Schoepf 1991, 1995; Singer 1994, 1998; Singer et al 1990, 1992). By the early to mid-1990s, cultural analysis had emerged as an important corrective to the perceived limitations of earlier behavioral approaches. At the same time, a new focus on political and economic analysis of the structural factors associated with an increased risk for HIV infection, and with both the structural barriers and facilitators for risk reduction, emerged as central to the evolving anthropological response to the epidemic (Farmer et al 1996; Feldman 1994; Singer 1994, 1998).

Because this research on structural factors in relation to HIV/AIDS has emerged in a number of different social settings, ranging from deeply impoverished rural areas in developing countries to the marginalized inner cities in the United States, the language that it has used, the conceptual tools that it has employed, and the specific focus of analysis have often varied (e.g., Bond et al 1997b; Farmer 1992; Kreniske 1997; Schoepf 1991, 1992a,b,c, 1995; Singer 1994, 1998). In spite of the differences in terminology and at times in research emphasis, this work has consistently focused on what can be described as forms of "structural violence," which determine the social vulnerability of both groups and individuals. In developing these concepts, the work considers the interactive or synergistic effects of social factors such as poverty and economic exploitation, gender power, sexual oppression, racism, and social exclusion (Farmer et al 1996; Singer 1998; Parker & Camargo 2000; Parker et al 2000b). And the research has typically linked this vulnerability to a consideration of the ways in which such structural violence is itself situated in historically constituted political and economic systems—systems in which diverse political and economic processes and policies (whether related to economic development, housing, labor, migration or immigration, health, education, and welfare) create the dynamic of the epidemic and must be addressed in order to have any hope of reducing the spread of HIV infection (Bond et al 1997a; de Zalduondo & Bernard 1995; González Block & Liguori 1992; Farmer et al 1996; Kammerer et al 1995; Long 1997; Porter 1997; Romero-Daza 1994; Romero-Daza & Himmelgreen 1998; Susser & Kreniske 1997; Symonds 1998). To respond to this growing perception of the importance of structural factors and structural violence in shaping sexual experience and vulnerability to HIV infection, attention has increasingly focused on the ways in which societies and communities structure the possibilities of sexual interaction between social actors—the ways in which they define the available range of potential sexual partners and practices, as well as the ways in which they impose both the sexual possibilities and options that will be open to differentially situated actors. With whom one may have sex, in what ways, under what circumstances, and with what specific outcomes are never simply random questions (Akeroyd 1997; de Zalduondo & Bernard 1995; McGrath et al 1992, 1993; Parker et al 1991; Rwabukwali et al 1994).[1] Such possibilities are defined through the implicit and explicit rules and regulations imposed by the sexual cultures of specific communities as well as the economic and political power relations that underpin these sexual cultures. They can never be fully understood without examining the importance of issues such as "class," "race" or "ethnicity" and the other multiple forms through which different societies organize systems of social inequality and structure the possibilities for social interaction along or across lines of social difference.

This awareness of the ways in which social orders structure the possibilities (and obligations) of sexual contact has drawn special attention to socially and culturally determined differentials in power—particularly between men and women (de Zalduondo & Bernard 1995; Gupta & Weiss 1993; Parker 1991; Schoepf 1992a,b; Sobo 1993, 1994, 1995a,b, 1998)—but also, in some instances, between different types of men (Carrillo 1999; González Block & Liguori 1992; Liguori et al 1996; Prieur 1998; Silva 1999; Tan 1995, 1999).

Because different societies organize sexual (as well as other forms of) inequality in specific ways, social and cultural rules and regulations place specific limitations on the potential for negotiation in sexual interactions. These rules and regulations, in turn, condition the possibilities for the occurrence of sexual violence, for patterns of contraceptive use, for sexual negotiation, for HIV/AIDS risk reduction

---

[1]These concerns have of course long been present in anthropological studies of sexuality in non-Western societies and, in particular, in the anthropological literature on kinship (e.g., Fortes 1967; Goody 1973; Leach 1961; Lévi-Straus 1969; Malinowski 1929, 1955).

strategies, and so on. The dynamics of gender power relations have thus become a major focus for contemporary research, particularly in relation to reproductive health and the rapid spread of HIV infection among women in many parts of the world (e.g., Farmer et al 1996; Ginsberg & Rapp 1995; Gupta & Weiss 1993; Schoepf 1992a,b, 1995; Ward 1991). Just as detailed cross-cultural and comparative investigation of the social construction of same-sex interactions provided perhaps the key test case for demonstrating the importance of cultural analysis in relation to sexuality and HIV/AIDS, issues related to gender and power have been central to a better understanding of the importance of structural factors in organizing sexual relations and HIV/AIDS-related vulnerability (Akeroyd 1997; de Zalduondo & Bernard 1995; de Zalduondo et al 1991; Farmer 1999; Farmer et al 1996; Farmer et al 1993; Gupta & Weiss 1993, Long 1997; Obbo 1995; Paiva 1995; Romero-Daza 1994; Schoepf 1992b,c; Sobo 1993, 1995a,b).

As Farmer's work, in particular, has demonstrated, the political economic factors that drive the HIV/AIDS epidemic in virtually all social settings are intertwined with gender and sexuality, whose hierarchies make women, and low-income women in particular, especially vulnerable to HIV infection (Farmer 1992). In spite of this, there have still been relatively few ethnographically grounded studies on the ways in which gender and sexuality as structural (rather than behavioral) factors shape the AIDS epidemic. Farmer, Lindenbaum and Delvecchio-Good attribute this neglect to the initial predominance of AIDS cases among gay men in the industrialized Western countries, the fact that sexuality is a topic poorly understood by nearly all social scientists, and the fact that AIDS intervention programs often rely on superficial "rapid ethnographic assessment" procedures rather than on more detailed ethnographic description and analysis (Farmer et al 1993). The inappropriateness of many AIDS interventions directed toward women increasingly led a number of anthropologists to look more closely at gender and sexuality systems with the hopes of developing more realistic and effective HIV risk reduction options for women (Kammerer et al 1995; Schoepf 1991, 1992a,b; Symonds 1998).

Over the course of the 1990s, this growing interest in understanding the role of gender and sexuality structures in promoting HIV vulnerability, particularly among heterosexually active women and men, has increasingly generated a number of impressive ethnographic analyses that are attentive to both cultural and political economic factors. For example, Kammerer et al examine the ways in which the mountain tribes of the northern Thailand periphery are being exposed to the threat of HIV (Kammerer et al 1995). The vulnerability of these hillside tribes to HIV is in large measure generated by state and capitalist penetration, which has led to a breakdown of the material base rural life and has caused young people to migrate to valley towns in order to work not only as prostitutes but also as maids, waiters, and construction workers. These socioeconomic transformations have affected hillside sexuality, which until recently was structured around core values of "shame, name and blame." The authors provide ethnographic descriptions of these core values in relation to HIV/AIDS and how the gender power relations and customary prescriptions and prohibitions of hillside sexuality make talking about sex and taking precautions against HIV transmission difficult.

Similarly, Symonds, writing on the Hmong in Northern Thailand, has examined how the epidemic of HIV/AIDS in Thailand, and the place of Hmong within it, can be explained only by a combination of inter-related factors: the commercial sex industry, the prevalence of injection drug use, the political economic changes that have forced the Hmong living in the highlands to rely on lowland markets, racism and discrimination against the Hmong by the Thai majority, and sexual double standards, which permits polygyny among men yet controls the sexuality of young women (Symonds 1998). Finally, Schoepf has used vignettes from the life histories of women from various socioeconomic classes in Kinshasa, Zaire to demonstrate that HIV is spreading not through exotic cultural practices but because of many people's normal responses to situations of everyday life, such as dealing with substantial economic hardship and uncertainty (Schoepf 1992c). Like Kammerer et al and Symonds, Schoepf has promoted a participatory and collaborative form of action research with vulnerable women as a means to help redefine the gendered social roles and socioeconomic conditions that have contributed to the rapid spread of HIV in many parts of the world (Schoepf 1992a,b; Schoepf et al 1988).

In turning to issues of power, attention has focused not only on gender but also on poverty, both in the context of developing countries (see Farmer 1992, 1995, 1999; Farmer et al 1996; Farmer et al 1993; Kreniske 1997; Paiva 1995, 2000; Schoepf 1991) and in the impoverished inner-city ethnic communities of the United States (Farmer et al 1996; Singer 1994, 1998; Sobo 1993, 1994, 1995a), particularly as poverty interacts with gender power relations. Especially in the U.S.-based urban ethnography of HIV and AIDS, the impact of race and racism has necessarily been linked to issues of both poverty and gender, creating a kind of synergistic effect (Baer et al 1997; Farmer et al 1993; Singer 1994, 1998), involving multiple forms of oppression and shaping the nature of HIV/AIDS-related risk due to injecting drug use and voluntary as well as involuntary sexual practices (Singer 1998; Sobo 1995a). Although it has received less attention (perhaps because of the homophobia that affects anthropology as much as any other discipline), the extension of gender power inequalities together with pervasive heterosexism have also increasingly been understood as interacting with other forms of structural violence, including both poverty and racism, in creating situations of extreme vulnerability in relation to gender nonconformity, to transgender and male sex work, to gay men from ethnic minority groups, and among young men who have sex with men generally (see Díaz 1998; Carrier et al 1997; Khan 1996; Lichtenstein 2000; Parker et al 1998; Silva 1999; Tan 1995, 1999; Whitehead 1997; Wright 1993, 1997).

Ultimately, work casting the body as both a symbolic and a material product of social relations—a construct that is necessarily conditioned by a whole range of structural forces—has provided an especially important way of reframing recent research on sexuality in relation to HIV and AIDS (e.g., Bishop & Robinson 1998; Manderson & Jolly 1997; Parker 1999). The potential implications of this understanding for prevention interventions and strategies are farreaching. In seeking to broaden the potential scope and impact of intervention strategies, a number of new approaches have been developed that have been heavily influenced by anthropologically and ethnographically grounded understandings of the political economy of HIV and AIDS. What have been described as structural interventions have come to the fore. For example, there are attempts to change the employment options for sex workers or improve the logistics of condom availability and distribution, with the ultimate goal of altering the structural conditions that may impede or facilitate the adoption of safer sex (Parker et al 2000a,b; Preston-Whyte et al 2000). Strategies aimed at "community mobilization" and the stimulation of activism or advocacy have also drawn attention, with a growing number of intervention studies now focusing on the dynamics of community organizing in different settings (Susser & Kreniske 1997). In some of the most innovative work currently being carried out, HIV/AIDS intervention research has increasingly drawn on theories of "social transformation" and "collective empowerment" in order to examine issues related to power and oppression. The research has increasingly turned from the psychological theorists of reasoned decision-making to the work of community activists and popular educators in seeking the basis for a transformative or dialogical educational process in which participants explore and question their own lives and realities. Through this exploration and questioning, the participants begin to undergo a process of collective empowerment and transformation in order to respond to the forces that threaten and oppress them (see Paiva 2000, Parker 1996b).

All of this recent work has called attention to the need for structural changes aimed at transforming the broader forces that structure HIV/AIDS vulnerability and at enabling the members of affected communities to more adequately respond to these forces. Perhaps most important, it has focused on the extent to which HIV/AIDS prevention (and prevention research, in anthropology as in other disciplines) must be understood as part of a broader process of social transformation aimed not merely at the reduction of risk but at the redress of the social and economic inequality and injustice that has almost universally been found linked to increased vulnerability in the face of HIV and AIDS.

CONCLUSION

Anthropologists were rather slow to respond to the initial impact of the HIV/AIDS epidemic during the early and mid-1980s, allowing an essentially biomedical and highly individualistic model of AIDS research and intervention that has continued up to the present time as the dominant approach to the epidemic. Nevertheless anthropological perspectives have taken a leading role in defining what have been perhaps the most important alternative currents of social research in response to AIDS. Since the late 1980s, and increasingly over the course of the 1990s, anthropological research on the cultural meanings that shape and construct sexual experience, and on the political economy of structural forces that impinge upon sexual life, have provided alternative models and paradigms for responding to the epidemic both locally and cross-culturally (Parker et al 2000a; Treichler 1999). Although these two approaches for the most part emerged independently, inspired by distinct tendencies within the discipline more broadly, by the end of the 1990s both cultural and political economic or structural approaches increasingly merged in offering an important counterpoint to the more biomedical and behavioral perspectives that continue to dominate the field and to receive the lion's share of funding and prestige. Although it is impossible to fully predict the ways in which HIV/AIDS research will develop in the future, the fact that the epidemic continues to expand in large part independent of all of the efforts thus far to control it, and the fact that it continues to take its greatest toll in the so-called developing world and among the most impoverished and marginalized sectors of all societies, suggests that the kinds of approaches that anthropologists have offered for the study of sexuality and HIV/AIDS will continue to be important. The kind of response that anthropology continues to make in relation to the epidemic will be an important indicator of the relevance of the discipline as we enter the new millennium.

Visit the Annual Reviews home page at www.AnnualReviews.org

LITERATURE CITED

Aggleton P, ed. 1996. *Bisexualities and AIDS: International Perspectives*. London: Taylor Francis

Aggleton P, ed. 1999. *Men Who Sell Sex: International Perspectives on Male Prostitution and HIV/AIDS*. London: UCL Press

Akeroyd A. 1997. Sociocultural aspects of AIDS in Africa: occupational and gender issues. See Bond et al. 1997a, pp. 11–30

Alonso AM, Koreck MT. 1989. Silences: "Hispanics," AIDS and sexual practices. *Differences* 1:101–24

Altman D. 1994. *Power and Community: Organizational and Cultural Responses to AIDS*. London: Taylor Francis

Avila M, Zuñiga P, de Zalduondo B. 1991. Diversity in commercial sex work systems: preliminary findings from Mexico City and their implications for AIDS interventions. See Chen et al. 1991, pp. 179–94

Baer H, Singer M, Susser I. 1997. *Medical Anthropology and the World System*. Westport, CT/London: Bergin Garvey

Bibeau G. 1991. L'Afrique, terre imaginaire du SIDA: la subversion du discours scientifique par le jeu des fantasmes. *Anthropol. Soc.* 15(2–3):125–47

Bishop R, Robinson LS. 1998. *Night Market: Sexual Cultures and the Thai Economic Miracle*. New York/London: Routledge

Bolognone D. 1986. AIDS: a challenge to anthropologists. *Med. Anthropol. Q.* 17(2):36 (Abstr.)

Bolton R. 1992. Mapping terra incognita: sex research for AIDS prevention—an urgent agenda for the 1990s. See Herdt & Lindenbaum 1992, pp. 124–58

Bolton R, Lewis M, Orozco G. 1991. AIDS literature for anthropologists: a working bibliography. *J. Sex Res.* 28(2):307–46

Bolton R, Singer M, eds. 1992. *Rethinking AIDS Prevention: Cultural Approaches*. Philadelphia: Gordon Breach Sci.

Bond G, Kreniske J, Susser I. Vincent J, eds. 1997a. *AIDS in Africa and the Caribbean*. Boulder: Westview

Bond G, Kreniske J, Susser I. Vincent J. 1997b. The anthropology of AIDS in Africa and the Caribbean. See Bond et al. 1997a, pp. 3–9

Bond K, Celentano D, Phonsophakul S, Vaddhanaphuti C. 1997. Mobility and migration: female commercial sex work and the HIV epidemic in Northern Thailand. See Herdt 1997b, pp. 185–215

Carballo M, Cleland J, Caraël M, Albrecht G. 1989. A cross-national study of patterns of sexual behavior. *J. Sex Res.* 26:287–99

Carrier J. 1989. Sexual behavior and the spread of AIDS in Mexico. *Med. Anthropol.* 10:129–42

Carrier J. 1995. *De Los Otros: Intimacy and Homosexuality among Mexican Men.* New York: Columbia Univ. Press

Carrier J. 1999. Reflections on ethical problems encountered in field research on Mexican male homosexuality: 1968 to present. *Cult. Health Sex.* 1(3):207–21

Carrier J, Magaña R. 1991. Use of ethnosexual data on men of Mexican origin for HIV/AIDS prevention programs. *J. Sex Res.* 28(2):189–202

Carrier J, Ngyen B, Su S. 1997. Sexual relations between migrating populations (Vietnamese with Mexican and Anglo) and HIV/STD infections in Southern California. See Herdt 1997b, pp. 225–50

Carrillo H. 1999. Cultural change, hybridity and male homosexuality in Mexico. *Cult. Health Sex.* 1(3):223–38

Chen LC, Amor JS, Segal SJ, eds. 1991. *AIDS and Women's Reproductive Health.* New York/London: Plenum

Chouinard A, Albert J, eds. 1989. *Human Sexuality: Research Perspectives in a World Facing AIDS.* Ottawa: Int. Dev. Res. Cent.

Clatts M. 1989. Ethnography and AIDS intervention in New York City: life history as an ethnographic strategy. In *Community-Based AIDS Prevention, Studies of Intravenous Drug Users and their Sexual Partners.* Rockville, MD: Natl. Inst. Drug Abuse

Clatts M. 1994. "All the king's horses and all the king's men": some personal reflections on ten years of AIDS ethnography. *Hum. Organ.* 53:93–95

Clatts M. 1995. Disembodied acts: on the perverse use of sexual categories in the study of high-risk behaviour. See ten Brummelhuis & Herdt 1995, pp. 241–55

Cleland J, Ferry B, eds. 1995. *Sexual Behavior and AIDS in the Developing World.* London: Taylor Francis

Conant F. 1988a. Evaluating social science data relating to AIDS in Africa. In *AIDS in Africa: Social and Policy Impact,* ed. N Miller, R Rockwell, pp. 197–209. Lewiston, NY: Edwin Mellen

Conant F. 1988b. Using and rating cultural data on HIV transmission in Africa. See Kulstad 1988, pp. 198–204

Daniel H, Parker R. 1993. *Sexuality, Politics and AIDS in Brazil.* London: Falmer

de Zalduondo BO. 1991. Prostitution viewed cross-culturally: toward recontextualizing sex work in AIDS research. *J. Sex Res.* 22:223–48

de Zalduondo BO, Avila M, Zuñiga P. 1991. Intervention research needs for AIDS prevention among commercial sex workers and their clients. See Chen et al. 1991, pp. 165–78

de Zalduondo BO, Bernard J. 1995. Meanings and consequences of sexual-economic exchange. See Parker & Gagnon 1995, pp. 155–80

Díaz RM. 1998. *Latino Gay Men and HIV: Culture, Sexuality, and Risk Behavior.* New York/London: Routledge

Dyson T. 1992. *Sexual Behaviour and Networking: Anthropological and Socio-Cultural Studies on the Transmission of HIV.* Liège: Derouax-Ordina

Farmer P. 1992. *AIDS and Accusation: Haiti and the Geography of Blame.* Berkeley/Los Angeles: Univ. Calif. Press

Farmer P. 1995. Culture, poverty, and the dynamics of HIV transmission in rural Haiti. See ten Brummelhuis & Herdt 1995, pp. 3–28

Farmer P. 1999. *Infections and Inequalities: The Modern Plagues.* Berkeley/Los Angeles: Univ. Calif. Press

Farmer P, Connors M, Simmons J, eds. 1996.

Women, Poverty and AIDS: Sex, Drugs and Structural Violence. Monroe, Maine: Common Courage

Farmer P, Lindenbaum S, Delvecchio-Good MJ. 1993. Women, poverty and AIDS: an introduction. *Cult. Med. Psychiatry* 17(4):387–97

Feldman D. 1985. AIDS and social change. *Hum. Organ.* 44(4):343–48

Feldman D, ed. 1994. *Global AIDS Policy.* Westport, Connecticut/London: Bergin Garvey

Feldman D, Johnson T, eds. 1986. *The Social Dimensions of AIDS: Method and Theory.* New York: Praeger

Feldman DA, Friedman SR, Des Jarlais DC. 1987. Public awareness of AIDS in Rwanda. *Soc. Sci. Med.* 24(2):97–100

Flowers N. 1988. The spread of AIDS in rural Brazil. See Kulstad 1988, pp. 159–73

Fortes M. 1967. *The Web of Kinship among the Tallensi.* London: Oxford Univ. Press

Gagnon JH, Parker RG. 1995. Conceiving sexuality. See Parker & Gagnon 1995, pp. 3–16

Geertz C. 1973. *The Interpretation of Cultures.* New York: Basic Books

Geertz C. 1983. *Local Knowledge.* New York: Basic Books

Ginsberg FD, Rapp R. 1995. *Conceiving the New World Order: The Global Politics of Reproduction.* Berkeley/Los Angeles: Univ. Calif. Press

González Block MA, Liguori AL. 1992. *El SIDA en los Estratos Socioeconómicos de México.* Cuernavaca, Mex.: Inst. Nac. Salud Pública

Goody J, ed. 1973. *The Character of Kinship.* Cambridge, UK: Cambridge Univ. Press

Gorman E. 1986. The AIDS epidemic in San Francisco: epidemiological and anthropological perspectives. In *Anthropology and Epidemiology: Interdisciplinary Approaches to the Study of Health and Disease*, ed. CR Janes, R Stall, SM Grifford, pp. 157–72. Dordrecht, Neth.: D. Reidel

Gorman E. 1991. Anthropological reflections on the HIV epidemic among gay men. *J. Sex Res.* 28(2):263–73

Gorman M. 1986. Introduction. *Med. Anthropol. Q.* 17(2):31–32

Gupta GR, Weiss E. 1993. Women's lives and sex: implications for AIDS prevention. *Cult. Med. Psychiatry* 17(4):399–412

Henriksson B. 1995. *Risk Factor Love: Homosexuality, Sexual Interaction and HIV Prevention.* Göteborg, Swed.: Göteborgs Univ.

Henriksson B, Mansson S. 1995. Sexual negotiations: an ethnographic study of men who have sex with men. See ten Brummelhuis & Herdt 1995, pp. 157–82

Herdt G. 1987. AIDS and anthropology. *Anthropol. Today* 3(2):1–3

Herdt G. 1997a. Intergenerational relations and AIDS in the formation of gay culture in the United States. See Levine et al. 1997, pp. 245–81

Herdt G, ed. 1997b. *Sexual Cultures and Migration in the Era of AIDS: Anthropological and Demographic Perspectives.* London: Claredon

Herdt G. 1997c. Sexual culture and population movement: implications for AIDS/STDs. See Herdt 1997b, pp. 3–22

Herdt G, Boxer A. 1991. Ethnographic issues in the study of AIDS. *J. Sex Res.* 28(2):171–87

Herdt G, Boxer A. 1992. Sexual identity and risk for AIDS among gay youth in Chicago. See Dyson 1992, pp. 153–202

Herdt G, Leap WL, Sovine M. 1991. Anthropology, sexuality and AIDS. *J. Sex Res.* 28(2):167–69

Herdt G, Lindenbaum S, eds. 1992. *The Time of AIDS: Social Analysis, Theory, and Method.* Newbury Park, CA: Sage

Hogsborg M, Aaby P. 1992. Sexual relations, use of condoms and perceptions of AIDS in an urban area of Guinea-Bissau with a high prevalence of HIV-2. See Dyson 1992, pp. 203–32

Irvine JM, ed. 1994. *Sexual Cultures and the Construction of Adolescent Identities.* Philadelphia: Temple Univ. Press

Jenkins CL. 1996. Homosexual context, heterosexual practice in Papua New Guinea. See Aggleton 1996, pp. 191–206

Kammerer CA, Hutheesing OK, Maneeprasert R, Symonds PV. 1995. Vulnerability to HIV infection among three hilltribes in Northern Thailand. See ten Brummelhuis & Herdt 1995, pp. 53–78

Kane S, Mason T. 1992. "IV drug users" and "sex partners": the limits of epidemiological categories and the ethnography of risk. See Herdt & Lindenbaum 1992, pp. 199–222

Kendall C. 1995. The construction of risk in AIDS control programs. See Parker & Gagnon 1995, pp. 249–58

Khan S. 1996. Under the blanket: bisexualities and AIDS in India. See Aggleton 1996, pp. 161–77.

Klein C. 1999. "The ghetto is over, darling": emerging gay communities and gender and sexual politics in contemporary Brazil. *Cult. Health Sex.* 1(3):239–60

Kreniske J. 1997. AIDS in the Dominican Republic: anthropological reflections on the social nature of disease. See Bond et al. 1997a, pp. 33–50

Kulstad R, ed. 1988. *AIDS 1988: AAAS Symposia Papers.* Washington, DC: Am. Assoc. Adv. Sci. 478 pp.

Lang N. 1986. AIDS: biocultural issues and the role of medical anthropology. *Med. Anthropol. Q.* 17(2):35–36

Larvie P. 1997. Homophobia and ethnoscape of sex work in Rio de Janeiro. See Herdt 1997b, pp. 143–64

Larvie P. 1999. Natural born targets: male hustlers and AIDS prevention in urban Brazil. See Aggleton 1999, pp. 159–77

Law L. 1997. A matter of "choice": discourses on prostitution in the Philippines. See Manderson & Jolly 1997, pp. 233–61

Leach ER. 1961. *Rethinking Anthropology.* London: Athlone

Levi-Strauss C. 1969. *The Elementary Structures of Kinship.* Boston, MA: Beacon

Levine MP, Nardi PM, Gagnon JH, eds. 1997. *Changing Times: Gay Men and Lesbians Encounter HIV/AIDS.* Chicago/London: Univ. Chicago Press

Lichtenstein B. 2000. Sexual encounters: black men, bisexuality, and AIDS in Alabama. *Med. Anthropol. Q.* 14(3):374–93

Liguori AL, González Block MA, Aggleton P. 1996. Bisexuality and HIV/AIDS in Mexico. See Aggleton 1996, pp. 76–98

Liguori A, Aggleton P. 1999. Aspects of male sex work in Mexico City. See Aggleton 1999, pp. 103–25

Lindenbaum S. 1997. AIDS: body, mind, and history. See Bond et al. 1997a, pp. 191–94

Lindenbaum S. 1998. Images of catastrophe: the making of an epidemic. See Singer 1998, pp. 33–58

Long L. 1997. Refugee women, violence, and HIV. See Herdt 1997b, pp. 87–103

Lyttleton C. 2000. *Endangered Relations: Negotiating Sex and AIDS in Thailand.* Amsterdam: Harwood Acad.

Magaña JR. 1991. Sex, drugs and HIV: an ethnographic approach. *Soc. Sci. Med.* 33(1):5–9

Malinowski B. 1929. *The Sexual Life of Savages in North-western Melanesia.* London: G. Routledge

Malinowski B. 1955. *Sex and Repression in Savage Society.* New York: Meridian Books

Manderson L, Jolly M, eds. 1997. *Sites of Desire/Economies of Pleasure: Sexualities in Asia and the Pacific.* Chicago: Univ. Chicago Press

McGrath JG, Rwabukwali CB, Schumann DA, Pearson-Marks J, Nakayiwa S, et al. 1993. Anthropology and AIDS: the cultural context of sexual risk behaviors among urban Baganda women in Kampala, Uganda. *Soc. Sci. Med.* 36(4):429–39

McGrath JG, Schumann DA, Rwabukwali CB, Pearson-Marks J, Mukasa R, et al. 1992. Cultural determinants of sexual risk behavior for AIDS among Baganda women. *Med. Anthropol. Q.* 6(2):153–61

Nachman SR, Dreyfuss G. 1986. Haitians and AIDS in South Florida. *Med. Anthropol. Q.* 17(2):32–33

Obbo C. 1988. Is AIDS just another disease? See Kulstad 1988, pp. 191–97

Obbo C. 1993. HIV transmission through social

and geographic networks in Uganda. *Soc. Sci. Med.* 36:949–55

Obbo C. 1995. Gender, age and class: discourses on HIV transmission and control in Uganda. See ten Brummelhuis & Herdt 1995, pp. 79–95

Paiva V. 1995. Sexuality, AIDS and gender norms among Brazilian teenagers. See ten Brummelhuis & Herdt 1995, pp. 97–114

Paiva V. 2000. Gendered scripts and the sexual scene: promoting sexual subjects among Brazilian teenagers. See Parker et al. 2000a, pp. 216–39

Parker R. 1999. *Beneath the Equator: Cultures of Desire, Male Homosexuality and Emerging Gay Communities in Brazil.* New York/London: Routledge

Parker R, Aggleton P, eds. 1999. *Culture, Society and Sexuality: A Reader.* London: UCL Press

Parker R, Camargo Jr K. 2000. Pobreza e HIV/ AIDS: aspectos antropológicos e sociológicos. *Cad. Saúde Pública* 16(Suppl. 1):89–102

Parker R, Khan S. Aggleton P. 1998. Conspicuous by their absence? Men who have sex with men (msm) in developing countries: implications for HIV prevention. *Crit. Public Health* 8(4):329–46

Parker RG. 1987. Acquired immunodeficiency syndrome in urban Brazil. *Med. Anthropol. Q.* (New Ser.) 1:155–72

Parker RG. 1988. Sexual culture and AIDS education in urban Brazil. See Kulstad 1988, pp. 269–89

Parker RG. 1991. *Bodies, Pleasures and Passions: Sexual Culture in Contemporary Brazil.* Boston: Beacon

Parker RG. 1994. Sexual cultures, HIV transmission, and AIDS prevention. *AIDS* 8(Suppl. 1):S309–14

Parker RG. 1996a. Behavior in Latin American men: implications for HIV/AIDS interventions. *Int. J. STD AIDS* 7(Suppl. 2):62–65

Parker RG. 1996b. Empowerment, community mobilization, and social change in the face of HIV/AIDS. *AIDS* 10(Suppl. 3):S27–31

Parker RG, Barbosa RM, Aggleton P, eds.

2000a. *Framing the Sexual Subject: The Politics of Gender, Sexuality, and Power.* Berkeley/Los Angeles/London: Univ. Calif. Press

Parker RG, Easton D, Klein C. 2000b. Structural barriers and facilitators in HIV prevention: a review of international research. *AIDS.* 14(Suppl. 1):S22–32

Parker RG, Gagnon JH, eds. 1995. *Conceiving Sexuality: Approaches to Sex Research in a Postmodern World.* New York/London: Routledge

Parker RG, Herdt G, Carballo M. 1991. Sexual culture, HIV transmission, and AIDS research. *J. Sex Res.* 28:77–98

Pollak M. 1988. Les homosexuels face au SIDA. Paris: A Métaillé

Porter D. 1997. A plague on the borders: HIV, development, and traveling identities in the Golden Triangle. See Manderson & Jolly 1997, pp. 212–32

Preston-Whyte E. 1995. Half-way there: anthropology and intervention-oriented AIDS research in KwaZulu/Natal, South Africa. See ten Brummelhuis & Herdt 1995, pp. 315–37

Preston-Whyte E, Varga C, Oosthuizen H, Roberts R, Blose F. 2000. Survival sex and HIV/AIDS in an African city. See Parker et al. 2000a, pp. 165–90

Prieur A. 1998. *Mema's House, Mexico City: On Transvestites, Queens and Machos.* Chicago: Univ. Chicago Press

Romero-Daza N. 1994. Multiple sexual partners, migrant labor and the makings for an epidemic: knowledge and beliefs about AIDS among women in highland Lesotho. *Hum. Organ.* 53:192–211

Romero-Daza N, Himmelgreen D. 1998. More than money for your labor: migration and the political economy of AIDS in Lesotho. See Singer 1998, pp. 185–204

Rubin G. 1997. Elegy for the Valley of Kings: AIDS and the leather community in San Francisco, 1981–1996. See Levine et al. 1997, pp. 101–44

Rwabukwali CB, Schumann DA, McGrath JG, Carroll-Pankhurst C, Mukasa R, et al. 1994. Culture, sexual behavior, and attitudes toward condom use among Baganda women. See Feldman 1994, pp. 70–89

Schoepf B. 1991. Ethical, methodological and political issues of AIDS research in central Africa. *Soc. Sci. Med.* 33:749–63

Schoepf B. 1992a. AIDS, sex and condoms: African healers and the reinvention of tradition in Zaire. *Med. Anthropol.* 14:225–42

Schoepf B. 1992b. Sex, gender and society in Zaire. See Dyson 1992, pp. 353–75

Schoepf B. 1992c. Women at risk: case studies from Zaire. See Herdt & Lindenbaum 1992, pp. 259–86

Schoepf B. 1995. Culture, sex research and AIDS prevention in Africa. See ten Brummelhuis & Herdt 1995, pp. 29–51

Schoepf B, Nkera R, Ntsomo P, Engundu W, Schoepf C. 1988. AIDS, women, and society in central Africa. See Kulstad 1988, pp. 176–81

Setel PW. 1999. *A Plague of Paradoxes: AIDS, Culture and Demography in Northern Tanzania.* Chicago: Univ. Chicago Press

Silva L. 1999. Travestis and gigolos: male sex work and HIV prevention in France. See Aggleton 1999, pp. 41–60

Sindzingré N, Jourdain G. 1987. Le SIDA: épidémiologie et anthropologie. *Polit. Afr.* 28:33–41

Singer M. 1994. AIDS and the health crisis of the U.S. urban poor: the perspective of critical medical anthropology. *Soc. Sci. Med.* 39:931–48

Singer M, ed. 1998. *The Political Economy of AIDS.* Amityville, NY: Baywood

Singer M, Flores C, Davidson L, Burke G, Castillo Z, et al. 1990. SIDA: the economic, social and cultural context of AIDS among Latinos. *Med. Anthropol. Q.* 4(1):72–114

Singer M, Jia Z, Schensul J, Weeks M, Page JB. 1992. AIDS and the IV drug user: the local context in prevention efforts. *Med. Anthropol.* 14:285–306

Sobo EJ. 1993. Inner-city women and AIDS: psychosocial benefits of unsafe sex. *Cult. Med. Psychiatry* 17:454–85

Sobo EJ. 1994. Attitudes toward HIV testing among impoverished urban African-American women. *Med. Anthropol.* 16:1–22

Sobo EJ. 1995a. *Choosing Unsafe Sex: AIDS-Risk Denial Among Disadvantaged Women.* Philadelphia, PA: Univ. Penn. Press

Sobo EJ. 1995b. Finance, romance, social support, and condom use among impoverished inner-city women. *Hum. Organ.* 54:115–28.

Sobo EJ. 1998. Love, jealousy and unsafe sex among inner-city women. See Singer 1998, pp. 75–103

Stall R. 1986. The behavioral epidemiology of AIDS: a call for anthropological contributions. *Med. Anthropol. Q.* 17(2):36–37

Susser I, Kreniske J. 1997. Community organizing around HIV prevention in rural Puerto Rico. See Bond et al. 1997a, pp. 51–64

Symonds PV. 1998. Political economy and cultural logics of HIV/AIDS among the Hmong in Northern Thailand. See Singer 1998, pp. 205–26

Tan ML. 1995. From *bakla* to gay: shifting gender identities and sexual behaviors in the Philippines. See Parker & Gagnon 1995, pp. 85–96

Tan ML. 1996. *Silahis*: looking for the missing Filipino bisexual male. See Aggleton 1996, pp. 207–25

Tan ML. 1999. Walking the tightrope: sexual risk and male sex work in the Philippines. See Aggleton 1999, pp. 241–61

Tan ML. 2000. AIDS, medicine, and moral panic in the Philippines. See Parker et al. 2000a, pp. 143–64

ten Brummelhuis H, Herdt G, eds. 1995. *Culture and Sexual Risk: Anthropological Perspectives on AIDS.* Amsterdam: Gordon Breach

Terto V. 2000. Male homosexuality and seropositivity: the construction of social identities in Brazil. See Parker et al. 2000a, pp. 60–78

Treichler PA. 1999. *How to Have Theory in an Epidemic: Cultural Chronicles of AIDS.* Durham, NC/London: Duke Univ. Press

Turner CF, Miller HG, Moses LE, eds. 1989.

AIDS: Sexual Behavior and Intravenous Drug Use. Washington, DC: Natl. Acad. Press

Ward M. 1991. Cupid's touch: the lessons of the family planning movement for the AIDS epidemic. *J. Sex Res.* 28(2):289–305

Whitehead T. 1997. Urban low-income African American men, HIV/AIDS, and gender identity. *Med. Anthropol. Q.* 11:411–47

Wilson C. 1995. *Hidden in the Blood: A Personal Investigation of AIDS in the Yucatan.* New York: Columbia Univ. Press

Wright JW. 1993. African-American male sexual behavior and the risk of HIV infection. *Hum. Organ.* 52:421–31

Wright JW. 1997. African American males and HIV: the challenge of the AIDS epidemic. *Med. Anthropol. Q.* 11:454–55

Annu. Rev. Anthropol. 2001. 30:181–207

EARLY AGRICULTURALIST POPULATION DIASPORAS? FARMING, LANGUAGES, AND GENES

Peter Bellwood

School of Archaeology and Anthropology, Australian National University, Canberra ACT 0200, Australia; e-mail: peter.bellwood@anu.edu.au

Key Words   spread of agriculture, Neolithic/Formative archaeology, farmer-hunter interactions, language family origins and dispersals, population expansions

■ **Abstract**   The consequences of early agricultural development in several regions of the Old and New Worlds included population growth, the spread of new material cultures and of food-producing economies, the expansions of language families, and in many cases the geographical expansions of the early farming populations themselves into territories previously occupied by hunters and gatherers. This chapter discusses some of the different outcomes that can be expected according to the differing perspectives of archaeology, linguistics, and biological anthropology. I argue that agriculturalist expansion lies at the root of many of the world's major language families, although this need not imply that farmers always replaced hunter-gatherers in the biological sense. History, enviromental variations, and prior cultural configurations dictated many of the outcomes, some of which played a fundamental role in the large-scale genesis of human cultural and biological patterning from Neolithic/Formative times into the world of today.

INTRODUCTION

This chapter discusses the multidisciplinary implications of a series of major changes from hunting-gathering to farming that occurred in various parts of the world, at varying times, often independently of each other. They are of particular interest because of their potential linkages with language family and population dispersals. They form major keystones in the explanation of the patterns of human variation, both cultural and biological, that characterized the pre-Columbian world and that still dominate in many parts of the world today. As far as the general likelihood of early agriculturalist (Neolithic/Formative) population dispersal is concerned, the time has come to take stock, to look dispassionately at the options, and to take a worldwide multidisciplinary view. Some guidelines and a feeling for issues that might respond to theoretical debate should help the momentum along.

0084-6570/01/1021-0181$14.00

THE ORIGINS AND DISPERSALS OF AGRICULTURAL SOCIETIES AND LANGUAGE FAMILIES

Human prehistory gives us a record of two very important, yet at first sight unrelated, examples of expansion. These are (*a*) the expansions of agricultural systems from hearth areas such as Southwest Asia, China, and Mesoamerica, and (*b*) the expansions of the world's major language families. Some of the latter are of course associated with predominantly hunter-gatherer populations, but the majority occur in agricultural latitudes and their component languages are spoken by people who were already agriculturalists at the dawn of history. Many of these widespread agriculturalist language families, such as Austronesian, Indo-European, Niger-Congo, Uto-Aztecan, and Afroasiatic, had reached their precolonial geographical limits (give or take a few hundred kilometres) long before the local existence of any written records—their spreads belong among prehistoric farmers/pastoralists and small-scale social formations, rather than among the great conquest empires and charismatic world religions of history. Could the early dispersals of agriculture and the early spreads of certain major language families be linked effects of the same underlying set of causes? Do these causes relate to the demographic growth and rapid expansion profiles of early farmers?

In recent years, a number of prehistorians have suggested that there are major linkages between the relevant cultural, linguistic, and biological data sets pertaining to early farming dispersal in different parts of the world (e.g., Bellwood 1984, 1984–1985, 1991, 1996a,b, 1997b, 2000a; Cavalli-Sforza & Cavalli-Sforza 1995; Diamond 1997a,b, Higham 1996; Renfrew 1987, 1991, 1992, 1994, 1996). The essential reasoning here, as clearly set out by Renfrew (e.g., 1996), is that the rise of farming, wherever and whenever it occurred, formed a veritable "unconformity" that ran spatially across the chronological course of history, an unconformity that always had the potential to form a line of weakness along which factors that caused spreading could have operated with vigor.

In addition, such spreads, viewed from the experience of recent historical diasporas, would always have had the potential for substantial degrees of isomorphism between cultural, linguistic, and biological variation (i.e., if they involved well-delineated ethnic groups). Furthermore, correlations between these variables may have continued long after dispersal had ceased. But let it be stressed, given current touchiness about this issue in the anthropological literature, that no one seriously claims *absolute* isomorphism between the data sets (archaeology, language, biology) in any particular early farming situation. Language shift, gene flow, and cultural borrowing can obviously operate in almost all human contexts, except perhaps in situations of *extreme* isolation. So the possibility of any 1:1:1 correlation between a gene pool, a culture, and a language, each changing only by internal variation of inherited source materials, can be dismissed right from the start.

Because of such real-world complications, the questions asked in this essay cannot be given simple answers. But it is possible to suggest that, in a world peopled entirely by hunters and gatherers, any groups who by some means developed and came to depend upon systematic methods of food production (of plants, of animals, and—best of all—of both) would have acquired a "demographic edge" over their neighbors, particularly if those neighbors did not also, by choice or circumstance, adopt the food-producing economy themselves. Increasing birth rates would have promoted a geographical budding-off of the agricultural populations as their numbers increased, as long as social or geographic circumscription did not intervene.

Bearing this in mind, there would appear to be two opposite outcomes in regions surrounding early foci of agricultural development, with a range of possibilities in-between. At one extreme, the hunter-gatherer neighbors of the agriculturalists could have adopted the agricultural economy themselves, thus inhibiting any tendencies by the existing farmers to spread into new territory. At the other extreme, they could have remained as hunter-gatherers facing eventual assimilation into the larger and expanding farming societies. If the former option prevailed, agriculture would have spread ultimately through many diverse linguistic and archaeological populations, previously hunter-gatherers, with similar levels of diversity probably continuing thereafter. If the latter option prevailed, agriculture would have spread mainly through the expansion of the farming populations themselves, together with their languages. Under such circumstances of farmer expansion from a homeland region, we would expect the imposition of relative homogeneity of language and material culture on the ensuing cultural and linguistic patterns, and possibly a corresponding spread of certain population-specific markers in genetics.

It is clear, however, that under pre-state social conditions, such absolute extremes are both most unlikely outcomes. Farmers will often seek new land; hunters will often, if allowed, familiarize themselves with farming techniques. Where exactly, within the continuum of reality, different historical trajectories will fall can be estimated from several sources of data:

1. Evidence for agricultural "homelands," and the time and space coordinates of agricultural system spread into regions beyond those homelands, combined with a consideration of the productive "power" of the various agricultural economies and their resulting long-term potentials for demographic expansion.

2. Evidence of pre-agricultural to agricultural continuity, or hiatus, in the archaeological record (in general terms, Mesolithic to Neolithic in the Old World, Archaic to Formative in the New).

3. Patterns of diversity/homogeneity through space in early agricultural material culture. In this regard, some early Neolithic/Formative cultural assemblages are remarkably widespread compared to preceding and succeeding patterns, and this is a counter-intuitive situation if one considers increasing sedentism and settlement endogamy to be factors differentiating early farmers from their more mobile hunter-gatherer predecessors (i.e., early farmers had good reason to be parochial).

4. Evidence for language family homelands, proto-language cultural vocabularies (especially agricultural cognate sets), rates of spread as derived from

family tree structures (to be discussed below), and inter-family borrowing histories.

5. Palaeoanthropological studies of ancient skeletal remains from the Mesolithic-Neolithic transition, together with genetic evidence for population histories in terms of multiple nuclear gene clines, mtDNA and Y chromosome haplogroup histories and their estimated coalescence times.

The historical and behavioral possibilities involved in any hunter-to-farmer transition, encompassing factors such as economic challenge and response, language continuity and language shift, population dispersal and gene flow, are so truly immense on a worldwide scale as to defy brief generalization. This paper aims only to examine some of the major archaeological, linguistic, and genetic data sets and to apply some linking theory derived from ethnographic and historical observation. Did ancient hunter-gatherers commonly adopt agriculture, as claimed, for instance, by Price & Gebauer (1992, Price 1995)? Did ancient (pre-state and pre-literate) populations shift their languages frequently? Were early farming populations relatively endogamous or exogamous with respect to neighboring hunter-gatherers? Did farmers and hunter-gatherers switch their economies back and forth so frequently that any attempt to differentiate the two lifestyles becomes pointless? These are all questions that require theoretical consideration if interpretations of episodes of prehistoric agricultural expansion are to carry conviction.

THE PERSPECTIVE FROM ARCHAEOLOGY: TEMPO, SPREAD, AND FRICTION

Try as they may, archaeologists alone can never prove that a population expansion occurred in prehistory because material culture is always capable of diffusing beyond the hands of its creators. But it is possible to test models created in the light of data from other disciplines and to debate how population dispersal might have been structured in specific situations and what kind of archaeological evidence could demonstrate its occurrence (Adams et al 1978; Anthony 1990, 1997; Burmeister 2000; Chapman & Hamerow 1997; Rouse 1986). Early agriculturalist expansion across continental space could have consisted, at one extreme, of continuous population growth along an expansion front, of the type defined by Ammerman & Cavalli-Sforza (1984) for Neolithic Europe as a wave of advance fueled by "demic diffusion." At another extreme, one might have a progression of saltatory jumps from one suitable environment to another, as suggested for Neolithic Greece by van Andel & Runnels (1995). These models assume that early agricultural populations entered landscapes either devoid of humans or with relatively sparse hunter-gatherer populations. Were they to enter landscapes already settled by other farmers or by dense and complex hunter-gatherer societies, then less expansive and more reticulate outcomes must be expected (Bellwood 1996b).

One problem for archaeologists is that any population dispersal, by virtue of imposing a chain of founder effects and spanning a range of environments, as well as offering a range of outcomes from increased wealth to increased deprivation, can impose changes on the societies concerned such that homelands need not always be patently obvious in the archaeological record. For instance, population dispersal can alter social structures by encouraging founder-based ideologies as new bases for social ranking (Anthony 1990, Bellwood 1996c for Austronesia; K.P. Smith 1995 for Iceland). On the other hand, Blust (1999) shows how Austronesian populations lost many cultural items as a result of adaptations during their dispersal history from Island Southeast Asia into Polynesia. Population dispersal can also lead to an important category of situations in which the descendants of partially agricultural societies enter adverse landscapes and are thereby obliged to specialize "back" into a hunting and gathering economy. Good examples of the latter include the Punan/Penan sago collectors of Borneo, the southern Maoris of New Zealand, also probably the Numic- (Uto-Aztecan) speaking peoples of the Great Basin (Bellwood 1997a, 2000a, in press; Hill 1999, Sather 1995). Many early Polynesian agriculturalist populations also specialized toward a hunting-gathering economy among the naïve bird faunas of Oceania (Anderson 1989, Steadman 1999), at least until avian extinction/extirpation occurred and obliged them to refocus on agriculture.

Such trajectories imply that many early Neolithic/Formative cultures did not initially carry their full homeland agricultural economy into new lands, particularly when those new lands were relatively marginal in agricultural suitability. Dispersal is surely a generator of stronger selective and foundership factors, and of more rapid change, than is merely staying at home, a conclusion reached also by linguists with respect to a greater rapidity of linguistic change among small migrant populations (Blust 1991, Fortescue 1997, Ross 1991). The lesson here for archaeology is that migrants do not merely clone themselves and their cultures indefinitely. So rejecting a dispersal-based explanation just because a homeland is not immediately obvious is not always justified.

But merely considering the possible structure of an early farmer dispersal (or lack thereof) will not prove or disprove that one occurred. For this we need to examine specifics and to consider aspects of cultural transmission through time. The loci of primary agricultural origin across the world are fairly well established within the archaeological community; few would quibble over the significance of the Fertile Crescent, central China (middle Yangzi and Yellow basins), highland Mesoamerica and the Peruvian Andes, or perhaps even the Eastern Woodlands of the USA (Harris 1996, Price & Gebauer 1995, B. Smith 1995). Less agreement would be forthcoming over the roles of West Africa and the Sahel/savanna, Amazonia, and the New Guinea Highlands. The issue here is not over the homelands of specific crops, since many crops originated in regions not known to have harbored independent transitions to agriculture (e.g., India, Southeast Asia). The issue concerns independence of the trajectory from foraging to farming; archaeological and botanical demonstration of this can be claimed only for Southwest Asia, with the other regions (including even China) still in the realm of extreme likelihood rather than certainty.

A number of questions now need to be asked, from a comparative perspective. First, how productive (food output per head of population) were the agricultural systems that evolved in the various regions? This is an important matter to consider for any demographic growth modeling. There can be no doubt that the remarkably multifaceted agropastoral economy that had evolved in Southwest Asia by the end of the Pre-Pottery Neolithic phase (c.7500 B.C.E.) wins in terms of sheer number of major domesticated cereals *and* animals. China, with its rice, bovids, pigs, and poultry comes a close second. Central Africa, with its millets and the adoption of caprines and bovids from the north, would probably come third. New Guinea and the Americas, with no significant meat animals at all (pigs are post-3000 BP in New Guinea) and a relatively greater emphasis on tubers as opposed to cereals, all come further down the scale. The fact that the complex civilizations and farming cultures of the Americas depended to a high degree on only one major cereal (maize) and essentially on *hunted* meat (localized stocks of camelids, dogs, guinea pigs, and turkeys notwithstanding) could have had a dramatic impact on many aspects of culture and history (e.g., Harris 1978, pp. 99–110). In terms of the overall extents of language family and agricultural system expansion from these homeland regions, I suspect a similar ranking applies. The evidence for early farming dispersal out of Southwest Asia and China is far more compelling across all disciplines than it is out of the New Guinea Highlands and the Andes.

A second question arises immediately, and this concerns tempos of spread. How long did it take for the agricultural complexes that developed in the various homeland regions to reach their prehistoric limits? I am a firm believer in the concept of a "Neolithic Revolution," insofar as it relates to the inception and economic domination of cereal *cultivation* in Mesoamerica, Southwest Asia, and China (Sherratt 1997). In specific circumstances, the concept remains very apt. But tempos of origin and subsequent trajectories of spread must be kept analytically separate. We have the following well-established spread times from source region to ultimate prehistoric geographical limit demonstrated by archaeology and careful use of chronological techniques, well-established regardless of who (expanding farmers or converting hunters) actually spread the farming way of life:

- Fertile Crescent to Britain, 3000 years (7000 to 4000 B.C.E.) over 3600 km (Price 2000);
- Yangzi Basin to Island Southeast Asia, 4000 years (6500 to 2500 B.C.E.) over 5000 km (Bellwood 1997a);
- Central Mesoamerica to the Southwest, 2000 years (3500 to 1500 B.C.E.) over 2500 km (Muro 1998, Benz & Long 2000);
- Pakistan into Peninsular India, 4000 years (7000 to 3000 B.C.E.) over 2000 km (Chakrabarti 1999).

On these scales, *average* rates of spread ranged between 0.5 and 1.25 km per year, which can surely be considered fairly slow. It is irrelevant here whether the agriculture was being spread by converting hunter-gatherers or range-expanding farmers—both groups would have become subject to population increase in good environments. Recent colonizing populations in low-density situations of good health and rich resources were frequently capable of doubling numbers every generation, and there is no reason why early farmers, whatever their origins, should have been different on the large scale. Something seems to have been applying a brake to the operation of free and untrammeled fecundity.

That something was presumably, on the continents at least, a combination of environmental variation and native hunter-gatherer resistance. The farming way of life clearly had to progress through some very complex environmental and social barrier zones. Environmentally, these included alterations of rainfall seasonality, as for instance in the changes from winter to summer (monsoon) rainfall in India and Sub-Saharan Africa, and the latitudinal factors of day-length and temperature variation, significant in the East African, East Asian, and American situations. Crosby (1986, p. 18) and Diamond (1997a, p. 176) have suggested that longitudinal (north-south) geographical axes led to slower spread than latitudinal ones, but while this may be generally true it does not work in all instances (compare South Asia with eastern and southern Africa). The conclusion at this point must be that, over the long term and the long distance, agriculture did not always spread quickly, whatever the axis.

However, the situation looks rather different if we focus on more specific situations (Figure 1). Intermediate-scale instances of rapid spread of both initial agriculture and the archaeological assemblages attached to it are in fact relatively common, and it is here that axes *can* matter because all such rapid spreads occurred in zones of rather high suitability for the agricultural systems concerned:

- Bismarck Archipelago to western Polynesia, 500 years (1300 to 800 B.C.E.) over a fairly daunting 4500 km, but mostly over water and along the same tropical latitude (Lapita archaeological complex—Kirch 1997);

- Hungarian Plain to Alsace, 400 years (5700 to 5300 B.C.E.) over 1000 km, again along the same general latitude and through the same zone of temperate climate (LBK [Danubian] archaeological complex—Keeley 1992, Bogucki 1996, Gronenborn 1999);

- Levant to northwestern Pakistan, 500 years or less (7500 to 7000 B.C.E.) over 2500 km, again along one latitude and in one winter rainfall climate zone (late Pre-Pottery Neolithic archaeological complex—Bar-Yosef 1998);

- East African Lakes to South Africa, 1000 years (1000 B.C.E. to C.E. 1) over 3500 km through one zone of predominantly monsoonal rainfall, albeit a north-south one in this instance (Chifumbaze complex—Phillipson 1985, 1993, Ehret 1998).

Average rates of spread in these cases were much faster than in the first more generalized group, ranging from 2.5 to 5 km per year in the continental cases, with the fastest (9 km per year) predictably in Oceania. In general, most spreads were predominantly latitudinal, except for that in Africa. Clearly, early agricultural

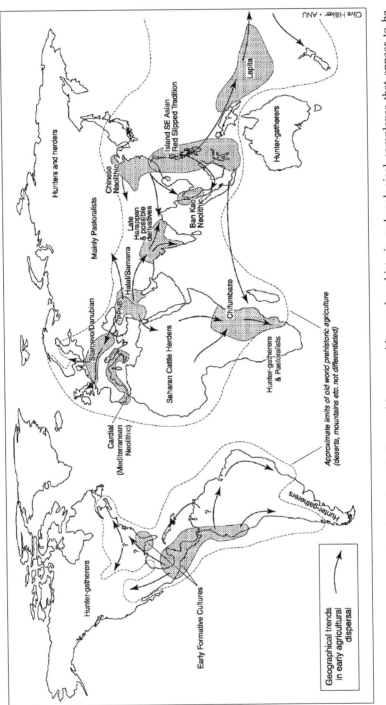

Figure 1 The distribution of prehistoric agriculture, with some widespread prehistoric archaeological complexes that appear to be associated with early agriculturalist expansion.

economies and their associated material cultures could spread extremely rapidly in those environments in which they had developed and/or to which they were well adapted. But environmental boundaries and transitions slowed down the process by creating friction against the easy and unopposed spread of early farming communities, and one may surmise that such "friction zones" served as likely arenas of major reticulation and reformulation within the linguistic and genetic realms, as well as in material (archaeological) culture. These friction zones, of course, occurred around the edges of the "spread zones" (after Nichols 1992) just listed, in regions such as northern and western Europe, lowland New Guinea, the Indus-to-Ganges transition from winter to summer rainfall climate, and the nonalluvial hilly terrains of southern China. We meet them also in the Americas—for example, the Amazonian interfluves and the eastern Great Plains. We can expect zones of friction to occur not just in environmentally unsuitable situations such as semi-deserts, dry grasslands, or coniferous forests, but also where hunter-gatherers lived in high densities, along productive coastlines for instance.

The above reasoning suggests that zones of rapid agricultural spread should reveal some degree of phylogenetic *interruption* to the continuous inheritance of material culture across the transition to agriculture. This should be the case regardless of whether existing hunters adopted farming rapidly and then spread geographically, or whether existing farmers migrated in. Rosenberg, for instance, actually lists hunter-gatherer–to–farmer transition periods in many parts of the world as the majority of his cases of rapid and discontinuous bouts of punctuated cultural evolution, when periods of "stress-generated systemic failure" (Rosenberg 1994, p. 322) stimulated the creation of new cultural formations. Continuity over the *whole* of a spread zone from Mesolithic/Archaic forebears would be a little unlikely from this perspective because spreading and continuity obviously contradict each other in their implications. On the other hand, friction zones should witness slower trajectories from hunter to farmer, with many apparent situations of regional continuity in culture and biology. It is here we might expect to see the clearest evidence of regional hunter-gatherer adoption of agriculture via the phases termed *availability*, *substitution*, and *consolidation* by Zvelebil & Rowley-Conwy (1986, Zvelebil 1998).

On the ground, of course, it is sometimes very difficult to ascertain if the change from Mesolithic to Neolithic or Archaic to Formative in a particular region does or does not reveal a phylogenetic break. Opinions on such matters differ greatly and often become quite heated, as in the debate over the Neolithic transition in Europe, where worlds often collide rather roughly. The extent of earliest Neolithic cultures in any situation clearly matters—if they are extremely widespread, as are the LBK and Lapita, then population movement will always deserve careful consideration. In my own research area, Island Southeast Asia, I have little doubt that the widespread and polythetic Neolithic cultural complex with its rice, pig, and dog bones, red-slipped or paddle-impressed pottery, polished stone adzes, shell and stone ornaments, barkcloth beaters, and occasional microblade industries and spindle whorls, marks a fundamental phylogenetic break, in both a material-culture and an economic sense, with the preceding late-Preceramic assemblages (Bellwood 1997a). The same applies to the contemporary Lapita complex in Melanesia (Spriggs 1996). In many other parts of the archaeological world such breaks have been claimed and counterclaimed with such an intensity that any attempt here to summarize would be fruitless. In terms of continuity, however, one important pitfall must be contemplated.

This is the pitfall of *ambiguous phylogeny*—the situation in which there *appears* to be regional continuity within an archaeological record, but in which the real homeland is actually another region, perhaps one quite distant, with a similar antecedent material culture. Ambiguous phylogeny becomes a problem in situations where the material culture of the immediately prefarming phase is complacent over very large regions in terms of stylistic variation, as it is for instance in much of Southeast Asia and the western Pacific (Spriggs 1996). In much of this region, small flake industries often continue apparently without a break from Preceramic into Neolithic assemblages, but since such flake tools are virtually universal prior to the common use of iron, this need mean little. Such a circumstance can only be taken to imply continuity if it is supported by other data sets.

A final consideration, while dealing with archaeological data, is that of ultimate causation of agricultural spread. Farmer population growth and hunter-gatherer adoption doubtless fueled the process to varying degrees, but one important factor may also be that of the *declining homeland environments* of early farmers. Some regions of early agriculture, in particular the Levant (Rollefson & Kohler-Rollefson 1993) and northern Greece (van Andel et al 1990), are known to have suffered environmental damage during the Neolithic, and one wonders whether this could have been a relevant factor in inducing spreads of agricultural populations. The other regions of early agriculture are less well understood in terms of environmental history, but southern coastal China (particularly Fujian), the Sahel, northern Mesoamerica and drier regions of the Andes could have been affected very early on by intensive cultivation, just as were Sumer, the Indus Valley, the Southwestern United States, and Easter Island in later cultural phases. Is it purely coincidental that the spread of Neolithic agriculture into the Nile Valley and into Europe (beyond Cyprus and Greece) occurred *not* with the first farming in the Levant (c. 8000 B.C.E.), but with fully agropastoral and pottery-using populations at about 6500 B.C.E. or later?

THE PERSPECTIVES FROM HISTORY AND ANTHROPOLOGY: ADOPTING AGRICULTURE

The historical record obviously tells us a great deal about the dispersal of farmers into new lands. It is not my intention here to argue whether the recent colonial occupations of the Americas and Australasia offer relevant comparisons for deep Neolithic prehistory, but there are two observations I think are of great importance. The first, most clearly stated by Crosby (1986), is that colonial-era migrants rapidly dominated where pre-existing populations were small, but migrants became increasingly less successful as prior populations became more complex and numerous and as the territorial goals became more tropical and disease-protected. Thus, Spanish ancestry dominates the genes and cultures of modern Argentina to a far greater extent than those of rural Mexico. British ancestry still dominates the genes and cultures (not to mention the surnames and place-names) of Australia to a far greater extent than those of India or Malaysia. The conclusion here must be that colonizing populations of farmers will always face relatively resistant native cultures, and in the resulting mix many factors will matter: local patterns of disease, relative demographic profiles, overlaps in territorial requirements, relative complexities of social organization, etc. In the case of Neolithic farmers entering hunter-gatherer territories, the situation might seem simple, until one begins to think about the complexity of linguistic, genetic, and social relationships between Aborigines and Europeans in many parts of modern Australia.

The second observation from the diasporas of recent history is one that goes against the feeling held by many anthropologists that race, language, and culture never correlate and always vary independently of each other ["It is customary to insist on the mutual independence of racial, cultural and linguistic factors" (Sapir 1918:10)]. For much of human prehistory, and in certain specific and well-known ethnographic situations such as lowland Melanesia, many regions of Africa, Madagascar, and the Caribbean, a substantial lack of isomorphism certainly holds good. But in many colonial-era cases of rapid long-distance migration, it manifestly did not. Naturally, intermarriage with prior inhabitants of a region will *always* occur, but the fact remains that, in inception, any successful colonizing expansion will have a core population within which biological variation, language, and material culture will sit together isomorphically to a very comfortable degree. Any such isomorphism, of course, may not last for long, but its long-term significance can still be very great indeed.

The anthropological (ethnographic) record also provides food for thought on three further issues. Admittedly, ethnography does not reveal any situations parallel to the initial spreads of farmers or language families (Fix 1999:150). It covers far too short a time span and deals for the most part with societies in retreat from colonial confrontations. But observations (expressed in the ethnographic present) from a fairly broad cross-section of the literature indicate that:

- Hunter-gatherer and agricultural economies rarely blend on a balanced basis over the long term (Murdock 1967, Hunn & Williams 1982). Many traditional hunter-gatherers certainly husband and protect resources. Most farmers hunt and gather if their environments allow such luxuries (Kent 1989), and clearly all farmers in the Americas continued throughout prehistory to be unusually dependent upon hunting. But 50:50 balances are rare, and those that occur generally carry a marginal air from the perspectives of agricultural expansion and demographic growth.

- Hunter-gatherers rarely adopt agriculture successfully. When they come into contact with farmers and are able to avoid assimilation, they often develop mutualistic trade- and labor-based networks of interaction (Peterson 1978).

One can of course suggest that modern hunter-gatherers, by definition and because of encapsulation (Woodburn 1982), only exist because they have not adopted agriculture; hence they are irrelevant for any consideration of the behavior of ancient hunter-gatherers, especially those in environments with high agricultural potentials. This observation, however, collides rather hard with one major objection.

The objection is that many recent hunter-gatherers in rich *potential* farmlands were in contact with farmers, were not encapsulated, yet never showed the slightest interest in adopting agriculture. These include the peoples of California and the Northwest Coast, and of course much of northern Australia. One can bring in many opinions here as to why agriculture was never adopted—desires for mobility and nonaccumulation of debts and property, lack of economic need (hunter-gatherer "affluence") and so forth—but facts remain facts. Neither northern Australia nor California were hostile environments for agriculture. These populations were probably behaving quite logically—why take on the scheduling demands of agriculture unless it was necessary? Such examples, of course, make us wonder just how frequently hunter-gatherers would have adopted agriculture in the deeper past, especially in the zones of rapid farming spread.

Because I have a more detailed survey of all these topics in preparation, I conclude this section simply by stating that, in the ethnographic record, hunters and gatherers have rarely adopted agriculture, and if they were to do so, particularly in rich environments suitable for farmer spread, then quick reactions would have been required. Mesolithic hunters in Baltic Europe doubtless had far longer to weigh up their options than did their contemporaries in the Danubian loesslands (Keeley 1992, Zvelebil 1998). Hunters in the friction zones marginal for agropastoralism might have occupied ethnographically unusual oscillating economic trajectories between farming and food production (see Kent 1992), but I certainly doubt that such situations could ever have been common. Any assumption that all hunters in prehistory would or could simply have adopted agriculture as soon as the word was whispered in their ears is probably misguided.

THE PERSPECTIVE FROM LINGUISTICS: NATIVE SPEAKERS VERSUS LANGUAGE SHIFT

Linguists debate issues such as language family homeland options and proto-language dispersal histories, but they rarely focus on the social conditions in which the dispersals might have occurred. In this regard they are the opposite of archaeologists, who place great stress on the ancient societies but often have unrealistic views about how languages are transmitted through space and time. As Nettle (1996, 1999) points out, very little literature exists on the formation of language groups in anthropology. For instance, many archaeologists favor convergence, creolization, lingua francas, and multilingualism as environments for the spreads of linguistic entities such as Proto-Indo-European (Zvelebil 1995), Proto-Bantu (Hall 1990), and Proto-Austronesian (Meacham 1984–1985). Such concepts, often linked with substantial episodes of language shift, allow archaeologists to escape the stigma attached to migration-based explanations. Indeed, language shift explanations for large-scale spread have also been proposed by a number of linguists (e.g., Nichols 1997, 1998 for Indo-European).

However, in the light of comparative historical and ethnographic observations, it seems that creolization, lingua francas, and multilingualism *alone* cannot be sufficient explanations for such enormous vernacular spreads as those required to understand the genetic foundations of, for instance, the early Indo-European, Bantu, and Austronesian languages (e.g., Mallory 1987, pp. 258–59, Vansina 1990, Ross 1997b). These families are not reputed, on an overall basis, to reveal massive traces of substratum residue or universal histories of creolization. The latter, apart from being in large part a postcolonial phenomenon attached to forced translocation, cannot account for the spread of language families that can be classified genetically (Mühlhäusler 1986, Thomason & Kaufman 1988). This need not imply that individual proto-languages can never have been pidgins or creoles, although my understanding of human history suggests to me that translocative situations conducive to pidgin formation would be most unusual in a Neolithic/Formative context. Pidginization, of course, must be distinguished from the more normal forms of contact-induced change discussed by many linguists (e.g., Thomason & Kaufman 1988, Dutton 1995, Ross 1996, 1997a).

Likewise, lingua francas and the languages of small ruling élites have not ever, in history, led to the spreads of single languages on anything like the required scale without substantial components of native speaker migration and settlement, as we know from the spreads of Latin, Hellenistic Greek, Spanish, Arabic (Pentz 1992), and English. The languages associated with noncolonizing conquest empires, such as Mongolian, Persian, and Nahuatl, did not replace all the vernacular languages in the regions conquered, and surely the reasons for the greater success of Quechua in this regard relate to the Inca policy of population translocation and the subsequent adoption of Quechua as a lingua franca by Spanish missionaries (Heath & Laprade 1982). The spreads of politically neutral national languages such as Bahasa Indonesia (Errington 1998) and Tok Pisin (Kulick 1992) represent circumstances specific to modern literate nations with central governments and positive language policies, hardly the assumed characteristics of Neolithic/Formative nonliterate and pre-state societies.

Multilingualism, finally, has traditionally been a vehicle for language *maintenance*, not replacement, as is clear in linguistically complex ethnographic situations in western Melanesia (Kulick 1992) and the Vaupes region of Amazonia. In the latter case, an almost unprecedented rate of linguistic exogamy does not cause large-scale language mixing or replacement (Sorenson 1982, Aikhenvald 1996). Multilingualism can lubricate the workings of contact-induced change and language shift, but it does not in itself promote the latter and can often militate against it (Sauder 1990). Language loyalty is also an extremely important factor because it can serve as an antidote to free-wheeling language shift (for interesting case studies, see Schooling 1990, Smalley 1994). Is it realistic to assume that language shift alone could have swept through vast areas of pre-state "Neolithic" social landscape, in the complete absence of any state-level mechanisms involving literacy, political unity, and the repression of ethnic identity?

For a more realistic reconstruction of language family dispersal history, it is necessary to recognize that language families are genetic entities, transmitted essentially and continuously through successive generations of native speakers. Overall, they are divergence rather than convergence phenomena; unrelated languages cannot converge into a genetically constituted family with a common proto-language. Presumably, they have originated in processes of language spread from homeland regions, ramifying through time via nodes (proto-languages) delineated by groupings of shared innovations (Blust 1995a,b, Peiros 1998).

However, languages rarely split irrevocably to form innovation-defined subgroups unless some long-distance movement or intermediate language extinction occurs. Following initial expansion, chains and meshes will form, along which innovations develop in overlapping sets (see Pawley & Ross 1995 on innovation-defined versus innovation-linked subgroups). Such chains can in time generate discrete subgroups, but if the initial spread is rapid and geographically extensive, then any such subgroups will show a rather frustrating rake-like phylogeny, which can be uninformative with respect to homeland and direction of dispersal (Ross 1997a, Pawley 1999). Language families with clearly bifurcating histories and obvious homelands are rare in reality, a circumstance which might suggest that most had fairly punctuated (rake-like) rather than gradualist (tree-like) origins and early dispersal histories, as perceived by Dixon (1997).

To explain such punctuation effects, it is necessary to resort to social explanations and of course to examine the archaeological record. Can the concepts of spread and friction zones be applied to language history, and if so, do the zones so defined correspond to any degree with those recognized from the archaeological record? It is essential to remember here that the comparative linguistic record for most parts of the world draws on living languages; thus historical leveling and replacements can alter the picture substantially (e.g., the expansions of Turkish in Anatolia, Sinitic languages in southern China, Arabic, English, Spanish, etc.), just as transformation processes can alter the archaeological record. But even with these provisos, it is apparent that many regions with very strong indications of contact-induced linguistic change or substratum interference tend to correlate with regions identified as friction zones in the archaeological discussion above. Such regions include northern India and peripheral regions of Europe within Indo-European (Masica 1978, Sverdrup & Guardans 1999, Wiik 2000), western Melanesia within Austronesian (Ross 1988, Pawley & Ross 1993, 1995, Dutton 1995), and southern China within Sino-Tibetan (Ballard 1981).

Conversely, in many archaeological spread zones, the dispersals of major language families have left few clear traces of any prior linguistic patterning—we

often seem to have a series of clean sweeps with no survival of linguistic isolates or major traces of substrata. Such is certainly the case with Austronesian
in most of Island Southeast Asia, with the Bantu languages in Africa, and with
Sinitic in central China. Of course, linguists have also toyed with the concepts
of spread and friction (otherwise residual) zones, in particular Johanna Nichols
(1992, 1997), with whom the concepts appear to have originated. Like Nichols, I
regard spread zones as canvases for rapid and relatively overwhelming language
movement and replacement (as we would expect from early farming dispersal,
among other reasons), whereas the residual zones of Nichols 1992 can have two
distinct types of origin. They can be end-of-the-line regions of inflow and substratum residue, as in the concept of the friction zone presented above. This is
the sense in which Nichols generally uses the term "residual zone." On the other
hand, many regions of great diversity at the level of whole language families—
areas such as the Middle East, Mesoamerica, East Asia in general, and central
Africa—cannot really be considered residual zones but rather are "upwelling" or
"starburst" zones of net population increase and outflow. These regions are all
agricultural homelands, and all have linguistic profiles that reflect language family
genesis and outflow rather than residual accretion (Bellwood 1991, 1994, 1996a,
1997b).

So, in terms of language dispersal, we have three concepts: (*a*) the homeland
starburst zone of language outflow and nonreplacement; (*b*) the spread zone of
rapid language flow and widespread replacement; and (*c*) the friction zone of
reticulation. Through these zones, the ancestral genetic components of the major
language families must have been transported *for the most part* in the mouths
of native speakers, and processes involving language shift would have operated
most frequently in the friction zones. But even in spread zones, societies would
have been permeable with respect to the incorporation of outsiders, perhaps in large
numbers in situations of low population density, with lack of conflict over land and
bilateral as opposed to tightly unilineal land ownership. From this perspective, early
language dispersals such as those of early Indo-European or early Austronesian
must have involved the movement of sizeable populations of native speakers,
however the criterion of "nativeness" might be spelt out in reality. As Ross (1997b,
p. 183) points out for Austronesian:

> ... it is indeed difficult to conceive of the movement of Austronesian lan-
> guages only or even largely in terms of language shift: what could have mo-
> tivated group after group to abandon its language in favor of an Austronesian
> one? We must infer that movements of people have played a large role in the
> dispersal of the Austronesian languages.

This background debate brings us around again to the central hypothesis—that
the *foundation* dispersals of the major agriculturalist language families (i.e., the
spread of their basal-node proto-languages) have a high chance of being directly
associated with the spread of initial farming populations through regions previously
occupied by hunter-gatherers. If this hypothesis has a fair chance of surviving closer

examination (it goes without saying that absolute proof will never be an option), then we would expect a number of correlations to occur:

- Language families with potential for this kind of origin should have strong proto-language cognate sets, with stable meanings, relating to crops, agricultural activities, and perhaps domestic animals, according to regional circumstances.

- They should have indications of an early spread over a large area, probably to be indicated by a rake-like basal phylogeny (i.e., two or more first-order subgroups that cannot be ordered hierarchically and that could have emerged from a prior innovation-linked continuum).

- They should have time-depths that correspond roughly with those for early agricultural dispersal from the archaeological record (issues of language-family time depths cannot be examined in detail here, but see Renfrew et al 2000 for a constellation of current views).

- They should have other material items reconstructible within their proto-language etyma that can be correlated with nonuniversal items in the archaeological record (for many examples of this kind of reconstruction in the Austronesian family, see Pawley & Ross 1994, Ross et al 1998, Kirch & Green 2001—horizon-like and sudden appearances are perhaps the most useful). The archaeological record should reveal homeland and dispersal histories for agriculture, and most importantly, it should place the homelands and directions of spread in a geographical framework similar to the (potentially linked) linguistic homelands and spreads.

A number of points require special comment here. First, it is extremely difficult to offer homelands for language families that began with far-flung proto-language dispersals (Fix 1999, p. 163, makes the same point for biological anthropology—that rapid population expansion tends to mask information on phylogeny). But in previous papers, Renfrew and I (see listed references) have suggested that agricultural homelands do correlate to a major degree with potential language family homelands and that the dispersal of these language families can be seen as radiative or flower-like, spreading out of a source region (see also Sherratt & Sherratt 1988). There is no doubt scope for disagreement here, particularly over homelands of very widespread families such as Indo-European or Uto-Aztecan, but I detect increasing agreement among linguists and archaeologists that, for instance, Proto-Indo-European originated in the vicinity of Anatolia (Dolgopolsky 1993, Gamkrelidze & Ivanov 1995, Mallory 1997, Renfrew 1999) as opposed to the Ukraine, and that Proto-Uto-Aztecan originated in Mesoamerica (Bellwood 2000a, Hill 1999) as opposed to Oregon or California. Both Anatolia and Mesoamerica are of course well-established foci of early agricultural development. The Ukraine and Oregon are not.

Finally, we must ask if it is purely coincidental that most language families would appear to belong to the past 8,000 years, not to the past 15,000, at least according to a very broad range of calculations from glottochronology to rule-of-thumb comparisons of modern languages with their ancient literary forebears. The only language family commonly given a time-depth of more than 8,000 years is Afroasiatic. The vast majority of others are reputed to be between 2,000 and 8,000 years old (Bellwood 2000a). Why? Is it because comparative linguistics has a rock-bottom limit of 8,000 years? Or is it because these language families *do* represent real flowerings imposed over a prior continuum of Palaeolithic/Mesolithic languages, which were not ordered into sharply bounded families and which, instead, reflected a vast mesh of intersecting relationships similar to the Pama-Nyungan hunter-gatherer languages of Australia? [I make this point without wishing to be drawn into the debate over Pama-Nyungan identity and origins (Dixon 1997, McConvell 1996, Evans & Jones 1997)]. If such flowerings did occur out of agricultural homeland regions, then this could provide the historical background for those shadowy macrofamilies, such as Nostratic and Austric, which currently generate so much heat among linguists (e.g., Renfrew & Nettle 1999).

THE PERSPECTIVE FROM BIOLOGICAL ANTHROPOLOGY: BONES, GENES, AND CHRONOLOGY

Early farming expansion implies dispersals of real populations. The only way to recover prehistoric people directly is through their bones—languages, archaeology, and the genetics of living populations can never offer more than proxy data for the on-the-spot prehistoric culture-wielding animal itself. Did the first farmers all radiate as distinct ethnic and racial groups from agricultural homelands? Did no one move at all, with only languages and agriculture passing from group to group? Or was there always a mixture, with farmer demic spread being most marked in the spread zones, but hunter-gatherer incorporation being most marked in the friction zones where farming was not always the ultimate panacea?

Palaeoanthropology should, in theory, be a major arbiter. However, it presents some major problems. Large skeletal assemblages are widely reported from Neolithic sites but are rare from Mesolithic ones, and when they are available from either side of the transition, they are usually not from the same site or immediate region. One interesting exception here is the large Hoabinhian and Neolithic sample from the shelter of Gua Cha in Malaysia (Bulbeck 2000), where, as one might expect, the evidence for population continuity is quite strong (the interior Malay Peninsular rainforests are undoubtedly a major friction zone with respect to agriculture). In Europe, Mesolithic samples are rare and small, and opinions on population continuity or lack thereof vary. For instance, Fox (1996) and Jackes et al (1997) offer opposing opinions for Portugal, a presumed friction zone, whereas Vencl (1988) favors Neolithic replacement in the spread zone of central Europe. For China, Brown (1998) points to major morphological change across the Mesolithic/Neolithic boundary. A large literature on palaeoanthropological aspects of the Jomon to Yayoi transition in Japan, recently reviewed by Hudson

(1999), indicates major morphological change associated with Yayoi immigration from Korea. To my knowledge, however, there have been very few large-sample studies of morphological variation in human bones dating to either side of the transition from single localities. Indeed, there is a major need for a synthesis of the palaeoanthropological record for the hunter-to-farmer transition on a world-wide basis.

Three other aspects of palaeoanthropology are also of direct relevance in the transition to farming: trends in health, fertility, and diet. With regard to health, there is no strong evidence to suggest that *early* farming was the universal slide into ill-health sometimes visualized as an epiphenomenon of the "affluent forager" syndrome, at least not until the emergence of crowd diseases and burgeoning population densities. However, the proviso here must be that large samples from relevant time periods are rare. That farmer health declined in general through later prehistory is not in debate (Larsen 1995) and is not here considered a relevant issue.

Major problems with determining the fertility profiles of cemetery populations (Wood et al 1992, Meindl & Russell 1998, p. 390) render comment on issues of early farmer demography and birth rates by a nonspecialist rather superfluous. But Tayles (1999) provides evidence for high birthrates among first farmers in Neolithic central Thailand. Even without direct skeletal evidence for fertility increases, the cemetery size and site-area increases in the Neolithic/Formative in regions such as the Levant, China, and Mesoamerica tend to make it fairly obvious that there were many more first farmers in agricultural homeland regions than there were last hunters (Hassan 1981). In terms of diet, a number of recent stable isotope studies on bone have also pointed to major changes toward increasing quantities of agricultural foods across the transition (e.g., Richards & Hedges 1999, Bonsall 1997).

But perhaps the main point to be derived from the palaeoanthropological liter-ature is that *both* population continuity *and* replacement can be identified across the hunter-to-farmer transition in different parts of the world; there is no right or wrong universal, and every situation needs to be examined on its own merits.

In terms of genetic history derived from living populations, we seem to be currently in a phase of impasse. The recombining nuclear DNA data for Europe, as analyzed from a multisystem standpoint, present a clinal situation suggestive of significant demic diffusion across the continent from southeast to northwest at some time in prehistory (Ammerman & Cavalli-Sforza 1984, Cavalli-Sforza et al 1994, Barbujani et al 1994, 1998, Cavalli-Sforza & Minch 1997, Chikhi et al 1998, Barbujani & Bertorelle 2001). These techniques in themselves of-fer no time depth or precise ties with early farmers and are basically phenetic rather than directly phylogenetic in implication, but they are nevertheless highly suggestive. As Cavalli-Sforza & Cavalli-Sforza (1995:149) point out, the first principal component of one particular European gene frequency analysis explains 28% of the total variation and must reflect population movement—so many genes could not produce such a cline as a result of natural selection alone, unless we follow the suggestion of Fix (1996, 1999) that the moving agropastoral system itself was supplying the selective basis for the gene frequencies via zoonotic diseases. Even from this viewpoint, however, Fix is unable to argue strongly for hunter-gatherer adoption of agriculture as opposed to farmer spread, and indeed Fix concludes that genetics alone cannot solve the problem. Furthermore, Krantz (1988, p. 93) offers the interesting observation that a constant incorporation of native hunter-gatherer genes into a spreading agricultural population of ultimate Southwest Asian origin would give the eventual Northwest European first farmers a genome between 70% and 94% of European derivation. So, even if demic diffusion did occur across Europe during the Neolithic, we can hardly expect the Neolithic British to have been exact clones of the denizens of Catalhoyuk in Anatolia.

The strongest claims *against* the reconstructions favoring demic spread in the European Neolithic come from studies of the nonrecombining portions of the genome—mitochondrial DNA and the Y chromosome. In Europe, current calculations of coalescence times for mtDNA haplotypes suggest origination in European Late Palaeolithic rather than Neolithic Southwest Asian chronological contexts (Sykes 1999, Richards et al 2000). But some very crucial issues here would seem to involve the precise mutation rates utilized for such calculations. Indeed, my impression of the nonrecombining DNA literature is that coalescence dates are getting ever younger and overlapping with the terminal Pleistocene and the beginning of the Holocene (e.g., Torroni et al 1998, Sykes 1999, Excoffier & Schneider 1999, especially Kayser et al 2001). I anticipate further movement toward an even younger direction in the near future. There is tremendous scope here for insight into early farming dispersal, particularly if the impressive starbursts of mtDNA lineages presented by Di Rienzo & Wilson (1991; see also Rogers & Jorde 1995) can be dated to the relevant timescale. Kayser et al (2000, 2001) suggest major phases of population expansion commencing 6000 BP for Austronesians and 2200 BP for Polynesians from Y chromosome data, and it has to be admitted that these dates do fit extremely well with the archaeological and linguistic data on Austronesian dispersal.

In the Pacific region, recent work on the nonrecombining genetic systems has focused attention on Austronesian origins in Island Southeast Asia and Taiwan, versus Papuan origins among more ancient populations in western Oceania (Richards et al 1998, Lum et al 1998, Merriwether et al 1999, Hagelberg et al 1999, Bing Su et al 2000, Kayser et al 2000, 2001). This research supports a general scenario of Austronesian horticulturalist expansion around the Papuan horticultural and arboricultural homeland region of New Guinea, combined later with a substantial Papuan take-over of Austronesian language and genotype in the western Pacific (Bellwood 1998, Kayser et al 2000, 2001). The latter brings up a perhaps obvious point, that a "native" genotype in an environment with a high incidence of diseases such as malaria will have some selective advantage over an immigrant genotype.

But although this perspective can explain why Melanesia is Melanesian, it cannot explain the much stronger Asian genetic heritage in neighboring and equally tropical western and central Indonesia, a heritage clearly visible in all genetic systems. Here we must fall back on cultural explanations, one of these being that migrating Austronesians replaced hunter-gatherers in Indonesia but were in turn absorbed by denser populations of existing arboriculturalists in lowland Melanesia (Bellwood 1997a, 1998).

Because the genetic field of population history is in a constant state of flux, as befits its new and revolutionary explosion into the arena of prehistory, I avoid further comment and merely raise the question of how modern gene distributions in living populations can really reflect on prehistoric "events" that occurred many millennia ago. As Bertranpetit (2000, p. 6927) points out, in discussing an apparent misfit between Y chromosome and palaeoanthropological chronologies for modern human expansion, inferences from molecules to populations are not straightforward. As Weiss (1998, p. 285) also points out, different population histories can generate the same genetic outcome.

If Polynesian or European mtDNA lineages indeed turn out to have Palaeolithic coalescence times (as claimed by Richards et al 1998, 2000), we still need to ask just where these lineages originally commenced their existences in geographical terms (Barbujani & Bertorelle 2001). There could be problems of masked phylogeny here similar to those in archaeology, especially if the traces of genetic events that might have seemed major at the time have become hidden by the vagaries of millennia of subsequent history.

CONCLUSIONS: HOMELANDS, SPREADING INTO FRICTION, AND BEYOND

In this paper I have obviously taken the position that Neolithic farmer dispersal was an important factor in establishing the current world pattern of languages and geographical races. I have also pointed to regions where such dispersal was minimized by hunter-gatherer adoption of agriculture and language (certainly Melanesia, maybe western and northern Europe, maybe northern India, but in all honesty I find it hard to point with great conviction to many other *large-scale* regions). Archaeologists have great difficulty in coming to agreement on this issue, as can be seen from the absolutely voluminous literature that has emanated in recent years on the Mesolithic to Neolithic transition in Europe, favoring both Neolithic "packages" and Mesolithic adoption. By contrast, American archaeology has been singularly quiet on this issue, mainly because a majority of North American archaeologists accept without question a hunter-gather adoption of agriculture in all situations and relatively few (with notable exceptions) take an interest in linguistic prehistory.

Many linguists, however, do support agriculture and language farmer-dispersal correlations for language family origins, to the extent that even the Trans-New

Guinea Phylum languages of western Melanesia are now being debated as another possible example of early farmer dispersal (Papuan Pasts 2000; and see Hagelberg et al 1999 for some mtDNA data that could support this). Some linguists remain negative about farmer dispersal (Campbell 1999, p. 221), as do some biologists (Oppenheimer 1997; see Bellwood 2000b for a discussion of this book). But other geneticists (Cavalli-Sforza & Cavalli-Sforza 1995, Barbujani et al 1998) seem to have no doubts about its efficacy as an explainer of the past.

In the future, increased knowledge and understanding will only come from careful multidisciplinary considerations of many strands of evidence (Renfrew 1992, 2000). This observation applies to archaeologists, linguists, palaeoanthropologists and geneticists alike; disciplinary superiority gets us nowhere. Right now, I sense a fairly even balance across the anthropological community for and against the concept of early farming dispersals, a circumstance which suggests to me that (*a*) there can be no absolute answer, and (*b*) reality combines both perspectives of agriculturalist dispersal and hunter-gatherer adoption. *But in any specific situation, reality will not be absolutely balanced*, and the sciences of prehistory need to treat every situation as of equal significance. Starburst zones, spread zones, friction zones, and also the "beyond" zones where migrating former-farmers were obliged to specialize into hunting and gathering, can be expected to give entirely different results with respect to phylogenetic versus reticulative transmission of genes, languages, and material cultures (Table 1). What works for central Europe might not work for coastal New Guinea or the Great Basin.

TABLE 1 Simplified character states for the four conceptualized zones of agricultural origin and spread

	Homeland/Starburst zones	Spread zones	Friction zones	Beyond (no agriculture)
Tempo of spread	Upwelling at varied rates	Fast	Slow	Variable
Extent of spread	Upwelling with radial spread	Great	Varies, generally limited	Variable
Suitability for agriculture	High	High	Low	Nil
Prior hunter-gatherer population densities	High (but hunters become farmers)	Low	Often high, especially along coastlines and rivers	Variable
Mesolithic-Neolithic continuity	Yes	Unlikely, except at entry point	Yes, to varying degrees	No

ACKNOWLEDGMENTS

I would like to thank Colin Groves and Malcolm Ross for their comments on this essay. All errors, alas, are surely mine.

Visit the Annual Reviews home page at www.AnnualReviews.org

LITERATURE CITED

Adams WY, van Gerven DP, Levy RS. 1978. The retreat from migrationism. *Annu. Rev. Anthropol.* 7:483–32

Aikhenvald A. 1996. Areal diffusion in northwest Amazonia—the case of Tariana. *Anthropol. Linguist.* 38:73–116

Ammerman AJ, Cavalli-Sforza LL. 1984. *The Neolithic Transition and the Genetics of Populations in Europe.* Princeton, NJ: Princeton Univ. Press

Anderson AJ. 1989. *Prodigious Birds.* Cambridge: Cambridge Univ. Press

Anthony D. 1990. Migration in archaeology: the baby, and the bathwater. *Am. Anthropol.* 92:895–914

Anthony D. 1997. Prehistoric migration as social progress. In *Migrations and Invasions in Archaeological Explanation,* ed. J Chapman, H Hamerow, pp. 21–32. Oxford: BAR Int. Seri. 664

Ballard CL. 1981. Aspects of the linguistic history of South China. *Asian Perspect.* 24:163–85

Barbujani G, Bertorelle G. 2001. Genetics and the population history of Europe. *Proc. Natl. Acad. Sci. USA* 98:22–25

Barbujani G, Bertorelle G, Chikhi L. 1998. Evidence for Paleolithic and Neolithic gene flow in Europe. *Am. J. Hum. Genet.* 62:488–91

Barbujani G, Pilastro A, de Domenica S, Renfrew C. 1994. Genetic variation in North Africa and Eurasia: Neolithic demic diffusion vs. Paleolithic colonization. *Am. J. Phys. Anthropol.* 95:137–54

Bar-Yosef O. 1998. On the nature of transitions. *Cambridge Archaeol. J.* 8:141–63

Bellwood P. 1984. The great Pacific migration.

Encycl. Br. Yrbk. Sci. Future for 1984, pp. 80–93

Bellwood P. 1984–1985. A hypothesis for Austronesian origins. *Asian Perspect.* 26:107–17

Bellwood P. 1991. The Austronesian dispersal and the origins of languages. *Sci. Am.* 265:88–93

Bellwood P. 1994. An archaeologist's view of language macrofamily relationships. *Oceanic Linguist.* 33:391–406

Bellwood P. 1996a. The origins and spread of agriculture in the Indo-Pacific region. In *The Origins and Spread of Agriculture and Pastoralism in Eurasia,* ed. D Harris, pp. 465–98. London: UCL Press

Bellwood P. 1996b. Phylogeny and reticulation in prehistory. *Antiquity* 70:881–90

Bellwood P. 1996c. Hierarchy, founder ideology and Austronesian expansion. In *Origins, Ancestry and Alliance,* ed. J Fox, C Sather, pp. 18–40. Canberra: Dep. Anthropol., Res. Sch. Pac. Asian Stud., Aust. Natl. Univ.

Bellwood P. 1997a. *Prehistory of the Indo-Malaysian Archipelago.* Honolulu: Univ. Hawaii Press

Bellwood P. 1997b. Prehistoric cultural explanations for widespread language families. See McConvell & Evans, pp. 123–34

Bellwood P. 1998. From Bird's Head to bird's eye view: long term structures and trends in Indo-Pacific prehistory. In *Perspectives on the Bird's Head of Irian Jaya, Indonesia,* ed. J Miedema, C Odé, R Dam, pp. 951–75. Amsterdam: Rodopi

Bellwood P. 2000a. The time depth of major language families: an archaeologist's perspective. In *Time Depth in Historical Linguistics,* ed. C Renfrew, A McMahon, L Trask, 1:

109–40. Cambridge: McDonald Inst. Archaeol. Res.

Bellwood P. 2000b. Some thoughts on understanding the human colonization of the Pacific. *People Cult. Oceania* 16:5–17

Bellwood P. 2001. Archaeology and the historical determinants of punctuation in language family origins. In *Areal Diffusion and Genetic Inheritance: Problems in Comparative Linguistics*, ed. R Dixon, A Aikhenvald. Oxford: Oxford Univ. Press. In press

Benz BL, Long A. 2000. Prehistoric maize evolution in the Tehuacan Valley. *Curr. Anthropol.* 41:459–65

Bertranpetit J. 2000. Genome, diversity and origins: the Y chromosome as a storyteller. *Proc. Natl. Acad. Sci. USA* 97:6927–29

Bing Su, Underhill P, Martinson J, Saha N, McGarvey S, et al. 2000. Polynesian origins: insights from the Y chromosome. *Proc. Natl. Acad. Sci. USA* 97:8225–28

Blust R. 1991. Sound change and migration distance. In *Current Trends in Pacific Linguistics*, ed. R Blust, pp. 27–42. Canberra: Pac. Linguist., Ser. C-117

Blust R. 1995a. The position of the Formosan languages: method and theory in Austronesian comparative linguistics. In *Austronesian Studies Relating to Taiwan*, ed. P Li, D Ho, Y Huang, C Tsang, C Tseng, pp. 585–650. Taipei: Acad. Sin., Inst. Hist. Philol., Symp. Ser. 3

Blust R. 1995b. The prehistory of the Austronesian-speaking peoples: a view from language. *J. World Prehist.* 9:453–510

Blust R. 1999. *On the explanation of similarity*. Pap. pres. at NSF Conf., *Entering New Landscapes*, Univ. FL, Gainesville, Feb.

Bogucki P. 1996. The spread of early farming in Europe. *Am. Sci.* 84:242–53

Bonsall C, Lennon R, McSweeney K, Stewart C, Harkness D, et al. 1997. Mesolithic and early Neolithic in the Iron Gates: a palaeodietary perspective. *J. Eur. Archaeol.* 5:50–92

Brown P. 1998. The first Mongoloids? : another look at Upper Cave 101, Liujiang and Minatogawa 1. *Acta Anthropol. Sin.* 17:260–75

Bulbeck D. 2000. Dental morphology at Gua Cha, West Malaysia. *Bull. Indo-Pac. Prehist. Assoc.* 19:17–41

Burmeister S. 2000. Archaeology and migration: approaches to an archaeological proof of migration. *Curr. Anthropol.* 41:539–68

Campbell L. 1999. Nostratic and linguistic palaeontology in methodological perspective. In *Nostratic: Examining a Linguistic Macrofamily*, ed. C Renfrew, D Nettle, pp. 179–230. Cambridge: McDonald Inst. Archaeol. Res.

Cavalli-Sforza LL, Cavalli-Sforza F. 1995. *The Great Human Diasporas*. Reading, MA: Addison-Wesley

Cavalli-Sforza L, Menozzi P, Piazza L. 1994. *The History and Geography of Human Genes*. Princeton, NJ: Princeton Univ. Press

Cavalli-Sforza L, Minch E. 1997. Paleolithic and Neolithic lineages in the European mitochondrial gene pool. *Am. J. Hum. Genet.* 61:247–51

Chakrabarti D. 1999. *India: An Archaeological History*. New Delhi: Oxford Univ. Press

Chapman J, Hamerow H, eds. 1997. *Migrations and Invasions in Archaeological Explanation*. Oxford: BAR Int. Ser. 664

Chikhi L, Destro-Bisol G, Bertorelle G, Pascali V, Barbujani G. 1998. Clines of nuclear DNA markers suggest a largely Neolithic ancestry of the European gene pool. *Proc. Natl. Acad. Sci. USA* 95:9053–58

Crosby AW. 1986. *Ecological Imperialism*. Cambridge: Cambridge Univ. Press

Diamond J. 1997a. *Guns, Germs and Steel*. London: Jonathan Cape

Diamond J. 1997b. The language steamrollers. *Nature* 389:544–46

Di Rienzo A, Wilson A. 1991 Branching pattern in the evolutionary tree for human mitochondrial DNA. *Proc. Natl. Acad. Sci. USA* 88:1597–1601

Dixon RMW. 1997. *The Rise and Fall of Languages*. Cambridge: Cambridge Univ. Press

Dolgopolsky A. 1993. More about the Indo-European homeland problem. *Medit. Lang. Rev.* 6:230–48

Dutton T. 1995. Language contact and change in Melanesia. In *The Austronesians*, ed. P Bellwood, J Fox, D Tryon, pp. 192–213. Canberra: Dep. Anthropol., Res. Sch. Pac. Asian Stud., Aust. Natl. Univ.

Ehret C. 1998. *An African Classical Age.* Charlottesville: Univ. Press Virginia

Errington J. 1998. *Shifting Languages.* Cambridge: Cambridge Univ. Press

Excoffier L, Schneider S. 1999. Why do hunter-gatherer populations not show signs of Pleistocene demographic expansion? *Proc. Natl. Acad. Sci. USA* 96:10597–602

Evans N, Jones R. 1997. The cradle of the Pama-Nyungans. See McConvell & Evans, pp. 385–417

Fix A. 1996. Gene frequency clines in Europe: demic diffusion or natural selection? *J. R. Anthropol. Inst.* 2:625–44

Fix A. 1999. *Migration and Colonization in Human Evolution.* Cambridge: Cambridge Univ. Press

Fortescue M. 1997. Dialect distribution and small group interaction in Greenlandic Eskimo. See McConvell & Evans, pp. 111–22

Fox CL. 1996. Physical anthropological aspects of the Mesolithic-Neolithic transition in the Iberian Peninsula. *Curr. Anthropol.* 37:689–94

Gamkrelidze TV, Ivanov VV. 1995. *Indo-European and the Indo-Europeans.* Berlin: Mouton de Gruyter

Gronenborn D. 1999. A variation on a basic theme: the transition to farming in southern central Europe. *J. World Prehist.* 13:123–210

Hagelberg E, Kayser M, Nagy M, Roewer L, Zimdahl H, et al. 1999. Molecular genetic evidence for the human settlement of the Pacific. *Philos. Trans. R. Soc. London Ser. B* 354:141–52

Hall M. 1990. *Farmers, Kings and Traders.* Chicago: Univ. Chicago Press

Harris D. ed. 1996. *The Origins and Spread of Agriculture and Pastoralism in Eurasia.* London: UCL Press

Harris M. 1978. *Cannibals and Kings.* London: Collins

Hassan F. 1981. *Demographic Archaeology.* New York: Academic

Heath S, Laprade R. 1982. Castilian colonization and indigenous languages: the cases of Quechua and Aymara. In *Language Spread*, ed. RL Cooper, pp. 118–47. Bloomington: Indiana Univ. Press

Higham C. 1996. Archaeology and linguistics in Southeast Asia: implications of the Austric hypothesis. *Bull. Indo-Pac. Prehist. Assoc.* 14:110–18

Hill J. 1999. *Why is Uto-Aztecan so big?* Presented at Dep. Anthropol. Colloq. Ser., Univ. Calif. Davis

Hudson M. 1999. *Ruins of Identity.* Honolulu: Univ. Hawai'i Press

Hunn ES, Williams NM. 1982. Introduction. In *Resource Managers: North American and Australian Hunter-Gatherers*, ed. NM Williams, ES Hunn, pp. 1–16. Boulder, CO: Westview

Jackes M, Lubell D, Meiklejohn C. 1997a. On physical anthropological aspects of the Mesolithic-Neolithic transition in the Iberian Peninsula. *Curr. Anthropol.* 38:839–46

Kayser M, Brauer S, Weiss G, Underhill P, Roewer L, et al. 2000. Melanesian origin of Polynesian Y chromosomes. *Curr. Biol.* 10:1237–46

Kayser M, Brauer S, Weiss G, Schiefenhovel W, Underhill A, Stoneking M. 2001. Independent histories of human Y chromosomes from Melanesia and Australia. *Am. J. Hum. Genet.* 68:173–90

Keeley LH. 1992. The introduction of agriculture to the western North European Plain. In *Transitions to Agriculture in Prehistory*, ed. AB Gebauer, D Price, pp. 81–96. Madison: Prehistory Press

Kent S ed. 1989. *Farmers as Hunters.* Cambridge: Cambridge Univ. Press

Kent S. 1992. The current forager controversy. *Man* 27:45–70

Kirch PV. 1997. *The Lapita Peoples.* Oxford: Blackwell

Kirch PV, Green RC. 2001. *Hawaiki: Ancestral Polynesia. An Essay in Historical Anthropology.* Cambridge: Cambridge Univ. Press

Krantz G. 1988. *The Geographical Development of European Languages.* New York: Peter Lang

Kulick D. 1992. *Language Shift and Cultural Reproduction.* Cambridge: Cambridge Univ. Press

Larsen CS. 1995. Biological changes in human populations with agriculture. *Annu. Rev. Anthropol.* 24:185–213

Lum JK, Cann R, Martinson J, Jorde L. 1998. Mitochondrial and nuclear genetic relationships among Pacific Island and Asian populations. *Am. J. Hum. Genet.* 63:613–24

Mallory J. 1989. *In Search of the Indo-Europeans.* London: Thames & Hudson

Mallory J. 1997. The homelands of the Indo-Europeans. In *Archaeology and Language I,* ed. R Blench, M Spriggs, pp. 93–121. London: Routledge

Masica C. 1978. Aryan and Non-Aryan elements in North Indian agriculture. In *Aryan and Non-Aryan in India,* ed. M Deshpande, P Hook, pp 55–152. Ann Arbor: Univ. Mich., Pap. South and Southeast Asia 14

McConvell P. 1996. Backtracking to Babel. *Archaeol. Oceania* 31:125–44

McConvell P, Evans N, eds. 1997. *Archaeology and Linguistics.* Melbourne, Aust.: Oxford Univ. Press

Meacham W. 1984–1985. On the improbability of Austronesian origins in South China. *Asian Perspect.* 26:89–106

Meindl R, Russell K. 1998. Recent advances in method and theory in paleodemography. *Annu. Rev. Anthropol.* 27:375–99

Merriwether D, Friedlaender J, Mediavilla J, Mgone C, Gentz F, Ferrell R. 1999. Mitochondrial DNA variation is an indicator of Austronesian influence in Island Melanesia. *Am. J. Phys. Anthropol.* 110:243–70

Mühlhäusler P. 1986. *Pidgin and Creole Linguistics.* Oxford: Blackwell

Murdock GP. 1967. *Ethnographic Atlas.* New Haven, CT: HRAF Press

Muro M. 1998 (1989). Not just another roadside attraction. *Am. Archaeol.* 2/4:10–16

Nettle D. 1996. Language diversity in West Africa. *J. Anthropol. Archaeol.* 15:403–38

Nettle D. 1999. *Linguistic Diversity.* Oxford: Oxford Univ. Press

Nichols J. 1992. *Language Diversity in Space and Time.* Chicago: Univ. Chicago Press

Nichols J. 1997. Modeling ancient population structures and movements in linguistics. *Annu. Rev. Anthropol.* 26:359–84

Nichols J. 1998. The Eurasian spread zone and the Indo-European dispersal. In *Archaeology and Language II,* ed. R Blench, M Spriggs, pp. 220–66. London: Routledge

Oppenheimer S. 1997. *Eden in the East.* London: Weidenfeld & Nicholson

Papuan Pasts 2000. *Conference on the cultural, linguistic and biological history of the Papuan speaking peoples,* Nov. 27–30, Res. Sch. Pac. Asian Stud., Aust. Natl. Univ.

Pawley AK. 1999. Chasing rainbows: implications of the rapid dispersal of Austronesian languages. In *Selected Papers from the Eighth International Conference on Austronesian Linguistics,* ed. E Zeitoun, P Li, pp. 95–138. Taipei: Inst. Linguist., Acad. Sin.

Pawley AK, Ross M. 1993. Austronesian historical linguistics and culture history. *Annu. Rev. Anthropol.* 22:425–59

Pawley AK, Ross M, eds. 1994. *Austronesian Terminologies, Continuity and Change.* Canberra: Pac. Linguist. Ser. C-127

Pawley AK, Ross M. 1995. The prehistory of the Oceanic languages. In *The Austronesians,* ed. P Bellwood, J Fox, D Tryon, pp. 39–74. Canberra: Dep. Anthropol., Res. Sch. Pac. Asian Stud., Aust. Natl. Univ.

Peiros I. 1998. *Comparative Linguistics in Southeast Asia.* Canberra: Pac. Linguist. Ser. C-142

Pentz P. 1992. *The Invisible Conquest.* Copenhagen: Natl. Mus. Denmark

Peterson J. 1978. *The Ecology of Social Boundaries.* Urbana: Univ. Ill. Press

Phillipson D. 1985. An archaeological reconsideration of Bantu expansion. *Muntu* 2:69–84

Phillipson D. 1993. *African Archaeology.* Cambridge: Cambridge Univ. Press. 2nd ed.

Price TD. 1995. Social inequality at the origins of agriculture. In *Foundations of Social*

Inequality, ed. TD Price, GF Feinman, pp. 129–51. New Yok: Plenum

Price TD, ed. 2000. *Europe's First Farmers.* Cambridge: Cambridge Univ. Press

Price TD, Gebauer AB. 1992. Foragers to farmers: an introduction. In *Transitions to Agriculture in Prehistory*, ed. AB Gebauer, D Price, pp. 1–10. Madison: Prehistory Press

Price TD, Gebauer AB, eds. 1995. *Last Hunters, First Farmers.* Santa Fe, NM: Sch. Am. Res.

Renfrew C. 1987. *Archaeology and Language.* London: Jonathan Cape

Renfrew C. 1991. Before Babel: speculations on the origins of linguistic diversity. *Cambridge Archaeol. J.* 1:3–23

Renfew C. 1992. World languages and human dispersals: a minimalist view. In *Transition to Modernity*, ed. JA Hall, IC Jarvie, pp. 11–68. Cambridge: Cambridge Univ. Press

Renfrew C. 1994. World linguistic diversity. *Sci. Am.* 270:747–60

Renfrew C. 1996. Language families and the spread of farming. In *The Origins and Spread of Agriculture and Pastoralism in Eurasia*, ed. D Harris, pp. 70–92. London: Univ. Coll. London Press

Renfrew C. 1999. Time depth, convergence theory, and innovation in Proto-Indo-European. *J. Indo-Eur. Stud.* 27:257–93

Renfrew C. 2000. At the edge of knowability: towards a prehistory of languages. *Cambridge Archaeol. J.* 10:7–34

Renfrew C, McMahon A, Trask L, eds. 2000. *Time Depth in Historical Linguistics.* Cambridge: McDonald Inst. Archaeol. Res. 2 Vols.

Renfrew C, Nettle D, eds. 1999. *Nostratic: Examining a Linguistic Macrofamily.* Cambridge: McDonald Inst. Archaeol. Res.

Richards M, Hedges R. 1999. A Neolithic revolution? New evidence of diet in the British Neolithic. *Antiquity* 73:891–96

Richards M, Macaulay V, Hickey E, Vega E, Sykes B, et al. 2000. Tracing European founder lineages in the Near Eastern mtDNA pool. *Am. J. Hum. Genet.* 67:1251–76

Richards M, Oppenheimer S, Sykes B. 1998. MtDNA suggests Polynesian origins in eastern Indonesia. *Am. J. Hum. Genet.* 63:1234–36

Rogers A, Jorde L. 1995. Genetic evidence on modern human origins. *Hum. Biol.* 67:1–36

Rollefson GO, Kohler-Rollefson I. 1993. PPNC adaptations in the first half of the 6th millennium BC. *Paléorient* 19:33–42

Rosenberg M. 1994. Pattern, process, and hierarchy in the evolution of culture. *J. Anthropol. Archaeol.* 12:75–119

Ross M. 1988. *Proto Oceanic and the Austronesian Languages of Western Melanesia.* Canberra: Pac. Linguist. Ser. C-98

Ross M. 1991. How conservative are sedentary languages? In *Current Trends in Pacific Linguistics*, ed. R Blust, pp. 433–57. Canberra: Pac. Linguist. Ser. C-117

Ross M. 1996. Contact-induced change and the comparative method: cases from Papua New Guinea. In *The Comparative Method Reviewed*, ed. M Durie, M Ross, pp. 180–217. New York: Oxford Univ. Press

Ross M. 1997a. Social networks and kinds of speech community event. In *Archaeology and Language I*, ed. R Blench, M Spriggs, pp. 209–62. London: Routledge

Ross M. 1997b. Comment. *Curr. Anthropol.* 38:182–84

Ross M, Pawley A, Osmond M, eds. 1998. *The Lexicon of Proto Oceanic. 1. Material Culture.* Canberra: Pac. Linguist. Ser. C, Vol. 152

Rouse I. 1986. *Migrations in Prehistory.* New Haven, CT: Yale Univ. Press

Sapir E. 1918. *Time Perspective in Aboriginal American Culture.* Canada, Dep. Mines, Geol. Surv. Mem. 90

Sather C. 1995. Sea nomads and rainforest hunter-gatherers. In *The Austronesians*, ed. P Bellwood, J Fox, D Tryon, pp. 229–68. Canberra: Dep. Anthropol., Res. Sch. Pac. Asian Stud., Aust. Natl. Univ.

Sauder G. 1990. *Europe Between the Languages.* Canberra: Aust. Acad. Humanit.

Schooling S. 1990. *Language Maintenance in New Caledonia.* Dallas, TX: Summer Inst. Linguist.

Sherratt A. 1997. Climatic cycles and behavioral revolutions. *Antiquity* 71:271–87

Sherratt A, Sherratt E. 1988. The archaeology of Indo-European: an alternative view. *Antiquity* 62:584–95

Smalley WA. 1994. *Linguistic Diversity and National Unity*. Chicago: Univ. Chicago Press

Smith B. 1995. *The Emergence of Agriculture*. New York: Sci. Am.

Smith KP. 1995. Landnám: the settlement of Iceland in archaeological and historical perspective. *World Archaeol*. 26:319–47

Sorenson AP. 1982. Multilingualism in the northwest Amazon. In *Sociolinguistics*, ed. J Pride, J Holmes, pp. 78–93. Harmondsworth: Penguin

Spriggs M. 1996. What is Southeast Asian about Lapita? In *Prehistoric Mongoloid Dispersals*, ed. T Akazawa, E Szathmary, pp. 324–48. Oxford: Oxford Univ. Press

Steadman D. 1999. The prehistoric extinction of South Pacific birds. In *The Pacific from 5000 to 2000 BP*, ed. J-C Galipaud, I Lilley, pp. 375–86. Paris: Inst. Rech. Dév.

Sverdrup H, Guardans R. 1999. Compiling words from extinct Non-Indoeuropean languages in Europe. In *Historical Linguistics and Lexicostatistics*, ed. V Shevoroshkin, P. Sidwell, pp. 201–57. Melbourne: AHL

Sykes B. 1999. The molecular genetics of European ancestry. *Philos. Trans. R. Soc. London Ser.* B354:131–40

Tayles N. 1999. *The Excavation of Khok Phanom Di. Vol. V: The People*. London: Soc. Antiquaries

Thomason SG, Kaufman T. 1988. *Language Contact, Creolization, and Genetic Linguistics*. Berkeley: Univ. Calif. Press

Torroni A, Bandelt H-G, D'Urbano L, Lahermo P, Moral P, et al. 1998. MtDNA analysis reveals a major late Paleolithic population expansion from southwestern to northeastern Europe. *Am. J. Hum. Genet.* 62:1137–52

Van Andel T, Zangger E, Demitrack A. 1990. Land use and soil erosion in prehistoric and historic Greece. *J. Field Archaeol.* 17:379–96

Van Andel T, Runnels C. 1995. The earliest farmers in Europe. *Antiquity* 69:481–500

Vansina J. 1990. *Paths in the Rainforest*. Madison: Univ. Wisc. Press

Vencl S. 1988. The role of hunting-gathering populations in the transition to farming: a central European perspective. In *Hunters in Transition*, ed. M Zvelebil, pp. 43–51. Cambridge: Cambridge Univ. Press

Weiss K. 1998. Coming to terms with human variation. *Annu. Rev. Anthropol.* 27:273–300

Wiik K. 2000. Some ancient and modern linguistic processes in northern Europe. In *Time Depth in Historical Linguistics*, ed. C Renfrew, A McMahon, L Trask, 2:463–80. Cambridge: McDonald Inst. Archaeol. Res.

Wood J, Milner G, Harpending H, Weiss K. 1992. The osteological paradox. *Curr. Anthropol.* 33:343–70

Woodburn J. 1982. Egalitarian societies. *Man* 17:431–51

Zvelebil M. 1995. At the interface of archaeology, linguistics and genetics: Indo-European dispersals and the agricultural transition in Europe. *J. Eur. Archaeol.* 3:33–70

Zvelebil M. 1998. Agricultural frontiers, Neolithic origins, and the transition to farming in the Baltic region. In *Harvesting the Sea, Farming the Forest*, ed. M Zvelebil, L Domanska, R Dennell, pp. 9–27. Sheffield: Sheffield Acad. Press

Zvelebil M, Rowley-Conwy P. 1986. Foragers and farmers in Atlantic Europe. In *Hunters in Transition*, ed. M Zvelebil, pp. 67–95. Cambridge: Cambridge Univ. Press

Annu. Rev. Anthropol. 2001. 30:209–26

ARCHAEOLOGICAL TEXTILES: A Review of Current Research

Irene Good

Peabody Museum, Harvard University, Cambridge, Massachusetts 02138;
e-mail: igood@fas.harvard.edu

Key Words   cloth, cordage, fiber analysis, perishables, pseudomorphs

■ **Abstract**   Archaeological textile studies are now recognized as a robust source of information for anthropological inquiry. Over the past two decades several important developments have taken place, enabling a more integrated approach to their study than in the past. Topics addressed range from the development of methods for analyzing degraded fibers to the comparative study of specific histories of textile and clothing traditions. Archaeological textile studies address relevant issues ranging from aesthetics and style to gender; from technological development to production and exchange economics. This chapter presents an overview of current research in the growing field of archaeological textile studies.

INTRODUCTION

The craft of using fiber to produce goods, ranging from floor mats to bridal dowry, addresses all three of the basic human needs: food, clothing, and shelter. Cordage, basketry, and matting, as well as woven cloth, have long been such an integral part of human adaptations that one can hardly pass through a day without using a metaphor that is ultimately derived from the production of fiber-related goods. The history of textile technology and its related crafts of spinning, plaiting, twining, and basketry is long and wide. We now know from direct evidence that the fiber arts were known in the Upper Palaeolithic on the Eurasian continent and came with the earliest inhabitants of the New World.

The advent of producing spun thread from plant fibers is now recognized as a technological revolution (Barber 1994; Adovasio 2001). Manipulating reeds, bark, basts, and seed down into cords, braids, baskets, nets, mats, and cloth bolstered our capacity to adapt *exponentially*. By fastening some of these manipulated elements into passive threads onto a frame, the history of the loom began.

Direct evidence for looms is rare, but we find early depictions on ceramics in the neolithic in Egypt, western Asia and in Europe (Broudy 1979). Looms diversified in their evolution in different regions of the world as distinct weaving traditions developed. Simple looms are not limited to producing simple woven cloth, however,

0084-6570/01/1021-0209$14.00

as particularly evidenced in the later prehistory of Peruvian textiles. Complexity in weave, design, and manufacture are, in a very general sense, attributes of wealth and prestige, as cloth is a very practical visual display of labor. Complexity in loom technology only increased mechanization, expanding the possible dimensions and qualities of cloth produced, but also reducing the relative effort to produce complex weaves. Although archaeological traces of early fiber use and textile production are sparse and tenuous, evidence for early technological developments in the textile arts in both the Old and New Worlds has been growing steadily for well over two centuries.

The study of ancient textiles goes at least as far back as the earliest antiquarians in Egypt. Bronze age cloth from the northern European bog-finds were among the most comprehensive nineteenth-century recordings of antiquity. Rare and fascinating to us, these tangible, delicate, intimate aspects of the archaeological record hold multiple layers of information about our past. The general recognition of the importance of textiles as an aspect of the archaeological record has become manifest, in large part because of the efforts of scholars such as James Adovasio, Patricia Anawalt, Elizabeth Barber, Junius Bird, Irene Emory, and Veronika Gervers, to name just a few. Over the past 20 years, the number and caliber of technical studies has risen dramatically, thanks to a new generation of scholars and scientists under their tutelage.

Perhaps more significant is a greater degree of integration of textile, basketry, and other fiber arts–related data into the main forum of current discussions in archaeological theory, which is having direct impact on basic theoretical assumptions and paradigms. This chapter presents a broad overview of some of the current trends in the study of archaeological textiles and related materials. Once treated as little more than chance finds and curiosities, textiles, fibers, cordage, and other "perishables" have now garnered notable attention in recent archaeological research, not only because of improved techniques in their recovery and analysis, but also because researchers are more aware of the value this kind of data holds in the overall interpretation of archaeological finds.

Another important contribution to this trend has been the accumulation of technical studies, which allows a coalescence of earlier archaeological textile data, in both area studies as well as in diachronic studies, to the point where synthesis is now possible. Research interests in fiber arts now range from clarifying and synthesizing the history of technologies (Webster & Drooker 2000; Barber 1999, 1991; Jørgensen 1999, 1992; Crowfoot et al 1992; Walton & Wild 1990) and ancient aesthetic traditions and their cross-cultural transfer (Rubinson 1990, Adovasio 2000, Anawalt 1992, 1998, Barber 1999), to palaeoeconomic studies (Brumfiel & Earle 1987, Costin 1993, Jakes & Ericksen 1997), gender studies (Brumfiel 1991; Costin 1995, 1996), and division of labor (Soffer et al 1998, 2000a,b), production (Sherratt 1981, Chapman 1983; Costin 1990, 1995, 1998; Brumfiel 1996; Kuttruff 1988), and fiber source procurement (Janaway & Coningham 1995, McCorrison 1997). These vantage points have become viable and informative lines of inquiry among art historians and archaeologists, as well as scholars of ancient history. Critical methodological issues such as developments in fiber identification and interpretation (Angel & Jakes 1990, Jakes 2000, Chen & Jakes 2001, Jakes et al 1990, Srinivasan & Jakes 1997, Good 1999, Janaway & Scott 1989, Boddington et al 1987), or the epistemological limitations of intrasite spatial distribution of small finds related to textile craft such as spindle whorls (Costin 1990), are also important and active pursuits.

A comprehensive approach to the study of ancient textiles and fiber perishables addresses physical construction (Fowler et al 2000, Deegan 1997, Adovasio & Maslowski 1980, Frazier 1989), coloration (Jakes et al 1990, Sibley & Jakes 1994, Sibley et al 1992), and content (Körber-Grohne & Küstler 1985, Good & Kim 1994, Good 1995a, Wild 1984) in the context of the implements (if any) from which they are derived (Alfaro 1990; Bird 1983; Good 1995b; H. Tu, unpublished observations). These in turn are viewed within their social and physical environmental contexts (Sibley et al 1996; Song et al 1996; I.L. Good, unpublished data). This integrated approach has become a highly productive avenue of discovery into understanding some of the social processes that underlie the agency of production, use, and exchange, in terms of the generation and regeneration of style, genre, and aesthetic, as well as technique, process, and valuation. We now are able to examine how these facets of human experience are interfaced with regionalization, cultural demarcation, and the expression of social boundaries (Barber 1991; Bernick 1987; Cassman 2000; Teague 2000; Good 1998, 1999). Observing these critical social processes through the diachronic perspective offered by archaeology has allowed us to obtain a more comprehensive and seasoned understanding of issues that are highly relevant to social science.

THE NATURE OF THE DATA

What exactly is a textile? Most textile scientists would agree that it can be defined as "a web of interlaced threads produced on a loom." However, there are numerous objects that do not fall easily into that precise a definition, and there are several classes of fiber artifact that derive from related but separate technologies (for current discussions of terminologies and definitions see Emery 1980, Fowler et al 2000, Adovasio et al 1999; see also Seiler-Baldinger 1994).

The main venues for organic preservation are extreme aridity, freezing, acidic microenvironments (such as those near a metal object), or nitrogen-rich bogs in which little or no oxidation can occur. Each set of conditions plays a role in the nature of the preservation and concomitant conservation problems and courses of action. The ideal soil pH depends on the type of fiber. Linen and other cellulosic fibers preserve better in alkaline conditions, whereas animal protein fibers such as wool preserve better in slightly acidic environments.

There are several ways in which cordage, netting, matting, basketry, felts, and textiles or their traces can be recovered archaeologically. They can range from actual intact objects, to degraded fragments of former objects or their components with intact fibers, to chemically degraded pseudomorphs, even mere traces in soil. Textile and basketry information can also be derived from impressions in clay and plaster, whether purposive or unintended, and from design and patterns found in representational art and other media. Finally, there is an encyclopedic source of textile information, from fiber procurement to regional specialized craft production and exchange, within its own social context, which has been recovered from ancient texts (e.g., Waetzoldt 1972, Kuhn 1982, Steinkeller 1995). Clearly, the resources at our disposal are abundant.

Intact Structures of Perishable Materials

Occasionally, complete articles of clothing are found in archaeological contexts (see for example, Crowfoot et al 1992, Vogelsang-Eastwood 1993, Broholm & Hald 1940, Zhao & Yu 1998). Much more common in archaeological contexts are fragmented textiles or other perishable objects that have nevertheless retained their structure (see Figure 1). Intact textiles have been recovered and recorded from excavations for well over a century. The famous Bronze Age burial mounds and bog finds in Denmark, for example, turned the attention of antiquarians toward textile finds and their importance. From the barrows of Borum Eshøj, first

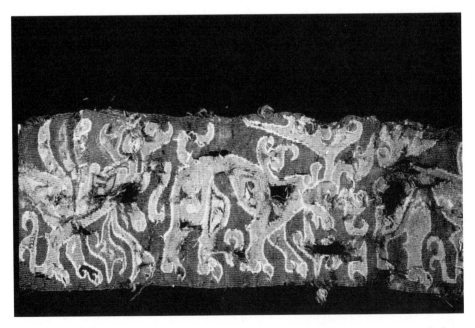

Figure 1   Scytho-Siberian "animal style" reindeer carefully executed in tapestry technique woolen panel from late first millennium B.C.E., Sampula, Xinjiang.

excavated in 1875, a very important corpus of textiles has been preserved. Although many of the objects were compromised owing to the circumstances of their discovery, the textile finds from this well-known site to this day remain part of a large inventory of curated Bronze Age costume from northern Europe. The Tarim Basin sites discovered during the early twentieth-century Sino-Swedish expeditions of Bergman and Hedin (1927–1935) and the British and Indian government expeditions led by Stein (1913–1916) and more recently by the Chinese (1976–1986) (Zhao & Yu 1998; Xia 1979; Wang 1986), as well as sites in the New World yielding large amounts of perishable remains, particularly in the American Southwest (Adovasio 1972, 1980; Adovasio & Gunn 1986) and Peru (Bird & Hyslop 1985), have collectively produced a considerable corpus of intact textile remains.

Exhaustive technical studies of textiles and clothing recovered from these excavations have begun to accumulate over the past several decades; some are recent studies of earlier excavations, for example of the corpus of cloth from the famous discovery of Tutankh-amun's tomb (Vogelsang-Eastwood 1993), and from the expedition to Pachacamac in Peru (Van Stan 1967). Others have been incorporated into final site reports, such as the several excavations in western Asia that recovered significant amounts of perishable fiber artifacts to warrant attention, such as those at Palmyra in Syria (Pfister & Bellinger 1945), at Gordion in Turkey (Ellis 1981; see also Bellinger 1962), and at Nahal Hemar in Israel (Schick 1988a,b). Textile specialists have written exhaustive documentation of the technical aspects of these finds, and later technical and textile historical syntheses have also been written (Andrews 1935; Sylwan 1937, 1941, 1949; O'Neale 1936; Simmons 1956; Hald 1980; Anawalt 2000). With each generation of interested specialists come new and more comprehensive techniques, so that techniques and methodological approaches can now address multiple levels of analysis (e.g., Ericksen et al 2000). With the advancement of analytical technology has come a plethora of scientific studies applying these new tools to the analysis of ancient perishable fiber artifacts (Jakes & Angel 1989; Jakes & Howard 1986; Good & Kim 1994; Chen & Jakes 2001; Chen et al 1996a,b, 1998, 2000).

Degraded Fiber Artifacts with Intact Fibers

A perishable object can be mechanically or chemically degraded, or both. Sometimes textile traces are found in soil but are too disintegrated to rescue. In each of these conditions, however, it is still possible to recover information about fibers and even threads, if present (see Figure 2). Threads often retain their shape from their former structure, under most conditions favorable to their preservation, making it possible to at least partially reconstruct the object structure. For example, construction along with fiber and spin information can often reliably relate partial finds to a larger cultural context and can inform us about technique, skill, craft specialization, choice, access to materials, and other basic factors that played

Figure 2   Image of *Linum* fiber single cell "ultimates" from third millennium B.C.E., Shahr-i Sokhta, Iran, using interference microscopy to highlight diagnostic dislocation scars.

a role in creating past social environments (see Deegan 1997; Johnson 1996; Kuttruff 1988; Good 1995a, 1999; Rodman 1992; DeRoche 2001; Anawalt 1988, 1997; Cassman 2000).

A related situation to this is the occurrence of traces of thread or other binding material in a composite find, such as a necklace of beads, where traces of thread are still encased within the holes of some of the beads. The careful study of this type of small find, along with the removal of matrix soil around the find during retrieval in the field and withholding cleaning until examination, are each valuable tactics to practice. Beads found from a child's grave in chalcolithic Nevasa in South Asia, for example, retained intact thread fragments made of mixed fibers of silk and bast (Gulati 1961). If this attribution and date are correct, the silk is one of the earliest examples on record outside of China. This kind of find also occurred at Roman Period Sardis in Turkey, where beads revealed traces of an exceptionally fine wool thread (Greenwalt 1990). This fine wool is one of a rare number of early examples of the development of fine wool fleece (Ryder 1969, 1983, 1987). These and other small pieces of evidence have been gradually filling in the gaps of our knowledge of fiber use in prehistory.

Thread and cordage can be studied for the direction and degree of spin, as well as for fiber content. Much attention has recently been given to this very perfunctory utilitarian category, resulting in some surprisingly profound revelations concerning handedness, spinning technique, and the tenacity of taught methods of spinning and plying (Minar 2000, Petersen 2000, Petersen & Adovasio 1999, Sibley et al 1989). The consideration of this kind of work in reshaping current perceptions of issues such as the division of labor and status differentiation in the Upper Palaeolithic and PalaeoIndian periods, now that more evidence has come to light (Adovasio 1998; Soffer et al 2000a,b). Even when extant fibers are lost, in certain conditions, traces of fibers and fiber objects can be recognized, if care is taken to look for them.

Pseudomorphs

A pseudomorph is a physical trace remain of a former fiber, thread, or textile. The term was first coined by Vollmer (1974). Much more common than textile finds, these delicate traces are occasionally found on calcined ceramic vessels, metal objects, and even on stone. Pseudomorphs, *sensu stricto*, contain not intact fibers but only their chemical breakdown products. Pseudomorphs occur primarily when textiles are in contact with metal objects. As the metal breaks down, the concomitant metal salts create a specific type of microenvironment that is ideal for the preservation of textiles. Pseudomorphs are highly useful for study because they often leave negative hollows of the fibers in casings of metal salts, much like a fossil cast, leaving behind the structure of the former cloth and hints of the threads and fibers (see Chen et al 1998, Janaway & Scott 1989, Boddington et al 1987). It is quite common, however, for these pseudomorphs actually to have trace amounts of chemically intact fiber preserved in the matrix. Biochemical study of preserved fibers in pseudomorphs has yet to become routine, although this approach is feasible for identifying fiber content and can be much more informative than chemical testing (see Good 1995a, 1999).

Impressions

Another form of indirect textile trace formation is in the negative; textile and reed matting impressions are commonly found in clay, mud, and plaster from architectural features. Textile impressions are also found in ceramics; in fact there are distinct pottery manufacturing traditions that require the use of cloth. The traces of the cloth are baked right into the pot. Various ceramic traditions from regions throughout the world use some kind of technique involving cord-marking or textile-impressed paddling; and some of these traditions have been carefully studied (Bird 1956, Hyland et al 2000, Shishlina et al 2000, Shishlina 1999, Harding et al 2000). Impressions have been recovered from Mesolithic and Upper Paleolithic sites in eastern Europe and Russia (Adovasio 1998, 2000). Sometimes microscopic amounts of actual fibers can be retained in the matrix containing the impression (see Figure 3). This humble class of artifact is currently transforming fundamental perceptions we have built about the past, particularly in our deep prehistory (Adovasio 1999).

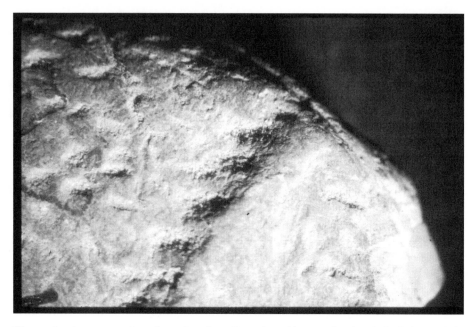

Figure 3   An apparently unintentional textile and cord impression in a baked clay nodule from late fourth millennium B.C.E., Anau, Turkmenistan.

Cloth and Clothing Design and Patterns Derived From Representational and Abstracted Art

It is an almost universal maxim that social groups, and individual social stations within groups, are marked via cloth, clothing, and modes of dress. The study of ancient dress, therefore, is of particular interest to anthropologically trained archaeologists. There are also indirect ways of reconstructing ancient cloth and clothing from less perishable archaeological remains. One aspect of this type of approach is to study actual dress and ornamentation as derived from representational art, from detailed statuary (see Figure 4) to small ceramic figurines. Particularly noteworthy in this regard are the finely executed statuary from Early Dynastic Mesopotamia made of basalt or diorite. The hard stone has preserved a great amount of detail from some of the rather exacting executions of dress. Human dress and adornment derived from figurines and other forms of representational art have been studied in many other instances (Tosi 1983; Kawami 1992, 1992; Koslin 1987, 2001), some on the level of a concerted effort to reconstruct costume (Anawalt 1988, 1992, 2000; Anawalt & Davis 2001; Gullberg & Åstom 1970; Soffer et al 2000a,b).

A second approach is that of inferring textile and basketry designs from artwork. Ceramic motifs in particular can help to ascertain the type of weave or possibly the type of loom. An example of this type of study is an examination of the traditional

Figure 4   Extant paint showing detail of textile decoration on marble statue from fifth-century B.C.E. Greece.

Turkoman carpet patterns derived from ceramics (Pinner 1982). A better-known example of this is that of the wall frescoes of Çatal Hüyük by Mellart (1975, 1962). Barber has examined Bronze Age wall frescoes in the Mediterranean and deduced much concerning weaving structures from patterned motifs (Barber 1991; see also Sibley et al 1991).

Discussion of Current Issues in Archaeological Textile Studies

There have been two major difficulties challenging the archaeological study of textiles. The first is a methodological one, and the second is interpretive. There are several factors that make the analysis of archaeological textiles especially difficult. One obvious factor is that of fiber degradation. There are myriad ways in which a fiber can degrade, making it necessary to have a diverse range of analytical tests available. Carbonization is one of the more common states in which archaeological textile fibers are recovered. Researchers have worked on the specific problem of carbonization with regard to perishable material remains in general (e.g., see Letts et al 1994). The problem of identifying carbonized fibers and otherwise degraded samples is what makes archaeological fiber analysis challenging, and caution must always be exercised in making identifications.

Fiber identifications can be inaccurate or inadequate, either because of difficulty distinguishing diagnostic features under poor conditions of preservation or because the information was not sought out. The vast majority of archaeological fibers are badly degraded or carbonized by the time they reach the specialist's laboratory, and the limitations of conventional light microscopy can deter proper identification. Without access to an array of analytical techniques such as scanning electron microscopy, phase contrast and interference microscopy, and chemical and biochemical methods, identifications are often lacking or even counterproductive. For example, the famous textiles from the Neolithic site Çatal Hüyük in southeastern Anatolia, dating to 6000 B.C.E., were originally thought to be woolen (Helbaek 1963). Only later analysis by Ryder (1965), however, revealed that they are of bast. The difficulty in their identification was because the fibers were opaqued by carbonization, which is problematic in conventional transmission light microscopy.

Proteins, lipids, and even DNA from cortical cells can be detected and identified from animal fibers in degraded condition (e.g., see Sibley & Jakes 1984). These types of analysis have begun to be carried out on archaeological fibers, in particular with wild and domesticated silks (Good & Kim 1994, 1995a). Biochemical testing can be applied to other animal fibers from archaeological textiles as well and has been done recently with success (Good 1999). Another biochemical test is polymerase chain reaction, where fragments of ancient DNA extracted from proteinaceous fibers are amplified. (For recent application of this type of test on ancient DNA, see Francolatti 1998; see also Pääbo et al 1989.) Each of these tests should be used as a corroborative tool for identification and should not be relied upon in isolation.

Perhaps the more consequential problem, however, is interpretive. Imprecise or inconclusive identifications can be misinterpreted, and then the misinterpretations become amplified into general archaeological literature. For example, a textile discovered in 1932 in a Hallstatt grave was thought to be Chinese silk even though the technical report clearly stated that the chemical tests were inconclusive (Hundt 1971). The general literature discussing the finds assumes Chinese origin to be a fact, and the interpretation of long-distance contacts revolves around this single assumption (cf. Wells 1980, p. 84; Wild 1984; Barber 1991, pp. 31–32). In another example, linen was identified among the textile finds at Gordion in Turkey and assumed imported, simply because virtually nothing was known at that time about fiber procurement in Iron Age Anatolia (Young 1958, Bellinger 1962).

Ascertaining the fiber in a fiber-perishable artifact will necessarily have a great bearing on the understanding of this critically important aspect of material culture history. The information required to make this judgment is not always consulted or is not always available. Even when the fiber identification is accurate, interpretation of it can be faulty. By using a multiple range of tests for identifications, along with a contextual and environmental approach to the interpretation of fiber perishables, a more precise knowledge of textile and fiber-related materials within a given area can be ascertained, thus allowing for more refined interpretation of finds.

CLOSING REMARKS

A concise yet truly comprehensive review of the current state of research in archaeological textiles, from the Upper Palaeolithic to historic periods, in the Old and New Worlds, is a truly daunting task. This chapter is limited to the review of some of the more salient aspects of recent trends, primarily from reports in English, although much relevant literature exists in many other languages, particularly from journals published in Russian, Norwegian, Danish, Spanish, Japanese, and Chinese.

Archaeological textiles and other perishable fiber artifacts are materials that are highly conducive to study from multiple approaches: from the perspective of a qualitative aesthetic discipline, as well as from a quantitative, deductive materials science investigation. The processes of their production have required complex, scheduled, highly labor-intensive human effort and have always been in constant demand (therein perhaps is the true significance of their being "perishables"), and perhaps even more than the processes of ceramic production, they tend to adhere to multiple semiotic and stylistic norms over time and place. Whereas fiber objects are a relatively small portion of the archaeological record, textiles have provided us with a relatively large portion of the information we have gained about the past. For this reason the study of archaeological textiles and other fiber products holds a unique position in anthropology.

Although they will never be as commonly recovered from archaeological sites as more durable materials, textiles and other ephemeral fiber objects and their related materials have been studied intensely for well over a century. There is also much in the way of related evidence at our disposal that does preserve well. Recent efforts in art history, textile history, and archaeology, as well as in textile science and chemistry, have helped to create momentum in bringing cohesion, meaning, and accessibility to this once arcane subject.

These cumulative data we now have at our disposal are amply suited for a new generation of comparative studies and syntheses for addressing some basic anthropological questions. Fresh textile and fiber perishables data can now be interpreted with the aid of a large interdisciplinary framework built from what we know, rather than simply documented in site report appendices and forgotten, as they often were just 20 years ago. This new trend will perhaps accelerate the process of bringing the subject of ancient fiber use into view as a serious subdiscipline of archaeology, routinely taught to students of archaeology, museum studies, and textile science, rather than being left to a handful of overwhelmed specialists.

It is important to continue with diligence the restudy and revision of weaker aspects of earlier technical studies when possible, for accurate data sets are an imperative prerequisite to producing meaningful interpretations. We must also strive for a balance between technical acumen and relevance, taking care to increase the level of integration between inference and assumption, rather than to compromise one over the other. We can now expect much more of these valuable "perishable" artifact data to come to the light of day, and we can also expect much more information to be revealed.

Visit the Annual Reviews home page at www.AnnualReviews.org

LITERATURE CITED

Adovasio JM. 1972. *Basketry as an indicator of archaeological frontiers: a case study from the Southwest.* Presented at Annu. Meet. Soc. Am. Arch., 37th, Miami

Adovasio JM. 1980. Prehistoric basketry of western North America and Mexico. In *Early Native Americans: Prehistoric Demography, Economy and Technology*, ed. D Browman, pp. 341–62. The Hague: Mouton

Adovasio JM. 1998. *Perishable industries and the colonization of the East European Plain.* Presented at Int. Congr. Anthropol. Ethnol. Sci., 14th, Williamsburg, VA

Adovasio JM. 1999. *Perishable artifacts, paleoindians and dying paradigms.* Presented at "Clovis Beyond—Peopling America." Conf., Santa Fe, NM

Adovasio JM. 2000. *Style, basketry and basketmakers: agency concretized in a perishable medium.* Presented at Annu. Chacmool Conf., 33rd, Calgary, Can.

Adovasio JM. 2001. *Perishable technology and Late Pleistocene/Early Holocene adaptations in the Americas.* Presented at Plants Perishables Prehist. Symp., SAA 66th Ann. Meet., New Orleans, LA, Apr. 18–22, 2001

Adovasio JM, Gunn JM. 1986. The antelope house basketry industry. In *Archeological Investigations at Antelope House*, ed. DP Morris, pp. 306–97. Washington, DC: Natl. Park Serv., US Dep. Inter.

Adovasio JM, Maslowski RF. 1980. Textiles and cordage. In *Guitarrero Cave*, ed. TF Lynch, pp. 253–90. New York: Academic

Alfaro C. 1990. Weaving systems in northwest Europe: Prehistoric to Roman. See Walton & Wild 1990, pp. 29–37

Anawalt PR. 1988. Pageantry of Aztec warfare as reflected in military attire. In *Smoke and Mist: Mesoamerican Studies in Memory of Thelma D. Sullivan*, ed. JK Josser, K Dakin, pp. 113–50. Oxford, UK: BAR Int. Ser. 402

Anawalt PR. 1992. A comparative analysis of the costumes and accoutrements of the *Codex Mendoza*. In *The Codex Mendoza*, ed. FF Berdan, PR Anawalt, 1:103–50. Berkeley: Univ. Calif. Press

Anawalt PR. 1997. Textiles as sacrifice: Aztec ritual capes. In *Sacred and Ceremonial Textiles: Proc. 5th Bienn. Symp. Text. Soc. Am., 1996*, pp. 131–40. Earleville, MD: Text. Soc. Am.

Anawalt PR. 1998. They came to trade exquisite things: ancient West Mexican-Ecuadorian contacts. In *Ancient West Mexico: Art and Archaeology of the Unknown Past*, ed. RF Townsend, pp. 233–50. New York: Thames Hudson; Chicago: Art Inst. Chic.

Anawalt PR. 2000. Textile research from the Mesoamerican perspective. See Drooker & Webster 2000, pp. 205–28

Anawalt PR, Davis V. 2001. Perished but not beyond recall: Aztec textile reconstruction via word, image and replica. In *Fleeting Identities: Perishable Material Culture in Archaeological Research*, ed. PB Drooker, pp. 187–209. Occasional Paper No. 28. Carbondale, IL: Cent. Archaeol. Investig., South. Ill. Univ.

Andrews FH. 1935. *Descriptive Catalogue of Antiquities Recovered by Sir Aurel Stein During His Explorations in Central Asia, Kansu and Eastern Iran.* New Delhi: Central Asian Antiq. Mus.

Angel A, Jakes KA. 1990. Preparing and analyzing fractured archaeological fibers. *J. Electron Microsc. Tech.* 20(14):1–5

Barber EW. 1991. *Prehistoric Textiles.* Princeton, NJ: Princeton Univ. Press

Barber EW. 1994. *Women's Work—the First*

20,000 Years. Princeton, NJ: Princeton Univ. Press

Barber EW. 1999. *The Mummies of Ürümchi*. New York: Norton

Bellinger L. 1962. Textiles from Gordion. *Bull. Needle Bobbin Club* 46:1–2

Bernick K. 1987. The potential of basketry for reconstructing cultural diversity on the northwest coast. In *Ethnicity and Culture: Proc. 18th Annu. Conf. Archaeol. Assoc. Univ. Calgary*, ed. R Auger, MF Glass, S MacEachern, PH McCartney, pp. 251–57. Calgary, Can.: Univ. Calgary Archaeol. Assoc.

Bird J. 1956. Fabrics, basketry and matting as revealed by impressions on pottery. In *WA Fairservis Jr: Excavations in the Quetta Valley, West Pakistan*. Anthropol. Pap. Am. Mus. Nat. Hist., New York. Appendix 2. 45(2):372–77

Bird J. 1983. Matched pair of archaeological looms from Peru. In *In Celebration of the Curious Mind*, ed. N Rogers, M Stanley, pp. 1–8. Loveland, CO: Interweave

Bird J, Hyslop J. 1985. *The preceramic excavations at Huaca Prieta, Chicama Valley, Peru, with textile sections by JB Bird, completed by MD Skinner*. Anthropol. Pap. Am. Mus. Nat. Hist., New York. 62(1)

Boddington A, Garland AN, Janaway R. 1987. *Death, Decay, and Reconstruction: Approaches to Archaeology and Forensic Science*. Manchester, UK: Manchester Univ. Press

Broudy E. 1979. *The Book of Looms—a History of the Handloom from Ancient Times to the Present*. Providence, RI: Brown Univ. Press

Broholm HC, Hald M. 1940. *Costumes of Bronze Age Denmark; Contributions to the Archaeology and Textile History of the Bronze Age*. Copenhagen: Ny Nordisk

Brumfiel EM. 1991. Weaving and cooking: women's production in Aztec Mexico. In *Engendering Archaeology: Women and Prehistory*, ed. JM Gero, MW Conkey, pp. 224–51. Oxford, UK: Blackwell

Brumfiel EM. 1996. The quality of tribute cloth: the place of evidence in archaeological argument. *Am. Antiq.* 61(3):453–62

Brumfiel M, Earle T. 1987. Specialization, exchange and complex societies: an introduction. In *Specialization, Exchange, and Complex Societies*, ed. E Brumfiel, T Earle, pp. 1–9. Cambridge, UK: Cambridge Univ. Press

Cassman V. 2000. Prehistoric ethnicity and status: the textile evidence. See Drooker & Webster 2000, pp. 253–60

Chapman JC. 1985. The secondary products revolution and the limitations of the neolithic. *Bull. Inst. Arch.* 19:107–22

Chen HL, Foreman DW, Jakes KA. 1996. X-ray diffractometric analyses of the microstructure of mineralized plant fibers. In *Archaeological Chemistry: Organic, Inorganic and Biochemical Analysis*, ed. MV Orna, pp 187–201. Am. Chem. Soc. Symp. Ser. 625, Wahsington, DC.

Chen HL, Foreman DW, Jakes KA. 2000. *Peak-fitting analysis of cellulose powder XRD spectra*. Preprints Poly. Mat. Sci. Engl. Sect. Am. Chem. Soc. Natl. Meet. 20th Washington, DC

Chen HL, Jakes KA, Foreman DW. 1998. Preservation of archaeological textiles through fibre mineralization. *J. Archaeol. Sci.* 20(25):1015–22

Chen HL, Jakes KA, Foreman DW. 1996. SEM, EDS and FTIR examination of archaeological mineralized plant fibers. *Text. Res. J.* 66(4):219–24

Chen R, Jakes KA. 2001. FTIR microspectroscopy as an effective tool for single fiber identification and fiber structural analysis. *Postprints Text. Specialty Group, Am. Inst. Conservation of historic and artistic works*, pp. 25–37. Vol. 10. Washington, DC: Am. Inst. Conserv. In press

Costin CL. 1990. Craft specialization: issues in defining, documenting and explaining the organization of production. In *Archaeological Method and Theory*, ed. M Schiffer, 3:1–56. Tucson: Univ. Arizona Press

Costin CL. 1993. Textiles, women, and political economy in Late Prehispanic Peru. *Res. Econ. Anthropol.* 14:3–28 Greenwich: JAI Press

Costin CL. 1995. Cloth production and gender relations in the Inka Empire. In *Research Frontiers in Anthropology—Advances in Archaeology and Physical Anthropology*, ed. PN Peregrine, CR Ember, M Ember. Englewood Cliffs, NJ: Prentice Hall

Costin CL. 1996. Exploring the relationship between gender and craft in complex societies: methodological and theoretical issues of gender attribution. In *Gender and Archaeology*, ed. RP Wright, pp. 111–40. Philadelphia: Univ. Penn. Press

Costin CL. 1998. Housewives, chosen women, skilled men: cloth production and social identity in the Late Prehispanic Andes. In *Craft and Social Identity*, ed. CL Costin, RP Wright, pp. 123–44. Arlington, VA: Arch. Papers Am. Anthropol., Assoc. No. 8

Crowfoot E, Pritchard F, Staniland K. 1992. *Textiles and Clothing c. 1150–c. 1450: Medieval Finds from Excavations in London*, Vol. 4. London: Mus. London

Davis-Kimball J, Murphy EM, Koryakova L, Yablonsky LT. 2000. *Kurgans, Ritual Sites, and Settlements: Eurasian Bronze and Iron Age*. Oxford: Brit. Archaeol. Res. Rep.: Int. Ser. 870: Oxford: Archaeopress

Deegan AC. 1997. Anasazi sandals of Hseyi-Hatsosi Canyon, Arizona: attributes and cultural context. *Cloth. Text. Res. J.* 15:12–19

DeRoche D. 2001. *European fabrics in Pennsylvania's Native American graves*. Presented at Text. Negot. Power Symp., SAA 66th Ann. Meet., New Orleans, LA, Apr. 18–22, 2001

Drooker P, Webster L, eds. 2000. *Beyond Cloth and Cordage: Current Approaches to Archaeological Textile Research in the Americas*. Salt Lake City: Univ. Utah Press

Emery I. 1980. *The Primary Structures of Fabrics—an Illustrated Classification*. Washington, DC: Text. Mus.

Ellis R. 1981. Appendix III. The textiles. In *Three Early Tumuli*, ed. R Young. Philadelphia, PA: Univ. Mus. pp. 294–310

Ericksen AG, Jakes KA, Wimberley VS. 2000. Prehistoric textiles: production, function and semiotics. See Drooker & Webster 2000, pp. 60–84

Fowler CS, Hattori EM, Dansie AJ. 2000. Ancient matting from Spirit Cave, Nevada. See Drooker & Webster 2000, pp. 119–52

Francolatti P. 1998. DNA analysis on ancient dessicated corpses from Xinjiang (China): further results. See Mair 1998, pp. 537–47

Frazier D. 1989. *A Guide to Weft Twining and Related Structures with Interacting Wefts*. Philadelphia: Univ. Penn. Press

Good IL. 1995a. On the question of silk in pre-Han Eurasia. *Antiquity* 69(266):959–68

Good IL. 1995b. Notes on a Bronze Age textile fragment from Hami, Xinjiang, with comments on the significance of twill. *J. Indo-Eur. Stud.* 23(3&4):319–45

Good IL. 1998. Bronze Age cloth and clothing of the Tarim Basin: the Chärchän evidence. See Mair 1998, pp. 656–68

Good IL. 1999. *The ecology of exchange: textiles from 3rd millennium BC Iran*. PhD diss. Univ. Penn. Ann Arbor: Univ. Mirofilms Int.

Good IL, Kim EJ. 1994. *The Silk Project Final Report*. Philadelphia: Univ. Penn. Res. Found.

Greenwalt CH. 1990. *Report of the Sardis Campaign of 1986*. Bull. Am. Sch. Oriental Res. (Suppl.) 26

Gulati AN. 1961. A note on the early history of silk in India. In *Technical Reports on Archaeological Remains III*, ed. J Clutton Brock, Vishnu-Mittre, AN Gulati, pp. 53–59. Deccan College Post-graduate and Research Institute, Dept. of Archaeology and Ancient Indian History. Publication 2. Poona, India: Deccan College

Gullberg E, Åstrom P. 1970. *The thread of Ariadne: a study in ancient Greek dress*. Stud. Mediterr. Archaeol. Vol. 7. Goteburg, Sweden: Paul Åstrom

Hald M. 1980. *Ancient Danish Textiles from Bogs and Burials*. Vol. 21. Copenhagen: Natl. Mus. Denmark, Arch. Hist. Ser.

Harding D, Olsen S, Jones Bley K. 2000. Reviving their fragile technologies: reconstructing perishables from pottery impressions from Botai, Kazakhstan. Presented at Annu. Meet. Soc. Am. Arch., 65th, Philadelphia, PA

Helbaek H. 1963. Textiles from Çatal Hüyük. *Archaeology* 67:39–46

Hoffman M. 1966. *The Warp-Weighted Loom. Stud. Nor.* 14. Oslo: Univ. Forlaget

Hundt HJ. 1971. On prehistoric textile finds. *Jahrbuch Römisch-Germanisches Zentralmuseum* 16:59–71

Hyland DC, Zhushlikhovskaya IS, Medvedev VE, Derevianko AP, Tabarev AV. 2000. *Pleistocene textiles in the Far East: impressions from the world's oldest pottery.* Presented at Annu. Meet. Soc. Am. Arch., 65th, Philadelphia, PA

Jakes KA. 2000. Microanalytical methods for the study of prehistoric textile fibers. See Drooker & Webster 2000, pp. 51–59

Jakes KA, Angel A. 1989. The determination of elemental distribution in ancient fibers. In *Archaeological Chemistry IV*, ed. RO Allen. pp. 451–64. Adv. Chem. Ser. No. 220, Washington, DC: Am. Chem. Soc.

Jakes KA, Ericksen AG. 1997. Socioeconomic implications of prehistoric textile production in the eastern woodlands, materials issues. In *Materials Issues in Art Archaeol.* 5th Annu. Symp., Dec. 3–5, 1996, Boston, MA, ed. P Vandiver, J Druzik, JF Merkel, J Stewart. 462:281–86. Pittsburgh, PA: Materials Res. Soc. Symp. Proc.

Jakes KA, Howard JH III. 1986. Replacement of protein and cellulose fibers by copper minerals and the formation of textile pseudomorphs. In *Historic Textile and Paper Materials: Conservation and Characterization*, ed. HL Needles, S Haig Zeronian, pp. 277–87. Adv. Chem. Ser. No. 212. Washington, DC: Am. Chem. Soc.

Jakes KA, Katon JE, Martoglio PA. 1990. Identification of dyes and characterization of fibers by infrared and visible microspectroscopy: application to Paracas textiles. In *Archaeometry 90: Proceedings of the 27th International Symposium on Archaeometry*, ed. E Pernicka, G Wagner, pp. 305–15. Basel: Birkhauser

Janaway RC, Coningham RAE. 1995. A review of archaeological textile evidence from South Asia. *South Asian Stud.* 11:157–74

Janaway RC, Scott BG. 1989. Evidence preserved in corrosion products: new fields. In *Artifact Studies.* London: UK Inst. Conserv. Occasional pap. No. 8. Leeds: Proc. Joint Conf. UKIC Arch. Sect. Council Brit. Archaeol. Sci. Comm.

Johnson WC. 1996. A new twist on an old tale: analysis of cordage impressions on late woodland ceramics from the potomac river valley. In *A Most Indespensible Art: Native Fiber Industries from Eastern North America*, ed. JB Petersen, pp. 144–59. Knoxville: Univ. Tenn. Press

Jørgensen LB. 1992. *Northern European Textiles until AD 1000.* Århus, Denmark: Univ. Press

Jørgensen LB. 1999. *Textiles in European archaeology:* Rep. 6th NESAT Symp. 7, Boras, Sweden, 1996. Goteborg : Goteborg University, Dept. Archaeol.

Kawami TS. 1992. Archaeological evidence for textiles in pre-Islamic Iran. In *The Carpets and Textiles of Iran—New Perspectives in Research. J. Soc. Iran. Stud. (special issue)* 25(1–2):7–18

Körber-Grohne U, Küstler H. 1985. *Hochdorf I.* Stuttgart: Konrad Theiss

Koslin D. 1987. Manifest insignificance—the consecrated veil of medieval religious women. *Proc. Text. Soc. Am.* pp. 141–47. Minneapolis, MN: Text. Soc. Am.

Koslin D. 2001. Dressed in humility—consecration of religious women. In *Robes of Honor—the Medieaval World of Investiture*, ed. S Gordon. New York: St. Martin's

Kuhn D. 1982. The silk workshops of the Shang Dynasty 16th–11th century BC. In *Explorations in the History of Science and Technology in China*, ed. L Guohao, Z Mengwen, C Tianqin, pp. 367–407. Shanghai: Chinese Classics

Kuttruff JT. 1988. *Textile attributes and production complexity as indicators of Caddoan status differentiation in the Arkansas Valley and southern Ozark regions.* PhD diss. Ohio State Univ., Columbus. Ann Arbor: UMI

Letts JB, Evans J, Fung M, Hilman G. 1994. A

chemical method of identifying charred plant remains using infrared spectroscopy. In *Corn and Culture in the Prehistoric New World*, ed. C Hasdorf, C Johannson, pp. 67–80. St. Paul: Univ. Minn. Press

Mair V, ed. 1998. *The Bronze Age and Early Iron Age People of Eastern Central Asia*. Washington, DC: Inst. Study Man

McCorrison J. 1997. The fiber revolution. *Curr. Anthropol.* 38(4):519–50

Mellart J. 1962. Excavations at Çatal Hüyük. *Anatolian Stud.* 12:41–65

Mellart J. 1975. *The Neolithic of the Near East*. New York: Scribner's

Minar CJ. 2000. Spinning and plying: anthropological directions. See Drooker & Webster 2000, pp. 85–100

O'Neale L. 1936. A survey of the woolen textiles in the Sir Aurel Stein collections. *Am. Anthropol.* 38:414–32

Pääbo S, Higuchi RG, Wilson AC. 1989. Ancient DNA and the polymerase chain reaction. *J. Biol. Chem.* 264(17):9709–12

Petersen JB. 1996. A most indespensible art: native fiber industries from Eastern North America. Knoxville: Univ. Tenn. Press

Petersen J, Wolford J. 2000. Spin and twist as cultural markers: a New England perspective on native fiber industries. See Drooker & Webster 2000, pp. 101–18

Petersen J, Adovasio JM. 1999. Fiber perishable impressions. In *Prehistoric Ceramic Artifacts*, ed. JB Petersen. pp. 277–312. Prehistory of the Bay Springs Rockshelters 4. Erie PA: Mercyhurst Archaeol. Inst. Rep. Investig. 2

Pfister R, Bellinger L. 1945. *The Excavations at Dura-Europos: Final Report 4, Part II: the Textiles*. New Haven, CT: Yale Univ. Press

Pinner R. 1982. Decorative designs on prehistoric Turkmenian ceramics. *Hali* 5(2):118–19

Rodman AO. 1992. Textiles and ethnicity: Tiwanaku in San Pedro de Atacama, North Chile. *Latin Am. Antiq.* 3(4):316–40

Rubinson K. 1990. The textiles from Pazyryk: a study in transfer and transformation of artistic motifs. *Exped. Mag.* 32(1):49–61

Ryder ML. 1965. Report of Textiles from Çatal Hüyük. *Anatolian Stud.* 15:176

Ryder ML. 1969. Changes in the fleece of sheep following domestication. In *The Domestication and Exploitation of Plants and Animals*, ed. P Ucko, G Dimbleby. London: Duckworth

Ryder ML. 1983. *Sheep and Man*. London: Duckworth

Ryder ML. 1987. The evolution of the fleece. *Sci. Am.* 257(1):112–19

Schick T. 1988a. *The cave of the warrior: a fourth millennium burial in the Judean desert. IAA Rep.*; *No. 5*. Jerusalem: Israel Antiq. Auth.

Schick T. 1988b. Nahal Hemar Cave: cordage, basketry and textiles. *'Atiqot* Engl. Ser. 18:31–43

Seiler-Baldinger A. 1994. *Textiles: a Classification of Techniques*. Washington, DC: Smithsonian Inst. Press

Sherratt A. 1981. Plough and pastoralism: aspects of the secondary products revolution. In *Pattern of the Past: Studies in Honour of David Clarke*, ed. I Hodder, G Issacs, N Hammond, pp. 261–305. Cambridge UK: Cambridge Univ. Press

Shishlina N. 1999. *Textiles of the Bronze Age Eurasian Steppe*. Vol. 109. Moscow: Pap. State Hist. Mus.

Shishlina NI, Golikov VP, Orfinskaya OV. 2000. Bronze Age textiles of the Caspian Sea Maritime Steppes. In *Origin of Textile Production and Use in the Bronze Age Western Eurasian Steppe*, ed. J Kimball-Davis, pp. 109–15. *Brit. Archaeol. Rep. No. 870*. Oxford, UK: Archaeo

Sibley LR, Jakes KA. 1984. Survival of protein fibers in archaeological contexts. *Sci. Archaeol.* 26:17–27

Sibley LR, Jakes KA. 1989. Etowah textile remains and cultural context: a model for inference. *Cloth. Text. Res. J.* 7(2):37–45

Sibley LR, Jakes KA. 1994. Implications of coloration in Etowah textiles from Burial 57. In *Archaeometry of Pre-Columbian Sites and*

Artifacts, ed. DN Scott, J Meyers, pp. 395–418. Los Angeles: J. Paul Getty Conservation Inst.

Sibley LR, Jakes KA, Larson LH. 1996. Inferring behavior and function from an Etowah fabric incorporating feathers. In *A Most Indispensable Art: Native Fiber Industries from Eastern North America*, ed. JB Peterson, pp. 73–87. Knoxville: Univ. Tenn. Press

Sibley LR, Jakes KA, Song C. 1989. Fiber and yarn processing by prehistoric people of North America: examples from Etowah. *Ars Textrina* 11:191–209

Sibley LR, Jakes KA, Swinker ME. 1992. Etowah feather remains from Burial 57: identification and context. *Cloth. Text. Res. J.* 10(3):21–28

Sibley LR, Swinker ME, Jakes KA. 1991. The use of pattern reproduction in reconstructing Etowah textile remains. *Ars Textrina* 15:179–202

Simmons P. 1956. Some recent developments in Chinese textile studies. *Bull. Mus. Far Eastern Antiq.* 28:19–44

Soffer O, Adovasio JM, Hyland DC. 1998. *Moravia: new insights into the origin and nature of the Gravettian.* Presented at Inst. Archaeol., Prague and Masaryk Univ., Brno, Czech Republic

Soffer O, Adovasio JM, Hyland DC. 2000a. The well-dressed Venus: women's wear, Ca. 27,000 BP. *Archaeol. Ethnol. Anthropol. Eurasia* 1(1):37–47

Soffer O, Adovasio JM, Hyland DC. 2000b. The 'Venus' figurines—textiles, basketry, gender and status in the Upper Paleolithic. *Curr. Anthropol.* 41(4):511–38

Song CA, Jakes KA, Yerkes RW. 1996. Seip Hopewell textile analysis and cultural implications. *Midcont. J. Archaeol.* 21(2):247–65

Srinivasan R, Jakes KA. 1997. Optical and scanning electron microscopic study of the effects of charring on Indian hemp (*Apocynum cannabinum* L.) fibres. *J. Archaeol. Sci.* 24:517–27

Steinkeller P. 1995. Sheep and goat terminology in UR III sources from Drehem. *Bull. Sumer. Agric.* 8:49–70

Sylwan V. 1937. Silk from the Yin Dynasty. *Bull. Mus. Far East. Antiq.* 9:119–26

Sylwan V. 1941. The woollen textiles of the Loulan People. *Rep. Sci. Exped. Northwest. Prov. China Leadersh. Dr. Sven Hedin.* Vol. 7. No. 2. Stockholm: Archaeology

Sylwan V. 1949. Investigation of silk from Edsen-Gol and Lop-Nor. *Rep. Sci. Exped. Northwest. Prov. China Leadersh. Dr. Sven Hedin.* Vol. 7. Stockholm: Archaeology

Teague L. 2000. Revealing clothes: textiles from the upper ruin, Tonto National Monument. See Drooker & Webster 2000, pp. 161–78

Tosi M. 1983. A bronze female statuette from Shahr-i Sokhta: chronological problems and stylistic connections. In *Prehistoric Sistan*, 307–17. Rome: Inst. Ital. Medio Estremo Oriente

Van Stan I. 1967. *Textiles from Beneath the Temple of Pachacamac, Peru.* Philadelphia, PA: Univ. Mus.

Vogelsang-Eastwood G. 1993. *Ancient Egyptian Clothing.* Leiden, Ger.: Brill

Vollmer J. 1974. Textile pseudomorphs on Chinese bronzes. In *Irene Emory Roundtable on Museum Textiles, 1974 Proceedings*, ed. PL Fiske, pp. 170–74. Washington, DC: Text. Mus.

Waetzoldt H. 1972. *Die Neo-Sumerische Textilindustrie.* Studi economici e tecnologici, n. 1. Istituto per l'Oriente, Rome

Wang B. 1986. Several bronze assemblages discovered in East Xinjiang. *Kaogu* 10:887–90

Walton P, Wild JP, eds. 1990. *Textiles in northern archaeology.* NESAT III Text. Symp. York. London: Inst. Archaeol.

Webster LD, Drooker PB. 2000. Archaeological textile research in the Americas. See Drooker & Webster 2000, pp. 1–24

Wells P. 1980. *Culture contact and culture change.* Cambridge, UK: Cambridge Univ. Press

Wild JP. 1984. Some early silk finds in northwest Europe. *Text. Mus. J.* 23:17–23

Xia N. 1979. New finds of ancient silk fabrics in

Sinkiang. In *Essays on Archaeology of Science and Technology in China.* (Engl. summary of pp. 69–97), pp. 145–47. Beijing: Inst. Archaeol., Chinese Acad. Sci.

Young RS. 1958. The Gordion Campaign of 1957: preliminary report. *Am. J. Archaeol.* 62:139–54

Zhao F, Yu Z. 1998. *Legacy of the Desert King: Textiles and Treasures From Niya Site on the Silk Road.* Hong Kong: ISAT

Annu. Rev. Anthropol. 2001. 30:227–60

THE ANTHROPOLOGY OF AFRO-LATIN AMERICA AND THE CARIBBEAN: Diasporic Dimensions

Kevin A. Yelvington

*Department of Anthropology, University of South Florida, Tampa, Florida 33620-8100;
e-mail: yelvingt@chuma1.cas.usf.edu*

Key Words African diaspora, blackness, history of anthropology, "race," ethnicity, nationalism, creolization

■ **Abstract** The contributions of a number of First and Third World scholars to the development of the anthropology of the African diaspora in Latin America and the Caribbean have been elided from the core of the discipline as practiced in North America and Europe. As such, the anthropology of the African diaspora in the Americas can be traced to the paradigmatic debate on the origins of New World black cultures between Euro-American anthropologist Melville J. Herskovits and African American sociologist E. Franklin Frazier. The former argued for the existence of African cultural continuities, the latter for New World culture creations in the context of discrimination and deprivation characteristic of the experiences of peoples of African descent, in light of slavery, colonialism, and postcolonial contexts. As a result, subsequent positions have been defined by oppositions in every subdisciplinary specialization and area of interest. Creolization models try to obviate this bifurcation, and newer dialogical theoretical perspectives build upon such models by attempting to combine revisionist historiography with social/cultural constructionist approaches to identity, especially around the concept of blackness understood in the context of cultural identity politics.

INTRODUCTION: THE PRESENCE OF THE ANTHROPOLOGICAL PAST

The current anthropological concern with processes of globalization, dispersion, migration, and transnationalism, citizenship; with colonialism, the historical development of cultures, cultural hybridity, cultural politics and the politics of culture, difference and disjuncture; with resistance, structure and agency can be presented as "new," "cutting edge," or "hot topics" only by eliding and implicitly dismissing foundational scholarship on the anthropology of the African diaspora in the Americas, such as that of W.E.B. Du Bois (1868–1963), St. Clair Drake (1911–1990), Zora Neale Hurston (1903–1960), Katherine Dunham (b. 1909), Jean Price-Mars (1876–1969), Rómulo Lachatañeré (1909–1952), or Arthur A. Schomburg

0084-6570/01/1021-0227$14.00

(1874–1938), to name only a few. The Haitian anthropologist Anténor Firmin (1850–1911), whose writings on "race" [Firmin 2000 (1885)] preceded those of Franz Boas and were in direct opposition to contemporaneous racist theorists like Gobineau, placed himself and his work squarely within a framework of diasporal exchanges but can nowhere be seen as an anthropological ancestor. Furthermore, recent works from a number of disciplines aimed at defining diaspora and elaborating and justifying its use as a theoretical concept do so from a parochial perspective that relegates the African diaspora in the New World to the status of a case study. Although this is not the forum to write or right such a history, whether revisionist or redemptionist, nor a place to cite chapters and ignored verse of anthropology's forgotten founders, a mention of this vanquished scholarship is in order here to understand the following remarks on the history of the study of the African diaspora in Latin America and the Caribbean, allowing us to pause long enough to wonder aloud what connection exists between the fact that these scholars themselves were of African descent and the minor role they played in anthropological canon-making (see for example Baker 1998; Drake 1980, 1990; Fluehr-Lobban 2000; Harrison 1992; and the chapters in Harrison & Harrison 1999).

The anthropology of the African diaspora in Latin America and the Caribbean was born out of the elision of these scholars and their scholarship and continues to be shaped by its paradigmatic formation as an anthropological specialization dating back to the 1930s. In the debate begun then, the opposing sides were exemplified by the work of Euro-American anthropologist Melville J. Herskovits (1895–1963) and African-American sociologist E. Franklin Frazier (1894–1962). Their debate has in many ways continued to define the terms of reference for the production of anthropological knowledge (Yelvington Forthcoming a). With the publication of *The Myth of the Negro Past* (1941), Herskovits is credited with legitimating the study of black cultures within anthropology. He aimed at exploding racist depictions of New World blacks by maintaining the Boasian conceptual separation of "race" and culture. He did so by utilizing a number of tropes and conceptual devices in order to trace what he saw as "Africanisms" (see Cole 1985) in religion, language, the family, and other cultural forms and institutions transported to the New World with the slaves from what he called the West African–Congo "cultural area." While in his early work on African Americans (e.g., Herskovits 1925) he emphasized the process of assimilation to American culture, by 1930 Herskovits was defining his project as that of "The Negro in the New World" (Herskovits 1930; cf. Jackson 1986). After early physical anthropological work on African Americans, he carried out ethnographic fieldwork on this research problem with his wife and collaborator Frances S. Herskovits (1897–1972) in Suriname, Dahomey, Haiti, Trinidad, and Brazil (Baron 1994, Gershenhorn 2000, Simpson 1973, Yelvington Forthcoming b).

Some of the concepts Herskovits employed have explicitly or unintentionally in different guises become part of the perspectives of subsequent generations of anthropologists of the African diaspora in the Americas, including "cultural tenacity," "retentions," "reinterpretation," and "syncretism," all under the overarching rubric of "acculturation." For Herskovits, even improvisation was an African trait, and "psychological resilience" he saw as a "deep-rooted African tradition of adaptation" (Herskovits 1948; cf. Apter 1991). Herskovits's position was a logical extension of Boasian historical and cultural particularism. He combined an advocacy of anthropology as a dispassionate scientific mode of inquiry with a radical cultural relativism. His thought was also (in)formed by the patronage of American folklorist Elsie Clews Parsons (1875–1941), whose work exemplified a similar quest for ultimate origins, as well as by his relations with those pioneering Latin American and Caribbean anthropologists and ethnologists whose study of the "African presence" in their societies predated Herskovits's interest. Their studies were congruent with his approach, occurring within the context of diverse local nationalist projects (distinct from Herskovits's) that were aimed at showing the black element in national culture and the black contribution to the nation, and that suggested public policies relating to blackness (see, among others, Bastide 1974; Coronil 1995; Corrêa 1998, 2000; Davis 1992; Fernandes 1958; Iznaga 1989; Moore 1994; Morse 1996; Palmié 2001; Peirano 1981; Shannon 1996; Simpson 1973; Yelvington Forthcoming b). These pioneers included Arthur Ramos (1903–1949) in Brazil and Fernando Ortiz Fernández (1881–1969) in Cuba [both followers of the Brazilian Raymundo Nina Rodrigues (1862–1906)], Price-Mars in Haiti, and Gonzalo Aguirre Beltrán (1908–1996) in Mexico. This "intellectual social formation" engaged in setting the field's parameters; Herskovits and Ramos, for example, worked to exclude the work of American anthropologist Ruth Landes (1908–1991), whose take on Afro-Brazil diverged somewhat from their own (Landes 1947; cf. Cole 1994, 1995, Healey 1998, Landes 1970, Yelvington Forthcoming b).

Herskovits felt that the disparaging of "the Negro past" and cultural heritage on the part of the dominant society sustained racism and the oppression of African Americans. In order to reverse this, he provided evidence for what he saw as Africanisms in New World Negro culture that reached back beyond, and endured through, the ignominy of slavery. These Africanisms were seen as survivals of African cultures that existed in more or less transmuted variants in the Americas existing beneath the surface cultural forms blacks had adapted. He believed he could chart the intensity of Africanisms, and specifically their origin in African "nations" or ethnicities (Herskovits 1933), versus other cultural legacies in various institutions and practices across the societies of the Americas (see Table 1).

Frazier (e.g., 1939), the Chicago School sociologist, utilized a more structural approach and argued that African slaves in the United States were dispossessed of their cultures in the enslavement process and were best viewed as disadvantaged Americans. Placing his work in opposition to Herskovits, Frazier maintained that "as regards the Negro family, there is no reliable evidence that African culture has had any influence on its development" (1939, p. 12). For him, "probably never before in history has a people been so nearly completely stripped of its social heritage as the Negroes who were brought to America." They had, "through force of circumstances," to "acquire a new language, adopt new habits of labor, and take

TABLE 1 Herskovits's "Scale of Intensity of New World Africanisms"[1]

	Technology	Economics	Social organization	Non-kinship institutions	Religion	Magic	Art	Folklore	Music	Language
Guiana (bush)[2]	b	b	a	a	a	a	b	a	a	b
Guiana (Paramaribo)	c	c	b	c	a	a	e	a	a	c
Haiti (peasant)	c	b	b	c	a	a	d	a	a	c
Haiti (urban)	e	d	c	c	b	b	e	a	a	c
Brazil (Bahia-Redife)	d	d	b	d	a	a	b	a	a	a
Brazil (Porto Alegre)	e	e	c	d	a	a	e	a	a	c
Brazil (Maranhão-rural)	c	c	b	e	c	b	e	b	b	d
Brazil (Maranhão-urban)	e	d	c	e	a	b	e	d	a	b
Cuba	e	d	c	b	a	a	b	b	a	a
Jamaica (Maroons)	c	c	b	b	b	a	e	a	a	c
Jamaica (Morant Bay)	e	c	b	b	a	a	e	a	a	a
Jamaica (general)	e	c	d	d	b	b	e	a	b	c
Honduras (Black Caribs)[3]	c	c	b	b	b	a	e	b	c	e

Trinidad (Port of Spain)	e	c	b	a	a	e	b	a	e
Trinidad (Toco)	e	c	c	c	b	e	b	b	d
Mexico (Guerrero)	d	b	b	c	b	e	b	?	e
Colombia (Chocó)	d	c	c	c	b	e	b	e	e
Virgin Islands	e	c	d	e	b	e	b	b	d
U.S. (Gullah Islands)	c	c	d	c	b	e	a	d	b
U.S. (rural South)	d	c	d	c	b	e	d	b	e
U.S. (urban North)	e	c	d	c	b	e	d	b	e

[1] Only the greatest degree of retention is indicated for each group. a: very African, b: quite African, c: somewhat African, d: a little African, e: trace of African customs, or absent, ?: no report.

[2] The derivations of the listings given in Table 1 are as follows:

Guiana, Brazil (Bahia and southern Brazil), *Trinidad,* and *Haiti;* field research and various published works bearing on the Negro peoples of these countries.

Brazil (north-urban and rural); unpublished reports of fieldwork by Octavio Eduardo in Maranhão.

Jamaica; first-hand contact with the Maroons and other Jamaican Negroes, though without opportunity for detailed field research; and for the general population, the volume *Black Roadways,* by Martha Beckwith.

Cuba, various works by F. Ortiz, particularly his *Los negros brujos,* and on R. Lachatañeré's *Manual de santería.*

Virgin Islands, the monograph by A.A. Campbell entitled, "St Thomas Negroes—a study of Personality and Culture" (*Psychological Monographs,* vol. 55, no. 5, 1943), and unpublished field materials of J.C. Trevor.

Gullah Islands, field-work by W.R. Bascom, some results of which have been reported in a paper entitled, "Acculturation Among the Gullah Negroes" (*American Anthropologist,* vol. 43, 1941, pp. 43–50).

United States, many works, from which materials of African derivation have been abstracted and summarized in my own work, *The Myth of the Negro Past.*

[3] Carib Indian influences are strong in this culture.

Source: Herskovits 1966: 53, 61.

over, however imperfectly, the folkways of the American environment." Thus, "of the habits and customs as well as the hopes and fears that characterized the life of their forebears in Africa, nothing remains" (1939, pp. 21–22).

The contrasting perspectives of Herskovits and Frazier have in a large part dictated the approaches of subsequent researchers in all fields of the anthropology of the African diaspora in the Americas (see the discussions in Abrahams & Szwed 1983, Whitten & Szwed 1970, Yelvington Forthcoming a). These successors produced more correctly, perhaps, overdrawn idealizations of their work. A debate in the pages of the *American Sociological Review* over the black family in Brazil indicates well their different approaches (Frazier 1942, 1943; Herskovits 1943). But Frazier adhered to a Herskovitsian view of acculturation (Frazier 1957, pp. 243–46): Citing Herskovits, he was willing to admit that African survivals existed in the Caribbean and Latin America, especially in religion (Frazier 1939, pp. 5–6), and he attributed the uniqueness of the United States in this regard (Frazier 1939, pp. 7–8, 1957, p. 336) to the contrasting effects of the differing slave regimes. On the other hand, Herskovits never diminished the power of the enslavement process in "stripping from the aboriginal African culture" their "larger institutions, leaving the more intimate elements in the organization of living" (Herskovits & Herskovits 1947, p. 7). Nevertheless, today scholars tend to be identified (even if they do not explicitly self-identify) with one of two competing camps: the neo-Herskovitsians versus "creationist" or "creolization" theorists. These latter emphasize cultural creativity, cultural blending and borrowing, cultural adaptations to local circumstances, and ethnogenetic processes.

In terms of a politics of reception, Frazier's views have fallen from anthropology's purview. Although Herskovits's notions of Africanisms were for the most part rejected by African-American intellectuals in the pre–Civil Rights era, today Herskovits's work continues to loom large and many anthropologists of the African diaspora in the Americas are liable to locate themselves within this tradition. Partisans may allow themselves a broad canvas in art or philosophy (Thompson 1983, cf. S. Price, Forthcoming) or they may confine themselves to a single practice or institution, such as family land in the Caribbean (e.g. Carnegie 1987a, cf. Besson 1987). A search for "pre-contact" culture in contexts that assume "contact" by definition fits, after all, anthropology's search for the pristine (Trouillot 1992). Thus, the anthropology of Afro-Latin America and the Caribbean is an example of what Bourdieu might call a "field" (*champ*), and is a discrete and integrated activity with its own "logic," within which the imposition of one group's set of taxonomies results in the production of a "natural order" that tends to uphold certain structured "ways of seeing." Furthermore, the relationship between the anthropology and the anthropologists' personal questions of identity is crucial (Frank 2001, Yelvington 2000). Scott rightly insists that "a critical anthropology of the African diaspora has to be constituted through a close attention to the history of its own categories and to the extent to which it assumes their transparency" (1999, p. 108). But this is rarely acknowledged as such by anthropologists of the African diaspora in Latin America and the Caribbean. This is because few working anthropologists are also historians of anthropology. Fewer still are anthropologists who attempt overtly and explicitly to place themselves and their theoretical approach within specific traditions. One notable exception is Harrison (Harrison 1992, Harrison & Nonini 1992), a Caribbeanist who sets her approach in relation to Du Bois's anthropology in calling for an anthropology of the African diaspora (Harrison 1988) and advocating anthropology as a tool of liberation (Harrison 1991).

The foregoing is not merely historical background to the anthropological study of the African diaspora in Latin America and the Caribbean; rather it signals the extent to which this anthropology continues to be framed by these foundational paradigms and politics (Szwed 1972). With this in mind, I provide an admittedly narrow focus in what follows, concentrating on the social and cultural anthropology of Afro-Latin America and the Caribbean inasmuch as this scholarship engages the concept of diaspora or shows how Afro-Americans are conscious of being in diaspora; my review has a bias toward recent work. This unfortunately leaves out a number of important studies of black communities in the Americas south of the Río Grande. To compensate, I attempt to make this review interdisciplinary in the sense that I refer (albeit too briefly) to work from other disciplines that is either anthropological in orientation or speaks directly to questions that have been pursued by social and cultural anthropologists—namely, the work of ethnomusicologists, historians, linguists, cultural theorists, and writers and literary critics.

GEOGRAPHIES OF BLACKNESS: DELINEATING DIASPORA

Even though Du Bois (e.g., 1939), Drake (e.g., 1982), and others operated within what can be called a diasporic frame of reference, their marginalization meant that the African diaspora in Latin America and the Caribbean has been defined in various theoretical terms and not always explicitly as "diaspora." More than four decades ago, when commenting on the Herskovits-Frazier debate, the Jamaican anthropologist M.G. Smith (1921–1993) called for an approach that combined social and cultural perspectives (1957). Perhaps the best exemplification of this is the widely cited work of Mintz & Price (1992 [1976]), who, taking up directly the question of survivals versus cultural creation, argue "it is less the unity of West (and Central) Africa as a broad culture area" than "the levels at which one would have to seek confirmation of this postulated unity," adding: "An African cultural heritage, widely shared by the people imported into any new colony, will have to be defined in less concrete terms, by focusing more on values, and less on sociocultural forms, and even by attempting to identify unconscious 'grammatical' principles, which may underlie and shape behavioral response" (1992, pp. 9–10). These principles are "basic assumptions about social relations" and "basic assumptions and expectations about the way the world functions phenomenologically." They posit that "certain common orientations to reality may tend to focus the attention of individuals from West and Central African cultures upon similar kinds of events, even though the ways for handling these events may seem quite diverse in formal terms," suggesting that "the comparative study of people's attitudes and expectations about sociocultural change . . . might reveal interesting underlying consistencies" (1992, p. 10). While Mintz & Price admit that these "underlying principles will prove difficult to uncover," they point to scholarship that attempts "to define the perceived similarities in African (and African-American) song style, graphic art, motor habits, and so forth," asserting that "if the perceived similarities are real, there must exist underlying principles (which will often be unconscious) that are amenable to identification, description, and confirmation." Thus, "in considering African-American cultural continuities, it may well be that the more formal elements stressed by Herskovits exerted less influence on the nascent institutions of newly enslaved and transported Africans than did their common basic assumptions about social relations or the workings of the universe" (1992, p. 11).

Drawing on work on the history of the slave trade, Mintz & Price emphasize the ethnic heterogeneity of New World slave populations, which, perhaps counterintuitively, they see as an invitation to inter-African syncretism and an interactive creolization process that began in the first moments of the creation of New World slave societies. They dispute the approach that infers historical connection between a single, specific culture in West Africa and one in the New World based on putative similarities (such as lexical items), arguing that, besides being at odds with historical data, such a model is committed to a view of culture as an undifferentiated whole: "Given the social setting of early New World colonies, the encounters between Africans from a score or more different societies with each other, and with their European overlords, cannot be interpreted in terms of two (or even many different) 'bodies' of belief and value, each coherent, functioning, and intact. The Africans who reached the New World did not compose, at the outset, *groups*. In fact, in most cases, it might even be more accurate to view them as *crowds*, and very heterogeneous crowds at that." The slaves could only become communities "by processes of cultural change": "What the slaves undeniably shared at the outset was their enslavement; all—or nearly all—else had to be *created by them*" (1992, p. 18). This being the main thrust of their model, Mintz & Price are careful to point to differences in slave regimes and relative concentration or dispersal of slaves belonging to the same ethnic/cultural group as historical questions; they do not dispute the influence of later-arriving African ethnic groups on the direction of a particular locale's Afro-American culture. They point to "immensely important continuities of many kinds with ancestral civilizations; and [they] must add that the history of Afro-America is marked by renewals of identification on many occasions." They say they "recognize that many aspects of African-American adaptiveness may themselves be in some important sense African in origin" (1992, pp. 94, 95).

The influence of the model has been wide, stimulating work in the "culture of slavery" (e.g., Palmié, 1995a) and on play and popular culture (e.g., Burton 1997). Price & Price, for example, drawing on their extensive work on Afro-American arts, followed up this more programmatic statement with a tour de force on Saramaka (Suriname maroon) aesthetics (1999). Citing the model with approval, Trouillot (1998, p. 9) cautions against theories that "seize creolization as a totality, thus one level too removed from the concrete circumstances faced by the individuals engaged in the process" and insists that the "historical conditions of cultural production" become "a fundamental and necessary part" of analyses. Maurer (1997) also criticizes notions of creolization and hybridity that rest upon metaphors of biological reproduction and genetic recombination. R. Price has strongly urged anthropologists to take account of parallel work by contemporary Caribbean writers such as Kamau Brathwaite, Maryse Condé, Édouard Glissant, George Lamming, and Derek Walcott (1998). These writers actively engage with and often criticize the anthropology (Scott 1999). The Martinican playwright and cultural critic Glissant writes:

> One of the most terrible implications of the ethnographic approach is the insistence on fixing the object of scrutiny in static time, thereby removing the tangled nature of lived experience and promoting the idea of uncontaminated survival. This is how those generalized projections of a series of events that obscure the network of real links become established. The history of a transplanted population, but one which elsewhere becomes another people, allows us to resist generalization and the limitations it imposes. Relationship (at the same time link and linked, act and speech) [needs to be] emphasized over what in appearance could be conceived as a governing principle, the so-called universal 'controlling force' (1989, p. 14).

On the other hand, Price & Price (1997) show how some intellectuals emphasize "creolism" (*créolité*) as part of elite ethnic and class politics.

The Mintz and Price creolization model comes out of and has inspired (both for and against) work in Afro-Latin American and Caribbean languages. Confronted with extreme, even bewildering, linguistic heterogeneity in the region (see Table 2), linguists and linguistically oriented anthropologists have poured a significant amount of effort into investigations of creoles, pidgins (Jourdan 1991), and the development of African-influenced languages in the New World (e.g., Perl & Schwegler 1998). There is little agreement on the very categories of analysis (see e.g., Schieffelin & Doucet 1994 on Haitian *kreyòl*). Mintz (1971) warned as early as a 1968 conference on pidgins and creoles held at the University of the West Indies in Jamaica that the characteristic shape of a language cannot be seen outside of its sociological context and the processes of historical change. Still, investigations are often couched in terms of locating "Africanisms" (Mufwene 1993). The continuity versus creativity debate is alive here too. This body of work has also imbibed all of the controversies associated with the study of pidgins and creoles generally, e.g., differentiating between pidgins and creoles themselves, monogenesis versus polygenesis debates, (African) substrata versus (European) superstrata versus universalist hypotheses of creole genesis (the latter of which includes Bickerton's controversial "bioprogram hypothesis," and the applicability of pidginization-creolization-decreolization creole continuum models), and the

TABLE 2   Caribbean language situations

Multilingual: Trinidad has standard and nonstandard forms of English, a French-based creole, nonstandard Spanish, Bhojpuri, Urdu, and Yoruba. Suriname has Dutch, Sranan, Saramaccan, Ndjuka, Javanese, and Hindi.

Bilingual: St. Lucia, Dominica, and Grenada have standard and nonstandard forms of English and a French-based creole. The Netherlands Antilles has Dutch and Papiamentu (with English and Spanish widely used).

Diglossia: In Haiti and the French West Indies, French and a French-based creole exist but are kept relatively separate.

Continuum: Guyana, Antigua, Jamaica, Montserrat, and St. Kitts have different graded levels of language beginning with a polar variety commonly called "creole" or "patois" and moving through intermediate levels to a standard norm of English at the other pole.

Monolingual: Barbados, Cuba, the Dominican Republic, and Puerto Rico have a standard and a nonstandard form of European languages (English in the first case, Spanish in the others).

Source: Alleyne 1985:166.

New or the Old World as the site of creole genesis (Jourdan 1991; cf. McWhorter 1997). Maroon societies are often the privileged site of investigations (e.g., Schwegler 1996; cf. Price 1975). A common problem occurs when linguists try to extend their model to "culture at large." Most models between the either/or poles (and polemics) have given way to those that in one way or another try to account for an interaction of influences (Jourdan 1991). Speech acts as both play and expressive culture incorporating ambiguity and indirection are located in a common Afro-American culture, whether conceived in retentionist or creationist terms (Abrahams 1983; cf. Wilson 1973). But many anthropologists have chosen to focus on issues of identity, language use, and language choice (Mentore 1993, Schnepel 1993), and on language use in religious practices (Bilby 1983), including Rastafarianism (Homiak 1995, Pulis 1993).

A number of recent treatments of the African diaspora in the New World (e.g., Martínez Montiel 1992, Rahier 1999a), especially by historians and historically oriented scholars (e.g., Byfield 2000, Conniff & Davis 1994, Hine & McLeod 1999, Jalloh & Maizlish 1996, Okpewho et al 1999, but see the earlier work in Harris 1982 and Crahan & Knight 1979), have surmounted the necessary but not sufficient procedure of documenting rather mechanically the origins and destinations of the slaves and the dispersals of peoples of African descent in the region that received roughly 90% of all enslaved Africans landed in the Americas (cf. Mintz 1974, pp. 1–32). New syntheses by historians of the slave trade emphasize the provenience, direction, and ethnic identities of enslaved Africans (e.g., Eltis 2000, Eltis & Richardson 1997, Lovejoy 2000a,b; see Table 3). Many new studies in this vein challenge the Mintz & Price model by affirming the power of various

African "nations"/ethnicities (variously defined) to shape particular New World slave societies (e.g., Thornton 1992, Palmer 1995, cf. Scott 1999). In promoting an "Africa-centred" focus, Lovejoy (2000b, pp. 16, 17) argues that Mintz and Price's model results in a "depersonalized" view of slaves, and he charges that their vision "telescopes" and represents a "hypostatization" of the creolization process. Eltis (2000, p. 245), however, finds their idea that enslaved Africans on the middle passage were a "crowd" rather than a cultural grouping to be "overdrawn" because of data that indicate the nonrandom arrivals of Africans in the Americas. Both Lovejoy and Eltis misrepresent the Mintz & Price model in the process. Anthropologists accepting colonial data on slave ethnicities as unproblematic do so by making unwarranted assumptions about the nature of colonial knowledge (Scott 1999). The most illuminating studies on the Americas in this genre are those dealing with specific times and contexts, such as Thornton's on African soldiers and ideologies in the Haitian Revolution (1991, 1993). In contrast, historians of the Americas such as Berlin (1998), Morgan (1998), and Palmié (1995a) tend to affirm the model by pointing, depending on the historical and regional context, to material showing inter-African creolization, resident-forced immigrant creolization, re-Africanization, recreolization, and the invention of tradition at work in the creation of ethnic/national labels and identities in the Americas. On this last score they have received backing from Africanist historians (Law 1997). Similar divisions exist in the archaeology of the African diaspora in the region (see Orser 1998).

Attempts at conceptualizing the diaspora come from many directions these days. But the work of major cultural studies theorists such as Hall (1990, 1999) and Gilroy (1993, cf. Helmreich 1993, Scott 1999) not so much obviates as complicates anthropological concerns. They both make important points against the racial and cultural essentializing of blackness and tout a perspective on cultural hybridity. The diaspora experience is defined "not by essence or purity, but by the recognition of a necessary heterogeneity and diversity; by a conception of 'identity' which lives with and through, not despite, difference; by hybridity. Diaspora identities are those which are constantly producing and reproducing themselves anew, through transformation and difference . . ." (Hall 1990, p. 235). The lack of politics in the notion of hybridity is never discussed. "Africa," Hall maintains, is never unmediated, unchanged, nor completely recoverable for Caribbean people and by extension blacks in the diaspora. It becomes a sort of base for this hybridity, giving it a singular, recognizable form: "Africa, the signified which could not be represented directly in slavery, remained and remains the unspoken, unspeakable 'presence' in Caribbean culture. It is 'hiding' behind every verbal inflection, every narrative twist of Caribbean cultural life. It is the secret code with which every Western text was 're-read.' It is the ground-bass of every rhythm and bodily movement. This was—is—the 'Africa' that 'is alive and well in the diaspora'" (1990, p. 230). Gilroy, too, opposes essentialism but tends to assume the formation of a black diaspora. The "Black Atlantic" is a singular, albeit "hybrid," cultural form now "continually crisscrossed by the movements of black people" (1993, p. 16),

TABLE 3 Estimates of regional distribution of slave exports to America from Africa, 1662–1867

Decade	Senegambia	Sierra Leone	Gold Coast	Bight of Benin	Bight of Biafra	West Central Africa	Southeast Africa	Total	Annual exports
1662–1670	3,232		12,174	23,021	34,471	9,695	91	82,684	9,187
1671–1680	5,842		20,597	22,753	24,021	15,794	309	89,316	8,932
1681–1690	10,834		15,333	71,733	21,625	32,760	5,392	157,677	15,768
1691–1700	13,376		17,407	103,313	12,115	30,072	190	176,473	17,647
1700–1709	22,230	34,560	31,650	138,590	23,130	109,780	0	359,940	35,994
1710–1719	36,260	6,380	37,540	138,690	51,410	132,590	0	402,870	40,287
1720–1729	52,530	9,120	65,110	150,280	59,990	179,620	0	516,650	51,665
1730–1739	57,210	29,470	74,460	135,220	62,260	240,890	0	599,510	59,951
1740–1749	35,000	43,350	83,620	97,830	76,790	214,470	0	551,060	55,106
1750–1759	30,100	83,860	52,780	86,620	106,100	222,430	0	581,890	58,189
1760–1769	27,590	178,360	69,650	98,390	142,640	266,570	0	783,200	78,320
1770–1779	24,400	132,220	54,370	111,550	160,400	234,880	0	717,820	71,782
1780–1789	15,240	74,190	57,650	121,080	225,360	300,340	0	793,860	79,386
1790–1799	18,320	70,510	73,960	74,600	181,740	340,110	0	759,240	75,924

1800–1809	18,000	63,970	44,150	75,750	123,000	280,900	0	605,770	60,577
1811–1815	19,300	4,200		34,600	33,100	111,800	8,700	203,000	40,600
1816–1820	48,400	9,000		59,200	60,600	151,100	59,600	328,300	65,660
1821–1825	22,700	4,000		44,200	60,600	128,400	43,200	259,900	51,980
1826–1830	26,700	4,900		70,500	66,700	164,400	58,100	333,200	66,640
1831–1835	27,400	1,100		37,700	71,900	102,800	3,000	240,900	48,180
1836–1840	35,300	5,700		50,400	40,800	193,500	99,400	325,700	65,140
1841–1845	19,100	200		45,300	4,400	112,900	20,300	181,900	36,380
1846–1850	14,700	700		53,400	7,700	197,000	66,700	273,500	54,700
1851–1855	10,300	300		8,900	2,900	22,600	12,800	45,000	9,000
1856–1860	3,100	300		14,000	4,400	88,200	11,300	110,000	22,000
1861–1865	2,700	0		2,600	0	41,200	2,700	46,500	9,300
1866–1867	0	0		400	0	3,000	0	3,400	1,700
Total	599,864	756,390	710,451	1,870,620	1,658,152	3,927,801	391,782	9,529,260	46,035

Source: Klein 1999:208–9.

typified by their common "desire to transcend both the structures of the nation state and the constraints of ethnicity and national paticularity" (1993, p. 19). But his examples are drawn from Anglophone societies and with these specifics are made to stand as "the" Black Atlantic. Whereas Hall, in the end, represents diaspora using familiar metaphors of contagion (Browning 1998), Gilroy disappoints anthropologists by his inattention to the "politics of politics" (Williams 1995).

Drawing from the historians, cultural theorists, and others, and engaging in developments within their own discipline, some anthropologists now seek to move beyond culturalist approaches to diaspora and beyond a mechanical and essentialized notion of culture in which culture becomes a reified, thing-like entity that may be "possessed," "maintained," or "lost," "decays," or is "resistant" in the face of "culture contact." These anthropologists seek to combine prior anthropological preoccupations with a concern with the constitutive practices of discourse and representations of blackness and diaspora. In addition, creolization, antisyncretism (Palmié, 1995b), and local constructions of African cultural "purity" and "authenticity" come in for analysis. If Africanisms are found, anthropologists ask, by what mechanism(s) are they transmitted? For the French ethnographer of Afro-America, Roger Bastide (1898–1974), the mechanism was "memory" (Bastide 1978). And what are Africanisms in the first place? The idea seemed deceptively essentializing and a hypostatization of culture to many. Sometimes glossed as "presence" (de Friedemann 1993; Martínez Montiel 1993, 1995), "vestiges" (Pollak-Eltz 1972), or the idea of an "African element," "African background," or "African heritage" in New World culture, it is not (and perhaps cannot be) precisely defined. As Whitten & Torres impatiently write, "anthropological understanding of black cultures and traditions in the New World has often bogged down in debates about how to scale Africanisms against Europeanisms" (1992, p. 22). These same authors develop the concepts of "blackness" and "black culture" that are placed within the context of power relations (Whitten & Torres 1998, p. 4). Blackness, understood as a kind of ethnicity ("race" and culture) arising from cultural "identity politics" (Hale 1997), is for Rahier part of processes of creolization: "These processes brought cultural fragments from various origins, as well as original creations, to mingle in particular ways, to be reshaped within various time-space contexts, and to become singular cultural traditions associated with blackness" (1999b, p. 290). But others prefer a more existential definition of blackness (Bastide 1974, p. 122).

If anthropological models of creolization derive from linguistics, that discipline also provides a new metaphor for the anthropology of diaspora—that of dialogue. Dialogism in anthropology has come to signify concern with language and with representation and authority/authorship in ethnographic texts, but there is no inherent reason it should be limited to these issues. The concept of dialogue as can be applied to the anthropology of diaspora does not imply an equality among participants in the process. It entails, rather, multiparty interactions of material, ideational, and discursive phenomena, among others, in complex relationships characterized more often than not by an unequal distribution of power; a dialogue not between fixed objects, but a process of mutual influence and conditioning that is itself already part of an ongoing dialogic process where "rhetorics of self-making" (pace Battaglia 1995) play a crucial role. Recent developments include the work of Matory (1999a,b), whose dialogic approach to the emergence of Yorùbá/Nagô-derived religion and identity in Brazil is based on the premise that Africa is historically "coeval" with the cultures of the Americas, rather than representative of some past or base line. This implies a central role for African agency: "Both African agency and African culture have been important in the making of African diaspora culture, but, more surprisingly, the African diaspora has at times played a critical role in the making of its own alleged African 'base line' as well" (1999a, p. 74). In the case at hand, he demonstrates the reciprocal influences between northeastern Brazil and late-nineteenth century colonial Lagos, Nigeria. He effectively argues that a mobile, educated class, transnational and culturally hybrid, moving back and forth across the Atlantic, created and propagated "Yorùbá" culture in Brazil that gets represented as "pure African" culturally and, at times, racially. He argues that, in turn, this process is related to and derivative of the cultural-nationalist "Lagosian renaissance" of the 1890s, itself the result not only of local colonial ethnic and class relations but of the influence of Afro-Brazilian "returnees."

Whether a dialogic approach is a "third way" or a kind of epistemic break is not yet clear (Yelvington Forthcoming a), but it is compatible with creolization models of culture and language as well as with Skinner's (1982) "dialectic" between diasporas and homelands. The dialogic concept is consistent with an approach to African cultural "continuities" as the process, "whereby sociocultures persist while undergoing change and even 'transformation,'" where continuity is defined as "a synthetic phenomenon with the property of appearing flexible and adaptive under some conditions and persistent and self-replicating under others," manifesting "both tradition and change at all times" (Smith 1982, p. 127). It is also an amenable overlay to the empirical, historical work on back-and-forth movements between African and New World societies that complement Gilroy's notion of the Black Atlantic (Sarracino 1988, Turner 1942, Verger 1968), and even an overlay to such activity at a more symbolic level involving the negotiations over "blackness" and "race" between Afro-Americans and Africans (Yelvington 1999). There are now a number of theorists of diaspora whose approaches could be broadly called dialogic. Gordon's important recent work (1998, Gordon & Anderson 1999) is an example. Through personal political engagement through/with ethnography, he explores the contradictory cultural constructions of "race," color, and nation on the Nicaraguan-Caribbean coast, showing how Creoles see themselves as part of "disparate diasporas," unexpectedly negotiating and naturalizing cultural practices and ideas that constitute what he calls "Creole common sense," neither automatically nor incontrovertibly accepting racialized notions of blackness. Gordon & Anderson (1999) distinguish between diaspora as a conceptual tool referring to a specific group of people and diaspora as a term to denote a kind of identity formation; they call for increased ethnographic attention to processes of diasporic identification (to the extent they exist). The idea of investigating the "borders" of diaspora (Clifford 1994) is relevant here. Within the broad confines of this approach, then, is a commitment to a social/cultural constructionism centered around investigating local manifestations of blackness in light of their articulations with historical and globalizing processes, with process, negotiation, and conflict in culture-making, which is often characterized by conflict, all grounded in world-system perspectives and historical particularities.

IDENTITY PLAYS: "RACE," ETHNICITY, CLASS, GENDER, AND NATION/TRANSNATION

The anthropological imagination is formed not only by disciplinary doctrine and institutional logics but by national(izing) processes of "race," ethnicity, class, gender, and nation/transnation. In his 1974 review of the status of Afro-American research in Latin America, Bastide complained that while "entire aspects of African civilization have been preserved in Latin America so clearly that no concept of 'reinterpretation' is needed to discover them," it was nevertheless more difficult to do research in South America than in North America because "miscegenation continues to occur" and because miscegenation's cultural twin, syncretism, has worked to the point where "cultural identity shifts from blacks and mulattos to the nation as a whole," so that "one will find African cultural traits in whites as well as European cultural traits in the descendants of Africans." He asked: "How can one establish a science if its very object cannot be clearly defined?" (1974, p. 111) What Bastide was lamenting was for Europeans and North Americans a diffuse and uncertain notion of blackness, not only with regard to what was supposedly happening "on the ground" but also within nationalist discourse and its interaction with ethnography. Anthropologists who focus on identity within diaspora have turned to these problems, at some times representing their subjects' conceptions of diaspora, at others promulgating their own criteria for diasporal definition and inclusion. A brief survey follows.

Blackness versus Mestizaje

Defining the subject of anthropological inquiry has hinged on accepted ethnological definitions. The picture in this region appears complicated. Colonial Latin American and Caribbean concepts of "race" and hence blackness are defined under the rubric of *mestizaje* (*métissage* in French), meaning miscegenation or "race"-mixing as well as a cultural blending. Colonial knowledge deployed elaborate systems and nomenclatures for the "racial" results of such mixing, which, fastforwarding to say the twenty-first century, stand mostly in contrast to North Atlantic ideas. Black and white "races," however, are thought of as polar opposites in both systems. Mestizaje is a foundational theme in the culture of the Americas, coupled with the ideology of *blanqueamiento* ("whitening"), and has been and is used to project different kinds of putative "nonracial" nationalisms that in general paradoxically make claims for an all-inclusive "mixed-race" national identity, hail the virtues of the miscegenation process, while at the same time entailing the hegemonic valorization of whiteness.

This discourse is a way to talk about society "improving" through mixture, diluting, as it were, black and Indian elements (e.g., Graham 1990, Harrison 1995, Stutzman 1981, Torres 1998, Wade 1993, 1997, Yelvington 1997). Blackness is stigmatized, and a plethora of "racial" terms leads identification away from blackness towards whiteness, rendering blacks invisible and blackness a shifting entity, hard to pin down from emic or etic perspectives (Godreau 2000). But at the same time "black culture," rendered as folkloric, becomes a topic of investigation by local ethnographers, with the effect of charting the disappearance of particular black cultural traits and narrating and domesticating black (popular cultural) contributions to the nation. A complementary discourse is one of contributions to the nation. With the colonial order turned upon its head in the late colonial and postcolonial setting, there is the construction of ethnic and cultural difference to prove and justify contribution, authenticity, and citizenship, often through cultural performance (Guss 2000, Segal 1993, Williams 1991); here "Africa" often serves in a symbolic system of the requisite distinction.

Perhaps the best known discourse of nationalism is the Brazilian variant, known as "racial democracy," promoted by Brazilian sociologist/social historian Gilberto Freyre (1900–1987), a student of Boas at Columbia University (see e.g., de Araújo 1994, Needell 1995). This discourse has had an effect on anthropology. Frazier's work in Brazil came at a time when African Americans were debating Brazil as a "racial paradise." Frazier, too, proclaimed that "Brazil has no race problem."

In the postwar context, UNESCO believed the myth enough to sponsor two teams under the direction of Swiss anthropologist Alfred Métraux (1902–1963) to try to verify racial democracy's existence (Bastide 1974, pp. 113–14, Fontaine 1980, pp. 123–24, Maio 2001). Subsequently, anthropologists have documented the operation of "fluid" racial systems (e.g., Harris 1970, Sanjek 1973). Harris (1970) in Brazil used a set of 72 drawings on cards to solicit "racial" identifications across class, gender, and region; he obtained 492 different categorizations, many of which are not translatable, and showed that there was large disagreement on the categories themselves (Figure 1). Anthropologists working in this realm have set out (as have scholars from other disciplines) directly to debunk the myth and simultaneously account for its existence within the context of racial formations (Goldstein 1999, Sheriff 2000, Twine 1998; cf. Ferreira da Silva 1998, Fry 2000, Segato 1998). On the other hand, Bourdieu and Wacquant (1999) want to see this debunking as a kind of U.S. cultural imperialism, claiming that U.S. scholars are simply importing their own concepts of "race," which are ill-fitting in the Brazilian context (cf. Fry 2000, Healey 2000, and the numerous reactions in *Theory, Culture & Society* 17(1) 2000). Blackness is a prominent theme in Latin American social movements (Álvarez et al 1998), and scholars now investigate the growth of new black consciousness/social movements in the region and their articulation with a globalizing blackness (Gomes da Cunha 1998, Grueso et al 1998, Sansone 1997; cf. Mintz 1984).

Anthropologists continue to find blackness (see Table 4) in "black places" like Bahia, Brazil, where scores of Ph.D. students have gone to look for African survivals; Bahia parallels various locales such as the Pacific coast of Colombia, Cuba, and Haiti, and Ponce, Puerto Rico, which serve functions analogous to those of the Sea Islands of South Carolina and Georgia for North American Afro-Americanists. Godreau (1999) deals with this in a sensitive way regarding her own research in Ponce. But anthropologists may ask, Where does that leave contemporary "mixed" groups and identities such as "Spanish" in Trinidad (Khan 1993), the Garífuna people of Central America (González 1988), or Afro-Mexicans (Lewis 2000)? Some anthropologists draw on the perspective of "ethnogenesis," or the process of a people coming into being and into thinking of themselves as a group.

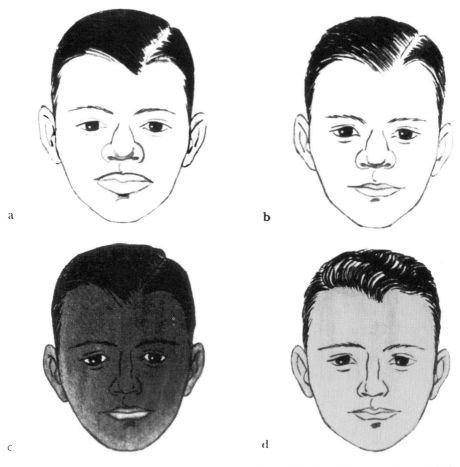

a

b

c

d

Figure 1   Drawings used to elicit responses on "race" in Brazil. Source: Harris 1970, pp. 3–4. Used with permission of the *Journal of Anthropological Research*.

That is, they focus on concepts of people(hood) in contrast to traits or elements of culture (Whitten 1996). Bilby (1996) for example uses the concept to show how maroons in Jamaica and the Guianas, the cultures seen as "more African" than others, are the result of a rapid creation of new societies out of multiple (African ethnic and New World situational) pasts. R. Price's powerful work on Suriname maroon historical consciousness and self-definition (1983, 1990; cf. Scott 1991) is the best-known example across disciplines. Price (1998) now extends this vision to a Martinique that is at once thoroughly creolized, subject to French assimilationist policies, and, in a nostalgist mood, engaged in "pastifying" the social relations of the present. The past proves to be a dynamic resource for identity, seen in the considerable effort thrown into the commemorating of slavery in some national contexts (Thomas 1999); elsewhere the past is "silenced"(Trouillot 1995).

a

b

c

d

Figure 1   *(Continued)*

TABLE 4   Populations of African descent in the Americas

Country	Population (thousands)		Percent of Total	
	Minimum	Maximum	Minimum	Maximum
Brazil	9,477	53,097	5.9	33.0
United States	29,986	29,986	12.1	12.1
Colombia	4,886	7,329	14.0	21.0
Haiti	6,500	6,900	94.0	100.0
Cuba	3,559	6,510	33.9	62.0
Dominican Republic	847	6,468	11.0	84.0
Jamaica	1,976	2,376	76.0	91.4
Peru	1,356	2,192	6.0	9.7
Venezuela	1,935	2,150	9.0	10.0
Panama	35	1,837	14.0	73.5
Ecuador	573	1,147	5.0	10.0
Nicaragua	387	559	9.0	13.0
Trinidad and Tobago	480	516	40.0	43.0
Mexico	474	474	0.5	0.5
Guyana	222	321	29.4	42.6
Guadeloupe	292	292	87.0	87.0
Honduras	112	280	2.0	5.0
Canada	260	260	1.0	1.0
Barbados	205	245	80.0	95.8
Bahamas	194	223	72.0	85.0
Bolivia	158	158	2.0	2.0
Paraguay	156	156	3.5	3.5
Suriname	146	151	39.8	41.0
St. Lucia	121	121	90.3	90.3
Belize	92	112	46.9	57.0
St. Vincent and the Grenadines	94	105	84.5	95.0
Antigua and Barbuda	85	85	97.9	97.9
Grenada	72	81	75.0	84.0
Costa Rica	66	66	2.0	2.0
French Guiana	37	58	42.4	66.0
Bermuda	38	39	61.0	61.3
Uruguay	38	38	1.2	1.2
Guatemala	*	*	*	*
Chile	*	*	*	*
El Salvador	**	**	**	**
Argentina	0	**	0	**
Total	64,859	124,332	9.0	17.2

* = presence of blacks acknowledged but no official figures given; ** = no figures available.
Source: Monge Oviedo 1992:19.

The Positionality of Blackness

Two decades ago, Fontaine (1980) issued a clarion call for political-economic and class perspectives on Afro-Latin America. It is probably fair to say that this call—beckoning the explicit formulation of relationships between diaspora and class—has been largely unheeded by anthropologists. The full potential of an approach within anthropology that considers differential insertion of communities of blacks into the global political economy in relation to transnational cultural flows, including constructions of diaspora, remains a chimera. The role of class in the identification with and commitment to blackness is not to be underestimated. In one study conducted in Cartagena, Colombia (Solaún et al 1987), 120 adults from four social classes were asked to identify the "race" of individuals depicted in 22 photographs. This exercise elicited the usual plethora of "racial" identifiers. When the respondents went on to describe themselves, only among the upper class was there a majority of self-reported *blancos* (whites). No blancos were found in the lower class, nor were *negros* (blacks) found in the upper class; among this class darker individuals referred to themselves as *morenos* (browns), which has dark and light implications. Hardly any respondents positively identified with blackness used negro when referring to themselves, nor used terms denoting African ancestry. Indeed, negro is not generally a polite term when used to describe others in Latin America; as a self-appellation it, as well as designations with "Afro-" as a prefix, have grown in popularity in black intellectual circles, however. Such is the situation under blanqueamiento: Fewer and fewer people remain on the side of the continuum that receives the most discrimination, thus affirming whiteness as the ideal. Macro work has sought to describe the "position" of blacks within national structures of racism, documenting the black presence but also "invisibility," discrimination, and human rights violations, as well as the advent of new black social movements, which sometimes exist in cooperation with Amerindian groups (Minority Rights Group 1995). Sometimes anthropologists are called on to justify claims to cultural distinction and heritage. The work of Jaime Arocha and the late Nina S. de Friedemann was important for the passing in Colombia of a 1993 law based on the 1991 constitution that gave recognition to the ethnic status of Afro-Colombians and identified their territorial and cultural rights (see e.g. Arocha 1998, de Friedemann & Arocha 1995).

Gendered Logics

Anthropology has shown the central place of gendered logics and distinctions in all aspects of an Afro-American society; S. Price's (1993) richly textured ethnography of the Saramaka is an important example. Historical anthropology has sought to document the social and legal conditions for "miscegenation" in relations of power between white men and black women (Martínez-Alier 1989). The articulation of gender ideologies and gendered practices with the central institution of kinship (and kinship-building) has preoccupied ethnographers seeking to chart diasporal connections and similarities. Herskovits had, as might be imagined, postulated that what were regarded as significant (and notorious, depending on political positioning) features of Afro-American family and kinship systems—female-headed households, extended families, and high rates of "illegitimacy"—were reinterpretations of African patterns. By contrast, M.G. Smith (1962), like Frazier, located the origins of the system in the slavery period, while R.T. Smith (e.g. 1988) has been concerned with the determining role of class differences. To an extent, then, diaspora vis-à-vis gender and kinship was mapped in slavery and lower-class status. Rather than in slavery per se, Stolcke locates the present family and kinship forms in "the interplay of the colour-class hierarchy, family ideals, and gender ideology" (1992, p. 140).

On the other hand, the prevalence of Afro-Caribbean women as marketeers with economic autonomy (a phenomenon documented during slavery) is hypothesized by Mintz & Price (1992, pp. 77–80) to be the result of certain African notions of the separateness of male and female roles reinforced in the plantation context. Women's visibility and influence in Afro-American religious cults has been noted (Brown 1991, Burdick 1998, Silverstein 1979, Wedenoja 1989; cf. Steady 1981), and the intersections of gender and blackness are prominent themes in the literature (e.g., Bolles 1996, McClaurin 1996). There is an emerging interest in issues of sexuality, beauty, and aesthetics within mestizaje/nationalism (Rahier 1998), and the definition of blackness from the "outside" as a commodity in the context of sex tourism (Fernández 1999). Black masculinity is now being theorized by Latin Americanists and Caribbeanists, as are the links between black homosexuality and transnationalism to the extent that not only a "global gay" but a "global black gay" identity is articulated (Murray 2000; cf. Sweet 1996).

Transcendental Blackness, Diaspora, and Nation/Transnation

Blackness is often seen to transcend nation-states (and history) from Africa to the New World in the form of African-derived and Afro-Christian religions such as *santería* in Cuba, *vodou* in Haiti, and *candomblé* and *umbanda* in Brazil and their adherents in North America—all of which have received an enormous amount of attention from anthropologists. Substantial agreement exists between the Afro-genetic and creation/creolization theorists in that area of culture demarcated as "religion" on the existence of "Africanisms," however conceived, as a subject of inquiry. Herskovits maintained that "it is in that general field of culture we may denominate as supernatural sanctions that peoples of African descent manifest the widest range of Africanisms, and the purest" (1948, p. 3). Recall that even Frazier was willing to admit "Africanisms" in religion (see 1957, p. 279).

General descriptions of Afro-American religious cults (e.g. Murphy 1994, Simpson 1978, cf. Glazier 2001) as well as case studies emphasize continuities (but cf. Besson & Chevannes 1996, Thoden van Velzen & van Wetering 1988). Some prominent themes include spirit possession (Wafer 1991; cf. Zane 1999), trance and altered states of consciousness (Bourguignon 1973), healing and medicinal knowledge and practices (Laguerre 1980, Littlewood 1993, Voeks 1997,

Wedenoja 1989), syncretism (de Heusch 1989, Houk 1995), but antisyncretism too (Palmié 1995b). Anthropologists have charted the movement of a single institution or deity from Africa to the New World (Barnes 1997, Brandon 1993), as well as black interaction with established (and new, evangelical) religions (Burdick 1993, 1999) and, in contrast, the "African" influence on the forms of Christian worship (Austin-Broos 1997, Kopytoff 1987). The role of colonial and postcolonial politics in the histories of African-derived religions is an emerging theme (Chevannes 1994, 1995, Harding 2000, Pulis 1999a, van Dijk 1993), and religion-as-resistance, certainly a Herskovitsian theme, is explored as well (Besson 1995, Chevannes 1994). Even when the global spread and popularization of Caribbean religion such as Rastafarianism is discussed, it is (still) sometimes conceived in terms of "formal and direct continuities" from African cultures (Savishinsky 1998).

The theme of flight is prominent in Afro-American consciousness and spirituality (McDaniel 1990); at the same time anthropologists have mapped out Afro-American religious dispersal (Greenfield 1994, Segato 1996). The efflorescence of identity in migration situations (Purcell 1993) is often tied to constructions of religious diaspora (Brown 1991; Pulis 1999b). Along these migration routes come public performances (Bettelheim 1979, Green 1999; cf. Scher 1999) and music (Duany 1994; Wade 2000) where the "Africa" (and thus diaspora consciousness) theme is prominent, for example in Bahian carnival groups (Agier 2000) and "black music" performers in Colombia (Wade 2000). Here, ethnomusicologists have made especially creative contributions (Austerlitz 1997, Averill 1997, Fryer 2000, Guilbault 1993, Moore 1997, Pacini Hernández 1995). The religious meanings and moorings inherent in these forms of popular public culture are also traced (Bettelheim 1979; cf. Bilby 1999).

The notion of transcendence is also entailed in questions of how national identities are imagined in light of the diaspora experience. Hall (1999, p. 2) asks of Caribbean national imaginations: "Where do their boundaries begin and end, when regionally each is culturally and historically so closely related to its neighbours, and so many live thousands of miles from 'home'? How do we imagine their relation to 'home', the nature of their 'belongingness'?" Anthropologists have shown these imaginations to be mediated by migration routes, social networks, family ideologies, national identities, and transnational creations of blackness within diaspora (Olwig 1993) and affected by articulation with U.S. blackness and African American identities (Duany 1998, Foner 1998, Greenbaum 2001, Ho 1991, Stepick 1998).

CONCLUSION

That the anthropology of the African diaspora in Latin America and the Caribbean has been elided from the core of the discipline is somewhat ironic in that many of the staple theoretical concepts in cultural anthropology in the past, such as acculturation, assimilation, and syncretism, in part derived from its practitioners, such as Herskovits and his followers. The result is that "new" perspectives in contemporary anthropological theory such as the globalization of cultures, hybridity, transnationalism, colonialism, and political economy, which have always been the concerns of Afro-Americanists, can only be presented as "new" in and through this elision. Yet this exile was a two-way street. Afro-Americanists have imbibed anthropology's concern for the pristine and exotic even while working in ethnographic and historical contexts where such a stance was an unlikely one—while at the same time not historicizing this concern. In other words, anthropologists of the African diaspora in the New World neither did nor do, by and large, relate anthropological ways of knowing about the African diaspora to the conditions of the production and reception of that knowledge. To the extent that this anthropology has consciously or unconsciously aligned itself with either side of the Herskovits-Frazier debate, it has suffered from a kind of "paradigm paralysis," not only with respect to the positionings (political as well as anthropological), but also with a view of culture as an undifferentiated whole with firm discernable borders. Approaches, such as the creolization model, laying claim to obviating the debate have been used to provide the foundation for newer perspectives and tools taken from current interests in the discipline as a whole (and from other disciplines). Some of the most interesting newer directions are charted not by a hyper-relativistic, hyper-reflexive postmodernism that eschews a commitment to truth-value, but are ones that attempt to steer paths through materialistic determinism and cultural production and through ethnography and revisionist historiography. In so doing, they have perhaps replaced for good prior explananda such as African "survivals," "retentions," and the like with new ones such as the concept of "blackness," understood less as a kind of ontology and more as a kind of cultural identity politics.

This raises a new set of issues, political as well as epistemological. To the extent that an older anthropology has been drawn on by disempowered communities of blacks in the New World to justify their place within nationalizing processes, and to the extent to which what have come to be classified as "essentialist" self-concepts lend themselves to effective "strategic essentialism," then this new anthropology has some hard choices to make. The controversies surrounding processual views of culture, the "invention of tradition" perspective, and those aligned perspectives that emphasize cultural hybridity, vis-à-vis the political effects of this kind of anthropological discourse on disempowered, subject peoples, is one of the most contentious and compelling issues at present in the discipline. Portraying "black culture" not as entailing some stable heritage inherited from the past but as made and remade under specific historical conditions, or choosing to emphasize choice and agency, means that there is always the possibility that black claims to cultural authenticity and distinctiveness might be subverted and with them a whole series of rights in highly politically divisive and contentious situations. Ironically, however, even to search for Africanisms means to show how much African culture has been lost. These issues are rarely explicitly discussed within the anthropology of the African diaspora in Latin America and the Caribbean, despite some of the major arguments coming from Latin Americanist anthropologists (Briggs 1996, Jackson 1989; cf. Hale 1997). Perhaps when the innovative nature and unique opportunities presented by Afro-American anthropology are fully realized the debate will be moved forward. The picture is extremely complicated, and there is no reason to believe it will not remain so for some time to come.

ACKNOWLEDGMENTS

I would like to thank Faye V. Harrison for her encouragement and support, for suggesting the focus on the diasporic dimensions of the anthropology of Afro-Latin America and the Caribbean, and for her comments on an earlier draft of what I've written here. I thank J. Lorand Matory for his advice and pertinent suggestions on sources and perspective. I also thank Kenneth M. Bilby, John D. French, Isar P. Godreau, and Richard Price, for their comments on an earlier draft of the article, Claire Insel for her editorial prowess and her patience, and Paul Eugen Camp for his technical assistance. And I would like to thank Bárbara C. Cruz for all of her *ayuda y apoyo*.

Visit the Annual Reviews home page at www.AnnualReviews.org

LITERATURE CITED

Abrahams RD. 1983. *The Man-of-Words in the West Indies: Performance and the Emergence of a Creole Culture*. Baltimore, MD: Johns Hopkins Univ. Press

Abrahams RD, Szwed JF. 1983. Introduction. In *After Africa: Extracts from British Travel Accounts and Journals of the Seventeenth, Eighteenth, and Nineteenth Centuries concerning the Slaves, their Manners, and Customs in the British West Indies*, ed. RD Abrahams, JF Szwed, pp. 1–48. New Haven, CT: Yale Univ. Press

Agier M. 2000. *Anthropologie du Carnaval: La Ville, la Fête et L'Afrique à Bahia*. Marseille, Fr.: Éditions Parenthèses

Alleyne MC. 1985. A linguistic perspective on the Caribbean. In *Caribbean Contours*, ed. SW Mintz, S Price, pp. 155–79. Baltimore, MD: Johns Hopkins Univ. Press

Álvarez SE, Dagnino E, Escobar A, eds. 1998. *Cultures of Politics/Politics of Cultures: Revisioning Latin American Social Movements*. Boulder, CO: Westview

Apter A. 1991. Herskovits's heritage: rethinking syncretism in the African diaspora. *Diaspora* 1(3):235–60

Arocha J. 1998. Inclusion of Afro-Colombians: unreachable national goal? *Latin Am. Perspect.* 25(3):70–89

Austerlitz P. 1997. *Merengue: Dominican Music and Dominican Identity*. Philadelphia: Temple Univ. Press

Austin-Broos DJ. 1997. *Jamaica Genesis: Religion and the Politics of Moral Orders*. Chicago: Univ. Chicago Press

Averill G. 1997. *A Day for the Hunter, a Day for the Prey: Popular Music and Power in Haiti*. Chicago: Univ. Chicago Press

Baker LD. 1998. *From Savage to Negro: Anthropology and the Construction of Race, 1896–1954*. Berkeley: Univ. Calif. Press

Barnes ST, ed. 1997 (1989). *Africa's Ogun: Old World and New*. Bloomington: Indiana Univ. Press. 2nd ed.

Baron R. 1994. *Africa in the Americas: Melville J. Herskovits' Folkloristic and Anthropological Scholarship*. PhD thesis, Univ. Penn.

Bastide R. 1974. The present status of Afro-American research in Latin America. *Daedalus* 103(2):111–23

Bastide R. 1978 [1960]. *The African Religions of Brazil: Toward a Sociology of the Interpenetration of Civilizations*. Baltimore, MD: Johns Hopkins Univ. Press. Transl. H Sebba (From French)

Battaglia D, ed. 1995. *Rhetorics of Self-Making*. Berkeley: Univ. Calif. Press

Berlin I. 1998. *Many Thousands Gone: The First Two Centuries of Slavery in North America*. Cambridge, MA: Belknap, Harvard Univ. Press

Besson J. 1987. Family land as a model for Martha Brae's new history. See Carnegie 1987b, pp. 100–32

Besson J. 1995. Religion as resistance in Jamaican peasant life: the Baptist Church, Revival worldview and Rastafari movement. See Chevannes 1995, pp. 43–76

Besson J, Chevannes B. 1996. The continuity-creativity debate.: the case of Revival. *Nieuwe West-Indische Gids* 70(3–4):209–28

Bettelheim J. 1979. Jamaican Jonkonnu and related Caribbean festivals. See Crahan & Knight 1979, pp. 80–100

Bilby KM. 1983. How the "older heads" talk: a Jamaican maroon spirit possession language and its relationship to the creoles of Suriname and Sierra Leone. *Nieuwe West-Indische Gids* 57(1–2):37–88

Bilby KM. 1996. Ethnogenesis in the Guianas and Jamaica: two maroon cases. In *History, Power, and Identity: Ethnogenesis in the Americas, 1492–1992*, ed. JD Hill, pp. 119–41. Iowa City: Univ. Iowa Press

Bilby KM. 1999. Gumbay, Myal, and the great house: new evidence on the religious background of Jonkonnu in Jamaica. *Afr. Caribb. Inst. Jamaica Res. Rev.* 4:47–70

Bolles AL. 1996. *Sister Jamaica: A Study of Women, Work, and Households in Kingston*. Lanham, MD: Univ. Press Am.

Bourdieu P, Wacquant L. 1999 (1998). On the cunning of imperialist reason. *Theory, Culture, Society* 16(1):41–58. Transl. DM Robbins, L Wacquant

Bourguignon E, ed. 1973. *Religion, Altered States of Consciousness and Social Change*. Columbus: Ohio State Univ. Press

Brandon G. 1993. *Santeria from Africa to the New World: The Dead Sell Memories*. Bloomington: Ind. Univ. Press

Briggs CL. 1996. The politics of discursive authority in research on the "invention of tradition." *Cult. Anthropol.* 11(4):435–69

Brown KM. 1991. *Mama Lola: A Vodou Priestess in Brooklyn*. Berkeley: Univ. Calif. Press

Browning B. 1998. *Infectious Rhythm: Metaphors of Contagion and the Spread of African Culture*. New York: Routledge

Burdick J. 1993. *Looking for God in Brazil: The Progressive Catholic Church in Urban Brazil's Religious Arena*. Berkeley: Univ. Calif. Press

Burdick J. 1998. *Blessed Anastácia: Women, Race and Popular Christianity in Brazil*. New York: Routledge

Burdick J. 1999. What is the color of the holy spirit?: Pentecostalism and black identity in Brazil. *Lat. Am. Res. Rev.* 34(2):109–31

Burton RDE. 1997. *Afro-Creole: Power, Opposition, and Play in the Caribbean*. Ithaca: Cornell Univ. Press

Byfield J, ed. 2000. Special Issue on the Diaspora. *Afr. Stud. Rev.* 43(1)

Carnegie CV. 1987a. Is family land an institution? See Carnegie 1987b, pp. 83–99

Carnegie CV, ed. 1987b. *Afro-Caribbean Villages in Historical Perspective*. Kingston: Afr.-Caribb. Inst. Jamaica

Chevannes B. 1994. *Rastafari: Roots and Ideology*. Syracuse: Syracuse Univ. Press

Chevannes B, ed. 1995. *Rastafari and other African-Caribbean Worldviews*. London: Macmillan

Clifford J. 1994. Diasporas. *Cult. Anthropol.* 9(3):302–38

Conniff ML, Davis TJ, eds. 1994. *Africans in the Americas: A History of the Black Diaspora*. New York: St. Martin's

Cole JB. 1985. Africanisms in the Americas: a brief history of the concept. *Anthropol. Hum. Q.* 10(4):120–26

Cole S. 1994. Introduction: Ruth Landes in

Brazil: writing, race, and gender in 1930s American Anthropology. In *City of Women*, R Landes. 2nd. ed., pp. vii–xxxiv. Albuquerque: Univ. New Mex. Press

Cole S. 1995. Ruth Landes and the early ethnography of race and gender. In *Women Writing Culture*, ed. R Behar, DA Gordon, pp. 166–85. Berkeley: Univ. Calif. Press

Coronil F. 1995. Introduction to the Duke University Press edition: transculturation and the politics of theory: countering the center, Cuban counterpoint. In *Cuban Counterpoint: Tobacco and Sugar*, F Ortiz. Transl. H de Onís (1947, from Spanish), pp. ix–lvi. Durham, NC: Duke Univ. Press

Corrêa M. 1998. *As ilusõs da liberdade: a escola Nina Rodrigues e a antropologia no Brasil*. Braganca Paulista: EDUSF

Corrêa M. 2000. O mistério dos orixás e das bonecas: raca e gênero na antropologia Brasileira. *Etnográfica* 4(2):233–65

Crahan ME, Knight FW, eds. 1979. *Africa and the Caribbean: The Legacies of a Link*. Baltimore, MD: Johns Hopkins Univ. Press

Davis DJ. 1992. *The Mechanisms of Forging a National Consciousness: a Comparative Approach to Modern Brazil and Cuba, 1930–1964*. PhD thesis, Tulane Univ.

de Araújo RB. 1994. *Guerra e paz: Casa-grande & Senzala e a obra de Gilberto Freyre nos anos 30*. Rio de Janeiro: Editora 34

de Friedemann NS. 1993. *La saga del negro: presencia africana en Colombia*. Bogotá: Inst. Genet. Hum., Facult. Med., Pontif. Univ. Javeriana

de Friedemann NS, Arocha J. 1995. Colombia. See Minority Rights Group 1995, pp. 47–76

de Heusch L. 1989 [1989]. Kongo in Haiti: a new approach to religious syncretism. *Man* (N.S.) 24(2):290–303. Transl. N Mellot (from French)

Drake S. 1980. Anthropology and the black experience. *Black Sch.* 11(7):2–31

Drake S. 1990. Further reflections on anthropology and the black experience, ed. WL Baber. *Transform. Anthropol.* 1(2):1–14

Drake S. 1982. Diaspora studies and pan-Africanism. See Harris 1982, pp. 341–402

Duany J. 1994. Ethnicity, identity and music: an anthropological analysis of the Dominican merengue. In *Music and Black Ethnicity: The Caribbean and South America*, ed. GH Béhague, pp. 65–90. New Brunswick, NJ: Transaction

Duany J. 1998. Reconstructing racial identity: ethnicity, color, and class among Dominicans in the United States and Puerto Rico. *Latin Am. Perspect.* 25(3):147–72

Du Bois WEB. 1939. *Black Folk: Then and Now; An Essay in the History and Sociology of the Negro Race*. New York: Henry Holt

Eltis D. 2000. *The Rise of African Slavery in the Americas*. Cambridge, UK: Cambridge Univ. Press

Eltis D, Richardson D, eds. 1997. *Routes to Slavery: Direction, Ethnicity and Mortality in the Transatlantic Slave Trade*. London: Frank Cass

Fernandes F. 1958. *A etnologia e a sociologia no Brasil: ensaios sobre aspectos da formação e do desenvolvimento das ciencias sociais na sociedade brasileira*. Sao Paulo: Edit. Anhambi

Fernández N. 1999. Back to the future?: women, race, and tourism in Cuba. In *Sun, Sex, and Gold: Tourism and Sex Work in the Caribbean*, ed. K Kempadoo, pp. 81–89. Lanham, MD: Rowman Littlefield

Ferreira da Silva D. 1998. Facts of blackness: Brazil is not (quite) the United States . . . and racial politics in Brazil? *Soc. Ident.* 4(2):201–34

Firmin A. 2000 [1885]. *The Equality of the Human Races (Positivist Anthropology)*. New York: Garland. Transl. A Charles (from French)

Fluehr-Lobban C. 2000. Anténor Firmin: Haitian pioneer of anthropology. *Am. Anthropol.* 102(3):449–66

Foner N. 1998. West Indian identity in the diaspora: comparative and historical perspectives. *Latin Am. Perspect.* 25(3):173–88

Fontaine P-M. 1980. Research in the political economy of Afro-Latin America. *Lat. Am. Research Rev.* 15(2):111–41

Frank G. 2001. Melville J. Herskovits on the

African and Jewish diasporas: race, culture and modern anthropology. *Identities* 8(2) In press

Frazier EF. 1939. *The Negro Family in the United States*. Chicago: Univ. Chicago Press

Frazier EF. 1942. The Negro family in Bahia, Brazil. *Am. Soc. Rev.* 7(4):465–78

Frazier EF. 1943. Rejoinder. *Am. Soc. Rev.* 8(4): 402–4

Frazier EF. 1957. *Race and Cultural Contacts in the Modern World*. New York: Alfred A. Knopf

Fry P. 2000. Politics, nationality, and the meanings of "race" in Brazil. *Daedalus* 129(2):83–118

Fryer P. 2000. *Rhythms of Resistance: African Musical Heritage in Brazil*. Middletown, CT: Wesleyan Univ. Press

Gershenhorn JB. 2000. *Melville J. Herskovits and the Racial Politics of Knowledge*. PhD thesis, Univ. North Carolina, Chapel Hill

Gilroy P. 1993. *The Black Atlantic: Modernity and Double Consciousness*. Cambridge, MA: Harvard Univ. Press

Glazier SD, ed. 2001. *Encyclopedia of African and African-American Religions*. New York: Routledge

Glissant É. 1989 [1981]. *Caribbean Discourse: Selected Essays*. Charlottesville: Univ. Press Virginia. Transl. JM Dash (from French)

Godreau IP. 1999. *Missing the Mix: San Antón and the Racial Dynamics of "Nationalism" in Puerto Rico*. PhD thesis, Univ. Calif., Santa Cruz

Godreau IP. 2000. La semántica fugitiva: "raza", color y vida cotidiana en Puerto Rico. *Rev. Cienc. Soc.* (Nueva Época) 9:52–71

Goldstein D. 1999. "Interracial" sex and racial democracy in Brazil: twin concepts? *Am. Anthropol.* 101(3):563–78

Gomes da Cunha OM. 1998. Black movements and the "politics of identity" in Brazil. See Álvarez, Dagnino, Escobar, pp. 220–51

González NL. 1988. *Sojourners of the Caribbean: Ethnogenesis and Ethnohistory of the Garifuna*. Urbana: Univ. Ill. Press

Gordon ET. 1998. *Disparate Diasporas: Identity and Politics in an African-Nicaraguan Community*. Austin: Univ. Texas Press

Gordon ET, Anderson M. 1999. The African diaspora: towards an ethnography of diasporic identification. *J. Am. Folklore* 112(445):282–96

Graham R, ed. 1990. *The Idea of Race in Latin America, 1870–1940*. Austin: Univ. Texas Press

Green GL. 1999. Blasphemy, sacrilege, and moral degradation in the Trinidad carnival: the Hallelujah controversy of 1995. See Pulis 1999b, pp. 189–213

Greenbaum SD. 2001. *More Than Black: Afro-Cubans in Tampa*. Gainesville: Univ. Press Fla. In press

Greenfield SM. 1994. Descendants of European immigrants in southern Brazil as participants and heads of Afro-Brazilian religious centres. *Ethnic Racial Stud.* 17(4):684–700

Grueso L, Rosero C, Escobar A. 1998. The process of black community organizing in the southern Pacific coast region of Colombia. See Álvarez et al. 1998, pp. 198–219

Guilbault J. 1993. *Zouk: World Music in the West Indies*. Chicago: Univ. Chicago Press

Guss DM. 2000. *The Festive State: Race, Ethnicity, and Nationalism as Cultural Performance*. Berkeley: Univ. Calif. Press

Hale CR. 1997. Cultural politics of identity in Latin America. *Annu. Rev. Anthropol.* 26:567–90

Hall S. 1990. Cultural identity and diaspora. In *Identity: Community, Culture, Difference*, ed. J Rutherford, pp. 222–37. London: Lawrence Wishart

Hall S. 1999. Thinking the diaspora: home-thoughts from abroad. *Small Axe* 6:1–18

Harding RE. 2000. *A Refuge in Thunder: Candomblé and Alternative Spaces of Blackness*. Bloomington: Indiana Univ. Press

Harris JE, ed. 1982. *Global Dimensions of the African Diaspora*. Washington, DC: Howard Univ. Press

Harris M. 1970. Referential ambiguity in the calculus of Brazilian racial identity. *SW J. Anthropol.* 26(1):1–14

Harrison FV. 1988. Introduction: an African diaspora perspective for urban anthropology. *Urban Anthropol.* 17(2-3):111–41

Harrison FV, ed. 1991. *Decolonizing Anthropology: Moving Further Toward an Anthropology for Liberation.* Washington, DC: Am. Anthropol. Assoc.

Harrison FV. 1992. The Du Boisian legacy in anthropology. *Crit. Anthropol.* 12(3):239–60

Harrison FV. 1995. The persistent power of "race" in the cultural and political economy of racism. *Annu. Rev. Anthropol.* 24:47–74

Harrison FV, Nonini D. 1992. Introduction to WEB Du Bois and anthropology. *Crit. Anthropol.* 12(3):229–37

Harrison IE, Harrison FV, ed. 1999. *African-American Pioneers in Anthropology.* Urbana: Univ. Ill. Press

Healey MA. 1998. "The sweet matriarchy of Bahia": Ruth Landes' ethnography of race and gender. *Dispositio/n* 23(50):87–116

Healey MA. 2000. Disseram que voltei americanisada: Bourdieu y Wacquant sobre la raza en Brasil. *Apuntes Investig. CECYP* 4(5):95–102

Helmreich S. 1993. Kinship, nation, and Paul Gilroy's concept of diaspora. *Diaspora* 2(2):243–9

Herskovits MJ. 1925. The Negro's Americansim. In *The New Negro*, ed. A Locke, pp. 353–60. New York: Albert Charles Boni

Herskovits MJ. 1930. The Negro in the New World: the statement of a problem. *Am. Anthropol.* 32(1):145–55

Herskovits MJ. 1933. On the provenience of New World Negroes. *Social Forces* 12(2):247–62

Herskovits MJ. 1941. *The Myth of the Negro Past.* New York: Harper

Herskovits MJ. 1943. The Negro in Bahia, Brazil: a problem in method. *Am. Soc. Rev.* 8(4):394–404

Herskovits MJ. 1948. The contribution of Afro-american studies to Africanist research. *Am. Anthropol.* 50(1):1–10

Herskovits MJ. 1966. *The New World Negro: Selected Papers in Afroamerican Studies,* ed. FS Herskovits. Bloomington: Ind. Univ. Press

Herskovits MJ, Herskovits FS. 1947. *Trinidad Village.* New York: Alfred A. Knopf

Hine DC, McLeod J, eds. 1999. *Crossing Boundaries: Comparative History of Black People in Diaspora.* Bloomington: Ind. Univ. Press

Ho CGT. 1991. *Salt-Water Trinnies: Afro-Trinidadian Immigrant Networks and Non-Assimilation in Los Angeles.* New York: AMS

Homiak JP. 1995. Dub history: soundings on Rastafari livity and language. See Chevannes 1995, pp. 127–81.

Houk JT. 1995. *Spirits, Blood, and Drums: The Orisha Religion in Trinidad.* Philadelphia: Temple Univ. Press

Iznaga D. 1989. *Transculturación en Fernando Ortiz.* Havana: Editor. Cienc. Soc.

Jackson J. 1989. Is there a way to talk about making culture without making enemies? *Dialect. Anthropol.* 14(2):127–43

Jackson WA. 1986. Melville Herskovits and the search for Afro-American culture. In *Malinowski, Rivers, Benedict and Others: Essays on Culture and Personality, History of Anthropology,* ed. GW Stocking, Jr., pp. 4:95–126. Madison: Univ. Wisc. Press

Jalloh A, Maizlish SE, eds. 1996. *The African Diaspora.* College Station, TX: Texas A&M Univ. Press

Jourdan C. 1991. Pidgins and creoles: the blurring of categories. *Annu. Rev. Anthropol.* 20:187–209

Khan A. 1993. What is "a Spanish"?: ambiguity and "mixed" ethnicity in Trinidad. In *Trinidad Ethnicity,* ed. KA Yelvington, pp. 180–207. Knoxville: Univ. Tenn. Press

Klein HS. 1999. *The Atlantic Slave Trade.* Cambridge, UK: Cambridge Univ. Press

Kopytoff BK. 1987. Religious change among the Jamaican maroons: the ascendance of the Christian God within a traditional cosmology. *J. Social Hist.* 20:463–84

Laguerre MS. 1980. *Afro-Caribbean Folk Medicine.* South Hadley, MA: Bergin Garvey

Landes R. 1947. *The City of Women.* New York: Macmillan

Landes R. 1970. A woman anthropologist in

Brazil. In *Women in the Field*, ed. P Golde, pp. 117–39. Chicago: Aldine

Law R. 1997. Ethnicity and the slave trade: "Lucimi" and "Nago" as ethnonyms in West Africa. *Hist. Afr.* 24:205–19

Lewis LA. 2000. Blacks, black Indians, Afromexicans: the dynamics of race, nation and identity in a Mexican moreno community (Guerrero). *Am. Ethnol.* 27(4):898–926

Littlewood R. 1993. *Pathology and Identity: The Work of Mother Earth in Trinidad.* Cambridge, UK: Cambridge Univ. Press

Lovejoy PE, ed. 2000a. *Identity in the Shadow of Slavery.* London: Continuum

Lovejoy PE. 2000b. Identifying enslaved Africans in the African diaspora. See Lovejoy 2000a, pp. 1–29

Maio MC. 2001. UNESCO and the study of race relations in Brazil: regional or national issue? *Lat. Am. Res. Rev.* 36(2):118–36

Martínez-Alier V. 1989 (1974). *Marriage, Class and Colour in Nineteenth-Century Cuba: A Study of Racial Attitudes and Sexual Values in a Slave Society.* Ann Arbor: Univ. Michigan Press. 2nd ed.

Martínez Montiel LM. 1992. *Negros en América.* Madrid: Editor. MAPFRE

Martínez Montiel LM, ed. 1993. *Presencia africana en Centroamérica.* Mexico City: Consejo Nac. Cult. Artes

Martínez Montiel LM, ed. 1995. *Presencia africana en Sudamérica.* Mexico City: Consejo Nac. Cult. Artes

Matory JL. 1999a. The English professors of Brazil: on the diasporic roots of the Yorùbá nation. *Comp. Studs. Soc. Hist.* 41(1):72–103

Matory JL. 1999b. Afro-Atlantic culture: on the live dialogue between Africa and the Americas. In *Africana: The Encyclopedia of the African and African American Experience*, ed. KA Appiah, HL Gates, Jr. New York: Basic Civitas Books, pp. 36–44

Maurer B. 1997. *Recharting the Caribbean: Land, Law, and Citizenship in the British Virgin Islands.* Ann Arbor: Univ. Mich. Press

McClaurin I. 1996. *Women of Belize: Gender and Change in Central America.* New Brunswick: Rutgers Univ. Press

McDaniel L. 1990. The flying Africans: extent and strength of the myth in the Americas. *Nieuwe West-Indische Gids* 64(1–2):28–40

McWhorter JH. 1997. *Towards a New Model of Creole Genesis.* New York: Peter Lang

Mentore G. 1993. Alienating emotion: literacy and creolese in Grenada. *Ethnic Groups* 10(4):269–84.

Minority Rights Group, ed. 1995. *No Longer Invisible: Afro-Latin Americans Today.* London: Minority Rights Group

Mintz SW. 1971. The socio-historical background of pidginization and creolization. In *Pidginization and Creolization of Languages*, ed. D Hymes, pp. 153–68. Cambridge, UK: Cambridge Univ. Press

Mintz SW. 1974. *Caribbean Transformations.* Chicago: Aldine

Mintz SW. 1984 [1977]. Africa *of* Latin America: an unguarded reflection. In *Africa in Latin America: Essays on History, Culture, and Socialization*, ed. M Moreno Fraginals, pp. 286–305. New York: Holmes Meier. Transl. L Blum (From Spanish)

Mintz SW, Price R. 1992. *The Birth of African-American Culture: An Anthropological Perspective.* Boston: Beacon

Monge Oviedo R. 1992. Are we or aren't we? *Rep. Am.* 25(4):19

Moore R. 1994. Representations of Afrocuban expressive culture in the writings of Fernando Ortiz. *Lat. Am. Music Rev.* 15(1):32–54

Moore R. 1997. *Nationalizing Blackness: Afrocubanismo and Artistic Revolution in Havana, 1920–1940.* Pittsburgh: Univ. Pittsburgh Press

Morgan PD. 1998. *Slave Counterpoint: Black Culture in the Eighteenth-Century Chesapeake and Lowcountry.* Chapel Hill: Univ. N.C. Press

Morse RM. 1996. Race, culture and identity in the New World: five national versions. In *Ethnicity in the Caribbean: Essays in Honor of Harry Hoetink*, ed. G Oostindie, pp. 22–38. London: Macmillan

Mufwene SS, ed. 1993. *Africanisms in Afro-American Language Varieties*. Athens: Univ. Georgia Press

Murphy JM. 1994. *Working the Spirit: Ceremonies of the African Diaspora*. Boston: Beacon

Murray DAB. 2000. Between a rock and a hard place: the power and powerlessness of transnational narratives among gay Martinican men. *Am. Anthropol.* 102 (2):261–70

Needell JD. 1995. Identity, race, gender, and modernity in the origins of Gilberto Freyre's *oeuvre. Am. Hist. Rev.* 100(1):51–77

Okpewho I, Davies CB, Mazrui AA, eds. 1999. *The African Diaspora: African Origins and New World Identities*. Bloomington: Ind. Univ. Press

Olwig KF. 1993. *Global Culture, Island Identity: Continuity and Change in the Afro-Caribbean Community of Nevis*. Philadelphia: Harwood Academic

Orser CE. Jr. 1998. The archaeology of the African diaspora. *Annu. Rev. Anthropol.* 22: 63–82

Pacini Hernández D. 1995. *Bachata: A Social History of Dominican Popular Music*. Philadelphia: Temple Univ. Press

Palmer CA. 1995. From Africa to the Americas: ethnicity in the early black communities of the Americas. *J. World Hist.* 6(2):223–36

Palmié S, ed. 1995a. *Slave Cultures and the Cultures of Slavery*. Knoxville: Univ. Tenn. Press

Palmié, S. 1995b. Against syncretism: "Africanizing" and "Cubanizing" discourses in North American òrìsà worship. In *Counterworks: Managing the Diversity of Knowledge*, ed. R Fardon, pp. 80–104. London: Routledge

Palmié S. 2001. *Wizards and Scientists: Explorations in Afro-Cuban Modernity and Tradition*. Durham, N.C.: Duke Univ. Press

Peirano MG e S. 1981. *The Anthropology of Anthropology: The Brazilian Case*. PhD thesis, Harvard Univ.

Perl M, Schwegler A, eds. 1998. *América negra: panorámica actual de los estudios lingüísticos sobre variedades hispanas, portuguesas y criollas*. Frankfurt: Vervuert

Pollak-Eltz A. 1972. *Vestigios africanos en la cultura del pueblo venezolano*. Caracas: Univ. Catól. Andrés Bello, Inst. Invest. Hist.

Price R. 1975. KiKoongo and Saramaccan: a reappraisal. *Bijdragen tot Taal, Land Volkenkd.* 131:461–78

Price R. 1983. *First-Time: The Historical Vision of an Afro-American People*. Baltimore, MD: Johns Hopkins Univ. Press

Price R. 1990. *Alabi's World*. Baltimore, MD: Johns Hopkins Univ. Press

Price R. 1998. *The Convict and the Colonel*. Boston: Beacon

Price S. 1993 (1984). *Co-Wives and Calabashes*. Ann Arbor: Univ. Michigan Press. 2nd ed.

Price S. Forthcoming. Seaming connections. See Yelvington Forthcoming a

Price R, Price S. 1997. Shadowboxing in the mangrove. *Cult. Anthropol.* 12(1):3–36

Price S, Price R. 1999. *Maroon Arts: Cultural Vitality in the African Diaspora*. Boston: Beacon

Pulis JW. 1993. "Up-full sounds": language, identity, and the world-view of Rastafari. *Ethn. Groups* 10(4):285–300

Pulis JW. 1999a. Bridging troubled waters: Moses Baker, George Liele, and the African American diaspora to Jamaica. In *Moving On: Black Loyalists in the Afro-Atlantic World*, ed. JW Pulis, pp. 183–221. New York: Garland

Pulis JW, ed. 1999b. *Religion, Diaspora, and Cultural Identity: A Reader in the Anglophone Caribbean*. Amsterdam: Gordon & Breach

Purcell TW. 1993. *Banana Fallout: Class, Color, and Culture among West Indians in Costa Rica*. Los Angeles: Center for Afro-American Studies, Los Angeles: Univ. Calif. Los Angeles

Rahier JM. 1998. Blackness, the racial/spatial order, migrations, and Miss Ecuador 1995–96. *Am. Anthropol.* 100(2):421–30

Rahier JM, ed. 1999a. *Representations of*

Blackness and the Performance of Identities. Westport, CT: Bergin Garvey

Rahier JM. 1999b. Blackness as a process of creolization: the Afro-Esmeraldian *décimas* (Ecuador). See Okpewho et al. 1999, pp. 290–314

Sanjek R. 1973. Brazilian racial terms: some aspects of meaning and learning. *Am. Anthropol.* 73(5):1126–43

Sansone L. 1997 The new blacks from Bahia: local and global in Afro-Bahia. *Identities* 3(4):457–93

Sarracino R. 1988. *Los que volvieron a África.* Havana: Editor. Cienc. Soc.

Savishinsky NJ. 1998. African dimensions of the Jamaican Rastafarian movement. In *Chanting Down Babylon: The Rastafari Reader,* ed. NS Murrell, WD Spencer, AA McFarlane, pp. 125–44. Philadelphia: Temple Univ Press

Scher PW. 1999. West Indian American Day: becoming a tile in the "gorgeous mosaic." See Pulis 1999b, pp. 45–66

Schieffelin BB, Doucet RC. 1994. The "real" Haitian Creole: ideology, metalinguistics, and orthographic choice. *Am. Ethnol.* 21(1): 176–200

Schnepel EM. 1993. The creole movement in Guadeloupe. *Int. J. Soc. Lang.* 102:117–34

Schwegler A. 1996. *"Chi ma nkongo": lengua y rito ancestrales en el Palenque de San Basilio (Colombia).* Frankfurt: Vervuert

Scott D. 1991. That event, this memory: notes on the anthropology of African diasporas in the New World. *Diaspora* 1(3):261–84

Scott D. 1999. *Refashioning Futures: Criticism after Postcoloniality.* Princeton, N.J.: Princeton Univ. Press

Segal DA. 1993. "Race" and "colour" in pre-independence Trinidad and Tobago. In *Trinidad Ethnicity,* ed. KA Yelvington, pp. 81–115. Knoxville: Univ. Tenn. Press

Segato RL. 1996. Frontiers and margins: the untold story of the Afro-Brazilian religious expansion to Argentina and Uruguay. *Crit. Anthropol.* 16(4):343–59

Segato RL. 1998. The color-blind subject of myth; or, where to find Africa in the nation. *Annu. Rev. Anthropol.* 27:129–51

Shannon MW. 1996. *Jean Price-Mars, the Haitian Elite and the American Occupation, 1915–35.* London: Macmillan

Sheriff RE. 2000. Exposing silence as cultural censorship: a Brazilian case. *Am. Anthropol.* 102 (1):114–32

Silverstein LM. 1979. Mãe de todo mundo: modos de sobrevivência nas communidades de candomblé da Bahia. *Relig. Soc.* 4:143–69

Simpson GE. 1973. *Melville J. Herskovits.* New York: Columbia Univ. Press

Simpson GE. 1978. *Black Religions in the New World.* New York: Columbia Univ. Press

Skinner EP. 1982. The dialectic between diasporas and homelands. See Harris 1982, pp. 17–45

Smith ME. 1982. The process of sociocultural continuity. *Curr. Anthropol.* 23(2):127–42

Smith MG. 1957. The African heritage in the Caribbean. In *Caribbean Studies: A Symposium,* ed. V Rubin, pp. 34–46. Mona, Jamaica: Inst. Soc. Econ. Stud., Univ. College West Indies

Smith MG. 1962. *West Indian Family Structure.* Seattle: Univ. Wash. Press

Smith RT. 1988. *Kinship and Class in the West Indies: A Genealogical Study of Jamaica and Guyana.* Cambridge, UK: Cambridge Univ. Press

Solaún M, Vélez M, Smith C. 1987. Claro, trigueño, moreno: testing for race in Cartagena. *Caribb. Rev.* 15(3):18–19

Steady FC, ed. 1981. *The Black Woman Cross-Culturally.* Cambridge, MA: Schenkman

Stepick A. 1998. *Pride Against Prejudice: Haitians in the United States.* Boston: Allyn Bacon

Stolcke V. 1992. The slavery period and its influence on household structure and the family in Jamaica, Cuba, and Brazil. In *Family Systems and Cultural Change,* ed. E Berquó, P Xenos, pp. 125–43. Oxford: Clarendon

Stutzman R. 1981. *El mestizaje:* an all-inclusive ideology of exclusion. In *Cultural Transformations and Ethnicity in Modern Ecuador,* ed. NE Whitten, Jr., pp. 45–93. Urbana: Univ. Ill. Press

Sweet JH. 1996. Male homosexuality and spiritism in the African diaspora: the legacies of a link. *J. History Sexuality* 7(2):184–202

Szwed JF. 1972. An American anthropological dilemma: the politics of Afro-American culture. In *Reinventing Anthropology*, ed. D Hymes, pp. 153–81. New York: Pantheon

Thoden van Velzen HUE, van Wetering W. 1988. *The Great Father and the Danger: Religious Cults, Material Forces, and Collective Fantasies in the World of the Surinamese Maroons*. Dordrecht, Holland: Foris

Thomas DA. 1999. Emancipating the nation (again): notes on nationalism, "modernization," and other dilemmas in post-colonial Jamaica. *Identities* 5(4):501–42

Thompson RF. 1983. *Flash of the Spirit: African and Afro-American Art and Philosophy*. New York: Random House

Thornton JK. 1991. African soldiers in the Haitian revolution. *J. Caribb. History* 25(1–2):58–80

Thornton JK. 1992. *Africa and Africans in the Making of the Atlantic World, 1400–1680*. Cambridge, UK: Cambridge Univ. Press

Thornton JK. 1993. "I am the subject of the King of Congo": African political ideology and the Haitian revolution. *J. World Hist.* 4(2):181–214

Torres A. 1998. La gran familia puertorriqueña "ej prieta de beldá" (The great Puerto Rican family is really really black). In *Blackness in Latin America and the Caribbean: Social Dynamics and Cultural Transformations*, ed. A Torres, NE Whitten, Jr., pp. II: 285–306. Bloomington: Ind. Univ. Press

Trouillot M-R. 1992. The Caribbean region: an open frontier in anthropological theory. *Annu. Rev. Anthropol.* 21:19–42

Trouillot M-R. 1995. *Silencing the Past: Power and the Production of History*. Boston: Beacon

Trouillot M-R. 1998. Culture on the edges: creolization in the plantation context. *Plantation Soc. Am.* 5(1):8–28

Turner LD. 1942. Some contacts of Brazilian ex-slaves with Nigeria, West Africa. *J. Negro Hist.* 27(1):55–67

Twine FW. 1998. *Racism in a Racial Democracy: The Maintenance of White Supremacy in Brazil*. New Brunswick: Rutgers Univ. Press

van Dijk FJ. 1993. *Jahmaica: Rastafari and Jamaican Society 1930-1990*. Utrecht: ISOR

Verger P. 1968. *Flux et reflux de la traite des nègres entre le Golfe de Bénin et Bahia de Todos os Santos, du XVIIe au XIXe siècle*. Paris: La Haye, Mouton

Voeks RA. 1997. *Sacred Leaves of Candomblé: African Magic, Medicine, and Religion in Brazil*. Austin: Univ. Tex. Press

Wade P. 1993. *Blackness and Race Mixture: The Dynamics of Racial Identity in Colombia*. Baltimore, MD: Johns Hopkins Univ. Press

Wade P. 1997. *Race and Ethnicity in Latin America*. London: Pluto

Wade P. 2000. *Music, Race, and Nation: Música Tropical in Colombia*. Chicago: Univ. Chicago Press

Wafer J. 1991. *The Taste of Blood: Spirit Possession in Brazilian Candomblé*. Philadelphia: Univ. Pa. Press

Wedenoja W. 1989. Mothering and the practice of "balm" in Jamaica. In *Women as Healers: Cross-Cultural Perspectives*, ed. CS McClain, pp. 76–97. New Brunswick: Rutgers Univ. Press

Whitten NE, Jr. 1996. Ethnogenesis. In *Encyclopedia of Cultural Anthropology*, ed. D Levinson, M Ember, pp. 2:407–11. New York: Henry Holt

Whitten NE. Jr., Szwed JF, eds. 1970. *Afro-American Anthropology: Contemporary Perspectives*. New York: Free

Whitten NE. Jr., Torres A. 1992. Blackness in the Americas. *Rep. Am.* 25(4):16–22

Whitten NE. Jr., Torres A. 1998. To forge the future in the fires of the past: an interpretive essay on racism, domination, resistance, and liberation. In *Blackness in Latin America and the Caribbean: Social Dynamics and Cultural Transformations*, ed. NE Whitten, Jr., A Torres, pp. I:3–33. Bloomington: Indiana Univ. Press

Williams BF. 1991. *Stains on My Name, War in My Veins: Guyana and the Politics of Cultural Struggle*. Durham, NC: Duke Univ. Press

Williams BF. 1995. Review of *The Black Atlantic: Modernity and Double Consciousness*, by Paul Gilroy. *Social Identities* 1(1): 175–92

Wilson PJ. 1973. *Crab Antics: The Social Anthropology of English-speaking Negro Societies of the Caribbean*. New Haven, CT: Yale Univ. Press

Yelvington KA. 1997. Patterns of ethnicity, class, and nationalism. In *Understanding Contemporary Latin America*, ed. RS Hillman, pp. 209–36. Boulder, CO: Lynne Rienner

Yelvington KA. 1999. The war in Ethiopia and Trinidad, 1935–1936. In *The Colonial Caribbean in Transition: Essays on Postemancipation Social and Cultural History*, ed. B Brereton, KA Yelvington, pp. 189–225. Gainesville: Univ. Press Fla.

Yelvington KA. 2000. Herskovits' Jewishness. *Hist. Anthropol. Newsl.* 27(2):3–9

Yelvington KA, ed. Forthcoming a. *Afro-Atlantic Dialogues: Anthropology in the Diaspora*. Santa Fe, N.M.: School Am. Research

Yelvington KA. Forthcoming b. The invention of Africa in Latin America and the Caribbean: political discourse and anthropological praxis, 1920–1940. See Yelvington Forthcoming a

Zane WW. 1999. *Journeys to the Spiritual Lands: The Natural History of a West Indian Religion*. New York: Oxford Univ. Press

Annu. Rev. Anthropol. 2001. 30:261–83

ANTHROPOLOGY OF TOURISM: Forging New Ground for Ecotourism and Other Alternatives

Amanda Stronza

Anthropological Sciences, Stanford University, Stanford, California 94305;
e-mail: Astronza@stanford.edu

Key Words   origins of tourism, impacts of tourism, alternative tourism, conservation, development

■ **Abstract**   Tourism is relevant to many theoretical and real-world issues in anthropology. The major themes anthropologists have covered in the study of tourism may be divided conceptually into two halves: One half seeks to understand the origins of tourism, and the other reveals tourism's impacts. Even when taken together, these two approaches seem to produce only a partial analysis of tourism. The problem is that most studies aimed at understanding the origins of tourism tend to focus on tourists, and most research concerning the impacts of tourism tend to focus on locals. The goal of future research should be to explore incentives and impacts for both tourists and locals throughout all stages of tourism. This more holistic perspective will be important as we explore the ways in which ecotourism and other alternative forms of tourism can generate social, economic, and environmental benefits for local communities while also creating truly transformative experiences for tourists.

> Tourism has some aspects of showbiz, some of international trade in commodities; it is part innocent fun, part a devastating modernizing force. Being all these things simultaneously, it tends to induce partial analysis only.
>
> Victor Turner, 1974

INTRODUCTION

Anthropologists and tourists seem to have a lot in common. Both spend time exploring the cultural productions and rituals of society, and both carry the status of outsider as they make forays into the lives of others. Though as anthropologists we may be loath to admit any relationship to the sandal-footed, camera-toting legions in our midst, the truth is that tourism can be an ideal context for studying issues of political economy, social change and development, natural resource management, and cultural identity and expression. Indeed, many of the major questions that concern cultural anthropologists appear in the study of tourism.

Using the lens of tourism, anthropologists have asked many questions. What are the cross-cultural meanings of work and leisure (MacCannell 1976; Nash 1981,

0084-6570/01/1021-0261$14.00

1996)? What are the connections between play, ritual, and pilgrimage (Cohen 1972, Graburn 1983, Turner 1982)? What are the dynamics and impacts of inter-cultural contact between tourists and locals (Machlis & Burch 1983, Nuñez 1989, Rossel 1988, Silverman 2001)? How is culture represented in tourist settings, and how is it perceived (Adams 1984, 1995; Bruner 1987; Bruner & Kirshenblatt-Gimblett 1994; Urry 1990)? How are cultural traditions changed or reinvented over time to match tourist expectations (Bendix 1989, Gamper 1981, Leong 1989), and what can distinguish the genuine from the spurious (Boorstin 1964)? How and why are ethnic stereotypes constructed and manipulated for tourism (Cohen 1979, Desmond 1999, MacCannell 1984, Van den Berghe 1994)? How do indigenous societies change as they become integrated with the tourism market (Mansperger 1995, Seiler-Baldinger 1988)? How do values about culture change once they are commodified (Cohen 1988, Greenwood 1977), and how do values about nature change (Davis 1997, Groom et al 1991, Orams 1999)? How can conserving natu-ral areas and cultural traditions for tourism lead to benefits for local communities (Eadington & Smith 1992, Honey 1999, Lindberg 1991)? What are the relations of power in the context of tourism that determine who wins and who loses (Stonich 2000, Young 1999), and why is local participation relevant to the success of tourism (Bookbinder et al 1998, Wunder 1999, Epler Wood 1998)? In seeking to answer these and other questions, many anthropologists have made tourism the main focus of their interpretation and analysis.

In this review, I highlight several of the key themes anthropologists have covered in the study of tourism. I suggest that the current literature on tourism may be divided conceptually into two halves, one that focuses on understanding the origins of tourism and one that aims to analyze the impacts of tourism. One of my main points is that both approaches, even when taken together, seem to tell only half the story. The problem is that many studies about the origins of tourism tend to focus on tourists, and much of the research directed at the impacts of tourism tend to analyze just the locals.

Exploring only parts of the two-way encounters between tourists and locals, or between "hosts and guests," has left us with only half-explanations. Although we have theories about the historical origins of tourism (Adler 1989, Towner & Wall 1991), why people travel as tourists in the modern era (MacCannell 1976), or why some tourists seek particular kinds of destinations and experiences over others (Cohen 1988), we lack an understanding of why people and host communities engage in tourism in particular ways. In the absence of analysis, we have been left with assumptions, and typically what we have assumed is that tourism has been imposed on locals, not sought, and not invited.

On the flip side, when we examine the impacts of tourism, our work has tended to focus more on locals than on tourists, and again, we have been left with only a partial analysis. For example, we have learned several things about the ways in which host communities tend to change in the aftermath of tourism. Local economies tend to become either strengthened from employment opportunities (Mansperger 1995) or made more dependent on tourist dollars (Erisman 1983);

local traditions and values can either become meaningless (Greenwood 1977) or more significant (Van den Berghe 1994) once they are commodified in tourism; and local residents can either bear the brunt of resource degradation (Stonich 2000) or become the primary stewards of resource protection (Young 1999) in the context of tourism. We know practically nothing, however, about the impacts of tourism on the tourists themselves. How are they affected by what they see, do, and experience during their travels?

These gaps in our understanding can also be characterized in terms of theory versus data for different kinds of analyses. In their assessments of what motivates tourists (i.e., the psychosocial factors, material conditions, etc.), several scholars have posited generalizeable theories (MacCannell 1976, Graburn 1983, Nash 1981). Yet, relatively little empirical data has been analyzed to support or refute such theories. Conversely, in the examination of the impacts of tourism, researchers have relied much more on data than on theory. Though the literature is well stocked with ethnographic case studies of tourism's impacts in host communities, we have yet to develop models or analytical frameworks that could help us predict the conditions under which locals experience tourism in particular ways.

I elaborate on these gaps in the literature with greater detail in the following pages. My main message is that we should be posing new kinds of questions in the anthropology of tourism, especially as we begin to consider the social, economic, and environmental merits of ecotourism and other alternative forms of tourism. In the past decade or so, the tourism industry has taken major shifts toward goals of economic and ecological sustainability, local participation, and environmental education. Just as the industry has changed, so too should our research objectives. I suggest that we devote more attention to two kinds of inquiry. On the host end, what are some of the factors that can explain particular kinds of local involvement in tourism? On the guest end, what are the differential effects of certain kinds of tourism on guests' attitudes and behaviors, both in the midst of their tour and once they have returned home?

Throughout the paper I refer primarily to tourism that involves people from Western developed parts of the world visiting either non-Western or economically underdeveloped parts of the world. Of course, the tourism industry includes many other types of travel and leisure, including family vacations to Disney World, group tours through art museums and battlefields, and honeymoons in Las Vegas. Some of my discussions are relevant to these other types of tourism, but mostly I make special reference to international tourism that brings people together from often highly disparate socioeconomic and cultural backgrounds.

ANTHROPOLOGY AND TOURISM

Until the 1970s, few anthropologists showed much academic interest in tourism. Though tourism was certainly relevant to the peoples and places many anthropologists were studying, few perceived it as a legitimate focus of analysis (Nash 1996).

One exception was Nuñez, who described weekend tourism in a Mexican village in 1963. In the past two decades, a whole field has emerged, complete with refereed journals, most notably *The Annals of Tourism Research*, conferences, university courses, and oft-cited seminal works. One of the best-known pioneering works in the academic study of tourism is by Smith (1989), first published in 1977. Her volume provided both a preliminary theoretical perspective and 12 case studies documenting the impacts of tourism. MacCannell (1976) has also been highly influential, especially for developing a theory of tourism in modern society. Several key scholars have published field-defining articles over the years (Cohen 1972, 1984; Crick 1989; Graburn 1983; Jafari 1977; Nash 1981; Nash & Smith 1991;) More recent introductory compendiums include those by Burns (1999), Chambers (1997, 1999), and Nash (1996).

Several factors make tourism especially relevant to anthropology. For one, tourism occurs in most, if not all, human societies. It is, at least, safe to say that people in nearly every society have been touched in some way by tourism. Many anthropologists have witnessed first-hand the changes wrought by tourism in their field sites. In fact, tourism seems to occupy at least a subsection in many studies that otherwise have little to do with tourism per se. Places off the beaten path—the kinds of places often of most interest to anthropologists—are increasingly opening to tourism as the international economy globalizes, and as transnational networks of transportation and communication are improved (Lanfant et al 1995). Today, tourists are gaining access to even the most remote destinations in the Amazon (Castner 1990, Linden 1991), the Himalayas (Jayal 1986, McEachern 1995), the Antarctic (Hall & Johnston 1995, Vidas 1993), and, yes, outer space (Rogers 1998).

The economic importance of tourism has also merited the attention of anthropologists. As Greenwood (1989) noted, tourism is "the largest scale movement of goods, services, and people that humanity has perhaps every seen" (p. 171). The World Tourism Organization (2000) estimated that the number of international tourists traveling in the world in 1999 was 664 million. The International Ecotourism Society (1998) calculated that tourism receipts represent one third of the world trade in services. Such figures point to the fact that tourism is a significant catalyst of economic development and sociopolitical change, processes that are central to the interests of many anthropologists. Especially among those concerned about sustainable development and conservation, ecotourism has become a special focus.

Finally, tourism has captured the attention of anthropologists because it often involves face-to-face encounters between people of different cultural backgrounds. Lett (1989) once credited tourism with bringing about "the single largest peaceful movement of people across cultural boundaries in the history of the world" (p. 275). When tourists and locals come together, both have the opportunity not only to glimpse how others live, but also to reflect on their own lives through the eyes of others. As a result, these cross-cultural interactions often cue "live performances" of some of the broadest theoretical issues in anthropology.

Generally, the kinds of questions anthropologists have posed about tourism have come from one of two stages in what has been called the "touristic process" (Nash 1981). Simply put, the touristic process is the flow of travelers from a "tourist generating" site, like the United States or Europe, to a travel destination, usually in some "periphery" country (Jafari 1977; for a critical discussion of how this flow has reversed in the age of "ex-primitives" and "postmoderns," see MacCannell 1992). Viewing tourism in this vector-like manner, researchers have typically examined the origins of tourism on one end, and the impacts of tourism on the other. Questions concerning the origins of tourism have included what makes a person a tourist, what motivates tourists to travel, and what determines the kinds of places and experiences tourists seek? Inquiries on the impacts of tourism have generally focused on the range of socioeconomic, psychological, cultural, and environmental changes that tourism has caused in host destinations.

ORIGINS OF TOURISM

Despite its relevance to people almost everywhere, anthropologists have had a hard time defining tourism (Cohen 1974, Nash 1981). Essentially, a tourist is "a temporarily leisured person who voluntarily visits a place away from home for the purpose of experiencing a change" (Smith 1989, p. 2). One topic of interest among scholars of tourism has been to trace the motives, social profiles, and activities of these "leisured persons" over time. Who are they? Where have they traveled, and what have they been seeking? (Pearce 1982). A recent historical overview comes from Lofgren (1999). The pages read much like a travelogue as Lofgren takes his readers on a tour of the Western holiday world, from the Grand Tour routes of the eighteenth century, to the "global beaches" of today. His goal is to show how two centuries of leisure travel have taught us to be tourists and to move, often according to social dictate, through different types of "vacationscapes."

The things tourists do and the experiences they seek have changed over time, just as they have varied from country to country, and across social categories of class, gender, and race. Several tourism scholars have sought to explain the psychosocial motives for some of these variations. MacCannell (1976) proposed that by following in the footsteps of tourists, one can begin to understand the value systems of the modern world. In fact, by taking tourists as his subject, MacCannell's purpose was to craft "an ethnography of modern society." Modernity, for MacCannell, is characterized by feelings of alienation, fragmentation, and superficiality. The search for authentic experiences is a reflection of modern tourists' desire to reconnect with "the pristine, the primitive, the natural, that which is as yet untouched by modernity" (Cohen 1988, p. 374; see also Dobkin de Rios 1994, Harkin 1995, Redfoot 1984).

Especially evocative in MacCannell's work is the idea that tourism can serve as a unifying force in modern societies, bringing people together to define collectively the places, events, and symbols that are deemed important and somehow meaningful (i.e., "not to be missed"). These might include the Grand Canyon, the Golden Gate Bridge, and the Eiffel Tower. The act of seeing these "in person" and then sharing the experience with others through photographs, souvenirs, and stories allows tourists to reassemble the disparate pieces of their otherwise fragmented lives. Through tourism, then, life and society can appear to be an orderly series of representations, like snapshots in a family album (but see Lippard 1999). Indeed, Kirshenblatt-Gimblett (1998) has interpreted the ways in which tourism stages and displays the world as a museum of itself. By touring the sites of this global "museum" tourists can ultimately affirm and reinforce what they think they already know about the world (Bruner 1991).

In a similar vein, Graburn (1989) characterized tourism as a kind of ritual process that reflects society's deeply held values about health, freedom, nature, and self-improvement. In this view, vacations can be interpreted as the modern, secular equivalent of the annual festivals and pilgrimages in more traditional, religious societies. Drawing on Durkheim, Graburn analyzed the ritual function of tourism in society, especially its role in building and maintaining a collective consciousness. The totems in the modern ritual of tourism appear on the pages of guidebooks, on websites, and on the surfaces of our souvenirs. Through the collective reverence of these totems, tourists are able to strengthen their connection to each other as well as to the larger society.

Turner & Turner (1978) theorized that leisure travel is indeed like a pilgrimage, one that can lift people out of the ordinary structures of their everyday lives. Tourism can offer freedom from work and other obligatory time, an escape from traditional social roles, and the liberty to spend one's time however one chooses. Like other ritual activities, tourism ushers its participants to a state of liminality, or unstructured "time out of time." In this way, modern tourism reflects the "antistructure" of life, an escape from something, rather than a quest for something (Turner 1969, 1982). Here then, the importance of authenticity is diminished as an explanation for what motivates tourists to travel (Bruner 1991).

In other studies related to the origins of tourism, anthropologists have sought to explain why some kinds of tourism arise in particular types of societies (Cohen 1972). In this line of research, tourism is conceptualized as a superstructural phenomenon, dependent on a range of material factors (Nash 1996). The question becomes what particular social, political, and environmental conditions in any given society give rise to certain types of leisure travel or particular types of tourists (Crandall 1980, Dann 1981)? What is it about Japanese society, for example, that compels its people to favor sightseeing in large groups?

Assessing Local Choices and Constraints

Though anthropologists have delved into the factors that motivate tourists to travel, they have trained less attention on examining the conditions under which people in host destinations become involved in tourism. A first step in filling this gap would be first to recognize that not all people in a host destination participate in tourism equally. Some members of a local area may participate directly, interacting with tourists on a regular basis as guides, performers, or artisans, whereas others may become involved only behind the scenes, working as support staff or as wholesalers of foods and supplies. From an economic perspective, local hosts will also differ in terms of how much time and energy they invest in tourism: Some will work as full-time wage laborers, whereas others will contract their labor occasionally or earn cash only through the sale of goods.

In teasing apart differences in how local hosts participate—or choose not to participate—in tourism, we may begin to analyze the range of factors that determine who gets involved, why, and in what ways. Only by asking these latter questions can we explore what tourism determines in people's lives and what factors in people's lives define their connection with tourism.

From case studies, we know that gender is one important variable that determines who within a host community participates in tourism. Swain (1989) found that gender roles among the Kuna Indians of Panama have shaped the local response to tourism. Specifically, Kuna women have produced mola artwork of fabric appliqué, thus maintaining a marketable image of ethnicity to tourists, while Kuna men control the political decisions that determine Kuna interactions with tourism. Wilkinson & Pratiwi (1995) found that women in an Indonesian village could not be involved in tourist guiding because it was not regarded favorably by villagers, the connotation being that women were perceived as prostitutes interested in contacting foreign tourists. Levy & Lerch (1991) learned more generally that women tend to work in less-stable, lower-paid, and lower-level jobs in the tourism industry of Barbados. Gender stereotypes can also result in women being the first ones in a host community contracted to work in tourism. Kinnaird & Hall (1994) found that the involvement of women in tourism in Ireland has been accepted in a society where, historically, women's work has been linked to the roles of wife, mother, and caretaker of others.

Assessing gender differences in how hosts participate in tourism is a step toward improving our understanding of the origins of tourism from the hosts' perspective (Swain 1995). However, many questions remain in terms of why and under what conditions local residents may choose to, or may be driven to, become involved in tourism. Our understanding would also improve if we examined the extent to which hosts act as decision-makers in shaping the kinds of tourism that will take place in their own communities.

The recommendation I make here is not new. In 1981, Nash suggested that while a local society may unavoidably be affected by tourism "it also may play a significant role in determining the kind of tourists it receives and the form of tourism they practice" (p. 462). Similarly, Chambers (1999) has pointed out that "too often we regard the local communities and regions that receive tourists as being the passive recipients of a tourist dynamic" (p. x), adding that our attempts to understand tourism solely on the basis of the motives and behaviors of tourists, "is certain to leave us with only a partial appreciation for what tourism has come to represent in our time" (p. 22).

IMPACTS OF TOURISM

In examining the impacts of tourism, anthropologists have often been devoted to writing ethnographic accounts of how tourism has affected host communities in a wide range of Western and non-Western settings (Jafari 1990). In general, anthropologists have conceptualized tourism as determining the fate of hosts in many ways, such as whether they will develop economically or not, whether they will feel pride or shame about themselves and their traditions, or whether they will have incentives to protect or destroy their environment.

Rarely have scholars' opinions about the effects of tourism on host communities been positive. Rossel's (1988, p. 1) comment that "tourists wreak havoc over the face of the social and cultural landscape" aptly reflects the overall sentiment from anthropologists. Indeed, as Crick noted, tourism has been blamed "for every value transformation under the sun" (1989, p. 308). An overarching disdain for tourism was especially prevalent in the years before ecotourism and other forms of alternative tourism gained recognition.

Economic Change

The pessimism about tourism has not been shared by all social scientists. Particularly during the 1970s, but also to some extent today (see Schwartz 1997), economists enthusiastically promoted tourism as an ideal strategy for development. Multilateral lending agencies funded touristic infrastructure in the Third World as a way to increase foreign exchange earnings and raise gross national product per capita. Especially in the so-called sand, sun, and sea regions, tourism was seen as having limitless growth potential (Crick 1989). As aid money was channeled south, the modernizationists of the 1970s applauded tourism as a powerful catalyst for helping the Caribbean and other places "take off" into flourishing service-based economies.

Despite the early hopes, tourism as a "passport" to macroeconomic development did not pan out quite as planned (de Kadt 1979). Rather than alleviate poverty, tourism seemed to be introducing new kinds of social problems, including currency black markets, drugs, and prostitution (see Oppermann 1998). In addition, tourism was associated with luxury spending, overcrowding, and pollution, all of which were compounding environmental degradation (Honey 1999). Meanwhile, the kinds of infrastructure governments and aid agencies were investing in—golf courses and high-rise hotels—were doing little to alleviate the educational, health, and welfare needs of local populations (Richter 1982). All the while, profits from tourism were being siphoned off to industry leaders in developed countries (Crick 1989). In short, tourism had become a vanguard of neocolonialism (Nash 1989).

At the level of the local economy, anthropologists were learning that tourism was wreaking other kinds of havoc. For one, wage labor opportunities created through tourism were disrupting subsistence activities of small producers.

Ethnographic case studies from host destinations around the world showed that wage labor introduced through tourism raises the opportunity costs of subsistence activities. Oliver-Smith (1989) described a case in Spain in which local hosts substituted their labor in farming with work in tourism. Mansperger (1995) analyzed how tourism among Pacific islanders led to the cessation of subsistence activities and made locals more dependent on the outside world. Seiler-Baldinger's (1988) research in the Upper Amazon attributed declines in health among locals to the fact that they moved away from subsistence activities to work in tourism. Rosenberg (1988) argued that tourism contributed to the demise of agriculture in a small mountain village in France, where grazing animals came to be used mainly for clearing ski slopes. The disruption of subsistence activities was not necessarily a problem in itself, but it became a problem when the flow of tourists was reduced, and people were left with no economic alternatives from which to sustain themselves. Unfortunately, this was (and still is) a relatively common phenomenon because the tourism industry is especially prone to boom-bust cycles.

A second problem anthropologists found with tourism-fueled development is that it often leads to increased wealth stratification in host communities, ultimately sparking or exacerbating social conflict. Among the Yapese, Mansperger found "the Chief is not sharing the entrance fees to the village . . . and money is making people stingy, therefore harming community spirit" (1995, p. 90). Vickers (1997) related a similar story among the Siona and Secoya of Ecuador, in which some individuals were working as native entrepreneurs, guiding tourists with outboard motors and even constructing their own lodges. Problems arose when those showing the most entrepreneurial spirit were perceived as seeking personal enrichment without regard for the welfare of the group. In these cases, as in many others, tourism seemed to contribute to increased social stratification and conflict.

Though the literature in the anthropology of tourism currently includes excellent descriptions of what can go wrong when tourism is introduced into local communities, the analysis so far has been strangely devoid of local voices. We have learned relatively little about how locals themselves perceive the array of pros and cons associated with tourism. Often our assumptions have been that locals were duped into accepting tourism rather than having consciously chosen such an option for themselves. Compounding the absence of local perspective has been a lack of rigor in terms of analyzing the pure effect of tourism on new problems and/or improvements in host communities. Although it may be true that tourism precipitates conflict in host communities, it also may be true that other factors in any given destination site, such as the construction of a road, or the proclamation of a new protected area, have caused conflicts. In general, anecdotal case studies of tourism often suffer the problem of reversed causality. For example, although tourism may cause increased wealth stratification in some communities, perhaps people who live in places where wealth differences are already marked are somehow more likely to become involved in tourism.

Social and Cultural Change

In addition to economic development, intercultural contact and the changes that result from it have been an especially pervasive theme in studying the impacts of tourism (Nash 1996). An early example came from Nuñez (1963, p. 347), who described tourism as a "laboratory situation" for testing how acculturation occurs when urban tourists representing "donor" cultures interact with host populations in "recipient" cultures. Though anthropologists may shy away from the now politicized term acculturation, the concept behind it is still present in public and academic discourses on tourism in indigenous communities. Acculturation is what many fear will happen with the intrusion of tourists, consumerism, and the "commodification of culture" (e.g., Chicchón 1995, McLaren 1997, Rossel 1988, Seiler-Baldinger 1988).

"Commodification of culture" has been used to describe a process by which things come to be evaluated primarily in terms of their exchange value, in a context of trade, thereby becoming goods (Cohen 1988). Greenwood (1977) used the concept of commodification in association with tourism to describe how the *alarde* festival in the Basque town of Fuenterrabia lost its cultural and symbolic meaning to locals once it had been opened to tourists and marketed like any other commodity. The concern among many tourism scholars has been whether a cultural item or ritual loses meaning for locals once it has been commodified. Does the item become material property of the highest bidder rather than a spiritually, ceremonially, or in some other way significant artifact of the host culture? In applying this question to Australian Aboriginal bark paintings, Hall (1994), for example, found that once the paintings had been marketed to international consumers, they were uprooted from their traditional social and cultural context, and thus lost significance for locals. Picard (1990) asserted that Balinese culture has been so commodified that the distinction between what is Balinese and what is attributable to tourism is no longer clear, even to the Balinese themselves.

Often entangled in discussions of commodification is the idea that people in host destinations will lose their cultural identity as a result of tourism. Many worry that tourism may cause hosts to forget their past or "lose their culture" as they adopt the new lifestyles and ways of being they learn from outsiders. Erisman has argued that the massive influx of foreign goods, people, and ideas to rural host destinations has a negative impact, which, ultimately, "erodes people's self-esteem" (1983, p. 350). In this view, tourism can lead to a kind of "cultural dependency" in which local people gain economic benefits, but only as they are catering to the needs of outsiders. Loss of identity occurs in this scenario as the local economy improves and hosts begin to act and think like tourists, whom they perceive as superior in every way. In other studies as well, commodities have been seen as an especially corruptive force among indigenous peoples. Reed (1995) noted that commodities are perceived as pulling people "deeper into the dark vortex of commercial activities and spewing them out on the other side of the ethnic boundary into the harsh light of national societies and the international economy" (p. 137).

Other scholars perceive tourism as affecting local identity through the conveyance of expectations. According to this view, tourists shape the outcome of touristic encounters by giving preference to locals who look and behave in ways that are authentically indigenous or ethnic. A problem here is that authenticity is a subjective concept, and tourists often define for themselves what is authentic, relying on popular stereotypes as points of reference rather than on historical or ethnographic facts (Adams 1984, Crick 1989). Boorstin (1964) described encounters between tourists and locals as "pseudo-events" that are based on what tourists choose to see rather than on what is really there. What tourists choose to see is, in turn, strongly influenced by the marketing efforts of tour operators (Silver 1993), the popular media (Urry 1990), and the state (Volkman 1990). In an analysis of travel brochures, Rossel (1988, p. 5) found "exaggerations, misleading statements, and lies" that provided a certain way of understanding the reality, and that offered the "tourist view." Adams (1984, p. 470) has argued that brochures and travel agents essentially provide tourists with a first glimpse of the locals through "prepackaged ethnic stereotypes," which later are either reified or dismantled during the tourists' journeys. Especially in developing countries, the state has also played a key role in framing ethnicity for tourism, partly as a way to build national solidarity, and partly as a strategy to attract foreign tourists (Matthews & Richter 1991).

In theory, tourists' stereotypes are transmitted to locals through what Urry (1990, 1996) has called "the tourist gaze." A simplistic rendering of this idea is that tourists wield power through the way they look at locals and expect them to appear and behave. In turn, locals acquiesce to the gaze by mirroring back images they hope will please tourists. The long-term implication is that locals will maintain, or at least act out, traditions they are sure will satisfy and attract more tourists. MacCannell (1984) has referred to this process as "reconstructing ethnicity." Indeed, locals may consciously try to match visitors' expectations of what is authentic, even if the results seem contrived or fake. Evans-Pritchard (1989) wrote of a Native American woman who felt she had to "look 'Indian' in order to be accepted as authentic by the tourists on whose dollars she depends" (p. 97). Cohen (1979, p. 18) described locals who "play the natives" to live up to the tourists' image.

This "playing up" has not always been described by anthropologists as a negative trend. If the tourist gaze does indeed have power to act as a mirror and, ultimately, transform the identity of the people gazed on, then, some scholars argue, tourism has as much potential to revive old values as it does to destroy them. Smith (1982), for example, has found that tourism may "serve to reinforce ethnic identity" (p. 26). Also, Mansperger (1995) suggested that tourism "can help native people maintain their identity" (p. 92). Van den Berghe (1994) wrote that tourism can lead to "a renaissance of native cultures or the recreation of ethnicity" (p. 17). Tourism then can become an empowering vehicle of self-representation, and locals may purposely choose to reinvent themselves through time, modifying how they are seen and perceived by different groups of outsiders (Cohen 1988).

Two studies from the 1980s exemplify well how locals may consciously alter their appearance to please tourists. In one, Gamper (1981) found that people in southern Austria began to change their clothes for tourism. In normal routines, locals were wearing outfits typical of any other place in Europe, but during the tourist season, people became conscious of the need to don traditional costumes. Yet even the costumes were adjusted. Though originally brown, black, and white, a bright red vest was added later because, as one informant explained, "[r]ed looks better on Kodachrome" (p. 439). In another study, Albers & James (1983) examined 600 postcard images of Native Americans issued between 1900 and 1970. They discovered that the images changed with the growth of tourism in the American West, and that representations of Indians were increasingly tailored to match tourists' expectations. The most striking change was the disappearance of images that showed Indians in their normal surroundings and everyday dress. Increasingly, the pictures conformed to a stereotypic image, "derived from the equestrian, buffalo-hunting, and tipi-dwelling Indians of the nineteenth century" (p. 136) (see also Mamiya 1992).

Turning Back the Gaze

Anthropologists have argued that host-guest interactions tend to be asymmetrical in terms of power, and that guests have the upper hand in determining how any given encounter will unfold. Further, ethnographic accounts have shown that the gaze of tourists can be especially influential in determining how hosts look, behave, and feel. Generally, hosts are portrayed in these interactions as passive, unable to influence events, as if they themselves were somehow physically locked in the gaze. Missing in these analyses is the possibility that locals can, and often do, play a role in determining what happens in their encounters with tourists. A notable exception is found in the ethnographic work of Silverman (2001), who has consciously foregrounded the abilities of the Iatmul people of Papua New Guinea "to act with intention and strategy," and to exercise creativity in the context of their interactions with outsiders (p. 105).

Also missing from many current analyses is an attempt to learn more about the dynamics of host-guest interactions by observing and talking with people on both sides of the encounter. Evans-Pritchard (1989) noted that academics have largely ignored the subject of how locals perceive outsiders. Although a vast literature exists on the subject of local responses to social changes wrought by tourists, relatively few studies have explored the attitudes and ideas of local residents toward outsiders.

Kincaid (1988) took an important step toward filling the gap by writing plainly and explicitly about her anger and resentment toward tourists who visit the Caribbean island of Antigua. Kincaid is an Antiguan herself, and her prose emanates from an insiders' perspective. It is not surprising that her depiction of Antigua is at odds with the ones often found in tourism brochures. She writes, "[T]he Antigua that I knew, the Antigua in which I grew up, is not the Antigua you, a tourist, would see now" (1988, p. 23). With acerbic wit, she assures Antigua's visitors, "[Y]ou needn't let that slightly funny feeling you have from time to time about exploitation, oppression, domination develop into full-fledged unease, discomfort; you could ruin your holiday" (p. 10). It is strange that comments such as these from people in host destinations, though laden with meaning, are largely absent from the literature.

In her own research, Evans-Pritchard found that Native Americans often use ethnic-based humor to ridicule tourists, burlesquing outsiders by "exaggerating the already overblown stereotypes of a group " (1989, p. 96; see also Laxson 1991). In another study, Howell (1994) observed that locals can reap enjoyment from toying with tourists who are "relatively ignorant of local conditions, and thus often appear incompetent, ridiculous, gullible, and eminently exploitable" (p. 152). In addition to "toying with tourists," locals may be active agents in determining what they want to preserve, purposely inventing traditions and/or folk art for tourists, yet entirely cognizant themselves of what is real or staged, authentic or spurious. Evans-Pritchard (1989) learned that Indian silversmiths often use traditional figures and symbols to create the right aesthetic effect for their pieces. Yet they also make up stories about the art, consciously capitalizing on the tourists' hopes to find meaning and cultural significance in everything they see. This enterprising behavior seems to contradict the notion that locals are passive victims, caught unaware as they lose themselves and their culture to commodification and the intrusive gaze of outsiders.

Even in cases where local hosts are changing aspects of their identity or their lives to appeal to tourists, they may not necessarily be losing their culture or their ability to judge for themselves what is spurious and genuine. To the contrary, local hosts may feel empowered by interactions with outsiders to redefine who they are and what aspects of their identity they wish to highlight or downplay. In the midst of reviving the past or inventing traditions, locals may be quite conscious of the fact that they are presenting cultural displays to tourists and not exposing the truly meaningful symbols and rituals of their private and "backstage" lives.

Davis (1997) used ethnographic methods to reveal how Sea World produces very carefully controlled experiences and images for visitors. In adopting a hosts' perspective—in this case, a large corporate host—Davis has presented a potential model for how other researchers might explore tourism in smaller host communities around the world. Questions might include, What are locals consciously doing to manipulate certain kinds of images or evoke particular feelings among their guests? An example of this kind of work is Adams (1995), who has examined how the Torajan people of Indonesia have manipulated tourism for their own political ends. For years, the Torajans have been studied and scrutinized both by tourists and anthropologists. Adams found that the local response to such global attention has been to capitalize on it as a means to achieve local objectives. Appropriately, Adams describes the Torajans as "active strategists" and "ingenious cultural politicians" in the context of tourism.

With only a few exceptions, research in the anthropology of tourism has over-looked the origins and motivations of tourism from the hosts' perspective. Although many anthropologists have eloquently portrayed the ways in which tourism has changed the lives of locals, we have neglected to turn the analysis around and to imagine how hosts might be affecting guests. This trend may change as we shift away from assuming that tourism is always imposed on passive and powerless people. Even in cases where the forced and exploitative nature of tourism is irrefutable, we may begin to probe more deeply into understanding how locals themselves are perceiving the imposition, rather than continuing to rely on our own perspectives as anthropologists.

ALTERNATIVE FORMS OF TOURISM

In the 1970s and 1980s, review articles on the study of tourism often asked why anthropologists were avoiding tourism as a legitimate subject of analysis. Today, the question might be the opposite: Why are anthropologists paying so much attention to alternative forms of tourism? Especially in the past decade, tourism has gained a much more positive reputation among social scientists, environmental conservationists, development practitioners, and indigenous rights activists. This is because an expanding group of new tourism companies, often in partnership with nongovernmental organizations, now claims to go easy on the environment and on indigenous peoples, even as they strive for profit. These companies label their excursions variously as "ecotourism," "community-based tourism," "cultural tourism," or simply "alternative tourism."

Generally defined, alternative tourism includes "forms of tourism that are consistent with natural, social, and community values, and which allow both hosts and guests to enjoy positive and worthwhile interaction and shared experiences" (Eadington & Smith 1992, p. 3). This new brand of tourism has grabbed the attention of scholars concerned with recent agendas to link conservation and development (e.g., Guillen 1998, Lamont 1999, Sills 1998, Stronza 2000, Wildes 1998). At least a couple of new journals, including the *Journal of Ecotourism* and the *Journal of Sustainable Tourism*, have begun to focus on the possibilities and limitations of alternative tourism. In general, the literature seems more balanced than did earlier research on tourism. At least anthropologists are not automatically condemning the impacts of tourism on local communities. If anything, perhaps the scale has tilted in the other direction. Now the tendency seems to be to applaud tourism as a panacea for achieving a wide array of social, economic, and environmental goals. Munt (1994) observed that "[w]hile mass tourism has attracted trenchant criticism as a shallow and degrading experience for Third World host nations and peoples, new tourism practices have been viewed benevolently" (p. 50).

Ecotourism has gained a lion's share of the attention aimed at alternative travel. An early publication on ecotourism commissioned by the U.S.-based environmental group, Conservation International, identified ecotourism as "a form of tourism inspired primarily by the natural history of an area, including its indigenous cultures" (Ziffer 1989). In the ideal scenario, ecotourists' nonconsumptive use of and appreciation for the natural and cultural resources of an area can contribute attention and revenue to local conservation efforts while also providing economic opportunities to local residents (Sherman & Dixon 1991). This linkage of goals has also meant that the applied research of anthropologists has become critical to the planning and implementation of tourism projects around the world.

Conservationists are both optimistic and skeptical that ecotourism may help protect nature while meeting the economic needs of local residents (Barkin 1996, Boo 1990, Cater & Lowman 1994, Honey 1999, Lindberg 1991, Lindberg & Enriquez 1994, Orams 1999, Whelan 1991). Relative to other activities, such as hunting, logging, or agriculture, ecotourism seems to have a low impact on ecosystems (Groom et al 1991, Kusler 1991), and ideally revenues from ecotourism may be channeled into conservation and local development needs. But critics counter that too much ecotourism, particularly if it is unmonitored and unregulated, may spoil natural areas and disturb both wildlife and people (Begley 1996, Giannecchini 1993). Some also fear that the rhetoric of ecotourism is a guise for business as usual. Vickers (1997) has stressed that "much of what passes for 'ecotourism' is comprised of business ventures whose aim is to maximize the profits of tourist agencies and professional guides" (p. 1). The implication is that the quest for profits occludes any intention to protect nature or improve the lives of local people.

In the midst of the debates over the good and bad of ecotourism, the themes of local participation and local ownership of touristic infrastructure have assumed new importance (Eadington & Smith 1992). Increasingly, local communities are joining in partnerships with government agencies, nongovernmental organizations, and private tour companies to plan tourism strategies and develop new attractions for visitors. As a result, local hosts are gaining much more control over how tourism affects their communities.

Despite the new attention on alternative tourism and local decision making in tourism, the same conceptual and analytical weakness found in studies on conventional tourism remain. Advocates of ecotourism, for example, are focused on the notion that appropriate kinds of tourism will lead to positive impacts for local communities and ecosystems, and that particular touristic inputs will result in the most desirable outcomes both for people and natural areas. The ecotourism literature is filled with guidelines and "best practices" for achieving success (Ceballos-Lascurain 1996). A collection of papers presented at the Yale School of Forestry's Conference on Ecotourism (Miller & Malek-Zadeh 1996), for example, focused on "strategies" and "parameters of success" for developing ecotourism projects. The ideas are generally prescriptive, arguing that if the ecotourism industry were to provide the right inputs, such as "a participatory approach," then the negative impacts of tourism on local hosts could be reduced. The emphasis remains, however, on what is external to a site, rather than on what the existing conditions might reveal about whether tourism will have a positive or negative impact on local residents.

Just as we lack an understanding of how hosts participate in the origins of conventional tourism, we also know relatively little about how and why local hosts get involved in ecotourism. Although locals may not be financing new infrastructure or negotiating directly with international travel agencies, they are nevertheless affecting what happens on the ground in many ecotourism sites. In cases where locals are opposed to ecotourism, for example, they may express their opposition by vandalizing infrastructure. Also, by hunting or clearing trails in areas around an ecolodge, locals can sabotage the image of pristine nature many ecotourism lodges promote. Bennett (1999) described a case in Panama in which members of the Kuna protested outsiders' investment in tourism by burning a hotel twice, and attacking one of the hotel owners. Belsky (1999) wrote about a similar example in the village of Maya Center in Belize, where the locals burned a handicraft center.

Local residents can also decide the fate of an ecotourism operation by playing competitor companies off on each other, setting the conditions under which they will tolerate or welcome the influx of tourists. If several companies are competing for the same acceptance of a community, they may become involved in battles over who can provide the best benefits, a situation in which the locals are determining, to some extent, the operating costs of the companies. In these ways, local hosts can influence the success or failure of tourism, regardless of the external inputs and intentions of outsider consultants.

From Both Sides Now

In current efforts to make tourism participatory and to involve local residents as decision makers in tourism projects, anthropologists can make a significant contribution to the field by focusing more attention on the reasons local residents choose to, or are able to, become involved in tourism. This information will be important if we consider that the right external inputs are probably necessary, but not sufficient for ensuring the benefits of tourism for locals. Prevailing conditions, such as the structure of local political and economic institutions, ethnic relations, gender stereotypes, and the subsistence labor obligations of local would-be hosts may be particularly relevant.

A few scholars have already advanced hypotheses about local conditions most conducive to successful community based tourism. For example, Smith (1989) wrote, "Tourism is especially favored where significant segments of the population have minimal education or technical skills, inasmuch as other industries may require extensive training" (p. xi). In 1996, King & Stewart (1996) hypothesized that "[p]ositive impacts of ecotourism are likely to be the greatest when the indigenous culture is already in a state of decline as a result of natural resources scarcity" (p. 299). These are precisely the kinds of assumptions we may want to explore in the future. Although we now have many solid descriptive analyses of what happens when tourism is introduced to communities, we lack comparison across sites to analyze both the internal and external factors that determine why we find certain kinds of interactions with tourism in particular settings.

As with conventional tourism, we also lack information about the impacts of ecotourism on tourists. Researchers have invested considerable effort into the impacts of ecotourism on hosts, and much hope is pinned on the possibility that ecotourism will provide the economic incentive for hosts to maintain and protect the natural sites and cultural traditions tourists come to see. Less effort has been invested in analyzing the incentives ecotourism offers to tourists to change their own perspectives and behaviors. This gap in the research exists despite the fact that a significant goal of ecotourism is to raise environmental and cultural awareness among tourists.

We do not know, for example, what kinds of travel heightens consciousness or educates people in particular ways. We do know a lot about how tourists feel in terms of their accommodations—most companies request posttravel evaluations— but we do not know how their thoughts, feelings, or behaviors change as a result of what they have seen in host destinations. We could ask many questions related to this issue. For example, do ecotourists consider running less tap water at home once they have seen how difficult it is for people to collect water in remote destinations they have visited? Do they begin to recycle more often? More fundamentally, do their values change? What kinds of impressions are generated from different kinds of touristic experiences? How can tourism and recreation be linked more explicitly with learning? Despite the relevance of these questions to the goals of alternative tourism, we are lacking studies that track the attitudes, much less the behaviors, of tourists before and after they have traveled to a host site. Two models for how we might proceed come from Orams (1997) and Jacobson (1995).

CONCLUSION

I have discussed the reasons tourism can be a fascinating subject of study for anthropologists. Despite its association with things shallow and frivolous, tourism is relevant to many theoretical and real-world issues in anthropology. For people in host destinations, tourism is often the catalyst of significant economic and social change, the context for cross-cultural encounters, and the stage-like setting for displays and recreations of culture and tradition. For the tourists, tourism can be a ritual form of escape from the structure of everyday life, or it can represent a symbolic quest for the kinds of authentic experiences that elude modern society. For anthropologists, tourism can be a lens through which to explore issues of political economy, social change and development, natural resource management, and cultural identity and expression. Current scholarship on tourism is somewhat lopsided. In examining the origins of tourism—what motivates tourists to travel, and what determines where they go—anthropologists have focused significant attention on tourists, almost to the exclusion of locals. As a result, we know little about the motivations of people in host destinations to become involved in tourism, or to promote certain kinds of tourism over others. Too often, we have assumed that tourism is imposed on hosts rather than invited.

In exploring the impacts of tourism, anthropologists have tilted in the opposite direction. Researchers have analyzed extensively, usually by way of ethnography, the impacts of tourism on hosts, and we have many case studies describing the effects of tourism on the economy and on the cultural identity of hosts. But we are lacking information about the impacts tourism can have on guests. Too often, we have assumed that hosts are relatively passive and that their disadvantaged position under the powerful gaze of tourists precludes locals from shaping the encounters with tourists.

An interest in alternative forms of tourism, particularly ecotourism, has boomed in recent years. Proponents have posited that the participation of local residents can be critical to maximizing economic, environmental, and social benefits of tourism. Despite this attention to the active role of local residents, researchers tend to emphasize the importance of external inputs, rather than on the prevailing motivations or constraints of locals, to enhance the success of tourism. Advocates for ecotourism have also suggested that tourism can be educational for tourists, and that the right kinds of touristic experiences can result in increased environmental awareness and cultural sensitivity among tourists. Although we are optimistic about the possibility of raising consciousness through tourism, few scholars have analyzed how tourists' attitudes actually do change as a result of particular kinds of experiences.

The goal of future anthropological research in tourism should be to fill the gaps in our current understanding. We should know the full story of what happens to both hosts and guests throughout all stages of their journeys and cross-cultural interactions. This will be especially true as we strive to develop the kinds of tourism that can generate a range of benefits for hosts as well as educational and transformative experiences for guests.

ACKNOWLEDGMENTS

I am grateful to Irma McClaurin, Marianne Schmink, Ricardo Godoy, and Russell Bernard for valuable comments on an earlier version of this paper. I have also benefited greatly from discussions with the students in my Fall 2000 course, "Anthropology of Tourism and Ecotourism" at Stanford.

Visit the Annual Reviews home page at www.AnnualReviews.org

LITERATURE CITED

Adams KM. 1984. Come to Tana Toraja, "Land of the Heavenly Kings": Travel agents as brokers in ethnicity. *Ann. Tour. Res.* 11:469–85

Adams KM. 1995. Making-up the Toraja? The appropriation of tourism, anthropology, and museums for politics in upland Sulawesi, Indonesia. *Ethnology* 34:143–54

Adler J. 1989. Origins of sightseeing. *Ann. Tour. Res.* 16:7–29

Albers PC, James WR. 1983. Tourism and the changing photographic image of the Great Lakes Indians. *Ann. Tour. Res.* 10:123–48

Barkin D. 1996. Ecotourism: a tool for sustainable development in an era of international integration? See Miller & Malek-Zadeh 1996, pp. 263–72

Begley S. 1996. Beware of the humans (ecotourism is hurting ecosystems). *Newsweek* 127:52–54

Belsky JM. 1999. Misrepresenting communities: the politics of community-based rural ecotourism in Gales Point Manatee, Belize. *Rural Sociol.* 64:641–66

Bendix R. 1989. Tourism and cultural displays: inventing traditions for whom? *J. Am. Folk.* 102:131–46

Bennett J. 1999. The dream and the reality: tourism in Kuna Yala. *Cult. Surviv. Q.* 23:33–35

Boo E. 1990. *Ecotourism: The Potentials and Pitfalls*, Vol. 1. Washington, DC: World Wildlife Fund

Bookbinder MP, Dinerstein E, Rijal A, Cauley H, Rajouria A. 1998. Ecotourism's support of biodiversity conservation. *Conserv. Biol.* 12:1399–404

Boorstin D. 1964. *The Image: A Guide to Pseudo-Events in America*. New York: Harper & Row

Bruner EM. 1987. Of cannibals, tourists, and ethnographers. *Cult. Anthropol.* 4:438–45

Bruner EM. 1991. Transformation of self in tourism. *Ann. Tour. Res.* 18:238–50

Bruner EM, Kirshenblatt-Gimblett B. 1994. Maasai on the lawn: tourist realism in East Africa. *Cult. Anthropol.* 9:435–70

Burns PM. 1999. *An Introduction to Tourism and Anthropology*. London: Routledge

Castner J. 1990. Pay your respects to the rainforest. *Sierra* 75:82–84

Cater E, Lowman G, eds. 1994. *Ecotourism: A Sustainable Option?* Chichester, UK: Wiley

Ceballos-Lascurain H. 1996. *Tourism, Ecotourism, and Protected Areas: the State of Nature-Based Tourism Around the World and Guidelines for its Development*. Gland, Switzerland: Int. Union Conserv. Nat.

Chambers E, ed. 1997. *Tourism and Culture: An Applied Perspective*. New York: State Univ. NY

Chambers E. 1999. *Native Tours: The Anthropology of Travel and Tourism*. Prospect Heights, IL: Waveland

Chicchón A. 1995. Gestión de Bases: Experiencias y propuestas sobre la participación de poblaciones indígenas en la operación turística en la Amazonía peruana. *Med. Ambient.*, Feb:19–21

Cohen E. 1972. Towards a sociology of international tourism. *Soc. Res.* 39:164–82

Cohen E. 1974. Who is a tourist?: a conceptual clarification. *Soc. Rev.* 22:527–55

Cohen E. 1979. The impact of tourism on the Hill Tribes of Northern Thailand. *Int. Asienforum* 10:5–38

Cohen E. 1984. The sociology of tourism: approaches, issues and findings. *Annu. Rev. Sociol.* 10:373–92

Cohen E. 1988. Authenticity and commoditization in tourism. *Ann. Tour. Res.* 15:371–86

Crandall R. 1980. Motivations for leisure. *J. Leis. Res.* 12:45–54

Crick M. 1989. Representations of international tourism in the social sciences: sun, sex, sights, savings, and servility. *Annu. Rev. Anthropol.* 18:307–44

Dann G. 1981. Tourist motivation: an appraisal. *Ann. Tour. Res.* 8:187–219

Davis SG. 1997. *Spectacular Nature: Corporate Culture and the Sea World Experience*. Berkeley: Univ. Calif. Press

de Kadt E, ed. 1979. *Tourism: Passport to Development?* New York: Oxford Univ. Press

Desmond J. 1999. *Staging Tourism*. Chicago: Univ. Chicago Press

Dobkin de Rios M. 1994. Drug tourism in the Amazon: why Westerners are desperate to find the vanishing primitive. *Omni* 16:6

Eadington WR, Smith VL, eds. 1992. *Tourism Alternatives: Potentials and Problems in the Development of Tourism*. Philadelphia: Univ. Penn. Press

Epler Wood M. 1998. *Meeting the Global Challenge of Community Participation in*

Ecotourism: Case Studies and Lessons from Ecuador, Work. Pap. No. 2. Washington, DC: Am. Verde, Lat. Am./Carib. Div., US-AID/TNC

Erisman HM. 1983. Tourism and cultural dependency in the West Indies. *Ann. Tour. Res.* 10:337–61

Evans-Pritchard D. 1989. How "they" see "us": Native American images of tourists. *Ann. Tour. Res.* 16:89–105

Gamper J. 1981. Tourism in Austria: a case study of the influence of tourism on ethnic relations. *Ann. Tour. Res.* 8:432–46

Giannecchini J. 1993. Ecotourism: new partners, new relationships. *Conserv. Biol.* 7:429–32

Graburn N. 1983. The anthropology of tourism. *Ann. Tour. Res.* 10:9–33

Graburn N. 1989. Tourism: the sacred journey. See Smith 1989, pp. 21–36

Greenwood DJ. 1977. Tourism as an agent of change: a Spanish Basque case. *Ann. Tour. Res.* 3:128–42

Greenwood DJ. 1989. Culture by the pound: an anthropological perspective on tourism as cultural commoditization. See Smith 1989, pp. 171–85

Groom MA, Podolsky RD, Munn CA. 1991. Tourism as a sustained use of wildlife: a case study of Madre de Dios, Southeastern Peru. In *Neotropical Wildlife Use and Conservation*, ed. JG Robinson, KH Redford, pp. 393–412. Chicago: Univ. Chicago Press

Guillen HA. 1998. *Sustainability of ecotourism and traditional agricultural practices in Chiapas, Mexico.* PhD thesis. Univ. Florida, Gainesville, Fla. 248 pp.

Hall CM. 1994. *Tourism and Politics: Policy, Power and Place.* West Sussex, UK: Wiley

Hall CM, Johnston ME, eds. 1995. *Polar Tourism: Tourism in the Arctic and Antarctic Regions.* New York: Wiley

Harkin M. 1995. Modernist anthropology and tourism of the authentic. *Ann. Tour. Res.* 25:650–70

Honey M. 1999. *Ecotourism and Sustainable Development: Who Owns Paradise?* Washington, DC: Island

Howell BJ. 1994. Weighing the risks and rewards of involvement in cultural conservation and heritage tourism. *Hum. Org.* 53:150–59

Int. Ecotourism Soc. 1998. *Ecotourism Statistical Fact Sheet.* North Bennington, VT: Int. Ecotour. Soc.

Jacobson SK, ed. 1995. *Conserving Wildlife: International Education and Communication Approaches.* New York: Columbia Univ. Press

Jafari J. 1977. Editor's page. *Ann. Tour. Res.* 5:6–11

Jafari J. 1990. Research and scholarship: the basis of tourism education. *J. Tour. Stud.* 1:33–41

Jayal MM, ed. 1986. *Conservation, Tourism, and Mountaineering in the Himalayas.* Dehra Dun: Natraj

Kincaid J. 1988. *A Small Place.* New York: Penguin

King DA, Stewart WP. 1996. Ecotourism and commodification: protecting people and places. *Biodivers. Conserv.* 5:293–305

Kinnaird V, Hall D. 1994. Conclusion: the way forward. In *Tourism: A Gender Analysis*, ed. V Kinnaird, D Hall, pp. 210–16. Sussex, UK: Wiley

Kirshenblatt-Gimblett B. 1998. *Destination Culture: Tourism, Museums, and Heritage.* Berkeley: Univ. Calif. Press

Kusler JA, ed. 1991. *Ecotourism and Resource Conservation: A Collection of Papers from the 1st International Symposium.* Berne, NY: Ecotour. & Resource Conserv. Proj.

Lamont SR. 1999. *The effects of ecotourism on plant resource use and management in Amazonian Peru.* PhD thesis. Miami Univ., Miami, FL. 252 pp.

Lanfant M-F, Allcock JB, Bruner EM, eds. 1995. *International Tourism: Identity and Change.* London: Sage

Laxson JD. 1991. How "we" see "them": tourism and Native Americans. *Ann. Tour. Res.* 18:365–391

Leong WT. 1989. Culture and the state: manufacturing traditions for tourism. *Crit. Stud. Mass Commun.* 6:355–75

Lett J. 1989. Epilogue. In *Hosts and Guests: An Anthropology of Tourism*, ed. V. Smith, pp. 275–79. Pittsburgh, PA: Univ. Penn. Press

Levy DE, Lerch PB. 1991. Tourism as a factor in development: implications for gender and work in Barbados. *Gend. Soc.* 5:67–85

Lindberg K. 1991. *Economic Policies for Maximizing Nature Tourism's Contribution to Sustainable Development.* Washington, DC: World Resour. Inst.

Lindberg K, Enriquez J. 1994. *An Analysis of Ecotourism's Economic Contribution to Conservation and Development in Belize.* Washington, DC: World Wildlife Fund

Linden E. 1991. Taking a guided tour through Eden. *Time* 137:80–81

Lippard LR. 1999. *On the Beaten Track: Tourism, Art and Place.* New York: New Press

Lofgren O. 1999. *On Holiday: A History of Vacationing.* Berkeley: Univ. Calif. Press

MacCannell D. 1976. *The Tourist.* New York: Schocken. 2nd ed.

MacCannell D. 1984. Reconstructed ethnicity tourism and cultural identity in third world communities. *Ann. Tour. Res.* 11:375–91

MacCannell D. 1992. *Empty Meeting Grounds: The Tourist Papers.* New York: Routledge

Machlis GE, Burch WR. 1983. Relations between strangers: cycles of structure and meaning in tourist systems. *Sociol. Rev.* 31:666–92

Mamiya CJ. 1992. Greetings from paradise: the representation of Hawaiian culture in postcards. *J. Commun. Inq.* 16:86–102

Mansperger MC. 1995. Tourism and cultural change in small-scale societies. *Hum. Org.* 54:87–94

McEachern J. 1995. *Prospects for Tourism in Manaslu.* Gland, Switz.: IUCN–World Conserv. Union

McLaren D. 1997. *Rethinking Tourism and Ecotravel: The Paving of Paradise and What You Can Do to Stop It.* West Hartford, CN: Kumarian

Matthews HG, Richter LK. 1991. Political Sciences and tourism. *Ann. Tour. Res.* 18:120–35

Miller JA, Malek-Zadeh E, eds. 1996. *The Ecotourism Equation: Measuring the Impacts.* New Haven, CT: Yale Univ. Press

Munt I. 1994. Eco-tourism or ego-tourism? *Race Class* 36:49–60

Nash D. 1981. Tourism as an anthropological subject. *Curr. Anthropol.* 22:461–81

Nash D. 1989. Tourism as a form of imperialism. See Smith 1989, pp. 171–85

Nash D. 1996. *Anthropology of Tourism.* New York: Pergamon

Nash D, Smith VL. 1991. Anthropology and tourism. *Ann. Tour. Res.* 18:12–25

Nuñez T. 1989. Touristic studies in anthropological perspective. See Smith 1989, pp. 265–79

Nuñez TA. 1963. Tourism, tradition, and acculturation: weekendismo in a Mexican village. *Ethnology* 2:347–52

Oliver-Smith A. 1989. Tourist development and struggle for local resource control. *Hum. Org.* 48:345–52

Oppermann M, ed. 1998. *Sex Tourism and Prostitution: Aspects of Leisure, Recreation, and Work.* New York: Cognizant Commun. Corp.

Orams M. 1999. *Marine Tourism: Development, Impacts and Management.* London: Routledge

Orams MB. 1997. The effectiveness of environmental education: Can we turn tourists into "greenies"? *Progr. Tour. Hospit. Res.* 3:295–306

Pearce PL. 1982. *The Social Psychology of Tourist Behavior.* Oxford: Pergamon

Picard M. 1990. Cultural tourism in Bali: cultural performance as tourist attractions. *Indonesia* 49:37–47

Redfoot D. 1984. Touristic authenticity, touristic angst, and modern reality. *Qual. Sociol.* 7:291–309

Reed R. 1995. Household ethnicity, household consumption: commodities and the Guaraní. *Econ. Dev. Cult. Change* 44:129–45

Richter L. 1982. *Land Reform and Tourism Development. Policy-making in the Philippines.* Cambridge, MA: Schenkman

Rogers T. 1998. Space tourism: a response to

continuing decay in US civil space financial support. *Space Policy* 14:79–81

Rosenberg H. 1988. *A Negotiated World.* Toronto: Univ. Toronto Press

Rossel P. 1988. *Tourism: Manufacturing the Exotic.* Copenhagen: IWGIA

Schwartz R. 1997. *Pleasure Island: Tourism and Temptation in Cuba.* Lincoln: Univ. Nebr. Press

Seiler-Baldinger A. 1988. Tourism in the Upper Amazon and its effects on the indigenous population. In *Tourism: Manufacturing the Exotic*, ed P Rossel, pp. 177–93. Copenhagen: IWGIA

Sherman PB, Dixon JA. 1991. The economics of nature tourism: determining if it pays. See Whelan 1991, pp. 89–131

Sills EO'D. 1998. *Ecotourism as an integrated conservation and development strategy: econometric estimation of demand by international tourists and impacts on indigenous households on Siberut Island, Indonesia.* PhD thesis. Duke Univ., Durham, NC. 324 pp.

Silver I. 1993. Marketing authenticity in third world countries. *Ann. Tour. Res.* 20:302–18

Silverman EK. 2001. Tourism in the Sepik River of Papua New Guinea: favoring the local over the global. *Pac. Tour. Rev.* 4:105–19

Smith V. 1982. Tourism to Greenland: renewed ethnicity? *Cult. Surviv. Q.* 6:27

Smith V, ed. 1989. *Hosts and Guests: The Anthropology of Tourism.* Philadelphia: Univ. Penn. Press. 2nd ed.

Stonich SC. 2000. *The Other Side of Paradise: Tourism, Conservation, and Development in the Bay Islands.* New York: Cognizant Commun. Corp.

Stronza A. 2000. *"Because it is Ours:" Community-Based Ecotourism in the Peruvian Amazon.* PhD thesis. Univ. Florida, Gainesville, Fla. 229 pp.

Swain MB. 1989. Gender roles in indigenous tourism: Kuna Mola, Kuna Yala, and cultural survival. See Smith 1989, pp. 83–104

Swain MB. 1995. Gender in tourism. *Ann. Tour. Res.* 22:247–66

Towner J. Wall G. 1991. History and tourism. *Ann. Tour. Res.* 18:71–84.

Turner V. 1969. *The Ritual Process: Structure and Anti-structure.* Chicago: Aldine

Turner V. 1974. *Dramas, Fields, and Metaphors: Symbolic Action in Human Society.* Ithaca, NY: Cornell Univ. Press

Turner V. 1982. *From Ritual to Theater: The Human Seriousness of Play.* New York: Perform. Arts J.

Turner V, Turner E. 1978. *Image and Pilgrimage in Christian Culture: Anthropological Perspectives.* New York: Columbia Univ. Press

Urry J. 1990. *The Tourist Gaze: Leisure and Travel in Contemporary Societies.* London: Sage

Urry J. 1996. Tourism, culture and social inequality. In *The Sociology of Tourism: Theoretical and Empirical Investigations*, ed. Y Apostolopoulos, S Leivadi, A Yiannakis, pp. 115–33. New York: Routledge

Van den Berghe P. 1994. *The Quest for the Other: Ethnic Tourism in San Cristóbal, Mexico.* Seattle: Univ. Wash. Press

Vaughan D. 2000. Tourism and biodiversity: a convergence of interests? *Int. Aff.* 76:283–98

Vickers WT. 1997. *The new invaders: Siona-Secoya responses to thirty years of tourism.* Presented at 20th Int. Congr. Latin Am. Stu. Assoc., Guadalajara, Mexico, April 18

Vidas D. 1993. *Antarctic Tourism: A Challenge to the Legitimacy of the Antarctic Treaty System?* New York: United Nations

Volkman TA. 1990. Visions and revisions: Toraja culture and the tourist gaze. *Am. Ethnol.* 17:91–111

Whelan T, ed. 1991. *Nature Tourism: Managing for the Environment.* Washington, DC: Island

Wildes FT. 1998. *Influence of ecotourism on conservation policy for sustainable development: the case of Costa Rica.* PhD thesis. Univ. Calif., Santa Barbara. 372 pp.

Wilkinson PF, Pratiwi W. 1995. Gender and tourism in an Indonesian village. *Ann. Tour. Res.* 22:283–99

World Tour. Org. 2000. *Tourism Highlights 2000.* Madrid: WTO. 2nd ed.

Wunder S. 1999. *Promoting Forest Conservation Through Ecotourism Income? A Case Study from the Ecuadorian Amazon Region.* Bogor, Indonesia: Cent. Int. Forest. Res.

Young EH. 1999. Balancing conservation with development in small-scale fisheries: Is ecotourism an empty promise. *Hum. Ecol.* 27:581–620

Ziffer K. 1989. *Ecotourism: The Uneasy Alliance.* Washington, DC: Conserv. Int.

Annu. Rev. Anthropol. 2001. 30:285–317

SOCIAL MOVEMENTS: Changing Paradigms and Forms of Politics

Marc Edelman

Hunter College and the Graduate Center, City University of New York, New York,
New York 10021; e-mail: medelman@shiva.hunter.cuny.edu

Key Words   collective action, protest, resistance, civil society, globalization

■ **Abstract**   Theories of collective action have undergone a number of paradigm shifts, from "mass behavior" to "resource mobilization," "political process," and "new social movements." Debates have centered on the applicability of these frameworks in diverse settings, on the periodization of collective action, on the divisive or unifying impact of identity politics, and on the appropriateness of political engagement by researchers. Transnational activist networks are developing new protest repertoires that challenge anthropologists and other scholars to rethink conventional approaches to social movements.

INTRODUCTION

The worldwide political effervescence of "the long 1960s" (Isserman & Kazin 2000) contributed to a paradigm crisis in social scientific thinking about collective action. This prolonged decade of extraordinary upheaval in New York, Chicago, Berkeley, Paris, Rome, Berlin, Tokyo, Mexico City, Prague, Beijing, and elsewhere was the most intense period of grassroots mobilization since the 1930s. Civil rights and antiwar movements, youth and student rebellions, mobilizations in defense of regional autonomy and the environment and for the rights of women, gays and lesbians, the elderly, the disabled, and a host of other emergent groups, identities, and causes converged with an unprecedented wave of anticolonial and antiimperial insurgencies in poorer regions of the globe. Social scientists of various orientations concerned with geopolitics and revolution had ready-made categories ("national liberation," "subversion") for analyzing events in the "Third World." But the turmoil in the developed North highlighted the inadequacy of existing social scientific frameworks and gave rise to new and rich debates.

Even though anthropologists were well represented as participants in this tide of unrest and their 1960s sensibilities contributed to new conceptualizations of "interstitial politics" and of power, gender, colonialism, and the state (Vincent 1990), they remained to a large extent on the periphery of social scientific theorizing about collective action. One notable exception was the Vietnam-era agrarian studies tradition

0084-6570/01/1021-0285$14.00

(Roseberry 1995) pioneered by Wolf (1969), a work that was an outgrowth of the teach-in movement. In part, anthropologists' marginal involvement in discussions of collective action reflected an academic division of labor that assigned them peasants, the urban (especially Third World) poor, ethnic minorities, and millenarian or syncretic religious sects and allocated other types of mobilization (and national-level phenomena) to sociologists, political scientists, or historians. Also important by the mid-1980s, in the United States at least, was anthropologists' fascination with "everyday" as opposed to organized resistance and with microlevel analyses of power à la Foucault (Burdick 1995). Ethnographic research on social movements, moreover, tended to resist "grand theoretical" generalizations because close-up views of collective action often looked messy, with activist groups and coalitions forming, dividing, and reassembling and with significant sectors of their target constituencies remaining on the sidelines.

This article tells four long stories in a short space. The first is an account of the post-1960s paradigm shift in social scientific studies of collective action, which, though overly abbreviated and canonical, is necessary for examining the state of the field today and particularly what transpired when theory traveled beyond Europe and North America. The second is an appraisal of how ideas about periodization shaped competing post-1960s analytical frameworks. The third concerns the centrifugal and centripetal, or fragmenting and unifying, impacts of identity politics, the disproportionate attention social scientists devote to movements they like, and their infrequent efforts to theorize right-wing movements. The fourth story involves new developments in social movements themselves, particularly an intensifying transnational activism, a disenchantment on the part of diverse activists with identity politics, and a resurgence of varied kinds of struggles against inequality.

One of the most striking features of the collective action field is its continuing intellectual compartmentalization. Debates have tended to occur along parallel and disconnected tracks, reflecting different disciplinary personal networks and forms of socialization and inquiry and a major divide separating case study and grand theory practitioners. One recent effort at synthesis notes that scholars of revolutions, strikes, wars, social movements, ethnic mobilizations, democratization, and nationalism have paid little attention to each other's findings (McAdam et al 2001). Students of right-wing movements rarely engage theories about other kinds of collective action. Despite frequent gestures toward transgressing academic boundaries (and notwithstanding occasional successes), anthropologists on the one hand and sociologists and political scientists on the other have had little impact on or awareness of each other's efforts to understand social movements.[1]

---

[1]One of the few non–regionally focused anthologies on social movements edited by U.S. anthropologists is indicative of this mutual unfamiliarity, despite the inclusion of case studies—virtually all first-rate—from a range of disciplines. While it may be true that "the study of protest outside the industrial North is largely under-theorized" (Boudreau 1996, p. 175), Fox & Starn (1997) suggest—seemingly unaware of a substantial literature

A short article of broad scope can obviously invoke only some theorists and works (and movements). I emphasize recent work and allude sparingly to the "classics" of the field and more briefly than I would prefer (or not at all) to various relevant issues. Anthropologists, for reasons noted above, are less well represented than scholars from other disciplines. Geographically, the emphasis of this review is on the Americas and Europe, not because significant social movements have not occurred elsewhere, but because these have been prominent sites of pertinent theoretical production. Academic books and specialized journals—including those devoted to collective action studies, such as *Mobilization* and *Research in Social Movements, Conflicts and Change*—have been key fora for many debates. Because activists and scholars engage each other (and sometimes are each other), some of the most provocative analyses of social movements' visions, strategies, and practices appear in nonacademic media: hybrid activist-scholarly publications, small journals of opinion, 'zines, web pages, organizing handbooks, and manuals by those who seek to control particular kinds of movements.

A CONVENTIONAL STORY OF SHIFTING PARADIGMS

In the early 1970s, functionalism still held sway in U.S. sociology. Park and the Chicago School had, since the 1920s, juxtaposed "social organization"— institutionalized, conventional patterns of everyday life—to "collective behavior," a category that included crowds, "sects," fashions, and mass movements, all of which they saw as simultaneously symptoms of societal disequilibria and harbingers of new patterns of social relations (Park 1967). Smelser (1962) rejected the notion of "disequilibria" as "too strong" and attributed collective behavior to tensions that exceeded the capacity of a social system's homeostatic mechanisms and that constituted a source of new bases of Durkheimian-style solidarity. Related psychological theories explained the rise of totalitarianism as a mass response to economic crises and "magnetic leaders" by individuals with a "mob mentality" (Arendt 1951) or an "authoritarian character" (Fromm 1941). These theories about totalitarianism were of limited use in analyzing turmoil in largely democratic, affluent polities in the 1960s. Olson (1965) advanced a notion that remains a point of departure for much theorizing. An economist, Olson rejected theories based on the irrationality of individuals [although he also stated it would "be better to turn to psychology" than to economics to understand "fanatic" or "lunatic fringe" movements "in unstable countries" (1965, pp. 161–62)]. Instead, he posited individuals

---

on contentious politics—that "we still know relatively little about the ample and charged territory between the cataclysmic upheaval of revolutionary war and the small incidents of everyday resistance, . . . social struggles where people enter into open protest yet do not seek the total overthrow of the social order" (p. 3). Moreover, apart from a few individuals in each group whose work genuinely engages historical documentation and scholarship, the vast literature by historians on collective action tends to be surprisingly underutilized.

so rational they would not participate in collective endeavors—a rather odd premise for the turbulent 1960s—because each could benefit from others' activity as a "free rider," pursuing low-risk self-interest at the group's expense. Like the "tragedy of the commons" model, which was later criticized (Prakash 1998) as divorced from culture or—alternatively—as a caricature of a historically specific *homo economicus*, this perspective explained collective action as the sum of strategic decisions by individuals, who could only be induced to join a group effort through incentives or sanctions. Given the stability of North America and Western Europe and the high risks many 1960s activists assumed—arrests, police beatings, ruined careers— "rational choice" did not appear to be a promising avenue of interpretation

Marxism, still in or close to the mainstream in European universities in "the long 1960s," viewed conflict in capitalist societies as revolving around the fundamental contradiction between the bourgeoisie and the proletariat. In all but the most heterodox Marxist (Thompson 1971) tendencies, class interest and historical agency derived unproblematically from class position (although classes "in" and "of" themselves raised less easily resolved issues of consciousness and hegemony). This framework too was of little use in making sense of movements in the 1960s that frequently had largely middle-class leadership and multiclass constituencies.

By the mid-1970s, two distinct perspectives emerged that attempted to fill the apparent theoretical vacuum: the "identity-oriented" or European paradigm [also widely termed new social movements (NSMs)] and the "resource mobilization" or American paradigm (Cohen 1985, Della Porta & Diani 1999, Foweraker 1995, Garner 1997, Laraña et al 1994, McAdam et al 1996a). Neither comprised an entirely coherent "school," but for heuristic purposes the differences between them constitute a suitable, if conventional, point of departure.

For Touraine (1988), among the first and most prolific advocates of a NSMs approach, the issue of social movements has two dimensions, loosely derived from aspects of Marx's and Weber's thought. The first is the notion of a "central conflict" in society; for Marx, this was the struggle between labor and capital in industrial society. But, Touraine argues, with the passage to a "postindustrial" society, labor-capital conflict subsides, other social cleavages become more salient and generate new identities, and the exercise of power is less in the realm of work and more in "the setting of a way of life, forms of behavior, and needs" (1988, p. 25). The main Weberian element in Touraine's approach is the concept of "the actor" as key protagonist of "social action." In postindustrial society, diverse collectivities have a growing capacity to act on themselves and to struggle for "historicity"—"the set of cultural, cognitive, economic, and ethical models . . . through which social practices are constituted" (1988, pp. 40–41). Touraine thus posits the "way of life" as the focus of contention; struggles that seek to affect the relations of domination characteristic of the "way of life" (with its forms of knowledge, mores, and investment) are "social movements." He explicitly excludes from this category, however, forms of "collective behavior" that "defend" the social order or "social struggles" directed at the state. Melucci (1989) argued that social movements have three important dimensions: actors' recognition of commonalities and shared identities, objectives, and understandings; adversarial relations with opponents who claim the same goods or values; and actions that exceed the tolerance limits of a social system, thereby pushing it to change. Melucci did a doctorate under Touraine in the 1970s at the École Pratique des Hautes Études, but this definition suggests a move beyond his professor's stress on the structural preconditions of forms of collective action in postindustrial society. Instead, adopting Habermas's (1981) terminology (though not his emphasis on "defensive" movements), Melucci pointed to how the state and market rationalize the private sphere, generating new social groupings and collective action that illuminates "the silent and arbitrary elements of the dominant codes" and "publicizes new alternatives" (1989, p. 63).

Touraine, Melucci, and other advocates of NSMs theory (Laclau & Mouffe 1985) delineated characteristics they saw as particular to the NSMs and that contrasted with the "old" labor or working-class movement. Although the "old" labor movement upheld class as the primary social cleavage, category of analysis, organizational principle, and political issue, the NSMs emerge out of the crisis of modernity and focus on struggles over symbolic, informational, and cultural resources and rights to specificity and difference. Participation in NSMs is itself a goal, apart from any instrumental objectives, because everyday movement practices embody in embryonic form the changes the movements seek. The NSMs diffuse "social conflictuality to more and more numerous relations." This proliferation of "points of antagonism" produces "new social subjects" whose "multiple social positions" complicate interpretations of political agency based on a single, privileged principle of identity (Laclau & Mouffe 1985).

If NSMs theorists in Europe tended to explain collective action as a response to "claims," grievances, or postindustrial society, on the other side of the Atlantic a growing coterie of social scientists pointed out that the mere existence of discontent, which was presumably omnipresent, could not explain how movements arose in particular times and places. Several authors in particular (McCarthy & Zald 1977, Zald 1992, McAdam et al 1996b) argued for a focus on "resource mobilization." This "strategy-oriented" paradigm (Cohen 1985) took Olson's rational-actor postulate as "one of its underlying problems" (McCarthy & Zald 1977, p. 1216) but professed to have solved the "free rider" puzzle by analyzing the resources—material, human, cognitive, technical, and organizational—that movements deployed in order to expand, reward participants, and gain a stake in the political system. Resource mobilization (RM) theory, with its focus on the construction of "social movement industries" made up of "social movement organizations," regarded collective action mainly as interest group politics played out by socially connected groups rather than by the most disaffected. Movement "entrepreneurs" had the task of mobilizing resources and channeling discontent into organizational forms. Resource availability and preference structures became the perspective's central foci rather than the structural bases of social conflict (as in Touraine's version of NSMs) or state and market assaults on the private sphere (as in Melucci's and Habermas's versions).

In underscoring the importance of mobilization processes and well-endowed organizations (and competition among the latter), the RM paradigm tended to disregard situations in which social movements, usually of the very poor, emerged with few resources or where overt organization—in contexts of extreme inequality, severe repression, and hopeless odds—endangered participants, producing "shadowy" (Piven & Cloward 1977), "submerged" (Melucci 1989), or "hidden" forms of resistance (Scott 1990) that might or might not lead to collective action (Burdick 1998). By viewing social movements as interest group politics, the paradigm understood "success" primarily as the achievement of policy objectives rather than in relation to broader processes of cultural transformation. RM proponents eventually conceded as well that their framework did not deal adequately with "enthusiasm, spontaneity, and conversion experiences" or the "feelings of solidarity and communal sharing" that rewarded movement participants (Zald 1992, pp. 330–31).

Several scholars influenced by the American paradigm advocated incorporating a focus on states and on "political opportunity structure" (POS) into the RM model's concern with the internal dynamics of organizations. The POS approach tended to examine movement strategizing in the context of the balance of opportunities-threats for challengers and facilitation-repression by authorities (Tarrow 1998). Some POS scholars who worked with European case materials emphasized a diachronic approach, studying the frequency of contentious events over long durations (with methods influenced by *Annales* historians' "serial" history and their distinction between "events," "conjunctures," and "*longues durées*") (Shorter & Tilly 1974, Tilly 1986). Other Europeanists (Tarrow 1989) examined the opening and closing of POSs over much shorter periods. A complementary approach involved analyzing conflicts occurring around the same time in relation to space, within a given region or nation (Shorter & Tilly 1974), or as part of a cross-national comparison (Gamson & Meyer 1996). This synchronic approach had antecedents, not always acknowledged, in European studies of early industrial-era protest, such as Hobsbawm & Rudé (1968), who analyzed, for 1830–1832, types of repression and disturbances according to frequency, geographical location, categories of persons targeted, and damages inflicted.

Critics noted that the POS perspective gave little attention to discursive aspects of identity, gender, the social construction of POS itself, or its local and international aspects (Abdulhadi 1998). They further charged that POS was too broad and imprecise, "a dustbin" (Della Porta & Diani 1999, p. 223) or "a sponge that soaks up virtually every aspect of the social movement environment . . . an all-encompassing fudge factor . . . [which] may explain nothing at all" (Gamson & Meyer 1996, p. 274). Increasingly, POS proponents came to see it as one element of a broader political process, which included greater emphasis on the cultural-historical sources of discontent, protest, and mobilization (and which was distinct from—and apparently incognizant of—the similarly named perspective that evolved out of Manchester anthropology). By the 1990s, proponents of the political process approach echoed Cohen's (1985) call for fusing the European and American paradigms and professed to have an "emerging synthesis." This included "political opportunities," "mobilizing structures," and "framing," a category encompassing the ways in which collective identities arose, as well as the interpretative, discursive, and dramaturgical practices that shaped movement participants' understandings of their condition and of possible alternatives (McAdam et al 1996a, 2001; Tarrow 1998). By the end of the decade, political process enthusiasts could claim that the model occupied a "dominant" (Garner 1997) or "hegemonic" (Giugni 1999) place in the study of social movements.

INTERROGATING THE CANON

It is remarkable how little attention has been devoted to understanding why contrasting approaches originated on different sides of the Atlantic. Melucci attributed the rise in the United States of RM theory, with its presumption of rationality and metaphors about "entrepreneurs," to the "unprecedented development of organization theory in the analysis of business and administration" and to the weakness of Marxist or radical thought in U.S. sociology (1989, p. 194). Della Porta & Diani (1999) indicate that in the 1980s, rising disillusion with a strong Marxist intellectual tradition in Europe contributed to a search for new non–class-based dimensions of conflict. Foweraker (1995), looking at the sociopolitical context of theory, suggests that in western Europe the "social democratic consensus," developed welfare states, and powerful labor organizations and corporatist traditions contributed to making NSMs look genuinely "new" and to producing explanations that stressed major societal transformations. In contrast, in the United States, in the absence of a strong labor movement or a social democratic class pact, outsider groups (the civil rights movement was the paradigmatic case for RM theorists) had to mobilize resources to gain representation in the political system (McAdam et al 2001, Morris 1999). A further cause of trans-Atlantic differences was the isolation in which theorists of the two traditions worked; only in the mid-1980s were there sustained contacts between and joint conferences of social movements scholars from Europe and North America (McAdam et al 1996a).

How did NSMs and POS theories fare when they traveled outside Europe and North America? Latin America, in particular, has been fertile territory for studies of collective action, though largely by scholars and scholar-activists influenced by NSMs (Escobar & Alvarez 1992, Alvarez et al 1998) or historical-structural perspectives (Eckstein 1989).[2] Even though RM and POS perspectives on movements'

---

[2]"Historical-structural" approaches "show ideology, values, traditions, and rituals to be of consequence and trace the importance of culture to group, organization, and community dynamics and to other features of social structure. Yet they never presume that protest is mechanically determined by social structure. They show the patterning of defiance to be contingent on historical circumstances" (Eckstein 1989, p. 3).

interactions with states were pertinent in Latin America (Foweraker 1995), they had less appeal outside developed northern democracies because it was difficult, especially under authoritarian regimes, to imagine political opportunity as a significant explanatory category; tellingly, in the few works on Latin America that make explicit use of a POS perspective, such as Schneider's (1995) ethnographic tour-de-force on Chile's urban poor under the Pinochet dictatorship, the theoretical framework is understated. Davis (1999, p. 586) argues that NSMs theory's emphasis on civil society appealed "to the lived experience and normative ideals of Latin American intellectuals." Also important, however, were the ties to Latin America of NSMs theorists in Europe. Touraine, who spent the mid-1950s at the University of Chile and developed his ideas about "historicity" in dialogue with Latin American sociologists in the early 1970s (Touraine 1973), has had continuing ties to the region. The writings of Laclau, a native of Argentina established in Europe who shifted from Althusserianism to a poststructuralism that drew selectively and idiosyncratically on Gramsci (Laclau & Mouffe 1985), have been widely read in Latin America since the early 1970s. It is likely, furthermore, that in the 1970s and 1980s visceral anti-U.S. sentiments (especially in Mexico and among exiles there) and a strong Europhile streak (particularly in Buenos Aires) predisposed Latin American intellectuals to embrace NSMs perspectives and to ignore those from U.S. academia. Anthropologists were drawn to NSMs perspectives for similar reasons, as well as for the central role that NSMs accorded to cultural practice as a force for political transformation (Alvarez et al 1998, Escobar & Alvarez 1992).

Within Latin America, recent studies of collective action cluster geographically, mirroring the concentration of earlier social scientific production in certain selected places. The 1994 Zapatista uprising in the southern Mexican state of Chiapas has inspired an extraordinary outpouring of scholarly work, much of it directed at informing a sympathetic public or mobilizing solidarity. Drawing on three decades of work on Chiapas, Collier (1994), produced less than a year after the Zapatistas' rebellion, remains an essential reference. Emphasizing agrarian rather than indigenous sources of insurgency, especially the constitutional modifications that effectively ended land reform, Collier describes how community factionalism and population growth generated an exodus of disaffected migrants to remote jungles in eastern Chiapas. Although the Zapatistas condemned the North American Free Trade Agreement (NAFTA) and warned of its deleterious consequences for Mexico's peasantry, linking the insurrection to NAFTA, Collier says, was a "pretext," because other grievances had kindled the movement during years of clandestine organizing. In 1994, the origins of the Zapatista National Liberation Army (EZLN) were unclear. Harvey (1998), whose research began nearly a decade before the uprising, details the multiple strands of peasant, indigenous, and student organizing that eventually coalesced in the EZLN. In analyzing the Zapatistas' struggle on behalf of Chiapas Indians and the Mexican poor in general, Harvey maintains that the construction of democracy in Mexico often depends on informal local and regional, rather than formal national-level processes.[3] Womack (1999) introduces a first-rate collection of primary documents on Chiapas and extends inquiry forward and backward in time. He relates the erratic course of EZLN-government negotiations and also traces the notorious intransigence, venality, and bigotry of contemporary highland elites to their conquistador ancestors' schemes to defraud the Crown of tribute and to racialize space in their urban centers. Drawing on a decades-long involvement with Chiapas, Nash (1997) indicates how Zapatista outreach campaigns are elements of a broader project of mobilizing civil society and of redefining modernist notions of democracy in a pluriethnic Mexico.

The Zapatista case is significant not only for its reverberations within Mexico, but also because it figures as a prototype for sometimes rhapsodic claims about a new period characterized by "informational" (Castells 1997) or "postmodern" (Nash 1997) movements and "democratic" (Touraine 2000) guerrillas. Most Zapatista internet activity is carried out by a small number of sympathetic individuals and nongovernmental organizations (NGOs), but their presence on the net has allowed them to communicate demands, foster alliances, and represent themselves as part of a global struggle against neoliberal capitalism. Among the most in-depth and singular treatments of this phenomenon is a U.S. Army–funded RAND Corporation study (Ronfeldt et al 1998) that provides a glimpse of how counterinsurgency planners view this new form of politics.

Apart from the high-profile Zapatistas, diverse Latin American struggles led social scientists to reconsider approaches to collective action and NSMs theory, in particular. Two outstanding anthologies (Escobar & Alvarez 1992, Alvarez et al 1998), among the few in which anthropologists (as well as Latin America–based scholars) are well represented, provide a useful guide to the field as it developed in the 1990s.

Despite the wide scope of these anthologies, which range from examinations of the state (Fals Borda 1992) and democratization (Calderón et al (1992) to cyberpolitics (Ribeiro 1998) and grassroots (Baierle 1998; Yúdice 1998) and transnational (Alvarez 1998) organizing, two broad areas are conspicuously absent, or nearly so. Peasant movements receive relatively short shrift, apart from Starn (1992). This is perhaps surprising, given that in Mexico outside Chiapas (Paré 1994, Williams 2001), in Central America (Edelman 1998, Edelman 1999), and elsewhere, these have been in the forefront of opposition to neoliberalism and that in Brazil social movements research has concentrated heavily on struggles of small farmers and the landless (Houtzager & Kurtz 2000, Maybury-Lewis 1994, Pereira 1997, Stephen 1997). Right-wing movements are another area largely ignored in these volumes, reflecting in all likelihood a reluctance on the part of

---

[3]This parallels Rubin's (1997) innovative work on the leftist Zapotec movement COCEI in Juchitán, Oaxaca. Both works critique state-centered understandings of Mexican politics (Castells 1997).

NSMs scholars to acknowledge that conservative responses are also an outcome of proliferating social tensions, rapid cultural change, the advance of democratization, and the progressive movements themselves (Calhoun 1994, Payne 2000, Pichardo 1997).

When NSMs perspectives traveled outside of social democratic Europe, the inclusion in their purview of major movements in Latin America—human rights and democratization, indigenous and minority peoples, Christian-based communities, the urban poor, street children—entailed a recognition of economic and power inequalities as key dimensions of collective action. This did not mean a resort to an obsolete, unidimensional class analysis, however, because the actors in motion went way beyond the traditional proletariat and because investigations of real movements nearly always uncovered participants from a range of class origins and intense contention over issues of identity and representation. This continued significance of class or distributive conflicts led many Latin Americanists to eschew NSMs terminology altogether and to speak instead of "popular" (literally, "people's") movements (Foweraker 1995).

PERIODIZATION DEBATES: SO WHAT'S NEW?

One irony of the stress on newness of NSMs was that emerging movements of women, environmentalists, gays and lesbians, and oppressed minorities, as well as anticolonial forces in the Third World, sought to uncover hidden histories of their political ancestors in order to fortify their legitimacy and forge new collective identities. This rediscovery of the complexity of old and first-wave social movements was part of wider efforts to theorize periodizations of collective action through examining "origins," "waves," "cycles," and "protest repertoires." The discussion of movements in terms of origins has occurred chiefly in relation to environmentalism. Two recent works highlight what is at stake (Grove 1995, Judd 2000). Efforts to theorize the Northern environmentalist movements that arose in the 1960s, while acknowledging their diversity, usually argued that affluence and urbanization produced an appreciation and need for natural amenities. Melucci, in an uncharacteristically blunt declaration, insinuated that contemporary environmental movements are offspring of a "new intellectual-political elite" living in a "gilded but marginalizing ghetto" (Melucci 1996, p. 165). Similar "postmaterialist" premises extended to explanations of nineteenth- and early twentieth-century conservation campaigns as projects of "enlightened elites" or even of "a gentry overwhelmed by industrialization" (Castells 1997, p. 121). Against this predominant outlook, Grove (1995) attributes the rise of environmentalism to Europe's encounter with the tropics and to the devastation caused by rapacious plantation economies. Judd, focusing on rural New England, also challenges the thesis of the elite origins of conservation, which he says derives from a "tendency to glean evidence of rising concern about forests from federal publications, national journals, or writings of prominent thinkers" (2000, pp. 90–91). In a meticulous study of local sources, he finds a pervasive conservation ethic, rooted in common uses of forest, pasture, and farmland, which superseded private property rights until well into the nineteenth century. After 1870, "conservation took on class overtones" (2000, p. 178) as genteel anglers, hunters, and federal bureaucrats took up the cause, reshaping notions about the place of "nature" in agrarian landscapes, as well as nature itself. The thesis of conservation's upper-class origins, Judd maintains, contributes to demagogic efforts today to paint environmentalism as an elite conspiracy unfairly implemented at great cost to the working poor.

Guha & Martínez-Alier (1997) trace early environmentalism to the destruction wrought by the industrial revolution at home and in colonial territories and to a heterogeneous collection of thinkers, such as Aldous Huxley, Mahatma Gandhi, and urbanist Lewis Mumford. The main contribution of the work, however, is its trenchant critique of developed-country overconsumption and its elaboration of commonalities and distinctions between movements. They find postmaterialist environmentalisms in the "empty-belly" South ("essentialist eco-feminism," which sees poor women as embodying intrinsic "naturalness," and "deep ecology" tendencies, which revere biotic integrity more than human needs), as well as ones in the "full-stomach" North (environmental justice movements), which deploy the language of class and, at times, race to organize. "Social conflicts with ecological content" include struggles against "environmental racism" (siting dumps in minority communities), "toxic imperialism" (waste disposal in poorer countries), "ecologically unequal exchange" (based on prices which do not reflect local externalities), the North "dumping" subsidized agricultural surpluses in the South (to the detriment of small farmers there), and "biopiracy" (corporate appropriation of genetic resources without recognition of peasant or indigenous intellectual property rights).

Within feminism, the periodization discussion has been cast in terms of "waves," a convention that reveals and conceals key continuities and ruptures in forms of exclusion and of women's collective action. The demands of different national "first-wave" women's movements are usually said to have centered on suffrage and political rights [although it is also clear that issues of sexuality and male violence were important in contexts as varied as Germany (Grossmann 1995) and Puerto Rico (Findlay 1998)]; "second-wave" movements in the 1960s and 1970s demanded equity in the workplace and domestic unit, exposed the political foundations of seemingly personal circumstances, and championed a range of new rights, from access to abortion to protection from sexual harassment; and "third-wave" feminists, generally born after 1963 and active in the 1990s and after, take cultural production and sexual politics as key sites of struggle, seeking to fuel micropolitical struggles outside of formal institutional channels.

Historians who located first-wave feminism in the mid-nineteenth to the early twentieth century usually did so provisionally, concerned that such clear-cut categorizations obscured significant antecedents as well as major variations between, say, the United States and Norway, or India and France (Sarah 1983); indeed, arguments for the inclusion of women in "the rights of man" reach back to the French Revolution (Scott 1996) and the early abolitionist movement (Keck & Sikkink 1998, Lerner 1998), although they were not always backed by collective action. Discussions about third-wave feminism, in contrast, reflect the emergence (in the United States, at least) of a deeply felt generational identity defined against both older second wavers and conservative postfeminists of the 1980s (Baumgardner & Richards 2000, Heywood & Drake 1997).

The waves formulation is problematical in that it privileges political generations and tends to mask variation among movement participants and organizations along lines of age, class, race, and sexual orientation, as well as between- and after-wave activity. In the United States, for example, linking the first and second waves were the elite-led National Women's Party (which provided many alumnae to the second wave) and the Communist-dominated Congress of American Women, which for 5 years following World War II boasted some 250,000 members (several of whom were leading historians of the first wave and activists of the second wave) before it dissolved during the 1950s red scare (Rosen 2000). Whittier (1995) points out that numerous local radical feminist collectives were active during the hostile 1980s interval between the second and third waves but that their rejection of mainstream politics often rendered them invisible to social movements scholars whose main focus was national organizations.

Political process theorists did not generally draw sharp distinctions between waves or between new and old movements but some nonetheless posited a significant break between the "parochial," defensive forms of collective action characteristic of Europe up to the mid-nineteenth century (charivaris, machine-breaking, field invasions, food riots) and the modern repertoire of contention that flowered after 1848 with the consolidation of nation-states. Tilly (1986, p. 392), for example, described the social movement as a challenge to the state that employs a protest repertoire of public meetings, demonstrations, and strikes and that attempts to bargain with established authorities on behalf of its constituency.

Tarrow (1998), also employing a political process perspective, shared Tilly's notion of a fundamental shift in protest repertoires around the mid-nineteenth century. For Tarrow, however, the principal concept for periodization was the "protest cycle" [which in later work (1998) he termed cycle of contention], a time of heightened activity typically involving more than one movement.

Although the claims of some 1980s NSMs enthusiasts that NSMs represented a fundamental rupture with a putative, unitary old movement were quickly recognized as "spurious" (Escobar & Alvarez 1992), even recent work sometimes maintains a marked new-versus-old distinction, arguing, for example, that the traditional Left did not consider the relation between culture and politics a "central question" (Dagnino 1998, p. 34). Such assertions, likely rooted in social scientists' curious underutilization of the "vast number of accounts by historians . . . on the cultural activities of political movements" (Eyerman & Jamison 1998, p. 12), became difficult to sustain as sympathizers of the 1960s movements recovered earlier, forgotten histories of activism. Some pointed to the identity-based dimensions of old working-class movements, which in the United States (Calhoun 1993, Flacks 1988, Freeman 2000; Mishler 1999) and elsewhere (Fisher 1999; Waterman 1998) took up such issues as child labor, work environments, women's status, housing, health, community life, education, and access to public services. The middle class, the supposedly distinctive source of new movements, was also prominent in many older ones, notably campaigns in Europe and the United States for abolition, prohibition, reproductive rights, and suffrage (Grossmann 1995, Lerner 1998, Pichardo 1997).

How, though, were these earlier versions of cultural politics forgotten in the initial enthusiasm about NSMs? Some scholars believe that "the specific tactics and methods of state repression" and their impact on movements "have received little systematic attention" (Carley 1997, p. 153).[4] Adam (1995) traces the sources of some NSMs theorists' "amnesia" about earlier militant traditions to both the crisis in Marxism, which allowed leftist scholars to "see" non-class-based activity they had previously overlooked, and to the impact of totalitarian regimes in Europe and the Cold War red scare in the United States, which destroyed diverse progressive movements.

Although some collective action theorists deplore the lack of "a theory that explains the relationship between preexisting protest traditions and the rise ... of new social movements" (Morris 1999, p. 536), evidence abounds of activist continuities from one era to another and across movements. Among the approaches in the literature on the United States are those that emphasize broad cultural transformations, the life trajectories of groups of activists, the role of institutions and organizations, and the reinventing of musical and other traditions. Flacks (1988, p. 181) notes that as the U.S. New Deal generation retreated politically in the 1950s and concentrated on family life, many tried to apply humanistic and democratic values in the home, producing offspring predisposed to question mainstream culture.

Together with a "vibrant semi-underground current of anarchistic mockery of conventional authority" (Flacks 1988, p. 181) embodied in the Beat poets, *Mad* magazine, risqué satirists like Lenny Bruce, and rock and rhythm-and-blues music, which discredited "the notion that creativity obeyed a color line" (Isserman & Kazin 2000, p. 19), this quiet cultural shift laid the groundwork for rebellion in the 1960s. Some accounts of the 1960s argue that future student activists "grew up with little or no contact with a previous generation that had been radicalized by the Depression" (Fraser et al 1988, p. 17). However, veteran radicals disillusioned with earlier traditions—Communism, pacifism, Trotskyism—had by that time often discarded old dogmas while retaining political ideals, contacts, and skills that contributed mightily to the civil rights, antinuclear, anti–Vietnam War,

---

[4]Hart (1996. p. 238), in a magnificent study of the Greek Resistance, makes a similar observation but then goes on to provide an impressive oral historical account of Cold War–era political repression. Usually, however, such assertions reflect intellectual and political isolation from those (Arditti 1999, Feldman 1991) who have made repression a central object of study.

and women's movements (Freeman 2000, Rosen 2000, Whittier 1995). Institutions that survived McCarthyism also served as bridges between the protest cycles of the 1930s and 1960s (Horton et al 1990). The rediscovery and nurturing of musical and other artistic traditions are important features of social movements' action repertoires and continuity (Eyerman & Jamison 1998), although expressive culture has also sometimes constituted a source of intramovement contention (Monson 1997).

IDENTITY-BASED AND ANTI-IDENTITY POLITICS

The "invention and creation of new rights" (Dagnino 1998, p. 50; Melucci 1989), rooted in the struggles of emergent social groups, clearly accelerated in "the long 1960s" along with the mass adoption and refashioning of views and practices that were earlier peculiar to small cultural and political avant-gardes (Flacks 1988, Fraser et al 1988, Isserman & Kazin 2000). For Castells (1997) as for his mentor Touraine, "identity" is a process through which social actors construct meaning on the basis of cultural attributes that are given priority over other potential sources of meaning. Calhoun (1994) historicizes the category in relation to the rise of individualism since the Protestant Reformation, the advent of nation-states, and Enlightenment appeals to nature as a "moral source." Whether and under what conditions the recent proliferation of particular identities produced opportunities for new alliances or merely political fragmentation remains much debated, as are the related tendencies of identity-based movements to oscillate between downplaying and celebrating differences from majority groups or to lose their political character altogether.

Among the dramatic shifts occurring out of struggles for new rights is the changing view of disability. Charlton (1998) chronicles how people considered disabled in southern Africa, Asia, and the Americas organized, often against the wishes of paternalistic, able-bodied advocates, to make notions of normality more inclusive and to "break with the traditional perception of disability as a sick, abnormal, and pathetic condition" (p. 10). Disability oppression has interrelated sources: poverty and powerlessness, resulting from both economic exclusion and underdevelopment (four fifths of the world's disabled live in poor countries); views of the disabled as degraded and aberrant, which legitimize exclusionary practices; and internalization by the disabled themselves of attitudes of self-loathing and self-pity, which hinder understanding of their situation and organizing around it. To perhaps a greater extent than with other movements, the aspirations of the disabled intersect with struggles against other forms of discrimination and for housing and veterans' rights, a ban on land mines, the democratization of technology and scientific knowledge, and the creation or preservation of workplace opportunities and social safety nets. They also, however, complicate the demands of other movements in ways outsiders seldom anticipate. Saxton (1998), for example, in a searing critique of assumptions about prenatal diagnosis and selective abortion, challenges the belief that the quality of life for disabled people is necessarily inferior and that raising a child with a disability is an undesirable experience.

> The reproductive rights movement emphasizes the right to have an abortion; the disability rights movement, the right *not to have to have* an abortion.
>
> (p. 375; emphasis in original).

Other identity-based social movements have found expanding mainstream conceptions of normality a source of internal contention. This is dramatically illustrated in the course of gay and lesbian politics since the 1969 Stonewall rebellion. Early gay liberation movements practiced consciousness raising, exalted long-repressed sexualities, contested the dominant sex/gender system, openly occupied public space, and struggled for nondiscrimination and the depathologization of homosexuality. The "assimilationist" advocacy groups that emerged out of more radical and inclusive gay liberation movements of the early 1970s engaged in a denial of difference intended to gain access to mainstream social institutions and in positing an artificially homogeneous "gay essence" intended to build political unity (Cohen 2001). With the advent of AIDS and rising homophobia in the 1980s, and a shift to confrontational tactics spurred by "the urgency of impending death" (Hodge 2000, p. 356), activists attempted to destabilize the "gay white middle-class identity," which had dominated the movement and to ally with a wider range of sexually, economically, and racially marginalized collectivities. In contrast to the assimilationists, this involved an assertion of fundamental difference with "heteronormativity," as well as a greater acknowledgment of how gay and lesbian identities were plural, socially constructed, and inflected by race, class, and national origin (Adam 1995, Stein 1997). This "queer" challenge to earlier gay activism professed to have resolved a central conundrum of identity politics by privileging "affinity," a shared opposition to class-, race-, and gender-based power and a common AIDS catastrophe rather than particular varieties of sexual desire. Some scholar-activists, however, maintain that academic "queer theory" is still mired in privilege, fails to follow the lead of the radical street movement, and gives scant attention to political-economic aspects of power at all levels, from the state and social class structure to the everyday practices that shape public space (Hodge 2000). The latter misgiving is shared by critics who question whether the category "queer" is an "overarching unifier" or just "another fraction in the overall mosaic of contemporary gay and lesbian organizing" (Adam 1995, p. 164).

The danger that identity-based politics could become a form of "narcissistic withdrawal" impelled by aspirations for individual self-realization and "political tribalism" (Melucci 1989, p. 209) has produced similar commentaries from various directions. Claims of difference can fortify demands for new rights, but they can imply an abdication of rights as well. In a scathing attack on "cultural" or "difference" feminism, di Leonardo (1998) points out that journalistic and New Age "women's culture tropes" ignore political-economic dimensions of gender oppression and presuppose an immanent and superior female morality and nurturing capability that is held up as an alternative to the destructive militarism and environmental ruin caused by aggressive, patriarchal men. The implication of such arguments is that women deserve a place in society not because of any inherent right but because of their innate capacity to make things better, a stance that no other oppressed group is required to take.

"Beneath the current black-female-student-chicano-gay-elderly-youth-disabled, ad nauseam, 'struggles,'" Reed (1999) proclaims in an acerbic yet cogent analysis of postsegregation African-American politics, "lies a simple truth: There is no coherent opposition to the present administrative apparatus" (p. 55). He attributes the "atrophy of opposition within the black community" to the breakdown of the civil-rights–era consensus, a media-anointed leadership so enamored of "authenticity" and "corporate racial politics" that it is incapable of acknowledging class and interest-group differentiation within the supposedly unitary "community," and an "academic hermeticism" that is isolated from political action and disinterested in distinguishing challenges to socioeconomic hierarchy from politically insignificant "everyday resistance" fads (1999, pp. 56, 151). Although it would not be hard to take issue with Reed's categorical gloom (or his indifference to other struggles in his ad nauseam inventory), his larger point—that class dynamics arise from and operate autonomously within and across identity-based collectivities—remains an unavoidable limitation on the emancipatory potential of movements defined in purely identity or difference terms.

A related pitfall of identity-based mobilizations is the facility with which many become little more than fodder for lucrative corporate marketing crusades. In an astute discussion of how branding practices have generated anticorporate activism, Klein (1999) maintains that "diversity" is now "the mantra of global capital," used to absorb identity imagery of all kinds in order to peddle "mono-multiculturalism" across myriad differentiated markets (p. 115).

Warren's (1998) insightful study of pan-Maya activists, however, highlights complications both of identity-based mobilization and of calls for a new class politics. Beginning in the mid-1980s, in the aftermath of genocide and in the midst of continuing civil war, alongside and sometimes against popular movements that demanded social rights (land, freedom to organize, an end to military impunity), pan-Maya intellectuals launched an unabashedly essentialist cultural project that includes revitalizing Indian languages, revalorizing ancient calendrical and numerical systems (and more generally, ethnically specific epistemologies, spiritualities, and leadership practices), and overturning received Ladino versions of history with new readings of indigenous and Spanish chronicles. Their movements claim a privileged authority in representing Mayan peoples, and strive for a "pluricultural" nation in which they have collective, as well as individual, rights. The pan-Maya movements' carving out of political space via essentialist practices leads Warren to argue for a middle ground in the analysis of identity politics, focusing on "the coexistence of multiple politics and histories...hidden by the antagonism of . . . anthropological constructions" (1998, p. 179).[5]

Transcending such constructions in the pursuit of a grounded analysis of multiple politics is a challenging task. Chhachhi & Pittin (1999) question approaches that either consider the primacy of one identity over another or simply "add together gender, ethnicity and class" (p. 68). Instead, they suggest viewing women's possibilities for action through the prism of time, space, and place in order to understand how their "very multiplicity of roles and plethora of pressures may provide both the impetus and the necessary networking" for them to press demands at various work sites (p. 74). They suggest that "the question of women's consciousness" remains an "underdeveloped" area in theorizing identity politics. A considerable ethnographic literature on women in situations of national conflict, however, suggests that this project is further along than Chhachhi & Pittin believe. Hart's (1996) oral historical account of women in the Greek Resistance, Abdulhadi's (1998) examination of Palestinian women's efforts to carve out autonomous space within a larger nationalist movement, Aretxaga's (1997) work on gender politics in Northern Ireland, and Arditti's (1999) study of grandmothers of the disappeared in Argentina are notably successful efforts to move beyond formulaic "additive" approaches and to comprehend how multiple identities emerge from and configure each other and political action, subjectivity, and memory. Debates continue over the limitations and potentialities of multiple politics (Stephen 1997), including mobilizing around motherhood and the extent to which this implies essentialist notions of womanhood (Gledhill 2000).

RIGHT-WING AND CONSERVATIVE MOVEMENTS

Even though identity-based movements sometimes walk a fine line between celebrating particularities and promoting exclusivity or intolerance, the former dimension has received vastly more attention than the latter. NSMs scholars have largely skirted the issue of right-wing collective action, in part due to Touraine's (and others') limiting of the field to movements that seek "historicity" and in

---

[5]In this she echoes feminists who call for "risking" essentialism in the formative stages of movements (Calhoun 1994). Although Warren locates the origins of pan-Maya movements in 1940s Catholic activism and in the crisis of the Guatemalan state in the 1980s, Forster's (1998) reconstruction of ethnic labor migration streams in the 1940s points to a proto–pan-Mayan blurring of specific indigenous identities in the piedmont plantation belt. Grandin (2000), who traces pan-Maya ideology to the nineteenth-century indigenist liberalism of K'iche' elites, argues that "the danger faced by many of the current proponents of Mayan nationalism has to do with their trading in the sort of universalisms that will render the creation of an indigenous identity meaningless to the majority of rural, poverty-stricken Maya" (pp. 228–29).

part because researchers overwhelmingly choose to study "attractive" movements with which they sympathize (Calhoun 1994, Hellman 1992, Pichardo 1997, Starn 1999). Political process theorists typically emphasized Western civic movements and largely sidestepped in-depth analysis of troubling questions raised by the "violent, sectarian, and self-enclosed identity movements" of the 1990s (Tarrow 1998, p. 204). Apart from some attempts to systematize concepts such as backlash and reaction (Hirschman 1991) or to view conservative movements as merely reactionary mirror-images of identity-based NSMs (Garner 1997), studies of the right constitute yet another parallel universe in collective action research, with inconsistent connections to larger traditions of social movement theory.

The exceptions suggest a variety of moves to specify the objects of study. For Ginsburg (1998), "conservatism" involves "a complex balancing act between a libertarian celebration of individualism, economic freedom, and capitalism, and a traditionalist emphasis on community, moral order, and the like" (pp. 47–48). She describes fieldwork with pro-choice and antiabortion activists—surely itself a balancing act—and charts the changing composition of the right-to-life movement, as evangelical Protestant men—many inclined to violence—displaced the moderate women who had been local leaders in North Dakota. Diamond (1995), in a far-reaching analysis of U.S. right-wing politics, objects that conservatism implies reticence about change and thus fails to capture what many self-described conservatives are about. "To be right-wing," she argues, "means to support the state in its capacity as *enforcer* of order and to oppose the state as *distributor* of wealth and power downward and more equitably in society" (p. 9, emphasis in original). Berlet & Lyons (2000), in a landmark study of American right-wing populism from Bacon's rebellion in 1676 to the militias of the 1990s, note that classifying populist movements (which make antielitist appeals to "the people") along a right-left spectrum is often misleading. In contrast to Diamond, they stress that some rightist movements have advocated downward distribution of wealth and power, though not to everyone, and that some reject the state altogether and have tried to overthrow it (pp. 5–6). In an examination of putschist military officers in Argentina, homicidal landowners in Brazil, and violent paramilitary bands in Nicaragua, Payne (2000) defines her object as "uncivil movements," which employ deliberate violence and threats, as well as more conventional tactics and appeals to threatened identities, to advance exclusionary policies in democratic polities. Echoing Melucci's discussion of NSMs, she declares that uncivil movements "emphasize identity over interests. They use cultural symbols to empower new movements" (p. 17).

The emergence of antiimmigrant movements in Europe is among the cases that indicate the urgency of grasping how the right deploys cultural politics. Stolcke (1995) contends that new "doctrines of exclusion" differ from older varieties of organicist racism in positing irreducible cultural differences and deeply ingrained propensities to fear and loathe strangers and to wish to live among people of the same national group. This new cultural fundamentalism eschews claims about innate inferiority in favor of a rhetoric of difference. It posits a supposedly generic human attribute—anxiety about the "other"—in order to construct an antiuniversalist politics, assiduously avoiding rhetoric too directly suggestive of fascist and Nazi racism. Stoler (1999), in a brief paper on the far-right Front Nationale (FN) in Aix-en-Provence, calls attention—like Stolcke—to a peculiar situation where racial discourse looms large and is simultaneously effaced or irrelevant. However, in contrast to frameworks that distinguish a new "cultural racism" from earlier "colonial racism," she indicates that the old racism also spoke "a language of cultural competencies, 'good taste' and discrepant parenting values" (p. 33), while the contemporary FN draws from a broader French cultural repertoire that includes a toned-down racism but also patriotic republicanism and anxieties about European integration and globalization. In the United States, a basic theme of right-wing populist narratives is "producerism," which "posits a noble hard-working middle group constantly in conflict with lazy, malevolent, or sinful parasites at the top and bottom of the social order" (Berlet & Lyons, p. 348). Although the Christian Right employs coded scapegoating to identify social problems with low-income communities of color, far-right white supremacists endorse an explicitly biological racism. Each tends to reinforce the other in public discourse. NSMs theorists, as well as government agencies, media, and human relations organizations, frequently brand right-wing movements "irrational" (Cohen 1985, pp. 666–67). Berlet & Lyons (2000) warn against such "centrist/extremist" interpretations, which see such movements as fringe phenomena. This, they argue, "obscures the rational choices and partially legitimate grievances that help to fuel right-wing populist movements, and hides the fact that right-wing bigotry and scapegoating are firmly rooted in the mainstream social and political order" (p. 14). They give only passing attention, however, to how the ownership and content of communications media shape notions of common sense and facilitate growth of right-wing movements. The impact of hate radio and internet sites seems to have been covered most by scholars interested in monitoring (Hilliard & Keith 1999), rather than theorizing (Castells 1997), reactionary movements.

Stock (1996) considers producerism almost synonymous with the "rural producer radicalism" that (along with a "culture of vigilantism") has been a constant of U.S. small-farmer politics for 200 years. Early twentieth-century reform liberalism, such as the Farmer-Labor Party of the 1920s, had ties to rural producer radicalism, but more recent "compensatory liberalism" neglected the values of many rural Americans. The U.S. farm crisis of the 1980s gave rise to armed right-wing groups (Stock 1996) and to antimilitarist, conservationist organizations influenced by Christian notions of land stewardship (Mooney & Majka 1995). Clearly, "the roots of violence, racism, and hatred can be and have been nourished in the same soil and from the same experiences that generated rural movements for democracy and equality" (Stock 1996, p. 148).

TRANSNATIONAL MOVEMENTS:
GLOBALIZATION-FROM-BELOW?

At the same time that some U.S. farmers turned to right-wing populism, others gravitated to movements—many of them transnational—influenced by environmentalism, feminism, and opposition to unfettered free trade (Mooney & Majka 1995, Ritchie 1996). From the mid-1980s to the mid-1990s, farmers' protests at GATT (General Agreement on Tariffs and Trade) meetings galvanized a growing international movement critical of the lack of democratic accountability of supranational institutions, of the terms under which agriculture was included in free-trade agreements, and of how neoliberal policies and industrial farming threatened rural livelihoods, human health, genetic diversity, and the resource base (Brecher et al 2000). Small-farmer opposition actions and transnational organizing flourished in areas where regional economic integration and supranational governance were making their weight felt at the local level. In France, farmer José Bové demolished a McDonald's, attracting worldwide attention and national acclaim for his denunciations of agribusiness, free trade, and "*la malbouffe*," a word he coined that may be roughly glossed as "junk food" (Bové et al 2000, pp. 77–84). The action of Bové and his collaborators was modeled in part on events in India, where peasants in Karnataka destroyed a Kentucky Fried Chicken outlet and ransacked facilities owned by the multinational seed company Cargill (Gupta 1998). In North America, the Canadian National Farmers Union spearheaded links with counterpart groups in Mexico and the United States in order to influence the NAFTA negotiations (Ritchie 1996). In Central America, peasant leaders forged contacts with European, Canadian, and Indian activists, created a regional transnational lobbying organization, and played a major role in the formation of a global small farmer network called the *Vía Campesina*/Peasant Road (Edelman 1998).

In 1993, Falk introduced the phrase globalization-from-below to refer to a global civil society linking "transnational social forces animated by environmental concerns, human rights, hostility to patriarchy, and a vision of human community based on the unity of diverse cultures seeking an end to poverty, oppression, humiliation, and collective violence" (1993, p. 39). Explicitly directed against elite and corporate-led "globalization from above," the multistranded opposition that Falk described involved diverse sectors organizing across borders and raising connections like those that small farmers made between livelihood, health, intellectual property, environment, human rights, and the expanding dominance of supranational governance institutions. The Barbados meetings in the 1970s and after that brought together native activists and anthropologists from throughout the Americas (Brysk 2000), the global women's meetings sponsored by the United Nations in the 1980s and 1990s (Alvarez 1998), the 1992 Earth Summit (Gupta 1998), the NGO forums held in tandem with World Bank, International Monetary Fund, (IMF) and Group of Seven Industrialized countries meetings, and a multitude of similar events connected issues and activists in postmaterialist and identity- and class-based movements as never before (Adam 1995, Brecher et al 2000, Charlton 1998).

Just a few years ago, one of the foremost observers of this process could state that the new internationalisms have been "subject to little strategic reflection" and have "as yet little or no theoretical status" (Waterman 1998, p. 4). Appadurai (2000) recently remarked that "the sociology of these emergent social forms—part movements, part networks, part organizations—has yet to be developed" (p. 15). Research on transnational organizing has, however, flourished in the mid- to late 1990s. Initially, it usually looked at organizations that crossed one or two adjacent borders, such as issue-oriented binational coalitions of U.S. and Mexican activists (Fox 2000), the sanctuary movement that aided Central American refugees (Cunningham 1999), or anti-NAFTA coalitions (Ayres 1998). Increasingly, scholars have examined globalization-from-below in terms of its antecedents, protest repertoires, geographic reach, and theoretical and strategic underpinnings. Risse-Kappen (1995) investigates how international governance structures legitimize transnational activists' efforts, increase their access to national polities, and bolster their capacity to form effective coalitions. Smith et al (1997) analyze a wide range of transnational activism and advance a broader project of relating contemporary organizing to previous cross-border efforts, earlier theories of collective action, and debates about global governance. Waterman (1998) provides a subtle discussion of emerging labor internationalisms, grounded in a thorough understanding of old working-class transnational solidarities. Keck & Sikkink (1998) focus on transnational advocacy networks, which they distinguish from coalitions, movements, and "civil society" by their "nodal" organization and their use of information, symbolic, leverage, and accountability politics. They employ a concept of "network" that potentially includes social movements, but also media, unions, NGOs, and intergovernmental and governmental organizations.

When the 1997 Nobel Peace Prize was awarded to the International Campaign to Ban Landmines and Jody Williams, the ICBL had to wait for nearly a year to receive its half of the award money because it had no bank account and no address and was not an officially registered organization anywhere in the world (Mekata 2000). Acephalous, horizontal, loosely networked alliances, of which the ICBL was emblematic, have emerged as major actors on the world scene and are frequently said to have important advantages vis-à-vis hierarchical organizations, particularly states, but also supranational governance and financial institutions. Although all-embracing definitions of the term network are common (Castells 1997), more restricted interpretations are most revealing as regards concrete instances of collective action. Among the most developed discussions of networks is the previously cited RAND study of the Zapatistas (Ronfeldt et al 1998). Distinguishing between "chain," "star" or "hub," and "all-channel" networks, depending on the degree and type of interconnection between nodes, the RAND authors are mainly interested in developing a counterinsurgency strategy to replace 1980s "low-intensity conflict" doctrine. Among their concerns are "swarming," when dispersed nodes of a network converge on a target (as human rights NGOs did in Chiapas), and "sustainable pulsing," when "swarmers" coalesce, disperse, and recombine for attacks on new targets (as in anti-Maastricht marches in Europe and, one supposes, more recent demonstrations in Seattle and elsewhere). According to RAND, combating networks requires mimicking their form with interagency and multijurisdictional cooperation. States seeking foreign investment are most vulnerable to "netwar" campaigns that may damage their image or generate perceptions of instability. Giant corporations that invest heavily in linking brand images to consumer identities may be similarly threatened by informational campaigns, such as the antisweatshop movement, that expose pernicious environmental and labor practices (Klein 1999, Ross 1997).

Fox (2000) specifies with greater clarity than most theorists differences between transnational movements, coalitions, and networks, according to the extent to which they engage in mutual support and joint actions and share organized social bases, ideologies, and political cultures (with movements united along the most dimensions and networks along the fewest). He cautions that although the concepts are often used interchangeably and the categories sometimes blur, such analytical distinctions are necessary to keep in view imbalances and political differences within what might otherwise appear from the outside to be cohesive "transnational movements." Like Keck & Sikkink (1998), he is circumspect regarding hypotheses about "global" civil society because in their "hard version" such assertions suggest that changing international political norms and new technologies have fundamentally and universally altered the balance of power between state and society.

Appadurai (2000) also points to the limited success that transnational networks have had in "self-globalization" and attributes it to "a tendency for stakeholder organizations concerned with bread-and-butter issues to oppose local interests against global alliances" (p. 17), something amply documented by other researchers (Edelman 1998, Fox & Brown 1998). His assertion that networks' greatest edge vis-à-vis corporations is that "they do not need to compete with each other" is perhaps less persuasive because networks and their nodes collaborate even as they vie for funding, supporters, and political access, and it is their loose, horizontal structure instead that confers advantages over hierarchical organizations, as the RAND group (Ronfeldt et al 1998) worries. Similarly, the notion that "one of the biggest disadvantages faced by activists working for the poor in fora such as the World Bank, the U.N. system, the WTO [World Trade Organization], [and] NAFTA . . . is their alienation from the vocabulary used by the university-policy nexus" (Appadurai 2000, p. 17) is belied by a range of investigations from various world regions that demonstrate levels of sophistication on the part of grassroots activists that sometimes exceed those of their elite antagonists (Edelman 1998, Fox & Brown 1998, Gupta 1998). Other power differentials, beyond purely discursive ones, clearly skew contention between activists and these formidable institutions.

"Civil society"—"global," "national," and "local"—continues nonetheless to generate considerable excitement and an outsized literature, most of it beyond the scope of this article. Scholars have devoted extensive attention to the genealogy and boundaries of the concept (Cohen 1995, Comaroff & Comaroff 1999, Walzer 1995), its Gramscian roots (Nielsen 1995), and—more germane in considering social movements—to conservative and progressive variants of "civil society" discourse (Macdonald 1994, White 1994) and to the complicated relations between movements and other organizational forms which make up civil society, particularly NGOs (Alvarez 1998, Edelman 1999, Fox & Brown 1998, Gill 2000), but also political parties (Schneider & Schneider 2001). The key watershed in discussions from a wide variety of viewpoints and regions is the end of the Cold War, which at times is attributed not just to the failure of centrally planned economies to keep pace with informational and technological innovations but also to civil society itself, either its rise in the East (Chilton 1995) or its activities in the West (Tirman 1999). The end of superpower competition opened political space not only in erstwhile socialist societies but also in capitalist states where corruption and authoritarianism in political life could no longer be justified by the struggle against international communism. Weller (1999) shuns the term civil society as Eurocentric and insufficiently attentive to informal community ties in his examination of institutions in Taiwan and China "intermediate" between the state and family. He nonetheless develops a suggestive thesis about how village temples and informal local associations, often led by women and mobilizing around idioms of traditional Chinese culture, energized national-level environmental struggles in Taiwan. He indicates that comparable groups on the mainland already back underreported protest movements and could evolve as components of a gradual process of democratization. Schneider & Schneider (2001) trace the emergence of antimafia civic movements in Sicily, which they locate in the expansion after World War II of urban, educated, outward-looking social groups and the erosion in the post–Cold War era of an anti-Communist landowner-Christian Democratic–organized crime alliance. Like Weller, who emphasizes the political polivalence of traditional Chinese institutions and the significance of local practices in a rapidly changing national and international context, the Schneiders demonstrate that the struggle to retake social space from the mafia and its allies entails contention in neighborhoods, kin groups, workplaces, schools, and state institutions, as well as nurturing alternative civic sensibilities and debunking assumptions about the ancient roots of the mafia in Sicilian society.

The end of the Cold War, while opening political space for all manner of civil society initiatives, also brought accelerated economic liberalization and pressure on welfare-state institutions in developed and developing countries. Even before the fall of the Berlin Wall, during the free-market triumphalism that swept much of the world in the 1980s, it became increasingly artificial to envision NSMs as unengaged with the state. Indeed, fiscal austerity and draconian "adjustments" in public-sector services made states key targets for forces seeking to safeguard historic social conquests and prevent further rollback of healthcare, education, housing, and transportation programs. It is by now commonplace to indicate how globalization generates identity politics (Castells 1997), how attacks on welfare-state institutions fire resistance movements (Edelman 1999), and how supranational governance institutions (NAFTA, IMF, World Bank, WTO) are part and parcel of each process (Ayres 1998, Ritchie 1996). It is less frequent to find analyses that link these trends to the expanding movement against corporate power and unfettered free trade which burst into public consciousness in 1999 during the Seattle demonstrations and riots against the WTO.[6]

At first glance the anti-free trade coalition of environmental, labor, and farm activists would seem an unlikely combination of social forces, demands, and political practices. Brecher et al (2000) argue that an "epochal change" is occurring, as disparate movements find common ground and press not just for new rights, but for adherence by corporations, states, and suprastate institutions to generally held norms. According to these authors,

> the apparent opposition among strengthening local, national, and global institutions is based on a false premise: that more power at one level of governance is necessarily disempowering to people at others. But today the exact opposite is the case. The empowerment of local and national communities and polities today *requires* a degree of global regulation and governance (p. 40).

Although duly cognizant of the divisions that afflict social movements, they point to successful campaigns to secure debt forgiveness for underdeveloped countries, to derail the proposed Multilateral Agreement on Investment, to secure ratification of a global climate treaty and a protocol regulating genetically engineered organisms, and to stall the WTO Millennium Round as examples of how grassroots pressure may establish and enforce new norms of conduct that better balance the public interest and special interests.

With a lucidity and empirical foundation far beyond anything by Habermas or Melucci, Klein (1999) examines how market-based invasions of public space and individuals' "life-worlds" have become an impetus for anticorporate activism. Global corporations' outsourcing of production had allowed them to concentrate on branding and on efforts to insinuate brand concepts into the broader culture via sponsorships, advertising, and "synergies" with the sports, arts, and entertainment worlds. In North America and elsewhere, this was taking place alongside privatization of services, forcing schools, neighborhoods, museums, and broadcasters to turn to corporations for support, thus commercializing what remained of the public sphere. Superstore-studded malls were reshaping communities into newly privatized pseudo-public spaces. Branding became so entangled with culture, space, and identities that consumers increasingly felt bombarded and

---

[6]The sudden media attention to anti–free-trade activism in the aftermath of the Seattle demonstrations raises the question of the effectiveness of social movements' use of disruptive and violent versus moderate tactics, about which there has long been substantial debate (Giugni 1999, Piven & Cloward 1977, Tarrow 1998).

complicit in and threatened by corporate wrongdoing. High-profile events in 1995–1996 that pitted environmental and human rights activists against some of the world's most powerful corporations—the "McLibel" trial of anti-McDonald's activists in England, Aung San Suu Kyi's denunciations of labor conditions in Burma, Nigerian Ken Saro-Wiwa's execution during the Ogoni people's mobilization against Shell Oil—led growing numbers to link particular problems to a broader corporate assault on democracy, on communities, on cultural production (concentration of culture industries, restrictions on artisanal foods), and on the environment. The new willingness of established human-rights and environmental organizations to protest corporate malfeasance further fed the "rising bad mood" regarding transnational corporations and supranational governance institutions.

CONCLUSION

Recent writings on collective action suggest several areas of potential cross-fertilization that could invigorate social movements research. Political process and NSMs theorists could benefit from a greater sensitivity to the historical and cultural processes through which some of their main analytical categories (frames, submerged networks, movement culture) are constructed, as well as a more genuine appreciation of the lived experience of movement participants and nonparticipants, something that is accessible primarily through ethnography, oral narratives, or documentary history. Ethnographic analyses of social movements have been most persuasive when they transcend the single-organization or single-issue focus of much collective action research in favor of broader examinations of the political and social fields within which mobilizations occur. Although ethnographers have often provided compelling, fine-grained accounts of collective action, they have been less consistent when it comes to developing dynamic analyses of either the larger political contexts in which mobilizations occur or the preexisting militant traditions and the organizing processes that constitute movements' proximate and remote roots. To anthropologists, some of the issues (rationality, free riders) that continue to engross the grand theorists of contentious politics may appear misplaced or peculiarly devoid of cultural content, but others of their concerns certainly merit greater attention (cycles of contention, protest repertoires) if anthropologists are to avoid reverting to their traditional disciplinary predilection for advancing ahistorical pseudo-explanations for phenomena with profound historical roots.

The role of ethnography in the study of social movements has been significant but seldom theorized. Ethnographers—like historians who work with documentary or oral sources—may have privileged access to the lived experience of activists and nonactivists, as well as a window onto the "submerged" organizing, informal networks, protest activities, ideological differences, public claim-making, fear and repression, and internal tensions, which are almost everywhere features of social movements. Some of these aspects raise questions that can be addressed only though ethnographic or ethnographically informed historical research. Weller's (1999) study of how environmentalism emerged from local temples in Taiwan, Whittier's (1995) specification of how lesbian communes contributed to keeping radical feminism alive in the 1980s, and the Schneiders' (2001) attendance at rural Sicilian picnics where mafiosi and antimafiosi feasted together, uneasily aware that they were antagonists in a larger cultural-political struggle, are merely a few examples of the kinds of processes available to ethnographic observers but largely invisible to those working at a temporal or geographical distance from the activities they are analyzing. As a collection of methods, however, ethnography alone—as traditionally conceived—is hardly sufficient for studying the deep historical roots or wide geographical connections of most contemporary mobilizations. Nor does ethnography necessarily innoculate researchers against the common pitfalls of overidentification with the movements they study, accepting activist claims at face value, or representing "movements" as more cohesive than they really are (Edelman 1999, Hellman 1992).

If anything has distinguished anthropological, as opposed to other, students of social movements, it may well be a greater preoccupation with the researcher's political engagement, from the "reinvented" anthropology of the early 1970s to the "barefoot" anthropology of the 1990s (Burdick 1998, p. 181). For some, the "committed" stance is an unproblematic matter of preexisting ethical-political principles, as when one U.S. anthropologist—newly arrived in South Africa—identified herself in a squatter camp as "a member of the ANC [African National Congress]" (Scheper-Hughes 1995, p. 414). An astute scholar of rural Mexico (Paré 1994, p. 15) observes,

> For many of us it turned out to be impossible to record acts of repression and forms of exploitation and to witness the difficulties the peasant organizations had in making their voice heard without taking sides. . . . Participation—whether directly in the organization, in advising groups, in collective analysis with the organizations themselves, in negotiations, in publicity, in solidarity, in communications, or in the government as a planner, functionary or technician—necessarily implies taking a position, a "committed" vision.

Ethnographers of social movements who share these sensibilities frequently indicate that their own political involvement (Charlton 1998, Cunningham 1999, Schneider 1995, Stephen 1997, Waterman 1998) or their location in groups perceived as sympathetic or suffering a similar oppression (Aretxaga 1997, Hart 1996) is precisely what permits them access to activist interlocutors. Yet unproblematic versions of this position potentially mask vital movement dynamics and may even limit researchers' political usefulness for activists. Real social movements are often notoriously ephemeral and factionalized (Brecher et al 2000, Tilly 1986), manifest major discrepancies among leaders and between leaders and supporters (Edelman 1999, Morris 1999, Rubin 1997), and—probably most important—rarely attract more than a minority of the constituencies they claim to represent (Burdick 1998). To which faction or leader does the ethnographer "commit"? What does that commitment imply about hearing dissenting or un-interested voices or grasping alternative histories, political projects, or forms of cultural transformation? If commitment is a sine qua non of social movements ethnography, how are we to understand movements about which we do not feel "intensely protective" (Hellman 1992, p. 55) or which we may, in fact, not like at all?

The tendency of collective action scholars to focus on groups and organizations with explicit programs for change is, as Burdick suggests, in effect an acceptance "of the claim of the movement to be a privileged site in the contestation and change in social values." Elevating the question of lack of participation to the same level of importance as mobilization, he charges that much "sociological writing on the 'freeloader' problem ring[s] a bit hollow and even a bit arrogant in its presumption ... that social movement organizational action is the only, or best, social change game in town" (1998, pp. 199–200). In a candid account of his efforts to place research findings at the service of his activist interlocutors, he argues that accompanying a movement may, for the ethnographer, most usefully entail "reporting the patterned testimony of people in the movement's targeted constituency who on the one hand held views and engaged in actions very much in line with movement goals, but who on the other hand felt strongly put off, alienated, or marginalized by one or another aspect of movement rhetoric or practice" (1998, p. 191). In order to accomplish this, though, it is not the movement itself that becomes the object of study, but rather the broader social field within which it operates (cf. Gledhill 2000).

The widening of social fields implied by the rise of transnational activism suggests that this challenge will be even harder to meet in the era of globalization-from-below. Over the past three decades, theorists have had to scramble to keep up with the rapidly evolving forms of contentious politics. From identity-based movements that allegedly eschewed engagement with the state, to mobilizations that targeted neoliberal efforts to decimate social-welfare institutions, to more recent struggles against corporate power and supranational governance and international financial institutions, "scholars have come late to the party" (Keck & Sikkink 1998, p. 4). Part of the difficulty is recognizing transformative moments as they are being lived and even what comprises "movement activity." The new anticorporate activism, for example, employs an action repertoire that combines decidedly postmodern elements (informational politics, cyber-attacks, and "swarming") with others that hark back to early nineteenth-century forms of direct action, albeit with global rather than local audiences (uprooting genetically modified crops, ransacking corporate franchises). Whether or not we are on the verge of a new cycle of NSMs, it is already evident that understanding today's mobilizations will require new conceptions of what constitutes ethnography, observation, participation, and certainly engagement.

ACKNOWLEDGMENTS

Many thanks to Jimmy Weir and Susan Falls for research assistance, to the numerous colleagues who provided bibliographical advice, and to John Burdick and Khaled Furani for helpful comments on an earlier draft of this review.

Visit the Annual Reviews home page at www.AnnualReviews.org

LITERATURE CITED

Abdulhadi R. 1998. The Palestinian women's autonomous movement: emergence, dynamics, and challenges. *Gend. Soc.* 12(6):649–73

Adam BD. 1995. *The Rise of a Gay and Lesbian Movement.* New York: Twayne. Rev. ed.

Alvarez SE. 1998. Latin American feminisms "go global": trends of the 1990s and challenges for the new millennium. See Alvarez et al 1998, pp. 293–324

Alvarez SE, Dagnino E, Escobar A, ed. 1998. *Cultures of Politics/Politics of Cultures: Re-Visioning Latin American Social Movements.* Boulder, CO: Westview

Appadurai A. 2000. Grassroots globalization and the research imagination. *Public Cult.* 12(1):1–19

Arditti R. 1999. *Searching for Life: The Grandmothers of the Plaza de Mayo and the Disappeared Children of Argentina.* Berkeley: Univ. Calif. Press

Arendt H. 1951. *The Origins of Totalitarianism.* New York: Harcourt, Brace & World

Aretxaga B. 1997. *Shattering Silence: Women, Nationalism, and Political Subjectivity in Northern Ireland.* Princeton, NJ: Princeton Univ. Press

Ayres JM. 1998. *Defying Conventional Wisdom: Political Movements and Popular Contention Against North American Free Trade.* Toronto: Univ. Toronto Press

Baierle SG. 1998. The explosion of experience: the emergence of a new ethical-political principle in popular movements. See Alvarez et al 1998, pp. 118–38

Baumgardner J, Richards A. 2000. *Manifesta: Young Women, Feminism, and the Future.* New York: Farrar, Straus & Giroux

Berlet C, Lyons MN. 2000. *Right-Wing Populism in America: Too Close for Comfort.* New York: Guilford

Boudreau V. 1996. Northern theory, southern protest: opportunity structure analysis in cross-national perspective. *Moblization* 1(2):175–89

Bové J, Dufour F, Luneau G. 2000. *Le Monde n'est pas une Marchandise: Des Paysans contre la Malbouffe.* Paris: Découverte

Brecher J, Costello T, Smith B. 2000. *Globalization from Below: The Power of Solidarity.* Boston: South End

Brysk A. 2000. *From Tribal Village to Global Village: Indian Rights and International Relations in Latin America.* Stanford, CA: Stanford Univ. Press

Burdick J. 1995. Uniting theory and practice in the ethnography of social movements: notes toward a hopeful realism. *Dialect. Anthropol.* 20:361–85

Burdick J. 1998. *Blessed Anastácia: Women, Race, and Popular Christianity in Brazil.* New York: Routledge

Calderón F, Piscitelli A, Reyna JL. 1992. Social movements: actors, theories, expectations. See Alvarez et al 1998, pp. 19–36

Calhoun C. 1993. "New social movements" of the early nineteenth century. *Soc. Sci. Hist.* 17(3):385–427

Calhoun C. 1994. Social theory and the politics of identity. In *Social Theory and the Politics of Identity*, ed. C Calhoun, pp. 9–36. Oxford, UK: Blackwell

Carley M. 1997. Defining forms of successful state repression of social movement organizations: a case study of the FBI's COINTELPRO and the American Indian movement.

Res. Soc. Move. Conflict Change 20:151–76

Castells M. 1997. *The Information Age: Economy, Society and Culture.* Vol. 2. *The Power of Identity.* Oxford, UK: Blackwell

Charlton JI. 1998. *Nothing About Us Without Us: Disability Oppression and Empowerment.* Berkeley: Univ. Calif. Press

Chhachhi A, Pittin R. 1999. Multiple identities, multiple strategies: confronting state, capital and patriarchy. In *Labour Worldwide in the Era of Globalization: Alternative Union Models in the New World Order,* ed. R Munck, P Waterman, pp. 64–79. London: Macmillan

Chilton P. 1995. Mechanics of change: social movements, transnational coalitions, and the transformation processes in Eastern Europe. See Risse-Kappen 1995, pp. 189–226

Chomsky A, Lauria-Santiago A, eds. 1998. *Identity and Struggle at the Margins of the Nation-State: The Laboring Peoples of Central America and the Hispanic Caribbean.* Durham, NC: Duke Univ. Press.

Cohen CJ. 2001. Punks, bulldaggers, and welfare queens: the radical potential of queer politics? In *Sexual Identities, Queer Politics,* ed. M Blasius, pp. 200–27. Princeton, NJ: Princeton Univ. Press

Cohen JL. 1985. Strategy or identity: new theoretical paradigms and contemporary social movements. *Soc. Res.* 52(4):663–716

Cohen JL. 1995. Interpreting the notion of civil society. See Walzer 1995, pp. 35–40

Collier GA [with E Lowery Quaratiello]. 1994. *Basta! Land and the Zapatista Rebellion in Chiapas.* Oakland, CA: Inst. Food & Dev. Policy

Comaroff JL, Comaroff J. 1999. Introduction. In *Civil Society and the Political Imagination in Africa,* ed. JL Comaroff, J Comaroff, pp. 1–43. Chicago: Univ. Chicago.

Cunningham H. 1999. The ethnography of transnational social activism: understanding the global as local practice. *Am. Ethnol.* 26(3):583–604

Dagnino E. 1998. Culture, citizenship, and democracy: changing discourses and practices of the Latin American left. See Alvarez et al 1998, pp. 33–63

Davis DE. 1999. The power of distance: retheorizing social movements in Latin America. *Theory Soc.* 28(4):585–638

Della Porta D, Diani M. 1999. *Social Movements: An Introduction.* London: Blackwell

Diamond S. 1995. *Roads to Dominion: Right-Wing Movements and Political Power in the United States.* New York: Guilford

di Leonardo M. 1998. *Exotics at Home: Anthropologies, Others, American Modernity.* Chicago: Univ. Chicago Press

Dudziak ML. 2000. *Cold War Civil Rights: Race and the Image of American Democracy.* Princeton, NJ: Princeton Univ. Press

Eckstein S, ed. 1989. *Power and Popular Protest: Latin American Social Movements.* Berkeley: Univ. Calif. Press.

Edelman M. 1998. Transnational peasant politics in Central America. *Latin Am. Res. Rev.* 33(3):49–86

Edelman M. 1999. *Peasants Against Globalization: Rural Social Movements in Costa Rica.* Stanford, CA: Stanford Univ. Press

Escobar A, Alvarez SE, eds. 1992. *The Making of Social Movements in Latin America: Identity, Strategy, and Democracy.* Boulder, CO: Westview

Eyerman R, Jamison A. 1998. *Music and Social Movements: Mobilizing Traditions in the Twentieth Century.* Cambridge, UK: Cambridge Univ. Press

Falk R. 1993. The making of global citizenship. In *Global Visions: Beyond the New World Order,* ed. JB Childs, J Brecher, J Cutler, pp. 39–50. Boston: South End

Fals Borda O. 1992. Social movements and political power in Latin America. See Escobar & Alvarez 1992, pp. 303–16

Feldman A. 1991. *Formations of Violence: The Narrative of the Body and Political Terror in Northern Ireland.* Chicago: Univ. Chicago Press

Findlay EJ. 1998. Free love and domesticity: sexuality and the shaping of working-class feminism in Puerto Rico, 1900–1917. See Chomsky & Lauria-Santiago 1998, pp. 229–59

Fisher D. 1999. "A band of little comrades": socialist Sunday schools in Scotland. In *Popular Education and Social Movements in Scotland Today*, ed. J Crowther, I Martin, M Shaw, pp. 136–42. Edinburgh: Natl. Org. Adult Learn.

Flacks R. 1988. *Making History: The American Left and the American Mind*. New York: Columbia Univ. Press.

Forster C. 1998. Reforging national revolution: campesino labor struggles in Guatemala, 1944–1954. See Chomsky & Lauria-Santiago 1998, pp. 196–226

Foweraker J. 1995. *Theorizing Social Movements*. London: Pluto

Fox JA. 2000. *Assessing Binational Civil Society Coalitions: Lessons from the Mexico-US Experience. Work. Pap. No. 26*. Santa Cruz: Chicano/Latino Res. Cent., Univ. Calif.

Fox JA, Brown LD, eds. 1998. *The Struggle for Accountability: The World Bank, NGOs, and Grassroots Movements*. Cambridge, MA: MIT Press

Fox RG, Starn O, eds. 1997. *Between Resistance and Revolution: Cultural Politics and Social Protest*. New Brunswick, NJ: Rutgers Univ. Press

Fraser R, Bertaux D, Eynon B, Grele R, Le Wita B, et al. 1988. *1968: A Student Generation in Revolt*. New York: Pantheon

Freeman JB. 2000. *Working Class New York: Life and Labor Since World War II*. New York: New Press

Fromm E. 1941. *Escape from Freedom*. New York: Holt, Rhinehart & Winston

Gamson WA, Meyer DS. 1996. Framing political opportunity. See McAdam et al 1996b, pp. 274–90

Garner R. 1997. Fifty years of social movement theory: an interpretation. In *Social Movement Theory and Research: An Annotated Bibliographical Guide*, ed. R Garner, J Tenuto, pp. 1–58. Lanham, MD: Scarecrow

Gill L. 2000. *Teetering on the Rim: Global Restructuring, Daily Life, and the Armed Retreat of the Bolivian State*. New York: Columbia Univ. Press

Ginsburg FD. 1998 [1989]. *Contested Lives: The Abortion Debate in an American Community*. Berkeley: Univ. Calif. Press. 2nd ed.

Giugni M. 1999. Introduction. How social movements matter: past research, present problems, future developments. See Giugni et al 1999, pp. xiii–xxxiii

Giugni M, McAdam D, Tilly C, eds. 1999. *How Social Movements Matter*. Minneapolis: Univ. Minn. Press

Gledhill J. 2000. *Power and its Disguises: Anthropological Perspectives on Politics*. London: Pluto Press. 2nd. ed.

Grandin G. 2000. *The Blood of Guatemala: A History of Race and Nation*. Durham, NC: Duke Univ. Press

Grossmann A. 1995. *Reforming Sex: The German Movement for Birth Control and Abortion Reform, 1920–1950*. New York: Oxford Univ. Press

Grove RH. 1995. *Green Imperialism: Colonial Expansion, Tropical Island Edens and the Origins of Environmentalism, 1600–1860*. Cambridge, UK: Cambridge Univ. Press

Guha R, Martínez-Alier J. 1997. *Varieties of Environmentalism: Essays North and South*. London: Earthscan

Gupta A. 1998. *Postcolonial Developments: Agriculture in the Making of Modern India*. Durham, NC: Duke Univ. Press

Habermas J. 1981. New social movements. *Telos* 49:33–37

Hart J. 1996. *New Voices in the Nation: Women and the Greek Resistance, 1941–1964*. Ithaca, NY: Cornell Univ. Press

Harvey N. 1998. *The Chiapas Rebellion: The Struggle for Land and Democracy*. Durham, NC: Duke Univ. Press

Hellman JA. 1992. The study of new social movements in Latin America and the question of autonomy. See Escobar & Alvarez 1992, pp. 52–61

Heywood L, Drake J, eds. 1997. *Third Wave Agenda: Being Feminist, Doing Feminism*. Minneapolis: Univ. Minn. Press

Hilliard RL, Keith MC. 1999. *Waves of Rancor: Tuning in the Radical Right.* Armonk, NY: Sharpe

Hirschman AO. 1991. *The Rhetoric of Reaction: Perversity, Futility, Jeopardy.* Cambridge, MA: Harvard Univ. Press

Hobsbawm E, Rudé G. 1968. *Captain Swing: A Social History of the Great English Agricultural Uprising of 1830.* New York: Pantheon

Hodge GD. 2000. Retrenchment from a queer ideal: class privilege and the failure of identity politics in AIDS activism. *Environ. Plan. D* 18:355–76

Horton M, Kohl J, Kohl H. 1990. *The Long Haul: An Autobiography.* New York: Doubleday

Houtzager PP, Kurtz MJ. 2000. The institutional roots of popular mobilization: state transformation and rural politics in Brazil and Chile, 1960–1995. *Comp. Stud. Soc. Hist.* 42(2):394–424

Isserman M, Kazin M. 2000. *America Divided: The Civil War of the 1960s.* New York: Oxford Univ. Press

Judd RW. 2000. *Common Lands, Common People: The Origins of Conservation in Northern New England.* Cambridge, MA: Harvard Univ. Press

Keck ME, Sikkink K. 1998. *Activists Beyond Borders: Advocacy Networks in International Politics.* Ithaca, NY: Cornell Univ. Press

Klein N. 1999. *No Logo: Taking Aim at the Brand Bullies.* New York: Picador USA

Laclau E, Mouffe C. 1985. *Hegemony and Socialist Strategy: Towards a Radical Democratic Politics.* London: Verso

Laraña E, Johnston H, Gusfield JR, eds. 1994. *New Social Movements: From Ideology to Identity.* Philadelphia: Temple Univ. Press

Lerner G. 1998. The meaning of Seneca Falls: 1848–1998. *Dissent* 45(4):35–41

Macdonald L. 1994. Globalising civil society: interpreting international NGOs in Central America. *Millennium J. Int. Stud.* 23(2):267–85

Maybury-Lewis B. 1994. *The Politics of the Possible: The Brazilian Rural Workers' Trade Union Movement, 1964–1985.* Philadelphia: Temple Univ. Press

McAdam D, McCarthy JD, Zald MN. 1996a. Introduction: opportunities, mobilizing structures, and framing processes—toward a synthetic, comparative perspective on social movements. See McAdam et al 1996b, pp. 1–20

McAdam D, McCarthy JD, Zald MN, eds. 1996b. *Comparative Perspectives on Social Movements: Political Opportunities, Mobilizing Structures, and Cultural Framings.* Cambridge, UK: Cambridge Univ. Press

McAdam D, Tarrow S, Tilly C. 2001. *Dynamics of Contention.* Cambridge, UK: Cambridge Univ. Press

McCarthy JD, Zald MN. 1977. Resource mobilization and social movements: a partial theory. *Am. J. Sociol.* 82(6):1212–41

Mekata M. 2000. Building partnerships toward a common goal: experiences of the international Campaign to Ban Landmines. In *The Third Force: The Rise of Transnational Civil Society,* ed. AM Florini, pp. 143–76. Washington, DC: Carnegie Endow. Int. Peace

Melucci A. 1989. *Nomads of the Present: Social Movements and Individual Needs in Contemporary Society.* Philadelphia: Temple Univ. Press

Melucci A. 1996. *Challenging Codes: Collective Action in the Information Age.* Cambridge, UK: Cambridge Univ. Press

Mishler PC. 1999. *Raising Reds: The Young Pioneers, Radical Summer Camps, and Communist Political Culture in the United States.* New York: Columbia Univ. Press

Monson I. 1997. Abbey Lincoln's straight ahead: jazz in the era of the civil rights movement. See Fox & Starn 1997, pp. 171–94

Mooney PH, Majka TJ. 1995. *Farmers' and Farm Workers' Movements: Social Protest in American Agriculture.* New York: Twayne

Morris AD. 1999. A retrospective on the civil rights movement: political and intellectual landmarks. *Annu. Rev. Sociol.* 25:517–39

Nash J. 1997. The fiesta of the word: the

Zapatista uprising and radical democracy in Mexico. *Am. Anthropol.* 99(2):261–74

Nielsen K. 1995. Reconceptualizing civil society for now: some somewhat Granscian turnings. See Walzer 1995, pp. 41–67

Olson Jr., M. 1965. *The Logic of Collective Action: Public Goods and the Theory of Groups. Harvard Econ. Stud.*, Vol. 124. Cambridge, MA: Harvard Univ. Press

Paré L. 1994. Algunas reflexiones metodológicas sobre el análisis de los movimientos sociales en el campo. *Rev. Mex. Sociol.* 61(2): 15–24

Park RE. 1967. *On Social Control and Collective Behavior: Selected Papers*, ed. RH Turner. Chicago: Univ. Chicago Press

Payne LA. 2000. *Uncivil Movements: The Armed Right Wing and Democracy in Latin America*. Baltimore, MD: Johns Hopkins Univ. Press

Pereira AW. 1997. *The End of the Peasantry: The Rural Labor Movement in Northeast Brazil, 1961–1988*. Pittsburgh: Univ. Pittsburgh Press

Pichardo NA. 1997. New social movements: a critical review. *Annu. Rev. Sociol.* 23:411–30

Piven FF, Cloward RA. 1977. *Poor People's Movements: Why They Succeed, How They Fail*. New York: Pantheon

Prakash S. 1998. Fairness, social capital and the commons: the societal foundations of collective action in the Himalaya. In *Privatizing Nature: Political Struggles for the Global Commons*, ed. M Goldman, pp. 167–97. London: Pluto

Reed A, Jr. 1999. *Stirrings in the Jug: Black Politics in the Post-Segregation Era*. Minneapolis: Univ. Minn. Press

Ribeiro GL. 1998. Cybercultural politics: political activism at a distance in a transnational world. See Alvarez et al 1998, pp. 325–52

Risse-Kappen T, ed. 1995. *Bringing Transnational Relations Back In: Non-State Actors, Domestic Structures and International Institutions*. Cambridge, UK: Cambridge Univ. Press .

Ritchie M. 1996. Cross-border organizing. In *The Case Against the Global Economy and for a Turn toward the Local*, ed. J Mander, E Goldsmith, pp. 494–500. San Francisco: Sierra Club

Ronfeldt D, Arquilla J, Fuller GE, Fuller M. 1998. *The Zapatista Social Netwar in Mexico*. Santa Monica, CA: RAND Corp. Arroyo Cent.

Roseberry W. 1995. Latin American peasant studies in a 'postcolonial' era. *J. Latin Amer. Anthro.* 1(1):150–77

Rosen R. 2000. *The World Split Open: How the Modern Women's Movement Changed America*. New York: Viking

Ross A, ed. 1997. *No Sweat: Fashion, Free Trade, and the Rights of Garment Workers*. London: Verso

Rubin JW. 1997. *Decentering the Regime: Ethnicity, Radicalism and Democracy in Juchitán, Mexico*. Durham, NC: Duke Univ. Press

Sarah E, ed. 1983. *Reassessments of "First Wave" Feminism*. Oxford, UK: Pergamon

Saxton M. 1998. Disability rights and selective abortion. In *Abortion Wars: A Half Century of Struggle, 1950–2000*, ed. R. Solinger, pp. 374–93. Berkeley: Univ. Calif. Press.

Scheper-Hughes N. 1995. The primacy of the ethical: propositions for a militant anthropology. *Curr. Anthropol.* 36(1):409–20

Schneider CL. 1995. *Shantytown Protest in Pinochet's Chile*. Philadelphia: Temple Univ. Press

Schneider JC, Schneider PT. 2001. *Reversible Destiny: Mafia, Antimafia, and the Struggle for Palermo*. Berkeley: Univ. Calif. Press

Scott JC. 1990. *Domination and the Arts of Resistance: Hidden Transcripts*. New Haven, CT: Yale Univ. Press.

Scott JW. 1996. *Only Paradoxes to Offer: French Feminists and the Rights of Man*. Cambridge, MA: Harvard Univ. Press

Shorter E, Tilly C. 1974. *Strikes in France 1830–1968*. Cambridge, UK: Cambridge Univ. Press

Smelser NJ. 1962. *Theory of Collective Behavior*. New York: Free

Smith J, Chatfield C, Pagnucco R. 1997.

Transnational Social Movements and Global Politics: Solidarity Beyond the State. Syracuse, NY: Syracuse Univ. Press

Starn O. 1992. 'I dreamed of foxes and hawks:' reflections on peasant protest, new social movements, and the *rondas campesinas* of northern Peru. See Escobar & Alvarez, pp. 89–111

Starn O. 1999. *Nightwatch: The Politics of Protest in the Andes.* Durham, NC: Duke Univ. Press

Stein A. 1997. Sisters and queers: the decentering of lesbian feminism. In *The Gender/Sexuality Reader: Culture, History, Political Economy*, ed. RN Lancaster, M di Leonardo, pp. 378–91. New York: Routledge

Stephen L. 1997. *Women and Social Movements in Latin America: Power from Below.* Austin: Univ. Texas Press

Stock CM. 1996. *Rural Radicals: Righteous Rage in the American Grain.* Ithaca, NY: Cornell Univ. Press

Stolcke V. 1995. Talking culture: new boundaries, new rhetorics of exclusion in Europe. *Curr. Anthropol.* 16(1):1–34

Stoler AL. 1999. Racist visions for the twenty-first century: on the cultural politics of the French radical right. *J. Int. Inst.* 7(1):1, 20–21, 33

Tarrow S. 1989. *Democracy and Disorder: Protest and Politics in Italy 1965–1975.* Oxford, UK: Clarendon

Tarrow S. 1998. *Power in Movement: Social Movements and Contentious Politics.* Cambridge, UK: Cambridge Univ. Press. 2nd ed.

Taylor DE. 2000. The rise of the environmental justice paradigm. *Am. Behav. Sci.* 43(4):508–80

Thompson E. 1971. The moral economy of the English crowd in the eighteenth century. *Past Present* 50:76–136

Tilly C. 1986. *The Contentious French.* Cambridge, MA: Harvard Univ. Press

Tirman J. 1999. How we ended the cold war: peace activists' demand for an end to nuclear madness played a decisive role. *Nation* 269(14):13–21

Touraine A. 1973. Las clases sociales. In *Las Clases Sociales en América Latina*, ed. R Benítez Zenteno, pp. 3–71. Mexico City, Mex.: Siglo XXI

Touraine A. 1988 [1984]. *Return of the Actor: Social Theory in Postindustrial Society.* Transl. M. Godzich. Minneapolis: Univ. Minn. Press (From French)

Touraine A. 2000. *Can We Live Together? Equality and Difference.* Stanford, CA: Stanford Univ. Press

Vincent J. 1990. *Anthropology and Politics: Visions, Traditions, and Trends.* Tucson: Univ. Ariz. Press

Walzer M, ed. 1995. *Toward a Global Civil Society.* Providence, RI: Berghahn Books

Warren KB. 1998. *Indigenous Movements and their Critics: Pan-Maya Activism in Guatemala.* Princeton, NJ: Princeton Univ. Press

Waterman P. 1998. *Globalization, Social Movements and the New Internationalisms.* London: Mansell

Weller RP. 1999. *Alternate Civilities: Democracy and Culture in China and Taiwan.* Boulder, CO: Westview

White G. 1994. Civil society, democratization and development. I. Clearing the analytical ground. *Democratization* 1(3):375–90

Whittier N. 1995. *Feminist Generations: The Persistence of the Radical Women's Movement.* Philadelphia: Temple Univ. Press

Williams HL. 2001. *Social Movements and Economic Transition: Markets and Distributive Conflict in Mexico.* Cambridge, UK: Cambridge Univ. Press

Wolf ER. 1969. *Peasant Wars of the Twentieth Century.* New York: Harper & Row

Womack J, Jr. 1999. *Rebellion in Chiapas: An Historical Reader.* New York: New

Yúdice G. 1998. The globalization of culture and the new civil society. See Alvarez et al 1998, pp. 353–79

Zald MN. 1992. Looking backward to look forward: reflections on the past and future of the resource mobilization research program. In *Frontiers in Social Movement Theory*, ed. AD Morris, C McMueller, pp. 326–48. New Haven, CT: Yale Univ. Press

Annu. Rev. Anthropol. 2001. 30:319–34

RADICAL WORLDS: The Anthropology of Incommensurability and Inconceivability

Elizabeth A. Povinelli

Department of Anthropology, University of Chicago, Chicago, Illinois 60637;
e-mail: epovinel@midway.uchicago.edu

Key Words   power, language, new social movements, liberal diaspora, ethics

■ **Abstract**   This essay seeks to provide an overview of the anthropology of radical alterity and social commensuration. I begin with critical theoretical discussions of incommensurability and undecidability in the context of radical interpretation. I then resituate these theoretical debates in liberal ideologies of language-use and public reason in order to suggest the delicate and dramatic ways in which institutionalized conventions of risk and pleasure commensurate social worlds. How do incommensurate worlds emerge and how are they sustained? In other words, how is the inconceivable conceived? How are these new ethical and epistemological horizons aligned or not in the complicated space and time of global capital and liberal democratic regionalisms and nationalisms? How do publics interpret and decide between competing social visions and practices in the shadow of the seemingly incompatible frameworks of post-foundationalist and fundamentalist enlightenments?

INTRODUCTION

Street-dwellers in Mumbai and ferals in Australia (Appadurai 2000, Rajagopal 2002), indigenous activists in São Paulo and queer activists in Vienna, Cape Town, and Jakarta (Bunzel 2000, da Cunha & Almeida 2000, Boellstorf 1999, Hoad 1999); new religious fundamentalists in the Christian and Islamic worlds (Mahmood 2001, Lattas 1998, Asad 1993, Harding 2000, Crapanzano 2000)[1]—a

---

[1]And their complex interactions, "Another and significant gay & lesbian area centres around the suburb of Newtown in Sydney's "Inner West". This is an area just west of the CBD. Newtown is an area of old Victorian terraces, either under-going renovation, or falling down due to neglect! It's an area in transition. There is a slow gradual process of gentri-fication. As a result, fags & dykes, ferals, aging hippies, old conservatives, young families, and yuppie professionals are all neighbours. A healthy mix really." AUSTRALIA Out and About in Sydney: Queer Capital of the S Pacific John—*Canberra Australia.* <http://www.viajartravel.com/travsydn.htm> See also http://www.ferals.com.au/

0084-6570/01/1021-0319$14.00   **319**

significant portion of anthropology now focuses on what Charles Taylor has called the emergence of new social imaginaries and Nancy Frazer calls subaltern counterpublics, but what I will call the emergence of radical worlds in the shadow of the liberal diaspora (Taylor 1999, 2002, Fraser 1993; see also Warner 2002, Negt & Kluge 1993). We might say that anthropology has now complemented and complicated classical social questions about how actual social worlds are reproduced and ruptured, by asking: How do incommensurate worlds emerge and how are they sustained in their incommensurability? In other words, how is the inconceivable conceived? How are these new ethical and epistemological horizons aligned or not in the complicated space and time of global capital and liberal democratic regionalisms and nationalisms? How do publics interpret and decide between competing social visions and practices in the shadow of the seemingly incompatible frameworks of post-foundationalist and fundamentalist enlightenments?

The topic of incommensurability and interpretation has occupied a wide range of scholars and artists outside of anthropology, including political scientists, economists, jurists, and artists in the literary and plastic fields (Cage 1992, Simon 1999, Knapp & Michaels 1997, Flagg 1996, Chang 1997, Posner 2000, Perloff 2000). Studies include such disparate topics as indeterminacy and investment adjustment costs; intentionality, linguistics, and the indeterminacy of translation; and romanticism and intimacy. And the authors of these studies include everyone from the US Federal Reserve Board members to postclassical musicians to political theorists of multicultural nationalism.

This essay seeks to provide an overview of the anthropology of radical alterity and social commensuration. I begin with critical theoretical discussions of incommensurability and undecidability in the context of radical interpretation. I then resituate these theoretical debates in liberal ideologies of language-use and public reason in order to suggest the delicate and dramatic ways in which institutionalized conventions of risk and pleasure commensurate social worlds—how they make radical worlds unremarkable.

RADICAL INTERPRETATION

Scholars in the philosophy of language have understood incommensurability to refer to a state in which an undistorted translation cannot be produced between two or more denotational texts. The concept of incommensurability is closely related to linguistic indeterminacy. Indeed, they are sometimes used interchangeably. Indeterminacy is also used in a more narrow sense to refer to the condition in which two incompatible "translations" (or, "readings") are equally true interpretations of the same "text." In other words, if indeterminacy refers to the possibility of describing a phenomenon in two or more equally true ways, then incommensurability refers to a state in which two phenomena (or worlds) cannot be compared by a third without producing serious distortion. W. V. Quine used as an example of this kind of problem the translation into the Arunta language of a theory first formulated in English. Assuming that English sentences have "their meaning only together as a body, then we can justify their translation into Arunta only together as a body. There will be no justification for pairing off the component English sentences with component Arunta sentences, except as these correlations make the translation of the theory as a whole come out right. Any translations of the English sentences into Arunta sentences will be as correct as any other, so long as the net empirical implications of the theory as a whole are preserved in translation. But it is to be expected that many different ways of translating the component sentences, essentially different individually, would deliver the same empirical implications for the theory as a whole; deviations in the translation of one component sentence could be compensated for in the translation of another component sentence. Insofar, there can be no ground for saying which of two glaringly unlike translations of individual sentences are right" (Quine 1960, p. 80).

Philosophers such as Gadamar, De Mann, and Derrida have vigorously argued about the degree of distortion in translations (and interpretations) across incommensurate semantic fields; about the risk of assigning and acting on these translations in ordinary life; and about the social productivity of foregrounding indeterminacy/undecidability as a progressive social ideal (Wittgenstein 1969, Quine 1969, Kuhn 1966, Putnam 1978, Steiner 1975, Gadamar 1982, De Mann 1979, Derrida 1985, Caputo 1993, Connolly 1999). The stakes of translation seem high, given, as Jim Hopkins has argued, that the ability to "spontaneously, continually, and with remarkable precision and accuracy" interpret one another "seems fundamental to our co-operative and cognitive lives" (Hopkins 1999, p. 255).

But, as Quine suggests above, analytic philosophers seem haunted by much more than the ordinary stakes of ordering and getting a coffee. The ability to commensurate two textual (and thus social) fields without distortion or the ability to decide between these two translations on the basis of truth and accuracy puts more than metaphysics at risk (though as Derrida and Spivak have noted, it also puts metaphysics at risk by dislocating it from its foundation; Derrida 1982, Spivak 1999). Indeed, Quine's student, Donald Davidson, has hinged the philosophical problem of truth and incommensurability to representations and understandings of colonial and postcolonial history insofar as his notion of "radical interpretation" finds its purest expression there. By "radical interpretation," Davidson means to ask how it is possible for speakers to interpret an utterance in the context of radical linguistic (and social) alterity (Davidson 1984d). How could the Hawaiians have understood James Cook, or Cook the Hawaiians, without producing serious distortions (Sahlins 1995, Obeyesekere 1997)? As he puts it, "Hesitation over whether to translate a saying of another by one or another of various non-synonymous sentences of mine does not necessarily reflect a lack of information: it is just that beyond a point there is no deciding, even in principle, between the view that the Other has used words as we do but has more or less weird beliefs, and the view that we have translated him wrong. Torn between the need to make sense of a speaker's words and the need to make sense of his patterns of belief, the best we can do is choose a theory of translation that maximizes agreement" (Davidson 1984a, p. 101).

Davidson answers his own question about the possibility of radical translation positively, by propping the possibility of radical interpretation on the "principle of charity," namely, that speakers and listeners assume that the other is acting according to a set of rational linguistic conventions like their own (Davidson 1984b, p. 277). This convention allows speakers and hearers constantly to readjust their "passing theories" about the meaning of words as they realize that others are not using them as the listener would. As a result, if our aim is to understand the speaker as she or he wishes to be understood, then we modify our own language assumptions in the direction of a speaker's own as, in the course of conversation, we realize that the two are divergent—that the semantic way the other uses "hippopotamus" is the way we use "orange" (Davidson 1984c, p. 153). In other words we negotiate charitably. Charity begins at home, however; and Davidson has also argued that "if we cannot find a way to interpret the utterances and other behaviors of a creature as revealing a set of beliefs largely consistent and true *by our own standards*, we have no reason to count that creature as rational, as having beliefs, or as saying anything" (Davidson 1984d, p. 137, my emphasis; for a trenchant critique see Cutrofello 1999). Contra Davidson, critical theorists have argued that indeterminacy/undecidability is the normal condition of communication and is productively exploited in domestic and international negotiations such as in the standoff in early 2001 between the United States and China over responsibility for the downing of an American spy plane. Maximizing agreement in this case and others depends on the nonsynonymous nature of lexemes and sentence-level texts and the uncharitable, performative nature of the dissemination and excess of those texts (Bataille 1985, Derrida 1972).

As the reference to James Cook and his Hawaiian interlocutors was meant to suggest, analytic philosophers and critical theorists are hardly the only scholars of language and culture interested in the problem of incommensurability and undecidability in contexts of radical interpretation. Since Benjamin Whorf proposed studying the ways that structures of languages influence (or, in its strong version, determine) the thoughts of those who use them, anthropologists and other students of culture have struggled to understand the significance of the semantic distortions and gaps that occur in translations across social and sociolinguistic fields (for discussion of the legacies of Whorfian linguistic relativity, see Schultz 1990, Lucy 1992, P Lee 1996).

The work of linguistically minded anthropologists initially focused on grammatical categories—classically, the influence of overt and covert grammatical markings on people's cognition. From this standpoint, precision and accuracy seem vital indeed to our everyday lives, given that "empty" gasoline drums could seem like lesser fire hazards (Whorf 1967). But more recently, linguistic anthropologists have foregrounded the problem that metalanguage poses to efforts to close semantic space in moments of radical translation (Lucy 1993, Jakobson 1962a, Silverstein 1981). John Lucy put it this way: "Whorf's account makes clear that there is a specific semiotic problem involved stemming from the formal characteristics of reflexive uses of language. When using language reflexively (as metalanguage) to characterize the referents of forms in the language (as object language), speakers typically use the very same set of categories to describe the linguistic forms and to describe the reality to which those forms have reference" (Lucy 1993, pp. 24–25). Distortions are then not merely across linguistic phenomena but across levels of "linguistic consciousness" (Sapir 1949, Jakobson 1962b). Distortions simply compound as the structural terrain of translation becomes more complicated. Lucy again: "In fact, the problem is doubly acute since the analyst's own language categories may be so strongly felt that other languages will be interpreted or described in terms of them—effectively short-circuiting the possibility of developing clearly contrasting cases" (Lucy 1993, p. 25).

One of my favorite examples of such distortions is found in T. G. H. Strehlow's classic *Aranda Phonetics and Grammar* (1944). Strehlow's text seems especially relevant insofar as it shows the migration of the distortions produced by metalinguistic problems into moral evaluation. Strehlow's task is to outline the major phonemic and grammatical features of Arunta. But Strehlow is significantly bothered by one feature of Arunta grammar, the supposed absence of gender distinctions. Strehlow initially presents this difference with distinct neutrality: "The Aranda nouns know no distinctions of gender: masculine, feminine and neuter are all meaningless terms to the Central Australian tribesman. Not even the common animals of the chase are differentiated according to sex" (Strehlow 1944, p. 59). However, linguistic difference quickly migrates to moral ascription. For Strehlow, the Arunta do not merely *lack* gender distinctions, the Arunta "*refused* to acknowledge in its grammar the primal distinction of the genders" (Strehlow 1944, p. 59, my emphasis). Putting aside the question of whether and how Arunta marks gender, we see the grammatical presuppositions and entailments of English motivating what Strehlow considers the basic conditions of human articulateness. Quine's query about whether it is possible to translate an English-based theory into Arunta is apposite, though somewhat differently approached. The metalinguistic sense Strehlow has of the necessity of nominal gender in English becomes a moral insistence on what "primal distinctions" humans must acknowledge to be human as such.

The concept of linguistic and cultural indeterminacy and foreclosure has a much broader scope than linguistic anthropology. A paradigmatic case in the anthropological literature was the debate between feminist anthropologists in the 1980s over the relevance of the concepts of nature, culture, and capital to other societies (Ortner 1974, MacCormack & Strathern 1980, Di Leonardo 1991, Gal 2001). Marilyn Strathern's *Gender of the Gift* is in many senses the ethnographic apotheosis of this debate (Strathern 1988). We see a renewed interest in this problematic in the more recent generation's interest in the Foucauldian concept of "singularities," the Derridean concept of "undecidability," the Gramscian focus on cultural hegemony, and perhaps most influentially, Walter Benjamin's invocation of translation in *The Task of the Translator* (Benjamin 1969). For instance, in a study influential in critical anthropology, William Pietz has argued that the cultural fetish—we might include under the sign of "cultural fetish" all trade in and around cultural difference—is the mark of the foreclosure that occurs in the process of radical translation. "Fetish is not of any one of the two cultures coming into contact. It is a concept-thing (an idea and a material thing at the same time) that arises in the gap that comes about at the moment of contact between the two cultures/languages. It becomes imbued with power to carry meaning across borders" (Pietz 1985, 1987, 1988; see also Taussig 1993, and for recent full-length ethnographies incorporating these critical traditions see Ivy 1995, Rabinow 1999, Rofel 1999, Morris 2000).

Indeed, however interestingly, much of the post-Whorfian literature has focused on the semantic and grammatical features of language that lead to linguistic and social distortions in the proximity of alterity. But, in focusing on how linguistic distortions influence the apprehension of the social world, these studies have bracketed how social interaction, and thus social power, determines linguistic distortion (commensurability, and incommensurability). And it is exactly the issue of power that has interested anthropologists studying radical and subaltern worlds. Talal Asad noted some time ago that insofar as "the languages of the Third World societies. . . are 'weaker' in relation to Western languages (and today, especially to English), they are more likely to submit to forcible transformation in the translation process than the other way around" (Asad 1986, pp. 157–58; see also Chakrabarty 2000, Trouillot 2000). To return to Quine and Strehlow, if gender was not a feature of Arunta noun phrases, how did it become so, rather than English losing this grammatical marking? A number of scholars have examined just these types of questions, including Miyako Inoue, who has studied the "birth" and subsequent history and social effects of a discernible "woman's role" and an associated "women's language" in post-Meiji Japan, and Lydia Lui, who has developed Asad's point in the context of "translated modernity" in China during the first forty years of twentieth century (Inoue 1994, Lui 1995; see also Hart 1999, Saussy 1999). More recently, Emily Apter and Gayatri Spivak have discussed the impact of machine translation on the global politics of social intelligibility and conceivability (Apter 2001, Spivak 2001).

To be sure, recent pragmatically inclined anthropological approaches to semiotics resituate Davidson's focus on interpretive commensuration away from semantics and toward an interactive sociology (Daniel 1984, Urban 1996, Silverstein & Urban 1996, B Lee 1997, Irvine & Gal 1999). If Davidson advocates a semantically grounded theory of translation that maximizes agreement, pragmatic approaches ground agreement in real-time social contestations over the presuppositional underpinnings of any interaction. By demonstrating that Davidsonian adjustment occurs at the level of language usage, these scholars re-embed social and linguistic commensuration and de-commensuration in their social and institutional contexts. They demonstrate that every domestic and foreign exchange is a struggle at multiple levels. At the simplest, the struggle is to characterize the social nature of the interaction (the socially inscribed who, what, and where of any event, even those that happen "nowhere"), and thus the terms of how and what are say-able in this context and how it relates to questions of social and subjective worth, and livability. If a listener orients her conventions of interpretation toward a speaker, we can now ask what institutions of capital, subjectivity, and state influence the degree of this orientation (Povinelli 2002a).

Insofar as pragmatic approaches socially saturate communication, they help us ask questions about the emergence and foreclosure of socially inconceivable and incommensurate worlds. For, whether implicitly or explicitly, interactional signals indicate to persons how they should calculate and calibrate the stakes, pleasures, and risks of being a certain type of form in a certain type of formed space. Drawn into the semiotic process are the formal and inform(ation)al institutional forces that dictate the varying degrees of pleasure and harm varying types of people face breaking frame—of having the wrong body, or wrong form of a body, or wrong attitude about that formed body in a (informed) formed world. Davidson's worry over interpretation in the context of radical interpretation is displaced from a semantico-logical problem into a social problem; namely, the delicate and dramatic ways in which institutionalized conventions of risk and pleasure commensurate social worlds—make radical worlds unremarkable (Povinelli 2001).

POWER AND THE PRACTICE OF COMMENSURATION

Others have already begun moving in this direction. In "Commensuration as a Social Process," Wendy Espeland & Mitchell Stevens note that although it is evident in routine decision-making and a crucial vehicle of rationalization, commensuration as a general social process has been given little consideration by sociologists (Espeland & Stevens 1998). Drawing on Marxist analysis of capital forms of commodification and Weberian analysis of modern bureaucracies, Espeland & Stevens argue that the efficiency of bureaucracies and economic transactions depends on a standardization between disparate things that reduces the relevance of context—or, as they put it, "commensuration transforms qualities into quantities, difference into magnitude" (Espeland & Stevens 1998). They call for a sociology of commensuration that would ask, What motivates people to commensurate? What forms of commensuration do they use? What are commensuration's practical and political effects? What are the tensions between ethical systems and the formal rationality of commensuration such as, though not their example, the body organ trade (see Cohen 1999, Scheper-Hughes 2000, Comaroff & Comaroff 1999). Indeed, the emergent scholarship on bioethics in anthropology and science studies is an excellent site for studying the practical and political effects of social commensuration (see Kleinman et al 1999).

The questions Espeland & Stevens propose are nowhere more vital than in the anthropology of radical worlds and, more specifically, the study of the challenge radical worlds pose to the liberal diaspora. Philosophical worries about the possibility of commensurating various variant moral and epistemological fields become national and international concerns. The Islamic diaspora into western Europe, the emergence of queer sexualities throughout the world, and other older forms of social life in new places or emergent forms of social life in any place push against the previously tacitly held understandings of a shared deontic and epistemic horizon (Handler 1988, Povinelli 2002b). National concerns do not stop at the doorstep of cultural and social movements. The emergence of new forms of economic association—adapting to and resisting globalizing capital—equally may challenge the grounds of older forms of liberal civil society (Gilmore 1999, Wright 1999, Nancy 1991, Agamben 1993). Primarily focusing on the emergence of new financial instruments, Lee and Lipuma have described a much broader anthropological task of studying "cultures of circulation" (Lee & Lipuma 2002). And yet, put crudely, the liberal national form seems continually to reconstitute some nominal, and normative, we-horizon out of these publicly celebrated or scorned, but in any case seemingly economically vital, flows of people, images, and things (Ong 1999, Malkki 1995, Rouse 1991). The question of how radical worlds emerge in this context is displaced by a seemingly more pressing question: How are these disparate social and cultural worlds made commensurate with the social idea(l) of nationalism and/or civil society without the use of repressive force? The problem of radical interpretation once again reappears. But now we ask what social practices and forms of social power are used to commensurate disparate ethical and epistemological systems in liberal national forms.

One answer seems clear enough. The power of a particular form of communication to commensurate morally and epistemologically divergent social groups lies at the heart of liberal hopes for a nonviolent democratic form of governmentality. Since Kant, great faith and store has been placed in public reason as a means of diluting the glue that binds people unreflectively to moral or epistemological obligations and, at the same time, as a means of fusing, defusing and refusing deontological and epistemological horizons (Foucault 1997). Public reason—a form of communication in which free and equal citizens present truth claims to other free and equal citizens who accept or reject these claims on the basis of their truth, sincerity, and legitimacy has been granted the power of refashioning social institutions by continually opening them to the current consensus about what constitutes the most legitimate form(s) of public life (Habermas 1989, Rawls 1993). In this view, the procedures of reason and judgment are seen as determining social epistemologies and moral obligations, of bending moral sensibilities and making them pliable; and, in so doing, making a shared cultural and moral community. Through public reason perspective becomes perspectival; moral obligation and its conditioning of freedom opens to a broader moral horizon, the I-you dyad to a we-horizon, most notably the we-horizons of the nation and the human, the national and the cosmopolitan. Orienting justifications to this horizon detaches the social from the bonds of particular persons and groups; it makes members freer. It universalizes historical reason and moral obligations not by finding some transcendental reference, but by recalibrating the scope of current consensus. At no time in history have these procedures of public reason seemed so necessary and so valuable as when they were emerging in the midst of the religious carnage of seventeenth-century Europe and as they are now called upon to mediate moral co-presence in an increasingly diasporic world.

In liberal democracies, the corrective function of public reason is not merely located in the give and take of discourse, but in the give and take of formal and informal institutions. In other words, the dynamic among the domains of liberal society—between the public sphere, civil society, various formal institutions of government—should ideally mimic the self-correcting movement of reasoned public debate. Take for instance the juridical branch in Australia. Jurists may well represent themselves as basing decisions on precedent and other genre-specific procedures of the juridical domain. But they also understand themselves to be continually realigning the relevance of the common law to contemporary public opinion of what constitutes public understandings of the good, the tolerable, the abhorrent, and the just (Povinelli 1998). Indeed, the actions of each "estate" are represented and understood to be liable to correction by another, and all, ultimately, to the franchised public.

Habermas has perhaps gone furthest in seeking to integrate the embedded dynamic of discursive and institutional self-correction. For him, the proceduralism of the democratic public sphere understands that the truth claims made by free and equal citizens are refracted against the "objective world (as the totality of entities about which true statements are possible)," the "social world (as the totality of legitimately regulated interpersonal relations," and the "subjective world (as the totality of experiences to which a speaker has privileged access and which he can express before a public)" (Habermas 1989, p. 120). The end-point however is roughly the same, some nonviolent means of commensurating divergent or diverging moral and epistemological worlds.

And yet, in the real-time of social life, democratic nations contain the violent suppression of Islamic fundamentalisms, David Koresh and Move members are burnt to the ground, queers are staked out in all senses of the term, and many, even voluntary, social practices are outlawed. Even public practices that seem aligned to reasoned public debate are the target of sometimes severe forms of governmental control (Hirschkind 2001, Daniel 1996, Feldman 1991, Aretxaga 1997). In other words, rather than edging toward a horizon of shared epistemic and moral values, these discursive and institutional gaps could be seen as always already allowing repressive acts. By the time the legislative branch catches up, the law has already sentenced a generation to death. What seems to be at stake then is how we come to characterize moments of social repression and social violence directed at left and right radical worlds as moving forward a nonviolent shared horizon, as the peaceful proceduralism of communicative reason, rather than as violent intolerance, i.e., the pragmatic aspects of communication. To do this we have to shift our perspective. We do not ask how a multicultural or plural nation (or world) is sutured at the end of some horizon of liberal, institutionally embedded, communication. We ask instead how the incommensurateness of liberal ideology and practice is made to appear commensurate.

The temporalizing function of the horizon of successful self-correction seems an essential part of the means by which the practice of social violence is made to appear and to be experienced as the unfurling of the peaceful public use of reason. Characterizations of liberal governmentality as always already stretching to the future horizon of apologetic self-correction figure contemporary real-time contradictions, gaps, and incommensurabilities in liberal democratic discourses and institutions as in the process of closure and commensuration. Any analysis of real-time violence is deflected to the horizon of good intentions, and more immediately, as a welcomed part of the very process of liberal self-correction itself. Richard Rorty's discussion of liberal irony is interesting on this point. Rorty's ideal liberal is not a dispassionate philosopher in search of the holy grail of Truth, Goodness, and Justice, but a poet privately plagued by self-doubt about her deepest moral convictions, about what appears to her as a set of commonsense intuitions. In his words, "the process of socialization which turned her into a human being by giving her language may have given her the wrong language, and so turned her into the wrong kind of human being" (Rorty 1989, p. 75). Her doubt is born from the knowledge that all truths are the contingent values of linguistic functions; that no one "vocabulary" is closer to reality than another; and that the values one cleaves to most dearly may well be harmful to others. Nevertheless, although Rorty's ideal liberal subject privately suffers her anxieties and doubts, she publicly passionately defends her values until the organic philosophers, poets, ethnographers, and literary critics—the minor philosophers of late modern times—demonstrate to her, not so much what she can gain by incorporating another set of values into her own, but how she can avoid inflicting pain and humiliation on others.

For Rorty, the pragmatic approach to the problem of metalanguage and radical interpretation is essential to his liberal eschatology. Because of the type of metalinguistic feedback discussed by Lucy and others, reflection on one's final vocabulary and its interpretive grounds simply binds a person more deeply into the structures of that language. So deep and wide are these final vocabularies and so saturated and mired is subjectivity within them that their commonsense appeal cannot be escaped through critical reflection on the propriety, validity, and truth of their interpretive groundings. Only an encounter with an Other can break the hermetic seal of linguistic subjectivity (Rorty 1989, p. 80).

It is important to note that the external cry of the pained subject is the necessary supplement of Rortian liberalism, producing not only the liberal subject's own sense of her good, but also nontotalitarian forms of propositional truth. For Rorty, new *semantic* world disclosures "provide fresh grist for the argumentative mill" providing the "novelties" that forestall a collapse into totalitarian regimes of truth (Rorty 1998, p. 319; Bakhtin 1986). Unfortunately, the grist Rorty feeds the mill are those multitudinous others whose pain we might be unintentionally causing. They provide what the liberal subject requires to think and change since the knowledge of the contingency of all moral vocabularies is not enough to cause him to flee his particular moral vocabulary. He could not flee even if he so chose because, in Rorty's pragmatic deconstruction, to be a human subject is to be and become a value through and of language. Linguistic values (semantic, logical forms) cohere the self. They constitute the subject and society *as such* and as specifically valued beings-in-the-world-of-others. Listening to the articulated cry of a pained minority subject is the only means by which liberals can know when they are inflicting harm, pain, and torture on others, and why this pain is unjustified; i.e., of the type, scale, and quality that makes it systematic. In effect Rorty differentiates two distinct and distinctive social roles within multicultural liberal national society. Liberals will listen to and evaluate the pain, harm, torture they might unwittingly be causing minority others. Nonliberals and other minority subjects will present their pained subjectivity to this listening, evaluating public (see Connolly 1983 for a trenchant critique).

But note, those radical worlds that turn inward or away or refuse to dilate to the sympathy of the Same are treated as Durkheim once described the treatment of those who seek to free themselves from the norms of all thought. "Does a mind seek to free itself from the norms of all thought? Society no longer considers this a human mind in the full sense, and treats it accordingly" (Durkheim 1995, p. 16). Any political theorist worth her or his salt knows that liberals work within the space between the currently tolerable and the truth and acknowledges a crucial—the critical—distinction between the true and the conceivable. In a recent short book Michael Walzer, who has thought long and hard about liberal political forms, reminds us of a certain set of commonplaces among liberal political theorists: that all liberals acknowledge that "we choose within limits"; that few would ever be so daring as to advance "an unconstrained relativism"; and that not every act should be tolerated (Walzer 1997). Having said this Walzer does what theorists of liberal pluralism, multiculturalism, and diasporic nationalism often do, he urges readers to set aside the intractable problems facing national and international life—both within liberalism and across liberal and nonliberal societies—and concentrate instead on levels and types of disagreement that can be resolved without physical violence. Begin with the doable and the conceivable will follow.

Absent however from Rorty and Walzer's discussion is the dual orientation of this message of liberal sympathy. If we take liberal theorists of liberal worlds seriously, the anthropological study of radical emergences and incommensurate social imaginaries is faced with a numbing recognition. If the message addressing the liberal public might be "begin with the doable," the message addressing radical worlds is "be other so that we will not ossify, but be in such a way that we are not undone, that is make yourself doable for us." And the message conveys the stakes of refusing to be doable, and, thereby, the stakes of forcing liberal subjects to experience the intractable impasse of reason as the borders of the repugnant—actual legal, economic, and social repression. It is in this way that the late liberal diaspora shifts the burden for social commensuration from the place it is generated (liberalism) to the place it operates on.

ACKNOWLEDGMENTS

I would like to thank the members of the Late Liberalism faculty group at the University of Chicago for conversations stimulating much of the content in this essay and E. Valentine Daniel and Michael Silverstein for their careful and insightful reading of this essay.

Visit the Annual Reviews home page at www.AnnualReviews.org

LITERATURE CITED

Agamben G. 1993. *Theory Out of Bounds*. Minneapolis: Univ. Minn. Press

Appadurai A. 1996. *Modernity at Large, Cultural Dimensions of Globalization*. Minneapolis: Univ. Minn. Press

Appadurai A. 2000. Spectral housing and urban cleansing: notes on millennial Mumbai. *Public Cult.* 12(3):627–51

Apter E. 2001. On translation in a global market. *Public Cult.* 13(1):1–12

Aretxaga B. 1997. *Shattering Silence: Women, Nationalism, and Political Subjectivity in Northern Ireland*. Princeton, NJ: Princeton Univ. Press

Asad T. 1986. The concept of cultural translation in British social anthropology. In *Writing Culture: The Poetics and Politics of Ethnography*, ed. J Clifford, GE Marcus. Berkeley: Univ. Calif. Press

Asad T. 1993. *Genealogies of Religion*. Baltimore, MD: Johns Hopkins Univ. Press

Bakhtin MM. 1986. The problem of speech genres. In *Speech Genres & Other Late Essays*, ed. C Emerson, M Holquist, pp. 60–102. Austin, TX: Univ. Tex. Press

Bataille G. 1985. *Visions of Excess: Selected Writings, 1927–1939*, transl. A Stoekl, CR Lovitt, DM Leslie Jr. Minneapolis: Univ. Minn. Press

Benjamin W. 1969. The task of translator. In *Illustration: Essays and Reflections*, ed. H Arendt, transl. H Zohn, pp. 69–82. New York: Schocken

Boellstorff T. 1999. The perfect path: gay men, marriage, Indonesia. *GLQ: J. Lesbian Gay Stud.* 5(4):475–511

Bunzel M. 2000. The Prague experience: gay male sex tourism and the neo-colonial invention of an embodied border. In *Altering States: Ethnographies of the Transition in Eastern Europe and the Former Soviet Union*, ed. D Berdahl, M Bunzl, M Lampland, pp. 70–95. Ann Arbor: Univ. Mich. Press

Cage J. 1992. *Indeterminacy: New Aspect of Form in Instrumental and Electronic Music*. Washington, DC: Smithsonian Folkways

Caputo JD. 1993. *Against Ethics, Contributions to a Poetics of Obligation with Constant Reference to Deconstruction*. Bloomington, IN: Ind. Univ. Press

Chakrabarty C. 2000. *Provincializing Europe: Postcolonial Thought and Historical Difference*. Princeton, NJ: Princeton Univ. Press

Chang R, ed. 1997. *Incommensurability, Incomparability, and Practical Reason*. Cambridge, MA: Harvard Univ. Press

Cohen L. 1999. Where it hurts: Indian material for an ethics of organ transplantation. *Daedelus* 128(4):135–65

Comaroff J, Comaroff JL. 1999. Occult economies and the violence of abstraction: notes from the South African postcolony. *Am. Ethnol.* 26(3):279–301

Connolly W. 1999. *Why I Am Not a Secularist*. Minneapolis: Univ. Minn. Press

Connolly WE. 1983. On Richard Rorty: two views. *Raritan* 3(1):124–35

Crapanzano V. 2000. *Serving the Word: Literalism in America from the Pulpit to the Bench*. New York: New Press

Cutrofello A. 1999. On the transcendental pretensions of the principle of charity. In *The Philosophy of Donald Davidson*, ed. LE Hahn, pp. 333–41. Chicago/La Salle: Open Court

Da Cunha MC, Almeida M. 2000. Indigenous people, traditional people and conservation in the Amazon. *Daedalus* 129(2):315–38

Daniel EV. 1984. *Fluid Signs: Being a Person the Tamil Way*. Berkeley: Univ. Calif. Press

Daniel EV. 1996. *Charred Lullabies, Chapters in an Anthropology of Violence*. Princeton, NJ: Princeton Univ. Press

Davidson D, ed. 1984a. On saying that. In *Inquiries into Truth and Interpretation*, pp. 93–108. Oxford, UK: Clarendon

Davidson D. 1984b. Communication and convention. In *Inquiries into Truth and Interpretation*, pp. 265–80. Oxford, UK: Clarendon

Davidson D. 1984c. Belief and the basis of meaning. In *Inquiries into Truth and Interpretation*, pp. 141–54. New York: Oxford Univ. Press

Davidson D. 1984d. Radical interpretation (1973). In *Inquiries into Truth and Interpretation*, pp. 125–39. Oxford, UK: Clarendon

De Mann P. 1979. *Allegories of Reading, Figural Language in Rousseau, Nietzsche, Rilke, and Proust*. New Haven, CT: Yale Univ. Press

Derrida J. 1972. *Dissemination*. Chicago: Univ. Chicago Press

Derrida J. 1982. The ends of man. In *Margins of Philosophy*, transl. A Bass, pp. 109–36. Chicago: Univ. Chicago Press

Derrida J. 1985. Des tours de Babel. In *Difference in Translation*, ed. transl. JF Graham. Ithaca, NY: Cornell Univ. Press

Di Leonardo M, ed. 1991. *Gender at the Crossroads of Knowledge, Feminist Anthropology in the Postmodern Era*. Los Angeles: Univ. Calif. Press

Durkheim E. 1995. *The Elementary Forms of Religious Life*, transl. KE Fields. New York: Free Press

Espeland WN, Stevens ML. 1998. Commensuration as a social process. *Annu. Rev. Sociol.* 24:313–43

Feldman A. 1991. *Formations of Violence : The Narrative of the Body and Political Terror in Northern Ireland*. Chicago: Univ. Chicago Press

Flagg B. 1996. Changing the rules: some preliminary thoughts on doctrinal reform, indeterminacy, and whiteness. *Berk. Women's Law J.* 11:250

Foucault M. 1997. *The Politics of Truth*, ed. S Lotringer, L Hochroth. New York: Semiotext(e)

Fraser N. 1993. Rethinking the public sphere: a contribution to the critique of actually existing democracy. In *Habermas and the Public Sphere*, ed. C Calhoun, pp. 109–42. Cambridge, MA: MIT Press

Gadamer H-G. 1982. *Truth and Method*, transl. G Barden, J Cumming. New York: Crossroad

Gal S. 2001. Movements of feminism: the circulation of discourses about women. In *Recognition Struggles*, ed. B Hobson. Cambridge, UK: Cambridge Univ. Press. Forthcoming

Gilmore R. 1999. You have dislodged a boulder: mothers and prisoners in the post Keynesian California landscape. *Transforming Anthropol.* 8(1,2):12–38

Habermas J. 1989. *The Theory of Communicative Action*. 2 vols. Transl. T McCarthy. Boston: Beacon

Handler R. 1988. *Nationalism and the Politics of Culture in Quebec*. Madison: Univ. Wisc. Press

Harding S. 2000. *The Book of Jerry Falwell: Fundamentalist Language and Politics*. Princeton, NJ: Princeton Univ. Press

Hart R. 1999. Translating the untranslatable: from copula to incommensurable worlds. In *Tokens of Exchange, the Problem of Translation in Global Circulation*, ed. LH Lui, pp. 45–73. Durham, NC: Duke Univ. Press

Hirschkind C. 2001. Civic virtue and religious reason: an Islamic counter-public. *Cult. Anthropol.* 16,1:3–37

Hoad N. 1999. The perfect path: gay men, marriage, Indonesia. *GLQ: J. Lesbian Gay Stud.* 5(4):559–84

Hopkins J. 1999. Wittgenstein, Davidson, and radical interpretation. In *The Philosophy of Donald Davidson*, ed. LE Hahn, pp. 255–85. Chicago/La Salle: Open Court

Inoue M. 1994. Gender and linguistic modernization: historicizing Japanese women's language. In *Cultural Performances: Proceedings of the Third Berkeley Women and Language Conference*, ed. M Bucholtz, AC Liang, LA Sutton, C Hines, pp. 322–33. Berkeley, CA: Berkeley Women Lang. Group

Irvine J, Gal S. 1999. Language ideology and linguistic differentiation. In *Regimes of Language*, ed. PV Kroskrity, pp. 35–84. Santa Fe, NM: School Am. Res.

Ivy M. 1995. *Discourses of the Vanishing: Modernity, Phantasm, Japan*. Chicago: Univ. Chicago Press

Jakobson R. 1962a. Metalanguage as a linguistic problem. In *Selected Writings VII*, pp. 113–21. Berlin: Mouton

Jakobson R. 1962b. On the linguistic approach to the problem of consciousness and the unconsciousness. In *Selected Writings VII*, pp. 148–62. Berlin: Mouton

Kleinman A, Fox RC, Brandt AM, eds. 1999. *Bioethics and Beyond*. Special Issue. *Daedalus* 128(4)

Knapp S, Michaels WB. 1997. Legal indeterminacy and legitimacy. In *Legal Hermenuetics, History, Theory, and Practice*, ed. G Leyh. Berkeley: Univ. Calif. Press

Kuhn T. 1966. *The Copernican Revolution*. Cambridge, MA: Harvard Univ. Press

Lattas A. 1998. *Cultures of Secrecy: Reinventing Race in Bush Kaliai Cargo Cults*. Madison: Univ. Wisc. Press

Lee B. 1997. *Talking Heads: Language, Metalanguage, and the Semiotics of Subjectivity*. Durham, NC: Duke Univ. Press

Lee B, Lipuma E. 2002. Cultures of circulation. *Public Cult.* 14(1): Forthcoming

Lee P. 1996. *The Whorf Theory Complex: A Critical Reconstruction*. Amsterdam/Philadelphia: John Benjamins

Lucy J. 1992. *Language Diversity and Thought, A Reformulation of the Linguistic Relativity Hypothesis*. Cambridge, UK: Cambridge Univ. Press

Lucy J. 1993. Reflexive language and the human disciplines. In *Reflexive Language: Reported Speech and Metapragmatics*, ed. J Lucy, pp. 9–32. Cambridge, UK: Cambridge Univ. Press

Lui LH. 1995. *Translingual Practice: Literature, National Culture, and Translated Modernity, China, 1900–1937*. Stanford, CA: Stanford Univ. Press

MacCormack C, Strathern M, eds. 1980. *Nature, Culture, and Gender*. Cambridge, UK: Cambridge Univ. Press

Mahmood S. 2001. Feminist theory, embodiment, and the docile agent: some reflections on the Egyptian Islamic revival. *Cult. Anthropol.* 6(2): Forthcoming

Malkki L. 1995. *Purity and Exile: Violence, Memory, and National Cosmology among Hutu Refugees in Tanzania*. Chicago: Univ. Chicago Press

Morris RC. 2000. *In the Place of Origins, Modernity and Its Mediums in Northern Thailand*. Durham, NC: Duke Univ. Press

Nancy J-L. 1991. *The Inoperative Community*, ed. P Connor, transl. P Connor, M Holland, S Sawhney. Minneapolis, MN: Univ. Minn. Press

Negt O, Kluge A. 1993. *Public Sphere and Experience, Toward an Analysis of the Bourgeois and Proletarian Public Sphere*, transl. P Labanyi, JO Daniel, Oksiloff. Minneapolis: Univ. Minn. Press

Obeyesekere G. 1997. *The Apotheosis of Captain Cook: European Mythmaking in the Pacific*. Princeton, NJ: Princeton Univ. Press

Ong A. 1999. *Flexible Citizenship: The Cultural Logics of Transnationality*. Durham, NC: Duke Univ. Press

Ortner S. 1974. Is female to male as nature is to

culture? In *Woman, Culture and Society*, ed. MZ Rosaldo, L Lamphere, pp. 67–88. Stanford, CA: Stanford Univ. Press

Perloff M. 2000. *The Poetics of Indeterminacy: Rimbaud to Cage*. Evanston, IL/London: Northwestern Univ. Press

Pietz W. 1985. The problem of the fetish, Part 1. *Res* 9:5–17

Pietz W. 1987. The problem of the fetish, Part 2. *Res* 13:23–34

Pietz W. 1988. The problem of the fetish, Part 3. *Res* 16:105–23

Posner EA. 2000. *Law and Social Norms*. Cambridge, MA: Harvard Univ. Press

Povinelli EA. 1998. The state of shame: Australian multiculturalism and the crisis of indigenous citizenship. *Crit. Inq.* 24(2):575–610

Povinelli EA. 2001. Sexuality at risk: psychoanalysis (meta)pragmatically. *Homosexuality and Psychoanalysis*, ed. T Dean, C Lane, pp. 387–411. Chicago: Univ. Chicago Press

Povinelli EA. 2002a. The vulva thieves: (*Atna nylkna*) modal ethics and the colonial archive. See Povinelli 2002b

Povinelli EA. 2002b. *The Cunning of Recognition: Indigenous Alterity and the Making of Australian Multiculturalism*. Durham, NC: Duke Univ. Press. Forthcoming

Putnam H. 1978. *Meaning and the Moral Sciences*. London: Routledge & Kegan Paul

Quine WV. 1960. *Word & Object*. Cambridge, MA: MIT Press

Quine WV. 1969. *Ontological Relativity and Other Essays*. New York: Columbia Univ. Press

Rabinow P. 1999. *French DNA: Trouble in Purgatory*. Chicago: Univ. Chicago Press

Rajagopal A. 2002. The violence of commodity aesthetics: hawkers, demolition raids and a new regime of consumption. *Social Text*. Forthcoming

Rawls J. 1993. *Political Liberalism*. New York: Columbia Univ. Press

Rofel L. 1999. *Other Modernities: Gendered Yearnings in China after Socialism*. Berkeley: Univ. Calif. Press

Rorty R. 1989. *Contingency, Irony and Solidarity*. Cambridge, UK: Cambridge Univ. Press

Rorty R. 1998. Habermas, Derrida, and the functions of philosophy. In *Truth and Progress*, pp. 307–26. Cambridge, UK: Cambridge Univ. Press

Rouse R. 1991. Mexican migration and the social space of postmodernism. *Diaspora* 2(2):8–23

Sahlins MD. 1995. *How "Natives" Think: About Captain Cook, For Example*. Chicago: Univ. Chicago Press

Sapir E. 1949. The unconscious patterning of behavior in society. In *Selected Writings of Edward Sapir in Language, Culture, and Personality*, ed. D Mandelbaum, pp. 544–59. Berkeley: Univ. Calif. Press

Saussy H. 1999. Always multiple translation, or, how the Chinese language lost its grammar. In *Tokens of Exchange, The Problem of Translation in Global Circulation*, ed. LH Lui, pp. 107–23. Durham, NC: Duke Univ. Press

Scheper-Hughes N. 2000. The global traffic in human organs. *Curr. Anthropol.* 41(2):191–224

Schultz EA. 1990. *Dialogue at the Margins: Whorf, Bakhtin, and Linguistic Relativity*. Madison: Univ. Wisc. Press

Silverstein M. 1981. The limits of awareness. *Sociolinguistic Work. Pap. No. 84*. Austin, TX: Southwest Educ. Dev. Laboratory

Silverstein M, Urban G, eds. 1996. *Natural Histories of Discourse*. Chicago: Univ. Chicago Press

Simon WH. 1999. Three limitations to deliberative democracy: identity politics, bad faith, and indeterminacy. In *Deliberative Politics: Essays on Democracy and Disagreement*, ed. S Macedo, pp. 49–57. New York: Oxford Univ. Press

Spivak G. 1999. *The Critique of Colonial Reason, Toward a History of the Vanishing Present*. Cambridge, MA: Harvard Univ. Press

Spivak G. 2001. Questioned on translation: adrift. *Public Cult.* 13.1:13–22

Steiner G. 1975. *After Babel*. New York: Oxford Univ. Press

Strathern M. 1988. *The Gender of the Gift*. Los Angeles: Univ. Calif. Press

Strehlow TGH. 1944. *Aranda Phonetics and Grammar*. Oceania Monogr., No. 7. Sydney: Aust. Natl. Res. Council

Taussig M. 1993. Maleficium: state fetishism. In *Fetishism as Cultural Discourse*, ed. E Apter, W Pietz, pp. 217–47. Ithaca, NY: Cornell Univ. Press

Taylor C. 1999. Two theories of modernity. *Public Cult.* 11(1):153–74

Taylor C. 2002. New social imaginaries. *Public Cult.* 14(1): In press

Trouillot MT. 2000. Abortive rituals. Historical apologies in the global era. *Interventions* 2(2):171–86

Urban G. 1996. *Metaphysical Community: The Interplay of the Senses and the Intellect*. Austin, TX : Univ. Tex. Press

Walzer M. 1997. *On Toleration*. New Haven, CT: Yale Univ. Press

Warner M. 2002. Counter-publics. *Public Cult.* 14(1): In press

Whorf BL. 1967. The relation of habitual thought and behavior to language. In *Language, Thought & Reality*, ed. JB Carroll, pp. 134–59. Cambridge, MA: MIT Press

Wittgenstein L. 1969. *On Certainty*. New York: Harper & Row

Wright M. 1999. The dialectics of still life: murder, women, and maquiladoras. *Public Cult.* 11(3):453–73

Annu. Rev. Anthropol. 2001. 30:335–61

INTERNATIONAL AIDS RESEARCH IN ANTHROPOLOGY: Taking a Critical Perspective on the Crisis

Brooke G. Schoepf

Institute for Health and Social Justice, Department of Social Medicine, Harvard University Medical School, Boston, Massachusetts 02115; e-mail: bgscs@netzero.net

Key Words   medical anthropology, Africa/global economy, interpretive anthropology, critical theory, social suffering

■ **Abstract**   Anthropological literature on AIDS in the international arena from the 1990s shows researchers' increasing attention to linkages between local sociocultural processes that create risk of infection and the lifeworlds of sufferers to the global political economy. Focus on Africa, where the heterosexual epidemic has attained catastrophic proportions, reveals some cultural particularisms but many more regularities in the social production of disease. Global inequalities of class, gender, and ethnicity are revealed, as poverty, powerlessness, and stigma propel the spread of HIV. Anthropologists' witness to suffering, their concern and engagement, are potent elements in the research process and in advocacy in national and international arenas. The combined strength of theory and practice in the field of international research on AIDS is a significant contribution to anthropology in the twenty-first century.

A BIOSOCIAL PERSPECTIVE

The dawn of the twenty-first century finds the world beset by the most devastating pandemic known. Since the slow-acting human immunodeficiency virus (HIV) began to spread silently across the globe in the late 1970s, an estimated 19 million people have died of AIDS, and more than 36 million currently are infected. Ninety percent of those with HIV and AIDS live in the Third World. Some 70%, an estimated 27 million people, are Africans; most have become infected through sex. Without access to anti-viral therapies, the majority will die within the next five years. Another 16 million Africans are believed already to have died of AIDS. While the epidemic has slowed or stabilized in a few areas, elsewhere in countries across sub-Saharan Africa infection rates are rising rapidly; nearly 4 million people are estimated to have acquired HIV infection in the year 2000 (UNAIDS 2000).

0084-6570/01/1021-0335$14.00   **335**

Reasons for different infection prevalence rates within sub-Saharan Africa are not yet understood. In some countries in West Africa, prevalence is estimated at less than 5% of adults; in the two worst affected countries, the rate is at more than 30%. Ten countries have rates estimated at 20%–30%. Botswana has the highest infection prevalence; South Africa, with more than four million seropositive people, has the highest number. Neither differences in sexual behavior nor differences in the virulence of locally predominant HIV-1 strains appears to account for the divergence; a hypothesized protective role for male circumcision remains unclear. Untreated conventional sexually transmitted infections (STIs) raise the likelihood of HIV infection; thus the absence of biomedical health services with effective antibiotic treatment poses a serious risk. (The role of socioeconomic and political conditions is discussed below.)

Research in molecular genetics finds the closest living relatives of HIV viruses in chimpanzees and African green monkeys. One model places a species leap from an ancestral chimpanzee virus to HIV-1 in the seventeenth century; another proposes that it is more recent—around 1930 (+/−30 years). Several hypotheses attempt to account for its increasing virulence in social terms related to increased population movements and ecological change. One suggests that prolonged social crises in Central Africa from the mid-1970s may be a contributing factor. HIV-1 now exhibits the fast-spreading characteristics of a well-established "virgin field" epidemic. A retrovirus, the HIV multiplies rapidly; mutation and recombination render the vaccine search difficult. Despite rapid progress in the biomedical sciences, much remains unknown about the HIV and AIDS.

AIDS is not just another disease; the HIV virus is not just one among many new microorganisms affecting humans. Biological and social conditions propel spread of the virus; the same elements combine to make HIV-prevention education and behavior changes difficult. Disease becomes evident only long after infection takes place (on average, ten years) and then presents as many different opportunistic infections. This makes the reality of AIDS difficult for lay-people, including political leaders, to grasp, especially in early stages of the epidemic. Complex cultural and psychological meanings also intervene in representations of AIDS. With transmission linked to body fluids—to semen and vaginal secretions, blood, and mothers' milk—to sex, reproduction, and death, AIDS in many cultures is freighted with extraordinary symbolic and emotional power, including ideas about social and spiritual "pollution."

Disease epidemics are social processes: Spread of infectious agents is shaped by political economy, social relations, and culture. A disease of modernity and global population movement, AIDS has struck with particular severity in communities struggling under the burdens of poverty, inequality, economic crisis, and war. Many people who know about the danger of sexual transmission, especially many girls and women, cannot avoid becoming infected because they cannot control the relations of power that put their lives at risk. The pandemic is much more than a series of personal and family tragedies. AIDS' deaths have depleted the workforce, lowered life expectancies, raised dependency ratios, and are likely to shred the already torn social fabric of numerous countries.

Worldwide, the virus is spreading at an accelerating pace. The Asian pandemic has begun to burgeon, with an estimated four million people already infected. Due to the large numbers of people potentially at risk, there is cause for deep concern. Unless the familiar patterns of fear, denial, stigma, and disempowering education campaigns, coupled with conditions of widespread poverty, inequality, and violence are ended, Africa's tragedy will be replicated elsewhere.

ANTHROPOLOGISTS AND AIDS

From slow beginnings in the mid-1980s, AIDS research by anthropologists has grown rich and diverse. In addition to medical anthropologists, researchers from three of anthropology's classic four fields, from numerous sub-disciplines, have examined aspects of the pandemic. This review focuses on contributions by anthropologists and their collaborators from other disciplines working in the international arena. It situates these studies within major theoretical and methodological approaches and controversies. It attempts to assess their significance for the field of anthropology at the dawn of the twenty-first century.

The rapidly expanding anthropological literature includes numerous edited collections (Bibeau & Murbach 1991, Dyson 1991, Bolton & Singer 1992, Herdt & Lindenbaum 1992, Farmer et al 1993, Feldman 1994, Brummelhuis & Herdt 1995, Dozon & Vidal 1995, Orubuloye et al 1995, Farmer et al 1996, Parker & Gagnon 1995, Bond et al 1997, Desclaux & Raynaut 1997, Herdt 1997, Ntozi et al 1997, Singer 1998, Becker et al 1999, Fay 1999, Desclaux & Taverne 2000), as well as journal articles and chapters in books devoted to area studies and to other subjects. Since they cannot all be reviewed here, I have chosen issues I consider pertinent to the contribution of AIDS research to anthropology. The small but growing number of full-length ethnographies of AIDS is a major advance of the second decade. These richly contextualized studies allow the voices of sufferers and people at risk to be heard, by incorporating narratives, texts of interviews, observations, and public speech. Most adopt a historically grounded "political economy-and-culture" strategy (Schoepf 1988, 1998, Singer 1998).[1]

Space and language facility limit consideration to English and French sources. Many of the cited works are collections with a diverse geographical purview. Other collections also contain data and analyses valuable for international research (see Berger & Ray 1993, Schenker et al 1996, Schneider & Stoller 1995, Aggleton et al 1999). Readers are directed to topical literature reviews (Schoepf 1991, 1993a,b, 1997; DeBruyn 1992; Ulin 1992; Farmer et al 1996; Baer et al 1997; Farmer 1997;

---

[1]References to much of my own research in medical anthropology, including that with the CONNAISSIDA Project from 1985, are found in Schoepf (1998) and Schoepf et al (2000). They are omitted here, as are many citations from the classics, in order to save space. Statements not footnoted are taken from my work, which examines most of the issues discussed here.

Seidel & Vidal 1997; Lindenbaum 1998; Singer 1998; Symonds & Schoepf 2000; Schneider & Stein 2001).

Because sub-Saharan Africa has been the most affected by AIDS to date and has been a site of controversy in scientific and popular media, and in the policy arena, this review features work by anthropologists in sub-Saharan Africa. An area studies focus assists in discerning the extent to which anthropological research on HIV/AIDS has compared and contrasted infection and disease across cultures within the same area and in wider fields. Struggles over meaning in scholarly and policy arenas are critically examined before moving to other areas. Scientists' construction of risk, identities, gender relations, inequality, poverty, and powerlessness are of crucial interest.

STRUGGLES OVER MEANING

Internationally, as in the United States, AIDS is "an epidemic of signification" (Treichler 1999). Responses have been moralizing and stigmatizing. Initially recognized among elites in many countries, HIV rapidly spread along "the fault-lines of society" to the poor and disinherited. Response to AIDS is political everywhere. Knowledge is socially situated, built on previous knowledges with the power to define how we know. In the case of AIDS in Africa, the defining power lay in the international biomedical arena, but these definitions met with enduring disease representations and practices, especially with respect to contagion and "disordered" sexuality in afflicted societies. The contradictions between situational need and response have been particularly sharp in Africa. This can be explained, at least in part, by discourses surrounding the appearance and spread of the new virus:

AIDS brings forth representations that support and reproduce already constituted gender, color, class, and national hierarchies. Societal responses to AIDS, including disease control policies, are propelled by cultural politics forged in the history of relations between Africa and the West (Schoepf 1988).

The cultural politics of AIDS are now well understood—their effects on the pandemic, somewhat less so (Symonds & Schoepf 2000). At the outset, epidemiologists in government agencies designated entire populations as "risk groups," obscuring differences among people assigned to the categories (Farmer 1988, Bolton 1992). A focus on risk groups implies that everyone not included within the boundaries of stigma is not at risk (Parker 1987, Lyttleton 1996). Common in public health discourse, such constructions are part of a "hegemonic process" that helps dominant groups to maintain, reinforce, re-construct, and obscure the workings of the established social order (Glick-Schiller 1992). In Gramsci's elaboration of the concept, hegemony does not simply flow from the class structure as an expression of power. Rather, it comes about through struggle between forces with opposing interests.

Full responsibility for moralizing discourses and the resulting social demobilization cannot be laid solely at the feet of biomedical policymakers, for the discourses and policy are embedded in the public culture of late twentieth-century Western societies. The currently dominant biomedical model incorporates capitalist economic assumptions about health resulting from individually chosen lifestyles. It leaves little scope for understanding how behaviors are related to social conditions, or how communities shape the lives of their members. The epidemiologists' focus on individual sexual behavior, their claim to exclusive value-neutral objectivity, and reliance on surveys as the sole method of "science" is very much their responsibility (Fee & Krieger 1993, Frankenberg 1994, Hunt 1996, Seidel & Vidal 1997, Bastos 1999). The late Dr. Jonathan Mann was self-critical:

> The focus on individual risk reduction was simply too narrow, for it was unable to deal concretely with the lived social realities . . . applying classical epidemiological methods to HIV/AIDS ensures–pre-determines–that 'risk' will be defined in terms of individual determinants and individual behavior. . . . (Mann 1996, p. 3).

The choice of epistemology was political rather than disciplinary. Critical traditions in epidemiology and public health long have employed a more social focus, beginning with Virchow who in 1848 wrote that to preserve health, medicine must intervene in social and political affairs (Hunt 1989). Some health planners, including epidemiologists and physicians, offered alternative views of AIDS, often writing in collaboration with social scientists about the social production of AIDS in Africa. Struggles over meaning were international and interdisciplinary, as African and western researchers contested the narrow paradigm and its implications. They were ignored.

Mann noted two reasons for this state of affairs. One was medical dominance: ". . . a desire by public health workers to 'own' the problem . . . by keeping the discourse at a medical and public health level. . . ." The second was to avoid ". . . the inevitable accusation that public health is 'meddling' in societal issues which 'go far beyond' its scope and competence and inevitably puts [researchers] . . . potentially 'at odds' with governmental and other sources of power in the society" (Mann 1996, p. 6).

Marginalization of the critical social sciences was deliberately maintained; political and economic inequalities that drive the pandemic were slighted; examples of empowering community-based prevention ignored. Reid (1992) charges that international AIDS policy-makers lacked "epistemic responsibility" in their neglect of gender inequality. Some effects of the dominant paradigm are considered in the next section.

DISCOURSES OF STIGMA AND RACISM

Once placed in a risk category, individuals are separated from other sources of identity, henceforward stigmatized and degraded by definition. Creation of alterity allows those in power to dehumanize, to scapegoat, to blame, and thus to avoid responsibility for sufferers (Douglas 1991). Accused witches, lepers, and other people who are assigned the status of "dangerous others" in various times and places are believed to be morally contagious and often sexually polluting. The results are broadly similar: Such people may be consigned to limbo and to social or corporeal death. The struggles of people with HIV and AIDS to resist this "othering" process were charted from the beginning of ethnographic research on AIDS (Parker 1987, Farmer 1988, Schoepf 1988).

Homosexual men, Haitians, and Africans were placed on the "other" side of the social fault line and stigmatized as "promiscuous"–a notion so imprecise and value-laden that it cannot be used scientifically (Pellow 1990, Bolton 1992, Lyons 1997). Stigma rapidly led to discrimination, in what Farmer calls a "geography of blame." Haitians were denied housing, dismissed from jobs, and required to undergo tests to enter the United States. In Europe, Africans were targeted. In Russia several African students were killed by mobs; others interrupted their studies and fled home (Osman Kabia, personal communication, May 2000).

Some early studies of culture and AIDS in Africa, undertaken at the behest of biomedical researchers, were less than competent. Novices to African studies produced rapid assessments and cobbled-together surveys. The worst literature searches tore bits of erotica from context (shades of the "bleeding traits" of yore!). Sweeping statements were made about a special "African sexuality," based on traditional marriage patterns different from those of Europe and Asia. Culture was designated as the culprit of HIV spread. Blaming cultural differences for situations clearly linked to inequality supports the status quo (Sobo 1999). US anthropologists may remember the 1960s' struggle against the "culture of poverty." Frankenberg (1995) describes the travails of anthropologists struggling with the categories imposed by epidemiologists in interdisciplinary teams. Anthropologists were "... token members on research projects [directed] by scientists who regarded 'culture' as an obstacle" (Obbo 1999, p. 69). Some, like myself, worked on small grants without salaries to maintain their independence.

Critics disputed the premises and methods of authors who misapplied genetics and ethology to human populations. They challenged racist representations surrounding heterosexual transmission of HIV. They showed how elements of *raciologie* used to justify slavery and colonial domination were adapted in AIDS discourse. They contested notions of culture as fixed and immutable, posing insurmountable barriers to protection from HIV. These critics included anthropologists, historians, biologists, and physicians. Emphasis on heterosexual transmission, published in scientific journals and sensationalized in the mass media, supported some critics' contention that AIDS was being blown out of proportion by Western governments. Some held that the sexual transmission paradigm had closed off the search for organic co-factors that made weakened bodies unable to fend off HIV infection. Some viewed concern with AIDS in Africa as a diversionary ploy by conservative Western politicians, strongly influenced by the moralizing of the Christian right. In the 1980s their policies contributed to deepening global economic and political crisis, and to the demise of the claim of the world's disinherited to health care as a human right, elaborated in the 1978 Alma Ata Declaration goal of "Health for All by the Year 2000."

Anthropologists objected that emphasis on promiscuity and sex with prostitutes reinforced the African perception that westerners continued to stigmatize their sexuality as "excessive," "diseased," and "dirty." Depiction of prostitutes as "a reservoir of infection," fueled local constructions of AIDS as "a disease of women," or of the "lower orders," from whom the "pure" required protection. This construction is found among some people in Africa, Asia, the Caribbean, and the United States (Brandt 1988, Taylor 1990, Lyttleton 1996, Fay 1999, Le Palec 1999). Not unexpectedly, stigma aroused defensive reactions among African officials, intellectuals, and journalists, making it difficult to conduct culturally sensitive qualitative research on sexuality (Schoepf 1991, 1995; Obbo 1999).

The official response reverberated in international policy circles. Bilateral funds for AIDS research and prevention were channeled through WHO and centralized in health ministries. The racism and moralizing texts were "words that kill" (Allen 1991) since prevention was retarded by reluctance to address the issues. Governments insisted on the assurance that programs be closely controlled, top-down, and vertical. With health ministries among the weakest in terms of budgets and policy implementation, this frequently meant that AIDS prevention remained confined to the capital (Eboko 2000). It also overdetermined the focus on politically powerless risk groups (Nzokia 1994, contributors to Fay 1999). Authoritarian states prevented mobilization of imaginative educational responses rooted in popular culture.

African Health Ministries, perennially short of funds and especially starved by Structural Adjustment Programs (SAPs), welcomed the centralized control of international AIDS money. International biomedical research offered western and African professionals opportunities for advancement in careers and for multiple roles in the national political economy (Nzokia 1994, Obbo 1999, Eboko 2000). Some of the silences within Africa that made it difficult to conduct social research on AIDS were linked to economic interests of policy makers. In Kenya, for example:

> politicians were reluctant to publicly acknowledge the full scale of the epidemic on the pretext that such publicity could cause irreparable damage to vital sectors of the economy such as tourism. Little acknowledgement was, however, made of private fortunes [being made] in such ventures, allowing personal interests to be tactfully couched in nationalistic phrases. (Nzokia 1994, p. 170).

The dominance of bio-power was limited by competing representations. Early popular responses constructed AIDS as an imaginary disease invented by westerners to discourage Africans from sex and procreation (Schoepf et al 1988, Stein & Zwi 1990, Hagenbucher-Sacripanti 1994, Le Palec & Diarra 1995, Smith 1996). Skepticism also was related to unfamiliarity with people with AIDS (PWAs). Women and youth, especially, suspected that churches and government officials sought to control their sexuality (Schoepf 1988, Romero-Daza 1994, Obbo 1995,

Setel 1999). When AIDS was recognized as real, it was declared to have come from "elsewhere." Not only in Africa, but elsewhere in the Third World, American military men, businessmen, and sex tourists were made into plausible sources; deliberate biological warfare seemed a possibility to many during the Cold War; a laboratory accident or a result of vaccine testing, all had their supporters. There were also fantasmic scenarios, some drawn from the wells of history. For example, Euro-American suggestions of monkey's blood, used in love magic or voodoo rites, were matched in Africa by attribution of AIDS' origin to European men who paid African women to have sex with dogs (or chimpanzees, or horses). The latter built on an old and widespread construction of STD origins (Schoepf 1991, Porter 1994, Le Palec & Diarra 1995, Fay 1999).

The stigmatizing "words that kill" not only retarded prevention campaigns: By fostering social isolation, they added to the suffering endured by sick people and their families. In several countries, "free women," living without male protection, were scapegoated, rounded up and deported to rural areas where they were unable to make a living or were even imprisoned and raped (Dozon & Fassin 1989, Baylies & Bujra 1999). Women whose HIV/AIDS was known or suspected were evicted from their homes and deprived of livelihoods and children. Some, accused as witches, were killed (Yamba 1997, Lawuyi 1998). Accusations are related to older representations of disease as "sent sickness," (see Farmer 1992 for Haiti) and "re-appropriations of tradition" (Lawuyi 1998) that emerged with socio-economic changes and movement of populations (Fisiy & Geschire 1996), a subject to be revisited below. Many people attributed contagion to sorcery and to practices identified with other conditions believed to be sexually transmitted and "polluting" (Hagenbucher-Sacripanti 1994, Mogensen 1995, Caprara 2000). Many African healers claimed to cure AIDS.

As the epidemic went on, however, deaths from this "long and painful sickness" mounted. A political-economic construction was elaborated and spread along the *radio trottoir*, or "sidewalk radio" that carries popular culture in Africa's cities. AIDS came to stand for "Acquired Income Deficiency Syndrome," a disease brought on by poverty, unemployment, and the strategies that poor people commonly adopted for survival.

MORE THAN A "KAP-Gap"

Anthropologists were invited to collaborate in surveys of knowledge, attitudes, and practices (KAP) sponsored by public health agencies from the mid-1980s. Qualitative methods were often confined to focus groups and rapid appraisals. Anthropological demographers, experienced in surveys of reproduction and migration, sought to devise methods, principally studies of sexual networking, that would yield valid data to explain the spread of HIV and aid in prevention. This extensive, well-funded work deserves a separate review (examples are found in Dyson 1991, Herdt 1997, *Health Transition Review*, *Migrations et Santé*, as well as in other cited collections. As a result of this research, it appears that measurable differences in sexual behavior are not correlated with differences in HIV incidence and prevalence. Surveys discovered that around the world increased knowledge of AIDS did not translate into widespread protection, which, of course, anthropologists familiar with studies of past public health campaigns had predicted. It gives no satisfaction to be proved correct in the face of overwhelming tragedy.

GLOBAL INTERCONNECTIONS

In the 1990s a growing number of anthropologists conducted processual ethnographies that linked individuals' life worlds to global structures and processes, showing how these are involved in spreading HIV. The importance of the macrolevel cannot be overstated, for not only has it created the conditions for the spread of infection, it has also created the conditions for response in both international and local arenas. In many countries of the South, the crisis deepened as terms of trade for tropical products worsened and development funding dwindled. Structural Adjustment Programs (SAPs) imposed by the institutions of international finance (IFIs) as a condition for further borrowing contributed to deepening poverty. SAP measures included devaluation, debt reimbursement, "liberalization" of markets, privatization, and compression of government budgets. Agricultural and health services, education and social programs, which the poor depended on governments to provide, were sacrificed. Urban unemployment grew, crops remained uncollected, and migration in search of work increased. The informal economic sector ceased to absorb new micro-enterprises. Many poor people lost their land to transnational firms that pay very low wages. Deepening poverty brought mass social dislocations, hunger, disease, and untold suffering.

Across the globe, structural violence set people on the move (Herdt 1997). This set the stage for sex with multiple partners, gender violence, and wide dissemination of STIs, including HIV (Heise et al 1994, Schoepf et al 2000). Farmer (1992) shows how the construction of a hydroelectric dam funded by USAID drove peasants from their lands, resulting in greater poverty, migration in search of livelihoods, and increased risk of AIDS. A similar process in Ghana drove women from uprooted, landless families to seek earning opportunities in Côte d'Ivoire, where the only work they found was as prostitutes, and many contracted HIV (Porter 1994). Other anthropologists show how strategies adopted for survival by the world's poor and excluded contribute to sexual risk (Schoepf et al 1988, Muecke 1992, de Zaldoundo & Bernard 1995, Kammerer et al 1995, Farmer et al 1996, Hammar 1996, Ackeroyd 1997, Hassoun 1997, Setel 1999, Eboko 2000, Schoepf et al 2000). As expected, AIDS spread along trade and migration routes, as had infectious diseases in the colonial past (Setel et al 1999). A new feature in the quest for exotic sexual adventures by the affluent is flourishing sexual tourism (contributors to Herdt 1997).

The growth of social violence stemming from poverty, hopelessness, and illegal trafficking is a major contributor to HIV transmission. Several studies focus on recent decade-long situations of unchecked violence and "dirty wars," in which civilians are targeted. They document the political economic contexts of violence and the common use of rape as a weapon of war (Bond & Vincent 1991, Baldo & Cabral 1990, Cloutier 1993, Leclerc-Madlala 1997). For example, ". . . extension of AIDS in Uganda is an unintended consequence of the macro-order of international political and economic relations. Yet, it has an immediate effect on the everyday activities of specific regions and localities, affecting how individuals conduct their daily lives" (Bond & Vincent 1991, p. 119).

Gender rapidly emerged as a significant concern in the representations of AIDS and in vulnerability to infection (Schoepf 1988, 1993a,b, 1998; Kisekka 1990; Bassett & Mhloyi 1991; Jochelson et al 1991; Goldstein 1992; Obbo 1993a,b, 1995; Bardem & Gobatto 1995; de Zalduondo & Bernard 1995; Hassoun 1997; Kane 1998; Bujra 2000). The structures of inequality, analyzed by anthropologists in societies around the world from the late 1960s, frame the contexts of women's risk. The social identities imparted with gender enculturation are found to contribute to relative powerlessness even for women with some control over economic resources. Families, especially fathers and guardians, may force girls into sex work. Several studies find that sex workers who identify themselves as such may be able to negotiate condom use with clients; prostitutes and other women, however, experience constraint in relationships they define as romantic, particularly those they hope will lead to marriage. Many women's resources were diminished by SAP policies that, although assumed to be gender-neutral, in fact increased the poverty of women already disadvantaged in comparison with men. The varieties of women's experience and their struggles for agency in the face of AIDS are the focus of much research (see reviews by DeBruyn 1992, Ulin 1992, Schoepf 1993a, Ackeroyd 1997, Seidel & Vidal 1997).

A major social fault line is drawn between people of high moral repute and stigmatized "others": working class men and women "on the move." They include transport workers, miners, domestic workers, farm workers, waitresses, prostitutes, job seekers, and other poor migrants (Hunt 1989, Jochelson et al 1991, 1994; Nzokia 1994, Herdt 1997, *Migrations et Santé* 1998). Painter (1999), who has worked for nearly two decades with migrants and their families in the Sahel, notes that migrants are represented as bringing sickness—constructed as social pollution and ritual danger—from "out there" in the case of returnees from other African countries, or from "over there," in Europe. International discourses were translated into familiar local concepts and actions. Elite men continued to deny their risk and responsibility as they subjected youth and women to moralizing discourses cast as "tradition" (Schoepf 1988, Obbo 1993b, 1995, Seidel 1993, Nzokia 1994). Young men found political reasons for rejecting condom protection (Fay 1999).

In the Caribbean, Latin America, Asia, and the Pacific, discourses of morality and transgression also resound, although the particular groups and their designated attributes differ (Kammerer et al 1995, Hammar 1996, Lyttleton 1996, Benoit 2000). In Thailand and China, distant ethnic minorities were the other; in Myanmar it was poor sex workers returning from Thailand. As fiscal crisis struck in Indonesia, government and religious leaders scapegoated both prostitutes and returning labor migrants who demanded jobs (Husson 1999). In Malaysia, the way that the state managed burials of people who died from AIDS triggered social exclusion of survivors (Vignato 1999). While on other continents, stigma and blame attach to men having sex with men, in sub-Saharan Africa the stigma against homosexuality is so powerful that this mode of transmission finds little ethnographic exploration, even as a minor theme.

Brummelhuis & Herdt (1995) embrace the creative tension of anthropology as it "lives" "between subjective experience and objective reality." They find that AIDS has shattered many anthropologists' particularistic conceptions of local societies in favor of contextual studies that examine their global interconnections as well as cultural disjunctions. The methodological stance is not new; they cite the late Eric Wolf (1980), who throughout his career urged that we study such interconnections. Many cultural anthropologists and physicians who heretofore eschewed this critical perspective have adopted it as a result of their experiences in AIDS research.

Epistemological support comes not only from anthropology's humanist tradition, but from feminist studies in Africa and "subaltern studies." Most research on AIDS avoids the excesses of postmodernist anthropology in which all is reduced to discourse (Herdt 1992). Instead of viewing the world as endlessly fractured and shifting, or seeking nonconflictual interpretations, some have attempted to identify "productive conflicts" that can lead to social change (Gorz, cited in Singer 1998). Singer provides an excellent statement of the theoretical underpinnings of the genre (also see Schoepf 1988, 1998). Studies using the approach appear likely to make lasting contributions to anthropology.

ETHNOGRAPHIES OF AIDS

This section examines some full-length ethnographies that chart changing popular understandings of HIV/AIDS. Most incorporate analysis of the structures of violence that create risk in everyday life and give voice to people at risk. While many anthropologists may be more interested in the study of meanings, symbols, healers, and sex, professional responsibility also demands attention to the embodiment of inequality represented by HIV and AIDS. Schoepf (1988, 1991, 1998), Farmer & Kim (1991), Herdt (1992), Farmer (1997, 1999), Obbo (1999), Schoepf & Symonds (2000), among others, are critical of researchers who omit analysis of political economic forces, thus leaving the impression that the pandemic is caused by unchanging cultural representations.

Book-length ethnographies are an important new contribution, beginning with Farmer (1992), whose path-breaking articles appeared earlier. They include participant-observation with people at risk in their communities, but such studies also show how the structural violence of poverty and other inequalities form the context of belief and action (Béat-Songué 1993, Cloutier 1993, Romero-Daza 1993, Strebel 1993, Bardem & Gobatto 1995, Sevede-Bardem 1997, Fritz 1998, Kane 1998, Setel 1999, Stewart 2000). They focus on women, youth, and gender relations as these are shaped by local African economic contexts. Depth interviews conducted with the same people or groups over time are less concerned with context (Pagezy 1991, Mogensen 1995, Vidal 1996). Vidal charts the "quest for therapy" among AIDS sufferers and their families. A diary of conversations kept over seven months offers a male perspective on sex, gender, and AIDS in rural Mali (Dumestre & Toure 1998). Others study the biomedical providers (Desclaux 1999) and "traditional healers" from whom sick people seek care (Hagenbucher-Sacripanti 1994, Caprasse 2000).

The ethnographies make extensive use of interviews, personal documents, and cultural performances, enriched by description of the contexts of their production. These enable a view of culture that is more than rules and hegemonic meanings, but also much more than simply a collection of individual experiences of sex and sickness (here I take issue with Vidal 1996). They often capture the tension between structure and agency, attempting to chart both their dramatic manifestations and their silent conflicts. For example, a chapter in Setel's (1999) study of young people on Mount Kilimanjaro is titled "Personhood and the Pragmatics of Desire"; the next is "The Acquired Income Deficiency Syndrome". Setel and others cited write poignantly of the tragedy of African youth in the time of AIDS, caught up in the existential crises of poverty and maldevelopment that overwhelms attempts to reduce sexual risk. The AIDS risk of children and youth affected by war has yet to be studied by anthropologists.

Kane's (1998) multisited postmodern ethnography follows the fractured movement of knowledge across domains. She contrasts approaches to research and policy through space and time, and shows how risk is situationally determined. Kane also acknowledges the stress created by deep, long-term involvement. Stress results not only from engagement with sufferers and their deaths. Much like physicians who suffer from therapeutic impotence in their inability to cure, anthropologists who believe they know how to effectively engage people in protecting themselves suffer from a kind of social and political impotence. Some suffer in silence; others write, use gallows humor, or scream; still others disengage.

RISK, STRUCTURE, AND AGENCY

Conditions of structural violence appear to leave little scope for agency among the poor (Farmer 1996, Farmer et al 1996). Responding belatedly to overwhelming evidence of gender inequality, the concept of "vulnerability" was used at WHO in 1990 to claim a social focus for international public health, a focus that had been missing in the first decade of AIDS. Seidel & Vidal (1997) argue that the term obscures the fact that many African women are able to demonstrate considerable negotiating strength in sexual relations. I agree. As a characterization, vulnerability denies the agency of the oppressed and the empowerment that many derive from participation in social movements. Moreover, a homogeneous construction of "vulnerability" obscures its causal conditions and thereby robs the social critique of its power. Even in situations of war, and genocide, with mass population displacements and refugee camps that exacerbate sexual violence and risk of AIDS, rich and poor, young and old, women and men, rich older women and poor younger women, accompanied and separated children experience different types of privations and different levels of risk. Thus researchers must disaggregate their data.

At the same time it is easy to exaggerate the agency of very poor women and children. The late twentieth century saw widespread use of mass rape as a weapon of war; children sold into slavery and the sex trade by poor parents; youth caught up in the violence associated with gold fields, diamond mines, and drug trafficking; millions of homeless children living on the streets; hundreds of thousands of children captured and impressed by rebel armies to commit atrocities. That these are conditions of life and death for many millions must not be overlooked when arguing for attention to agency, negotiation, and choice (Heise et al 1994, Richards 1996, Benjamin 1998, Rwegera 1999, Bujra 2000, Luis & Roets 2000). In the time of AIDS, many poor peoples' survival strategies have resulted in their destruction. Anthropologists have barely begun to take the measure of these global conditions of social risk (Caplan 2000, Green & Sobo 2000).

Witnessing

Humanist dimensions of anthropology also are implicated in the research process. Like the experiential community-based disease prevention methods, lived experiences of sufferers and their families shed light on the interfaces between structure and agency. They show how stigma and fear of death spoil identies, and how, through collective struggles, people can sometimes create new, valued identities for themselves (Farmer 1992, Berer & Ray 1993, Vidal 1996, Desclaux & Raynaut 1997, Kerouedan & Eboko 1999). Several of these studies chart the evolution of associations of people living with HIV and AIDS.

Many anthropologists are personally as well as professionally engaged, for AIDS has brought about the deaths of informants, colleagues, students, lovers, family members and friends. "Witnessing" of social suffering (Farmer & Kleinman 1989) is a potent subtext to many research rationales. Some view this as an activity that surpasses their professional role as anthropologists, but what francophone writers call the "*accompaniment*" of sufferers has clinical applications (Vidal 1996). Witnessing may be part of the research process in a time of tragedy, for writing "... about absence and loss, makes present through revealing and re-inscribing the historical and human processes implicated in the making of that absence and loss" (Muteshi 1998, p. 73). Accompanying people who are in deep distress is not easy. Few anthropologists have written about their personal "burnout" (but see Vidal 1996, Kane 1998), or their anger at too much needless death and suffering.

Writing also may bring healing to anthropologists (Sydel Silverman, personal communication 1999).

Applied Research

The urgency of AIDS prevention appears to have legitimated applied anthropology among symbolic and other "pure" anthropologists. The best anthropological research on prevention is both applied and theoretical, privileging interconnections rather than bowing to the familiar dichotomy. The responses of people at risk, and of those living with infection are not self-evident. Coping strategies vary, and the voices of those who are silenced, their "views from below," are critical to policy and planning (Schoepf et al 1988, Heritier-Augé 1993, Obbo 1995, Farmer 1996, Stein 1996, Vidal 1996, Fay 1999, Le Palec 1999, Setel 1999). Rather than seeking to understand the contexts and constraints of their lives, much public health discourse presented prostitutes and youth as irrational in their risk-taking (Cloutier 1993, Fay 1999, Bujra 2000). The same was true of HIV-positive women who sought to have children on the grounds that one might NOT be infected (indeed chances are more than even that an infant will not be), and not bearing children is often grounds for divorce. The powerful legacy of conservative Christianity in mission health services fueled moralist, blaming discourses among health professionals in Uganda (Seidel 1993, Whyte 1996). Some, like the mainly muslim nurses in Burkina Faso studied by Desclaux (1999), blamed mothers for transmitting HIV to infants whom they suspected, on the basis of symptoms, were seropositive. Many women, however, only become aware of their own serostatus when a sick child is tested or dies from AIDS. For women who fear to engage male partners in condom negotiation, to disclose a positive diagnosis or to seek treatment for genital infections they recognize as sexually transmitted is not irrational. To do so may bring immediate risks including violence and repudiation by male partners, loss of home, children, and livelihood, loss of self-esteem, and loss of status in communities (Stein 1996, Wallman & Banteybe 1996, Caplan 2000).

Social impact studies chart the effects of AIDS deaths on families, on production, and on societies (Hunter 1990, Obbo 1992, UNAIDS 2000). As in the United States, African women bear the brunt of caring for the sick and orphaned, even though many are sick themselves and burdened by economic responsibilities. Extended family and community coping capacities may work well early in the epidemic. As it progresses, however, they often become overstretched and the social fabric of solidarity tears (Vidal 1996, Raynaut & Muhongayire 1995). Sometimes the anger and depression expressed by people with AIDS, the hardships of caring for them with inadequate resources (no soap, towels or sheets, and water that must be carried) and the social stigma heaped upon them by neighbors, drive their families from them (Vidal 1996). Anthropologists argue against the reification of the idea of "community," clan, and extended family, pointing to social, economic, and religious differences that divide local actors, and charting their role in shaping AIDS discourse (Whyte 1996, Ackeroyd 1997, Bujra & Baylies 1999). The isolation, worry, and deprivation suffered by young daughters caring for asylum-seeking refugee parents with AIDS, and for younger siblings, in London shows how the vulnerability of refugee status is compounded by the indifference of the host nation (Chinouya-Mudari & O'Brien 1999).

Anthropologists, some trained as physicians, have used research to advocate for changes in health care practices and policies, often with scant success (Vidal 1996). New research on issues of HIV testing, confidentiality, disclosure, and counseling of PWAs sheds light on biomedical practice (Desclaux 1997, Desclaux & Raynaut 1997). Recent work on the issue of breast milk transmission (Desclaux & Taverne 2000) adds to the healthy tradition of policy critique that emerged in the second decade. A critical new policy issue is access to life-prolonging drugs. Farmer (1998, 1999) and Kim (2001) hope to extend their recent demonstration of successful treatment of multi-drug resistant tuberculosis that led WHO to change its policy, to show how to deliver antiretroviral therapies for poor AIDS sufferers.

Action-Research and "Empowerment"

Some applied research on AIDS has embraced theoretical, ethical, and epistemological concerns that draw upon literature of "empowerment." (Schoepf et al 1991, Berer & Ray 1993, Schoepf 1993b, DeBruyn et al 1995, Schneider & Stoller 1995). Action-research, properly so-called, is a transdisciplinary method designed to foster social change. It uses carefully crafted, structured group-dynamics exercises that incorporate ethnographic knowledge. Participatory problem-posing generates new data and ideas for action that are tested in the community. In development literature, action-research designates the use of this method to generate collective strategies that enhance the capacity of poor people to take charge of social relationships and to improve the conditions of their lives by creating culture change. Group dynamics methods cannot substitute for socio-economic change. But they can offer space for reflection and action to the limits of agency, and they provide hope so that people can "keep on keeping on." Because action-research requires "trainers" to act in teams, it offers the space for the researchers' own replenishment of courage and hope.

An example from India shows the role of action-research in fostering women's agency. Heise & Elias (1995) compared responses of two groups of women to a film on AIDS. The first group acted withdrawn and embarrassed, and expressed fear of raising the subject with husbands. This is exactly what one would expect from the ethnographic review by Nag (1996). The second group reacted quite differently, however. Engaged by the film's information, they felt confident and entitled to discuss condoms with husbands. They recommended holding a community meeting on AIDS. The latter group was comprised of women who had taken part in a community organization for the previous six years. When a new situation arose, they were able to enact their empowerment in the new domain. India's strong tradition of local development organizations that use this Freierian pedagogy linking analysis of political economy, culture, and social dynamics is less widespread in Africa. Essential social support services (see Weeks et al 1993) also are absent, or limited in their resources.

In response to the AIDS crisis, a number of anthropologists proposed to constitute AIDS action-research teams to work with groups of people variously situated in society to discover how they constructed disease and risk, and how they would go about creating protective strategies over time. Bolton & Singer note the importance of the method:

> Prevention works best when it promotes change through individual and community empowerment strategies informed by holistic understanding of the local context, when it acknowledges the positive contributions of local cultural values to the process of change, and when it incorporates an array of options that permit individuals to transform their lives in ways that enhance their physical, emotional, and material well-being. (1992, p. 5).

Studies of interactive group prevention efforts in Africa include Schoepf et al 1991; Strebel 1993; Preston-Whyte 1995a,b; Rwegera 1995; Seidel & Coleman 1999; Ahlberg et al 1999; Baylies & Bujra 1999; Bujra & Baylies 1999. The terms "empowerment" and "action-research" have been subjected to misuse, however. Some interactive community-based methods rely on dramatic performances without facilitated discussion. These may be experienced as liberating when they shatter dominant discourses. Without incorporation into the action-research method, however, they may constitute "rituals of rebellion" that can be harnessed by community officials to "traditionalist" political goals (see Preston-Whyte & Darymple 1996). Not all those who conduct what they call "action-research" have actually obtained training in the method. Such training would seem a logical next step in the education of anthropologists who undertake transdisciplinary participatory research on AIDS prevention.

MEDICAL PLURALISM AND THE QUEST FOR THERAPY

A growing number of studies chart what Janzen called "the quest for therapy," and they document the ways in which people "live the disease" and struggle against social exclusion. The harsh reality of HIV/AIDS, its prolonged wasting, and the frightening inevitability of tragic outcomes influences both quests by sufferers and their families, and communities' capacity to cope with disease. Many "traditional healers" (THs), and others who are aware of biomedicine's therapeutic impotence, represent AIDS as an "old African disease" that THs may claim to cure (Hagenbucher-Sacripanti 1994, Vidal 1996, Caprasse 2000).

Some aspects of patient care are assumed by THs because biomedical practitioners do not or cannot assume it . THs may or may not be more effective in treating opportunistic infections; this is a research question. Their medicinals may be less expensive, although THs therapies are rarely less costly in the long run. However, many THs offer credit and delayed payment schemes, which biomedical services do not, and provide answers to the question "why me?" that are considered by many to be more satisfactory. Still, many patients go back and forth, finding little satisfaction in either system (Dozon 1995, Vidal 1996, Desclaux & Raynaut 1997).

One common assumption is that healers provide psychosocial therapy not available from the biomedical health system. This is not always the case. Patients may be relegated to the margins while the healer gets on with the business of seeking a "sorcerer" who can be held responsible for "sending sickness." The result may be further suffering for patients, rather than sense or solace. The role of healers in hastening the death of lingering AIDS sufferers is spoken of by anthropologists *en coulisse* (offstage) but is not reported in the literature.

In Asia, too, strong traditions of medical pluralism lead people to THs of various kinds. This is particularly the case when biomedicine fails, violates confidentiality, or is coercive and leads to stigma for patients and families (Bertrand 1998, Vignato 1999). In this arena, too, the tensions between structure and agency are evident, as not all of those who consult healers without recourse to biomedicine would do so were social conditions different.

Discourses and practices of witchcraft have a stellar role in classical anthropology. The persona of the witch fascinates. The powers of political leaders were and may still be related to leaders' perceived ability to control "occult forces." Counter-claims by opponents are a familiar idiom of political competition. The role of African healers in "witch finding" has received renewed attention from anthropologists in the context of economic crisis and AIDS (Fissiy & Geschire 1996, Yamba 1997). THs may accuse PWAs or others and may scapegoat them for deteriorating social and economic conditions. Women are frequently accused in the deaths of husbands and children. Culturally constructed ideas of witches may lead to the death of accused persons just as surely as does AIDS (Yamba 1997, Lawuyi 1998). Accusation scenarios can be seen to change over time as the epidemic progresses (Taylor 1992, Farmer 1992, Vidal 1996). Regardless of stated beliefs, few sufferers refuse effective biomedical treatment when available and affordable.

Treatment effectiveness is also a question of research ethics and human rights. A number of consultants advocate a role for healers in AIDS prevention and treatment. Their claims resonate in the agencies as a way to provide cheap care in the private sector, with expenses borne by patients and families. Anthropologists whose ethnographies contain observations of what healers actually do and say to patients and their families are more cautious. "Studies of healers' practices should not be construed as indicating scientific validation, nor should anthropologists be lulled into putting their work at the service of the publicity machines used by healers to attract clients" (Dozon 1995, p. 193, author's translation).

Health is a human right according to the 1951 UN Universal Declaration, and the 1969 OAU Declaration of Human and People's Rights. With public health systems a shambles, even in countries with little HIV/AIDS, however, the goal of "Health for All by the Year 2000," agreed upon by world leaders at Alma Ata in 1978, is a farce today.

The care available must be related to biomedical advances. New therapies with protease inhibitors prolong life for those who can afford them. It will not do to allow public health services to be ground down and then declare that locally offered care meets human rights standards. Today, many people are unable to afford simple antibiotics, the prices of which have skyrocketed with SAP-imposed devaluation. They are condemned to needless suffering and early death from opportunistic infections. Only the wealthy few can afford AIDS drugs, even at sharply reduced prices. Moreover, administration of antivirals requires effective health care systems. An ethical stance on AIDS and human rights includes advocacy for triple therapies and the means to deliver them safely to poor Africans as well as to the wealthy (Farmer 1998, 1999; Obbo 1999; Kim 2001). It also requires advocacy for increased research into vaccine development against HIV strains prevalent in Africa and for accelerated testing of microbicides that women can use for protection. All are related to the pharmaceutical industry's profits and patents, which pits property rights against the right to health.

The danger is that the World Bank and WHO may propose reliance on THs as "culturally appropriate" agents of privatized health care. There is a precedent: USAID, at the urging of some medical anthropologists, in 1979 adopted the slogan "Primary Health Care (PHC): Traditional Healers are already there!" The slogan resonated with leaders' nationalist rhetoric about authenticity, even as they went abroad for treatment not available at home. Such biomedical services as were available were mainly concentrated in cities. PHC, with its emphases on prevention and community participation in rural areas, was starved for funds. An estimated 70% of Africans have no other recourse than THs because biomedical care of a reasonable standard is neither accessible nor affordable. In a situation without choice between alternatives, discourse about reliance on THs is a hegemonic ploy that anthropologists should not facilitate.

THE STATE

Anthropologists have been charged in the past with inattention to the state and its coercive powers. AIDS researchers, however, find that the pandemic cannot be understood without reference to the capture of the state in many areas of the world by conservative forces seeking to control sexuality and pleasure (Seidel 1993, contributors to Feldman 1994, Bond et al 1997).

The process of class consolidation and shrinking foreign assistance, coupled with insistence on debt reimbursement, undermined the capacity of states in Africa to provide public services. This has had serious consequences. Many states in Africa found themselves in what Eboko (2000), in a play on the French term for AIDS, calls a "*syndrome d'immunodéficience politique acquise*," as economic crisis and SAPs sharply reduced resources available to leaders for redistribution. Collaborating in the pauperization of more than half the population, the state "fed the risks more than it fought them" (Eboko 2000, p. 235). Youth whose aspirations were thwarted contested the legitimacy of the state, and with it, official public health messages about AIDS (Fay 1999). The continuing crisis of the state is a crisis for people, as well, especially for PWAs (Kerouedan & Eboko 1999).

Policies of the World Bank, now the leading lender for AIDS and health services, stand accused as a major contributor to the pandemic and a major obstacle to the health of the poor (Millen & Lederer 1998, Kim et al 2000, Schoepf et al 2000, Millen et al 2001). At issue are cost-benefit considerations (Brunet-Jailly 2001) versus human rights and social justice. Anthropologists who believe that private interests must be subordinated to the public good have an opportunity to deepen analysis of the policy arena, particularly of international institutions that have become quasi-states.

From Structural to Corporeal Violence

AIDS is not the only dangerous outcome of increasing inequality, social exclusion, and hopelessness. Many people who feel themselves excluded from society, especially youth, have responded to exhortations to violence by leaders competing for control of the state (Richards 1996, Eboko 2000, Schoepf et al 2000). Unless efforts to create "sustainable rural livelihoods" (a catch phrase for the new century) are successful on a national scale, the youth of other areas could become prey for unscrupulous politicians and warlords bent on maximum destruction. This has occurred in Angola, Rwanda, Uganda, Mozambique, Sudan, Somalia, Liberia, and Sierra Leone. Poverty and unemployment are a deadly combination when over half of the excluded are youth.

South Africa now has the world's highest number of persons who are HIV-positive. The causes are familiar ones, magnified by apartheid and the protracted struggle to achieve majority rule. AIDS policy issues and politics are analyzed by Schneider & Stein (2001). Anthropologists find that in the former bantustans, as well as in urban townships where young people took part in the political struggle, the hopes of many to resume schooling, find jobs, and found families are still unfulfilled. The hopelessness of youth in KwaZulu-Natal, their sense of powerlessness about AIDS as "an inevitable part of growing up," are frequently expressed in violence, including rape and the threat of spreading HIV (Leclerc-Madlala 1997). Lawuyi (1998) analyzes the violence of rural youth in the Transvaal as a particularly virulent type of "re-traditionalization" in the absence of hoped-for social transformation.

Such dismal scenarios are neither inevitable, nor irreversible. South Africa has a vigorous legacy of the Mass Democratic Movement, in which youth organizations can be mobilized (Schneider & Stein 2001). In Uganda, where similar attitudes were expressed a decade ago (Schoepf, fieldnotes, Kampala, February 1992), HIV prevalence among youth has been reduced. Prevention involved a vigorous campaign that includes condoms and delayed sexual debut, as well as punishment meted out to men who coerce girls to have sex (UNAIDS 2000). In Tanzania and Zambia, youth talk about sex and HIV risk in their organizations (Bujra & Baylies

1999). Thailand's campaign also has been acclaimed as successful. In South Africa, civic organizations of labor, health workers, and youth are stronger than in many parts of the world due to their leadership in the anti-apartheid struggle. Many are accustomed to democratic leadership styles. There is also a critical press that has contested leaders' obtuseness. It remains to be seen if these forces for change can place the struggle against HIV in a political context so that government will make implementation of measures to save South Africa's youth an urgent priority.

As many anthropologists, along with other critical social scientists and physicians cited in this review have documented through research and practice, transformation of the living conditions of the world's poor majority are required to stop the AIDS pandemic.

CONCLUSION

AIDS is truly a disease of the global system, emblematic of permanent crisis in the South. In communities with deepening poverty, hunger, and deteriorating health infrastructure, the HIV virus battens on bodies weakened by malnutrition and infectious and parasitic disease, and social bodies weakened by inequality, debt, structural violence, and war. Anthropological literature on AIDS in the international arena from the 1990s shows researchers' increasing attention to linkages between local sociocultural processes that create risk of infection and the life-worlds of sufferers to the global political economy. Focus on Africa, where the heterosexual epidemic has attained catastrophic proportions, reveals some cultural particularisms but many regularities in the social production of disease. In many ways AIDS encapsulates the global body politic. Global inequalities of class, gender, and ethnicity are revealed, as poverty, powerlessness, and stigma propel the spread of HIV. The bodies on which states and wealthy leaders inscribe both their power and their powerlessness are those of women, youth and poor men.

Anthropological research on AIDS has stimulated reflection on the hegemonic discourses that support power structures and justify social inequalities of gender, race, and class. The cultural logics that provide meaning and support personhood, the pragmatics of desire and delight, all have been overturned by this unprecedented social disorder. The best anthropological research on AIDS refuses to reify culture, treating phenomena commonly designated as "cultural constraints to change" as the results of complexly linked aspects of social life. It shows how structural and corporeal violence result in social suffering and contribute to risk of AIDS, and demonstrates the key role of power and inequality in determining the health of populations. Anthropologists' witness to suffering, their concern and engagement, are potent elements in the research process, and in advocacy in national and international arenas.

Sydel Silverman, recently retired President of the Wenner Gren Foundation for Anthropological Research, challenges anthropologists to continue to advance anthropology's "grand vision for the understanding of humankind" (Silverman 2000,

p. 1). She honors anthropologists' marginal status as a source of critical imagination, conferring the ability to see what others take for granted. This tradition would appear to be alive and struggling in the time of AIDS, as many anthropologists' research promotes critical appraisal of intellectual currents that affect the world's processes and problems. The combined strength of theory and practice in the field of international research on AIDS is a significant contribution to anthropology in the twenty-first century.

ACKNOWLEDGMENTS

I wish to acknowledge the collaboration of colleagues in the Connaissida Project: Pascal Ntsomo Payanzo, Alphonse wa Nkera Rukarangira, Claude Schoepf, and Veronique Engundu Walu from 1985. I wish to acknowledge our funders, principally Scott B. Halstead at the Rockefeller Foundation from 1987–1990 and Sydel Silverman at the Wenner Gren Foundation for Anthropological Research for 1988 and 1991. Without their support and encouragement, my interest in HIV/AIDS prevention in Africa would not have become operational. Other valued colleagues, Christine Obbo from 1986, Paul Farmer from 1988, Jim Yong Kim, Joyce V. Millen, and Patricia V. Symonds from 1991, provided valuable insights and reassured me that our approach to AIDS was on target. Opinions and errors of fact are my responsibility. Two Connaissida collaborators have died, Noella Ngirabakunzi in the 1994 genocide in Rwanda, and Beatrice Makyla in Zaire in 1992 of a long and painful illness. In memoriam.

Visit the Annual Reviews home page at www.AnnualReviews.org

LITERATURE CITED

Ackeroyd AV. 1997. Sociocultural aspects of AIDS in Africa: occupational and gender issues. See Bond et al. 1997, pp. 11–30

Aggleton P, Hart G, Davies G, ed. 1999. *Families and Communities Responding to AIDS.* London: Univ. College London Press. 217 pp.

Ahlberg BM, Kimani V, Kirumbi L, Kaara M, Krantz I. 1999. Male circumcision: practice and implication for transmission and prevention of STD/HIV in Central Kenya. See Becker et al. 1999, pp. 599–612

Allen G. 1991. Race-based genetic research: 'Ideas that can kill'. *The Scientist* (14 May): 19–21

Baer HA, Singer M, Susser I. 1997. AIDS: a disease of the world system. In *Medical Anthropology and the World System: A Critical Perspective*, ed. HA Baer, M Singer, I Susser, pp.159–80. Westport: Bergin Garvey. 277 pp.

Baldo M, Cabral AJ. 1990. Low intensity wars and social determinations of the HIV transmission: The search for a new paradigm. See Stein & Zwi 1990, pp. 34–43

Bardem I, Gobatto I. 1995. *Maux d'amour, vies de femmes.* Paris: L'Harmattan. 167 pp.

Bassett MT, Mhloyi M. 1991. Women and AIDS in Zimbabwe: the making of an epidemic. *Int. J. Health Serv.* 21:143–56

Bastos C. 1999. Global response to AIDS. Bloomington: Univ. Ind. Press. 225 pp.

Baylies C, Bujra J, et al. 1999. Rebels at risk: young women and the shadow of AIDS in Africa. See Becker et al. 1999, pp. 319–41

Béat-Songué P. 1993. *Sida et prostitution au Cameroun*. Paris: L'Harmattan. 99 pp.

Becker C, Dozon J-P, Obbo C, Toure M. ed. 1999. *Vivre et Penser le Sida en Afrique/ Experiencing and Understanding AIDS in Africa*. Paris: Karthala. 707 pp.

Benjamin J. 1988. Issues of power and empowerment in refugee settings: Rwandan women's adapted behavior at Benaco refugee camp. *Refuge* 17(4):17–22

Benoit J, Desclaux A, eds. 1996. *Anthropologie et Sida: Bilan et Perspectives*. Paris: Karthala. 381 pp.

Berer M, Ray S. 1993. *Women and HIV/ AIDS: an international resource book*. London: Pandora. 383 pp.

Bertrand D. 1998. AIDS and treatment by traditional healers in Cambodia. *Curare* 21(2):195–200

Bibeau G, Murbach R. eds. 1991. L'Univers du Sida. *Anthropol. Soc.* 15(2–3):5–247

Bolton R. 1992. Aids and promiscuity: muddles in the models of HIV prevention. *Med. Anthropol.* 14:145–223

Bolton R, Singer M, eds. 1992. Introduction, pp. 139–43. In *Rethinking HIV Prevention: Cultural Approaches, Medical Anthropology* 14:139–363

Bond G, Kreniske J, Susser I, Vincent J. eds. 1997. *AIDS in Africa and the Caribbean*. Boulder: Westview. 234 pp.

Bond G, Vincent J. 1991. Living on the edge: structural adjustment in the context of AIDS. In *Changing Uganda: Dilemmas of Structural Adjustment and Revolutionary Change*, ed. H-B Hansen, M Twaddle, pp. 113–29. London: James Currey. 403 pp.

Bond G, Vincent J. 1997. AIDS in Uganda: the first decade. See Bond et al. 1997, pp. 85–97

Brandt AM. 1988. AIDS: from social history to social policy. In *AIDS: The Burdens of History*, ed. E Fee, D Fox, pp. 147–71. Berkeley: Univ. Calif. Press

Brummelhuis Ht, Herdt G, eds. 1995 *Culture and Sexual Risk*: Amsterdam: Gordon & Breach. 337 pp.

Brunet-Jailly J. 2001. Quels critères pour une juste répartion des soins? *Esprit* 271(Jan): 98–114

Bujra J. 2000. Risk and trust: unsafe sex, gender and AIDS in Tanzania. See Caplan 2000

Bujra JM, Baylies C. 1999. Solidarity and stress: gender and local mobilization in Tanzania and Zambia. See Aggleton et al. 1999, pp. 35–52

Caplan P, ed. 2000. *Risk Revisited*. London: Pluto. 258 pp.

Caprara A. 2000. *Transmettre la maladie*. Paris: Karthala. 211 pp.

Chinouya-Moudari M, O'Brien M. 1999. African refugee children and HIV/AIDS in London. See Aggleton et al. 1999, pp. 21–34

Cloutier L. 1993. *Harlem City Ardeb-Djoumal: stratégies de santé des femmes de N'Djamena (Tchad)*. PhD diss. Québec: Université Laval

de Bruyn M. 1992. Women and AIDS in developing countries. *Soc. Sci. Med.* 34(3):249–62

de Bruyn M, Jackson M, Wigermars M, Knight VC, Berkvens R. 1995. *Facing the Challenges of STDs, HIV/AIDS: A Gender-Based Response*. Amsterdam: Royal Tropical Inst.

Desclaux A, ed. 1997. *Le Depistage du VIH et le Conseil en Afrique au Sud du Sahara*. Paris: Karthala. 326 pp.

Desclaux A. 1999. Des infirmières face au sida: Impact de l'épidémie sur les rôles professionnels dans un service de pédiatrie du Burkina Faso. See Becker et al. 1999, pp. 541–57

Desclaux A, Raynaut C, ed. 1997. *Urgence, précarité et lutte contre le VIH-sida en Afrique*. Paris: L'Harmattan. 326 pp.

Desclaux A, Taverne B, eds. 2000. *Allaitement et VIH en Afrique de l'Ouest*. Paris: Karthala. 560 pp.

de Zalduondo B, Bernard JM. 1995. Meanings and consequences of sexual-economic exchange: gender, poverty and sexual risk behavior in urban Haiti. See Parker & Gagnon 1995, pp. 157–82

Douglas M. 1991. Witchcraft and leprosy: two strategies for rejection. In *Epidemics: Perspectives in Cultural Studies. Work. Pap.*

No.21, pp. 70–89. Cambridge: MIT Cult. Stud. Proj.

Dozon J-P. 1995. Médecine traditionnelle et sida. Les modalités de sa prise en charge par un tradipraticien ivoirien. See Dozon & Vidal 1995, pp. 187–95

Dozon J-P, Vidal L, eds. 1995. *Les Sciences Sociales Face au Sida: Cas Africains Autour d'un Exemple Ivoirien.* Paris: ORSTOM Editions. 300 pp.

Dyson T, ed. 1991. *Sexual Behaviour and Networking: Anthropological and Sociocultural Studies on the Transmission of AIDS.* Liege: Editions Derouaux-Ordina. 385 pp.

Eboko F. 2000. Risque-sida, sexualité et pouvoirs. La puissance de l'Etat en question. In *Le Désarroi Camerounais*, ed. G Courade, pp. 235–62. Paris: Karthala. 277 pp.

Farmer PE. 1988. Bad blood, spoiled milk: bodily fluids as moral barriers in rural Haiti. *Am. Ethnol.* 15(1):62–83

Farmer PE. 1992. *AIDS and Accusation: Haiti and the Geography of Blame.* Berkeley: Univ. Calif. Press. 331 pp.

Farmer PE. 1996. On suffering and structural violence: a view from below. *Daedalus* 125(1):261–83

Farmer PE. 1997. AIDS and anthropologists: ten years later. *Med. Anthropol. Q.* 11(4): 516–25

Farmer PE. 1998. Inequalities and antivirals. *Pharos* 61:34–38

Farmer PE. 1999. Pathologies of power: rethinking health and human rights. *Am. J. Publ. Health* 89(10):1486–96

Farmer PE, Connors M, Simmons J, ed. 1996. *Women, Poverty, and AIDS: Sex, Drugs, and Structural Violence.* Monroe, ME: Common Courage. 456 pp.

Farmer PE, Kim JY. 1991. Anthropologists, accountability and the prevention of AIDS. *J. Sex Res.* 28(2):203–21

Farmer PE, Kleinman A. 1989. AIDS as human suffering. *Daedalus* 118(2):135–60

Farmer PE, Lindenbaum S, Good M-J, eds. 1993. Women, poverty and AIDS. *Cult., Med. Psychiatry* (Special Issue) 17(4)

Fassin D. 2000. *Les Enjeux Politiques de la Santé: Etudes Sénégalaises, Equatoriennes et Françaises.* Paris: Karthala. 344 pp.

Fay C. 1999a. Du "culturel", de "l'universel" ou du "social"? Penser le sida et la prevention au Mali. See Becker et al. 1999, pp. 277–99

Fay C, ed. 1999b. *Le Sida des Autres. Autrepart* 12. Paris: Editions de l'Aube, IRD. 158 pp.

Feldman D, ed. 1994. *Global AIDS Policy.* Westport, CT: Bergin & Garvey. 245 pp.

Fisiy C, Geschire P. 1996. Witchcraft, violence and identity: different trajectories in postcolonial Cameroon. In *Postcolonial Identities in Africa*, ed. R Werbner, T Ranger. Pp. 193–221. London: Zed. 292 pp.

Frankenberg R. 1994. The impact of HIV/AIDS on concepts relating to risk and culture within British community epidemiology: candidates or targets for prevention? *Soc. Sci. Med.* 38(10):325–35

Frankenberg R. 1995. Learning from AIDS: the future of anthropology. In *The Future of Anthropology: Its Relevance to the Contemporary World*, ed. A Ahmed, C Shore, pp. 110–33. London: Athalone

Fritz K. 1998. Women, power, and HIV risk in rural Mbale district, Uganda. diss. New Haven, CT: Yale Univ. Press

Glick-Schiller N. 1992. What's wrong with this picture? The hegemonic construction of culture in AIDS research in the United States. *Med. Anthropol. Q.* 6(3):237–54

Goldstein D. 1992. Welcome to the mainland, welcome to the world of AIDS: cultural viability, localization and contemporary legend. *Contemp. Legend* 2:23–40

Green G, Sobo E. 2000. *The Endangered Self.* London: Routledge

Hagenbucher-Sacripanti F. 1994. *Représentations du Sida et Médecines Traditionnelles dans la Région de Pointe-Noire (Congo).* Paris: ORSTOM Editions

Hammar L. 1996. Bad canoes and bafalo: the political economy of sex on Daru Island, Western Province, Papua New Guinea. *Genders* 23:212–43

Hassoun J. 1997. *Femmes d'Abidjan Face au Sida.* Paris: Karthala. 202 pp.

Heise LL, Elias C. 1995. Transforming AIDS

prevention to meet women's needs: a focus on developing countries. *Soc. Sci. Med.* 40(7):931–43

Heise LL, Raikes A, Watts CH, Zwi AB. 1994. Violence against women: a neglected public health issue in less developed countries. *Soc. Sci. Med.* 39(9):1165–79

Herdt G. 1992. Introduction. See Herdt & Lindenbaum 1992, pp. 3–26

Herdt G, ed. 1997. *Sexual Cultures and Migration in the Era of AIDS: Anthropological and Demographic Approaches.* Oxford: Clarendon. 256 pp.

Herdt G, Lindenbaum S, eds. 1992. *Social Analysis in the Time of AIDS.* Newbury Park, CA: Sage. 341 pp.

Heritier-Auge F. 1992. Ce mal invisible et sournois. In *L'Homme Contaminé: La Tourmente du Sida.* Paris: Autrement, Série Mutations 130:148–57

Hunt CW. 1989. Migrant labour and sexually transmitted diseases: AIDS in Africa. *J. Health Soc. Behav.* 30(4):353–73

Hunt CW. 1996. Social vs. biological: theories on the transmission of AIDS in Africa. *Soc. Sci. Med.* 42(9):1283–96

Husson L. 1999. Etat, islam et sida en Indonésie: un épineux ménage à trois. See Fay 1999b, pp. 53–72

Jochelson K, Mothibeli M, Leger J. 1991. Human immunodeficiency virus and migrant labor in South Africa. *Int. J. Health Serv. Res.* 21:157–73

Kammerer C, Hutheesing O, Maneeprasert R, Symonds P. 1995. Vulnerability to HIV infection among three hill tribes in Northern Thailand. See Brummelhuis & Herdt 1995, pp. 53–75

Kane S. 1998. *AIDS Alibis: Sex, Drugs, and Crime in the Americas.* Philadelphia: Temple Univ. Press. 215 pp.

Kerouedan D, Eboko F. 1999. *Politiques publiques du sida en Afrique.* Bordeaux: Centre d'Etude d'Afrique Noire (CNRS). Trav. et Doc. 61-62. 73 pp.

Kim JY. 2001. Achieving simple justice for the world's most vulnerable populations. Plenary address, Global Assembly: Advancing the Human Right to Health, Iowa City: Univ. Iowa April 22

Kim JY, Millen JV, Irwin A, Gershman J, eds. 2000. *Dying for Growth: Global Inequality and the Health of the Poor.* Monroe, ME: Common Courage. 585 pp.

Lawuyi OB. 1998. Acts of persecution in the name of tradition in contemporary South Africa. *Dialectical Anthropol.* 23:81–95

Leclerc-Madlala S. 1997. 'Infect one, infect all,' Zulu youth response to the AIDS epidemic in South Africa. *Med. Anthropol.* 17:363–80

LePalec A. 1999. Le sida, une maladie des femmes. See Becker et al. 1999, pp. 343–62

LePalec A, Diarra T. 1995. Révélations du sida à Bamako. Le "traitement" de l'information. See Dozon & Vidal 1995, pp. 109–21

Lindenbaum S. 1998. Review of Herdt, ed. 1997. *Am. Anthropol.* 100(3):830–31

Long LD. 1997. Refugee women, violence and HIV. See Herdt 1997, pp. 87–103

Lugalla JLP, Emmelin MAC, Mutembi AK, Comoro CJ, Kilewo JZJ, et al. 1999. The social and cultural contexts of HIV/AIDS transmission in Kagera Region (Tanzania). *J. Afr. Asian Stud.* 34(4):377–402

Luis JM, Roets L. 2000. Prostitution and the law in South Africa: the state as pimp. *J. Contemp. Afr. Stud.* 18(1):21–38

Lyttleton C. 1996. Health and development: knowledge systems and local practice in rural Thailand. *Health. Transition Rev.* 6(1):25–48

Mann JM. 1996. Human rights and AIDS: the future of the pandemic. See Schenker et al. 1996, pp. 1–7

McFadden P. 1992. Sex, sexuality and the problems of AIDS in Africa. In *Gender in Southern Africa: Conceptual and Theoretical Issues,* ed. R Meena. Harare: SAPES. 201 pp.

Millen JV, Lederer B. 1998. Banking on disaster. *POZ* July:98–101,119

Millen JV, Mate K, Irwin A, Gershman J. 2001. *The World Development Rep. 2000/2001:* implications for health care. *The Health Exchange,* Feb.:21–22

Mogensen HO. 1995. *AIDS is a Kind of*

Kahungo that Kills. Oslo: Scand. Univ. Press. 135 pp.

Muecke M. 1992. Mother sold food, daughter sells her body: cultural continuity of prostitution. *Soc. Sci. Med.* 35(7):891–901

Muteshi JK. 1998. A refusal to argue with 'inconvenient evidence': women, proprietorship and Kenyan law. *Dialectical Anthropol.* 23:55–81

Nag M. 1996. *Sexual Behaviour and AIDS in India.* New Delhi: Vikas

Naur M. 2001. Indigenous knowledge and HIV/AIDS: Ghana and Zambia. Washington, DC: World Bank, IK Notes 30 (March) 1–4

Ntozi J, Anarfi J, Calwell J, Jain S, eds. 1997. Vulnerability to HIV infection and effects of AIDS in Africa and Asia/India. *Health Transition Rev.* 7 (Suppl.)

Nzokia C. 1994. AIDS policies in Kenya: a critical perspective. In *AIDS: Foundations for the Future*, ed. P Aggleton, P Davies, G Hart, pp. 159–75. London: Taylor & Francis. 214 pp.

Obbo C. 1992. Needs, demands and resources in relation to primary health care in Kampala. Kampala: Save the Children Fund

Obbo C. 1993a. HIV transmission through social and geographical networks in Uganda. *Soc. Sci. Med.* 36(7):949–55

Obbo C. 1993b. HIV Transmission: men are the solution. *Popul. Environ.* 14(3):211–43

Obbo C. 1995. Gender, age and class: discourses on HIV. See Brummelhuis & Herdt 1995, pp. 79–95

Obbo C. 1999. Social science research: understanding and action. See Becker et al. 1999, pp. 67–78

Oppong C. 1995. A high price to pay for education, subsistence or a place in the job market. See Orubuloye et al. 1995, pp. 35–56

Orubuloye IO, Caldwell JC, Caldwell P, Jain S, eds. 1995. The third world AIDS epidemic. *Health Transition Rev.* (Suppl.) 5. 305 pp.

Pagezy H. 1993. *Sida et Modification des Comportements Sexuels: le Cas des Reclusions de Longue Durée chez les Mongo du Sud du Zaire.* ANRS: Paris. 231 pp.

Painter TM. 1999. Livelihood, mobility and AIDS prevention in West Africa. See Becker et al. 1999, pp. 645–65

Parker RG. 1987. Acquired immunodeficiency syndrome in urban Brazil. *Med. Anthropol. Q.* NS 1(Jun 2):155–75

Parker RG. 1996. Empowerment, community mobilization and social change in the face of AIDS. *AIDS* 10(Suppl.):27–32

Parker RG, Gagnon JH, eds. 1995. *Conceiving Sexuality: Approaches to Sex Research in a Postmodern World.* New York: Routledge. 307 pp.

Pellow D. 1990. Sexuality in Africa. *Trends in Hist.* 4(4):71–96

Porter RW. 1994. AIDS in Ghana: priorities and policies. See Feldman 1994, pp. 90–106

Preston-Whyte E. 1995. 'Bring us the female condom': HIV intervention, gender and political empowerment in two South African communities. *Health Transition Rev.* 7(Suppl.):209–22

Preston-Whyte E. 1996. Gender and the domestic cycle: a dual perspective for planning AIDS and HIV interventions in South Africa. *Afr. Anthropol.* III(1):113–31

Preston-Whyte E, Darymple L. 1996. Participation and action: reflections on community-based AIDS interventions in South Africa. In *Participatory Research in Health*, ed. K de Konig, M Marten, pp. 108–18. London: Zed

Raynaut C, Muhongayire F. 1995. Chronique d'une mort annoncée: problèmes d'éthique et de méthode (cas rwandais). See Dozon & Vidal 1995, pp. 235–54

Reid E. 1992. Gender, knowledge and responsibility. In *AIDS in the World*, ed. J Mann, D Tarantola, T Netter. pp. 657–66. Cambridge: Harvard Univ. Press. 1012 pp.

Richards P. 1996. *Fighting for the Rain Forest: War, Youth and Resources in Sierra Leone.* Oxford: IAI with James Currey; Porthmouth, NH: Heineman. 300 pp.

Romero-Daza N. 1994. Multiple sexual partners, migrant labor and the makings of an epidemic: knowledge and beliefs about AIDS among women in highland Lesotho. *Hum. Org.* 5:192–211

Rwegera D. 1995. Expérience de recherche-action après d'immigrés africains dans la région parisienne. See Dozon & Vidal 1995, pp. 149–58

Rwegera D. 1999. Le Sida en situation extrême. See Becker 1999, pp. 669–76

Schenker II, Sabar-Friedman G, Sy F, eds. 1996. AIDS Education: Interventions in Multicultural Societies. New York: Plenum. 259 pp.

Schneider B, Stoller N, eds. 1995. Women Resisting AIDS: Feminist Strategies of Empowerment. Philadelphia, PA: Temple Univ. Press. 339 pp.

Schneider H, Stein J. 2001. Implementing AIDS policy in post-apartheid South Africa. Soc. Sci. Med. 52(5):723–31

Schoepf BG. 1988. Women, AIDS and economic crisis in Central Africa. Can. J. Afr. Stud. 22(3):625–44

Schoepf BG. 1991. Ethical, methodological and political issues of AIDS research in Central Africa. Soc. Sci. Med. 33(7):749–63

Schoepf BG. 1993a. Action-research on AIDS with women in Kinshasa. Soc. Sci. Med. 37(11):1401–13

Schoepf BG. 1993b. Gender, development and AIDS: a political economy and culture framework. In The Women and International Development Annual III, ed. R Gallin, A Ferguson, J Harper. pp. 55–85. Boulder, CO: Westview

Schoepf B. 1997. Review of Sexual Behavior and AIDS, ed. J Clellan, B Ferry. Am. Anthropol. 99(2):431–32

Schoepf B. 1998. Inscribing the body politic: women and AIDS in Africa. In Women and Biopower: What Constitutes Resistance? eds. M Lock, P Kaufert, pp. 98–126. New York/London: Cambridge Univ. Press. 364 pp.

Schoepf BG, Rukarangira wN, Schoepf C, Walu E, Payanzo N. 1988. AIDS and society in Central Africa: a view from Zaire. In AIDS in Africa: Social and Policy Impact, ed. N Miller, R Rockwell. pp. 211–35. Lewiston, ME: Mellen. 332 pp.

Schoepf BG, Schoepf C, Millen JV. 2000. The-oretical therapies, remote remedies: SAPS and the political ecology of health in Africa. In Dying for Growth: Global Inequality and the Health of the Poor, ed. JY Kim, JV Millen, J Gershman, A Irwin, pp. 91–125, 440–57. Monroe, ME: Common Courage Press. 585 pp.

Schoepf BG, Walu E, Rukarangira wN, Payanzo N, Schoepf C. 1991. Gender, power and risk of AIDS in Central Africa. In Women and Health in Africa, ed. M Turshen, pp. 187–203. Trenton: Africa World Press. 250 pp.

Seidel G. 1993. The competing discourses of HIV/AIDS in sub-Saharan Africa: discourses of rights and empowerment vs. discourses of control and exclusion. Soc. Sci. Med. 36(3):175–94

Seidel G, Coleman R. 1999. HIV, gender, support and uses of storytelling in rural KwaZulu-Natal. See Aggleton et al. 1999, pp. 53–56.

Seidel G, Vidal L. 1997. The medical, gender and development, and culturalist discourses on HIV/AIDS in Africa and their implications. In The Anthropology of Public Policy, ed. C Shore, B Wright, pp. 59–87. London/New York: Routledge

Setel PW. 1999. A Plague of Paradoxes: AIDS, Culture, and Demography in Northern Tanzania. Chicago: Univ. Chicago Press. 308 pp.

Setel PW, Chinwa WC, Preston-Whyte E, eds. 1997. Sexual networking, knowledge and risk: confronting AIDS and STDs in Eastern and Southern Africa. Health. Transition Rev. 7(Suppl.):3

Setel PW, Lewis M, Lyons M, eds. 1999. Histories of Sexually Transmitted Diseases and HIV/AIDS in Sub-Saharan Africa. Westport, CT: Greenwood. 267 pp.

Sevéde-Bardem I. 1997. Précarités Juvéniles en Milieu Urbain Africain (Ouagadougou). Paris: L'Harmattan. 256 pp.

Silverman S. 2000. Report of the outgoing president. In The Wenner Gren Foundation for Anthropological Research, Annual Report 1999, pp. 1–7. New York: Wenner Gren Found.

Singer M, ed. 1998. *The Political Economy of AIDS*. Amityville, NY: Baywood. 236 pp.

Smith B. 1996. AIDS: religion and medicine in rural Kenya. See Schenker et al. 1996, pp. 239–49

Sobo E. 1999. Cultural models and HIV/AIDS: new anthropological views (editorial). *Anthropol. Med.* 6(1):5–12

Stein J. 1996. Coping with HIV infection: the theory and the practice. *Afr. Anthropol.* III:67–83

Stein Z, Zwi A. eds. 1990. *Action on AIDS in Southern Africa. Rep. Maputo Conf. on Health*. New York: CHISA. April. 143 pp.

Stewart KA. 2000. *Socio-economic determinants of HIV/AIDS in adolescents in rural Western Uganda*. PhD thesis, p. 318. Gainesville: Univ. Florida

Strebel A-M. 1993. *Women and AIDS: a study of issues in the prevention of HIV infection*. PhD thesis, 244 pp. South Africa: Cape Town.

Symonds PV, Schoepf BG. 2000. HIV/AIDS: the global pandemic and struggles for control. *Rev. Anthropol.* 28:189–209

Taylor CC. 1990. AIDS and the pathogenesis of metaphor. In *Culture and AIDS: The Human Factor*, ed. D Feldman, pp. 55–65. Westport, CT: Praeger. 208 pp.

Treichler P. 1999. *How to Have Theory in an Epidemic: Cultural Chronicles and AIDS*. Durham, NC: Duke Univ. Press. 451 pp.

Ulin P. 1992. African women and AIDS: negotiating behavioural change. *Soc. Sci. Med.* 34 (1):63–73

UNAIDS. 2000. World AIDS Day: AIDS Epidemic Update. Geneva: UNAIDS. (1 December). <http://www.unaids.org>

Varga CA. 1997. Sexual decision-making and negotiation the midst of AIDS: youth in KwaZulu/Natal, South Africa. See Setel et al. 1997, pp. 45–67

Vidal L. 1996. *Le Silence et le Sens: Essai d'Anthropologie du Sida*. Paris: Anthropos/Economica. 217 pp.

Vignato S. 1999. Le corps exclu: notes sur le sida en Malaisie. See Fay 1999b, pp. 87–103

Wallman S, Bantebye-Kyomuhendo G. 1996. *Kampala Women Getting By in the Time of AIDS*. London: James Currey. 340 pp.

Weeks MR, Singer M, Grier M, Hunte-Marrow J, Haughton C. 1993. AIDS prevention and the African-American injection drug user. *Transforming Anthropol.* 4(1–2):39–51

Whyte MA. 1996. Talking about AIDS: the biography of a local AIDS program within the Church of Uganda. See Schenker et al. 1996, pp. 221–38

Wolf ER. 1980. *Europe and the People Without History*. Berkeley: Univ. Calif. Press. 503 pp.

Yamba CB. 1997. Cosmologies in turmoil: witchfinding and AIDS in Chiawa, Zambia. *Africa* 67(2):200–23

Annu. Rev. Anthropol. 2001. 30:363–85

KURU, PRIONS, AND HUMAN AFFAIRS:
Thinking About Epidemics

Shirley Lindenbaum

Department of Anthropology, Graduate Center, City University of New York,
New York 10036; e-mail: lindenbaum@mindspring.com

Key Words   epidemic structures, social forms, disease causation, counter
narratives, agenda for anthropology

■ **Abstract**   The study of epidemics provides a unique point of entry for examining
the relationships among cultural assumptions, institutional forms, and states of mind.
The Black Death is said to have contributed to the emergence of nation states, the rise
of mercantile economies, and the religious movements that led to the Reformation.
It may also have brought about new ways of understanding God, the meaning of
death, and the role of authority in religious and social life. Cholera induced a public
health approach that stressed quarantine, and venereal diseases led to contact tracing.
Western medicine, however, failed to cure the epidemics that resulted from imperial
expansion into the Americas, Asia, Africa, and Europe. The focus of this essay is
on the impact of two contemporary epidemics considered to be caused by prions, a
newly recognized infectious agent: kuru in Papua New Guinea and bovine spongiform
encephalopathy (associated with variant Creutzfeldt-Jakob disease) in Europe. A close
look at epidemics constitutes a sampling device for illuminating relationships among
illness, social forms, and social thought. Theories of disease causation provide ways
of thinking about the world and sets of directions for acting in it.

INTRODUCTION

The unexpected emergence of AIDS in the early 1980s, which signaled the return
of the industrialized nations to what we had assumed was a vanished world of
infectious disease, drew anthropologists along with many others to consider the
nature of epidemics (Farmer 1992, 1999; Herdt & Lindenbaum 1992; Kane 1998;
Singer 1998; Treichler 1999; Bastos 1999 to cite but a few anthropological studies).
The AIDS epidemic initially led many scholars to compare it with past epidemics,
especially the bubonic plague (the Black Death) in Europe between 1348 and 1350,
following the death of millions of Asians in the preceding decade (McNeill 1976).
Historians attribute the spread of the Black Death, in part, to the emergence of
nation states, the rise of mercantile economies, and the religious movements that
led to the Reformation (Campbell 1931, McNeil 1976, Tuchman 1978). The Black

0084-6570/01/1021-0363$14.00

Death may also have brought about new ways of understanding God, the meaning of death, and the role of authority in religious and social life (Jonsen & Stryker 1993, p. 5).

The comparison of AIDS with past epidemics also suggested ways in which epidemics left a beneficial imprint on social institutions. Cholera, for example, initiated a public health approach that stressed quarantine, and venereal diseases led to contact tracing (Jonsen & Stryker 1993, p. 6). On the other hand, Western medicine is pictured as failing to cure the epidemics that resulted from imperial expansion into the Americas, Asia, Africa, and Europe (Watts 1997).

In their public character, dramatic intensity, and unity of time and place, epidemics are well suited to the concerns of moralists, as well as to scholars seeking to understand the relationships among ideology, social structure, and the construction of particular selves (Rosenberg 1992, p. 279). Severe misfortune and illness precipitate a crisis, mobilizing communities to produce a pageant of ritual responses in which common values are stressed and the actors reaffirm fundamental social conventions and conformist dictates (Turner 1957). Epidemics are thus lightning rods for eliciting the particular terrors that monitor the social forms and cultural values of different communities (Lindenbaum 1998).

Recent research on the nature of epidemics suggests that the shock of pestilence elicits quite similar responses in very different historical and geographical contexts (Slack 1992, p. 3). Many historical forms of pestilence were seen by their contemporaries as being transmitted from person to person. Even when theories about their origin combined notions of miasma and contagion, they were said to arise in the stench of filthy local conditions. Once recognized, the social response usually involved flight. Disease carriers were identified as scapegoats and stigmatized—foreigners in Renaissance Italy and modern Hawaii, immigrants to the United States (Kraut 1994), and "polluters" of different kinds—untouchables in India, ex-slaves in Africa, or Jews at the time of the Black Death. Epidemics have elicited religious and ritual responses that promised effective action—processions in Merovingian Paris and Renaissance Europe, and ecstatic or prophetic cults in Athens and Africa. In addition, outbreaks of epidemic illness are often associated with social upheavals, war, famine, migration, and sometimes pilgrimage (Slack 1992, pp. 2–8).

In 1998 it was still possible to say that AIDS may be the most widely discussed disease in the history of medicine (Lindenbaum 1998, p. 34), and until recently the AIDS epidemic continued to occupy center stage. That was before the arrival of bovine spongiform encephalopathy (BSE) and the variant form of Creutzfeldt-Jakob disease (vCJD) in humans, both considered to be caused by an infectious agent the nature of which has been the subject of heated debate.

The focus of this essay is on two contemporary epidemics: kuru in Papua New Guinea and bovine spongiform encephalopathy (associated with variant Creutzfeldt-Jakob disease) currently moving like a tsunami across Europe. In the text that follows, I discuss BSE and vCJD as a single, related epidemic. A close look at the epidemics of kuru and BSE/vCJD constitutes a sampling device for illuminating the relationships among illness, social forms, and social thought. Theories of disease causation are not only ways of thinking about specific diseases, but ways of thinking about the world and sets of directions for acting in it (Rosenberg 1992, p. 304).

Kuru, BSE (and vCJD)

When the first cases of BSE, the new neurological disease in cattle, were identified in Britain in 1986, veterinarians noted that the brain pathology was similar to that seen in scrapie, a fatal neurological disease in sheep, endemic in British flocks and known in Europe since the middle of the eighteenth century. Scrapie had provided the stimulus for earlier research on kuru, a fatal neurological disorder in humans affecting people in Papua New Guinea. W. J. Hadlow, a veterinarian working on scrapie, had pointed to the remarkable similarities in the clinical and pathological features of kuru and scrapie. Moreover, the disease of sheep was transmissible by inoculation, leading Hadlow to suggest that kuru, like scrapie, might be experimentally transmissible (Hadlow 1959). By 1957, the epidemiology of kuru had been mapped, revealing its high incidence in certain families and hamlets, its localization to the Fore (pronounced "Foray") and adjacent peoples with whom they intermarried, and its predilection for children and adult women (Gajdusek & Zigas 1957). A genetic basis for the disease was soon proposed. Kuru was said to be a hereditary disorder determined by a single autosomal gene, dominant in females but recessive in males (Bennett et al 1958, 1959). It became apparent, however, that a fatal genetic disorder could not reach the incidence kuru then had among the South Fore without killing off the host population, unless the gene for kuru conferred a selective survival advantage. There was no evidence to support this notion (Mathews 1971).

Anthropological evidence gathered in 1962 by Glasse and Lindenbaum indicated that kuru was of recent origin and that many people could provide vivid accounts of their first encounter with the disease. According to the Fore, kuru first entered the Fore region from the north some time in the early 1920s, arriving in the South Fore in the late 1920s and early 1930s, and in some border areas as late as the 1940s (Glasse 1962). Ethnographic research also suggested that the arrival of kuru was related to the earlier adoption of the consumption of deceased relatives, which began in the north at the turn of the century, and at later moments in the south (Glasse 1963, 1967, Lindenbaum 1979). Accounts of the consumption of the first kuru victims in a certain location also described cases some years later among those who had eaten the victim (Mathews et al 1968, Klitzman et al 1984).

Following Hadlow's observation of the remarkable similarities in the clinical and pathological features of kuru and scrapie, Gajdusek and coworkers began work with primates, and in 1966 they announced that after incubation periods of up to 50 months, chimpanzees injected with brain material from deceased kuru patients had developed a clinical syndrome akin to kuru (Gajdusek et al 1966). Kuru, like scrapie, appeared to be a viral disease of extraordinarily long incubation, transmitted by cannibalism.

The three diseases (kuru, BSE, and vCJD) gained conceptual unity with Prusiner's suggestion that the infectious agent causing certain degenerative disorders in humans and animals might consist of a protein (Prusiner 1982), a notion that initially elicited widespread skepticism. The idea of a proteinaceous agent for the prion diseases, or transmissible spongiform encephalopathies (TSEs), had been suggested earlier by Alper and coworkers, who found that ultraviolet radiation that destroys all nucleic acids does not destroy scrapie infectivity in sheep (Alper et al 1967). Griffith (1967) soon proposed that infectivity of scrapie could be due to the altered conformation of a normal cellular protein. In 1982 Prusiner achieved biochemical purification of the scrapie agent (*Science* 216, pp. 136–44), and coined the term "prion" to distinguish the infectious pathogen from viruses or viroids (the term said to be used for small virus-like particles often used in TSE research when the infective agent is not known). Prions were defined as small proteinaceous infectious particles that resist inactivation by procedures that modify nucleic acids (Collinge & Prusiner 1992, p. 7).

The prion diseases now include scrapie (in sheep and goats), bovine spongiform encephalopathy (BSE) in cattle, transmissible mink encephalopathy (in mink), chronic wasting disease (CWD) in mule deer and elk, as well as Gerstmann-Straussler-Scheinker syndrome (GSS), fatal familial insomnia, Creutzfeldt-Jakob disease (CJD), and kuru in humans (Collinge & Prusiner 1992, pp. 6–7). BSE has caused the death of domestic cats in Europe, as well as the death of exotic ruminants in English zoos. Bison, nyala, gemsbok, orynx, greater kudu, and eland have all been shown to die from BSE, as did Major, a popular lion, despite his treatment with conventional medicines, a magnetic collar, and faith healing (De Bruxelles 2000).

Prion diseases are unique in that they are inherited disorders and yet often transmissible experimentally to laboratory animals (Anderton et al 1992, p. 3). They can also cause sporadic disease in which neither inheritance nor transmission between individuals is evident (Prusiner 1995, p. 48). The diseases slowly attack brain tissue, often leaving microscopic spongelike holes characterized by accumulations of abnormal forms of the prion protein (PrP) that occur naturally in brain tissue. Recent studies in mice show that the infectious prion accumulates in the absence of any clinical signs (Hill et al 2000), a finding with important implications for public health, both with respect to iatrogenic transmission from apparently healthy humans, and dietary exposure to cattle and other species exposed to BSE prions.

Recent theories concerning the origin of the BSE epidemic now propose that the disease was derived not from sheep infected with conventional scrapie, but from the recycling in cattle feed of cattle remains infected with BSE itself. The first case may have originated in a cow that developed the disease as a consequence of a gene mutation. The looser regulation in the rendering process of meat products, once thought to be a cause, is also discounted, since rendering practices were never capable of completely inactivating the infectious agent. The social circumstances contributing to the spread of BSE are thus said to result from the unforeseen dangers associated with industrialized farming, as well as the ineptitude of a government bureaucracy and the collusion of government agencies charged with monitoring the beef industry. The findings of a British government inquiry, the Phillips Report, were published on 27 October, 2000 (*Guardian* 2000). More recently, additional farming practices have been identified as a potential danger. BSE is said to have arisen in British herds in the 1980s when the Ministry of Agriculture ordered cattle farmers to treat their animals for warbler fly infection with high doses of Phosmet, an organophosphate that captures copper. At the same time cattle feed was supplemented with chicken manure from birds dosed with manganese to increase their egg yield. The prion proteins in cows' brains were both deprived of copper and dosed with manganese, causing the prions to become distorted (Monbiot 2000, Purdey 1996a,b, 1998).

Kuru, BSE, and vCJD have contributed to a new field of scientific research that lies at the intersection of genetics, cell biology, and virology. They also provide a compelling case for the inclusion of the human sciences in the study of epidemics, reclaiming the legacy of Rudolph Virchow, the German pathologist whose studies of typhus in Upper Silesia in 1848, cholera in Berlin, and an outbreak of tuberculosis in Berlin during 1848 and 1849 led him to develop a theory of epidemics that emphasized the social circumstances contributing to the spread of illness (Waitzkin 2000, p. 62). The study of epidemics contributes to our understanding of the human, organizational, and cultural contexts in which disease thrives or fails to gain a foothold (Rosenberg 1992, p. 303).

Kuru and Human Affairs

As social phenomena, epidemics are said to have a familiar dramaturgic form. They "start at a moment in time, proceed on a stage limited in space and duration, following a plot line of increasing and revelatory tension, move to a crisis of individual and collective character, then drift toward closure" (Rosenberg 1992, p. 279). The kuru epidemic appears to follow this plot line of progressive revelation (Act 1), agreement among different actors on an explanatory framework (Act 2), a sense of crisis that elicits individual and collective political and ritual action (Act 3), and a gradual drift toward closure (Act 4).

Act 1 began for the Fore in the late 1920s and early 1930s with the emergence of the first puzzling cases. Thought at first to be a benign shaking disorder called cassowary disease resulting from assault by ghosts of the dead, they fed the sufferers a homeopathic mixture of pork and casuarina bark. (The victim's tremor resembled the swaying fronds of casuarina trees, and by further analogue, cassowary quills). For a short time they also called the condition *negi nagi*, indicating silly or foolish behavior, thinking that they were observing a form of temporary derangement and bodily tremor caused by anthropomorphic spirits. When they saw that the victims were uniformly dying, they concluded that living sorcerers were to blame (Act 2), a diagnosis that assigns etiology to the malevolence of male competitors beyond a limited range of kinship and residence. This statement about the nature of perceived dangers and unacceptable behaviors is a sociomedical diagnosis that continues to this day. Calling the illness "kuru," a word denoting shaking or fear, again incorporating both biology and culture, is an apt description of the victim's tremors and a term that has a certain political and social resonance.

Act 3 began in the late 1950s and 1960s when the epidemic reached its height and the Fore began to speak of a social and moral crisis. The sexual bias in kuru mortality, which had resulted in male-female ratios of 3:1 in some hamlets, left many men without wives and many infants without mothers. Daily activities now included the investigation of suspected sorcerers, the policing of hamlets and political boundaries, and propitiatory rituals directed at exposing the killers. Large-scale ceremonies provided a forum for purging by confession, and for an appeal to halt the aggression that they believed had raised the spectre of demographic extinction and internal disruption so great that society itself was in danger (Lindenbaum 1979).

By the 1990s, cases of the disease were extremely rare, and the sense of crisis had passed. There are currently about 4 cases a year (J. Whitfield, personal communication). Fore now say that the arrival of Christianity and "development" directs their attention to more pressing matters, and that the older generation no longer conveys knowledge of sorcery to young men (S. Lindenbaum, unpublished data). Act 4 thus ends not with a bang but a whimper, providing the Fore with an opportunity for retrospection and moral judgment, in the classical rendering of the finale (Rosenberg 1992, pp. 286–87).

For non-Fore observers, Act 1 opened in August 1953 when a government patrol officer noted the violent shivering and spasmodic jerking of a young girl seated by a fire. The Fore said that she was a victim of sorcery and would be claimed by death within a few weeks (Lindenbaum 1979, p. 9). The first medical evaluation of kuru in 1955 suggested "acute hysteria in an otherwise healthy woman" thought to be precipitated by the threat or fear of sorcery, a diagnosis discounted by Gajdusek based on evidence of advanced neurological disease (quoted in Lindenbaum 1979, p. 14). Act 1 continued with the clinical description of the disease and spatial mapping of the epidemic (Gajdusek & Zigas 1957).

Act 2, with its plot line of revelatory tension, unfolds with Hadlow's contribution concerning scrapie. The drama took a sensational turn with the transmission of the infectious agent to laboratory primates (Gajdusek et al 1966) and introduced additional actors and themes. Anthropological data concerning the recent arrival of kuru, the adoption and then abandonment of cannibalism, and the demonstration that Fore genealogies were social, not entirely biological constructs, opened the door for a nongenetic interpretation of the disease (Lindenbaum 1979, Chapters 2, 4). The 1966 transmission of kuru to laboratory primates, as well as epidemiological evidence gathered between 1970 and 1977, showed that no cases of kuru had occurred among people born after the cessation of cannibalism, and this fact strengthened the hypothesis that kuru was a disease transmitted by cannibalism and caused by an infectious agent of extremely long incubation.

The early years of kuru research, however, continued to provide an abundance of hypotheses—infectious etiology, possible plant toxins, metallic poisoning (Reid & Gajdusek 1969, Sorenson & Gajdusek 1969), and a return to the supposition that the genetic constitution of the kuru-affected populations could not be dismissed (Simmons et al 1972, Plato & Gajdusek 1972). Cannibalism was given low priority or discounted, perhaps because Gajdusek's 1957 data on Fore cannibalism were inaccurate (Lindenbaum 1982), or because he thought the idea was too exotic (Rhodes 1997, p. 103). Act 2 thus introduced a greatly enlarged cast of characters and theories of disease causation more varied than those considered by the Fore. To this point, Fore and non-Fore plot lines differed mainly in scale and complexity.

Act 3 brings the Fore and non-Fore observers onto the same stage. Together they attended curing ceremonies and funerals, the observers experiencing but part of the anguish, since the crisis was not theirs. Conference papers and publications written for a non-Fore audience attempted to provide empathetic descriptions of the social and psychological impact of kuru on individuals and families; they described changes in Fore social life resulting from the epidemic and the colonial encounter (Glasse (Lindenbaum) 1962, Gajdusek & Alpers 1972). This was perhaps another form of ritual witnessing, admittedly in the distancing languages of anthropology and medicine.

Kuru Act 4 is the longest-playing scene in the scientific drama. By 1974 "the sinister trio" of kuru, scrapie, and classical Creutzfeldt-Jakob disease were considered to belong to the category of subacute spongiform viral encephalopathies (*Lancet* 1974), later called the transmissible spongiform encephalopathies. The nature of the infectious agent remained elusive until the early 1980s when Prusiner published his work on the prion protein and kuru joined the list of prion diseases. (Prusiner received the 1997 Nobel Prize in Physiology and Medicine for his work on prions 21 years after Gajdusek was made Nobel Laureate for demonstrating that TSEs were transmissable.) As a prion disease transmitted orally, kuru now provides an ideal model for studies of vCJD. Anthropological studies (in conjunction with medical research) have been recently revived, particularly in relation to regional variations in mortuary practices, population genetics, and susceptibility and resistance to infection. In light of research indicating that prion diseases may result from abnormalities of copper metabolism (Wadsworth et al 1999, Purdey 1998), studies in Papua New Guinea also include an examination of copper and magnesium levels in plants, soil, and water (J. Whitfield, personal communication).

As the incidence of the disease gradually declines, the epidemic provides an occasion for retrospective thought and moral judgment in the form of autobiography (Zigas 1990, Klitzman 1998), popular science (Rhodes 1997, Cooke 1998), reflections on the way in which sorcery beliefs affected patterns of human interaction (Sorenson 1976), anthropological texts that retell the kuru story from different theoretical perspectives (McElroy & Townsend 1979, Keesing 1991, Park 2000), and the provocative suggestion that the connection between kuru and cannibalism is questionable because it is said that there is no satisfactory first-hand account of cannibalism as a socially approved custom in any part of the world (Arens 1979). A historian examined the multiple and cross-disciplinary contributions to kuru research that led to its successful scientific outcome, as well as the international disputes, differential rewarding of credit, and the moral and ethical issues raised by medical research in an era not well policed by ethical guidelines (Nelson

1998). Papers from a conference on prion diseases in humans and animals were supplemented by historical reflections from Hadlow, Alpers, Gibbs, Glasse & Lindenbaum (Prusiner et al 1992). As scholars increasingly study the way in which scientific knowledge is produced, kuru research has been examined to show how anthropologists and medical scientists, each with their grammar of practice, gain explanatory power and cultural authority through their interaction (Anderson 1992), and how the transaction of kuru material (brains, blood, and bodies) with their different meanings for the Fore, for Gajdusek, and for laboratory workers in Australia and the United States, lend themselves to observations about the creation of value and the circulation of goods in global science (Anderson 2000).

This much-telescoped account of the engagement of Western scholarship with kuru is tailored to reveal a scientific drama that runs parallel to that of the Fore. (The vast medical literature on kuru can be located on the National Library of Medicine PubMed website http://www.ncbi.nlm.nih.gov). With the decline in the epidemic, and Fore attention turning to other matters, Act 4 properly ends here. The kuru story, however, finds new life on another stage.

During the early years of the epidemic, kuru was extensively documented with cinema records, some now assembled as a research tool (Gajdusek et al 1970). Kuru has also been the subject of recent documentaries produced for television, as an example of medical sleuthing (WGBH-TV 1985) and contemporary cannibalism (Pangolin 1998, Café 2000). Journalists wrote about the disease during the 1960s, the Australian press insensitively dubbing kuru "the laughing death" just as the British press would later refer inappropriately to dying animals as "mad cows."

Kuru continues to excite popular imagination in the form of a short story (Berkun 2000), a comedy, said to be based "very very loosely on what was a true story" (Glisson 1991), and a wave of popular literature stimulated by the parallel with BSE. While some authors correctly cite original documents (Rhodes 1997), others make little effort at literature review, or misread published accounts (Cowley 2001), and include many errors, such as the statement that the initial symptoms of CJD, GSS, and kuru "are self-neglect such as failure to groom, bathe or eat properly" (Crawford 1998, p. 11), a misconception that appears to be based on data concerning TSEs in animals not humans, and that most patients are "in their late 50s at onset," a misreading of the history of the epidemic. It is also proposed that kuru and transplant tissues are dangerous because they are uncooked (Brouwer 1998, p. 31), although Fore cooking procedures as well as laboratory simulation of Fore cooking temperatures are well documented; that the disease attacks victims at atypically younger and younger ages (the reverse is the case); and an imaginative portrait of burial preparations in which women are said to suction "the brain from the dead person's skull, licking the straw as they worked" and "sharing it with their children" (Brouwer 1998, p. 30). The many misstatements in popular publications, as well as in scientific journals, suggest that anthropological contributions to scientific research are often overlooked (Goodfield 1997), a symptom perhaps of the more general subordination of the human sciences to the natural sciences

(Nelson 1998, Nelkin 1995). The persistent misreading of existing epidemiologic and ethnographic data also lends itself to meta-analysis (Farmer 1992, p. 2), as do alternate theories of disease causation and counter-narratives (discussed below). The elaboration of Act 4, better seen as an epilogue, reveals an enduring engagement with the story of the epidemic, but the Fore are no longer active participants.

BSE, vCJD, and Human Affairs

An attempt to cast the story of BSE and vCJD in dramaturgic form is perhaps a test of the assumption that epidemics, like the theories that explain them, are tied to particular social forms. Analysis of the kuru epidemic reveals Fore consensus concerning etiology, intervention, and therapeutic response. This shared understanding stems from a relatively egalitarian social order that retains a fair degree of harmony between world view and assumptions about appropriate behavior and the way the body functions. By way of contrast, the BSE/vCJD epidemic produces a more complex set of understandings and responses in the context of a more fragmented social order.

Act 1 introduces the epidemic as a disease of cattle. On 22 December, 1984, a British veterinarian was called to examine a cow with arched back and weight loss, later identified as the first known case of BSE. In November 1986, scientists working for the Ministry of Agriculture formally identified the new cattle disorder. In June 1988, BSE became a notifiable disease, and in July, the feeding of sheep and cattle remains to cattle or sheep was effectively banned. Farmers with BSE-affected cattle were given 50% compensation for their slaughtered animals. In November 1989, the ban on specified bovine offal in human food came into force. In March 1990, the European Commission exacted the first restrictions on cattle exports applying to cattle under six months, and in April it made BSE a notifiable disease.

In May 1990, the British chief medical officer reassured the public that beef was safe to eat, as did the Minister of Agriculture, who appeared on television encouraging his four-year old daughter to bite into a beefburger. Later in 1990, however, the British government established the national CJD surveillance unit in Edinburgh to monitor vCJD cases and to investigate the possible link with BSE. By March 1993, BSE rates had started to decline, and the new chief medical officer again reassured the public that British beef was safe to eat. Adhering to the classical format of progressive revelation, Act 1 continues as officials track the new cattle disease for the next two years. (The Mad Cow web page, www.mad-cow.org, from January 3, 1999, to the present provides a detailed chronology of the epidemic. Other websites include www.bse.org.uk and www.doh.gov.uk/cjd).

Act 2 witnessed a growing consensus concerning the transmission of the disease, with disclosures about industrial farming. Precautionary measures taken to prevent the introduction of cattle offal into human foods, as well as the Minister for Agriculture's theatrical consumption of beef before an anxious television audience, had already begun to reflect a mood of increasing tension.

Act 2 was scarcely under way when players from Acts 3 and 4 burst on stage.

The government's announcement on Wednesday March 20, 1996, that the recent death of a 20-year old man, as well as 9 other recently diagnosed cases among young people was due to exposure to BSE, triggered a well-publicized crisis. Reversing the position the government had held for a decade, the announcement caused public hysteria, particularly in light of the loss of trust in the ability of the government to keep the food supply free of contamination. In the decade leading up to the BSE/vCJD crisis, British consumers had faced a number of food scares—Salmonella in eggs, Listeria in cheese, *Escherichia coli*, antibiotics, and hormones in meat, and pesticide residues and benzene compounds in other foods (Jacob & Hellstrom 2000, p. 305). The day after the announcement, five European countries banned the importation of British beef, and 10,000 British schools dropped beef from their menus. By Friday, McDonald's had stopped serving British beef, and by Monday, Burger King and Wendy's had also eliminated British beef from their offerings. The World Health Organization endorsed the British government's conclusion that vCJD was best explained by its connection to BSE, that is from eating beef in the late 1980s before the introduction of controls to prevent contaminated beef entering the food chain (Greger 1996). BSE was viewed as the most serious threat ever posed to British agriculture. Attempts at statistical modeling to predict the eventual scale of vCJD ranged from 100 to several million cases (Collinge 1999, p. 354, p. 318), reflecting the many uncertainties surrounding the epidemic. By October 2000, 80 people in Britain had died of the disease, and five victims were reported to be still alive (Pallister 2000, p. 6). By January 2001, governments in Britain (and Europe) began to search for storage sites and for ways to subsidize the construction of incinerators to burn the mountains of dead cattle (Stecklow 2001). During December 2000 the BSE crisis spread throughout Europe, and there were fears of its entry into the United States.

The epidemic in Britain had not yet reached closure before the public was provided with moral judgments and lessons to be learned (the mark of Act 4). Critics pointed to government errors in risk management that must be prevented to avoid similar mistakes occurring in future scares concerning agricultural technology. The process of research and decision-making was said to have been dominated by scientists, industrialists, and civil servants, a group accused in the past of giving too little attention to health risks and too much to the needs of farmers and commerce. The closeted activities of the Ministry of Agriculture, Fisheries and Food received special criticism (*Nature* 1996). The need to inform the public of potential health hazards, as well as the need of the media for sensational headlines, was seen as threatening to compromise the scientific process (Ashby 1996, p. 109).

The crisis in Britain simultaneously ignited an explosion of apocalyptic prose (characteristic of Act 3) concerning BSE, vCJD, and kuru. Journalists wrote about the dangers of "a terrifying new plague" (Rhodes 1997), and "the shocking legacy of a 20th Century disease" (Cooke 1998). A former dairy inspector and physician warned of the danger of a BSE epidemic in the United States (Hulse 1996), and a cattle rancher, now the president of the International Vegetarian Union, expressed his concerns in writing (Lyman 1998) and on the Oprah Winfrey Show. A jury subsequently found Lyman, Winfrey, and Harpo Productions not liable for damages in a lawsuit filed by a group of Texas cattlemen who had charged them with "food disparagement" (Croft 2000).

Mad cow disease was fast attaining the status of "a global populist issue" and an "icon of our time" (McCalman 1998, p. ii). In the United States, a documentary told the story of "The Brain Eaters" (Nova 1998), citing BSE and kuru as examples of the dangers that arise when animals and humans consume their own species. Television in France and England provided graphic images of the deterioration of 17-year old Arnaud Eboli and 14-year old Zoe Jeffries, both afflicted with vCJD. The death of Zoe Jeffries is said to have been watched by millions of viewers (BBC News 2000). The sense of crisis had been sustained since the government revelation of March 20, 1996. Given the uncertainties surrounding the mode of transmission and the length of incubation, Act 3 may last for some time. Incubation periods for kuru range from 4 years (the earliest recorded case) to 50 years, with a mean of 12 years (Whitfield 2000, p. 54). Moreover, in this case, the crisis is ours.

Several seasons later, the French drama opened, closely following the British plot line. Act 1 began in March 1996 with a European Union ban on British beef. The French view BSE as a British epidemic. Act 2 revealed the participants attempting to reach agreement on an explanatory framework. The French agricultural minister hinted at a "mysterious third way" of spreading the disease, other than through animal-based feed and from cow to calf (www.mad-cow.org. 23 April 2000). By June 2000, 18 cases of BSE had been identified in France, but the government continued to assure the public that mad cow disease was confined to the United Kingdom. Nevertheless, a program to screen cattle began in mid June. Act 2 came to a close with a general sense that the source of the epidemic lay in Britain, and that British agricultural practices were to blame.

Act 3 opened abruptly in mid October 2000 with the arrest of a farmer who was trying to sell a diseased cow for slaughter. The authorities intercepted the cow, but a thousand tons of suspect meat from the same herd had already entered the market. On October 24, the Carrefour supermarket chain said that the meat had been distributed to 39 stores, mostly in northern France (Daley 2000). Television stations broadcast documentaries about vCJD, beef sales dropped, and France was said to be experiencing a psychosis. In a ritual echo of the British Agricultural Minister's performance four years earlier, the French Farm Minister declared that "I eat beef, my children eat beef, and all the scientists who are mad cow disease experts eat beef, and so do their children" (Reuters, 8 Nov. 2000).

As in England, public confidence in the ability of the government to protect the safety of foods had been undermined by the discovery of tons of rotten duck about to be shipped off for sale, and by subsequent alerts over Listeria bacteria in sausages and ice cream (Reuters, 22 Nov. 2000). Many people still retained memories of the 1985 scandal over tainted blood, in which more than 4000 people contracted AIDS from contaminated blood or blood products (Butler 1994). Just as the ban on consumption of British beef had dealt a blow to national identity, the French psyche was damaged by the recommendation that certain national delicacies—pâté, sweetbreads, and sausages made from cow intestines—were to be avoided (Lichfield 2000).

By the end of the year the public was experiencing a confusing mix of moral judgment, collective action, and political ritual. The French Agricultural Minister said that Britain would be "judged morally" for introducing mad cow disease to France (Bishop 2001); the government launched a counter-offensive in support of the beef industry; and opposition benches in parliament, with an eye to challenging the presidency in 2002, proposed a policy of urgent caution. The family of a third French vCJD victim joined two other families in filing a novel lawsuit challenging French, British, and European Union authorities for mishandling outbreaks of BSE in the 1980s and 1990s (Reuters, 23 Nov. 2000. Meat workers, demanding compensation, barricaded the roads around Paris, Bordeaux, Toulouse, and Lyon (*New York Times*, 9 Jan. 2001), and cattle raisers sponsored a "sane cow barbecue" in the Luxembourg Gardens in an attempt to persuade the public that the danger lay in meat from dairy herds, not beef cattle (Reuters, 10 Dec. 2000).

As in Britain, the classical narrative structure appears to be violated: Acts 3 and 4 had opened before Act 2 had run its course. The cacophony of voices, as well as the media reenactment of the many acts of protest and political theater, convey a sense of self-conscious display and detachment. By way of contrast, the sequence of events in the kuru epidemic had been more orderly and predictable. In their small-scale, relatively homogeneous communities, the Fore assemblies held to discuss the epidemic reinforced a common set of understandings about the nature of their predicament. Produced with an eye on the Australian Administration, which they feared would punish them for excessive and continued use of sorcery, the assemblies manifested an element of self-consciousness. Nevertheless, they were not postmodern happenings (Lindenbaum 1998, p. 45).

Postmodern Epidemics, Postmodern Societies?

The question of whether an epidemic might be considered postmodern in an era of postmodernity had been raised earlier for AIDS (Rosenberg 1992, p. 292). In the rapidity of its spread and the parallel rapidity of its identification as a unified clinical entity, AIDS differed from syphilis, tuberculosis, and rheumatic fever, which only gradually emerged as clinical entities, observations that apply well to BSE/vCJD. As with AIDS, it could also be said that BSE and vCJD seem postmodern phenomena in the self-conscious, reflexive, and bureaucratically structured detachment with which we regard them (Rosenberg 1992, pp. 289–90).

The collapse of the traditional four-part dramatic structure also captures the postmodern sense of the compression of spatial and temporal worlds (Harvey 1990, p. 240). It would be hard to overestimate the role of the internet in this collapse of space and time, and in the creation of a virtual (and real) community of scholars, as well as among the families of vCJD sufferers who have joined internet support groups. By the end of February 2001, the mad cow web page alone had registered almost a million hits. Newspapers, journals, and television also broadcast a torrent of information about the spread of BSE, new cases of vCJD, farmers' protests, the statements of politicians and their opponents, and critical analyses of the government's role in handling the crisis in Britain, France, and Germany. The "classical" narrative structure appears to have been destabilized by instantaneous exposure to data, analysis, and political activism.

Specialists on prion disease also provided readable accounts of the prion diseases for nonspecialists (Ridley & Baker 1998). Several publications presented a multidisciplinary approach to the crisis (Ratzan 1998, McCalman et al 1998), the latter a self-conscious exercise in bridging the "fragmentation and hyperspecialization of modern knowledge" said to have "given rise to the pervasive late twentieth century cultural paradigm of postmodernity" (1998, p. ii). In addition, the online edition of the Oxford English Dictionary now had an entry for mad cow disease, a French film-maker explored mad cow disease from the perspective of Hindus who hold a different image of the cow (Balmes 1997), and a composition for clarinet and chamber ensemble composed by John Adams in 1996 had a segment called "Hoedown (Mad Cow)", said to be a version of the traditional Western hoedown that addresses the fault lines of international commerce from a distinctly American perspective (Program notes 1997). A sense of postmodern pastiche and irony is compounded by references to mad cows, mad scientists, mad bureaucrats, and rogue and ghost proteins. Calling cows mad gives them human attributes and suggests that cows are viewed here as human surrogates, as does the paired image of the staggering cow and the dying vCJD victim in both video and print (Leach 1998, p. 127). This may provide cover for the compulsion to joke about the disease in cows, though not humans, concerning dementia, disability, and cannibalism. It may also be the stimulus for a poem entitled "Mad Cows and Englishmen" (Marsden & Dealler 2000), and a witty essay about mad cow disease from the viewpoint of the cow (Wallace-Crabbe 1998, p. 167). Mad cow jokes can be found on a number of websites, such as The Chemical Cow Home Page http://sis.bris.ac.uk/~mm7372.

Postmodernity or Risk Society?

Risk emerged as the key word for social analysis of the prion diseases and contemporary society, an approach foreshadowed in Garrett's warning of the dangers to public health in a world out of balance (Garrett 1994). Poor risk communication was also a theme in much of the popular literature. Mad cow disease was said to be "one of the most expensive and tragic examples of poor risk management in the last twenty-five years" (Powell & Leiss 1988), and a lesson about the ways in which "pessimism, paranoia, and a misguided media are leading us toward disaster" (Cohl 1997). For ecofeminists, BSE was a salutary example of the globalization of nonsustainable and hazardous food production, and of industrial agriculture's overstepping of the ecological boundaries that recognize the difference between herbivores and carnivores (Shiva 2000). The editors of *PRWATCH*, a quarterly newsletter that focuses on manipulative and misleading practices of the public relations industry, cite BSE as another example of the need for regulations to counter the power of the modern "agribusiness" lobby (Rampton & Stauber 1997). Political scientists used the crisis in Britain to show that institutional arrangements had predisposed decision-makers to adopt a counter-productive approach to handling situations of scientific uncertainty (Jacob & Hellstrom 2000), reinforcing the Phillips Report that "at the heart of the BSE story lie questions of how to handle hazard" (Pallister 2000). A health policy analyst judged that the British government had erred in failing to enact more aggressive interventions to protect public health, even though the risk to humans from BSE was unknown (Lanska 1998).

In France, sociologists expressed their views in the daily press. Bruno Latour was critical of a division of labor that allowed risk evaluators (experts) and managers of risk (politicians) to exclude public participation in final decisions about the hierarchy of risks (Latour 2000). Denis Duclos considered the European response to mad cow disease in France to be a political diversion, allowing the French government to avoid dealing with Corsican terrorism, the price of oil, and the falling Euro. This "artificial psychosis" allowed the disaster to be blamed generically on human beings without naming scapegoats, provided a way of questioning the general workings of society, and revealed how we can destroy ourselves through the industrial destruction of other forms of life (Duclos 2000). In Portugal, the BSE crisis revealed a different balance between science and politics. The divide between scientists and policy-makers is said to have widened at a time when so-called "risk societies" demonstrate the need for greater local scientific input to political decision-making (Goncalves 2000).

The social theorist Ulrich Beck cites BSE as a textbook example of the workings of what he calls "risk society" (1999, p. 48), a new kind of society or "second modernity" in which the very idea of controllability, certainty or security, so fundamental in the first modernity, collapses. He challenges the belief that "the environmental hazards we face today can still be captured by nineteenth-century, scientific models of risk assessment and industrial assumptions about danger and safety" (Beck 1999, p. 148). Giddens also suggests that one distinguishing feature of late modernity is the increasing unknowability of the risks produced by technological innovations partly through unanticipated consequences (cited in Miller 1999, p. 1241).

A British writer and medical practitioner challenges Beck's concept of risk society that links the issue of BSE and vCJD to the nuclear leak at Chernobyl and the dangers of genetic engineering. Elevating risk society caution to become the prime directive of human action would thus prevent any form of scientific or social experimentation (Fitzpatrick 1998, p. 57). A media analyst similarly uses the case of BSE to argue that the social production of risks in the public domain is not the inevitable consequence of late modernity or postmodernity, as Beck and Giddens would have it, but the product of the pursuit of definitional and material advantages in the context of already existing definitional and material conditions. The neglect of questions of agency has led theorists to present risks as inevitable concomitants of technological and cultural developments, overlooking identifiable processes of "realpolitik." of nameable agencies of power and capital, thus leaving them in the grip of political quietism (Miller 1999).

Beck's analysis of risk society had also used BSE to reveal the new political economy of uncertainty in a world characterized by the anarchy of international relations (Beck 1999). Aaltola, however, resists the temptation to formulate the relation between epidemics and international relations in new terms, noting that throughout history epidemics have had a direct impact on political interaction by vindicating, weakening, testing, and molding international relations. The present interaction between disease and politics is said to differ in degree in the sense of increasing the tempo of international interactions and the increasing scale of global threats, pointing to the risk of an increasing intensity of lethal epidemic diseases. The effects of the BSE epidemic on international relations were said to follow essentially "the same course of activity that has been observed in similar situations over the last two millenia" (Aaltola 1999, p. 236).

The discussion of risk society centers on the relationship of culture to nature, an old topic in anthropology. Risk society is said to be characterized by the loss of a clear distinction between nature and culture brought about by industrialization and by "the hazards that endanger humans, animals and plants alike" (Beck 1999, p. 145). Luttwak, a Bolivian cattle rancher and director of geo-economics at the Washington-based Center for Strategic and International Studies, notes that the BSE drama calls attention to the habitual malpractice of the cattle industries in Europe and North America, which resist the pace and limits set by nature. Moreover, bovines, unlike humans and pigs, are said to be pure herbivores. Their four-part ruminant stomachs break down cellulose in grass but cannot easily digest cereals and other concentrates containing high levels of protein without triggering a variety of diseases. Nearly all beef cattle in Europe and North America thus survive in a state of chronic, low-level sickness, treated with large doses of antibiotics (Luttwak 2001).

The theme that vCJD represents "the revenge of nature" and that such problems have arisen because we have "denatured cattle" (Rifkin 1996) is resisted by Fitzpatrick, who notes that there is no such thing as a "natural" method of farming. "Agriculture is by definition a violation of nature" (Fitzpatrick 1998, p. 60). Taking a position that departs from that of Luttwak, Fitzpatrick proposes that the controversy about turning cows into cannibals overlooks the fact that, like most mammals, cows are omnivores, capable of digesting animal as well as plant protein, and the feeding of animal protein to cattle long predates modern intensive farming. Despite his view that we face less threat from nature than at any time in human history, however, Fitzpatrick allows that "the popularity of the notion that the source of all our problems lies in the very attempt to increase human control over nature reveals the deep despondency of modern society and its extraordinary collapse of confidence in itself" (1998, p. 62). The BSE/vCJD epidemic thus appears to evoke the "spirit" of the era. It is also the product of societies fragmented and realigned in ways that to many observers seem unfamiliar.

An Agenda for Anthropology

This review reveals a tumultuous international discussion about what are perceived to be new kinds of epidemics, new social forms, and new states of consciousness. Participants in the discussion represent a variety of disciplines in medicine and the human sciences, but anthropology is not among them. During the 1960s historians appear to have responded to a call for further research into the social history of epidemics (Slack 1992, p. 1). A wave of important studies of past epidemics soon followed (Crosby 1972, McNeill 1976, Cipolla 1979, Brandt 1985, Rosenberg 1962, Ranger & Slack 1992, Watts 1997, Herlihy 1997). As descendants of W. H. R. Rivers, Evans-Pritchard, and Victor Turner, however, anthropologists studying health and illness turned first to the intricacies and subtleties of non-Western health beliefs and behaviors. Anthropologists also came late to the study of the AIDS epidemic perhaps because, in addition to textual and media analysis, ethnographic research depends on long-term fieldwork. By the time they began to analyze their data, they faced a field dominated by models of human motivation and behavioral change that obscured the way risk behavior is shaped by social and economic contexts (Singer 1998, pp. 14–15).

Just as the kuru epidemic profited from a multidisciplinary conversation, many aspects of the BSE/vCJD epidemic lend themselves to anthropological investigation. Study of the impact of the epidemic on individuals, families, and communities could convey the essence of the calamity in a way that is not furnished by television or the internet, which provide a false sense of immediacy and community mediated by the screen of technology. Day-to-day field research in afflicted communities can avoid the construction of social suffering at a safe distance without the social responsibility of real engagement (Kleinman et al 1997, p. xviii).

An ethnography of changing European diets could illuminate the links among commerce, agriculture, and ideologies about food and health, traceable to the mad cow epidemic. In the wake of wartime penury, for example, the French became Europe's biggest meat eaters, and steakhouse restaurants appeared in major cities and in suburban shopping malls (August 2000). Responding to growing consumer resistance, however, three-star restaurants, representatives of agro-business, and even McDonalds have a new-found interest in "reasoned agriculture," organic foods, and the creation of a vegetable cuisine, a shift with huge implications for the global production and marketing of food.

Long-term field research can also unravel the chains of relationships that prompt behaviors often framed in terms of risk, an epidemiological category that plucks behavior from context, and one that led to many misunderstandings during the first decade of the AIDS epidemic (Kane & Mason 1992). By examining behaviors embedded in complexes of relationships, ethnographers can trace the chains of risk that link local and more distant contexts, moving from individuals in families and communities to the fast food industry, perhaps even to the illicit traffic in beef and beef products investigated by the mad cow unit of the French police force (Comtex Newswire 2000). A political and economic reading of the epidemic would further inquire into the benefits that flow from damaging alliances between certain industries and government agencies. In addition to the well-documented collusion between the beef industry and the British Ministry for Agriculture, Food and Fisheries, some consider the agro-chemical industry responsible for the disasters falling upon Mark Purdey, the organic farmer who first suggested that BSE was associated with the use of phosmet to treat warbler fly infection. Originally dismissed for his heretical views (as was Prusiner), Purdey's research has now been published in a mainstream medical journal (Purdey 1996a,b, 1998) and is being rigorously tested by others (Wadsworth et al 1999; see also "Copper Consensus" on the Mad Cow Home Page). Following a newspaper article about his research, however, his farmhouse burnt down, his telephone lines were cut, and he is said to be trailed when he travels around the country to talk about his theory. Some propose that the death of his veterinarian and his first lawyer in road accidents, as well a car crash involving his second lawyer, may not be coincidence (Kail 2001). While this may suggest unwarranted paranoia, fear of industry retaliation seems to have been responsible for the absence of a press release or media report of a study of the risk of transmission to humans of chronic wasting disease in Colorado wild deer and elk. The "Mad Cow" Webmaster summarized the study and provided editorial comments (Raymond et al 2000).

Theories of disease causation that reject orthodox views lend themselves to anthropological analysis. Counter-narratives and structures of blame have been noted in other epidemics, where they are seen to be commentaries about cultural values and the perceived state of social relations (Arnold 1987, Farmer 1992, Lindenbaum 1998). Alternate hypotheses about the BSE/vCJD epidemic reflect anxieties about the environment, industry, the government, and the intrusion of outsiders. They include the suggestion that BSE might be carried in cow's milk, in the soil (from cow dung), in water supplies (in some cases resulting from the spillage of BSE waste into floodwaters), and in dust particles emitted from rendering plants (www.mad-cow.org. Dec. 15, 2000). Echoing similar fears expressed during the AIDS epidemic, the families of vCJD victims have suggested that the government is covering up the military's accidental release of a secret disease (J. Whitfield, personal communication). Social class is rarely mentioned except to note that infected meat is most likely to be found in the cheaper cuts of beef and is possibly associated with the introduction of self-service meals in some schools during the 1980s (Derbyshire 2000). It has also been proposed that there is no infectious agent responsible for kuru, BSE, or vCJD, which are stress-caused diseases in both humans and animals (T. Doré, unpublished data). Epidemics release marginal ideas and unmask opposed interests kept subdued in less critical times.

The study of epidemics provides a critical commentary on complex political and economic relationships at home and abroad. The spread of the BSE epidemic from Britain to continental Europe led to the erection of barricades to prevent beef from crossing national borders, to political pressure from opposition parties critical of their government's handling of an issue of concern for public health, and to European governments blaming foreign governments for their own domestic predicaments, a sign of the fragility of the European Union. The epidemic also provides a case study of the way in which a new brand of venture capitalists fund scientific research to study the role of proteins or to produce test kits that detect mad cow disease in animals before slaughter (Olsen 2001). Acquiring the licenses for research that hold the promise of huge profits, venture capitalists leave to governments the basic research that may be too expensive or too risky.

As this essay has shown, epidemics appear to share certain aspects of narrative structure, as well as a number of sociological features. Since they are mirrors held up to society, however, we need to distinguish the unique from the apparently universal in each epidemic, an exercise that the advocates of contemporary history propose as a contribution to health policy (Berridge 1992). Certain epidemics (and diseases) fade in and out of consciousness in ways that depend on more than matters of biology or demography (Rosner & Markowitz 1991, Crosby 1989). BSE/vCJD and kuru, already the subject of intense international discussion, have laid claim to our future attention. Analysts of risk society have identified a contemporary sense of anxiety about protecting our domestic space from the dangerous world outside the door. The fear of ingesting rogue proteins, or genetically modified (Frankenstein) foods, as well as our ambivalence about human and animal cannibalism, appear to express a more general sense of unease concerning control of our lives, framed in terms of society's relationship to nature, said to be "the central debate in the coming years" (Duclos 2000). As this review attempts to show, the study of epidemics provides a unique point of entry for examining the relationships among cultural assumptions, particular institutional forms, and states of mind.

Visit the Annual Reviews home page at www.AnnualReviews.org

LITERATURE CITED

Aaltola M. 1999. International relations and epidemics: a short expedition to places inhabited by states and mad cows. *Med. Confl. Surviv.* 15(3):235–54

Alper T, Cramp WA, Haig DA, Clarke MC. 1967. Does the agent of scrapie replicate without nucleic acid? *Nature* 214:764–66

Alpers M, Gajdusek DC. 1965. Changing patterns of Kuru: epidemiological changes in the period of increasing contact of the Fore people with Western civilzation. *Am. J. Trop. Med. Hyg.* 14(5):852–79

Anderson W. 1992. Securing a brain: the contested meanings of Kuru. In *So Human a Brain. Knowledge and Values in the Neurosciences*, ed. A Harrington, pp. 193–203. Boston, MA: Birkhauser

Anderson W. 2000. The possession of Kuru: medical science and biocolonial exchange. *Comp. Stud. Soc. Hist.* 42(4):713–44

Anderton B, Collinge J, Powell J, Prusiner S. 1992. An introduction to prion research. In *Prion Diseases of Humans and Animals*, ed. SB Prusiner, J Collinge, J Powell, B Anderton. Chichester, UK: Ellis Horwood

Arens W. 1979. *The Man-Eating Myth. Anthropology and Anthropophagy*. New York: Oxford Univ. Press

Arnold D. 1987. Touching the body: perspectives on the Indian plague, 1896–1900. *Subaltern Stud.* V:55–90

Ashby J. 1996. Mad cows, bats and baby milk. *Nature* 382:109

August, M. November 21, 2000. *Top French*

chefs unaffected by mad cow fears. http://www.mad-cow.org

Balmes T. 1997. *Maharaja Burger: Mad Cows, Sacred Cows.* Paris: Quark Prod.

Bastos C. 1999. *Global Responses to AIDS.* Bloomington: Indiana Univ. Press

BBC News. Oct 30, 2000. http://www.mad-cow.org

Beck U. 1999. *World Risk Society.* Cambridge, UK: Blackwell

Bennett JH, Rhodes FA, Robson HN. 1958. Observations on Kuru: a possible genetic basis. *Aust. Ann. Med.* 7:269

Bennett JH, Rhodes FA, Robson HN. 1959. A possible genetic basis for Kuru. *Am. J. Hum. Genet.* 11:169

Berkun N. 2000. *Mad Cow disease.* http://www.skidmore.edu/studentorgs/svc/essays/madcow.htm

Berridge V. 1992. AIDS, history and contemporary history. In *The Time of AIDS*, ed. G. Herdt, S. Lindenbaum, pp. 41–64. Newbury Park, CA: Sage

Bishop P. January 9, 2001. France blames Britain for its BSE. *Telegraph.* http://www.mad-cow-org/UKCJD/;CJD_news30.html

Brandt AM. 1985. *No Magic Bullet. A Social History of Venereal Diseases in The United States Since 1880.* New York: Oxford Univ. Press

Brouwer E. 1998. Sheep to cows to man: a history of TSEs. In *The Mad Cow Crisis*, ed. SC Ratzan, pp. 26–34. New York: New York Univ. Press

Butler D. 1994. French ministries face public trial in HIV blood affair. *Nature* 370:243

Café Productions 2000. Forbidden Rites—"Cannibalism." London

Campbell AM. 1931. *The Black Death and Men of Learning.* New York: Columbia Univ. Press

Cipolla CM. 1979. *Faith, Reason, and the Plague in Seventeenth Century Tuscany.* New York: Norton

Cohl HA. 1997. *Are We Scaring Ourselves to Death? How Pessimism, Paranoia, and a Misguided Media Are Leading Us Toward Disaster.* New York: St. Martin's Griffin

Collinge J. 1999. Variant Creutzfeldt-Jakob disease. *Lancet* 354:317–23

Collinge J, Prusiner S. 1992. Terminology of prion diseases. In *Prion Diseases of Humans and Animals*, ed. SB Prusiner, J Collinge, J Powell, B Anderton, pp. 5–12. Chichester, UK: Ellis Horwood

Comtex Newswire. Nov 14, 2000. *France: mad cow case triggers wave of fear.* http://www.mad-cow.org

Cooke J. 1998. *Cannibals, Cows and the CJD Catastrophe.* Sydney, Aust.: Random House

Cowley G. 2001. Cannibals to cows: the path of a deadly disease. *Newsweek*, Mar. 12

Crawford LM. 1998. BSE: A veterinary history. In *The Mad Cow Crisis*, ed. SC Ratzan, pp. 9–14. New York: New York Univ. Press

Croft A. February 12, 2000. *Reuters Online Service.* http://www.mad-cow.org.

Crosby AW. 1972. *The Columbian Exchange. Biological and Cultural Consequences of 1492.* Westport, CT: Greenwood

Crosby AW. 1989. *America's Forgotten Pandemic. The Influenza of 1918.* Cambridge, UK: Cambridge Univ. Press

Daley S. 2000. Arrests spur French fears over spread of mad cow. *New York Times*, Nov. 3. p. A7

De Bruxelles S. November 16, 2000. Major the 3rd lion suffered from BSE. *Times*, 15 Nov. http://www.mad-cow.org.

Derbyshire D. 2000. School food may have spread CJD. *Telegraph*, 17 July. http://www.mad-cow.org/UKCJD/CJD_news9.html

Duclos D. 2000. At the sign of the panicked cow. *Le Monde Diplomatique*, 16 Dec.

Farmer P. 1992. *AIDS and Accusation. Haiti and the Geography of Blame.* Berkeley, CA: Univ. Calif. Press

Fitzpatrick M. 1998. How now mad cow? See McCalman et al. 1998, pp. 37–65

Gajdusek DC, Alpers M. 1972. Genetic studies in relation to Kuru. 1. Cultural, historical and demographic background. *Am. J. Hum. Genet.* 24:1–38 (Suppl.)

Gajdusek DC, Gibbs CJ, Alpers M. 1966. Experimental transmission of a Kuru-like syndrome to chimpanzees. *Nature* 209:794–96

Gajdusek DC, Sorenson ER, Meyer J. 1970. A comprehensive cinema record of disappearing Kuru. *Brain* 93:65–76

Gajdusek DC, Zigas V. 1957. Degenerative disease of the central nervous system in New Guinea: the endemic occurrence of "Kuru" in the Native population. *New Engl. J. Med.* 257:974

Garrett L. 1994. *The Coming Plague: Newly Emerging Diseases in a World Out of Balance.* New York: Penguin

Glasse S (Lindenbaum) 1962. The Social Effects of Kuru. *Dept. Pub. Health Territ. P. N. G.* pp. 1–48

Glasse S (Lindenbaum) 1963. The Social Life of Women in the South Fore. *Dept. Pub. Health Territ. P. N. G.* pp. 1–13

Glasse S (Lindenbaum) 1964. The social effects of Kuru. *P. N. G. Med. J.* 7:36–47

Glasse R. 1962. The Spread of Kuru among the Fore. *Dept. Pub. Health Territ. P. N. G.*

Glasse R. 1963. Cannibalism in the Kuru region. *Dept. Pub. Health Territ. P. N. G.*

Glasse R. 1967. Cannibalism in the Kuru region of New Guinea. *Trans. NY Acad. Sci.* 29(6):748–54

Glisson TL. 1991. A comic stew with bite. *St. Petersburg Times*, June 21, p. 27

Goncalves ME. 2000. The importance of being European: the science and politics of BSE in Portugal. *Sci. Technol. Hum. Values* 25(4):417–48

Goodfield J. 1997. Cannibalism and Kuru. *Nature* 387:841

Greger M. 1996. Interview with Michael Greger!!!. http://www/mad-cow.org/greg.html

Griffith JS. 1967. Self replication and scrapie. *Nature* 215:1043–44

Hadlow WJ. 1959. Scapie and Kuru. *Lancet* 2:28

Harvey D. 1990. *The Condition of Postmodernity.* Cambridge, MA: Blackwell

Herdt G, Lindenbaum S, eds. 1992. *The Time of AIDS. Social Analysis, Theory and Method.* Newbury Park, CA: Sage

Herlihy D. 1997. *The Black Death and the Transformation of the West*, ed. SK Cohn. Cambridge, MA: Harvard Univ. Press

Hill AF, Joiner S, Linehan J, Desbruslais M, Lantos PL, et al. 2000. Species-barrier-independent prion replication in apparently resistant species. *Proc. Natl. Acad. Sci. USA* 97(18):10248–53

Hulse VM. 1996. Mad Cows and Milk Gate. Ashland, OR: Marble Mountain

Jacob M, Hellstrom T. 2000. Policy understanding of science, public trust and the BSE-CJD crisis. *J. Hazard. Mater.* 78:303–17

Jonsen A, Stryker J. 1993. *The Social Impact of AIDS in the United States.* Washington, DC: Natl. Acad. Press

Kail P. January 17, 2001. *The Chemical Industry Plays Dirty.* http://www.freezerbox.com/archive/20001/01/bse

Kane S. 1998. *AIDS Alibis. Sex, Drugs and Crime in the Americas.* Philadelphia, PA: Temple Univ. Press

Kane S, Mason T. 1992. *"IV Drug Users" and "Sex Partners" : The Limits of epidemiological categories and the ethnography of risk.* In *The Time of Aids*, ed. G. Herdt, S. Lindenbaum. Newbury Park, CA: Sage

Keesing R. 1991. *Cultural Anthropology. a Contemporary Perspective.* New York: Holt, Rinehart & Winston

Kleinman A, Das V, Lock M, eds. 1997. *Social Suffering.* Berkeley, CA: Univ. Calif. Press

Klitzman R. 1998. *The Trembling Mountain. A Personal Account of Kuru, Cannibals, and Mad Cow Disease.* New York: Plenum

Klitzman R, Alpers M, Gajdusek DC. 1984. The natural incubation period of Kuru and the episodes of transmission in three clusters of patients. *Neuroepidemiology* 3:20

Kraut AM. 1994. *Silent Travellers. Germs, Genes and the "Immigrant Menace."* New York: Basic Books

Lancet. 1974. Kuru, Creutzfeldt-Jakob, and Scrapie. 11:1551–52

Lanska DJ. 1998. The mad cow problem in the UK: risk perceptions, risk management, and health policy development. *J. Pub. Health Policy* 19(2):160–83

Latour B. 2000. La sagesse des vaches folles. *Le Monde*, 23 Nov.

Leach J. 1998. Madness, metaphors and

miscommunication: the rhetorical life of mad cow disease. In *The Mad Cow Crisis*, ed. SC Ratzan, pp. 119–30. New York: New York Univ. Press

Lindenbaum S. 1979. *Kuru Sorcery: Disease and Danger in the New Guinea Highlands.* Palo Alto, CA: Mayfield

Lindenbaum S. 1982. Review of Kuru: Early Letters and Fieldnotes from the Collection of D. Carleton Gajdusek, ed. JD Farquar, DC Gajdusek. *J. Polyn. Soc.* pp. 150–52

Lindenbaum S. 1998. Images of catastrophe: the making of an epidemic. In *The Political Economy of AIDS*, ed. M Singer, pp. 33–58. Amityville, NY: Baywood

Lichfield J. May 10, 2000. French Pâté and Sausage hit by BSE rule. http://www.mad-cow.org/UKCJD/CJD˙news8.html

Luttwak E. 2001. Sane cows, or BSE isn't the worst of it. *London Rev. Books*, 8 Feb., pp. 26–7

Lyman HF. 1998. *Mad Cowboy: Plain Truth from the Cattle Rancher Who Won't Eat Meat*. New York: Scribner

Marsden C, Dealler S. 2000. Mad Cows and Englishmen. http://spare.airtime.co.uk.bse/poem.htm

Mathews JD. 1971. *Kuru: a puzzle in culture and environmental medicine*. PhD thesis. Univ. Melbourne

Mathews JD, Glasse R, Lindenbaum S. 1968. Kuru and cannibalism. *Lancet* 2:449

McCalman I. 1998. Introduction. See McCalman et al. 1998, pp. i–ix

McCalman I, Penny W, Cook M. 1998. Mad Cows and Modernity, Canberra, Aust.: Hum. Res. Cen. Monogr. Ser. 13

McElroy A, Townsend P. 1979. *Medical Anthropology in Ecological Perspective*. North Scituate, MA: Duxbury

McNeill WH. 1976. *Plagues and Peoples*. Garden City, NY: Doubleday

Meikle J. 2000. Denial, failure and the betrayal of the public. *Guardian Oct.* 27:1

Miller D. 1999. Risk, science and policy: definitional struggles, information management, the media and BSE. *Soc. Sci. Med.* 49(9):1239–55

Monbiot G. 2000. Copper-bottomed answer to mad cow disease? *Guardian Weekly Dec.* 6:19

Nature. 1996. Lessons from BSE for public confidence, 28 Mar., p. 271

Nelkin D. 1995. *Selling Science. How the Press Covers Science and Technology*. New York: Freeman

Nelson H. 1998. Kuru: the pursuit of the prize. See McCalman et al. 1998, pp. 125–66

New York Times, November 3, 2000. Arrests Spur French Fears Over Spread of Mad Cow

New York Times. January 9, 2001. France: mad cow protests

Nova 1998. The brain eaters. Feb 10. Boston

Olsen E. 2001. A small Swiss company takes on mad cow disease. *New York Times*, Jan 31, p. W1

Pallister D. 2000. "Culture of secrecy" misled the public about risk of eating Beef. *Guardian Oct.* 27:6

Pangolin Pictures. 1998. Kuru: to tremble with fear. New York

Park MA. 2000. *Introducing Anthropology. An Integrated Approach*. Palo Alto, CA: Mayfield

Plato CC, Gajdusek DC. 1972. Genetic studies in relation to kuru. *Am. J. Hum. Genet.* 24:86–94 (Suppl.)

Powell D, Leiss W. 1998. *Mad Cows and Mother's Milk*. Montreal, Canada: McGill-Queen's Univ. Press

Program Notes. Oct. 19, 1997. Chamber Music Society, Lincoln Center, NY

Program Notes. Oct. 27, 1997. Chamber Music Society, Lincoln Center, NY p. 20B

Prusiner SB. 1982. Novel proteinaceous infectious particles cause scrapie. *Science* 216:136–44

Prusiner SB. The Prion diseases. *Sci. Am.* Jan. pp. 48–57

Prusiner S, Collinge J, Powell J, Anderton B, eds. 1992. *Prion Diseases Of Humans and Animals*. Chichester, UK: Ellis Horwood

Purdey M. 1996a. The UK epidemic of BSE: slow virus or chronic pesticide-initiated modification of the prion protein? Part 1: Mechanisms for a chemically induced pathogenesis/transmissibility. *Med. Hypoth.* 46(5): 429–43

Purdey M. 1996b. The UK epidemic of BSE: slow virus or chronic pesticide-initiated modification of the prion protein? Part 2: An epidemiological perspective. *Med. Hypoth.* 46(5):445–54

Purdey M. 1998. High-dose exposure to systemic phosmet insectide modifies the phosphatidylinositol anchor on the protein prion: the origins of new variant transmissible spongiform encephalopathies? *Med. Hypoth.* 50(2):91–111

Rampton S, Stauber J. 1997. *Mad Cow U.S.A. Could the Nightmare Happen Here?* Monroe, Maine: Common Courage

Ranger T, Slack P, eds. 1992. *Epidemics and Ideas. Essays on the Historical Perception of Pestilence.* Cambridge, UK: Cambridge Univ. Press

Ratzan SC, ed. 1998. *The Mad Cow Crisis. Health and the Public Good.* New York: New York Univ. Press

Raymond GJ, Bossers A, Raymond LD, O'Rourke KI, McHolland LE, et al. 2000. Evidence of a molecular barrier limiting susceptibility of humans, cattle and sheep to chronic wasting disease. *EMBO J.* 19(17):4425–30. http://www.mad-cow.org/00/sep/00_sci_news.html

Reid LH, Gajdusek DC. 1969. Nutrition in the Kuru region 11. A nutritional evaluation of traditional Fore diet in Moke Village in 1957. *Acta. Trop.* XXV1 36:4:331–45

Reuters. 2000. http://www.mad-cow.org. Posted: Nov 8

Reuters. 2000. Third French Family to Launch Madcow lawsuit. http://www.mad-cow.org. Posted: Nov. 23

Reuters. 2000. "What is safe to eat?" consumers ask amid BSE scare. http://www.mad-cow.org/. Posted: Nov. 25

Reuters. 2000. http://www.mad-cow.org/. Dec. 10

Rhodes R. 1997. *Deadly Feasts. Tracking The Secrets of a Terrifying New Plague.* New York: Simon Schuster

Ridley RM, Baker HF. 1998. *Fatal Protein. The Story of CJD, BSE, and Other Prion Diseases.* Oxford: Oxford Univ. Press

Rifkin J. 1996. *Beyond Beef: The Rise and Fall of the Cattle Culture.* London: Thorstons

Rosenberg CE. 1962. *The Cholera Years. The United States in 1832, 1849 and 1866.* Chicago, IL: Chicago Univ. Press

Rosenberg CE. 1992. *Explaining Epidemics and Other Studies in the History of Medicine.* Cambridge, UK: Cambridge Univ. Press

Rosner D, Markowitz G. 1991. *Deadly Dust. Silicosis and the Politics of Occupational Disease in Twentieth-Century America.* Princeton, NJ: Princeton Univ. Press

Shiva V. 2000. Mad cows and sacred cows. In *Stolen Harvest: the hijacking of the food supply.* Cambridge, MA: South End

Simmons RT, Graydon JJ, Gajdusek DC, Alpers M, Hornabrook RW. 1972 Genetic studies in relation to Kuru, no. 2. *Am. J. Hum. Genet.* 24:39–71 (Suppl.)

Singer M, ed. 1998. *The Political Economy of AIDS.* Amityville, NY: Baywood

Slack P. 1992. *Introduction. In Epidemics and Ideas,* ed. T. Ranger, P. Slack, pp. 1–20. Cambridge UK: Cambridge Univ. Press

Sorenson ER. 1976. *The Edge of the Forest. Land, Childhood and Change in a New Guinea Protoagricultural Society.* Washington, DC: Smithsonian Inst. Press

Sorenson R, Gajdusek DC. 1969. Nutrition in the kuru region. 1. Gardening food handling, and diet of the Fore people. *Acta. Trop.* XXV1 4:281–30

Stecklow S. 2001. Powder kegs: in battling Mad Cow Britain spawns heaps of pulverized cattle. *Wall Str. J.* Jan. 8

Treichler P. 1999. *How to Have Theory in an Epidemic.* Durham, NC: Duke Univ. Press

Tuchman B. 1978. *A Distant Mirror. the Calamitous 14th Century.* New York: Knopf

Turner VW. 1957. *Schism and Continuity in an African Society.* Manchester, UK: Manchester Univ. Press

Wadsworth JD, Hill AF, Joiner S, Jackson GS, Clarke AR, et al. 1999. Strain-specific prion protein conformation determined by metal ions. *Nature Cell Biol.* 1:55–9

Waitzkin H. 2000. *The Second Sickness.* Boston: Rowman Littlefield

Wallace-Crabbe C. 1998. Mad Cow disease: a bovine viewpoint. See McCalman et al. 1998, pp. 167–86

Watts S. 1997. *Epidemics and History. Disease, Power and Imperialism.* New Haven, CT: Yale Univ. Press

WGBH-TV Boston. 1985. Quest for the killers. Pt. 1. Kuru

Whitfield J. 2000. *Kuru.* MA thesis. London Sch. African & Oriental Stud.

Zigas V. 1990. Laughing Death. The Untold Story of Kuru. Clifton, NJ: Humana

Annu. Rev. Anthropol. 2001. 30:387–422

BIOARCHAEOLOGY OF THE AFRICAN DIASPORA IN THE AMERICAS: Its Origins and Scope

Michael L. Blakey

*Department of Anthropology, College of William and Mary, Williamsburg, Virginia 23187
and Department of Anatomy, College of Medicine, Howard University, Washington,
DC 20059; e-mail: mlblak@wm.edu*

Key Words   African Americans, archaeology, paleopathology, biohistory, slavery

■ **Abstract**   The results of over 70 years of African Diasporic bioarchaeology
are discussed and explained as emerging from distinct interests and traditions of
African Diasporan studies, sociocultural anthropology, history, physical anthropology, and archaeology, in that chronological order. Physical anthropology is the core
discipline of African-American bioarchaeology, yet it has been the least informed by
cultural and historical literatures. Forensic approaches to bioarchaeology construct
a past that fails to be either cultural or historical, while biocultural approaches are
emerging that construct a more human history of African Diasporic communities.
The involvement of African Americans, both as clients and as sources of scholarship, has begun to transform bioarchaeology as in the example of the New York
African Burial Ground. The social history of the field examined here emphasizes
the scholarship of diasporans themselves, and critiques a bioarchaeology that, until recently, has had little relevance to the people whose history bioarchaeologists
construct.

INTRODUCTION

The origins, development, and current scope of African diasporic bioarchaeology
are examined below. The review are organized as a social history, emphasizing
the auxiological interaction of diverse traditions of scholarship with the social,
political, and economic forces by which that field of study developed. The major
research findings of selected studies are reviewed, and the vast majority of the
literature in African-American bioarchaeology is referred to.

The review attempts to (*a*) describe the scope of theory and method used by
bioarchaeologists and anthropological biohistorians, (*b*) present their research results on the temporal, regional, and industrial diversity of the historic African
Diaspora in the Americas, and (*c*) explain how this field has been shaped by social
historical phenomena. The reviewer's vantage is that of a physical anthropologist,
a science historian, and an African American who has participated in formative
bioarchaeological research on the diaspora during the past two decades.

0084-6570/01/1021-0387$14.00   **387**

I believe it is the act of relating bioarchaeology to the longer and broader development of diasporan studies, and an evaluation of the field's relationship to African Americans themselves, that most distinguishes this perspective. The African Diaspora, as the term developed, is more a concept than either a technical specialization or a geographical area of study. It is interdisciplinary and motivated by emic concerns. According to Harris (1993), the "African diaspora concept subsumes the global dispersion (voluntary and involuntary) of Africans throughout history; the emergence of a cultural identity abroad based on origin and social conditions; and the psychological or physical return to the homeland, Africa. Thus viewed, the African Diaspora assumes the character of a dynamic, continuous and complex phenomenon stretching across time, geography, class, and gender."

African-American biohistory "has evolved into the study of both the biological and sociocultural factors that have . . . influenced the health, fertility, morbidity and mortality of Afro-Americans in the New World within an historical context. Afro-American biohistory is a meeting ground for the many disciplines that focus on the health and disease of African slaves and their descendants in the Americas" (Rankin-Hill 1997). Principal among these disciplines are history, archaeology, and biological anthropology. Although Rankin-Hill uses the term to encompass both historical and historical archaeological studies, my practical use here of the term biohistory refers to research that relies primarily on written records or anatomical collections; the term bioarchaeology I reserve for studies that focus on excavated archaeological populations. Overall, the traditions of American history, archaeology, and physical anthropology have continued to merge for the development of these specializations.

By the above definitions, African-American bioarchaeology and biohistory might have been subsumed under the broad umbrella of diasporic studies, but for interesting reasons that has not happened. They have evolved separately. Juxtaposed and periodically cross-fertilizing, these separate but related research domains also reflect different ethnic and social vantages on the black experience, emphasizing different ranges of methodology and motivations. Diasporic studies developed directly from the history of African-American and other diasporic scholarship, which rarely incorporated the tools of archaeology and biology. Bioarchaeology developed from two anthropological subdisciplines that, like biohistory, have evolved from traditions of Euro-American and other "white" scholarship, rarely incorporating the social science, humanistic, and activist understandings of diasporan studies. Both traditions, however, developed within a common world of intellectual, social, and political change that connected and divided them.

These segmented trends fostered by a "racially" segregated American society have recently been merged into a single study of the eighteenth-century African Burial Ground in the City of New York, for which I am principal investigator. This review looks backward to the origins and evolution of the intellectual trends that have coalesced only at the end of the twentieth century with a single project to garner national attention. It comments on the equally recent emergence of biocultural and publicly engaged anthropology whose liberal-left formulation achieved a new compatibility with diasporan intellectual traditions, thus allowing the present merger and synthesis. And then there remains a distinct forensic tradition that racializes and dehistoricizes the diasporic experience.

ORIGINS OF AFRICAN DIASPORA STUDIES

Studies of the African Diaspora were probably begun by Catholic priests, commissioned by the Spanish Crown, who deviated from their assignment of investigating Native Americans with forays into the cultures and languages of Africans enslaved in the West Indies. At the end of the legal British trade in human captives from Africa, British studies were also commissioned (Drake 1993, Herskovits 1941), which, taken with the detailed commercial data on enslaved Africans throughout the Americas, are heavily relied on for knowledge of the diaspora during slavery. As an example, an important new database at Harvard University has amassed many of the diverse colonial records on the American slave trade.

Yet the accounting of chattel is less than a human history. The record of the human experience of Africans in the Americas during slavery is sparse, afforded mainly by the initial writings of people who had themselves been enslaved. Its Anglophone beginning (1772–1815) is as narratives about slavery (with comments on life in Africa), of the humanity of blacks and the inhumanities foisted on them by whites, in the works of freed and escaped captives such as Morrant, Gronniosaw, Cugoano, Equiano, and Jea (Gates & Andrews 1998), often arguing their cases with moral fervor.

Later, the narratives of abolitionist and statesman Frederick Douglass (1950) exemplified his life in slavery and damned the institution in a more analytical vein. In 1854, in a speech to scholars at Western Reserve University, he also attacked the racial determinism, craniometry, and racist Egyptology of Morton, Agassiz, Nott, and Gliddon (Nott & Gliddon 1854). With Douglass's "The Claims of the Negro Ethnologically Considered" (1950), an African-American genre of critical, dialectical, environmentalist, vindicationist, and activist scholarship had begun that would form a fundamental distinction of Diasporan scholarship. And it would emerge in opposition to the new genre of physical anthropology and African (Egyptian) archaeology, which Douglass claimed to be merely an attempt to justify slavery. Other African Americans were going to Africa and bringing back reports to elevate an understanding of Africa and its relationship to U.S. blacks for either missionary or nascent Pan-Africanist motives (see Delany 1861, Crummell 1861). Haitian leader and scholar Anténor Firmin (1885) wrote a 600-page anthropological treatise, *De l'égalite des Races Humaines*, in 1885, countering arguments of de Gobineau's adherents among the members of the Societe d'Anthropologie de Paris, which Firmin had penetrated as one of two black members (Firmin 2000). No white American, British, or French anthropologist of the nineteenth century opposed racial determinism and ranking (Fluehr-Lobban 2000, Gould 1996).

The American Negro Academy that Crummell founded in 1897 served as a think tank of and for African Americans whose interest was in the uplifting of a global black race. W.E.B. Du Bois, a charter member of the Academy, would publish the first empirical urban ethnography in 1899. Du Bois went on for more than seven decades as the dean of African-American social historical research, with application to Pan-Africanist, civil rights, and socialist organizing. [Du Bois and Firmin met at the first Pan-African Congress in Paris, in 1900 (Fluehr-Lobban in Firmin 2000)]. The Atlanta University Studies, which Du Bois began in 1898, were a comprehensive program of sociological and historical research on blacks; his editorship of the NAACP's *Crisis* applied social science to the civil rights effort at the beginning of the twentieth century (Harrison & Nonini 1992; see Harrison 1992 and others in this special issue of *Critique of Anthropology* devoted to Du Bois' influence in anthropology). His Jamaican-American contemporary of the early twentieth century, Marcus Garvey, a student of African and biblical history and head of the Universal Negro Improvement Association, was concerned with the building of an ideology and organization for diasporic self-help and African repatriation.

The African-American research was nearly always critical, in that it began from the observation that white racism had distorted the historical record that reinforced a sense of whites' entitlement, obscured their inequities, and inculcated a sense of inferiority in blacks. Du Bois (1915) begins an early study of Africa and its diaspora by saying that the "time has not yet come for a complete history of Negro peoples. Archaeological research in Africa has just begun, and many sources of information in Arabian, Portuguese, and other tongues are not fully at our command; and too it must frankly be confessed, racial prejudice against darker peoples is still too strong in so-called civilized centers for judicial appraisement of the peoples of Africa." The problem of an ideologically distorted Africana past continued to inspire a search for information by Diasporan scholars, creating an enormous body of "vindicationist" literature.

During the first part of the twentieth century, Zora Neal Hurston (Hemenway 1977, Mikell 1999) conveyed the complexity of African-American and Caribbean cultures through literary works based on ethnology and folklore. The Haitian Marxist ethnologist Jacques Roumain (Fowler 1972) helped found the Negritude movement, which paralleled the Harlem Renaissance in Francophone Africa and the Caribbean, writing about Haiti in a humanistic vein similar to Hurston's. Another Haitian scholar activist, Jean Price Mars, founded the Society of African Culture and helped found *Presence Africaine*, the scholarly organ of black Francophone intellectuals. It was here in 1955 that Senegalese scholar Cheikh Anta Diop first published portions of what would become, among African and diasporic readers (Anta Diop 1974), the most influential classical archaeological and linguistic analysis of the Africanity of ancient Egypt. Another African-American anthropologist, Katherine Dunham, through the vehicle of dance, studied and performed the common and deviating threads of African diasporic culture and religion in Brazil, Haiti, Cuba, and the United States. African-American anatomist and physical anthropologist W. Montague Cobb focused on issues of evolution, race, racism, and health care in the United States in the middle third of the century, also combining his biology with humanism and politics (Rankin-Hill & Blakey 1995; see also Caroline Bond Day physical anthropologist, under Hooton in Ross et al 1999). Fernando Ortiz conducted both bioarchaeological and ethnographic work on the African influences of Cuba (1929, 1947). Black anthropologist Irene Diggs, having worked with both Ortiz and Du Bois, covered a broad range of U.S. and Latin American subjects (see Bolles 1999). African-American historian William Leo Hansberry had been the first to write a thesis in African studies at Harvard before taking a faculty position at Howard, where in the early 1920s he advocated for African studies and archaeology programs. It was Melville Herskovits, however, who would start the first African studies program at Northwestern University following a brief visiting position at Howard, where he studied "race crossing" (Herskovits 1928). In 1916, historian Carter Woodson, also at Howard University, established the *Journal of Negro History*. The organization for which the *Journal* was principal organ, the Association for the Study of Negro Life and History (today the Association for the Study of African-American Life and History), began "Negro History Week" (today Black History Month) in order to disseminate the history of peoples of African descent. Work by the Fisk- and Harvard-educated historian John Hope Franklin (1947) should also be noted among these pre-1960s contributions to diasporic studies.

This is but a small sample of the prolific contributors of that period, suggestive of the breadth and focus of domestic and international work toward diasporic studies. With the exception of the enigmatic Hurston, all were involved in political activism, and many were involved in the Pan-Africanist movement, which sought to free the continent of colonialism and to unite it and its diasporic peoples. Their scholarly efforts were to preserve and report on African cultural persistence and creativity on the continent and in the Americas, to revise what they saw as Eurocentric distortions of the Africana world, and to foster an understanding of common cultural identity, albeit at times incorporating an essentialized racial identity, not unlike contemporary European romanticists.

White archaeologists and physical anthropologists had initiated no such journals and research organizations by the 1960s, nor did they publish in black journals. But some Euro-American social and cultural anthropologists and historians did use the *Journal of Negro History* and *Phylon* (edited by Du Bois at Atlanta University).

Franz Boas's work on and interest in African cultures gave an important foundation for American scholarship in this area. His empirical and cultural determinist approaches were both welcomed by and in conflict with African-American scholarship, based on how the Boasians did and did not relate to civil rights goals (Willis 1972, Baker 1998). Colonial European anthropology of Africa was abundant but had limited the involvement of American anthropologists until the postcolonial and Cold War era breached the proprietary wall [for an example of this change point in a meeting between Evans Pritchard, Melville Herskovits, and a young Elliot Skinner at Oxford, see Mwaria (1999, p. 280)]. Boas' student Melville Herskovits

(1930, 1941), along with Roger Bastide (1967), was among the first of non–African Americans to take an interest in a "hemisphere-wide synthesis" of black life in the diaspora. In the Boasian vein, their work focused on the persistence of African culture, acculturation, and miscegenation, without devoting serious study to social and economic discrimination (Drake 1993).

Herskovits, like many diasporan scholars, poignantly recognized that much of what had been written about African Americans constituted a "myth of the Negro past." In sum, this mythology conspired to present blacks as "a man without a past" who, being without cultural contributions of his own, had been readily and completely acculturated by Europeans. Herskovits intended to expose and correct the myth by undertaking the study of "Africanisms" among diasporic peoples (1941).

Yet the liberal white (and prominently Jewish) tradition of scholarship represented by Boas and Herskovits was also distinguished by a patronizing and instrumental approach to black scholars who were often already advanced in their Diaspora interests. Although Boas took the conventional approach of using Hurston to gain access to craniometric data from black communities (Willis 1972, Drake 1980), Herskovits deterred black students from studying in Africa because it was too similar to their own culture (Mwaria 1999, p. 280). A counterintuitive rationale from the perspectives of most African Diasporan intellectuals, the anthropological characterization of the etic perspective as objective had served to empower the voices of white anthropologists concerning the non-white world where they worked. Despite these American social constraints, these major Euro-American cultural anthropologists commonly referred to the publications of the African Diasporan intellectuals, and vice versa.

These conflicts of liberal racism might be partly why intellectual cross-fertilization with diasporans at Northwestern and Columbia (see Sanday 1999, p. 248) tended to proceed through literary interaction, whereas collective use of primary data by black and white scholars occurred at Chicago during the same period. It is also important that the sociologists and social anthropologists at Chicago were willing to examine social and economic inequality, in contrast to the cultural focus at Northwestern and Columbia. Under the influences of W. Lloyd Warner and black graduate students such as St. Clair Drake (Bond 1988, Baber 1999), E. Franklin Frazier (1939) (Edwards 1968), and Allison Davis (Browne 1999), Du Boisian sociology was melded to British social anthropology with an eye toward policy correctives for "the race problem." Drake & Clayton (1945) is an excellent example of this synthesis (also see Harrison 1992). Herskovits' elucidation of the "myth of the Negro past" and its alternative (i.e., that the Negro had a cultural history) was meant, however, to debunk the ideological legitimation of social and economic inequity as its contribution to Myrdal's study (1945), a study being coordinated by the Chicagoans.

By the 1960s, some Euro-American cultural anthropologists were beginning to expand their thinking to include both a diasporic scope and a critique of inequality. Norman Whitten and John Szwed organized the first anthropological symposium on the diaspora, with white and black contributors, leading three years later to the publication of *Afro-American Anthropology: Contemporary Perspectives* (Whitten & Szwed 1970). Along with the work of Mintz (1974) (who had a degree from Columbia and who studied with Herskovits) in the Caribbean (1951, 1974) and Marvin Harris and others who undertook the State of Bahia–Columbia University Community Study Project in Brazil (Hutchinson 1957), one began to see studies of the socioeconomic effects of diasporic exploitation conducted by Euro-American anthropologists three generations down the Boasian lineage.

Throughout the early development of research on the African Diaspora, the members of that diaspora who framed that research approached the subject with both interdisciplinary and activist bents, whether missionary, integrationist, Marxist, or Pan-Africanist (Harris 1993, Harrison & Harrison 1999). Drake (1980) describes this African-American intellectual tradition as "vindicationist" and meant to correct the omissions and distortions of the mainstream Eurocentric tradition. The research of some Euro-American anthropologists in the Boasian lineage was useful in those efforts. The interethnic collaboration at Chicago had policy implications. Yet black scholars maintained a front-line stance, as they had since the antislavery movement, in asserting the need to increase this work against the prevailing "denigration" of the black experience that was systematically perpetrated by Western education. Frederick Douglass had elucidated an ideological myth of the Negro past nearly 100 years before Herskovits, and African-American efforts to destroy the myth continued to evolve into intellectual, organizational, and activist dimensions within the future black world.

Those mentioned above are a small and prominent sample of the major sources of in-depth research on people of African descent between the mid–nineteenth century and 1960. Their research, humanistic expression, and political activism attended the global emergence of the African diaspora from slavery, colonialism, and segregation. It deliberately contributed to an understanding of people of African descent and their relation to the world that would empower those transitions and adjustments. In 1965, as an outgrowth of its International Congress of African Historians convened in Tanzania, UNESCO publications in several languages referenced the "African Diaspora" as a recurring theme (Harris 1993).

During the late 1960s and 1970s, scores of black studies programs and departments sprang up at recently desegregated U.S. colleges and universities as black students physically took over campus buildings for that purpose. During the 1980s and 1990s, the emphasis on "black studies" became more resoundingly diasporic. And although there are many Euro-American and other scholars working in African-American studies programs at predominantly white institutions in the United States, they remain the most likely academic home of black faculty, and the sociocultural refuge of black students, to be found in those institutions.

The articulation and disarticulation between these developments and the field of bioarchaeology is a major theme addressed below. This summary of intellectual history provides a reference point against which to contrast the development of an African Diasporic bioarchaeology that, though recently impacted by black and cultural scholarship, began along a segmented trajectory of white ecological and racial scholarship that has structured the study of black people very differently. That structuring has taken place, in fact, virtually without recognition of the longer-developed intellectual traditions described above. Archaeology and physical anthropology have experienced even less interaction with the black intellectual traditions than did American sociocultural anthropology. I turn now to the white (or in their unmarked guise "mainstream") traditions of physical anthropology and archaeology, whose branches will also penetrate African Diasporic research during the 1970s.

PHYSICAL ANTHROPOLOGY AND THE NEGRO

African-American bioarchaeology as it has usually been practiced combines skeletal biology (principally the specialization in paleopathology or the study of health and disease in ancient populations) and historical archaeology (the archaeology of the post-Columbian era in the Americas). Skeletal biology has a longer concern with people of African descent in the Americas than has archaeology. For most of that time, physical anthropology followed a different trajectory from other research. This is mainly because physical anthropology has had little, if any, concern for culture or history. Its principal concern for racial differences meant that African-descent populations, constructed as "Negroes," "Negroids," or biologically "black," were an important group for comparisons with "Caucasoids," "Caucasians," or "whites" as a biological standard of normalcy. This racist nineteenth- and early twentieth-century history of physical anthropology has been extensively critiqued (e.g., Gould 1996, Blakey 1996, Smedley 1993, Armelagos & Goodman 1998). It is now simple to summarize that apart from interspecific differences, physical anthropologists classified human populations racially and created hierarchical rankings of races. Whether these were evolutionary or preevolutionary rankings, European-descent groups (Caucasoids) were placed at the top, Africans (Negroids) at the bottom, and Asians and Native Americans (Mongoloids) usually intermediate. Although racial classifications were at times more diverse, from the time of Linnaeus' eighteenth-century taxonomy to the UNESCO Statement on Race in 1951, this hierarchy was typical of Euro-American and European physical anthropology. It was typical of the thinking and policies of the general white population of which physical anthropologists were part.

The emphasis on race was part of a broader conceptualization of objective science defined by natural historical explanations of variations in natural biological categories (e.g., race). The cognizant point was to develop a science of "man" grounded in the same principles as zoology, biology, anatomy, and medicine, from which fields most physical anthropologists initially derived. But the resulting science was clearly not "objective." Physical anthropology served as a means of ideological production that naturalized and, thus, justified colonialism, racial segregation, eugenics, class, and gender inequity. The United States, which had no African colonies to understand and manage, instead needed simply to maintain the centuries-old subjugation of a black racial caste. American Negroes were considered synonymous with former slaves, who were expected to be thankful for the opportunities Christianity and acculturation had afforded for them to emerge above their assumed absence of prior civilization, to be helpful to white patrons. The dearth of mainstream research and education on Africa and diasporic cultures (along with the conceptual removal of Egypt from Africa) meant that unlike European identity, Negroid identity was left to stand as naked as a chimp. There were no contradictions between "the myth" and physical anthropological study of blacks because the biological category of race dehistoricized and naturalized the identities of those to whom it was applied. Physical anthropology was the primary author of the myth. The containment of vindicationist studies within the Diasporan communities themselves helped maintain the myth as an essential component in Euro-America's construction of white identity.

The Smithsonian Institution's leading physical anthropologist, Aleš Hrdlčika, was assigned the task of reviewing all of the work on "the Negro" in 1927 for the National Research Council Committee on the Negro (Hrdlička 1927). His bibliography included sociological works of Du Bois and Frazier and the historical work of Woodson and other African-American writers among a majority list of white scholarship analyzing what was then termed the Negro problem. Hrdlička viewed the previous work as shoddy, not rigorous, and "tinged with more or less bias for or against the Negro" (p. 207) and proposed that future research should focus on the Negro brain (the organ in which he specialized), which, after all, was the "real problem of the American Negro." He then continued work on measurements of the skulls of 26 living African Americans found at Howard University and fudged his data so that "the full-blood Negro" appeared to be of inferior 'mentality' (Hrdlička 1928; Blakey 1996, pp. 76–77). In fact, since Morton's time, the study of the Negro had been done almost entirely on anatomical collections of the recently deceased or on living populations [for an example showing the deleterious effects of miscegenation in Jamaica, see Davenport & Steggerda (1929)].

Earnest Hooton (Harvard) would follow Hrdlička as America's most influential physical anthropologist, beginning in 1930. The Pecos Canyon study by Hooton (1930) also established what has variously been called the statistical (Armelagos et al 1971), paleoepidemiological (Buikstra & Cook 1980), or demographic (Aufderheide & Rodreguez-Martin 1998, p. 7) approach, which initiated the development of modern paleopathology, in which vein most bioarchaeology is currently conducted. Paleoepidemiology would characterize the core of African-American bioarchaeological studies that emerged during the 1980s, but not before.

There were exceptions to the dominant racial deterministic trend in early physical anthropology. Studies of the new documented anatomical populations (macerated cadavers from the dissecting rooms of medical schools) began en force during the 1930s. As it happened, the largest collection, at [Case] Western Reserve University, was completed by T. Wingate Todd, a liberal Scottish physical anthropologist who had been an officer among Colored troops in Canada (Cobb 1939a). Todd's analysis of the Hamann-Todd collection's crania showed environmental causes of differences in black and white cranial development, from which he deduced an equal potential for achievement in these "races," in a unique presentation he made at a meeting of the National Association for the Advancement of Colored People (Todd 1930).

Todd's liberal environmental analyses were furthered by Cobb (his former student and an African-American physical anthropologist at Howard), who used data from skeletal collections and living populations to show that biology did not determine the athletic acumen of blacks or whites (Cobb 1936). Furthermore, Cobb was one of the first physical anthropologists to use available demographic data, within a synthesized evolutionary and social historical paradigm, to show the high adaptability of African Americans against the adversities of slavery and racial segregation in the United States (Cobb 1939b). Cobb would later put his approach to physical anthropology and social medicine to service in the U.S. Civil Rights movement in the diasporan tradition of activist scholarship (Rankin-Hill & Blakey 1994). But these studies seem to have had little impact on the development of anthropology.

Measurements of the skull meant to show a racial evolutionary basis of social inequality (having evolved from prescientific phrenology) continued as the focus of the physical anthropology of Negroes until World War II. Craniometry would then continue as the focus of descriptive racial taxonomic studies in colonial Africa (Tobias 1953, Oschinsky 1954, Villiers 1968) and in American studies of racial admixture (Pollitzer 1958) and in forensic studies for the identification of crime victims and missing persons.

CONCEPTION OF AFRICAN DIASPORIC BIOARCHAEOLOGY

Physical anthropology stood at the doorstep of modern paleopathology during the 1930s, when African Diasporic bioarchaeology began. African-American scholarship was not involved, nor was a keen interest in the Africana world. Instead, the field would grow from the physical anthropologist's main interest in race, applied to African Diasporic skeletons accidentally discovered by archaeologists who were looking for presumably extinct pre-Columbian Indians.

In 1938, a team of Oxford archaeologists, funded by Northwestern and Columbia Universities, excavated some of the first bioarchaeological sites in the African diaspora (Buxton et al 1938). In 1939, T. Dale Stewart, who had long been Hrdlička's assistant curator at the Smithsonian Institution, responded to this article and to correspondence with E. M. Shilstone, who had made a related find in the British colony of Barbados (Stewart 1939). Stewart's position at the U.S. National Museum made him a likely expert on the racial identification of the curious remains of the one, male, African-looking skull found in an apparently Arawak (Taino) midden in Barbados and the two "Negro" skulls that were found on Water Island, St. Thomas, U.S. Virgin Islands. His analysis was that the skeletal remains were more consistant with a "Negro" than a "Negroid" classification. It was actually the cultural data of dental versus cranial modification that were most convincing of African ancestry. Buxton et al (1938) commented on a similar situation reported by Duerden for a Jamaican site in 1897, in which the craniometric methods seemed unreliable for explaining Africans among the remains of the Arawak. In all cases, the African burials were assumed to be later intrusions, although the stratigraphy was not sufficiently careful to discount contemporaneity of African and Taino burials. The St. Thomas individuals (an adult male and female) were buried in association with red ochre mounds and stone artifacts, and with a pot over the face of one of the "Negro" individuals. Nor is it at all clear from these publications why the site is assumed to be pre-Columbian (the authors actually refer to pre-1700) simply because there were Taino artifacts; Tainos were actually present in the Caribbean in early colonial and genocidal times. The remains were curated at the University Museum at Oxford, but the temporal relationships may never be resolved. There would not be another diasporic study until 35 years later and under similarly accidental circumstances.

A notable comparison is found in the work by Ortiz (1927), and in later work by Rivero de la Calle (1973), on several cases of dental filing or modification (*mutilación*) in Cuban skeletal remains. Although the general assessment of the skeleton is limited, the historical, ethnographic, and folkloric context is extensively revealed with the analysis of the significance of this practice. The practice of *mutilación* was associated with Maroons (*cimarrones*) and religious enclaves. These are also the only examples of dental modification evaluated as a possible local practice, rather than as having occurred among Africans brought to the Americas subsequent to the modification of their teeth. Prior to the 1970s, no North American skeletal researchers considered the sociocultural context of African diasporic skeletons.

In 1974, two skeletons were found at site 2-AVI-1-ENS-1 at Hull Bay, St. Thomas, which Smithsonian physical and forensic anthropologists assessed to be "Negroid" (Ubelaker & Angel 1976). Skeleton B was associated with coffin nails and therefore reasonably of the colonial period. But skeleton A was definitely associated with an indigenous pottery fragment (Elenoid period, dated 800–1200) and no colonial artifacts. Radiocarbon dating only resolved that the skeletons were not recent, which was important for the forensic concerns of the investigation. In this example of another accidental bioarchaeological encounter with an African skeleton, the racing, age, sex, and stature methodology continues to be important for forensic identification, yet the further assessment of pathology (skeleton A showed a slight infection, whereas skeleton B evinced extensive infection and partly healed fractures) marks a more modern approach than found in the earlier St. Thomas study 36 years prior to it. None of the Smithsonian forensic examinations attempts to explore the population, history, or social condition of Afro-Caribbean people.

In 1976, another Smithsonian publication by Angel examined secular changes between colonial and modern American skeletons. The study compared 82 archeological skeletons (1675–1879) with 182 modern forensic and donated skeletons. Angel anticipated increased body size in both European-American and African-American populations owing to increased genetic heterosis and "improvements in disease-control, diet, and living conditions" (p. 727). It is a traditional study in its reliance on physical anthropological and anatomical literature, early military data on stature, and evolutionary interpretations. The study showed remarkably little skeletal change, albeit greater in the black population than in whites. Life expectancy does increase, as does a pelvic indicator of nutritional adequacy, whereas poorer dental health and the increased frequency of traumatic fractures were seen to reflect modern stresses. The increased interest in the biological effects of socioeconomic environment during the 1970s is certainly suggested by the Angel paper, despite his continuing reliance on the use of evolutionary principles. With Angel, the Smithsonian had taken a significant step forward from an earlier preoccupation with the racial evolution of "Old American" white (Hrdlička 1925) or "full-blood Negro" (Hrdlička 1927) crania in U.S. history. Still, there was scant use of social history and culture.

In 1977, the skeletons of two enslaved African-American men (burial 3 was 30–40 years of age and burial 5 was 40–45 years of age) of circa 1800 were reported from a 3000-year-old burial mound on St. Catherines Island of the Sea Islands off the Georgia coast. These skeletons, too, were found accidentally during a long-term study of the island's native archaeology by the American Museum of Natural History. The analysis (Thomas et al 1977) was, however, less forensic and more pertinent to historical interpretation than were the Smithsonian studies. Racial identification was made, as in the other studies, along with a modern paleopathological assessment. One man (burial 3) had a recently fractured leg that had become infected, which probably led to his death. The other "was probably shot to death by a military-type weapon" (p. 417). Both men showed evidence of arduous labor by virtue of their robustness. David Hurst Thomas, an archaeologist, and his associates also encountered the fancy burial of the slaveholder's son in a separate location, showing him to be physically young, gracile, and lacking in evidence of hard work (Thomas et al 1977). His evidence of childhood illness and poor dental health were similar to the African-American skeletons. These comparisons were used to examine the relative quality of life and condition of the two plantation groups, bringing to bear both written and oral historical sources. The researchers had no answer for why burials 3 and 5 had been made in a much older Native American burial mound.

The study involved an inadequate number of burials for statistical generalizations and only a rudimentary historical and cultural analysis. But this study does engage such an analysis and is advanced over the previous accidental studies by suggesting new motivations in addition to its use of the new paleopathology. These authors were examining people, not a race, and probing the conditions of slavery. They reinterred the remains, rather than curate them, and made recommendations about historic burial sites that regard both public sensibilities and scientific concerns for improved rigor and cultural interpretation:

We do not, of course, advocate wholesale archaeological investigation of historic graveyards. Prevalent social and religious customs are to be respected in matters of this sort. But we do urge that as graveyards are required to be moved to make way for progress, archaeological mitigation should include adequate research designs to raise some of the germane questions regarding past human behavior and belief systems . . . (Thomas et al 1977, p. 418).

These meager examples appear to be the only African diasporic bioarchaeological studies published prior to 1978, when sample sizes and geographical ranges would increase, historical and cultural interpretation would become more sophisticated, and "customs . . . respected in matters of this sort" would begin to overwhelm bioarchaeology. What would be responsible for these dramatic changes?

GROWTH FACTORS

The emergence of an active research interest in African-American sites required that major changes take place, which they did under the National Historic Preservation Act of 1966. This Act required the funding of archaeological work to mitigate the effects of all federal construction projects, including buildings and highways, in order to preserve cultural heritage. These Cultural Resources Management (CRM) projects caused the growth of private archaeological consulting firms, which would quickly become the main source of archaeological employment in the United States. CRM also meant that contract funding was available for site excavation and descriptive reporting for sites that were encountered accidentally. Road and building projects produced a random sample of U.S. sites and therefore regularly encountered African-American cemeteries. If one simply wanted to keep the revenue of a CRM firm going, one would take the opportunity to acquire a contract for the excavation of the African-American sites that were popping up everywhere. Here was a target of opportunity, but it was also an opportunity for the launching of African-American and historical archaeology, which might begin to reveal the "partly mythical basis" of U.S. national identity (Schuyler 1976).

The first work on a plantation site, the Kingsley Plantation in Florida, was excavated by Fairbanks in 1967. Against the grain of the "new archaeology," which emphasized natural ecological determinants, Fairbanks took a more historical approach. According to Ferguson (1992, p. xxxviii), "Fairbanks was not bowing to professional pressure or pleas for a new and more objective archaeology; he was addressing black demands for more attentiveness to black history, and without that political pressure African-American archaeology would have developed much more slowly, if at all." I agree with Ferguson that this new specialty resulted from a combination of "the structure of the law, together with the pressure of black political and social protest." But this did not mean that the archaeological community respected blacks' intelligence.

Although sustained black protest had created both an interest in and market for black history, archaeologists (and bioarchaeologists) showed little or no interest in the huge corpus of scholarship on this subject that African Americans themselves had generated (less even than white sociocultural anthropologists had shown during the days of legal segregation!). Archaeologists did not take courses in the African-American studies departments that were multiplying during the period of the 1970s–1990s, when the archaeological shift took place. These departments remained marginal to the university education of whites. Nor did most archaeologists excavating black sites collaborate with African Americanists, most of whom were black, who had the most extensive knowledge of African Diasporic history and culture. Nor did archaeologists participate in the Association for African American Life and History, or any other scholarly associations African Americans had long established for the purposes that archaeology was just beginning to serve.

This lack of regard for the intellectual fundamentals of the subject to which archaeologists were now shifting would continue to produce important limiting effects on African-American archaeology and African-American studies. Notably, plantation archaeologist Theresa Singleton (Smithsonian and Syracuse University) and African-American studies specialist Ronald Bailey (Northeastern University) organized a week-long meeting at the University of Mississippi in 1989, which had as a goal to bring practitioners of both fields together in dialogue. It is not sociologically surprising that the only black PhD archaeologist working on plantation sites, Singleton, would be the one to notice that something was wrong and try to bring African-American studies and archaeology together to talk.

In an extensive review, Singleton & Bograd (1995) found that African-American archaeology had expanded since the 1960s to include greater regional and industrial diversity of southern sites, to address issues of race and ethnicity, acculturation, inequities, and resistance (p. 23). But their exhaustive survey also revealed that most of the literature "is largely descriptive, it relies too heavily upon flawed analytical techniques or very narrow perceptions of ethnicity, and it has been slow to incorporate African-American perspectives in developing this research" (p. 30). "That race predominates in discussions of plantation life or defines the presentation of blacks' lives following emancipation may in part reflect white archaeologists' and white America's preoccupation with race. There is a tendency to presume that race, or ethnicity, is significant, which is not to say that race is not important. Rather it is to assert that white preoccupations are not always the same as black preoccupations" (p. 31). The reviewers suggest that the superior direction being achieved by some researchers is to consider ethnicity as a "process" that is both foisted on and creatively utilized by African Americans, rather than as the widespread "archaeology of 'the other,'" consisting of static typologies that identify a group with objects. In most cases, the absence of type objects comes to constitute evidence of acculturation and assimilation when other plausible interpretations exist (see Schuyler 1980). I suspect that this typological approach is tethered to both the American "myth of the Negro past" and Herskovits' search for Africanisms. According to Singleton & Bograd (1995), "[t]he tenor of many ethnicity studies is problematic. One problem is that they tend to take a perspective from the outside, how archaeologists and others define ethnics or cultural groups, rather than how ethnics define themselves" (pp. 23–24). Similar issues were raised for African archaeology (Andah 1995). The ability to define another people has been a major means and measure of social control, with or without archaeology. It is against such disempowerment that diasporan scholars had been writing.

The Euro-American archaeologists and bioarchaeologists of the 1970s and 1980s were influenced by the new historiography of plantation life that had also been fostered by the social changes of the 1960s. The Black Consciousness and Black Studies movements (Drake 1993) had succeeded steadily in producing a market for history books and lectures, while the Civil Rights movement had created an openness to interest in blacks and American racism. The historical works of Jordan (1968) and Genovese (1972) followed the peculiarly early work of the left-leaning Aptheker (1943) as examples of an emerging Euro-American interest in African-American historiography that explained the origins of American racism and the condition of blacks. A historical and demographic study by Gutman (1976) opposed the influential report by Senator Daniel Moynihan (1965). Moynihan had attributed urban black poverty to the legacy of a dysfunctional slave family and African matriarchy, which Gutman showed to have little historical basis. But it was Fogel & Engerman's economics treatise, *Time on the Cross* (1974), that stirred a major debate about whether or not working class whites were as oppressed as enslaved blacks, who they claimed were adequately nourished. Like Moynihan, Fogel & Engerman (1974) further raised the specter of apology when blacks were found to have been worse off in many respects after the Reconstruction than during slavery. The critiques of this work by Gutman (1975) and David et al (1976) were devastating to it. This critical historiography drew on the prior work of black scholars. Add to these the work by Curtin (1969), which estimated the death toll of the "middle passage" in the millions (millions more than most whites wanted to acknowledge and millions fewer than estimated by some black scholars) as major historical grist for the mill of scholarly and politicized debate.

Physical anthropologists began to pick up on the data about the demography, nutrition, and health of enslaved African Americans that were being generated to test these various questions regarding the quality of life among the enslaved. Curtin's work and the body of work by Steckel on problems of nutrition, disease, and mortality on plantations (1986) followed work by Stamp (1956) in showing the dire demographic and health consequences of American slavery. Higman's extensive Trinidadian data on the demography of the slave trade even found its way to the *American Journal of Physical Anthropology* (1979). Apologetic theories by Kiple & King (1981) and Savitt (1978) attributing slavery and racism to black genetic immunities to disease also resonated with the evolutionary bent of physical anthropologists. The biological data generated by these biohistorical debates interested physical anthropologists, who were poised to enter the discussion with the bones and teeth of the enslaved people themselves. Yet Rankin-Hill (1997) seems correct in saying that "little has been accomplished [by the historians and economists] in expanding the conceptual limits of [biohistory]. In fact, much of the emphasis has been on the intricacies of quantification and data manipulation, and not on different approaches to interpreting and/or examining the data generated" (p. 12). The essential research question behind all these studies was, did whites do anything particularly bad toward blacks during slavery that caused their current condition?

This I believe is the stage on which the nascent bioarchaeology of the 1980s was set. Political events spurred a broader societal interest in blacks. A marketplace and government-funding venues opened for research and publications in African-American archaeology in particular and historical archaeology in general. And a biohistorical literature came to prominence that spoke to biological anthropologists, who had seized on epidemiological and demographic approaches.

Racial biological studies had lost vitality for research after the Nazi era had ended, apart from forensics at least. Physical anthropologists were looking for new ways of applying their methods to societal issues (Blakey 1996, Armelagos & Goodman 1998). Biocultural approaches that sought to use biological stress indicators as evidence of social inequality and change began to emerge during the 1970s (see Goodman & Leatherman 1998, Blakey 1998b). The data of the biohistorians, if applied to bioarchaeological contexts, were ideal for biocultural studies. The students of paleopathologist George Armelagos and others at the University of Massachusetts in the forefront of biocultural anthropology had a particular impact on the evolving shape of African-American bioarchaeology.

Finally, the hurricane-like sweep of successful efforts by Native Americans in the 1980s to control the disposition of their skeletal remains and sacred objects culminated in NAGPRA legislation in 1990 (Thomas 2000). The writing was on the wall. American physical anthropologists were losing access to a major source of professional reproduction: Native American bioarchaeological research. The field of African-American bioarchaeology was an open niche.

THE BIRTH OF AFRICAN-AMERICAN BIOARCHAEOLOGY

In 1985 there was a sufficient amount of African-American research among physical anthropologists for Ted Rathbun (University of South Carolina) and Jerome Rose (University of Arkansas) to organize the first symposium on "Afro-American Biohistory: The Physical Evidence" at the Annual Meeting of the American Association of Physical Anthropologists. Reference to blacks at these meetings in such ethnic and historical, rather than racial, terms was novel itself. The symposium was published as a special issue of the *American Journal of Physical Anthropology*, in 1987, with one paper (Blakey 1988) routed to a later issue of the journal. Rose coauthored the histological study of the Cedar Grove Cemetery site (Rose 1985, Martin et al 1987) with Debra Martin and Ann Magennis. This may have been the first African-American cemetery covered by the National Historic Preservation Act, which had initially applied only to the site's Indian component. This post-Reconstruction black Arkansas population was shown by all indications to have been highly stressed (Rose 1985). The work regime for these freed and free men and women "had not changed since slavery" and the "general quality of life for southwest Arkansas Blacks had deteriorated significantly since emancipation due to the fall of cotton prices and legalized discrimination" (p. v). This was a direct response to Fogel & Engerman (1974). The recent study of the Freedman's Cemetery of Dallas, Texas examines Reconstruction and post-Reconstruction bioarchaeology in greater historical depth (Peter et al 2000).

Also included in the 1985 symposium were bioarchaeological studies of a South Carolina plantation near Charleston showing evidence of malnutrition and disease in a sample of 27 individuals who died between 1840 and 1870 (Rathbun 1987). Dental and skeletal growth disruption was found to be highest for male children, 80% of whom had evidence of anemia and infection. Most men and women had evinced bone reactions to infection, with relatively high exposure to lead and strontium concentrations, indicative of a diet high in plant foods. No clear evidence of syphilis was found (Rathbun 1987). The study contains a useful review of the biohistorical and archaeological literature, again showing the close connection to debates in history and archaeology at that time (also see Rathbun and Scurry 1991). The site was being removed because of the development of private land, where the law did not require mitigation. The research team was able to convince the landowner to allow research prior to reburial.

The demography and pathology of individuals from the eighteenth- and early nineteenth-century St. Peter Street cemetery in New Orleans give evidence of arduous labor among younger males, and comparatively less such evidence among many females and older adults interpreted as house servants (Owsley et al 1987). Census data is given on variation in mortality by occupation in eighteenth-century New Orleans. The further racial analysis of this study, attributing lower life spans to "racial admixture," along with the dearth of social and historical analysis, shows continuity with older racial traditions preserved by the forensic influences of the University of Tennessee on this study.

A subsequent study by Owsley and colleagues (1990) compares the 149 black and white skeletons from Cypress Grove Cemetery (1849–1929) of Charity Hospital of New Orleans with other sites. This site, too, resulted from the legally required mitigation of a federal highway project. Similarities were found with the St. Peter Street cemetery as well as with the infection rates of a pauper's cemetery used by whites in New York state. The extensive evidence of cut bone showed that blacks and whites who died at Charity often were dissected prior to burial. As is consistent with the forensic approach often used in CRM bioarchaeology, the extensive data are descriptive and not integrated with community history. The accompanying volume prepared by archaeologists provides historical description (Beavers et al 1993), which deals mainly with the city health and medical context of the Hospital.

Several biohistorical studies in an anthropological vein were also presented at the Afro-American Biohistory Symposium. Hutchinson (1987), an anthropological geneticist using Harris County, Texas, slave schedules of 1850 and 1860 (and a credible range of biohistorical literature), explains its marked population growth as a function of importation despite little natural increase. She shows that enslaved persons who were recorded as "black" tended to be older (higher life expectancy on small farms than on large farms), while those termed mulattoes were on average older than blacks on large plantations, possibly due to mulatto house servitude on large plantations where black field hands were exposed to the worst conditions. Alternatively, hypothesized immunities to yellow fever (a la Kiple & King 1981) might have contributed to differences in life expectancy between blacks and mulattoes (Hutchinson 1987).

Also combining the traditional evolutionary and biodeterministic tendencies of the field with a new bioculturalism is the work of Wienker (1987) on an early twentieth-century logging company town in Arizona. Pointing to the health care inadequacies for blacks in a town deeply segregated, the study takes great interest in the possibility that dark pigmentation might have deleterious effects in the temperate Arizona highlands.

A clearer break toward a nonbiodeterministic view, as seen in Rose (1985), Martin et al (1987), and Rathbun (1987), is also found in the symposium paper by Blakey (1988). This paper traces ethnogenesis and demographic change in an Afro–Native American ethnic group (Nanticoke-Moors) in rural Delaware from the colonial period until 1950. The study uses a political economic analysis of 406 cemetery headstones, archival data, and oral history. It proposes that community responses to racial policies and industrialization brought about a single community's segmentation into different socially constructed races. Although genetically similar, Nanticoke-Moors experienced different educational and economic options, depending on their "racial" affiliations. Among the results were the increased isolation required for the maintenance of Indian identity, with increasingly higher life expectancy among the industrializing African American–identified kin than among Indian-identified kin who maintained a farming economy. Notably, this study took little account of the biohistorical debates [though it utilizes Eblen (1979)] and relates instead to historical and ethnographic literature on African-American/Native American relations in the eastern seaboard region.

During the mid-1980s, a major collaboration between the Smithsonian Institution and John Milner Associates (a contract archaeology concern) also contributed to the Afro-American Biohistory Symposium. The First African Baptist Church (FABC) cemetery in downtown Philadelphia had been used mostly by free African Americans between 1823 and 1841. In the path of subway expansion, archaeological mitigation was required for the site. John Milner Associates excavated 140 skeletons, a far larger African-American archaeological population than from any previous African-American site. The FABC was also unique as a northern black bioarchaeological site, and rare as an urban one (the St. Peter Street cemetery in New Orleans was the other urban exception). The fact that it was in the hands of J. Lawrence Angel, a preeminent physical anthropologist at the Smithsonian, raised the status of African-American bioarchaeology, as surely as did the Rathbun-Rose symposium itself. Angel, who had first established his reputation on the paleopathology of ancient Greece, had turned to the study of secular change in the European and African-American skeleton from the colonial period to the present (Angel 1976). Along with his assistant, Jennifer Kelley, and the principal archaeologist, Michael Parrington, and with the collaboration of Lesley Rankin-Hill and Michael Blakey (who together coordinated and completed the project following Angel's death), Angel availed the collection to a loose team of researchers while conducting core research himself.

The population appeared to be stressed by inadequate nutrition, arduous labor, pregnancy and childbearing, unsanitary conditions, limited exposure to the sun, and extensive exposure to infectious diseases. Nutritional and growth indicators showed conditions that were little better than for enslaved blacks of the Catoctin Iron Works of Maryland, 1790–1820, although evidence of arthritis and violence-related fractures was rarer at the Philadelphia site (Angel et al 1987). The hunt for genetic traits persisted, as per the tradition of physical anthropology, so that the observation of 30% of individuals with *os acromiale* (nonunion of part of the shoulder joint) was interpreted as a familial trait, when it might have been evaluated as the result of persistent mechanical, labor-induced stress during adolescent development (Rankin-Hill 1997, p. 152).

The comparative analysis of Angel & Kelley (1987) was further developed in a second symposium paper (Kelley & Angel 1987), for which they had assembled 120 colonial African and African-American skeletons from 25 sites in Maryland (Catoctin), Virginia, and the Carolinas, as well as forensic cases from the Smithsonian's collections. As in the other studies, nutritional stresses were evident in the skeleton, including anemia (which these authors overly attribute to sicklemia). Adolescents and many adults (male and female) showed exaggerated development of lifting muscles (deltoid and pectoral crests of the humeri) and early degeneration of the vertebral column and shoulder. Evidence of trauma to the skull as well as "parry" fractures of the lower arm suggest an unusually high incidence of accidents and violence at Catoctin Furnace, particularly. The use of historical references is rudimentary.

The First African Baptist Church skeletons were reburied in Eden Cemetery, Philadelphia, by the modern congregation in 1987. At a time when Native Americans were calling for reburial of 18,000 remains at the Smithsonian, the Institution's initial interest in announcing the FABC ceremony was administratively quashed. The impressions of African Americans regarding this research were mixed. Four years later, the New York community would explode over a similar project.

John Milner Associates continued to develop the preliminary work of Parrington and elaborations of the foundation study done with Angel (Parrington & Roberts 1984, 1990). Blakey and associates of Howard's Cobb Laboratory published articles on childhood malnutrition and disease based upon analyses of dental developmental disruption (enamel hypoplasia) (Blakey et al 1992, 1994, 1997). The dental defects in the FABC population were at frequencies similar to those found in the Maryland and Virginia populations Angel had compared, pointing to a degree of childhood malnutrition and disease in the recently free north similar to that in the plantation south (Blakey et al 1994). Hypoplasia frequencies were between 70% and 100%, which were among the highest in any human population studied by anthropologists.

Rankin-Hill (1997) published the first book that synthesized a breadth of African-American bioarchaeological and biohistorical data for the interpretation of the FABC. Rankin-Hill's extensive treatment of modern paleopathological and demographic methods and the use of general and site-specific historical sources is extensive. She presents the most developed theoretical formulation for African-American bioarchaeology, which includes the political and economic factors interacting with the physiology and health of early African Americans. Too comprehensive to be adequately summarized here, she examines the multiple stressors, cultural buffers, and skeletal effects of physiological stress in the lives of Philadelphia laborers and domestic workers.

The influence of the University of Massachusetts is tangible, as the graduate institution of Rose, Martin, Magennis, Rankin-Hill, and Blakey. It can be distinguished from the other centers of the development of this specialty (along with South Carolina) by its unabashed advocacy and development of biocultural theory [fully developed by Goodman & Leatherman (1998) and Rankin-Hill (1997)]. Early biocultural models were developed from the synthesis of the human adaptability interests of R. Brooke Thomas, the biocultural paleopathology of George Armelagos, and the historical demography of Alan Swedlund during the late 1970s and 1980s at Massachusetts. These models were honed and evolved by their students to incorporate political and economic factors that would expose the biological effects of oppression. The influences of left-leaning faculty in archaeology, cultural anthropology, and the Departments of Economics and African-American Studies influenced the physical anthropologists, all of whom were exchanging information at a time when walls were being erected between subdisciplines at many other anthropology departments.

The involvement of African Americans was also unusual at the University of Massachusetts, which included one faculty member (Johnnetta Cole), a third of the black physical anthropology students in United States (Rankin-Hill & Blakey), and the only black paleopathologists during this crucial period. African-American traditions of critical, activist, and humanistic scholarship were introduced into the departmental discourse. The progressive motivations of the 1960s and early 1970s were fresh in mind at Massachusetts, as was the abysmal record of physical anthropology regarding race. Research on the political history of physical anthropology was exceptionally active there, and the emphasis was on the development of new theory.

The Smithsonian Institution and the University of Tennessee were steeped in the racial tradition, commonly reinforced by their emphasis on forensic work for the Federal Bureau of Investigation, police departments, and the court system. In fact, the prominent forensic anthropologist at Tennessee, William Bass, trained most of the leading skeletal biologists at the Smithsonian (excepting Stewart and Angel, who were of an earlier generation but nonetheless forensic in orientation). The degree-granting institution, Tennessee, had no black students of physical anthropology. A technical emphasis on human identification grew in isolation from social, cultural, and political theory there.

The dichotomy of biocultural vs forensic approaches of paleopathology is well appreciated among practitioners today. The distinct marks made by each trajectory on African-American bioarchaeology should become more evident. The clashes between biocultural and forensic approaches that occurred during the 1990s (Goodman & Armelagos 1998), highlighted by the African Burial Ground phenomenon in New York City, are understandable from this vantage (see Epperson 1999, La Roche & Blakey 1997).

Some very interesting diasporic bioarchaeology was also conducted by researchers outside the United States by the end of the 1980s. The most sophisticated (more so than most U.S. studies) is the work of Mohamad Khudabux (1989, 1991), sponsored by the Universities of Surinam, Kuwait, and Leiden. These studies refer extensively to much of the recent U.S. skeletal literature discussed above, and to Higman's (1979) archival data on statures of different African ethnic groups enslaved in the Caribbean. The study of the 38 African skeletal remains (57 burials) of the Waterloo Plantation (1793–1861) in costal Surinam is striking for its combination of modern paleopathological methods (from the Workshop of European Anthropologists), use of historical documents, and political economic analysis. The overarching question of the study is whether the skeletal data would confirm the eighteenth- and nineteenth-century chronicles pointing to poorer health and quality of life among the enslaved Africans of the Caribbean than among those of the United States. The data generally do so confirm, but the detailed analysis is all the more interesting.

The higher life expectancy than at sugar plantations was attributed to the less extreme arduousness of cotton work. The study makes statural comparisons with Caribbean and North American sites, with a consideration of the influences of both genetics and diet. Uniquely, the Surinam study describes variation in African cultural origins during the course of the trade, including Ewe-, Fon-, Yoruba-, and Akan-speaking societies, and thus gives a cultural texture to bioarchaeology that racial assessment otherwise obscures.

This study's evidence demonstrates the skeletal effects of heavy work, poor housing, and poor nutrition, as does the contemporary research on North America. A definite pattern for Surinam, which the authors effectively generalize to much of the Caribbean during the active trade, is the small proportion of women on Surinam plantations. At Waterloo, there were approximately twice the number of skeletons of enslaved men as of enslaved women, and historical documents showed a less extreme but consistently low sex ratio for Surinam as a whole. They show the clearest possible evidence of syphilis in 27% of the population (with vault stellate lesions). Skeletal manifestations at this level point to a majority (possibly all) of the population being infected by treponema, most of which appears to be syphilis.

What stands above most U.S. observations of this colonial disease in blacks is the incorporation of a dynamic historical context. Documentation shows that syphilis was introduced to Africans by the frequent rape and "abuse of women" on slaving ships, and the widespread concubinage of female house servants, which spread contagion. Since the sex ratio was so low, as was a woman's control of her own body, it is clearly implied that European and African males would have shared women. Khudabux and his associates (1989, 1991) show that when the transatlantic trade was outlawed and Surinam needed to foster fertility among the Africans enslaved there, the ravages of syphilis had become so great that it would be a long time before its population could grow, which ironically hindered Surinam's economic development.

U.S. anthropologists were also examining Caribbean bioarchaeological data during the late 1980s and 1990s. The historical archaeological report of Handler & Lange (1978) spurred many subsequent skeletal studies of Newton Plantation in Barbados. Since the archaeological excavation of the skeletons had been more convenient than systematic, skulls comprised the bulk of the collection and dental studies were emphasized. These studies revealed high frequencies of enamel hypoplasia, indicating high nutritional and disease stresses in early childhood (Corruccini et al 1985). Their findings included three individuals with Moon's molars and Hutchinson's incisors, which they extrapolated to a 10% syphilis rate for the living plantation population (Jacobi et al 1992). Studies of trace elements showed very high lead contents, which suggested a high intake of rum distilled in leaded pipes (Corruccini et al 1987b; also see Aufderheide et al 1985 on lead in African American skeletal populations). They also show dental modification ("tooth mutilation"), high frequencies of tooth root hypercementosis associated with chronic malnutrition and periodic, seasonal rehabilitation (Corruccini et al 1987a), and high childhood mortality (Jacobi et al 1992, Corruccini et al 1982).

Undertaken by Handler, a cultural and historical anthropologist, one finds a stronger historical bent in these studies. Yet the work of the physical anthropologists discussed above is modestly integrated with the more cultural and historical work reported in specialized articles. Site reports can overcome this segmentation. An example of a better integrated, small study is found in Armstrong & Fleischman (1993), who evaluated four African skeletons from the Seville Plantation, Jamaica, combining paleopathology, history, and archaeological analysis. The elegant simplicity of these house burials (showing cultural continuity between the Asante, plantation laborers, and Maroons) and their symbolic goods accentuates their evocative individual biological characterizations, but the sample is inadequate for populational analysis.

A good example of the forensic approach is also shown in the Caribbean. The Harney Site Slave Cemetery, on private land in Montserrat, was being destroyed by swimming pool construction when archaeologist David Watters obtained the owner's cooperation in salvaging some of the skeletal remains. The site was so much disturbed that artifacts could not be established as grave goods, although a few pottery sherds were found, including imported and "Afro-Montserratian" unglazed wares. As at Newton Plantation, graves were in west-east/head-foot orientation (Watters & Peterson 1991). The remains of 17 "black slaves" found during construction (only 10 of which were in situ burials) were sent to the University of Tennessee for study (Mann et al 1987). Degenerative joint disease was moderate and related mainly to aging. The authors point to a "harsh lifestyle" with periodic severe malnutrition and common illnesses, leading to early death (see also Jones et al 1990 on the Galways Plantation burials in Montserrat).

The lack of local historical context is striking. West Indies shipping data from one historical source is mentioned along with two comparisons with the Newton Plantation skeletal study. The remaining literature is solely forensic or skeletal biological. There is no discussion of the conditions of life on the Bransby Plantation (or of Montserrat as a whole), where the interred had previously lived and worked. The repeated references to their study of the "Negroid traits" of the "black slaves" (Mann et al 1987; see also Watters & Peterson 1991) showed an irritating continuity with the Smithsonian-Tennessee studies in which "racial" identification substituted for the construction of a human cultural and historical identity.

THE NEW YORK AFRICAN BURIAL GROUND PHENOMENON

By the 1990s, two tendencies of African diasporic bioarchaeology had become well-defined. The biocultural approach combines cultural and social historical information with the demography and epidemiology of archaeological populations to verify, augment, or critique the socioeconomic conditions and processes experienced by past human communities. In its most derived form, political economic theory structures the interpretation of data that are also critically and publicly evaluated. The forensic approach uses the descriptive variables favored by police departments for individual identifications (race, sex, age, and stature) along with pathology assessments in order to describe the biological condition of persons buried in archaeological sites. Although the majority of the technical observations, measurements, and assessments of the skeleton are the same for both approaches, they differ in the extent to which forensics evaluates biology descriptively and racially, without relying on (or constructing) social, cultural, and historical information that is required of biocultural approaches. The result of forensic work is the construction of an acultural and ahistorical group of individuals by attending to a positivistic scientism that views the discounting of culture as equaling objectivity (see Armelagos & Goodman 1998, Blakey 1998b). The result of biocultural work is a biological reflection of the social history of a community of people articulated with broad political-economic forces (see Goodman & Leatherman 1998). Given that we are dealing with only the past few centuries of history, the choice of either approach changes our current identities and understanding of the events that shape us today.

The rediscovery and excavation of the African Burial Ground in New York City between 1991 and 1992 during federal building construction brought the differences between these approaches emphatically to a head. A biocultural and African Diasporic research program took over the analysis of the skeletal remains excavated by forensic anthropologists and contract archaeologists (Cook 1992), whose knowledge of the African Diaspora was meager. The site, dating between the late 1600s and 1794, from which 408 skeletons were removed, would later be recognized as the earliest and largest American colonial population of any kind available for study. The cemetery became a source of deep public interest and concern, especially among African Americans, who protested and held massive prayer vigils at the site during excavation. The efforts mainly of the African-American "descendant community" successfully nominated the site a National Historic Landmark and brought its disposition under their influence with the help of mainly African-American legislators. The U.S. General Services Administration (GSA) responsible for the site persisted unsuccessfully to oppose African-American control, extensive biocultural research, and the law (Harrington 1993, La Roche & Blakey 1997). There had not been such public outcry about an African-American cemetery's desecration since the "doctor's riots" at the New York African Burial Ground and its adjacent pauper's field in 1788. And never before had the African-American public taken such an interest in their bioarchaeology.

The forensic anthropologists' emphasis on racial traits, their obvious ignorance of the study population's culture and history, and their cooperation with the federal governments' efforts to fend off African Americans' involvement were responded to with deepening repugnance by many of the black people who witnessed the excavation. Researchers at the W. Montague Cobb Biological Anthropology Laboratory at Howard, along with collaborators from eight other universities and contract firms, would take over all postexcavation research with the backing of the descendant community. The fact that the research was conducted within a diasporan university and with an African-American clientage brought the tradition of African Diasoporan scholarship squarely into the core of the research program. The availability of diaspora expertise in various departments within Howard University (especially the diaspora program in the History Department), along with the imbalance of the University's research vs curricular resources in anthropology, encouraged the use of many disciplines to reveal the diverse human dimensions of the research problem. These characteristics were compatible with the biocultural approach. The project's director had been working with indigenous people's organizations, the World Archaeological Congress, and the American Anthropological Association for several years on the ethics and epistemology of repatriation and public engagement.

Combining these influences, the African Burial Ground Project formed as a biocultural, diasporic, interdisciplinary project that utilized critical theory and activist scholarship/public engagement. The research design called for the full range of the latest methods in skeletal recordation [using the manuscript by Haas (1994), then in preparation], molecular genetics, and chemical isotope studies. Specialists from Africa, the Caribbean, and North America were involved among the 25 PhD researchers in order to capture the effects of those areas in which the dead Africans of the Burial Ground had spent portions of their lives, just as the diverse disciplines (from art history to chemistry) would capture and reveal human complexity in the recounted lives of those buried. The public would review and have input into the research design (Howard University and John Milner Associates 1993), and a federal advisory (steering) committee consisting mainly of African-American activists and cultural workers would ultimately approve it. The principle research questions concerned the population's origins, transformation, quality of life, and resistance to slavery. An Office of Public Education and Interpretation would be directed by an urban anthropologist, Sherrill Wilson, which provided a continuous exchange of information, with more than 100,000 lay people and educators. A monument, interpretive center, and reburial ceremony have been funded and are planned for this unique, iconesque cemetery and archaeological site.

The African Burial Ground Project's initial findings have been striking. The historically and culturally informed craniometric data (27 individuals) and mitochondrial DNA (40 individuals) identified possible Asante, Benin, Tuareg, Ibo, Yoruba, and Senegambians. Central African states whose members were frequently captured and taken to the Americas (Jackson 1997) are missing from current DNA comparative databases because few geneticists had been interested in the origins of the African diaspora (Kittles et al 1999, Jackson et al 2000; M.E. Mack & M.L. Blakey, manuscript in preparation). The Project is proceeding in cooperation with African embassies to fill in missing comparative data that should allow identification of many West Central African backgrounds as well (Jackson et al 2000). Historians have examined the dynamic history of the slave trade in Africa and the Caribbean that routed these people to New York (Medford et al 2000). Archaeologists and historians have examined diverse burial practices of these specific, named societies in Africa and among their colonial American descendants. The archaeological record revealed a modest number of symbolic African artifacts, the most striking of which may be Akan (Ansa 1995, Perry et al 1999, Holl 2000). Craniometric analysis of specific populations rather than race also points to the Akan-speaking states (Shujaa & Keita 2000). These artifacts represent origins and resistance to the dehumanization and ethnocide carried out by the colonial English and Dutch as they wrestled for social control by attempting to destroy the culture of the enslaved.

Historians have examined the working, dietary, legal, and other conditions to which individuals in the cemetery might have been exposed in every region where these Africans had spent a part of their lives. Uniquely, their report (Medford et al 2000 and in preparation) is a study of the people connected to many places, not a study only of the site or even of New York slavery. Studies of chemical isotopes are being experimented with as sourcing data for tracking the geographical movements of individuals at different points during their lives, informed by geologists, geneticists, archaeologists, and historians (Goodman et al 2000).

An example of results in reports currently in preparation bears on fertility and the lives of women. Since the completion of skeletal recordation and assessment in 1999, it has been shown that young women had particularly high mortality related to their importation directly from Africa (unlike most men, who were first "seasoned" in the Caribbean) and conditions in New York. The female majority among New York Africans seems to have resulted from a combination of colonial European efforts to stem rebellions against slavery (of which there were two in New York City during the cemetery's use, in which the Akan were represented), efforts to reduce prices, and a lesser demand for the extreme stamina required for Caribbean sugar production, for which men were more often selected (Howson et al 2000). These women were exposed to desperate conditions on the ships—cold weather, malnutrition and disease, hard labor, and reproductive risks—which were stressing them simultaneously. Mortality was especially high among 15- to 20-year-old females and 15- to 25-year-old males, the ages of most new arrivals and the subjects of intensive work regimes.

Treponemal disease (much of which was probably yaws rather than syphilis) was not as prevalent as in the Caribbean and did not include cases of cloaca and cranial lesions associated with advanced syphilis (lower than in Barbados and dramatically lower than in Surinam) (Null et al 2000). Skeletal evidence of enlarged muscle attachments and muscle tears was found in most men and women. Several fractures of the spine and skull base were associated with axial loading of the head, as enslaved Africans would have been burdened with heavy loads (Hill et al 1995, Terranova et al 2000).

Skeletal demography combined with colonial census data from New York pointed to a population of low fertility (below replacement), more like the Caribbean than Virginia, despite the fact that, unlike the Caribbean, most were female and venereal disease seemed low (Rankin-Hill et al 2000). Those women who survived, and were sufficiently healthy to reproduce, bore children in a high-risk environment, where 21% of the burials were infants, likely equating to a well over 50% infant mortality when differential preservation of infant bones is considered. In fact, the Project's mortality data from the archival records of Trinity Church show that the infants of the enslaver's class had far lower mortality, as did 15- to 25-year-olds. English women and men lived to old age (55–60+ years of age) about five to ten times more often than African men and women, respectively (Blakey et al 2000). Most dead children show evidence of anemia (porotic hyperostosis) and infectious disease. Hypoplasia (reflecting childhood malnutrition and disease) were significantly more frequent among those without dental modification than among the 26 individuals whose filed teeth gave evidence suggestive of African childhoods (Mack et al 2000). During this period, when the legal trade was very active, enslaved Africans were worked at the expense of their fertility, merely to be replaced, unlike nineteenth-century efforts to enhance the domestic reproduction of African-American people for sale (See Figure 1).

Figure 1   Burial #315, a women in her 30s with skeletal evidence of arduous labor, nutritional inadequacy, and infection. Her crossed arms are consistent with an Asante practice representing completion, fullness, neutralization, and transition. Photograph by Dennis Seckler, courtesy of the African Burial Ground Project, Howard University, Washington, DC.

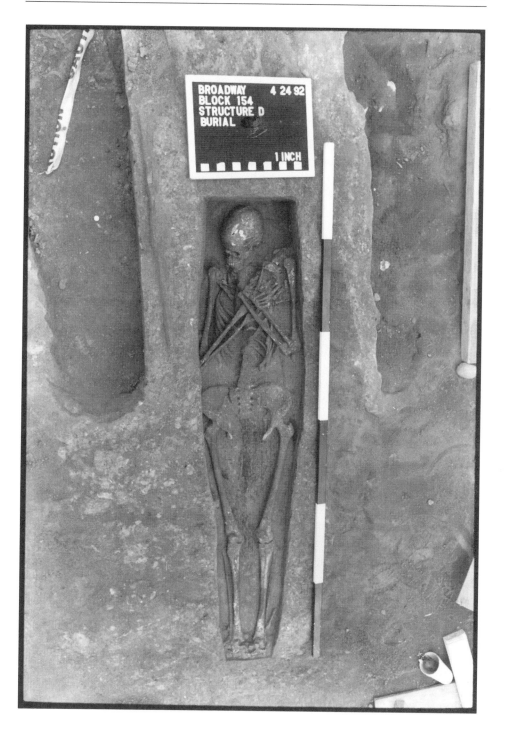

The vivid contrasting of a human face of slavery with its dehumanizing conditions I believe accounts for much of the strong public feeling regarding this work (Blakey 1998a), as it appears in six documentary films, hundreds of news articles, and scores of radio interviews. The power of the most primary of evidence of northern slavery, the bones of the people themselves, has overturned the mythology of the free north according to introductory textbooks, and the Project's approach to public engagement has helped advance general archaeological theory (Thomas 1998, p. 551; Pearson 1999, p. 179; Johnson 2000, pp. 168–70). The ready accessibility of the site and the Cobb Laboratory to the public for education, cultural programs, and religious observances has been important. The simple fact that this research is conducted at an African-American institution deliberately seeking to work on behalf of African Americans' interest in their own past, to "tell our own story," has engendered feelings of empowerment (Harrington 1993). The idea of restoring an understanding of African origins has consistently been of keen public interest for the general redefinition and psychosocial well-being of African Americans, consistent with the long-standing goals of diasporic scholarship cultivated within the black world for over a century. For the first time, bioarchaeology has been brought into that world, with a struggle to do so on that world's own terms. Elsewhere, African Americans succeeded in influencing the historical interpretation and educational uses of Freedman's Cemetery data in Dallas, while limiting the amount of skeletal research to far less than was allowed for the African Burial Ground (Peter et al 2000:3–19).

Of extraordinary interest to African Americans is the ability achieved by this project using DNA to establish a database for showing affiliations between the skeletons and specific African societies (Saheed 1999, Staples 1999). As a result of public interest, the Project realized that if this could be done with respect to the skeletal remains, the same comparative database might someday soon allow any living African American to estimate his or her ancestry within a reasonable probability. The technical ability to restore the knowledge of lineages that had been deliberately severed in the attempt to make their ancestors into chattel should contribute to more intimate ties between the African Diaspora and the African "homeland," with consequences for foreign relations. The physical evidence comparing the physical quality of life under slavery versus African societies has lead to an emergent discussion of human rights, apologies, and reparations (Congressional Black Caucas Task Force on the World Conference Against Rausm briefing by Blakey 19 June 2001; UN Human Rights Commission briefing Blakey 1998a) for slavery. Surely this research relates to the point made by Singleton & Bograd (1995) about differences in Euro-American and African-American questions for archaeology.

In January of 2001 and after several attempts of legislators and community groups to hold them accountable to a memorandum of agreement, the GSA refused to fund the extensive DNA and chemical sourcing studies. These studies had been set forth in the research design that the GSA had approved under public scrutiny in 1994. The years of wrangling with the federal government brought physical anthropologists and archaeologists into a politically active campaign as advisors on behalf of a descendant community, seeking consistency between project goals and GSA agreements. Thus, as seen in engaged anthropological work concerning the treaties or human rights of living people, a great deal of time and energy are expended apart from the actual conduct of research when positions are taken in such a socially significant arena. In this case, the bioarchaeologists stand in an opposite relation to the culturally affiliated communities than do the forensic anthropologists suing for control of so-called Kennewick Man (Thomas 2000). Despite these differences, the resources and visibility accruing to the African Burial Ground Project are advantageous. Although the distinctive scope of work in progress is promising, it remains to be seen what long-term implications this project may have upon completion.

CONCLUSIONS

Biocultural approaches are amenable to the kinds of broad interdisciplinary syntheses, diasporic scope, critique, and public engagement that are compatible with the traditions of scholarship of diasporic people themselves. The New York African Burial Ground Project has stimulated more than an unprecedented interest in bioarchaeology among African Americans. It has brought about unprecedented and sustained national and international interest in an African Diasporic bioarchaeology that reveals the human complexity and contributions of African Americans. This project helps expose the "myth of Euro-American entitlement," i.e., the idea of egalitarian and freedom-loving European forefathers who, all by themselves, built the nation that their descendants can feel especially entitled to enjoy.

The forensic approaches, although salvaging descriptive data that might not otherwise have become available, have demonstrated little ability to interest the public in diasporic bioarchaeology. The racialized and often ahistorical descriptions produced are so reminiscent of the early years of physical anthropology as to be at best puzzling, at worst repugnant to many African Americans, most strikingly demonstrated in New York in the 1990s. Diasporic scholarship was known to many members of the African American lay public in New York, often through recent "Afrocentric" books, study groups, tours, and seminars. For them, something was wrong with the expertise they initially saw at the site. Yet forensics seemed to be a compatible method with government clients whose interests are antithetical to extensive and community-empowering research projects that can slow construction schedules, halt site destruction, undermine their sense of authority, and expose national myth. The fact that CRM contract announcements often request "forensic" expertise rather than bioarchaeological or skeletal biological expertise is simply harmful. These are communities, not crime scenes.

African Diasporic bioarchaeology has been thrown into heated debate about who should participate in the shaping of the past and how it should be done (McDavid & Babson 1997). It is now known that choices can be made by anthropologists themselves. It is possible to work with communities and successfully struggle for a study of mutual interest to scholars and the public, albeit with the risk of seeing memorials built without study in some cases. We should live with this. At a minimum, the results of previous forensic contract work should be brought into an academic setting and reworked into more sophisticated interdisciplinary products. The question of for whom and for what these products are intended remains essential to their form and contribution.

ACKNOWLEDGMENTS

I am very thankful for the research assistance of David Harris, who obtained copies of all of the literature in African Diasporic bioarchaeology for this review. Thanks also to the many helpful colleagues who sent me their site reports. The African Burial Ground Project's emergent results are the collective products of over 100 technicians and senior researchers who have at some time worked with us. The principals associated with the findings and methods represented here include Mark Mack, Lesley Rankin-Hill, M. Cassandra Hill, Warren Perry, Edna Medford, Sherrill Wilson, Fatimah Jackson, Jean Howson, Len Bianchi, Shomarka Keita, Kweku Ofori Ansa, Augustin Holl, Christopher DeCorse, Linda Heywood, Selwyn Carrington, Michael Gomez, John Thornton, Susan Goode-Null, Alan Goodman, Christopher Null, Kenya Shujaa, Rachel Watkins, Emylin Brown, Ruth Mathis, Jean-Marie Cerasale, and many student technicians.

Visit the Annual Reviews home page at www.AnnualReviews.org

LITERATURE CITED

Andah BW. 1995. Studying African societies in cultural context. See Schmidt & Patterson 1995, pp. 149–82

Angel JL. 1976. Colonial to modern skeletal change in the U.S.A. *Am. J. Phys. Anthropol.* 45:723–36

Angel JL, Kelley JO, Parrington M, Pinter S. 1987. Life stresses of the free black community as represented by the First African Baptist Church, Philadelphia, 1823–1841. *Am. J. Phys. Anthropol.* 74:213–29

Ansa KO. 1995. Identification and validation of the Sankofa symbol. *Update* 1:3

Anta Diop C. 1974. *The African Origin of Civilization: Myth or Reality.* Chicago: Lawrence Hill Books

Aptheker H. 1943. *American Negro Slave Revolts.* New York: International

Armelagos GJ, Goodman AH. 1998. Race, racism, and anthropology. See Goodman & Leatherman 1998, pp. 359–78

Armelagos GJ, Mielke JH, Winter J. 1971. *Bibliography of Human Paleopathology. Res.*

Rep. No. 8. Amherst, MA: Dep. Anthropol., Univ. Massachusetts

Armstrong DV, Fleishman M. 1993. *Analysis of Four Burials from African Jamaican House-Yard Contexts at Seville. Rep. Jamaican Natl. Hist. Trust., Archaeol. Rep. 65.* Syracuse, NY: Syracuse Univ.

Aufderheide AC, Rodreguez-Martin C. 1998. *The Cambridge Encyclopedia of Human Paleopathology.* Cambridge, UK: Cambridge Univ. Press

Baber WL. 1999. St. Clair Drake: scholar and activist. See Harrison & Harrison 1999, pp. 191–212

Baker LD. 1998. *From Savage to Negro: Anthropology and the Construction of Race, 1896–1954.* Berkeley: Univ. Calif. Press

Bastide R. 1967. *Les Ameriques Noires, Les Civilisations Africaines dans le Nouveau Monde.* Paris: Payot

Beavers RC, Lamb TR, Greene JR. 1993. *Burial Archaeology and Osteology of Charity Hospital/Cypress Grove II Cemetery, New*

Orleans, Louisiana. Vol. 1: *Archaeology and History*. New Orleans, LA: Dep. Anthropol., Univ. New Orleans

Blakey ML. 1988. Social policy, economics, and demographic change in Nanticoke-Moor ethnohistory. *Am. J. Phys. Anthropol.* 75:493–502

Blakey ML. 1996 [1987]. Skull doctors revisited: intrinsic social and political bias in the history of American physical anthropology, with special reference to the work of Aleš Hrdlička. In *Race and Other Misadventures: Essays in Honor of Ashley Montagu in His Ninetieth Year*, ed. L Reynolds, L Lieberman, pp. 64–95. New York: General Hall

Blakey ML. 1998a. The New York African Burial Ground Project: an examination of enslaved lives, a construction of ancestral ties. *Transform. Anthropol.* 7:53–58

Blakey ML. 1998b. Beyond European enlightenment: toward a critical and humanistic human biology. See Goodman & Leatherman 1998, pp. 379–406

Blakey ML, Jenkins SB, Jamison D, Leslie TE. 1997. Dental indicators of fetal and childhood health in the archaeological remains of a nineteenth century African-American community. In *Pathways to Success*, eds. LR Sloan, BJ Starr, pp. 177–94. Washington, DC: Howard Univ. Press

Blakey ML, Leslie TE, Reidy JP. 1992. Chronological distribution of dental enamel hypoplasia in African American slaves: a test of the weaning hypothesis. *Am. J. Phys. Anthropol. Suppl.* 14:50 (Abstr.)

Blakey ML, Leslie TE, Reidy JP. 1994. Frequency and chronological distribution of dental enamel hypoplasia in enslaved African Americans: a test of the weaning hypothesis. *Am. J. Phys. Anthropol.* 95:371–84

Blakey ML, Mack ME, Medford EG, Wilson SD, Hankin A. 2000. Political economy of mortality of enslaved Africans. *Am. J. Phys. Anthropol. Suppl.* 30:108 (Abstr.)

Bolles AL. 1999. Ellen Irene Diggs: coming of age in Atlanta, Havana, and Baltimore. See Harrison & Harrison 1999, pp. 168–90

Bond GC. 1988. A social portrait of John Gibbs

St. Clair Drake: an American anthropologist. *Am. Ethnol.* 15:762–82

Browne DL. 1999. Across class and culture: Allison Davis and his works. See Harrison & Harrison 1999, pp. 168–90

Buchner CA, Breitburg E, Williams C, Williams E. 1999. *At Rest, Again: The Ridley Graveyard (40WM208) Archaeological Relocation Project, Williamson County, Tennessee*. Report submitted to the Tennessee Department of Transportation, Environmental Planning Office, Nashville, 238 pp. Memphis: Panamerican Consultants

Buikstra JE, Cook DC. 1980. Paleopathology: an American account. *Annu. Rev. Anthropol.* 9:433–70

Buxton LHD, Trevor JC, Julien AH. 1938. Skeletal remains from the Virgin Islands. *Man* 38:49–51

Cobb WM. 1936. Race and runners. *J. Health Phys. Ed.* 7:1–9

Cobb WM. 1939a. Thomas Wingate Todd: an appreciation. *Am. J. Phys. Anthropol. Suppl.* 25:1–3

Cobb WM. 1939b. The Negro as a biological element in the American population. *J. Negro Ed.* 8:336–48

Cook K. 1993. Black bones, white science: the battle over New York's African Burial Ground. *Village Voice* 4 May:23–27

Corruccini RS, Aufderheide AC, Handler JS, Wittmers LE Jr. 1987a. Patterning of skeletal lead content in Barbados slaves. *Archaeometry* 29:233–39

Corruccini RS, Handler JS, Jacobi K. 1985. Chronological distribution of enamel hypoplasias and weaning in a Caribbean slave population. *Hum. Biol.* 57:699–711

Corruccini RS, Handler JS, Mutaw RJ, Lange FW. 1982. Osteology of a slave burial population from Barbados, West Indies. *Am. J. Phys. Anthropol.* 59:443–59

Corruccini RS, Jacobi KP, Handler JS, Aufderheide AC. 1987b. Implications of tooth root hypercementosis in a Barbados slave skeletal collection. *Am. J. Phys. Anthropol.* 74:179–84

Crummell A. 1861. *The Relations and Duties on*

the Free Colored Men in America and Africa. Hartford

Curtin P. 1969. *The Atlantic Slave Trade: A Census.* Madison: Univ. Wisc. Press

Davenport CB, Steggerda M. 1929. *Race Crossing in Jamaica.* Washington, DC: Carnegie Inst.

David PA, Gutman HG, Sutch R, Temin P, Wright G. 1976. *Reckoning with Slavery: A Critical Study in the Quantitative History of American Negro Slavery.* New York: Oxford Univ. Press

deVilliers H. 1968. *The Skull of the South African Negro: A Biometrical and Morphological Study.* Johannesburg, S. Afr.: Witwatersrand Univ. Press

Delany MR. 1861. *Official Report of the Niger Valley Exploring Party.* New York

Douglass F. 1950 [1854]. The claims of the Negro ethnologically considered. In *The Life and Writings of Frederick Douglass*, ed. PS Foner, pp. 289–309. New York: International

Drake StC. 1980. Anthropology and the Black experience. *Black Sch.* 11:2–31

Drake StC. 1993. Diaspora studies and pan-Africanism. See Harris 1993, pp. 451–514

Drake StC, Clayton HR. 1945. *Black Metropolis: A Study of Negro Life in a Northern City.* New York: Harcourt, Brace

Du Bois WEB. 1899. *The Philadelphia Negro: A Social Study.* Philadelphia: Univ. Penn. Press

Du Bois WEB. 1915. *The Negro.* New York: Holt

Eblen JE. 1979. New estimates of the vital rates of the United States black population during the nineteenth century. In *Studies in American Historical Demography*, ed. MA Vinovskis, pp. 339–57. New York: Academic

Edwards GF. 1968. *E. Franklin Frazier on Race Relations.* Chicago: Univ. Chicago Press

Epperson TW. 1999. The contested commons: archaeologies of race, repression, and resistance in New York City. In *Historical Archaeologies of Capitalism*, ed. MP Leone and PB Potter Jr, pp. 81–110. New York: Plenum

Ferguson L. 1992. *Uncommon Ground: Archaeology and Early African America, 1650–1800.* Washington, DC: Smithsonian Inst.

Firmin A. 1885. *De L'égalité des Races Humaines.* [*The Equality of the Human Races*]. Transl. A Charles, 2000. New York: Garland (From French)

Fluehr-Lobban C. 2000. Antenor Firmin: Haitian pioneer of anthropology. *Am. Anthropol.* 102:449–66

Fogel RW, Engerman SL. 1974. *Time on the Cross: The Economics of American Negro Slavery.* Boston: Little, Brown

Fowler C. 1972. *A Knot in the Thread: The Life and Work of Jacques Roumain.* Washington, DC: Howard Univ. Press

Franklin JH. 1947. *From Slavery to Freedom: A History of Negro Americans.* New York: McGraw Hill

Frazier EF. 1930. The Negro slave family. *J. Negro Hist.* 15:198–259

Frazier EF. 1939. *The Negro Family in the United States.* Chicago: Univ. Chicago Press

Gates HL, Andrews X. 1998. *Pioneers of the Black Atlantic.* Cambridge, MA: Harvard Univ. Press

Genovese ED. 1972. *Roll, Jordan, Roll: The World the Slaves Made.* New York: Vintage Books

Goodman AH, Leatherman TL, eds. 1998. *Building a New Biocultural Synthesis: Political-Economic Perspectives on Human Biology.* Ann Arbor: Univ. Mich. Press

Goodman AH, Armelagos GJ. 1998. Race, racism, and anthropology. In *Building a New Biocultural Synthesis: Political-Economic Perspectives on Human Biology*, ed. A Goodman, TL Leatherman, pp. 359–78. Ann Arbor: Univ. Mich. Press

Goodman AH, Martin DL, Armelagos GJ, Clark G. 1984. Indicators of stress in bones and teeth. In *Paleopathology at the Origins of Agriculture*, ed. X Cohen, GJ Armelagos. Orlando, FL: Academic Press

Goodman AH, Reid JR, Mack ME, Jones J, Spaulding C, et al. 2000. Chemical analyses of the places of birth and migration of the

Africans of colonial New York. *Am. J. Phys. Anthropol. Suppl.* 30:162

Gould SJ. 1996 [1981]. *The Mismeasure of Man.* New York: Norton

Guatelli-Steinberg D, Lukacs JR. 1999. Interpreting sex differences in enamel hypoplasia in human and non-human primates: developmental, environmental, and cultural considerations. *Yearb. Phys. Anthropol.* 42:73–126

Gutman HG. 1975. *Slavery and the Numbers Game: A Critique of* Time on the Cross. Urbana: Univ. Illinois Press

Gutman HG. 1976. *The Black Family in Slavery and Freedom, 1750–1925.* New York: Vintage Books

Haas J. 1994. *Standards for Data Collection from Human Skeletal Remains. Proc. Semin. Field Mus. Nat. Hist. Res. Ser. No. 44.* Fayetteville, AK: Arkansas Archaeol. Surv.

Handler JS, Lange FW. 1978. *Plantation Slavery in Barbados: An Archaeological and Historical Investigation.* Cambridge, MA: Harvard Univ. Press

Harrington S. 1993. Bones and bureaucrats. *Archaeology* 6:28–38

Harris JE, ed. 1993 [1982]. *Global Dimensions of the African Diaspora.* Washington, DC: Howard Univ. Press

Harrison FV. 1992. The Du Boisian legacy in anthropology. *Crit. Anthropol.* 12:239–60

Harrison FV, Nonini D. 1992. Introduction [to the special issue on WEB De Bois and anthropology]. *Crit. Anthropol.* 12:261–80

Harrison IE, Harrison FV, eds. 1999. *African American Pioneers in Anthropology.* Urbana: Univ. Illinois Press

Hemenway RE. 1977. *Zora Neale Hurston: A Literary Biography.* Urbana: Univ. Illinois Press

Herskovits MJ. 1928. *The American Negro: A Study of Racial Crossing.* New York: Knopf

Herskovits MJ. 1930. The Negro in the new world: statement of a problem. *Am. Anthropol.* 32:145–56

Herskovits MJ. 1941. *The Myth of the Negro Past.* New York: Harper & Bro.

Higman BW. 1979. Growth in Afro-Caribbean slave populations. *Am. J. Phys. Anthropol.* 50:373–86

Holl AFC. 2000. *Toward an Archaeology of Urban Slavery: The Spacial Analysis of the New York African Burial Ground (ca. 1650–1796).* La Jolla, CA: Dep. Anthropol., Univ. Calif.

Hooton EA. 1930. *The Indians of Pecos Pueblo: A Study of their Skeletal Remains.* New Haven, CT: Yale Univ. Press

Howard Univ., John Milner Assoc. 1993. *Research Design for Archaeological, Historical, and Bioanthropological Investigations of the African Burial Ground (Broadway Block),* New York, New York. 14 Dec.

Howson JE, Goode-Null SK, Blakey ML, Brown EL, Rankin-Hill LM. 2000. Political economy of forced migration and sex ratio. *Am. J. Phys. Anthropol. Suppl.* 30:184

Hrdlička A. 1925. *The Old Americans.* Baltimore: Williams & Wilkins

Hrdlička A. 1927. Anthropology and the Negro: historical notes. *Am. J. Phys. Anthropol.* 10:205–35

Hrdlička A. 1928. The full-blood American Negro. *Am. J. Phys. Anthropol.* 12:15–30

Hutchinson HW. 1957. *Village and Plantation Life in Northeastern Brazil.* Seattle: Univ. Wash. Press

Hutchinson J. 1987. The age-sex structure of the slave populations in Harris County, Texas: 1850–1860. *Am. J. Phys. Anthropol.* 74:231–38

Jackson FLC. 1997. Concerns and priorities in genetic studies: insights from recent African American biohistory. *Seton Hall Law Rev.* 27:951–70

Jackson FLC, Jackson KM, Jackson LF, Khan S, Heywood L, et al. 2000. Strategies for overcoming the current limitations on comparative genetic studies of the African Atlantic Diaspora. *Am. J. Phys. Anthropol. Suppl.* 30:187–88

Jacobi KP, Cook DC, Corruccini RS, Handler JS. 1992. Congenital syphilis in the past: slaves at Newton plantation, Barbados, West Indies. *Am. J. Phys. Anthropol.* 89:145–58

Jones DG. 1990. *Preliminary Excavations at*

a *Burial Ground at Galways Plantation, Montserrat, West Indies*. Boston, MA: Dep. Archaeol., Boston Univ.

Jordan WD. 1968. *White Over Black: American Attitudes Toward the Negro, 1550–1812*. New York: Norton

Keita S, Shujaa K. 2000. A preliminary affinity analysis of crania from the New York African Burial Ground Project. *Am. J. Phys. Anthropol. Suppl.* 30:194

Kelley JO, Angel JL. 1987. Life stresses of slavery. *Am. J. Phys. Anthropol.* 74:199–211

Khudabux MR. 1989. Signs of physical strain as indications of health status during growth in a Negro slave population in Surinam (S.A.). *Advances in Paleopathology*, ed. L Capasso, S Carmiello, G Di Tota. *J. Paleopathol.*: Monographic Publication—1, Cheiti, Italy p. 131–34

Khudabux MR. 1991. *Effects of life conditions on the health of a Negro slave community in Suriname, with reference to similar effects in local pre-Columbian Indians*. PhD thesis. Gravenhage, Pasmans Offsetdrukkeru (Dep. Anatomy), Rijksuniversiteit te Leiden, Leiden, Ger. 143 pp.

Kiple KF, King VH. 1981. *Another Dimension to the Black Diaspora: Diet, Disease, and Racism*. Cambridge, UK: Cambridge Univ. Press

Kiple KF, Kiple VH. 1977. Slave child mortality: some nutritional answers to a perennial puzzle. *J. Soc. Hist.* 10:284–309

Kittles RA, Doura M, Sylvester N, Jackson FLC, Blakey ML. 2000. From African to African American, insight on the formation of African American mtDNA variation. *Am. J. Phys. Anthropol. Suppl.* 30:197 (Abstr.)

Kittles RA, Morris G, George M, Dunston G, Mack M, et al. 1999. Genetic variation and affinities in the New York burial ground of enslaved Africans. *Am. J. Phys. Anthropol. Suppl.* 28:170 (Abstr.)

La Roche CJ, Blakey ML. 1997. Seizing intellectual power: the dialogue at the New York African Burial Ground. *Hist. Archaeol.* 31:84–106

Mack ME, Blakey ML, Goodman AH. 2000. Dental evidence of health in African-born and American-born children. *Am. J. Phys. Anthropol. Suppl.* 30:184

Mann RW, Meadows L, Bass WM, Watters DR. 1987. Skeletal remains from a black slave cemetery, Montserrat, West Indies. *Ann. Carnegie Mus.* 56:319–36

Martin DL, Magennis AL, Rose JC. 1987. Cortical bone maintenance in an historic Afro-American cemetery sample from Cedar Grove, Arkansas. *Am. J. Phys. Anthropol.* 74:255–64

McDavid C, Babson DW, special eds. 1997. In the realm of politics: prospects for public participation in African-American and plantation archaeology. *Hist. Archaeol.* 31:1–152

Medford EG, Perry W, Heywood L, Thornton J, Agorsah K, et al. 2000. Historical and archaeological evidence of the origins of enslaved Africans in colonial New York. *Am. J. Phys. Anthropol. Suppl.* 30:226 (Abstr.)

Mikell G. 1999. Feminism and Black culture in the ethnography of Zora Neale Hurston. See Harrison & Harrison 1999, pp. 51–69

Mintz SW. 1951. *Canamelar: the contemporary culture of a Puerto Rican proletariat*. PhD dissertation. Columbia Univ.

Mintz S. 1974. *Caribbean Transformations*. Chicago: Aldine

Moynihan DP. 1965. *The Negro Family in America: The Case for National Action*. Washington DC, Dept. of Labor, Office of Planning and Research (March 1965)

Mwaria C. 1999. The continuing dialogue: the life and work of Elliot Skinner as exemplar of the African-American/African dialectic. See Harrison & Harrison 1999, pp. 274–92

Myrdal G. 1944. *An American Dilemma*. Public Affairs Pamphlet, Public Affairs Committee, No. 95

Nott JC, Gliddon GR. 1854. *Types of Mankind: Or Ethnological Researches, Based upon the Ancient Monuments, Paintings, Sculptures, and Crania of Races, and upon their Natural, Geographical, Philological, and Biblical History*. Philadelphia, PA: Lippincott, Grambo

Null C, Blakey ML, Carrington SHH, Jackson FLC. 2000. Infectious disease in enslaved Africans of colonial New York: descriptive indicators and the treponema question. *Am. J. Phys. Anthropol. Suppl.* 30:239

Ortiz F. 1927. Los Afrocubanos dientimellados. *Cuba Odontol.* 2:207–16

Ortiz F. 1929. Los Afrocubanos dientimellados. *Arch. Folk. Cuba.* 4:5–24

Ortiz F. 1947. *Cuban Counterpoint: Tobacco and Sugar.* New York: Knopf

Oschinsky L. 1954. *The Racial Affinities of the Baganda and other Bantu Tribes of British East Africa.* Cambridge, UK: Heffer

Owsley DW, Mann RW, Lanphear KM. 1990. *Osteological Examination of Human Remains from the Charity Hospital/Cypress Grove II Cemetery, New Orleans, Louisiana: Final Report of Investigations*, Vol. 2. Washington, DC: Smithsonian Inst., Dep. Anthropol.

Owsley DW, Orser CE Jr, Mann RW, Moore-Jansen PH, Montgomery RL. 1987. Demography and pathology of an urban slave plantation from New Orleans. *Am. J. Phys. Anthropol.* 74:185–97

Parrington M, Roberts DG. 1984. The First African Baptist Church Cemetery: an archaeological glimpse of Philadelphia's early nineteenth century free Black community. *Archaeology* 37:26–32

Parrington M, Roberts DG. 1990. Demographic, cultural, and bioanthropological aspects of a nineteenth century free Black population in Philadelphia, Pennsylvania. In *A Life in Science: Papers in Honor of J. Lawrence Angel*, ed. JE Buikstra, pp. 138–70. Kampsville, IL: Cent. Am. Archaeol.

Pearson MP. 1999. *The Archaeology of Death and Burial.* Phoenix Mill, UK: Sutton

Peter DE, Prior M, Green MM, Clow VG, eds. 2000. *Freedman's Cemetery: A Legacy of a Pioneer Black Community in Dallas, Texas.* Vol. 1. Plano, TX: Geo-Marine. Spec. Publ. No. 6

Pollitzer WS. 1958. The Negroes of Charleston (S.C.): a study of hemoglobin types, serology, and morphology. *Am. J. Phys. Anthropol.* 16:241–63

Rankin-Hill LM. 1997. *A Biohistory of 19th-Century Afro-Americans: The Burial Remains of a Philadelphia Cemetery.* Westport, CT: Bergin & Garvey

Rankin-Hill LM, Blakey ML. 1994. W. Montague Cobb (1904–1990): physical anthropologist, anatomist, and activist. *Am. Anthropol.* 96:74–96

Rankin-Hill LM, Blakey ML, Carrington SHH, Howson JE. 2000. Political economy of fertility and population growth among enslaved Africans in colonial New York. *Am. J. Phys. Anthropol. Suppl.* 30:259

Rathbun TA. 1987. Health and disease at a South Carolina plantation: 1840–1870. *Am. J. Phys. Anthropol.* 74:239–53

Rathbun TA, Scurry JD. 1991. Status and health in colonial South Carolina: Belleview Plantation, 1738–1756. In *What Mean these Bones: Studies in Southeastern Bioarchaeology*, ed. ML Powell, PS Bridges, AMW Mires, pp. 148–64. Tuscaloosa: Univ. Alabama Press

Rivero de la Calle M. 1973. La mutilación dentaria en la población Negroide de Cuba. *Ciencias* 4:3–21

Rose JC, ed. 1985. *Gone to a Better Land: A Biohistory of a Rural Black Cemetery in the Post-Reconstruction South.* Res. Ser. No. 25. Fayetteville, AK: Arkansas Archaeol. Surv.

Ross HB, Adams AM, Williams LM. 1999. Caroline Bond Day: pioneer Black physical anthropologist. See Harrison & Harrison 1999, pp. 37–50

Saheed M. 1999. "Code" blooded: breakthrough work by Howard Univ. scientists may soon allow Blacks in the diaspora to trace their genetic links to a specific African village. *Final Call* Dec. p. 1

Sanday PR. 1999. Skeletons in the anthropological closet: the life and work of William S. Willis, Jr. See Harrison & Harrison 1999, pp. 243–64

Schmidt PR, Patterson TC, eds. 1995. *Making Alternative Histories: The Practice of Archaeology and History in Non-Western Settings.* Santa Fe, NM: Sch. Am. Res.

Schuyler RL. 1976. Images of America: the contribution of historical archaeology to national identity. *Southwest. Lore* 42:27–39

Schuyler RL. 1980. *Archaeological Perspectives on Ethnicity in America: Afro-American and Asian American Culture History*. Farmingdale, NY: Baywood

Shujaa K, Mack ME, Terranova CJ. 2000. Growth and development of enslaved Africans in colonial New York. *Am. J. Phys. Anthropol. Suppl.* 30:281

Singleton TA, (ed). 1999. "I, Too, Am America": Archaeological Studies of African-American Life. Charlottesville: Univ. Virginia Press

Singleton TA, Bograd M. 1995. *The Archaeology of the African Diaspora in the Americas. Historical Archaeology, Guides to the Archaeological Literature of the Immigrant Experience in America*, No. 2. Soc. Hist. Archaeol. Tucson, AZ

Smedley A. 1993. *Race in North America: Origins and Evolution of a World View*. Boulder, CO: Westview

Stamp KM. 1956. *The Peculiar Institution: Slavery in the Ante-Bellum South*. New York: Vintage Books

Staples B. 2000. History lessons from the slaves of New York. *New York Times*. Sept. 1, p. 18

Steckel RH. 1977. *The Economics of U.S. Slave and Southern White Fertility*. PhD thesis. Univ. Chicago, Chicago, IL

Steckel RH. 1986. A dreadful childhood: the excess mortality of American slaves. *Soc. Sci. Hist.* 10:427–67

Stewart TD. 1939. Negro skeletal remains from Indian sites in the West Indies. *Man* 39:49–51

Terranova CJ, Null C, Shujaa K. 2000. Musculoskeletal indicators of work stress in enslaved Africans in colonial New York: functional anatomy of the axial appendicular skeleton. *Am. J. Phys. Anthropol. Suppl.* 30:301

Thomas DH. 1998. *Archaeology*. Fort Worth, TX: Harcourt Brace

Thomas DH. 2000. *Skull Wars: Kennewick Man, Archaeology, and the Battle for Native American Identity*. New York: Basic Books

Thomas DH, South S, Larson CS. 1977. Rich man, poor man: observations on three antebellum burials from the Georgia coast. *Anthropol. Pap. Am. Mus. Nat. Hist.* 54:393–420

Tobias PV. 1953. The problem of race determination: limiting factors in the identification of the South African races. *J. Forensic Med.* 1:113–23

Todd TW. 1930. An anthropologist's study of Negro life. Address delivered before the Assoc. for the Stud. of Negro Life and Hist., No. VIII, Oct. 27. Cleveland, OH: Brush Found.

Ubelaker DH, Angel JL. 1976. Analysis of the Hull Bay skeletons, St. Thomas. *J. Virgin Islands Arch. Soc.* 3:393–420

Watters D, Petersen J. 1991. The Harney Site slave cemetery, Montserrat: archaeological summary. *Rep. Archaeol. Anthropol. Inst. Netherlands Antilles* 9:317–25

Whitten NE Jr, Szwed JR, eds. 1970. *Afro-American Anthropology: Contemporary Perspectives*. New York: Free Press

Willis WS Jr. 1972. Skeletons in the anthropological closet. In *Reinventing Anthropology*, ed. D Hymes, pp. 121–52. New York: Pantheon

Annu. Rev. Anthropol. 2001. 30:423–56

ADAPTATIONS TO ALTITUDE:
A Current Assessment

Cynthia M. Beall
*Department of Anthropology, Case Western Reserve University, Cleveland,
Ohio 44106-7125; e-mail: cmb2@po.cwru.edu*

Key Words Tibet, Andes, hypoxia, oxygen transport

■ **Abstract** The high-altitude Andean and Tibetan Plateaus offer natural experimental settings for investigating the outcome of the past action of evolution and adaptation as well as those ongoing processes. Both Andean and Tibetan high-altitude natives are descended from sea-level ancestors; thus both initially encountered chronic, lifelong high-altitude hypoxia with the same homeostatic "toolbox" that evolved at sea level for responding to brief and transient hypoxia. Yet now they differ phenotypically in many traits thought to be important for offsetting chronic high-altitude hypoxia. Compared on the basis of mean values of five traits, the characteristics of Tibetan high-altitude natives differ more than those of Andean high-altitude natives from the ancestral or unselected response to chronic hypoxia exhibited by acclimatized lowlanders. This suggests that different evolutionary processes have occurred in the two geographically separate areas, although it is not clear why or how those processes differed. Answers to those questions require better knowledge of the prehistory of human populations on the plateaus, as well as information on new phenotypes and the relationship between phenotype and genotype.

INTRODUCTION

The high-altitude Andean and Tibetan Plateaus offer natural experimental settings for investigating the outcome of the past action of evolution and adaptation as well as those ongoing processes. High-altitude hypoxia is a severe physiological stress caused by lowered barometric pressure. High-altitude hypoxia is unavoidable, and a biological response has been the only option until very recently because behavioral responses could not create a non-hypoxic microclimate. Theoretically, a chronic stress requiring a biological response is a likely situation for adaptation to improve homeostatic response to that stress. For this reason, high-altitude-adapted populations have the potential to provide information on the dynamics of evolution and adaptation in humans: For example, how long can homeostatic responses be sustained? When during the lifecycle do adaptations occur? How much within-population variation can be tolerated? How much phenotypic change can occur without a change in genotypic frequencies? And how fast can allele and genotypic frequencies change?

The high-altitude native populations of the Andean and Tibetan Plateaus are hypothesized to illustrate the outcome of evolutionary processes because they have been living at high altitudes for millennia, and there has been opportunity for natural selection to act. Evidence accumulating over the past 20 years or so demonstrates that the indigenous inhabitants of the Andean and Tibetan Plateaus differ quantitatively in some respiratory, circulatory, and hematological traits that are thought to offset the stress of high-altitude hypoxia. Both Andean and Tibetan high-altitude natives are descended from sea-level ancestors, and thus both initially encountered chronic, lifelong high-altitude hypoxia with the same homeostatic toolbox that evolved at sea level for responding to brief and transient hypoxia. Yet they may have diverged phenotypically since then. That is, the natural experiment of moving two different populations to high altitude for thousands of years may have resulted in two different outcomes. The purpose of this review is to evaluate evidence that the two populations do indeed exhibit quantitatively different suites of traits at high altitude; to examine whether these influence function; and to consider why they differ, particularly whether evolutionary processes can be inferred.

The general approach will be to explain the ancestral or unselected response to acute exposure to high-altitude hypoxia and the response over the longer term of years of acclimatization, and then compare the Andean and Tibetan high-altitude natives with those models to see whether either has diverged. The evolutionary logic is that visitors to high altitude engage ancient homeostatic mechanisms that evolved at sea level to counter brief episodes of hypoxia encountered in everyday life. In contrast, populations residing at altitude for millennia on the Andean and Tibetan Plateaus have been exposed to the opportunity for natural selection to evolve more effective or different mechanisms to counter lifelong chronic hypoxia. Homeostatic responses to hypoxia at sea level counter deficiencies of oxygen in the blood rather than in the ambient air. Hypoxia is encountered during everyday life when there is a temporary airway obstruction, or if breathing slows substantially, for example during sleep, and may occur occasionally with blood loss or anemia. Responses to ventilatory hypoxia are fast and measured over the course of seconds to minutes, while responses to circulatory hypoxia are slower and are usually measured over the course of days to weeks. Sea-level hypoxic stress is transient, but high-altitude hypoxic stress is chronic. Therefore, an important consideration is whether responses that evolved to counter transient stress can be sustained under chronic stress. This can be examined in acclimatized lowlanders, people who have spent years at high altitude and belong to low-altitude populations that have not been exposed to the opportunity for natural selection by chronic hypoxia. Examples of such populations are residents of European descent in Colorado, USA, and La Paz, Bolivia, and of Han Chinese descent in Lhasa, Tibet Autonomous Region, China. The other important consideration is whether populations with generations of exposure have different, more effective responses. This can be examined in the indigenous populations of the Andean Plateau, the Aymara and Quechua, and those of the Tibetan Plateau including the Tibetans, Bods, and Sherpas.

HIGH-ALTITUDE HYPOXIA

Hypoxia is less than the normal sea-level amount of oxygen in the inspired air or in the body. High-altitude hypoxia results from a decrease in barometric pressure with increasing altitude (Figure 1). The consequent decrease in the partial pressure of oxygen in inspired air leads to less oxygen in the alveoli of the lung to diffuse to the pulmonary bloodstream for transport to body tissues where a constant supply of oxygen is required for mitochondrial metabolism. For example, a liter of inspired air contains 21% oxygen at all altitudes; but at 4000 m (13,200 ft), that liter has just 63% of the number of oxygen molecules compared with sea level. Thus, homeostatic processes must sustain a sufficient flow of oxygen to the mitochondria starting from a smaller pool of molecules in the lung. Those homeostatic processes may be conserved from sea-level ancestors, or they may be the result of evolution and adaptation in colonizing populations.

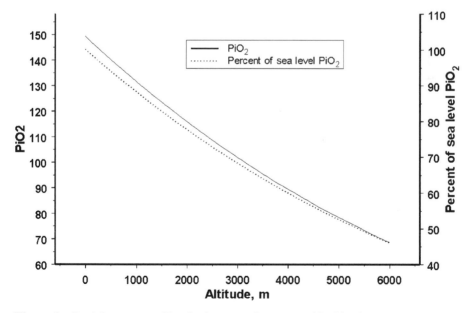

Figure 1   Partial pressure of inspired oxygen decreases with altitude

OXYGEN SATURATION

A physiological measure of the degree of arterial hypoxia is oxygen saturation, the percent of hemoglobin that is carrying oxygen. It falls within seconds of exposure. The unselected response to high altitude is an immediate, profound drop in the oxygen saturation of acutely exposed sea-level natives. For example, young men traveling from sea level to Pike's Peak, Colorado, at 4300 m exhibited an abrupt fall in oxygen saturation to 81% that improved over the following weeks but did not return to sea-level oxygen saturation of 97% (Reeves et al 1993). The variation among individuals was very large on the first day, when the range was from 68% to 92%, and as compared to their sea-level range of from 95% to 99% (Reeves et al 1993, p. 1118, Figure 1). Acclimatization was incomplete in the sense that sea-level baseline values were not achieved. This leads to the expectation that acclimatized lowlanders have lowered oxygen saturations. Figure 2 presents the mean values of samples of acclimatized lowlanders drawn from populations such as Europeans or Han Chinese across a range of altitude. It illustrates a regular decrease in oxygen saturation with increasing altitude.

If indigenous populations had the same oxygen saturations as acclimatized lowlanders, it would be evidence that natural selection had not acted to improve this link in the chain of oxygen transport. Andean highlanders have saturations lower than sea-level samples; the decrease with altitude is irregular. Figure 2 indicates higher saturation levels than those of the acclimatized lowlanders at altitudes up to about 4000 m, but lower saturations at altitudes above that. In contrast, the Tibetans show a steady decline in oxygen saturation with altitude. Figure 2 summarizes findings describing over 3000 people from 45 samples. The fact that multiple sources were used means there is likely to be some experimental noise. A large comparative study using the same techniques was conducted at the same altitude of about 4000 m in two rural villages, the first in Andean Bolivia and the second in the Tibet Autonomous Region. The study found that the Andean highlanders had 2.6% higher oxygen saturation than did the Tibetans (Beall et al 1999b, Beall et al 1997c). Andean highlanders may be less stressed hypoxically at a given altitude at least up to about 4000 m, but more explicitly comparative samples are needed to further support this idea. The data summarized in Figure 2 demonstrate that all three populations—altitude-acclimatized lowlander and Andean and Tibetan high-altitude natives—have arterial hypoxia as measured by oxygen saturation. Indeed, this measure is commonly used to quantify hypoxic stress. However, oxygen saturation is a complex phenotype that reflects many influences.

Oxygen saturation varies with demographic characteristics. Andean and Tibetan adult males have higher oxygen saturation than do females. Figure 2 was limited to samples of people from 15 to 50 years of age because those younger and older have lower saturations (Beall 2000, Beall et al 1992a, Beall & Goldstein 1990b). Characteristics of infants are of particular interest because the lower saturation levels could create the possibility of differential survival and natural selection during the life cycle stage already characterized by relatively high mortality rates.

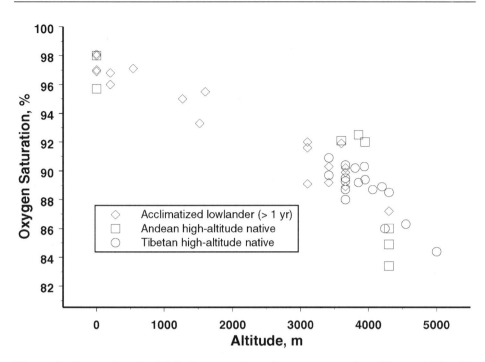

Figure 2   Scatterplot of published mean values of oxygen saturation of hemoglobin with altitude. It is based on samples of ten or more people, natives or long-term residents with an average of more than a year at altitude, with an average age between 15 and 50 years. (Sources include Antezana et al 1994; Beall et al 2000, 1999, 1997, 1992; C.M. Beall unpublished data; Beall & Goldstein 1990; Brutsaert et al 2000; Chen et al 1997; Curran et al 1995; Decker et al 1991; Ge et al 1995; Huang et al 1992, 1984; Jansen et al 1999; Kryger et al 1978; Lawler et al 1988; Leon-Velarde et al 1994, 1991; Marcus et al 1994; Martin et al 1989; Moore et al 1990, 1982; Reeves 1993; Schlaepher et al 1992; Sun et al 1996; Tucker et al 1984; Weil et al 1978; Zhuang et al 1993, 1992.)

Infants in two unselected populations, Europeans in Colorado and Han Chinese in the Tibet Autonomous Region, had different developmental trajectories of oxygen saturation during the first four months of life. Infants of European descent born at 3100 m in Colorado showed a large drop in the first week followed by a two-month period of gradually increasing oxygen saturation to a stable level maintained from two to four months of age. In contrast, infants of Han Chinese descent born at 3658 m showed a decline in saturation throughout the first four months of life (Carpenter et al 1998, Niermeyer et al 1995). Both samples of infants from unselected populations contrasted with Tibetan infants born at 3658 m, whose saturation level dropped in the first several days and then stabilized within a week to levels maintained through the first four months of life. The three different patterns illustrate that the degree of arterial hypoxia varies widely early in life and also illustrate that unselected populations may differ qualitatively. It is not known whether the contrasts between the European babies in Colorado and the Chinese babies in Tibet are due to the different altitudes at which the studies were conducted or due to different responses to altitude.

Exercise increases oxygen demand and causes oxygen desaturation at high altitudes. Comparative studies demonstrate that submaximal exercise causes more desaturation in unselected populations than in their Andean and Tibetan counterparts (Brutsaert et al 2000, Zhuang et al 1996). Those findings may indicate that diffusion of oxygen into the blood is limited during heavy exercise, but the limit has been partly overcome in members of the population that have been subject to the opportunity for natural selection.

HYPOXIC PULMONARY VASOCONSTRICTION

An immediate response to hypoxia in inspired air is pulmonary vasoconstriction, a narrowing of the blood vessels in the lung where oxygen diffuses into the bloodstream. One adaptive explanation is that hypoxic pulmonary vasoconstriction evolved at sea level as a local homeostatic mechanism to redistribute blood from temporarily poorly ventilated and oxygenated to better ventilated and oxygenated portions of the lung in order to restore oxygen diffusion and blood oxygen content (Harris 1986). Another adaptive explanation is that hypoxic pulmonary vasoconstriction evolved as a mechanism to achieve the fetal pattern of blood flow (when blood is not oxygenated in the lungs) and that vasoconstriction is immediately released upon exposure to the relative hyperoxia of extrauterine life to achieve the postnatal pattern of blood flow through the lungs (Ward et al 1989, p. 156). According to this explanation, the retention of the vasoconstrictive response later in life has no adaptive function but remains because there has been no selection against it. Either way, at high altitude, where the entire lung is chronically hypoxic, this response could lead to a general narrowing of blood vessels and cause an increase in pulmonary artery blood pressure as cardiac output flows into the narrower vessels.

The ancestral or "unselected" pulmonary vasoconstrictive response is illustrated by increases in the pulmonary artery blood pressure of sea-level natives traveling to high altitude. For example, acute exposure to 3700 m altitude increased pulmonary artery pressure 85% within hours of arrival from sea level (Moret et al 1972). The hypoxic vasoconstrictive response appears to be maintained indefinitely in the unselected population of European descent at 3100 m in Colorado as revealed by measures of about 50 people. Mean pulmonary artery pressures were slightly elevated in one study and were roughly double normal sea-level values in another (Hartley et al 1967, Grover et al 1967, 1963, Vogel et al 1962). In addition, "Chronic hypoxia tends to bring out the latent differences among normal individuals in terms of pulmonary vascular reactivity" (Grover 1963, p. 2). About 20% of 28 high school students studied at 3100 m were "hyper-reactors" (i.e. retained vasoreactivity), whereas another proportion were "hypo-reactors" when exposed to additional hypoxia or exercise.

Andean high-altitude natives also maintain the vasoconstrictive response. The pulmonary artery pressures of over 200 Andean highlanders at altitudes from 3700 to 4540 m have been reported, and all were above the normal sea-level range. Considerable variation appeared in studies of mean pulmonary artery pressure, although there was no evidence of an altitude gradient in pulmonary artery pressure (Penaloza et al 1963, Sime et al 1963, Rotta et al 1956, Hultgren et al 1965a,b, Moret et al 1972, Lockhart et al 1976, Spielvogel et al 1969). A few minutes of relief from hypoxia by breathing 35% or 100% oxygen partly reversed the pulmonary artery hypertension (Sime et al 1971, Hultgren et al 1965a, Moret et al 1972, Spielvogel et al 1969), while a few minutes of additional hypoxia raised pulmonary artery pressure. These findings indicated that the reflexive pulmonary vasoreactivity was intact and that vasoconstriction was ongoing.

A few minutes of relief from hypoxia lowered pulmonary artery pressures, but not as low as sea-level values. This is because there had been anatomical changes in the pulmonary vessel. The small pulmonary arteries of Andean highlanders are described as "muscularized" because they have bands of muscle plus two layers of elastic lamina, while those of lowlanders have just a single elastic lamina (Heath & Williams 1989). The additional layers of tissue cause the lumen of the arterioles to narrow further and thus provide higher resistance to blood flow and higher pulmonary artery pressure than those caused by vasoconstriction alone. The reversibility of this anatomical modification has been demonstrated. Ten days at sea level was insufficient to allow Colorado residents' pulmonary artery pressures to fall to sea-level values (Hartley et al 1967), while two years of residence at sea level was sufficient for a sample of Andean highlanders (Sime et al 1974).

The muscularization of the pulmonary arteries is achieved by delaying and curtailing the neonatal reduction to mature levels of pulmonary artery pressure that usually occurs in the first few days and the attainment of adult-like anatomy that usually occurs in the first weeks of life. At high altitude, the decrease takes longer and ends at a higher mature level (Sime et al 1963, Carpenter et al 1998, Gamboa & Marticorena 1971 and 1972). Pulmonary artery pressure illustrates the challenges of defining the various modes of adaptation. The hypoxic pulmonary vasoreactivity is immediately reversible and for that reason could be called an acclimatization. However, it changes a developmental pattern that results in distinctive mature anatomy of the pulmonary artery and for that reason could be called a developmental adaptation. One response is reversible with just a few minutes of oxygen and the other after years at sea level.

There are intriguing albeit less extensive data about hypoxic pulmonary vaso-constriction from Tibetan populations. Just two studies of 27 people have been reported. One reported characteristic a mean pulmonary artery pressure as high as in the Andes (Yang et al 1987). However, the other reported a mean within the normal sea-level range (Groves et al 1993). Reporting on just five men it found that pulmonary artery pressure increased in response to further hypoxia but did not respond to hyperoxia. Those findings suggested that the normal hypoxic va-soreactive response was intact and was centered at the sea-level mean. Anatomical evidence from Tibetan infants and adults describing pulmonary arteries normal in appearance but lacking the structural changes associated with Andean pulmonary hypertension support the finding of low pulmonary artery pressure (Sui et al 1988, Gupta et al 1992). Those findings are evidence that at least some Tibetans may have lost the sea-level sustained vasoconstrictive response and the concomitant morphological changes of the acclimatized and the Andean populations. This is tentative evidence of Andean-Tibetan differences in this early link in the chain of oxygen transport. The molecular mechanism for vasoconstriction is downregulation of pulmonary synthesis of the vasodilator, nitric oxide (Dweik et al 1998). There may be Andean-Tibetan differences in the constitutive production of NO or in the sensitivity of nitric oxide synthase enzymes to hypoxic downregulation.

If the adaptive function of hypoxic vasoconstriction is to improve oxygen diffusion into the blood, then these findings predict that Andean highlanders have more oxygen in their blood. Andean highlanders' average arterial partial pressure of oxygen (p_aO_2) at 3700 m ranges from 57 to 64 torr (Spielvogel et al 1969, Lockhart et al 1976, Winslow et al 1989), whereas Tibetans' average p_aO_2 at 3658 m was 52–54 torr (Zhuang et al 1996, Groves et al 1993). This is consistent with the suggestion that Andean highlanders may have higher oxygen saturation in that altitude range. Altogether, this evidence suggests that there has been a change from the ancestral unselected response of sustained hypoxic vasoconstriction to allow Tibetans to maintain normal sea-level values of pulmonary artery pressure and vasoreactivity under chronic hypoxia.

A cost of very strong and/or sustained hypoxic pulmonary vasoconstriction may be greater susceptibility to high-altitude pulmonary edema (HAPE, a severe response to acute exposure that is characterized by fluid in the lungs) for those on the upper end of the distribution. Acutely exposed adults who had previously experienced HAPE had very high pulmonary artery pressures during a subsequent exposure to hypoxia (e.g., Busch et al 2001, Duplain et al 2000, Scherrer et al 1996), although their pulmonary artery pressures did not differ from those of controls at sea level. In addition, those prone to HAPE had lower exhaled nitric oxide concentrations at altitude, but not at sea level (Duplain et al 2000).

Another cost of maintaining high pulmonary artery pressure is an increased incidence among Andean infants of patent ductus arteriosus, a fetal blood vessel joining the aorta and the pulmonary artery that usually closes functionally and anatomically after birth when the systemic blood pressure far exceeds the pulmonary artery pressure. However, there appear to be no adverse consequences of the chronic mild pulmonary hypertension after infancy (Sime et al 1963). A study comparing Han Chinese and Tibetan children along an altitude gradient found no ethnic differences in the prevalence of patent ductus arteriosus and atrial septal defect but did find a higher prevalence at altitude (Miao et al 1988). Those data argue against generally low pulmonary artery pressures among Tibetan infants and children. The hypothesized mechanisms in play were failure to constrict the ductus due to high pulmonary vascular resistance and inhibition of closure of the foramen ovale due to right heart pressures.

RESTING VENTILATION

An increase in ventilation occurs within seconds of exposure to hypoxia and the fall in oxygen saturation. This is considered adaptive because it moves more air and oxygen through the lungs in a given time to offset the hypoxia in the air. The unselected response is illustrated by a sample of young men who traveled to Pike's Peak, Colorado, at 4300 m. Their resting ventilation increased from 6.8 L/min at sea level to 8.7 L/min on the first day and to 10.5 L/min by the eighth day (Moore et al 1987). That response leads to the expectation that acclimatized lowlanders have high resting ventilation, when they generally do not. There is no clear trend toward high average resting ventilation at higher altitudes among Europeans and Han Chinese residents who have resided for more than a year at high altitudes (Figure 3). Instead, they have resting ventilations similar to

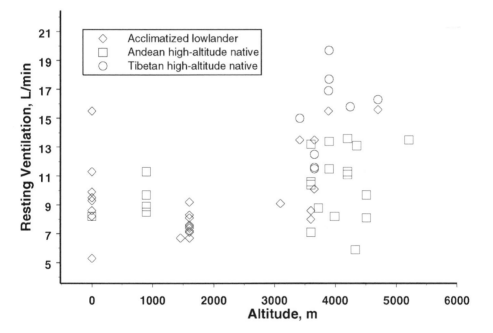

Figure 3   Scatterplot of published mean values of resting ventilation with altitude. It is based on samples of ten or more people, natives or long-term residents with an average of more than a year at altitude, with an average age over 15 years. (Sources include Beall et al 1997, 1992; Brutsaert et al 2000; Chiodi 1957; Cudkowicz et al 1972; Curran et al 1995; Filuk et al 1988; Frisancho et al 1999; Ge et al 1995, 1994; Georgopoulos et al 1989; Hackett et al 1980; Holtby et al 1988; Huang et al 1984, 1981; Hultgren et al 1965; Kryger et al 1978; Marcus et al 1994; Moore et al 1987; Nishimura et al 1987; Peterson et al 1981; Poulin et al 1993; Regensteiner et al 1990, 1988; Schoene 1982; Sime et al 1971; Sun et al 1990; Vargas et al 1998; White et al 1983; Zhuang et al 1993.)

sea-level residents at sea level, although a few samples have high means. Similarly, Andean highlanders exhibit little relationship between altitude and ventilation, although there is more variability in the Andean samples. These data suggest that the increase in ventilation of acutely exposed lowlanders is not sustained by either acclimatized lowlanders or by Andean highlanders.

In contrast, Tibetans do have high resting ventilation and it increases with altitude. That is, Tibetans are more similar to sea-level natives acutely exposed to hypoxia. The mean ventilation values of all the Tibetan samples are higher than the sea-level range and are similar to or above that of acutely exposed lowlanders. Figure 3 summarizes 50 samples describing nearly 1400 people. An analysis of covariance of the 28 samples above 3000 m, where all three populations have been studied, tested for the effects of population of origin while controlling for altitude. At a mean altitude of 3896 m, the estimated mean ventilation of Tibetan samples was 15.0 L/min as compared with 10.5 L/min among Andean samples and 11.7 L/min among acclimatized lowlanders ($F_{population} = 8.4$, $p < .05$). A comparative study at 4000 m confirmed the marked population difference and found that a Tibetan sample had 50% higher resting ventilation than its Andean counterpart (Beall et al 1997a). These findings suggest that some homeostatic response or responses have changed to allow Tibetans, but not others, to sustain high resting ventilation under chronic high-altitude hypoxia. There are no data as to whether the two high-ventilation phenotypes result from the same mechanisms.

There is little information about other influences on ventilation at high altitude. Males had higher ventilation than females, and there was no age-related increase in ventilation during childhood in Andean and Tibetan samples (Beall et al 1997c). Pregnancy was associated with increased ventilation (Beall & Goldstein 1990; Moore et al 1982a, 1986a).

HYPOXIC VENTILATORY RESPONSE

The reflexive increase in ventilation induced by hypoxia is called the hypoxic ventilatory response (HVR). HVR is studied by inducing a known experimental hypoxic stress and measuring the increase in ventilation. There are several ways to quantify the HVR. The measure used here is the change in ventilation divided by the change in oxygen saturation. HVR can be measured at any altitude; at high altitude it is simply added to ambient hypoxia. The HVR is interpreted as adaptive because it initiates the increase in ventilation. The unselected HVR response to acute exposure to high altitude is illustrated by young men who traveled to the Barcroft Laboratory, California, at 3810 m (12,600′). Their average HVR nearly doubled during the first nine days at altitude and then started to decrease (Sato et al 1994). The downturn at the end of a few days of acute exposure at high altitude appears to have been the beginning of a longer process. Acclimatized lowlanders have very low HVR (Figure 4), a phenomenon sometimes described as "acquired blunting" of HVR. Samples of acclimatized adult Europeans at 3100 m in Colorado

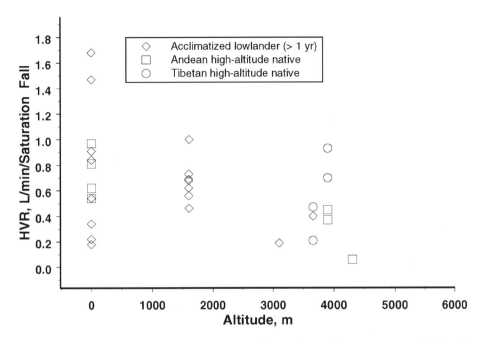

Figure 4   Scatterplot of published mean values of hypoxic ventilatory response (HVR) with altitude. It is based on samples of ten or more people, natives or long-term residents with an average of more than a year at altitude, with an average age over 15 years. (Sources include Beall et al 1997; Curran et al 1995; Kryger et al 1978; Littner et al 1984; Marcus et al 1994; Moore et al 1987, 1986, 1984; Nishimura et al 1989; Peterson et al 1981; Regensteiner et al 1990, 1988; Sato et al 1992; Schoene 1982; Vargas et al 1998; White et al 1983; Zhuang et al 1993.)

and Han Chinese at 3658 m in Tibet were blunted in proportion to the length of adult residence at high altitude (Weil et al 1971, Zhuang et al 1993). Because 9–10-year-old children in Colorado had normal, sea-level HVRs, it is thought that acclimatized individuals develop a "blunted" or lower HVR over long periods of residence after childhood at high altitude (Byrne-Quinn et al 1972).

The few Andean data points in Figure 4 indicate that Andean highlanders also have blunted HVR. Andean highlanders have low HVR compared with populations at intermediate and low altitudes and show no evidence of a trend with altitude. In contrast, Tibetan HVR is in the normal to high sea-level range. Figure 4 summarizes data on 25 samples describing nearly 1000 people, including 8 samples describing about 400 people above 3000 m. (There are too few samples to conduct an analysis of covariance with acceptable statistical power.) The results of a comparative study at 4000 m confirmed the visual impression of Figure 4 and found that Tibetan mean HVR was more than double that of the Andean highlanders (Beall et al 1997a). Thus, none of the three high-altitude populations sustains the very high HVR of acutely exposed lowlanders; however, the Tibetans maintain HVR in the normal sea-level range, while the acclimatized lowlanders and the Andean highlanders have very low HVR. These findings suggest that some homeostatic response has changed to allow Tibetans, but not others, to maintain HVR in the normal sea-level range under chronic hypoxia.

An early study suggested that the blunted HVR of Andean highlanders was acquired during adolescence, roughly the same time that susceptibility to blunting was apparently acquired in Colorado (Lahiri et al 1976). However, recent studies did not corroborate these findings (Vargas et al 1998, Beall et al 1997a). Two studies (Vargas et al 1998, Beall et al 1997a) found that Andean high-altitude natives as young as eight years old have low HVR values and therefore contrast with the Colorado children who retained normal HVR at 9 to 10 years of age. Andean high-altitude babies responded to experimentally induced hypoxia no differently than did sea-level babies (Mortola et al 1992). Therefore, any blunting seems likely to occur early in life. Some have argued that Tibetans also acquire blunted HVR with prolonged exposure to high altitude. The inference rests on the interpretation of outlier values in two studies (Curran et al 1995, Hackett et al 1980) and is not consistent with other data.

HEMOGLOBIN CONCENTRATION

Studies of hematological adjustments to hypoxia focus on hemoglobin, the molecule that transports oxygen. An increase in hemoglobin concentration is interpreted as adaptive because it offsets the lower oxygen saturation and partly restores the arterial oxygen content. Arterial oxygen content is primarily a function of the oxygen saturation and hemoglobin concentration. Upon acute exposure to high altitude, hemoglobin concentration gradually increases. For example, the average hemoglobin concentrations of young men visiting Pike's Peak increased from 14.0 gm/dL at sea level to 14.9 and then 15.7 gm/dL after 10 days and 20 days at 4300 m (Grover et al 1998). Acclimatized lowlanders maintain this response and exhibit an elevation proportional to altitude (Figure 5). Andean highlanders exhibit the same pattern. Hemoglobin concentration illustrates that the same quantitative phenotype may result from different mechanisms. The increase in hemoglobin concentration during the first days to weeks is due to hemoconcentration resulting from a decrease in plasma volume and blood volume. After a few days at altitude, the subjects produced new red blood cells, and an increase in the proportional volume of red blood cells accounts for the higher hemoglobin concentration (Pugh 1964, Ward et al 2000).

In contrast, Tibetans do not maintain a large elevation of hemoglobin concentration. Indeed, as high as 4000 m the mean hemoglobin concentration of many Tibetan samples is not elevated and is within 5% of the sea-level mean. At very high altitudes, over 4500 m, Tibetans have hemoglobin concentrations elevated above sea level, but even at those altitudes the concentrations remain lower than those

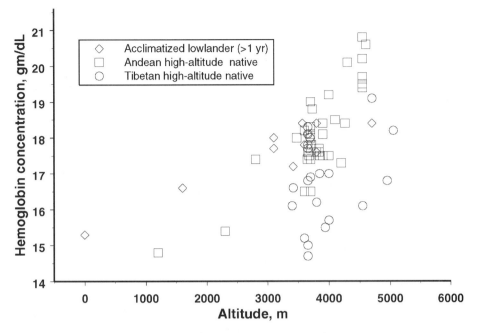

Figure 5   Scatterplot of published mean values of hemoglobin concentration with altitude. It is based on samples of ten or more men, natives or long-term residents with an average of more than a year at altitude, with an average age over 15 years. (Sources include Adams & Shrestha 1974; Adams & Strang 1975; Arnaud et al 1981; Banchero et al 1966; Beall et al 1998, 1990, 1987; Beall & Goldstein 1990; Beall & Reichsman 1984; Bharadwaj et al 1973; Brutsaert et al 2000; Cudkowicz et al 1972; Droma et al 1991; Eaton et al 1969; Frisancho 1975; Garruto 1976; Ge et al 1995, 1994; Guleria et al 1971; Huang et al 1992; Hultgren et al 1965; Hurtado 1945; Larrick & Topgyal 1985; Leon-Velarde et al 1991; Mazess 1969; Moore et al 1990; Morpurgo et al 1972; Okin et al 1966; Penaloza et al 1963; Ruiz 1973; Samaja et al 1979; Santolaya et al 1973; Schoene et al 1990; Spielvogel 1997; Sun et al 1990; Tarazona-Santos et al 2000; Tufts et al 1985; Velasquez 1972; Vincent et al 1978; Winslow et al 1990, 1988, 1981; Zhuang et al 1996, 1993.)

of their Andean counterparts. Figure 5 summarizes over 70 samples describing more than 5000 men. An analysis of covariance using the 53 samples taken above 3000 m controlled for altitude and tested for the effect of population on hemoglobin concentration. At a mean altitude of 3859 m, the estimated mean hemoglobin concentration of Tibetan men was 16.9 gm/dL as compared with 18.1 for Andean and 18.2 for acclimatized men ($F_{population} = 9.0$, $p < .05$). Comparative studies confirm that contrast (Beall et al 1998, Winslow et al 1989). Females exhibit the same population differences as males, although there are fewer comparative samples (e.g., Beall et al 1998, Moreno-Black et al 1984, Okin et al 1966). Thus, acclimatized lowlanders and Andean highlanders maintain a large increase in hemoglobin concentration over sea-level values and do so starting at fairly low altitudes, while Tibetans generally do not maintain a large increase unless the hypoxic stress is very severe.

Hemoglobin concentration varies substantially at any one altitude. The high hemoglobin concentration among acclimatized lowlanders and Andean highlanders is expressed in children and adolescents (Treger et al 1965, Garruto 1976). Some studies report an increase in hemoglobin concentration with age during adulthood in Andean samples (Tufts et al 1985, Leon-Velarde et al 1997). Adult males have higher hemoglobin concentrations than those of adult females. Rural populations tend to have lower hemoglobin concentration than do urban ones at similar altitudes, even when the subjects are screened for health and iron nutrition (Beall et al 1990).

Nutritional factors have been considered as a potential influence on hemoglobin concentration. Studies that screened for iron deficiency found that it does not explain the lower Tibetan hemoglobin concentrations (Beall & Reichsman 1984, Beall et al 1998). Iron availability may limit the erythropoietic response by limiting the capacity to increase the production of iron-containing hemoglobin. For example, three months of iron and folate supplementation for Andean women at 4800 m increased their mean hemoglobin concentration to 19.2 gm/dL from 17.7 gm/dL (Berger et al 1997), a value already elevated over the sea-level reference. However, similar supplementation at 3600 m had no effect, indicating sample differences in iron availability. Such differences may contribute to some of the variation among samples at a given altitude. Another nutritional influence on hemoglobin concentration is body mass index (BMI). Higher BMI correlates with higher hemoglobin concentration in Andean, but not Tibetan, samples (e.g., Tufts et al 1985, Beall et al 1998). Additionally, smokers at 3000 m have higher hemoglobin concentration than do nonsmokers (Ramirez et al 1991).

The molecular basis of the increase in hemoglobin concentration is an increase in synthesis of the hormone, erythropoietin. Erythropoietin increase is detectable within hours of arrival at high altitudes and initiates differentiation of precursors to red blood cells. New mature red blood cells are delivered to the circulation some two to five days later (Hillman 1995, Spivak 1995). Erythropoietin increases sharply by severalfold in the first days of acute exposure to high altitude and then decreases over the course of a week or two at the same high altitude to reach a level slightly higher than that at sea level (e.g., Abbrecht & Littell 1972, Milledge & Cotes 1985). There is no regular association between erythropoietin concentration and altitude or between erythropoietin concentration and hemoglobin concentration among Andean and Tibetan high-altitude natives. Sea-level values range from 9 to 27 mIU/mL (Cotes et al 1986, Boning et al 1996), while Andean and Tibetan high-altitude natives span virtually the same range from 8 to 28 mIU/ml (Winslow et al 1989, Leon-Velarde et al 1994). A comparative study of erythropoietin and hematocrit (the volume percent of blood occupied by red blood cells, a measure correlated closely with hemoglobin concentration) in Andean and Tibetan samples found no significant difference in erythropoietin concentration despite significantly higher Andean hematocrit levels. For a given level of hematocrit, Andean erythro-poietin concentration was 72% higher, which suggests that the Andean highlanders were responding as if they were anemic (Winslow et al 1989).

Paradoxically, the Andean elevation appears to be an overshoot in the sense that it often results in an arterial oxygen concentration higher than sea-level reference values. For example, the mean calculated arterial oxygen content of Andean men in one sample was 24.4 ml/100ml blood as compared with 21.2 at sea level (Beall 2000a) and 19.2 for Tibetan men at the same altitude of around 4000 m. The relative costs and benefits of the Andean erythropoiesis have been considered, although the costs and benefits for the relative Tibetan lack of erythropoiesis have not. Some have argued that the elevated hemoglobin concentration of Andean highlanders serves no adaptive purpose and may instead exact a cost because high blood viscosity can cause poor microcirculation. An experiment at 4300 m that entailed decreasing hemoglobin concentration by phlebotomy or hemodilution found no improvement in maximal exercise capacity (Winslow & Monge 1987, p. 182). On the other hand, a study of Andean men with a wide range of "natural" levels of hemoglobin concentration found that there was an optimal hemoglobin concentration that was higher than that at sea level. Men at 3700 m with a mean hemoglobin concentration about 20% higher than at sea level had higher maximal exercise capacity than men with lower or higher hemoglobin concentration (Tufts et al 1985).

ANDEAN-TIBETAN DIFFERENCES

This overview of some of the most widely studied traits indicates several population differences in the adaptive response to chronic high-altitude hypoxia. The most clear-cut Andean-Tibetan differences as evaluated on the basis of mean adult values of a trait were found for the following three traits.

1. Resting ventilation. Tibetans retain the high resting ventilation of acute expo-sure in contrast to acclimatized lowlanders and Andean highlanders, whose ventilation rates resemble more closely sea-level populations at sea level.

2. Hypoxic ventilatory response. Tibetans maintain sea-level HVR in the nor-mal sea-level range, while acclimatized lowlanders and Andean highlanders have very low HVR.

3. Hemoglobin concentration. Tibetans maintain hemoglobin concentration near sea-level values at altitudes as high as 4000 m and have elevated hemoglobin concentrations at higher altitudes, while acclimatized lowlan-ders and Andean highlanders maintain substantially elevated hemoglobin concentrations proportional to altitude and starting at altitudes as low as 1600 m.

Less clear-cut Andean-Tibetan differences, possibly owing to limited evidence, as evaluated on the basis of mean adult values were found for the following two traits.

4. Oxygen saturation. Andean highlanders may have higher oxygen saturation than acclimatized lowlanders and Tibetan high-altitude natives.

5. Hypoxic pulmonary vasoconstriction. Tibetans may have normal sea-level values of pulmonary artery pressure, while acclimatized lowlanders and Andean highlanders have elevated pulmonary artery pressures.

Thus, compared on the basis of mean values of traits and considered in terms of differences from an ancestral, unselected response to chronic hypoxia as exhibited by acclimatized lowlanders, Tibetans diverge more than Andean highlanders.

Explanatory Hypotheses

Several hypotheses have been suggested to explain these contrasts. Hochachka and colleagues hold that these traits reflect ancient adaptation to endurance performance that just happen to respond to high-altitude hypoxia, too. They view the population contrasts as inconsequential, trivial adjustments that are expected because of a long history of separate evolution estimated to be at least 40,000 years in length (Hochachka & Monge, 2000, Hochachka 1998). Moore and colleagues have argued that the Tibetans are better adapted because adaptation is time dependent and Tibetans have been at altitude for longer. They offer dates of 25,000 years or possibly upwards of 50,000 years for the length of habitation of the Tibetan Plateau (Moore et al 1998, Niermeyer et al 1995, Moore et al 1992). Beall and colleagues suggest that Andean and Tibetan highlanders have adapted differently as a result of different microevolutionary processes in the two continents (Beall et al 1999b, Beall 2000a). This hypothesis and that of longer habitation on the Tibetan Plateau are not mutually exclusive; however, this hypothesis does not suggest that one population is better adapted.

The length of habitation of the two plateaus is important for understanding how the populations came to differ. The earliest chronometrically dated site at high altitude on the Andean Plateau dates to around 11,000 years ago (Aldenderfer 1999), whereas the earliest chronometrically dated site on the Tibetan Plateau dates to around 7000 years ago (Chang 1992). The date for the Andean Plateau is based on much more archaeological evidence than that for the Tibetan Plateau, where little work has been conducted. The assertion that Tibetans have been on the Plateau for 25,000–50,000 years or longer is based mainly on interpreting the looks of undated stone tools gathered on the surface of the ground. New archaeological work on the entry routes and time of occupation of the Tibetan Plateau is necessary. An indirect source of information on the antiquity of the Tibetan population is genomic analysis. Analyses of Tibetan Y-chromosome haplotypes suggested a split from a low-altitude ancestral population in northern China about 6000 years ago (Su et al 2000, Qian et al 2000). The earliest date is always subject to revision with later discoveries; however, current evidence does not suggest that the length of habitation of the two plateaus is substantially different.

Benefits and Costs

Another approach to evaluating the various hypotheses is to consider the relative benefits and costs of the two patterns to determine if one is superior. The two most common measures of benefit have been maximal physical work capacity and birth weight.

Physical work capacity decreases markedly upon acute exposure to high altitude. For example, maximal work capacity of young men and women who traveled to Pike's Peak at 4300 m decreased about 25% in the first five days (Mazzeo et al 1991, Braun et al 2000). The relatively few studies of acclimatized lowlanders report a wide range of maximal work capacities (Figure 6). A potential important confounding factor making these comparisons difficult to interpret is habitual activity and training level (e.g., Brutsaert et al 1999, Weitz 1984, Frisancho et al 1995). Andean and Tibetan highlanders also exhibit a wide range of maximal work capacities. Comparative studies indicate that the indigenous populations have higher

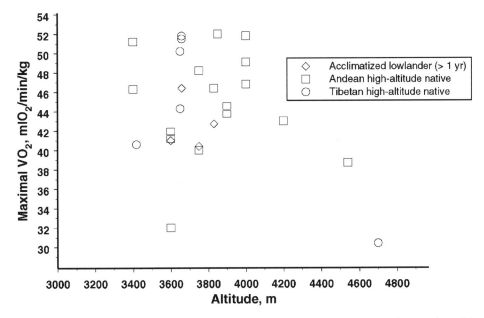

Figure 6   Scatterplot of published mean values of maximal physical work capacity with altitude above 3000 m. It is based on samples of ten or more men, natives or long-term residents with an average of more than a year at altitude, with an average age over 15 years. (Sources include Antezana et al 1992; Baker 1969; Brutsaert et al 2000; Frisancho 1995; Frisancho et al 1973; Ge et al 1995, 1994; Hochachka et al 1991; Huang et al 1992; Hurtado 1964; Kollias et al 1968; Maresh et al 1983; Mazess 1969a,b; Schoene et al 1990; Spielvogel et al 1996; Sun et al 1990; Weitz 1984.)

maximal physical work capacity than do acclimatized lowlanders. One study at 3700 m comparing Andean high-altitude natives with Europeans born and raised there found a 20% higher maximal physical work capacity (Brutsaert et al 1999). Another study at 3658 m comparing Tibetans with Han Chinese residents reported an 11% percent higher maximal physical work capacity (Sun et al 1990). These data and the information in Figure 6 suggest that Andean and Tibetan highlanders do not differ functionally as measured by maximal physical work capacity and that both have higher functionality than acclimatized lowlanders. A variety of factors have been suggested as important in determining the higher physical work capacity of the two indigenous populations, including larger lung volumes, higher ventilation during exercise, and greater pulmonary diffusing capacity (e.g., Schoene et al 1990, Sun et al 1990, Brutsaert et al 1999).

Birth weight is directly relevant to differential fertility and mortality. At sea level, birth weight is a classic example of stabilizing selection because infants with very low and very high birth weights have higher infant mortality, while those with intermediate birth weights have the best chance of surviving (Karn & Penrose 1951). A steady decrease in mean birth weight is proportional to altitude in the United States (Figure 7). Essentially all U.S. women are descended from low-altitude populations and therefore this represents the unacclimatized response. The birth weights of unacclimatized samples outside the United States are consistent. Birth weight is influenced by factors in addition to altitude. For example, the birth weight at 3100 m in Colorado rose to 3.2 kg in 1977–1978 from 2.7 kg in 1949–1951 (Cotton et al 1980, Lichty et al 1957). The existence of a secular trend toward higher birth weight in that site is a reminder of potential unmeasured influences on this and other traits. Andean and Tibetan babies' birth weights are generally higher than those of acclimatized babies at altitudes where there are samples from all populations. Comparative studies confirm that the indigenous Andean and Tibetan high-altitude native women give birth to heavier babies than do unacclimatized women (e.g., Moore et al 2001, Haas 1980). An analysis of covariance on the 35 samples above 3000 m controlled for altitude and tested for the effects of population. It found the Andean and Tibetan altitude-adjusted mean birth weights were 3.2 and 3.1 kg, respectively, as compared with 3.0 and 2.8 for U.S. and other populations, respectively ($F_{population} = 4.2$, $p < .05$). These data suggest that the Andean and Tibetan population have equal functional capacity as measured by birth weight.

Heavier babies are generally hypothesized to have an advantage for survival, although high mortality is associated with very high birth weight babies at both sea level and altitude (Karn & Penrose 1951, Beall 1981). Studies of factors associated with heavier birth weight have focused on two general aspects of oxygen transport in the fetus. One aspect was physiological adjustments during pregnancy that sustain arterial oxygen content, and another was blood flow to the uteroplacental unit. Unacclimatized populations of European women at 3100 m in Colorado and Han Chinese women in Lhasa, Tibet, apparently emphasize different aspects. Women in Colorado with higher arterial oxygen content during the third trimester of

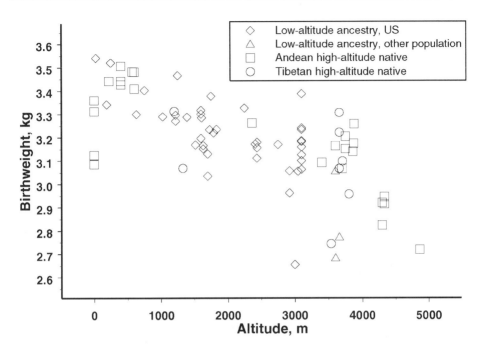

Figure 7 Scatterplot of published mean values of birth weight with altitude. It is based on samples of ten or more babies whose mothers were natives or long-term residents with an average of more than a year at altitude. (Sources include Beall 1981; Cotton et al 1980; Grahn & Kratchman 1963; Haas 1980; Haas et al 1977; Jensen & Moore 1997; Leibson et al 1989; Lichty et al 1957; Lubchenco et al 1963; Macedo-Dianderas 1966; McClung 1969; McCullough et al 1977; Moore et al 1990, 1986, 1984, 1982, 1980; Mortola et al 2000; Niermeyer et al 1995, 1993; Saco-Pollitt 1981; Smith 1997; Thilo et al 1991; Unger et al 1988; Usher & McLean 1969; Weinstein & Haas 1977; Wiley 1994; Yancey et al 1992; Yip 1987; Zamudio et al 1993.)

pregnancy gave birth to heavier babies. The higher arterial oxygen content was due to greater increase in ventilation, higher oxygen saturation, and hemoglobin concentration (Moore et al 1982b). However, among Han Chinese women in Tibet, ventilation, hemoglobin, and arterial oxygen content did not correlate with heavier babies, although oxygen saturation did (Moore et al 2001). The Han Chinese women who redistributed a larger proportion of blood flow from the common iliac artery to the uterus had heavier babies, whereas there was no association between measures of uterine blood flow and birth weight in Colorado (Zamudio et al 1995b). These findings suggest that there may not be a single unacclimatized response to high-altitude pregnancy, perhaps because of other biological or environmental influences. Among Andean high-altitude native women the increase in hypoxic ventilatory response over their non-pregnant values was the strongest correlate of birth weight. It probably acted to maintain ventilation, oxygen saturation, and arterial oxygen content, although these traits were not correlated with birth weight (Moore et al 1986a). Blood flow was not measured. Among Tibetan women, ventilation and hypoxic ventilatory response were associated with heavier birth weight, and there was no association with oxygen saturation, hemoglobin concentration, or arterial oxygen content, or with measures of utero-placental blood flow (Moore et al 2001). However, contrasting the sample of Tibetan women with the sample of Han Chinese women showed that, as a group, the Tibetan women had substantially lower arterial oxygen content and higher re-distribution of common iliac blood flow to the uterine artery. The conclusion was that the indigenous Tibetan population relied more on vascular and circulatory adjustments, and the result was heavier babies (Moore et al 2001).

Two costs associated with high-altitude pregnancy and birth are experienced by acclimatized Colorado women. There is an increased risk of pregnancy-associated hypertension, a condition associated with increased maternal and infant mortality and morbidity. One study reported a prevalence of 16% pregnancy-associated hypertension at 3100 m as compared with 3% at 1260 m (Palmer et al 1999). The high prevalence has been interpreted as the outcome of adaptations by some women that enhance maternal oxygen transport (such as hemoconcentration or a relatively low proportion of iliac artery blood flow redirected toward the uterine artery), but simultaneously predispose them to the risk of hypertension during pregnancy (Zamudio et al 1995a). Another possible cost is an increase in the prevalence of neonatal jaundice. One study reported a prevalence of 39% at 3100 m as compared with 16% at 1600 m (Leibson et al 1989). Jaundice is caused by high levels of a hemoglobin breakdown product, bilirubin, and is usually viewed as a disorder of transition from the intrauterine to the extrauterine environment. However, there is also the possibility that the high levels of bilirubin perform an antioxidant function during the neonatal period when antioxidant enzymes are not functionally mature (Brett & Niermeyer 1990).

Still another way to address the question of whether Tibetans are better adapted is to evaluate the overall costs of the two suites of traits. Currently, relevant data come only from the Andes, where there is a widely known syndrome called chronic mountain sickness (CMS). CMS is interpreted as a loss of adaptation in a previously adapted individual and is characterized by very low oxygen saturation, hypoven-tilation, very high hemoglobin concentration, and high pulmonary artery pressure (Winslow & Monge 1987). The risk factors are not known, although some studies suggest an increased risk with older age and higher BMI. It seems reasonable to hypothesize that healthy Andean highlanders at the low or high end of the dis-tribution of one or more of these traits are at increased risk; however, this has not been investigated. The question of costs associated with the Tibetan pattern of adaptation has simply not been considered. It seems reasonable to hypothesize that Tibetans at the low end of the hemoglobin and saturation distributions would have such low arterial oxygen content that function could be adversely affected. However, this has not been investigated.

Evidence for Natural Selection

The Andean-Tibetan population differences could have resulted from evolution by natural selection or may be maintained by natural selection. The question must be addressed indirectly because the genetic loci influencing these quantitative traits are not known. A starting point is the knowledge that natural selection requires genetic variance. The genotypes associated with these quantitative phenotypes are unknown; indirect analyses revealed Andean-Tibetan population contrasts with evolutionary implications. Quantitative genetics techniques analyze the phenotypic variation in a sample to evaluate the likelihood that genetic factors contribute to the variation. Quantitative genetic techniques are applied to continuously varying traits such as oxygen saturation that are probably influenced by more than one unknown locus and allele, as well as by individual characteristics such as age and sex and by environmental factors such as smoking. These techniques require fairly large data sets containing biological relatives and allow testing hypotheses about potential sources of phenotypic variance, including variance resulting from genetic factors. A frequently reported summary value is the heritability (h^2) calculated as the proportion of total phenotypic variance that is attributable to genetic relationships among relatives. Theoretically, heritability can assume values from zero to one—that is, from none to all of the phenotypic variance being attributable to genetic factors. Heritabilities are specific to the population from which the sample was drawn, just as estimates of the mean are specific to the population from which the sample was drawn. Heritability values do not provide information about mean values.

Table 1 presents the heritability, calculated as the genetic variance divided by (1-variance due to covariates) of six traits. Andean and Tibetan populations have similar, moderate heritabilities for two traits, body mass index and systolic blood pressure, which are unrelated to oxygen transport and included for reference. There are interesting population contrasts for the oxygen transport traits.

TABLE 1 Comparison of heritability (h^2) estimates in two high-altitude populations

Trait	Andean h^2	Tibetan h^2
Body mass index (BMI)	0.42	0.34
Systolic blood pressure	0.17	0.25
Oxygen saturation	ns[a]	0.40, major gene
Resting ventilation	ns	0.32
Hypoxic ventilatory response	0.22	0.35
Hemoglobin concentration	0.89	0.64

[a]ns = not significant

Hemoglobin concentration is the trait with by far the greatest potential for natural selection in both samples and particularly so in the Andean. There is no information on the Darwinian fitness of people with different hemoglobin concentrations to address the hypothesis of either directional selection or stabilizing selection in either population. It is noteworthy that oxygen saturation and resting ventilation had no significant genetic variance in the Andean sample. A major gene is an inferred allele with a large quantitative effect at a segregating autosomal locus (Weiss 1993). The major gene for oxygen saturation detected in Tibetan samples from 3850 to 4065 m and 4850 to 5450 m has the effect of conferring a 5%–6% higher saturation (Beall et al 1997c, Beall et al 1994). For example, at 4000 m some genotypes average 88.5% oxygen saturation, while others average just 83% saturation. That is, those individuals have less arterial hypoxia despite living in the same ambient hypoxia. Because it seems likely that higher oxygen saturation would be beneficial, these findings suggest the hypothesis that higher oxygen saturation is associated with higher fertility or lower mortality among Tibetans. The chromosomal location of the gene and the biochemical nature of the inferred alleles remain unknown. Both populations have moderate heritability for HVR.

The absence of genetic variance in oxygen saturation and resting ventilation in the Andean sample has implications for ongoing natural selection because natural selection requires genetic variance, and therefore there is no potential for natural selection to act on this trait in the Andean sample. It is unusual for a trait simply to lack genetic variance. The absence of genetic variance does not mean that genetic factors have no influence on this trait—it means that variance in the trait is not accounted for by genetic factors. Perhaps there is actually no genetic variance (the population is at or near fixation for relevant allele) or perhaps some other genetic or environmental factor prevents its expression. The reduction in population size after the Spanish Conquest would be expected to affect all traits and not just the oxygen transport traits. The reduction therefore seems unlikely to account for the absence of genetic variance of some traits in the Andean sample. Currently, there is no information to evaluate these alternative hypotheses.

Another approach to identifying the existence of genetic influences confirmed the existence of genetic influences on resting ventilation and HVR with a study of the offspring of Tibetan mothers and Han Chinese fathers. The offspring resembled Tibetans in having high ventilation and Han Chinese in having low HVR (Curran et al 1997). The authors suggested that the traits may be simple Mendelian traits or could be mitochondrially influenced because the offspring were not intermediate between the two parental populations.

To address the question of genetic adaptation, it will be essential to expand to new phenotypes and to expand analyses to incorporate more levels of biological organization. In particular, it will be important to integrate understanding of physiological phenotypes and genetic variance with cellular, molecular, and genetic information. A promising avenue of research involves the dozens of genetic loci regulated by the transcription factor called HIF-1 (hypoxic inducible factor one) (Semenza 2000, Guillemin & Krasnow 1997). HIF-1 is expressed in response to hypoxia in a wide range of cells and initiates the transcription of genes relevant to many of the traits we have considered here. For example, HIF-1 activates the transcription of the tyrosine hydroxylase gene, which catalyzes the synthesis of the neurotransmitter, dopamine, that underlies the increase in breathing. HIF-1 activates the transcription of the erythropoietin gene, which underlies the increase in hemoglobin concentration. HIF-1 also activates the transcription of many other genes that produce measurable gene products, and these would be appropriate for studies of adaptation to high-altitude hypoxia.

SUMMARY AND CONCLUSIONS

There are contrasts between Andeans and Tibetans in the mean values of a number of physiological traits associated with offsetting the stress of high-altitude hypoxia. These include resting ventilation, hypoxic ventilatory response, hemoglobin concentration, and perhaps oxygen saturation and hypoxic pulmonary vasoconstriction.

No consistent pattern appeared of high-altitude natives either retaining or modifying the ancestral or unselected responses to hypoxia, as expressed upon acute exposure or maintained during years of acclimatization to high altitude. Both patterns were found. Acclimatized lowlanders retain indefinitely the low oxygen saturation and the hypoxic pulmonary vasoconstriction, but not the elevated ventilation and HVR of the acutely exposed. Andean high-altitude natives appear quantitatively similar to acclimatized lowlanders in these traits. Compared with Andean high-altitude natives, Tibetans differ quantitatively from acclimatized lowlanders in more traits. At first glance that might suggest the absence of the action of natural selection in the Andean population. However, quantitatively similar phenotypes do not necessarily result from the same mechanisms. High hemoglobin concentration is due to hemoconcentration during early exposure and to erythropoiesis during acclimatization. The blunted hypoxic ventilatory response apparently is acquired after the age of ten years among acclimatized Europeans in Colorado, but before the age of eight years among Andean high-altitude natives. Paradoxically, the pattern of contrasts in these traits does not seem to affect the functional measures evaluated so far. The Andean and the Tibetan samples both have better function than acclimatized lowlanders when evaluated on the basis of physical work capacity and birth weight. It seems likely that other, so far unmeasured, traits account for the better function and also suggests that perhaps other measures of function would be informative. Thus, it is not clear whether the Tibetan changes from the ancestral response are changes in the direction of improved adaptation or are just change. Tibetans had higher genetic variance than Andean highlanders on all the oxygen transport traits, which indicates generally greater potential for natural selection. Hemoglobin concentration and oxygen saturation seem most tractable for future study owing to the very high heritability in both populations and the major gene among Tibetans.

From the standpoint of seeking to explain how and why Andean and Tibetan highlanders have diverged, there are interesting implications of the wide variation within samples of acutely exposed lowlanders and among acclimatized samples, i.e., the samples expressing phenotypes that were not selected for response to chronic hypoxia. For example, samples from the acutely exposed express variation in the degree of desaturation, the degree of hypoxic vasoconstriction, and the degree of increased ventilation. The samples from acclimatized subjects from Colorado, Bolivia, and the Tibet Autonomous Region exhibit variation in traits such as oxygen saturation during early life and physiological adjustments to pregnancy. If similar variations occurred during the separate colonizations of the Andean and Tibetan Plateaus, and if there were a genetic basis to the variation, then chance events could have influenced the characteristics of the founder populations and initiated the phenotypic divergence seen today. It is also significant that population contrasts may differ depending upon the stage of the life cycle. For example, Han Chinese infants had dramatically lower oxygen saturation than Tibetan infants, although adults from the two populations differed little in oxygen saturation. Natural selection may vary in force throughout the life cycle, and its action in the ancestral colonizing populations may have varied depending upon their age structure.

Understanding the evolutionary basis of the Andean and Tibetan phenotypes will require developing an understanding of the relationships between phenotypes and genotypes as well as expanding efforts to include newly identified, relevant phenotypes. This effort will require understanding the sociocultural and behavioral factors such as smoking, nutritional status, and rural-urban residence that influence these traits. While humans cannot adapt culturally to create a nonhypoxic microclimate, many sociocultural and behavioral factors can influence expression of oxygen transport traits. There is self-selection among subjects staying at altitude and being available for participating in study. Furthermore, nowadays humans can adapt culturally to create at least temporarily nonhypoxic microclimates. For example, supplemental oxygen is provided immediately to newborns at high altitude in Colorado, and oxygen enrichment can be provided to acutely exposed high-altitude workers. These are potential confounding factors for future comparative studies.

To understand past and present evolutionary processes in the two populations, it will be necessary to have reliable archaeological information on the time of occupation of both plateaus and genetic information on the likely source of the early colonizers and their relationship to present-day inhabitants. It will be necessary to understand the relationship between the measured phenotypes and the underlying genotypes, and new phenotypes will need to be identified. High-altitude environments and their resident and indigenous populations will continue to provide an informative natural laboratory for questions about human evolution and adaptation, which will require input from archaeologists and cultural and physical anthropologists.

Visit the Annual Reviews home page at www.AnnualReviews.org

LITERATURE CITED

Albrecht PH, Littell JK. 1972. Plasma erythropoietin in men and mice during acclimatization to different altitudes. *J. Appl. Physiol.* 32:54–8

Adams WH, Shresta SM. 1974. Hemoglobin levels, vitamin B12, and folate status in a Himalayan village. *Am. J. Clin. Nutr.* 27:217–19

Adams WH, Strang LJ. 1975. Hemoglobin levels in persons of Tibetan ancestry living at high altitude (38,952). *Proc. Soc. Exp. Biol. Med.* 149:1036–39

Aldenderfer M. 1999. The Pleistocene/Holocene transition in Peru and its effects upon human use of the landscape. *Quat. Int.* 53/54: 11–19

Antezana AM, Rechalet JP, Antezana G, Spielvogel H, Kacimi R. 1992. Adrenergic system in high altitude residents. *Int. J. Sports Med.* 13:S96–100

Antezana A-M, Kacimi R, Le Trong J-L, Marchal M, Abousahl I, et al. 1994. Adrenergic status of humans during prolonged exposure to the altitude of 6,542 m. *J. Appl. Physiol.* 76:1055–59

Arnaud J, Quilici JC, Riviere G. 1981. High-altitude hematology: Quechua-Aymara comparisons. *Ann. Hum. Biol.* 8:573–78

Baker PT. 1969. Human adaptation to high altitude. *Science* 163:1149–56

Banchero N, Sime F, Penaloza D, Cruz J, Gamboa R, Marticorena E. 1966. Pulmonary pressure, cardiac output, and arterial oxygen saturation during exercise at high altitude and at sea level. *Circulation* 33:249–62

Beall C. 2000a. Tibetan and Andean patterns of adaptation to high-altitude hypoxia. *Hum. Biol.* 72:201–28

Beall C, Worthman CM, Stallings J. 1999a. Oxygen saturation and the response to submaximal exercise among Tibetans at 3900 m. (Abstr.). *Am. J. Phys. Anthropol.* 28:88–89 (Suppl.)

Beall CM, Reichsman AB. 1984. Hemoglobin levels in a Himalayan high altitude population. *Am. J. Phys. Anthr.* 63:301–6

Beall CM. 1981. Optimal birthweights in Peruvian populations at high and low altitudes. *Am. J. Phys. Anthropol.* 56:209–16

Beall CM. 2000b. Oxygen saturation increases during childhood and decreases during adulthood among high altitude native Tibetans residing at 3800–4200 m. *High Altitude Med. Biol.* 1:25–32

Beall CM, Almasy LA, Blangero J, Williams-Blangero S, Brittenham GM, et al. 1999b. Percent of oxygen saturation of arterial hemoglobin of Bolivian Aymara at 3900–4000 m. *Am. J. Phys. Anthropol.* 108:41–51

Beall CM, Blangero J, Williams-Blangero S, Goldstein MC. 1994. A major gene for percent of oxygen saturation of arterial hemoglobin in Tibetan highlanders. *Am. J. Phys. Anthropol.* 95:271–76

Beall CM, Brittenham GM, Macuaga F, Barragan M. 1990. Variation in hemoglobin concentration among samples of high-altitude natives in the Andes and the Himalayas. *Am. J. Hum. Biol.* 2:639–51

Beall CM, Brittenham GM, Strohl KP, Blangero J, Williams-Blangero S, et al. 1997a. Ventilation and hypoxic ventilatory response of Tibetan and Aymara high altitude natives. *Am. J. Phys. Anthropol.* 104:427–47

Beall CM, Brittenham GM, Strohl KP, Blangero J, Williams-Blangero S, et al. 1998. Hemoglobin concentration of high-altitude Tibetans and Bolivian Aymara. *Am. J. Phys. Anthropol.* 106:385–400

Beall CM, Brittenham GM, Strohl KP, Decker MJ, Goldstein MC, et al. 1997b. Ventilation and hypoxic ventilatory response of Tibetan and Aymara high altitude natives. *Am. J. Phys. Anthropol.* 104:427–47

Beall CM, Goldstein MC. 1990. Hemoglobin concentration, percent oxygen saturation and arterial oxygen content of Tibetan nomads at 4,850 to 5,450 M. In *Hypoxia: The Adaptations*, ed. JR Sutton, G Coates, JE Remmers, pp. 59–65. Toronto: Decker

Beall CM, Goldstein MC, The Tibetan Academy of Social Sciences. 1987. Hemoglobin concentration of pastoral nomads permanently resident at 4,850–5,450 meters in Tibet. *Am. J. Phys. Anthropol.* 73:433–38

Beall CM, Reichsman AB. 1984. Hemoglobin levels in a Himalayan high altitude population. *Am. J. Phys. Anthropol.* 63:301–6

Beall CM, Strohl K, Blangero J, Williams-Blangero S, Brittenham GM, Goldstein MC. 1997c. Quantitative genetic analysis of arterial oxygen saturation in Tibetan highlanders. *Hum. Biol.* 69:597–604

Beall CM, Strohl KP, Gothe B, Brittenham GM, Barragan M, Vargas E. 1992a. Respiratory and hematological adaptations of young and older Aymara men native to 3600 m. *Am. J. Hum. Biol.* 4:17–26

Beall CM, Worthman CM, Stallings J, Strohl KP, Brittenham GM, Barragan M. 1992b. Salivary testosterone concentration of Aymara men native to 3600 m. *Ann. Hum. Biol.* 19:67–78

Berger J, Aguaya VM, San Miguel JL, Lujan L, Tellez W, Traissac P. 1997. Definition and prevalence of anemia in Bolivian women of childbearing age living at high altitudes: the effect of iron-folate supplementation. *Nutr. Rev.* 55:247–56

Bharadwaj H, Singh AP, Malhotra MS. 1973. Body composition of the high altitude natives of Ladakh: a comparison with sea level residents. *Hum. Biol.* 45:423–34

Boning D, Maassen N, Jochum F, Steinacker J, Halder A, et al. 1996. After-effects of a high altitude expedition on blood. *Int. J. Sport Med.* 18:179–85

Braun B, Mawson J, Muza S, Dominick S, Brooks G, et al. 2000. Women at altitude: carbohydrate utilization during exercise at 4,300 m. *J. Appl. Physiol.* 88:246–56

Brett JA, Niermeyer S. 1990. Neonatal jaundice: a disorder of transition or an adaptive process? *Med. Anthropol.* 4:149–61

Brutsaert TD, Araoz M, Soria R, Spielvoge H, Haas JE. 2000. Higher arterial oxygen saturation during submaximal exercise in Bolivian Aymara compared to European sojourners and Europeans born and raised at high altitude. *Am. J. Phys. Anthropol.* 113:169–82

Brutsaert TD, Spielvogel H, Soria R, Caceres E, Buzenet G, Haas JD. 1999. Effect of developmental and ancestral high altitude exposure to VO$_2$ peak of Andean and European/North American natives. *J. Appl. Physiol.* 110:435–55

Busch T, Bartsch P, Pappert D, Grunig E, Hildebrandt W, et al. 2001. Hypoxia decreases exhaled nitric oxide in mountaineers susceptible to high altitude pulmonary edema. *Am. J. Respir. Crit. Care Med.* 163:368–73

Byrne-Quinn E, Sodal IE, Weil JV. 1972. Hypoxic and hypercapnic ventilatory drives in children native to high altitude. *J. Appl. Physiol.* 32:44–46

Carpenter TC, Niermeyer S, Durmowicz AG. 1998. Altitude-related illness in children. *Curr. Probl. Pediatr.* 28:181–98

Chang K-C. 1992. China. In *Chronologies in Old World Archaeology*, ed. RW Ehrich, Chicago/London: Univ. Chicago Press. 3rd ed.

Chen Q-H, Ge R-L, Wang X-Z, Chen H-X, Wu T-Y, et al. 1997. Exercise performance of Tibetan and Han adolescents at altitudes of 3,417 and 4,300 m. *J. Appl. Physiol.* 83:661–67

Cosio G. 1972. Características hemáticas y cardiopulmonares del minero Andino. *Boloficina Sanit. Panam.* 72:547–57

Cotes PM, Dore CJ, Yin JAL, Lewis SM, Messinezy M, et al. 1986. Determination of serum immunoreactive erythropoietin in the investigation of erythrocytosis. *New Engl. J. Med.* 315:283–87

Cotton FK, Hiestand M, Philbin GE, Simmons M. 1980. Re-evaluation of birth weights at high altitude. *Am. J. Obstet. Gynecol.* 138:220–22

Cudkowicz L, Spielvogel H, Zubieta G. 1972. Respiratory studies in women at high altitude

(3,600 m or 12,200 ft and 5,200 m or 17,200 ft). *Respiration* 29:393–426

Curran L, Zhuang J, Sun SF, Moore LG. 1997. Ventilation and hypoxic ventilatory responsiveness in Chinese-Tibetan residents at 3,658 m. *J. Appl. Physiol.* 83:2098–104

Curran LS, Zhuang J, Droma T, Land L, Moore LG. 1995. Hypoxic ventilatory responses in Tibetan residents of 4400 m compared with 3658 m. *Respir. Physiol.* 100:223–30

Decker MJ, Redline S, Arnold JL, Masny J, Strohl KP. 1991. Normative values of oxygen saturation over time. *Ambul. Monit.* 4:297–304

Droma T, McCullough RS, McCullough RE, Zhuan J, Cymerman A, et al. 1991. Increased vital and total lung capacities in Tibetan compared to Han residents of Lhasa (3,658 m). *Am. J. Phys. Anthropol.* 86:341–51

Duplain H, Sartori C, Lepori M, Egli M, Allemann Y, et al. 2000. Exhaled nitric oxide in high altitude pulmonary edema. *Am. J. Crit. Care Med.* 162:221–24

Dweik RA, Laskowski D, Abu-Soud HM, Kaneko FT, Hutte R, Stuehr DJ. 1998. Nitric oxide synthesis in the lung: regulation by oxygen through a kinetic mechanism. *J. Clin. Invest.* 101:660–66

Eaton JW, Brewer GJ, Grover RF. 1969. Role of red cell 2,3-diphosphoglycerate in the adaptation of man to altitude. *J. Lab. Clin. Med.* 73:603–11

Favier R, Spielvogel H, Desplanches D, Ferretti G, Kayser B, Hoppeler H. 1995. Maximal exercise performance in chronic hypoxia and acute normoxia in high-altitude natives. *J. Appl. Physiol.* 78:1868–74

Filuk RB, Berezanski DJ, Anthonisen NR. 1988. Depression of hypoxic ventilatory response in humans by somatostatin. *J. Appl. Physiol.* 65:1050–54

Frappell PB, Leon-Velarde F, Aguero L, Mortola JP. 1998. Response to cooling temperature in infants born at altitude of 4,330 meters. *Am. J. Respir. Crit. Care Med.* 158:1751–56

Frisancho AR. 1975. Functional adaptation

to high altitude hypoxia. *Science* 187:313–19

Frisancho AR, Frisancho HG, Milotich M, Brutsaert T, Albalak R, et al. 1995. Developmental, genetic, and environmental components of aerobic capacity at high altitude. *Am. J. Phys. Anthropol.* 96:431–42

Frisancho AR, Martinez C, Velasquez T, Sanchez J, Montoye H. 1973. Influence of developmental adaptation on aerobic capacity at high altitude. *J. Appl. Physiol.* 34:176–80

Frisancho AR. 1999. Developmental components of resting ventilation among high and low altitude Andean children and adults. *Am. J. Phys. Anthropol.* 109:295–301

Gamboa R, Marticorena E. 1971. Presión arterial pulmonar en el recien nacido en las grandes alturas. *Arch. Inst. Biol. Andina* 4:55–66

Gamboa R, Marticorena E. 1972. The ductus arteriosus in the newborn infant at high altitude. *VASA* 1:192–95

Garruto RM. 1976. Hematology. In *Man in the Andes. A Multidisciplinary Study of High-Altitude Quechua,* ed. PT Baker, MA Little, pp. 261–82. Stroudsburg, PA: Dowden, Hutchinson & Ross

Garruto RM, Dutt JS. 1983. Lack of prominent compensatory polycythemia in traditional native Andeans living at 4,200 meters. *Am. J. Phys. Anthro.* 61:355–66

Ge R, He Lun G, Chen Q, Li HL, Gen D, et al. 1995. Comparisons of oxygen transport between Tibetan and Han residents at moderate altitude. *Wilderness Environ. Med.* 6:391–400

Ge R-L, Chen Q-H, Wang L-H, Gen D, Yang P, et al. 1994. Higher exercise performance and lower VO_{2max} in Tibetan than Han residents at 4,700 meters altitude. *Am J. Appl. Physiol.* 77:684–91

Georgopoulos D, Walker S, Anthonisen NR. 1989. Increased chemoreceptor output and ventilatory response to sustained hypoxia. *J. Appl. Physiol.* 67:1157–63

Grahn D, Kratchman J. 1963. Variation in neonatal death rate and birth weight in the

United States and possible relations to environmental radiation, geology and altitude. *Am. J. Hum. Genet.* 15:329–52

Grover RF, Vogel JHK, Averill KH, Blount SG. 1963. Pulmonary hypertension. Individual and species variability relative to vascular reactivity. *Am. Heart J.* 66:1–3

Grover RF, Selland MA, McCullough RG, Dahms TE, Wolfel EE, et al. 1998. B-Adrenergic blockade does not prevent polycythemia or decrease in plasma volume in men at 4300 meters altitude. *Eur. J. Appl. Physiol.* 77:264–70

Groves BM, Droma T, Sutton JR, McCullough RG, Cullough REM, et al. 1993. Minimal hypoxic pulmonary hypertension in normal Tibetans at 3,658 meters. *J. Appl. Physiol.* 74:312–18

Guillemin K, Krasnow MA. 1997. The hypoxic response: huffing and HIFing. *Cell* 89:9–12

Guleria JS, Pande JN, Sethi PK, Roy SB. 1971. Pulmonary diffusing capacity at high altitude. *J. Appl. Physiol.* 31:536–43

Gupta ML, Rao KS, Anand IS, Banerjee AK, Boparai MS. 1992. Lack of smooth muscle in the small pulmonary arteries of native Ladakhi: Is the Himalayan highlander adapted? *Am. J. Respir. Crit. Care Med.* 145: 1201–4

Haas JD. 1980. Maternal adaptation and fetal growth at high altitude in Bolivia. In *Social and Biological Predictors of Nutritional Status, Physical Growth, and Neurological Development*, ed. LS Greene, FE Johnston, pp. 257–90. New York/London: Academic

Haas JD, Baker PT, Hunt EE. 1977. The effects of high altitude on body size and composition of the newborn infant in southern Peru. *Hum. Biol.* 49:611–28

Hackett PH, Reeves JT, Reeves CD, Grover RF, Rennie D. 1980. Control of breathing in Sherpas at low and high altitude. *J. Appl. Physiol.* 49:374–79

Harris P. 1986. Evolution, hypoxia and high altitude. In *Aspects of Hypoxia*, ed. D Heath, pp. 207–16. Liverpool, UK: Liverpool Univ. Press

Hartley LH, Alexander JK, Modelski M,

Grover RF. 1967. Subnormal cardiac output at rest and during exercise in residents at 3,100 meters altitude. *J. Appl. Physiol.* 23:839–48

Heath D, Williams DR. 1989. *High-Altitude Medicine and Pathology*. London: Butterworths

Hillman RS. 1995. Acute blood loss anemia. In *Hematology*, ed. E Beutler, MA Lichtman, BS Coller, TJ Kipps, pp. 704–8. New York: McGraw-Hill. 3rd ed.

Hochachka PW. 1998. Mechanism and evolution of hypoxia-tolerance in humans. *J. Exp. Biol.* 201:1243–54

Hochachka PW, Monge CC. 2000. Evolution of human hypoxia tolerance physiology. In *Oxygen Sensing: Molecule to Man*, ed. S Lahiri, NR Prabhakar, RE Forster II, pp. 25–44. New York: Kluwer Academic/Plenum

Hochachka PW, Stanley C, Matheson GO, McKenzie DC, Allen PS, Parkhouse WS. 1991. Metabolic and work efficiencies during exercise in Andean natives. *J. Appl. Physiol.* 70:1720–30

Holtby SG, Berezanski DJ, Anthonisen NR. 1988. Effect of 100% O_2 on hypoxic eucapnic ventilation. *J. Appl. Physiol.* 65:1157–62

Huang SY, Alexander JK, Grover RF, Maher JT, McCullough RE, et al. 1984a. Hypocapnia and sustained hypoxia blunt ventilation on arrival at high altitude. *J. Appl. Physiol.* 56:602–6

Huang SY, Alexander JK, Grover RF, Maher JT, McCullough RE, et al. 1984b. Increased metabolism contributes to increased resting ventilation at high altitude. *Respir. Physiol.* 57:377–85

Huang SY, Sun S, Droma T, Zhuang J, Tao JX, et al. 1992. Internal carotid arterial flow velocity during exercise in Tibetan and Han residents of Lhasa (3,658 m). *J. Appl. Physiol.* 73:2638–42

Huang SY, White DP, Douglas NJ, Moore LG, McCullough RE, et al. 1984c. Respiratory function in normal Chinese: comparison with Caucasians. *Respiration* 46:265–71

Hultgren HN, Kelly J, Miller H. 1965a. Effect of oxygen upon pulmonary circulation in acclimatized man at high altitude. *J. Appl. Physiol.* 20:239–43

Hultgren HN, Kelly J, Miller H. 1965b. Pulmonary circulation in acclimatized man at high altitude. *J. Appl. Physiol.* 20:233–38

Hurtado A. 1964. Animals in high altitudes: resident man. In *Handbook of Physiology. Section 4: Adaptation to the Environment*, ed. DB Dill, pp. 843–59. Washington, DC: Am. Physiol. Soc.

Hurtado A, Merino C, Delgado E. 1945. Influence of anoxemia on the hemopoietic activity. *Arch. Int. Med.* 75:284–324

Jansen GF, Krins A, Basnyat B. 1999. Cerebral vasomotor reactivity at high altitude in humans. *J. Appl. Physiol.* 86:681–86

Jensen GM, Moore LG. 1997. The effect of high altitude and other risk factors on birth weight: independent or interactive effects. *Am. J. Public Health* 87:1003–7

Karn M, Penrose L. 1951. Birth weight and gestation time in relation to maternal age parity and infant survival. *Ann. Eugenics* 16:147–64

Kashiwazaki H, Suzuki T, Takemoto T-I. 1988. Altitude and reproduction of the Japanese in Bolivia. *Hum. Biol.* 60:831–45

Khan Q, Heath D, Smith P, Norboo T. 1988. The histology of the carotid bodies in highlanders from Ladakh. *Int. J. Biometeorol.* 32:254–59

Kollias J, Buskirk ER, Akers RF, Prokop EK, Baker PT, Picon-Reategui E. 1968. Work capacity of long-time residents and newcomers to altitude. *J. Appl. Physiol.* 24:792–9

Kryger M, McCullough R, Doekel R, Collins D, Weil JV, Grover RF. 1978. Excessive polycythemia of high altitude: role of ventilatory drive and lung disease. *Am. Rev. Respir. Dis.* 118:659–67

Lahiri S, Delaney RG, Brody JS, Simpser M, Velasquez T, Motoyama EK, Polgar C. 1976. Relative role of environmental and genetic factors in respiratory adaptation to high altitude. *Nature* 261:133–35

Larrick JW, Topgyal S. 1985. Hemoglobin levels in high altitude Tibetan natives of northwest Nepal. *Int. J. Biometeor.* 29:7–10

Lawler J, Powers SK, Thompson D. 1988. Linear relationship between VO_2 max and VO_{2max} decrement during exposure to acute hypoxia. *J. Appl. Physiol.* 64:1486–92

Leibson C, Brown M, Thibodeau S, Stevenson D, Vreman H, Cohen R, Clemons G, Callen W, Moore LG. 1989. Neonatal hyperbilirubinemia at high altitude. *Am. J. Dis. Child.* 143:983–87

Leon-Velarde F, Arregui A, Vargas M, Huicho L, Acosta R. 1994. Chronic mountain sickness and chronic lower respiratory tract disorders. *Chest* 106:151–55

Leon-Velarde F, Monge CC, Vidal A, Carcagno M, Criscuolo M, Bozzini CE. 1991. Serum immunoreactive erythropoietin in high altitude natives with and without excessive erythrocytosis. *Exp. Hematol.* 19:257–60

Leon-Velarde F, Ramos MA, Hernandez JA, de Idiaquez D, Munoz LS, et al 1997. The role of menopause in the development of chronic mountain sickness. *J. Appl. Physiol.* 272:R90–94

Lichty JA, Ting RY, Bruns PD, Dyar E. 1957. Studies of babies born at high altitude. *Am. J. Dis. Child.* 93:666–77

Lindgarde F, Lilljekvist R. 1984. Failure of long-term acclimatization in smokers moving to high altitude. *Acta Med. Scand.* 216:317–22

Littner M, Young E, McGinty D, Beahm E, Riege W, Sowers J. 1984. Awake abnormalities of control of breathing and of the upper airway occurrence in healthy older men with nocturnal disordered breathing. *Chest* 86:573–79

Lockhart A, Zelter M, Mensch-Dechene J, Antezana G, Paz-Zamora M, et al. 1976. Pressure-flow-volume relationships in pulmonary circulation of normal highlanders. *J. Appl. Physiol.* 41:449–56

Lubchenco LO, Hansman C, Dressler M, Boyd E. 1963. Intrauterine growth as estimated from liveborn birth weight data at 24 to 42 weeks of gestation. *Pediatrics* 32:793–800

Marcus CL, Glomb WB, Basinski DJ, Ward

SLD, Keens TG. 1994. Developmental pattern of hypercapnic and hypoxic ventilatory responses from childhood to adulthood. *J. Appl. Physiol.* 76:314–20

Marc-Vergnes J, Antezana G, Coudert J, Gourdin D, Durand J. 1974. Débit sangin et métabolisme énergetique du cerveau et équilibre acido-basique du liquide céphalo-rachidien chez les résidents en altitude. *J. Physiol. Paris* 68:633–54

Maresh CM, Noble BJ, Robertson KL, Sime WE. 1983. Maximal exercise during hypobaric hypoxia (557 Torr) in moderate-altitude natives. *Med. Sci. Sports Exerc.* 15:360–35

Mazess RB. 1969a. Exercise performance at high altitude in Peru. *Fed. Proc.* 28:1301–6

Mazess RB. 1969b. Exercise performance of Indian and White high altitude residents. *Hum. Biol.* 41:494–518

Mazzeo RS, Bender PR, Brooks GA, Butterfield GE, Groves BM, et al. 1991. Arterial catecholamine responses during exercise with acute and chronic high altitude exposure. *J. Appl. Physiol.* 261:E419–24

McClung J. 1969. *Effects of High Altitude on Human Birth. Observations on Mothers, Placentas, and the Newborn in Two Peruvian Populations.* Cambridge, MA: Harvard Univ. Press

McCullough RE, Reeves JT, Liljegren RL. 1977. Fetal growth retardation and increased infant mortality at high altitude. *Arch. Environ. Health* 32:36–39

Miao C-Y, Zuberbuhler JS, Zuberbuhler JR. 1988. Prevalence of congenital cardiac anomalies at high altitude. *JACC* 12:224–28

Milledge JS, Cotes PM. 1985. Serum erythropoietin in humans at high altitude and its relation to plasma renin. *J. Appl. Physiol.* 59:360–64

Miyachi M, Shibayama H. 1992. Ventilatory capacity and exercise-induced arterial desaturation of highly trained endurance athletes. *Ann. Physiol. Anthropol.* 11:263–67

Moore LG. 1982a. The incidence of pregnancy induced hypertension is increasing among Colorado residents. *Am. J. Obstet. Gynecol.* 144:123–29

Moore LG. 1990. Maternal O_2 transport and fetal growth in Colorado, Peru and Tibet high-altitude residents. *Am. J. Hum. Biol.* 2:627–37

Moore LG, Brodeur P, Chumbe O, D'Brot J, Hofmeister S, Monge C. 1986a. Maternal hypoxic ventilatory response, ventilation, and infant birth weight at 4,300 m. *J. Appl. Physiol.* 60:1401–6

Moore LG, Curran-Everett L, Droma TS, Groves BM, McCullough RE, et al. 1992. Are Tibetans better adapted? *Int. J. Sport Med.* 13:S86–88

Moore LG, Cymerman A, Huang S, McCullough RE, McCullough RG, et al. 1987a. Propranolol blocks metabolic rate increase but not ventilatory acclimatization to 4300 m. *Respir. Physiol.* 70:195–204

Moore LG, Harrison GL, McCullough RE, Micco AJ, Tucker A, et al. 1986b. Low acute hypoxic ventilatory response and hypoxic depression in acute altitude sickness. *J. Appl. Physiol.* 60:1407–12

Moore LG, Huang SY, McCullough RE, Sampson JB, Maher JT, et al. 1984a. Variable inhibition by falling CO_2 of hypoxic ventilatory response in humans. *J. Appl. Physiol.* 56:207–10

Moore LG, Jahnigen D, Rounds SS, Reeves JT, Grover RF. 1982a. Maternal hyperventilation helps preserve arterial oxygenation during high altitude pregnancy. *J. Appl. Physiol.* 52:690–94

Moore LG, McCullough RE, Weil JV. 1987b. Increased HVR in pregnancy: relationship to hormonal and metabolic changes. *J. Appl. Physiol.* 62:158–63

Moore LG, Newberry MA, Freeby GM, Crnic LS. 1984b. Increased incidence of neonatal hyperbilirubinemia at 3,100 m in Colorado. *Am. J. Dis. Child.* 138:157–61

Moore LG, Niermeyer S, Zamudio S. 1998. Human adaptation to high altitude: regional and life cycle perspectives. *Yearb. Phys. Anthropol.* 41:25–64

Moore LG, Rounds SS, Jahnigen D, Grover RF, Reeves JT. 1982b. Infant birth weight is related to maternal arterial oxygenation at high altitude. *J. Appl. Physiol.* 52:695–99

Moore LG, Zamudio S, Zhuang J, Sun S, Droma T. 2001. Oxygen transport in Tibetan women during pregnancy at 3,658 m. *Am. J. Phys. Anthropol.* 114:42–53

Moreno-Black G, Quinn V, Haas J, Franklin J, Beard J. 1984. The distribution of hemoglobin concentration in a sample of native high altitude women. *Ann. Hum. Biol.* 11:317–25

Moret P, Covarrubias E, Coudert J, Duchosal F. 1972. Cardiocirculation adaptation to chronic hypoxia: III. Comparative study of cardiac output, pulmonary and systematic circulation between sea level and high altitude residents. *Extr. Acta Cardiol.* 27:596–619

Morpurgo G, Battaglia P, Carter ND, Modiano G, Passi S. 1972. The Bohr effect and the red cell 2-3 DPG and Hb content in Sherpas and Europeans at low and at high altitude. *Experientia* 28:1280–83

Mortola JP, Frappell PB, Frappell DE, Villena-Cabrera N, Villena-Cabrera M, Pena F. 1992. Ventilation and gaseous metabolism in infants born at high altitude, and their responses to hyperoxia. *Am. Rev. Respir. Dis.* 148:1206–9

Mortola JP, Rezzonico R, Fisher JT, Villena-Cabrera N, Vargas E, et al. 1990. Compliance of the respiratory system in infants born at high altitude. *Am. Rev. Respir. Dis.* 142:43–48

Niermeyer S, Shaffer E, Thilo E, Corbin C, Moore LG. 1993. Arterial oxygenation and pulmonary arterial pressure in healthy neonates and infants at high altitude. *J. Ped.* 123:767–72

Niermeyer S, Yang P, Drolkar S, Shanmina, Zhuang J, Moore L. 1995. Arterial oxygen saturation in Tibetan and Han infants born in Lhasa, Tibet. *New Engl. J. Med.* 333:1248–52

Nishimura M, Suzuki A, Nishimura Y, Yamamoto H, Miyamoto K, et al. 1987. Effect of brain blood flow on hypoxic ventilatory response in humans. *J. Appl. Physiol.* 63:1100–6

Okin JT, Treger A, Overy HR, Weil JV, Grover RF. 1966. Hematologic response to medium altitude. *Rocky Mount. Med. J.* 63:44–47

Palmer S, Moore L, Young D, Cregger B, Berman J, Zamudio S. 1999. Altered blood pressure course during normal pregnancy and increased preeclampsia at high altitude (3100 meters) in Colorado. *Am. J. Obstet. Gynecol.* 180:1161–8

Penaloza D, Sime F, Banchero N, Gamboa R, Cruz J, Marticorena E. 1963. Pulmonary hypertension in healthy men born and living at high altitudes. *Am. J. Cardiol.* 11:150–57

Peterson DD, Pack AI, Silage DA, Fishman AP. 1981. Effects of aging on ventilatory and occlusion pressure responses to hypoxia and hypercapnia. *Am. Rev. Respir. Dis.* 124:387–91

Poulin MJ, Cunningham DA, Patterson DH, Kowalchuk JM, Smith WDF. 1993. Ventilatory sensitivity to CO_2 in hyperoxia and hypoxia in older aged humans. *Am. J. Appl. Physiol.* 2209–16

Pugh LGCE. 1966. A programme for physiological studies of high altitude peoples. In *The Biology of Human Adaptability* ed. PT Baker, JS Weiner, pp. 521–32. Oxford: Clarendon

Pugh LGCE. 1964. Blood volume and hemoglobin concentration at altitudes above 18,000 ft. (5500 m.). *J. Physiol.* 170:344–54

Qian Y, Qian B, Su B, Yu J, Ke Y, et al. 2000. Multiple origins of Tibetan Y chromosome. *Hum. Genet.* 106:453–54

Ramirez G, Bittle PA, Colice GL, Foulis PR, Agosti SJ. 1991. Biochemical adaptations to moderately high altitude living. *J. Wilderness Med.* 2:287–97

Reeves JT, McCullough RE, Moore LG, Cymerman A, Weil JV. 1993. Sea level PCO-2 relates to ventilatory acclimatization at 4,300 m. *J. Appl. Physiol.* 75:1117–22

Regensteiner JG, Pickett CK, McCullough RE, Weil JV, Moore LG. 1988. Possible gender differences in the effect of exercise on hypoxic ventilatory response. *Respiration* 53:158–65

Rotta A, Canepa A, Hurtado A, Velasquez T, Chavez R. 1956. Pulmonary circulation at sea level and at high altitudes. *J. Appl. Physiol.* 9:328–36

Ruiz L. 1973. *Epidemiología de la hipertensión arterial y de la cardiopatía isquémica en las grandes alturas.* Tesis dr. Lima: Univ. Peruana Cayetano Heredia

Saco-Pollitt C. 1981. Birth in the Peruvian Andes: physical and behavioral consequences in the neonate. *Child Dev.* 52:839–46

Samaja M, Veicsteinas A, Cerretelli P. 1979. Oxygen affinity of blood in altitude Sherpas. *J. Appl. Physiol.* 47:337–41

Santolaya R, Araya CJ, Vecchiola CA, Prieto PR, Ramirez RM, Alcayaga AR. 1981. Hematocrito, hemoglobina y presión de oxígeno arterial en 270 hombres y 266 mujeres sanas residentes de altura (2,800 mts). *Rev. Hosp. Roy H. Glover* 1:17–24

Sato M, Severinghaus JW, Bickler P. 1994. Time course of augmentation and depression of hypoxic ventilatory responses at altitude. *J. Appl. Physiol.* 77:313–16

Scherrer U, Vollenweider L, Delabays A, Savcic M, Eichenberger U, et al. 1996. Inhaled nitric oxide for high altitude pulmonary edema. *New Engl. J. Med.* 334:624–29

Schlaepher T, Bartsch P, Fisch H. 1992. Paradoxical effects of mild hypoxia and moderate altitude on human visual perception. *Clin. Sci.* 83:633–36

Schoene RB. 1982. Control of ventilation in climbers to extreme altitude. *J. Appl. Physiol.* 53:886–90

Schoene RB, Roach RC, Lahiri S, Peters RM, Hackett PH, Santolaya R. 1990. Increased diffusion capacity maintains arterial saturation during exercise in the Quechua Indians of Chilean altiplano. *Am. J. Hum. Biol.* 2:663–68

Semenza GL. 2000. HIF-I and human disease: one highly involved factor. *Genes Dev.* 14:1983–91

Sime F, Banchero N, Penaloza D, Gamboa R, Cruz J, Marticorena E. 1963. Pulmonary hypertension in children born and living at high altitudes. *Am. J. Cardiol.* 11:143–49

Sime F, Penaloza D, Ruiz L. 1971. Bradycardia, increased cardiac output, and reversal of pulmonary hypertension in altitude natives living at sea level. *Br. Heart J.* 33:647–57

Sime F, Penaloza D, Ruiz L, Gonzales N, Covarrubias E, Postigo R. 1974. Hypoxemia, pulmonary hypertension, and low cardiac output in newcomers at low altitude. *J. Appl. Physiol.* 36:561–65

Smith C. 1997. The effect of maternal nutritional variables on birth weight outcomes of infants born to Sherpa women at low and high altitudes in Nepal. *Am. J. Hum. Biol.* 9:751–63

Spielvogel H. 1997. Body fluid homeostasis and cardiovascular adjustments during submaximal exercise: influence of chewing coca leaves. *Eur. J. Appl. Physiol.* 75:400–6

Spielvogel H, Caceres E, Koubi H, Sempore B, Sauvain M, Favier R. 1996. Effects of coca chew on metabolic and hormonal changes during graded incremental exercise to maximum. *J. Appl. Physiol.* 80:643–49

Spievogel H, Otero-Calderon L, Calderon G, Hartmann R, Cudkowicz L. 1969. The effects of high altitude on pulmonary hypertension of cardiopathies, at La Paz, Bolivia. *Respiration* 26:369–86

Spivak JL. 1995. Erythrocytosis. In *Hematology. Basic Principles and Practice*, ed. R Hoffman, EJ Benz, SJ Shattil, B Furie, HJ Cohen, LE Silberstein, pp. 484–91. New York: Churchill Livingstone

Su B, Xiao C, Deka R, Seielstad MT, Kangwanpong D, et al. 2000. Y chromosome haplotypes reveal prehistorical migrations to the Himalayas. *Hum. Genet.* 107:582–90

Sui GJ, Liu YH, Cheng XS, Anand IS, Harris E, et al. 1988. Subacute infantile mountain sickness. *J. Pathol.* 155:161–70

Sun S, Oliver-Pickett C, Ping Y, Micco AJ, Droma T, et al. 1996. Breathing and brain blood flow during sleep in patients with chronic mountain sickness. *J. Appl. Physiol.* 81:611–18

Sun SF, Droma TS, Zhang JG, Tao JX, Huang SY, et al. 1990. Greater maximal O_2 uptakes and vital capacities in Tibetan than Han residents of Lhasa. *Respir. Physiol.* 79:151–62

Tarazona-Santos E, Lavine M, Pastor S, Giori

G, Pettener D. 2000. Hematological and pulmonary responses to high altitude in Quechuas: a multivariate approach. *Am. J. Phys. Anthropol.* 111:165–76

Thilo EH, Berman ER, Carson BS. 1991. Oxygen saturation by pulse oximetry in healthy infants at an altitude of 1610 m. (5280 ft). *Am. J. Dis. Child.* 145:1137–40

Torrance JD, Lenfant C, Cruz J, Marticorena E. 1970/71. Oxygen transport mechanisms in residents at high altitude. *Respir. Physiol.* 11:1–15

Treger A, Shaw DB, Grover RF. 1965. Secondary polycythemia in adolescents at high altitude. *J. Lab. Clin. Med.* 66:304–14

Tucker A, Stager JM, Cordain L. 1984. Arterial O_2 saturation and maximum O_2 consumption in moderate-altitude runners exposed to sea level and 3,050 m. *J. Am. Med. Assoc.* 252:2867–71

Tufts DA, Haas JD, Beard JL, Spielvogel H. 1985. Distribution of hemoglobin and functional consequences of anemia in adult males at high altitude. *Am. J. Clin. Nutr.* 42:1–11

Unger C, Weiser JK, McCullough RE, Keefer S, Moore LG. 1988. Altitude, low birth weight, and infant mortality in Colorado. *J. Am. Med. Assoc.* 259:3427–32

Usher R, McLean F. 1969. Intrauterine growth of liveborn Caucasian infants at sea level: standards obtained from measurements in 7 dimensions of infants born between 25 and 44 weeks of gestation. *J. Pediatr.* 74:901–10

Vargas M, Leon-Velarde F, Monge CC, Palacios J-A, Robbins PA. 1998. Similar hypoxic ventilatory responses in sea-level natives and high-altitude Andean natives living at sea level. *J. Appl. Physiol.* 84:1024–29

Velasquez MT. 1972. *Análisis de la función respiratoria en la adaptación a la altitud.* Tesis dr. Univ. Nat. Mayor San Marcos

Vincent J, Hellot MF, Vargas E, Gautier H, Pasquis P, LeFrancois R. 1978. Pulmonary gas exchange, diffusing capacity in natives and newcomers at high altitude. *Respir. Physiol.* 34:219–31

Vogel JHK, Weaver WF, Rose RL, Blount SG Jr, Grover RF. 1962. Pulmonary hypertension on exertion in normal man living at 10,150 feet (Leadville, Colorado). *Med. Thorac.* 19:269–85

Ward MP, Milledge JS, West JB. 1989. *High Altitude Medicine and Physiology.* Philadelphia: Univ. Penn. Press

Ward MP, Milledge JS, West JB. 2000. *High Altitude Medicine and Physiology.* London: Oxford Univ. Press

Weil JV, Byrne-Quinn E, Sodal IE, Filley GF, Grover RF. 1971. Acquired attenuation of chemoreceptor function in chronically hypoxic man at high altitude. *J. Clin. Invest.* 50:186–95

Weil JV, Jamieson G, Brown DW, Grover RF, Balchum OJ, Murray JF. 1968. The red cell mass-arterial oxygen relationship in normal man. *J. Clin. Invest.* 47:1627–39

Weinstein RS, Haas JD. 1977. Early stress and later reproductive performance under conditions of malnutrition and high altitude hypoxia. *Med. Anthropol.* 1:25–54

Weiss KM. 1993. *Genetic Variation and Human Disease. Principles and Evolutionary Approaches.* Cambridge, UK: Cambridge Univ. Press

Weitz CA. 1984. Biocultural adaptations of the high altitude Sherpas of Nepal. In *The People of South Asia. The Biological Anthropology of India, Pakistan, and Nepal,* ed. JR Lukacs, pp. 387–420. New York/London: Plenum

White DP, Douglas NJ, Pickett CK, Weil JV, Zwillich CW. 1983. Sexual influence on the control of breathing. *J. Appl. Physiol.* 54:874–79

Wiley AS. 1994. Neonatal and maternal anthropometric characteristics in a high altitude population of the western Himalaya. *Am. J. Hum. Biol.* 6:499–510

Winslow RM, Chapman KW, Gibson CC, Samaja M, Monge C, et al. 1989. Different hematologic responses to hypoxia in Sherpas and Quechua Indians. *J. Appl. Physiol.* 66:1561–69

Winslow RM, Chapman KW, Gibson CC, Samaja M, Blume FD, Goldwasser E. 1988.

Hematologic response to hypoxia in Sherpas and Quechua Indians. *FASEB J.* 2:A1721

Winslow RM, Chapman KW, Monge CM. 1990. Ventilation and the control of erythropoiesis in high-altitude natives of Chile and Nepal. *Am. J. Hum. Biol.* 2:653–62

Winslow RM, Monge C. 1987. *Hypoxia, Polycythemia, and Chronic Mountain Sickness.* Baltimore, MD: Johns Hopkins Univ. Press

Winslow RM, Monge CC, Statham NJ, Gibson CG, Charache S, et al. 1981. Variability of oxygen affinity of blood: human subjects native to high altitude. *J. Appl. Physiol.* 51:1411–16

Winslow RM, Monge C, Winslow NJ, Gibson CG, Whittembury J. 1985. Normal whole blood Bohr effect in Peruvian natives of high altitude. *Respir. Physiol.* 61:197–208

Yancey MK, Moore J, Brady K, Milligan D, Strampel W. 1992. The effect of altitude on umbilical cord blood gases. *Obstet. Gynecol.* 79:571–74

Yang JS, He ZQ, Zhai HY, Yang Z, Zhang HM, et al. 1987. A study of the changes in pulmonary arterial pressure in healthy people in the plains and at high altitude under exercise load. *Chin. J. Cardiol.* 15:39–41

Yip R. 1987. Altitude and birth weight. *J. Pediatr.* 111:869–76

Zamudio S, Droma T, Norkyel KY, Acharya G, Zamudio JA, et al. 1993. Protection from intrauterine growth retardation in Tibetans at high altitude. *Am. J. Hum. Biol.* 91:215–24

Zamudio S, Palmer SK, Dahms TE, Berman JC, Young DA, et al. 1995a. Alterations in uteroplacental blood flow precede hypertension in preeclampsia at high altitude. *J. Appl. Physiol.* 79:15–22

Zamudio S, Palmer SK, Droma T, Stamm E, Coffin C, et al. 1995b. Effect of altitude on uterine artery blood flow during normal pregnancy. *J. Appl. Physiol.* 79:7–14

Zamudio S, Palmer SK, Regensteiner JG, Moore LG. 1995c. High altitude and hypertension during pregnancy. *Am. J. Hum. Biol.* 7:183–93

Zamudio SPD, Leslie KK, White M, Hagerman DD, Moore LG. 1994. Low serum estradiol and high serum progesterone concentrations characterize hypertensive pregnancies at high altitude. *J. Soc. Gynecol. Invest.* 1:197–205

Zhuang J, Droma T, Sun S, Janes C, McCullough RE, et al. 1993. Hypoxic ventilatory responsiveness in Tibetan compared with Han residents of 3,658 m. *J. Appl. Physiol.* 74:303–11

Zhuang J, Droma T, Sutton JR, Groves BM, McCullough RE, et al. 1996. Smaller alveolar-arterial O_2 gradients in Tibetan than Han residents in Lhasa (3658 m). *Respir. Physiol.* 103:75–82

Annu. Rev. Anthropol. 2001. 30:457–79

AIDS AND CRIMINAL JUSTICE

Stephanie Kane[1] and Theresa Mason[2]

[1]Department of Criminal Justice, Indiana University, Bloomington, Indiana 47405, and
[2]Abt Associates Inc., Cambridge, Massachusetts 02138; e-mail: stkane@indiana.edu,
terry_mason@abtassoc.com

Key Words   heroin and crack addiction, prostitution, jails and prisons,
ethnography and HIV risk behavior, poverty and health

■ **Abstract**   This article reviews scholarship at the intersection of anthropology, criminal justice, and AIDS. Street ethnography is presented in a political and historical context, focusing on the distinctive ways that anthropologists have contributed to discussions of illegal drug and sex markets in poor urban neighborhoods. The review also considers subjects that may be explored by anthropologists in the future, including imprisonment as an institutional HIV risk factor that intensifies individual behavioral risk and the criminalization of intentional HIV transmission. This research area raises critical questions about how culture and law shape viral risk.

THE POLITICS OF STREET ETHNOGRAPHY

For anthropologists doing ethnography "in the streets" of poor urban U.S. neighborhoods, it as if the intersection of AIDS and criminal justice were magnetically repulsive. There is a relevant and definable corpus of writings by anthropologists to which we hope this review does justice. The corpus fits into or easily overlaps with cannons in urban, medical, and feminist anthropology. However, it must be said at the outset that criminal justice issues inhabit this corpus only to the extent that they cannot be ignored. The geographic and cultural center of this academic intersection is the United States. The result is a skewed view of the epidemic—with a U.S. tilt—that reflects funding sources as well as scholarly interests. The study of prostitution and AIDS conveys a more global sense of the pandemic; however, researchers in this area also tend to downplay the criminal justice dimension of lives they observe and in their analyses of culture and disease (see below). Before delving into a review of the published literature, grouped into sections on illegal drug/sex markets and prisons, we explore the context and consequences of this odd but significant disciplinary face-off.

There are good reasons for both antipathy to and acknowledgement of criminal justice by anthropologists doing AIDS research and intervention. First and foremost is ethnographers' identification with the urban poor subject, a process central to ethnographic inquiry. Ethnographers who work with people dependent on illegal transactions that are simultaneously incited and punished with globalized zeal by armed police must maneuver within the resulting highly charged environment. The overweening influence of law enforcement in the lives of people directly connected to the underground drug trade as low-level entrepreneurs or consumers requires the researcher's attention at the level of theory at least. However, strategic access by researchers to the urban poor in the drug scene requires that ethnographers appear—and be—as removed from police as possible. The icons of criminal justice—police, prosecutors, judges, wardens, and corrections officers—are not in the article titles based on research "in the streets." Still, they haunt the edges of the texts.

Another source of the backstage presence of law enforcement in the ethnography of drugs and HIV risk is economic and bureaucratic. Most such ethnography has been funded by the National Institute on Drug Abuse, including ethnography for HIV prevention. The National Institute of Drug Abuse (NIDA) has been part of the National Institutes of Health since 1992. NIDA was established in 1974 and sponsors research on all public health facets of drug addiction and drug "abuse"—biomedical as well social, on both prevention and treatment (NIDA 2001). The term abuse is a loaded descriptor that signifies the political burdens this particular area of public health research endures. NIDA is the agency that represents the public health end of the federal stance toward what is known as the "drug problem" in the United States. The polarization between public health and criminal justice policy paradigms regarding illegal drug use and users is reflected in fundable research frameworks. NIDA funds public health research and the National Institute of Justice funds criminal justice research on drug use.

The oppositional public policy structure of legal/illegal, public health/criminal justice, prevention/imprisonment shapes the ethnographer's work. And within public health, epidemiology, with its behaviorally defined, socially meaningless, and politically contested categories (e.g., injecting drug users, female sex partners of drug users, men who have sex with men), has dominated the field of HIV prevention research (Clatts & Mutchler 1989, Kane & Mason 1992, Glick Schiller 1994, Singer 1994).

Interdisciplinary work settings demand a reflexive and critical awareness of the differences in the way anthropologists and behavioral scientists generally conceive of culture. In his study of the tensions and insights of anthropologists working in team settings, Frankenberg (1993, 1995) finds epidemiology to be an imposing scaffold of knowledge production in the anthropology of AIDS.

Concepts such as risk groups or transmission categories are politically loaded when applied to such social phenomena as the HIV/AIDs epidemic (Glick Schiller 1992, Farmer et al 1996a). Furthermore, they are analytic abstractions that are socially as well as causally distant from the mundane realities where ethnographers usually begin to do their thinking. And yet these concepts have pervasive influence as analytical frameworks in the field of HIV prevention as well as research. "What's wrong with this picture?" asks Glick Schiller (1992). Her comprehensive response to her own question dissects the appropriation of oversimplified notions of culture in health research in this field. Complex economic and social power dynamics are often masked or distorted as statistical associations between dichotomous variables. Race/ethnicity as variables reify culture and map risk group labels onto vastly differentiated categories of people ("Hispanic," "black," "men who have sex with men"). The result, Glick Schiller continues, is a cultural construction of the epidemic in terms that reflect and recreate dominant versus subordinate or deviant group discourse. This discourse glosses over the more specific geographic and behavioral as well as more global contexts constituting risk (Glick Schiller 1992). It is ironic, that anthropologists plying their constructivist and contextualizing notions of culture commonly find that what many biomedical colleagues and policy professionals actually hear is a notion of culture more akin to the causal and reductionist models familiar from debates about the culture of poverty and about specific ethnic minority cultures (Glick Schiller 1992; Dressler 1991, pp. 38–65).

There are strong historical parallels and overlaps in this regard between HIV/ AIDS social discourse and fear-driven and stigmatizing U.S. policy discourse concerning other sexually transmitted diseases and currently illegal drug sales and use in the United States (Brandt 1988; Musto 1973, 1988; Clatts & Mutchler 1989; Crimp 1989; Goldstein 1991; Cook & Colby 1992; Farmer 1992; Leonard 1993; Reinarman & Levine 1997) and in Britain (Watney 1994, Young 1996). These discursive currents discourage citizens from seeking legal protection, encouraging instead an aversion to law (Musheno 1994, p. 243; Burris 1999).

The Netherlands offer the most constructive contrast to the punitive and fear-driven U.S. policies. There, harm-reduction models have predominated—rather than totalizing prohibitions—in the interrelated spheres of drug use, prostitution, and HIV prevention and sexuality (Plant 1990, Mol et al 1992, Cohen 1997).

There is also a cognitive and political dimension to the magnetic repulsion between anthropologists who study AIDS and the personnel and institutions of the criminal justice system. It is the unnerving contradiction between a "justice" side that seems weak compared with the "criminal" side: criminal, the epitome of outsider adjectives (Becker 1963); justice, that blind woman statue with a scale weighed down by the suffering of over three million people under correctional supervision (Beck et al 2000). The blind woman is a sorry signifier.

In the arena of drugs and prostitution in the United States, rituals of arrest and court hearings are like constantly spinning turnstiles between the streets, the jails, and prisons. Anthropologists interviewing people in the streets are not really far from the jails and prisons in terms of the experience of those whom they study, many of whom have just gotten out or are soon to be in. Others have lovers, spouses, friends who are locked up. One can easily sense the ramifying effects of imprisonment within communities affected by drugs and AIDS.

Still, direct experience makes all the difference in ethnographic research. With the exception of Juvelis (1998), our search revealed no experienced anthropologists publishing in-depth research on AIDS in prisons or jails, this despite the fact that the problem is entrenched and severe and that the prison industry is growing (see below). Anthropologists studying AIDS are not the only observers who are scarce in prison settings. Prisons do not generally extend invitations to social science researchers, who may be critical of management practices and conditions. The relative absence of scrutiny by outsiders may be a symptom of what some criminologists have identified as the prison's crisis of legitimacy as a model of punishment (Garland 1996, Duster 1997).

There are published reports of qualitative studies as part of HIV/AIDS prevention efforts with prisoners, pre- and postrelease. However, the studies are not by anthropologists and hence we have not included them here. Still, collaborations between prisons, nonprofit organizations, and social scientists for the purposes of HIV prevention do exist. The Center for AIDS Prevention Studies affiliated with the University of California at San Francisco has conducted focus groups with inmates at San Quentin State Prison in Marin County, California. This and similar studies do not constitute ethnography, but they indicate the potential for such research to shape educational efforts and to influence risk for inmates and for their postrelease partners. Several of these Center for AIDS Prevention Studies' prison intervention and evaluation projects have been reported (Grinstead et al 1997, 1999). The interventions include inmate peer education, prerelease education for inmates generally, another for HIV-positive inmates, and HIV prevention for women visiting incarcerated partners.

Criminologists are beginning to explore the relationship of culture and forms of punishment more deeply (Garland 1990, Sloop 1996, Irwin & Austin 2000). Anthropologists have much to contribute to these discussions. For prisoners who become HIV infected or who die of AIDS in prison, the epidemic becomes an aspect of their punishment. This fact should be understood in terms of the wider social and cultural context that has linked them to this health emergency. The nineteenth-century model of prisons as total institutions designed to capture not only prisoners' bodies but also their souls or personalities is still in play (Goffman 1963). Criminologists who themselves survived as prisoners remind the overprotected world outside the walls that prisoners sustain a sense of their preprison selves. Whatever the pressures, preprison experiences and cultural knowledge remain the basis for organizing lives within (Irwin 1970). These processes are susceptible to ethnographic analysis. Were they feasible, such studies could become an important resource for AIDS intervention programs in prisons (for example, see Whitehead 2001).

MORPHING OF THE ETHNOGRAPHIC TROPES, OR OH, WHAT A PUNITIVE STREAK IN AMERICA CAN DO

"Being in the life" has its romantic side for those who are involved. It has moments of sensual glamour and poetry. There is the sharp albeit briefly transcendent experience of the high. The romance is part of the traditional draw of the street. People look to drugs and sex in all their myriad legal and illegal, soulful and soul-less forms. Poets and storytellers in prison recite poetry and tell toasts about being in the life. The old heads teach aesthetics and philosophy to the young. They let a generation of folklorists record their verbal art for posterity (Abrahams 1963, Jackson 1974, Dance 1978). The poetry of the streets and the prisons, and its collection and analysis by folklorists, is one of the early roots of the anthropology of AIDS, one that fits neatly into the emerging field of cultural criminology (Ferrell 1999). But the street does not stay romantic for long. In any case, HIV can thrive on romance, ignorance, hate, or defeat. It is secretive by nature. It settles slowly, allowing viral replicants to ride along from body to body, bloodstream to bloodstream. It thrives through our intricately interconnected human species.

Ethnographic research in HIV/AIDS began with a deceptively straightforward paradigm that focused on the social context of modes of transmission. The paradigm was immediately complicated by a number of on-the-ground epidemiological complexities that jumbled separate transmission modes together. A short list would include individual simultaneous use of a variety of drugs and modes of administration, the overlap of drug-related and sexual risk, and ambiguities surrounding HIV risk among prostitutes (the fabled signifier of sexual danger). This last risk has generally turned out in the United States to be related more to sex workers' own injection habits or the injection habits of their personal partners than to the numbers of client sexual interactions (Cohen et al 1988, Day 1988). The battle against ideological distortion motivated much research and writing. This was the era when television was pushing crack babies for public consumption, when prostitution misdemeanors became felonies, and when the prison industrial complex exploded.

Heroin Injectors and Their Subculture

In the late 1960s and 1970s, drugs were framed as an epidemic, not a war. In 1968, Agar began research on urban heroin addicts (1973). In that brief moment of opportunity, the prison windows opened a crack and the rehabilitation model seemed plausible. He worked in the National Institites of Mental Health Clinical Research Center in the federal prison/hospital in Lexington, KY.

Addicts were pretty much worthless humans in the public imagination in those days, too. Agar's general question was (1973, pp. xi–xii): What would happen if we abandoned a priori judgements (of failure or criminality) and studied addicts as "a legitimate community with an alternative culture, different but equally valid compared to other American subcultures?" It is not likely he would get far with that argument with policy makers or advocates for the poor today. However, the relativist tone clicked with the sociological moment. Lindesmith (1968, p. 149), who began interviewing heroin addicts in the 1940s, conceptualized the drug habit as the organizational basis of a drug subculture [see also Preble & Casey's (1969) classic street ethnography about heroin addicts "taking care of business"]. Ethnographers began to explain addicts' working culture. Although perhaps ill chosen and misbegotten, addicts had careers, and street ethnography, the qualitative study of crime and drug use in "natural settings," gained a foothold in social science (Weppner 1977).

The theory required the addict, or rather, the addict's image, to play a certain role. In their work, Feldman & Beschner (1979, p. 3) introduce that subject: "Within the street culture, the addict could be seen as resourceful and clever, enjoying pursuits that gave his life meaning and adventure." Agar also participated in this multidisciplinary team study, one of the first organized around a particular drug and its associated subculture. The image of a resourceful and clever addict was animated in patterned ways in cities across America—an artful dodger arising out of social disorganization. The notion of a group of people who organized their lives around a shared set of meanings and practices related to buying and shooting up drugs produced a conceptual terrain—a subculture—with its own linguistic and moral codes. This terrain made possible among public health and other officials later on in the AIDS era the idea of needle sharing as symbolic exchange and ritual, something between convenience and gift giving between running buddies or friends. This exemplifies one kind of appropriation and a classic misuse of "subculture" in policy discourse.

After concern about the drug epidemics of the 1960s and 1970s faded, there was a lull in multidisciplinary team research. By the time street ethnographers were called on to research how drug use fueled the AIDS epidemic in the 1980s, drugs had become a rationale for war. Ritual needle sharing entered the conversational frame as soon as intravenous drug users (IVDUs) became a target. Intervention was conceived as a mechanism for transforming subcultural codes regarding injection behavior. The aim was to change the ritual dynamics of sharing (DesJarlais et al 1986).

A practical logic was at work in assumptions behind prevention messages: Addicts don't want to kill themselves or each other, they just want to get high or at least be able to function. Once they learn that HIV can be transmitted through dirty needles, every rational person will try to have his or her own needle or to clean a used one. With education, an unclean, used needle will no longer sustain the aura of a gift. The culture is key: If you change the culture (rules, codes, values, habits) of IVDUs organized into social networks, you will also change the networks of HIV risk.

Once transported into the AIDS epidemic, the emphasis on ritual behavior obscured the practical concerns that motivated the reuse of needles. Most important, it obscured the ways in which enforcement of paraphernalia laws was crucial in constituting and reproducing the practice. If caught with a needle in most U.S. cities, it was not only symbolic to be charged by police with a crime. To not have an extra $2 to buy a clean needle was not only symbolic. To lend your needle to someone because you owe them for the last time you were dope sick is not only symbolic. The emphasis on internal cultural rituals implicit in subcultural analyses tended to obscure the pivotal role of law enforcement in intensifying HIV risk behavior (Mason 1989, Carlson et al 1994, Clatts et al 1994, Koester 1994).

This understanding led anthropologists to focus their participant observation more precisely, developing a visually objective practice of watching people buy and shoot drugs. Ethnographers documented variations by neighborhood, city, and region, by ethnic/racial/cultural style, habit, social organization, and history (Page et al 1990, Kane 1991, Singer et al 1992, Carlson et al 1994, Koester 1994). At a NADR (National AIDS Demonstration Research, the NIDA-funded national program) meeting in Chicago, anthropologist Stephen Koester pointed out that the focus had been on showing people how to rinse used needles with bleach once, then in water twice. However, he had noticed that people tended to rinse their needles in the same glass of water. Also when people "cooked" the heroin in a spoon over a flame, they tended to use the same piece of cotton as a filter for undissolved lumps. "Should these things also be talked about?" he asked the other experts around the table.

At some point it seeped into consciousness that not everybody was an IVDU. Some people just skin popped, for example. So IVDUs became IDUs, injecting drug users. Later, experts announced that bleach might not be as rapidly effective as thought in killing the virus. The politics of government-funded needle exchange was fierce. Scientific evidence of its value as a harm-reduction tool has been pushed aside by both Republican and Democratic administrations. Finding political will to fight for making clean syringes legally and easily available became the responsibility of citizens acting at state and local levels (for discussion, see Raymond 1990, Singer et al 1991, Fernando 1993, Henman et al 1998).

Many addicts did change their needle-use behaviors to reduce the chance of HIV transmission. The state, for the most part, has never changed its destructive law enforcement policies. Who is the criminal?

Demon Crack

Televised orphan babies in the intensive care units of public hospitals marshal public wrath and point it toward their zombie mothers. They are caught in the structures of dejection (Ronell 1992, p. 58) that we have come to associate with drugs and the war on the poor. In her work, Roberts (1997) discusses the creation of a new bio-underclass. Panic over "crack babies" epitomizes this creation: descending hordes of ruined black children requiring special services, children expected to grow up to be criminals. As a review of the medical evidence recently showed, the image of the crack baby is not based on fact; indeed, 36 studies conducted over 16 years show that when women's smoking and alcohol use were factored in, pregnant women's cocaine use did not increase the developmental risk of their children up to age 6 (Frank et al 2001). The demonization of crack-using women has led to more than 200 women in 30 states having been arrested for using the drug during pregnancy, a clear misapplication of the quest for social order (Chien et al 2000).

If chaos is the norm, should not disordered order, as much as ordered disorder, be the object of research? asks Taussig (1992, p. 17). In the ethnography of AIDS we tend to look at the latter. We study the meaning and context of that which is labeled disorder (drug abuse) and often suggest ways of instituting a different kind of order, one that is more user friendly. But we rarely study the meaning and context of order (law enforcement) or suggest ways of instituting order of a different kind. Why?

Consider the contrast between the crack baby/crack whore set of images and this next set, which followed on the heels of the former (and the waning of the crack epidemic) by a few years. The first image set is in the mode of reproduction and race: Crack babies and crack whores evoke vehement public cries for order to dominate disorder; the images feeding the impulse for more police! more weapons! more war! The second set portrays lethal police brutality through two New York City incidents linked in time and memory that evoke vehement public cries to control the disorder perpetrated by the forces of order: The police are out of control!

In a ritual of power, four policemen arrested Abner Louima, a Haitian immigrant standing on the street in front of Club Rendez-Vous in Flatbush, Brooklyn, NY, on August 10, 1997 (Kocieniewski 1997). Although innocent of any crime, he was beaten and tortured in the police station and dropped off at an emergency room to die. The police then covered up the act. Then on February 4, 1999, in the course of employing the urban guerilla warfare tactics that Mayor Giuliani routinized in certain neighborhoods, police shot 41 bullets into Amadou Diallo, a West African immigrant employed as a street peddler who was standing in the entranceway of his apartment building. He held a wallet in his hand (Flynn 1999).

A member of the police gang engaged in the ritual of power in the Louima case was convicted and written off as an exception who will not be tolerated—the pathology individuated (Fried & Harden 1999). The police gang that attacked a human being with a barrage of bullets was acquitted, the event written off as an accident in a routine that needs some adjustment—the pathology of the system diffused (McFadden 2001). Williams (1991) might well consider this a case of spirit murder in its racist form. She writes: "One of the reasons I fear what I call spirit murder—disregard for others whose lives qualitatively depend on our regard—is that it produces a system of formalized distortions of thought. It produces social structures centered on fear and hate, a tumorous outlet for feelings elsewhere unexpressed" (p. 73). Her definition includes cultural obliteration, prostitution, abandonment of the elderly and the homeless, and genocide as some other guises of spirit murder.

The two sets of images—crack babies/crack whores and police brutality—are both indexes of the structure of violence that has been inner city poverty. The anthropology of AIDS should give weight to the dynamically unequal relations of power they symbolize.

Peaking in the 1980s, the crack epidemic stretched distortions to the limit. The new brand of horror attracted enormous media and political play. It also brought virgin users onto the scene at an accelerated rate (Levine & Reinaerman 1987). Anthropologists deployed their skills to challenge the deviant imagery associated with crack addiction and to combat its punishing effects. The demonic is a medieval mode of theorizing crime, still active after all these years. Ethnographic frames of interpretation can provide counterpoint, recognizing ideological distortions that commonly remain unexamined (for examples, see Hamid 1991a–d, 1992; Fullilove et al 1992, Maher & Curtis 1992; Koester & Schwartz 1993; Dunlap et al 1994; Bourgois 1995a,b, 1996; Maher & Daly 1996; Sterk 1999, 2000). A bird's eye view, albeit fictionalized, of crack's pharmacological power is found in the novel by Shell (1995).

Anthropologists have approached this conjuncture of plagues, this structure of dejection, with holistic fervor, analyzing history, political economy, social organization, and the cultural politics of race, gender, and class. Read against this vivid background, the specific sex-related risks associated with HIV transmission among crack addicts—which pertain to the high frequency of unprotected sexual encounters and to some extent the mode of administration (through mouth sores associated with smoking)—can be put into perspective (Wallace et al 1997).

Prostitution

The subject of prostitution links inner city AIDS research to theories of gender and sexuality (Rubin 1975, Caplan 1987, Weston 1998, Parker & Aggleton 1999), to a transnational arena of field sites (Day 1988, Plant 1990, White 1990, Herdt et al 1991, Parker 1991, de Zalduondo 1991, Gil et al 1996, Bond et al 1997, Brummelhuis 1997, Caldwell et al 1997, Carrier et al 1997, Larvie 1997, Law 1997, Maticka-Tyndale et al 1997, Orubuloye 1997, Kane 1998a, Bishop & Robinson 1998, Pellow 1999, Enloe 2000, Nencel 2001), and to activist literature from prostitutes and gay rights organizations that do not always welcome the interests of scholarly and/or feminist intrusions (Millett 1971, Delacoste & Alexander 1987, McClintock 1993, Colter et al 1996). Approaches used in data collection and analysis turn toward perspectives of women, gays, and transgendered persons and generate insights about the processes of negotiation and cultural constraints crucial to the transformation of AIDS knowledge to active risk reduction (Kane 1990, Taylor 1990, Carrier & Magaña 1992, Shedlin & Oliver 1993, Castañeda et al 1996, Waddell 1996, Weeks et al 1998, Kammerer et al 2000). Other work established alternative cultural models of prostitution as legitimate work (Schoepf 1992, Hammar 1996, Pheterson 1996). Others analyzed the symbolic and historical significance of men's dreadful delight in prostitutes' bodies (Gilman 1988, Walkowitz 1992, Bell 1994, Kane 1998b).

Research on women who use drugs and sell sex brought gender balance to street ethnography, which before AIDS had traditionally been a masculine, heterosexual endeavor focused more narrowly on drug use. The work relies on a mixture of life history and sociocultural analysis of the dimensions of risk, engendering and enriching the picture of being in the life (Rosenbaum 1981; Taylor 1993; Maher 1997; Pettiway 1997; Sterk 1999, 2000). In her Camden, NJ research, Leonard (1990) posed as a street prostitute just long enough to elicit rare data on risk behavior from johns driving up in cars. The bold design of her methods stand out.

At the same time that anthropologists tied their research to the public health sectors, legislatures began expanding the law's coercive powers over prostitutes. There is a common scenario being played out across the United States. Its legal basis has been twisting its way through the criminal justice system since the very beginning of the AIDS epidemic:

Prostitutes are losing legal rights to their own body fluids. Like prisoners, they are fast becoming an exception relative to the Constitution; their Fourth Amendment rights have been taken away (Zink 1992). The police cannot go into a business and extract information without cause and a warrant, but in many states, they can arrest a woman soliciting sex on the street, take her to the station, and force her to give blood for an HIV antibody test and to officially receive the results. Illegal search and seizure does not apply. If she is HIV positive, they can arrest her a second time and charge her with a felony instead of the usual misdemeanor.

There is a lack of cultural analysis of these legal practices. The exceptions are studies of mass-mediated and legal representations of cases of intentional HIV transmission, including those of prostitutes (Kane 1998a, 2001; Flavin 2000). These latter studies are based on disembodied legal texts and unpredictable, sensationalized journalistic accounts. The logistics of participant observation in such cases are prohibitive. Most cases do not surface in the media at the national level; most are not tried in court. If tried, they do not rise to the level of appeals and, hence, do not result in a published legal decision. To the difficulties of discovering events scattered randomly over a wide geography and the time delay between arrests and discovery are added all the obstacles to observing such events and interviewing incarcerated persons. As a result of these obstacles, the groundedness ethnographers rely on eludes researchers studying mass-mediated criminal law in action. Perhaps future ethnographers could incorporate this criminal justice issue if and when it arises in situ [for an overview of the large and growing field of civil and criminal AIDS law, see Webber (1997)].

Criminalization of HIV Transmission

Understanding how the criminal justice system and public health entwine may lead to a productive analysis of how institutions shape everyday life more generally. The public impulse for criminalization (Dalton 1993) articulates repressed fears about transmission from HIV-positive to HIV-negative persons. This repression has perhaps been inadvertently encouraged by mainstream public health prevention messages that were fixated on the uninfected. HIV-negative persons were advised, nay, admonished, to protect themselves by assuming everyone was potentially infected. A dichotomy between prevention and treatment was set up early, with prevention help provided for the uninfected, with treatment for the infected.[1]

---

[1] Recent media coverage of debates in South Africa concerning whether to invest in HIV prevention versus treatment appear to be replicating this dichotomous thinking.

The result was an educational vacuum regarding how to handle sexuality for HIV-positive people, for whom it was presumed permanently passe. The responsibilities of the infected toward the uninfected were likewise neglected (Collins et al 2000). The public impulse to criminalize filled the vacuum.

There are signs that this fragmented approach to thinking about primary and secondary prevention, and prevention versus treatment, may be changing. There are a number of major studies and federally funded programs focusing on secondary prevention for HIV infected people, including the Prevention for HIV-Positive Person's Programs funded by the Centers for Disease Control and Prevention, a demonstration project currently underway in several states (Collins et al 2000). Indeed, the Centers for Disease Control and Prevention now lists increasing links with prevention services, along with care and treatment services for HIV-infected people, as one of their top four national goals (2001). In time, these efforts may serve to reduce the public impulse for criminalizing HIV infected people.

It is difficult for ethnographers to research the factors affecting how the state and its institutions respond to, and make use of, social crises. In 1988, legal scholars Sullivan & Field wrote that it is crucial to realize the specific manner in which AIDS has been used to extend the coercive power of the state. The poor and the addicted are most easily punished because their punishment is most easily ignored. Their Fourth Amendment rights to be free of government intrusion, such as mandatory blood tests and forced quarantines, are taken away stealthily; the necessary public discussions regarding the wider implications of allowing the state to reduce individual liberty have not taken place.

Zink (1992, pp. 818–19) argues that the extreme urgency, indeed hysteria, generated by the need to combat this disease calls for careful constitutional consideration of all laws passed under the guise of dealing with the AIDS crisis. She quotes Supreme Court Justice Marshall's dissenting opinion in another case weakening the Fourth Amendment, *Skinner v. Railway Executive Ass'n* [489 U.S. 602, 635 (1989)], where he cautions that

> [h]istory teaches that grave threats to liberty often come in times of urgency, when constitutional rights seem too extravagant to endure. The World War II relocation camp cases *Hirabayashi v. United States*, *Korematsu v. United States* and the Red Scare and the McCarthy-Era internal subversion cases, *Schenck v. United States*, *Dennis v. United States*, are only the most extreme reminders that when we allow fundamental freedoms to be sacrificed in the name of real or perceived exigency, we invariably come to regret it.

Given Justice Marshall's warning as a framework for understanding, we must nevertheless acknowledge that HIV-positive prostitutes who engage in vaginal or oral sex without condoms may present a danger to clients, and through clients to wider social networks, including other prostitutes. There are epidemiological, economic, and psychological bases for such concerns. At the same time, we must challenge the sensationalism that tends to drive the production of new criminal law and question whether the intensification of criminal law is the best approach to this problem. Hence, we urge anthropologists to search for alternatives at the same time that they participate and inform the processes by which new laws are written, enacted, and enforced.

Ethnographic analysis lends itself well to understanding the factors affecting different kinds of negotiations involved in revealing HIV status. One such factor is violence against women who either ask men to use condoms or disclose their HIV status to men with whom they have sexual relationships (Doyal 1995, Quirk & De Carlo 1998). Another is the well-grounded fear that the state will assume custody of HIV-infected women's children because of drug use. There is a growing trend to criminalize women for being addicted and/or HIV positive while pregnant. Thirty-four states have already prosecuted women for either one or the other under the charge of child abuse (Chien et al 2000). Sobo's (1995, 1997) research on self disclosure has provided an important beginning in our understanding of this testy issue. She analyzed when and why people in a variety of circumstances choose to disclose their HIV status to sexual intimates, considering moral issues, rather than criminal law, as a shaper of behavior. That kind of understanding may be useful to counselors and doctors in clinical settings, as well as to defense attorneys, prosecutors, and legislators. The nexus of disease, technology, law, and communication in which the subject of privacy and disclosure is situated also provides an interesting context for developing theories about social agency and legal consciousness.

Like the interpersonal and structural violence that greatly oppresses women who work sex on the street, the issue of criminalization of intentional HIV trans-mission is a significant, but little studied, aspect of what Treichler (1987) named an epidemic of signification. Criminal justice issues are part of the overwhelming volume of meaning, all fighting to become the official AIDS story in the public arena. Treichler called for an epidemiology of signification, i.e., the comprehen-sive mapping and analysis of multiple meanings. This project, she says, is crucial to a democratic rendering of events and possible solutions. Ethnographers have taken up her challenge with great assurance where anthropology intersects public health, but where anthropology intersects criminal justice there are no maps, yet.

Imprisonment is a Risk Factor, Too

Our prisons are overflowing with men and women whose lives are actively being rendered worthless through a lucrative and growing criminal justice industry—a phenomenon Duster (1997) calls the "growth and darkening of U.S. prisons." Even rural jails are overcrowded with inmates with histories of drug injection and poor health care (Kane & Dotson 1997). Poor people's risk of HIV infection is intensified, first, by the conditions they face on the street and, second, by those they face in prison. The statistics are as follows.

Nearly 1.2 million men and women were in the custody of state and fed-eral prisons at year end 1997. Of these, 94% were men, with 48% white and

49% black persons (Beck et al 2000). The overall rate of confirmed AIDS cases was more than five times the rate in the U.S. population as a whole; between 1991 and 1996, one in three inmates died of AIDS-related causes. Of those who had been tested in state prisons, 2.2% of men and 3.4% of women were infected. Those convicted on drug offenses had the highest HIV-positive rate (2.9%); of all state inmates 2.8% of blacks, 2.5% of Hispanics, and 1.4% of whites reported that they were HIV positive (Maruschak 1999). "Sentenced to prison, sentenced to death?" questions Jürgens (1994) after a study of AIDS in U.S. and Canadian prison systems.

With 10.8% of its state prison inmates infected with HIV in 1997, New York leads the nation (Maruschak 1999). Wallace (1990) related the state's high AIDS rate to urban desertification, or the contagious physical and social abandonment of urban areas (see also Fullilove 1995). The high rates of HIV infection in prisons and in the neighborhoods that prisons predominately draw from must be related not only to wider social conditions, but also to conditions within prisons (Juvelis 1992, 1995, 1998; Kane 1995). There is a predisposition to ignore HIV-related risk in prison and a history to this predisposition. Gambling on the efficacy of rehabilitation went out with the 1960s. Victory went to the forces within the prison system who favored the custody model of management. Since then, prison administrators reach ever more greedily for the bottom line. They build computerized human warehouses, train armed patrols to control the perimeter, and offer the bare legal minimum of education, counseling, and medical care inside, i.e., they aim just a technical hair above cruel and unusual punishment (from which the Eighth Amendment of the Constitution still theoretically protects prisoners).

Anthropologists have few opportunities to do research in prisons, but it is tempting to think about what our approach would be if opportunities arose. The question of whether sex is an instinct—whether we are driven to have sex—has not been settled by the essentialists and constructionists. But perhaps less subject to dispute is the idea that one's sexuality is an elemental and/or fundamental part of one's personhood and cannot easily be repressed. Foucault's (1980) historic insight is that we miss the point if we only see the side of the state that represses sexuality. The state is, indeed, a parasite on our sexuality. It busies itself inciting our desires. If it is outlawed, our sexuality is not merely repressed. It may also be aroused.

Although the commissioners on high might outlaw sex, they cannot deny sexuality and, therefore, should not deny the necessity of meeting health standards. This requires the distribution of condoms via a mechanism that is anonymous and easy to tap into. But they do forbid condom distribution, even in New York state prisons, which are epicenters of the epidemic. Forget needle or bleach distribution. At the same time, there is no doubt that in prison sex is commonplace, both consensual and coerced. Shooting drugs is more rare than out on the street, but if people shoot drugs, they are more likely to use infected needles (Hammett & Maruschak 1999).

We suggest here that imprisonment itself be considered an HIV risk factor. If an inmate engages in drug or sex-related risk behaviors in prison, the likelihood of infection increases because of the lack of prevention tools (condoms, needles, bleach) in prison. In other words, all things being equal, imprisonment increases the level of risk associated with any instance of risk behavior. In this case, it is officials who must engage in risk reduction behavior and integrate some flexibility into the custody model. Of course, meeting health standards theoretically requires that prison administrators also implement effective and confidential treatment programs for those who are HIV infected and who have AIDS.

Marquart et al (1999) argue that the drug war has "led to the incarceration of numerous offenders who are low criminal risks but represent major public health risks on release. Criminal justice policies penalizing drug users may be contributing factors to the spread of HIV infection in the wider society." Note that this logic is analogous to that which spurred surveillance and research on injecting drug users and their sex partners, who were also seen as threatening links to the general (heterosexual) population. It has not worked to jump-start large-scale outreach to prisoners, however. Their existence is hidden from public consciousness. Canada did a much better job of studying the issue of AIDS in prison and coming up with harm-reduction policies. But to the disappointment of the Canadian AIDS Society and Canadian HIV/AIDS Legal Network, which sponsored prison AIDS research and intervention, administrators were successful in ignoring their recommendations (Jürgens 1995).

The criminal justice system is a racist and intolerant system. As Mann (1997) says, "[W]e don't need more wars," and we do not need any more research to prove that the system is both racist and intolerant. In 1996, Kane organized a panel on the new Indiana "Battery by Body Waste Law," inviting the legislators and sheriffs who drafted the law to exchange views with a legal activist from a prominent gay organization. The exchange revealed that the law was written to show the police and corrections officers that the lawmakers cared about them. The law misrepresented the routes of HIV transmission (by suggesting that spitting, biting, or throwing excrement put victims at a not improbable risk of infection). As it turned out, the lawmakers' purpose was not AIDS prevention at all. Instead, legislators merely saw an opportunity to use fear of AIDS as a platform for fortifying institutional alignments.

There is no sure ground yet between anthropology and criminal justice. But the comprehensive critical analyses of how political economy shapes the health of people living in poverty, including illegal drug users, provide the foundation for developing an anthropology of AIDS that confronts criminal justice issues more directly (Farmer 1992; Singer 1994; Carlson 1996; Farmer et al 1996b; Waterston 1993, 1999; Kane 1998a).

When scholarly understanding is combined with activist dedication, important pathways for creating social change become possible. The long-standing collaboration among anthropologists—including Steven Schensul, Jean Schensul, and Merrill Singer—and community activists through the Hispanic Health Council, a community-based health institute in the Puerto Rican community of Hartford, CT, exemplifies the way in which research in medical anthropology can combine with political action to successfully discern and advocate the health needs of the poor (Singer 1995). Paul Farmer and the professionals and activists, among them anthropologists, of Partners in Health are also guiding lights. Farmer and his colleagues have incorporated the anthropology of AIDS into a healing global vision complete with hillside clinics and urban field stations. These offer positive models for anthropologists and medical practitioners alike.

CONCLUSION

The profession of anthropology has had rather ignominious beginnings in the social science of crime. Back in the nineteenth and early twentieth century, when pathologizing theory was in vogue (not unlike today), the father of phrenology, Cesare Lombroso, Italian physician and anthropologist, claimed that he could empirically identify born criminals by the shape of their cranial features by the shape of their cranial features (Rafter 1992). This history is taught in few if any graduate courses in anthropology today.

On an American Anthropological Association 2000 panel on "legal" and "illegal" economies in relation to moral orders of globalization, Allen Feldman commented on the quandaries faced by anthropologists who study criminals today. When he reached Philippe Bourgois' paper on addicts who use needle exchange programs, Feldman asked how the ethnographic gaze aggravated this situation and what the space formed by ethnography was. Most pertinent to this subject, he asked if ethnography required criminalization to function.

The last question reverses an assumption we commonly make: the assumption of critical distance imposed between ethnographic practice and law enforcement. It is an assumption that rarely disrupts the analytic core of our findings. Feldman's questions demand that we reconsider. We push cops out of the frames of systematic street observation; we have not intervened in the expansion of the prison industrial complex. Are these tactics of avoidance a basis for critical distance or have we fallen into a trap, making a living off the routines of coercive state power by studying its effects? Information and technology are channeled in specific directions and the flows of symbolic and material capital do not favor the citizenry who live in those parts of the country zoned for urban removal, dead or alive. Nothing is random here.

Compared with anthropology, the academic field of criminal justice may seem much more implicated in the forces of oppression at issue. Like the police, criminologists need crime and its related social problems or it would be out of business. For anthropologists with a holistic perspective, crime and its control are just one set of complex factors. But we may be more implicated in allowing and indirectly profiting from the coercive forces of the state than we imagine. Like academics who invest their retirement money in mutual funds strong in technology but who think they are innocent of weapons sales and manufacture around the world, the simplicity of our motives is an illusion.

One way or another, we are destined to play our professional roles in the "third worlding of America" (Koptiuch 1991). Although we can craft our representations with care, intelligence, and respect and orient them toward the world, we cannot control their effects, not even in local contexts. On the other hand, one cannot reach resolution without going through contradiction first (Levi-Strauss 1963). A focus on epidemiological significance at the level of cotton, spoon, and flame has as undeniable value as intervention insight. Ultimately, this level of analysis has its limits. The expanding criminal justice apparatus and its convergence with the HIV/AIDS epidemic needs more attention from anthropologists, despite the difficulties of such an undertaking. The public discourse concerning crime and punishment is impoverished. Public health and criminal justice remain for the most part at odds. The human suffering is too great, the silences too loud.

ACKNOWLEDGMENTS

Stephanie Kane thanks Carol Greenhouse, William Leap, Shirley Lindenbaum, and Phil Parnell for their steadfast and inspiring intellectual support; Sydel Silverman of the Wenner Gren Foundation for her open-minded vision of where anthropologists may usefully tread; colleagues in the Department of Criminal Justice at Indiana University for their multidisciplinary exchanges, and the students of the "Sex, Drugs and AIDS" seminars for lively discussions and research. She gives special thanks to C. Jason Dotson, whose conversation and word craft inform every page of this essay. Theresa Mason is grateful to Michael Agar for mentoring; to Wayne Weibel for the initial opportunity to do street ethnography; to Myron Johnson and the other Heroes, outreach colleagues, for their street point of view; to Ted Hammett of Abt Associates, a consistent supporter; and to Steve Koester, Reyes Ramos, and, in more recent years, Margaret Connors, Nina Kammerer, and Kevin Batt for stimulating exchanges.

Visit the Annual Reviews home page at www.AnnualReviews.org

LITERATURE CITED

Abrahams R. 1963. *Deep Down in the Jungle: Negro Narrative Folklore from the Streets of Philadelphia*. Chicago: Aldine

Agar MH. 1973. *Ripping and Running: A Formal Ethnography of Urban Heroin Addicts*. New York: Seminar

Beck AJ, Bonczar TP, Ditton PM, Gilliard DK, Wolf Harlow C, et al. 2000. *Correctional Populations in the United States, 1997*. Washington, DC: Bur. Justice Stat., US Dep. Justice

Becker HS. 1963. *Outsiders: Studies in the Sociology of Deviance*. New York: Free Press

Bell S. 1994. *Reading, Writing and Rewriting the Prostitute Body*. Bloomington: Indiana Univ. Press

Bishop R, Robinson LS. 1998. *Night Market: Sexual Cultures and the Thai Economic Miracle*. New York: Routledge

Bond KC, Celentano DD, Phonsophakul S, Vaddhanaphuti C. 1997. Female commercial sex work and the HIV epidemic in Northern Thailand. See Herdt 1997b, pp. 185–215

Bourgois P. 1995a. *In Search of Respect: Selling Crack in El Barrio.* New York: Cambridge Univ. Press

Bourgois P. 1995b. The political economy of resistance and self-destruction in the crack economy: an ethnographic perspective. *Ann. NY Acad. Sci.* 749:97–118

Bourgois P. 1996. In search of masculinity: violence, respect and sexuality among Puerto Rican crack dealers in East Harlem. *Br. J. Criminol.* 36(3):412–27

Brandt AM. 1988. AIDS and metaphor: social meaning of epidemic disease. *Soc. Res.* 55(3):413–32

Brummelhuis HT. 1997. Mobility, marriage, and prostitution: sexual risk among Thai in the Netherlands. See Herdt 1997, pp. 167–184

Burris S. 1999. Studying the legal management of HIV-related stigma. *Am. Behav. Sci.* 42(7):1229–43

Burris S, Dalton HL, Miller JL, Yale AIDS Law Project. 1993. *AIDS Law Today: A New Guide for the Public.* New Haven, CT: Yale Univ. Press

Caldwell JC, Anarfi JK, Caldwell P. 1997. Mobility, migration, sex, STD's and AIDS: an essay on sub-Saharan Africa with other parallels. See Herdt 1997b, pp. 41–54

Caplan P, ed. 1987. *The Cultural Construction of Sexuality.* New York: Routledge

Carlson RG. 1996. The political economy of AIDS among drug users in the United States: beyond blaming the victim and powerful others. *Am. Anthropol.* 98(2):266–78

Carlson RG, Falck RS, Siegal HA. 2000. Crack cocaine injection in the heartland: an ethnographic perspective. *Med. Anthropol.* 18:305–23

Carlson RG, Siegal HA, Falck MA. 1994. Ethnography, epidemiology, and public policy: needle-use practices and HIV-1 risk reduction among injecting drug users in the Midwest. See Feldman 1994, pp. 185–214

Carrier J, Nguyen B, Su S. 1997. Sexual relations between migration populations (Vietnamese with Mexican and Anglo) and HIV/STD infection in Southern California. See Herdt 1997b, pp. 225–50

Carrier JM, Magaña JR. 1992. Use of ethnosexual data on men of Mexican origin for HIV/AIDS prevention programs. See Herdt & Lindenbaum 1992, pp. 243–58

Castañeda X, Ortíz V, Allen B, García C, Fernández Avila M. 1996. Sex masks: the double life of female commercial sex workers in Mexico City. *Culture, Med. Psychiatr.* 20(2):229–47

Center for AIDS Prevention Study [CAPS]. 2001. *What are HIV + persons' HIV prevention needs?* Cent. AIDS Prev. Res., Univ. Calif., San Francisco. http://www.caps.ucsf. edu/poz.html

Centers for Disease Control and Prevention. January 2001. *HIV Prevention Strategic Plan Through 2005.* http://www.cdc. gov/hiv/dhap.htm

Chien A, Connors M, Fox K. 2000. The drug war in perspective. In *Dying for Growth: Global Inequality and the Health of the Poor,* ed. JY Kim, YV Millen, A Irwin, J Gershman, pp. 293–332. Monroe, ME: Common Courage

Clatts MC, Davis WR, Deren S, Goldsmith D, Tortu S. 1994. AIDS risk behavior among drug injectors in New York City: critical gaps in prevention policy. See Feldman 1994, pp. 215–35

Clatts MC, Mutchler KM. 1989. AIDS and the dangerous other: metaphors of sex and deviance in the representation of disease. *Med. Anthropol.* 10:105–14

Cohen J, Alexander P, Wofsy C. 1988. Prostitutes and AIDS: public policy issues. *J. AIDS Public Pol.* 3(2):16–20

Cohen PDA. 1997. Crack in the Netherlands: effective social policy is effective drug policy. See Reinarman & Levine 1997, pp. 214–24

Collins C, Morin SF, Shriver MD, Coates TJ. 2000. *Designing Primary Prevention for People Living with HIV.* AIDS Policy Cent., Cent. AIDS Prev. Stud. AIDS Res. Inst., Univ. Calif., San Francisco. Policy Monogr. Ser.

Colter EG, Hoffman W, Pendleton E, Redick

A, Serlin D. (Dangerous Bedfellows) 1996. *Policing Public Sex: Queer Politics and the Future of AIDS Activism*. Boston: South End

Cook TE, Colby DC. 1992. The mass-mediated epidemic: the politics of AIDS on the nightly network news. In *The Making of a Chronic Disease*, ed. E Fee, D Fox, pp. 84–122. Berkeley: Univ. Calif. Press

Crimp D, ed. 1989. *AIDS: Cultural Analysis, Cultural Activism*. Cambridge: MIT Press

Dalton HL. 1993. Criminal law. See Burris et al. 1993, pp. 242–62

Dance DC. 1978. *Shuckin' and Jivin': Folklore from Contemporary Black Americans*. Bloomington: Indiana Univ. Press

Day S. 1988. Prostitute women and AIDS: anthropology. *AIDS* 2:421–28

Delacoste F, Alexander P. 1987. *Sex Work: Writings by Women in the Sex Industry*. Pittsburgh, PA: Cleis

DesJarlais DC, Friedman S, Strug D. 1986. AIDS and needle sharing within the IV drug use subculture. In *The Social Dimensions of AIDS: Methods and Theory*, ed. D Feldman, T Johnson, pp. 141–60. New York: Praeger

de Zalduondo BO. 1991. Toward recontextualizing sex work in AIDS intervention research. See Herdt et al. 1991, pp. 223–48

Downe PJ. 1997. Constructing a complex of contagion: the perception of AIDS among working prostitutes in Costa Rica. *Soc. Sci. Med.* 44(10):1575–83

Doyal L. 1995. *What Makes Women Sick: Gender and the Political Economy of Health*. New Brunswick, NJ: Rutgers Univ. Press

Dressler WW. 1991. *Stress and Adaptation in the Context of Culture: Depression in a Southern Black Community*. Albany: State Univ. NY Press

Dunlap D, Johnson B, Manwar A. 1994. A successful female crack dealer: case study of a deviant career. *Deviant Behav.* 15:1–25

Duster T. 1997. Pattern, purpose, and race in the drug war: the crisis of credibility in criminal justice. See Reinarman & Levine, pp. 260–87

Enloe C. 2000. *Maneuvers: The International Politics of Militarizing Women's Lives*. Berkeley: Univ. Calif. Press

Farmer P. 1992. *AIDS and Accusation: Haiti and the Geography of Blame*. Berkeley: Univ. Calif. Press

Farmer P, Connors M, Fox K, Furin J. 1996a. Rereading social science. See Farmer et al. 1996b, pp. 147–206

Farmer P, Connors M, Simmons J, eds. 1996b. *Women, Poverty and AIDS: Sex, Drugs, and Structural Violence*. Monroe, ME: Common Courage

Feldman DA, ed. 1994. *Global AIDS Policy*. Westport, CT: Bergin Garvey

Feldman HW, Beschner G. 1979. Introduction. In *Angel Dust: An Ethnographic Study of PCP Users*, ed. WH Feldman, MH Agar, G Beschner, pp. 1–18. Lexington, MA: Lexington

Fernando MD. 1993. *AIDS and Intravenous Drug Use: The Influence of Morality, Politics, Social Science, and Race in the Making of a Tragedy*. Westport, CT: Praeger

Ferrell J. 1999. Cultural criminology. *Annu. Rev. Sociol.* 25:395–418

Flavin J. 2000. (Mis)representing risk: headline accounts of HIV related assaults. *Am. J. Crim. Justice* 25(1):119–36

Flynn K. 1999. Police killing draws national notice. *NY Times*, Feb. 8, Sect. B, p. 5

Foucault M. 1980. *The History of Sexuality*, Vol. 1: *An Introduction*. New York: Vintage

Frank DA, Augustyn M, Grant Knight W, Pell T, Zuckerman B. 2001. Growth, development and behavior in early childhood following pre-natal cocaine exposure. *JAMA* 285(12):1613–25

Frankenberg R. 1993. Risk: anthropological and epidemiological narratives of prevention. In *Knowledge, Power and Practice in Medicine and Everyday Life*, ed. S Lindenbaum, M Lock, pp. 219–42. Berkeley: Univ. Calif. Press

Frankenberg R. 1995. Learning from AIDS: *the future of anthropology*. In *The Future of Anthropology*, ed. AS Ahmed, CN Shore, pp. 110–33. Atlantic Highlands, NJ: Athlone

Fried JP, Harden B. 1999. The Louima case: the overview; officer is guilty in torture of Louima. *NY Times*, June 9, Sect. A, p. 1

Fullilove MT, Lown A, Fullilove RE III. 1992. Crack 'hos' and skeezers: traumatic experiences of women crack users. *J. Sex Res.* 29 (2):275–87

Fullilove RE III. 1995. Community disintegration and public health: a case study of New York City. In *Assessing the Social and Behavioral Science Base for HIV/AIDS Prevention and Intervention.* Workshop Summary, pp. 93–116. Washington, DC: Natl. Acad.

Garland D. 1990. *Punishment and Modern Society: A Study in Social Theory.* Chicago: Univ. Chicago Press

Garland D. 1996. The limits of the sovereign state: strategies of crime control in contemporary society. *Br. J. Criminol.* 36(4):445–71

Gil VE, Wang MS, Anderson AF, Lin GM, Wu ZO. 1996. Prostitutes, prostitution, and STD/HIV transmission in Mainland China. *Soc. Sci. Med.* 42(1):141–52

Gilman S. 1988. *Disease and Representation: Images of Illness from Madness to AIDS.* Ithaca, NY: Cornell Univ. Press

Glick Schiller N. 1992. What's wrong with this picture? The hegemonic construction of culture in AIDS research in the United States. *Med. Anthropol. Q.* 6:237–54

Glick Schiller N. 1994. Risky business: the cultural construction of AIDS risk groups. *Soc. Sci. Med.* 38:1337–46

Goffman EL. 1963. *Stigma: Notes on the Management of Spoiled Identity.* Englewood Cliffs, NJ: Prentice Hall

Goldstein R. 1991. The implicated and the immune: responses to AIDS in the arts and popular culture. In *A Disease of Society: Cultural and Institutional Responses to AIDS,* ed. D Nelkin, DP Willis, SV Parris, pp. 17–42. New York: Cambridge Univ. Press

Grinstead OA, Faigeles B, Zack B. 1997. The effectiveness of peer HIV education for male inmates entering state prison. *J. Health Edu.* 28(6):S31–37

Grinstead OA, Zack B, Faigeles B, Grossman N, Blea L. 1999. Reducing postrelease HIV risk among male prison inmates: a peer-led intervention. *Crim. Just. Behav.* 26:468–80

Hamid A. 1991a. From ganja to crack: Caribbean participation in the underground economy of Brooklyn, 1976–1986. Part 1: Establishment of the marijuana economy. *Int. J. Addict.* 26(6):615–28

Hamid A. 1991b. From ganja to crack: Caribbean participation in the underground economy of Brooklyn, 1976–1986. Part 2: Establishment of the cocaine (and crack) economy. *Int. J. Addict.* 26(7):729–38

Hamid A. 1991c. Crack: new directions in drug research. Part 1: Differences between the marijuana and cocaine (crack economy). *Int. J. Addict.* 26(8):825–36

Hamid A. 1991d. Crack: new directions in drug research. Part 2: Factors determining the current functioning of the crack economy—a program for ethnographic research. *Int. J. Addict.* 26(9):913–22

Hamid A. 1992. Drugs and patterns of opportunity in the inner city: the case of middle-aged, middle-income cocaine smokers. In *Drugs, Crime and Social Isolation: Barriers to Urban Opportunity,* ed. AV Harrell, GE Peterson, pp. 209–40. Washington, DC: Urban Inst.

Hammar L. 1996. Bad canoes and bafalo: the political economy of sex on Daru Island, Western Province, Papua New Guinea. *Genders* 23:212–43

Hammett TM, Maruschak LM. 1999. Update: HIV/AIDS, STDs, and TB in correctional facilities, 1996/1997. Washington, DC: Natl. Inst. Justice Cent. Dis. Cont. Prev.

Henman AR, Paone D, DesJarlais DC, Kochems LM, Friedman SR. 1998. Injection drug users as social actors: a stigmatized community's participation in the syringe exchange programmes of New York City. *AIDS Care* 10(4):397–408

Herdt G, ed. 1997. *Sexual Cultures and Migration in the Era of AIDS: Anthropological and Demographic Perspectives.* Oxford, UK: Oxford Univ. Press

Herdt G, Leap W, Sovine M, eds. 1991. Sex, AIDS, and anthropology. *J. Sex Res.* 28(2): 167–69

Herdt G, Lindenbaum S, eds. 1992. *The Time of*

AIDS: Social Analysis, Theory, and Method.
Newbury Park, CA: Sage

Irwin J. 1970. *The Felon.* Englewood Cliffs, NJ: Prentice Hall

Irwin J, Austin J. 2000. *It's About Time: America's Imprisonment Binge.* Belmont, CA: Wadsworth

Jackson B. 1974. *"Get Your Ass in the Water and Swim Like Me": Narrative Poetry from Black Oral Tradition.* Cambridge, MA: Harvard Univ. Press

Jürgens R. 1994. Sentenced to prison, sentenced to death? HIV and AIDS in prisons. *Crim. Law Forum* 5(2/3):763–88

Jürgens R. 1995. *HIV/AIDS in Prisons: A Discussion Paper.* Montreal, Quebec, Can.: Can. AIDS Soc. & Can. HIV/AIDS Legal Netw.

Juvelis JA. 1992. AIDS in prisons and jails. *Practicing Anthropol.* Summer:13–16

Juvelis JA. 1995. Stress factors: HIV and prisoners. See Kane 1995, pp. 6–10

Juvelis JA. 1998. *Access to primary health care for HIV+ African Americans: politics, economics, and "race."* PhD thesis. Univ. S. Florida, Tampa. 158 pp.

Kammerer N, Mason T, Connors M, Durkee R. 2001. Transgenders, substance abuse and HIV/AIDS: from risk group to risk prevention. In *Transgenders and HIV: Risks, Prevention, and Care,* ed. W Bockting, S Kirk. New York: Hayworth. In press

Kane S. 1990. AIDS, addiction and condom use: sources of sexual risk for heterosexual women. *J. Sex Res.* 27(3):427–44

Kane S. 1991. HIV, heroin, and heterosexual relations. *Soc. Sci. Med.* 32:1037–50

Kane S, ed. 1995. AIDS and prisons. *AIDS Soc. Int. Res. Policy Bull.* 6(3)

Kane S. 1998a. *AIDS Alibis: Sex, Drugs and Crime in the Americas.* Philadelphia, PA: Temple Univ. Press

Kane S. 1998b. Reversing the ethnographic gaze: experiments in cultural criminology. In *Ethnography at the Edge: Crime, Deviance and Field Research,* ed. J Ferrell, S Hamm, pp. 132–45. Boston: Northeastern Univ. Press

Kane S. 2001. Mythic prostitutes, AIDS and criminal law. *Ethnologies* 23(1):255–87

Kane S, Dotson CJ. 1997. HIV risk and injecting drug use: implications for rural jails. *Crime Delinq.* 43(2):169–85

Kane S, Mason T. 1992. "IV drug users" and "sex partners": the limits of epidemiological categories and the ethnography of risk. See Herdt & Lindenbaum 1992, pp. 199–222

Kocieniewski D. 1997. Injured man says Brooklyn officers tortured him in custody. *NY Times,* Aug. 13, Sect. B, pp. 1, 3

Koester S. 1994. Copping, running and paraphernalia laws: contextual variables and needle risk behavior among injection drug users in Denver. *Hum. Organ.* 53:287–95

Koester S, Schwartz J. 1993. Crack, gangs, sex and powerlessness: a view from Denver. In *Crack Pipe as a Pimp: An Ethnographic Investigation of Sex-for-Crack Exchanges,* ed. M Ratner, pp. 187–203. New York: Lexington

Koptiuch K. 1991. Third-worlding at home. *Soc. Text* 28:87–99

Larvie P. 1997. Homophobia and the ethnoscape of sex work in Rio de Janeiro. See Herdt 1997b, pp. 143–66

Law L. 1997. A matter of "choice": discourses on prostitution in the Philippines. In *Sites of Desire, Economies of Pleasure: Sexualities in Asia and the Pacific,* ed. L Manderson, M Jolly, pp. 233–61. Chicago: Univ. Chicago Press

Leonard AS. 1993. Discrimination. See Burris et al. 1993, pp. 242–62

Leonard TL. 1990. Male clients of female street prostitutes: unseen partners in sexual disease transmission. *Med. Anthropol. Q.* 4:41–55

Levine HG, Reinerman C, eds. 1987. *The Crack Panic.* San Francisco: Inst. Sci. Anal.

Levi-Strauss C. 1963. *Structural Anthropology.* New York: Doubleday

Lindenbaum S, Lock M, eds. 1993. *Knowledge, Power and Practice in Medicine and Everyday Life.* Berkeley: Univ. Calif. Press

Lindesmith AR. 1968. *Addiction and Opiates.* Chicago: Aldine

Maher L. 1997. *Sexed Work: Gender, Race and Resistance in a Brooklyn Drug Market*. New York: Oxford Univ. Press

Maher L, Curtis R. 1992. Women on the edge of crime: crack cocaine and the changing contexts of street-level sex work in New York City. *Crime Law Soc. Change* 18:221–58

Maher L, Daly K. 1996. Women in the street level drug economy: continuity or change? *Criminology* 34(4):465–91

Mann CR. 1997. We don't need more wars. *Valparaiso Law Rev. Symp.* 31(2):565–78

Marquart JW, Brewer VE, Mullings J, Crouch BM. 1999. The implications of crime control policy on HIV/AIDS-related risk among women prisoners. *Crime Delinq.* 45(1):82–98

Maruschak LM. 1999. *HIV in Prisons, 1997.* Washington, DC: Bur. Justice Stat., US Dep. Justice

Mason T. 1989. *The politics of culture: drug users, professionals, and the meaning of needle sharing.* Presented at 48th Meet. Soc. Appl. Anthropol., Santa Fe, April

Maticka-Tyndale E, Elkins D, Haswell-Elkins M, Rujkarakorn D, Kuyyakanond T, Stam K. 1997. Contexts and patterns of men's commercial sexual partnerships in northeastern Thailand: implications for AIDS prevention. *Soc. Sci. Med.* 44(2):199–213

McClintock A. 1993. Sex workers and sex work. *Soc. Text* 37:1–10

McFadden RD. 2001. Police department rejects punishment for officers in Diallo shooting. *NY Times*, Apr. 27, Sect. A, p. 1

Millett K. 1971. *The Prostitution Papers: A Candid Dialogue.* New York: Basic Books

Mol R, Otter E, van der Meer A. 1992. *Drugs and AIDS in the Netherlands: The Interests of Drug Users.* Amsterdam: Interest Group Drug Users MDHG

Musheno M. 1994. Socio-legal dynamics of AIDS: constructing identities, protecting boundaries amidst crisis. *Law Policy* 16(3):235–48

Musto DF. 1973. *The American Disease: Origins of Narcotics Control.* New Haven, CT: Yale Univ. Press

Musto DF. 1988. Quarantine and the problem of AIDS. In *AIDS: The Burdens of History*, ed. E Fee, DM Fox, pp. 67–85. Berkeley: Univ. Calif. Press

Nencel L. 2001. *Ethnography and Prostitution in Peru.* London: Pluto

NIDA. 2001. *Index of articles from NIDA. The Body: An AIDS and HIV Information Resource.* http://www.thebody.com/nida/nidapage.html

Orubuloye IO. 1997. Sexual networking, use of condoms, and perception of STDs and HIV/AIDS transmission among migrant sex workers in Lagos, Nigeria. See Herdt 1997b, pp. 216–24

Page JB, Chitwood DD, Smith PC, Kane N, McBride DC. 1990. Intravenous drug use and HIV infection in Miami. *Med. Anthropol. Q.* 4:56–71

Parker R. 1991. *Bodies, Pleasures, and Passions: Sexual Culture in Contemporary Brazil.* Boston: Beacon

Parker R, Aggleton P. 1999. *Culture, Society and Sexuality: A Reader.* Philadelphia, PA: UCL

Pellow D. 1999. Sex, disease and culture change in Ghana. In *Histories of Sexually Transmitted Diseases and HIV/AIDS in Africa*, ed. P Settel, M Lewis, M Lyons, pp. 17–42. Westport, CT: Greenwood

Pettiway LE. 1997. *Workin' It: Women Living Through Drugs and Crime.* Philadelphia, PA: Temple Univ. Press

Pheterson G. 1996. *The Prostitution Prism.* Amsterdam: Amsterdam Univ. Press

Plant M, ed. 1990. *AIDS, Drugs and Prostitution.* New York: Tavistock/Routledge

Preble E, Casey J. 1969. Taking care of business: the heroin user's life on the street. *Int. J. Addict.* 4:1–24

Quirk K, De Carlo P. 1998. *What are Women's Prevention Needs? CAPS Fact Sheet.* San Francisco: Cent. AIDS Prevent. Stud., Univ. Calif.

Rafter N. 1992. Criminal anthropology in the United States. *Criminology* 30(4):525–36

Raymond CA. 1990. U.S. cities struggle to implement needle exchanges despite apparent success in European cities. In *AIDS: The Impact on the Criminal Justice System*, ed. M Blumberg, pp. 188–94. Columbus, OH: Merrill

Reinarman C, Levine HG. 1997. *Crack in America: Demon Drugs and Social Justice.* Berkeley: Univ. Calif. Press

Roberts D. 1997. *Killing the Black Body: Race, Reproduction, and the Meaning of Liberty.* New York: Pantheon

Ronell A. 1992. *Crack Wars: Literature, Addiction, Mania.* Lincoln: Univ. Nebraska Press

Rosenbaum M. 1981. *Women on Heroin.* New Brunswick, NJ: Rutgers

Rubin G. 1975. The traffic in women: notes on the "political economy" of sex. In *Toward an Anthropology of Women*, ed. RR Reiter, pp. 157–210. New York: Monthly Review

Schoepf BG. 1992. Women at risk: case studies from Zaire. See Herdt & Lindenbaum 1992, pp. 259–86

Shedlin MG, Oliver D. 1993. Prostitution and HIV risk behavior. *Adv. Popul.* 1:157–72

Shell R. 1995. *Iced.* New York: Penguin

Singer MC. 1994. AIDS and the health crisis of the U.S. urban poor: the perspective of critical medical anthropology. *Soc. Sci. Med.* 39:931–48

Singer MC. 1995. Beyond the ivory tower: critical praxis in medical anthropology. *Med. Anthropol. Q.* 9:80–106

Singer MC, Irizarry R, Schensul JJ. 1991. Needle access as an AIDS prevention strategy for IV drug users: a research perspective. *Hum. Organ.* 50:142–53

Singer MC, Jia Z, Schensul JJ, Weeks M, Page JB. 1992. AIDS and the IV drug user: the local context in prevention efforts. *Med. Anthropol.* 14:285–306

Sloop JM. 1996. *The Cultural Prison: Discourse, Prisoners, and Punishment.* Tuscaloosa: Univ. Alabama Press

Sobo E. 1995. *Choosing Safe Sex: AIDS-Risk Denial Among Disadvantaged Women.* Philadelphia: Univ. Penn. Press

Sobo E. 1997. Self-disclosure and self-construction among HIV-positive people: the rhetorical uses of stereotypes and sex. *Anthropol. Med.* 4(1):67–87

Sterk C. 1999. *Fast Lives: Women Who Use Crack Cocaine.* Philadelphia, PA: Temple Univ. Press

Sterk CE. 2000. *Tricking and Tripping: Prostitution in the Era of AIDS.* Putnam Valley, NY: Soc. Change

Sullivan KM, Field MA. 1988. AIDS and the coercive power of the state. *Harvard Civil Rights Civil Libert. Law Rev.* 23:139–97

Taussig M. 1992. *The Nervous System.* New York: Routledge

Taylor A. 1993. *Women Drug Users: An Ethnography of a Female Injecting Community.* Oxford, UK: Clarendon

Taylor CC. 1990. Condoms and cosmology: the 'fractal' person and sexual risk in Rwanda. *Soc. Sci. Med.* 31(9):1023–28

ten Brummelhuis H, Herdt G. 1997a. Mobility, marriage, and prostitution: sexual risk among Thai in the Netherlands. See Herdt 1997b, pp. 167–84

Treichler PA. 1987. AIDS, homophobia, and biomedical discourse: an epidemic of signification. *Cult. Stud.* 1(3):263–305

Waddell C. 1996. HIV and the social world of female commercial sex workers. *Med. Anthropol. Q.* 10(1):75–82

Walkowitz JR. 1992. *City of Dreadful Delight: Narratives of Sexual Danger in Late-Victorian London.* Chicago: Univ. Chicago Press

Wallace JI, Porter J, Weiner A, Steinberg A. 1997. Oral sex, crack smoking, and HIV infection among female sex workers who do not inject drugs. *Am. J. Public Health* 87(3):470

Wallace R. 1990. Urban desertification, public health and public order: 'planned shrinkage', violent death, substance abuse and AIDS in the Bronx. *Soc. Sci. Med.* 31(7):801–13

Waterston A. 1993. *Street Addicts in the Political Economy.* Philadelphia, PA: Temple Univ. Press

Waterston A. 1999. *Love, Sorrow and Rage: Destitute Women in a Manhattan Residence.* Philadelphia, PA: Temple Univ. Press

Watney S. 1994. *Practices of Freedom: Selected Writings on HIV/AIDS*. Durham, NC: Duke Univ. Press

Webber D. 1997. *AIDS and the Law*. Aspen, CO: Aspen. 3rd ed.

Weeks MR, Grier M, Romero-Daza N, Pulgisi-Vasquez M, Singer M. 1998. Streets, drugs, and the economy of sex in the age of AIDS. *Women Health* 27(1–2):205–29

Wepper RS. 1997. *Street Ethnography: Selected Studies of Crime and Drug use in Natural settings*. Beverly Hills, CA: Sage

Weston K. 1998. *Longslowburn: Sexuality and Social Science*. New York: Routledge

White L. 1990. *The Comforts of Home: Prostitution in Colonial Nairobi*. Chicago: Univ. Chicago

Whitehead T. 2001. *Cultural Systems Analysis group contracts fact sheet*. http://www.bsos.umd.edu/anth/cusag/cusag 4.html

Williams P. 1991. *The Alchemy of Race and Rights: Diary of a Law Professor*. Cambridge, MA: Harvard Univ. Press

Young A. 1996. *Imagining Crime*, pp. 175–206. Thousand Oaks, CA: Sage

Zink K. 1992. Love V. Superior Court: mandatory testing and prostitution. *Golden Gate Univ. Law Rev.* 22:795–819

Annu. Rev. Anthropol. 2001. 30:481–504

ANTHROPOLOGY IN FRANCE

Susan Carol Rogers

Department of Anthropology, New York University, New York 10003;
e-mail: scr1@nyu.edu

Key Words   Europeanist anthropology, folklore, French society, history of
anthropology, research institutions

■ **Abstract**   In France as elsewhere, anthropology developed as an autonomous
discipline concerned with the study of faraway primitive or "exotic" societies, but it has
shifted its purview, especially over the past several decades, to also include societies
closer to home in both time and space. Consideration of the substantial literature
produced over the past 30 years by French anthropologists conducting research in
France illustrates the specificities of national disciplinary traditions in perceiving and
meeting this challenge. Anthropology's position within the institutional framework of
contemporary French academic and scholarly life, as well as the intellectual traditions
that have been brought to bear on the ethnological study of France (especially the
legacies of Durkheimian social thought and folklore studies) are shown to have helped
shape both the production of anthropological knowledge of and in France and debates
about its pertinence to the discipline's future.

INTRODUCTION

This turn of century, with its images of the global village, has brought challenges
to all of those anthropologies (including American, British, French) that were
born as autonomous disciplines concerned with the study of primitive or "exotic"
societies early in the twentieth century, toward the end of colonial imperialism's
heyday, and came of age in a postcolonial world riven by the Cold War. Just as
certainly, discernible differences appear across national traditions in the ways that
these challenges have been perceived and met. In this essay on French anthropology, I focus mainly on the anthropology of France, including a discussion of its
emergence (especially in the 1970s) and provide a necessarily selective overview
of more recent work.[1] This focus is not altogether representative of French anthropology in general which, by most measures, remains dominated by the study
of "the exotic." On the other hand, almost all of the French ethnological research

---

[1] Relatively little research has been conducted in France by foreign ethnologists, and I shall
not discuss it here. See Reed-Danahay & Rogers 1987; Rogers 1991, 1998 for considerations
of American ethnology of France; Beitl et al 1997 on German and Austrian research during
the 1930s; Grillo 1985 and MacDonald 1989 for examples of British ethnology.

0084-6570/01/1021-0481$14.00   **481**

conducted in postindustrial or western societies has been focused on France,[2] and it is arguably this segment of the discipline that most clearly brings to light a number of the quandaries shaping anthropology as it is currently being redefined in France, and—by contrast if not analogy—in the English-speaking world as well.

A 1986 special issue on the current state of the discipline published by *L'Homme*, France's premier journal of anthropology, offers a glimpse of French perceptions of anthropology's turn-of-the-century situation. This issue was organized to mark the twenty-fifth anniversary of the journal's founding by Claude Lévi-Strauss, two years after his 1959 election to a chair in Social Anthropology at the Collège de France and his establishment of the Laboratory of Social Anthropology there. By the mid-1980s, both Lévi-Strauss and the research group he founded were still productive (as they continue to be today), but the grand theoretical schemas that had defined French anthropology in the previous decades—especially Lévi-Straussian structuralism but also Marxism—had largely faded from the scene, without having been replaced by any similarly compelling intellectual agenda or singular disciplinary leader.

The authors contributing to the 1986 volume were invited to reflect on the present and future coherence of the discipline, in view of two related developments. First, the kinds of societies studied by anthropologists had shifted, partly due to the disappearance or inaccessibility of lifeways "traditionally" associated with anthropological research and largely because the ethnographic map had been extended to cover most of the world, including societies considered to be highly developed or modern. Second, this weakening of the "*grand partage*" that had once defined anthropology in terms of the particular places or types of societies in its purview implied a reworking of relationships with the other *sciences humaines*. (Pouillon 1986, pp. 21–22).[3]

Although the scholars contributing to this collection generally agreed that the ultimate purpose of anthropology is to grasp the fundamental characteristics of human society through ethnological consideration of the diversity of human societies, several fundamental sources of malaise are evident. For example, several authors (Sindzingre 1986, Bernand & Digard 1986, Smith 1986) develop elaborate arguments to demonstrate that the diversity both of analytical frames deployed by anthropologists and of the themes or culture areas they treat is a sign

---

[2]A few French ethnologists have conducted research elsewhere in Europe, especially in southern Europe (e.g., Augustins 1989, Handman 1983, Bromberger 1995). See note 12. There has also been a small amount of attention paid to the European Union (notably Abélès 1996, Bellier 1995). Although funds have been available for research in Eastern Europe, few French anthropologists have conducted fieldwork there. The United States has, almost without exception (Le Menestrel 1999) drawn no French ethnological research.

[3]The French category *sciences humaines*, a legacy of the Durkheimian project, is only roughly equivalent to "social sciences," as usually understood in English. At the center of the French category are history, sociology, human geography, and anthropology. Other social sciences are sometimes, but not always, considered to be among the *sciences humaines*.

of vitality rather than dissolution. This stance suggests that the lack of any discernible theoretical, topical, or geographical unity in the discipline was considered a serious problem by many. Another area of tension concerns definitions of the anthropological enterprise in terms of the kinds of society that are its object of study. One author argues that ethnology must be defined by the study of societies most different from our own (e.g., "primitive," corresponding to stateless, non-literate) (Testart 1986). Another claims with disapproval that the discipline has been drawn exclusively to the exotic (Panoff 1986), and a third asks what is the significance of the shift of the ethnological object from one defined in terms of distance in evolutionary time (primitive societies) to one defined in terms of distance in space (exotic societies) (Paul-Levy 1986). Yet another (Lenclud 1986) argues that the whole array of conventional ways of classifying societies (simple/complex, cold/hot, holistic/individualistic, mechanical solidarity/organic solidarity, gemein-schaft/gesellschaft, traditional/rational, stateless/state, nonliterate/literate, primitive/developed, traditional/modern) amounts to mutually inconsistent—albeit potentially useful—conceptualizations of societal difference. But, he asserts, if there is a fundamental empirical basis for this kind of binary distinction between societies, a discipline claiming to be concerned with human society in general can hardly afford to systematically eliminate from its purview all those on one side of such pairs. Alternatively, if such divisions, however heuristically useful, do not correspond to any inherent distinctions among human societies then there is no legitimate justification for the a priori elimination of any societies from the anthropological project. The development of an ethnology of societies closer to home, he goes on, does not undermine the coherence of the discipline but is simply the logical extension of the universalizing project of anthropology. Further, it does not mean that "classical" ethnology should be abandoned; on the contrary, the specificities of societies like our own will only be discernible in light of an understanding of those that are most different. Indeed, Lenclud, like several others (Belmont 1986, Pétonnet 1986), suggests that one important function of the anthropological enterprise may be the kind of reenchantment of our world offered by just this perspective. Again, the vehement defense in this article—like many in the collection—of an expansion of the ethnological enterprise beyond the primitive or exotic suggests that a strong counter-argument prevails.

In his introduction to the volume, Pouillon, citing Lévi-Strauss citing Mauss transposing Durkheim, notes that sociology (the study of modern societies) might best be understood as a branch of anthropology (the study of human society) (Pouillon 1986, p. 18). If ethnology is redefined as a synonym for anthropology, concerned with all human societies, rather than as that branch of the science of society concerned with the primitive (or exotic), then the distinction between ethnology and sociology—not to mention those other social sciences that developed as the study of one or another dimension of modern societies—becomes unclear, if not meaningless. Some of the authors here respond to this dilemma by suggesting that ethnology should be defined not by its object of study (particular kinds of societies) but rather by the concepts it brings to the study of social organization or societal difference. Some argue that although a given topic or setting—for example, illness (Augé 1986) or French politics (Abélès 1986)—may apparently be shared across disciplinary boundaries, the kinds of questions posed by anthropologists and the nature of insights forthcoming from their work remain both distinctive and legitimate. This line of argument implies that the discipline's essential cohesion as well as its difference from other disciplines becomes more apparent, rather than dissolving, as it moves to places and themes already occupied by those others. Some authors, on the other hand, caution that concepts developed in one kind of social context are not necessarily transposable to another (e.g., Terray 1986). Pushed to its logical limit, this claim, ultimately resting on the *grand partage* challenged by Lenclud and others, would suggest that concepts developed in societies of concern to "classical" ethnology (e.g., those associated with ritual or kinship analysis) are most likely to lose any real meaning when applied to other kinds of societies. In this view, the "ethnology" of modern societies might well be indistinguishable from sociology (or other social sciences), while the conceptual and methodological tools developed within anthropology would remain truly pertinent only to the study of the primitive or exotic societies for which they were invented. Alternatively, such a claim can be used to argue that an anthropology of "modern" societies might function to refine those tools, inviting salutary reconsideration of when and how they may be useful (e.g., Cuisenier & Segalen 1993). Finally, this line of argument is sometimes meant as a caution about illegitimate applications to our own society of such "ethnological" concepts as tribes or ritual by the ill-informed (especially, though not exclusively, nonanthropologists) (e.g., Abélès 1986, see also Althabe et al 1992).

Two more recent collections of essays on the current state of French anthropology include contributions by many of the same scholars. One, entitled "Anthropology today: new fieldsites, new objects," was published in a general-audience magazine on the social sciences (*Sciences Humaines* 1998), and one appeared in a magazine published by a national research institute (CNRS) and directed to professional researchers (*Sciences de l'Homme et de la Société* 1999; see also Godelier 2000). Both suggest that the definition of the discipline as well as the shape and likelihood of its future remain troublesome on essentially the same terms. Implicitly or explicitly, these two publications illustrate the lively debates—perhaps meriting the label of on-going identity crisis—within turn-of-the-century French anthropology as it faces the dispersion of analytical frames and topical specialties, the implications of the inclusion of modern western societies in its purview, questions about the continued pertinence of "classical" themes and concepts, and the nature or desirability of its autonomy with respect to other social science disciplines (see also Althabe 1992, Augé 1994, Bromberger 1997).

This discussion has occurred, of course, within a specifically French institutional framework, which has largely shaped the dynamics of the discipline's development. Before turning to the particular case of the anthropology of France, then, I sketch some of the important characteristics of this context.

INSTITUTIONAL CONTEXT

I should note at the outset that I use the terms "anthropology" and "ethnology" interchangeably to refer to social anthropology. In France, anthropology is not a four-field discipline: Archaeology and physical anthropology are generally defined as separate disciplines, while linguistic anthropology does not exist as such. None of these fields will be considered here. *Ethnologie*, meanwhile, has unambiguously to do with social anthropology, while *anthropologie* is sometimes (and increasingly) used as a synonym, sometimes refers to analyses at a higher order of generalization than that implied by *ethnologie* (i.e., a concern with the human condition generally, rather than consideration or comparison of particular societies), and sometimes (decreasingly) is taken to refer to physical anthropology (Smith 1986). *Ethnographie* has generally lost its association with a specific discipline, coming more commonly to refer loosely to certain kinds of qualitative research methods, potentially no less pertinent to sociology or other social sciences than to anthropology.

A second general point to note is the relatively small size and geographical concentration of the French anthropology field: it includes no more than about four hundred university or research positions nationwide (Fournier 1998), concentrated mainly in Paris, with a few centers in such provincial cities as Toulouse, Aix-en-Provence, Lyon, Strasbourg, and Lille. We are concerned here with a demographic and geographic scale corresponding to one or several small villages divided into hamlets. That is, most French anthropologists may at least potentially know *of* each other, even if their institutional structure is such that they are unlikely to personally know each other or to be familiar with the totality of work produced in the discipline.

In France, there are two main scholarly career tracks, both publically funded: teaching positions in universities or other institutions of higher education, and research positions in such institutions as the National Center of Scientific Research (CNRS), the Institute for Development Research (IRD, formerly ORSTOM), or the Institute for Medical Research (INSERM). Anthropology is unusual among the social sciences in France in its relative absence from higher education, and the commensurately greater importance for the discipline of research positions. It is taught in only about half of the 55 French institutions of higher education providing instruction in the social sciences, often as one of several specialties available within a sociology program. Anthropology degrees (undergraduate or graduate) are offered in only about one quarter (14) of these institutions (Fournier 1998). In all, there are about 150 permanent faculty positions in anthropology nationwide, while a substantially larger number of professional anthropologists hold full-time research positions (especially within CNRS).

This modest academic presence largely accounts both for the small size of the discipline (measured in terms of professional positions) and, because political pressures and institutional inertia make research positions considerably easier than academic posts to eliminate or redistribute to other disciplines, for its exceptional vulnerability to further shrinkage by attrition. This weak institutional position helps account for the on-going liveliness of debates around the discipline's identity, justification, and relationship to other social sciences. Such debates are motivated by pragmatic institutional as well as abstract epistemological concerns.

Another consequence of the relative absence of anthropology from French university curricula is that many professional anthropologists acquire substantial training in another discipline before undertaking anthropology at a fairly advanced stage of their postsecondary studies. At least until the 1970s, an especially important route was through philosophy. A number of the anthropologists completing their studies prior to that period passed the *agrégation* (a national examination roughly equivalent to Ph.D. comprehensive exams) in philosophy before beginning a specialty in anthropology. With the expansion of the university system in the 1960s and 1970s, most social sciences (notably sociology) acquired a substantially larger place in university curricula. Since then, many anthropologists—especially those interested in the study of "modern societies"—have begun their training with studies in sociology or another social science, taking a degree in anthropology only toward the end of their cursus. This pattern has undoubtedly contributed both to the blurring of boundaries between anthropology and other social sciences, and to the persistent distinction between "classical" anthropology and the anthropology of "modern societies."

French patterns of employment for anthropologists also mean that, unlike its American counterpart, French ethnology has developed since World War II primarily as a research rather than as a university-based discipline. Although some permanent researchers teach occasionally or regularly, their primary institutional affiliations and obligations lie elsewhere. The dominant model is the CNRS; hired through and ultimately accountable to a national anthropology commission composed of peers, most French anthropologists are grouped into research "laboratories," usually defined by geographic area or topical focus and sometimes cutting across disciplines, where they are generally free to pursue their own scholarly interests. Affiliation with one or another laboratory is apt to mark one's place on the social map of French ethnology and to reduce the likelihood of active ties with those colleagues in other research groups. At the same time, the collaborative activity formally undertaken by a given laboratory is quite variable but rarely goes beyond the periodic group seminar or occasional collective volume. The noncollaborative nature of most CNRS research groups in anthropology is partly attributable to the fact that very few new groups have been established over the past several decades, as well as to the more perennial absence of any on-going externally imposed collective obligations (of the kind required, for example, of university departments), and the solitary nature of much ethnological research. The result is that the CNRS laboratory organization, applied to anthropology, generally has more to do with maintaining distinctions among research groups than with furthering a shared purpose within them. At its best, this model gives free reign to individual creativity, fostering excellent scholarship reinforced by substantial informal contact with colleagues sharing one's research interests. At its worst, it creates a context that invites the entrenchment of routine, short-circuiting the synergy potentially generated by contact between established and neophyte scholars or across the boundaries of geographic and topical specialties. For better or for worse, this kind of organization, in the absence of widely shared analytical styles or especially powerful intellectual leaders, lends itself to a diversity of research agendas far outstripping what might otherwise be expected of a relatively small scholarly community.

Finally, in France both higher education and scholarly research are matters of the centralized state. The university system and the CNRS, and therefore the large majority of anthropologists, fall under the direct jurisdiction of the Ministry of Education or the Ministry of Research,[4] while other ministries control more specialized institutions of higher education and research institutes. As a result, the general contours of education and research policy—and often quite specific decisions about the allocation of teaching positions or research funding—are closely linked to high-level national politics. This means that persons in or aspiring to powerful positions within anthropology (like other disciplines) must cultivate connections and influence within the halls of political power in the French state. By the same token, French academics and scholars potentially have access to considerable public visibility. French newspapers, for example, regularly publish commentaries, interviews, and book reviews by anthropologists and other scholars, and their books are likely to be advertised and available to a public well beyond the academy. Scholarly journals—those publishing work within a particular discipline (such as *l'Homme, Journal des Anthropologues, Gradhiva, Ethnologie Française, Terrain* for anthropology), no less than those drawing from a broad range of scholars (for instance *Le Débat, Les Temps Modernes*)—are regularly sold in the bookstores of major cities. Although the university classroom provides a relatively less important forum for anthropology in France than it does in the United States, the French audience is more likely to include both a political elite and a broad educated public.

ETHNOLOGY OF FRANCE: EMERGENCE

Throughout the twentieth century, French anthropologists, like their British and American counterparts, have occasionally conducted research in their own or other familiar societies (Hertz 1913, Dumont 1987 [1951], Bernot & Blancard 1953) and have perhaps more frequently made authoritative statements about such settings. In all three anthropological traditions, however, it was only in the 1970s that there emerged a strong and self-conscious move to broaden the purview of legitimate ethnological research to routinely include western societies. Several particularities of the French case stand out. First, although British and American anthropologists

---

[4]Education and research have sometimes been combined within a single Ministry, but in the current government each of these state-sponsored functions has its own Ministry.

have generally conceptualized this move in spatial terms (especially with reference to western societies), French anthropologists have come most often to perceive it in temporal terms (especially with reference to contemporary societies, or the ethnology of the present). Secondly, although British and American anthropologists have been as likely to turn their attentions to a range of European societies as to their own, French anthropologists engaged in broadening the scope of ethnology have—at least until quite recently—focused almost exclusively on the study of France. Finally, although literary-based cultural studies has been an important interlocutor (positively or negatively) in the emergence of British and American anthropologies "at home," it has generally been other *sciences humaines* (especially history and sociology) that have played this role in France (cf. Marcus 1999). Although some of the motivations for the late–twentieth century broadening of the ethnological enterprise are undoubtedly shared across anthropological traditions, then, each has also been significantly shaped by its own national trajectory (Rogers 1999).

Contemporary French anthropology of France is arguably the child of two estranged parents of unequal social standing: ethnology and folklore (Chiva 1987, Segalen 1989b, Cuisinier & Segalen 1993, Bromberger 1987). Twentieth century French ethnology, conventionally defined by an intellectual genealogy running from Durkheim (1858–1917) to Mauss (1872–1950) to Lévi-Strauss (1908–), began as a museum-based discipline and became a research-based enterprise by mid-century. Twentieth century French folklore has remained a museum-based domain, and has been associated with a less well-established genealogy that includes Arnold Van Gennep (1873–1957), André Varagnac (1896–1984), and Georges-Henri Rivière (1897–1985). Both lineages have been premised on a radical distinction between pre-literate (primitive, simple, cold) societies and those that are literate (modern, complex, hot). The Durkheimian project is familiar enough: Ethnology was understood to make a crucial contribution to a larger and universalizing science of society through the study of the first type of society, promising an understanding of fundamental structures of social life.[5]

Folklore, on the other hand, was generally understood to be concerned with the practices and beliefs of common people in literate societies (especially in rural Europe), and by some definitions it was further limited to those elements of culture that might be considered survivals of a pre-industrial past (Belmont 1986; Cuisinier & Segalen 1993, p. 19). In the view of Durkheim and his intellectual descendents, ethnology could be further distinguished from folklore by the scientific rigor of the former and the antiquarian triviality of the latter (Barthelemy & Weber 1989, p. 127). In part because of folklore's (and Van Gennep's) marginalization with respect to the Durkheimian vision of social science, folklore in general never acquired the scholarly standing in France that it did elsewhere in Europe, remaining

---

[5]Lévi-Strauss's articulation of this position, a passage from his essay on "The place of anthropology in the social sciences" is frequently cited in the discussions evoked above (Lévi-Strauss 1967, p. 344).

associated primarily with museums (especially the national Museum of Popular Arts and Traditions as well as a number of provincial museums) and provincial learned societies. Nor did folklore acquire the same political weight in nineteenth and early twentieth century French nation-building as was the case elsewhere, largely because the diverse customs of rural folk offered a weak—and potentially reactionary—counter to claims about the rational or Revolutionary roots of the nation (Belmont 1986, Bromberger 1996). Indeed, the Vichy regime's embrace of folklore during World War II both further crippled the future of French folklore studies and blackened or deleted altogether subsequent perceptions of its past (Fabre 1998, Weber 2001).

The legacy of French folklore studies and the history of its relationship to ethnology were revisited in the 1970s and 1980s by a number of scholars committed to establishing the legitimacy of ethnological approaches to the study of France. The historical depth and legitimacy—as well as the political color—of sharp distinctions between "primitive" ethnology and French folklore have been challenged, for example, through consideration of their shared institutional foundations. In particular, the Trocadero Musée d'Ethnographie, founded in 1878, included a French Room displaying collections from the provinces, as well as displays collected in primitive or exotic societies. It was only in 1937, under the auspices of the left-wing Popular Front government, that its two offshoots were inaugurated: a Musée de l'Homme (concerned mainly with collections from non-European societies) and the Musée des Arts et Traditions Populaires (concerned with French folk culture). Rivière, founding director of the latter had worked closely at the older museum with, and was strongly influenced by, not only Paul Rivet, founding director of the Musée de l'Homme, but also other key figures in the development of French anthropology, most notably, Marcel Mauss (Cuisenier & Segalen 1993, Chiva 1987). Further, the work of such scholars associated with folklore as Van Gennep (Belmont 1974) and Rivière (Chiva 1985) is shown not only to have been scientifically rigorous but to have subscribed to or anticipated analytical frames and empirical standards that unambiguously merit the ethnological label. Belmont subtitles her book on Van Gennep "Father of French Ethnography," for example, while an article on Rivière opens with the phrase "Georges Henri Rivière was an ethnologist" (Desvallées 1987). Finally, the career trajectories of various key players are frequently evoked to establish the permeability of distinctions between the (folkloric) study of France and ethnology, and the marriageability of the two. For example, Van Gennep's pre-1924 publications were all based on ethnological materials from primitive societies (Belmont 1974), Rivière began his anthropological career at an ethnographic museum, Louis Dumont's first publication was a study of a popular festival in southern France (Dumont 1987 [1951]), and the Southeast Asianist Lucien Bernot began his career with a French village study, published by the Institut d'Ethnologie (Bernot & Blancard 1953). In general, the argument is less that folklore is, after all, a legitimate form of study, than that significant bodies of research conducted under that rubric in France beginning in the first half of the twentieth century can legitimately be considered ethnology.

As it emerged in the 1970s, French anthropology of France was in fact a marriage of these two traditions. Concerned almost exclusively with reconstituting, through oral histories and archival materials, earlier lifeways in one or another rural French setting, this body of work dealt with the stuff of folklore: the traces of oral tradition, belief, ritual, material culture, and technology to be found in French peasant societies. At the same time, it was consistent with the conventions defining ethnology: Deploying both temporal (albeit archaic rather than primitive) and spatial (albeit provincial rather than exotic) distance, these ethnologists identified not-hot (albeit tepid rather than truly cold) and relatively simple societies within France. In the local monographs they produced, they ably demonstrated the pertinence of such well-established ethnological domains and the conventional tools for analyzing them as kinship, ritual, sorcery, collective and private property, concepts of time and space, processes of social cohesion (e.g., Favret-Saada 1977, Verdier 1979, Karnoouh 1980, Zonabend 1980, Assier-Andrieu 1981, Claverie & Lamaison 1982, Segalen 1985).[6] Most of the scholars producing such work were affiliated with one of two research groups: the Centre d'Ethnologie Française at the Musée des Arts et Traditions Populaires, where there was a commitment to demonstrating that research on France could in fact be properly ethnological[7] or the Laboratoire d'Anthropologie Sociale at the Collège de France, where some researchers were interested in demonstrating that real anthropologists could legitimately work on France.[8]

In addition to offering a way of reconciling the study of France with the established conventions of French ethnology, this style of research was clearly situated with respect to other disciplines that have longer roots in the study of French society. On the one hand, it found a powerful ally in the French history establishment, by then dominated by *Annales* history concerned with the social analysis of ordinary life, especially in the diverse rural societies largely comprising pre-Revolutionary France. Many *Annales* historians found in this version of ethnology a fruitful interlocuter able to offer, around a shared interest in rural French societies of the past, a new source of research problems, insights, and explanation, as well as a legitimizing association with a bona fide social science (Burguière 1978, Goy 1986). On the other hand, this style of research was easily distinguishable from sociological approaches to the study of French

---

[6]Note that although most of these books were published in the early 1980s, they were based on research conducted in the 1970s and generated a considerable journal literature, as well as more informal discussion, during that decade.

[7]It is certainly relevant that the title of the journal published by this group was renamed *Ethnologie Française* in 1971, succeeding a series of journals published since 1882, all having instead *folklore, traditions populaires,* and/or *ethnographie* in their titles (*Ethnologie Française* 1997).

[8]But note Abélès' impression as a young researcher joining this group during the 1970s that "the most prestigious researchers ... were all working on more exotic sites. [France] was left to the women, and work there was treated more as a curiosity than as something truly serious" (Abélès 1999, p. 405).

society, even from the then-lively field of rural sociology. During the 1970s, French rural sociologists were primarily concerned with the dramatic changes sweeping rural France since World War II (Mendras 1970, Jollivet 1974, Lamarche 1980). In contrast, although ethnologists sometimes included a final chapter on recent changes (e.g., Assier-Andrieu 1981), they generally focused their attention on the reconstruction of earlier and slower-moving rural societies, emphasizing their distinctiveness rather than their connections to the French nation or state. On the whole, modernity and processes of local or large-scale change (in rural as well as urban settings) were left to sociologists, while ethnologists focused on deep structure and the recoverable traces of a relatively stable and small-scale past (almost exclusively in rural settings). The ethnological enterprise was thus established on French soil via selective interweaving of (largely discredited) folklore and honorable ethnological conventions, astute flirtation with a legitimizing history establishment, and a clear distinction from sociology (Rogers 1995).

This arrangement lasted barely a decade. By the end of the 1980s, folklore was a dead issue. Rural France had been replaced on the French anthropological agenda by the "ethnology of the present." The flirtation with history had largely ended, and distinctions between sociological and anthropological approaches to the study of France were blurred. Debates about the cohesion of the discipline and legitimate objects of anthropological research were rife.

ETHNOLOGY OF FRANCE: IN THE PRESENT

The development of the ethnology of France over the past two decades has been immeasurably furthered and shaped by the establishment in 1980 of a *Mission de Patrimoine Ethnologique* (Division of Ethnological Heritage) within the French Ministry of Culture (Chiva 1990, Langlois 1999, Fabre 2000). This agency was initiated by Isac Chiva (then the associate director of Lévi-Strauss's *Laboratoire d'Anthropologie Sociale* and formerly an associate of G-H Rivière at the *Musée des Arts et Traditions Populaires*) and other anthropologists interested in promoting ethnological approaches to the study of France. Formally independent of the research institutes and teaching units that hire anthropologists, the *Mission* has injected substantial resources into this domain by providing competitive grants for ethnological research in France and outlets for the publication of its results. Its role has been a proactive one. A governing board composed of anthropologists, as well as representatives of CNRS, the national Museum Service, and other high civil servants defines a research theme each year for which it invites proposals, funding about 500 projects over the past 20 years. Since 1983, it has published the journal *Terrain*, now one of the principle four or five anthropology journals in France. Each of its biannual issues is organized around a theme, grouping fieldwork-based articles meant to appeal to both a professional and a general audience (see Appendix). Although articles based on research elsewhere in Europe or in more "exotic" settings have increasingly appeared in recent years, this publication focuses principally on France. Finally, the *Mission* publishes several books each year, including both ethnographic monographs (e.g., Vialles 1987, Moulinié 1998) and edited collections (e.g., Voisenat 1995, Fabre 1997, Bromberger & Chevallier 1999).[9]

As a glance at the Appendix, listing the titles of theme issues of the journals *Ethnologie Française* (since 1971) and *Terrain* (since 1983) suggests, it is no easy matter to summarize the considerable output of ethnological research undertaken in France over the last two decades. Covering a dizzying array of topics, it has been conducted by researchers affiliated with various research groups including the two noted above, but also a number of others, such as the more recently established Laboratoire d'Anthropologie des Institutions et des Organisations Sociales (LAIOS), Centre d'Anthropologie des Mondes Contemporaines (CAMC), and the Laboratoire d'Anthropologie Urbaine, all in Paris, as well as a number of provincial research centers, including the Centre d'Anthropologie in Toulouse and the Institut d'Ethnologie Méditerranéenne et Comparative in Aix. This scholarly production has also been fed by a considerable number of persons with recent graduate training but no permanent employment as anthropologists.

The main thrust of earlier ethnology of France is easy enough to summarize with reference to its focus on the reconstruction of archaic and small-scale rural societies and its clear relationships to history, sociology, and general anthropology. It is perhaps only a slight oversimplification to argue that it now tends to be focused on the social processes, observable in a wide range of settings, by which social difference, cohesion, and complex forms of integration are produced, expressed, and maintained. Further, such research stands in a variety of relationships to the conventions associated with "classical" anthropology and the other social sciences.

For example, although peasant villages have generally been abandoned as pertinent fieldsites, some ethnologists have focused on other kinds of relatively well-defined marginal groups: for example, residents of housing projects (Pétonnet 1985, Lepoutre 1997), Parisian homeless persons (Gaboriau 1993), gypsies (Williams 1993), ethnic minorities (Hassoun 1997, Raulin 2000). Based on participant observation research of varying intensity, such studies generally explicitly reject widely shared visions of the subject group as isolated, chaotic, or trapped by static culture. Instead, they aim to explore the ways in which their subjects construct a social universe that is both internally coherent and actively engaged with the larger French context. Drawing on well-established conventions of ethnological inquiry in their analyses of social relationships expressed, for example, in ritual practices, patterns of exchange, uses of language and names, and the meanings of everyday objects, this work challenges a body of sociological research concerned

---

[9]Of the items listed in the attached bibliography, most of those published by the Editions de la Maison des Sciences de l'Homme are part of a *Mission* series. A few of these have also been published in English translation by Cambridge University Press.

with the social disintegration widely perceived in contemporary France. In the latter body of scholarship, formal institutions are given a more central role; the social disarray and exclusion generally associated with such groups is apt to be given as a social problem and to be analyzed in terms of the breakdown of French institutions of integration (e.g., Dubet 1991, Donzelot 1991, Wieviorka 1991).

The study of marginal groups has not provided the only locus for such reconsiderations of widely held ideas about social cohesion and difference in contemporary French society through analyses of social relations expressed in the symbolic and material practices of everyday life. Indeed, although the establishment of distance between the researcher and his or her subjects is often invoked as epistemologically and methodologically crucial to the ethnological enterprise, French ethnologists of France have not focused predominantly on groups located at a maximum (lower) social distance from themselves. For many, the move from the countryside and into the present rested on assertions that the usefulness of ethnological tools of analysis extends beyond the archaic, exotic, or downtrodden (e.g., Althabe et al 1993). Deploying a range of strategies similar to those noted above, for example, Weber (1989) draws on a community study to argue that a distinctive working class persists in France, despite claims to the contrary; Chalvon-Demersay (1998) analyzes the dynamic by which social distinctions are both asserted and masked in a Parisian neighborhood undergoing gentrification; Le Wita (1988) explores the mechanisms by which the Parisian bourgeoisie both reproduces and denies the distinctiveness of its culture; Bellier (1993) analyzes the social dynamics within the elite Ecole Nationale d'Administration to uncover the processes by which an esprit de corps is forged among the high civil servants it trains; Hassoun (2000) examines the production of social relationships among pit traders on the Paris stock exchange.

Further, a clear opposition is not necessarily to be found between ethnological and sociological research of this kind. Indeed, among those monographs written in the last two decades on one or another social category, the distinction between those produced by ethnologists and those by sociologists is sometimes barely perceptible. On one hand, the analysis of social reproduction, in terms borrowed from sociologist Pierre Bourdieu, has been key to many ethnologists.[10] On the other, many French sociologists since the 1980s, frequently inspired by Chicago School sociology or the work of Goffman and Garfinkel, deploy ethnographic methods to render fine-grained, actor-centered case studies (e.g., Pinçon & Pinçon-Charlot 1989, 1993; Beaud & Pialoux 1999).[11] Some scholars in either

---

[10]French ethnologists generally borrow quite a different version of Bourdieu's thought than do American anthropologists. See Bahloul's comments on this transatlantic reinterpretation (1991).

[11]Note for example, that in a recent textbook on sociological research methods, only three of nine chapters are concerned with formal or quantitative methods of analysis; the first three chapters are on ethnographic observation, participant-observation, and local studies respectively, while a later chapter treats life histories (Mendras & Oberti 2000).

discipline consider the distinction between the two to be insubstantial, and calls for the erasure of the boundary have occasionally been made (notably Bouvier 1995, 2000).

The study of family and kinship illustrates a somewhat different configuration of intra- and inter-disciplinary relationships. In their effort to demonstrate the amenability of French settings to ethnological analysis, a number of the ethnologists conducting research in rural France in the 1970s incorporated the analysis of kinship systems into their studies, using those tools most associated with the prestigious heart of French anthropology. Without a doubt, says one (perhaps wishfully), "research on descent and alliance among French populations, past and present, significantly contributed to the integration of the ethnology of France within the general discipline" (Lamaison 1987, p. 112, my translation). With the move out of an archaic countryside and into the present, however, kinship analysis, almost alone among the ethnological tools of the trade used initially in French settings, has largely disappeared from the ethnology of France. General discussions of kinship studies in France, for example, draw heavily on work concerned with peasant societies and become notably thinner with regard to the rest (e.g., Zonabend 1987, Salitot et al 1989, Segalen 1992). It would appear that the conceptual tools developed in kin-based societies were found difficult to apply plausibly in settings largely organized around other kinds of social relations. At the same time, the field of family sociology, resting on quite a different problematic, largely dominates the study of family systems and relationships in France (e.g., Singly 1991). Claims about the pertinence of the French setting to a full understanding of kinship (Zonabend 1994) or of anthropological concepts to an understanding of French family and kinship (Weber 2000) are occasionally made. But with few exceptions, notably work (especially in historical anthropology) on fictive or ritual kinship (Cadoret 1995; Fine 1994, 1998), a domain generally neglected by family sociologists, kinship has dropped from the purview of the ethnology of France. It is significant that in recent public debates around legislation permitting homosexual marriage, the expertise of family sociologists and of anthropologists of the exotic (including Lévi-Strauss himself) was solicited by journalists and lawmakers, but not that of ethnologists of France (Borrillo et al 1999). On another register, the recent special issue on kinship of *L'Homme*, a 700-page tribute marking the fiftieth anniversary of the publication of Lévi-Strauss's *Elementary Structures of Kinship*, included only two articles on France, one on genealogical memory in a rural setting (Zonabend 2000) and one by a nonanthropologist (Fassin 2000). For at least some ethnologists of France, this amounted to exclusion from anthropology's inner sanctum, symptomatic of the discipline's persistent resistance to acknowledging contemporary France as a legitimate site of ethnological research.

One challenge to anthropological conventions posed by ethnological research in France (or vice versa), frequently invoked by its practitioners, concerns the ideal of holism or the strategy of focusing on "total" social facts that may illuminate a given society in its entirety. Research agendas for the ethnological analysis of

France-as-a-whole, for example through some facet of its national heritage (*patrimoine*) have occasionally been proposed (e.g., Fabre 1996, 2000).[12] In practice, however, most of the ethnological research conducted in France concerns particular socially or territorially defined segments of French society. It might be argued that the pervasive concern in this literature to illuminate the formation or expression of social difference and collective identity is itself an important social fact about contemporary France. Nonetheless, very little of the ethnological research conducted in France claims to be about France as a whole. In this sense, the *grand partage* would seem to hold firm: Some types of societies are amenable to anthropology's holistic approach, but others, more complex or less distant, lend themselves better to a focus on their discrete dimensions or segments. Alternatively, it is sometimes argued that anthropology's claim to capture a whole society in the round is a hopeless delusion, in exotic settings no less than in France (e.g., La Pradelle 2000). One exception is Abélès' work on French institutions purporting to draw together the society as a whole. In his analyses of social relations among politicians and between constituents and their elected representatives (1989, 2000), he captures the logic of French territorial integration and governance, as well as key characteristics of French national identity. Explicitly differentiating his approach from the quantitative methods and concern with more narrowly political phenomena that are generally characteristic of political science research (1989, p. 13–14), he grounds his work in classical anthropological strategies for uncovering definitive elements of a society's social organization through analysis of its political institutions and practices.

If relatively few of the French ethnologists conducting research in France claim to extend their analysis beyond one or another segment of French society, some aim to transcend the French case altogether, to explore the nature of social relations in the contemporary world. For example, La Pradelle's study of a small-town market in southern France (1996) and Bromberger's analysis of soccer matches (1995) both focus on well-defined spaces in which sociologically diverse persons are drawn together to share in a spectacle shown to operate as a kind of modern ritual, similar in some ways to the classic Durkheimian ritual of social integration and collective identity, but also revealing of certain characteristics of social relations held to be specific to life in today's world (see also Augé 1992). While many ethnologists of France have been concerned to show that the social processes at work in France are, after all, similar enough to those found

---

[12]D. Fabre's interest in an ethnology of France-as-a-whole is undoubtedly related to the fact that he has been considerably more insistent than many ethnologists of France on the importance of cross-national comparison. The research group he directs (in Toulouse) has been closely involved with research and researchers in other European countries, especially Italy and Spain. This commitment is reflected in the collective volumes he has edited (e.g., 1996, 2000). An interest in southern European cross-national comparisons is also characteristic of research conducted by members of the group headed by C. Bromberger in Aix-en-Provence but is generally less evident among the Parisian laboratories.

in societies more conventionally associated with the ethnological enterprise to render legitimate the repatriation of ethnological tools of analysis, some have used the French case to reassert a temporal divide. In the latter view, social processes observable in contemporary France are different from those to be found in the primitive settings of classical ethnology and promise to offer the keys for an anthropology of the world (exotic or familiar) in which we all now find ourselves.

CONCLUSIONS

The world that generated anthropology as an autonomous discipline concerned with the study of the primitive or exotic has, by many measures, been relegated to the dustbin of history. This fact is perhaps especially obvious in France, where the fragility of the discipline's institutional standing is matched only by its national and international renown. There, the substantial bodies of ethnological research conducted in France over the past several decades—considerably more than could be adequately covered in these few pages—represent one kind of effort to reposition the discipline under these circumstances. This development has been shaped in large measure by the powerful institutional support and substantial material resources invested by the Ministry of Culture's *Mission de Patrimoine Ethnologique*. It has also been shaped by a ranked distinction that remains salient for some French anthropologists between, on the one hand, "real" anthropologists, defined most frequently in terms of their subjects' distance in space (exotic) and, on the other, anthropologists conducting research in France, usually defined by their subjects' proximity in time (contemporary, the present). This asymmetry of definition is perhaps best explained by the ongoing efforts of the latter to establish their work as a legitimate new development of the discipline, rather than as simply the addition of another geographically defined ethnographic case. As we have seen, ethnologists of France have most frequently been concerned to demonstrate that well-established analytic and conceptual tools developed in "exotic" settings may effectively illuminate social processes within French society. Alternatively, French settings have sometimes been used as sites for adapting anthropological tools to the kinds of social relations thought characteristic of today's world. Either way, the underlying argument is that social processes observable in France are fundamentally similar to those found elsewhere. French settings are thus used to demonstrate the ongoing pertinence of an ultimately universalizing anthropological enterprise for understanding the collective processes by which people integrate themselves into coherent groups and differentiate themselves from others.

Such demonstrations have not always been convincing to others in the discipline, and it remains equally unclear what the ethnology of France might add to better-established forms of knowledge about such societies, especially those forms produced within other social sciences. As we have seen, ethnologists have at times reproduced an old division of labor by retreating to those corners of French society left unexamined by scholars in other disciplines. When they venture onto ground occupied by others, sometimes borrowing tools and concepts across disciplinary lines, they produce analyses that have alternately challenged, complemented, or closely resembled those associated with other disciplinary traditions.

When they claim that their research in France constitutes an ethnology of the present, French ethnologists are ultimately situating their work in our time rather than in a particular place. This stance arguably distinguishes their work from that produced within other French social sciences, more likely to be ultimately concerned with France in particular (in its historical, social, political ... dimensions). Indeed, analysis of specific settings with reference to a broadly comparative framework—consistent with an ultimate concern to grasp human society in general—is undoubtedly one of anthropology's most powerful and distinctive characteristics. To the extent that the ethnology of the present draws exclusively on the study of contemporary settings in France, however, there is a considerable risk of universalizing specific characteristics of the French case, and losing the comparative perspective that defines and distinguishes anthropology.

If French ethnologists involved in developing an anthropology of "contemporary society" sometimes seem perilously overfocused on French locales, they have nonetheless vigorously resisted the autobiographical mode they associate with Anglo-American "post-modern" anthropology. Brief personal accounts of fieldwork experience are occasionally included in ethnographic monographs, but sustained reflexivity has not been a French ethnological mode. Whether conducted at home or abroad, ethnological research is not presented as being about an individual self. By the same token, it generally does not rest on a vision of the contemporary world as an inherently incoherent one. Rather, for all its diversity of themes and analytic frames, French anthropology remains largely concerned with understanding the social processes engaged in creating an orderly universe around collective meanings, social cohesion, and perceptions of difference.

ACKNOWLEDGMENTS

My understanding of anthropology in and of France comes from the many opportunities I have been given, beginning with my initial rural French fieldwork in 1971, to work as the American student, collaborator, colleague, or visiting professor of more French anthropologists and other social scientists than I can list by name here. My debt to them, for their hospitality, time, and encouragement over many years, is enormous. For their suggestions and comments on this paper, I would especially like to thank Marc Abélès, Gérard Althabe, Jean-Pierre Hassoun, Benoit de l'Estoile, Anne Raulin, Emmanuelle Saada, Florence Weber, and T.O. Beidelman. Responsibility for any errors, misstatements, or distortions, is entirely mine.

APPENDIX

The table below, listing the titles (my translation) of theme issues published by the two French journals principally concerned with the ethnology of France, offers an overview of the range and evolution of topics treated within this domain. Note that *Ethnologie Française*, founded as such in 1971, is the quarterly journal of the *Société d'Ethnologie Française* (SEF) and is published by the research group *Centre d'Ethnologie Française*, housed at the *Musée des Arts et Traditions Populaires* (MATP). Many of its theme issues correspond to colloquia organized by SEF or exhibits and collections at MATP. *Terrain* was established in 1983 as a publication of the *Mission du Patrimoine Ethnologique* at the Ministry of Culture. Many of its theme issues reflect the annual research themes for which the *Mission* has awarded competitive grants. Sharing a focus on ethnological approaches to the study of France, the two journals publish the work of largely overlapping networks of scholars, mainly composed of anthropologists, but also including other social scientists.

Year	*Ethnologie Française* (since 1971)	*Terrain* (since 1983)
1973	Rural Architecture	
1973	Language diversity in France	
1974	Research in Chardonneret [a rural community]	
1976	The body (language and images)	
1977	Immigrant workers	
1978	Anthropology of art	
1979	Maritime ethnology	
1980	Provinces and provincials in Paris	
1980	Food habits in France	
1981	Official and popular religion	
1981	Kinship and marriage in peasant societies	
1982	Cultural anthropology in urban settings	
1983	Contemporary popular imagery	Folk environmental knowledge
1983	Ostensions [a religious ritual] in the Limousin region	
1984	The production of symbols among workers	Industrial anthropology
1984	Recent research in ethnomusicology	Urban ethnology
1985	Furniture: classic approaches and formal analysis	Family and kinship

Appendix   *(Continued)*

Year	*Ethnologie Française* (since 1971)	*Terrain* (since 1983)
1985		Cultural identity and regional ties
1986	Household linens and underwear	Man and the natural environment
1986		Foreign communities in France
1987	Georges-Henri Rivière	Contemporary rituals
1987	Chance and societies	Living in houses
1988	Ethnology and racisms	Man and animals
1988	Regionalisms	
1989	Textiles	Family consumption practices
1989	Physical appearance	Drinking
1989	Crisis of landscape?	
1990	Bourgeois cultures	Proving the unbelievable
1990	Animal figures	Appearing in public
1990	Between the oral and the written	
1990	The paradoxes of color	
1991	American anthropologists: views of France	Skill
1991	Violence, brutality and barbarism	Nations in Europe
1991	Apprenticeships	
1992	The body, illness and society	The body
1992	Words of outrage	Fire
1993	Mythical textures	Death
1993	Immigration, identities, integration	Power: clientelism revisited
1993	Science and parascience	
1994	Thinking about heredity	Emotions
1994	Uses of images	Uses of money
1994	Anthropology in Italy	
1995	Heritages [Patrimoines] in question	The making of saints
1995	Motivation in the social sciences	Sports
1995	Romania: national construction	
1996	Material culture and modernity	Dreaming
1996	Ritualization of daily life	Love
1996	Russia	
1997	Food habits and cultural identity	Mirrors of colonialism
1997	Practices, rituals	Living in time
1997	Which ethnologies? France, Europe 1971–1997	

(Continued)

Appendix   (*Continued*)

Year	*Ethnologie Française* (since 1971)	*Terrain* (since 1983)
1997	Germany: questions	
1998	AIDS: mourning, memory, new rituals	Looking
1998	Metamorphosis	Pure bodies
1998	Asterix: myth and images	
1998	Gifts: at what price?	
1999	Street music and playgrounds	Beauty
1999	Portugal: from Tage to the China Sea	Authenticity?
1999	Museum, nation: after the colonies	
1999	Words and institutions	
2000	Time	Do animals think?
2000	Spain: anthropology and cultures	Dance
2000	Ins and outs of transmission	
2000	New religious movements	

Visit the Annual Reviews home page at www.AnnualReviews.org

LITERATURE CITED

Abélès M. 1986. L'anthropologie et le politique. See *L'Homme* 1986, pp. 207–34

Abélès M. 1989. *Jours Tranquilles en 89: Ethnologie Politique d'un Département Français*. Paris: Odile Jacob. 365 pp. Transl.: 1991. *Quiet Days in Burgundy: A Study of Local Politics*. A McDermott. Cambridge: Cambridge Univ. Press. 279 pp.

Abélès M. 1996. La Communauté Européene: une perspective anthropologique. *Soc. Anthropol.* 4:33–45

Abélès M. 1999. How the anthropology of France has changed anthropology in France: assessing new directions in the field. *Cult. Anthropol.* 14:404–8

Abélès M. 2000. *Un Ethnologue à L'Assemblée*. Paris: Odile Jacob. 283 pp.

Althabe G. 1992. Vers une ethnologie du présent. See Althabe et al. 1992, pp. 247–57

Althabe G, Fabre D, Lenclud G, eds. 1992. *Vers une Ethnologie du Présent*. Paris: Edit. Maison Sci. l'Homme. 259 pp.

Althabe G, Marcadet C, de La Pradelle M, Sélim M. 1993. *Urbanisation et Enjeux Quotidiens: Terrains Ethnologiques dans la France Actuelle*. Paris: Harmattan. 199 pp.

Assier-Andrieu L. 1981. *Coutumes et Rapports Sociaux: Etude Anthropologique des Communautés Paysannes du Capcir*. Paris: Editions CNRS. 215 pp.

Augé M. 1986. L'anthropologie de la maladie. See *L'Homme* 1986, pp. 77–88

Augé M. 1992. *Non-Lieux: Introduction à une Anthropologie de la Surmodernité*. Paris: Seuil. 156 pp. Transl. 1995. *Non-Places: Introduction to an Anthropology of Surmodernity*. Transl. J Howe. New York: Verso. 122 pp.

Augé M. 1994. *Pour une Anthropologie des Mondes Contemporains*. Paris: Aubier. 196 pp. Transl.: 1999. *An Anthropology for Contemporaneous Worlds*. A Jacobs. Stanford, CA: Stanford Univ. Press. 144 pp.

Augustins G. 1989. *Comment se Perpétuer? Devenir des Lignées et Destins des Patrimoines dans les Paysanneries Européennes.* Nanterre: Soc. d'Ethnol. 433 pp.

Bahloul J. 1991. France-USA: ethnographie d'une migration intellectuelle. *Ethnol. Française* 21:49–55

Barthelemy T, Weber F, eds. 1989. *Les Campagnes à Livre Ouvert: Regards sur la France Rurale des Années Trente.* Paris: Presses de L'Ecole Normale Supérieure. 262 pp.

Beaud S, Pialoux M. 1999. *Retour sur la Condition Ouvrière: Enquête aux Usines Peugeot de Sochaux-Montbéliard.* Paris: Fayard. 468 pp.

Beitl K, Bromberger C, Chiva I, eds. 1997. *Mots et Choses de L'Ethnographie de la France: Regards Allemands et Autrichiens sur la France Rurale dans les Années 30.* Paris: Edit. Maison Sci. L'Homme. 241 pp.

Bellier I. 1993. *L'ENA Comme si Vous y Etiez.* Paris: Seuil. 350 pp.

Bellier I. 1995. Moralité, langue et pouvoirs dans les institutions européénes. *Soc. Anthropol.* 3:235–50

Belmont N. 1974. *Arnold Van Gennep: Le Créateur de l'Ethnographie Française.* Paris: Payot. 187 pp.

Belmont N. 1986. Le folklore refoulé ou les séductions de l'archaisme. See *L'Homme* 1986, pp. 287–98

Bernard C, Digard JP. 1986. De Téhéran à Tehuantepec: l'ethnologie au crible des aires culturelles. See *L'Homme* 1986, pp. 54–76

Bernot L, Blancard R. 1953. *Nouville, un village français.* Paris: Inst. d'Ethnol. 447 pp.

Borrillo D, Fassin E, Iacub M, eds. 1999. *Au-Delà du PaCS: L'Expertise Familiale à l'Epreuve de l'Homosexualité.* Paris: Presses Univ. France. 273 pp.

Bouvier P. 1995. *Socio-Anthropologie du Contemporain.* Paris: Galillée. 176 pp.

Bouvier P. 2000. *La Socio-Anthropologie.* Paris: Colin. 218 pp.

Bromberger C. 1987. Du grand au petit: variations des échelles et des objets d'analyse dans l'histoire récente de l'ethnologie de la France. See Chiva & Jeggle 1987, pp. 67–94

Bromberger C. 1995. *Le Match de Football: Ethnologie d'une Passion Partisane à Marseille, Naples et Turin.* Paris: Edit. Maison Sci. l'Homme. 406 pp.

Bromberger C. 1996. Ethnologie, patrimoine, identités: y a-t-il une spécificité de la situation française? See Fabre 1996, pp. 9–23

Bromberger C. 1997. L'ethnologie de la France et ses nouveaux objets: crise, tatonnements et jouvence d'une discipline dérangeante. *Ethnol. Française* 27:294–313

Bromberger C, Chevallier D, eds. 1999. *Carrières des Objets: Innovations et Relances.* Paris: Edit. Maison Sci. l'Homme. 224 pp.

Burguière A. 1978. The new Annales: a redefinition of the late sixties. *Review* 1:195–205

Cadoret A. 1995. *Parenté Plurielle: Anthropologie du Placement Familial.* Paris: L'Harmattan. 230 pp.

Chalvon-Demersay S. 1998. *Le Triangle du XIVe: Des Nouveaux Habitants dans un Vieux Quartier de Paris.* Paris: Edit. Maison Sci. L'Homme. 173 pp.

Chiva I. 1985. Georges-Henri Rivière: un demi-siècle d'ethnologie de la France. *Terrain* 5:76–83

Chiva I. 1987. Entre livre et musée: émergence d'une ethnologie de la France. See Chiva & Jeggle 1987, pp. 9–33

Chiva I. 1990. Le patrimoine ethnologique: l'exemple de la France. *Encyclopaedia Universalis* 24:229–41

Chiva I, Jeggle U, eds. 1987. *Ethnologies en Miroir: La France et les Pays de Langue Allemande.* Paris: Edit. Maison Sci. L'Homme. 396 pp.

Claverie E, Lamaison P. 1982. *L'Impossible Mariage: Violence et Parenté en Gévaudan 17e, 18e, 19e Siècles.* Paris: Hachette. 363 pp.

Cuisenier J, Segalen M. 1993 [1986]. *Ethnologie de la France.* Paris: Presses Univ. de France. 127 pp.

de La Pradelle M. 1996. *Les Vendredis de Carpentras: Faire son Marché en Provence ou Ailleurs.* Paris: Fayard.

de La Pradelle M. 2000. La ville des anthropologues. In *La Ville et L'Urbain: L'Etat des*

Savoirs, ed. T Paquot, M Lussault, S Body-Gendrot, pp. 45–52. Paris: La Découverte. 442 pp.

de Singly F, ed. 1991. *La Famille: L'Etat des Savoirs*. Paris: La Découverte. 448 pp.

Desvallées A. 1987. Les musées de l'homme, du temps, de l'espace. *Ethnol. Française* 1987(1):59–60

Donzelot J, ed. 1991. *Face à l'Exclusion: Le Modèle Française*. Paris: Esprit. 227 pp.

Dubet F. 1991. *Les Lycéens*. Paris: Seuil. 410 pp.

Dumont L. 1987 [1951]. *Tarasque: Essai de Description d'un Fait Local d'un Point de Vue Ethnographique*. Paris: Gallimard. 258 pp.

Ethnologie Française. 1997. Filiation de la revue *Ethnologie Française*. *Ethnol. Française* 27:402–3

Fabre D, ed. 1996. *L'Europe entre Cultures et Nations*. Paris: Edit. Maison Sci. L'Homme. 343 pp.

Fabre D, ed. 1997. *Par Ecrit: Ethnologie des Ecritures Quotidiennes*. Paris: Edit. Maison Sci. L'Homme. 396 pp.

Fabre D. 1998. L'ethnologie française à la croisée des engagements (1940-1945). In *Résistants et Résistance*, ed. JY Boursier, pp. 319–400. Paris: L'Harmattan. 408 pp.

Fabre D. 2000. L'ethnologie devant le monument historique. In *Domestiquer L'Histoire: Ethnologie des Monuments Historiques*, ed. D Fabre, pp. 1–29. Paris: Edit. Maison Sci. L'Homme. 222 pp.

Fassin E. 2000. Usages de la science et science des usages: à propos des familles homoparentales. *L'Homme* 154–5:391–408

Favret-Saada J. 1977. *Les Mots, la Mort, les Sorts: La Sorcellerie dans le Bocage*. Paris: Gallimard. 332 pp. Transl.: 1980. *Deadly Words: Witchcraft in the Bocage*. C Cullen. New York: Cambridge Univ. Press. 273 pp.

Fine A, 1994. *Parrains, Marraines: La Parenté Spirituelle en Europe*. Paris: Fayard. 389 pp.

Fine A, ed. 1998. *Adoptions: Ethnologie des Parentés Choisies*. Paris: Edit. Maison Sci. L'Homme. 311 pp.

Fournier M. 1998. Profession: ethnologue. *Sci. Hum.* 23:60–63

Gaboriau P. 1993. *Clochard*. Paris: Julliard. 235 pp.

Godelier M. 2000. Le métier de chercheur. *Sci. l'Homme Soc.* 58:12–18

Goy J. 1986. Histoire rurale. In *Dictionnaire des Sciences Historiques*, ed. A Burguière. pp. 609–15. Paris: Presses Univ. France. 693 pp.

Grillo RD. 1985. *Ideologies and Institutions in Urban France: The Representation of Immigrants*. Cambridge, UK: Cambridge Univ. Press. 328 pp.

Handman ME. 1983. *La Violence et la Ruse: Hommes et Femmes dans un Village Grec*. Aix: Edisud. 209 pp.

Hassoun JP. 1997. *Hmong du Laos en France: Changement Social, Initiatives et Adaptations*. Paris: Presses Univ. France. 215 pp.

Hassoun JP. 2000. Le surnom et ses usages sur les marchés à la criée du MATIF: controle social, fluidité relationelle et représentations collectives. *Genése* 41:5–40

Hertz R. 1913. Saint-Besse, étude d'un culte alpestre. In *Revue de l'Histoire des Réligions* 67:115–80 Transl.: 1983. St. Besse: a study of an Alpine cult. In *Saints and their Cults*, ed. S Wilson, pp. 115–180. Cambridge, UK: Cambridge Univ. Press

Jollivet M. 1974. *Sociétés Paysannes ou Luttes de Classes au Village*. Paris: Colin. 272 pp.

Karnoouh C. 1980. Le pouvoir et la parenté. See Lamarche et al 1980, pp. 141–210

Lamaison P. 1987. La parenté 2: filiation et alliance. See Chiva & Jeggle 1987, pp. 109–121

Lamarche H. 1980. Pouvoir et rapports de production. See Lamarche et al. 1980, pp. 17–58

Lamarche H, Karnoouh C, Rogers SC. 1980. *Paysans, Femmes et Citoyens: Luttes pour le Pouvoir dans un Village Lorrain*. Le Paradou: Actes Sud. 216 pp.

Langlois C. 1999. Recent developments in French anthropology of France and the role of the Mission du Patrimoine Ethnologique. *Cult. Anthropol.* 14:409–16

Le Menestrel S. 1999. *La Voie des Cadiens: Tourisme et Identité en Louisiane.* Paris: Belin. 431 pp.

Lenclud G. 1986. En être ou ne pas en être: l'anthropologie sociale et les sociétés complexes. See *L'Homme* 1986, pp. 151–63

Lepoutre D. 1997. *Coeur de Banlieue: Codes, Rites et Langages.* Paris: Odile Jacob. 362 pp.

Lévi-Strauss C. 1967. *Structural Anthropology.* Transl. C Jacobson, BG Schoepf. New York: Anchor Books. 413 pp.

Le Wita B. 1988. *Ni Vue Ni Connue: Approche Ethnographique de la Culture Bourgeoise.* Paris: Edit. Maison Sci. L'Homme. 200 pp. Transl.: 1994. *French Bourgeois Culture.* JA Underwood. Cambridge, UK: Cambridge Univ. Press. 168 pp.

L'Homme 1986. *Anthropologie: Etat des Lieux.* Paris: Navarin. 411 pages [reedition of *L'Homme, Revue Française d'Anthropologie* no. 97–98, 1986]

MacDonald M. 1989. *We are Not French! Language, Culture and Identity in Brittany.* New York: Routledge. 384 pp.

Marcus G. 1999. How anthropological curiosity consumes its own places of origin. *Cult. Anthropol.* 14:416–22

Mendras H. 1970. *La Fin des Paysans: Innovations dans les Sociétés Rurales Françaises.* Paris: Colin. Transl.: 1970. *The Vanishing Peasant: Innovation and Change in French Agriculture.* J Lerner. Cambridge, MA: MIT Press. 289 pp.

Mendras H, Oberti M. 2000. *Le Sociologue et son Terrain: Trente Recherches Exemplaires.* Paris: Colin. 294 pp.

Moulinié V. 1998. *La Chirurgie des Ages: Corps, Sexualité et Représentations du Sang.* Paris: Edit. Maison Sci. L'Homme. 342 pp.

Pannoff M. 1986. Un valeur sûre: l'exotisme. See *L'Homme* 1986, pp. 321–31

Paul-Levy F. 1986. A la fondation de la sociologie: l'idéologie primitiviste. See *L'Homme* 1986, pp. 299–320

Pétonnet C. 1985. *On est tous dans le Brouillard: Ethnologie des Banlieus.* Paris: Galilée. 331 pp.

Pétonnet C. 1986. La pâleur noire: couleur et culture aux Etats-Unis. See *L'Homme* 1986, pp. 183–204

Pinçon M, Pinçon-Charlot M. 1989. *Dans les Beaux Quartiers.* Paris: Seuil. 255 pp.

Pinçon M, Pinçon-Charlot M. 1993. *La Chasse à Courre: Ses Rites et ses Enjeux.* Paris: Payot. 308 pp.

Pouillon J. 1986. Introduction: de chacun à tout autre, et réciproquement. See *L'Homme* 1986, pp. 11–22

Raulin A. 2000. *L'Ethnique est Quotidien: Diasporas, Marchés et Cultures Métropolitaines.* Paris: L'Harmattan. 229 pp.

Reed-Danahay D, Rogers SC. 1987. Introduction to "Anthropological research in France: problems and prospects for the study of complex society." *Anthropol. Q.* 60:51–55

Rogers SC. 1991. L'ethnologie nord-américaine de la France: l'entreprise ethnologique "près de chez soi." *Ethnol. Française* 21:5–12

Rogers SC. 1995. Natural histories: the rise and fall of French rural studies. *French Hist. Stud.* 19:381–97

Rogers SC. 1998. Strangers in a crowded field: American anthropology in France. In *Europe in the Anthropological Imagination*, ed. S Parmen, pp. 1–33. Garden City, NJ: Prentice-Hall. 274 pp.

Rogers SC. 1999. Interesting friends and *faux amis*: introduction to new directions in French anthropology. *Cult. Anthropol.* 14:396–404

Salitot M, Segalen M, Zonabend F. 1989. Anthropologie de la parenté et sociétés contemporaines. See Segalen 1989a, pp. 79–88

Sciences de l'Homme et de la Société. 1999. Dossier: l'anthropologie. *Sci. l'Homme Soc.* 57:3–18

Sciences Humaines. 1998. Anthropologie: nouveaux terrains, nouveaux objets. *Sci. Hum.* 23 (*hors série*):3–63

Segalen M. 1985. *Quinze Générations de Bas-Bretons: Parenté et Société dans le Pays Bigouden Sud 1720–1980.* Paris: Presses Univ. France. 405 pp.

Segalen M, ed. 1989a. *L'Autre et le Semblable: Regards sur l'Ethnologie des Sociétés*

Contemporaines. Paris: Presses du CNRS. 240 pp.

Segalen M. 1989b. Introduction. See Segalen 1989a, pp. 7–14

Segalen M. 1992. La parenté: des sociétés "exotiques" aux sociétés modernes. See Althabe et al. 1992, pp. 175–93

Sindzingre N. 1986. L'anthropologie: une structure segmentaire? See *L'Homme* 1986, pp. 25–53

Smith P. 1986. Le souci anthropologique. See *L'Homme* 1986, pp. 373–88

Terray E. 1986. L'état, le hasard et la nécessité: réflexions sur une histoire. See *L'Homme* 1986, pp. 234–48

Testart A. 1986. L'objet de l'anthropologie sociale. See *L'Homme* 1986, pp. 147–50

Verdier Y. 1979. *Façons de Dire, Façons de Faire: La Laveuse, la Couturière, la Cuisinière*. Paris: Gallimard. 347 pp.

Vialles N. 1987. *Le Sang et la Chair: Les Abatoirs des pays de l'Adour*. Paris: Edit. Maison Sci. L'Homme. 168 pp. Transl.: 1994. *Animal to Edible*. JA Underwood. Cambridge, UK: Cambridge Univ. Press. 142 pp.

Voisenat C, ed. 1995. *Paysage au Pluriel: Pour une Approche Ethnologique des Paysages*. Paris: Edit. Maison Sci. L'Homme. 241 pp.

Weber F. 1989. *Le Travail A-Côté: Etude d'Ethnographie Ouvrière*. Paris: Inst. Natl. Recherche Agronomique and Ecole des Hautes Etudes Sci. Soc. 212 pp.

Weber F. 2000. Pour penser la parenté contemporaine: maisonnée et parentèle, des outils de l'anthropologie. In *Une Ethnographie de la Vie Quotidienne: Enjeux et Debats*, pp. 80–110. Mem. Habilit. Rech. Paris: Univ. Paris VIII

Weber F. 2001. L'ethnologie française sous Vichy: note sur quelques publications récentes. *Rev. Synthèse*. In press

Wieviorka M. 1991. *L'espace du racisme*. Paris: Seuil. 251 pp. Transl.: 1995. *The Arena of Racism*. C Turner. London: Sage. 148 pp.

Williams P. 1993. *"Nous, On N'en Parle Pas:" Les vivants et les morts chez les Manouches*. Paris: Edit. Maison Sci. L'Homme. 110 pp.

Zonabend F. 1980. *La Mémoire Longue: Temps et Histoire au Village*. Paris: Presses Univ. France. 314 pp. Transl.: 1984. *The Enduring Memory: Time and History in a French Village*. A Forster. Manchester, UK: Manchester Univ. Press. 218 pp.

Zonabend F. 1987. La Parenté 1: origines et méthodes de la recherche et usages sociaux de la parenté. See Chiva & Jeggle 1987, pp. 95–107

Zonabend F. 1994. Laboratoire d'Anthropologie Sociale: équipe d'anthropologie de la parenté. *Terrain* 23:178–80

Zonabend F. 2000. Les maitres de parenté: une femme de mémoire en Basse-Normandie. *L'Homme* 154–5:505–23

Annu. Rev. Anthropol. 2001. 30:505–26

BIODIVERSITY PROSPECTING:
Lessons and Prospects

Katy Moran,[1] Steven R. King,[2] and Thomas J. Carlson[3]

[1]The Healing Forest Conservancy, Washington, DC 20007-2243; [2]Ethnobotany and Conservation and [3]Medical Ethnobotany, Shaman Pharmaceuticals, Inc., South San Francisco, California 94080; e-mail: MoranHFC@AOL.com; SKing@Shaman.com; TCarlson@Socrates.Berkeley.edu

Key Words ethnobotany, indigenous peoples, intellectual property rights, pharmaceuticals, U.N. Convention on Biological Diversity

■ **Abstract** Introduction of the U.N. Convention on Biological Diversity and the growth of biotechnology processes have recently led anthropologists into the rapidly moving, ethically and philosophically challenging field of bioprospecting or exploring biological diversity for commercially valuable genetic and biochemical resources. Is bioprospecting an innovative mechanism that will (a) help produce new therapeutics and preserve traditional medical systems, (b) conserve both biological and cultural diversity by demonstrating their medical, economic, and social values, and (c) bring biotechnology and other benefits to biodiversity-rich but technology poor countries? Or is bioprospecting yet another form of colonialism—"bioimperialism"—wherein the North rips off the South's resources and intellectual property rights? This article reviews the current literature on bioprospecting that lies somewhere between current polemics and calls for more anthropological research into the bioprospecting process.

BRIEF HISTORY OF BIOPROSPECTING

To alleviate the loss of the flora and fauna of our planet, at the U.N. Earth Summit in Rio de Janeiro, Brazil, the Convention on Biological Diversity (CBD) (http://www.biodiv.org) was opened for signature on June 5, 1992. Objectives of the CBD are (a) the conservation of biodiversity, (b) the sustainable use of its components, and (c) the equitable sharing of the benefits resulting from the commercial use of genetic resources.

Perhaps the most critical component of the CBD for biodiversity-rich countries is sovereignty over bioresources by nation states, as the treaty recognizes their right to regulate and charge outsiders for access to their biodiversity. No longer are biotic resources considered "common heritage," the pre-CBD paradigm that provided open access to bioresources. The "grand bargain" of the CBD is to balance how all interest groups involved can gain from the use of biodiversity by recognizing the economic, sociocultural, and environmental values of bioresources and the costs of preserving them (Orlove & Brush 1996, Moran 1998a, *Nature* 1998). Since the CBD was introduced nine years ago, however, few of the 178 signatory nations have introduced legislation requiring benefit-sharing for access to their national bioresources by outsiders with commercial interests (ten Kate & Laird 1999).

At the same time, commercial users of bioresources voluntarily attempt to comply with convention provisions in order to gain access to the raw bioresources that can be developed into products. These arrangements to explore biological diversity for commercially valuable genetic and biochemical resources have come to be called biodiversity prospecting or bioprospecting (Reid et al 1993). Although the unfortunate term suggests a new form of biocolonial appropriation, with all its attendant controversy, it has, nevertheless, become the most-used term for these transactions.

The commercial collecting of biological species is certainly not new, but their value has increased owing to the demand for genetic and biochemical raw materials for biotech products (Farnsworth 1988, McChesney 1996). Bioprospecting products include pharmaceuticals, botanical medicines, agribiotech, horticulture, cosmetics, and personal care products (ten Kate & Laird 1999). Agribiotech is briefly reviewed here, but only in relationship to pharmaceuticals because it generates a different set of policy debates, such as biosafety and world food security (Cleveland & Murray 1997). This chapter is confined to reviewing bioprospecting for terrestrial plant medicines and the use of ethnobotany and benefit-sharing in natural products drug discovery, as we are experienced in these sectors. Brief examples of existing bioprospecting endeavors are presented throughout this review.

BIOPROSPECTING STAKEHOLDERS

During the decade since the CBD was introduced, the treaty has catalyzed new relationships. Biodiversity-rich countries, indigenous societies with their knowledge of the use of such bioresources as medicines, and companies that seek to discover new therapeutics through medicinal plants and indigenous knowledge now share common interests, and, often, conflicts. The value of plants for medicines is more widely recognized and the intellectual property rights (IPRs) connected with their use have been debated worldwide. Indeed, IPRs have become the metaphor to describe indigenous ownership of traditional knowledge also, generating options for contractual mechanisms to ensure benefits return to source cultures and countries (Brush 1993, Greaves 1994, King et al 1996, Gupta 1996, Mays et al 1997, Gollin 1999, Riley & Moran 2001).

Governments and Their Agencies

Most biodiversity-rich countries are located in the tropics of the south, but technology-rich countries, with resources to develop biodiversity, are primarily in the temperate north (Kloppenburg & Balick 1995). Most southern nations are burdened with poverty, oppressive external debt, impoverished university systems, and a dearth of scientists and technology. Few have been able to collect, identify, inventory, and screen their rich biological assets, let alone develop them into products. Thus, the CBD allows northern interests to access the biodiversity of southern countries through commitments to share the technology and benefits that arise from its commercial use (Porter 1992, Glowka 1998). It is the responsibility of each CBD contracting party to devise a national biodiversity policy to document how this will work in their country, including a legal framework to implement it. Because many countries now have only a patchwork of legal provisions, such as collecting or export permits, the International Union for the Conservation of Nature, the World Conservation Union, recently published a guide (Glowka 1998). The United Nations Development Programme also offers CBD nations a guide (Prescott et al 2000), which includes case studies from the Democratic Republic of Congo, the Sultanate of Oman, the Republic of Niger, and the province of Quebec.

Although the U.S. Senate has yet to ratify the CBD, the government is active in a multicountry bioprospecting program in which conservation and development goals are linked to the bioprospecting process. Three federal agencies, the National Institutes of Health, the National Science Foundation, and the Department of Agriculture, support the program, called the International Cooperative Biodiversity Groups (ICBG), in 12 developing countries, the United States and the United Kingdom. Goals are to improve health through the discovery of new drugs from natural sources, to conserve biodiversity while developing local capacity to manage natural resources, and to promote sustainable economic development, particularly in communities of the developing tropics. Most ICBG have some ethnomedical component to their field efforts (Rosenthal 1999).

Although each ICBG is unique, all are coordinated by U.S. academic principal investigators, with programs in anthropology, ethnobotany, natural products chemistry, or drug development. As required by grants, each has a commercial pharmaceutical partner and a counterpart institution in the host country, and each works with local national and international nongovernmental organizations (NGO). The total budget for 1999 was $3.7 million, which includes contributions from all collaborating partners. The U.S. government has continued involvement in the projects through scientific advisory committees with representatives from each federal agency (Rosenthal 1999).

Biotech Industry

Since Watson and Crick's discovery of the double helix, no legal biotech case has been as influential as Diamond v Chakrabarty, in which new genetically engineered life forms were deemed patentable. The court found that a genetically modified bacterium fit Thomas Jefferson's language in the Patent Act of 1793, making a new "composition of matter" patentable (U.S. Congr. 1991). In the United States, legal, scientific, political, and economic mindsets during the 1980s shaped emerging biotechnology firms. Major federal granting agencies, such as the

National Science Foundation and the National Institutes of Health, implemented policies that encouraged corporate-university collaboration in extremely difficult and expensive biotechnology research. At Genentech of South San Francisco, for example, using biotech processes, university researchers learned how to produce huge supplies of insulin to treat diabetics. Secured by patents, venture capital supported the research as investment opportunities, creating biotech firms dedicated to research and development for a profit (U.S. Congr. 1991, Cassier 1999, Rabinow 1994).

The majority of the biotech industry is not involved in bioprospecting because most companies today favor the use of cheaper, faster, synthetic technologies over exploring for natural products (Gollin 1999, Farnsworth 1988). But biotechnology spawns ethical, social, and legal debates at the margins of pharmaceutical bioprospecting in which anthropologists have been active. They include the collaboration of big business and big science, the ethics of genetic engineering, and the patentability of life forms (Bruce & Bruce 1998). Biotechnology overlaps with ideas about genetics and racism, culture and ethnicity (Bradby 1996). Projects involving mapping of the human genome, such as Iceland's national human genome project, also have implications for anthropological studies (Palsson & Rabinow 1999). Crook (2000) debates the public safety and genetic pollution some associate with genetically modified organisms versus the ability of genetically modified organisms to alleviate world hunger and environmental degradation. Clark & Juma (1991) draw on case studies from the African Centre Technology Studies and outline an international research agenda for using biotechnology for sustainable development in developing countries.

Since the CBD was introduced, however, no pharmaceutical bioprospecting product developed by using traditional knowledge has been commercialized; no economic profit has been realized. Drug development requires expensive and time-consuming studies and clinical trials in order to secure government regulatory approval before any drug may be marketed. In the United States, a product typically takes from 10 to 15 years to materialize, after an investment of some $300 million by the company and investors who take the financial risk to discover, develop, test, and market a new drug. For a new company, infrastructure such as buildings, equipment, and research scientists' salaries must be paid before any product generates any revenues (U.S. Congr. 1993, Baker et al 1995).

To raise such huge amounts of money to fund capital-intensive drug research and development (R&D), companies—other than financially stable, large pharmaceutical companies—depend on venture capital, stock offerings, partnerships, and the like—investments by outsiders into a company's high-risk but potentially high-gain ventures (U.S. Congr. 1991). Investors range from individuals to organizations, and their investments are secured by patents. Patents provide intellectual property protection for the invention of the company, enabling investors to regain the funds they risked for R&D if and when a product is commercialized. It is unlikely that any company or any investor would risk capital to discover or develop a drug without their multimillion dollar investment being protected from competing companies by a patent (U.S. Congr. 1991; see also http://www.cid.harvard.edu/cidbiotech/homepage.html).

Only a small number of bioprospecting research expeditions begin by using ethnobotany as a discovery methodology (Cox & Balick 1994). The work soon evolves into economic botany, as the laboratory focus shifts to the plant's chemistry, biological activity, and general pharmacology/toxicology (Balick 1990). During the drug discovery processes, the active chemical constituents of the biological materials are elucidated, often modified, then patented (Tempesta & King 1994). In biotech companies, this patented information becomes a commodity in itself, in the form of chemical compounds or tissue samples that can be outlicensed, or "rented," to other commercial interests, with the company profiting from each circulation. Libraries of extracts, compounds extracted from plants collected at random, or plants used as medicines are licensed to biotech companies or large pharmaceutical firms that screen in high volume—often up to 100,000 compounds per week (Balick et al 1996).

In the United States, drug development includes preclinical studies in animals to assess which molecule produces the highest level of pharmacological activity and the lowest level of toxicology. Phase I human clinical studies determine the safety of the drug candidates in healthy volunteers. In phase II trials, increased numbers of actual patients help test and determine dosage and formulation. Final proof of safety and efficacy is produced in phase III clinical trials. If the data are adequate, a new drug application is submitted to the Food and Drug Administration. It can take up to 2 years before the Food and Drug Administration supplies permission to market a drug. Every country has its own unique requirements for marketing drugs and does not necessarily accept data from other countries (ten Kate & Laird 1999).

Horrobin & Lapinskas (1998) narrate the enormous problems faced by a company attempting to develop herbal medicinal resources. Anderson (2000) states that it is "[a] valuable corrective to the one-sided presentations so typical of anthropological writing in which corporations are represented as villains. In these complex matters, all sides deserve a hearing, and the wise ethnobotanist will not judge prematurely."

Science and Medicine

There are, however, more bioprospecting stakeholders than provider countries (including local, state, regional, and national governments) and user industries (including both small start-up and multinational biotech companies). Major stakeholders include both the domestic and international research communities, including botanical gardens and universities. For their screening programs, a majority of companies outsource plant samples from brokers that collect, taxonomically identify, ship, and resupply materials to users (ten Kate & Laird 1999).

International research institutions are obligated to the national access legislation in countries where they perform these broker functions. To insure consistency with the CBD, after a lengthy deliberative process, the Common Policy Guidelines for Participating Botanic Gardens were institutionalized by most gardens (ten Kate & Laird 1999). International plant research spans a continuum from pure to applied research and reflects the increasing commercial value of bioresources and the vitality of biodiversity for human health. Today, one fourth of pharmaceutical products are based on, or derived from, plants (Farnsworth 1988). In developing countries, 80% of the population depend on plant medicines for their primary health care (Farnsworth 1988, ten Kate 1995, Balick et al 1996). Work by Grifo & Rosenthal (1997) is the result of a conference sponsored by the National Institutes of Health, the National Science Foundation, and the National Association of Physicians for the Environment held at the Smithsonian Institution to explore the human health consequences of biodiversity loss.

Prendergast (1998) demonstrates the wide range of anthropological interests in economic botany. A review of ethnopharmacology by Etkin (1988) documents the field's ecological perspective, both biobehavioral and multidisciplinary. In contrast to general compilations that document the medical use and constituents of plant substances, Etkin shows that biobehavioral studies explore both biological and behavioral parameters that contextualize human-plant interactions and their impact on human health.

Many ethnobotanists active in bioproprospecting have urged professional associations of scientists to develop codes of conduct to guide members through the new ground rules brought about by the CBD. They include, among others, the American Society for Pharmacognosy, the Society for Applied Anthropology, the International Society of Ethnobiology, and the Society for Economic Botany, most of which have posted draft guidelines on their websites (Prance 1991, Berlin & Berlin 1994, Cox & Balick 1994, King et al 1996, Brush & Stabinsky 1996, Cleveland & Murray 1997).

Civil Society

Benthall (2000) broadly defines civil society as "all associational forms in society other than the state or the market" and sees it as the prerequisite and foundation for a democratic society. Many nonprofit development agencies base grants to governments that are buttressed by a strong and vibrant civil society, as they serve to buffer the challenges of reform and social change (Comarrof & Comarrof 1999). Widely accessible and affordable technology has revolutionized global communications in recent years and made it possible for civil society activists to join forces for maximum impact. Nontraditional international actors mobilize information strategically to help create new issues and to persuade, pressure, and gain leverage over much more powerful organizations (Zarembo 2001).

Some forms of civil society, however, have devastating effects—anthropologists find them "ethnocentric and insidious" and difficult to distinguish from other self-interested groups (Hitchcock 1994). The new communications freedom also brings up questions of representativeness—if anyone can speak, who speaks for whom and who decides this? Problems have arisen in local discussions on bioprospecting, which often originate in forums hosted by an NGO with a specific agenda. Forum results, often a statement by an individual or a small group who support that agenda, are then circulated around the world via the Internet as representative opinions of a larger group. Slick NGO networks skew the debate by presenting their version of public opinion in a determined direction (Hann & Dunn 1996; see also http://www.rafi.org, http://www.grain.org/index.htm).

To level the playing field in bioprospecting negotiations, many countries and culture groups have successfully sought outside expertise from intermediaries (Guerin-McManus et al 1998). Typically, intermediaries have some vested interest in promoting an equitable exchange on mutually agreed-to terms for access to genetic resources. NGOs representing civil society in such areas as conservation, development, human rights, health, and other nonprofit organizations, foundations, and pro bono law firms play growing roles in fostering, facilitating, and evaluating bioprospecting partnerships (Mays et al 1997). Many intermediaries speak the local language, have worked and often lived in the host community, and have earned its trust (Green 1998). They play different roles in access and benefit-sharing arrangements with source countries and other stakeholders, often becoming partners in the relationship.

Some of the conservation organizations active in bioprospecting issues are Conservation International in Suriname (http://www.conservation.org; see also Guerin-McManus et al 1998), the International Union for the Conservation of Nature globally (Glowka 1998), and the World Resources Institute in Costa Rica (Reid et al 1993). The Bioresources Development and Conservation Programme (http://www.Bioresources.org) is a Nigerian NGO organized in 1991 as the focal point for collaborative bioprospecting research relationships, such as the ICBG. Goals are to build technical skills in Nigeria so bioresources are a viable vehicle for sustainable development. Bioprospecting programs generate pharmaceutical leads that target therapeutic categories for tropical diseases suffered in Nigeria, such as malaria, leishmaniasis, and trypanosomiasis (Iwu 1996a,b).

The National Biodiversity Institute, INBio, a private, nonprofit, public interest association, was established by the Costa Rican Ministry of Environment and Energy in 1991 (Reid et al 1993). Its aim is to promote sustainable development of biotic resources through a strategy of "save, know, use." INBio has a Central research institute in San Jose and 28 research stations and employs almost 200 people. In 1991, INBio and the multinational pharmaceutical company Merck and Co. entered into a landmark million-dollar, 2-year contractual relationship, later renewed, to develop Costa Rica's rich biological resources through bioprospecting (Reid et al 1993). Since then, INBio has signed commercial research agreements with Bristol-Myers Squibb, INDENA for phytochemicals, Phytera for the development of cell cultures from plants and medicines, and the British Technology Group for the development of a bionematicide from a tropical legume (ten Kate & Laird 1999).

Indigenous Cultures

Ethnoscience is also recognized as valuable (Ford 1978, Linden 1991, Berlin 1992, Moerman 1996, Iwu 1996a,b) but is used by only a small segment of bioprospectors (Farnsworth 1988). According to Schultes (1988):

> The accomplishments of aboriginal people in learning plant properties must be a result of a long and intimate association with, and utter dependence on, their ambient vegetation. This native knowledge warrants careful and critical attention on the part of modern scientific methods. If phytochemists must randomly investigate the constituents of biological effects of 80,000 species of Amazon plants, the task may never be finished. Concentrating first on those species that people have lived and experimented with for millennia offers a short-cut to the discovery of new medically or industrially useful compounds.

Although they are based on natural products, indigenous medicines are not "found" in nature. They are products of traditional knowledge. Elisabetsky (1991) explains:

> To transform a plant into a medicine, one has to know the correct species, its location, the proper time of collection (some plants are poisonous in certain seasons), the solvent to use (cold, warm or boiling water; alcohol, addition of salt, etc.), the way to prepare it (time and conditions to be left on the solvent), and finally, posology (route of administration, dosage).

For pharmaceuticals, concentrating bioprospecting efforts on the traditional use of plants focuses leads for screening and can result in a more efficient and less expensive drug discovery process (Elisabetsky & Castilhos 1990). Likewise, leads from the traditional process of plant preparation for healing provide clues to the type of chemical compounds in plants under investigation (Schultes & Raffauf 1990). Of the 120 active compounds isolated from higher plants and used today in Western medicine, 74% have the same therapeutic use as in native societies (Farnsworth et al 1985). Rather than randomly collecting and screening plants, it can be a more efficient strategy for some companies to use indigenous knowledge as a lead to pinpointing promising plants for new medicines (King et al 1997). Organisms can be chosen for bioassays through leads unique to the area and cultures where they are located (McChesney 1996).

Shaman Pharmaceuticals, Inc. (http://www.shaman.com) is a small, California-based company that focuses on the discovery and development of novel pharmaceuticals from plants with a history of native use (Burton 1994, King et al 1996, Carlson et al 1997a, Oubre et al 1997). This ethnobotanical/chemotaxonomic approach produced a highly focused selection of plant candidates for screening and development, notably *sangre de grado*, commonly used for a variety of ailments throughout Latin America (Carlson & King 2000). Meza and colleagues (Meza 1999, Meza et al 1998) developed a manual and a technical book for the sustainable sourcing of *sangre de grado*, an abundant, pioneer plant that produces a red latex (Carlson & King 2000). Resulting from ecological and management studies funded by and conducted during Shaman Pharmaceuticals' operations in Latin America, the manual is a practical guide for the propagation, cultivation, and sustainable management of the source for raw materials for Shaman's leading drug candidate (King et al 1997).

EVOLVING BIOPROSPECTING ISSUES

Intellectual Property Rights

Intellectual property rights (IPRs) spring from European philosophical traditions that create rights over intangible information. In today's industrialized world, their underlying rationale is that IPRs are commercial monopoly rights for a limited time period that provide incentives for further investment in developing future innovations. IPRs are often defined and protected in the form of patents, plant breeders' rights, trade secrets, copyrights, and trademarks, and patent law is most commonly used to protect the right to benefit financially from scientific innovations (Axt & Corn 1993, Mays et al 1997, Glowka 1998, Gollin 1999).

There are confusing misconceptions about, as well as genuine philosophical objections to, patents, including the morality of patents relating to life-forms (Greely 1998, Bruce & Bruce 1998). In the United States, for example, no living or dead plant found in nature can, itself, be legally patented (35 U.S. Code #101). But if there has been a horticultural or genetic change created by a plant breeder, a novel horticultural form of a rose, for example, it is an invention and can be patented by the innovator. Patents on living organisms in pharmaceutical bioprospecting are uncommon. Typically, patents are granted for scientific advances during the isolation and modification of chemical derivatives and analogs of compounds originally isolated from a plant for an identified use (Rosenthal 1999). Another misconception is that patents relating to traditional knowledge infringe on performing indigenous cultural practices, but, in fact, indigenous rights to use their tangible and intangible cultural resources in both traditional and innovative ways are not affected by patents (Wagner 1987, Rosenthal 1999).

Some bioprospecting source countries think that patents on products create monopolies at the expense of those providing the original material. A recent patent challenge on tumeric, however, demonstrates that the system can work and that patent claims that are not truly novel can be overturned (Gollin 1999, Pollack 1999, *Science* 1999). Companies see patents on natural products derivatives as protection from competing companies and an essential mechanism to recoup their R&D investments. They seek global expansion of a legal framework for proprietary rights to the new drugs they develop (UNCTAD 2000, ten Kate & Laird 1999).

Article 8(j) of the CBD requires contracting parties to (*a*) respect, preserve, and maintain the knowledge, innovation, and practices of indigenous and local communities embodying traditional lifestyles; (*b*) promote their wider application with the approval and involvement of their holders; and (*c*) encourage equitable sharing of benefits derived from their use. Because these provisions are directed to states, implementation is subject to their national legislation.

The Agreement of Trade-Related Aspects of Intellectual Property Rights of the World Trade Organization sets minimum requirements for the protection of IPRs, including novelty, non-obviousness, and usefulness. Indigenous knowledge, however, fails the novelty requirement, so most countries' IPR regimes do not provide for its protection or for benefit-sharing from bioprospecting (Axt & Corn 1993). The World Intellectual Property Organization (http://www.wipo.org) is now completing a status report to address this omission and influence evolving legislation on indigenous IPRs (UNCTAD 2000, Blankeney 1999).

The policy of the ICBG program is that when traditional knowledge is involved in a patentable invention, if the provider cannot be recognized as an inventor, the contribution should be treated as valuable "know how." In any related publications and in the patent, the contribution must be credited as prior art. Prior art citations formalize the contribution of such knowledge but do not claim any monopoly rights to use. In fact, the absence of a prior art citation may constitute grounds to deny or invalidate a patent (Rosenthal 1999).

New processes, consistent with other forms of IPR, also attempt to ensure equitable sharing of benefits from bioprospecting while protecting it from exploitation and extinction (Hitchcock 1994, Simpson 1997). Glowka (1998) describes such endeavors: traditional resource rights are bundles of rights that can be used for protection, compensation, and conservation (Posey & Dutfield 1996); community registers, or peoples' biodiversity registers, are data banks of local knowledge within India (Anuradha 1997); community intellectual rights from the Third World Network is primarily defensive because it protects communities from commoditization of their knowledge and resources (Singh Nijar 1996); and know-how licenses were used in an ICBG by the Aguaruna in the Peruvian Amazon as contractual legal instruments applied to intellectual property (Tobin 1997).

Although IPR discussions under the auspices of the CBD continue, many companies, including Shaman, the ICBG commercial partners, and others, have developed contractual legal instruments under which bioprospecting is conducted that reflects the spirit of the CBD. Contracts typically define objectives of the partnership, terms of material transfer, the rights and responsibilities of collaborators, and the types and amounts of benefits (Rosenthal 1999). Contractual agreements among bioprospecting partners are widely considered the mechanism of choice to gain access to genetic resources and traditional knowledge and to deliver benefits to source culture groups and countries. In contrast to patent law, contracts can be designed to fit differing relationships between collaborators (Laird 1993, Rubin & Fish 1994, Shelton 1995, Putterman 1996, Hunter 1998).

Cleveland & Murray (1997) point out some neglected theoretical and empirical aspects of the current IPR debate. The article primarily discusses IPRs for agricultural biotechnology, rather than pharmaceutical bioprospecting, which generates a very different set of policy debates. More informative is the wide range of comments that follow the Cleveland & Murray article. Alcorn states that the authors fail to acknowledge that issues of "indigenous peoples" are far different from those of "local people," groups that are lumped together throughout the CBD. They fail to acknowledge the validity of being indigenous, argues Alcorn, and to capture the real conflicts and defining differences between competing perspectives. Fowler agrees and adds that IPR processes must differentiate between agricultural and pharmaceutical bioresources. He states that CBD IPRs "favor bilateral deals" for pharmaceutical benefit-sharing, whereas agricultural debates focus on multilateral arrangements for benefit-sharing. Authors of this review argue later about the importance of distinguishing between agricultural and pharmaceutical bioprospecting issues (Moran 2001).

Gupta comments on the article by calling for full disclosure on where and how source plant material is acquired under patent applications. Brush thinks that failures to resolve IPR disputes demonstrate the wide gulf between international discussions and the willingness of nations to act. Because rights are socially mediated, Brush argues, a "new class of rights" must be negotiated in the appropriate political arena. Downes, an environmental lawyer, comments that the inflammatory charges of "biopiracy" need more anthropological research for empirical evidence to cut through such rhetoric (Cleveland & Murray 1997).

Greaves (1994), in an early and important anthropological volume addressing IPR issues in which bioprospecting case studies are presented, addresses the current debate on the merits of intellectual property systems to protect cultural knowledge and biological diversity. Compensation to indigenous peoples, it is argued, could both internationally validate their knowledge of the biodiversity they manage and provide them with an equitable reward for sharing it, thereby compensating biological stewardship and encouraging conservation (Brush 1993). An early issue of the *Cultural Survival Quarterly* (Clay 1991), as well as a recent issue, is dedicated to IPRs. Riley & Moran (2001) provide a compendium of articles on tools that work to protect indigenous IPRs. The titles suggest how IPR has evolved among anthropologists in just a decade. An interdisciplinary analysis of the value and use of medicinal plants and traditional knowledge in the pharmaceutical industry, focusing on economic rationales for biodiversity conservation is documented by Swanson (1995).

During the past decade, regional coalitions and federations of indigenous peoples worldwide have joined forces in a spirit of solidarity to discuss IPRs and related issues (N. Am. Congr. Latin Am. 1994). Federations have committed their discussions into charters, declarations, and other statements, then disseminated them for public use (Varese 1996). The Charter of the Indigenous-Tribal Peoples of the Tropical Forests was promulgated in Malaysia in 1992. Article 44 of the Charter states that the traditional technologies of members can make important contributions to humanity, including developed countries: They claim control over the development and manipulation of their traditional medicinal knowledge (Colchester 1994). Coalitions and federations comprise groups such as the Coordinating Body for the Indigenous Peoples' Organization of the Amazon Basin in Amazonian countries, where more than 200 tribes are located, the South and Meso American Indian Information Center, and the World Rainforest Movement (Morris 1992). Many of these groups participated in two workshops on traditional knowledge and biodiversity, held in Spain and sponsored by the CBD, to put forward mechanisms to achieve the objectives of Article 8(j) (Burgiel et al 1997, UNEP 1997). International human rights instruments supply additional fundamental principles for IPR legislation, including the U.N. Working Group on Indigenous Populations and the intergovernmental process initiated by the U.N. Commission on Human Rights mandated to consider the Draft U.N. Declaration on the Rights of Indigenous Peoples (Shelton 1995, Anaya 1996, Blankeney 1999, Bowen 2000).

At the time of its incorporation as a for-profit corporation in 1989, Shaman Pharmaceuticals, Inc., also founded and continues to financially support the Healing Forest Conservancy (http://www.shaman.com/Healing_Forest.html), a nonprofit foundation established specifically to develop and implement a process to return benefits to Shaman's 30 collaborating countries and some 60 culture groups after a product is commercialized. Benefits from commercial products will be shared equally among all countries and culture groups that participate in Shaman's drug discovery process, no matter where the plant or knowledge originated. The Healing Forest Conservancy developed a constitution, a legal instrument available on the worldwide web, under which indigenous groups legally organize to receive monetary benefits (Moran 1998b). The company uses Agreements of Principles, legally enforceable contracts, to establish the terms under which Shaman conducts research. Culture groups' rights to prior informed consent, confidentiality, privacy, and fair compensation form the philosophical underpinnings of the company and its principles for research. Several publications supply detailed descriptions of Shaman's operations globally, including its lengthy prior informed consent process (Burton 1994, Carlson et al 1997b, Richter & Carlson 1998, Duncan 1998).

Benefit Sharing

The third goal of the CBD, "the equitable sharing of the benefits resulting from the use of genetic resources," has taken many forms: monetary benefits for source countries include bioprospecting fees and fees for each sample, a percentage of the research budget dedicated to locally preferred use, development of alternative income-generating schemes, and a commitment by the company to obtain future plant supplies in the source country. To date, INBio's bioprospecting agreements have contributed more than $3 million to conservation areas, universities, and other groups affiliated with INBio. Resources totaling over $210,000 were provided to Nigeria from 1990 to 1996 by Shaman (ten Kate & Laird 1999).

Nonmonetary benefits include the acknowledgment of contributions in publications or joint authorship, joint research, training and increased scientific capacity, free access to technology, equipment and products, and research results and coownership of IPRs. Since 1993, over 1400 developing country collaborators from 12 countries have received formal training in degreed as well as technical training programs from the ICBG. Both INBio and Shaman have made capacity-building contributions in collaborating countries as well (ten Kate & Laird 1999, King & Carlson 1995, Rosenthal 1999).

There is no "model" for the process of benefit-sharing, but trust funds have become the method of choice to return monetary benefits from bioprospecting to culture groups. In the form of a foundation, nonprofit corporation, or common-law trust, such trusts operate as permanent endowments, revolving or sinking trust funds in hard currency to avoid inflation shrinkage, either off-shore or in the country of origin (Moran 1998b).

The Fund for Integrated Rural Development and Traditional Medicine, an independent trust fund, was established by the Bioresources Development and Conservation Programme as the financial mechanism to distribute bioprospecting benefits among Nigerian stakeholders for sustainable development in rural areas. The board, balanced to reflect these interest groups, is composed of leaders of traditional healers' associations, senior government officials, representatives of village councils from various ethnic groups, and technical experts from scientific institutions. The predominance of traditional solidarity systems, such as tribal associations and professional guilds of healers, supplies a social structure to ensure community participation. Diverse culture groups in Nigeria receive funds through traditional healers' organizations and villages consistent with their governing customs. Town associations, village heads, and professional guilds of healers are empowered to make decisions regarding projects in their localities. Those funded follow the criteria of promoting conservation of biodiversity and drug development, as well as the socioeconomic well-being of rural cultures. At the local level, technical skills gained from benefit-sharing help standardize and promote phytomedicines, disseminating and sharing information that benefits traditional healers and the health of the communities they serve (Iwu 1996a, Moran 1998b, Laird 2000).

LESSONS AND PROSPECTS

Roles for Anthropologists

Can bioprospecting produce new drugs, preserve traditional medical systems, and deliver capacity-building technologies to the developing world while conserving biodiversity? Despite the fact that no pharmaceutical company has yet marketed any bioprospecting product, the above efforts have already brought considerable monetary and nonmonetary benefits to developing country collaborators. Drug discovery, for the ICBG and INBio, for example, is only one bioprospecting objective, and time will tell whether all ambitious goals can be met (Rosenthal 1999).

As the world moves from free to controlled access to genetic resources, the "common heritage" of the past is now called biopiracy. Caught up in North/South politics, there have been calls for today's bioprospectors to pay the price for yesterday's paradigm. Such rhetoric threatens opportunities for economic development, technology transfer, and capacity-building in tropical countries; potential breakthroughs in medicine and abandonment of research that may never be completed as the extinction rate of biocultural diversity accelerates (Shiva 1997, Kimbrell 1997; see also http://www.grain.org/index.htm, http://www.rafi.org).

More anthropological studies that sort out, describe, and analyze bioprospecting's ethical issues and stakeholders' behaviors are needed (Durant et al 1996, Fundación Sabiduria Indígena & Kothari 1997, Skinner 1999). Empirical data open the process to constructive criticism and enable the bioprospecting dialogue to evolve beyond the rhetoric that dominates much of today's discussion of this complex process. Also, the health, development, and conservation components of bioprospecting are basic to applied anthropology. In such multidisciplinary collaboration, nonsocial scientists often find their bioprospecting attempts caught up in problems they cannot resolve because of little or no preparation or experience in the social processes, or they fail to recognize that every society has mechanisms useful to conservation, including grass-roots affiliations, that are rarely noticed or prioritized by outsiders.

Differentiate Between Indigenous Peoples and Local Communities

What has not yet been adequately addressed by the CBD is how the on-the-ground stewards of biodiversity, the "indigenous and local communities embodying traditional lifestyles" referred to in Article 8(j), can share in bioprospecting benefits (Cleveland & Murray 1997). One reason this critical issue remains unresolved is that the wording of the CBD is ambiguous and confusing. It lumps indigenous peoples and local communities together throughout the document without separating them into discrete groups (Moran 2001).

With some exceptions, indigenous peoples have minority status within modern nation states. They primarily seek collective rights and self-determination for use of their biological and cultural resources. This is different from local communities—typically small farming communities that have socioeconomic aspirations similar to those of the national culture. Most farmers identify with the nation states in which they live, typically speak the national language, and practice the religion of the majority (Palmer 1996, Maybury-Lewis 1997). Lumping indigenous peoples into farmers' groups directly undermines indigenous efforts for self-determination and creates concerns that they will be immersed under farmers' movements and their specific concerns subordinated to those of the more powerful and numerous farmers' groups (Moran 2001).

Indigenous knowledge of the use of plants for medicines is typically generational, often sacred, and always deeply imbedded in culture (Reichel-Dolmatoff 1976), whereas farmers' manipulation of germplasm for improved crops is usually individual and more secular. Changes to improved crops are brought about by human manipulation, but the chemicals within wild plants are valuable by themselves in the use of natural compounds for medicines. Likewise, when developing new products, the processes are different. To improve crops, useful genes are transferred or put into plants to create new varieties. The discovery of new medicines, however, particularly pharmaceuticals, comes about by a series of steps to take useful chemicals out of a medicinal plant. Although distributing benefits from these agricultural and medicinal products requires completely different processes, the CBD wording binds them together. This haphazard process of labeling societies allows those with vested interests to exploit the very concerns that the CBD was created to resolve (Moran 2001).

Share Risks and Benefits Throughout the Bioprospecting Process

Shaman Pharmaceuticals, Inc., was restructured because of costs of future clinical trials for the company's first drug, which subsequently was launched as a dietary supplement, not a pharmaceutical. In the case of Shaman, however, the company's benefit-sharing principles are still intact, and considerable revenues can be generated from the botanical income stream while pharmaceutical research continues. In 1997, for example, the U.S. dietary supplement market for herbals or botanicals was nearly $4 billion (King et al 1999; see also http://www.ShamanBotanicals. com).

A major lesson of the Shaman case comes from the time, costs, and risks associated with drug discovery, a burden shouldered primarily by the company, but with critical implications for benefit-sharing to source countries and culture groups. Spreading the risks and benefits among all stakeholders increases opportunities for bioprospecting benefits and lessens risk. Royalties may never materialize because of the tremendous costs, long time frame, unpredictability and volatility of the market, and the many other potential pitfalls of drug discovery. Some sort of up-front benefits, monetary or nonmonetary, as well as "milestone" payments up to the time for royalties are essential during the bioprospecting process (Putterman 1996, Fundación Sabiduría Indígena & Kothari 1997).

Share Benefits Within Nation States Equitably

Article 8(j) signals an important international acknowledgment that traditional knowledge is valuable to modern society. However, the CBD, which formalizes the sovereignty of nations over their biodiversity, merely "encourages" equitable sharing of benefits arising from traditional knowledge, innovations, and practices. The CBD has not yet established mechanisms to accomplish this equitably within nations.

The political climate of the governments under which indigenous groups live is critical to the CBD's success. Because they are huge stakeholders, governments must include indigenous peoples in national discussions on interpreting and implementing the CBD, as is required for all signatories. If states are to be effective at preserving the worlds' biocultural diversity, all stakeholders must participate. The process must be democratic, built from the bottom up, not imposed from the top down. This also means guarding against paternalism and letting indigenous groups determine for themselves the extent to which they choose to participate. Different culture groups hold different beliefs about entrepreneurship, which can be a double-edged sword when introduced into nonmarket economies (Pritchard 1998). At the same time, however, many communities seek greater access to markets. These differences should never be an excuse to exclude indigenous groups from the sustainable use of biodiversity, for this is their, and only their, decision to make.

Acknowledge All Contributions

Missing in all this is recognition and acknowledgment of the contribution from indigenous societies in the discovery of new medicines that have historically benefited humankind. Recognition validates indigenous systems within countries and internationally, just as it does for Western scientists. It also spotlights the unique identity of traditional cultures groups at a time when they are organizing to pursue self-determination (Daes 1993, Fundación Sabiduria Indígena & Kothari 1997).

Sustainable Use of Phytomedicines, Herbal Medicine, or Dietary Supplements

The international conservation community is neglecting the huge impact of the herbal medicine industry on medicinal plants sold not as processed pharmaceuticals (King et al 1999). Concerned representatives from a small portion of the fast-growing phytomedicine industry now attempt conservation and sustainable use measures, but virtually no companies are addressing the third goal of the CBD—benefit-sharing with source groups and countries. Herb and phytomedicine companies pay a low price for large volumes of medicinal plant biomass from tropical ecosystems, package it in their own facilities, then sell the products at an inflated price in northern countries (Leaman et al 1998). Despite the CBD, the industry still enjoys a period of uncontrolled, undocumented, and poorly managed free access to medicinal plants and cultural knowledge throughout the world (Brevoort 1995, King et al 1999).

Importance of Biocultural Diversity Conservation Globally

Too often, when the importance of biodiversity conservation is discussed for its value to human health, it refers to the health of residents of industrialized nations. The attitude is that biodiversity must be preserved to enlarge the pharmacopoeia of Western medicine, which provides therapeutics primarily for Western societies. Less discussed is the vitality of biodiversity to the health of 80% of the world, populations that depend solely on medicinal plants for their primary health care (Berlin et al 1999, Iwu 1993, Farnsworth 1988). Preserving biodiversity for the benefit of human health means preserving it for those in the tropics already using it, as well as for distant populations that may know it only in some refined or synthetic form, at some unspecified future date.

Finally, discussions of biodiversity and its local, national, and international medical utility should never be disaggregated from the rich, complex, and diverse cultural and biological matrix from which it evolved. One of the most important goals of biodiversity prospecting is to help conserve the vast diversity of languages, cultures, peoples, and other organisms that inhabit this earth. One of the challenges that faces anthropologists, ethnobotanists, physicians, entrepreneurs, and development professionals is to creatively utilize biodiversity prospecting as one of many tools to maintain and manage the fertile, but fragile, diversity of people, plants, cultures, and ecosystems that are under constant threat of extinction.

Visit the Annual Reviews home page at www.AnnualReviews.org

LITERATURE CITED

Anaya SJ. 1996. *Indigenous Peoples in International Law*. New York: Oxford Univ. Press

Anderson EN. 2000. Book reviews/related fields. *Am. Anthropol.* 102(1):213–14

Anuradha RV. 1997. In search of knowledge and resources: Who sows? Who reaps? *Rev. Eur. Commun. Int. Environ. Law* 6:263

Axt JR, Corn LM. 1993. *Biotechnology, Indigenous Peoples, and Intellectual Property Rights*. Washington, DC: Congr. Res. Serv.

Baker J, Borris R, Carte B, Cordell G, Soejarto D, et al. 1995. Natural product drug discovery and development: new perspectives on international cooperation. *J. Nat. Prod.* 58:1325–57

Balick MJ. 1990. Ethnobotany and the identification of therapeutic agents from the rainforest. In *Bioactive Compounds from Plants*, ed. DJ Chadwick, J Marsh, pp. 22–39. New York: Wiley

Balick MJ, Elisabetsky E, Laird SA, eds. 1996. *Medicinal Resources of the Tropical Forest: Biodiversity and Its Importance to Human Health*. New York: Columbia Univ. Press

Benthall J. 2000. Civil society's need for de-deconstruction. *Anthropol. Today* 16(2):1–3

Berlin B. 1992. *Ethnobiological Classification: Principles of Categorization of Plants and Animals in Traditional Societies*. Princeton, NJ: Princeton Univ. Press

Berlin B, Berlin EA. 1994. Anthropological issues in medical anthropology. In *Ethnobotany and the Search for New Drugs. Ciba Found. Symp. No. 185*, ed. G Prance, pp. 240–58. New York: Wiley

Berlin B, Berlin EA, Ugalde JCF, Barrios LG, Puett D, et al. 1999. The Maya ICBG: drug discovery, medical ethnobotany, and alternative forms of economic development in the highland Maya region of Chiapas, Mexico. *Pharmaceut. Biol.* 37(Suppl.):127–44

Blankeney M. 1999. *Roundtable on Indigenous Populations and Traditional Knowledge*. Geneva: World Intellect. Prop. Org.

Bowen J. 2000. Should we have a universal concept of "indigenous peoples" rights? Ethnicity and essentialism in the twenty-first century. *Anthropol. Today* 16(4):3–7

Bradby H. 1996. Genetics and racism. See Marteau & Richards 1996.

Brevoort P. 1995. The US botanical market. *HerbalGram* 36:49–57

Bruce D, Bruce A. 1998. *Engineering Genesis: The Ethics of Genetic Engineering in Non-Human Species*. London: Earthscan

Brush SB. 1993. Indigenous knowledge of biological resources and intellectual property rights: the role of anthropology. *Am. Anthropol.* 95:653–86

Brush S, Stabinsky D, eds. 1996. *Valuing Local Knowledge: Indigenous People and Intellectual Property Rights*. Washington, DC: Island

Burgiel S, Prather T, Schmidt K. 1997. Summary of the workshop on traditional knowledge and biological diversity. *Earth Negotiat. Bull.* 9(75):1–40

Burton TM. 1994. Magic bullets: drug company looks to "witch doctors" to conjure products. *Wall Street J.*, July 7, p. 1, 8

Carlson TJ, Cooper R, King SR, Rozhon EJ. 1997a. Modern science and traditional healing. *R. Soc. Med. Sp. Pub. Phytochem. Div.* 200:84–95

Carlson TJ, Iwu M, King SR, Obialor C, Ozioko A. 1997b. Medicinal plant research in Nigeria: an approach for compliance with the Convention on Biological Diversity. *Diversity* 13(1):29–33

Carlson TJS, King SR. 2000. Sangre de drago: a phytomedicine for the treatment of diarrhea. *Health Notes Rev. Complement. Integr. Med.* 7(4):315–20

Cassier M. 1999. Research contracts between university and industry: cooperation and hybridisation between academic research and industrial research. *Int. J. Biotechnol.* 1(1):82–104

Clark N, Juma C. 1991. *Biotechnology for Sustainable Development: Policy Options for Developing Countries.* Nairobi: Afr. Cent. Technol. Stud.

Cleveland DA, Murray SC. 1997. The world's crop genetic resources and the rights of indigenous farmers. *Curr. Anthropol.* 38:477–515

Colchester M. 1994. *Salvaging Nature: Indigenous Peoples, Protected Areas and Biodiversity Conservation. UN Res. Inst. Soc. Dev. Discuss. Pap. 55.* Geneva: World Rainforest Movement

Comarrof JL, Comaroff J. 1999. *Civil Society and the Political Imagination in Africa: Critical Perspectives.* Chicago: Univ. Chicago Press

Cox PA, Balick MJ. 1994. The ethnobotanical approach to drug discovery. *Sci. Am.,* June:60–65

Crook T. 2000. Length matters: a note on the GM debate. *Anthropol. Today* 16(1):8–11

Clay J, ed. 1991. Intellectual property rights: the politics of ownership. *Cult. Surv. Q.* 15(3):1–52

Daes EI. 1993. *Study on the Culture and Intellectual Property of Indigenous Peoples. Work. Group Indig. Popul.* E/CN.4/Sub.2/Geneva/28 July

Duncan DE. 1998. A shaman's cure. *Life Sp.*

Issue Med. Miracles Next Millenn., Fall 26–37

Durant J, Hansen A, Bauer M. 1996. Public understanding of the new genetics. See Marteau & Richards 1996.

Elisabetsky E. 1991. Folklore, tradition, or know-how? *Cult. Surv. Q.,* Summer (15):9–13

Elisabetsky E, Castilhos ZC. 1990. Plants used as analgesics by Amazonian *cabaclos* as a basis for selecting plants for investigation. *Int. J. Crude Drug Res.* 28:49–60

Etkin NL. 1988. Ethnopharmacology: biobehavioral approaches in the anthropological study of indigenous medicines. *Annu. Rev. Anthropol.* 17:23–42

Farnsworth NR. 1988. Screening plants for new medicines. In *Biodiversity,* ed. EO Wilson, FM Peters, pp. 83–97. Washington, DC: Natl. Acad.

Farnsworth NR, Akerele O, Bingel AS, Soejarto DD, Guo Z. 1985. Medicinal plants in therapy. *Bull. World Health Org.* 63(6):965–81

Ford RI. 1978. *The Nature and Status of Ethnobotany. Anthropol. Pap. No. 67.* Ann Arbor: Univ. Mich., Mus. Anthropol.

Fundación Sabiduría Indígena, Kothari B. 1997. Rights to the benefits of research: compensating indigenous peoples for their intellectual contribution. *Hum. Org.* 5(2):127–37

Glowka L. 1998. *A Guide to Designing Legal Frameworks to Determine Access to Genetic Resources.* Gland, Switzerland: Int. Union Conserv. Nat., World Conserv. Union

Gollin MA. 1999. New rules for natural products research. *Nat. Biotechnol.* 17:921–22

Greaves T, ed. 1994. *Intellectual Property Rights for Indigenous Peoples: A Source Book.* Oklahoma City, OK: Soc. Appl. Anthropol.

Greely HT. 1998. Legal, ethical, and social issues in human genome research. *Annu. Rev. Anthropol.* 27:473–502

Green EC. 1998. *Ethnobotany, intellectual property rights and benefit sharing: the ICBG project in Suriname.* Presented at

Annu. Meet. SfAA Symp. on Coming to Terms with IPR, San Juan, Puerto Rico, April 23

Grifo F, Rosenthal J. 1997. *Biodiversity and Human Health.* Washington, DC: Island

Guerin-McManus M, Famolare L, Bowles I, Stanley AJ, Mittermeier R, et al. 1998. Bioprospecting in practice: a case study of the Suriname ICBG project and benefit-sharing under the Convention on Biological Diversity. In *Case Studies on Benefit Sharing Arrangements,* 4th Conf. Parties Conv. Biol. Divers., Bratislava, May, http://www.biodiv. org/chm/techno/genres.html

Gupta AK. 1996. The Honey Bee Network: voices from grassroots innovators. *Cult. Surv. Q.* 20(1):57–60

Hann C, Dunn E. 1996. *Civil Society: Challenging Western Models.* New York: Routledge

Hitchcock RK. 1994. International human rights, the environment and indigenous peoples: international environmental law and policy. *Colo. J. Int. Law Policy* 5(1):1–22

Horrobin D, Lapinskas P. 1998. The commercial development of food plants used as medicines. See Prendergast et al. 1998, pp. 75–81

Hunter CJ. 1998. Sustainable bioprospecting: using private contracts and international legal principles and policies to conserve raw medicinal materials. *Boston Coll. Environ. Aff. Law Rev.* 25:129–75

Iwu M. 1993. *Handbook of African Medicinal Plants.* Boca Raton, FL: CRC. 435 pp.

Iwu MM. 1996a. Biodiversity prospecting in Nigeria: seeking equity and reciprocity in intellectual property rights through partnership arrangements and capacity building. *J. Ethnopharmacol.* 5(1):209–19

Iwu MM. 1996b. Development of genetic resources: Bioresources Development and Conservation Programme experience in West and Central Africa. In *Science in Africa: Utilizing Africa's Genetic Affluence through Natural Products Research and Development,* pp. 99–112. Washington, DC: Am. Assoc. Adv. Sci. Sub-Saharan Afr. Progr.

Kimbrell A. 1997. Breaking the law of life. *Resurgence* 182:10–12

King SR, Carlson T, Moran K. 1996. Biological diversity, indigenous knowledge, drug discovery and intellectual property rights. See Brush & Stabinsky 1996, pp. 167–85

King SR, Carlson TJ. 1995. Biomedicine, biotechnology, and biodiversity: the Western Hemisphere experience. *Interciencia* 20(3): 134–39

King SR, Meza E, Ayala F, Forero LE, Penna M, et al. 1997. Croton lechleri and sustainable harvest and management of plants in pharmaceuticals, phytomedicines and cosmetic industries. In *Int. Symp. on Herbal Medicine,* ed. DS Wosniak, S Yuen, M Garrett, TM Shuman, pp. 305–33. San Diego: Int. Inst. Hum. Resourc. Dev., Coll. Health & Hum. Serv., San Diego State Univ.

King SR, Meza E, Carlson T, Chinnock J, Moran K, et al. 1999. Issues in the commercialization of medicinal plants. *Herbalgram* 47:46–51

Kloppenburg J, Balick MJ. 1996. Property rights and genetic resources: a framework for analysis. In *Medicinal Resources of the Tropical Forest: Biodiversity and Its Importance to Human Health,* ed. MJ Balick, E Elisabetsky, SA Laird, pp. 174–81. New York: Columbia Univ. Press

Laird S. 1993. Contracts for biodiversity prospecting. See Reid et al. 1993, pp. 99–130

Laird SA, ed. 2000. Equitable partnerships in practice: the tools of the trade. In *Biodiversity and Traditional Knowledge, A People and Plants Programme Conservation Manual.* London: Earthscan

Leaman D. 1997. Environmental protection concerns of prospecting for and producing plant-based drugs. In *Int. Symp. on Herbal Medicine,* ed. DS Wosniak, S Yuen, M Garrett, TM Shuman, pp. 352–78. San Diego: Int. Inst. Hum. Resourc. Dev., Coll. Health & Hum. Serv., San Diego State Univ.

Linden E. 1991. Lost tribes, lost knowledge. *Time,* Sept. 23, pp. 46–56

Marteau T, Richards M, eds. 1996. *The Troubled Helix: Social and Psychological Implications of the New Human Genetics.* Cambridge, UK: Cambridge Univ. Press

Maybury-Lewis, D. 1997. *Indigenous Peoples, Ethnic Groups, and the State.* Boston: Allyn & Bacon

Mays T, Duffy-Mazan K, Cragg G, Boyd M. 1997. A paradigm for the equitable sharing of benefits resulting from biodiversity research and development. See Rosenthal 1997, pp. 267–80

McChesney J. 1996. Biological diversity, chemical diversity and the search for new pharmaceuticals. In *Medicinal Resources of the Tropical Forest: Biodiversity and Its Importance to Human Health*, ed. M.J. Balick, T. Elisabetsky, S. Laird, pp. 11–18. New York: Columbia Univ. Press

Meza T, ed. 1999. *Conservando la Biodiversidad Cultural: Sangre de grado y el Reto de la Producción Sustenable en el Peru.* Lima: Propaceb

Meza E, Ayala F, Castaoel M, Forero LE, Penna M, et al. 1998. *El Manejo Sostenible de Sangre de Drago o Sangre de Grado, Material Educativo.* San Francisco: Shaman Pharmaceut. & Healing Forest Conserv.

Moerman DE. 1996. An analysis of the food plants and drug plants of Native North America. *J. Ethnopharmacol.* 52:1–22

Moran K. 1998a Moving on: less description, more prescription for human health. *EcoForum* 2(4):5–9

Moran K. 1998b. *Mechanisms for benefit-sharing: Nigerian case study for the Convention on Biological Diversity.* 4th Meet. Conf. of Parties, Sec. Conv. Biol. Divers., Bratislava, Slovakia, May, http://www.biodiv.org/chm/techno/gen-res.html

Moran K. 2001. Indigenous peoples and local communities embodying traditional life styles: definitions under Article 8(j) of the Convention on Biological Diversity. In *Ethnobotany and Drug Discovery*, ed. MM Iwu. Neth.: Elsevier Sci. BV. In press

Morris K. 1992. *International Directory and Resource Guide.* Oakland, CA: South & Meso Am. Ind. Inf. Cent.

Nature. 1998. The complex realities of sharing genetic assets. *Nature* 392:525

N. Am. Congr. Latin Am. 1994. Gaining ground: the indigenous movement in Latin America. *N. Am. Congr. Latin Am.* 24(5):14–43

Orlove BS, Brush SB. 1996. Anthropology and the conservation of biodiversity. *Annu. Rev. Anthropol.* 25:329–52

Oubre AY, Carson T, King SR, Reaven G. 1997. From plant to patient: an ethnomedical approach to the identifications of new drugs for the treatment of NIDDM. *Diabetologia* 40:614–17

Palmer P. 1996. Partnerships and power: an indigenous community in Costa Rica develops on its own terms. *Ecoforum* 20(3):12–13

Palsson G, Rabinow P. 1999. Iceland: the case of a national human genome project. *Anthropol. Today* 15(5):14–18

Pollack A. 1999. Patenting life: a special report; biological products raise genetic ownership issues. *NY Times*, Nov. 26, p. 1, c4

Porter G. 1992. *The False Dilemma: The Biodiversity Convention and Intellectual Property Rights.* Washington, DC: Environ. & Energy Study Inst.

Posey DA, Dutfield G. 1996. *Beyond Intellectual Property: Toward Traditional Resource Rights for Indigenous Peoples and Local Communities.* Ottawa: Int. Dev. Res. Cent.

Prance GT. 1991. What is ethnobotany today? *J. Ethnopharmacol.* 32:209–16

Prendergast HDV, Etkin NL, Harris DR, Houghton PJ. 1998. Plants for food and medicine. In *Proc. Joint Conf. Soc. Econ. Bot. Int. Soc. Ethnopharmacol.*, pp. 438. Kew, Richmond, UK: Sci. Publ. Dep., R. Bot. Gard.

Prescott J, Gauthier B, Sodi JMS. 2000. *Guide to Developing a Biodiversity Strategy from a Sustainable Development Perspective.* Quebec, Can.: Inst. Energie Environ. Francophonie, Minist. Environ. Quebec, UN Dev. Progr., UN Environ. Progr.

Pritchard S. 1998. *Indigenous Peoples, the*

United Nations and Human Rights. London: Zed Books

Putterman DM. 1996. Model material transfer agreements for equitable biodiversity propsecting. *Colo. J. Int. Law Policy* 7:141–77

Rabinow P. 1994. *Making PCR: A Story of Biotechnology.* Chicago: Univ. Chicago Press

Reichel-Dolmatoff G. 1976. Cosmology as ecological analysis: a view from the rainforest. *Man J. R. Anthropol. Inst.* 11(3):307–18

Reid WV, Laird SA, Meyer CA, Gamez R, Sittenfeld A, et al. 1993. *Biodiversity Prospecting: Using Genetic Resources for Sustainable Development.* Washington, DC: World Resourc. Instit.

Richter RK, Carlson TJS. 1998. Report of biological assay results on tropical medicinal plants to host country collaborators. *J. Ethnopharmacol.* 62:85–88

Riley M, Moran K, ed. 2001. Culture as commodity: intellectual property rights. *Cult. Surv. Q.* 24(4):1–57

Rosenthal J, ed. 1999. *Pharmaceutical Biology. Drug Discovery, Economic. Development and Conservation: The International Cooperative Biodiversity Groups.* The Netherlands: Swets & Zeitlinger

Rubin S, Fish S. 1994. Biodiversity prospecting: using innovative contractual provisions to foster ethnobotanical knowledge, technology and conservation. *Colo. J. Int. Environ. Law Policy* 5:23–58

Schultes RE. 1988. Primitive plant lore and modern conservation. *Orion Nat. Q.* 3:8–15

Schultes RE, Raffauf RF. 1990. *The Healing Forest: Medicinal and Toxic Plants of the Northwest Amazonia.* Portland, OR: Dioscorides

Science. 1999. Plant patent killed. *Science* 286:1675

Shelton D. 1995. Fair play, fair pay: preserving traditional knowledge and biological resources. *Int. Yearb. Int. Law* 6(77)

Shiva V. 1997. *Biopiracy: The Plunder of Nature and Knowledge,* Boston: South End

Simpson T. 1997. *Indigenous Heritage and Self-Determination: The Cultural and Intellectual Property Rights of Indigenous Peoples.* Copenhagen: Int. Work Group Indig. Aff. 229 pp.

Singh Nijar G. 1996. In *Defence of Local Community Knowledge and Biodiversity: A Conceptual Framework and the Essential Elements of a Rights Regime.* Penang, Malaysia: Third World Nework

Skinner J. 1999. Anthropological ethics. *Anthropol. Today* 15(3):23–24

Swanson T, ed. 1995. *Intellectual Property Rights and Biodiversity Conservation: An Interdisciplinary Analysis of the Values of Medicinal Plants.* Cambridge, UK: Cambridge Univ Press

Tempesta M, King SR. 1994. Ethnobotany as a source for new drugs. In *Annual Reports in Medicinal Chemistry,* ed. E Venuti, pp. 325–30. Berkeley, CA: Academic

ten Kate K. 1995. *Biopiracy or Green Petroleum? Expectations and Best Practice in Bioprospecting.* London: Overseas Dev. Admin.

ten Kate K, Laird S. 1999. *The Commercial Use of Biodiversity: Access to Genetic Resources and Benefit-Sharing.* London: Earthscan. 398 pp.

Tobin B. 1997. Know-how licenses: recognizing indigenous rights over collective knowledge. *Bull. Work. Group Trad. Resourc. Rights* (Winter)

UN Conv. Trade Dev. (UNCTAD). 2000. *Outcome of the Expert Meeting, D/B/COM. 1/EM.13/L.1,* 9 November. http://www.unctad.org/en/special/c1em13do.htm

UN Environ. Progr. (UNEP) Rep. 1997. *Workshop on Traditional Knowledge and Biodiversity, Nov. 24–28,* Madrid. http://www.unep.org/

US Congr., Off. Technol. Assess. 1991. *Biotechnology in a Global Economy.* Washington, DC: US Gov. Print. Off.

US Congr., Off. Technol. Assess. 1993. *Pharmaceutical R&D: Costs, Risks and Rewards.* Washington, DC: US Gov. Print. Off.

Varese S. 1996. The new environmentalist movement of Latin American indigenous people. See Brush & Stabinsky 1996, pp. 122–42

Wagner AB. 1987. Human tissue research: Who owns the results? *J. Patent Trademark Off. Soc.*, June:329–52

Zarembo A. 2001. Magnet for globophobes: Chipas is happy to attract protest, non profit. *Newsweek Intl.* April 9

Annu. Rev. Anthropol. 2001. 30:527–50

WORLD ENGLISHES

Rakesh M. Bhatt

University of Illinois, Urbana-Champaign, Illinois 61801; e-mail: rbhatt@uiuc.edu

Key Words language spread, language contact, language variation, language change, English language studies

■ **Abstract** This essay is an overview of the theoretical, methodological, pedagogical, ideological, and power-related issues of world Englishes: varieties of English used in diverse sociolinguistic contexts. The scholars in this field have critically examined theoretical and methodological frameworks of language use based on western, essentially monolingual and monocultural, frameworks of linguistic science and replaced them with frameworks that are faithful to multilingualism and language variation. This conceptual shift affords a "pluricentric" view of English, which represents diverse sociolinguistic histories, multicultural identities, multiple norms of use and acquisition, and distinct contexts of function. The implications of this shift for learning and teaching world Englishes are critically reviewed in the final sections of this essay.

INTRODUCTION

This article focuses on major current theoretical and methodological issues related to what has been characterized as "World Englishes." In the past three decades, the study of the formal and functional implications of the global spread of English, especially in terms of its range of functions and the degree of penetration in Western and, especially, non-Western societies, has received considerable attention among scholars of English language, linguistics, and literature; creative writers; language pedagogues; and literary critics. It is in this context that the late Henry Kahane remarked: "English is the great laboratory of today's sociolinguist" (1986, p. 495). There is now a growing consensus among scholars that there is not one English language anymore: rather there are many (McArthur 1998), most of which are disengaged from the language's early Judeo-Christian tradition. The different English languages, studied within the conceptual framework of world Englishes, represent diverse linguistic, cultural, and ideological voices.

The field of study of world Englishes—varieties of English used in diverse sociolinguistic contexts—represents a paradigm shift in research, teaching, and application of sociolinguistic realities to the forms and functions of English. It rejects the dichotomy of US (native speakers) vs THEM (nonnative speakers) and emphasizes instead WE-ness (McArthur 1993, 1998, Kachru 1992a). Referring to the logo acronym of the journal *World Englishes* (1984), WE, McArthur (1993, p. 334) interpreted the field most succinctly when he observed "there is a club of equals here." The pluralization, Englishes, symbolizes the formal and functional variations, the divergent sociolinguistic contexts, the linguistic, sociolinguistic, and literary creativity, and the various identities English has accrued as a result of its acculturation in new sociolinguistic ecologies (Kachru 1965, Strevens 1992). The pluralism is an integral part of world Englishes, and the field has, especially in the past three decades, critically examined theoretical and methodological frameworks based on monotheistic ethos of linguistic science and replaced them with frameworks that are faithful to multilingualism and language variation (Kachru 1983, 1986, Lowenberg 1984, 1988, Chisimba 1984, 1991, Magura 1984, 1985, Mesthrie 1992, Bamgbose 1982, Bamgbose et al 1995). This conceptual-theoretical shift has extended the empirical domain of the study of English. English is regarded less as a European language and an exclusive exponent of Judeo-Christian traditions and more as a pluricentric language representing diverse sociolinguistic histories, multicultural identities, multiple norms of use and acquisition, and distinct contexts of function (Smith 1981, 1983, 1987, Ferguson 1982, Kachru 1982, Kachru & Quirk 1981). Linguistic and literary creativity in English is determined less by the usage of its native speakers and more by the usage of nonnative speakers, who outnumber native speakers 4:1 (Crystal 1995, McArthur 1992).

The world Englishes paradigm raises several interesting questions about theory, empirical validity, social responsibility, and ideology (Kachru 1990). An inquiry into world Englishes invites (*a*) theoretical approaches to the study of English that are interdisciplinary in orientation, (*b*) methodologies that are sensitive to multilingual and multicultural realities of language-contact situations, and (*c*) pedagogies that respond to both intra- and international functions of English (Bailey & Görlach 1982, Ferguson 1982, Cheshire 1991, Kachru 1982, Foley et al 1998). The philosophical-theoretical assumptions underlying the study of world Englishes are grounded in what has come to be known as liberation linguistics (Labov 1972, Kachru 1991, Bhatt 1995a, Milroy & Milroy 1985, Mesthrie 1992, Lippi-Green 1994, 1997). Liberation linguistics, as a general term for several forms of linguistic beliefs and practices that accent the sociopolitical dimensions of language variation, is rooted in contexts of social injustice and seeks to transform these contexts radically in the interest of the speakers of the "other tongue"—the nonnative speakers (Bhatt 2001a,b, Kachru 1997, Denière 1993, Parakrama 1990, 1995, Viswanathan 1989, Phillipson 1992, Pennycook 1994, 1998, Canagarajah 1999). The liberation linguistic-theoretic assumptions have displaced and discredited the trinity of ENL (English as a native language), ESL (English as a second language), and EFL (English as a foreign language) and has presented instead a model of diffusion of English that is defined with reference to historical, sociolinguistic, and literary contexts (McArthur 1992, 1993, Kachru 1986).

SPREAD AND STRATIFICATION

The Spread of English

The transformation of a tribal language to Standard English in the nineteenth century is well documented (Platt et al 1984, McCrum et al 1986, Machan & Scott 1992, Burchfield 1994, Crystal 1995). Its spread is arguably "the most striking example of 'language expansion' of this century if not in all recorded history. It has far exceeded that other famous case, the spread of Latin during the Roman Empire" (Platt et al 1984, p. 1). And now, at the dawn of the twenty-first century, we are witnessing John Adams' prophecy coming true: that English will become the most respected and universally read and spoken language in the world (Kachru 1992a).

The global spread of English is popularly viewed in terms of two diasporas: In the first, English was transplanted by native speakers, and in the second, English was introduced as an official language alongside other national languages (Knowles 1997, Kachru 1992a). After the initial expansion toward Wales in 1535, Scotland in 1603, and (parts of) Ireland in 1707, the first diaspora of English took place—the movement of English-speaking populations to North America, Canada, and Australia and New Zealand. Each of these countries adopted English as the language of the new nation, which resulted in English becoming one of the major languages of the world, along with Arabic, French, German, Hindi, Russian, and Spanish, though it was still not, as it is now, a global language, numerically or functionally.

The global status of English became established in its second diaspora. This diaspora brought English to "un-English" sociocultural contexts—to South Asia, Africa, and Latin America—which resulted in a significant alteration of the earlier sociolinguistic profile of the English language. It was in this second diaspora that English came into contact with genetically and culturally unrelated languages: in Asia with Indo-Aryan and Dravidian languages, in Africa with languages of the Niger-Congo family, and in Southeast Asia with Altaic languages. The contact of English with such diverse languages resulted in the development of regional-contact varieties of English, e.g., Indian English, Malaysian English, Singaporean English, Philippine English, Nigerian English, and Ghanian English (Kachru 1965, Foley 1988, Lowenberg 1986, Bautista 1997, Bamgbose 1982, Sey 1973). It was also in this second diaspora that a new ecology for the teaching of English was created, in terms of linguistic input, methodology, norms, and identity.

Several attempts have been made to model the spread and diffusion of English as a global language (Kachru 1988, Görlach 1991, McArthur 1987, Crystal 1997). Kachru's (1988) concentric circle model (Figure 1) captures the historical, sociolinguistic, acquisitional, and literary contexts of the spread and diffusion of English.

In this model, the inner circle refers to the traditional bases of English, where it is the primary language, with an estimated 320–380 million speakers (Crystal 1997).

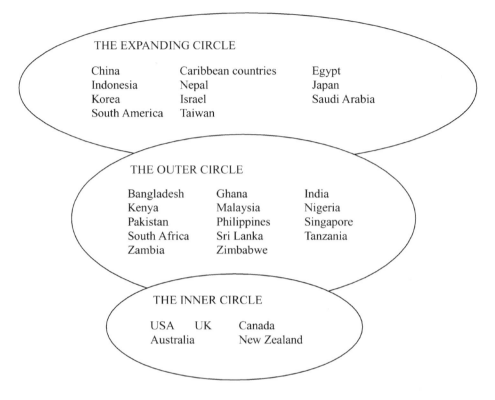

Figure 1   The concentric circle model. [Adapted from Kachru (1997).]

The outer circle represents the spread of English in nonnative contexts, where it has been institutionalized as an additional language, with an estimated 150–300 million speakers. The expanding circle, with a steady increase in the number of speakers and functional domains, includes nations where English is used primarily as a foreign language, with an estimated 100–1000 million speakers (Crystal 1997).

The impact and extent of spread is not easily quantifiable because many varieties of English are used for both inter- and intranational functions. Table 1 presents a list of countries where English is used as an "official" (loosely defined) language.

Exponents of Stratification

The stratification of English, especially varieties in the outer circle, has been interpreted in two ways: as a polylectal continuum (Platt 1975, Platt & Weber 1980, Platt et al 1984, Mufwene 1994, 1997) and as a cline of English bilingualism

TABLE 1   Countries in which English has official status[a]

Antigua and Barbuda	Irish Republic	Seychelles
Australia	Jamaica	Sierra Leone
Bahamas	Kenya	Singapore
Barbados	Lesotho	South Africa
Botswana	Liberia	Sri Lanka
Brunei	Malawi	Surinam
Cameroon	Malta	Swaziland
Canada	Mauritius	Tanzania
Dominica	New Zealand	Trinidad and Tobago
Fiji	Nigeria	Uganda
Gambia	Papua New Guinea	United Kingdom
Ghana	Philippines	United States of America
Grenada	St. Christopher and Nevis	Zambia
Guyana	St. Lucia	Zimbabwe
India	St. Vincent and the Grenadines	

[a]Adapted from Crystal (1985, p. 357).

(Kachru 1983, Pakir 1991, Bamgbose 1982). In terms of a lectal range, Platt & Weber (1980), following Bickerton's (1975) model of creole continuum, describe Singapore English (Singlish), identifiable with a spectrum of varieties spanning from the standard variety of the lexifier—identified as acrolect—to the basilect, its polar opposite. The sociolinguistic accounts of South African Indian English (Mesthrie 1992), Caribbean English (Winford 1997), and Liberian Englishes (Singler 1997) offer more evidence for the continuum model: In each case, the basilect is the variety of English used by people with little contact with English and no formal education, whereas the acrolect, which shows little difference from the colonial form of English, is the variety used mainly by educated people.

The cline of bilingualism, on the other hand, is related to the users and uses. One end of this cline represents the educated variety of English; the other end represents, among others, Nigerian Pidgin (Bamiro 1991), basilect in Malaysia and Singapore (Pakir 1991, Lowenberg 1991), and butler English (Hosali & Aitchison 1986). These varieties are not only spoken, they are also used in literature to characterize various types of interlocutor identities, socioeconomic classes, and the local cultural ethos.

There is also a functional aspect of this cline, as found most visibly in the context of outer-circle varieties of English (Quirk et al 1972, Kachru 1983). Kachru (1983), for example, has identified four functions of English in South Asia:

(*a*) instrumental—English as a medium of learning in educational systems; (*b*) regulative—English in administrative and legal systems; (*c*) interpersonal— English as a link language between speakers of mutually unintelligible languages or dialects in sociolinguistically plural societies, and as a language of elitism and modernization; and (*d*) imaginative—English in various literary genres.

Linguistic Imperialism or Language Pragmatics

The third phase of English expansion, the second diaspora, has recently generated controversies about the processes and consequences of the introduction of English into what clearly were un-English contexts. The rapid spread of English during the third phase has been explained at least from two different, though not mutually exclusive, perspectives. According to one perspective, the spread of English in nonnative contexts was actively promoted, via English language teaching (ELT) agencies such as the British Council, as an instrument of the foreign policies of major English-speaking states. This theory, known as English linguistic imperialism (Phillipson 1992), argues that English is universally imposed by agencies of linguistic coercion, such as the British Council and TESOL (Teachers of English to Speakers of Other Languages), which introduce and impose a norm, Standard English, through which is exerted the domination of those groups that have both the means of imposing it as "legitimate" and the monopoly on the means of appropriating it (cf. also Pennycook 1994, 1998). Accordingly, linguistic imperialism results in the emergence, on the one hand, of an asymmetric relationship between producers and consumers that is internalized as natural, normative, and essential and, on the other hand, of a heteroglossic (hierarchical) arrangement of languages, pervaded by hegemonic value judgments, material and symbolic investments, and ideologies that represent interests only of those in power [for detailed critiques of this perspective of the spread of English, see Kibbee (1993), Brutt-Griffler (1998), Davies (1996), Canagarajah (1999)].

The other perspective on the spread of English is the econocultural model, proposed by Quirk (1988) and defended in Brutt-Griffler (1998). Industrial revolution, trade practices, and commercial exploitation of the late eighteenth- and early nineteenth-century England created conditions where one language had to develop as the language of the world market, the "commercial lingua franca." With England and the United States at the epicenter of industrial capitalism of the nineteenth century, it was natural that English became the language of global commerce. Especially after World War II—with the establishment of the United Nations, World Bank, UNESCO, UNICEF, World Health Organization, and, a few years later, the Commonwealth and the European Union—it was inevitable that the general competence in English in different political, social, cultural, and economic markets would continue to grow rapidly (Mazrui & Mazrui 1998, Brutt-Griffler

1998). The success of the spread of English, tied to the economic conditions that created the commercial supremacy of the United Kingdom and the United States, is guaranteed under the econocultural model by linguistic pragmatism not linguistic imperialism.

The educational system in the colonies was the most important instrument of the reproduction of English symbolic capital because schools[1] had the monopoly over the reproduction of the market on which the value of linguistic competence depends (Bourdieu 1977, Goke-Pariola 1993). In colonial South Asia and West Africa, where education was the only source for the acquisition of cultural capital[2] and apprenticeship into the "fellowships of discourse" (à la Foucault 1972)[3], the principal medium of that initiation was English. The recognition of English as symbolic capital is most clearly evidenced, for example, in the second phase—after the missionary phase—of the spread of English in South Asia, which was the result of the demand and willingness of local people to learn it (Kachru 1986). It is unsurprising, therefore, that prominent political leaders in colonial India, or, as Goke-Pariola (1993) reports, Nigerians in many parts of that country, contested the use of indigenous languages in the schools because it was perceived as denying them the linguistic capital necessary for the accumulation of both economic and political powers.

When the colonizers left, they left behind the linguistic habitus and the peculiar market conditions their intervention had created; but their departure did create a new ecology for the teaching of English in terms of (nonnative) linguistic input, local (Indian, Nigerian, etc.) norms, multiple identities, communicative competencies and methodologies that respect language variation.

---

[1]It is in schools, argues Giroux (1981, p. 24), that the production of hegemonic ideologies "hides" behind a number of legitimating forms. Some of the most obvious include "(1) the claim by dominant classes that their interests represent the entire interests of the community; (2) the claim that conflict only occurs outside of the sphere of the political, i.e., economic conflict is viewed as non-political; (3) the presentation of specific forms of consciousness, beliefs, attitudes, values and practices as natural, universal, or even eternal."

[2]Cultural capital here refers to the "system of meanings, abilities, language forms, and tastes that are directly or indirectly defined by dominant groups as socially legitimate" (Apple 1978:496, Bourdieu 1991).

[3]The function of "the fellowships of discourse" is, according to Foucault (1972, pp. 225–26), "to preserve or to reproduce discourse, but in order that it should circulate within a closed community, according to strict regulations, without those in possession being dispossessed by this very distribution. An archaic model of this would be those groups of Rhapsodists, possessing knowledge of poems to recite or, even, upon which to work variations and transformations. But though the ultimate object of this knowledge was ritual recitation, it was protected and preserved within a determinate group by the, often extremely complex, exercises of memory implied by such a process. Apprenticeship gained access both to a group and to a secret which recitation made manifest, but did not divulge. The roles of speaking and listening were not interchangeable."

LANGUAGE NATIVIZATION AND
BILINGUAL'S CREATIVITY

As the English language spread, through linguistic imperialism and linguistic pragmatism, to nonnative contexts and came into close, protracted contact with genetically and culturally unrelated languages, it went through a process of linguistic
experimentation and nativization by the people who adopted it for use in different functional domains, such as education, administration, and high society (cf.
Kachru 1992a). Nonnative English speakers thus created new, cultural-sensitive
and socially appropriate meanings—expressions of the bilingual's creativity—by
altering and manipulating the structure and functions of English in its new ecology.
As a result, English underwent a process of acculturation in order to compete in
local linguistic markets that were hitherto dominated by indigenous languages.
Given the linguistic and cultural pluralism in Africa and South Asia, linguistic innovations, creativity, and emerging literary traditions in English in these countries
were immediately accepted.

Linguistic Creativity

To understand the structural variation in English across cultures, two questions need
to be answered (Bhatt 1995a): What is the structure of "nonnative" Englishes, and
how did they come to be the way they are? With respect to these questions, a beginning has already been made toward explorations into the structure of outer-circle
varieties of English. Y. Kachru (1985) has provided valuable methodological as
well as theoretical insights into the structure of Indian English discourse. Mesthrie's
(1992) work on South African Indian English and Bhatt's (1995a,b, 1997, 2000)
and Sridhar's (1992) work on Indian English provide a framework for syntactic
descriptions that has implications for cross-language transfer and bilingual competence. Mohanan (1992), Chaudhary (1989), Hancin-Bhatt & Bhatt (1993), and
Bhatt (1995a,b) have provided accounts of various aspects of the sound patterns
of Indian English. The theoretical approaches adopted in all these studies have a
clear methodological agenda—to describe the structure of a "nonnative" variety
in its own terms, not as descriptions of aborted "interlanguages."

Bilingual's creativity in world Englishes, especially in the outer circle, is best
captured using the methodological premise that a descriptively adequate grammar
of English, in "nonnative" contexts, must address the relationship between the
forms that English manifests and its speakers' perception of reality and the nature
of their cultural institutions. This premise yields an interpretation of language use
constrained by the grammar of culture (cf. Bright 1968, Hymes 1974, D'souza
1988). The theoretical insights in the works of Halliday (1973), Kachru (1992a),
Sridhar (1992), and Bhatt (1995a, 2000) provide a framework of linguistic description that not only allows the simplest interpretation of English language
use across cultures, it also accommodates, in the most economical way, linguistically significant generalizations of the grammatical structure of world Englishes.

Consider the use of undifferentiated tag questions in Indian English to demonstrate how the theoretical assumptions and methodological insights discussed above provide socially realistic descriptions of the bilingual's grammar in the world Englishes context. In English, tag questions are formed by a rule that inserts a pronominal copy of the subject after an appropriate modal auxiliary. A typical example is "John said he'll work today, didn't he?"

Tags have also been analyzed as expressing certain attitudes of the speaker toward what is being said in the main clause, and in terms of speech acts and/or performatives. Functionally, tags in English behave like epistemic adverbials, such as probably, presumably, etc.: (*a*) "It's still dark outside, isn't it?" (*b*) "It's probably dark outside."

Kachru (1983, p. 79) and Trudgill & Hannah (1985, p. 111) discuss the use of what they call undifferentiated tag questions as one of the linguistic exponents of Indian English: (*a*) "You are going home soon, isn't it?" (*b*) "You have taken my book, isn't it?" Their description, however, leaves out the important pragmatic role the undifferentiated tags play in the Indian English speech community. In most cases, the meaning of the tag is not the one appended to the meaning of the main proposition; it is usually the tag that signals important social meaning. In fact, tags in Indian English are a fascinating example of how linguistic form (of the tag) is constrained by cultural constraints of politeness. Bhatt (1995b) has in fact argued that undifferentiated tags in Indian English are linguistic devices governed by the politeness principle of nonimposition: They serve positive politeness functions (à la Brown & Levinson 1987), signaling deference and acquiescence. Notice, for example, the contrast between Indian English—(*a*) "You said you'll do the job, isn't it?" and "They said they will be here, isn't it?"—and Standard British English/American English—(*b*) "You said you'll do the job, didn't you? and "They said they will be here, didn't they?" In contrast to the *b* examples above, Indian English speakers find the *a* examples nonimpositional and mitigating. This intuition is more clearly established when an adverb of intensification/assertion is used in conjunction with the undifferentiated tag: (*a*) "Of course you said you'll do the job, isn't it?" (*b*) "Of course they said they'll be here, isn't it?" The result is, predictably, unacceptable.

In a culture where the verbal behavior is severely constrained, to a large extent, by politeness regulations, where nonimposition is the essence of polite behavior, it is not surprising that Indian English has replaced Standard British English tags with undifferentiated tags. To understand why Indian English has chosen to use the undifferentiated strategy, the notion of grammar of culture (Bright 1968, D'souza 1988) becomes relevant.

Undifferentiated tags are not exclusive instances of the interplay of grammatical and cultural rules in Indian English, where one finds the linguistic form constrained by the grammar of culture. The influence of the grammar of culture on linguistic expressions in Indian English can also be seen in the use of the modal auxiliary "may." In Indian English, "may" is used to express obligation politely—"This furniture *may* be removed tomorrow"; "These mistakes *may* please be corrected"—in contrast to Standard British English—"This furniture is to be removed tomorrow"; "These mistakes should be corrected" (Trudgill & Hannah 1985, p. 109).

The linguistic checklist of innovations in the outer-circle varieties of English is endless. Several studies on linguistic acculturation and creativity in English in the outer circle have convincingly demonstrated that world Englishes have their own syntactic and logical structure, constrained both by cognitive-economy considerations and by social-functional requirements (Platt & Weber 1980, Kachru 1983, Sridhar 1992, Mesthrie 1992, 1997, Bokamba 1992, Bhatt 1995a,b, 2000, Bao 1995).

Sociolinguistic Creativity

There is also a sociolinguistic dimension of bilingual creativity, viewed in terms of acculturation and nativization of the use of English in the outer circle. The study and analysis of English language use in outer-circle varieties resulted in the following types of cross-cultural and cross-linguistic research: (*a*) discourse analysis, discourse strategies, and stylistic innovations (Richards 1979, Smith 1981, 1987, Gumperz 1982, Magura 1984, Y. Kachru 1985, 1995, 1997, Valentine 1988, 1991); (*b*) speech acts (Y. Kachru 1991, 1993, D'souza 1988, 1991); (*c*) code mixing and code switching (Bhatia & Ritchie 1989, Kamwangamalu 1989, Myers-Scotton 1993a,b, Bhatt 1997); (*d*) genre analysis (V. Bhatia 1997); and (*e*) language planning (Kandiah & Kwan-Terry 1994).

An illustration of the sociolinguistic dimension of bilingual's creativity—the manipulation of linguistic resources in language use to generate new meanings—is best exemplified by code switching (style shifting) reported by Mesthrie (1992). A young South African Indian English-speaking attendant at the security section of the airport asked him, "You haven' got anything to declare?" Mesthrie argues that in using the nonacrolectal variety, the security guard at the airport was defusing the syntax of power ("Do you have anything to declare?") in favor of mesolectal solidarity (Mesthrie 1992, p. 219). Other sociolinguistic functions of code switching and mixing in world Englishes, such as exclusion, politeness, identity, and elitism, have been discussed by Kachru (1983) and Myers-Scotton (1993b).

The other face of nativization of sociolinguistic uses of world Englishes is presented by code mixing in culture-specific interactions, in the news media, in matrimonial advertisements, in obituaries, and so on. The matrimonial columns reflect, as Kachru (1986) has convincingly argued, Asian and African sensitivity to color, caste hierarchy, regional attitudes, and family structure. It is not uncommon, for instance, to find matrimonial advertisements in South Asian English newspapers using highly contextualized English lexical items with semantic nativization, as shown in two Hindu examples from 1 July 1979 (Kachru 1986).

> Wanted well-settled bridegroom for a Kerala fair, graduate Baradwaja gotram, Astasastram girl . . . . Subsect no bar.

> Non-Koundanya well qualified prospective bridegroom below 20 for graduate Iyengar girl, daughter of engineer. Mirugaserusham. No dosham. Average complexion. Reply with horoscope.

The rhetorical-communicative styles of South Asian English, as in the above examples, show that both the text and the context must be nativized in order to derive an interpretation that is faithful to the new situations in which world Englishes function. Furthermore, the successful, contextually appropriate interpretation of the above examples requires bilingual as well as bicultural competence.

The cross-cultural attitudes about the forms and functions of world Englishes show a cline: from acquisitional deficit to pragmatic success. On one end of this attitudinal cline are the linguistic Cassandras, members of the inner circle (Quirk 1990, 1996, Honey 1983, 1997) launching paradigms of marginality, for primarily economic gains (Kachru 1996, Romaine 1997, Bhatt 2001a).

The other end of this attitudinal cline is captured rather faithfully in a conversation that takes place between a farmer and an Indian in Vikram Seth's novel, *A Suitable Boy*.

> "Do you speak English?" he said after a while in the local dialect of Hindi. He had noticed Maan's luggage tag.
> "Yes," said Maan.
> "Without English you can't do anything," said the farmer sagely.
> Maan wondered what possible use English could be to the farmer.
> "What use is English?" said Maan.
> "People love English!" said the farmer with a strange sort of deep-voiced giggle. "If you talk in English, you are a king. The more people you can mystify, the more people will respect you." He turned back to his tobacco.

But, what about the attitude toward nativization by nonnative speakers? Here the venerable Chinua Achebe (1966, p. 22) sums it up most eloquently: "I feel the English language will be able to carry the weight of my African experience. But it will have to be a new English, still in communion with its ancestral home but altered to suit its new African surroundings."

Achebe's observation about the appropriateness of indiginized varieties of English for articulating linguistic voices in nonnative contexts is supported by the results of empirical investigations on attitudes of nonnative speakers toward exocentric (native) and endocentric (nonnative) models (Llamzon 1969, Bamgbose 1971, Sey 1973, Kachru 1976).

Literary Creativity and Canonicity

The nativization and alteration of English ensured its use as a medium for indigenous expression. As Iyengar (1962, p. 3) puts it: "Indian writing in English is but one of the voices in which India speaks. It is a new voice, no doubt, but it is as much Indian as the others." These endorsements of the relationship between underlying thought patterns and language design are perhaps best exemplified by

Achebe (1969). Achebe provides two short passages of the same material, one written in the indiginized/Africanized style and the other in native English style. In the passage, the Chief Priest is telling one of his sons why it is necessary to send him to Church. The first of the two passages below, the Africanized version (Achebe 1969), reflects faithfully the underlying thought patterns of the cultural context of language use.

1. I want one of my sons to join these people and be my eyes there. If there is nothing in it you will come back. But if there is something then you will bring back my share. The world is like a mask, dancing. If you want to see it well, you do not stand in one place. My spirit tells me that those who do not befriend the white man today will be saying, "had we known", tomorrow.

2. I am sending you as my representative among these people—just to be on the safe side in case the new religion develops. One has to move with the times or else one is left behind. I have a hunch that those who fail to come to terms with the white man may well regret their lack of foresight.

An analysis of these new/indigenous varieties reveal that the innovations in their structure and use are, as discussed above, a linguistic response to the constraints of the grammar of their respective native cultures (Bright 1968, D'souza 1987). It is in these new Englishes, as Achebe ably demonstrates, that we observe today the most active processes of a bilingual's creativity: translation, transcreation, style shifting, code switching, etc. (Bhatia & Ritchie 1989, Bhatt 1997, Bokamba 1992, Kachru 1983, 1986, 1992a, 1994, Y. Kachru 1993, Lowenberg 1988, Mesthrie 1992, Smith 1981, 1987, Sridhar 1992, Thumboo 1992, Baumgardner 1993, 1996). English is used as a medium to present canons unrelated to traditional Judeo-Christian associations or the European cultural heritage of the language. Thus, the English language has become "multicanon" (Kachru 1991), a notion that attempts to accommodate the current sociolinguistic reality in world Englishes, where speakers of a wide range of first languages communicate with one another through English.

THE SACRED COWS OF ENGLISH

The global spread of English, its diffusion and penetration at various societal levels and functional domains, has had a very important consequence: Some of the traditional, taken-for-granted linguistic understandings of users and uses of English have been questioned and challenged (Kachru 1988). A sustained academic campaign for a non-Eurocentric approach to the study of world Englishes resulted in the sacrifice of five types of sacred cows: the acquisitional, sociolinguistic, pedagogical, theoretical, and the ideological.

Acquisitional Sacred Cow

Acquisitional questions relate to the relevance of concepts such as interference, error, interlanguage, and fossilization, to the users and uses of English in the outer circle. As discussed in the previous section, the use of undifferentiated tag questions by Indian English speakers is not a reflex of incomplete acquisition, a fossilized interlanguage, but a manifestation of a steady-state cultural grammar of English in outer-circle contexts.

Fossilization theory, a non–target language stage, suffers from the assumption of what Bley-Vroman (1983) terms a comparative fallacy. Comparative fallacy refers to the researcher imposing the structure of the target language onto an interlanguage. Several scholars have argued, rather convincingly, that the structure of the interlanguage at various stages should be considered on its own terms, not from the structural perspective of the target language (cf. Bley-Vroman 1983, White 1989, 1996, Schwartz 1995, Schwartz & Sprouse 1996, Sridhar 1994). As Schwartz (1995, p. 8) puts it: "If there's one thing we often know about developing Interlanguages, it's that they don't have the structure of the target grammar—so why such a fuss about the syntax of the target language . . . ." However, in Selinker's (1972, 1993) interlanguage theory, there can be no talk of fossilization without reference to such constructs as target language, native speakers, and errors (Davies 1989, 1991). These constructs, although invalid for acquisitional accounts of non-native varieties, perform an ideological function; the constructs provide a "habit of thought" that normalizes and universalizes a paradigm of linguistic inquiry that privileges "knowledge of language" in the possession only of native speakers.

Theoretical Sacred Cow

The theoretical concerns relate to three vital concepts: the speech community, the native speaker, and the ideal speaker-hearer. The conceptualization of speech community varies from Bloomfield's definition ("a speech community is a group of people who interact by means of speech") to the rather complex definitions of John Gumperz and Robert Le Page (Hudson 1980, pp. 25–30; see also Silverstein 1996a).

The standard definition of a second language is one that is acquired in an environment in which the language is spoken natively (Larsen-Freeman & Long 1991). This definition completely marginalizes the empirical fact that more second language acquisition takes place in "nonnative" contexts than in "native" contexts (cf. Ferguson 1982, Sridhar 1994). The native/nonnative distinctions, Bhatt (2001a,b) argues, get validated by the kind of intellectual imperialism whereby a particular model of language, possessed by "an ideal native speaker-hearer in a completely homogeneous speech community" (à la Chomsky 1986) assumes a paradigmatic status in the linguistic sciences as a whole (see also Silverstein 1996b). This idealization produces "the illusion of linguistic communism" and ignores and trivializes the sociohistorical and economic conditions that have established a particular set of linguistic practices as dominant and legitimate. The voices of reason are seldom ignored. Paikeday's (1985) all too familiar conclusion about the theoretical status of the term native speaker is conveniently ignored:

> I am convinced that "native speaker" in the sense of the sole arbiter of grammaticality or one whose intuitions of a proprietary nature about his or her mother tongue and which are shared only by others of his own tribe is a myth propagated by linguists, that the true meaning of the lexeme "native speaker" is a proficient user of a specified language, and that this meaning satisfies all contexts in which linguists, anthropologists, psychologists, educators, and others use it, except when it directly refers to the speaker's mother tongue or first-acquired language without any assumptions about the speaker's linguistic competence.

In the context of world Englishes, the codification of the native/nonnative distinction in standard textbooks universalizes its legitimacy and contributes to the success of Standard English ideology. And at the same time, this codification excludes the oppositional discourse (Rampton 1990, Sridhar 1994, Singh 1995).

Pedagogical Sacred Cow

The research in the past two decades has clearly demonstrated that world Englishes have their own structural norms, their own characteristic features, and even their own communicative styles (e.g., see Bailey & Görlach 1982, Kachru 1982, 1983, 1986, Mesthrie 1992, Smith 1987, Trudgill & Hannah 1985). However, the pedagogical paradigms—methods, models, and materials—have not shown any sensitivity to local sociolinguistic contexts.

Should the inner-circle norm be the model for teaching English in outer-circle contexts, or should it be the local variety? The theoretical relevance of this question is discussed by Savignon & Berns (1984), Tickoo (1991), Nelson (1992, 1995), Smith (1992), and Kachru (1992a). Their views entail a radical restructuring of (classroom) resources, (teacher) training, and (teaching) materials. Such a step, perhaps antidogmatic in ESL pedagogical practices, is the right step toward practicing socially realistic and contextually sensitive pedagogy.

Sociolinguistic Sacred Cow

The sociolinguistic concerns relate to the issue of "pluricentricity" of English, the various national, regional, and local identities English has acquired as a result of language contact and change. The most important outcome of pluricentricity, Kachru (1988) argues, has been the demythologization of the traditional English canon and the establishment of new canons with their own linguistic, literary, and cultural identities.

Ideological Sacred Cow

The teaching of English, with the entire framework and institutions that support it worldwide, is a critical site where the dominant ideology, Standard English,

TABLE 2   Labels used to symbolize the power of English[a]

Positive	Negative
National identity	Antinationalism
Literary renaissance	Anti–native culture
Cultural mirror (for native cultures)	Materialism
Vehicle for modernization	Vehicle for Westernization
Liberalism	Rootlessness
Universalism	Ethnocentricism
Secularism	Permissiveness
Technology	Divisiveness
Science	Alienation
Mobility	Colonialism
Access code	

[a]From Kachru (1996, p. 142).

is constantly evolving and continuously bargaining with regional ideologies for power (Dua 1994). As a language that conveniently disregards the essentially circumstantial, random relationships between itself and the universe, the dominant ideology must present itself as possessing some kind of inherent, inevitable tie with the value it represents. In so doing, subjects of a society are actively taught to believe that the adoption of ideology can bring about social changes for their benefit. There are works of many scholars, such as Quirk (1990, 1996), Honey (1983, 1997), and Medgyes (1992, 1994), that illustrate how English language teaching in outer-circle contexts is surreptitiously forced to serve to inculcate only the culture, ideologies, and social relations necessary to promote and sustain the status quo.

This ideological landscape is changing now as outer-circle varieties compete for functional domains that belonged exclusively to inner-circle varieties. The ideological and symbolic power of English in outer circle has two sides, positive and negative, as shown in Table 2.

TEACHING WORLD ENGLISHES: CRITICAL ISSUES

Codification and Standard English Ideology

The standardization of English has allowed the interpretation of sociolinguistic, educational, and acquisitional problems as consequences of liberal linguistic thinking, general grammatical ignorance, and other similar contraventions of English linguistic norms. Conforming to these norms, e.g., Standard English, then becomes the solution to the problems (cf. Quirk 1988, 1990, 1996). The success of standardization depends largely on the ideological strategies and rhetorical operations used to devalue indigenous (nonnative) varieties against the standard (native) variety.

It is the function of the (Standard English) ideology that the ELT profession recognizes "ambilingualism" as the goal of second language acquisition, "fossilization" as the ultimate fate of second language learners, and "interlanguage" as the variety spoken by nonnative speakers. These constructs—ambilingualism, interlanguage, fossilization—provide a habit of thought. Soon after being introduced, they are understood as mathematical axioms, above debate; the assumptions shared are not propositions to be defended or attacked (cf. Bhatt 2001b, Kachru 1988, 1996). The assumptions form part of the "tacit dimension" of scholarly understanding. In reality, however, these assumptions consecrate linguistic and cultural privilege. Even where learners meet the criterion of functional bilingualism, trivial dichotomies such as proficiency/competence and standard/nonstandard are created by the profession and then used as an alibi for maintaining linguistic ethnocentrism disguised with concerns over intelligibility among the English-using population (Bhatt 1995a, 2001b, Kachru & Nelson 1996, Lippi-Green 1997). The learners are thus confined to lifelong apprenticeship in the second language without any hope for sociolinguistic emancipation (Tollefson 1991, 1995).

The system of ideological management—the strategic and regulatory practices required to manage language variation (Bhatt 2001b)—provides the tools, the theoretical-methodological constructs, such as native/nonnative, standard/nonstandard, fossilization/ultimate attainment, and target language/interlanguage, needed to naturalize and essentialize homogenization and standardization. The success of the management paradigm manifests in different forms of attitudinal internalizations, especially among the ELT professionals (cf. Honey 1983, Quirk 1990, Johnson 1992, Medgyes 1992, 1994). The common strategy employed by the ELT professionals to manage and minimize language variation is to present it as an unfortunate outcome of liberal pedagogy and liberation linguistics that presumably locks second language learners to substandard use of English (Bhatt 2001a,b).

The liberation ideology confronts and competes with the dominant Standard English ideology and produces competing sets of "values" (Bourdieu 1991), creating strong pressure in favor of the nonstandard-language varieties (Canagarajah 1993, 1996). These nonstandard varieties are marginalized by the grammarians, the lexicographers, and the teachers—the agents of linguistic coercion—mainly for two reasons: (a) The recognition of language variation threatens, as Milroy & Milroy (1999) argue, the ideological link between "grammar" and authority, and (b) the standard language can continue to function as the norm through which is exerted the domination of those groups that have both the means of imposing it as legitimate and the monopoly on the means of appropriating it (Bourdieu 1977). The recent debate on Ebonics and the politics of diglossia in the United States (Pullum 1997, Rickford 1997), often polemical, bear testimony to the success of the Standard English ideology.

Communicative Competence and Intelligibility

The traditional monotheistic methodologies used for teaching English worldwide fail to honor the range of social functions and identities that world Englishes carries out in diverse sociocultural contexts. Second language teaching methodologies must, therefore, be culture sensitive, as perhaps is the case with the approach known as ethnography of communication (Hymes 1974, 1996). The key concept in this approach is communicative competence, the "appropriate" use of linguistic conduct. What is appropriate for a situation in one culture may not be so in another culture. It is important, then, that learning, teaching, and using world Englishes require familiarization with not only the conversational context but also the broader sociocultural context in which the utterance is located (Berns 1990). Earlier pedagogical paradigms, with their monolingual and monocultural bias, are untenable (cf. Sridhar 1994, Y. Kachru 1994).

The linguistic realization of different speech acts—greeting, leave taking, complimenting, requesting—in Indian or Zambian English is quite different from American or British English (D'souza 1991, Y. Kachru 1991, Berns 1990). The models of teaching and learning need therefore to reflect the sociocultural ethos of the context of teaching/learning, which has wide implications for a theory of second language pedagogy and for its application (McKay & Hornberger 1996).

Another issue, connected to the issue of communicative competence, is that of intelligibility. The issue touches the very core of the debatable distinction between language and dialect, that, over time, different dialects of English will become mutually unintelligible. Quirk (1985, p. 3), for example, writes of "the diaspora of English into several mutually incomprehensible languages." For Quirk (1985, p. 6), all English-using nations must accede to "a form of English that is both understood and respected in every corner of the globe where any knowledge of any variety of English exists."

Nelson (1984, 1995), Smith & Nelson (1985), and Smith (1992) have argued against the monolithic view of intelligibility and have argued instead that a better understanding of this concept is revealed in its use as a continuum—from intelligibility (word/utterance recognition) to comprehensibility (word/utterance meaning; locutionary force) to interpretability (meaning behind word/utterance; illocutionary force). "Understanding," an interactional concept in this model, is lowest at the level of intelligibility and highest at the level of interpretability. There are, for instance, several examples of English text that are readily intelligible and comprehensible but not necessarily interpretable. The matrimonial examples, discussed above, from the vantagepoint of the inner circle will fail at the level of interpretability. Smith (1988, p. 274) forcefully argues that, contrary to what is being taught to students from grammar textbooks, "interpretability is at the core of communication and is more important than mere intelligibility or comprehensibility."

CONCLUSIONS

This essay focused on the theoretical, conceptual, descriptive, ideological, and power-related concerns of world Englishes. The rise of a tribal language to a global language in a millennium dominated by Latin and, later, French, the languages of intellectual expression and cultural erudition, is unprecedented. Sociolinguistic inquiries into this unprecedented spread of the English language have yielded significant understandings of the linguistic processes and products of language contact and language change. There is more awareness today about how language use interacts with global economic, demographic, and cultural trends. Graddol's (1997) provocative survey of the future of English shows conflicting trends of language use: English is increasingly required for high-skill jobs everywhere in the world; it is the most widely studied foreign language; it dominates satellite TV programming and yet its functions in youth culture are more symbolic than communicative; its share of internet traffic is declining; and its economic significance in many countries is challenged by regional economics.

The historical, sociolinguistic, and ideological accounts of homogeneity and hegemony of Standard English within the world Englishes paradigm have yielded a broader understanding of the social and discursive relationships between (and within) speech communities, the institutional acquisition and use of linguistic resources, and the relationship between language and systems of domination and subordination (Phillipson 1992, Parakrama 1995, Pennycook 1998, Blommaert & Verschueren 1998, Bhatt 2001a,b, Ramanathan 1999, Skutnabb-Kangas 2000, Woolard 1985, Woolard & Schieffelin 1994).

The interdisciplinary theoretical and methodological framework of world Englishes has provided an understanding of the productive relationship between cultural studies and English studies. Literary creativity in world Englishes, as Dissanayake (1985) argues, is able to reappropriate and repossess fictional discourse that had come under the influence of regimes of colonial authority.

Finally, the pedagogical concerns in world Englishes provide, as argued by Kachru & Nelson (1996), an insightful understanding of the relationships between linguistic and language-teaching theory, methodology, and applications. Second language curriculum, testing procedures, and resource materials must be constructed after careful study of variation, and the pragmatics of variation, for effective second language pedagogy (McKay & Hornberger 1996, Lowenberg 1992, Davidson 1993).

In conclusion, then, the field of world Englishes reevaluates, critiques, and displaces the earlier tradition of cross-cultural and cross-linguistic acquisition and use of English, its teaching, and its transformations. World Englishes, in its most ambitious interpretation, attempts to decolonize and democratize applied linguistics.

Visit the Annual Reviews home page at www.AnnualReviews.org

LITERATURE CITED

Achebe C. 1966. *Things Fall Apart*. London: Heinemann

Achebe C. 1969. *Arrow of God*. New York: Doubleday

Apple M. 1978. The new sociology of educa-tion: analyzing cultural and economic repro-duction. *Harvard Educ. Rev.* 48:495–503

Bailey R, Görlach M, eds. 1982. *English as a World Language*. Ann Arbor: Univ. Mich. Press

Bamgbose A. 1971. The English language in Nigeria. In *The English Language in Africa*, ed. J Spencer, pp. 35–48. London: Longman

Bamgbose A. 1982. Standard Nigerian English: issues and identification. See Kachru 1982, pp. 99–111

Bamgbose A, Banjo A, Thomas A, eds. 1995. *New Englishes: A West African Perspective*. Ibadan, Nigeria: Mosuro

Bamiro E. 1991. Nigerian Englishes in Nigerian English literature. *World Engl.* 10:7–17

Bao ZM. 1995. 'Already' in Singapore English. *World Engl.* 14:181–88

Baumgardner R. 1993. *The English Language in Pakistan*. Karachi, Pakistan: Oxford Univ. Press

Baumgardner R, ed. 1996. *South Asian English: Structure, Use, and Users*. Urbana: Univ. Ill. Press

Bautista M, ed. 1997. *English is an Asian Language: The Philippine Context*. Sydney, Aust.: Macquarie Libr.

Berns M. 1990. *Contexts of Competence: Social and Cultural Considerations in Communicative Language Teaching*. New York: Plenum

Bhatia TK, Ritchie W, eds. 1989. Symposium on constraints on code-switching. *World Engl.* 15:261–439

Bhatia V, ed. 1997. Genre analysis and world Englishes. *World Engl.* 16(3):313–426

Bhatt RM. 1995a. Prescriptivism, creativity, and world Englishes. *World Engl.* 14:247–60

Bhatt RM. 1995b. The uprooted, the indentured, and the segregated: South African Indian English. *J. Pidgin Creole Lang.* 10:381–96

Bhatt RM. 1997. Code-switching, constraints, and optimal grammars. *Lingua* 102:223–51

Bhatt RM. 2000. Optimal expressions in Indian English. *Engl. Lang. Linguist.* 4:69–95

Bhatt RM. 2001a. Language economy, standardization, and world Englishes. In *The Three Circles of English*, ed. E Thumboo. Singapore: Univ. Press. In press

Bhatt RM. 2001b. *Venerable Experts and Vulnerable Dialects: Discourse of Marginalization in ESL and ELT*. Urbana Univ. Ill. Ms

Bickerton D. 1975. *Dynamic of a Creole*

System. Cambridge, UK: Cambridge Univ. Press

Bley-Vroman R. 1983. The comparative fallacy in interlanguage studies: the case of systematicity. *Lang. Learn.* 33:1–17

Blommaert J, Verschueren J. 1998. *Debating Diversity*. New York: Routledge

Bokamba EG. 1992. The Africanization of English. See Kachru 1992b, pp. 125–47

Bourdieu P. 1977. *Outline of a Theory of Practice*. Cambridge, UK: Cambridge Univ. Press

Bourdieu P. 1991. *Language and Symbolic Power*. Cambridge, MA: Harvard Univ. Press

Bright W. 1968. Toward a cultural grammar. *Indian Ling.* 29:20–29

Brown P, Levinson S. 1987. *Politeness: Some Universals in Language*. Cambridge, UK: Cambridge Univ. Press

Brutt-Griffler J. 1998. *The development of English as an international language: a theory of world language*. PhD thesis. Ohio State Univ., Columbus, Ohio, 237 pp.

Burchfield R, ed. 1994. *The Cambridge History of the English Language*, Vol. 5. Cambridge, UK: Cambridge Univ. Press

Canagarajah AS. 1993. Critical ethnography of a Sri Lankan classroom: ambiguities in student opposition to reproduction through ESOL. *TESOL Q.* 27:601–26

Canagarajah AS. 1996. "Nondiscursive" requirements in academic publishing, material resources of periphery scholars, and the politics of knowledge production. *Writ. Commun.* 13:435–72

Canagarajah AS. 1999. *Resisting Linguistic Imperialism in English Teaching*. Oxford, UK: Oxford Univ. Press

Chaudhary S. 1989. *Some Aspects of the Phonology of Indian English*. Ranchi, India: Jayaswal

Cheshire J, ed. 1991. *English Around the World: Sociolinguistic Perspectives*. Cambridge, UK: Cambridge Univ. Press

Chisimba M. 1984. *African varieties of English: text in context*. PhD thesis. Univ. Illinois, Urbana-Champaign. 214 pp.

Chisimba M. 1991. Southern Africa. See Cheshire 1991, pp. 435–45

Chomsky N. 1986. *Knowledge of Language.* New York: Praeger

Crystal D. 1985. How many millions? The statistics of English today. *Engl. Today* 1:7–9

Crystal D. 1995. *The Cambridge Encyclopedia of the English Language.* Cambridge, UK: Cambridge Univ. Press

Crystal D. 1997. *English as a Global Language.* Cambridge. UK: Cambridge Univ. Press

Davidson F. 1993. Testing English across cultures: summary and comments. *World Engl.* 12:113–25

Davies A. 1989. Is international English an interlanguage? *TESOL Q.* 23:447–67

Davies A. 1991. *The Native Speaker in Applied Linguistics.* Edinburgh: Edinburgh Univ. Press

Davies A. 1996. Ironising the myth of linguicism. *J. Multilin. Multicult. Dev.* 17: 487–96

Denière M. 1993. Democratizing English as an international language. *World Engl.* 12:169–78

Dissanayake W. 1985. Towards a decolonized English: South Asian creativity in fiction. *World Engl.* 4:233–42

D'souza J. 1987. South Asia as a sociolinguistic area. PhD thesis. Univ. Illinios, Urbana-Champaign. 242 pp.

D'souza J. 1988. Interactional strategies in South Asian languages: their implications for teaching English internationally. *World Engl.* 7:159–71

D'souza J. 1991. Speech acts in Indian English fiction. *World Engl.* 10:307–16

Dua HR. 1994. *The Hegemony of English.* Mysore, India: Yashoda

Ferguson C. 1982. Foreword. See Kachru 1982, pp. xii–xvii

Foley J, ed. 1988. *New Englishes: The Case of Singapore.* Singapore: Singapore Univ. Press

Foley J, Kandiah K, Zhiming B, Gupta AF, Alsagoff L, Lick HC. 1998. *English in New Cultural Contexts: Reflections from Singapore.* Singapore: Oxford Univ. Press

Foucault M. 1972. *The Archaeology of Knowledge and the Discourse on Language.* Transl.

AM Sheridan Smith. New York: Pantheon Books

Giroux HA. 1981. *Ideology, Culture, and the Process of Schooling.* Philadelphia, PA: Temple Univ. Press

Goke-Pariola A. 1993. Language and symbolic power: Bourdieu and the legacy of Euro-American colonialism in an African society. *Lang. Commun.* 13:219–34

Görlach M. 1991. *Englishes: Studies in Varieties of English.* Amsterdam: John Benjamins

Graddol D. 1997. *The Future of English?* London: Br. Counc.

Gumperz JJ. 1982. *Discourse Strategies.* Cambridge, UK: Cambridge Univ. Press

Halliday MAK. 1973. *Explorations in the Functions of Language.* London: Arnold

Hancin-Bhatt BJ, Bhatt RM. 1993. On the nature of L1 filter and cross language transfer effects. In *New Sounds' 92*, ed. J Leather, A James, pp. 18–28. Amsterdam: Univ. Amst.

Honey JRS. 1983. *The Language Trap.* Sussex, UK: Natl. Counc. Educ. Stand.

Honey JRS. 1997. *Language Is Power.* London: Faber & Faber

Hosali P, Aitchison J. 1986. Butler English: a minimal pidgin? *J. Pidgin Creole Lang.* 1:51–79

Hudson R. 1980. *Sociolinguistics.* Cambridge, UK: Cambridge Univ. Press

Hymes D. 1974. *Foundations of Sociolinguistics: An Ethnographic Approach.* Philadelphia: Univ. Penn. Press

Hymes D. 1996. *Ethnography, Linguistics, Narrative Inequality.* London: Taylor & Francis

Iyengar KRS. 1962. *Indian Writing in English.* Bombay: Asia Publ. House

Johnson H. 1992. Defossilizing. *ELT J.* 46:180–89

Kachru BB. 1965. The *Indianness* in Indian English. *Word* 21:391–410

Kachru BB. 1976. Models of English for the third world: white man's linguistic burden or language pragmatics? *TESOL Q.* 10:221–39

Kachru BB, ed. 1982. *The Other Tongue: English Across Cultures.* Oxford, UK: Pergamon

Kachru BB. 1983. *The Indianization of English: The English Language in India.* Delhi: Oxford Univ. Press

Kachru BB. 1986. *The Alchemy of English: The Spread, Functions and Models of Non-Native Englishes.* London: Pergamon

Kachru BB. 1988. The spread of English and sacred linguistic cows. See Lowenberg 1988, pp. 207–28

Kachru BB. 1990. World Englishes and applied linguistics. *World Engl.* 9:3–20

Kachru BB. 1991. Liberation linguistics and the Quirk concerns. *Engl. Today* 25:3–13

Kachru BB. 1992a. The second diaspora of English. See Machan & Scott 1992, pp. 230–52

Kachru BB, ed. 1992b. *The Other Tongue.* Urbana: Univ. Illinois Press

Kachru BB. 1994. Englishization and contact linguistics. *World Engl.* 13:135–54

Kachru BB. 1996. The paradigms of marginality. *World Engl.* 15:241–55

Kachru BB. 1997. World Englishes and English-using communities. *Annu. Rev. Appl. Linguist.* 17:66–87

Kachru BB, Nelson CL. 1996. World Englishes. See McKay & Hornberger 1996, pp. 71–102

Kachru BB, Quirk R. 1981. Introduction. See Smith 1981, pp. xiii–xx

Kachru Y. 1985. Discourse analysis, non-native Englishes and second language acquisition research. *World Engl.* 4:223–32

Kachru Y, ed. 1991. Symposium on speech acts in world Englishes. *World Engl.* 10(3):295–340

Kachru Y. 1993. Social meaning and creativity in Indian English speech acts. In *Language, Communication, and Social Meaning,* ed. JE Alatis, pp. 378–87. Washington, DC: Georgetown Univ. Press

Kachru Y. 1994. Monolingual bias in SLA research. *TESOL Q.* 28:795–800

Kachru Y. 1995. Contrastive rhetoric and world Englishes. *Engl. Today* 11:21–31

Kachru Y. 1997. Culture and argumentative writing in world Englishes. In *World Englishes* 2000, ed. LE Smith, M Forman, pp. 48–67. Manoa: Univ. Hawaii Press

Kahane H. 1986. A typology of the prestige language. *Language* 62:495–508

Kamwangamalu N. 1989. A selected bibliography of studies on code-mixing and code-switching. *World Engl.* 8:433–40

Kandiah T, Kwan-Terry J, eds. 1994. *English and Language Planning: A Southeast Asian Contribution.* Singapore: Times Acad.

Kibbee DA. 1993. Perspective 2. In symposium on linguistic imperialism. *World Engl.* 12:342–47

Knowles G. 1997. *A Cultural History of the English Language.* London: Arnold

Labov W. 1972. *Sociolinguistic Patterns.* Philadelphia: Univ. Penn. Press

Larsen-Freeman D, Long M. 1991. *An Introduction to Second Language Acquisition Research.* London: Longman

Lippi-Green R. 1994. Accent, standard language ideology and discriminatory pretexts in the courts. *Lang. Soc.* 23:163–98

Lippi-Green R. 1997. *English with an Accent.* London: Routledge

Llamzon T. 1969. *Standard Filipino English.* Manila: Ateneo Univ. Press

Lowenberg PH, 1984. *English in the Malay Archipelago: nativization and its functions in a sociolinguistic area.* PhD thesis. Univ. Illinois, Urbana-Champaign. 216 pp.

Lowenberg PH. 1986. Sociolinguistic context and second language acquisition: acculturation and creativity in Malaysian English. *World Engl.* 5:71–83

Lowenberg PH, ed. 1988. *Language Spread and Language Policy.* Washington, DC: Georgetown Univ. Press

Lowenberg PH. 1991. Variation in Malaysian English: the pragmatics of language in contact. See Cheshire 1991, pp. 365–75

Lowenberg PH. 1992. Testing English as a world language: issues in assessing non-native proficiency. See Kachru 1992b, pp. 108–21

Machan T, Scott C, eds. 1992. *English in its Social Contexts: Essays in Historical Sociolinguistics.* New York: Oxford Univ. Press

Magura B. 1984. *Style and meaning in Southern African English*. PhD thesis. Univ. Ill., Urbana-Champaign. 242 pp.

Magura B. 1985. Southern African Black English. *World Engl.* 4:251–56

Mazrui A, Mazrui A. 1998. *The Power of Babel: Language and Governance in the African Experience*. Chicago: Univ. Chicago Press

McArthur T. 1987. The English languages? *Engl. Today,* July/Sept:9–11

McArthur T. 1992. *The Oxford Companion to the English Language*. Oxford, UK: Oxford Univ. Press

McArthur T. 1993. The English language or the English languages? In *The English Language*, ed. WF Bolton, D Crystal, pp. 323–41. London: Penguin

McArthur T. 1998. *The English Languages*. Cambridge, UK: Cambridge Univ. Press

McCrum R, Cran W, MacNeil R. 1986. *The Story of English*. London: Faber & Faber

McKay S, Hornberger N, eds. 1996. *Sociolinguistics in Language Teaching*. Cambridge, UK: Cambridge Univ. Press

Medgyes P. 1992. Native or non-native: who's worth more? *ELT J.* 46:340–49

Medgyes P. 1994. *The Non-native Teacher*. London: Macmillan

Mesthrie R. 1992. *English in Language Shift*. Cambridge, UK: Cambridge Univ. Press

Mesthrie R. 1997. A sociolinguistic study of topicalization phenomena in South African Black English. In *English Around the World*, ed. E Schneider, 119–40. Amsterdam: Benjamins

Milroy J, Milroy L. 1985. *Authority in Language*. London: Routledge

Milroy J, Milroy L. 1999. *Authority in Language*. London: Routledge. 2nd ed.

Mohanan KP. 1992. Describing the phonology of non-native varieties of a language. *World Engl.* 11:111–28

Mufwene S. 1994. New Englishes and the criteria for naming them. *World Engl.* 13:21–31

Mufwene S, ed. 1997. Symposium on English-to-Pidgin continua. *World Engl.* 16(2):181–279

Myers-Scotton C. 1993a. *Duelling Languages*. Oxford, UK: Clarendon

Myers-Scotton C. 1993b. *Social Motivations for Code-Switching: Evidence from Africa*. Oxford, UK: Clarendon

Nelson C. 1984. *Intelligibility: the case of nonnative varieties of English*. PhD thesis. Univ. Illinois, Urbana-Champaign. 164 pp.

Nelson C. 1992. Bilingual writing for the monolingual reader: blowing up the canon. *World Engl.* 11:271–75

Nelson C. 1995. Intelligibility and world Englishes in the classroom. *World Engl.* 14:273–79

Paikeday TM. 1985. *The Native Speaker is Dead!* Toronto: Paikeday

Pakir A. 1991. The range and depth of English-knowing bilinguals in Singapore. *World Engl.* 10:167–79

Parakrama A. 1990. *Language and Rebellion: Discoursive Unities and the Possibility of Protest*. London: Katha

Parakrama A. 1995. *De-hegemonizing Language Standards*. London: MacMillan

Pennycook A. 1994. *The Cultural Politics of English as an International Language*. London: Longman

Pennycook A. 1998. *English and the Discourses of Colonialism*. London: Routledge

Phillipson R. 1992. *Linguistic Imperialism*. Oxford, UK: Oxford Univ. Press

Platt J. 1975. The Singapore English speech continuum and its basilect "Singlish" as a Creoloid. *Anthropol. Linguist.* 17:363–74

Platt J, Weber H. 1980. *English in Singapore and Malaysia: Status, Features, Functions*. Kaula Lampur: Oxford Univ. Press

Platt J, Weber H, Ho ML. 1984. *The New Englishes*. London: Routledge

Pullum GK. 1997. Language that dare not speak its name. *Nature* 328:321–22

Quirk R. 1985. The English language in a global context. In *English in the World: Teaching and Learning the Language and Literatures*, ed. R Quirk, H Widdowson, pp. 1–6. Cambridge, UK: Cambridge Univ. Press

Quirk R. 1988. The question of standards in the international use of English. See Lowenberg 1988, pp. 229–41

Quirk R. 1990. Language varieties and standard language. *Engl. Today* 21:3–10

Quirk R. 1996. *Grammatical and Lexical Variance in English*. London: Longman

Quirk R, Greenbaum S, Leech G, Svartvik J. 1972. *A Grammar of Contemporary English*. London: Longman

Ramanathan V. 1999. "English is here to stay": a critical look at institutional and educational practices in India. *TESOL Q.* 33:211–31

Rampton MBH. 1990. Displacing the "native speaker": expertise, affiliation, and inheritance. *ELT J.* 44:97–101

Richards J. 1979. Rhetorical and communicative styles in the new varieties of English. *Lang. Learn.* 25:1–25

Rickford J. 1997. Commentary: suite for ebony and phonics. *Discover* Dec:82–87

Romaine S. 1997. The British heresy in ESL revisited. In *Language and its Ecology*, ed. S Eliasson, E Jahr, pp. 417–32. Berlin: Gruyter

Savignon S, Berns M. 1984. *Initiatives in Communicative Language Teaching*. Reading, MA: Addison-Wesley

Schwartz B. 1995. *Transfer and L2A: Where are we now?* Presented at 2nd Lang. Res. Forum, Ithaca, NY

Schwartz B, Sprouse R. 1996. L2 cognitive states and the full transfer/full access model. *Second Lang. Res.* 12:40–72

Selinker L. 1972. Interlanguage. *Int. Rev. Appl. Linguist.* 10:209–31

Selinker L. 1993. *Rediscovering Interlanguage*. London: Longman

Sey KA. 1973. *Ghanian English: An Exploratory Survey*. London: Macmillan

Silverstein M. 1996a. Encountering language and languages of encounter in North American ethnohistory. *J. Linguist. Anthropol.* 6(2):126–44

Silverstein M. 1996b. Monoglot "standard" in America: standardization and metaphors of linguistic hegemony. In *The Matrix of Language: Contemporary Linguistic Anthropol-*

ogy, ed. D Brenneis, RKS Macaulay, pp. 284–306. Boulder, CO: Westview

Singh R, ed. 1995. On new/non-native Englishes. *J. Pragmat.* 24:283–333

Singler J. 1997. The configuration of Liberia's Englishes. *World Engl.* 16:205–32

Skutnabb-Kangas T. 2000. *Linguistic Genocide—or Worldwide Diversity and Human Rights*. Mahwah, NJ: Erlbaum

Smith LE, ed. 1981. *English for Cross-Cultural Communication*. London: Macmillan

Smith LE, ed. 1983. *Readings in English as an International Language*. London: Pergamon

Smith LE, ed. 1987. *Discourse Across Cultures*. London: Prentice Hall

Smith LE. 1988. Language spread and issues of intelligibility. See Lowenberg 1988, pp. 265–82

Smith LE. 1992. Spread of English and issues of intelligibility. See Kachru 1992b, pp. 75–90

Smith LE, Nelson CL. 1985. International intelligibility of English: directions and resources. *World Engl.* 4:333–42

Sridhar SN. 1992. The ecology of bilingual competence: language interaction in indigenized varieties of English. *World Engl.* 11:141–50

Sridhar SN. 1994. A reality check for SLA theories. *TESOL Q.* 28:800–5

Strevens P. 1992. English as an international language: directions in the 1990s. See Kachru 1992b, pp. 27–47

Thumboo E. 1992. The literary dimension of the spread of English. See Kachru 1992b, pp. 255–82

Tickoo M, ed. 1991. *Language and Standards: Issues, Attitudes, Case Studies*. Singapore: SAEMEO Region. Lang. Cent.

Tollefson J. 1991. *Planning Language, Planning Inequality: Language Policy in the Community*. London: Longman

Tollefson J, ed. 1995. *Power and Inequality in Language Education*. Cambridge, UK: Cambridge Univ. Press

Trudgill P, Hannah J. 1985. *International English*. London: Arnold

Valentine T. 1988. Developing discourse types in non-native English: strategies of gender in Hindi and Indian English. *World Engl.* 7:143–58

Valentine T. 1991. Getting the message across: discourse markers in Indian English. *World Engl.* 10:325–34

Viswanathan G. 1989. *Masks of Conquest: Literary Study and British Rule in India.* London: Faber & Faber

White L. 1989. *Universal Grammar and Second Language Acquisition.* Amsterdam: Benjamins

White L. 1996. Universal grammar and second language acquisition: current trends and new directions. In *Handbook of Second Language Acquisition*, ed. W Ritchie, T Bhatia, pp. 85–120. New York: Academic

Winford D. 1997. Re-examining Caribbean English creole continua. *World Engl.* 16:233–79

Woolard K. 1985. Language variation and cultural hegemony: toward an integration of sociolinguistic and social theory. *Am. Ethnol.* 12:738–48

Woolard K, Schieffelin B. 1994. Language ideology. *Annu. Rev. Anthropol.* 23:55–82

Annu. Rev. Anthropol. 2001. 30:551–72

LOCATIONS FOR SOUTH ASIAN DIASPORAS

Sandhya Shukla

Department of Anthropology, Columbia University, New York, NY 10027;
e-mail: srs52@columbia.edu

Key Words migration, nationalism, postcolonial formations, race and ethnicity, identity

■ **Abstract** This review explores the cultural consequences of migrations from the Indian subcontinent for interdisciplinary inquiries into difference and belonging. It poses the question of whether the constructed term South Asian can adequately bridge the divide between more internationalist conceptions of diaspora and nationalist accounts of racial and ethnic formation, and if so, whether it creates new epistemologies for the consideration of migration in highly globalized political and economic arrangements. In arguing that multiple formations of nationality take place in diasporic culture, this review also intervenes in debates in anthropology about the geographical and conceptual boundaries of community. Finally, in suggesting that gender, sexuality, and generation might profoundly fissure South Asian and other diasporas, the article raises the question of the implicit limits of any category of location or identity.

INTRODUCTION

The subject of diaspora immediately elicits basic questions of origins and locations. Where do people come from? Where do they pause, rest, live? What routes have they traveled? And yet the real and imagined worlds of all peoples, especially migrant peoples, have proven far too complex and contradictory to be easily serviced by any attempt to respond in the singular to such compelling questions. In fact, diasporic cultures, of South Asians and others, resist singularity of location, or of origin, for that matter. And so it is not surprising that the published collections of work on South Asian diasporas are markedly broad in geographical reach, across nations and continents (Clarke et al 1990, Van der Veer 1995, Bates 2001, Rukmani 1999, Petievich 1999). Diaspora, by definition, is dispersion, which effectively compresses time and space such that it enables the experiences of many places at what would appear to be one moment. And today such multiplicity and simultaneity have become particularly pronounced (Appadurai 1996, Sassen 1998, Schiller et al 1994, Kearney 1995). Homeland, land of settlement, space for travel, all undergo significant reworking through the concept and object of diaspora.

This article seeks to map out the social and theoretical arrangements of South Asian diasporas. In assuming the task of explaining a category that is by no means seamlessly constructed, I pay special attention to the various strands that comprise

0084-6570/01/1021-0551$14.00

this subject matter, regionally, generationally, and conceptually. Creating a sense of being Indian abroad or participating in pan-Islamic productions of culture, for example, may each autonomously and differently relate to "South Asian diasporas" while contributing to a broader epistemology of nationality and subjectivity. This is to say that within the very topic of diaspora there is an immanent tension between the specific and the general that may be variously rendered as the local and the global, the particular and the universal, or the national and the regional.

One way to think about a constitutive dynamic of these South Asian, and other, diasporas, is through Jones's (1968) notion of a "changing same." Jones has considered African American music as simultaneously reprising African traditions and evincing an embeddedness in their national context of the United States. The meaning of the music Jones interprets lies very much in its performance, which is every time a new occurrence, but which also makes vivid other imaginative worlds from which it gained a particular energy. Gilroy (1993) has used the "changing same" to describe his own project of explaining black diasporic cultures. I would suggest that this concept enables an intervention into anthropological debates about cultural continuity and change. It illuminates, for our purposes, the apparent paradox of the amazing persistence of South Asian traditions and forms of expression around the world and the increased visibility of innovative renderings of national, regional, and religious identities under the sign of "South Asianness," "Indianness," or even "Islam." Things stay the same and they change in South Asian as well as other diasporas. To faithfully maintain the duality of that fundamental truism, though, is to resist the reduction of any cultural moment to national or homeland difference.

A movement between different orders of South Asian diasporas can be charted in disciplinary terms, too. Situated within a range of imagined and real nations, South Asian diasporas embody a set of disconnections between place, culture, and identity (Gupta & Ferguson 1997). Just as life experiences, imaginative inclinations, and psychic investments lie outside observed geographical boundaries, they are expressed through word and text in a variety of forms. Imaginaries, in social life or fictional narrative, are a central fact of diasporas through time and in this article are explored as taking shape not only in anthropology but across other fields of study as well.

In the ways that South Asian diasporas are comprised of stories about culture, identity, and nation, they offer an often misleading coherence or stability to categories that have real power in the lives of many peoples, but nonetheless that need considerable unraveling. And so it is Foucault's (1972) basic charge of taking discursive formations seriously that animates this closer look at diasporas.

HISTORIES AND CONCEPTS

The assertion of peoplehood that is basic to the expression of South Asian diasporas produces a range of analytic dilemmas, not least of which is a kind of essentializing of character, identity, and inclination. In some sense this is the fundamental problematic of subjectivities that are cast in the languages of race and ethnicity (Cohen 1978). It is difficult to describe difference—inside or outside a broadly constituted entity such as nation or transnation—without reifying the boundaries of that difference through color, caste, religion, or, even more ambiguously, "culture." Such issues premise important critiques of anthropology as well as of more interdisciplinary fields, such as ethnic studies (Lowe 1996).

But in its ever-present indication of the experience of displacement, the term diaspora is able to signify, constantly, multiplicity: of origins, cultures, nations, forms (Cohen 1997). And the grouping of "South Asian," too, as a geographical reference that does not have nation or religion in its root meaning, constructs a highly provisional language, a kind of theory itself, for thinking about how people see themselves as part of broader social formations. The term South Asian diasporas connotes peoples who have at some time in the past come from all the countries that comprise the Indian subcontinent, yet without the emphasis on forced expulsion that Jewish or black diasporas have conveyed (Boyarin 1992, Gilroy 1993). Although time and origins may remain maddeningly ambiguous for this topic, they also constitute rich analytical terrain for the consideration of South Asian subjectivity because the obvious constructedness itself of South Asian diasporas allows for interesting possibilities, for alliances and allegiances across national boundaries that help us create new conceptual models for the complex renderings of affect and experience.

As peoples from South Asian countries move around the world, they carry a repertoire of images and experiences from the past and present that meet alternative narrative productions in new places of settlement. Postcolonialism, racial and ethnic formation, and globalization might be seen as three kinds of structuring narratives with which South Asian diasporas come into contact and are shaped by. With particularized meanings for individual contexts of Britain, the United States, or the Caribbean, for example, the frameworks of postcolonialism, racial-ethnic formation, and globalization nonetheless all, and often in dialogue, address the transnational networks in which South Asian migrants are embedded. Again we rehearse the constitutive tensions of diaspora.

In its emphasis on the relationship between India and the world, postcolonial theory has established one important axis on which the development of South Asian subjectivities turn (Loomba 1998, Gandhi 1998). The realities, memories, and rebuttals to British colonialism have profoundly affected diasporic peoples and their cultures. In idea and deed, colonialism, then, has created a language in which to understand the development of nationalisms, at home and abroad. And although anthropological work on South Asian migrant cultures has been more inclined to utilize transnationalism or diaspora as explanatory rubrics, I would suggest here that postcolonialism can be of service, too. In the ways that postcolonial, or colonial discourse, studies have emerged from more literary spaces (Bahri & Vasudeva 1996), these fields also contain questions related to genre and textuality more generally that illuminate the imaginaries central to South Asian diasporic cultural production and experience.

Racial formation and ethnicity function analagously, as broad social frameworks in which South Asian diasporas come to life and are made visible (Fryer 1984, Gillespie 1995, Khoshy 1998, Leonard 1992, Sivanandan 1982, Kumar 2000, Prashad 2000, Shukla 1997, Fisher 1980, Desai 1963, Daniels 1989, Williams 1988, Vertovec 1992). Historically, and more globally, South Asian diasporas can be linked to crucial shifts in the development of capitalism and explanatory discourses of difference; in both the political and military domination of the eastern and southern hemisphere, as well as in the insertion of their peoples into European and North American systems of labor, can be found the origins of the racialization of South Asian diasporas. And the specificities are intriguing. In many Caribbean countries, such as Trinidad and Guyana, South Asians occupy particular ethnic positions within hybrid and vigorously multicultural societies (Khan 1994, Munasinghe 2001). South Asian communities in Fiji and South Africa alternately embrace and reject their own racial exceptionalism within very racially conflictive national-social arrangements (Lemon 1990, Thiara 2001, Gillion 1962). And in the United States and Britain, the sites of many insurgent movements on behalf of racial identities and the public production of ethnicity as a mode of social stratification, South Asians have played various central and peripheral roles (Prashad 2000, Shukla 1997, Leonard 1992, Helweg & Helweg 1990, Ballard 1994). The persistence of various forms of homeland-derived identities, such as Indianness, Hindutva, or Pan-Islamicism, within differently articulated social formations abroad testifies to the difficulty of decoupling the national from the international, or the local and the global, in diasporic forms.

Given the wide geographic coordinates of South Asian diasporas, recent efforts to describe shifts in the world economy that have resulted in more financial and political integration as part of a process called globalization are also particularly relevant here (King 1991, Sassen 1998). Diasporas have become ideal sites to explore the cultural effects of globalization, and South Asian diasporas comprise, in many ways, the paradigmatic case. The juncture of two facts render South Asian diasporas analytically ripe for globalization theorists: the emergent third-world technologically based economy of India and the often crucial role that Indian migrant financiers around the world play in a range of transnational capital formations (Lessinger 1992, Shukla 1999, Nayyar 1994, Khandelwal 1995). The primary difficulty with seeing South Asian diasporas through a lens shaped by theories of globalization is the contemporary, presentist nature of the analysis when in fact the field of study must entail a longer historical trajectory that begins even before British colonialism.

The shortcomings attending any singular perspective on these diasporas emerge as much from disciplinary limits as they do from conceptual problems. In as much as postcolonialism has been thought to be the purview of literature, identity formation the preoccupation of the field of racial and ethnic studies, and globalization a problematic within sociology, we have lacked a sustained dialogue among the theories and concepts that have emerged from specific academic locations. One premising argument of this review is that diasporic forms, particularly those that have emerged from and through South Asian experiences, are a stage for the bringing together of varied models for thinking through subjectivity, and an occasion to draw those approaches out of their confined spaces of literary criticism, the social sciences, history, and ethnic studies. This kind of interdisciplinarity emerges through the disconnections between place and identity, the negotiations between the local and the global, and the highlighting of the importance of the imaginary in any evocation of "experience" that are not only produced from within South Asian diasporas but are also central to how anthropology is being reworked, methodologically and theoretically (Gupta & Ferguson 1997, Ong 1999). The differences created, inside a nation, transnation, and internation, by South Asian diasporas gesture, then, toward the old and new differences lying at the very door of anthropology.

THE WORK OF SOUTH ASIANS

Perhaps one of the most acute dissonances within South Asian diasporas is the social life of class. Indentured sugar workers from the Indian subcontinent in the early 1900s in Mauritius (Carter 1996) would seem to have little, if anything, in common with contemporary nonresident Indians in Hong Kong who are able to draw on huge sources of capital. And my goal here is hardly to make the case that these experiences should or should not be seen as part of an enforced trajectory. But those variances themselves pose important issues for the content of this topic.

Although peoples from the Indian subcontinent could be found in spaces around the ancient world, in Greece and Rome (Arora 1991, Begley & Daniel 1991), and onward, this essay begins in a more modern period, with British colonialism and, therefore, implicitly builds a trajectory of experiences through shifts in world capitalism. Between 1830 and 1920, a large proportion of Indians living abroad served as indentured labor in Mauritius, Malaya, Burma, Ceylon, Reunion, Jamaica, Trinidad, Martinique, British Guiana, Natal, and other places (Anderson 2000, Breman & Daniel 1992, Carter 1995, Gillion 1962, Kale 1998, Kondapi 1951, Lal 1980, Laurence 1994, Northrup 1995, Tinker 1993). From the outset, indentured, and later, free wage, labor posed a problem to originary meanings for the term diaspora as a forced dispersion. But work itself, and especially the kinds of work in which Indians were engaged in the colonies, has always implied varying levels of choice and compulsion; one could certainly see these movements out of India as compelled by the disadvantaged economic circumstances at home (and the detrimental effects of British colonialism) and simultaneously seized on, as opportunities, by those with a particular ability to desire and execute departure. The diverse backgrounds of workers and the multiple processes of proletarianization in which they became imbricated put a brake on the inclination to make some general conclusion about the subjectification of workers from the Indian subcontinent through time. Breman & Daniel (1992) make an analagous observation in their important discussion of the fissured category of the "coolie." And though for our purposes Indians served as important sources for plantation labor, it needs also to be mentioned that peoples from all over Asia occupied similar categories; the resulting social and cultural complexity within sites of British imperialism does not simply accrue to South Asian diasporas but to a whole range of other displaced populations as well.

South Asian workers, their families, and their descendants were made to occupy a complex intermediary role in the structures of race relations in these societies, a role that has had tremendous political and social consequences into the present. In South Africa, the half-life of Indian indentured labor has taken shape through the machinations of apartheid, and it has made for complicated alliances and conflicts through time with black Africans as well as white Afrikaners and British (Bhana 1992, Thiara 2001, Lemon 1990). And in Fiji, relations between Indians and native peoples continue to approach various crisis points when political and social control are up for negotiation. The representation of Indian women, and their sexuality, became a site of anxiety as the pros and cons of indenture, and then free movement of labor to colonial outposts, were the subject of intense colonial debates (Kelly 1991).

In Trinidad and Guyana, where Indian populations have reached equivalent numbers to black African groups, an important issue has been the persistence of South Asian (Indian or Hindu, mainly) religious, kinship, culinary, musical, or other social traditions in the face of tremendous diversity and apparent mixtures within a broader rubric of what writer Wilson Harris (1999) has called "cross-cultural," as opposed to multicultural, societies. In some ways, this may be a recasting of the familiar problematic of integration into host societies. But the issue bears special significance in the debates on South Asian diasporas because it calls into question the basis for the presumed connections between peoples: "culture," origin, or something else altogether?

In his 1961 study, Klass (1961) elaborated the cultural connections that Indians maintained with "homeland traditions." For Klass, this was testament to a kind of cultural survival, an issue of particular importance to anthropological work of that period. Yet such insights are not easily bounded by time; in fact, a more recent study by Myers (1998) of Hindu music makes similar points about how devotional songs in Trinidad, connected to their counterparts in India, chart the geographical movement of peoples. More interesting than the truth claims of these studies are the consequences of thinking about Indian cultures as unities in the face of an array of spectacularly diverse elements external to them. It is precisely this type of historical and social experience that has served as the evidence, in the past and into the present, for stories of ethnicity, for anthropological considerations of difference, and for cultural politics in a range of contexts (Cohen 1978, Glazer & Moynihan 1963). But it matters a great deal how the lens for looking at a culture is constructed theoretically and what the direction is of the gaze. And in large part, the languages of cultural integrity and continuity have governed that process.

But recent work in cultural studies (Hall 1996, Lowe 1996, Joseph 1999), especially, has brought into being theoretical concepts like "hybridity," which highlight the cultural mixtures, ambivalences of peoplehood, and constructedness of race and ethnicity that are particularly central to South Asian diasporas all over the world and that have a particular resonance in the diverse social spaces of the Caribbean. In Trinidad, for example, South Asian cultures in diaspora have undergone transformation vis a vis African traditions dating back to the slave economy. Whether some elements of those cultures remain unchanged, in political or social terms, is a question that recasts hybridity itself as, possibly, a cultural mixture comprised of individual, and discrete, parts (Khan 1994, Munasinghe 2001). And here, again, we return to ethnicity paradigms: the melting pot or the salad bowl is one rendering of that problematic (Glazer & Moynihan 1963).

Leonard (1992) has treated these issues in her study of Punjabi Indian workers who migrated to California and the Pacific Northwest in the early 1900s. Like their counterparts in the sugar colonies, these Indians were certainly marked by an imbrication in agricultural labor arrangements. But their position in developing racial landscapes was special, taking shape as it did within, on the one hand, Anglo-Mexican-East Asian arrangements in the U.S. west coast and, on the other, black-white national discourses of citizenship. Dating back to the early 1900s, and in many ways lasting until the present, Indian migrants' racial otherness in the United States was liminal and ambiguous. Inclusion in the category of "Asian" was uncertain for Indian workers whose national and cultural histories, as well as smaller numbers and dispersed populations, created other languages for group boundary construction and social integration. Leonard focuses on an interesting case in which significant numbers of Indian men who stayed in the United States married Mexican women and created bicultural families and somewhat hybrid social formations. Leonard's simultaneous emphasis on extraordinary moments of social mixture and studied persistence of "Punjabi" and "Mexican" cultural traditions in a North American landscape represents the intrinsic tensions of diaspora. And the desires of a second generation of Punjabi-Mexican Americans to identify as Indian, as related to their fathers' status as landowners, for the sake of class privilege, underscores the continual correspondences between class and ethnicity created by hierarchies of nation-state formation.

The process by which class has been indexed to diasporic ethnicity has acquired complex forms in the case of South Asian migrants working and living in England. Contradictions between a homeland and settlement orientation are cast into specific forms of relief in an epistemological context of making empire and postcolony. Appearing first as "underclass" laborers, Indians went to England as lascars, sailors who had worked on British ships transporting goods (Visram 1986), as ayahs, or nannies, and as valets and household servants; these peoples' movements, in fact, took the routes of the British empire, in material, financial, as well as reproductive terms. Those who stayed on in London after their terms of utility had been completed became the subject of racialized social reform projects, as missionary Salter (1873) evidences. Very early in the trajectory of South Asians in Britain, then, the collusion of the apparati of colonialism abroad, and the developing machinery of the state domestically, would define the subjectivity of the diasporic migrant.

The incorporation of these experiences of labor, oppressive and highly racialized, within the cultural and intellectual productions of South Asian diasporas remains an ambivalent proposition. In more contemporary evocations of diaspora, in fact, the silences around an older set of reference points can be seen to reflect class, caste, and regional biases; a certain financially successful, upper-caste and India-centric image of South Asians abroad can only be destabilized by a juxtaposition with stories and experiences that do not contain such privilege. And to be sure, much scholarship and cultural production has made a great deal of the disjunctures in a historical trajectory of migration. The specificity of this dilemma, within Indian or South Asian diasporic communities, may in a general way simply compel a return to the basic problematic of ethnicity, of difference and sameness, and of the essentially tenuous, and at times heuristic, nature of what coheres the subject of study.

TRAVEL AND AN EXHILIC IMAGINARY

One way of metaphorically rendering the movement that gives rise to diasporic experience is travel. Often counterposed to migration as a theoretical tool in understanding diasporas, travel has often been relegated to the sphere of literary studies, just as migration has hovered within the collective concerns of the social sciences. But I would suggest that an imaginary is central to the way diasporic experience is articulated, within and outside of actual communities, and further argue that no one language of displacement, like that of settlement, should dominate an understanding of the field. Wherein travel implies an impermanency to the experience of moving abroad, it does so not only in actual terms, relating to the question of whether or not peoples are able and willing to return to their homeland, but also in psychic terms that seem to quite vividly depict those who live outside of what might be perceived of as "home." Clifford (1997) has productively joined the terms travel and diaspora not only to elucidate what happens imaginatively and materially when ethnographic subjects move or have moved, but also to illumine the complexities for researcher and researched alike, inherent in the anthropological project to understand the worlds that have come about through such tremendous social shifts.

Fischer (1986) has compellingly argued for critically reading autobiographical and other ethnic texts as part of new ethnographic projects. And Seyhan writes, in a way that seems particularly compelling for our topic, that "possibility of self-representation is intricately linked to a collective memory and represents explicitly or implicitly conflicts with past and present contexts" (1996, pp. 187–88). Intrinsic tensions of the diasporic experience are represented, if not assuaged, as South Asian subjects engage in processes of translation with a variety of literary-cultural consequences.

Travel is the unifying theme of two important works by writer-anthropologist Amitav Ghosh. In the quasi-historical novel *Shadow Lines* (Ghosh 1995), Ghosh explores the postwar period more generally, beginning with a preindependence migration, detailing life in India and Britain through the 1950s and 1960s, and ending with England in the 1970s. Divided into two sections entitled "Going Away" and "Coming Home," the novel is peopled by characters who travel between the worlds of England and India, actually and symbolically. The notions of "going away" and "coming home" function ironically in this text, as provisional points in a more circular movement between places of the mind and spirit, much as they do for South Asian migrants whose "home" is a matter of some debate and who create all sorts of connections with a real and imagined world outside of the ones they live in. In this sense, too, "Indianness" or "South Asianness" is detached from its presumed place in the subcontinent. An ultimately futile search for origins is the conceit of *In an Antique Land* (Ghosh 1992)—a text that charts Ghosh's desire, in the midst of ethnographic fieldwork in Egypt, to learn more about an Indian slave written about in the middle 1100s by Jewish and Egyptian merchants. The presence of an Indian, both the slave and Ghosh himself, in the state of travel affords a rethinking of Indian diasporas; here there is no possibility of the relinquishment of a national-cultural identity, simply a rearranging of the coordinates in which it is articulated. Narrative resolution in both texts lies in hybridity, the sense that all cultures are in some kind of contact, although here, as in the cases of South Asian diasporas in the Caribbean and in the 1900s in North America, that hybridity leaves some character of the elements intact. Ghosh remains Indian, just as the slave did, but within a wider imaginative circuitry. These are the "routes" that Clifford has written about so compellingly.

Nation is multiply transgressed and reinscribed in an explicitly autobiographical text, *My Own Country: A Doctor's Story* (Verghese 1994), about a Christian Keralite doctor from Ethiopia who attends medical school in India and moves to the United States to work with AIDS patients in Tennessee. Verghese's story contains travels that challenge simple homeland–land of settlement dichotomies; the autobiographical subject is not simply from India, but instead, commutes between various points in the broader circuitry of diaspora that, importantly, are not those of the more familiar metropoles of Bombay, New York, and London. His subsequent and intense intimacies with other men, particularly those suffering from AIDS, create an alternative setting for affiliation and attachment outside of the ethnic community. Verghese multiply renders his "country" as America, as small-town Tennessee, and as a more transnational world. Such multiplicity might be seen as essential to the creation of a range of South Asian diasporic artifacts that have sought to come to terms with the contradictions of exile (Dangor 1997, Nelson 1992).

OLD AND NEW NATIONS OF DIASPORA

Despite the international reach of South Asian diasporas, a basic building block remains the nation, in some form or another. In fact, nation is the script not only of the cultures created, but also of the presence of South Asians in non-South Asian countries. In a postwar world, where diverse "multicultural" societies are understood to be the integrated ideal of western countries, being from another nation confers a sense of identity and creates the means for membership into a broader set of social arrangements. This interpretation casts into question the validity, even in the past, of assimilative processes that were thought to undergird national formations, particularly of the United States.

For Indians in their respective diasporas, the language of nationality has been ultimately tied to and created within the ideologies, as well as actual power structures, of colonialism. This was as true after 1947 as it was before, and it is possible to argue for real continuities in national feeling through various social and political shifts. Yet of course the content, as well as the power, of the national force changes, in ways that reveal the essential tenuousness of the unities. As colonial subjects were assigned to the British administrative category of India, their subjectivity as Indian was manifested in an anticolonial nationalism, a production in which even the diversity acknowledged and managed by the colonial project could be strategically suppressed. And the power of this nationalism was also in its ability to move transnationally through Indian migrant communities. The Ghadar Party, a revolutionary anticolonial group originally formed in the United States, but with influence and alliances throughout myriad sites of Indian migrant concentration, was in many respects an exemplary diasporic formation (Bose 1965, Ganguly 1980, Mathur 1970, Puri 1983, Raucher 1974). And Indian independence, in fact, became a conceptual site to consider broader questions of the power relations between nations and among social groups formed through inequities and western domination, the latter of which eventually led to the creation of third-worldist sensibilities, and to the alliance of postwar nationalisms, in the nonaligned movement. An account by Puri (1983) of the Ghadar Party, in fact, makes a great deal of the broad connections made with others around the world, noting in particular the members of revolutionary political groups in Russia, China, Mexico, Ireland, and Egypt called "fellow Ghadarites."

It is interesting that much of the existing scholarship on the Ghadar Party has been published in India, rather than in the United States or England. Partly, this fact resonates with the earlier discussion about more working-class experiences fading from the view of postwar narrativization of ethnic insurgency. But we might also consider the ways in which such a historiographical silence reflects alternative and, to some extent, competing ideas about Indian nationalism that have come to be spatially and temporally bounded. The internationalist reach and the necessary alliances of the political (and social) formation of the Ghadar Party may be particularly germane to the desire among scholars located in the subcontinent to recover a progressive form of Indian nationalism, one that critiques western imperialism. But in diasporic articulations from largely first-world nations that have, in the postindependence period, become associated with the homeland of India, and that have directed themselves largely to "Indianness," as opposed to a more subcontinental South Asianness, that moment when nationality was being asserted from abroad as indexed to political developments of a more global nature may not be part of a functional historical memory. This is to say that just as there are many forms of Indian nationalist memory at home (Chatterjee 1993), there are varied renderings abroad for purposes that have to do with how "ethnic" groups become constituted in countries of settlement.

As a basic organizing logic for diasporic communities, nation has expansive and, often, apparently contradictory meanings. And after independence in 1947, nation and state were indissolubly linked, even as each of those categories became variously occupied by the project of a new India, a new Pakistan and independent Sri Lanka and Bangladesh. Especially in the case of India, an intense anticolonial nationalist sentiment undergirded the formation of the institutional apparatus of the state and the forms of consent produced among largely Hindu but also Muslim and Christian populations; in this respect, it is useful to resist conceiving of a familiar divide between the nation as imagined and the state as materially constructed, for a more abstract rendering of both entities took shape at home and abroad. In fact, the fluidity between the concept of the nation and the possibilities for the Indian state is a fundamental and distinctive characteristic of the "Indianness" created in diaspora. Through the close connection between nation and state, we can also see new (and old) translations of difference from "home" into social differentiation abroad. Region, language, caste, and religion all become fertile sites for subjectification after 1947, in ways both anchored to and autonomous from nation-state projects and are arguably less resuppressed in the postindependence period (Daniel 1984).

Yet the constructed memory of the trauma of colonialism has been a central part of nationalist communities, as well as of their articulation to other possibilities of self and group, such as integration in places outside of India. India's (and Pakistan's) place in a world of nations in the past, present, and future has conferred special identities of opposition, manifested in the geopolitical projects of anticolonialism, nonalignment, and, eventually, neoliberalism. At times, being an Indian, Pakistani, or Bangladeshi subject became tied to various political movements that posed critiques of western domination in a world system. Cheddi Jagan, prime minister of Guyana, whose Indianness signified simultaneously ethnic minority status within the country and a connection to a progressive third worldism based in histories of economic and social development that made his ancestors coolie laborers, is an interesting diasporic subject in this regard (Williams 1991, Singham & Hune 1986). Subsequent struggles over the role of Indian citizens in emergent nationalist arrangements, not only in Guyana but also, most spectacularly, in Trinidad and Fiji during the 1960s and into the present, telescoped historical experiences of colonialism and nationalism in India into other time periods.

An identity based in opposition relates not only to colonialism, but also to its aftermath. Although the complex of "India" could conjure forth progressive critiques of domination, it could also allude to political and social oppression, particularly concerning those "minority" positionalities. Perhaps the most profound of these is Islam. The dominance of Hindus within particular visions of Indian nationalism, the contested nature of the partition of the Indian subcontinent in 1947, and the ensuing hostilities between postindependence India and Pakistan produced deep divisions that became organized under the sign of religion. Largely the development of Pakistani nationalism, too, has operated as religious opposition, to India as well as to a developing global order, much as have nationalisms of other Muslim-majority countries. In this sense, Pakistani migrant communities are articulated as much to the broader diasporic production of Islam, and to an imagined religious homeland of Mecca, as they are to any nation-state. Here the difference that emerges from some kind of absence (of state power, of control of national boundaries) is transformed into a difference of religious community across state boundaries. In some sense, then, in these non-Indian, post-1947 diasporas, a broad national heterogeneity is accounted for and negotiated.

The desire for a Punjabi-Sikh homeland, a Khalistan, creates another account of nationality, diaspora, and identity (Axel 2001, Mahmood 1996, Tatla 1999). Positioned against the Indian nation-state, Sikhs fighting for independence may see themselves as in a state of exile both at home and abroad. Political (and forced) exile testifies to a rather different form of diasporic experience; in as much as the Khalistan movement is transnational in its very nature, it cannot be easily captured by any category of migration that maintains a division between homeland and land of settlement. For her book on Sikh militants, in fact, Mahmood (1996) conducted her fieldwork entirely among subjects living in North America, noting that geography and culture are effectively decoupled through the extraordinary transplantation of Sikh households and communities in the United States and Canada that seems to reproduce what is from home. Yet the fascinating claiming of west coast gurudwaras from the Ghadar movement originally directed at Indian national independence by activists for Sikh independence may again raise questions related to Jones's (1968) idea of the "changing same," namely is this or is this not a different instantiation of culture and politics? Perhaps this is best responded to from within the realm of representation, as Axel's work (2001) has done.

Nonetheless, the problematic of claimed territory within existing states that the Sikh case develops (Tatla 1999) is one that has general importance for the analysis of diasporas. Based on an intensive study of the Tamil diaspora, Fuglerud (1999) concludes that there is a highly internalized logic to the social experience of refugees in a variety of places, such that the formations seem to be almost untouched by their appearance in specific locales, such as Norway or Canada, or for that matter, Sri Lanka. Regardless of whether or not comparative ethnographic work in all the many sites of a Tamil diaspora would bear out this conclusion, the similarity between Fuglerud's and Mahmood's points here is intriguing and might be best interpreted through the overlapping figures of the political exile and refugee, especially as they are positioned against that of the migrant.

Difference as simultaneously willed oppositionality and external minoritization is another way to think about the tensions that subcontinental cultural identities have produced in new lands of settlement. And in fact, as noted by Ahmed & Donnan (1994a), globalization has especially accelerated desires for Islam. Perhaps the most dramatic of illustrative events is the diasporic effects of the controversy over the publication of *The Satanic Verses* (Rushdie 1988). What is important for our purposes here is the tremendous response elicited from British Muslims, largely migrants from Pakistan and Bangladesh. In spectacularized events to support the Iranian Ayatollah's death warrant, Muslims in London and other British cities burned books as well as effigies of Rushdie and expressed a sense of profound victimization by the text itself (Samad 1992). These moments became, in the western media, symbolic of religious intolerance and fundamentalism; in the classic overwriting of Islam, the Ayatollah became conflated with Muslim immigrants from the Indian subcontinent. In their analyses of the controversy, both Asad (1990) and Werbner (1996), though in different ways, refocus attention on Muslim migrant subjects through the construction of those communities that sought to express disagreements with Rushdie through multiple readings of the text and of their selves. What Werbner has noted for another similarly representative moment, the Gulf crisis, is also relevant for the Rushdie affair, that this kind of moment is a window on the confluences of "enclaved" community formation and more diasporic forms of citizenship, a rendering of a local-global problematic (Werbner 1994).

The Rushdie affair, and its effects on diasporic cultures, illustrates how the process by which ethnic communities claim a text has to do not only with whether it is actually read by community members but also with what it and its author represent. This is to say that certain diasporic-ethnic "reading practices" may bring together text and context in new ways, precisely because they command psychic and even bodily identification.

That constitutive local-global tension of diasporic formations finds expression in the social architecture of specific migrant communities. One highly studied community space is Southall, London. A well-traveled symbol of "Indian community" or "Punjabi community," Southall has achieved legendary importance throughout the diaspora for its ability to crystallize the conflicts between migrant and host societies. Just as importantly, migrant groups have engaged in political struggles over how to define their own space, as well as how to respond to racism. And most of the recent anthropological work significantly departs from older models of ethnic studies in which the coming to consciousness of a certain kind of ethnic identity is made to overlap with the trajectory of development of a geographically bounded community. Instead, migrant-racial communities are deconstructed from the very outset, leading to a complex notion of the lived experience of not one but many diasporas. Baumann (1996), in fact, actively works against "reified culture" by identifying within the boundaries of Southall five "ethnic" communities: Sikh, Hindu, Muslim, Afro-Caribbean, and White. In so doing, he also challenges the content of popular images circulated through South Asian diasporas of Southall as a Punjabi and, by extension, Indian place. Despite the emphasis on conceiving of ethnic minority boundaries as being broken down by movements to and from homeland, there is surprisingly little work done on how ethnic groups themselves are porous to one another. This research gap appears not only in work on South Asian and other ethnic minority groups in England, it also appears in the United States, which has a long tradition of detailed studies of ethnic minorities in polyglot sites. This is why the emphasis on differentiation within recent work on Southall is important. In her exploration of the experience of television and video among young South Asian people in Southall, Gillespie (1995) identifies another cultural site that has profound fissuring possibilities: technology. Both the open-ended narratives embodied in television and the transnational (and transcommunity) transmission possibilities of communal watching anticipate a truly transformed diasporic subjectivity, although Gillespie's specific concern is the contestations of generational shifts in British Asian ethnic communities and their representation.

Simultaneously a "Little India" and a British "ethnic community," Southall is able to wonderfully capture the contradictions of nation in a globalized world, contradictions South Asian diasporas more generally bring into sharper focus. Boundaries of time and space are continually transgressed by social formations that come into being through imaginative and political renderings of themselves elsewhere. For the Sikh community in Southall, the fantasy of a Khalistani homeland creates a language for comprehending not only issues of subjectivity but also forms of political violence and surveillance perpetrated by the Indian state (Axel 2001). And in my own work (Shukla 1999) on Southall and Jackson Heights, Queens, another "Little India" in the United States, I have engaged in a consideration of how the consumption of "Indianness" creates forms of cultural citizenship that resonate with, on the one hand, profound desire for India and, on the other, practical membership in the British and U.S. nations. The apparent paradox created from such moves is assuaged by discourses of multiculturalism and the national script basic to its execution. Here we again return to the point that South Asian diasporas have served as ideal vehicles (*a*) for intervening in anthropological debates about ethnography, (*b*) of taking seriously the breakdown of geography as a centrally defining force in people's lives, and (*c*) for giving descriptive power to narratives of rupture in social life that work on globalization has asserted to be a cultural dominant of our times.

Globalization has in no way diminished the intensity of nationalism; in fact, there is a powerful argument to be made about the increase in nationalism through very contemporary negotiations of global and local spheres of culture, politics, and economy. For the case of South Asian diasporas, it is impossible to overstate the importance of the rise of the Indian nation-state in a postwar and postindependence period. In fact, it is through diaspora that one could track nationalism, and this, certainly, is tied to changes in technology, communication, and community associated with globalization. This has certainly taken shape in the conceptual correspondences made between religion and nation. Bhatt (2000) has powerfully argued that Hindutva movements have been able to negotiate the relationship of diasporic subjects to their homeland through nationalist-religious stories of prevalence and preservation taking shape in worldwide organizations of Vishwa Hindu Parishad and Rashtriya Swayamsevak Sangh. Yet these broader groupings have differential effects, and the ability of diasporic fables to encompass questions of minoritization in England and the United States is testament to their supple awareness of local-global dynamics and an acceptance of the contradictory nationalisms that migrant communities live within. In more general terms, given these complexities in acknowledged paradoxical moments, it seems important to read the rise of traditionalism, in religion and culture, within open narratives of globalization (Rajagopal 2001). Even the nonresident Indian who has emerged out of the programs of the Indian nation-state to encourage investment, and who is a prototype for transnational capitalist classes (Lessinger 1992), freely operates in a space created by the cultural past and extreme modernity, a kind of practice that Ong (1999) has termed flexible citizenship.

DIASPORAS AS NONNATIONAL?

Nationality acquires different meanings and effects when our gaze is directed to nations other than India, just as diaspora takes different shapes through non–first world spaces. South Asians from countries of the Caribbean and in eastern and southern Africa present special challenges to linear trajectories of immigration and even to homeland-centered narratives of diaspora, particularly when these peoples become further dislocated. The 1972 expulsion of South Asians from Uganda precipitated, on the one hand, a national political crisis within Britain about how and where to resettle former colonial subjects and, on the other, a profound anxiety within South Asian communities about migration, belonging, and citizenship (Layton-Henry 1992, Bhachu 1985, Mamdani 1973, Marett 1989). In some cases, a connection with a distant Indian homeland was deliberately reconstructed, while in others, formations articulated to other national-racial spaces emerged (Joseph 1999).

The increased flow of people of South Asian origin from the Caribbean into first-world countries, more evidence of what has been called "twice-migration" (Bhachu 1985), rearranges the coordinates of class and ethnic formation in diaspora. If the scholarship on indentured and free migration has become somewhat dichotomized as attending to "third-world" and "first-world" perspectives, the globalization that produces all sorts of new migrations intervenes and challenges us to consider, for example, the impact of working-class Guyanese Asian immigrants in Queens on the cosmopolitan Indian diaspora. Joseph (1999) has productively turned to issues of performance in order to elucidate the multiplicity, and even agency, basic to some lesser-known dislocations that are a part of South Asian diasporas.

The contemporary political dominance of the nation-state of India within the subcontinental region finds a kind of double standard in the significant majority of works on Indian formations within the literature on South Asian diasporas. And that fact ultimately generates the question of the extent to which assumptions and experiences specific to India unduly influence the proposed content and meaning of more diverse formations. Particularly with regard to categories of subjectivity, national shifts of emphasis can make a great deal of difference. Whether the presumed South Asian subject is a "worker," a "migrant," a "refugee," or an "exile," as the cases of Sikhs and Tamils have suggested, depends on the routes and temporality of diasporic movement and determines the production of class, racial, and ethnic positionality (Daniel 1996). Leaving the broader rubric of South Asian diasporas as open as possible, and as dynamically constructed by tensions of the general and the particular, is but a temporary solution to some of these basic dilemmas. Important conflicts between traditional notions of culture and increasingly nontraditional forms of identity have taken place within diasporic formations of gender, sexuality, and youth. Feminist organizations, particularly in North America and Britain, have been disposed to conceive of themselves as "South Asian" or "black" (Bhattacharjee 1992) and, in so doing, level critiques simultaneously at the particularistic and nationalistic conceptions of culture effected by what Kasinitz (1992) has termed the ethnicity entrepreneurs and the hierarchical relationships of gender and class within migrant communities. In this production, the category of gender enables a fracturing of nation, such that the diaspora can be experienced in more liberatory ways, as an opening for transformed subjectivity that is not merely tied to its links to a past history.

Sexuality, too, as a theoretical field, has provided an important space for critique of boundaries—of community, nation, and even transnation—as the fluidity of identity and the accompanying reconstruction of notions of self and group become the means to create new unities that significantly depart from older forms (Gopinath 1992). Here we might think of how it is not only diaspora itself that works against nation, but rather the identities that emerge from the dispersions, discontinuities, and ambiguities of diasporic citizenship that can destabilize already formed unities like those of the state. In fact, queer diasporas call into question the heteronormativity essential to all nation-building projects and also that same nationalism that might create certain forms of diasporic attachment.

Many have argued for the importance of musical cultures as a fertile arena for subjectivity. But unlike Myers (1998), whose material on Hindu religious songs in Trinidad seems to demonstrate cultural continuity of form and content, much recent work has focused on hybrid South Asian musical practices and their cultures, such as bhangra in Britain and North America especially (Maira 1999, Back 1995/1996) and chutney music in Trinidad and other parts of the Caribbean. As Gilroy (1993) has argued for the black diaspora, so too do Sharma et al. (1996) suggest for South Asian diasporas, that music can be a centrally important cultural site for reconceiving of identity, culture, and solidarity because of its ability to transform itself, as well as be transmitted, across national boundaries. In Trinidad, when Indian women perform local musics, as Niranjana has shown, they create spaces for new dialogues on the nature of gender, sexuality, and nation.

The broader dilemma of how to express a community's hope and desires and package it for the outside world, or how to move from explorations of the self to the group, centers on the issue of representation, an issue that preoccupies all groups constructed through difference, both inside and outside a nation (Radhakrishnan 1996). And in turn, "ethnic literature," or "diasporic literature," comes to terms not only with the difference of a group but also with what social effects that difference has in a range of social arrangements (Women of South Asian Descent Collective 1993, Bahri & Vasudeva 1996). In this respect, the Rushdie affair brought the fundamental question of representation to the fore, brought it, in fact, to a crisis point. But this issue cannot be wholly relegated to the field of literary studies. As Werber (1996) has suggested, it addresses central concerns of anthropology, having to do with textuality and cultural translation, perhaps the very mainstay of ethnographic analysis. As South Asian diasporas are made vivid through a broad array of cultural forms, some familiar, such as music and literature, and others newer, such as television and the internet, they bring to the field interesting methodological questions about how to proceed with cultural analysis for a rapidly changing, geographically dispersed, and multimedia set of communities. Various cultural producers have increasingly turned to film to represent changing South Asian cultures in diaspora. Chadha's British film, *Bhaji on the Beach* (1994), was explicit in its portrayal of multiple generations of British Punjabi women who in varied ways contest gender and cultural expectations and also travel to a liminal site, Blackpool, England, for a climactic working out of social tensions. Prasad's recent film, *My Son the Fanatic* (1998), reversed the familiar generational conflict by portraying a Pakistani immigrant taxi driver in love with a white prostitute whose British Pakistani son becomes a Muslim fundamentalist. The popularity of diasporic film and other expressive forms, such as art (Queens Museum of Art 1997) and dance, reflect a new concern with the visual, as well as, perhaps, a resistance to narrative closure. I would also suggest that this set of productions exhibits interests in representing diasporic culture for wider publics, and relatedly, expresses a desire to contemplate forms of belonging, in old (homeland) and new (settlement) nations. The recent proliferation of work on South Asian diasporas within anthropology as well as literary and cultural studies may have the unintended effect of leading us to think of the theoretical vocabulary for such formations as new. But although it is important to regard the tremendous transformations in migrant cultures, we might also take the subject of South Asian diasporas as an occasion to inspire a revisiting of some older anthropological debates about the national boundedness of culture. It is interesting, for example, that the classic study of East Indians in Trinidad by Klass (1961) was prefaced by comments by Conrad Arensberg that drew out Indian subjects' cultural connections with India and the challenges that such "transnationalism" (though the word was not then used) posed to multiethnic and multiracial societies of the Caribbean. In fact, Klass (1961) and Herskovits & Herskovits (1947) before him were deeply conscious of diasporas that challenged simple models of integration in Trinidad. What, then, does it mean in general terms for such multiplicity to be understood in more historical terms and as a model for subsequent developments of migrant culture?

In exploring such questions, South Asian diasporas may produce a conversation between older and newer anthropological work on the subject of group diversity. Exploring what it means to be Asian, Asian American, Muslim, Tamil, or Indian

American cannot be separated from an acknowledgment of the persistence of Indianness around the world or the production of subcontinental antagonisms in diasporic sites. In this sense, too, South Asian diasporas are a stage for South Asian studies to come into dialogue with ethnic studies and for national productions of knowledge to be thrown into question.

If the category of "South Asian" makes the most sense in constructed political alliances in the subcontinent or in the solidarities of new identities in diasporas, it also comes into direct conflict with the hyperproduction of more nationalist groupings that evacuate the term of its meaning for a range of communities. New forms of technology have not established a position in this debate, they have aided and abetted both kinds of subjectivity. A broader analytical question that emerges from this social impasse is whether the ethnographic field is able to accommodate subject matter (as well as communities) that only provisionally hold together. When "South Asian" defines a field of inquiry, does it create a new knowledge, or does it simply do the work of description? These are questions implicit in a variety of historical renderings of, not least of all, material in the present.

ACKNOWLEDGMENTS

I would like to thank E. Valentine Daniel and Thomas Klubock for their encouragement and counsel.

Visit the Annual Reviews home page at www.AnnualReviews.org

LITERATURE CITED

Ahmed A, Donnan H. 1994a. Islam in the age of postmodernity. See Ahmed & Donnan 1994b, pp.1–20

Ahmed A, Donnan H, eds. 1994b. *Islam, Globalization and Postmodernity.* New York: Routledge

Anderson C. 2000. *Convicts in the Indian Ocean: Transportation from South Asian to Mauritius, 1815–53.* New York: St. Martin's

Appadurai A. 1996. *Modernity at Large: Cultural Dimensions of Globalization.* Minneapolis/London: Univ. Minn. Press

Arora UP, ed. 1991. *Graeco-India, India's Cultural Contects* [sic] *with the Greek World.* New Delhi: Ramanand Vidya Bhavan

Asad T. 1990. Ethnography, literature and politics: some readings and uses of Salman Rushdie's *The Satanic Verses. Cult. Anthropol.* 239–69

Axel BK. 2001. *The Nation's Tortured Body: Violence, Representation and the Formation of a Sikh "Diaspora."* Durham NC/London: Duke Univ. Press

Back L. 1995/1996. X amount of Sat Siri Akal! Apache Indian, reggae music and the cultural intermezzo. *New Form.* 27:128–47

Bahri D, Vasudeva M, eds. 1996. *Between the Lines: South Asians and Postcoloniality.* Philadelphia: Temple Univ. Press

Ballard R, ed. 1994. *Desh Pardesh: The South Asian Presence in Britain.* London: Hurst

Bates C, ed. 2001. *Community, Empire and Migration: South Asians in Diaspora.* New York: Palgrave

Baumann G. 1996. *Contesting Culture: Discourses of Identity in Multi-Ethnic London.* Cambridge, UK: Cambridge Univ. Press

Begley V, Daniel R, eds. 1991. *Rome and*

India: the Ancient Sea Trade. Madison: Univ. Wisc. Press

Bhachu P. 1985. *Twice Migrants: East African Sikh Settlers in Britain*. London/New York: Tavistock

Bhatt C. 2000. Dharmo Rakshati Rakshitah: Hindutva movements in the UK. *Ethn. Racial Stud.* 23:559–93

Bhattacharjee A. 1992. The habit of ex-nomination: nation, woman, and the Indian immigrant bourgeoisie. *Public Cult.* 5:19–44

Bhana S. 1992. *Gandhi's Legacy: The Natal Indian Congress, 1894–1994*. Pietermaritzburg: Univ. Natal Press

Bose AC. 1965. Indian nationalist agitations in the U.S.A. and Canada till the arrival of Har Dayal in 1911. *J. Ind. Hist.* 43:227–39

Boyarin J. 1992. *Storm from Paradise: the Politics of Jewish Memory*. Bloomington: Indiana Univ. Press

Breman J, Daniel EV. 1992. Conclusion: the making of a coolie. *J. Peasant Stud.* 19(3/4): 268–95

Carter M. 1995. *Servants, Sirdars and Settlers: Indians in Mauritius 1834–1874*. Delhi/New York: Oxford Univ. Press

Carter M. 1996. *Voices from Indenture: Experiences of Indian Migrants in the British Empire*. London/New York: Leicester Univ. Press

Chadha G. 1994. *Bhaji on the Beach*. Film.

Chandan A. 1986. *Indians in Britain*. New Delhi: Sterling

Chatterjee P. 1993. *The Nation and Its Fragments: Colonial and Postcolonial Histories*. Princeton, NJ: Princeton Univ. Press

Clarke C, Peach C, Vertovec S, eds. 1990. *South Asians Overseas: Migration and Ethnicity*. Cambridge, UK/New York: Cambridge Univ. Press

Clifford J. 1997. *Routes: Travel and Translation in the Late Twentieth Century*. Cambridge, MA/London: Harvard Univ. Press

Cohen R. 1978. Ethnicity: problem and focus in anthropology. *Annu. Rev. Anthropol.* 7:379–403

Cohen R. 1997. *Global Diasporas: An Introduction*. Seattle: Univ. of Wash. Press

Daniel EV. 1984. *Fluid Sings: Being a Person the Tamil Way*. Berkeley: Univ. Calif. Press

Daniel EV. 1996. *Charred Lullabies: Chapters in an Anthropography of Violence*. Princeton: Princeton Univ. Press

Daniels R. 1989. *History of Indian Immigration to the United States: An Interpretive Essay*. New York: Asia Soc.

Dangor A. 1997. *Kafka's Curse*. New York: Pantheon

Desai R. 1963. *Indian Immigrants in Britain*. London: Oxford Univ. Press

Fischer M. 1986. Ethnicity and the post-modern arts of memory. In *Writing Culture: The Politics and Poetics of Ethnography*, ed. J Clifford, G Marcus, pp. 194–233. Berkeley: Univ. Calif. Press

Fisher M. 1980. *The Indians of New York City*. Columbia, MO: South Asia Books

Foucault M. 1972. *The Archaeology of Knowledge and the Discourse on Language*. New York: Pantheon

Fryer P. 1984. *Staying Power: The History of Black People in Britain*. London: Pluto

Fuglerud O. 1999. *Life on the Outside: The Tamil Diaspora and Long Distance Nationalism*. London: Pluto

Gandhi L. 1998. *Postcolonial Theory: A Critical Introduction*. New York: Columbia Univ. Press

Ganguly A. 1980. *Ghadar Revolution in America*. New Delhi: Metropolitan Book

Gardner K. 1993. Desh-Bidesh: Sylheti images of home and away. *Man* 28:1–15

Ghosh A. 1989. The diaspora in Indian culture. *Public Cult.* 2:73–78

Ghosh A. 1992. *In an Antique Land: History in the Guise of a Traveler's Tale*. New York: Vintage Books

Ghosh A. 1995. *The Shadow Lines*. New Delhi: Oxford Univ. Press

Gillespie M. 1995. *Television, Ethnicity and Cultural Change*. London/New York: Routledge

Gillion K. 1962. *Fiji's Indian Migrants; a History to the End of Indenture in 1920*. Melbourne/New York: Oxford Univ. Press

Gilroy P. 1993. *The Black Atlantic*. Cambridge, MA: Harvard Univ. Press

Glazer N, Moynihan D. 1963. *Beyond the Melting Pot*. Cambridge, MA: MIT Press

Gopinath G. 1992. Nostalgia, desire, diaspora: South Asian sexualities in motion. *Positions* 5:

Gordon L. 1989. Bridging India and America: the art and politics of Kumar Goshal. *Amerasia* 15:68–88

Gordon M. 1964. *Assimilation in American Life: The Role of Race, Religion and National Origin*. New York: Oxford Univ. Press

Gupta A, Ferguson J, eds. 1997. *Culture, Power, Place: Explorations in Critical Anthropology*. Durham, NC/London: Duke Univ. Press

Hall S. 1996. New ethnicities. In *Stuart Hall: Critical Dialogues in Cultural Studies*, ed. D Morley, K Chen. London/New York: Routledge

Harris W. 1999. The art of the imagination. *J. Caribb. Lit.* 2:17–25

Helweg A, Helweg U. 1990. *An Immigrant Success Story: East Indians in America*. London: Hurst

Herskovits M, Herskovits F. 1947. *Trinidad Village*. New York: Knopf

Jensen J. 1988. *Passage from India*. New Haven, CT: Yale Univ. Press

Jones L. 1968. *Black Music*. New York: Morrow

Joseph M. 1999. *Nomadic Identities: The Performance of Citizenship*. Minneapolis: Univ. of Minn. Press

Kale M. 1998. *Fragments of Empire: Capital, Slavery, and Indian Indentured Labor Migration in the British Caribbean*. Philadelphia: Univ. Penn. Press

Kaplan C. 1996. *Questions of Travel: Postmodern Discourses of Displacement*. Durham, NC/London: Duke Univ. Press

Kasinitz P. 1992. *Caribbean New York: Black Immigrants and the Politics of Race*. Ithaca, NY: Cornell Univ. Press

Kearney M. 1995. The local and the global: the anthropology of globalization and transnationalism. *Annu. Rev. Anthropol.* 24:547–65

Kelly JD. 1991. *A Politics of Virtue: Hinduism, Sexuality, and Counter-Colonial Discourse in Fiji*. Chicago: Univ. Chicago Press

Khan A. 1994. Juthaa in Trinidad: food, pollution, and hierarchy in a Caribbean diaspora community. *Am. Ethnol.* 21:245–69

Khandelwal M. 1996. Indian immigrants in Queens, New York City: patterns of spatial concentration and distribution, 1965-1990. See van der Veer 1995, pp. 178–96

Khoshy S. 1998. Category crisis: South Asian Americans and questions of race and ethnicity. *Diaspora* 7:285–320

King AD, ed. 1991. *Culture, Globalization and the World-System*. London: Macmillan

Klass M. 1961. *East Indians in Trinidad: A Study of Cultural Persistence*. New York/London: Columbia Univ. Press

Kondapi C. 1951. *Indians Overseas 1838–1949*. New Delhi: Indian Counc. World Aff.

Kumar A. 2000. *Passport Photos*. Berkeley: Univ. Calif. Press

Lal BV. 1980. Approaches to the study of Indian indentured emigration with special reference to Fiji. *J. Pac. Hist.* 15:52–70

Laurence KO. 1994. *A Question of Labour: Indentured Immigration into Trinidad and British Guiana*. New York: St. Martin's

Layton-Henry Z. 1992. *The Politics of Immigration*. Oxford, UK: Blackwell

Lemon A. 1990. The political position of Indians in South Africa. See Clarke et al. 1990, pp. 131–48

Leonard K. 1992. *Making Ethnic Choices: California's Punjabi Mexican Americans*. Philadelphia: Temple Univ. Press

Lessinger J. 1992. Nonresident-Indian investment and India's drive for industrial modernization. In *Anthropology and the Global Factory; Studies of the New Industrialization in the Late Twentieth Century*, ed. FA Rothstein, M Blim, pp.62–82. New York/Westport, CT: Bergin & Garvey

Loomba A. 1998. *Colonialism/Postcolonialism*. London/New York: Routledge

Lowe L. 1996. *Immigrant Acts: On Asian American Cultural Politics*. Durham, NC/London: Duke Univ. Press

Mahmood CK. 1996. *Fighting for Faith and Nation: Dialogues with Sikh Militants.* Philadelphia: Univ. Penn. Press

Maira S. 1999. Identity dub: the paradoxes of an Indian American youth subculture (New York mix). *Cult. Anthropol.* 14(1):29–60

Mamdani M. 1973. *From Citizen to Refugee: Uganda Asians Come to Britain.* London: Frances Pinter

Marett V. 1989. *Immigrants Settling in the City.* Leicester, UK: Leicester Univ. Press

Mathur LP. 1970. *Indian Revolutionary Movement in the United States.* New Delhi: Chand

Munasinghe V. 2001. *Callaloo or Tossed Salad? East Indians and the Cultural Politics of Indentity in Trinidad.* Ithaca, NY: Cornell Univ. Press

Myers H. 1998. *Music of Hindu Trinidad: Songs from the India Diaspora.* Chicago: Univ. Chicago Press

Nayyar D. 1994. *Migration, Remittances and Capital Flows: The Indian Experience.* Delhi: Oxford Univ. Press

Nelson E, ed. 1992. *Reworlding: The Literature of the Indian Diaspora.* New York: Greenwood

Niranjana T. Left to the imagination: Indian nationalisms and female sexuality in Trinidad. *Public Cult.* 11:223–43

Northrup D. 1995. *Indentured Labor in the Age of Imperialism 1838–1914.* Cambridge, UK/New York: Cambridge Univ. Press

Ong A. 1999. *Flexible Citizenship: The Cultural Logics of Transnationality.* Durham, NC/London: Duke Univ. Press.

Orsi RA. 1985. *The Madonna of 115th Street: Faith and Community in Italian Harlem, 1880–1950.* New Haven, CT/London: Yale Univ. Press

Parekh B. Some reflections in the Hindu diaspora. *New Community* 20(4):603–20

Prashad V. 2000. *The Karma of Brown Folk.* Minneapolis: Univ. Minn. Press

Petievich C, ed. 1999. *The Expanding Landscape: South Asians and the Diaspora.* New Delhi: Manohar

Prasad U. 1998. *My Son the Fanatic.* Film

Puri H. 1983. *Ghadar Movement: Ideology, Organization and Strategy.* Amritsar, India: Garu Nanak Dev Univ.

Queens Museum of Art. 997. *Out of India: Contemporary Art of the South Asian Diaspora, December 8, 1997–March 22, 1998.* New York: Queens Museum of Art

Radhakrishnan R. 1996. Is the ethnic "authentic" in the diaspora? In *Diasporic Mediations: Between Home and Location*, pp. 203–14. Minneapolis/London: Univ. Minn. Press

Rajagopal A. 2001. *Politics After Television: Religious Nationalism and the Reshaping of the Indian Public.* Cambridge, UK: Cambridge Univ. Press

Raucher A. 1974. American anti-imperialists and the pro-India movement, 1900–1932. *Pac. Hist. Rev.* 43:83–110

Rukmani TS, ed. 1999. *Hindu Diaspora: Global Perspectives.* Montreal, Canada: Chair Hindu Stud., Concordia Univ.

Rushdie S. 1988. *The Satanic Verses.* New York: Viking

Salter J. 1873. *The Asiatic in England: Sketches of Sixteen Years' Work Among Orientals.* London: Seely, Jackson & Halliday

Samad Y. 1992. Book burning and race relations: political mobilisation of Bradford Muslims. *New Commun.* 18:507–19

Sassen S. 1998. *Globalization and Its Discontents: Essays on the New Mobility of People and Money.* New York: New Press

Schiller N, Basch L, Blanc C. 1994. *Nations Unbound: Transnational Projects, Postcolonial Predicaments, and Deterritorialized Nation-States.* New York: Gordon Breach

Seyhan A. 1996. Ethnic selves/ethnic swings: invention of self, space, and genealogy in immigran writing. In *Culture/Contexture: Explorations in Anthropology and Literary Studies*, ed. EV Daniel, J Peck, pp. 175–94. Berkeley: Univ. of Calif. Press

Sharma S, Hutnyk J, Sharma A. 1996. Introduction. In *Dis-Orienting Rhythms: The Politics of the New Asian Dance Music*, ed. S Sharma, J Hutnyk, A Sharma, pp.1–11. London/New Jersey: Zed Books

Shukla S. 1997. Building diaspora and nation:

the 1991 "Cultural festival of India." *Cult. Stud.* 11:296–315

Shukla S. 1999. New immigrants, new forms of transnational community: post-1965 Indian migrations. *Amerasia J.* 25:19–36

Singham AW, Hune S. 1986. *Non-Alignment in an Age of Alignments.* Westport, CT: Hill

Sivanandan A. 1982. *A Different Hunger: Writings on Black Resistance.* London: Pluto

Tatla DS. 1999. *The Sikh Diaspora: The Search for Statehood.* London: UCL

Thiara R. 2001. Imagining? Ethnic Identity and Indians in South Africa. In *Community, Empire and Migration: South Asians in Diaspora*, ed. C Bates, pp. 123–52. New York: Palgrave

Tinker H. 1993. *A New System of Slavery; the Export of Indian Labour Overseas, 1830–1920.* London: Hansib

Van der Veer P, ed. 1995. *Nation and Migration: The Politics of Space in the South Asian Diaspora.* Philadelphia: Univ. Penn. Press

Verghese A. 1994. *My Own Country: A Doctor's Story.* New York: Vintage

Vertovec S. 1992. *Hindu Trinidad: Religion, Ethnicity and Socio-Economic Change.* London: Macmillan

Visram R. 1986. *Ayahs, Lascars and Princes: Indians in Britain 1700–1947.* London: Pluto

Von Eschen P. 1997. *Race Against Empire: Black Americans and Anticolonialism, 1937–57.* Ithaca, NY: Cornell Univ. Press

Watson JF, Kaye JW. 1872. *The People of India; a Series of Photographic Illustrations of the Races and Tribes of Hindustan*, Vols. 1–8. London: India Mus.

Werbner P. 1994. Diaspora and millennium: British Pakistani global-local fabulations of the Gulf War. See Ahmed & Donnan 1994b, pp. 213–36

Werbner P. 1996. Allegories of sacred imperfection: magic, hermeneutics, and passion. In *The Satanic Verses. Curr. Anthropol.* 37:S55–86

Williams B. 1991. *Stains on My Name, War in My Veins: Guyana and the Politics of Cultural Struggle.* Durham, NC/London: Duke Univ. Press

Williams R. 1988. *Religions of Immigrants from India and Pakistan: New Threads in the American Tapestry.* Cambridge, UK/New York: Cambridge Univ. Press

Women of South Asian Descent Collective. 1993. *Our Feet Walk the Sky: Women of the South Asian Diaspora.* San Francisco: Aunt Lute Books

Annu. Rev. Anthropol. 2001. 30:573–96

A BIOARCHAEOLOGICAL PERSPECTIVE ON THE HISTORY OF VIOLENCE

Phillip L. Walker

Department of Anthropology, University of California, Santa Barbara, California 93106;
e-mail: walker@sscf.ucsb.edu

Key Words warfare, archaeology, skeletal trauma, prehistoric homicide

■ **Abstract** Traumatic injuries in ancient human skeletal remains are a direct source of evidence for testing theories of warfare and violence that are not subject to the interpretative difficulties posed by literary creations such as historical records and ethnographic reports. Bioarchaeological research shows that throughout the history of our species, interpersonal violence, especially among men, has been prevalent. Cannibalism seems to have been widespread, and mass killings, homicides, and assault injuries are also well documented in both the Old and New Worlds. No form of social organization, mode of production, or environmental setting appears to have remained free from interpersonal violence for long.

INTRODUCTION

Injuries and deaths caused by interpersonal violence are a major worldwide health problem. Such violence occurs in many different social situations, ranging from attacks by serial killers on strangers to the highly organized bombing raids of multinational government coalitions. In the United States, injuries and deaths from gang warfare and spousal abuse are viewed as health problems of epidemic proportions, and violence is the leading cause of premature death among young adults (Cornwell et al 1995, Whitman et al 1996).

What have anthropologists contributed to our understanding of the causes and cultural correlates of violence? A survey of the anthropological literature shows that in spite of its social and economic significance, few anthropologists have focused on this topic (Ferguson 1997, p. 344; Krohn-Hansen 1994). As Keeley (1996) points out, the contribution of anthropologists to our understanding of the causes of violent conflict in earlier, nonindustrialized societies (an area of great theoretical significance that we are ideally positioned to explore) is miniscule in comparison to the vast literature historians and sociologists have generated in their explorations of warfare and violence in modern industrialized societies. This is unfortunate because anthropology's broad, cross-cultural, historical perspective has the potential to yield key insights into the complex web of

0084-6570/01/1021-0573$14.00

intricately related biological and sociocultural factors that shape our modern violent propensities.

Among anthropologists, bioarchaeologists are ideally positioned to explore the causes of violence in earlier societies. Human remains from archaeological sites are a unique source of data on the environmental, economic, and social factors that predispose people to both violent conflict and peaceful coexistence. The controversy over the effects that expansion of Western societies had on patterns of warfare in non-Western cultures provides a good example of bioarchaeology's relevance. Some anthropologists believe that patterns of warfare documented by ethnohistorians and ethnographers in formerly "isolated" non-Western societies of the New World and elsewhere are a reflection not so much of precontact cultural patterns as of the social disruption and economic inequalities created by the trade goods and diseases that inevitably accompany contact with Westerners (Dunnell 1991, Ferguson 1995, Walker 2001b). From this perspective, the warfare historically documented in modern non-Western societies is little more than a reflection of the violent competition and insatiable desire for the accumulation of material wealth that taints the modern world. Some researchers consequently dismiss the ethnographic and ethnohistoric records as largely irrelevant to understanding earlier patterns of violence and speculate that the warfare that did exist in premodern societies was a rarely deadly, typically ineffective, ritualized form of culturally mediated dispute resolution designed to efficiently maintain social boundaries while minimizing fatalities. Although there are those who strongly disagree with the factual basis of this neo-Rousseauian view of premodern passivity (Keeley 1996), it is an argument that resonates with many people and is difficult to counter without reference to bioarchaeological data from our distant, preindustrial past.

Skeletal studies have the potential to greatly expand our understanding of the human potential for both violent and nonviolent behavior. Historical documents and ethnographic records provide a narrow view of the spectrum of human capacities for selfless kindness and utter cruelty. The number of historically documented groups is minuscule in comparison to the enormous number of extinct societies for which we have no written records. When historical descriptions of warfare and violence are available, it is difficult (some say impossible) to disentangle their factual basis from the observer's cultural biases concerning this highly emotionally and politically charged aspect of life. Human skeletal remains, in contrast, provide direct evidence of interpersonal violence in both prehistoric and historically documented societies that, in many respects, is immune to the interpretive difficulties posed by literary sources (Walker 1997, 2001b). Several flint arrow points embedded in a person's spine are not symbolic constructs (Figure 1, see color insert). They say something indisputable about physical interactions that occurred between those bones and those stones. Of course, an infinite number of more-or-less likely alternative explanations could be given for such injuries (homicide, burial ritual, hunting accident, scientific hoax, extraterrestrial intervention, and so on), but the fact remains that the vertebrae have arrow points embedded in them. A single piece of evidence such as this concerning past human behavior has limited evidentiary value. However, when many such examples are assembled and viewed within their larger archaeological and paleoecological context, it is possible to greatly constrain the range of plausible alternative behavioral explanations. Through such laborious bioarchaeological research, we can gradually obtain a better, more-useful understanding of the violence that afflicts the modern world.

DEFINITION OF VIOLENCE

Evaluating skeletal evidence of ancient violence is made difficult by both the technical problems of interpreting injuries and some fundamental definitional issues related to the distinction between accidental and intentional injuries. In medicine, "injury" means the damage or wound caused by trauma, and "trauma" refers to an accidental or inflicted injury caused by "harsh contact with the environment" (Stedman 1982). Although seemingly straightforward in their reference to physical damage, the concepts of trauma and injury are often extended to encompass psychological as well as physical injuries.

The distinction commonly made between accidental and intentional traumatic injuries is even more problematic because of the causal implication of human malevolence. Accidental injuries are those caused by unplanned events that happen unexpectedly. The concept of "violent injury," on the other hand, often carries with it, in its vernacular use, the implication of human intentionality. This seemingly clear-cut causal distinction can easily become obscured. Although most people use "violence" to imply a harmful interaction between people (i.e., "interpersonal" violence), epidemiologists show little concern for this fundamental distinction and typically include accidental deaths along with homicides and suicides in their classificatory schemes under the heading of "violent injuries" (Holinger 1987; Lancaster 1990, p. 341; Murray & Lopez 1996).

Even if we can agree that a key element of any definition of violence is that it refers, as in some international human rights statements (United Nations 1993), to the behavior of people relative to each other in ways that are likely to cause personal harm or injury, there is room for argument over the degree of intentionality required for an act of violence to have occurred. For example, it can be argued that all injuries resulting from the marginalization of one group by another through territorial expansion, social dominance, or economic exploitation meet the definition of violence if the dominant groups shows callus disregard for the safety and physical well-being of the people they have marginalized.

There is also the problem of cultural contingency: The term violence means different things in different cultures and even to members of the same culture (Krohn-Hansen 1994). In many societies, beating children and spouses to discipline them is socially sanctioned because it is considered beneficial, not harmful, to the recipients of the beatings. On the other hand, it is common in the social sciences and humanities to expand the concept of violence to embrace "any unjust or cruel state of affairs or maltreatment of another human being" (Straus 1999).

Because of the limited physical evidence available to document interpersonal violence in earlier societies, there are few opportunities to make subtle distinctions such as these in bioarchaeological studies. Instead, the complex array of behaviors that result in accidental and intentional injuries is reduced to skeletal remains or occasionally mummified tissues and the archaeological context within which these human remains are found. Owing to these evidentiary limitations, it is wise to restrict use of the term violent injury in bioarchaeology to skeletal injuries for which there is strong circumstantial evidence of malevolent intent (e.g., the presence of several arrow points embedded in the skeleton of a man in a mass grave with other injured young men whose skulls show cutmarks consistent with scalping) and to reserve the term accidental injury for cases lacking such clear evidence of malevolent intent.

INTERPRETING SKELETAL INJURIES

Traumatic injuries are some of most common pathological conditions seen in human skeletons. Osseous changes associated with trauma include unhealed fractures, calluses from old injuries, remodeling subsequent to joint dislocations, and the ossifications that occur within injured muscles, tendons, and the connective tissue sheath (periosteum) that encapsulates bones. Interpreting this evidence of ancient trauma requires a complicated decision-making process (Figure 2). Of great significance from a behavioral perspective is distinguishing among injuries suffered before death (antemortem), around the time of death (perimortem), and after death (postmortem) through soil movement and other site formation processes. Antemortem and perimortem injuries are of considerable anthropological interest because of the implications they have for human behavior.

Antemortem fractures are comparatively easy to identify because the well-defined callus of new bone that usually forms around the fracture persists long after the trauma that produced it (Figure 3, see color insert). If a fracture shows no signs of healing, it is safe to say that it is either a perimortem injury, postmortem damage caused by site-formation processes, or postrecovery damage from archaeological excavation or museum curation. It is comparatively easy for a well-trained osteologist to distinguish fractures that occurred long after death from perimortem injuries. Fractures in the bones of the living and recently dead tend to propagate at an acute angle to the bone's surface in a pattern comparable to that seen in other plastic materials (Figure 4, see color insert). After death, collagen loss makes a bone much more brittle. As a result, breaks in old bones caused by soil movement and other site-formation processes tend to propagate at right angles to the bone's surface, like those seen in a broken piece of chalk (Villa & Mahieu 1991) (Figure 5, see color insert). Often, postmortem fractures in old bones also can be identified because of a color difference between the bone's surface (usually darker) and that of the area exposed by the fracture (usually lighter). This surface

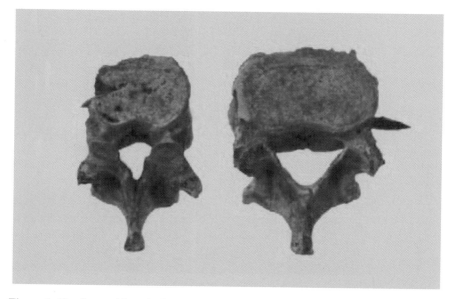

Figure 1 Vertebrae with embedded arrow points from a prehistoric homicide victim from a southern California site (Ven-110). The trajectories of the arrows indicate that someone standing behind her shot this woman in the back.

Figure 3 Well-healed fracture calluses on the ribs of a modern American woman who was chronically beaten by her husband and eventually killed by him.

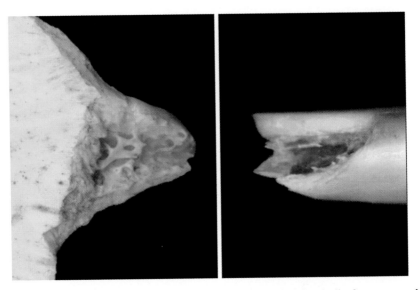

Figure 4 Perimortem fractures. (*Left*) Fracture in the base of the skull of a woman who received massive cranial trauma when she was hit by a railroad train. Note oblique angle of fracture. (*Right*) Perimortem fracture in the shaft of an infant's leg bone (tibia) received during a fatal beating. The helical shape of this spiral fracture is typical of child abuse cases.

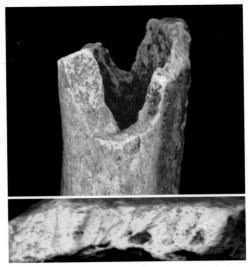

Figure 5 Postmortem fracture in the shaft of a femur that occurred long after death. Note that the bone fractured at right angles to the surface instead of obliquely. The parallel lines in the fractured surface (*upper left*) are from rodent gnawing (*bottom inset*: enlargement of this area). The superimposition of the tooth marks upon an old break shows that the gnawing occurred long after death.

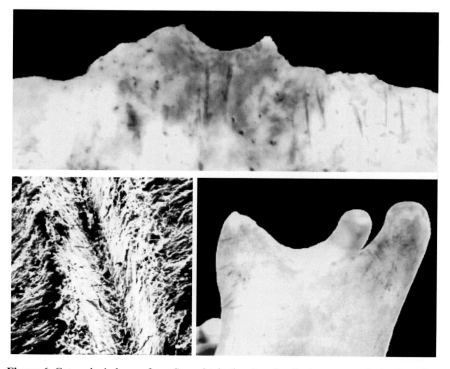

Figure 6 Cutmarks in bones from Saunaktuk, the site of an Inuit massacre in the Canadian arctic. (*Top*) Vertical lines are decapitation cutmarks in the base of the skull of a child. The facture line at the top was made with a heavy bladed tool, which was used to chop off the back of the child's head. This was probably done after decapitation. (*Lower right*) Cutmarks on the mandible of an adult from the same site in areas of muscle attachment. (*Lower left*) Scanning electron microscope image of one of the cutmarks showing a straight-sided groove typical of those made by metal tools.

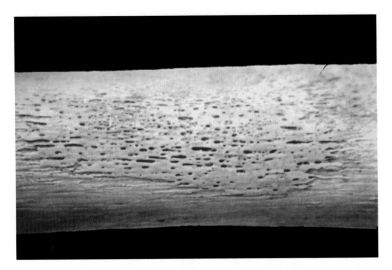

Figure 7 Area of subperiosteal new bone formation on the fibula of a child who was chronically beaten and eventually killed by her parents. Plaques of new bone such as this form through calcification of blood that accumulates in traumatized areas under the connective tissue sheath that covers bones. The well-defined margins and porosities indicate that the injury was in the process of healing at the time of death.

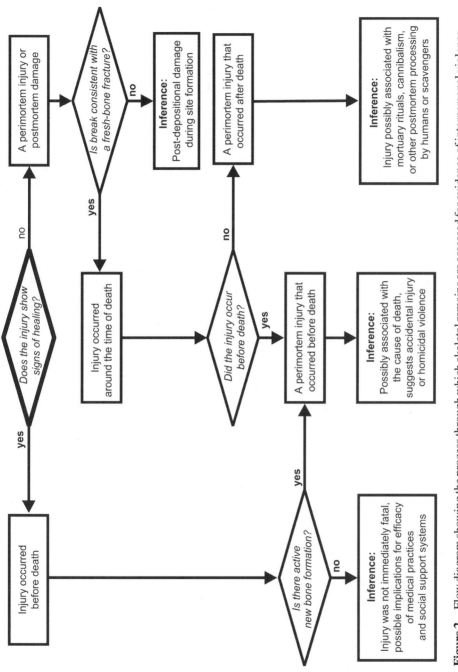

Figure 2   Flow diagram showing the process through which skeletal remains are assessed for evidence of interpersonal violence.

discoloration, which is produced through prolonged contact with the surrounding soil, makes it possible to distinguish cutmarks made around the time of death by weapons or other tools from damage that occurred long after death, such as during archaeological excavation or museum curation (Frayer 1997, White & Toth 1989).

Signs of healing, of course, are unequivocal evidence that the injury occurred before death. Osseous responses to injury, however, are not immediate. In forensic work on modern trauma victims, it is often possible to differentiate antemortem-perimortem and postmortem-perimortem injuries because there is little bleeding around antemortem injuries sustained after the heart stops beating. Although staining from decomposed blood is sometimes seen in ancient mummified remains, the absence of such evidence in most archaeological situations means that fractures in the bones of the living and recently dead are essentially identical in appearance. It may be impossible, for instance, to decide if a perimortem cranial fracture is the result of a lethal blow to the head or rough treatment of the corpse after death. Although such issues sometimes cannot be resolved, the type of perimortem injury is often telling. A skeleton riddled with arrow wounds strongly suggests malevolent intent, even if some of the injuries were inflicted posthumously as a gesture of disrespect.

Reconstructing the behavioral implications of antemortem and perimortem injuries is a two-stage process (Lovell 1997). First, the proximate, or most direct cause of the injury needs to be considered. The mechanical properties of bone are well known, and these, along with clinical experience and common sense, provide a basis for reconstructing the mechanical cause of an injury. The diagnostic features of fractures produced by blunt objects, bladed weapons, and high-velocity projectiles are the focus of much forensic work, and principals guiding their interpretation are well understood (Spitz 1993). After the range of probable proximate causes is delimited, a second, more-difficult analytical phase aimed at reconstructing the cultural context of an injury can begin. This search for the injury's "ultimate cause" requires detailed consideration of both intrinsic biological variables, such as age and sex, and extrinsic factors, relating to the physical and sociocultural context. Considering an injury from a population perspective is essential. When viewed in isolation, a person's injuries often are open to many different interpretations. However, if the same injuries are seen in many of the person's colleagues, a likely behavioral explanation is often suggested.

Arcane technical issues surrounding the interpretation of injuries such as those just discussed can be of great interpretive significance. For example, most people now believe that misidentification of carnivore activity and postmortem damage as lethal perimortem blows led the famous paleontologist Raymond Dart to construct a dismal, culturally influential image of our early australopithecine ancestors as vicious predators (Cartmill 1993). Based on his osteological studies, Dart (1953, p. 209) concluded that the earliest humans were

> confirmed killers: carnivorous creatures that seized living quarries by violence, battered them to death, tore apart their broken bodies, dismembered them

limb from limb, slaking their ravenous thirst with the hot blood of victims and greedily devouring livid writhing flesh.

Evaluating such claims within the broadest possible frame of reference is a key element of the bioarchaeological method. An individual's injuries are often open to multiple, sometimes even paradoxical interpretations (e.g., violent death and dismemberment vs. veneration of the deceased through careful preparation of their cleansed bones for afterlife adventures). However, when viewed within their larger archaeological and paleoecological context in conjunction with a large number of such instances, many previously viable alternative explanations become increasingly improbable.

This approach of progressively developing more and more contextual information so that the number of reasonable alternative hypotheses can gradually be reduced is well illustrated by a series of recent studies of scattered, highly fragmented collections of ancient human bones from the American Southwest. Although such collections have been reported for many years, they were typically dismissed as residues from secondary burial or carnivore activity. More recently, detailed bioarchaeological studies have been conducted that place these collections within a broader, more-informative archaeological context. In his meticulous analysis of osteological material from the Mancos site, White (1992) demonstrated a clear correspondence between the pattern of cutmarks, percussion damage, fractures, burning, and body part representation in a collection of highly fragmented human remains and the damage pattern present in associated faunal remains discarded as refuse from culinary activities. Several similar collections have been described that show the same pattern of massive perimortem breakage and percussion damage with evidence of subsequent processing, cutmarks, and burning that strongly suggest consumption of human flesh by other humans (Billman et al 2000, Turner & Turner 1999).

The gustatory motivations for such harsh treatment of the dead have been doubted, and alternative hypotheses, including "witch destruction," have been offered as alternatives to cannibalism (Darling 1998, Dongoske et al 2000, Martin 2000). Although the motivations for treating human corpses like the carcasses of game animals are undoubtedly complex, the inference that human flesh was actually consumed has recently been dramatically reinforced by contextual evidence from an unexpected source. Chemical analysis of human excrement from the Cowboy Wash in the Four Corners area of southwestern Colorado, an area where there is strong osteological evidence for cannibalism at a number of sites, has been shown to contain traces of a myoglobin, a human muscle protein, that could have gotten there only through the ingestion of human flesh (Marlar et al 2000). These studies provide an excellent example of the power of the bioarchaeological approach to understanding the human past: Through the progressive accumulation of evidence from disparate sources, it is possible to gradually bring into clearer focus what really happened during the history of our species.

MODERN INTERPERSONAL VIOLENCE

There is an enormous modern trauma literature that is directly relevant to understanding the behavioral significance of the injuries seen in ancient skeletal remains. Data on the physical manifestations of modern interpersonal violence provide a baseline against which bioarchaeological evidence for ancient violence can be measured. Although uncritically projecting what we know about modern trauma into the past is potentially misleading, modern trauma patterns do provide a rich source of comparative data that allows ancient injuries to be placed within meaningful behavioral and cultural-historical contexts.

Age and sex are important dimensions of the modern violence pattern. Put simply, the perpetrators and victims of modern assaults tend to be young men. Throughout their lives, men are much more likely than women to suffer from all types of traumatic injuries, especially those associated with interpersonal violence (Baker 1992). Males commit 84% of the assaults in which the victim reports to hospital emergency rooms (Rand & Strom 1997). For homicides committed in the United States between 1976–1992, the median age of the assailant (87% of whom were males) was 20 years and that of the victims (78% of whom were males) was 25 years (Fox 1994). In an exaggerated form, owing to the selectivity of military recruitment practices, the demographic profile of modern warfare mortality parallels that seen in civilian homicides, with a predominance of young male victims in their early twenties: 40% of the German solders killed in World War I were 20–24 years old (Lancaster 1990, p. 330). Recruitment practices also guarantee that male warfare casualty rates exceed those associated with civilian violence. For example, only 9% of the hospital admissions for chest wounds in the recent Yugoslavian conflict were women (Ilic et al 1999).

The social context of civilian violence shows significant sex differences. In 57% of attacks on females, the assailant is a family member or intimate partner. For males, in contrast, only 17% of the attackers are family members or intimate partners (Craven 1997, Rand & Strom 1997). Homicides show the same pattern, with 49% of the females victims killed by relatives or intimate partners and only 15% of the males (Fox 1994). Intimate partner violence contributes importantly to these sex differences. In the United States during 1994, females were five times more likely to be victimized by intimate partners than were males (Craven 1997). For homicides in which the victim-offender relationship was known, an intimate killed 31% of the murdered females and 4% of the murdered males (Craven 1997).

There also appear to be sex-dependent gender differences in homicide patterns (see Walker & Cook 1998). This is suggested by the fact that same-sex homicides account for 6% of all intimate partner homicides committed by men and only 1% of the same-sex intimate partner homicides committed by women (Fox 1994). This is a substantial bias toward greater violence among gay males, even if one considers the demographic surveys that suggest the ratio of male-to-female homosexual couples is about 3:2 (Croes 1996).

Levels of interpersonal violence have varied significantly in modern societies. This is of considerable theoretical interest for bioarchaeologists because of the sampling problems similar temporal variation in earlier societies would pose. Modern accidental and intentional injury rates show clear daily, weekly, and annual oscillations, and of course there are the well-documented outbreaks of intense violence that erupt sporadically owing to widespread warfare and civil unrest. In the United States, homicides are more likely to occur late at night and early in the weekend (Baker 1992, Fox 1994, Swann et al 1981), and there is clear homicide seasonality, with low rates during the inclement winter months and a modest midsummer increase. Homicides also increase during December and January, a phenomenon possibly associated with social activity during the holiday season (Fox 1994). Longer-term trends over a period of decades are especially clear during the twentieth century among nonwhite males in the United States. Homicide rates were low early in the century, began increasing rapidly during the 1920s, and peaked during the economic depression of the early 1930s. After that, they decreased among civilians until World War II, when they increased briefly. During the last half of the twentieth century, homicide rates increased again to reach unprecedented levels (nearly doubling among nonwhite males) during the 1970s and 1980s (Holinger 1987).

Civilian data such as these neglect the important effects of warfare-related deaths. There have been more than 160 wars and armed conflicts since 1945 (Summerfield 1997). Although they are often relatively small in comparison, warfare-related mortality from malnutrition and disease, deaths, and injuries directly related to military activity can cause dramatic short-term increases in trauma among both combatants and civilians (Summerfield 1997, Toole 1995, Toole & Waldman 1993).

Such short-term fluctuations in violence are problematic from a bioarchaeological point of view. Episodes of mass killing may leave few traces in the archaeological record because systematic disposal of the dead is often impossible, and sometimes even actively prevented, during times of widespread social unrest. On the other hand, the discovery of mass graves of war dead can inflate the evidence we have for violence. Seasonal cycles of violence-associated patterns of economic or ceremonial activity can also be problematic because of their potential to create a distorted picture of violence in mobile groups that use different cemeteries on a seasonal basis. Most cemeteries, however, contain the comingled remains of people who died in various seasons over a period of decades, if not centuries. This is an important impediment to the documentation of prehistoric violence because short-term fluctuations are obscured by the long time spans and low temporal resolution that characterizes most archaeological skeletal collections.

MODERN ASSAULT INJURY PATTERNS

The injury patterns documented in the clinical literature provide revealing analogies that can help us understand the behavioral implications of similar injuries in the past. Modern clinical research is also of great relevance to the fundamental methodological issue of distinguishing between ancient accidental and intentional injuries. Fortunately, the location of an injury often provides a clue to its cause. For example, anthropologists commonly refer to fractures of the ulnar shaft as "parry fractures" because they frequently occur when an assault victim raises his forearm to deflect a blow to the head. Fractures of the distal radius near the wrist, in contrast, are much less likely to be assault injuries. They often occur when the arms are thrust forward to break an accidental fall. The problem with such causal inferences is that the same types of skeletal injuries can be produced by both accidental and intentional trauma. Parry fractures are not always assault injuries; sometimes accidental twisting of the arm breaks the ulna (Lovell 1997). Thus we cannot simply assume without additional supporting contextual information that similar injuries in ancient skeletons reflect interpersonal violence.

Modern civilian morbidity and mortality reports reveal some clear interpersonal violence-related injury patterns that might be echoed in earlier societies. A Department of Justice study of the people admitted to U.S. hospital emergency departments during 1994 provides a good overview of the assault injuries currently suffered by people in the United States (Rand & Strom 1997). For the most part, these assault injuries (58.4%) did not involve weapons. Nineteen percent were inflicted with an object, such as a rock or a stick, that an assailant held or threw. Modern assault victims show a distinctive distribution of skeletal injuries with high facial trauma rates (Walker 1997). In a study of 539 adult English assault victims, facial injury accounted for 83% of all fractures, 66% of all lacerations, and 53% of all hematomas (Shepherd et al 1990). Of the victims, 26% sustained at least one fracture, and nasal fractures were the most frequently observed skeletal injury (27%). The upper limb was the next most common injury site (14% of all injuries). These injuries most often resulted from assaults involving punching (72%) and kicking (42%). Only 6% of the victims received knife wounds. Broken drinking glasses, a weapon apparently favored by inebriated English pub patrons, produced a surprisingly large proportion (11%) of the injuries.

Although modern assailants of both men and women appear to intentionally target the face, in England at least, women are much more likely than men to sustain fractured facial bones that would be detectable archaeologically (Shepherd et al 1988). In a study of 294 consecutive assault victims, 15% of whom were women, a significantly higher proportion of the women (56%) than the men (26%) had facial fractures ($x^2 = 7.8$, $p = 0.005$). The reasons for this higher rate in females are unclear; it could reflect either sex differences in facial bone strength or culturally conditioned, gender-related differences in the severity of beatings. Whatever their cause, such differences show that the frequency of skeletal injuries seen in archaeological materials may sometimes be related in a somewhat indirect way to the actual frequency of assaults.

The question of why the face and especially the nose are targeted by modern assailants is an interesting one. Archaeological data suggest that this nasal fixation is not a genetically programmed human universal but instead is highly culturally contingent. It seems likely that the ritualized, socially sanctioned fighting that occurs in such sports as boxing influences the assault patterns seen in the larger society outside of the sports arena (Walker 1997). This hypothesis is supported by coroner records from England that show a striking correlation between the rise of modern boxing and an increase in the proportion of homicides caused by hitting and kicking (Walker 1997, p. 171). Thus offensive techniques learned through viewing and participating in violent sports may shape in important ways the patterns of violence seen outside of this highly ritualized context.

The major consequences technological change can have for patterns of interpersonal violence are abundantly documented in the modern trauma literature. Many people attribute the marked increase in U.S. homicides during the late 1980s, especially among the young, to increased availability and use of firearms (MMWR 1996). This trend is paralleled by less-frequent use of knives for homicides (Fox 1994). Such changes can sometimes be abrupt. In Durban, South Africa, the ratio of fatal stab wounds to gunshot wounds reversed within the 5-year period between 1987 and 1992. Between 1985 and 1995, stab wounds declined by 30% and gunshot wounds increased by more than 800% (Muckart et al 1995). Comparable, technology-related changes have recently been documented in remote areas of highland Papua New Guinea, where an earlier pattern of direct confrontation with bushknives and axes has been replaced, with devastating results, by increased use of bows and arrows and firearms (Mathew 1996).

The apparent propensity of British drinkers to use drinking glasses as weapons (Shepherd et al 1990, p. 76) underscores the role that cultural factors can have in determining weapon choice and also, to some extent, the patterning of assault injuries (Walker 1997). Another example is the apparent tendency of police to avoid hitting the faces of their victims because of the public sanctions such highly visible injuries might stimulate (Aalund et al 1990). Cultural sensitivity of this kind can also be seen among Chinese gang members, who prefer knives to guns in certain situations. When attacking other gang members, they use long knives and make multiple lacerations, or "chops," in the flesh of their victims instead of stabbing them (Yip et al 1997). Often the intention is to wound rather than kill. The massive cranial trauma associated with the recent adoption of the baseball bat as a weapon of choice for certain types of urban violence is another example of a highly culturally contingent violence pattern (Berlet et al 1992, Groleau et al 1993, Ord & Benian 1995).

The social context of an assault clearly influences the weapon an assailant selects. A Massachusetts study, for instance, shows that knives are more likely to be used as weapons during arguments with acquaintances and that firearms are more likely to be used against strangers (MMWR 1995). My analysis (P. L. Walker, unpublished observations) of U.S. homicide reports (Fox 1994) reveals significant differences between ethnic groups in the weapon selected for killing spouses that cannot be readily explained by weapon availability, given the household context that is typical for such murders. Between 1976–1992, the weapon of choice for Native American women who killed their spouses was a knife (46% of all such homicides). Native American men, in contrast, rarely killed spouses with knives (20% of all such homicides); they usually used firearms (40%). Among Americans of European ancestry, a different pattern is seen, with firearms the weapon of choice for spouse killings by both men (56%) and women (67%).

One important lesson for bioarchaeologists from the modern trauma literature is that most assaults cause soft-tissue injuries that would not be detected in ancient skeletal material. Only 16.6% of the assault injuries in the United States are classified as "muscular/skeletal" (Rand & Strom 1997), and many of these would not be observable in archaeological remains. An additional 5% involve gunshots, but a large proportion of these projectiles only wound soft tissue. According to my calculations, in frontal view, a person's skeleton occupies about 60% of the target area a body presents to an assailant. This means that about half of the time a projectile randomly shot at a person would not impact bone. Thus, we can safely assume that the frequency of injuries detected in ancient skeletal remains is just the "tip of the iceberg" in terms of the actual incidence of injuries.

ASSAULTING THE MYTH OF OUR PACIFISTIC PAST

Considering the many methodological problems I have described, what can we say based on currently available data about the prevalence of violence in earlier societies? First, it is fair to say that there has been a historical bias toward overreporting spectacular cases, such as skulls with embedded projectile points, gaping saber wounds, and gruesome scalping marks. People seem to have a deep-seated fascination with violence, especially if the victim was a stranger (thus the enormous popularity of cinéma-vérité television shows featuring emergency rooms and trauma victims). This prurient interest perhaps explains in part the impressive number of paleopathological case reports devoted to describing the wounds of individual trauma victims (Elerick & Tyson 1997). This "case" approach to the documentation of ancient violence dominated the field of paleopathology during most of the twentieth century and reflects the diagnostic interests and lack of population perspective of the physicians who did much of this earlier work. These problems of possible overreporting and lack of a population perspective mean that most of the paleopathological literature provides little basis for estimating the prevalence of past violence. We know that throughout the prehistoric world, many people died at the hands of others, but almost nowhere are data available for even roughly estimating how the frequency of such assaults varied through space and time (Walker 1997).

In spite of these limitations, case reports do have much to teach us about the history of human aggression. They show us that the roots of interpersonal violence penetrate deep into the evolutionary history of our species. Bones bearing cutmarks inflicted by other humans are surprisingly common considering the paucity of early hominid remains. The anatomical position of stone tool marks on the cheekbone of a Plio-Pleistocene specimen from the Sterkfontein site in South Africa suggests that they were inflicted by someone who cut through this person's muscles during the process of removing the jaw from the rest of the head (Pickering et al 2000).

Similar marks on the forehead of one of the earliest members of our species show that as early as 600,000 years ago, people living at the Bodo site in Ethiopia were defleshing the heads of other people (White 1986). The number of such specimens is small, and the limitations of associated contextual information make it difficult to determine what motivated this early practice of cutting into the flesh of the dead; cannibalism, anatomical curiosity, and ritual manipulation of body parts are all possibilities.

Speculation over the extent to which early humans killed and consumed each other has long been a part of the anthropological literature. In the 1930s, Franz Weidenreich suggested, based on the abundance of cranial vaults with fractured bases and the paucity of infra-cranial remains, that *Homo erectus* specimens from the Zhoukoudien site were the victims of brain extraction during cannibal feasts (Weidenreich 1943). This evidence of cannibalism has always been controversial, and the ongoing dispute will be difficult to resolve because many of the original specimens were lost during World War II. Some prehistorians still accept Weidenreich's evidence as compelling (Lanpo & Weiwen 1990, Walpoff 1996), whereas others have reinterpreted the condition of the Zhoukoudien bones as postmortem damage from porcupine gnawing and other site formation process (Binford & Ho 1985, Binford & Stone 1986).

By the Middle Paleolithic, evidence of skeletal trauma increases markedly, perhaps in part because of the availability of much larger skeletal samples. Healed fractures are especially common among the Neanderthals. Many of these injuries appear to have been accidental and perhaps are explained by the dangers of a predatory adaptation that involved hunting big game with simple tools (Berger & Trinkaus 1995, Gardner 2001, Richards et al 2000, Trinkaus & Zimmerman 1982). Some of these injuries may also be a result of interpersonal violence. Although no bones have been found with embedded points or undisputed weapon wounds, one early *Homo sapiens* specimen from Israel (Skhul IX) has a perimortem injury suggestive of a lethal attack: A spear was thrust through the upper leg and into the pelvic cavity (McCown & Keith 1939).

Cutmarks and other signs of postmortem processing possibly associated with cannibalism have been reported in several collections of Neanderthal remains. The tool marks on a few of these specimens can be explained in much less dramatic, noncannibalistic ways. Scratches on the cranium of the Engis 2 child thought by some to be cutmarks (Russell & Lemort 1986) appear instead to be recent damage from the tools used to prepare and measure the specimen (White & Toth 1989). Since its discovery more than 50 years ago, the isolated Circeo I cranium from Guattari Cave with its damaged base and purported faunal associations has traditionally been viewed as an example of a Neanderthal mortuary ritual involving brain extraction. Recent reexamination of this specimen along with new studies of the associated faunal assemblage, however, suggests that spotted hyenas are most likely responsible for the condition of the skull (Stiner 1991, White & Toth 1991).

It is also important to remember that even in cases where a strong case for cannibalism can be shown, this does not necessarily mean that someone was murdered to obtain their flesh. Although rare, ritual consumption of portions of the bodies of people who died from natural causes has been reported ethnographically, and the phenomenon of starvation cannibalism among famine victims is a well-documented modern phenomenon (Keenleyside et al 1997, Petrinovich 2000).

The earliest evidence of European cannibalism comes from 800,000-year-old human remains recovered at the Spanish site of Atapuerca. The Atapuerca skeletons are highly fragmented and are scored with cutmarks that have been interpreted as evidence of decapitation and defleshing (Fernandez-Jalvo et al 1999). Some of the long bones show perimortem damage consistent with marrow extraction, and the entire human bone assemblage appears to have been treated like food refuse. The cutmarks and fragmentary condition of the Krapina Neanderthal remains from Croatia have often been interpreted as evidence of cannibalism (Gorjanovíc-Kramberger 1906, Ullrich 1978). Others suggest that Neanderthal morticians could have made the cutmarks and attribute the fractures to nonhuman causes, such as natural rock falls or excavation damage (Russell 1987a,b; Trinkaus 1985). The evidence for Neanderthal cannibalism has been greatly strengthened through recent studies of the spatial distributions, tool marks, and skeletal element frequencies on human and animal remains from Moula-Guercy, a French cave site. These studies show strikingly similar patterns of perimortem damage that suggest both the human and the ungulate bones deposited at the site are food refuse (Defleur et al 1999). Bones from La Baume Fontebregoua, a French Neolithic site, show a similar correspondence between fragmentary human remains and faunal collections of food refuse (Villa 1992, Villa et al 1986). These data suggest that the practice of cannibalism was not confined to Neanderthals. Instead, it seems to have persisted through the transition from hunting and gathering to farming.

By Mesolithic times, evidence of mortal injuries strongly suggestive of homicide begins to increase markedly. This is in part a by-product of increased use of bows and arrows, a weapon whose small points embed securely in a victim's bone (Figure 1). When multiple arrow wounds are present, it is unmistakably evidence of homicide (e.g. Boule & Vallois 1937).

Ofnet, a 7720-year-old Mesolithic site in Bavaria, provides the first clear evidence of mass murder (Frayer 1997). The Ofnet collection consists of 38 skulls. Many of these show beveled fractures at the back of the head that strongly suggest perimortem bludgeoning. There is no evidence of cannibalism and few indications of butchering. However, decapitation is suggested by perimortem cutmarks on many of the cervical vertebrae recovered with the skulls. This evidence of mass killing among hunter-gatherers is important because it shows that the development of sedentary agricultural communities is not a prerequisite for organized, large-scale, homicidal activity. It seems clear that Mesolithic hunter-gatherers, like their modern counterparts (e.g Knauft 1987), sometimes lived in societies where fear of becoming a homicide victim was a fact of everyday life.

A recent survey of traumatic injuries in ancient Italy shows some interesting post-Mesolithic trends (Robb 1997). Although the samples are small, clear changes can be seen between the Neolithic and Iron Age. Cranial injuries, which in modern-day people are often a result of interpersonal violence, and infra-cranial injuries, which are more often associated with occupational activity, follow different trajectories. The frequency of infra-cranial injuries increased over time. Cranial injuries, in contrast, were common during the Neolithic, diminished during the Eneolithic, and increased again during the Bronze and Iron ages. The high frequency of cranial injuries among Neolithic farmers is interesting because it is at odds with the traditional view of Neolithic Italians as peaceful compared with later groups, whose iconography glorifies weapons and male warriors (Robb 1997). In other words, the cultural celebration of violence seems to have had an inverse relationship to its frequency.

Probing the antiquity of the modern hegemonic position of men as both the perpetrators and the victims of interpersonal violence is made difficult by the technical problems of accurate sex determination (Walker 1995), and the small sizes of earlier collections, which, when partitioned by sex, often prove inadequate for statistical comparisons. The Ofnet material is interesting in this regard because it is the earliest collection of homicide victims from a single site that is large enough for meaningful demographic analysis. Women and children predominate among the massacre victims. This could be interpreted in several ways: The bodies of men could have been disposed of elsewhere, they could have escaped, or they could have been away from their families at the time of the attack. This last scenario fits well with the pattern seen in the skeletal remains from Saunaktuk, an Inuvialuit (Eskimo) village in the Canadian artic that contains the bones of many women and children with perimortem injuries, which suggests violent death, dismemberment, and probable cannibalism (Walker 1990) (Figure 6, see color insert). The Inuvialuit have recorded this incident in oral histories that describe an attack by Dene (Indians) that occurred when most of the Inuvialuit men were away hunting whales. During the attack, the people who remained at the village are said to have been tortured in various ways before being slaughtered (Melbye & Fairgrieve 1994).

When ancient collections from large geographical areas and spans of time are pooled, the modern pattern of more male traumatic injuries begins to emerge. Angel (1974) pooled 11 samples from the eastern Mediterranean ranging in age from the early Neolithic to recent times and found a tendency for females to have fewer fractures throughout, especially of the head and neck. Robb (1997) has done a similar survey of Italian collections. He found that after the Neolithic period, the frequency of male cranial trauma increases markedly over that of females, and by the Iron age, trauma of all kinds was much more common among males than females (Robb 1997). Robb concludes that these injury patterns are not a direct result of violence in warfare; instead, he attributes them to the development of gender roles that prescribed violent behavior for males and reinforced a sexual division of labor in which women were not expected to perform activities considered heavy or dangerous, including warfare.

PREHISTORIC NATIVE AMERICAN VIOLENCE

It could be argued that these data suggesting a long history of mass killing, homicide, and male-dominated interpersonal violence in the Old World have little relevance to the question of the effects European contact had on patterns of Native American warfare and violence. After their arrival in the New World, Native Americans could have evolved their own, less-violent, culturally mediated systems for dispute resolution that diverged significantly from the pathological trajectory followed by Western societies. Fortunately, there are many large, well-studied, New World collections directly relevant to this issue.

The 9000-year-old Kennewick find, one of the earliest Native American skeletons, has a large leaf-shaped projectile point, probably propelled by a spear thrower, healed into the bone of his pelvis as well as a small, well-healed cranial fracture (Chatters 2000). Although it is conceivable that both of these injuries were accidental, interpersonal violence is a much more likely interpretation of the spear-thrower wound. Similar injuries, including embedded points and cranial injuries, have been found in other early Native American remains (Dickel et al 1988; J. Chatters, personal communication). These data suggest that the first Americans brought with them patterns of violence similar to those documented in contemporaneous Old World populations, and that those patterns persisted despite low population densities and the availability of vast expanses of uninhabited land.

Archaic period (ca. 6000–500 BC) skeletal collections from western Tennessee provide additional evidence of interpersonal violence among early New World populations. Embedded projectile points, cutmarks, and missing bones suggest that homicide, scalping, decapitation, and forearm-trophy taking were common practices among these early hunter-gatherers (Smith 1997). Out of 439 interments from the Kentucky Lake Reservoir sample, 10 individuals, all males, show evidence of warfare-related interpersonal violence, including 6 people, mostly from one site, with embedded projectile points. At one cemetery, 20.4% of the people show evidence of perimortem violence. This figure includes six people apparently killed in a massacre, whose bodies were haphazardly thrown into a mass grave.

The prevalence of wounds inflicted by clubs, spears, and arrows clearly shows that levels of prehistoric Native American violence varied both regionally and through time. This is consistent with ethnographic evidence of marked tribal differences in warfare patterns. Many of the tribes of central California, for example, practiced highly ritualized forms of combat, with special weapons and rules remunerating injured opponents, that minimized fatalities; others, such as the Mojave, are well known ethnographically for their cultural emphasis on lethal conflict (Kroeber 1925, McCorkle 1978, Stewart 1947).

Bioarchaeological studies of patterns of interpersonal violence among native Californians clearly show that such differences have considerable time depth. The low frequency of cranial injuries in prehistoric central Californians (2.7%–3.5% of adults affected) is different from the extremely high frequency seen in roughly contemporaneous people living in the Santa Barbara Channel area, where 17% have antemortem cranial injuries (Jurmain & Bellifemine 1997, Lambert 1997, Walker & Thornton 2001). Patterns of violence seem to have varied even within a single region. For example, in the Santa Barbara Channel area, nonlethal cranial injuries are more common on the Channel Islands than on the mainland. This may be the result of a ritualized form of dispute resolution that evolved because conflict avoidance through population movement is not feasible for geographically circumscribed island populations (Walker 1989).

Levels of violence in the Santa Barbara Channel area varied significantly through time. Nonlethal cranial injuries and lethal projectile wounds gradually increased in frequency with the growth of the coastal population. Their frequency peaked during the Middle period and then appears to have declined somewhat thereafter (Lambert 1994, 1997; Walker et al 1996) (Figure 1). The age and sex distributions of people with fatal projectile point wounds is similar to that seen in modern homicide victims, with nearly 20% of the 15- to 26-year-old males having projectile point injuries (Lambert 1997, p. 96).

Although the causes of the exceptionally high rates of Middle period violence are undoubtedly complex, with many different cultural, historical, and ecological dimensions, there is strong evidence that resource stress was a significant factor. Paleopathological data show that living conditions declined markedly at the end of the Middle period in the Channel Island area (Lambert 1993, Walker & Lambert 1989). This was a time of climatic instability and drought-induced increases in competition over resources throughout the western United States (Jones et al 1999, Walker & Lambert 1989). Throughout California there is archaeological evidence of population movement, reorganization of trade networks, and increased warfare during the Middle period (Moratto & Fredrickson 1984, pp. 213–14, 564; Walker & Lambert 1989).

Another potentially significant variable is the introduction of the bow and arrow, which began to replace spears and spear throwers in warfare throughout California beginning around AD 500 (Moratto & Fredrickson 1984). The bow and arrow has a greater killing distance than the spear thrower and is well suited for use in raiding and ambush attacks. Its introduction would have created a short-term disequilibrium in offensive capabilities and consequent social disruptions, comparable to those seen among modern tribal societies with the introduction of firearms (e.g., Mathew 1996).

Bioarchaeological studies of warfare and violence in late prehistoric period Native American communities in the eastern United States show inter- and infraregional variation in levels of violence, similar to those documented in California (Kuemin Drews 2001, Smith 2001). At some sites, there is little or no evidence of interpersonal violence, whereas at others, a significant proportion of the burials appear to be those of homicide victims. For example, an analysis of 264 burials from an Oneota cemetery in Illinois dating to about AD 1300 suggest that chronic warfare caused at least one third of all adult deaths (Milner et al 1991).

Data from other fourteenth-century sites show that this was a time of extreme violence. Excavations at Crow Creek, a large palisaded village site on the Missouri River, uncovered the remains of at least 486 victims of a mass killing dating to AD 1325 (Willey & Emerson 1993). The bones of men, women, and children are present, and nearly 95% of the intact skulls bear scalping marks. Many of these victims were decapitated and dismembered. The conclusion that this massacre was a result of intervillage warfare is reinforced by ongoing research that has produced evidence of similar massacres at two fourteenth-century villages within striking range of Crow Creek (Pringle 1998).

CONCLUSIONS

What have we learned from bioarchaeological studies of these hapless victims of ancient violence? The first, and perhaps most painful, lesson is one of human equality. Everywhere we probe into the history of our species we find evidence of a similar pattern of behavior: People have always been capable of both kindness and extreme cruelty. The search for an earlier, less-violent way to organize our social affairs has been fruitless. All the evidence suggests that peaceful periods have always been punctuated by episodes of warfare and violence. As far as we know, there are no forms of social organization, modes of production, or environmental settings that remain free from interpersonal violence for long.

On the other hand, the many obvious differences between patterns of modern and ancient violence should be of considerable theoretical interest to anthropologists. The technologies we have created to maim and kill each other have gradually advanced from stones and spears, which required intimate physical contact between the assailant and the victim, to modern depersonalized killing techniques, in which unwitting victims appear as illuminated pixels on computer screens. This ability to kill at a distance has greatly transformed the demography of warfare; the ritualized battles of the past in which young men slaughtered young men are being replaced by rooms full of technicians of both sexes trained in "surgical bombing" and "target neutralization." Unfortunately, as the many victims of modern warfare well know, none of this has appreciably reduced the toll of death and human suffering that warfare still takes.

Modern urban environments have proven to be an ideal refuge for the persistence of old patterns of male-dominated violence in the form of gang warfare and armed robberies. The social anonymity and isolation of modern urban life has also created opportunities for new forms of violence that, as far as we know, did not exist in the past. Although "serial killers" who delighted in murdering other people undoubtedly existed in the past, their careers are likely to have been abruptly terminated by execution if they were foolish enough to redirect their homicidal urges closer to home and away from the socially sanctioned killing of outlaws and dehumanized "others."

The "battered-child syndrome" is a similar example of a modern pattern of violence that lacks a clear ancient analog. This is a severe form of physical abuse in which parents chronically beat their young children, often until death. Like serial killing, the battered child syndrome seems, at least in part, to be a product of the lack of surveillance and weakened social control associated with modern urban anonymity. Such abusive behavior leaves clear skeletal stigmata that my colleagues and I have looked for in vain in many large prehistoric skeletal series (Walker 1997, 2001a) (Figures 4 and 7, see color inserts). It seems likely that treating children in this way was simply impossible in earlier societies. When people lived in large kin-based groups, where every action was publicly scrutinized and privacy unheard of, the repeated abuse of infants in this way would inevitably elicit intervention from relatives.

A final lesson from our violent past is the complexity that is apparent in its causes. First, arguing over the extent to which nature or nurture is responsible for cross-cultural regularities, such as the apparent long-standing dominance of males as perpetrators and victims of violent acts, is a sterile exercise. The question makes no more sense than arguing about whether the length or the width of a rectangle makes a greater contribution to its area (Petrinovich 2000). We are products of both our biological and cultural heritages, and their contributions are, for all practical purposes, inseparable. Proponents of simplistic materialist/ecological models that reduce warfare to competition over land and food will find little comfort in the evidence for frequent violent conflicts among earliest immigrants to the New World. These people lived at low densities and had ample opportunity to avoid violence by moving away from it but apparently were unable to do so. On the other hand, explanations that myopically focus on the quest for prestige, mates, or gender-based "binaristic" thinking (Cooke 1996) as prime movers of violence are equally suspect.

One sobering pattern that emerges from a survey of past violence is the close relationship repeatedly seen between large-scale outbreaks of violence and climatic instabilities. Crop failures and a greatly diminished zone of arable land induced by climate cooling during the fourteenth century have been suggested as stimulants for the warfare and mass killing documented at Crow Creek. Similar climatically induced conflicts appear to have occurred on the Colorado Plateau and other areas of the western United States (Jones et al 1999, LeBlanc 1999). Many of us are fortunate enough to live comfortably in culturally buffered environments, where modern climatic perturbations do not perceptibly interfere with our food supply or plunge us into the dangerous world of drought-induced warfare and civil unrest. This shows the fallacy of making simplistic equations between climatic change and warfare. However, we know from paleoenvironmental records that major climatic fluctuations on a scale unheard of during recent times are a fact of the earth's history. Dealing with the violent potential of such a worldwide climatic catastrophe is a challenge future generations surely will face.

Visit the Annual Reviews home page at www.AnnualReviews.org

LITERATURE CITED

Aalund O, Danielsen L, Sanhueza RO. 1990. Injuries due to deliberate violence in Chile. *Forensic Sci. Int.* 46:189–202

Angel JL. 1974. Patterns of fracture from Neolithic to modern times. *Anthropol. Kozlemenyek* 18:9–18

Baker SP. 1992. *The Injury Fact Book.* New York: Oxford Univ. Press. 344 pp.

Berger TD, Trinkaus E. 1995. Patterns of trauma among the Neanderthals. *J. Archaeol. Sci.* 22:841–52

Berlet AC, Talenti DP, Carroll SF. 1992. The baseball bat: a popular mechanism of urban injury. *J. Trauma* 33:167–70

Billman BR, Lambert PM, Leonard BL. 2000. Cannibalism, warfare, and drought in the Mesa Verde region during the twelfth century A.D. *Am. Antiq.* 65:145–78

Binford LR, Ho CK. 1985. Taphonomy at a distance: Zhoukoudian, "The cave home of Beijing man?" *Curr. Anthropol.* 26:413–42

Binford LR, Stone NM. 1986. Zhoukoudian: a closer look. *Curr. Anthropol.* 27:453–75

Boule M, Vallois HV. 1937. Anthropologie. In *Téviec: Station-Nécropole Mésolithique du Morbihan*, ed. M Saint-Just Péquart, H Vallois, pp. 111–223. Paris: Arch. Inst. Paléontol. Hum.

Cartmill M. 1993. *A View to a Death in the Morning: Hunting and Nature Through History.* Cambridge, MA: Harvard Univ. Press

Chatters JC. 2000. The recovery and first analysis of an early holocene human skeleton from Kennewick, Washington. *Am. Antiq.* 65:291–316

Cooke M. 1996. *Women and the War Story.* Berkeley: Univ. Calif. Press

Cornwell EE III, Jacobs D, Walker M, Jacobs L, Porter J, Fleming A. 1995. National Medical Association Surgical Section position paper on violence prevention. A resolution of trauma surgeons caring for victims of violence. *JAMA* 273:1788–89

Craven D. 1997. *Sex Differences in Violent Victimization, 1994. Spec. Rep. Publ. NCJ-164508.* Washington, DC: US Dept. Justice, Bur. Justice Stat.

Croes MM. 1996. Samenwoners van gelijk geslacht. *Samenwoners Gelijk Geslacht* 44:24–26

Darling JA. 1998. Mass inhumation and the execution of witches in the American Southwest. *Am. Anthropol.* 100:732–33

Dart RA. 1953. The predatory transition from ape to man. *Int. Anthropol. Linguist. Rev.* 1:201–17

Defleur A, White T, Valensi P, Slimak L, Cregut-Bonnoure E. 1999. Neanderthal cannibalism at Moula Guercy, Ardeche, France. *Science* 286:128–31

Dickel DN, Aker CG, Dickel DN, Aker CG, Barton BK, Doran GH. 1988. An orbital floor and ulna fracture from the early Archaic of Florida. *J. Paleopathol.* 2:165–70

Dongoske KE, Martin DL, Ferguson TJ. 2000. Critique of the claim of cannibalism at Cowboy Wash. *Am. Antiq.* 65:179–90

Dunnell RC. 1991. Methodological impacts of catastrophic depopulation. In *Columbian Consequences: The Spanish Borderlands in Pan-American Perspective*, ed. DH Thomas, pp. 561–80. Washington, D.C.: Smithsonian Inst.

Elerick DV, Tyson RA. 1997. *Human Paleopathology and Related Subjects: An International Bibliography.* San Diego, CA: San Diego Mus. Man. 716 pp.

Ferguson RB. 1997. Violence and war in prehistory. See Martin & Frayer 1997, pp. 321–55

Ferguson RB. 1995. *Yanomami Warfare: A Political History.* Santa Fe, NM: Sch. Am. Res. 449 pp.

Fernandez-Jalvo Y, Diez JC, Caceres I, Rosell J. 1999. Human cannibalism in the early Pleistocene of Europe (Gran Dolina, Sierra de Atapuerca, Burgos, Spain). *J. Hum. Evol.* 37:591–622

Fox JA. 1994. *Uniform Crime Reports of the*

United States: Supplementary Homicide Reports, 1976–1992. Boston, MA: Northeastern Univ., Coll. Crim. Justice

Frayer DW. 1997. Ofnet: evidence for a mesolithic massacre. See Martin & Frayer 1997, pp. 181–216

Gardner JC. 2001. An analysis of the pathology of the Krapina Neandertals. *Am. J. Phys. Anthropol.* 35:68 (Abstr.)

Gorjanovíc-Kramberger D. 1906. *Der Diluviale Mensch von Krapina in Kroatien.* Weisbaden, Ger.: Kreidel

Groleau GA, Tso EL, Olshaker JS, Barish RA, Lyston DJ. 1993. Baseball bat assault injuries. *J. Trauma* 34:366–72

Holinger PC. 1987. *Violent Deaths in the United States: An Epidemiological Study of Suicide, Homicide and Accidents.* New York: Guilford. 274 pp.

Ilic N, Petricevic A, Tanfara S, Mimica Z, Radonic V, et al. 1999. War injuries to the chest. *Acta Chir. Hung.* 38:43–47

Jones TL, Brown GM, Raab LM, McVickar JL, Spaulding WG, et al. 1999. Environmental imperatives reconsidered. *Curr. Anthropol.* 40:137–70

Jurmain R, Bellifemine VI. 1997. Patterns of cranial trauma in a prehistoric population from central California. *Int. J. Osteoarchaeol.* 7:43–50

Keeley LH. 1996. *War Before Civilization: The Myth of the Peaceful Savage.* New York: Oxford Univ. Press. 245 pp.

Keenleyside A, Bertulli M, Fricke HC. 1997. The final days of the Franklin expedition: new skeletal evidence. *Arctic* 50:36–46

Knauft BM. 1987. Reconsidering violence in simple human societies. *Curr. Anthropol.* 28:457–98

Kroeber AL. 1925. *Handbook of the Indians of California.* Washington, DC: US Gov. Print. Off. 995 pp.

Krohn-Hansen C. 1994. The anthropology of violent interaction. *J. Anthropol. Res.* 50:367–81

Kuemin Drews NJ. 2001. Warfare in the late prehistoric Southeast: a multi-site osteological analysis from west-central Tennessee. *Am. J. Phys. Anthropol.* 35 (Suppl.): 93

Lambert PM. 1993. Health in prehistoric populations of the Santa Barbara Channel Islands. *Am. Antiq.* 58.:509–21

Lambert PM. 1994. *War and peace on the western front: a study of violent conflict and its correlates in prehistoric hunter-gatherer societies of coastal southern California.* PhD diss., Santa Barbara, CA: University of California. 259 pp.

Lambert PM. 1997. Patterns of violence in prehistoric hunter-gatherer societies of coastal southern California. See Martin & Frayer 1997, pp. 77–109

Lancaster HO. 1990. *Expectations of Life: A Study in the Demography, Statistics, and History of World Mortality.* New York: Springer-Verlag. 605 pp.

Lanpo J, Weiwen H. 1990. *The Story of Peking Man: From Archaeology to Mystery.* New York: Oxford Univ. Press. 270 pp.

LeBlanc SA. 1999. *Prehistoric Warfare in the American Southwest.* Salt Lake City: Univ. Utah Press

Lovell NC. 1997. Trauma analysis in paleopathology. *Yearb. Phys. Anthropol.* 40:139–70

Marlar RA, Leonard BL, Billman BR, Lambert PM, Marlar JE. 2000. Biochemical evidence of cannibalism at a prehistoric Puebloan site in southwestern Colorado. *Nature* 407:74–78

Martin DL. 2000. Man corn: cannibalism and violence in the prehistoric American Southwest. *Am. Antiq.* 65:199

Martin D, Frayer D, eds. 1997. *Troubled Times: Violence and Warfare in the Past.* Toronto: Gordon & Breach

Mathew PK. 1996. Changing trends in tribal fights in the highlands of Papua New Guinea: a five-year review. *Papua New Guinea Med. J.* 39:117–20

McCorkle T. 1978. Intergroup conflict. In *Handbook of North American Indians: California,* ed. RF Heizer, pp. 694–700. Washington, DC: Smithsonian Inst.

McCown TD, Keith A. 1939. *The Stone Age Men of Mount Carmel: The Fossil Human*

Remains from the Levalloiso-Mousterian. Oxford, UK: Clarendon

Melbye J, Fairgrieve SI. 1994. A massacre and possible cannibalism in the Canadian Arctic—new evidence from the Saunaktuk site (Ngtn-1). *Arctic Anthropol.* 31:57–77

Milner GR, Anderson E, Smith VG. 1991. Warfare in late prehistoric west-central Illinois. *Am. Antiq.* 56:581–603

MMWR. 1995. Emergency department surveillance for weapon-related injuries—Massachusetts, November 1993–April 1994. *Morbid. Mortal. Wkly. Rep.* 44:160, 163–69

MMWR. 1996. Trends in rates of homicide—United States, 1985–1994. *Morbid. Mortal. Wkly. Rep.* 45:460–64

Moratto MJ, Fredrickson DA. 1984. *California Archaeology.* Orlando, FL: Academic. 757 pp.

Muckart DJ, Meumann C, Botha JB. 1995. The changing pattern of penetrating torso trauma in KwaZulu/Natal—a clinical and pathological review. *S. Afr. Med. J.* 85:1172–74

Murray CJL, Lopez AD. 1996. *The Global Burden of Disease: A Comprehensive Assessment of Mortality and Disability from Diseases, Injuries, and Risk Factors in 1990 and Projected to 2020.* Cambridge, MA: Harvard Univ. Press. 990 pp.

Ord RA, Benian RM. 1995. Baseball bat injuries to the maxillofacial region caused by assault. *J. Oral Maxillofac. Surg.* 53:514–17

Petrinovich LF. 2000. *The Cannibal Within.* New York: de Gruyter. 232 pp.

Pickering TR, White TD, Toth N. 2000. Brief communication: cutmarks on a Plio-Pleistocene hominid from Sterkfontein, South Africa. *Am. J. Phys. Anthropol.* 111:579–84

Pringle H. 1998. Crow Creek's revenge. *Science* 279:2039

Rand M, Strom K. 1997. *Violence-Related Injuries Treated in Hospital Emergency Departments. Spec. Rep. Publ. NCJ-156921.* Washington, DC: US Dept. Justice, Bur. Justice Stat.

Richards MP, Pettitt PB, Trinkaus E, Smith FH, Paunovic M, Karavanic I. 2000. Nean-

derthal diet at Vindija and Neanderthal predation: the evidence from stable isotopes. *Proc. Natl. Acad. Sci. USA* 97:7663

Robb J. 1997. Violence and gender in early Italy. See Martin & Frayer 1997, pp. 111–44

Russell MD. 1987a. Bone breakage in the Krapina hominid collection. *Am. J. Phys. Anthropol.* 72:373–79

Russell MD. 1987b. Mortuary practices at the Krapina Neandertal site. *Am. J. Phys. Anthropol.* 72:381–97

Russell MD, Lemort F. 1986. Cutmarks on the Engis 2 calvaria? *Am. J. Phys. Anthropol.* 69:317–24

Shepherd JP, Gayford JJ, Leslie IJ, Scully C. 1988. Female victims of assault. A study of hospital attenders. *J. Craniomaxillofac. Surg.* 16:233–37

Shepherd JP, Shapl M, Pearce NX, Scully C. 1990. Pattern, severity, and aetiology of injuries in victims of assault. *J. R. Soc. Med.* 83:161–62

Smith MO. 1997. Osteological indications of warfare in the Archaic period of the western Tennessee Valley. See Martin & Frayer 1997, pp. 241–65

Smith MO. 2001. Intergroup violence: a comparison between Dallas phase and Mouse Creek phase frequencies and patterns. *Am. J. Phys. Anthropol.* 35 (Suppl.):139

Spitz WU. 1993. *Medicolegal Investigation of Death: Guidelines for the Application of Pathology to Crime Investigation.* Springfield, IL: Thomas. 829 pp.

Stedman TL. 1982. *Steadman's Medical Dictionary.* Baltimore, MD: William & Wilkins

Stewart KM. 1947. Mojave warfare. Southwest. *J. Anthropol.* 3:257–78

Stiner MC. 1991. The faunal remains from Grotta Guattari: a taphonomic perspective. *Curr. Anthropol.* 32:103–17

Straus MA. 1999. The controversy over domestic violence by women: a methological, theoretical, and sociology of science analysis. In *Violence in Intimate Relationships,* ed. B Ximena, E Arriaga, S Oskamp, et al., pp. vii, 17–44. Newbury Park, CA: Sage

Summerfield D. 1997. The social, cultural and political dimensions of contemporary war. *Med. Confl. Surviv.* 13:3–25

Swann IJ, MacMillan R, Strong I. 1981. Head injuries at an inner city accident and emergency department. *Injury* 12:274–78

Toole MJ. 1995. Mass population displacement. A global public health challenge. *Infect. Dis. Clin. N. Am.* 9:353–66

Toole MJ, Waldman RJ. 1993. Refugees and displaced persons. War, hunger, and public health. *JAMA* 270:600–5

Trinkaus E. 1985. Cannibalism and burial at Krapina. *J. Hum. Evol.* 14:203–16

Trinkaus E, Zimmerman MR. 1982. Trauma among the Shanidar Neandertals. *Am. J. Phys. Anthropol.* 57:61–76

Turner CG, Turner JA. 1999. *Man Corn: Cannibalism and Violence in the Prehistoric American Southwest.* Salt Lake City: Univ. Utah Press

Ullrich H. 1978. Kannibalismus und leichenzerstuckelung beim Neandertaler von Krapina. In *Krapinski Pracovjek i Evolucija Hominida*, pp. 293–318. Zagreb: Jugoslav. Akad. Znan. Umjet.

United Nations. 1993. *Declaration on the Elimination of Violence Against Women. Resolution 48/104.* New York: UN Dept. Public Inf.

Villa P. 1992. Cannibalism in prehistoric Europe. *Evol. Anthropol.* 1:93–104

Villa P, Bouville C, Courtin J, Helmer D, Mahieu E, et al. 1986. Cannibalism in the Neolithic. *Science* 233:431–37

Villa P, Mahieu E. 1991. Breakage patterns of human long bones. *J. Hum. Evol.* 21:27–48

Walker PL. 1989. Cranial injuries as evidence of violence in prehistoric southern California. *Am. J. Phys. Anthropol.* 80:313–23

Walker PL. 1990. *Appendix 5: Tool Marks on Human Bone from Saunaktuk.* Yellowknife, Northwest Terr.: Prince of Wales North. Heritage Cent.

Walker PL. 1995. Problems of preservation and sexism in sexing: some lessons from historical collections for paleodemographers. In *Grave Reflections: Portraying the Past Through Skeletal Studies*, ed. A Herring, S Saunders, pp. 31–47. Toronto: Can. Scholars

Walker PL. 1997. Wife beating, boxing, and broken noses: skeletal evidence for the cultural patterning of interpersonal violence. See Martin & Frayer 1997, pp. 145–75

Walker PL. 2001a. *Is the Battered-Child Syndrome a Modern Phenomenon?* Presented at 10th Eur. Meet. Paleopathol. Assoc., Göettingen, Ger.

Walker PL. 2001b. A Spanish borderlands perspective on La Florida bioarchaeology. In *Bioarchaeology of La Florida: Human Biology in Northern Frontier New Spain*, ed. CS Larsen. Gainesville: Univ. Florida Press. In press

Walker PL, Cook DC. 1998. Gender and sex: vive la difference. *Am. J. Phys. Anthropol.* 106:255–59

Walker PL, Drayer F, Siefkin S. 1996. *Malibu Human Skeletal Remains: A Bioarchaeological Analysis.* Sacramento, CA: Resource Manage. Div., Dept. Parks & Recreat.

Walker PL, Lambert PM. 1989. Skeletal evidence for stress during a period of cultural change in prehistoric California. In *Advances in Paleopathology*, ed. L Capasso, pp. 207–12. Chieti, Italy: Solfanelli

Walker PL, Thornton R. 2001. Health, nutrition, and demographic change in native California. In *The Backbone of History: Health and Disease in the Western Hemisphere*, ed. R Steckel, J Rose. Cambridge, UK: Cambridge Univ. Press. In press

Walpoff MH. 1996. *Human Evolution.* New York: McGraw Hill. 927 pp.

Weidenreich F. 1943. *The Skull of Sinanthropus Pekinensis; A Comparative Study on a Primitive Hominid Skull.* Pehpei, Chungking: Geol. Surv. China. 484 pp.

White TD. 1986. Cut marks on the Bodo cranium: a case of prehistoric defleshing. *Am. J. Phys. Anthropol.* 69:503–10

White TD. 1992. *Prehistoric Cannibalism at Mancos 5MTUMR-2346.* Princeton, NJ: Princeton Univ. Press. 462 pp.

White TD, Toth N. 1989. Engis: preparation

damage, not ancient cutmarks. *Am. J. Phys. Anthropol.* 78:361–68

White TD, Toth N. 1991. The question of ritual cannibalism at Grotta Guattari. *Curr. Anthropol.* 32:118–38

Whitman S, Benbow N, Good G. 1996. The epidemiology of homicide in Chicago. *J. Natl. Med. Assoc.* 88:781–87

Willey P, Emerson TE. 1993. The osteology and archaeology of the Crow Creek massacre. *Plains Anthropol.* 38:227–69

Yip KM, Tam TY, Hung LK. 1997. Multiple chop wounds in Hong Kong. An epidemiological study of an unusual injury. *Arch. Orthop. Trauma Surg.* 116:295–98

SUBJECT INDEX

CUMULATIVE INDEXES

CONTRIBUTING AUTHORS, VOLUMES 22–30

Voland E, 27:347–74

Walker PL, 30:573–96
Weiss KM, 27:273–300
Weston K, 22:339–67

Whyte SR, 25:153–78
Wishnie M, 29:493–524
Wodak R, 28:175–99
Wolf AP, 22:157–75
Wolfe TC, 29:195–216

Woolard KA, 23:55–82
Worthman CM, 24:593–616

Yelvington KA, 30:227–60
Yoffee N, 24:281–311

CHAPTER TITLES, VOLUMES 22–30

Overviews

Archaeology

Biological Anthropology

Linguistics and Communicative Practices

Regional Studies

Sociocultural Anthropology

HISTORY, THEORY, AND METHODS

ECONOMICS, ECOLOGY, TECHNOLOGY, AND DEVELOPMENT

AFFECT, COGNITION, AND MEANING

MEDICAL ANTHROPOLOGY, NUTRITION, AND DEMOGRAPHY

Theme I: Aids

Theme I: Capitalism and the Reinvention of Anthropology

Theme I: Human Genetic Diversity

Theme I: Millennium

Theme II: Demographic Anthropology

Theme II: Diasporas